The Greek Epic Cycle and Its Ancient Reception

The poems of the Epic Cycle are assumed to be the reworking of myths and narratives which had their roots in an oral tradition predating that of many of the myths and narratives which took their present form in the *Iliad* and the *Odyssey*. The remains of these texts allow us to investigate diachronic aspects of epic diction as well as the extent of variation within it on the part of individual authors – two of the most important questions in modern research on archaic epic. They also help to illuminate the early history of Greek mythology. Access to the poems, however, has been thwarted by their current fragmentary state. This volume provides the scholarly community and graduate students with a thorough critical foundation for reading and interpreting them.

MARCO FANTUZZI teaches Greek literature at Columbia University, New York, and at the University of Macerata. His publications include: *Achilles in Love*, 2012; *Tradition and Innovation in Hellenistic Poetry* (with R. Hunter), 2004; *Ricerche su Apollonio Rodio: diacronie della dizione epica*, 1988; *Bionis Smyrnaei Adonidis epitaphium*, 1985; *Brill's Companion to Greek and Latin Pastoral*, ed. (with T. Papanghelis), 2006; and *Struttura e storia dell'esametro greco*, ed. (with R. Pretagostini) 1995–6; forthcoming commentary on the *Rhesus* ascribed to Euripides. Among his present research interests are Greek tragedy, Hellenistic poetry, Greek and Latin metrics, and ancient literary criticism and scholarship.

CHRISTOS TSAGALIS is Professor of Greek at the Aristotle University of Thessaloniki. His research interests encompass Homer, Hesiod, historiography, and the Greek epigram. His books include *From Listeners to Viewers: Space in the* Iliad, 2012; *The Oral Palimpsest: Exploring Intertextuality in the Homeric Epics*, 2008; *Inscribing Sorrow: Fourth-Century Attic Funerary Epigrams*, 2008 and *Epic Grief: Personal Laments in Homer's* Iliad, 2004. Among his current research interests is the publication of a commentary on the surviving fragments of genealogical and antiquarian Greek epic. He has edited, among other volumes, *Brill's Companion to Hesiod* (with F. Montanari and A. Rengakos), 2009; *Homeric Hypertextuality* and *Theban Resonances in Homeric Epic*, special issues of the journal *Trends in Classics*, 2010 and 2014.

The Greek Epic Cycle and Its Ancient Reception

A Companion

Edited By

MARCO FANTUZZI AND CHRISTOS TSAGALIS

CAMBRIDGE
UNIVERSITY PRESS

University Printing House, Cambridge CB2 8BS, United Kingdom

One Liberty Plaza, 20th Floor, New York, NY 10006, USA

477 Williamstown Road, Port Melbourne, VIC 3207, Australia

314-321, 3rd Floor, Plot 3, Splendor Forum, Jasola District Centre, New Delhi - 110025, India

79 Anson Road, #06-04/06, Singapore 079906

Cambridge University Press is part of the University of Cambridge.

It furthers the University's mission by disseminating knowledge in the pursuit of education, learning and research at the highest international levels of excellence.

www.cambridge.org
Information on this title: www.cambridge.org/9781108730266

© Cambridge University Press 2015

This publication is in copyright. Subject to statutory exception and to the provisions of relevant collective licensing agreements, no reproduction of any part may take place without the written permission of Cambridge University Press.

First published 2015
Reprinted 2016
First paperback edition 2018

A catalogue record for this publication is available from the British Library

Library of Congress Cataloging in Publication data
The Greek Epic Cycle and its ancient reception : a companion / edited by Marco Fantuzzi, Christos Tsagalis.
    pages   cm
Includes bibliographical references and index.
ISBN 978-1-107-01259-2 (hardback)
1. Epic poetry, Greek – History and criticism.   2. Lost literature – Greece.   3. Cycles (Literature)
I. Fantuzzi, Marco, editor.   II. Tsagalis, Christos, editor.
PA3105.G75   2015
883´.0109 – dc23   2015002311

ISBN 978-1-107-01259-2 Hardback
ISBN 978-1-108-73026-6 Paperback

Cambridge University Press has no responsibility for the persistence or accuracy of URLs for external or third-party internet websites referred to in this publication, and does not guarantee that any content on such websites is, or will remain, accurate or appropriate.

Contents

List of illustrations   [*page* viii]
List of contributors   [xi]
Editorial note   [xiii]

Introduction: *Kyklos*, the Epic Cycle and Cyclic poetry   [1]
MARCO FANTUZZI AND CHRISTOS TSAGALIS

PART I APPROACHES TO THE EPIC CYCLE

1 Coming adrift: The limits of reconstruction of the cyclic poems   [43]
JONATHAN BURGESS

2 Oral traditions, written texts, and questions of authorship   [59]
GREGORY NAGY

3 The Epic Cycle and oral tradition   [78]
JOHN M. FOLEY (†) AND JUSTIN ARFT

4 The formation of the Epic Cycle   [96]
MARTIN L. WEST

5 Motif and source research: Neoanalysis, Homer, and Cyclic epic   [108]
WOLFGANG KULLMANN

6 Meta-Cyclic epic and Homeric poetry   [126]
MARGALIT FINKELBERG

7 Language and meter of the Epic Cycle   [139]
ALBERTO BERNABÉ

8 Narrative techniques in the Epic Cycle   [154]
ANTONIOS RENGAKOS

9 Wit and irony in the Epic Cycle   [164]
DAVID KONSTAN

10 The Trojan War in early Greek art   [178]
    THOMAS H. CARPENTER

    PART II EPICS

11 *Theogony* and *Titanomachy*   [199]
    GIAMBATTISTA D'ALESSIO

12 *Oedipodea*   [213]
    ETTORE CINGANO

13 *Thebaid*   [226]
    JOSÉ B. TORRES-GUERRA

14 *Epigonoi*   [244]
    ETTORE CINGANO

15 *Alcmeonis*   [261]
    ANDREA DEBIASI

16 *Cypria*   [281]
    BRUNO CURRIE

17 *Aethiopis*   [306]
    ANTONIOS RENGAKOS

18 *Ilias parva*   [318]
    ADRIAN KELLY

19 *Iliou persis*   [344]
    PATRICK J. FINGLASS

20 *Nostoi*   [355]
    GEORG DANEK

21 *Telegony*   [380]
    CHRISTOS TSAGALIS

    PART III THE FORTUNE OF THE EPIC CYCLE IN THE ANCIENT WORLD

22 The aesthetics of sequentiality and its discontents   [405]
    MARCO FANTUZZI

23 The Epic Cycle, Stesichorus, and Ibycus   [430]
    MARIA NOUSSIA-FANTUZZI

24 Pindar's Cycle   [450]
    IAN RUTHERFORD

25 Tragedy and the Epic Cycle   [461]
    ALAN H. SOMMERSTEIN

26 The Hellenistic reception of the Epic Cycle   [487]
    EVINA SISTAKOU

27 Running rings round Troy: Recycling the 'Epic Circle' in Hellenistic and Roman art   [496]
    MICHAEL SQUIRE

28 Virgil and the Epic Cycle   [543]
    URSULA GÄRTNER

29 Ovid and the Epic Cycle   [565]
    GIANPIERO ROSATI

30 Statius' *Achilleid* and the *Cypria*   [578]
    CHARLES MCNELIS

31 The Epic Cycle and the ancient novel   [596]
    DAVID F. ELMER

32 The Epic Cycle and imperial Greek epic   [604]
    SILVIO BÄR AND MANUEL BAUMBACH

Works cited   [623]
Index of principal passages   [668]
Index nominum et rerum   [673]

Illustrations

10.1 Cycladic relief pithos from Mykonos. Seventh century BC. Neck: Trojan horse. Shoulder: Massacre of women and children. Mykonos Archaeological Museum, inv. 2240.   [*page* 180]

10.2 Detail of Figure 10.1. Drawing by L. C. Lancaster.   [182]

10.3 Hoplite shield with shield-band. Drawing by L. C. Lancaster.   [183]

10.4 Panel of an Argive shield-band from Olympia, perhaps showing Achilles in pursuit of Troilus. Sixth century BC. Drawing from E. Kunze, *Archaische Schildbänder, Olympische Forschungen*, Band II, Berlin, 1950, Pl. 5, 1b.   [185]

10.5 Scene of Attic black-figure volute krater (François Vase) showing Achilles' pursuit of Troilus. Sixth century BC. Drawing from A. Furtwängler and K. Reichhold, *Griechische Vasenmalerei*, Munich, 1900–32, Pl. 1.   [187]

10.6 Panel of an Argive shield-band from Olympia showing the Rape of Cassandra. Sixth century BC. Drawing from Kunze, Pl. 7, 1e.   [188]

10.7 Panel of an Argive shield-band from Olympia showing the suicide of Ajax. Sixth century BC. Drawing from Kunze, Pl. 55, xxvi *x*.   [192]

10.8 Apulian red-figure volute krater from Ceglie del Campo showing the murder of Thersites by Achilles. Fourth century BC. Boston, Museum of Fine Arts, inv. 1900.03.804.   [194]

27.1 Drawing of a 'Homeric cup', with inscription associating the scenes with the '*Little Iliad* according to the poet Lesches' (Berlin, Staatliche Museen, Antike Sammlungen, inv. 3371, now lost). After Sinn (1979: 94, no. MB 27). Reproduced by kind permission from the Institut für klassische Archäologie und Museum für Abgüsse klassischer Bildwerke, Ludwig-Maximilians-Universität, Munich.   [499]

27.2 Reconstruction of the painting of Penthesilea arriving at Troy from the east wall of the west wing of the eponymous room of the Casa del Criptoportico (Pompeii II.2.2). After Aurigemma (1953: 951, Fig. 965). Reproduced by kind permission from the Institut für

List of illustrations   ix

klassische Archäologie und Museum für Abgüsse klassischer Bildwerke, Ludwig-Maximilians-Universität, Munich.   [502]

27.3 Drawing of the east wall of oecus h in the Casa di Octavius Quartio (Pompeii II.2.2), with the Heracles frieze above, and the smaller Iliadic frieze below. After Aurigemma (1953: 975, Fig. 990). Reproduced by kind permission from the Institut für klassische Archäologie und Museum für Abgüsse klassischer Bildwerke, Ludwig-Maximilians-Universität, Munich.   [503]

27.4 Obverse of the *Tabula Iliaca Capitolina* [1A], as it survives today. Author.   [506]

27.5 Line drawing of the *Tabula Iliaca Capitolina* [1A] by Feodor Ivanovich. After Jahn 1873: Tafel I.   [507]

27.6 Reconstruction of the *Tabula Iliaca Capitolina* [1A]. Author.   [508]

27.7 Cyclical arrangement of scenes on the *Tabula Iliaca Capitolina* [1A], with suggested clockwise viewing of the Iliadic scenes. Author.   [522]

27.8 Cyclical arrangement of scenes on the *Tabula Iliaca Capitolina* [1A], with suggested anticlockwise viewing of the Iliadic scenes. Author.   [522]

27.9 Reconstruction of the obverse of the *Tabula New York* [2NY]. Author.   [523]

27.10 Drawing of the obverse of the *Tabula Sarti* [6B]. After Jahn 1873: Tafel III.   [524]

27.11 Reconstruction of the obverse of the *Tabula Veronensis II* [9D]. Author.   [525]

27.12 Reconstruction of the obverse of the *Tabula Froehner* [20Par]. Author.   [526]

27.13 Reconstruction of the reverse 'magic square' of the *Tabula New York* [2NY, upper left] and *Tabula Veronensis I* [3C, upper right]. Author.   [527]

27.14 Reverse of the *Tabula New York* [2NY]. Metropolitan Museum of Art, Fletcher Fund, 1924 (24.97.11); photograph © The Metropolitan Museum of Art, New York.   [528]

27.15 Obverse of the *Tabula New York* [2NY]. Metropolitan Museum of Art, Fletcher Fund, 1924 (24.97.11); photograph © The Metropolitan Museum of Art, New York.   [529]

27.16 Drawing of a 'Homeric cup' juxtaposing scenes from the *Iliad* and *Aethiopis* (Sinn 1979: 92 no. 23). After Robert (1896: 26, no. D).   [531]

27.17 Ground plan of the Casa del Criptoportico (Pompeii I.6.2), after Corlàita Scagliarini 1974–6: 34, Fig. 30, following Spinazzola (1953: 455, Fig. 517). [534]

27.18 Reconstruction of the north wing of the eponymous cryptoporticus in the Casa del Criptoportico (Pompeii I.6.2); the drawing shows the view across to the western wing of the room (with the Trojan cycle occupying the upper grey frieze). After Spinazzola (1953: 459, Fig. 523). Reproduced by kind permission from the Institut für klassische Archäologie und Museum für Abgüsse klassischer Bildwerke, Ludwig-Maximilians-Universität, Munich. [536]

27.19 Image of Hermes with Aeneas and Anchises, from the south wall of the west wing of the Casa del Criptoportico (Pompeii I.6.2). After Aurigemma (1953: 955, Fig. 971). Reproduced by kind permission from the Institut für klassische Archäologie und Museum für Abgüsse Klassischer Bildwerke, Ludwig-Maximilians-Universität, Munich. [537]

27.20 Reconstruction of the stucco frieze from the Casa di Sacello Iliaco (Pompeii I.6.4), showing the arrangement of scenes. After Brilliant (1984: 64, Fig. 2.5). [539]

27.21 Plan of the Iliadic and Heracles scenes in the Casa di Octavius Quartio (Pompeii II.2.2). Author. [540]

Contributors

JUSTIN ARFT *University of Missouri*

SILVIO BÄR *University of Oslo*

MANUEL BAUMBACH *Ruhr University, Bochum*

ALBERTO BERNABÉ *Complutense University, Madrid*

JONATHAN BURGESS *University of Toronto*

THOMAS H. CARPENTER *Ohio University*

ETTORE CINGANO *University of Venice "Ca' Foscari"*

BRUNO CURRIE *Oriel College, Oxford*

GIAMBATTISTA D'ALESSIO *University of Naples "Federico II"*

GEORG DANEK *University of Vienna*

ANDREA DEBIASI *University of Padua*

DAVID F. ELMER *Harvard University*

MARCO FANTUZZI *University of Macerata and Columbia University*

PATRICK J. FINGLASS *University of Nottingham*

MARGALIT FINKELBERG *Tel Aviv University*

JOHN M. FOLEY (†)

URSULA GÄRTNER *University of Potsdam*

ADRIAN KELLY *Balliol College, Oxford*

DAVID KONSTAN *New York University*

WOLFGANG KULLMANN *Albert Ludwing University of Freiburg (Professor Emeritus)*

CHARLES MCNELIS *Georgetown University*

GREGORY NAGY *Harvard University*

MARIA NOUSSIA-FANTUZZI *Aristotle University of Thessaloniki*
ANTONIOS RENGAKOS *Aristotle University of Thessaloniki*
GIANPIERO ROSATI *Scuola Normale Superiore, Pisa*
IAN RUTHERFORD *University of Reading*
EVINA SISTAKOU *Aristotle University of Thessaloniki*
ALAN H. SOMMERSTEIN *University of Nottingham*
MICHAEL SQUIRE *King's College, London*
JOSÉ B. TORRES-GUERRA *University of Navarra*
CHRISTOS TSAGALIS *Aristotle University of Thessaloniki*
MARTIN L. WEST *All Souls College, Oxford*

Editorial note

English translations of Greek and Latin texts are consistently from the Loeb Classical Library, where available, unless otherwise stated. Transliterations of the Greek are sometimes adopted, in the hope of expediting the reading experience – but only for single words or short phrases which have been already quoted for the first time in Greek.

With regard to the mythological *Library* ascribed erroneously by Photius to 'Apollodorus the Grammarian', namely the famous Apollodorus of Athens, we have consistently referred to its author as Ps.-Apollodorus, in agreement with a widespread convention. Of course the author of the *Library* may have been a different Apollodorus.

As there is so much inconsistency among classicists in the spelling of proper names, the editors decided to let each contributor develop their own system as long as they applied it consistently within their chapter. There may be a certain inconsistency in the abbreviated references used throughout the volume, but this should not affect clarity for those readers who wish to follow them up.

The volume was delivered to Cambridge University Press in the summer of 2014, and only occasionally could the authors or the editors refer to more recent bibliography (we are sorry, in particular, that none of us could acknowledge M. Davies, *The Theban Epics*, Harvard, 2015).

Introduction: *Kyklos*, the Epic Cycle and Cyclic poetry

MARCO FANTUZZI AND CHRISTOS TSAGALIS

KYKLOS: TRACING A METAPHOR

The term *kyklos* is notorious for its ambiguity. The word encompasses various interpretations, most of them metaphorical: apart from the proper sense 'circle', it can designate any circular body like a wheel, a trencher, a place of an assembly or the people standing in a ring, the vault of the sky, the orb or disk of a celestial body, the wall around a city, a round shield, the eyeballs, an olive wreath, a collection of legends or poems, a circular dance, a rounded period, a globe, a kind of anapaest, the ring composition. Whatever sense one adopts, it can be generally agreed upon that the meaning of *kyklos* as a 'cycle' of epic poems must be metaphorical.

We will now offer a synopsis of five possible interpretations of the term *kyklos* with respect to the Epic Cycle. In particular, the word *kyklos* has been employed so as to denote: (a) an idea of uniformity and continuity; (b) a notion of 'ring form'; (c) the concept of completeness; (d) an encircling or framing function; and (e) a poetics based on manufacturing a perfected whole.

(a) The notion of uniformity and continuity is inherent in an emblematic passage from Photius' *Bibliotheca* (319a30), which quotes Proclus – but Proclus may have reflected an older introductory justification to a compilation of summaries of the Cyclic poems that possibly were Proclus' source:[1] λέγει [scil. ὁ Πρόκλος] δὲ ὡς τοῦ ἐπικοῦ κύκλου τὰ ποιήματα διασῴζεται καὶ σπουδάζεται τοῖς πολλοῖς οὐχ οὕτωι διὰ τὴν ἀρετὴν ὡς διὰ τὴν ἀκολουθίαν τῶν ἐν αὐτῶι πραγμάτων ('Proclus says that the poems of the Epic Cycle are preserved and paid attention to not so much for their value as for the orderly sequence of the events narrated in it').

This passage makes clear that down to Proclus' day the epic cycle was studied for its narrative linearity, i.e. because it offered a sequential presentation of mythical events stretching from the 'love mixing' of Ouranos

---

[1] West (2013: 25). It is a widespread conjecture that Proclus' summaries presupposed an older epitome or a plurality of older epitomes: cf. e.g. Burgess and West, below in this volume, respectively pp. 48 and 105. On the identity of Proclus, see below, p. 35.

and Gaia to Odysseus' death and the end of the race of heroes. This narrative concatenation must have created a notion of uniformity that surpassed the individuality of the various epic poems from which the Epic Cycle was formed, and offered the readers a convenient, continuous and linear storyline.

The Cyclic poems' original shape will have substantially resembled that outlined in Proclus' summaries.[2] The summary of each poem begins with a thematic 'bridge' to the last episode or episodes of the previous epic in the list.[3] What seems at first sight like a repetition necessitated by the elliptical form of Proclus' summary may, in fact, reflect a recapitulation device that the original Cyclic poems expanded sometimes into a whole episode. Besides, Proclus' transitions from one poem to the other punctually stress that each poem 'succeeds' to another.[4] This 'cyclic impulse' was a basic feature not only of the archaic epic poems which were later named after it.[5] The

---

[2] Not without original overlappings and contradictions, however, which the epitomizers probably took care to mend: see here below and West, below in this volume, p. 98.

[3] *Cypria* (end): capture of Briseis and Chryseis and catalogue of Trojans and Allies – *Iliad* (beginning): strife between Achilles and Agamemnon on Briseis and Catalogue of Ships and Catalogue of Trojans and Allies; *Iliad* (end): death of Hector – *Aethiopis* (beginning): mention of Hector's funeral; the Trojans ask Penthesileia to help them to make up for the loss of Hector; *Aethiopis* (end): *stasis* between Odysseus and Ajax about the arms of Achilles – *Ilias parva* (beginning): *stasis* between Odysseus and Ajax about the arms of Achilles; *Ilias parva* (end): Trojan horse enters the city – *Iliou persis* (beginning): Trojan horse enters the city; *Iliou persis* (end): Achaeans insult Athena by raping Cassandra – *Nostoi* (beginning): Athena makes Agamemnon and Menelaus fight over the question of whether or not they must appease the goddess before sailing away; *Nostoi* (end): murder of Agamemnon by Clytaemnestra – *Odyssey* (beginning): the gods recall Agamemnon's fate; *Odyssey* (end): decision reached about the burial of the suitors – *Telegony* (beginning): burial of the suitors by their relatives.

Repetitions in the beginnings and endings of Trojan Cyclic epics are however a rather complex phenomenon: a line must be drawn between original overlappings (which may go back to oral epic tradition in the manner of narrative doublets and dwindling pendants) and editorial reworking, the former aiming at connecting an epic that narrates a distinct phase of the war to the next one, the latter trying to create a more smooth and linear narrative progression.

[4] At the beginning of the *Cypria*, 'to this succeed (ἐπιβάλλει τούτοις) . . . the so-called *Cypria*' (Proclus is referring here to the Cyclic poem preceding the Trojan Cycle in the broader Epic Cycle, i.e. the *Thebaid* or the connected *Epigonoi* or the *Alcmeonis*. See below, pp. 30–1, 102); for the *Aethiopis*: 'to the aforementioned material succeeds Homer's *Iliad* (ἐπιβάλλει δὲ τοῖς προειρημένοις Ἰλιὰς Ὁμήρου), after which are the five books of the *Aethiopis*'; for the *Ilias parva*: 'next (ἑξῆς) are the four books of the *Ilias parva*'; for the *Iliou persis*: 'to these succeed (ἕπεται δὲ τούτοις) the two books of the *Iliou persis*'; for the *Nostoi*, 'to these connect (συνάπτει δὲ τούτοις) the five books of the *Nostoi*'.

[5] See Scodel (2012: 514–15): 'The discussion of the Cycle has too often been framed in terms based on written texts, where we expect a sequel or introduction to fit itself precisely to the text that precedes it. This is not the standard we should apply to early Greek epic. The general shape of these poems gives the impression that they were composed with a view to telling a single story, but that the poets did not recognize the versions of others as possessed of any absolute authority. I would suggest that we understand the 'cyclic impulse' as a basic (though not, of

same 'cyclic impulse' can also be observed in classical historiography, where at least Hecataeus, Herodotus, Thucydides, Xenophon and Theopompus represent a chain of authors each of whom continues his narrative from the endpoint of his predecessor's account or tries to fill in the gap between that endpoint and the 'official' beginning of his own history.[6] This meticulous effort to create a thematic 'bridge' linking the start of one's own work to the end of his predecessor's bears a striking similarity to Proclus' summaries of the Trojan Cyclic epics.

In this light, we may see in the 'repeated' episodes featuring at the end of one Trojan Cyclic epic and the beginning of the next a reflection of the effort to communicate to the audience that the poem they are going to hear places itself within a chain of poems dealing with the same general topic, i.e. the Trojan War, its background, and its aftermath: the individual poem only makes sense if the audience is to recall that the epic they are about to hear *continues* a unified storyline lying beyond the boundaries of the poem at hand. The same may have been the case for the Theban part of the Epic Cycle. The *Epigonoi* begin with a verse – νῦν αὖθ' ὁπλοτέρων ἀνδρῶν ἀρχώμεθα, Μοῦσαι ('But now, Muses, let us begin on the younger men')[7] – that may presuppose a preceding poem or oral tradition on a previous generation of heroes. There may be yet another instance of this formulaic structure opening a poem that considered itself the continuation of another: the end (1019–20) of the Hesiodic *Theogony* and the beginning (1–2) of the *Catalogue of Women* point to this direction.[8] Along similar lines, Burgess has drawn attention to what he calls 'verse joints' aimed at creating an artificial link between the end of a poem and the beginning of the next: the condensed proem of the *Iliad* known to Aristoxenus[9] may have served as a bridge between the *Cypria* and this *Iliad*, and the two verses connecting the *Aethiopis* to the *Iliad*, which we know in two different

---

course, universal) characteristic of archaic epic.' See also West (2002a), whose discussion of a Corinthian epic cycle partly rests on the idea of complementarity between its three constituent epics, the *Titanomachy*, the *Corinthiaca*, and the *Europia*.

[6] Canfora (1971 = 1999). See § 2a below.
[7] *PEG* F 1 (= D., W.). See Cingano, below in this volume, pp. 244–5.
[8] On both *Epigonoi* and *Catalogue*, see Cingano, below in this volume, pp. 254–5.
[9] *Anecdoton Osanni* in *Lexicon Vindob.* ed. Nauck p. 273 (= *Vitae Homeri, App. Rom.* B pp. 454–5 West): Ἀριστόξενος δ' ἐν α' Πραξιδαμαντείων [F 91a Wehrli X 198] φησὶ κατά τινας ἔχειν· ἔσπετε νῦν μοι Μοῦσαι Ὀλύμπια δώματ' ἔχουσαι, / ὅππως δὴ μῆνίς τε χόλος τ' ἔλε Πηλεΐωνα / Λητοῦς τ' ἀγλαὸν υἱόν· ὃ γὰρ βασιλῆϊ χολωθείς ('Aristoxenus in book 1 of the *Praxidamanteia* says that, according to some, it [the non-Homeric *Iliad*] begins thus: "Tell me now Muses, who have your homes at Olympos, how wrath and anger seized the son of Peleus and the splendid son of Leto; for he [Achilles] being angry against the king"'). See Kelly, below in this volume, pp. 329–30.

variants,[10] indicate that these 'artificial' links between one epic and the preceding one within a group of thematically linkable poems may have been created in rhapsodic performance and thus were perhaps convenient for the rhapsodes and agreeable to their audiences.[11]

(b) The metaphor of *kyklos* to express an early notion of circularity inherent in the events of world history or human fate can be detected in Herodotus' famous 'wheel' of human life (1.207.2). Croesus, just defeated, and thus reduced from the greatest power to total misery as a captive, warns his vanquisher Cyrus: 'learn this first of all: there is a *kyklos* of the human affairs, and as it revolves (περιφερόμενος) it prevents the same people from enjoying success consistently'. Herodotus' *kyklos* describes a series of events which in his view involve a patterned evolution from a beginning to an acme and later an end which reiterates the situation of the beginning. Cities or nations that are small can become great and powerful for a while, just to return to their initial humbleness/smallness later on; so the Lydian empire emerged from an originally insignificant position to great power with Gyges and Croesus, but it was with them that it sank to misery again.[12]

The *scholia Parisina* to the very last verse of the *Argonautica* by Apollonius of Rhodes specifically state that the Argonauts who return to Iolcos have completed a *kyklos*: ὅθεν οὖν ἀνήχθησαν τὴν ἀρχὴν οἱ ἥρωες εἰς Σκυθίαν ἐπὶ τὸ δέρας ἀποπλεύσαντες, ἐκεῖσε ὥσπερ διά τινος κύκλου κατήχθησαν ἐπανελθόντες ('from which place the heroes departed in the beginning when they sailed to Scythia in search of the Fleece, there [scil. to the same place] they returned by means of a kind of *kyklos*'). In this context, it is clear that the term *kyklos* refers to the external shape of the Argonautic epic, which may be called cyclical since the Argonauts returned to the very place they had sailed from at the beginning of the epic.[13] Apollonius may also have aimed at creating – in addition to the 'cyclic' use of time in his main narrative – an externally cyclical shape.[14] Likewise, it may be claimed that the last poem of the Epic Cycle, the *Telegony*, which ends with the immortalization of heroes, may be seen as a 'return' to the beginning of the first epic, the *Theogony*, which was about the creation of the divine world. In fact at the end of the *Telegony*, after Telemachus is married to Circe and Telegonus to Penelope, they are all immortalized and the same is the case with Odysseus who is transferred to the Isles of the Blessed. Thus, the Epic Cycle may have

---

[10] See Fantuzzi (2012: 268–70); Rengakos, below in this volume, pp. 312–13.
[11] Burgess (2001: 16, 140–1); also Rengakos, below, pp. 158–9.
[12] See below, p. 32.
[13] Adam (1889: 92).   [14] See in particular Rengakos (2004: 304).

ended in a way that denoted a kind of 'return' to a state of being in which the divine and human worlds coalesced. Like a circle, this compositional 'ring' would end exactly where it began.

(c) According to the scholia on Gregory of Nazianzos,[15] Aristotle also presupposed the question of how the epics belong to a 'cycle' or 'circle'. The scholiast reached the conclusion that in *Anal. post.* 77b32 the notion of cyclicality derives from the use of the same mythical material in a variety of epic poems.[16] *Kyklos* here would designate an encircled whole that is complete in its comprehensiveness.[17] The problem with this interpretation is that attempts at defining in what the completeness of the Epic Cycle consisted vary enormously: since at least two of the three subsections (i.e., the Theban and Trojan sets of poems) of the Epic Cycle are complete in themselves, the term *kyklos* was also easily applicable to them, not only to the wider nexus of poems that far surpassed in size these constituent sections. See for instance the first-century BC *Tabula Borgiana*, *IG* xiv.1292 (= 10K Sadurska), which may be designating at least the *Danaids*, the *Oedipodea* and the *Thebaid* as belonging to a Theban Epic Cycle,[18] and thus 'performs for other epic poems the sort of pictorial synthesis that the *Tabula Capitolina* acts out for the Trojan Cycle'.[19] On the other end of the spectrum, this idea of completeness perhaps also underlies the prose work of Dionysius the *kyklographos*, who drafted a mythological compilation in seven books called *kyklos historikos*. His compilation was a sort of encyclopedia of the mythical material found in epic, a formal corpus of heroic saga ('Corpus der Heldensage').[20] Perhaps it was similar to the fourth-century BC *Tragōidoumena* by Asclepiades of

---

[15] Σ Greg. Nazianz. *in laud. Bas. Magn.* 12 (ed. Jahn, *Patr. Gr.* 36, 914c Migne) = *Cyclus epicus PEG* T 29: καὶ Ἀριστοτέλης ἐν τῆι λογικῆι τάδε φησί· 'τὰ ἔπη κύκλος', καθὸ πᾶσα ποίησις περὶ τοὺς αὐτοὺς μύθους καταγίνεται καὶ περὶ τὰς αὐτὰς ἱστορίας ὥσπερ διά τινος περιάγεται κύκλου ('and Aristotle in the *Organon* says the following: "epic verse is a cycle", in so far as all [this] poetry deals with the same myths and the same stories as if it rotates in a circle').

[16] See also Arist. *Categ.* 11a8–11, where the circle is described as a kind of shape that does not have either variation or degree, i.e. that is complete in itself.

[17] See Scafoglio (2004: 42–3).

[18] Wilamowitz (1884: 333–4) suggested that both the *Epigonoi* and the *Alcmeonis* were also included in the damaged part (after line 12) of this inscription; see also *Cyclus epicus PEG* T 2 (= *Tit.* T 3 D.). Davies (1986: 97) is very skeptical of this interpretation, since --]μαχίας in line 9 – preceding the reference to the Theban epics – may well be designating the *Titanomachy* (Τιτανομαχίας), which would void Wilamowitz's suggestion. Other, even wilder, guesses include Severyns' suggestion (1928: 122) that there might have been an epic featuring Heracles that would have been placed between the *Titanomachy* and the *Cypria*, since they both contained some reference to Heracles (the latter by means of Nestor's digression).

[19] Squire (2011: 44; also 47 n. 49).

[20] Dionysius' work was divided into sections (μέρη) and had the form of a mythological encyclopedia. See Clem. *Protr.* 14; Athen. 9.481e; Rzach (1922: 2347).

Tragilos, a student of Isocrates, which were probably another mythological collection in six books consisting of the summaries of the myths treated in tragedy.

Likewise, we have the idea of *enkyklios paideia* as quite generally a canon of recognized writers that exceeds mere epic poetry. This may have been a rather late development but, as John Philoponus indicates *à propos* of *kyklos* in Aristotle,[21] it is based on the same notion of completeness that seems to be inherent in the meaning of the word *kyklos*. Be that as it may, the idea of completeness does seem to be closely connected to the notion of a 'cycle', regardless of whether the term was used for smaller sub-cycles or for the larger Epic Cycle or for even wider collections of material of thematic relevance.

(d) The term *kyklos* has also been employed with respect to an encircling or framing function. According to a scholium to Clement's *Protrepticus* (2.30.5 [303.35 Stählin]), κυκλικοὶ δὲ καλοῦνται ποιηταὶ οἱ τὰ κύκλωι τῆς Ἰλιάδος ἢ τὰ πρῶτα ἢ τὰ μεταγενέστερα ἐξ αὐτῶν τῶν Ὁμηρικῶν συγγράψαντες ('Those poets are called cyclic who have written about the events encircling the *Iliad*, either preceding or following from the Homeric ones'). In this case, the word *kyklos* is neither associated with the notion of 'unity' nor of 'ring form' nor of 'completeness', which are discussed above, but with that of 'enfolding', 'encasing' or 'enveloping'. This meaning presupposes the existence of a notional centre, in this case the *Iliad*, around which the *kyklos* is drawn.[22]

(e) A different kind of interpretation is suggested by those who believe that the term *kyklos* derives ultimately from an Indo-European metaphor for poetics. Building on the work of Schmitt,[23] Nagy[24] has pointed out the combination of the verb *takṣ-* 'join, fit together', which commonly refers to the handiwork of a carpenter, with the object *vāc*, which means 'poetic voice', in a passage of the *Rig-Veda* (1.130.6). He also stressed that in the very same passage the verb *takṣ-* takes as object the word *rátha*, which means 'wheel' and is used metonymically for 'chariot'. Greek poetic traditions

---

[21] Ioann. Philop. ad Arist. *Anal. post.* 77b 32 (156, 12 Wallies): ἢ κύκλον λέγει τὰ ἐγκύκλια λεγόμενα μαθήματα, οὕτω καλούμενα ἢ ὡς πᾶσαν ἱστορίαν περιέχοντά πως ἢ ὡς πάντων (ῥητόρων τε καὶ φιλοσόφων, τῶν τε καθόλου (καὶ τῶν add. Immisch) κατὰ μέρος add. Ra) περὶ αὐτὰ εἰλουμένων ('or he calls a cycle the so-called general education, which is called in this way either because it somehow contains the whole story or because everyone (orators and philosophers, both on the whole and in part) is drawn together around them'). On *kyklos* in Aristotle, see below, p. 30.

[22] On the use of the adverb κύκλωι, see *Etym. Magn.* 544.12–26 s.v.

[23] (1967: 296–8). The first to develop this idea was Darmesteter (1878: 319–21); on the Indo-European poet as a professional, see Campanile (1977: 35–54).

[24] (1996a: 89–90).

share such metaphors that envision the poet as craftsman, either explicitly (τέκτων ἐπέων[25] 'joiner of words') or implicitly (ἤραρε τέκτων[26] 'the joiner [*téktōn*] joined together [*ar-* in *arariskō*]'). Furthermore, the word *kyklos*/*kykla* (neuter plural) 'chariot(s) wheel'[27] (which in Homeric diction is invested with the same meaning as the word *harmo* in Linear B tablets) can metonymically replace *harma* ('chariot') in Homeric Greek. Therefore, Nagy argued that the meaning of *kyklos* as the 'sum total of epic by the master Homer is a metaphor that pictures the crafting of the ultimate chariot-wheel by the ultimate carpenter or "joiner"'.[28] This interpretation is further reinforced by the fact that the analogy between the activity of the carpenter and that of the poet is based on their shared conservation and unerring application of the rules of their art: 'a well-made song is similar to a chariot, which the carpenter can manufacture only by repeating and preserving a science much older than himself, a science that ignores individualism and innovation or regularly puts them into an almost imperceptible use'.[29] Seen from this angle, the metaphor implicit in the word *kyklos* may be preserving in fossilized form an old Indo-European metaphor pertaining to the close association between singer/song and carpenter/chariot, the more so since the very idea of *kyklos* as the 'sum total of epic'[30] was at an early stage linked to the prototypical *tektōn epeōn*, Homer himself.[31]

THE EVOLUTION OF THE EPIC CYCLE

The term '(Epic) Cycle' seems to be documented already in Aristotle as defining epic poetry or some epic poems (including Homer).[32] This use of the word as a canon of epic poetry may well be derived either from a

---

[25] Pind. *Pyth.* 3.112–4: 'We know of Nestor and Lykian Sarpedon, still the talk of men, from such echoing verses as wise craftsmen (τέκτονες οἶα σοφοί) constructed.' See also Alcm. *PMGF* 13a.8–10: 'a rival for Alcman the Laconian, the builder (τέκτονι) of elaborate maiden-songs'; *HHomHerm*. (4) 25: 'Hermes it was who first crafted (τεκτήνατ') the singing tortoise' (transl. by West 2003: 115); Pind. *Nem.* 3.4–5: 'the builders (τέκτονες) of honey-sounding revels'; Soph. *TrGF* F 159 (*Daedalus*): 'chief of the builders of verse' (τεκτόναρχος); Paus. 10.5.8: 'and first fashioned (τεκτάνατ') a song of ancient verses'; Bacchyl. 14.12–16: 'The voice of the phorminx and clear-sounding choruses are not befitting (ἁρμόζει) for the battle that causes grievous woes, nor is the ring of rattling bronze with festivities.' On the use of poetological phraseology pertaining to handiwork, see Nünlist (1998: 98–102).

[26] *Il.* 4.110; 23.712.   [27] *Il.* 23.340; see also *Il.* 5.722 for the plural form κύκλα.

[28] Nagy (1996a: 90).   [29] Campanile (1977: 36).   [30] Nagy (1996a: 90).

[31] For a complete list of the poems attributed by various authors to Homer, see *Cyclus epicus PEG* T 10 (= *3^A D.).

[32] See especially below, p. 30.

Peripatetic reading list[33] or it may have been a Hellenistic creation resulting from the tendency of the Alexandrian Museum to establish canons of ancient literary genres.[34] But long before the fourth century, there already existed some notion of a connected series of epic poems that were either all associated with the Trojan War (and giving a complete 'circular' view of this war) or encompassed a broader mythical history that included the establishment of the divine world and the greatest wars of the heroic age (both Trojan and Theban).[35] In fact, it is important to note that since the Cyclic epics were based on earlier epics that were orally composed, Cyclic poetry emerged from the same performance culture as Homeric poetry.[36] The Epic Cycle as a static list of texts containing material that stretches from the creation of the divine world to the end of the age of heroes will have emerged as only one step in the gradual evolution of a performance culture that was once very much alive and did not necessarily pursue the same selective drift as the later list.

Based on these observations, we will posit an evolutionary model for the development of the Epic Cycle that includes six stages or phases. In the first stage, Cyclic poetry constitutes a mythological 'supertext',[37] on which Homeric epic, early lyric and in particular choral poetry regularly feed. At this stage the Epic Cycle is a sort of gallery of oral traditions, not a clear-cut construct. The second stage finds expression in a Cyclic performance culture that is centered and contextualized in, but not limited to, the Panathenaic festival at Athens. At this stage, we can see how the performance of portions of these epics may have been accommodated to the time-frame of a single day set aside for musical and rhapsodic contests.[38] The third stage reflects two important changes in the evolution of the Epic Cycle: the first pertains to the creation of a fixed copy of the Cyclic poems, which was rapidly arranged into a written form, the second to their new function as a reading list, a series of texts arranged according to the relative chronology of the events they narrated. This reading list must have contained the Trojan epics but, very likely, included the Theban epics as well. A further stage in the

---

[33] Cf. West (2003: 3). [34] See below, pp. 9, 29.
[35] See West (1983) for the distinction between a prototypical Trojan Cycle and the broader Epic Cycle first documented with certainty by Athenaeus.
[36] Cyclic lays or oral traditions that are pre-Homeric must be kept distinguished from the written Cyclic epics that are post-Homeric as well as from the creation of a unified canon of epic poetry, the Epic Cycle, which may go back to the fourth century BC. See Reichel (2011: 69 n. 3).
[37] Dowden (1996: 51).
[38] See Burgess (2004b: 8). On a reconstruction of the Panathenaea, see Neils (1992: 13–27). On rhapsodic contests in Sicyon, see below, pp. 11–12, and Torres-Guerra and Debiasi, below in this volume, respectively pp. 241 and 278–80.

evolution of the Epic Cycle would have taken place during the Hellenistic period, when the Alexandrian poets' studies of the Homeric text and their assiduous use of cyclic material re-created the Cycle as the canonical reading list of non-Homeric poetry. At some point, most probably in the Hellenistic period, the series of individual poems narrating different phases of the war at Troy may have undergone a sort of editorial reworking, which modified (especially) their beginnings and endings to reduce overlaps and better streamline the *akolouthia* of the narrated events. It would probably have been only at this point that the original reading list was reshaped into the organic corpus that we can see behind Proclus' summaries.

The next stage involved the creation of prose summaries of the actual poems of the Epic Cycle. This is a definite indication that Cyclic poetry was no longer widely read, perhaps because it had been eclipsed by the pre-eminence of its Homeric counterpart. These prose summaries were mainly used in mythological compendia and began to exercise their own influence on the notion of the Epic Cycle with which we are familiar today. From this extended period stretching from the Imperial age to the early phases of Late Antiquity derives the most informative and authoritative piece of information about the content of the Epic Cycle, i.e. the summaries of Proclus.

Last, we can posit a sixth stage taking place during the Middle Ages, when the Trojan War summaries of Proclus were excerpted and included in manuscripts of the *Iliad*, in order to supply readers with background information. It is at this point that the evolution of the Epic Cycle is completed. The initial, notional, oral 'supertext'[39] has finally become an excerpt added to the margins of the text of the *Iliad*. One can hardly fail to notice the irony of this outcome, since this last phase functions as a metaphor for the ultimate subjugation of Cyclic poetry to Homeric poetry: having gradually lost its independence, it continued its life only in service of its mighty counterpart.

A NOTIONAL EPIC CYCLE

The idea of an early or notional Epic Cycle should not strike us as odd. The existence of a Sumerian Bilgames cycle or a Hurrian-Hittite Kumarbi cycle or even a Heracles cycle, which are all highly likely, suggest that something

---

[39] See Burgess (2005: 345): 'The Epic Cycle represents a literary manifestation of a longstanding notional arrangement of early Greek myth.'

of the same sort could have also existed in a loose form for the Theban and Trojan War myths. The basic difference though is that whereas Near Eastern cycles and the saga of Heracles were attached to a specific figure, each of the Theban and Trojan War cycles grew around a major event.[40] It is exactly this point of divergence that may have exercised considerable pressure to create a notional Epic Cycle, i.e. the fact that these two major events (the Theban War and its aftermath and the Trojan war and its aftermath) contained a series of interrelated episodes that almost 'asked for' a basically linear presentation.

Even a cursory reading of the summary of the *Cypria* shows that 'almost every event... was causally bound to the events which preceded and followed it'.[41] This observation is of crucial importance for an exploration of early notions of the Epic Cycle. Since the oral traditions relating the events of the Trojan War outside the time-frame of the Homeric epics covered the entire mythical span from the Apple of Discord to the death of Odysseus, an aetiological dimension may well be one of their recurring features. In this context, it is important that in the minds of the ancient Greeks the Trojan tradition formed a coherent whole, a continuous mythical tale with a clear-cut beginning and end. Evidence for this early notion of a Trojan War cycle can be found in lyric poetry[42] as well as – first and foremost – in the Homeric epics. The *Iliad* and *Odyssey* offer a series of allusions to all the epics belonging to the Trojan section of the Epic Cycle, which makes it not unthinkable that some early notion of a gallery of oral traditions pertaining to the Trojan War did indeed exist. For example, the *Odyssey* contains a highly condensed summary of the entire Trojan expedition and its aftermath with references to events featured in the *Cypria*, the *Iliad*, the *Aethiopis*, the *Ilias parva*, the *Iliou persis* and the *Nostoi*.[43] Nestor's elliptical 'Epic Cycle' (*Od.* 3.103–200) reflects what at the time of the shaping of the *Odyssey* must have been known as a set of mythical events pertaining to the Trojan War expedition. His version is highly abbreviated (it excludes those *Nostoi* that were not of prime importance to the subject matter of the *Odyssey*), and it covertly reflects not only the audience's knowledge of these stories but also their familiarity with their forming a coherent thematic whole. Further evidence lies in the fact that the alternative versions of Odysseus' return featuring

---

[40] See West (2011b: 30–1) and his contribution to this volume, pp. 96–7.
[41] Scaife (1995: 174). [42] See Noussia-Fantuzzi, below in this volume, pp. 430–2.
[43] *Cypria*: 3.105–106 (Teuthrania and twelve other towns plundered by Achilles; see West (2011b, 43)); *Iliad*: 3.110 (death of Patroclus); *Aethiopis*: 3.109, 3.111–112 (death of Antilochus); *Ilias parva*: 3.109 (death of Ajax the Telamonian – this could also have been part of the *Aethiopis*), 3.120–129 (Achaeans debate what to do and Odysseus' plan prevails); *Iliou persis*: 3.130 (sack of Troy); *Nostoi*: 3.131–200 (strife in the Greek army, divine punishment, returns of the various Achaean leaders).

in the *Odyssey*'s false tales display a cyclic nature or impulse, since they reproduce narratives that present not only thematic but mainly qualitative analogies with the poems of the Cycle, and in particular the *Nostoi*.

There was a developing tendency within epic, then, to consider the great Panhellenic war against Troy and its aftermath as a continuous and single mythical entity. Furthermore, a significant number of Stesichorus' poems (*Iliou persis, Oresteia, Nostoi, Helen*) also stem from narratives pertaining both to the Homeric epics and the Epic Cycle, and it is thus possible that a pre-Stesichorean choral tradition reflected an early notion of a Trojan War cycle.[44]

The same remark on an aetiological element that establishes the continuity of the Trojan events applies to the Theban sub-cycle as well, since the early mythical history of Thebes is intricately entwined with the subsequent expeditions of the Seven and the Epigonoi. In particular, we are in a position to suggest that the Theban epics (probably the *Thebaid* and the *Epigonoi*) were considered at least by the end of the seventh century as forming a poetic sub-cycle of mythical traditions pertaining to the two expeditions against Thebes. According to Herodotus (5.67.1), after the completion of the war against the Argives, Cleisthenes, who was tyrant of Sicyon, banned the performance of *Homēreia epea* in Sicyon because of the praise they bestowed on the Argives and Argos. We have deliberately refrained from translating the Greek phrase *Homēreia epea*, which constitutes an interpretive conundrum: does Herodotus mean the Homeric epics or the Theban ones? An echo of either the *Thebaid* or the *Epigonoi* has been traced in Tyrtaeus,[45] and the attribution of the Theban epics to Homer is attested for the archaic and even the classical period. Callinus of Ephesus specifically assigns the *Thebaid* to Homer;[46] Homer is credited by Simonides of Ceos with a narrative of Meleager's victory in spear-throwing at the funeral games of Pelias, which may have been in the *Thebaid*,[47] and by Pindar[48] with a narrative of the way Odysseus managed to seem worthier than Ajax to inherit the arms of Achilles, which may have been a passage of the *Aethiopis* or the *Ilias parva*. Last but not least Herodotus expresses his doubts as to the attribution of the

---

[44] On questions pertaining to the influence of this tradition on an early fixation of the Homeric poems, see Burkert (1987: 43–62).
[45] Tyrt. *IEG* F 12: γλῶσσαν δ' Ἀδρήστου μειλιχόγηρυν ἔχοι ('he has the soft-voiced tongue of Adrastus').
[46] Call. *IEG* F 6 (= Paus. 9.9.5): see Bethe (1891a: 147–8); Torres-Guerra, below in this volume, p. 228.
[47] Simon. *PMG* F 564.4 (= Athen. 4.172e). See Cingano (1985: 38 n. 25) with further bibliography.
[48] *Nem.* 7.20–8.

Epigonoi to Homer,[49] which attests to a debate concerning the authorship of the Theban epics that continued well into the fifth century BC.[50] Given (i) that the Argives and Argos are not specifically praised in Homer nor does the label 'Argives' have connotations different from national terms like 'Danaans' and 'Achaeans', (ii) that Cleisthenes replaced in Sicyon the cult of Adrastus, who was a symbol of Argive might, with the cult of the Theban Melanippus, i.e. a man most hateful to Adrastus, since he had killed Adrastus' brother Mecisteus and his son-in-law Tydeus[51] and (iii) that the initial verse of the *Thebaid* (Ἄργος ἄειδε, θεά, πολυδίψιον, ἔνθεν ἄνακτες… 'Sing, goddess, of thirsty Argos, from where the lords…') explicitly points to Argos,[52] it is likely that Cleisthenes did ban the Theban epics and that Herodotus is either attributing them directly to Homer or designating them as composed by rhapsodes specializing in 'Homeric' poetry.[53] If this line of thought holds true, we can surmise that a Theban epic as a whole (and perhaps not just one poem) could be performed in Sicyon before Cleisthenes (600–570 BC), i.e. during the seventh century BC. In this light, it may be claimed that Theban epic had already acquired, like its Homeric counterpart, some form of unity, as performance conditions and hero cult also strongly suggest.[54]

Seen from this vantage point, the idea of an interconnection between the various oral epics narrating different parts of the same myth seems to have been an almost built-in feature: the notion of unity and sequence was already there. But how did the association of the Theban *with* the Trojan sub-cycle come about? Ultimately, after all, they do not pertain to the same myth. Are there any early attestations of this association? Hesiod's *WD* (156–73) provides strong evidence for a very early pairing of these two traditions:

> Αὐτὰρ ἐπεὶ καὶ τοῦτο γένος κατὰ γαῖα κάλυψεν,
> αὖτις ἔτ' ἄλλο τέταρτον ἐπὶ χθονὶ πουλυβοτείρηι
> Ζεὺς Κρονίδης ποίησε, δικαιότερον καὶ ἄρειον,
> ἀνδρῶν ἡρώων θεῖον γένος, οἳ καλέονται
> ἡμίθεοι, προτέρη γενεὴ κατ' ἀπείρονα γαῖαν.   160

---

[49] Herod. 4.32–33: ἔστι δὲ καὶ Ὁμήρωι ἐν Ἐπιγόνοισι, εἰ δὴ τῶι ἐόντι γε Ὅμηρος ταῦτα τὰ ἔπη ἐποίησε ('and Homer also mentions them [the Hyperboreans] in the *Epigonoi*, if that is really a work of his').
[50] Wilamowitz-Moellendorff (1884: 352). See the discussion in Cingano (1985: 38).
[51] Herod. 5.67.3: ἐπηγάγετο δὲ τὸν Μελάνιππον ὁ Κλεισθένης (καὶ γὰρ τοῦτο δεῖ ἀπηγήσασθαι) ὡς ἔχθιστον ἐόντα Ἀδρήστωι, ὅς τόν τε ἀδελφεόν οἱ Μηκιστέα ἀπεκτόνεε καὶ τὸν γαμβρὸν Τυδέα ('Cleisthenes carried Melanippus back with him (I have to report this) because he was most hateful to Adrastus, since he had killed both his brother Mecisteus and his son-in-law Tydeus').
[52] *PEG* F 1 (= D., W.).   [53] See Huxley (1969: 48–9); Cingano (1985: 31–40).
[54] On Cleisthenes and Theban epic in sixth-century Sicyon, see also Debiasi, below in this volume, p. 278.

καὶ τοὺς μὲν πόλεμός τε κακὸς καὶ φύλοπις αἰνή
τοὺς μὲν ὑφ' ἑπταπύλῳ Θήβῃ, Καδμηίδι γαίῃ,
ὤλεσε μαρναμένους μήλων ἕνεκ' Οἰδιπόδαο,
τοὺς δὲ καὶ ἐν νήεσσιν ὑπὲρ μέγα λαῖτμα θαλάσσης
ἐς Τροίην ἀγαγὼν Ἑλένης ἕνεκ' ἠυκόμοιο. 165
ἔνθ' ἦ τοι τοὺς μὲν θανάτου τέλος ἀμφεκάλυψε
τοῖς δὲ δίχ' ἀνθρώπων βίοτον καὶ ἤθε' ὀπάσσας
Ζεὺς Κρονίδης κατένασσε πατὴρ εἰς πείρατα γαίης.
καὶ τοὶ μὲν ναίουσιν ἀκηδέα θυμὸν ἔχοντες
ἐν μακάρων νήσοισι παρ' Ὠκεανὸν βαθυδίνην, 170
ὄλβιοι ἥρωες, τοῖσιν μελιηδέα καρπὸν
τρὶς ἔτεος θάλλοντα φέρει ζείδωρος ἄρουρα.

> When the earth covered up this race too, Zeus, Cronus' son, made another one in turn upon the bounteous earth, a fourth one, more just and superior, the godly race of men-heroes, who are called demigods, the generation before our own upon the boundless earth. Evil war and dread battle destroyed these, some under seven-gated Thebes in the land of Cadmus while they fought for the sake of Oedipus' sheep, others brought in boats over the great gulf of the sea to Troy for the sake of fair-haired Helen. There the end of death shrouded some of them, but upon others Zeus the father, Cronus' son, bestowed life and habitations far from human beings and settled them at the limits of the earth; and these dwell with a spirit free of care on the Islands of the Blessed beside deep-eddying Ocean – happy heroes, for whom the grain-giving field bears sweet fruit flourishing three times a year.

The race of heroes occupies the fourth place in Hesiod's myth of races. It follows upon the golden, silver and bronze races, and it is placed before the iron one, in which the poet himself belongs. It is important to remember that Hesiod has informed his internal audience, his brother Perses, that he intends to 'recapitulate correctly and skilfully' how gods and humans came from the same origin. In other words, the entire section on the myth of races aims at tracing a continuous and uninterrupted sequence leading from the golden to the iron race, i.e. from the beginning of human history to the present era. This idea of a unified and coherent narrative of divine-human evolution probably had a long prehistory. We thus find the end of the race of heroes embedded within the larger framework of a continuous narrative sequence. Within it, the pairing of the Theban and Trojan wars is instructive. The priority of the former[55] is not only guaranteed by the fact

---

[55] It should be noted that in most mythological compendia and summaries (like Proclus) the Theban epics or Theban myth is dealt with before the Trojan one. The same seems to be the case in the Hesiodic *Catalogue of Women*.

that it is mentioned first in this passage, but mainly through the undisputable influences of the Theban myth on the Homeric *Iliad* (and to a smaller extent the *Odyssey*). When combined with the transfer of heroic figures (Diomedes, Sthenelus, Euryalus) and themes from the Theban to the Trojan saga,[56] this Hesiodic passage becomes a clear testimony to these two mythical subcycles' early association with each other. It is notable that this early pairing of the two poetic traditions is expressed in specifically 'epic' terminology (note that their protagonists are explicitly identified as 'heroes', i.e. subjects of epic poetry). We can therefore assume that the mythical traditions of Thebes and Troy as expressed in epic poetry must by the archaic period (at the latest) have been considered as forming a unity: this particular unity is, however, not one pertaining to a single theme, but one that covers the end of a whole mythical era, that of the age of heroes.[57]

Let us return to the reason that may have caused this association. We are now in a position to argue that certain characteristics shared by Hesiod's all-encompassing mythological poetry as well as by Cyclic epic attest to the gradual onset of that ideological and cultural revolution known as Panhellenism (at this early stage, we may call it Proto-Panhellenism). The emerging tendency to see different traditions as part of just one Epic Cycle is consonant with the general tendency of Panhellenism to downplay local traditions and create a continuous and coherent picture of the heroic age, centered around the two great wars characterized by Panhellenic participation, one on the mainland (Theban) and one against a foreign people (Trojan).[58]

A 'PANATHENAIC' CYCLE

The second stage in the evolution and shaping of the Epic Cycle is associated, mainly but not solely, with the Panathenaic festival at Athens.[59] Since it is widely assumed that only Homeric poetry was performed during

---

[56] See Torres-Guerra (1995a); Kullmann (2002a: 162–76).

[57] The Epic Cycle may also have included a *Theogony* (reflecting Orphic beliefs?; see West (1983: 125–6)) and a *Titanomachy*, which came before the Theban and Trojan sections; see West, below in this volume, pp. 101–2, and D'Alessio, also below.

[58] The creation of a cycle or sub-cycle of epic poems is reinforced both by external and internal factors. The former include performance conditions such as a festival or even larger cultural phenomena like that of Panhellenism, while the latter comprise the epics' aetiological and deterministic nature and high degrees of interconnectedness. On the existence of a Hesiodic cycle based on the interconnectedness of various Hesiodic poems, see Nelson (2005: 333–4).

[59] On the Panathenaea as a context for the performance of Cyclic epic, see Nagy, below in this volume, pp. 62–5.

the Panathenaea in Athens, it is necessary to reconsider the information available to us and address two fundamental questions with respect to the matter at hand: first, how did epic poetry fit in with the specific temporal and organizational constraints of this festival? And second, do our sources point to a continuous, line-by-line performance of Homeric narrative or rather to a discontinuous but thematically coherent relay-performance by multiple rhapsodes?

If only the first day of the eight-day Panathenaic festival was devoted to musical contests and rhapsodic performances, then it is virtually unthinkable that the Homeric poems could have been recited in their entirety. Both time and human limitations show that this scenario cannot stand to reason. The *Iliad* and the *Odyssey* – comprising approximately 27,000 verses – require about twenty-four hours of continuous and uninterrupted recitation to be performed from beginning to end. It is very unlikely that rhapsodes would be performing the Homeric poems without intermissions or that there would be audiences following such a long contest. The same argument applies to other Trojan epics. After all, the complete sequence from the *Cypria* to the end of the *Telegony* includes twenty-nine books. In this light, as Burgess rightly reminds us, the most reasonable solution is that epic poetry was performed in portions and that each rhapsode would pick up the story from the point, not the verse, where the previous rhapsode stopped. The thematic unity of the Trojan sub-cycle guaranteed that both rhapsodes and audience members could easily make the leap from one episode to the other, even if this process unavoidably resulted in some level of discontinuity. There are a handful of factors that strengthen this line of thought.

The existence of an earlier stage or phase during which the Epic Cycle represented a connected whole of epic traditions facilitated the filling-in of narrative gaps by means of a mythologically oriented *pars pro toto* principle. The kind of episodes that were selected by rhapsodes may have been determined by their importance, audience reception and fame, but variation between one Panathenaic festival and another should not be excluded. The particular taste of a given guild may also have played its role, and we should certainly not exclude the possibility that sometimes a rhapsode may have been faced with a difficult choice, if the previous rhapsode had just recited his favored episode. Creative stitching-together is a well-known practice that may in fact be attested in the *Homeric Hymn to Apollo* (cf. Hes. F 357 M.-W.), which 'has thematic unity but is discontinuous in the sense that it has two distinct parts'.[60] Befitting these observations, ancient

---

[60] Burgess (2004b: 15).

sources strongly suggest that the sequence of rhapsodes performing poetry attributed to Homer at some point came to be seen as cause for the reintegration of formerly 'scattered' Homeric epic.[61] Accordingly, the role played by figures like Lycurgus in Sparta and the Peisistratids in Athens with respect to the introduction of Homeric poetry to their respective cities is always presented in the light of the *unification* of Homeric epic that was previously recited in portions.[62] Information of this sort indicates that the relay performance by rhapsodes and their ability to connect formerly disparate parts of epic poetry was a standard practice. At some point, these stories turned into foundational myths explaining 'Homer' and 'Homeric poetry' in their 'fixed' state.

Further support for the inclusion of the Cyclic epics in the performance repertoire of the early Panathenaic festival is offered by some of the poems' linguistic features and thematic additions,[63] in particular by the Attic features that can be observed in the extant fragments of the Cyclic poems. This evidence cannot, however, be used without taking into account a number of other elements, thematic and comparative, that clearly point to a much earlier dating of the Cyclic epics. Thematic accretions[64] show that Cyclic epic traditions existed long before these accretions were made, and the comparative evidence of Stesichorean poetry, which points to the existence of independent traditions concerning distinct phases of the Trojan War saga, should not be ignored. When all factors are considered, then Lesky's and Griffin's argument about a late seventh-century origin for the Cyclic epics still stands. Yet the intrusion of Atticisms, along with the thematic accretions

---

[61] Σ Pind. *Nem.* 2.1d. See Nagy (1996a: 83–4).

[62] Ps.-Plat. *Hipparchus* 228b-c; Ael. *VH* 13.14; Plut. *Life of Lycurgus* 4.4. See also Diog. Laert. 1.57.

[63] Davies (1989a: 89) notes that in his influential 1977 article 'The Epic Cycle and the Uniqueness of Homer', Griffin refers to Wackernagel's dating of the Epic Cycle around the fifth century BC, but prefers, following Lesky, a late seventh-century date. Then, Davies (1989a: 90–100) himself reconsiders the linguistic arguments of Wackernagel (and Wilamowitz) and argues for a date just before the beginning of the fifth century.

[64] See Debiasi (2004: 132 n. 58, 206–207); for further examples, see Burgess (2001: 152, 247 n. 75). Consider the following formulation by Nagy (2010a: 320): 'Before the fifth century... Homer was viewed in Athens as the poet who created the epic Cycle as well as the two epics that we know as the *Iliad* and the *Odyssey*. Such a preclassical point of view can be situated in the era of the Peisistratidai, in the second half of the sixth century BCE, when the epics of the epic Cycle were still being performed in Athens: evidence for Athenian performances at that time can be found in patterns of Athenian accretions embedded in both the form and the content of such epics as the *Aithiopis* and the *Iliou persis* and the *Ilias parva*. For example, in the case of the *Iliou persis* attributed to Arctinus of Miletus, there is mention of the rescue of the mother of Theseus by the Athenian hero's two sons Akamas and Demophon after the capture of Troy (*Il. pers.* arg. lines 271–2 Severyns); there is another such mention of these figures in the *Ilias parva* attributed to Lesches of Lesbos (*PEG* F 20 = F 23 D., F 17 W. ap. Pausanias 10.25.8).' On the performance of epic poetry at the early Panathenaea, see Nagy (2010a: 69–73).

that are also of Attic provenance, strongly indicates that the Cyclic epics, like their Homeric counterparts, were especially prominent in Athens. In the light of the fact that Homer was considered the poet of not only the *Iliad* and the *Odyssey* but also of a good deal of Cyclic poetry,[65] these Attic features (thematic accretions and linguistic elements alike) reflect exactly this stage in the evolution of Cyclic poetry. In fact, it may not be a coincidence that *PEG* F 1 (= D., W.) of the *Cypria*, which may have been performed regularly in the relay performance of Cyclic and Homeric epic in the early phases of the Panathenaea, is 'particularly rich in "late" linguistic features',[66] since it would have been liable to the most frequent influence exercised by rhapsodes.[67]

In addition to these arguments, studies of the period's artistic conventions have recently made a rather compelling case that supports our argument.[68] In particular, the existence of a type of iconographical representation called 'cyclic' or 'syntagmatic',[69] in which the same topic is depicted in multiple, separate images 'following each other sequentially in time', points to a working analogy with the aforementioned practice of rhapsodic performance.[70]

---

[65] See below, pp. 21–8.

[66] The proem of the *Cypria* is indeed a special case but not for the reasons suggested by Davies (1989a: 98).

[67] For an overview on the language of the extant Cyclic fragments and the questions pertaining to the date of the relevant epics from a linguistic point of view, see Bernabé, below in this volume. See also Janko (1982: *passim*) who draws attention to the fact that a significant number of the so-called Atticisms are not real Atticisms and that the extremely limited number of actual cyclic verses that survive constitute serious drawbacks when arguing for the lateness of the Cyclic epics.

[68] Although there is a heated debate on our ability to link iconographic representations with specific Homeric or Cyclic poems, two things stand beyond doubt: first, that 'cyclic' representations are much more popular in art than their Homeric counterparts, and, second, that there is a striking correspondence between the 'cyclic' scenes depicted and the content of the relevant episodes in the actual Cyclic epics. In our view, such widespread correspondence shows that 'these poems accurately continued a stable tradition about the Trojan War' (Burgess 2001: 43).

[69] Some scholars have even argued that artists were inspired, at least at times, neither by their general knowledge of myth nor by some visual source like painting, but by oral performances of a given epic. In fact, iconographical discrepancies between representations of the same theme in archaic vase paintings may be explained in such terms; see Stewart (1983: 63, with n. 30); Scaife (1995: 177–8).

[70] See Burgess (2004b: 9–10). There are two other types of iconographical representation, i.e. monoscenic and synoptic iconography. In the former only one time and place is being depicted, while in the latter a single image includes different time frames and actions. On cyclic or syntagmatic iconography, see Robert (1881: 46–7); Weitzmann (1970: 12–36); Stansbury-O'Donnell (1999: 136–55). On the early example of Theseus' cups employing cyclic iconography, see Neils (1987: 143–8); Neils & Woodford (1994: nos. 32–60). On Hellenistic

The so-called 'Panathenaic Regulation', i.e. the performance of epic poetry at the Panathenaea by rhapsodes in a sequence, is generally assumed to apply to Homeric poetry alone, the more so since ancient sources clearly refer to 'Homer' and 'Homer's *epea*'. But, as we have seen in the case of the Theban poems, the term 'Homer' or 'Homeric poetry' was used for *any* kind of epic poetry attributed to Homer, which included not only the *Iliad* and the *Odyssey* but also the Theban epics and Cyclic poetry.[71] Further indirect evidence for this phenomenon is the importance attributed by major fifth-century Athenian tragedians to Cyclic poetry. Athenaeus' famous statements that Aeschylus considered his plays to be 'slices from Homer's banquet'[72] and that 'Sophocles was pleased (ἔχαιρε) with the Epic Cycle',[73] as well as Euripides' predilection for Cyclic rather than Homeric themes, indicates that fifth-century Attic tragedy was especially familiar with and fond of Cyclic poetry. This phenomenon is easy to account for if Cyclic poetry was indeed included in the relay performance tradition of the Panathenaic festival. Since there was a growing impact of this festival on Athenian cultural life, Cyclic poetry under the name of Homer would have been particularly cherished and diffused among fifth-century poets and audiences,[74] and became such an important part of Athenian cultural life, because or after it had played an important part in the most important cultural event of the Panathenaea in the previous decades.[75] It is also plausible that within this environment a vivid discussion began with respect to archaic epic under the name of Homer. The Panathenaic festival may have paved the way for the future qualitative reappraisal of the *Iliad* and the *Odyssey* versus the other Cyclic epics, for it had actually created a 'living workshop' for their comparison. Listening to the performance of portions from all these poems would no doubt have facilitated the growth of evaluative thinking with respect to their qualities.[76] This process required an extended period of time, until Aristotle and his school tipped the scales

examples like the Homeric bowls, see Sinn (1979); on Roman examples like the *Tabulae Iliacae*, see Sadurska (1964); Valenzuela Montenegro (2004); Squire (2011); on both Homeric bowls and *Tabulae*, Squire, below in this volume, pp. 497–9 and 502–12.

[71] See Pfeiffer (1968: 44 n. 3, 73).   [72] Athen. 8.347e = Aesch. *TrGF* 112a.
[73] Athen. 7.277e = Soph. *TrGF* T 136. See below in this volume, p. 408.
[74] We are not arguing that fifth-century poets became familiar with Cyclic epic through the Panathenaea. We are simply maintaining that the epic poetry performed at a certain period in the Panathenaea would be more diffused and treasured by audiences and this, to a certain extent, influenced choices of subject matter made by poets.
[75] See Nagy (1996a: 37–9; 2010a: 50–8, 69–73, 330).
[76] See Finkelberg (1998: 140).

in favor of the *Iliad* and *Odyssey* and thereby took an important step toward turning the Epic Cycle into a separate group of non-Homeric poems.[77]

THE HISTORICAL CYCLE

It has been convincingly argued that epic poetry was one of the principal models for Greek historiography.[78] The influence of the former on the latter was both intensive and extensive: general historical concepts like Greek national consciousness, the struggle between East and West, questions of causality, method, and truth, the structuring of time[79] and space in narration, the emphasis on warfare, literary devices like catalogues and *ekphrasis*-type descriptions, as well as narrative technique (the combination of simple narration (*diegesis*) and speeches (*mimesis*), and disclosure of the characters' inner world (internal focalization))[80] had already been developed by archaic Greek epic and were to serve as a model for Greek historiographical writing.[81]

Apart from these influences that archaic Greek epic is known to have exercised on Greek historiography, there is also a striking parallel between the tendency of each of the Cyclic epics to begin where a previous epic had ended, and the trend of the Ionian-Attic historians to begin their historical accounts from the point where their predecessor left off. Describing the latter phenomenon in terms of the former, Luciano Canfora has tellingly employed the term 'historical cycle' ('ciclo storico').[82] As we have already pointed out above, Canfora referred to a series of historians, including Hecataeus, Herodotus, Thucydides, Xenophon and Theopompus, who try to create a link with the work of one of their predecessors.

There is, however, a notable difference: except for Xenophon and Theompompus, who begin their *Hellenica* where Thucydides left off, all other historians have no single common topic that is being narrated. Rather, there is a wider chronological *akolouthia tōn pragmatōn* in the sense that

---

[77] For a detailed discussion of all the points in this paragraph, see Fantuzzi, below in this volume.
[78] The volume on Greek historiography in the *Greek and Rome Surveys* (Marincola 2001), for instance, correctly starts with Homer. According to Strabo 1.2.6 the most ancient historians such as Cadmus, Pherecydes and Hecataeus 'dissolved the metre but preserved most of the qualities of poetry'.
[79] Rengakos (2006: 209).
[80] See Huber (1965: 29–52); Fornara (1983: 31); Erbse (1992); Lendle (1992: 62); de Jong (1999: 217–75).
[81] See Rengakos (2006: 183).   [82] Canfora (1971) = (1999).

these historians struggle to show that their work is somehow linked to the work of a famous predecessor who has dealt with equivalent material. Herodotus begins his work by stating that he intends to refrain from discussing the more remote phase of the conflict between the Greeks and the barbarians. In this way he creates a formal link to genealogical literature, whose continuator he is.[83] Along similar lines, the *Pentecontaetia* in Thucydides' history begins with a rather insignificant event, i.e. the capture of Sestos by the Athenians. This has been recognized as a clear effort to create a bridge to the end of Herodotus' history.[84] Xenophon's *Hellenica* begin with the famous *meta de tauta*, a clear indication not only that Xenophon intends to continue Thucydides' history but also that he takes it for granted that his readers are familiar with the scope of the work of his predecessor. For Theopompus the narrative continuity between Herodotus and Thucydides was readily apparent. According to Jacoby,[85] the fact that Theopompus picks up the narrative where Thucydides had stopped (T 19) – taken together with his compilation of an *Epitome of Herodotus* in two books – shows that he was aiming to place his work within a larger narrative sequence. However, his minute presentation of a much shorter period (twelve books covering eighteen years, from 411 to 394 BC) than the one narrated by Xenophon (seven books covering fifty years, from 411 to 362 BC) indicates – given that Theopompus had seen the publication of both Xenophon's *Hellenica* and of the *Hellenica Oxyrhynchia* – that he was aiming to rival rather than endorse other writers who had continued Thucydides' history.

Another crucial point made by Canfora concerns the reasons that may have caused this historiographical trend. He argues that the agonistic framework within which these historians operated, their struggle to find a specific point of departure for their narrative, and the fact that they may have considered the work of their predecessor unfinished are the three key factors that have stimulated the tendency to begin where a previous historian had ended his work. Returning to the Epic Cycle, we can maintain that these same three factors also contributed to creating the notable points of overlap between the Cyclic poems. We do not need to say much about the agonistic framework within which epic poetry did indeed develop and blossom.[86]

---

[83] Canfora (1971 = 1999: 76–7).
[84] See Wilamowitz (1893: 26–7); Jacoby (1909: 100 and n. 2); Canfora (1971 = 1999: 77).
[85] (1909: 104 n. 2).
[86] Outside Athens, see e.g. Herod. 5.67.1: 'Cleisthenes, when he was at war with Argos, put an end to the contests of the rhapsodes at Sicyon (ἔπαυσε ἐν Σικυῶνι ἀγωνίζεσθαι τῶν Ὁμηρείων ἐπέων εἵνεκα), because in the Homeric poems Argos and the Argives were so constantly the theme of song' (τὰ πολλὰ πάντα ὑμνέαται).

The struggle to find a point of departure is a typical motif in epic poetry, traces of which are easily discernible in the proems of the two extant Homeric epics.[87] And the fact that these features of the Epic Cycle are no longer visible in Proclus' summaries may simply be due to the operation of Proclus or earlier compilers who smoothed over such other features of the breaks in the service of enhancing the exclusive sense and target of continuity.

AUTHORS AND AUTHORSHIP

The poems comprising what is first attested in Athenaeus (7.277e) as the 'Epic Cycle' existed long before this global term was used to designate a collection that included them. Both before and after the time the collection was arranged and the name came to be applied to it, the single poems were frequently quoted in isolation. In the archaic age all of them were most probably ascribed to Homer, but at least from the beginning of the sixth century they started to be attributed to different individual authors. Later on, all biographical speculation was abandoned, and while the poems continued to be attributed to different authors, these authors were now usually quoted as anonymous. According to the diachrony correctly schematized by Wilamowitz, all these poems 'in 500 BC are by Homer; in 350 only the *Iliad* and the *Odyssey* are by Homer, and all the other poems are conjecturally ascribed to this or that author, and a few still to Homer as well; at about 150 all the conjectures are discarded and the poems become all anonymous... the mass of poems which were once uniformly Homeric had been apportioned among an uncertain number of authors, but now they became a unity again, but this unity consisted in its negation'.[88]

Wilamowitz's scepticism on the historicity of the Cyclic authors is perhaps a bit radical (it is evident that at least Arctinus continued to be quoted as the author of the *Aethiopis* and the *Iliou persis*).[89] But there is no doubt that the attribution of authorship to the Cyclic poems was very shaky. One major difference between the *Iliad* and the *Odyssey* on the one hand, and the Cyclic poems on the other, is that nobody among the ancients doubted the authorship of the first two poems, but doubts about the Cyclic poems started to occur as early as the fifth century. Back in the sixth century, Callinus had still insisted that Homer also composed

---

[87] See Tsagalis (2005: 61–2).
[88] Wilamowitz (1884: 353–4); see also Allen (1908: 88); Graziosi (2002: 166).
[89] Cf. Merkelbach (1969: 139–41).

the *Thebaid*.[90] Differently, in order to explain a variance between the *Iliad* and the *Cypria* regarding the trip of Paris' and Helen's ship back to Troy from Sparta (*PEG* T 4 / F 14 = F 11 / T 5 D., F 14 W.), Herodotus (2.117) states without hesitation that this 'makes quite clear that the *Cypria* is not by Homer but by someone else' (the opposite, namely the idea that the *Cypria* and the other poems of the 'Cycle' are by Homer, and the *Iliad* by someone else, does not even cross Herodotus' mind). Herodotus' approach to this variance also shows that he had so high an opinion of Homer – the Homer of the *Iliad* – as to exclude the possibility that he could contradict himself.[91] A similar stance makes sense in a passage where Herodotus argues that the Hyperboreans do not exist, despite the fact that Hesiod and the *Epigonoi* deal with them. He introduces the latter poem as 'of Homer', but promptly adds the qualification 'if Homer really composed this poem', which saves Homer from a more substantial charge of unreliability (4.32 = *Epig. PEG* F 2 = F 2 D., F 5 W.).[92] A mistake in the *Epigonoi* is enough for Herodotus to suspect that this poem may not be by Homer. This says as much about the feebleness with which Homeric authorship is ascribed to the Cyclic *Epigonoi* as it does about the greatness of Homer.

The doubts about Homeric authorship certainly proliferated after Herodotus, and there consequently proliferated the ascriptions of the Cyclic poems to individual authors different from Homer. But we see from many hints that all these different ascriptions did not manage to become a widely accepted standard. Homer's long shadow kept casting doubt on alternative 'paternities'. Close in time to Herodotus, Pindar (F 265 (= *PEG* T2 = T1D. = p. 64 W.)) 'is the authority' (as Aelian maintains) for the story that Homer 'gave away' the *Cypria* to his daughter as her dowry. This anecdote features again with a slight modification in Photius and the *Suda*, *PEG* T 1 (= T 2 D.) and T 7 (= T 3 D., p. 66 W.): Homer is supposed to have given the *Cypria* as a dowry for his daughter to his son-in-law Stasinus (this Stasinus is in fact most commonly remembered as the author of the *Cypria*). Pindar may certainly have focused *also* on the fact that the *Cypria*, with all its weddings and love stories (Peleus and Thetis, Helen and Menelaus, Helen and Paris, Helen and Achilles) as well as the key role played by Aphrodite, was 'the most apt as

---

[90] The name 'Callinus' is a conjecture in the relevant passage of Pausanias (*Theb. PEG* T 2; see Torres-Guerra, below in this volume, p. 228), but Pausanias quotes Callinus six other times as a source (Allen (1924: 61)), which makes him a likely candidate.

[91] An opinion that is probably rooted in the same viewpoint about the Panhellenic relevance of Homer that led Hipparchus to the attempt at standardizing a Homer *ne varietur* for the Panathenaea: cf. Graziosi (2002: 198–9).

[92] Cf. Graziosi (2002: 195); Cingano, below in this volume, pp. 244–5.

a wedding gift'; besides, Pindar may *also* have used this anecdote to demonstrate that Homer was generous.[93] But Aelian narrates Pindar's anecdote just after remembering that the Argives 'invited both Apollo and Homer when they made sacrifices' to the god, a fact that is supposed to prove that they 'accorded Homer the first place as a poet, and made all others second to him'. In this context a story proving the generosity of Homer's soul would be less pertinent than a story proving that Homer was such a great poet that he could afford to give away one of his poems (this is independent of the question whether Pindar stated that the poem went to Homer's daughter or to her husband Arctinus – the idea of dowry-gift certainly presupposes that the poem's final destination was a husband).[94] Therefore, Pindar's anecdote may at least *also* be a reflection of the various ascriptions to authors other than Homer of the poems of the Epic Cycle originally supposed to be Homeric. The fact that they were 'given away' as 'presents' by the original owner of the whole original patrimony of epic narratives symbolizes the legitimate but limited authorships of the new authors: the ancient biographers, and Pindar as an occasional 'historian' of epic before them, may have preserved in this story the nostalgic idea of a unified Ur-corpus traditionally ascribed to Homer.

The story acknowledges Stasinus' right to the poem, but this newer 'author' would only have 'possessed' at a secondary level what Homer had possessed first, and only later given away. This idea of secondary possession seems in fact close to the modern metaphorical idea of a re-worker/re-performer, more than a real plagiarist. A story of *actual* plagiarism would have been that of Thestorides of Phocaea, also known as the author of the *Cypria*: according to the *Life of Homer* ascribed to Herodotus (chap. 15 = *Ilias parva PEG* T 8 = T 1 D.) Homer entrusted to him a written recording of the *Ilias parva* and the *Phocais*, but Thestorides 'formed the plan of going away from Phocaea, because he wanted to appropriate Homer's poetry' and settled in Chios, where he started to pass the two poems as his own.[95]

Stasinus' secondary authorship of the *Cypria* was not only weak in comparison with Homer's primacy, but it also encountered a number of rival 'secondary' candidates: Athenaeus and Photius ascribe the poem to Hegesinus of Salamis/Hegesias (*PEG* T 7 = T 3 D., p. 66 W. and *PEG* T 8 = T 12 / F 4 D., F 5 W.), whereas a second-century BC inscription recently found at Halicarnassus (*SEGO* 01/12/02 Merkelbach-Stauber) and perhaps Athenaeus (*PEG* T 8 = T 12 / F 4 D., F 5 W. and *PEG* T 9 =

---

[93] Graziosi (2002: 187–9).
[94] Merkelbach (1969: 141 n. 2) remarked that the name of Stasinus must have been implied, though it was not expressed by Aelian.
[95] See Nagy, below in this volume, pp. 69–77; also Cassio (2003: 38–40).

F 7 D. = F 10 W.) suggest Kyprías of Halicarnassus. Nor was the *Cypria*'s case an isolated one: an *Amazonia* (= *Aethiopis*) was ascribed to Homer (although the title *Aethiopis* only goes with Arctinus), the *Ilias parva* mainly to Lesches, but also to Homer, Cinaethon of Sparta, Diodoros of Erythrae or Thestorides of Phocaea; the *Nostoi* to Homer, Agias or Eumelus. By contrast, the *Telegony* seems to have been known only as the work of Eugammon of Cyrene,[96] and certainly the *Aethiopis* and the *Iliou persis* are regularly quoted as works of Arctinus.[97] However even in this case Homer's original overarching control over the whole archaic epic production influenced the way the ancients fictionalized the personality of Arctinus: Artemon of Clazomenae, a pre-Hellenistic scholar of perhaps the fourth century,[98] took care to specify in his work *On Homer* (*FgrHist* 443 F 2) that Arctinus was a 'student' (μαθητής) of Homer.

The most paradoxical level of interchangeability between Homer and other epic authors was perhaps reached with the anecdotes on the *Capture of Oechalia*, an epic poem celebrating one of Heracles' deeds, which never belonged to the Epic Cycle, at least according to our ancient sources. Most commonly, it seems, the poem was ascribed to Creophylus, whose birthplace was contested: Samos or Chios.[99] Creophylus was supposed to have hosted Homer in his house, and thus received from Homer as a gift in return for Creophylus' hospitality the 'ascription' (ἐπιγραφή) of the poem (Strabo: *PEG* T 8 = T 3 D., p. 172 W. and *Suda*: *PEG* T 6 = T 5 D., p. 174 W.).[100] According to this version, Creophylus was either Homer's son-in-law or

---

[96] If *PEG* T 2 (= T 4 D.) has to be corrected, as is commonly believed, and Eusebius did not ascribe the *Telegony* to Cinaethon.

[97] This may have depended on the fact that Arctinus was a more solid figure of literary history than the other Cyclic poets; he is the only poet of the Epic Cycle to get a rather circumstantial life in *Suda*.

[98] *FgrHist* iii.b (Komm.) pp. 290–1.

[99] Panyassis, another epic author who wrote on Heracles and lived in the first half of the fifth century, was said to have tried to 'steal' the poem from Creophylus, and to circulate it under his name – this anecdote (probably late: attested in Clement of Alexandria: *PEG* T 7 = T 8 D.) may have symbolized the similarity of subject matter (Heracles' deeds) between the works of Creophylus and Panyassis; in the third century Pha(e)nias of Eresus wrote similarly about Lesches and Stasinus (see below).

[100] The anecdote seems to have been conceived perhaps as the aition of the foundation of the guild of bards called 'Creophyleioi' (the same metaphor of the rhapsodic 'continuation' of Homer may of course be applied to Stasinus): cf. Burkert (1972: 67–80); Graziosi (2002: 187 and 190). Just as the anecdote on the *Cypria* as a wedding poem presented by Homer as a dowry to Stasinus, the anecdote on Creophylus is constructed around a gift of hospitality. Both in the epic and in the anecdote that grew around its composition, a breach of the hospitality probably formed the core of the plot (in the epic, Heracles, hosted by Eurytus at Oechalia, falls in love with his daughter Iole; when Eurytus later refuses to marry her to him, Heracles sacks Oechalia): see Graziosi (2002: 191–2).

just his friend (Plat. *Rep.* 10.600b and Σ: *PEG* T 3 = T 1 D. and *PEG* T 4 = T 7 D.). Other ancient scholars pointed to a radically different kind of relation with Homer, and described Creophylus as Homer's teacher (Strabo 14.639). Callimachus, possibly reshaping the anecdote of the gift in rationalistic terms, supports the idea that Creophylus was in fact the unappreciated author of the poem, both to express his surprise that it could in seriousness be considered 'Homeric' and to criticize with subtle irony poets whose imitation of Homer was so close that they not only risked annihilating their own identity, but were even happy with this result[101] (the epigram is transmitted by Strab. 14.638 = *HE* 1293ff. = *PEG* T 7 = T 2 D., p. 172 W.):

Τοῦ Σαμίου πόνος εἰμὶ δόμωι ποτὲ θεῖον ἀοιδόν
   δεξαμένου, κλείω δ' Εὔρυτον ὅσσ' ἔπαθεν,
καὶ ξανθὴν Ἰόλειαν, Ὁμήρειον δὲ καλεῦμαι
   γράμμα· Κρεωφύλωι, Ζεῦ φίλε, τοῦτο μέγα.

I am the work of the Samian, who once received in his house the divine bard, and I celebrate what Eurytus endured and the flaxen-haired Iole. But I am called a writing of Homer – dear Zeus, a great compliment for Creophylus!

Not unusually for his poetics, Callimachus seems to have intended to contribute with this epigram not only to the debate on the birthplace of Creophylus (the ethnic label in its emphatic position at the beginning of the poem even replaces the name of Creophylus) but also to the one on the authorship of the poem, which the thriving biographical activity of the Hellenistic scholars and the increasing bibliographic needs of the Library of Alexandria will certainly have stimulated.[102] After many centuries of epigrams inscribed on statues, this epigram gave voice to a book, and should be imagined as conceived for the colophon of a papyrus roll. Epigraphical conventions marked the utterances of a speaking object as a very reliable voice, and the single possible witness from an otherwise unrecoverable past. In an age of hot debate about the (Homeric or un-Homeric) authorship of archaic epic poems, it was a typically Callimachean insight that the book itself could proclaim who its author was and what was the great achievement of this author (merging himself into Homer's identity). But at the same time the author of the epigram does not miss the opportunity to hint at his

---

[101] The tone of the epigram, however, is not aggressive, and the disparaging hint only faint: cf. Eichgrün (1961: 69) and Cameron (1995: 400–1).
[102] Cf. Burkert (1972: 75).

skepticism about the greatness of this achievement. Similarly, the talking cock monument of Callim. *AP* 6.149 = *HE* 1161ff. confirms the affirmations of the dedicator, but it also humorously makes clear that if an object 'speaks', it can only and unavoidably be the biased spokesman of the dedicator. The papyrus roll of which the epigram pretends to be the colophon can only record/advertise the viewpoint of Creophylus, who was happy to merge his identity into the name of Homer. However, the dative *Kreōphylōi* on the one hand openly ascribes this statement to its author, on the other ambiguously delimits the applicability of the same statement. 'For Creophylus it is a great achievement to disappear into the name of Homer', says the colophon. 'But only for him', will imply Callimachus, if the last phrase is interpreted, as it suggests itself, as a comment by the author of the epigram.

The bio-bibliographical struggle that Callimachus' epigram playfully bypasses by recording (though destabilizing) the authoritative voice of the book itself must have attracted the efforts of many more scholars than just Artemon and Phaenias.[103] For example, the Macedonian cups with Homeric scenes dating from the first half of the second century record pacifically title and author – just one author – in the case of the *Ilias parva* MB 27 ∼ 28(?) ∼ 31 ∼ 32(?) (pp. 94–7 Sinn) = *PEG* T 1 (= T 7ii D.) and *PEG* T 2 (= T 7i D.): Lesches; and in the case of the *Nostoi* MB 36 (p. 101 Sinn) = *PEG* T 4 (= T 2 D., F 10 W.): Agias. The cups MB 23 ∼ 24 ∼ 25 (pp. 92–3 Sinn) = *Aeth. PEG* T 11, with scenes we know from the end of *Il.* 24 and the *Aethiopis*, mention neither the poem nor the author, but this may be due to the fact that they draw perhaps from more than one poem;[104] in the case of MB 34 (p. 98 Sinn) = *Iliou persis PEG* T 4 we are not sure whether the title *Iliou katalēpsis* refers to the epic *Iliou persis* or to the Stesichorean poem with the same title, or to both.[105]

Although scholarly attempts at naming the authors of the archaic epic poems and constructing anecdotes around their lives and their relations with Homer must have proliferated in the Hellenistic age, their results never became standard. In the meantime we can surmise that the 'Epic Cycle' became more and more a widespread collection or at least a reading list of archaic epic myths. And thus, while a few scholars kept re-proposing doubly or triply feeble ascriptions, the professionals of literary erudition usually just cut the Gordian knot of the Cyclic poems' authorship(s). It is impossible to decide whether the uncertainty of the poems' ascriptions and the flimsy historical dimension of the supposed authors facilitated this situation, but it is a fact that at some point of the late Hellenistic or early

---

[103] See below, pp. 28, 313. [104] Cf. Fantuzzi (2012: 268). [105] So *PEG* p. 87.

Imperial age indistinct general labels like *kyklikoi* or *neōteroi* prevailed. In cases where a reference to a specific poem of the Cycle was intended, anonymous references such as 'the author of the *Cypria*/*Aethiopis*/etc.' became standard (the first instance of this appears to be at Arist. *Poet.* 1459b1: ὁ τὰ Κύπρια ποιήσας καὶ τὴν μικρὰν Ἰλιάδα ('the author who made the *Cypria* and the *Ilias parva*')). In other words, also when the Cyclic poems were not referred to as the work of the 'Cyclic poets', they still seem to have been considered 'chapters' of the Epic Cycle: the individuality of their authors became negligible, and the collective identity of the Cycle was adopted as a satisfactory identity for all the epic poems. In fact, at least from the age of Herodotus onwards, these archaic epic poems appear to have been considered by some critics as the works of anonymous 'non-Homer(s)' – a negative anonymous identity which Aristotle's *Poetics* may have helped bring about with his analysis of some Cyclic (or Cyclic-to-be) poems as a group of texts mainly unified by their being aesthetically different from Homer.[106]

The direct inference 'Cyclic author = anonymous' – ὁ δὲ ποιητὴς αὐτῶν ἄδηλος. εἷς γάρ ἐστι τῶν κυκλικῶν ('the poet of the *Cypria* is uncertain. *In fact* he is one of the Cyclic authors') – which we find in a scholiast to Clement from Alexandria (*Cypr. PEG* T 10 = T 10 D., p. 66 W.), seems almost a paradox in its being so categorical, and it belongs to a scholar of the late antique or Byzantine world. But it nonetheless represents the standard viewpoint on which ancient commentators, from every age and on every genre of texts from the Hellenistic age onwards, converged in considering the authorship of the Cyclic poems. The quotations of fragments or titles of the poems of the Epic Cycle in the scholia to ancient authors are almost forty, and of all these only six give for granted the name of an author.[107] The vast majority of the references consist of agnostic periphrases of the title (such as 'the one who made/composed/wrote/arranged...')[108] or generalizing

---

[106] See Fantuzzi, below in this volume, pp. 410–16.

[107] Eumelus, *Tit. PEG* F 2 (= F 1^B D., F 1 W.); Stasinus, *Cypr. PEG* F 1 (= D., W.); Lesches, *Ilias parva PEG* F 5 ap. Σ Pind. *Nem.* 6.85 (= D., W.), F 19 (= D., F 28 W.), F 21 (= F 20 D, 29 W.); Arctinus, *Il. pers. PEG* F 4 (= F 1 D., F 2 W.).

[108] 'The one who has written (γράψας) the *Titanomachy*' *Tit. PEG* F 7 (= F 4 D., F 11 W.); 'the one who has made (ποιήσας) the *Gigantomachy*' *Tit. PEG* F 10 (= F 9 D., F 12 W.); 'the one who has made (ποιήσας) the Cyclic *Thebaid*' *Theb. PEG* F 3 (= D., W.); 'the ones who have written (γεγραφότες) the *Thebaid*' *Epig. PEG* F 3 (= D., F 4 W.); 'the story is according to the one who has made (ποιήσαντι) the *Cypria*' *Cypr. PEG* F 3 (= D., F 4 W.); 'the one who has arranged (συντάξας) the Cyprian histories' *Cypr. PEG* F 12; 'the one who has written down together (συγγράψας) the *Cypria*' *Cypr. PEG* F 15 (= F 13 D., F 16 W.); 'the *Cypria*', without author *Cypr. PEG* F 24 (= F 17 D., F 20 W.); 'the poets (ποιηταί) of the *Cypria*' *Cypr. PEG* F 27 (= F 21 D., F 23 W.); 'the one who has made (ποιήσας) the *Cypria*' *Cypr.* F 34; 'who writes (γράφων) the *Aethiopis*' *Aeth. PEG* F 5 (= F 1 D., F 6 W.); 'the one who has made

references to 'the Cyclic authors (*kyklikoi*)' and 'the more recent authors (*neōteroi*)' that destroy the individuality not only of the authors but also of the titles of the single poems.[109] They thus show how attentive the ancient commentators were in emphasizing their radical uncertainty about the authorship of the Cyclic poems. Exactly the same caution in referring to the authorship of archaic epic poems can be seen in Athenaeus. He has been the treasure-house of about a dozen of quotations from poems of the Epic Cycle. Only in one case does he straightforwardly quote an individual author (Lesches, perhaps (text uncertain)), for the *Ilias parva*, *PEG* F 23 = dub. F 3 D., F 31 W.); in four cases he adopts periphrases ('the author of etc.') of the kind that can be found in the scholiasts;[110] in four other cases he suggests at least two contrasting authorships such as 'Eumelus or Arctinus'.[111]

THE INVENTION OF THE EPIC CYCLE

The biographical fiction of a contest in which Lesches, the supposed author of the *Ilias parva*, defeated Arctinus, the poet to whom the *Aethiopis* and the *Iliou persis* were ascribed, seems to go back to the Peripatetic scholar Pha(e)nias of Eresus (F 33 Wehrli, *Aeth. PEG* T 5 = p. 108 W.). It is appealing to interpret this contest as symbolizing the fact that the time-span of the

---

(πεποιηκότι) the *Ilias parva*, whom some identify as Thestorides of Phocaea, some others (like Hellanicus) as Cinaethon of Lacedaemon; still others as Diodorus of Erythrae' *Ilias parva PEG* T 10 (= T 10 D., F 6 W.); 'the one who has made (πεποιηκώς) the *Il parva*' *Ilias parva PEG* F 2 (= D., W.); 'the poet (ποιητής) of the *Ilias parva*' *Il parva PEG* F 5 (= D., W.); 'the one who has written (γράψας) the *Ilias parva*' *Ilias parva PEG* F 7 (= F 8 D., F 8 W.); 'the one who has made (πεποιηκότι) the *Il parva*' *Ilias parva PEG* F 28 (= F 1 D., F 1 W.); 'the Cyclic poet who has assembled (συντεταχότα) the *Persis*' *Il. pers. PEG* F 6 (= F 3 D. = W.); the one who has made (πεποιηκότα) the *Sack*' *Il. pers. PEG* F 6 (= F 4 D., F 6 W.); 'the poet (ποιητής) of the *Returns*' *Nost. PEG* F 2 (= F 2 D., F 13 W.); 'the one who has made (ποιήσας) the *Returns*' *Nost. PEG* F 7 (= F 6 D., F 6 W.).

[109] *kyklikoi Tit. PEG* F° 14; *neōteroi Tit. PEG* F° 15; *kyklikoi/neōteroi Theb. PEG* F 8 (= F 6 D., F 11 W.); *kyklikoi Theb. PEG* F 9 (= F 5 D., F 9 W.); *kyklikoi Cypr. PEG* F 13 (= F 12 D., F 12 W.); *neōteroi Cypr. PEG* F 20; *neōteroi Cypr. PEG* F 22; *neōteroi Cypr. PEG* F 23; *kyklikoi / neōteroi Aeth. PEG* F 3 (W.); *kyklikoi PEG* F 4 (p. 74 D., F 4 W.); ἐν τῶι κύκλωι 'in the Cycle' *Nost. PEG* F 9 (= p. 75 D., F 8 W.); *neōteroi Tel. PEG* F 4 (= F 5 W.).

[110] *Tit. PEG* F 8 (= F 7 D., F 10 W.) 'the one who has made the *Titanomachy*'; *Theb. PEG* F 2 (= D., W.) 'the one who has made the Cyclic *Thebaid*'; *Cypr. PEG* F 17 (= F 15 D., F 18 W.) 'the poet of the *Cypria*'; *Nost. PEG* F 11 (= F 8 D., F 12 W.) 'the one who has made the *Return of the Atreidai*'.

[111] *Tit. PEG* T 2 (= T 2 D., F 14 W.) and *PEG* F 6 (= F 5 D., F 8 W.), *Cypr. PEG* T 8 (=T 12 / F 4 D., F 5 W.) and *PEG* T 9 (= F 7 D., F 10 W.). A few other quotations in Athenaeus are conjecturally ascribed to poems of the Epic Cycle, but left by Athenaeus without specification of the authorship: *Theb. PEG* F 4 (= 'Hom.' 3 D., F 8 W.); *Tel. PEG* F 1 (= 'Hom.' 10 D., F 1 W.).

myth with which Lesches dealt was besieged and engulfed on both sides by the chronological sections occupied by Arctinus.[112] This possibility becomes even more inviting if we remember that there were, actually, narrative territories contested between the *Ilias parva* and the *Iliou persis*: Proclus' summary includes the debate among the Trojans on what to do with the Wooden Horse both at the end of the *Ilias parva* and at the beginning of the *Iliou persis*, and in the fourth century Aristotle appears still to have considered as belonging to the *Ilias parva* some episodes that according to Proclus were included in the *Iliou persis*.[113] That this biographical fiction points to the delicate drawing of 'borders' between the events treated by Arctinus and Lesches is also an especially attractive hypothesis, as it was constructed in an age (the late fourth and early third century) when the compilation of an Epic Cycle had already been accomplished or was about to be accomplished: just as the Epic Cycle is built around the Homeric *Iliad* and *Odyssey*, so also the repertoire of Arctinus appears in this anecdote to be built around that of a besieged Lesches, and Lesches' victory in the context 'justifies' his right to hold on to his space.

We have to distinguish properly between, on the one hand, the chronology of the title '(Epic) Cycle' for the compilation of the poems under this name, which is probably only Hellenistic, and, on the other, the idea that the narration of a series of events was accomplished by a series of poems dealing with these events in more than one installment from beginning to end. The latter is certainly not late, but archaic, as the actual composition of the six Cyclic poems of the Trojan War, plus the *Iliad* and the *Odyssey*, demonstrates, and the survival of a few explicit connective links between them confirms.[114] We are much less sure about the date of the birth of the Epic Cycle as an organic compilation, where sequentiality soon became a more obvious value, and contradictions were more easily noticed – though the elimination of overlaps and dissonances probably occurred only or mainly at the stage of the summaries.[115] It is very difficult to conceive of archaic rhapsodes that managed to standardize a fixed form of one or more 'Epic Cycle(s)'[116], and most of the scholars who surmise the existence of an Epic Cycle in the fourth century deem it to be not so much a compilation, but a canon (Welcker) or a reading list arranged by Aristotle or his school (West).

---

[112] Cf. Nagy (1990b: 76); for a hint in this direction, see already Allen (1908: 88).
[113] See below, pp. 32–3. As Burgess (1996: 87) correctly comments, 'the manufacturing of the Epic Cycle seems to have truncated the *Ilias parva* so that it does not also narrate the sack of Troy'.
[114] On the episode- and verse-links between Cyclic poems, see above, pp. 3–4 (also for Aristoxenus' proem of the *Iliad*).
[115] See below, pp. 32–34.   [116] Cf. Burgess (2001: 12–15).

In fact two passages from Aristotle's *Organon* (*Soph. elench.* 171a7 and *Anal. post.* 77b32) are usually assumed to mention *kyklos* as a synonym of (respectively) *hē Homērou poiēsis* and *ta epē*,[117] and thus may constitute a *terminus ante quem* for the word *kyklos*.[118] In both passages, however, it is probable that *kyklos* does not designate the poems of the Epic Cycle as something distinguished from the Homeric poems (*Soph. elench.* 171a7, in particular, excludes this distinction). In Aristotle the word may simply point to the complete continuum of the narrative of the Trojan War from beginning to end – a continuum that, as such, includes both Homer and the poems of the Epic Cycle, despite the fact that Aristotle clearly distinguished between *Iliad*/*Odyssey* on the one hand, and the Cyclic poems on the other in the *Poetics*.[119]

At such an early stage the poems of the Cycle would have been probably kept in their original format. Editorial adjustments of the poems are difficult to assume before the Hellenistic age, with which we usually associate the beginning of proper editorial activity and poetry-books. The use of the general category 'cyclic poetry' in Callimachus' epigram *AP* 12.43.1 = *ep.* 28.1 Pf. = *HE* 1041[120] might then result from a new familiarity with editorial compilation of the Cyclic poems, and this epigram is thus a reasonable *terminus post quem* for it.[121] At least by Athenaeus' day, the notion of the Epic Cycle had definitely grown to include more than a Trojan Epic Cycle, as it certainly included a *Titanomachy* (7.277d) and a *Thebaid* (11.465e). It thus ranged from events concerning the origins and surely the

---

[117] These two works apparently apply different ideas of the Homeric authorship: the *Sophistic refutations*, which are usually thought to have been written before the *Analytica post.*, may share the idea, widespread in the classical age, that all archaic epic is by 'Homer', whereas the latter work speaks of 'epic' in general, without attributing it to Homer. According to Schwartz (1940: 5 nn. 2 and 8), this internal inconsistency of Aristotle may be due to a new position Aristotle would have taken up in the *Poetics* about the non-Homericity of the poems of the Epic Cycle; but the uncertain chronology of Aristotle's works makes this interpretation aleatory.

[118] The thesis that Aristotle's mention does not concern at all epic the Epic Cycle has been argued by Immisch (1894) and by Parmentier (1914: 369–94), with whom at least Severyns (1926: 135) seems to agree, but has never been widely accepted. Even more obscure is the occurrence of the word *kyklos* in *Rhet.* 1417a12. While appreciating the brevity of Odysseus' mention of his adventures to Penelope in *Od.* 23.310–41, Aristotle compares – it seems for this narrative velocity – 'Phayllos with the *kyklos*' (ὡς Φαῦλλος τὸν κύκλον). For a new interpretation of this passage, see West (2013: 24), and below in this volume, p. 104.

[119] For Aristotle's *Poetics* and the poems of the Epic Cycle, see Fantuzzi, below in this volume, pp. 512–13.

[120] If, as we believe, Callimachus is really speaking of the Epic Cycle: see Fantuzzi, below in this volume, pp. 418–19.

[121] Cf., again, Burgess (2001, 15–16).

wars of the gods[122], to the Theban War (*Thebaid*, and probably *Oedipodea*, *Alcmeonis*, and *Epigonoi*),[123] the Trojan War (*Cypria*, *Aethiopis*, *Ilias parva*, *Iliou persis*,[124] as well as of course the *Iliad* and *Odyssey*), and the homecomings (*Nostoi*) of the Greek heroes who had participated in it, as well as the events of Odysseus' life after his return (*Telegony*).[125] Since it concluded with the last events of the life of the last hero to return home at the end of the war of Troy, the most recent major war of the Greek mythical tradition, the Epic Cycle familiar to Athenaeus appears to have reflected a precise selection. It collected poems dealing with the beginning, evolution, and end of the myths of the gods and heroes as opposed to the 'modern' age which recorded/constructed these gods and these heroes. Furthermore, the Epic Cycle was apparently concerned with wars that constituted climaxing moments in the struggles between the gods or the wars between heroes for hegemony. Their results were possibly believed to reflect in the structure of the pantheon and the geopolitical reality of the historical 'men as we are now'.[126] There is also little doubt that according to Athenaeus' catalogue the poems concerning the war of Troy were practically a small Cycle within the larger Epic Cycle.[127]

Maybe some of these orientations did not belong only to Athenaeus or other late scholars. We can fairly assume that the written poetic fixation of the oral traditions that covered all the phases of the Trojan War (but not, as far as we know, some of the other myths) was the prototypical model for the large later collection of Trojan and a few extra-Trojan poems under the name of 'Epic Cycle'. Based on these criteria for inclusion, it is perhaps telling that the poetic tradition on the Argonautic expedition, though still

---

[122] The mention in Proclus and the *Etymologicum magnum* (*PEG Th.* p. 10 = *Ep. cycl.* T 1 D.) of the theogonic intercourse of Ouranos and Gaia may lead to suppose that a *Theogony* belonged in the Epic Cycle, but this mention focuses in reality on the birth of the Hundred-handers, the three giants who helped the Olympian gods in subduing the Titans, and thus may have rather just prefaced the *Titanomachy*. Another alternative would be that the first (theogony-oriented) book of the *Titanomachy* may have been dropped out when this poem was included in the Epic Cycle. See D'Alessio, below in this volume, pp. 202–3.

[123] For contiguity of subject matter with the *Thebaid*: Davies (1986: 96 n. 45); West (2003b: 10–11).

[124] All of them are secured to the Epic Cycle by the summaries of Proclus.

[125] Other poems have been supposed from time to time to be included in the Epic Cycle, such as, most frequently, *Danais/Danaides*, *Amazonia/Atthis*, *Aegimius*, *Mynias/Phocais* and *Capture of Oechalia* between the Theban and the Trojan Wars. See Davies (1986: 96–7) for a review of which poems have been included in the Epic Cycle, and by whom (and the correct acknowledgement, p. 97, that the *Danais* is the best candidate, as this title is mentioned together with other Cyclic poems in one of the Iliac tablets, the *Tabula Borgiana*); see Severyns (1928: 165–208) for a thorough discussion of their fragments and testimonies.

[126] *Il.* 5.304, etc. [127] See West (1983: 129).

well known to the Homeric bards (cf. *Od.* 12.68), was possibly never fixed in writing and certainly was never mentioned by ancient sources as belonging to the Epic Cycle. The Epic Cycle also refrained from including legends focusing on the deeds of individual heroes. Heracles for instance got no room in it, though on this hero at least Chreophylus and Pisander wrote poems in the archaic age, as did Panyassis in the first half of the fifth century; nor was there any room for Theseus, though he had his own *Theseis*, or more than one, between the end of the sixth and the fourth century.

Whether one sees the Epic Cycle as a book collection of epics or as a reading list of ancient myths, its plan and pattern may thus have mattered much more than it is commonly assumed, and it is pretty much in tune with the Herodotean metaphor of *kyklos* in 1.207.2.[128] This metaphor had conveyed the idea of non-openness (that is: a non-openness to linear, unpredictable evolutions, and thus consequently a predictable completeness) inherent in a specific series of human actions and situations, stressed by ring composition of beginning and end. It had thus presupposed an ideological interpretation of some historical events as connected to each other according to a predictable pattern, and in its task of ideologizing these events it even reminds us of Aristotle's idea of the perfect action of tragedy: Aristotle's tragedy, like Herodotus' *kyklos* of human affairs, had to be interpretable as a pattern – usually a pattern of ascent to the greatest power and consequent fall – and had to have a beginning and an end. We cannot be sure that the Epic Cycle earned its name originally because it recalled the tropic sense of *kyklos* as a patterned sequence of events, but this may have become sooner or later the sense, or one of the possible senses of *kyklos* in 'Epic Cycle'. A confirmation in this direction comes from the way Proclus presents the 'cyclicity' of the Epic Cycle in terms of *akolouthia tōn . . . pragmatōn* (ap. Phot. *Bibl.* 319a, quoted already above). The term *akolouthia* emphasizes the idea of compact sequentiality, with no substantial lacuna (and thus interruption of continuity) or overlapping and/or no contradiction between the events being narrated. Proclus himself obsessively emphasizes the idea of sequentiality with an introductory phrase in every summary that reminds that the poem succeds to another ('to this succeed . . .').[129] Can we assume that what we may call the aesthetics of sequentiality was already shared at some level by the individual original poems that were later joined into this collection?

We think that the answer should be 'yes', but not at the same level of obsessive consistency reached by Proclus. We have clues that the sequentiality of events in some version of the poems of the Epic Cycle was far less accurate

---

[128] See above, p. 4. [129] See above, p. 2 n. 4.

and smooth than the narrative displayed by Proclus' summaries. Aristotle seems to have read an *Ilias parva* including episodes (= potential tragedies, in his perspective) that for us form part of the *Iliou persis* ('sack of Troy' and 'departure of the Greeks').[130] Likewise Pausanias, who in his description of a series of paintings concerning the sack of Troy bases his interpretation of the images on the narrative of 'Lesches *en Iliou persidi*' (*Ilias parva PEG* F 10 = F 12 D. = F 15 W.) – a phrase that, in the absence of any known ascription of the *Iliou persis* to Lesches, seems to point to a section of Lesches' *Ilias parva* dealing with the destruction of Troy.[131] Moreover, events like Menelaus' dropping his sword when he sees again Helen's breast or Neoptolemus' taking Andromache as his prisoner and killing Astyanax are quoted as belonging to the *Ilias parva* (*PEG* F 19 = F 19 D., F 28 W. and F 21 = F 20 D., F 30 W.), but would be expected to be part of the *Iliou persis* (unless they were anticipations). Besides, there were certainly some repetitions in the poems of the Epic Cycle. For instance both the *Cypria* and the *Iliad* include a catalogue of the Trojans.[132] The summary of Proclus mentions the Trojans' debate about accepting the Wooden Horse both at the end of the *Ilias parva* and at the beginning of the *Iliou persis*.[133] Some of these repetitions were also contradictory. Polyxena died of wounds inflicted by Odysseus and Diomedes during the sack of Troy according to the *Cypria* (*PEG* F 34), but in Proclus' summary of the *Iliou persis*, she is killed at the grave of Achilles.

In spite of these hints at the original epics' at times incongruous nature, Proclus' summary of the Trojan Cycle displays virtually no contradictions between the events it includes. For instance, the contradiction between the *Cypria* and the *Iliad* on the route taken by Paris' and Helen's ship back to Troy (detour to Sidon, as in the *Iliad*, or three-day straightforward trip from Sparta to Troy as described in the *Cypria* according to Herodotus?) has completely disappeared in Proclus' summary: his *Cypria* in fact presents the same detour to Phoenicia which we find in the *Iliad*.[134] Likewise, we know from *PEG* F 5 (= F 1 D., F 6 W.) that Ajax committed suicide in the *Aethiopis*, but in Proclus' summary the *Aethiopis* seems only to have anticipated the fight for Achilles' arms, whereas the *Ilias parva* narrated both the fight and Ajax's suicide: did Proclus eliminate another repetition

---

[130] On the overlapping between some version of Lesches' poem and the standard version of the *Iliou persis*, see Burgess (2001: 22–4).
[131] Cf. Monro (1884: 317–18).
[132] See Burgess (1996: 86–90). But cf. Monro (1884: 7).
[133] See also above, p. 29.
[134] The agreement of the version in the summary of Proclus with Ps.-Apollodorus may lead to suspect that the Iliadic adjustment of the *Cypria* took place before Proclus; cf. Burgess (2001: 20).

or had it been eliminated before, e.g. when the compilation of the Epic Cycle was arranged? It is impossible to ascertain who was responsible for this perfect sequentiality and lack of contradictions. It is plausible however that the rhapsodes who first coped with the task of joining together the subjects of performances from different epics started the work,[135] and the work was later accomplished by the scholars who put together the Epic Cycle in the fourth century and the Hellenistic editors, or by Proclus and the other scholars before him who epitomized the original poems in prose.

THE CYCLE AS A PROSE SUMMARY

Although the earliest prose summaries of mythical material circulated under the name *kyklos* (such as, plausibly, the one of Dionysius the Cyclograph) go probably back to the Hellenistic period,[136] it is in the Imperial era and in Late Antiquity that most of the summaries, mainly but not solely in prose,[137] were created. The compilation of summaries presupposes and to a certain extent rests on a gradual waning of interest in reading the actual

---

[135] Burgess (2001: 13).

[136] Cf. Wilamowitz (1884: 360–1); Lang (1893: 327–8); Monro (1883: 326–7); Severyns (1928: 397); Burgess (2001: 16–17). On Dionysius see above, pp. 5–6. But see now West's hypothesis about Phayllos, below in this volume, p. 104.

[137] A notable example of this trend is the compilation, called *kyklos*, by the citharode Menecles of Teos who visited Priansos in Crete as an envoy around the middle of the second century BC (*I.Cret.* i.xxiv.1): εἰσ<ή>νεγκε δὲ κύκλον ἱστορημέναν ὑπὲρ Κρήτας κα[ὶ τ]ῶν ἐν [Κρήτ]αι γεγονότων θεῶν τε καὶ ἡρώων, [ποι]ησάμενο[ς τ]ὰν συναγωγὰν ἐκ πολλῶν ποιητᾶ[ν κ]αὶ ἱστοριαγράφων (sic) ('he introduced a historical cycle concerning Crete and the gods and heroes of Crete, compiling his collection from many poets and historians'). The inscription makes it plainly clear that Menecles collected his material from a range of sources on the basis of their connection to the island of Crete. We are not explicitly told how this material was organized, but the use of the word *kyklos* points to a compilation arranged on the basis of the sequentiality of the events; the combination of Cretan gods and Cretan heroes also reminds us of the association of theogonic and heroic myth in the Epic Cycle. See Chaniotis (1988a: 348–9; 1988b: 154–6); Burgess, below in this volume, p. 43. Another compilation of local concern is attested in a decree from Cnossos recorded in an inscription of the late second century BC from Delos (*I.Cret.* i.viii.12; *I.Délos* 1512), in which the epic and melic poet Myrinos of Amisos is said to have given public lectures (ἀκροάσεις) and composed a collection (prose or verse ?) of encomiastic information on Crete and the Cretan ethnos 'according to the poet [scil. Homer]' (παρὰ τὸν ποιητάν). See Chaniotis (1988a: 341–2; 2010: 262–3). Difficult to assess the range of Myrinos' sources: only the hints in the 'Homeric' *Hymn to Apollo* (391–479) and *Od.* 19.172–9 (Guarducci (1935–50: i.68)), or also Cyclic material?

We also also know via Ioannes Philoponus (ad Arist. *An. post.* 77b32 = *Comm. in Arist. Graec.* xiii.3.156f. Wallies) of a certain Pisander, who lived in the third century AD, and compiled 'a mythological commentary in verse that successfully rivaled the Epic Cycle' (Burgess 2001, 17). See the discussion of Severyns (1928: 75–6); *Cyclus epicus* PEG T 28 = T 2 D. On the passage of Philoponus, Monro (1883: 323–5); Wilamowitz (1925: 281).

poems of the Cycle. This did not happen overnight. It was a steady process that, according to Severyns, involved three intermediate steps: first, the Cyclic poems were read less and less; then, since allusions to the Cyclic epics started to be less widely comprehensible, the scholiasts began to cite them no longer on their own but together with other minor authors dealing with the same topic; and last, all references to the Cyclic poets or the *neōteroi* were replaced by quotations of logographic or mythographic sources.[138]

The two major sources of information with respect to the Cyclic epics are Ps.-Apollodorus' *Bibliotheca* and its *Epitome* and the second book of Proclus' *Chrestomathy* (whether Proclus was a second-century grammarian, as it is usually believed nowadays,[139] or a fifth-century Neoplatonic philosopher). The actual *Chrestomathy* is lost, but Photius' *Bibliotheca* summarizes the first two books of Proclus' four-book work (codex 239, pp. 318b–22a Bekker). In particular Proclus' abstracts of the poems of the Trojan Cycle was reproduced in some MSS of the *Iliad*.[140] The two works show stark similarities in content and, sometimes, diction, but each of them includes details or features that are absent from the other. This observation excludes the possibility of interdependence and leads us to conclude that they both draw on a common mythographic source that covered material ranging from the *Cypria* to the *Telegony*. This lost source may have been abridged a number of times, which would explain the differences between Ps.-Apollodorus and Proclus, who may well be deriving their material from different abridgments of the same source.[141] This does not mean that Ps.-Apollodorus and Proclus carry equal weight in our attempts to reconstruct the content of the Trojan War Cycle, for while the *Bibliotheca/Epitome* is a general mythological handbook containing information that clearly does not pertain *only* to the Epic Cycle, Proclus offers a summary of the actual epics. Proclus indicates this in the most explicit way, i.e. by stating the individual works, their authors, and the number of books into which they were divided. It is conceivable that 'Proclus summarized a rough and ready verse narration of the Trojan War (of late classical or early Hellenistic date) that was created from extensive excerpts (perhaps books) of the Cycle poems'.[142] Pseudo-Apollodorus

---

[138] Severyns (1928: 75–80).
[139] As most recently reproposed with new arguments by West (2013: 7–11). See also Welcker (1865: 3–7; 1882: 499–504); Hillgruber (1990: 397–404). For the opposite identification of Proclus with the neo-Platonic scholar, see Bethe (1891b: 593–633); Scafoglio (2004a; 2004b).
[140] See below, pp. 36–8.   [141] See Davies (1986: 104–6).
[142] Burgess, below in this volume, p. 57. As recently observed by West (2013: 7), 'when we consider the orderly plan of Proclus' work as it appears from Photius, it is difficult to avoid the feeling that the section of the Epic Cycle stands out as something of an erratic block. It was logical, after reviewing the canon of five best epic poets, to take note of the mass of lesser epic

may well include genuinely cyclic material omitted from Proclus' summary, but each case should be judged on its own, the more so since the problem of determining the sources he is drawing on remains a complex and vexing one.

THE CYCLE AS AN EXCERPT ACCOMPANYING THE *ILIAD*[143]

The final step in the Epic Cycle's long evolution took place when unknown hands (possibly a grammarian or grammarians) added Proclus' summary – which originally formed part of his *Chrēstomatheia grammatikē*[144] – to a number of MSS of the *Iliad*.

Some time well before the tenth century AD an unknown scholar heavily interested in the part of Proclus' *Chrestomathy* that discussed epic poetry decided to copy seven fragments – the *Life of Homer* and the six fragments pertaining to the six Trojan Cyclic epics (*Cypria, Aethiopis, Ilias parva, Iliou persis, Nostoi, Telegony*), that were placed much later in Proclus' work than the *Life of Homer* – from the exemplar of Proclus' *Chrestomathy* he had in front of him, and to place them in the beginning of a now lost MS of the *Iliad*.

This was the very first time that the head of a now lost codex of the *Iliad*, which following Severyns we may call Π (*codex primigenius*), featured the seven fragments from Proclus' *Chrestomathy* that had been copied, apparently with no substantial modifications, from the exemplar this unknown scholar had in his possession. This event was of enormous importance for the survival of the Epic Cycle, since, after their separation from a

---

in which so much of traditional mythology was embodied. But the series of detailed summaries of all the poems seems out of keeping with the manner of treatment followed in the work as a whole, insofar as we can judge it from Photius' description. It looks very much as if Proclus imported it from a different source from those that supplied the main framework of his discussion.'

[143] This section of the Introduction is heavily indebted to Davies (1986: 101–4). The groundwork was laid by Rzach *RE* xi.2347–435 and Severyns (1953: 122). A great debt is also owed to the meticulous researches of Severyns, who devoted no less than five volumes (*Recherches* i–v) to the study of Proclus' *Chrestomathy* and the elucidation of the relation between codex 239 of Photius' *Bibliotheca* and the MSS of the *Iliad* in which parts of Proclus' summaries survive (Severyns' conclusions, in brief, in 1953: 341–6). See however also the more recent studies of Hägg (1975) and Treadgold (1980).

[144] Or *Chrēstomatheias grammatikēs eklogai* according to Severyns (1938: 65–9; 1953: 248). Since the term χρηστομάθεια means 'desire of learning' (Ps.-Long. *subl*. 44.1), it was easily extended to refer as a title to a work that contained a 'summary of useful knowledge' (LSG s.v.). See also Helladius' Χρηστομάθειαι.

soon-to-disappear exemplar of Proclus' *Chrestomathy*, the summaries of the Trojan section of the Epic Cycle started a new life as prolegomena to the *Iliad*. It is due to this event that the survival of Cyclic poetry (if only in the form of summaries) was linked to that of Homer's *Iliad*. As it has been eloquently observed, 'as part of the original *Chrestomathy* it emanated from an author who wanted to give, and proceeded to the hands of a reader who desired to obtain, exact information as to the authors and contents of the relevant epics. As part of a Homeric MS its primary function became to convey the connection of episodes in the legends of Troy preparatory to a reading of the *Iliad*. The man who wants and needs to know this will not wish to be bothered with information concerning the names of the authors. Still less will he care to be troubled by doublets; and least of all by contradictions of the Iliadic narrative he just about to enjoy. He merely requires a simple coherent story to fill in the background detail.'[145]

The reliability of the form in which we have Proclus' summaries from the Iliadic MSS (the *Cypria* summary from a dozen MSS, none of high antiquity, the summaries of the other poems only from the Venetus A (Marcianus Gr. 454) of the tenth century AD) has been debated. Doubts regarding the accuracy of the information offered by Proclus himself are further aggravated by the fact that we are unaware of the extent of the changes introduced by the anonymous excerptor or excerptors who took the summaries from Proclus' work and added them to the Iliadic MSS. However scholars have shown that we are fortunate enough at least to possess 'their original order ... with *no* retouching to match these fragments to their new context as prolegomena to the *Iliad*'.[146] This is clearly shown by the fact that the phrase ἐπιβάλλει τούτοις is placed before the beginning of the *Cypria* summary and that it is also employed in slightly[147] or considerably[148] altered form before the summaries of the other epics. The verb should be taken in its intransitive meaning with the noun Κύπρια as its subject ('the *Cypria* comes after these'). In this case, the plural pronoun τούτοις cannot

---

[145] Davies (1986: 103–4).   [146] Again Davies (1986: 102).
[147] See the phrase ἐπιβάλλει δὲ τοῖς προειρημένοις that is placed before the summary of the *Aethiopis*; see above p. 2 n. 4.
[148] See the phrases ἕπεται τούτοις and συνάπτει δὲ τούτοις that are placed before the summaries of the *Iliou persis* and the *Nostoi* respectively. This argument is further reinforced by the fact that in the summaries of the other two epics (the *Ilias parva* and the *Telegony*) the syntax used (ἑξῆς δ' ἐστὶν Ἰλιάδος μικρᾶς βιβλία τέσσαρα / μετὰ ταῦτά ἐστιν Ὁμήρου Ὀδύσσεια· ἔπειτα Τηλεγονίας βιβλία δύο 'There follow four books of the *Ilias parva* / after these there is Homer's *Odyssey*; then two books of the *Telegony*') has as its subject the number of books of the epic poem to be summarized, which shows that Proclus is simply varying the verb he employs, keeping the number of books of each poem or the actual name of the poem (as in the case of the *Cypria*) as the subject.

refer to the (singular) *Vita Homeri* that precedes the *Cypria* in the Venetus A. Instead, it must refer to the summary of the last epic (i.e. τοῖς ἔπεσι, a plural noun), i.e. the last poem of the Theban section of the Epic Cycle, which would have preceded the Trojan section in Proclus' *Chrestomathy*.[149] Also other parts of the phrase with which the *Cypria* are introduced – ... Κύπρια ἐν βιβλίοις φερόμενα ἕνδεκα, ὧν περὶ τῆς γραφῆς ὕστερον ἐροῦμεν, ἵνα μὴ τὸν ἑξῆς λόγον νῦν ἐμποδίζωμεν ('... *Cypria*, transmitted in eleven books; we will speak of the spelling later in order not to hinder the order of the present account') – prove that the summaries must have been transcribed from Proclus almost mechanically, as the anticipation of the issue of the title spelling can only be explained by assuming that Proclus anticipates here a discussion elsewhere in the *Chrestomathy* on the problem whether we should read Κύπρια proparoxytone (as a title: '*Cypria*',) or Κυπρία (as a genitive of the name of the author 'by Cyprias').[150]

Some time after this *codex primigenius* (certainly before the tenth century AD), we need to postulate that among the descendants of Π the archetype from which our entire tradition stems was conceived (ω). After ω the manuscript tradition bifurcates: there is a more 'scientific or scholarly' branch (*a*) preserving all seven fragments transmitted by ω and going back to Π, and a more 'school-masterly' branch (*f*) that excludes five of the fragments (*cdefg*), includes only the *Cypria* summary and the *Life of Homer*, and has for them a very dry title omitting any mention of the *Chrestomathy* and other relevant bibliographic detail: Πρόκλου περὶ Ὁμήρου ('Life of Homer, by Proclus') b. Τοῦ αὐτοῦ περὶ τῶν Κυπρίων λεγομένων ποιημάτων ('On the so-called *Cypria*, by the same').

Branch *a* would have originated by a codex α, which was annotated by a scholar who was tentatively identified by Severyns with Arethas of Caesarea.[151] This scholar (Arethas?) himself had perhaps no access to an exemplar of Proclus' *Chrestomathy*, but probably thanks to the codex 239 of Photius' *Bibliotheca*, which he may have known[152], he was able to find out that the seven fragments placed at the head of his codex α came from Proclus' *Chrestomathy*. If it is true that the editorial presentation of these fragments introduced in α by this scholar (Arethas?) is reflected in the

---

[149] Davies (1986: 102) rightly points out that this observation is further corroborated by both the fact that there is no 'contrived transition between the *Vita Homeri* and the summary of the *Cypria*' and that the summary of the *Cypria* contains features, like Nestor's digression, which are rather incomprehensible and would have been omitted if the original content had been changed by the excerptor.

[150] See most recently West (2013: 6).   [151] But see Wilson ap. Davies (1986: 103 n. 74).

[152] According to Severyns, Arethas was in touch with Photius, but this has been more recently denied: see Wilson (1983: 120).

Venetus A,[153] then this scholar would have written in his codex headings and sub-headings for the seven fragments. The headings and sub-headings which with the exception of the text of the *Cypria* summary we can still see in the Venetus A – the same that could be found at the beginning of α in Severyns' reconstruction – are also accompanied by the grouping of the summaries into two sets of almost equal size: the first group comprises fragments *ab* (the *Life of Homer* and the summary of the *Cypria*: 169 lines in Severyns' numbering); the second contains fragments *cdefg* (the summaries of the *Aethiopis, Ilias parva, Iliou persis, Nostoi, Telegony*: 160 lines in Severyns' numbering). The result which we can see in the Venetus A is as follows:

	Πρόκλου χρηστομαθίας γραμματικῆς τῶν εἰς δ' διῃρημένων τὸ ᾱ
Life a	Ὁμήρου χρόνοι βίος χαρακτὴρ ἀναγραφὴ ποιημάτων
Cypria b	missing
Other Cyclic epics	Πρόκλου χρηστομαθίας γραμματικῆς τὸ δεύτερον
c	Αἰθιοπίδος ε̄ Ἀρκτίνου
d	Ἰλιάδος μικρᾶς δ̄ Λέσχεω
e	Ἰλίου πέρσιδος β̄ Ἀρκτίνου
f	Νόστων ε̄ Ἀγίου
g	Τηλεγονίας β̄ Εὐγάμμωνος
	Section one of Proclus' *Chrestomathy* that is divided into four books
Life a	Time, life, character of Homer and titles of his poems
Cypria b	missing
Other Cyclic epics	Section two of the epitome of excerpts from Proclus' *Chrestomathy*
c	From Arctinus' *Aethiopis* in five books
d	From Lesches' *Ilias parva* in four books
e	From Arctinus' *Iliou persis* in two books
f	From Agias' *Nostoi* in five books
g	From Eugammon's *Telegony* in two books

As can be seen from this list of headings and sub-headings, Venetus A still contains (among many other things) a *Vita Homeri* followed by a summary of five of the six epics included in the Trojan section of the Epic Cycle, i.e. the *Aethiopis, Ilias parva, Iliou persis, Nostoi* and *Telegony*. The only missing

---

[153] According to Severyns (1953: 245–52). But see Irigoin (1962: 64–5 and 80); Lemerle (1986: 261–2); Davies (1986: 103 n. 74).

summary (it is missing not because of an 'editorial' choice by the scribe, but because the first quire of the MS is mutilated), that of the *Cypria*, is given by a dozen other MSS of the *Iliad* belonging to branch *f*. But none of these other MSS also includes the summaries of the other Cyclic poems. The reason explaining the suppression of these five fragments of Proclus' summaries contained in ω may be that the *Life of Homer* and the *Cypria* cover the biographical data on the author and the mythical facts a student needed to know in order to understand the beginning of the action of the *Iliad*. This dry fact turned the hyper-abridged version of family *f* into the prime candidate to be used in teaching: for most medieval readers the summary of the *Cypria*, reduced to the role of an introduction to the *Iliad*, seems to have been enough.

PART I

Approaches to the Epic Cycle

1 | Coming adrift: The limits of reconstruction of the cyclic poems

JONATHAN BURGESS

What is the 'Epic Cycle'? The Greek is *epikos kyklos*, which literally means 'epic circle'. *Kyklos* in its most primary meaning refers to an object of circular dimensions (e.g. wheel, shield), but it could also be applied metaphorically to a compilation of literary material.[1] The 'Epic Cycle', simply put, is a collection of epic verse.[2] Unfortunately the Epic Cycle is now lost, except for various kinds of fragments, testimony and summaries. Our challenge is to sort through this evidence and reconstruct the Epic Cycle as best we can. Many learned and rewarding attempts to do so can be found in this *Companion*. But all attempts, not least my own, ultimately result from guesswork that depends on arbitrary assumptions.

MODELS OF RECONSTRUCTION

The Epic Cycle included theogonic beginnings and the heroic wars at Thebes and Troy. The Trojan War and its aftermath have attracted the most attention, both in antiquity and in the modern world, because of its relevance to the Homeric poems. Indeed the Epic Cycle's useful contextualization of the *Iliad* and the *Odyssey* has led to the common conception of it as something secondary to 'Homer', both in chronology and value. For hermeneutic purposes I will call this the 'Homer-centric' model, which has been dominant from antiquity onward. In its starkest form, this model posits that a series of poems were composed on the basis of the Homeric poems, though falling far short of their poetics, in order to surround them with prequels and

---

[1] A certain Phayllos compiled a 'cycle' of unknown material (Arist. *Rhet.* 3.16.7; see Introduction, above in this volume, p. 30 n. 118); Dionysius the 'Cyclograph' composed a prose work compiling all Greek myth that was called the *Kyklos* (see Monro (1883: 326–7) and above, pp. 5–6); the citharode Menecles of Teos compiled a 'cycle' of Cretan legend in the mid second-century BC (Guarducci 1935–50: i.xxiv.1; above, p. 34 n. 137); and the sixth-century AD Agathias compiled what the *Suda* calls a 'new cycle' of epigrams (see Cameron and Cameron 1966). The metaphoric usage can imply common circulation of material (cf. Callim. *ep.* 28 Pf.; see Fantuzzi, below in this volume, pp. 417–19), a circuit of pedagogical training (see de Rijk 1965), and other spatial, temporal or material connotations (Nagy (1996a: 38, 89–91); Burgess (2004b: 9–10, 2005: 347)). On its Indo-European etymology, see Beekes (2010: 798–9).

[2] See Introduction, above in this volume, for the various ancient usages of *kyklos*.

sequels.[3] A different model, which I will label 'Systemic,' would link the Epic Cycle broadly with various material about the Trojan War in ancient literary and artistic traditions. In its starkest form, this model suggests that the Cycle poems represent mythological and epic traditions that were earlier than the Homeric poems. Adherents to both models have dedicated themselves to the scholarly sleuthing required to make sense out of the scanty evidence. But these two models vary widely on their conception of how the Epic Cycle relates to the Homeric poems and what role they generally played in early epic.

The Homer-centric model often motivates an antiquarian approach to the Epic Cycle, leading to a dutiful if unenthusiastic categorization of relevant minutiae. If the Cycle poems are considered unworthy successors to the *Iliad* and *Odyssey*, given their apparently inept employment of Homeric technique, they nonetheless are of interest as potential sources for more inspired portrayals of the Trojan War in later art and literature. From this description, it may sound like the Homer-centric approach goes to an awful lot of trouble for poems it does not respect. But the model paradoxically cherishes the Cycle poems as prime examples of what the Homeric poems are not. Their inferiority serves to set off the uniqueness of the Homeric poems. This aesthetic component of the Homer-centric model has not just one but two trump cards: the *Iliad* and *Odyssey*. These poems, as opposed to the Cycle epics, *have* survived, the seeming result of Darwinian justice. The Homeric distinction in plot arrangement and expression was celebrated in antiquity by Aristotle (*Poet.* 8 and 23) and Homeric scholars (as evident in *scholia*), and the ancient world would seem to have agreed: papyri quantify the popularity of the Homeric poems, as they do not for the Cycle poems. We might easily imagine that no other epic poems could have even begun to match the *Iliad* and *Odyssey*, impressed as we are by their sensitive poetics, monumental size, and humane profundity.

How does the Systemic model vary from this Homer-centric one? Instead of focusing on the *Iliad* and *Odyssey*, it looks to place both the Homeric and Cyclic poems within widespread traditions of long-term duration in ancient Greek culture. For the past one hundred years Homeric studies has been revolutionized by the Parry-Lord oralist approach that employed fieldwork of contemporary performance practice to demonstrate the traditional and thus oral basis of Homeric epic.[4] Anthropological approaches have

---

[3] Cf. *Cyclus Epicus PEG* T 11 for a scholiastic portrayal of 'Cyclic' as compositions surrounding the *Iliad* in a circle. Perhaps the most striking Homer-centric image of antiquity is the painting cited at Ael. *VH* 13.22, in which Homer vomits verses that other poets draw up.

[4] See Nagy, below in this volume, p. 67.

also explored the nature of epic performance and reception, challenging a Homer-centric conception of early epic.[5] Since ancient comprehension of the oral nature of early epic was dim at best, the ancient portrayal of Homer as exclusively original, with other epics derivative, can be put aside. The apparently non-Homeric characteristics of Cyclic poetry, whether in content (more inclusive of the fantastic and local), length (shorter) or scope of plot (more episodes) can be judged authentic representation of early epic, not inept mimicking of Homeric poetics. In its straightforward narration of the expansive action of heroic myth, the cyclic might be treasured as traditional rather than parasitic.[6]

If the value of cyclic epic is thereby raised, this does not necessarily counter the modern consensus that the Cycle poems were composed later than the *Iliad* and *Odyssey*. But just as an anthropological understanding of performance culture has displaced the centrality of textualization for the Homeric poems, it might also limit the conclusions to be reached about Cyclic fragments. In Homeric studies controversy has raged as to whether surviving Homeric textual traditions faithfully represent an 'original' *Iliad* and *Odyssey*, or even go back to a time when these were being created. The Cyclic poems as well can be portrayed as late fixations of previous manifestations of performance traditions, or at best snapshot recordings of one version of a poem. If a Cyclic fragment seems linguistically late in comparison with Homeric norms,[7] this is certainly of great academic interest. But of what ultimate import? Does it justify the portrayal of the Cycle poems as secondary or second-rate, or does it simply testify to the trivia of 'book history'? One textual fixation, or a late-generation copy, could conceivably fail to reflect an early manifestation of a poem. If a version of one epic is textually later than a version of another epic, yet the first epic is organically earlier than the second, the significance of linguistic analyses quickly deflates.

The Homer-centric scholar, unimpressed by speculation that fails to account for the evidence at hand, can counter that the advent of literacy accurately recorded the literary history of the early archaic age. Indeed, literacy may have been the means by which Homer reached new heights of artistic sophistication.[8] And if literacy quickly transformed early Greek

---

[5] One could place the start of this trend in Homeric studies with Robert Wood; see Sachs (2010).
[6] Lack of capitalization for 'cyclic' signals throughout that I am not directly referencing the poems collected in the Epic Cycle.
[7] See Bernabé, below in this volume, pp. 139–40.
[8] Many favour the literate transcription of gifted oral compositions. For the idea that Homer inspired literacy, see Wade-Gery (1952); Powell (1991).

culture, then that might suggest how the *Iliad* and *Odyssey* could have galvanized the creation of satellite poems. Post-Homeric poets, perversely employing the new technology to imitate rather than innovate, could have mined recorded and available Homeric texts. The evident singularity of the *Iliad* and *Odyssey* seems to call for an explanation, at any rate, and a scenario of early literacy and textual influence is a possible solution.

Plausibility is another matter, the Systemic scholar might object. It is awkward for the Homer-centric assumption of early Homeric dominance that early Greek artists were far more interested in representing cyclic rather than Homeric content.[9] This does not testify to an early influence of specific Cycle poems, but it does confirm the ongoing importance of the stories that they narrated. There is no question that the Homeric poems eventually became tremendously central to Greek culture, but textual recordings of the Cycle poems, whatever their original importance, themselves seem to have achieved some degree of influence as epic traditions died out. Warming to the topic, the Systemic scholar continues, 'Where and how often they were performed in the later archaic age is not clear – have you read that rarely cited 2004 article by Burgess? – but the Cycle poems served as important documents for classical age artists and dramatists.'[10]

'Yes,' interrupts the Homer-centric scholar, 'it was already conceded that the Cycle fertilized the sprouting forth of more fortunate expressions of their contents.'

'If I *may* continue,' the Systemic advocate cuts in, 'though you have correctly noted the eventual neglect of the Cycle poems in antiquity, the ongoing endurance of cyclic myth in literary and artistic traditions calls into question your portrayal of an overwhelming Homeric sovereignty.'[11]

'All peripheral testimony to Homer's continuing sway,' mutters the Homer-centric critic.

Of course, my quarrelling 'Homer-centric' and 'Systemic' scholars are entirely hypothetical (that they would even communicate with one another will seem especially fantastic). And simple adherence to either the Homer-centric or Systemic model in reconstructing the Epic Cycle is rare. An excellent example is the school of thought in Homeric studies known as neoanalysis, which has continuously generated interest in the Cycle poems

---

[9] See Carpenter, below in this volume. The early literary influence of Homer, on the other hand, is often assumed (though rarely demonstrated; see ch. 2 of Burgess (2001b)).

[10] See e.g. Noussia-Fantuzzi and Sommerstein, below in this volume.

[11] The anti-Homeric literature of late antiquity (on which, see now Kim (2011)) to some degree reflects fatigue with the complacent orthodoxy of an isolated, cycle-free Homer. Comparable is the Hellenistic turn toward Hesiodic, as opposed to Homeric, aesthetics.

over the last half-century.[12] Neoanalysts posit that the Homeric poems, especially the *Iliad*, were greatly influenced by cyclic verse. It has sometimes been suggested that specific Cycle poems preceded the *Iliad*, but Neoanalyst argument more commonly speaks of cyclic prototypes, whether written or oral. In any event, in Neoanalyst methodology the surviving evidence for the Epic Cycle is diligently gathered, as well as bolstered by cyclic content in literary and artistic traditions, in order to identify cyclic motifs present in Homeric verse. It is claimed, with the methodology of the once-popular Homeric 'Analyst' school of thought, that apparent 'hiccups' in the logic or flow of the Homeric poems are evidence of compositional indebtedness. But the heart of Neoanalysts belongs to the anti-Analysis Unitarian school of thought, which insists that the *Iliad* and *Odyssey* were artistically unified. This puts the 'neo' in neoanalysis. Though Neoanalysts point out 'problems', they consider them only inconsequential evidence for the masterful transformation of cyclic material by Homer. So in a sense Neoanalysts employ both the Homer-centric and Systemic models, gathering evidence by means of the latter in order to serve the ideology of the former.

Actual reconstructions of the Epic Cycle vary widely, whatever the model to which a scholar owes allegiance. The general lack of evidence and the unreliability of what we do have make the process very difficult. The basic facts of who composed the Cycle poems, and when, are in dispute; certainty is even lacking as to what poems were in the Cycle and how they were entitled. It is the task of the rest of this chapter to rehearse some of the difficulties of using our sources. I will proceed by discussing different categories of our evidence for the Epic Cycle, employing representative samples for illustration. At the end of this survey I will return to the question of how to reconstruct the Epic Cycle by giving a critique of my own method of doing so.

WORKING WITH SOURCES

The most informative source is an ancient summary of the poems in the Trojan War section of the Epic Cycle. This is provided by a bibliophile named Proclus. It is important from the start to recognize that we do not possess this summary directly from Proclus, whoever he was (his identity and date are disputed). The summaries are recovered from the *Iliad* manuscript

---

[12] The monumental Neoanalyst work is Kullmann (1960); see Willcock (1997) for a survey and bibliography.

tradition, where they served the Homer-centric role of providing context for the Homeric epic. Summaries of five poems – the *Aethiopis*, the *Ilias parva*, the *Iliou persis*, the *Nostoi* and the *Telegony* – are preserved in the oldest surviving complete manuscript of the *Iliad*, the famous Venetus A, while a summary of the *Cypria* is preserved in other manuscripts. Information about the larger work from which summaries were excerpted (but not the summaries themselves) is provided by a ninth-century AD scholar named Photius. Among other things, Photius indicates the wider scope of the Epic Cycle, from the beginning of the cosmos to the death of Odysseus, and reports on some comments by Proclus. For example, Proclus reportedly says that Cycle poems are preserved in his day not for their worthiness but for their mythological content[13] (a very Homer-centric attitude).

The similarity of the wording in the summaries of Proclus to the account of the Trojan War by Ps.-Apollodorus the mythographer (which is more detailed, perhaps providing us with further evidence for the Cycle poems) has cast suspicion on Proclus – was he simply revising pre-existing summaries by Ps.-Apollodorus or others? But this is over-sceptical, given that Proclus, according to Photius, speaks as if he and contemporaries have access to the poems themselves.[14] In any event, Proclus briefly indicates the sequence of the poems (e.g., 'next comes', 'following is'), including where the Homeric poems slot in, though these are not summarized. As well, the Cyclic authors are named and the number of books given. What follows is a readable, bare-bones summary of the episodes in each poem. Proclus is thus the starting point for reconstructing the Epic Cycle. Without him, we would have no comprehensive understanding of the Trojan Cycle poems, beyond the minimal information suggested by the their titles and rare surviving fragments.

But nothing is simple with the Epic Cycle, and problems immediately arise. Even beyond the question of whether Proclus knew the original poems, and aside from our frustration at not having all of what he says about the Cycle, other testimony challenges how comprehensive Proclus is. For example, Pausanias indicates that the *Ilias parva* narrated the sack of Troy, though the summary by Proclus stops with the introduction of the Wooden Horse.[15] It is not immediately clear why the summary by Proclus is not harmonious with other evidence, but clearly all available evidence, and not just Proclus, is required for reconstruction of the Epic Cycle.

---

[13] See Introduction, above in this volume, pp. 1, 36–9.
[14] See Davies (1986: 104–9; 1989a: 7–8).
[15] *PEG* F 10–18, 20–22 (= F 12–18, 21–3 D. = F 15–27 W.). The testimony of Pausanias is discussed further below.

For testimony about the poems, let us start with their titles, which is a much more ambiguous topic than is commonly realized. Early epic poems did not require the literate and scholarly convention of a title. Orally performed poems announced their topic at their beginnings. For the *Iliad* the Muse is called upon to sing 'the wrath of Achilles', and for the *Odyssey* it is 'the much-travelled man' (the proems then proceed to work out a precise starting point). Our titles for the Homeric poems are not documented until the classical period, and then they are rather uninspired. '*Iliad*' comes from the Greek adjective meaning 'of Ilion' (a by-word for Troy) and so means '[the poem] of Ilion'. This could have easily served the Cycle poems *Cypria*, *Aethiopis*, *Iliou persis* and (obviously) *Ilias parva* (surely an academic distinction from the [big] *Iliad*, not an original acknowledgment of secondary status).

The titles of Cycle poems are equally uninformative, and they also are documented long after their poems' composition.[16] What's especially problematic is that many different titles survive in our testimony. Some may be alternative titles, perhaps arising before convention set in; some may refer to sections or additions to the Cycle poems; some are perhaps the names of other poems that covered the same material; some may simply result from confusion. To restrict ourselves to the Trojan War, the title '*Palamedeia*' refers to the character Palamedes, who is prominent in the *Cypria*. The title of the *Cypria* itself existed in minor variants, such as the alternative adjective *Cypriaka*, alone or modifying various words for 'epic', 'writings' or 'story'. Whatever *Cypria* ('Cyprian [poem]') means is not obvious – composed at Cyprus is the consensus view, but it arguably could reference Aphrodite or events occurring at the island. Consider also the title '*Amazonia*', which refers to the Amazon Penthesileia who is featured in the *Aethiopis* (which title references the Aethiopians led by Memnon). *Ilias parva* and *Nostoi* ('*Returns*') are such vague titles that multiple poems may have been saddled with them; in Bernabé's edition a section is entitled *Iliades parvae*, or '*Little Iliads*'. Of possible relevance is ancient testimony that refers to the 'poets' of Cycle poems.[17] The title '*Return of the Sons of Atreus*' might serve as an alternative for the Cyclic *Nostoi*, though it could well have been a different poem that restricted itself to Agamemnon and Menelaus. We also

---

[16] After Herodotus on the *Epigonoi* and *Cypria* (2.117, 4.32), Aristotle in the *Poetics* mentions the *Cypria* and *Ilias parva*, as well as the *Thebaid*- and *Heracleid*-type of epic poem (chs. 8, 23).

[17] The *Oedipodea*: PEG F 1 (= D., W.); the *Thebaid*: *Epigonoi* PEG F 3 (= F 3 D. = F 4 W.); the *Cypria* PEG F 27 (= F 21 D. = F 23 W.); the *Nostoi*: PEG T 2 (= p. 152 W.). On the *Telegony* and the *Thesprotis*, see Tsagalis, below in this volume, pp. 380–1, 388–9, 399–401.

hear of a *Thesprotis*, which refers to a geographical location featured in the *Telegony*.[18]

Scholars trying to reconstruct the Epic Cycle have resisted the implications of such testimony, for it threatens the whole undertaking of reconstruction. How does one keep all the worms in the can if poems had multiple titles, or multiple poems had the same title, or – more problematically – such evidence hints at a more extensive cyclic tradition than later evidence like Proclus indicates?[19] It should also be stressed that the early testimony refers to individual poems, with no hint that they existed as part of a Cycle.

As for ancient understanding of the authorship of the Cycle poems, it seems to be a combination of guesswork and befuddlement. For example, Athenaeus refers to the poet of the *Cypria* as 'some Cyprian or Stasinus or whoever he likes to be called' (*PEG* T 9 = F 7 D. = F 10 W.). 'Cyprian' might be emended to 'Cyprias', since Athenaeus elsewhere (*PEG* T 8 = T 12 / F 4 D.) reports that Cyprias was a candidate for authorship. By a change of accent the title of the Cycle poem could be understood as 'of Cyprias', as in 'the poem of Cyprias' as opposed to 'the Cyprian poem'. It appears that Proclus took this theory seriously,[20] and a Hellenistic verse inscription from Halicarnassus boasts of a native poet Cyprias who wrote an epic about the Trojan War.[21] Absurd as the Cyprias theory may seem, it underscores ancient disagreement about authorship of early epic poems and also points to a certain eagerness on the part of different locales to lay claim to Cyclic epics, whatever their modern reputation.

More commonly the *Cypria* was ascribed to Stasinus of Cyprus, who could be deemed the consensus author. But some thought Homer composed it (and gave it to his son-in-law Stasinus, the story went), or Hegesias of Cyprus. One sympathizes with Athenaeus in throwing up his hands, or with the scholiast who stated bluntly that the author was 'unknown' (*PEG* T 10 = D.), or another who referred to the 'poets' of the *Cypria* (*PEG* F 27 = F 21 D. = F 23 W.). Many, like Aristotle, wisely avoided the issue by referring anonymously to 'the one who wrote the *Cypria*' (*PEG* F 5 = D. = F 6 W.).

---

[18] For details on these titles, see Burgess (2001: 198 n. 31).

[19] For entertainment of the possibilities, see Murray (1934: 341–3); Huxley (1969: *passim*); *PEG* pp. 72, 93. For containment, cf. West (1971: 67–9); Davies (1989b: 6).

[20] His summary of the *Cypria* promises a discussion of the title elsewhere, and though this has not survived, Photius indicates that Proclus thought the accent should be changed (*PEG* T 7 = p. 33 D.; West (2003a: 66–7)).

[21] See Burgess (2002), with an argument for variant versions of the *Cypria*.

If testimony about the authors of the Cycle poems is uncertain, perhaps it at least preserves an indication of the poems' geographical origin. It is been maintained that the Cycle was more oriented toward local concerns than the Panhellenic Homeric poems.[22] If so, then we would expect items of local interest to be featured in the poems. What was 'Cyprian' about the *Cypria* is not immediately clear (or how and why Halicarnassus would claim it), and the local relevance of the *Ilias parva* (attributed to Lesches of Mytilene),[23] the *Iliou persis* (attributed to Arctinus of Miletus), and the *Nostoi* (attributed to Agias of Troezen) is not obvious. But it seems significant that the *Telegony* was ascribed to a Cyrenean poet and featured a character named Arcesilaus, the name (in different dialect form) of the kings of Cyrene. And the *Aethiopis*, which placed the afterlife of Achilles on Leuce ('White Island'), was also ascribed to Arctinus of Miletus, which colonized the northern Black Sea, where an island called 'Leuce' was central to cult worship of Achilles.[24]

The ancient dating for the Cycle poems (as opposed to the Epic Cycle, which is a later development)[25] has inspired as little confidence. This is partly because some Cyclic authors are placed in the eighth century BC, which is awkward for the Homer-centric model. But the ancient chronology is haphazard – the birth or acme of Arctinus (sometimes said to be the student of Homer) is dated variously in the eighth century BC.[26] Over the past one hundred years scholars have applied intensive linguistic analysis to the surviving fragments in an attempt to date the poems,[27] with the placement of Cycle poems as late as the second half of the sixth century. It is no disrespect to the admirable skill of such assessments, however, to wonder about the conclusions. The most thorough dating of early epic by linguistic method places the *Cypria* in the seventh century BC, though this poem is often seen as especially late on the basis of the same evidence.[28] The nature of the database presents a problem for this type of comparative methodology; in terms of quantity the *Iliad* and *Odyssey* overwhelm even the Hesiodic corpus, and surviving verse of the Epic Cycle adds up to something less than 150 lines. Comparative linguistic analysis must also

---

[22] Nagy (1990b: 70–9), and Nagy, below in this volume, pp. 63–5.
[23] For speculation on the relevance of early epic to Lesbos, see West (2002b).
[24] This does not necessitate the conclusion that the mythological concept of Leuce was introduced after colonization of the Black Sea; see Burgess (2009: chs. 7, 8).
[25] See West, below in this volume, pp. 96–106.
[26] See *PEG* pp. 65–6.   [27] See Bernabé, below in this volume, pp. 139–41.
[28] Janko (1982: 200 and *passim*). I do not necessarily accept this alternative dating for the *Cypria*. See Burgess (2001: 52–3) for a survey of controversy over Janko's arguments (restated at Janko (2011), emphasizing the relative not absolute nature of his dating), with B. Jones (2010; 2011).

confront issues of archaism, dialect, geographical variance and idiolect; the method's requirement of uniform linguistic progression does not make it so historically. Though resemblance between Homeric and Cyclic phraseology is usually seen as literate imitation, it has also been proposed that the fragments display oral qualities.[29] In any event, as noted above, adherents of the Systemic model will find the dating of a particular recording of Cyclic verse of less import than larger questions of epic and mythological traditions.

Iconography is extremely helpful for investigation of cyclic traditions,[30] and it proves that cyclic material was popular at an early date, though iconography, whether relatively early or late, should not be employed for the dating of specific Cyclic poems. For example, it is senseless to claim that the *Aethiopis* is post-Homeric because images of Penthesileia appear subsequently to a posited date for the Homeric poem – Penthesileia appears in artwork contemporaneously with and probably earlier than Hector, the Iliadic hero.[31] On the whole, the iconographical evidence suggests that early artists and poets worked independently within the same mythological traditions; artists were not interested in illustrating epic poems.

Herodotus is our earliest certain commentator of Cycle poems, twice raising the question of whether Homer was the author of a Cyclic work, as if this ascription was standard (2.117, 4.32).[32] His reasoning on the *Cypria* is particularly fascinating. Not quoting from the *Cypria*, but with some phraseology that seems derived from epic verse, he claims that in the Cyclic poem Paris enjoyed a smooth and direct sail back to Troy with Helen, though the *Iliad* indicates a more circuitous route. The historian is evidently thinking of *Il.* 6.289–91, where Paris is said to have obtained garments from Sidon on his way back with Helen. The problem is that Proclus, employing his characteristically plain style, states that Paris and Helen in the *Cypria* were driven by a storm to Sidon, which Paris sacked. Our essential source for the Epic Cycle (Proclus) thus is inharmonious with our earliest direct testimony for the content of a Cycle poem. How do we explain the contradiction?[33] Some have suspected the credibility of Proclus; some have posited multiple versions of the *Cypria*;[34] others have posited

---

[29] See Burgess (2005: 349) for bibliography. [30] See Carpenter, below in this volume.
[31] Doubt is present because early art often lacks inscriptions and can be fragmentary. See Burgess (2001: chs. 1, 2) for the history of interpreting uncertain images as Homeric.
[32] On Herodotus and the *Cypria*, see also Introduction, above in this volume, pp. 21–2; Nagy, below, pp. 61–2; Currie, below, p. 287.
[33] See *PEG* pp. 52–3 for bibliography and a survey of solutions.
[34] Cf. Finkelberg (2000); Burgess (2002).

manipulation of the poem or the summary, perhaps due to the influence of the *Iliad*. This mysterious crux is not readily solved. It is perhaps best to be satisfied with the observation that the boundary between Homeric and cyclic epic is less firm than is commonly supposed – the journey in Homer appears more 'cyclic' than that in Herodotus' *Cypria*. Homeric and Cyclic epics partook of shared mythological traditions, within which variability organically existed.

What of actual verse of the Epic Cycle, as opposed to testimony about it? Among the few surviving fragments exists the following attributed to the *Ilias parva*:

> But the illustrious son of great-hearted Achilles was conveying the wife of Hector down to the hollow ships. As for her child, taking him from the breast of the fair-tressed nurse he had hurled him from the tower, gripping him by the foot, and dark death and strong fate had seized him. And he chose Andromache for himself, the fair-girdled wife of Hector, whom the best of the pan-Achaeans gave to him indeed to have, when they bestowed a prize appropriate in recompense to the man, and as for him, the famous offspring of horse-taming Anchises, Aeneas, he put him on the sea-crossing ships, to bear off as prize from all the Danaans, exceptional from others.[35]

The Greek is awkward to translate in spots, as commentators have noted. Many have complained as well at how plain this account of murder and enslavement seems. The Epic Cycle covered an enormous amount of material in relatively short epics, at least on the evidence of the Proclus summaries, and it is probable that it contained much less character speech than in the Homeric poems. At times Cyclic narration might have been comparable to, say, the *Hesiodic Catalogue*, where genealogical material is covered quickly with brief expansions here and there on particular mythological episodes.[36] But this fragment, the longest surviving one of the *Ilias parva*, does indeed seem very brief in its narration of the post-sack experiences of three prominent characters. In the *Iliad* allusions to the death of the prince are made with some of the same phraseology, but much more movingly.[37]

---

[35] *PEG* F 21 (= F 20 D. = F 29 W.). For the Greek text and a discussion of this passage, see also Kelly, below in this volume, p. 335.

[36] On the other hand, it would be mistaken to let our sense of Cyclic poetics be coloured by the practical terseness of Proclus, who nevertheless indicates that there were many tangential narrative expansions in the Cycle, like the multiple myths related by Nestor in the *Cypria*, or the mythological *ekphrasis* of a bowl in the *Telegony*. See now the important study of Cyclic 'inset narratives' at Marks (2010).

[37] See Griffin (1977: 51–2).

And later literature would present the post-Troy adventures of Andromache and Aeneas very powerfully (and for Aeneas very differently).

But there is more to say. The shared phraseology may point back to pre-Homeric tradition rather than attest to Homeric influence.[38] Some of the awkwardness of expression could result from the passage's interest in the complex system of dividing heroic spoils.[39] The narratology of the passage is also uncertain. At first glance it seems to present a breathless jumble of information: the leading off of Andromache, the killing of Astyanax, the allotment of Andromache, the placement of Aeneas on the ships. Spatially the initial capture of Andromache and the killing of Astyanax must occur at the city of Troy, whereas the division and embarkation of captives must take place at the Greek camp by the ships. Chronologically, the capture of Andromache and death of Astyanax must take place first, whereas the process of moving and distributing the captives must have involved a series of events. It may seem that our poet starts with the transfer of Andromache to the ships, then blurts out the death of Astyanax, before suddenly reporting on the division of spoils at the ships. Yet we might have a different impression if we knew what preceded this passage. Could it have been a narration of the capture of Andromache and the death of Astyanax? Our lines perhaps then continued with the fortunes of Andromache, with a flashback cross-reference to the previous account of the prince's death (so my translation suggests). The focus of the fragment would really then be on the division of spoils, with an assumption of audience knowledge that we do not possess.

Interpretation is thwarted by the fact that our ancient testimony for the lines is itself contradictory. The Byzantine scholar Tzetzes, commenting on Lycophron, quotes the full passage, attributing it to Lesches as author of the *Ilias parva*. Yet a scholiast to Euripides quotes lines 6–11 and attributes them to Simias of Rhodes, a Hellenistic poet. Even if we dismiss this as a mistake,

---

[38] Burgess (2010). Formulaic and metrical variance in the fragment certainly exists from a Homeric standpoint, but should not necessarily be explained as deterioration. For example, where ἐυπλόκαμος (3) is employed instead of the Homeric ἐύζωνος (*Il.* 6.467) as an epithet for the nurse, repetition is avoided with line 6 of the fragment (assuming the fragment is a unity). What is more, *euzōnos* 'generally marks sexual partners over whom men compete in war or games,' as Ready (2005: 148) argues, which would thus indeed suit Andromache best in this fragment. Ready notes the one Homeric exception to the epithet's significance is its use for the nurse in *Iliad* 6. He may be right in supposing the nurse is here assumed to be a war captive, but I would argue that the contextual anomaly of the epithet (as opposed to formulaic/metrical norms of the Homeric database) assists the passage's meta-epic allusion (see Finkelberg, below in this volume) to the death of Astyanax (Burgess (2010)).

[39] See Ready (2007), with comments on Andromache as a prize at 35–6. In accordance with his interpretation, the verb of line 6 should be the active form used by Tzetzes, a reading I employ in my translation.

we are reminded once again of the fragile nature of our ancient testimony. Bernabé's brackets indicate that some scholars have deleted these lines. In the edition of Davies there is a small space between the sections; West separates them into two fragments, arguing that Tzetzes quotes two different passages of the *Ilias parva*. There have been various other explanations: that the lines have been jumbled, for example, or that Simias reworked a passage from the *Ilias parva*, or that the attributions of these lines to Lesches and/or Simias, secondhand as they are, are corrupt and confused.[40] In other words, a lot of castles have been built on shifting sands in the critical discussions.

Proclus is of no help here, for his summary of the *Ilias parva* ends with the introduction of the Wooden Horse into the city. As noted above, the testimony of Pausanias confirms that the Cyclic poem went on to describe the sack. Pausanias describes a now lost wall painting (by the fifth-century BC artist Polygnotus) at Delphi. According to Pausanias, Polygnotus used the *Iliou persis* (sic) by 'Lescheos' (sic) as a source. Valuable as this evidence is for the occurrence of Astyanax's death in the *Ilias parva*, let us note that it is rather round-about: a second-century AD traveller describes a fifth-century BC painting by making frequent references to the (mistakenly titled) work of Lesches (named in an unorthodox form).[41]

As one can see from my discussion of the *Ilias parva* fragment, analysis of Cyclic poetry depends greatly on scholarly editions of the Epic Cycle. The current generation has been well served by several: the editions by Bernabé and Davies came out in the 1980s, and now we also have the Loeb edition by West, which among other things helpfully foregrounds the important testimonial context of fragments in its facing-page translations. The Bernabé edition is chock-full of ancient material, and abetted by a multiple-levelled apparatus that includes brief Latin notes. Since the edition by Davies was to be succeeded by a commentary, its arrangement is minimalist in comparison, and accordingly easier to use.[42] Some would deem it superior in judgment, notably Davies himself in an opinionated yet fair review of the rival edition (1989b). What the details of his discussion make very clear is that an edition needs to address endless issues about testimony and fragments (where to draw the line between these, for example?). And even where editors agree on what constitutes a testimony or fragment of the Epic Cycle, they will necessarily employ a different numeration system for their different

---

[40] See Peralc (2010), with extensive bibliography. Cf. Burgess (2010; 2012) for an oralist approach to the Astyanax section of the fragment.
[41] F 21 D. = 18 W.; in the apparatus of *PEG* F 21.
[42] Though the commentary has not appeared, Davies has published both a detailed (1986) and general account (1989c) of his views on the Epic Cycle. See now West (2013).

arrangements.[43] Though the differences in arrangement and interpretation can be disconcerting, consultation of all three editions should be used in serious study of Cyclic material.

My title borrows a phrase from Davies' review of Bernabé's edition, but where he takes aim at a rival, it is my position that every reconstruction of the Epic Cycle 'soon comes adrift' (Davies 1989b: 5). Perhaps the least invidious way of demonstrating this is to provide a critique of my own reconstruction of the Cycle (Burgess 2001). In general my views adhere to the Systemic model outlined above. Though I am indebted to Neoanalyst arguments, ultimately my conclusions diverge from the centripetal, Homer-centric ideology of neoanalysis. Instead of viewing the Cycle poems as inferior poems that preserve obscure source material for Homer, I find them representative of mythological and epic traditions that pre- and post-date the *Iliad* and the *Odyssey*.

Such an approach might seem to reify a remarkably stable 'cyclic' tradition. Yet Greek myth certainly underwent metamorphosis at different times and in different locations, sometimes due to the creativity of individual poets. For example, the *Ilias parva* apparently portrayed Neoptolemus as the murderer of Astyanax, as we saw above, but in the *Iliou persis* the culprit was Odysseus (according to Proclus). A Systemic perspective might find here intriguing issues (e.g., that the Greeks debate what to do in the Odysseus version might reflect socio-political developments).[44] But a Homer-centric approach could judge such variation as willful and trivial innovation on the part of minor poets. My arguments of a 'cyclic' tradition might therefore be overoptimistic about its stability, especially when my oralist approach to early epic denies it a textualized centre.

Perhaps it is Proclus who provides the functional approximation of a center in my reconstruction of the Epic Cycle. I accept his summaries as a reliable reflection of Cyclic verse, as far as they go. Nonetheless I have stressed the apparent discrepancies between Proclus and other testimony concerning the parameters of the Cycle poems. Most agree that the beginnings and endings in the Proclus summaries are sometimes wrong, as apparently

---

[43] A useful table of comparative numeration for contemporary and older editions is provided at the back of the West edition (2003a).

[44] See Eur. *Tro.* 719ff. for the debate, to which Pausan. 10.25.18 alludes. It is intriguing that Clement attributes to Stasinus (the usual suspect for the *Cypria*) a line of verse stating 'Foolish is the one who kills the father and spares the sons' (*PEG* F 33 = F 25 D. = F 31 W.), which despite its proverbial generalization would seem to suit best the death of Astyanax in the context of the Trojan War. On the basis of this and other testimony I have proposed that the *Cypria* narrated the whole of the Trojan War (1996: 90–1); indications of agreement by others have so far eluded me.

shown for the *Ilias parva* by the testimony of Pausanias. My explanation is that Proclus summarized a rough-and-ready verse narration of the Trojan War (of late classical or early Hellenistic date) that was created from extensive excerpts (perhaps books) of the Cycle poems. It has also been argued that 'bleeding chunks' of longer Proclus summaries were transferred to the *Iliad* manuscript tradition.[45] In any event, Proclus is accepted in my reconstruction of the Cycle as reliable for what he does summarize, which would be much less certain if other summaries were the basis of his account (see above). As for the ancient testimony that contradicts Proclus on the extent of content in the Cycle, I have proposed that some ancient authorities (like Pausanias) had access to manuscripts of the whole poems that survived after the creation of a verse Cycle.[46] This shores up the authority of ancient testimony that I want to employ in my various arguments.

Keep my apparent desire for Cyclic cohesion in mind as we move back in time to the archaic age. To some degree I maintain an optimistic attitude toward the surviving evidence. The unnerving multiplicity of Cyclic titles, for instance, does not prevent me from grouping fragments and testimony together in accordance with conventions derived from Proclus. On the other hand my Epic Cycle can seem rather open-ended, as when I speak of early cyclic traditions as oral and fluid. I also allow rather extensive consequences to the common conclusion that Proclus does not always reflect the true extent of Cycle poems – e.g., that the *Cypria* covered the whole war. What is more, I deny that the poems were created with knowledge of each other, or even of the *Iliad* and *Odyssey*. That's because I posit a widespread, long-standing performance culture of epic which featured countless performances. All this speculation is and must remain largely undocumented.

As for the actual Cycle poets themselves, like many modern scholars I reject ancient testimony about specific authors. This is a common enough reaction to the contradictory evidence discussed above, but it also is harmonious with the de-emphasis of individual poets in the Systemic model. Why do I not accept the early dating given to some of the Cycle poets by our ancient sources, if I deny the secondary nature of Cyclic verse? Consenting to dates but not the authors attached to them would hardly be fair play. Nor would accepting early ancient dating of the Cycle poems but rejecting even earlier ancient dating of Homer. Ancient indications of the geographical

---

[45] Davies (1986: 102).
[46] Like Proclus, Pausanias has been unjustly accused by Wilamowitz and others of not directly reading the authors that he cites; see Habicht (1985).

origins of the poetry are considered possible in my reconstruction, however, since one could argue, with a Systemic perspective, that local content was considered especially memorable.

What about the precious fragments themselves, which might be thought central to any academic treatment of the Cycle? My arguments might seem to sidestep controversies about their content, whether linguistic or aesthetic. For in my view these poems – the authority of whose textual preservation should not be over-stressed anyway – merely represented a larger system of cyclic traditions. I am nevertheless frequently tempted to engage in controversy over the more intriguing fragments (e.g. my comments above on the possibly pre-Homeric or anthropological nature of phraseology in the *Ilias parva* fragment). The fragments are what we have to work with; one cannot interpret the Epic Cycle without addressing them. But the process of exploring their nature is complicated by an oralist approach.

For reconstruction of the Epic Cycle, then, difficult choices arise at every turn, and final decisions are usually motivated by one's vision of what the Epic Cycle represents. Consistency of argument is achieved only with great difficulty; gaps in the evidence, sometimes made wider by our method, must be met by leaps of faith. My own confessions of arbitrary judgment and overarching assumptions are in no way an admission of error – far from it. Rather, my purpose is to include myself in a general warning against all theories about the Cycle, here in this Companion and elsewhere. There is little hope of solving the mysteries about the Epic Cycle that antiquity has bequeathed to us, and less hope that any hypothesis will satisfy all. What we can do is be self-conscious about our own assumptions in reaching conclusions concerning the Cycle's many puzzles.

2 | Oral traditions, written texts, and questions of authorship

GREGORY NAGY

INTRODUCTION

The three parts of the title are interconnected topics.

The first part, referring to oral traditions, is all-important, since oral poetry shaped not only the Epic Cycle but also the Homeric *Iliad* and *Odyssey*. The formulation I have just offered is supported by the main line of argumentation I offer here. As we will see, I argue that the oral poetic traditions of the Cycle cannot be divorced from corresponding traditions that we find in the *Iliad* and *Odyssey*.

As for the second part of the title, referring to written texts, I must note from the start: there exists no proof for saying that the technology of alphabetic writing was needed for either the composition or the performance of the Homeric poems.[1] Further, in the case of the Cycle, the textual evidence is simply too meager in comparison with the corresponding evidence of the *Iliad* and *Odyssey*; so, again, there exists no proof for saying that the composition of epics in the Cycle was somehow dependent on the technology of writing.[2] Quite the contrary, it can be shown that these epics, like the *Iliad* and *Odyssey*, did in fact originate from oral traditions.

And now we come to the third part of the title, referring to questions of authorship. As we will see, such questions cannot be addressed in terms of written texts until we address them in terms of oral traditions. That is because, as I will argue, the attribution of authorship to obscure figures such as Arctinus of Miletus and Lesches of Mytilene or to even more obscure figures such as Thestorides of Phocaea can be understood only in terms of oral traditions. And such attributions of authorship, as I will also argue, depended on the idea that Homer was the author of only the *Iliad* and the *Odyssey*. That idea, which took final shape only at a relatively later stage in the history of ancient Greek epic traditions, brings us back full circle to what I have already announced as the main line of my argumentation:

---

[1] Nagy (1990b: 18; 1996a: 3). For an alternative view, see West (2011b).
[2] For an alternative line of argumentation, see West (2013).

that the oral poetic traditions of the Epic Cycle cannot be divorced from corresponding traditions that we find in the Homeric *Iliad* and *Odyssey*.

AN EARLIER MEANING FOR THE TERM 'CYCLE'

Essential for all three topics signaled in the title is the earliest reconstructable meaning of the word *kyklos* as applied to the epic Cycle.[3] In terms of such an application, *kyklos* refers to all poetry composed by Homer.[4] Such a meaning of *kyklos* as the sum total of Homeric poetry goes back to a metaphorical use of the word in the sense of 'chariot wheel'. In Homeric diction, *kyklos* actually means '"chariot wheel"' (*Il.* 23.340, plural *kykla* at 5.722). The metaphor of comparing a well-composed song to a well-crafted chariot wheel is explicitly articulated in the poetic traditions of Indo-European languages (as in *Rig-Veda* 1.130.6); more generally in the Greek poetic traditions, there is a metaphor comparing the craft of the *tektōn* 'joiner, master carpenter' to the art of the poet (as in Pind. *Pyth.* 3.112–114).[5]

Connected with this idea is the meaning of Ὅμηρος as a *nomen loquens*. Etymologically, the form can be explained as a compound **hom-āros* meaning 'he who fits/joins together', composed of the prefix *homo-* '"together"' and the root of the verb *ar-ar-iskein* "fit, join".[6] In terms of this etymological explanation, *Homēros* is a metaphor: Homer is 'he who fits [the song] together'.[7]

So the etymology of *Homēros*, in the sense of 'fitting together', is an aspect of the overall metaphor of the *kyklos* as a 'chariot wheel': a master poet 'fits together' pieces of poetry that are made ready to be parts of an integrated whole just as a master carpenter or joiner 'fits together' or 'joins' pieces of wood that are made ready to be parts of a chariot wheel.[8]

---

[3] What I argue in this paragraph recapitulates what I say in Nagy (2010a: 255–6), which is a summary of more extensive argumentation presented in Nagy (1990b: 70–81).

[4] For more on this earlier sense of *kyklos* with reference to all poetry composed by Homer, see Pfeiffer (1968: 73) and Nagy (1996a: 38). See also West (2013: 22–3), with reference to Proclus, *Life of Homer* 9. I agree with West (2013: 1, 8) that Proclus is to be dated to the second century AD.

[5] Nagy (1999: 297–300), interpreting the evidence assembled by Schmitt (1967: 296–8). On the sense of *kyklos* as 'chariot wheel', see also Introduction, above in this volume, pp. 6–7.

[6] Chantraine (2009) s.v. '*arariskō*'. For an alternative explanation of the meaning of *Homēros*, see West (1999: 372). For a commentary on this explanation, see Nagy (2010a: 60 n. 1).

[7] Nagy (1999: 296–300).

[8] Nagy (1996b: 74–5). See also Nagy (2010a: 254–64), where I argue that this etymology of Homer's name is compatible in meaning with the etymology of the noun *homēros* in the sense

A LATER MEANING FOR THE TERM 'CYCLE'

Whereas Homer in earlier times was considered to be the poet of an Epic Cycle that included what we now know as the *Iliad* and *Odyssey*, these two epics gradually become differentiated from the Cycle in later times. In the course of such a differentiation, the *Iliad* and the *Odyssey* eventually became the only epics that were truly Homeric, while the Cycle became non-Homeric.[9]

Such a differentiation between the Homeric *Iliad* and *Odyssey* on the one hand and a non-Homeric Cycle on the other hand is most clearly visible in sources dating from the fourth century BC. For example, when Aristotle in his *Poetics* (1459a) refers to the *kyklos* in the sense of 'Epic Cycle', he is referring to a body of epic poetry that was explicitly not composed by Homer.[10]

TRADITIONS ABOUT THE AUTHORSHIP OF EPICS

In Aristotle's time as also in still later times, the epics of the Cycle were attributed to poets other than Homer. For example, two epics of the Cycle, known as the *Aethiopis* and the *Iliou persis*, were attributed to an Ionian named Arctinus from the city of Miletus (*Aeth.* arg. lines 173–4 and *Ilias Pers.* arg. lines 239–40 Severyns). Similarly, the *Ilias parva* was attributed to an Aeolian named Lesches from the island of Lesbos (*Ilias parva* arg. lines 206–7 Severyns: his native city in Lesbos is specified as Mytilene); alternatively, the *Ilias parva* was attributed not to Lesches the Aeolian but instead to an Ionian, Thestorides of Phocaea (Σ Eur. *Tro.* 822).[11] To be contrasted is the mindset of earlier times, when the entire Epic Cycle had been attributed to Homer.[12]

The tendency to exclude the Epic Cycle from authorship by Homer is visible already in the second half of the fifth century, as we see from the argument offered by Herodotus (2.116.1–117.1) against the idea that the author of another epic of the Cycle, the *Cypria*, could have been Homer. What Herodotus leaves unsaid, as I have argued elsewhere, is that he is

---

of 'hostage', which derives from the same compound *hom-āros* meaning 'he who fits/joins together'. For an alternative explanation, see West (1999). But see also Debiasi (2012: 474 n. 21) who points out that such an explanation can be reconciled with the etymology that I propose.

[9] This paragraph recapitulates what I argue in Nagy (2010a: 69–70).
[10] Nagy (2010a: 320).   [11] Allen (1912: 126).
[12] Nagy (1996a: 38, 89–91); relevant comments by Burgess (2001: 15 and 200 n. 44).

following here an Athenian way of thinking.[13] For Athenians in the fifth century BC, though not necessarily for other Greeks of that time, Homer was the author of no epic other than the *Iliad* and the *Odyssey*. Such a way of thinking, as I have also argued elsewhere, indicates that the repertoire for performing epic at the premier festival of the Athenians, the Panathenaea, was restricted to the *Iliad* and the *Odyssey* during the fifth century.[14]

PANATHENAIC AND PANIONIC CONTEXTS FOR EPIC PERFORMANCE

Already in the pre-classical period, there was a tendency to exclude the Epic Cycle from authorship by Homer. During most of the sixth century BC in Athens, when this city was ruled by a dynasty of so-called tyrants known as the Peisistratidai, the epics of the Cycle were becoming marginalized while the *Iliad* and the *Odyssey* were becoming central in the performances of epic at the festival of the Panathenaea.[15] A climactic moment in this process was the establishment of the so-called Panathenaic Regulation in Athens toward the end of the sixth century BC: the terms of this regulation make it clear that the sole repertoire of epic performance at the festival of the Panathenaea in Athens had by now become the Homeric *Iliad* and *Odyssey*.[16]

So far, we have considered the emerging centrality of the Homeric *Iliad* and *Odyssey* at the expense of the Epic Cycle in the pre-classical era of epic as performed at the festival of the Panathenaea in Athens during the sixth century BC. But this emerging centrality can be dated even further back in time. I have in mind here an earlier pre-classical era of epic performance as it evolved at the festival of the Panionia at the Panionion of the Ionian Dodecapolis, in the late eighth and early seventh century. Already at that time, the two central epics performed at the festival of the Panionia were prototypical versions of the *Iliad* and the *Odyssey*.[17] As Douglas Frame has shown, a lasting trace of this centrality is the fact that each of these two epics is divisible into six performance units, adding up to twelve performance units representing each one of the twelve cities of the Ionian Dodecapolis.[18]

---

[13] Nagy (2010a: 75–8).   [14] Nagy (2002: 9–35).   [15] Nagy (2010a: 320; 1990b: 72).
[16] Nagy (2010a: 22–8), with reference to such primary passages as Ps.-Plat. *Hipparch.* 228b–c; Dieuchidas of Megara, *FgrHist* 485 F 6 (via Diog. Laert. 1.57); Lycurg. *Leoc.* 102.
[17] Nagy (2010a: 22).
[18] Frame (2009: 550–621), who shows that each one of these twelve performance units corresponds to four ῥαψῳδίαι 'rhapsodies' or 'books' of the Homeric *Iliad* and *Odyssey* as we know them ('books' 1–4, 5–8, 9–12, 13–16, 17–20, 21–4).

Herodotus (1.142.3) lists these twelve Ionian cities in the following order: Miletus, Myous, Priene, Ephesus, Colophon, Lebedos, Teos, Clazomenae, Phocaea, Samos, Chios, and Erythrae.[19] It is in the historical context of these twelve cities that the centrality of the *Iliad* and *Odyssey* and the marginalization of the Cycle can be explained, and it is this Panionic organization of Homeric performance in the late eighth and early seventh century that became the model for the Panathenaic Regulation in Athens in the late sixth century.[20] As I argue at length elsewhere, the Panathenaic Regulation was basically an Ionian tradition imported to Athens from the island state of Chios by way of a corporation of Chiote epic performers known as the 'sons of Homer', the *Homēridai*.[21]

THE RELATIVITY OF PANHELLENISM IN HOMERIC AND CYCLIC TRADITIONS

To be contrasted with the Panionian prototypes of the *Iliad* and *Odyssey* are the two Ionian epics attributed to Arctinus of Miletus, the *Aethiopis* and the *Iliou persis*, which do not fit the broader social framework of the Ionian Dodecapolis but rather the narrower one of Miletus as a single city that had once dominated the confederation of the Dodecapolis but was thereafter gradually eclipsed by other Ionian cities that belonged to that confederation; one of those other cities was the island state of Chios, the home of the *Homēridai*, which had escaped most of the misfortunes that befell Miletus in the course of that city's struggles against the Lydian Empire and, subsequently, against the Persian Empire.[22] In terms of this contrast, I need to make two points about such epics as the *Aethiopis* and the *Iliou persis*, both attributed to Arctinus of Miletus:

(1) The contents of such epics belonging to the Cycle tend to be more localized and therefore more conservative than the contents of the *Iliad* and *Odyssey*.[23]
(2) Conversely, the contents of the *Iliad* and *Odyssey* can be described as more Panhellenic.

The description 'more Panhellenic' can be explained in terms of an emerging differentiation between the Cycle on one hand and the *Iliad* and *Odyssey* on the other. The Panhellenization of the Homeric tradition

---

[19] Commentary in Nagy (2010a: 216–17).   [20] Nagy (2010a: 22).
[21] Nagy (2010a: 59–65, 68–9, 95–6, 313).   [22] Nagy (2010a: 322–4).   [23] Nagy (2010a: 321).

entailed a differentiation from older layers of Panhellenic epic tradition (as represented by the epic Cycle), and these older layers were gradually sloughed off in the process of Homeric streamlining. Such an explanation would account for not only the artistic superiority of the *Iliad* and *Odyssey* but also the thematic archaism of the Cycle. The older layers represented by the Cycle kept developing alongside the emerging core of the Homeric tradition and, being the more local versions, had the relative freedom to develop for a longer time, albeit at a slower pace, toward a point of textual fixation that still seems like a case of arrested development in contrast with the ultimate Homeric form. The Panhellenization of the Homeric tradition entailed a differentiation from the Cycle. The older aspects of Panhellenic poetry as represented by the epic Cycle were gradually sloughed off by Homeric poetry in a process that could be described as 'streamlining'.

In terms of such an explanatory model, we can account for both the artistic superiority of the *Iliad* and *Odyssey* and the archaism of the narratives represented by the Cycle. The older aspects of epic poetry represented by the Cycle kept developing alongside the emerging newer core of the Homeric tradition that became the *Iliad* and *Odyssey*. These older Cyclic aspects, more localized than the newer Homeric core, were more fluid and could thus develop for a longer period of time, though the pace of development would have been slower than that of the *Iliad* and *Odyssey*. By the time the Cycle reached a point of fixation, its content must have seemed more old-fashioned than the corresponding content of the Homeric *Iliad* and *Odyssey*, even though these two epics must have reached their point of fixation at an earlier time. That is why I say that the Cycle must have seemed like a case of arrested development by comparison with Homeric poetry.[24]

My description of the Homeric *Iliad* and *Odyssey* as relatively 'more Panhellenic' in content applies to Hesiodic poetry as well.[25] The term 'Panhellenic' can be used in a relativized sense, despite its inherently absolutized meaning as 'common to all Greeks'. To relativize 'Panhellenic' is to recognize that the Panhellenization of Homer and Hesiod, just like other aspects of Panhellenism, cannot be described in absolute terms of universalization. Despite the totalizing ideology implicit in the term 'Panhellenic', the Panhellenization of Homer and Hesiod was not an absolute: it was merely a tendency toward a notional absolute.[26] And, just as the concept of Panhellenism was in fact relative, and so also the concept of a Panhellenic Homer or a Panhellenic Hesiod was relative, since it depended on – and this relativism resulted from – regional variations in the various appropriations of these

[24] Nagy (1990b: 73). [25] Nagy (2009b: 275). [26] Nagy (1996a: 38–40).

poetic figures Homer and Hesiod by the various Greek communities that claimed them as their own.

MARGINALIZATIONS OF THE CYCLE

While the *Iliad* and the *Odyssey* were becoming centralized and ever more Panhellenic in the pre-classical period, first in the context of the Panionic festival of the Ionian Dodecapolis during the late eighth and early seventh centuries BC and thereafter in the context of the Panathenaic festival at Athens during the sixth century BC, the epics of the Cycle were becoming ever more marginalized, even though the basic content of its narratives could still keep on being readjusted to the contents of the *Iliad* and *Odyssey*.[27] By the time of the classical period, however, the marginalization of the Cycle had reached a point where no further readjustments could even be possible. By this time, the epics of the Cycle were phased out of the epic program of the Panathenaea in Athens, leaving the *Iliad* and *Odyssey* as the sole representatives of Homeric poetry at that festival.[28]

The classical version of the Homeric *Iliad* and *Odyssey* as performed at the festival of the Panathenaea, derived from the pre-classical version as performed at the festival of the Panionia, tended to neutralize any potential incompatibilities with older and more localized epic versions still evident in the Epic Cycle. A case in point is the Panathenaic elision of the hero Scamandrius, who had a role in Ionian as well as Aeolian versions of stories about the capture of Troy: in some of these versions, Scamandrius was a bastard son of Hector, distinct from the son named Astyanax, whose mother was Andromache (Σ Eur. *Andr.* 10; see also Strabo 13.1.52 (607)).[29] By contrast, the identities of Scamandrius and Astyanax are merged in the Panathenaic *Iliad* (6.402).[30]

When it comes to Ionian versions of epic poetry, I have already mentioned as prime examples the pair of epics known as the *Aethiopis* and the *Iliou persis*, both attributed to Arctinus of Miletus. Both of these epics promoted the Ionian traditions of the city of Miletus. Another such example is the *Ilias parva* attributed to Lesches of Mytilene, which promoted the Aeolian traditions of the island of Lesbos. By contrast, the Panathenaic version of the

---

[27] Nagy (1990b: 72). [28] Nagy (2010a: 320–1).
[29] Nagy (2010a: 67–8, 70, 71–2, 80–2, 85, 321–2, 323). [30] Nagy (2010a: 204–6).

Homeric *Iliad* tended to neutralize both the Ionian and the Aeolian versions of epic traditions associated respectively with Miletus and Lesbos.[31]

THE ORAL POETICS OF THE EPIC CYCLE AND BEYOND

As I have argued so far, the oral poetics of the Epic Cycle cannot be divorced from the corresponding oral poetics of the *Iliad* and *Odyssey*. We have not yet considered, however, the characteristics of oral poetry as reflected in the surviving texts attributed to Homer and to the poets of the Cycle – as also to Hesiod. In order to proceed, I need to review the essentials of oral poetic *composition, performance, reception,* and *transmission.*[32]

In any oral tradition, the process of composition is linked to the process of performance, and any given composition can be recomposed each time it is performed. The performer who recomposes the composition in performance may be the same performer who composed it earlier, or it may be a new performer, even a succession of new performers. The point is, such recomposition-in-performance is the essence of transmission in oral traditions. This kind of transmission is the key to a broader understanding of reception. Unlike what happens in literature, where reception by the public happens only after a piece of literature is transmitted, reception in oral traditions happens during as well as after transmission. That is because the process of composition in oral traditions allows for recomposition on each new occasion of performance for a public that sees and hears the performer. In oral traditions, there is an organic link between reception and performance, since no performance can succeed without a successful reception by the public that sees and hears the performer or performers.

THE QUESTION OF TEXTUALIZATION

It has been claimed that the dissemination of Homeric – and Hesiodic – poetry was a result of textualization.[33] In terms of such a claim, which can be applied also to the Epic Cycle, the new technology of alphabetic writing would have been used as early as the eighth century BC for the purpose of recording and disseminating such poetry.[34] There is simply no evidence,

---

[31] Nagy (2010a: 147–217).
[32] What follows is an abridged version of the formulation in Nagy (2009b: 282–3).
[33] For example, Most (2006a: xxxiv–xxxvi).   [34] Most (2006a: xx–xxii).

however, to indicate that writing had in fact been used for such a purpose in this early period – or for the purpose of actually composing the poetry.[35] The same can be said more generally about the archaic period extending from the eighth through the sixth centuries BC: even in this later period, there is no evidence for any widespread dissemination of any texts of poetry.[36]

By contrast, the early dissemination of Homeric, Cyclic, and Hesiodic poetry can be explained in terms of oral poetics.[37] In oral poetry, as I have already pointed out, composition and performance are aspects of the same process. So, when a composition is performed at different times and in different places, it can be recomposed in the process of composition-in-performance. And the ongoing recomposition-in-performance needs to be viewed diachronically as well as synchronically.[38] From a synchronic point of view, the poet who performs a poem can claim to own it as his own composition in the process of recomposing it in performance. From a diachronic point of view, however, the ownership can readily be transferred from poem to poem, from poet to poet. And such transference can promote the dissemination of both the poetry and the name of the poet.

As for the relatively later phases in the dissemination of Homeric, Cyclic, and Hesiodic poetry, the technology of writing finally enters the picture. In terms of reconciling written transmission with earlier oral transmission, however, it is important to distinguish different stages in the writing down of such poetry. These different stages can be formulated in terms of *transcript*, *script*, and *scripture*.[39]

THE QUESTION OF AUTHORSHIP

The authorship of each epic of the Cycle needs to be viewed in terms of oral traditions. That is because, as I already said at the beginning, the attribution of authorship to obscure figures such as Arctinus of Miletus and Lesches of Lesbos or to even more obscure figures such as Thestorides of Phocaea

---

[35] On the poetics of epigrams, which are attested already in the eighth century BC, see Nagy (1996a: 14, 35–6): it is argued there that the poetry of epigrams shows a clear separation between the processes of composing and inscribing.

[36] Nagy (1996a: 34–7).

[37] What follows is a summary of the argumentation in Nagy (1990a: 38–47) and (2009b: 281–7), relying on the fundamental work of Parry (collected writings first published in 1971) and Lord (1960/2000).

[38] On the distinction between synchronic and diachronic approaches to the analysis of a given structure in the study of oral poetics: Nagy (2003: 1), with reference to Saussure (1916 = 1972: 117).

[39] Nagy (1996b: 110–13) and (2009a: 5).

can only be understood in terms of oral traditions. And such attributions of authorship, as I also said at the beginning, depended on the idea that Homer was the author of only the *Iliad* and the *Odyssey*. We have already considered the reasons for the evolution of such an idea, but we have yet to consider the actual differentiation of the authors of the Epic Cycle from the authorship of Homer.

This differentiation of the Cycle from Homeric poetry is reflected in myths about the lives of Homer, Hesiod, and poets of the Cycle. In what follows, I will consider a variety of such myths, concentrating on one myth in particular.

THE *LIFE OF HOMER* AND OTHER *LIVES OF POETS* AS SOURCES

A primary source for the myths we are about to consider is a body of narratives known as the *Lives of Homer*. I will consider here two such *Lives*: one of them is *Vita 1*, sometimes known as the *Herodotean Life*, and the other is *Vita 2*, the *Contest of Homer and Hesiod*, which is sometimes called the *Certamen* for short.[40] Before I start my analysis, I will offer here some general observations about the *Lives*.[41]

The narratives of these *Lives* are myths, not historical facts, about Homer. To say that we are dealing with myths, however, is not at all to say that there is no history to be learned from the *Lives*. Even though the various Homers of the various *Lives* are evidently mythical constructs, the actual constructing of myths about Homer can be seen as historical fact. These myths about Homer in the *Lives* can be analyzed as evidence for the various different ways in which Homeric poetry was appropriated by various different cultural and political centers throughout the ancient Greek-speaking world. And these myths, in all their varieties, have basically one thing in common: Homeric

---

[40] I offer the following system for referring to these *Lives*, with page numbers as printed by Allen (1912):

Vita 1 = *Vita Herodotea*, 192–218
Vita 2 = *Certamen*, 225–38

There is is now also another system for numbering the *Lives*, introduced by West (2003b). For a new edition of *Vita 1* and *Vita 2*, see Colbeaux (2005). In the case of the *Certamen*, I must add, it draws extensively from a lost work, the *Mouseion* of Alcidamas, who flourished in the first half of the fourth century BC.

[41] The next two paragraphs are based on Nagy (2010a: 30).

poetry is pictured as a medium of performance, featuring Homer himself as the master performer.

Such myths about the lives of Homer and other poets can be read as sources of information about the reception and the transmission of oral poetry – even about the composition and the performance of such poetry. More generally, these myths provide information about the three main questions that are posed in my title: oral traditions, written texts and authorship. The information is varied and layered, requiring a combination of synchronic and diachronic analysis.

A STORY ABOUT HOMER AND THESTORIDES

This story is embedded in the overall narrative of *Vita 1*, which is the so-called Herodotean *Life of Homer*. Highlighted in the story are the poet Homer and the poet Thestorides of Phocaea, who is elsewhere credited with the authorship of an epic in the Cycle, the *Ilias parva* (Σ Eur. *Tro.* 822 = *Ilias parva PEG* T 10).[42] This myth, as we will see, activates the idea of making *transcripts* as well as *scripts* of an oral composition in performance, to be followed by the idea of turning such an authentic composition into a kind of *scripture*.[43]

According to the story, Homer has been wandering from city to city in Asia Minor, and he has just arrived at the Ionian city of Phocaea:

> Arriving in Phocaea, he [= Homer] made a living the same way as he had before, performing verses [ἔπεα] while sitting around in men's meeting places [λέσχαι].[44] During this time there was in Phocaea a man called Thestorides, who taught young people the knowledge of letters [γράμματα]. He was not an honest man. When he found out about Homer and his songmaking [ποίησις], he got into a conversation with him and made him the following offer: he said that he [= Thestorides] would guarantee support and subsidy for him [= Homer] if he [= Homer] would be

---

[42] The analysis that follows recapitulates my earlier analysis in Nagy (2010a: 37–42) of the story of Thestorides in *Vita 1*. For another study of this story, see Cassio (2003), whose interpretations differ from mine. On Thestorides of Phocaea, see also Introduction, above in this volume, pp. 23–4.
[43] Earlier, I have already drawn attention to these terms *transcript*, *script*, and *scripture*, with reference to Nagy (1996b: 110–13) and (2009a: 5).
[44] The setting for Homeric performances here, *leschai* 'men's meeting places', is relevant to the argumentation that follows.

willing to have a transcription made [ἀναγράψασθαι]⁴⁵ of the verses [epos plural] that he [= Homer] had made [ποιεῖν] and of other verses that he [= Homer] was about to make [ποιεῖν] and attribute them to him [= Thestorides] always. When Homer heard this, he decided that he should do it, since he was lacking even the bare necessities of life and was needy of support and subsidy. (*Vita* 1.192–202)

In the logic of the wording in this passage, as we will see, Homer's own act of composing – in the past, present, and future – does not depend on someone else's act of writing down his compositions.

Having accepted the deal offered by Thestorides, Homer stays in Phocaea and 'makes' the *Ilias parva* and the *Phocais*, but it is Thestorides who has it all written down:

> Spending his time in the house of Thestorides, he [= Homer] made [ποιεῖν] the *Ilias parva* [literally, the 'Smaller *Iliad*'], which begins this way:
> I sing Troy and the land of the Dardanoi, famed for horses.
> Many things for the sake of this land did the Danaoi suffer, those attendants [θεράποντες] of Ares.
> He [= Homer] also made the so-called *Phocais*, which the people of Phocaea say Homer had made [ποιῆσαι] in their city. And when Thestorides had the *Phocais* and all his [= Homer's] other things written down [ἐγράψατο]⁴⁶ from Homer, he [= Thestorides] made plans to depart from Phocaea, wishing to appropriate [ἐξιδιώσασθαι] the songmaking [= ποίησις] of Homer. (*Vita* 1.202–10)

So we see here that the narrative differentiates two poetic events: (1) Homer 'makes' poetry (*poiein*) *and* (2) Thestorides 'has a transcription made' of the poetry (*graphesthai*). And there are further differentiations. As we see from the narrative, Thestorides plans to depart from Phocaea as soon as he gets his transcript of Homeric poetry. Why? Because he wants to turn the transcript into a script. And why is that? As the narrative continues, the answer becomes clear: Thestorides aspires to be a rival Homer not only as a composer but also as a performer. What Thestorides wants from Homer is a

---

⁴⁵ I interpret the middle aorist of *ana-graphesthai* here as 'have [somebody] transcribe', where the grammar does not specify who will initiate the transcription; at a later point in the narrative, it becomes clear that it is Thestorides who initiates the transcription (*Vita* 1.208 *ho Thestoridēs egrapsato* 'Thestorides had [the poems] transcribed'); see Nagy (2010a: 38).

⁴⁶ So here we see, as I anticipated in the previous note, that the prospect of *ana-graphesthai* 'have [somebody] transcribe', as formulated in the original deal, has now become a done deal as Thestorides proceeds with the act of *graphesthai* 'having [someone] transcribe' the poetry of Homer.

script that will enable him to perform the poetry composed by Homer. Only by way of actually performing can Thestorides display the compositions that he claims to be his own. I will now summarize here the relevant part of the continuing narrative.[47]

In *Vita* 1.210 and following, Thestorides sails from Phocaea to the island of Chios, where he goes about performing (1.215 and 222) the verses or *epē* (= plural of *epos*) of Homer as if they were his own. Meanwhile, back in Phocaea, Homer finds out about this misappropriation and angrily resolves to make every effort to travel to Chios in order to set things straight (1.224–5). He lives through many adventures while trying to make his way to Chios (1.225–75). After finally arriving on the island (1.275–6), Homer 'makes' (*poiein*) new poems there (1.335). Thestorides hears about the presence of the composer and, to avoid being exposed as a pseudo-Homer, that is, as an unauthorized performer who claims the compositions of Homer, he abruptly leaves Chios (1.336–8). Throughout this narrative, the scripted performances of Thestorides are being contrasted with the unscripted compositions of Homer.

The narrative here makes the motive of the pseudo-Homer explicit: Thestorides intends to appropriate the poetry of Homer by performing it somewhere else, in the absence of Homer. But Homer refuses to let himself become an absent author. As the narrative continues, it becomes clear that Homer's authorizing presence is essential for any occasion when his compositions are being performed. By contrast, the scripted performances of Thestorides are all unauthorized by Homer. In terms of the narrative up to now, only the unscripted performances of the genuine composer are authorized.

I continue with my summary of the narrative of *Vita 1*. While Thestorides is living in the city of the island of Chios, pretending to be Homer, the real Homer is living in the countryside of the island after having arrived there, and he is composing 'rustic' poetry like *The Battle of the Frogs and Mice* (1.332–5); such poetry establishes Homer's reputation on the island. That is why, when Thestorides hears that Homer is living in the countryside of Chios, he flees from the city of Chios and from the island altogether (1.332–8). Thestorides feared the consequences of a performative confrontation with Homer, because he would then be exposed as a pseudo-Homer.

By now we have seen that Homer cannot afford to be an absent author. He can be an author only to the extent that his real or notional

---

[47] Nagy (2010a: 38–9).

presence authorizes the occasion of performance. In the narrative logic of *Vita 1*, Homer embodies the ongoing fusion of the composer with the performer. In other words, we see here a poetics of presence, not a poetics of absence.[48]

I return once more to the story in *Vita 1*. Once Thestorides has removed himself, Homer moves to the city of Chios, establishing himself as a master performer, and audiences throughout the island become *thaumastai* 'admirers' of his (1.342).[49] While he stays in the city of Chios, Homer is composing the *Odyssey* (1.350–2) and the 'big' *Iliad* (1.379–84). Homer's fame grows exponentially throughout Ionian Asia Minor, and his admirers urge him to tour the Helladic mainland (1.372–6). Though Homer is described as eager to make such a tour (1.376–7), he implicitly stays in Chios for a longer period as he continues to make verses that center on the glorification of Athens (1.378–99). After he finishes these embellishments, Homer can now finally leave Chios and set sail to tour the rest of Hellas (1.400), and he arrives at the island of Samos as a transitional stopover (1.401).

At this point, there is a bifurcation of the *Life of Homer* traditions. According to one main version (as narrated in *Vita 1*), Homer travels from Samos to the island of Ios, and he dies there before he can ever reach the Helladic mainland (1.484–516).[50] To be contrasted is the other main version, as narrated in *Vita 2*, which tracks Homer's itinerary through the great Helladic cities of Athens (2.276–8), Corinth (2.286–7), and Argos (2.287–315); after a most successful performance at Delos (2.315–22) he travels to the island of Ios, where he dies (2.322–28).[51]

Once Homer dies, what will happen to his principle of refusing to let himself become an absent author? If Homer's authorizing presence is essential for any occasion when his compositions are being performed, who will authorize the performances of Homer once he is dead? My answer is, the authorizers will be the *Homēridai*, natives of Chios, who are the notional sons of Homer.[52] At the Panathenaea, for example, the performances of Homeric poetry are authorized by the *Homēridai* of Chios (Plat. *Ion* 530d).[53] To be contrasted are the scripted performances of Thestorides, which are unauthorized by Homer.

---

[48] Nagy (2010a: 32–3). As I point out in that analysis, I seek to find common ground with the work of Graziosi (2002) on ideas of Homer as author. By contrast, Graziosi (2002) argues for a poetics of absence.

[49] This word *thaumastai* refers to Homeric reception throughout *Vita 1*: see Nagy (2010a: 37, 48–51).

[50] Commentary in Nagy (2010a: 64).   [51] Commentary in Nagy (2010a: 46–7).

[52] Nagy (2010a: 28).   [53] Nagy (2010a: 61–2).

Are we to understand, then, that the *Homēridai* have a script, as it were, of Homer's compositions? No, they have something more, and that is the scripture of Homer as the one true author, as opposed to the script of Thestorides as the false author. Just as the unscripted performances of the genuine composer were authorized by Homer, so also the performances of his legitimate heirs are authorized by him, authored by him, and the words of this author become scripture for the *Homēridai*.

The prototype for such a notional scripture is set up already in the narrative of *Vita 1*.[54] As we have seen, Thestorides is described as a teacher of grammata 'letters' (1.185, 223). As for Homer, once he is finally established in the city of Chios, he becomes a teacher of *epē* 'verses' (= plural of *epos*; 1.341). This distinction between a teacher of *epē* and a teacher of grammata 'letters' seems to elevate Homer from his former status as teacher of grammata in Smyrna – a status he inherits from a character named Phemius (1.50–2). This is not to say, however, that the word grammata implies, in and of itself, a distinction between *written* and *oral*. As we see in an earlier part of the narrative (1.37–8), even the undifferentiated usage of grammata includes the performing arts, *mousikē*. In *Vita 2* as well, we see that Homer himself is again described as a teacher of grammata (2.16).

But the fact remains that graphein 'to write' is not used either in *Vita 1* or in *Vita 2* to refer to the composition of poetry by Homer. Homer is said to 'make', *poiein*, whatever he composes, not to graphein it.[55] This pattern is backed up by the testimony of other sources.[56] In the works of Plato and Aristotle, for example, we see Homer as an artisan who 'makes', poiei, and who is not pictured as one who 'writes', graphei.[57] Only in later sources such as Plutarch and Pausanias is Homer finally seen as an author who *graphei* whatever he composes.[58] In such later sources, composition can be metaphorized as written composition, and, at least to that extent, we may think of Homer as a writer. Nevertheless, as we have seen, earlier sources like *Vita 1* and *Vita 2* simply do not metaphorize performance as an act of performing written texts.[59]

As we have seen, then, in the story of Homer and Thestorides as narrated in *Vita 1*, the narration requires the real or notional presence of Homer for authorizing the performance of Homer. And this narrative requirement holds up even in later periods of Homeric reception as narrated in the *Life of*

---

[54] Nagy (2010a: 38–9). [55] Nagy (2010a: 33–47; 2004). [56] Nagy (2010a: 31–2).
[57] Plat. *Phd.* 94d, *Hipp. Min.* 371a, *Rep.* 2.378d, *Ion* 531c–d. Also Arist. *De an.* 404a, *EN* 3.1116a and 7.1145a, *GA* 785a, *Po.* 1448a, *Pol.* 3.1278a and 8.1338a, *Rh.* 1.1370b, *HA* 513b. For an early example of *poiein* with Homer as subject, see Herodotus 2.53.2.
[58] Plut. *De amore* 496d, *Quaest. Conv.* 668d; Paus. 3.24.11, 8.29.2. [59] Nagy (2010a: 33).

Homer narratives. Even in such later contexts, where the poems attributed to Homer are described explicitly as his own writings, the narrative still requires the notional performance of these poems, and the model performer must still be Homer himself.[60]

COMPETITIONS IN THE PERFORMANCES OF EPICS

By now we have seen that Thestorides of Phocaea, according to *Vita 1*, is a pseudo-Homer who claims credit for composing the *Ilias parva* by virtue of performing this epic, which had actually been composed by the real Homer. Earlier on, however, we had seen that this Thestorides of Phocaea was in other contexts actually credited with the authorship of the *Ilias parva* (Σ Eur. *Tro.* 822). How, then, can we explain such different perspectives? The answer is, it all depends on whether Homer was viewed as the author of the *Iliad* and *Odyssey* exclusively. In terms of the narrative of *Vita 1*, this is clearly not the case, since Homer is the author of the *Ilias parva* as well. Such a Homer, as we have seen, is a pre-classical Homer, and such a poetic figure has to fight off the rival claims of other poetic figures in an ongoing struggle for getting credit as the author of any given epic in the Cycle. By contrast, the classical Homer is the author of only the *Iliad* and *Odyssey* as performed at the festival of the Panathenaea in Athens. From such a classical perspective, then, Thestorides of Phocaea may legitimately be viewed as the author of the *Ilias parva*, since Homer makes no rival claim to its authorship. But here we run into a problem: there do exist other rival claims to the authorship of the *Ilias parva*. As I will now argue, such rival claims indicate the existence of competing traditions in performing epics like the *Ilias parva*.

As we have already seen, the authorship of the *Ilias parva* is attributed not only to Homer or to Thestorides of Phocaea: according to a rival tradition, it can be attributed to another poet, named Lesches, who originates from the Aeolian city of Mytilene on the island of Lesbos (*Ilias parva* arg. lines 206–7 Severyns). This Aeolian poet Lesches of Mytilene, according to a myth reported by Phaenias of Eresus, who flourished in the fourth century BC (F 33 ed. Wehrli, by way of Clem. Al. *Strom*. 1.131.6), engaged in a poetic contest with the Ionian poet Arctinus of Miletus, and the contest was won by Lesches the Aeolian. In this case, it is no accident that our source is an author who originated from Eresus. This city, just like the city of Mytilene, is located on the Aeolian island of Lesbos. And the myth reported by Phaenias

---

[60] Nagy (2010a: 33).

about a competition in performance, it can be argued, is an aetiology for the existence of rival epics: Lesches of Mytilene is credited with the authorship of one of these epics, the *Ilias parva*, while Arctinus of Miletus is the accredited author of two other epics about the Trojan War, the *Aethiopis* and the *Iliou persis*.[61]

Even the name of Lesches of Mytilene indicates a context of competition in performance. His name Λέσχης is a *nomen loquens*, derived from the word *leschē*, which as we have already seen means 'men's meeting place'. And we have already seen this word referring to an actual context for the competitive performances of epic by Homer. It was in fact at a *leschē* where Homer's performances of epic had first captured the attention of his poetic rival, Thestorides of Phocaea, who as we have seen went on to steal Homer's *Ilias parva*:

> Arriving in Phocaea, he [= Homer] made a living the same way as he had before, performing verses [ἔπεα] while sitting around in men's meeting places [λέσχαι]. (*Vita* 1.192–4)

The *leschē*, as a place for competitive performances of poetry, is an arena for poetic reception, determining the acceptance or the rejection of the competing poet. At an earlier stage in Homer's life as narrated in *Vita* 1, back when his name was not yet Homer but Melesigenes, we see our poet performing the same way as he now performs in Phocaea. Back then, Homer's performances of epic were also in a *leschē*. Back then, he was performing in Cyme, which is an Aeolian city just like Mytilene, the city of Lesches. Here is the telling description of Homer's performance at Cyme:

> *Melēsigenēs* [= Homer] used to sit in the meeting-places [λέσχαι] of the elders in Cyme and perform [ἐπεδείκνυτο] the verses [ἔπεα] made [ποιεῖν] by him. With his words he gave pleasure to his audiences [τοὺς ἀκούοντας]. And they became his admirers [θαυμασταί]. But he, knowing that the people of Cyme accepted [ἀποδέχονται] his songmaking [ποίησις], and attracting [ἕλκων] his audiences into a state of familiarisation [συνήθεια] . . . (*Vita* 1.141–6)

During his stay here in the Aeolian city of Cyme, which is then immediately followed by his stay in the Ionian city of Phocaea, Homer is said to have 'performed' (= *epideiknynai* = 'made an *epideixis* of') the verses or *epea* (= plural of *epos*) that he had 'made' (*poiein*). His audiences, 'hearing' (*akouontes*) him perform, 'accepted' (*apodechontai*) his song-making

---

[61] Nagy (1990b: 19 n. 10, 28 n. 61, 74–5).

(*poiēsis*). The 'acceptance' or reception by the audience is correlated with their familiarization (*syn-ētheia*) to the song-making; this familiarization is in turn correlated with Homer's drawing power, his ability to attract audiences.[62] The successful reception of Homer here is conveyed by saying that his audiences in the Aeolian city of Cyme became his 'admirers'.[63] We have already noted earlier this particular way of referring to Homeric reception in Chios.

In sum, Homer's competitive performances at *leschai* are comparable to the performance of Lesches (or Λέσχεως: Pausanias) of Mytilene in the myth about his competition with the performance of Arctinus of Miletus. And such competition, juxtaposing the *Ilias parva* of the Aeolian Lesches with the *Aethiopis* and *Iliou persis* of the Ionian Arctinus, is in turn comparable to the ultimate poetic competition between Homer and Hesiod as narrated in *Vita 2*, the *Contest of Homer and Hesiod*.[64]

EPILOGUE

This study has collected traces of an old poetic rivalry between (1) epics now recognized as belonging to the Cycle and (2) the two epics of the Homeric *Iliad* and *Odyssey*, which were becoming the dominant epic repertoire of the festival of the Panionia already in the late eighth and early seventh centuries BC. The eventual dominance of the Homeric *Iliad* and *Odyssey* is signaled by the obsolescence of the Cycle in the epic repertoire of the festival of the Panathenaea in Athens during the sixth century BC, in the era of the Peisistratidai. As we will now see, however, epics of the Cycle were still being performed at that festival even in such a relatively late era.

In the surviving plot outlines of the Cycle, we see occasional references to distinctly Athenian agenda, indicating that the performance traditions of the Cycle were still alive in Athens during the sixth century.[65] For example, in the case of the *Iliou persis* attributed to Arctinus of Miletus, there is mention of the rescue of the mother of Theseus by the Athenian hero's two sons Acamas and Demophon after the capture of Troy (*Il. Pers.* arg. lines 270–1 Severyns); there is another such mention of these figures in the *Ilias parva* attributed to Lesches of Mytilene (*PEG* F 20 = F 23 D. = F 17 W. via Pausanias 10.25.8).[66]

---

[62] On the implications of 'reception' inherent in the word *apodechesthai* 'accept', see Nagy (1990b: 217–18, 221–2).
[63] Nagy (2010a: 36–7). [64] Nagy (1990b: 76). [65] Nagy (2010a: 320).
[66] Debiasi 2004: 132 n. 58, 207; for further examples of such Athenian accretions, see Burgess (2001: 152, 247 n. 75).

Still, the obsolescence of the Cycle in Athens is clearly indicated by a significant absence in a set of Athenian narratives about the text of the *Iliad* and *Odyssey*. I have in mind here the stories of the so-called Peisistratean Recension.[67] As we read in the most succinct version of these stories (retold in the *Suda* and reprinted in 258 lines 37–43 ed. Allen), Homer had recited the *Iliad* and *Odyssey* in bits and pieces while wandering throughout Asia Minor and beyond, and it was these bits and pieces that Peisistratus of Athens had assembled, thus constituting the integrity of the *Iliad* and *Odyssey* as a unified corpus of epic.[68] So what is the significant absence in such stories about the Peisistratean Recension? It is simply this: the epics of the Cycle are missing. The mythical framework of these stories is limited to the Homeric *Iliad* and *Odyssey*. There is no room any more for any bits and pieces that may come from cities like Mytilene in Lesbos or from Miletus, once the most dominant of all the cities of the Ionian Dodecapolis. By now, any bits and pieces of the Cycle can safely be attributed to marginal poets of an unrecoverable past, such as Lesches of Mytilene or Arctinus of Miletus. Even that notorious Thestorides of Phocaea can by now be safe, since he will no longer need to be suspected of becoming a pseudo-Homer.

[67] For a collection of stories about the Peisistratean Recension, with analysis, see Nagy 2010a: 314–25.
[68] Commentary on this summary in Nagy 2010a: 317–18.

3 | The Epic Cycle and oral tradition

JOHN M. FOLEY (†) AND JUSTIN ARFT

This chapter offers an alternative to textualist models and the assumptions that underlie them by weighing other ways in which epic stories can relate to one another and by querying the very notion of an organized, integral cycle as customarily construed. Briefly stated, we advocate the concept of a 'constellation' rather than an anthology, basing our model on the real-life ecology of living, observable oral epic traditions. That is, we interpret the remnants of the ancient Greek Epic Cycle as reflecting a loosely related consortium of flexible narratives rather than a sequenced, textually interactive collection of artifacts. Scholars may of course choose to impose a latter-day order upon the materials at hand, an order based on sequence, influence, and other mainstay textual features, but that does not necessarily mean that those materials were in fact composed (or received) according to such an externally imposed framework.

We contend that the surviving texts – Homer's *Iliad* and *Odyssey* and all of the Cycle fragments and summaries – represent possible instances of the epic stories surrounding the Trojan War and related events, instances that at some point took shape as fixed and stable (even if partial) entities, but which once existed as malleable story-patterns that featured and fostered variation within limits.[1] With this kind of pre-textual history behind them, overlap and even contradiction would have been natural and expectable, since the narratives were not reacting primarily to one another but were instead emerging from a multiform tradition. We ballast this proposal about the ancient Greek Epic Cycle by surveying several oral epic traditions from around the world that behave similarly, that is, which operate by generating instances that show primary allegiance to their tradition as a whole rather

---

[1] Rule-governed morphology, or variation within limits, has been recognized as a fundamental characteristic of oral traditions (and works that stem from oral traditions) since Milman Parry's seminal article on Homer and Homeric style in 1930, and for that matter by fieldworkers and philologists well beforehand (Foley 1988: 1–18). See further Lord (1960) and the bibliography of the so-called Oral-Formulaic Theory (http://oraltradition.org/bibliography/), with updates through 1992, after which time the original theory starts to merge with other approaches to oral tradition. For a discussion of the structure and meaning of phraseology, typical scenes, and story-pattern in Homer, see Foley (1999a). For further insights, see especially Nagy (1990b; 1996a; 2009a) and Jensen (2011).

than to any other single story-performance in particular. Toward the close of the chapter we offer some observations on the joint model of neoanalysis and oral traditional poetics that has been gaining momentum in Cycle scholarship.

TEXTUALIST PERSPECTIVES ON THE CYCLE

Aristarchus and other second-century BC editors of Homer were not collecting oral traditions. They sought text, and not just any variant text but the best or most common one. Aristarchus and the other librarians initiated a process designed to settle on the text of Homer. Their procedures were complicated, and their aesthetic motives cannot be entirely recovered, but it is quite clear that a single, standard and correct text of Homer was to emerge from outlying variants.[2] Within this ongoing process of sifting texts, an aesthetic concern for the 'real' Homer emerges as well.[3] Altogether, the overall goal is clear: a single, true Homer could be fashioned from multiform variation.

Although Aristarchus stands as a fairly clear historical point of no return for a fully textualized Homer, the basic notion of 'Homer' and 'not-Homer' was at work throughout the classical period.[4] This impulse to find uniformity in 'Homeric' tradition bore an important implication for the Cycle in particular – the Cycle and Homer would come to be seen in opposition rather than in relation to one another.[5] Rather than seeking the nuanced ways in which the Cycle and Homer were related and may have derived from a similar or shared oral tradition, the de facto otherness of the Cycle was (and still is) justified by invoking any number of aesthetic or temporal binaries.

Subsequently, the approach to the *Iliad*, *Odyssey*, and the Epic Cycle fragments has often been defined by the necessity to seek and interpret a fixed, uniform, singly authoritative text.[6] For any number of reasons, whether it remained more oral in transmission or more local in performance[7] – or simply lost favor in the shadow of a freshly textualized Homer – the Epic Cycle material, at one time distinct in its traditional expression, became

---

[2] See Nagy (2009a: 1–21). [3] See Nagy (2009a: 37–43).
[4] Nagy (2010b). [5] Nagy (2009a: 292).
[6] See Burgess (2001: 17–18) for the effects of a Hellenistic textual orientation on the subsequent fate of the Cycle.
[7] On the local versus 'Panhellenic' nature of the Cycle, see Marks (2010: 13) and Nagy (1999: 5–9) and above in this volume, pp. 63–5. For issues of performance and the Epic Cycle, see Burgess (2004b).

entangled in the textual-interpretive tradition of Homer and was judged accordingly by those who considered the uniform Homeric text as superior. No doubt this view of qualitative difference has led to an attitude perhaps best expressed by T. W. Allen that both 'enough and too much has been written about the Epic Cycle'.[8]

Yet, as this volume attests, we are clearly not done with the Cycle. Textual criticism is but one of many approaches to the traditions of the ancient and contemporary world: various critical stances on textuality and textual transmission, in addition to evolving methodologies for understanding oral traditional poetics, have provided even more entry points into the Homeric tradition. For the *Iliad* and *Odyssey* in particular, the work of Milman Parry, Albert Lord, and subsequent scholars has enabled us to see beyond the text into the oral traditional realities of Homeric tradition.[9] The Epic Cycle, however, has only very recently come under the same sort of examination. Despite recent reconsiderations, a textual focus still defines the default position on the Cycle.

Once upon a time, the 'Cycle' was not regarded as separate from 'Homer'. Even in Aristotle's distinction, this term may have referred to the entire epic repertoire of oral tradition from which the Cyclic materials, the *Iliad* and the *Odyssey* ultimately derive.[10] It is not until the later period of textualization that the Cycle becomes synonymous with 'not-Homer'. Once segregation from Homer is in force, the distinction is further emphasized by conferred notions of quality and aesthetics, beginning with Aristotle and continuing today.[11] The Cyclic materials are seen as post-Homeric[12] in large part due

---

[8] (1908a: 64).   [9] See note 1 above.

[10] For further discussion on the Epic Cycle's synonymity with Homer, see Nagy (1996b: 74–5) and (2010b) on the Cyclic material as equivalent to Homer in general. Within the fragments and testimonia themselves, there are numerous attributions of Cyclic materials as the work of Homer. For a few such instances, consult West (2003a: 54–5, 58–9, 64–5, 66–7, and 108–9).

[11] On the quality of the Cycle in relation to Homer, see Arist. *Poet.* 1459a37–b16 regarding the unity of narrative action and plot and the superior 'language' and 'thought' of Homer. See Nagy (2010b: nn.13–14) and (2009a: 291–3) on Aristotle's and Plato's judgments on the Cycle in relation to tragedy. Davies (1989c: 2–3) follows the argument about the Cycle's lack of unity and is hesitant to date the Cyclic material before 550 BC. He also contends that the Cycle's narrative style is inferior, and where Homer favors finer motifs the Cyclic material favors human sacrifice, 'barbaric customs', and 'phantasms' (7–9). Joachim Latacz (1996: 77) falls in line with these scholars, citing the inferiority and lateness of the Cycle. See also Nagy, above in this volume, p. 61, and Fantuzzi, below in this volume, pp. 410–16.

[12] Dating the fragments from internal evidence requires interpreting both philological evidence and contextual clues, especially when terms like νεώτεροι are used to describe the Cyclic 'authors'. West translates *neōteroi* as 'post-Homeric' (2003a: 103, 114, 131, 171). For a more complete discussion on the *neōteroi* as an Aristarchan editorial category, see Nagy (2009a: 291–3). Further, Nagy (2009a) attributes the Aristarchan regard for the non-Homeric quality

to their supposedly 'inferior' quality and are then ultimately viewed as attempts to fill in the gaps of the Trojan War story left by the *Iliad* and *Odyssey*.[13] It is critical to note that these views emerge in a period of growing textuality in Ancient Greece. These very conceptions, not just of a text but especially of a uniform text and a 'correct' fixed version, drive the assumptions regarding the lateness of the Cycle and its alleged inferiority as much as or more than the evidence itself. That is, an ideology of text[14] generates a priori assumptions that influence what can be concluded from the textual remnants of the Epic Cycle. From this standpoint, quibbles about the date or quality of the Cycle are not just simple disagreements but rather alternate positions in an overall understanding of oral tradition, textual transmission and even culture and language itself. Homer was first, best and most complete, so goes the argument, and because our concept of the overall story assumes a linear, integral whole, the Epic Cycle fragments represent an attempt to supply the missing parts.

Of the scholarship that aims to highlight the non-Homeric aspects of the Cycle and related conclusions, Jasper Griffin's 1977 article is perhaps the most fundamental.[15] Ingrid Holmberg[16] and Jonathan Burgess[17] offer careful rebuttals of his views (both the arguments for post-Homeric dating and for aesthetic inferiority), and further remarks on the role and dynamics of oral tradition will follow later in this chapter. For the moment, however, the most valuable guideline to consider in light of these arguments is simple

---

of the Cycle directly to Aristotle, consistent with Athenian attribution of the *Iliad* and *Odyssey* exclusively to Homer (291–3). Prior to this Athenian era however, Homer becomes seen as an 'author' of the entire epic tradition (2009a: 356–9). For a recent linguistic analysis on the late dating of the Epic Cycle, see Davies (1989a). Jonathan Burgess responds to this argument simply by noting that the latest form of a word in text does not indicate the lateness of an entire tradition (2001: 10–12); see also Bernabé, below in this volume, pp. 139–41.

[13] The Epic Cycle fragments and testimonia include references throughout to their sequence and arrangement within epic tradition, particularly in Proclus' summaries (West 2003a: 66–7, 110–11, 120–1 and 142–3). For secondary scholarship on the Cycle as gap-filling, see Kirk (1965: 28–9); Davies (1989c: 3); and West (2003a: 11). See Burgess (2001: 135–48) for a more complete discussion of arguments and possible solutions concerning the Epic Cycle's narrative 'fit' within the sequence of the larger Trojan War narrative.

[14] On this perspective see Foley (2012): 'The Ideology of Text', also available at www.pathwaysproject.org/pathways/show/Ideology of the Text.

[15] Griffin's basic argument here and in 1980 (114, n. 23; 166–7) is that Homer is distinct from the Cyclic material on moral and aesthetic grounds. Citing Griffin's work, several scholars follow this argument, including Davies (1981: 56), Janko (1998: 6), Alden (2000: 7–10) and Lloyd-Jones (2002: 12–13). Nagy (1999: 7–8 n. 4) cites Griffin 1977 as authoritative in regards to the non-Homeric aspect of the Cycle, but denies any basis for aesthetic comparison. Jensen (1980: 36) further asserts that simplicity or aesthetics cannot point to either an early or a late date relative to Homer.

[16] (1998: 470–4). [17] (2001: 157–71).

enough and allows us to step away from interpretive strategies limited by textual ideology: we must avoid confusing the artifact with the tradition.[18]

Given the extreme dearth of fragmentary material available from the Epic Cycle, it seems nearly impossible to make an informed aesthetic comparison to the *Iliad* and *Odyssey* or, even more basically, to judge the quality of an entire tradition from a handful of secondary references and late summaries of that tradition. But a measured perspective can still produce a few tenable conclusions. Just as the Homeric texts represent a process of textualization more than they do the tradition itself, so too do the Epic Cycle fragments. Correspondingly, just as we have been able to peer more deeply into Homer via oral traditional poetics, we can and should do the same for the Epic Cycle. In other words, once we begin to see Homer and the Cycle as derived from an oral tradition that operates according to a discernible system of ancient Greek poetics, we need not cling to imagining the 'correct' version of the story or even to insisting on a precise date for the textual remains. Correctness and dating are the concerns of the textualist, who must understand a single fixed text only in relation to another fixed text. The view from oral traditional poetics, as we shall see, offers a complementary heuristic.

ORAL TRADITIONAL POETICS

We begin with a disclaimer: oral traditional poetics views neither the Homeric epics nor the Epic Cycle (nor for that matter the Hesiodic poems or the Hymns) as simply transcribed oral performances. Given the endemic uncertainties and the fruits of comparative research, it would be naive and irresponsible to assume that writing could have played no part in the active composition, as well as transmission, of any of these works. Evidence from early medieval English manuscripts and from the transcription of acoustically recorded South Slavic epic shows that scribes can and do (re-)compose formulaically even as they ply their text-making trade.[19] Moreover, literate

---

[18] For an argument against drawing conclusions from such scant textual fragments, see Burgess (2001: 12–17 and especially 13), where he crucially distinguishes between the textual creature that is the fragment and the tradition it represents: 'In my view this manufacture of the Epic Cycle would involve the interference with fixed texts by individuals who stood outside any authentic compositional or performance tradition for these poems... the textual boundaries for the Cycle poems that are found in Proclus cannot be the dimensions of their oral traditions or the fixed texts arising from them.' Davies (1989b: 5) makes this distinction as well, but in the same breath criticizes the Epic Cycle as aesthetically inferior to Homer (7–9).

[19] On Anglo-Saxon scribes 'copying' formulaically as evidenced in the multiple texts of 'Cædmon's Hymn', see O'Keeffe (1990: 23–46). On the phenomenon of 're-singing' an

authors can and do use their fluency in traditional language to create original works, sometimes aimed at print publication, that nonetheless betray a fundamental dependence on oral tradition.[20] As awareness grows of how oral traditions function in real-world situations (as opposed to how they are theoretically imagined to work in situations we can no longer recover),[21] the dynamic interaction of 'orality' and 'literacy' – these overgeneralized abstractions always constituting a crude, unsustainable binary – has become an interesting and important focus.

With this background in mind, we address four key principles at the core of oral traditional poetics. First, a poetic tradition consists not of artifacts but of instances. As poems are made and re-made, they become fixed, tangible things only when they are recorded or (if composed in writing) epitomized as singular, freestanding texts. Whenever we are dealing with what Foley labels 'Voices from the past',[22] such as the Homeric poems or medieval European epics, we are dealing with instances that were generated from a large and malleable body of narrative. Textualization obscures the precise history and ontogeny of surviving works – even those awash in variants – and supports the false premise that oral-derived, traditional works can be treated simply as artifacts.[23] This misapprehension has important implications for the tools we use to analyze and understand 'Voices from the past', calling into question such standby concepts as intertextuality, for example. If instances owe their primary allegiance to the poet's shaping of a shared tradition

---

acoustically recorded performance as part of the process of 'verbatim', pen-in-hand transcription, consider the case of Nikola Vujnović (himself a guslar, or epic singer), who assisted Milman Parry and Albert Lord during their field expeditions in the 1930s (see Foley 2004b: 145–91).

[20] In the nineteenth century, for example, Bishop Petar II Petrović Njegoš used the oral poetic language he internalized as a boy in a Montenegrin village to pen both folk and learned poetry based on oral tradition (see Lord 1986: 29–34; Foley 2002: 50–51). Or consider the case of Elias Lönnrot, highly literate collector, editor and publisher of the Finnish Kalevala, who acquired a singer-like fluency in the traditional idiom; as Lauri Honko puts it (1998: 175), 'The fact is that Lönnrot internalised the epic tradition in a most comprehensive way and developed, by listening to the poems and discussing them with the singers, an epic register which enabled him to "speak" so easily in epic idiolect that it was no problem for him to insert a few lines to integrate two or more poems. He was actually more correct in his handling of metre and parallelism than most of the oral singers. But his medium was writing, and what he wrote was to be read, not sung.' Note that both Njegoš's and Lönnrot's creations fall into the category of 'Written oral poetry' (Foley 2002: 38–9, 50–2), not at all a contradiction in terms.

[21] For discussions of the Homeric epics in the context of comparative research on modern oral epic studied directly in situ, see Foley (2004a) and (2005b); Honko (1998: 169–217); Jensen (2011).

[22] (2002: 45–50).

[23] For the initial use of the term 'oral-derived' and a brief explanation, see Foley (1990: 5–8).

rather than to other pseudo-artifacts, then the combination of 'inter' and 'text' cannot yield a fully viable diagnostic.

Second, within an oral tradition, and in oral-derived works as well, we emphasize the difference between repetition and recurrence.[24] To repeat is to do something again, with the rhetorical force of the second and subsequent repetitions stemming from their imitation or echoing of the initial item. On the other hand, to recur is to arise idiomatically – not because of a specific prior occurrence, but rather because the element or pattern is itself associated with the compositional and artistic task and redolent with inherent, embedded meaning.[25] Thus formulas and typical scenes and story-patterns do not repeat in oral traditional epic. Homer does not resort to 'rosy-fingered dawn' at any given juncture because he deployed the phrase recently and wishes to capitalize on that salient usage. Nor do the elaborate scenes of feasting in the *Odyssey* or lamentation in the *Iliad* depend primarily on parallel instances that happen to precede them. The *Odyssey* as a whole is one very prominent recurrence of the Return pattern that proliferates throughout Indo-European story traditions.[26] Formulas and typical scenes and story-patterns index the epic tradition, serving as lemmata to a finally untextualizable body of story. In this sense they do not repeat; they idiomatically recur as the poet (re-)makes the poem-instance.

Third, and this principle follows from the first and second as well as (like them) finds confirmation in numerous living oral traditions, oral traditions and oral-derived works operate on an algorithm of *pars pro toto*, the part standing for the whole. Leaving aside the original Parry–Lord explanation of mere utility, we affirm that the compositional units and patterns typical of Homer and other 'Voices from the past' exhibit traditional referentiality. This principle, which is no more or less than a special case of idiomatic language, 'entails the invoking of a context that is enormously larger and more echoic than than the text or work itself, that brings the lifeblood of generations of poems and performances to the individual performance or text. Each element in the phraseology or narrative thematics stands not for that singular instance but for the plurality and multiformity that are beyond the reach of textualization.'[27] Formulas conjure complex characterizations

---

[24] The distinction between repetition and recurrence is discussed at length in Foley (2012); an online version of that discussion is available at www.pathwaysproject.org/pathwaysshow/Recur_Not_Repeat.

[25] For example applications of this principle to the ancient Greek, South Slavic, and medieval English traditions, see Foley (1995).

[26] On the Return story-pattern, typical scenes, and phraseology in the *Odyssey*, see, respectively, Foley (1999a: 115–67, 169–99, 201–37).

[27] Foley (1991: 7).

and familiar items; typical scenes provide recurring frames of reference for particular, individualized events; story-patterns encode a rough map for the narrative as a whole, complete with built-in prolepses. The recurring part implies the traditional whole.

Fourth, oral traditional poetics understands instances that recur and stand *pars pro toto* for the epic tradition at large as reflecting a system or network of linked nodes.[28] By their very nature, in other words, oral traditional and oral-derived poems cannot ever constitute a conventional anthology, a tidy collection of free-standing entities organized according to an implicit or explicit table of contents. Poem-instances can of course be forced into a facsimile anthology according to whatever scheme one wishes, with an editorial apparatus conferring a sequence and interrelationship that are entirely invented. Such an approach may square with the presumption of unmediated textuality, since it collates the surviving poem-instances according to a taxonomy that our literary and academic culture expects and readily understands. But such order is illusory: oral traditional and oral-derived works are linked to one another, to be sure, but neither the linkages nor the nodes themselves are fixed and final, nor for that matter singular or authoritative. Poem-instances are linked to one another via pathways in a network, but their relationship is not, strictly speaking, intertextual. Homer seems to conceive of just such a navigable web of story when he describes what the *aoidos* actually does (*Od.* 8.479–81): 'For among all mortal men the singers / have a share in honor and reverence, since to them / the Muse has taught the pathways, for she loves the singers' tribe (οἴμας Μοῦσ' ἐδίδαξε, φίλησε δὲ φῦλον ἀοιδῶν).'

LIVING CYCLES

Instead of assuming an organized set of items consisting of the *Iliad*, *Odyssey*, and various prequels and sequels, let us consider what reports from *in situ* fieldwork can tell us about oral epic narratives in living traditions. Because they were so extensively collected, we will concentrate on the Moslem songs recorded by Milman Parry and Albert Lord in the 1930s in the Former Yugoslavia.[29] Brief attention will also be given to Russian, Arabic, African, Central Asian, and Indian epic traditions in order to present a broad

---

[28] On the model of linked nodes for oral tradition and digital/internet technology, see Foley (2012) and the Pathways Project at www.pathwaysproject.org/pathways/show/HomePage.
[29] For published samples from their collecting trips, see M. Parry *et al.* (1954) and Foley (2004b). A digest of the Parry Collection of South Slavic epic performances is available in Kay (1995).

comparative view of relationships among poem-instances. The idea is to offer a model based on observed, experienced reality rather than to resort to (textually based) theorizing. *Nota bene*: we straightforwardly affirm that this model is put forward as an analogy and does not claim direct derivation from the extant evidence on the ancient Greek Epic Cycle. Nonetheless, it can portray how oral epic operates across various cultural contexts, and, as we shall see, these extremely diverse traditions operate quite similarly.

South Slavic oral epic

The *junačke pjesme* (heroic songs) that Parry and Lord encountered in the six regions where they and their native colleague Nikola Vujnović interviewed guslari (epic singers) and recorded their performances were far from an anthology or ordered matrix of tales.[30] Stories varied from one singer and instance to the next, and existed in loose aggregations across the hit-or-miss repertoires of different performers. Nor did epic tales even have titles as such until they were assigned formal designations by the investigators, and then as an imposed strategy to itemize them after the fact. Singers would customarily refer to a particular narrative not as a thing but as a series of pathways: for example, Halil Bajgorić described one story as follows: 'Velagić Selim spied on Janok, and then carried off Albanian Agha Ibro's sister, Ibro and Halil freed her.'[31] Focal characters were well known and featured prominently in the tradition, with such figures as an Agamemnon-like leader of troops named Mustajbey of the Lika, a Diomedes-like paragon called Djerdelez Alija, and the comical, infamous trickster Tale of Orašac who always proved so necessary to success in battle. But the song-performances collected by Parry, Lord, and Vujnović did not speak directly to one another, and they were most certainly not related intertextually. Instead, they existed within a composite constellation or network, any aspect of which might be instantiated in a performance (though differently in each recurrence, of course), with the performed part implying the always-immanent traditional whole.

Within the network, narratives took their shape from story-patterns or tale-types, such as Return, Rescue, Wedding, or Siege of City. The generic map within each subgenre was both coherent enough and flexible enough

---

See also the Collection website: http://chs119.chs.harvard.edu/mpc/. For more on comparative research on cycles, see Foley (1999b).

[30] On the collecting expeditions, see especially Lord (1954); Mitchell and Nagy (2000).
[31] Foley (2004b: 23).

to serve as a vehicle for a practically limitless variety of principal characters, geographical contexts, political alliances, and any other story-specific details associated with the particular tale. Thus the Return story, for example, essentially the story of the *Odyssey* and perhaps the *Nostoi*, typically involved a long-absent hero held in captivity who eventually wins his way homeward, always in disguise, only to find his wife or fiancée being courted by suitors whom he must defeat either athletically or martially or both. We learn about his adventures in a flashback, and the story opens with the hero in captivity; in other words, the story 'starts in the middle' by presuming a preceding epochal battle – with the hero's army led by the duplicitous Mustajbey – that led to the particular hero's capture. The hero's mate finally recognizes him through a shared secret – a musical, vocal, or other *sêma* – and the resulting *anagnorisis* produces either a Penelopean reunion or a Clytaemnestran tragedy. This story-pattern thus furnishes a frame of reference, complete with idiomatic implications and narrative prolepses, for many hundreds of epic performances in the Milman Parry Collection and elsewhere. And none of them speaks directly to any other particular instance, nor do they line up like 'chapters' in the 'book' of the epic tradition.

Russian oral epic

The Russian *byliny* collected primarily in the eighteenth and nineteenth centuries are commonly classified geographically, on the basis of the principalities from which they derive, into three groups. Further interrelationships then derive from that categorization. As Felix Oinas (1978) has demonstrated, the Kievan cycle features Vladimir, Grand Prince of Kiev, and the three heroes Il'ja Muromec, Dobrynja Nikitič, and Aleša Popovič. The Novgorod cycle focuses on Sadko and Vasilij Buslaev, while the Galician–Volhynian cycle encompasses the adventures of Djuk Stepanovič as its central hero. (The so-called mythological *byliny* are understood as existing outside the cycle organization.) In all three cases that are pertinent to our discussion, the intra-cycle dynamic is anything but textual: different singers, different heroes, different historical and political climates, and not least different audiences have produced a mélange of narratives and narrative types. Although far more material survives from the Russian epic tradition than from the ancient Greek, what scholars have encountered is once again a constellation of stories that are roughly geographical and character-centric in their organization. To put it straightforwardly, the three so-called cycles of *byliny* are diverse in subject and structure, and as such do not at all answer the model of an anthology.

Arabic oral epic

Similarly, the Sirat Bani Hilal epics, a complex network of stories spread across the Arabic-speaking world in multiple contexts, are often construed as a cycle. But within that loose confederation of tale-performances, different performance arenas can yield quite different results. As Dwight Reynolds explains, basing his comments on extensive fieldwork, each of these contexts 'entails a different relationship between the performer, the patron of the event, other participants, and the content of the performance'.[32] Reflecting the similar situations in other epic traditions, the performance-instances are not static or fossilized, but continuously evolve in response to individual and group attitudes and, on the larger canvas, to social and historical change. The outcome of this process – again, not a collection of artifacts but a rule-governed process – is inherently neither predictable nor easily sorted into categories. In Reynolds' words, 'the very content of the epic reflects generations of negotiations of social status, patronage, the role of the poet in the world, and images of manhood, womanhood, and honor as expressed in the portrayal of heroes and heroines, villains and saints'.[33] Even if the cycle were somehow collected exhaustively (an impossible notion that depends on a textual predisposition) and from a single time and place, its contents would reflect these long-standing and ongoing negotiations as well as the endemic ability to morph and to idiomatically imply their tradition. Like the South Slavic epics and the *byliny*, the Sirat Bani Hilal cycle demonstrates inherent, functional heterogeneity.

African oral epic

Because the first investigators of African epic presumed a European, at root a Homeric, model for understanding and collecting heroic stories from various regions, it was initially thought that epic simply did not exist in most or all regions of this vast continent. Later studies have exposed that misinterpretation, and many oral epics from dozens of African traditions

[32] (1995: 209).   [33] (1995: 212).

have now been recorded, transcribed, translated, and published.[34] This burst of fieldwork and reassessment has demonstrated a tremendous diversity of epic traditions and performers, and in turn a broad variety in their performances. At the same time, scholars have provided copious evidence that the textual paradigm of freestanding works complete in themselves and in an anthology-like relationship to one another does not apply to African epic. In discussing the epics of central Africa, for example, Stephen Belcher explains that 'the subject of the performance is not the "full" story . . . Rather, in each performance selected episodes are presented, drawn from a tradition that can be seen as endless – a bottomless reservoir, an ocean of story from which the performer draws as needed to suit the occasion and his inspiration. The corpus of the tradition breaks down into episodes that may be linked almost arbitrarily.'[35] In other words, the performer's (and audience's) navigation of the African epic network or constellation assumes a much wider and deeper context, with each performance taking on its own shape as well as maintaining fidelity to what remains implied, even if unspoken in any one particular performance.

Central Asian oral epic

Turkic oral epic stretches across many ethnicities and territories in Central Asia, involving a great variety of singers, audiences and performance situations. Full-length epics have been recorded from Karakalpak, Uzbek, Kazakh, and Kirghiz bards, among others, and it is well to recall that the foundational fieldwork and research undertaken by Wilhelm Radlov, which was to influence the Parry–Lord approach so significantly, was in fact centered on Kirghiz oral epic.[36] Of the epics that have been collected and published (only a very few of the ever-dwindling number still extant), the Uzbek Alpamish, which reaches 14,000 lines in the most famous performance-instance,[37] follows the same overall story-pattern of Return that we find in the South Slavic epics and elsewhere. In this multi-ethnic setting, the popular tales of the hero Köroğlu particularly well illustrate the constellation-like shape and fluid dynamics that underlie Central Asian epic. As Karl Reichl observes of this massive network of stories, '. . . apart from the general

---

[34] See e.g. Biebuyck and Mateene (1969); Johnson (1980); Johnson *et al.* (1997).
[35] Belcher (1999: 29).
[36] See the reports of his research in Radloff, *Proben der Volksliteratur der türkischen Stämme*, of 1885; for an English translation of the preface to volume 5, see Radloff (1885 = 1990).
[37] Reichl (2000: 22).

structure of the cycle, the individual branches are independent of one another and strung together in an open-ended series of episodes and adventures'.[38] Thus the plasticity and non-textuality of the cycle allows for variant realizations, or *dastans* as they are called in the relevant languages, among the various ethnic groups as well as by individual singers of epics. What one group includes in a *dastan* may well not appear in another region's cycle-version because different versions of the 'whole' cycle have different, sometimes contradictory, contents.

Indian oral epic

The Rajasthani Epic of Pābūjī presents a fascinating example of *pars pro toto* composition and reception. In one type of realization, the story is performed piecemeal in front of a *paṛ*, a painted cloth that iconographically depicts major episodes from a master narrative that is never recounted in its entirety.[39] The epic performers, or *bhopos*, adapt their singular instances of the epic tradition to a 12-hour time-frame, further individualizing their presentations according to their own particular tastes and those of the audience via a process they call 'reading the *paṛ*'. As John Davies Smith explains,[40] the result is hardly the kind of complete, fixed and sequential story-structure that textual ideology leads us to expect: '... in normal performance the epic story is not unitary and coherent, but fragmented and incoherent'. This compositional procedure means that each instance of the Pābūjī epic amounts to a singular navigation of the much larger, untextualizable network of episodes, with some of them realized (in multiform fashion) in any given performance and some left immanently implied. In this respect Smith notes that his 1976 recording of a unique, induced performance lasting 36 hours was probably the first and only 'complete' performance of the narrative,[41] and of course even that artificially lengthy song-instance amounted to

---

[38] (1992: 322).

[39] For the performer and audience 'the *paṛ* depicts the places in which the narrative occurs: it is a representation of epic geography, a sort of epic map' (Smith 1991: 57). Cf. Daniel Biebuyck's observation on the *pars pro toto* nature of the African Mwindo Epic performance: 'The interesting point is that the narrator would never recite the entire story in immediate sequence, but would intermittently perform various select passages of it' (Biebuyck and Mateene (1969: 14)).

[40] (1991: 17–18).

[41] Cf. Biebuyck's similar experience with the Mwindo Epic: 'Mr. Rureke [the performer] ... repeatedly asserted that never before had he performed the whole story within a continuous span of days' (Biebuyck and Mateene (1969:14)).

the contingent product of oral traditional poetics and variation within limits.

ORAL TRADITIONAL POETICS, NEOANALYSIS, AND THE CYCLE

With oral traditional poetics and these several examples of living epic traditions in mind, let us close by considering the recent burst in scholarship on the Epic Cycle that has often been understood as a composite application of the approach through oral tradition and the methods of neoanalysis.[42] We will concentrate on some of the fruits of this composite research below, but first it should be noted that neoanalysis, although prescribing an earlier date for the Epic Cycle relative to Homer, has done so by asserting that the Cycle fragments represent pre-Homeric texts or textual prototypes, from which Homer, a single genius, transferred fixed motifs or 'quoted' narrative plots. Neoanalysis has, in other words, advocated a view that is not rooted in Homeric primacy, thus allowing us to imagine a new kind of relationship between the Cycle and Homer. Nevertheless, its methods are still dependent on textualist thinking, and that allegiance necessarily presupposes a textual Epic Cycle.

As early as 1979, treatment of the Cycle from outside of the perspective of either neoanalysis or a literary, unitarian reading began to emerge. In a brief but poignant response to 'a majority of Homerists', Gregory Nagy claimed that the Epic Cycle stems not from a predecessor text but from an epic tradition.[43] In reaction to neoanalytic conclusions about the Cycle, Minna Skafte Jensen concluded that the fragmentary materials represent a larger performance tradition surrounding the 'Trojan cycle', and that the nature of the Cyclic material, even if somehow simpler than the *Iliad* or *Odyssey*, cannot support the claim of Homeric primacy.[44] While Jensen admits that neoanalysis had been effective in pointing out the 'richness' of the larger Trojan War tradition, she also finds that 'the interpretations tend to read into the text what is not there' (36). A variety of voices echo such ideas through the 1990s,[45] with Laura Slatkin's *The Power of Thetis* (1991)

---

[42] For a review and bibliography of neoanalytic scholarship to date, see Clark (1986). For more recent contributions on neoanalysis and the Epic Cycle, see especially Edwards (1990) and Burgess (2001: 61–4, 132–5). See also Kullmann, below in this volume.
[43] See Nagy (1999: 42–3, n. 3).   [44] (1980: 30–6).
[45] See Edwards (1990: 312–16); Beye (1993: 29); Nagy (1996a: 74).

considered an essential contribution to the understanding of the Epic Cycle in the context of shared tradition, performance, and audience.[46]

Also important in this discussion was a growing sense of the Cycle as emerging from an oral tradition contemporary to the tradition of Homer and the hermeneutic imperatives involved in this perspective. The most relevant and recent developments in the conversation about orality in the Epic Cycle began in 1996 with Jonathan Burgess,[47] who established a framework for viewing the *Cypria* as part of a larger tradition[48] and, in responding to the neoanalytic 'vengeance theory', credited neoanalysis as 'stimulating' and providing 'valuable observations', but ultimately reliant on 'untenable assumptions'.[49] Ingrid Holmberg went on to reaffirm some of the perceived limitations of these assumptions and ultimately recommended an oral traditional lens for understanding the Cycle.[50]

In 2000, Margalit Finkelberg turned to the concept of multiformity as a direct means of interpreting the Epic Cycle.[51] This suggestion sparked a conversation that reinvoked oral traditional poetics and further highlighted the need for a complementary critical perspective as a means of interpreting the Cycle. Nagy (2001) responded to this need directly by drawing from comparative evidence for textualization of oral epics, urging the growing recognition that the Epic Cycle must be understood as a tradition under the same pressures of textualization as the *Iliad* and *Odyssey* themselves.

---

[46] See espec. 1–16 and 28–46. While Slatkin has been credited for innovatively combining neoanalytic and oral traditional methodologies, it should be noted that many of the ideas she presents regarding audience, performance, and the relationship between traditions can be derived from attention to traditional referentiality and comparative oral poetics as well (Kelly 2006: 2, n. 4; Burgess 1997: 1, n. 2; Finkelberg 2003: 68; Burgess 2006: 152, n. 9).

[47] See Burgess (1996; 1997).

[48] (1996: 96). As Burgess notes, 'being a lost poem, the *Cypria* cannot be appreciated as poetry, but through fragments, testimonia, and summaries it can be valued as a window into ancient myth about the Trojan War'.

[49] (1997: 13).

[50] (1998: 470–2). See also Holmberg 1998: 470–1: 'Some, if not all, of the perceived inadequacies and inconsistencies of the epic cycle can be attributed to the mode of composition in an oral tradition. Both the *Iliad* and the *Odyssey* and the rest of the epic cycle were part of the oral tradition in which narratives were composed or recomposed by an individual bard according to the contingencies of the occasion and of his audience.'

[51] See Finkelberg (2000: 8–9): 'However that may be, it is hard to avoid the conclusion that the Greek tradition dealing with the first stages of the Trojan War fits in perfectly with Lord's definition of multiformity: while the general framework of the story about the beginning of the war remains the same, the details are subject to quite substantial fluctuation. This seems to indicate that, as far at least as variability is concerned, the Greek tradition does not differ from other heroic traditions: it is no more rigid than the medieval or South Slavic tradition and its variability cannot be reduced to the wording alone.'

Almost concurrently, Burgess's *The Tradition of the Trojan War in Homer and the Epic Cycle* (2001) provided a benchmark for any subsequent treatments of the Cycle in relation to Homer, oral tradition, and neoanalysis,[52] as well as summarized the conversation in comprehensive fashion up to this point. First and most importantly, he contends that the Epic Cycle does in fact draw upon a larger Trojan War tradition in the same manner that the *Iliad* and *Odyssey* do, and that the proliferation of the *Iliad* and *Odyssey* was not as monumental in the archaic period as initially thought. This point of view allows for more serious consideration of a fluid, multiform tradition that is shaped not solely by authors and texts, but largely by the interactive dynamics of the morphing tradition itself.

Perhaps the most interesting and important development in the joint neoanalytic and oral traditional treatments of the Epic Cycle – as Steve Reece calls it, 'oral-tradition with a neo-analytic twist'[53] – is a growing concern with how the mechanics of influence, allusion and even 'intertextuality' operate between the Cycle on the one hand and the *Iliad* and *Odyssey* on the other. Burgess (2006, 2009, 2012) and Christos Tsagalis (2008, 2011) stand at the forefront of this initiative, drawing from a broad variety of theoretical and methodological approaches. On the one hand, Burgess (2006) identifies various layers in the mythic traditions of the Cycle and Homer, then considers the relationships between these layers as well as the possibility of oral story components migrating from one tradition or poem to another. At the centre of this model is the concept of 'motif transference',[54] by means of which patterns from Cyclic myth are transferred into Homeric epic, but not as 'quotations'. For Burgess, a certain amount of specificity and stability are required of an element to be able to migrate integrally from one body of myth to another tradition or even poem (154–6). Further, it is through motif transference that Homer uniquely invokes Cyclic myth and epic in 'an allusive manner', resulting in the *Iliad* and *Odyssey* being 'meta-Cyclic', as he puts it (149). According to this model, the Homeric epics reach their full meaning by alluding to the Cyclic material (149).[55]

---

[52] On Burgess's brief and elegant handling of the Epic Cycle and the neoanalytic position, see (2001: 61–4 and 132–5).

[53] (2011: 110–12).

[54] Burgess is clear that he seeks to improve upon a model set forth by previous neoanalysis (148) and intends to show how neoanalytic tools can be useful to interpretations of the Cycle and orality (152). See also Burgess (2009) for a more detailed model of this process involving the relationship between Achilles and Patroclus in the *Iliad*.

[55] Jensen notes that this particular model is not supported by comparative evidence but still stands as a 'thoroughly oral and highly sophisticated process of intertextuality' (2011: 267).

With this proposal Burgess has moved beyond the assertion that Homer and the Epic Cycle are oral-derived and draw from a common tradition by establishing an intertextual model to explain how tradition 'A' moves into tradition 'B'. Underlying this model are assumptions of both fixity and movement, thus requiring a fixer and a mover. More specifically, he explains the process as follows (166): 'Often it is more plausible to posit intertextuality between a poem (or its performance tradition) and mythological traditions variously expressed in different media and notionally known throughout the culture. This intertextuality involves paradigmatic correspondence between motifs outside of Homeric poetry and within it, most strikingly in the phenomenon described above as "motif transference".' Although he is careful to stay within the realm of traditional performance and agrees that the term intertextuality is itself problematic, his application of this revised neoanalytic model, based as it is in allusion and movement between traditions and bodies of myth, in some ways runs counter to the multiform dynamics and compositional fluidity of a shared oral tradition.

Christos Tsagalis accepts Burgess' view of motif transference as a type of intertextuality[56] and, although modifying the term 'meta-Cyclic' to 'meta-epic' after Finkelberg, he embarks on an interpretive project for which a particular notion of intertextuality is crucial for understanding the many traditional layers and allusive force of Homer (xii). From this perspective, then, the *Iliad* and *Odyssey* are understood as constantly responding to competing performance traditions in an attempt to reshape or even 'best' them (xi–xxiii). Parallel to Burgess' proposition that Homer engages the non-Homeric tradition in a 'meta-Cyclic' manner, Tsagalis also finds Cyclic vestiges throughout Homer that are linked via intertextuality and allusion.

In many ways, Burgess (2012) and Tsagalis (2011) are both extremely attentive to the oral traditional nature of Homer and the Epic Cycle and avoid positing fixed textual traditions responding to one another. In some aspects, then, this meta-Cyclic or meta-epic view of Homer, whether predicated on motif transference or a revised version of intertextuality,[57] responds to the oral-traditional background of Homer and the Cycle. This approach also lends a much higher degree of priority to the Cycle by suggesting that the Homeric poems rely on Cyclic material to realize their full meaning. Nonetheless, we believe that there are problematic ramifications to understanding the Cycle in this way. First, in positing such movement between traditions via motif transference, the perceived gulf between the

---

[56] Tsagalis (2008a: xii, n. 9).
[57] See Burgess (2012) for a recent discussion of intertextuality without text.

Cycle and Homer is widened. Second, the conversation regarding intertextuality lends itself to mechanical models for influence and exchange between traditions that do not strike us as entirely tenable for oral-derived traditional works. In such oral-derived texts, interactions are much too complex, multidirectional, fluid, and dynamic for a purely intertextual model to fully explain. Further, traditional referentiality and an absence of textual fixity – typical features of oral and oral-derived narratives – undercut the notion that the elements and patterns that constitute a tradition can migrate from one poem to the other by a simple transference of units. Within an oral traditional environment, the instances (the textual remnants) represent singular realizations generated from a multiform tradition.

CONCLUSIONS

In summary, then, we view the Epic Cycle and the Homeric poems as instances stemming ultimately from an oral epic tradition of ancient Greek narrative. In advocating a 'constellation' or network model, and after making due allowance for what cannot be confidently determined because of the fragmentary nature of the Cycle remains, we do not support the imposed parameters of (supposed) quality or temporal sequence, nor do we see intertextuality per se as a tenable base assumption. At the same time, by invoking oral traditional poetics – as construed above in a set of four principles and as illustrated by analogy to several living epic traditions – we do not insist that any of the texts under consideration are transcriptions of oral performances in whole or in part. First and foremost, they are texts. But as research on a multitude of verbal art traditions has shown decisively over the past thirty years and more, a non-textual poetics can survive into the world of writing and print as a register of language that supports a particular kind of composition and reception. During our discussion we have called such oral-derived works 'Voices from the past'.[58] In the end, we understand Homer's grand poems and the fragmentary Epic Cycle as surviving remnants of a much larger oral epic tradition, most of whose riches either never reached textuality (for whatever reason) or have since perished.

---

[58] See Foley (2002: 45–50, 166–71, 177–83); also 'The rhetorical persistence of traditional forms' (Foley 1995: 60–98).

4 | The formation of the Epic Cycle

MARTIN L. WEST

The question of how the Epic Cycle was formed may be treated as a threefold one. Firstly, at what stage of the epic tradition did poems covering those areas of mythology first appear? Secondly, when and by what stages did a sense develop that a sequence of such poems, taken together, told a continuous story, so that if there was a gap a new poem might be composed to fill it? Thirdly, when and how did an Epic Cycle come to be formally recognized as a larger whole, and what was its literary or bibliographical status?

THE SUBJECT RANGE OF PRE-HOMERIC EPIC

It is generally accepted that the history of Greek epic reaches back into the Mycenaean period. Poems about a Trojan War perhaps began to be composed in the twelfth century. The legend of the Argo's voyage may have been the subject of song at the same period or not much later. There must have been many other strands of heroic poetry embodying and embellishing local memories of past events. After the middle of the eighth century, when Ionian epic evidently enjoyed a great flowering, we begin to have a clearer sense of some of the themes that were then current among epic singers. For example, from a series of allusions in Hesiod's *Theogony* it can be inferred that there were various songs about the deeds of Heracles, though perhaps no comprehensive *Heraclea* covering his whole career.[1] Each of these songs had an independent existence. They did not have to be recited or heard together or in a particular order. But they could be said to have constituted a Heracles cycle, in the loose sense in which scholars sometimes speak of a Sumerian Bilgames cycle or a Hurrian–Hittite Kumarbi cycle: that is, a set of poems attached to a particular figure, but not (so far as we know) intended to be taken in a particular order or perceived as forming a larger whole.

In the same way there must have been a set of poems relating to Thebes, and another relating to Troy. So long as epic remained purely oral their

---

This chapter is a variant recension of West (2013: 16–26), augmented by some material from other parts of the same book so that it can stand on its own.
[1] West (2011b: 30–1).

contents were in flux, continually evolving, but each established theme had an identity that persisted through the changing performances. In the course of the seventh century some poets took to writing their compositions down and in the process, in certain cases, allowed them to grow to a prodigious length. Two have come down to us: the *Iliad* and the *Odyssey*. Neither of them is Cyclic in conception; that is, neither is designed to form a segment of a vaster narrative continuum. Each is a free-standing poem, complete in itself. But each presupposes familiarity with the larger story of the Trojan War, and each contains numerous allusions to episodes that belong to the time before the action of the *Iliad* or between that of the *Iliad* and Odysseus' return to Ithaca, episodes that we know were treated in their proper places in the poems of the Cycle.[2] This does not mean that the Cyclic epics as current in the classical period, the *Cypria*, the *Aethiopis* and the rest, existed before the *Iliad* and *Odyssey*. But it means that poems existed containing much of the same material, not necessarily in written form and not necessarily corresponding to the later ones in coverage.

As the *Iliad* and *Odyssey* are not Cyclic (in the sense defined above) but free-standing, the same will have been true of other poems existing at the time: each will have told a self-contained story forming part of the larger tale of the Trojan War and not necessarily leading straight on from or to one of the others. The structure of the material itself, as it appears in the later tradition, betrays its origin in a set of unconnected poems. There had probably been one dealing with the Judgment of Paris and the abduction of Helen, ending with the wedding at Troy, and another telling of the gathering of the Achaeans at Aulis, perhaps continuing to their arrival in the Troad and the initial battle that they fought there. The *Iliad* poet himself evidently had a poem about the Aulis gathering in his repertoire; he has adapted his Catalogue of Ships from it.[3] Another poem, or more than one, told how the war was brought to an end after Philoctetes was fetched from Lemnos and Odysseus conceived the stratagem of the Wooden Horse. But there was nothing of any substance to bridge the gap between the first year and the tenth.

THE EMERGENCE OF THE CYCLIC APPROACH

Aristotle in his *Poetics* (1459a37-b7) picks out the *Cypria* and the *Ilias parva* as examples of epics whose πρᾶξις 'action', unlike the *Iliad* and *Odyssey*, is πολυμερής 'formed of many parts', and thus contains material for many

---

[2] Kullmann (1960: 5–11); West (2011b: 32–5). [3] West (2011b: 32–3, 85, 86, 107–8, 112).

tragedies. He has lit upon a feature of the two poems that is plain to us from Proclus' summaries. They lacked structural unity, and the reason is that they were composed to cover particular sections of the whole story of Troy that were not already covered by other epics.

It is sometimes thought that all the Cyclic epics were composed on this principle, and that consequently they were all episodic in structure and lacking in organic unity. But it is a mistake to treat them as a homogeneous group. It must first be observed that some of them overlapped in content, though this has been concealed in Proclus' summaries, which have been tailored to make a continuous narrative without duplications. Both the *Aethiopis* and the *Ilias parva* contained Ajax's suicide, and both the *Ilias parva* and the *Iliou persis* had full accounts of the sack of the city. This at once refutes the notion that each of the epics was designed to cover an allotted span of events so as to create one continuous story.

The *Aethiopis* was composed as a continuation of the *Iliad* – not a sequel, but an actual continuation, meant to complete the story of Achilles by telling of his death, of which there were many premonitions in the *Iliad*, and the events that were integrally linked to his death: the funeral games in his honour, the awarding of his arms to Odysseus and the suicide of Ajax.[4] The poet drew on an existing, pre-Iliadic account of the death of Achilles (which did not involve Memnon), and he also incorporated an independent *Einzellied* about an encounter between Achilles and the Amazon Penthesileia. This had previously had no particular context: Penthesileia's sudden arrival at Troy arises out of nothing that has gone before, and her defeat does nothing to bring Achilles' death any closer; on the contrary, it delays it, because it leads to Thersites' taunting of Achilles and Achilles' killing of Thersites, which necessitates his going away to Lesbos for purification. That was the ending of the Penthesileia story; it led on to nothing else. Achilles simply had to return to Troy and resume his warrior role. The whole episode could have been placed at any time in the war.

Arctinus (if that was the *Aethiopis* poet's name) appears as an epigone, building on the *Iliad* and other existing poetry. But his aim was only to make an *Ilias aucta*, completing the story of Achilles, not to carry the tale on towards the *Iliou persis* or to link up with some other epic that did so. The same poet is credited with the *Iliou persis*, a shorter epic that covered the end of the war. It did not begin where the *Aethiopis* ended but with the Trojans' discovery of the Wooden Horse. The Horse stratagem was integral to the story of the sack, and a poem about the sack had to begin, if not with the

---

[4] West (2011b: 428–30). See also Rengakos, below in this volume, pp. 315–17.

building of the Horse, then with the Trojans' finding it. Demodocus' song as summarized in *Od.* 8.499–520 had a very similar scope to the *Iliou persis*. The *Iliou persis*, then, was composed as a free-standing epic with thematic unity. It could be characterized as an *Einzellied*.

The same could not be said of the *Ilias parva*, which was, as Aristotle saw, a concatenation of potential *Einzellieder* (six anyway) without organic connection: the awarding of Achilles' arms and suicide of Ajax; the fetching of Philoctetes and his defeat of Paris; the fetching of Neoptolemus and his defeat of Eurypylus; Odysseus' entry into Troy disguised as a beggar and his meeting with Helen; the theft of the Palladium; the Wooden Horse and the sack. Their sequence is only partly determined by organic logic, as may be seen from other accounts where they come in a different order: in PRylands 22 (*PEG* 75) the Palladium episode precedes Neoptolemus' encounter with Eurypylus; in Sophocles, Quintus and others the bringing of Neoptolemus and his killing of Eurypylus precede the bringing of Philoctetes. Lesches, if that was the poet's name, set himself the task of telling the remainder of the Troy story after the death of Achilles, which must have been previously established as a major event that concluded a phase in the war. He must have drawn on a number of antecedent poems, whether oral or written, stitching them together to make a continuous narrative. This was a truly Cyclic enterprise in the sense defined earlier. If he did not limit himself to bridging the gap between the death of Achilles and the point where the *Iliou persis* started, it was presumably because he did not know the latter poem (which is not to say that it did not yet exist).

The *Cypria*, Aristotle's other prime example of a non-unitary, episodic epic, is an even more blatant product of Cyclic endeavour. Its eleven books took in everything from Zeus' first design for the war to the point where the *Iliad* begins. The *Iliad* was a given for the poet, and he took pains to fit in as many as he could of the events that were referred back to or presupposed in the *Iliad*.[5] Of course he had other sources too, including poetic accounts of the wedding of Peleus and Thetis, the Judgment of Paris and the abduction of Helen, the gathering of the Achaeans at Aulis, the mistaken invasion of Teuthrania and the ensuing debacle, and so on.[6]

It is clear that Stasinus, if that was his name, conceived his work not as something forming a complete whole in itself but as the first part of a tale that continued in the *Iliad*, and beyond the *Iliad* to the end of the war. His

---

[5] Welcker (1849: 149); Nitzsch (1852: 99–100).
[6] Most of these are already alluded to in the *Iliad*. The Teuthrania episode is not, but we now know from POxy. 4708 that it was current as early as Archilochus.

introduction (*PEG* F 1 = D., W.) was an introduction to the war as a whole, explaining why Zeus brought it about and what was the point of all the death and devastation that it involved. This was in effect an introduction to the whole Trojan Cycle.

The story of the war might have been considered complete with the sack of Troy. But there were legends about the fortunes of certain major heroes in the immediate aftermath of the war: the drowning of the Locrian Ajax in direct consequence of his sacrilegious conduct at the sack; the saga of Odysseus' homecoming, as related in the *Odyssey*; the murder of Agamemnon and his avenging by Orestes. These provided the basis for a more comprehensive epic on the Achaeans' returns from Troy, the *Nostoi*. It did not include the return of Odysseus (though he was mentioned in passing), doubtless because a separate *Odyssey* was already current and the poet did not want to duplicate it. So this again was a Cyclic undertaking, filling in areas that were not covered by existing poems. The return of the two Atridae was made the framework of the epic as a whole. It began with the dispute that separated them, and it ended with Menelaus' belated arrival home following Orestes' killing of Clytaemnestra and Aegisthus. The murder and avenging of Agamemnon formed the main heroic subject matter of the narrative. The returns of other heroes were accommodated within this frame. It is evident that the *Nostoi* was not just a loose sequence of separate stories but was carefully structured so as to integrate in one design several lines of action that proceeded concurrently in different places.[7] This is one of several features that it shared with the *Odyssey*. Both contained underworld episodes and touching scenes of reunion and recognition with grandfathers of the family (Odysseus with Laertes; Neoptolemus with Peleus). The *Odyssey* poet for his part takes pains to set Odysseus' return against the background of the other heroes' returns (1.11–14, 326–7, etc.). He adverts repeatedly to the story of Agamemnon. Telemachus learns about it and about some of the other heroes' returns from Nestor in 3.130–312, and they are supplemented by Menelaus' account of his own adventures in 4.351–586. There is extensive agreement between what is said in these passages and Proclus' summary of the *Nostoi*. It looks as if the two epics were being developed at the same time and with mutual interaction (if not actually by the same poet). The *Odyssey* poet was deeply engaged with the *Nostoi* tradition and helping to shape it.

When Odysseus finally reached home, the last of the heroes to do so, it might again seem that the story of the Trojan War was complete. Yet

[7] See Bethe (1929: 281–3).

the *Odyssey* itself, through Teiresias' prophecy in 11.118–37 (~ 23.248–87), presages further events in Odysseus' life, including some tale about his death. A later poet, Eugammon of Cyrene, developed these hints, together with elements of local Epirotic saga, folktale and romantic invention, into a sequel to the *Odyssey*, the *Telegony*, that covered the rest of Odysseus' life after his return from Troy, his death, and what became of Penelope and his sons. The poem was clearly episodic, with only the unity conferred by the person of the protagonist. It belongs unequivocally in the Cyclic category.

FROM TROJAN CYCLE TO PROCLUS' CYCLE

There are grounds for dating Eugammon to the 560s, and it is a reasonable assumption that by about 550, or at any rate by 520, the complete Trojan Cycle was current: *Cypria, Iliad, Aethiopis, Ilias parva, Iliou persis, Nostoi, Odyssey, Telegony*. This is not to say that anyone at that time thought of these poems as forming a set or series.[8] But they existed as stable texts, providing collectively a complete account of every stage of the Trojan War, from its first conception in heaven to the final destinies of the heroes.

This Trojan Cycle formed a major part of the universal Epic Cycle that Proclus knew. Yet it did not situate itself within a wider mythological canvas. Stasinus' introduction to the *Cypria* entirely shuts out earlier events of the Heroic Age. He makes no allusion to the Theban Wars. His story begins with a vague ἦν ὅτε 'once upon a time', a time when the Earth was burdened by overpopulation, and everything that follows is directed solely towards instigating the Trojan War. It is as if there were no historical context, no other mythology.

Proclus' Cycle had a more comprehensive scope. Photius gives only a bare outline of it, but from what he reports we know that it was made up from the works of various poets, whose names and places of origin were given, that it began with a theogony,[9] and that it went on to the death of Odysseus at the hands of Telegonus. So the sequence of Troy poems from *Cypria* to *Telegony*, for which Proclus' summaries have come down to us by another route,

---

[8] Nor indeed does anyone later speak of a Trojan Cycle distinct from the larger Epic Cycle. The central title ΤΡѠΙΚΟΣ on the Tabula Capitolina (Sadurska 1964: 29) (Valenzuela Montenegro (2004: 32); Squire, below in this volume, pp. 520–1) has sometimes (as by Heyne (1797: 370); Wilamowitz (1884: 333, 360)) been taken to stand for *Trōikos kyklos* 'Trojan Cycle', but the noun to be supplied is perhaps rather *pinax* 'tablet' (Wüllner (1825: 4)).

[9] 'The fabled union of Heaven and Earth, from which they say he begot three hundred-handed sons and three Cyclopes'. This matches a theogony current under the name of Orpheus, see West (1983: 125–6). See also D'Alessio, below in this volume, pp. 199–202.

made up the last portion of the whole Cycle. We cannot tell how many other poems it included between the initial theogony and the *Cypria*.[10] It can be inferred from Athenaeus 277c–e that it included the *Titanomachy* ascribed to Eumelus or Arctinus,[11] and two or three sources cite 'the Cyclic *Thebaid*' (to distinguish it from the *Thebaid* of Antimachus). A story that Photius says came from the Epic Cycle is conjecturally assigned to the *Epigonoi* (*PEG* F 5 = p. 74 D. = F 3* W.). So we may assume that the Cycle included the series of Theban epics, *Oedipodea*, *Thebaid*, *Epigonoi*, and perhaps *Alcmeonis*. On the so-called *Tabula Borgiana* (*IG* 14.1292; Sadurska 1964: 61; Valenzuela Montenegro (2004: 265) *Cyclus epicus*, *PEG* T 2), in some kind of list of epics with author-names and line-tallies, the *Oedipodea* and *Thebaid* are preceded by a title *Danaides* and followed a couple of lines later by an uncertainly read reference to 'the Cycle'. What else might Proclus' Cycle have had in it? Poems on the Calydonian boar-hunt, the voyage of the Argo, the stories of Io and Perseus? Pisander's Heracles epic? A *Theseis*?

We can at least say that it seems to have been confined to archaic epics and did not include Panyassis, Antimachus, or anything later. Nor, so far as we can see, did it contain any of the Hesiodic poems. Otherwise we cannot tell whether anything was excluded or whether it was made up of the whole available corpus of pre-classical epic, organized in sequence so as to provide a continuous narrative from the beginning of the world to the end of the Heroic Age.

This organization did not occur spontaneously. Something of the kind had happened with the Troy epics because the natural coherence of the subject matter invited it: the sequence of poems determined itself, and it was obvious where there were gaps in the story to be filled. With the Theban epics too the sequence followed necessarily from the subject matter. The first line of the *Epigonoi*, 'But now, Muses, let us begin on the younger men',[12] shows that it was conceived from the start as a sequel to a *Thebaid*. Among the whole mass of epics available to the organizer of the Cycle there may have been other small aggregations or mini-cycles. But for the most part he had to do the arranging and create a single sequence.

What was his purpose, and what did he actually have to do to achieve it? Did he make an edition of the entire Cycle? That seems unlikely; there is no good evidence that the Cycle was ever edited as a whole.[13] It has

---

[10] See Welcker (1865: 31–8).
[11] Cf. also Philo of Byblos, *FgrHist* 790 F 2 ap. Eus. *Praep. Evang.* 1.10.40 = *Titan. PEG* T 1 (= D.).
[12] For the Greek text and a discussion, see Cingano, below in this volume, pp. 244–5.
[13] See Wilamowitz (1884: 368).

sometimes been thought that traces of such an edition are to be seen in the alternative incipit of the *Iliad* known to Aristoxenus, which began ἔσπετε νῦν μοι Μοῦσαι ('Now tell me, Muses')[14] or in the alternative ending that led into the *Aethiopis*. But the alternative opening was more likely designed to follow a prefatory hymn, while the alternative ending is actually the original opening of the *Aethiopis*, which as I have said was composed from the start as a continuation of the *Iliad*.[15] The scholia to the *Odyssey* twice cite variant readings from ἡ κυκλική ('the Cyclic edition'), but it is not clear whether the copy so designated had anything to do with the Epic Cycle or was just a 'run of the mill' one, which is also a possible meaning of the adjective. If the former, it might simply have been a text found shelved with the other Cyclic poems; it would not be surprising if Hellenistic collectors or librarians sometimes put sets together.

But the original arranger of the Cycle need not have done so. What he needed to do – and it was really all he needed to do – was publish a protocol containing his list of poems and explaining that this was the Epic Cycle, made up of epics which, if read in the prescribed sequence, would provide a comprehensive account of the mythical age as represented by the oldest poets.[16] Each title was furnished with basic bibliographical details: the author's name and the length of the work. John Philoponus records that 'some have written about the Cycle registering how many poets there have been, and what each one wrote, and how many lines each poem had, and their order, which ones are to be read first and second and so on'.[17] Philoponus doubtless has Proclus in view, but the specifications he says were supplied surely went back to the original organizer of the Cycle.

The effect of the enterprise was to bring the disparate mass of early epic poems into order and to provide readers interested in their content with a guide to help them find their way. It was indeed for their subject matter rather than for their poetic virtues that they were generally consulted. Photius reports from Proclus the observation that 'the poems of the Epic

---

[14] *Appendix Romana* B 1 (West 2003b: 454); Aristoxenus F 91a Wehrli; taken by Bethe (1929: 384) as a continuation from the *Cypria*.
[15] See West (2011b: 81 and 428–30).
[16] This was clearly seen by Heyne (1797: 353–4): 'Neque umquam tale corpus plurium poetarum aliter confectum [esse constat], quam ut grammaticus aliquis eorum recensum seu indicem faceret, et singulari forte libello aut in opere grammatico ederet; nec facile omnes, quorum magnus fuit numerus, qui Genealogias deorum, Titanomachias, Gigantomachias, Argonautica, Thebaica, Heracleas, et sic porro, tum in rebus Iliacis, qui Νόστους scripserunt, tali indice enumerati fuerunt.'
[17] Philoponus on Arist. *Anal. post.* 77b32, p. 157. 11 Wallies = *Cyclus epicus PEG* T 28 = T 2 D.). See also Introduction, above in this volume, p. 103.

Cycle are preserved and studied by most people not so much for their quality as for the consecration of the matters it contains (διὰ τὴν ἀκολουθίαν τῶν ἐν αὐτῶι πραγμάτων)', in other words for a continuous account of all that was supposed to have happened.[18]

At what period is the codification of the Cycle likely to have been made? Such an operation is hardly conceivable before the fourth century BC. It is very well conceivable in the second half of the fourth century, when the systematization of knowledge in many spheres was in full swing, especially in the school of Aristotle. In the field of literature we may think of Lycurgus' ordinance establishing an official archive of the plays of the three great tragedians (Plut. *Oratorum vitae* 841f), and of Aristotle's own redaction of the dramatic and dithyrambic *Didaskaliai*. Clearchus collected proverbs and riddles. Demetrius of Phalerum made the first corpus of Aesopic fables (Diog. Laert. 5.80). The synoptic approach to mythology implicit in the aggregate Cycle may be seen as paralleling the rise of the genre of universal history pioneered by Ephorus.[19]

It is in Aristotle that we find the first allusions to an epic cycle, or to *the* Epic Cycle. In two of his logical works he refers to the false syllogism 'a *kyklos* (circle) is a shape; epic poetry is a *kyklos*; therefore epic poetry is a shape'.[20] In his *Rhetoric* (1417a12), giving examples of how the orator in relating the facts of a case should pass summarily over those parts that have no emotive power, he refers to Odysseus' succinct rehearsal of his adventures to Penelope (*Od.* 23.310–41) and then adds καὶ ὡς Φάϋλλος τὸν Κύκλον· καὶ ὁ ἐν τῶι Οἰνεῖ πρόλογος 'and as Phayllus (does with) the *Kyklos*; and (as is) the prologue of (Euripides') *Oineus*'. We know nothing of who this Phayllus was – the name is not uncommon – but he was evidently known at the time for having reduced something called the *Kyklos* to a concise factual summary.[21] In view of the other Aristotelian passages we can hardly doubt that it was an epic *Kyklos*; and if Aristotle uses the definite article with it, the inference is that he knew only one such Cycle. Why should we doubt that it was the Epic Cycle acknowledged by later writers? The exact phrase 'Epic Cycle' had perhaps not yet been coined, as the adjective ἐπικός is not attested before the first century BC, but it might have been known earlier as ὁ κύκλος τῶν ἐπῶν 'the Cycle of the Epics', or some such title. However that

---

[18] See Introduction, above in this volume, pp. 2–3, 32.
[19] On a 'historical cycle', see Introduction, above in this volume, pp. 19–21.
[20] *Soph. el.* 171a10, where it is 'the poetry of Homer'; *Anal. post.* 77b32. Cf. Schwartz (1924: 154–5; 1940: 5–6); Pfeiffer (1968: 73); Introduction, above in this volume, p. 30.
[21] On Phayllos, see also Introduction, above in this volume, p. 30; Burgess, above in this volume, p. 43.

may be, it appears to have been established as a literary quantity by the third quarter of the fourth century, even if it was less an editorial reality than a bibliographic construct.

The educated inquirer could then, if all the epics were available to him, find his epic mythology presented in the poets' words and laid out in a logical order. But most would have had difficulty in assembling all the texts, and even if they did, it was a daunting amount of verse to read through. Since (as Proclus was to note) it was the substance rather than the poetry that interested people, it was a natural step to cater for this interest by making a prose epitome of the whole Cycle, retaining the bibliographical details about the individual poets and works but reducing the narrative to the essentials. The dozens of volumes could thus be replaced for most purposes by a single one, easy to acquire and easy to handle and consult. The need for such a compendium would have been apparent from the start, and the currency of one no later than the Hellenistic period has long been inferred from the textual agreements between Proclus' summaries of the Trojan epics, the corresponding parts of Ps.-Apollodorus' *Bibliotheca*, and the captions of the Roman *Tabulae Iliacae*.[22]

Now, it appears from Aristotle that such an epitome already existed in his time, and he names its author: Phayllus. There is no reason why this should not have been the definitive one from which Proclus and Ps.-Apollodorus ultimately depended. Indeed, there is some likelihood that the Cycle and the epitome were created together and that Phayllus was responsible for both. Launching the Cycle as an ensemble meant, as I have said, promulgating a document that set out the details of the constituent epics. That would have taken up perhaps a couple of columns of writing, too brief a text to be issued as a book on its own. It must surely have been embodied in a larger publication: perhaps a treatise on literary history, but more probably, I submit, a work devoted to the Epic Cycle and consisting mainly of the epitomes, each headed by the information about the poem's author and length.[23]

A single author was named for each epic: Stasinus for the *Cypria*, Homer for the *Iliad* and *Odyssey*, Arctinus for the *Aethiopis* and *Iliou persis*, Lesches for the *Ilias parva*, Agias for the *Nostoi*, Eugammon for the *Telegony*, and we can probably add Cinaethon for the *Oedipodea* and Antimachus of

---

[22] Wilamowitz (1884: 332–6); Wagner (1886: 147–9); Hartmann (1917: 9); Bethe (1929: 207–10).

[23] On the *Tabula Borgiana* the length of the epics mentioned is given in lines, and this corresponds to what Philoponus says in the passage quoted above. Proclus, however, gives the lengths of the Troy epics in books. This may represent a later replacement for the stichometrical data; it is uncertain how early the book divisions were made.

Teos for the *Epigonoi*. These unequivocal attributions are reproduced in derivative sources: the Macedonian 'Homeric cups' (third to second century BC), the Roman Tabulae Iliacae (from the time of Augustus or Tiberius) and Proclus' summaries of the Troy epics.[24] Most of the poets' names are unattested before 350 BC,[25] and up to that time the Cyclic poems were often attributed wholesale to Homer, albeit not without controversy (Wilamowitz 1884: 351–4). After 350 Arctinus and the others are the authors commonly named, though we find occasional scholarly discussions of rival names, and many writers preferred to use non-committal expressions such as 'the man who composed the *Cypria*'. The change that takes place in the fourth century no doubt reflects the influence of Phayllus' initiative. We cannot identify the sources from which he gathered the poets' names, but they cannot have been unanimous or decisive. He created a set of ascriptions that unsophisticated people could accept as official. The bluff assertiveness with which he did so recalls that of certain Peripatetic writers on literary history, such as Heraclides Ponticus in his account of early Greek music, or Theophrastus' comrade Phaenias of Eresos, who set his fellow Lesbians Lesches and Terpander in a chronological relationship with each other and with the Milesian Arctinus (F 33 Wehrli).

SUMMARY: THE STAGES OF DEVELOPMENT

In conclusion it may be a convenience to provide a chronological summary of the stages of development postulated on the basis of the foregoing arguments.

750–600	Emergence/perpetuation of oral poems on multifarious heroic themes, some of them sharing a common focus such as the Trojan War, Heracles, etc.
660–600	Fixing of some large-scale and lesser epics in writing, including the *Iliad, Aethiopis, Iliou persis, Odyssey*.

---

[24] Although Proclus discussed alternative ascriptions for the *Cypria*, he did so in a different passage of his *Chrestomathy* and drawing on a different source.

[25] Stasinus was apparently known to Pindar (F 265). It is possible that Hellanicus named Lesches as the author of the *Ilias parva* and that his name has fallen out in Σ Eur. *Tro.* 822 = Hellan. *EGM* F 202c. Arctinus was known to Artemon of Clazomenae (*FgrHist* 443 F 2), whom Jacoby regards as pre-Hellenistic.

600–550	Creation or remodelling of other poems to bridge gaps in the sequence: *Nostoi*, *Ilias parva*, *Cypria*. Or to extend it: *Telegony*. This completed an unofficial Trojan Cycle.
550–350	Epics transmitted individually by recitation and increasingly as books.
350–320	Phayllus organizes a substantial number of epics into a formal, comprehensive Cycle, writes a Protocol defining it, and provides a prose epitome.
320–AD 200	The epitome widely used by mythographers and others; the original poems (apart from the *Iliad* and *Odyssey*) increasingly neglected, though at least some of them continue to be obtainable in places.
After AD 200	The poems no longer current; their contents known only from the epitome and derivative texts. New epics composed on 'Posthomerica' (Triphiodorus, Quintus) and 'Antehomerica' (Colluthus).

5 | Motif and source research: Neoanalysis, Homer, and Cyclic epic

WOLFGANG KULLMANN

INTRODUCTION

The Homeric *Iliad* narrates only a specific episode of the Trojan War but, as becomes clear from numerous allusions, nonetheless takes for granted its audience's familiarity with the legend of the whole war. It is impossible to understand the *Iliad* without knowledge of its mythical background. At the time of composition of the *Iliad*, this was probably known only in the form of orally performed lays or minor epics, being recorded in comprehensive written form only towards the end of the seventh century in the Cyclic epics. The date of the first written version of the *Iliad* is contested. My own assumption is that, after a long period of work carried out in stages, it was completed in writing by the author in the first half of the seventh century; Martin West,[1] among others, is of a similar opinion. It is obvious that there are close connections between the allusions to Trojan legends in the *Iliad* and the subject matter of the Cyclic epics: it is to these that the research of neoanalysis is directed. The most important source for the content of these lost epics can be found in the summaries of Proclus' *Chrestomathy*: for the *Cypria* these are preserved in various Homeric manuscripts, but for the other Cyclic epics only in the manuscript Venetus A. Complementary information can be found in the fragments, in the *Odyssey* and in Ps.-Apollodorus' *Bibliotheca*, a handbook of mythography. But in the latter case it is not certain that the information invariably goes back to the Cyclic epics. In our opinion, the main literary difference between the *Iliad* on the one hand and, on the other, the Cyclic epics or the pre-Homeric oral epic tradition preserved in these epics lies in the dramatic and psychologically deeper composition of the *Iliad*, with its numerous and continuous threads of motif, independent of the limited length of an oral presentation, and in the chronological style of narrative of the epic tradition as found in the Cycle. Oralists like Burgess also emphasize the differences of style and call that of the *Iliad* 'meta-Cyclic'.[2]

---

[1] Kullmann (1958: 546; 1981 = 1992: 88, 98–99; 2012: 114); West (2011b: 215–19).
[2] Burgess (2009: 4). See also Finkelberg, below in this volume.

Proclus' summaries are cited according to my own numeration by paragraphs.[3] For the *Cypria* and the *Aethiopis*, which in terms of mythical chronology directly frame the *Iliad*, we will give a translation to ease comparison.

CYPRIA

(§ 1) Zeus consults with Themis on the Trojan War. (§ 2) When the Gods celebrate the wedding of Peleus, Eris appears and incites a dispute over their beauty between Athena, Hera and Aphrodite, (§ 3) who are led by Hermes according to the order of Zeus to Mount Ida to have their beauty judged by Alexander. And he, led on by the (prospect of) marriage to Helen, gives preference to Aphrodite [*called the Judgment of Paris on account of Alexander's second name*]. (§ 4) Then, on the advice of Aphrodite, ships are built. (§ 5) And their future is foretold by Helenus. (§ 6) And Aphrodite invites Aeneas to go with him [*sc. Alexander*]. (§ 7) And Cassandra prophesies what is going to happen. (§ 8) And Alexandros lands in Lacedaemon and is hospitably received by the Tyndarids, (§ 9) and thereafter in Sparta by Menelaus; and Alexander hands presents to Helen when he receives hospitality. (§ 10) And then Menelaus goes to Crete, after instructing Helen to see that the guests have everything they need until their departure. (§ 11) But in the meantime Aphrodite brings Alexander and Helen together. And after intercourse they load up the largest possible amount of treasure and depart at night. (§ 12) But Hera sends them a storm. And, driven to Sidon, Alexander conquers the city. (§ 13) And he sails to Ilion and arranges marriage to Helen. (§ 14) In the meantime Castor, and with him Polydeuces, are caught as they rob Idas and Lynceus of their cattle. (§ 15) And Idas kills Castor but Lynceus and Idas are killed by Polydeuces. (§ 16) And Zeus grants them (*sc. Castor and Polydeuces*) immortality on alternate days. (§ 17) And after that, Iris reports to Menelaus what has happened at home. (§ 18) And he comes to his brother and they confer about the campaign against Ilion. (§ 19) And Menelaus proceeds to Nestor. (§ 20) And Nestor tells him in a digression how Epopeus seduced Lycus' daughter and how thereafter his city was destroyed, and the stories of Oedipus, of Heracles' madness and the stories about Theseus and Ariadne. (§ 21) Then they assemble the leaders by travelling through Greece. (§ 22) And they recognized that Odysseus was only pretending to be mad because he did not want to take part in the campaign, and on Palamedes' advice they took Telemachus away from him to give him a thrashing. (§ 23) And then they come together at Aulis and make a sacrifice. And the stories are told, of what happened with

---

[3] The Greek text with numbering of paragraphs can be found in Kullmann (1960: 52–7; 2002b: 156–61).

the snake and the sparrows. And Calchas makes predictions about what will come of this. (§ 24) Then they put to sea and reach Teuthrania and were about to destroy it in the belief that it was Ilion. (§ 25) Telephus comes to help (*scil. his compatriots*) and kills Thersander, son of Polynices, and is himself wounded by Achilles. (§ 26) On departing from Mysia, they are attacked by a storm and dispersed. (§ 27) Achilles lands on Scyros and marries Lycomedes' daughter Deidameia. (§ 28) Then Telephus proceeds to Argos on account of an oracle, and Achilles heals him under the condition that he should be their guide for the journey to Ilion. (§ 29) And when the fleet had gathered for a second time in Aulis, Agamemnon hunted down a stag and boasted that he outdid even Artemis. The goddess, however, in her rage obstructed their departure by bringing about storms. (§ 30) When Calchas had explained the goddess's rage and called on them to have Iphigenia sacrificed to Artemis, they fetch her under the pretence that she is to be married to Achilles, and try to sacrifice her. (§ 31) But Artemis carries her off to the Taurians and makes her immortal, putting a deer on to the altar in her place. (§ 32) Then they depart to Tenedos. (§ 33) And while they are holding a feast, Philoctetes is bitten by a water-snake and abandoned on Lemnos because of the bad smell. (§ 34) And Achilles falls out with Agamemnon, because he was invited too late. (§ 35) When they then seek to disembark at Ilion, they are pushed back by the Trojans. (§ 36) And Protesilaus meets his death through Hector. (§ 37) Then Achilles drives them back, after killing Cycnus, the son of Poseidon. And the dead are carried off. (§ 38) And they send an embassy to the Trojans to demand the return of Helen and her treasure. (§ 39) But when the others do not yield, they embark on the siege. (§ 40) Then they advance into the hinterland and also destroy the surrounding cities. (§ 41) And then Achilles desires to see Helen, and Aphrodite and Thetis bring them together at a meeting point. (§ 42) Then Achilles holds back the Achaeans, who are engaged in preparing to return home. (§ 43) And then he drives off Aeneas' cattle, (§ 44) and he destroys Lyrnessos and Pedasos and numerous cities in the neighbourhood. (§ 45) And he kills Troilus. (§ 46) And Patroclus brings Lycaon to Lemnos and sells him there. (§ 47) And from the spoils Achilles gets Briseis as his prize of honour, Agamemnon Chryseis. (§ 48) Then follows the death of Palamedes. (§ 49) And then comes Zeus' plan to relieve the Trojans' plight by making Achilles leave the Greek alliance. (§ 50) And the catalogue of those who fought on the side of the Trojans.

AETHIOPIS

(§ 51) The Amazon Penthesileia appears in order to fight on the Trojan side, a daughter of Ares and a Thracian by birth. (§ 52) And when she excels in battle, Achilles kills her. (§ 53) The Trojans however bury her. (§ 54) And Achilles kills Thersites, when reviled by him and reproached for his alleged love relationship with Penthesileia. (§ 55) Then thereafter a revolt rises amongst the Achaeans because of the death of Thersites. (§ 56) After that Achilles sails to Lesbos and makes a sacrifice to Apollo, Artemis and Leto and is absolved of the murder through the agency of Odysseus. (§ 57) And Memnon, son of Eos, appears in armour made by Hephaestus to help the Trojans; (§ 58) and Thetis prophesies to her son the matters relating to Memnon. (§ 59) And in the hand-to-hand fighting, Antilochus is killed by Memnon, (§ 60) then Achilles kills Memnon; (§ 61) and to him Eos gives the immortality which she had asked from Zeus. (§ 62) Achilles, however, drives the Trojans back and is killed by Paris and Apollo when he charges towards the city; (§ 63) and when around his fall a violent battle arises, Ajax gathers him up and carries him to the ships, while Odysseus fends off the Trojans. (§ 64) Then they bury Antilochus and lay out the body of Achilles; (§ 65) and Thetis appears with the Muses and her sisters and carries out the lamentation for her son; (§ 66) and after that Thetis snatches her son from the pyre and takes him to the White Island. (§ 67) The Achaeans however pile up a burial mound and put on an athletic competition; (§ 68) and a quarrel arises over the arms of Achilles between Odysseus and Ajax.

THE HISTORY OF THE PROBLEM

In the mid twentieth century, the relationship between the *Iliad* and the Epic Cycle came to the foreground of research on epic poetry, above all through the publications of Kakridis in 1944 and 1949 and Pestalozzi in 1945. Pestalozzi sought to prove that the second part of the *Aethiopis*, called 'Memnonis' by him and by others later, which tells the story of Achilles' death and to which the *Iliad* only alludes, is on account of the priority of certain motifs a pre-Homeric epic and the model for the *Iliad*. Independently of this, Kakridis[4] came to the conclusion that a precondition for the *Iliad* is that there must be an 'Achilleis', which could be identical with the Memnon story in the *Aethiopis*. Gruppe, who already in 1906[5] held the entire *Aethiopis* to be pre-Homeric, went unnoticed. Kakridis coined the term 'neoanalysis' for the method of research of motifs that resulted from these considerations, because it is in his opinion capable to resolve difficulties of interpretation while still assuming the unity of the *Iliad*, and so dispense with that assumption of layers of different provenance which was

---

[4] Kakridis (1944: 113–27; 1949: 83–95).   [5] Gruppe (1906: i.680).

characteristic of the old Analytical school. In the meantime, the term has come to be used independently of its genesis. 'Neoanalysis' is understood to mean especially the method of explaining sections of the *Iliad* as semi-rigid adaptations of motifs taken over from older epic contexts;[6] and, increasingly broadly, the examination of the relationship of the content of the *Iliad* (and where applicable also of the *Odyssey*) to the epic tradition as a whole. Criteria for the *transference of motifs* (*Motivübertragung*) are above all the cases of partial 'friction', of details that are unsuitable or without function in their new use, e.g. the funeral games in honour of Patroclus, a *hetairos* of Achilles, instead of, as in the original, for Achilles himself. *Allusions* and the illumination of their mythological background belong to the study of sources.

The method was given particular definition through a study by Schadewaldt, 'Einblick in die Erfindung der *Ilias*. *Ilias* und *Memnonis*'.[7] He endorsed Pestalozzi's thesis, deepened the latter's line of argument and strove for an interpretation of motif transference. He emphasized that the derivative character of the *Iliad* passages implied no value judgements. In his view, lesser originality often goes together with greater depth of meaning.[8]

In my own book on the sources of the *Iliad* (*Quellen der* Ilias),[9] I came to the view that the question of the relationship in content between the *Iliad* and the second part of the *Aethiopis* is only part of a more general problem. There are allusions in the *Iliad* to the legend of the Trojan War *as a whole*. As a start, these should be collected systematically and compared with our independent tradition of the Trojan legend, to be found above all in the Cyclic epics, insofar as these can still be reconstructed, even though these epics are post-Homeric. The examination is to be conducted independently of the question of how a possible priority of Cyclic motifs will be interpreted from a poetical point of view. Hence, the objective of the work was to be the determination of a pre-Homeric *canon of mythological facts* (*Faktenkanon*).[10] In line with today's insights, its transformation into poetry must essentially have taken place in oral epic, and before Homer.

---

[6] On motif-transference, see below, pp. 113–25 *passim*.   [7] Schadewaldt (1952 = 1965).
[8] Schadewaldt (1952 = 1965: 162).   [9] Kullmann (1960).
[10] See Kullmann (1960: 12–13 and *passim*). The final section in Kullmann, 'Die Ergebnisse im Spiegel der bestehenden Homertheorien', relates to hypotheses which prevailed more than half a century ago. The preceding examination had been conducted independently of these theories. The hypothesis that some of the Cyclic epics, or parts of them, are in themselves pre-Homeric can no longer be considered seriously today; a second one, however (1960: 361), can: that independent oral or written sources were used for the Cyclic epics which Homer himself also used.

MOTIF RESEARCH (*MOTIVFORSCHUNG*)

The Memnon story in the *Aethiopis* and the *Iliad*

It is the thesis that motifs from the Memnon story were taken over into the narrative of the *Iliad* that has attracted the greatest interest. Each narrative features a friend of Achilles, whose adversary then meets his own death at the hands of Achilles, in turn sealing also the fate of the latter, which is however narrated only in the *Aethiopis*. In the view of the Neoanalysts, roughly speaking, this transference displays itself in two ways:[11]

1. Memnon (Procl. §§ 57–61) is in the *Iliad* replaced as Achilles' adversary by Hector; Achilles' friend Antilochus, who is killed by Memnon (Procl. § 59), by Patroclus.
2. The 'Patroclea' within the *Iliad* (that is, in particular, large parts of Books 16–17, 22–23) is modelled on an 'Achilleis' (that is, on a pre-Homeric work of oral poetry, which corresponds in terms of subject matter with the Memnon section of the *Aethiopis*, also called the 'Memnonis'). The second assumption has found greater acceptance. But we begin with a detailed treatment of the first.

Procl. § 57 Memnon is not mentioned in the *Iliad*, but is definitely there at *Od.* 11.522 (compare also Phainops ~ Aethiops ~ Memnon: Schoeck (1961: 54 n. 6)). His appearance is a final bid for the Trojan side and there was no reason to mention this in the *Iliad*. His armour, made by Hephaestus, which is mentioned by Virgil in *Aen.* 8.383–4 (following the *Aethiopis* story)[12] is probably seen in the *Aethiopis* and its oral sources as a defensive counter to the armour given to Peleus by the gods and passed on to Achilles. For the 'second' armour, made for Achilles by Hephaestus in the *Iliad*, is a late feature in the legend, added in connection with the story of Patroclus' death in Achilles' armour which will become Hector's booty, and corresponds to Memnon's armour also made by Hephaestus.[13] This is shown by **Procl. § 68**: when Odysseus and Ajax quarrel over Achilles' arms, there is only a single armour of Achilles, presumably the old, inherited one. Worn by Patroclus in the *Iliad*, it fell as booty to Hector, who wore it and was then stripped

---

[11] Cf. the comparisons in Schadewaldt (1952 = 1965: 172–85); Currie (2006: 24–39). See also Rengakos, below in this volume, p. 316.
[12] See Fraenkel (1932: 242).
[13] Pestalozzi (1945: 43); Schadewaldt (1952 = 1965: 171); Kullmann (1960: 307).

of it again by Achilles. The new armour of the *Iliad* would have made the quarrel over the arms superfluous.[14]

Procl. § 58 The prophecy by Thetis, attested for the *Aethiopis*, seems to be the primary one, as against Thetis's prophecy in *Il.* 18.95–6. For the latter stands in contradiction to those passages in the *Iliad* that anticipate Achilles' early death as predestined by fate. This predestination seems already to be a reflection of the prophecy in the Memnon story.[15] It is a matter of debate whether in the *Aethiopis* Achilles used this prophecy as an opportunity to withdraw completely from the battle (*contra* Burgess 1997). Possibly Achilles at first only sought to avoid the battle with Memnon. In support of a complete withdrawal from battle could be cited the fact that the same thing is envisaged at *Il.* 11.794–7 and 16.36–9, where it seems out of place.[16]

Procl. § 59, *Od.* **3.111–12, 4.187–8, 24.78–9, supplemented by Pind. *Pyth.* 6.23–42** Antilochus hurries to help his father Nestor, when in the fighting Paris has killed a horse of Nestor's chariot; and, for the sake of his father, he suffers a sacrificial death at the hands of Memnon. The motif of the threat to Nestor is taken up in *Il.* 8.80–171. There too Paris kills a trace-horse of Nestor, but this proves inconsequential, as Nestor is saved by Diomedes. Real tragedy turns into near-tragedy.[17] The value of Pindar's testimony for the *Aethiopis* is confirmed by Virgil's recourse to the *Aethiopis* in *Aen.* 10.789–820 (sacrificial death of Lausus).[18] Virgil takes account of the content of this epic elsewhere too (e.g. at *Aen.* 1.489–93; Camilla ~ Penthesileia). A similar transference of motif can be seen at 16.462–76, in connection with the mortal trace-horse (Pedasus) of Patroclus who is under threat from Sarpedon. Finally, Antilochus gets into difficulties through Maris, the brother of Sarpedon's companion Atymnius whom he has killed, but is then saved by his own brother Thrasymedes: this scene in *Il.* 16.317–29 is a reversal of the later death of Antilochus in the relevant episode of the *Aethiopis*, in which no one stands by him.[19]

Procl. § 60 and vase paintings Hector's death (*Il.* 22.297–305) corresponds to that of Memnon. After the death of Antilochus, Achilles kills Memnon. The motif of retribution is evidently not presented in such an

---

[14] Kullmann (2005: 16; 2011: 102); cf. Edwards (1991: 140–1); Currie (2006: 28–9); cf. below, p. 120, on Procl. § 69.
[15] Currie (2006: 30–1); Kullmann (2012: 102).
[16] Pestalozzi (1945: 41–5; 1959: 167); Kullmann (1960: 309–10); Currie (2006: 30).
[17] Pestalozzi (1945: 9–11); Schadewaldt (1952 = 1965: 163); Kullmann (1960: 31–2, 314); Heitsch (1990 = 2001: 210–31); Willcock (1997: 179–81); cf. Burgess (2009: 74); *contra* West (2003c: 10–11); in favour Kullmann (2005: 23); cf. Wilamowitz (1920: 45); Burgess (2009: 74).
[18] Fraenkel (1932: 243–8); *contra* Kelly (2006: 1–25).
[19] Reinhardt (1961: 357); Kullmann (1965 = 1992: 188; 2005: 22).

emotional way in the *Aethiopis* as in the *Iliad*. There, with some poetical skill, Antilochus is kept out of the Patroclus episode through Nestor's advice at 17.377–83,[20] while in *Iliad* 23 he provides a kind of backdrop, with fine characterization, for Achilles' act of vengeance for the sacrificial death of his inferior in the heroic ranking order, Antilochus. The death of Memnon is preceded by a weighing of fates, substantiated by vase-paintings where the scenes showing two heroes with divine mothers suggest this interpretation.[21] This motif of the weighing is used in an imprecise way at *Il.* 8.68–72, where the topic is the general fate of the Trojans and the Achaeans.[22] A closer parallel is *Il.* 22.209–13, which involves the fate of Achilles and Hector. But since already, at 22.167–207, Zeus has decided in advance on Hector's death, the motif has no function here.[23] In order to prove, nevertheless, that the weighing scene is secondary in the case of Memnon, West[24] assumes that an original version of the *Iliad*, which included the death of Achilles, did not yet contain the earlier verses (22.167–207), and that the poet of the *Aethiopis* used this 'Ur-*Iliad*', replacing Hector by Memnon. So then the poet of the *Iliad* would have retroactively devalued his motif of weighing – why? West's thesis is thus founded on complex and unsubstantiated premises. What speaks against it is that, in the Memnon context, the weighing involves two sons of goddesses, whereas Hector is not equal in rank with Achilles, so that the weighing is inadequate (*Il.* 22.177–85). In addition, there is Hera's warning to Zeus against sparing his son Sarpedon, in order to avoid creating a precedent (16.440–9), where it is obviously the entreaties of Eos and Thetis that are already in mind.[25]

Procl. § 61 The immortality that is asked for the semi-divine Memnon has no counterpart in Hector's case.

Procl. § 62, Ps.-Apollod. *Epit.* 5.3 A call to storm the city of Troy in *Il.* 22.81–4 seems to have been a motif from the Memnon story, taken over from the situation after Hector's death but then, in semi-rigid form, converted into an unfulfilled idea.[26]

There is a non-tragic parallel for the fatal injury to Achilles from Paris's arrow, in the wounding by Paris of 'Achilles' substitute' Diomedes at *Il.* 11.375–8.[27] The prophecy of a possible death given to Achilles beforehand, probably already a pre-Homeric motif (cf. *Il.* 9.410ff.), is mirrored in the

---

[20] Kullmann (2012: 101). [21] Kossatz-Deissmann (1981: *LIMC* I 1, 172–175).
[22] See Kullmann (1960: 316–18). [23] Kullmann (1960: 317–18). [24] West (2011b: 388).
[25] Schoeck (1961: 25); Currie (2006: 39–41).
[26] Schadewaldt (1952 = 1965: 168–9); Kullmann (1960: 39, 324); Burgess (2009: 90).
[27] Kakridis (1961: 293 n. 1); Kullmann (1984 = 1992: 313); Edwards (1991: 18); Janko (1992: 409); Burgess (2009: 74–5).

prophecy of the death of the 'minor warrior' Euchenor at 13.660–72, also given in advance.[28]

Procl. § 63, Ps.-Apollod. *Epit.* 5.4, *Od.* 24.39–92 In *Il.* 18.26–7 Achilles, overwhelmed by grief at Patroclus' death, is given this description: 'And he himself lay in the dust, the great one, stretched out greatly.' Because of its partial agreement with the formula in *Od.* 24.40, this is considered to relate originally to the dead Achilles.[29] In the *Odyssey*, there follows the addition 'forgetful of the art of horsemanship', which is also applied, in the quotation at *Il.* 16.775–6, to the death of the charioteer Cebriones; but it is equally well suited to Achilles, the chariot-fighting owner of the immortal horses Xanthos and Balios.

The isolation of Odysseus in 11.401–2 and Ajax's coming to his rescue in 11.485–8, is a reflection of the fighting retreat of Ajax and Odysseus carrying the body of Achilles in its armour. The scene is a reversal of the situation in the Memnon story in which Ajax, carrying Achilles' body, is protected by Odysseus.[30] The emphasis on Ajax's defensive strength and powers of resistance in 11.544–74, 13.126–8, 13.701–11 and 15.415–18 seems to be the re-interpretation of a single episode into a characteristic one, serving to 'psychologize' the figure of Ajax.[31] Further reflections of the Memnon story can be found in the description of the retreat with Patroclus' body (see below).

Procl. § 66 There is no corresponding scene in Homer for the transportation of Achilles' body to the 'White Island' in the Black Sea (in *Od.* 11 Achilles is in Hades). According to West,[32] the motif is an invention of the epic poet Arctinus of Miletus, the starting point for the colonization of the Black Sea region.[33]

Let us now examine the second parallelism (that the 'Patroclea' within the *Iliad* is modelled on an 'Achilleis').

Procl. § 60 Patroclus partially takes on the role of Achilles. This is symbolized externally by his taking over the latter's armour. He kills the semi-divine Lycian Sarpedon, as Achilles kills the semi-divine Memnon (16.479–503).[34]

Procl. § 61 The immortality of Memnon becomes in the case of Sarpedon a transfer by Sleep and Death, at Zeus' instigation, to his tomb in Lycia

---

[28] Strasburger (1954: 75–6); Kullmann (1960: 320); cf. Σ A *Il.* 13.663.
[29] Pestalozzi (1945: 18); Kakridis (1949: 84–8); Schadewaldt (1952 = 1965: 168); Kullmann (1960: 38–9, 330); Dowden (1996: 59); Willcock (1997: 177); Danek (1998: 468–70); Currie (2006: 40); Burgess (2009: 84–5).
[30] Kullmann (1960: 326–7).   [31] Kullmann (1960: 327).   [32] West (2003c: 13).
[33] See also Burgess (2009: 126–31).
[34] Pestalozzi (1945: 13–15, 44–5); Schadewaldt (1952 = 1965: 169); Kullmann (1960: 318); Janko (1992: 312–14).

where he had a grave cult, which points to references outside the *Iliad*. In the *Iliad* Sarpedon has a status which stands halfway between those of Hector and of Memnon. He is not granted full immortality, probably also because Patroclus' victory must not be judged of higher value than that of Achilles over Hector. Zeus' son Sarpedon is nevertheless the equivalent of Achilles' adversary Memnon.

Procl. § 62 Patroclus meets his death through Hector and Apollo, as Achilles will be killed by Paris and Apollo (16.818–55). His death occurs because, like Achilles, he has dared to advance too far against Troy (16.698–709).[35]

Procl. § 63, Ps.-Apollod. *Epit.* 5.4, *Od.* 5.309–12, 24.39–92, *LIMC* I 2, 140 (Chalcidian amphora) The difficult recovery of Patroclus' body (17.268–734) corresponds to the difficult recovery of the body of Achilles. As Glaucus, in the *Aethiopis* and on the Chalcidian vase, is killed by Ajax in the attempt to take possession of Achilles' fought-over body, so too is Hippothous at Ajax's hands in the fight over the dead Patroclus.[36]

Procl. § 65, *Od.* 24.47–9: Thetis and the Nereids lament the death of Patroclus, just as with that of Achilles (18.35–69). It is obvious that the tribute to Achilles' dead *hetairos* cannot be the model for the tribute to Achilles himself.[37] Thetis' and the Nereids' lament (18.40–65) for Patroclus is also inappropriate, because when Achilles' cries are heard, they cannot know yet that Patroclus has died, or that through his death the death of Achilles is also brought closer.[38] The open appearance of the goddesses amongst the Myrmidons also contravenes the Homeric convention that deities move among humans only in disguised or different form, unless they are revealing themselves to an individual.[39] These incongruities are clear signs for the transference of motifs.

Procl. § 67, Ps.-Apollod. *Epit.* 5.5 As for Achilles, so in honour of Patroclus athletic games are organized as a tribute to the dead (*Il.* 23): in this, the priority of the Achilles story is obvious.[40] There, according to Ps.-Apollodorus, Eumelus won the chariot race, Diomedes the running race, Ajax the discus-throwing and Teucer the archery contest. In Homer

---

[35] See above. Cf. Burgess (2009: 95).
[36] Gruppe (1906: 682 n. 5); Pestalozzi (1945: 20); Schadewaldt (1952 = 1965: 170); Kullmann (1960: 328); Kossatz-Deissmann (1981: 183–4); Burgess (2009: 39–40, 82).
[37] Kakridis (1949: 65–75); Pestalozzi (1945: 32); Schadewaldt (1952 = 1965: 166); Edwards (1991: 149).
[38] Kullmann (1960: 36, 332); Willcock (1997: 177–8; 2009: 83–5).
[39] Kullmann (1956: 83–105; 2011b: 91).
[40] Pestalozzi (1945: 33); Schadewaldt (1952 = 1965: 162); Kullmann (1960: 334); Currie (2006: 25).

the chariot race and the archery contest are elaborately modified. Athena breaks the chariot yoke of the favourite Eumelus and favours Diomedes, and in the archery contest, by a cursory alteration of the source, a chance happening is included, with obvious illogicality, in the competition rules: Achilles intends to give first prize to whoever hits the dove, and the second to whoever hits 'only' the cord. So Meriones wins victory over Teucer, while in the Achilles story it was probably someone else, perhaps Meriones, who hit the cord, thereby releasing the dove that Teucer then shot down in flight.[41]

It is remarkable how this 'handling of the sources' in the description of the contests is, as it were, concealed by the poet of the *Iliad* through the 'preparatory' characterization of Antilochus (23.301–48, 23.755–6).[42] Or, put differently: the author of the *Iliad* strives to link his story as closely as possible to the tradition's canon of facts.

West[43] advocates a different thesis: that the *Aethiopis*, in the sections involving Achilles, is built on an 'Ur-*Iliad*' by the poet of the *Iliad*, which originally extended to the death of Achilles but whose concluding part was then abandoned in favour of Book 24: but the theory breaks down, first with the role of Antilochus in the *Iliad*, which is entirely oriented towards his fate in the Memnon story; then with the takeover of the motif of an armour made by Hephaestus, with the description of problems with chariots that recall the sacrificial death of Antilochus, with the awkward presentation of the archery event in the competitions, and finally with the close literary correspondence between Patroclus and Antilochus in the *Odyssey*, which seems to have been composed before the *Aethiopis*.[44]

Burgess objects to the argument that a hero like Patroclus should be modelled on two prototypes, Achilles and Antilochus.[45] But this concise form of words should not be taken to mean that the taking over of a motif is always linked to a meaningful literary allusion. Here the insights of the theory of oral poetry are useful. The transference of motifs is a purely technical process, just like the adoption of formulaic lines. It can either be a conscious allusion, or take place unconsciously; it can either relate to an entirely specific point, or be more far-reaching.[46] It arises in many other legendary contexts as well. In the present case, there is doubt as to whether Achilles has withdrawn altogether from the fighting, or whether he has for the moment kept out of the way of Memnon. Further, the motifs

[41] Wilamowitz (1920: 69); Schadewaldt (1966: 136 n. 3); Kullmann (1960: 334).
[42] Kullmann (1960: 316; 2011); Willcock (1997: 181–3).   [43] West (2003c: 9, 12; 2011b: 388).
[44] Kullmann (1960: 42); Currie (2006: 27).   [45] Burgess (1997: 15).
[46] Burgess (2009: 65–71) differs here too, in postulating the existence of a specific and conscious 'Trojan War motif transference'.

of friendship and revenge are developed quite differently in the two epic narratives. The heroic friendship between Patroclus and Achilles, going back to their childhood, is different in kind from the friendly sympathy that Achilles shows to the youthful Antilochus who, as his smiling reaction to Antilochus shows, reminds him of his own honour-conscious nature.[47] The motif of vengeance is developed less forcefully in the Memnon story than in the *Iliad*. Yet these and other motifs in the Memnon story remain influential for the overall structure of the *Iliad*.[48]

Whether Hector is a pure invention of the *Iliad* poet, as held by Schadewaldt,[49] is unclear. Certainly he appears in Procl. § 36 as the vanquisher of Protesilaus. But since at *Il.* 2.701 the victor is merely called 'a Dardanian man', it must remain uncertain whether the *Cypria* really identified him as Hector. Perhaps this equation goes back to Sophocles (*Poimenes*, *TrGF* F 497) or another source, and Proclus then merely applied this post-Homeric identification to the unknown Trojan of the *Iliad* (and perhaps of the *Cypria*). In any event, the figure of Hector seems not to belong to the tradition. Patroclus, as son of the Argonaut Menoetius (Ps.-Apollod. *Bibl.* 1.9.16) probably is pre-Homeric.[50]

TRANSFERENCE OF MOTIFS FROM *ILIAS PARVA* AND *ILIOU PERSIS*

Many Neoanalyst treatments fail to take into account the fact that the relationship of the *Iliad* to the tradition extends beyond the takeover of motifs from the Memnon theme. The impression is that the poet of the *Iliad* had before him the saga as a whole, and that for him it was not structured in lays or minor epics. This points to a wide proliferation of different performances by singers. Thus, a number of details in Book 23 recall the way in which topics were handled in the *Ilias parva* and *Iliou persis*.[51] The Locrian Ajax, among the spectators at the chariot race, is portrayed as quarrelsome (23.473–81), which seems to be a psychological inference from his role in the Palladion outrage: **Procl. § 93** ('And Ajax the son of Oileus tears Cassandra away, at the same time carrying off the wooden statue of Athena'). The winner of the boxing competition, Epeius, is aware of his unwarlike nature (23.670–1), which is a premonition of the substitute role allocated to him by Athena, as architect of the Wooden Horse (cf. 15.70–1; *Od.* 8.492–3):

---

[47] Rengakos (2007: 101–9).
[48] Kullmann (1960: 4; 1984 = 1992: 149; 2012: 109); Currie (2006: 38–9).
[49] Schadewaldt (1952 = 1965: 177).   [50] Kullmann (2009: 211).
[51] Kullmann (1960: 336–55; 2012: 106).

Procl. § 81 ('and Epeius makes the Wooden Horse, in accordance with Athena's decision'), **Ps.-Apollod. Epit. 5.14, Stesichorus,** *PMGF* **F 200**). The wrestling match between Odysseus and Telamonian Ajax (23.700–37) ends indecisively, perhaps under the influence of the pre-Homeric motif of the contest for the arms,[52] to which *Od.* 11.543–4 also alludes: **Procl. § 69** ('and the judgment over the arms takes place, and Odysseus wins them in accordance with Athena's will'), **Ps.-Apollod. Epit. 5,6**. In the running race, Odysseus wins against the Locrian Ajax, 'whom Athena harmed' (23.774), again anticipating **Procl. § 93.**

All in all, it emerges that the *Iliad* and its content fill a niche in the saga of the Trojan War as a whole, and are placed in front of the story of Memnon and Achilles, at the same time modifying, to a greater or lesser degree, motifs from that story. The point of reference is not however a specific 'Memnonis' or 'Achilleis', but the overall picture of the Trojan story, as can be brought out yet more clearly by the relationship with the content of the other Cyclic epics.

SOURCE RESEARCH (*QUELLENFORSCHUNG*)

Cypria, Amazonia, Ilias parva, Iliou persis, Nostoi

In the *Iliad* there are, to say the least, frequent allusions to the content of most of the other Cyclic epics too, of a kind that is important for the research into sources.

Cypria[53]

Procl. § 1, *Cypr. PEG* **F 1 (= D., W.)** The deliberations, withheld from the company of the other gods, seem devoted to the plan of using the Trojan War as a way of relieving the Earth of its burden of mortals. In my opinion, this plan is alluded to at *Iliad* 1.5.[54] *Cypria PEG* **F 2 (= D., W.)** The *Cypria*, like the *Iliad*, assumes the 'gratitude variant' of the story of Thetis' wedding, whereby Thetis rejected the advances of Zeus, for the sake of Hera who had brought her up.[55] The armour of Achilles is a wedding present from the gods to Peleus: 16.140–4, 16.381–2, 17.194–7, 17.443–9, 18.84–5.

---

[52] Cf. above, pp. 113–14 on Procl. § 68.
[53] See also Currie, below in this volume.
[54] Kullmann (1955a = 1992) and (2011: 79) with further references. *Contra*, among others, Schadewaldt (1966: 143).
[55] Lesky (1937: 297–8); Kullmann (1960: 370); *Il.* 18.85, 18.429–34, 24.59–62, 24.534–40.

Procl. § 2 and 3 The beauty contest is not mentioned in the *Iliad* but its result, the Judgment of Paris, is cited at 24.28–30 and determines the alignment of the deities in the *Iliad* (cf. e.g. 4.5–12, 4.24–9, 5.418–25).[56] **Procl. § 11** The 'rape' of Helen is often alluded to in the *Iliad*.[57] **Procl. § 12** The detour of Paris *via* Sidon – differently in Herodotus (= *Cypr. PEG* F 14 = F 11 D. = F 14 W.) – is mentioned at 6.289–91. **Procl. § 14–16, *Cypr. PEG* F 8 (= F 6 D. = F 9 W.), F15 (= F 13 D. = F 16 W.)** The Dioscuri were probably referred to in the *Cypria* in the context of the rescue of the 12-year-old Helen from the hands of Theseus, when Theseus' mother Aithra was taken along as Helen's slave (cf. *Il.* 3.144). The story is probably old, as is suggested by Helen's vain search for them at *Il.* 3.236.[58] **Procl. § 19–20, *Cypr., PEG* F 17 (= F 15 D. = F 18 W.)** The dove cup of Nestor (11.632–7) may have played a role on the occasion of Menelaus' visit to Nestor.[59] **Procl. § 21** The recruitment of the leaders of the army is referred to at 7.127–8, 9.252–9, 9.338–9, 9.438–43, 11.765–803. **Procl. § 22** This is unmentioned in Homer: see below under § 48. **Procl. § 23** On the arrival at Aulis and Calchas' prophecy, cf. 2.28–30, 16.221–7 and the parallel motifs with the Catalogue of Ships. **Procl. §§ 24–31, cf. § 76, § 77, § 79, § 91** The Teuthranian expedition and the second departure from Aulis are consciously blocked out of the *Iliad*, to further the conception of the Trojan campaign as a pre-colonial episode.[60] Only Helen's acknowledgment that this is her twentieth year at Troy (24.765–6) and the vague allusion to Calchas' pronouncement for the sacrifice of Iphigeneia (1.106), along with the mention of Neoptolemus on Skyros at 19.326–37; 24.466–7 (interpolated according to West,[61] a subsequent addition by the poet according to Kullmann[62]) betray knowledge of these stories and their continuation in the post-Homerica. **Procl. §§ 32–3, Ps.-Apollod. *Epit*. 3.23–7** That the Achaeans call in at Tenedos is known to the *Iliad* too: Hekamede, the booty prize of Nestor, is said to come from there (11.624–7). According to Ps.-Apollod. *Epit*. 3.26, Tenes was slain there by Achilles, something that the *Iliad*, probably deliberately, passes over in silence. Philoctetes, as at *Il.* 2.721–5, was bitten by a snake at a banquet and, at Agamemnon's command, taken back to the island of Lemnos, now to their rear, by Odysseus. **Procl. § 34, *Od*. 8.75–82, Strabo 1.2.4** On Tenedos, a dispute breaks out between Agamemnon and Achilles, because the latter was so late in being invited; perhaps also a quarrel between Achilles and Odysseus, as to how best to capture Troy. It is unclear whether the dispute referred to in the *Odyssey* really took place on Tenedos and featured in the *Cypria*, and whether

---

[56] Reinhardt (1997: 180–2); Kullmann (1960: 238–9); Kirk (1985) 338–9; Hirschberger (2008: 15–18).
[57] Kullmann (1960: 248–53). [58] Kullmann (2012: 94). [59] Kullmann (1960: 257 n. 2).
[60] Kullmann (1960: 189–203; 2009: 4–6; 2012: 20). [61] (2011b: 359). [62] (2011b: 103).

Il. 9.312–13 is a reflection of this second quarrel.[63] **Procl. § 35–6,**[64] **Procl. § 38 (The Embassy)** *Il.* 3.58–75 is a transfer of motif (peaceful settlement of the dispute through single combat between Menelaus und Paris), likewise Antenor's proposal for the return of Helen at 7.345–53. **Procl. § 39** The inspection of the army by Agamemnon at *Il.* 4.220–1 mirrors the beginning of the siege. **Procl. § 40** See below on Procl. § 44. **Procl. § 42:** The 'testing' (*peira*) of the Achaean army at 2.72–210 reflects the low fighting spirit of the Achaeans in the nineteenth year of hostilities.[65] **Procl. § 43, Ps.-Apollod. *Epit.* 3.32** The driving off of the cattle is confirmed by Aeneas' own report at 20.83–102, as well as by the words that Achilles directs at him at 20.187–98. **Procl. § 44** On the capture of (a) Lyrnessos, (b) Pedasos, (c) surrounding towns, (d) Lesbos, (e) Thebe, compare (a) 2.691, 19.59–60, 19.291–6, 20.89–93, 20.188–94; (b) 20.92; (c) 1.125, 2.226–8, 9.328–33, 9.365–7, 18.339–42; (d) 9.129–30, 9.271–2, 9.664–5; (e) 1.366–7 (Chryseis), 2.691 (in general), 6.415–17, 9.188, 23.826–9 (Andromache), 16.152–4 (the horse Pedasos). The tradition will have included, at least, the destruction of Thebe, but not necessarily the capture of Chryseis, still less this as Andromache's place of origin. **Procl. § 45, Ps.-Apollod. *Epit.* 3.32, *Cypr. PEG* F 41 (= F 25 W.)** The death of Troilus at the hands of Achilles is known to the *Iliad* (24.255–7), but Achilles' cruelty on that occasion is probably deliberately suppressed in the *Iliad*.[66] **Procl. § 46** Priam's son Lycaon, whose abduction for sale to Lemnos is reported, must probably be traditional; otherwise, the donning of his cuirass by Paris at 3.332–3 and Apollo's appearance in his guise at 20.81–5 would be inexplicable. On the other hand, his unexpected appearance at 21.34–8 gives the impression of an improvisation on the poet's part, along with the offer, as one of the prizes at the funeral games, of his cost price as a slave (23.740–6). **Procl. § 47, *Cypr. PEG* F 27 (= F 21 D. = F 23 W.), F 28 (= F 22 D. = F 24 W.)** Procl. § 47 gives an impression of being so pointedly added with regard to the *Iliad*, where Chryseis plays a central part in Book 1. An instance like 2.226–8 (speech of Thersites) suggests that the poet rather assumes a general picture of expeditions, which may mirror the experiences of colonization; whether, in addition, Chryseis and Briseis had special roles in the tradition is uncertain. Chryseis is captured in Thebe. The separation of her homeland (Chryse) from her place of capture is the premiss for the action of the *Iliad*, but is given no motivation there. According to *Cypr. PEG* F 28 (= F 22 D. = F 24 W.), she was in Thebe because she was sacrificing to Artemis there. It is possible, but not certain, that the *Cypria* here preserved

---

[63] Kullmann (1960: 91–3, 110, 272); Nagy (1999: 22–5). [64] See above, p. 119.
[65] Kullmann (1955b = 1992: 38–63). [66] Kullmann (2012: 113).

a traditional item of legend. Briseis was captured, according to *Cypr. PEG* F 27 (= F 21 D. = F 23 W.), in Pedasos and not in Lyrnessos as at *Il.* 2.688–93, 19.59–60, 19.291–6; this too may perhaps be the old version.[67] **Procl. § 22, § 48, § 107,** *Cypr. PEG* **F 29–30, Ps.-Apollod.** *Epit.* **6.7** Palamedes and the old city of Nauplia are passed over in the *Iliad*, clearly because the new image of Odysseus in the *Iliad* (and the *Odyssey*) would otherwise have been damaged.[68] **Procl. § 49** The plan of Zeus is paralleled as a motif by that of Thetis, approved by Zeus, to support Achilles in his abstention from fighting. Whether it is meant as a transition to the *Iliad* is unclear and debated. **Procl. § 50, Ps.-Apollod.** *Epit.* **3.34** Ps.-Apollodorus shifts the appearance of the heroes named in the Trojan Catalogue to the ninth year of the war. Penthesileia and Memnon could join them. It cannot be excluded that such a catalogue appeared in the *Cypria* and, already in the time before the *Iliad* existed, made the transition to the content of the *Aethiopis*.[69]

Apart from a few obscure passages at the end of Proclus' excerpts, everything speaks for the view that the composer of the *Cypria* uses pre-Homeric legend, quite independently of the *Iliad*, as the basis for his account. This is especially clear at two points, which deviate from the *Iliad* in exemplifying older legend: the first is the Teuthranian expedition. My once widely contested theory of 1960 that this pre-dates the *Iliad*[70] was confirmed by the new Archilochus Papyrus published in the year 2005.[71] Archilochus uses a traditional epic battle scene at Teuthrania as an *exemplum* for his own lost shield. Since he was composing only a little later than the conjectural date for the creation of the *Iliad*, it is now clear that the references in the *Iliad* to the 20-year duration of the war really do go back to an old bardic tradition. Likewise, the attention given to Palamedes, with its accompanying, more negative picture of Odysseus, is a sign of the relative antiquity of the content of the *Cypria*. So in this respect we reach the same conclusion as in the case of the *Aethiopis*.

Amazonia

The apparent reflections in the *Iliad* of the Penthesileia story, as narrated according to **Procl. § 51–6** in the first part of the *Aethiopis*, are contested.[72] After the slaying of Penthesileia (**Procl. § 52**), Thersites, the son of the

---

[67] Kullmann (1960: 288 n. 1).
[68] Kullmann (1965 = 1992: 174; 2011: 113); Danek (1998: 139, 237).
[69] Kullmann (1960: 171–3, 302). [70] Kullmann (1960: 189–203).
[71] Obbink (2005: 18–42). [72] See Kullmann (1960: 303–6).

Aetolian Agrius, reviles Achilles for his alleged love for Penthesileia (involving, according to the scholia to Sophocles, *Phil.* 445, necrophilia) and is killed by him (**Procl.** § 54). In *Il.* 2.220, Thersites is hated not only by Odysseus, but also by Achilles, which is intelligible only as an anticipation of the *Aethiopis* story. The poet makes the slanderer into a notorious complainer, with no ancestry. He would have acquired his physical defects in the Calydonian boar-hunt, when Meleager threw him from a crag for his refusal to join the fray (Pherecydes *FgrHist* 3 F 123). Thus they too are traditional.

Ilias parva[73] / *Iliou persis*[74]

Allusion is also made, in the *Iliad* as in the *Odyssey*, to the most important motifs from the Fall of Troy as described in these epics, and knowledge of them is assumed.

Procl. § 72 The fetching of Philoctetes (*Il.* 2.724–5). **Procl.** § 75 Helen's marriage with Deiphobus after the death of Paris: allusions in *Od.* 4.276, 8.517–18. **Procl.** § 76 The fetching of Neoptolemus: probably assumed at *Il.* 19.326–37. **Procl.** § 78–9 The slaying of Eurypylus is narrated at *Od.* 11.519–22. **Procl.** § 81 The Wooden Horse.[75] **Procl.** § 82 Odysseus as a scout in Troy (*Od.* 4.242–64). **Procl.** § 90 The Fall of Troy is taken for granted throughout the *Iliad*.[76] **Procl.** § 91 Slaying of Priam by Neoptolemus (*Il.* 6.448–51, 20.306). **Procl.** § 93 Crime of the Locrian Ajax.[77]

Nostoi[78]

Procl. § 107 ('Then the storm at the Capherean Rocks and the downfall of the Locrian Ajax is described'), **Ps.-Apollod.** *Epit.* 6.7 See above, p. 123. While the attack by Palamedes' father Nauplius on the returning Achaeans is omitted in the *Odyssey*, Ajax's death on Tenos is dealt with in *Od.* 4.499–510.[79]

Procl. § 112 (Assassination of Agamemnon), **Nost.** *PEG* F 10 (= T 2 D. = F 10 W.) At *Il.* 1.29–32, 1.109–13 the intention of Agamemnon to take Chryseis with him to Argos is a transference of motif from the actual

---

[73] See also Kelly, below in this volume.
[74] See also Finglass, below in this volume.
[75] See above, pp. 119–20.
[76] For twenty-one prominent passages, see Kullmann (1960: 343–8).
[77] See above, pp. 119–20.
[78] See also Danek, below in this volume.
[79] Kullmann (2012: 113).

taking of Cassandra. On Agamemnon's murder, cf. *Od.* 1.28–9, 1.298–300, 3.193–4, 3.234–5, 3.254–61, 3.303–4, 4.91–2, 4.512–37, 11.405–12, 11.453, 13.383–4, 24.96–7.[80] The content of the *Nostoi*, too, was known to both Homeric epics.

In general, an established canon of facts for the events of the Trojan War (*Faktenkanon*) is proved to have been already in existence before the creation of the *Iliad*, one which later formed a comprehensive basis for the Epic Cycle, and to which the *Iliad* alludes. In the face of the entire phenomenon of the Trojan saga, one must assume that a complete mythological picture, built up in a proliferation of oral performances by bards, was available to a large section of the audience. It was into this panorama that the *Iliad*, influenced by motifs from the Memnon story, was created and inserted.

---

[80] Kullmann (2002a: 174–5).

6 | Meta-Cyclic epic and Homeric poetry

MARGALIT FINKELBERG

In recent years, scholars who sought to combine Neoanalytic *Quellenforschung* with the theory of oral composition have become aware of the fact that Homer uses epic tradition, first and foremost that represented in the poems of the Trojan Cycle, in a rather idiosyncratic way: he does not just evoke the Cycle tradition or borrow its motifs but, rather, deliberately reshapes it, making it serve his own agenda.[1] This strongly suggests that, rather than behaving as two traditional poems among many, the *Iliad* and *Odyssey* claimed a special status within the tradition to which they belonged. To render this new awareness as regards the position of Homer vis-à-vis other traditional poetry, the terms 'metaepic' and 'meta-Cyclic' have been proposed in scholarly literature.[2]

HOMER'S ACKNOWLEDGMENT OF THE CYCLE TRADITION

It is universally accepted today that the *Iliad* and *Odyssey* lean heavily upon the nomenclature of Trojan subjects dealt with in the poems of the Epic Cycle. The recognition of this fact has been one of the major contributions of neoanalysis to Homeric scholarship. At the same time, this should not be taken to mean that, as the pioneers of neoanalysis initially supposed, Homer directly addressed the very poems that were known as 'Cyclic' in later periods[3] and that eventually formed the basis of Proclus' summary.

---

[1] See Finkelberg (2003a), a response to the question 'What are the most interesting new directions in oral tradition studies (with specific reference to your special field)?', circulated among students of oral poetries by the journal *Oral Tradition* in 2003. The studies I referred to on that occasion were Slatkin (1991), Ballabriga (1998), Danek (1998), Malkin (1998) and Burgess (2001).

[2] Finkelberg (1998: 154–5): 'Homer's transformation of the traditional saga into raw material for his poems endowed the latter with the status of metaepics'; Burgess (2012: 170): 'The Homeric poems are 'meta-Cyclic' in the sense that they transform Cyclic motifs and phraseology into new contexts'. Cf. Finkelberg (2002), (2003b), (2011a); Burgess (2009: 4, 66); see now also Tsagalis (2011: 218–28).

[3] *Kyklikoi*: see Σ *Il.* 3.242, 5.126, 18.486, 19.332, 23.346, 660–1, 19.326; *Od.* 11.547; cf. *scriptor Cyclicus* in Hor. *Ars Poetica* 136.

The sources on which Homer drew must have belonged to pre-Homeric Trojan tradition of which the poems of the Cycle were post-Homeric representatives. To quote Gregory Nagy, 'Paradoxically the textual fixation of the Homeric poems is older than that of the Cycle... and yet the inherited themes of the Cycle appear consistently older than those of the Homeric poems.'[4] The range of the identifiable 'Cyclic' subjects to which Homer refers is quite impressive. These references may come either as direct reminiscences of Cyclic episodes (both the *Iliad* and the *Odyssey*) or as re-enactments of events narrated in the poems of the Cycle (the *Iliad* only).

Reminiscences

Reminiscences as such are of course a widespread epic device whose range of application exceeds the story of the Trojan War.[5] They were probably not specific to Homer.[6] However that may be, Homer widely uses reminiscences evoking the Cycle tradition in order to fill gaps in his own account of the Trojan War. This is most conspicuous in the case of the *Odyssey*.

Two themes stand at the centre of the *Odyssey* attention – the Fall of Troy, the subject of the Cyclic *Aethiopis*, *Ilias parva* and *Iliou persis*, and the Returns, the subject of the Cyclic *Nostoi*.[7] The *Aethiopis* is evoked in the story about Achilles' funeral told by Agamemnon in the Underworld; the *Ilias parva* in Odysseus' meeting with Ajax in the Underworld described by Odysseus in *Odyssey* 11 and in the story of Odysseus' entering Troy as a spy told by Helen in *Odyssey* 4; *Iliou persis* in the story of the Wooden Horse told by Menelaus in *Odyssey* 4 and by Odysseus in *Odyssey* 11; this same story is also the subject of Demodocus' third song in *Odyssey* 8.[8] The *Nostoi*

---

[4] Nagy (1990b: 72). See now also West (2013: 17).

[5] See e.g. Nestor's reminiscences of his youthful exploits (*Il.* 1.260–73, 7.132–57, 11.668–761, 23.629–43), Phoenix' reminiscences of his past (*Il.* 9.447–95), or Eumaeus' reminiscences of his early life (*Od.* 15.389–484).

[6] Cf. the following passage from Proclus' summary of the *Cypria*: 'And Menelaus comes to Nestor. Nestor in a digression relates to him of how Epopeus, who raped the daughter of Lycurgus, had his city sacked, and the story of Oedipus, and the madness of Heracles, and the story of Theseus and Ariadne' (*Cypr.* arg. lines 114–17 Severyns). Although what is dealt with here are mythological paradigms rather than reminiscences proper, the episode suggests that reminiscences, including those of Nestor, might have emerged in the Cycle epics on other occasions.

[7] See Kullmann, above in this volume, pp. 124–5.

[8] Achilles' funeral: *Od.* 24.35–92, *Aeth.* arg. lines 196–9 Severyns; Odysseus and Ajax: *Od.* 11.541–64, *Aeth.* arg. lines 201–3 Severyns, *Ilias parva* arg. lines 208–10 Severyns; Odysseus the spy: *Od.* 4.235–64, *Ilias parva* arg. lines 224–7 Severyns; the Wooden Horse: *Od.* 4.265–89; 11.504–37; 8.499–520, *Ilias parva* arg. lines 230–2 Severyns, *Il. pers.* arg. lines 241–4 Severyns.

are evoked in Nestor's reminiscences of the aftermath of the Trojan War and his story of Agamemnon's death in *Odyssey* 3, in Menelaus' reminiscences in *Odyssey* 4 and in Agamemnon's ghost's account of his own death in *Odyssey* 11; this is also the subject of the song performed by Phemius in *Odyssey* 1.[9] As a result, the *Odyssey*, besides being a poem of the return of the last of the heroes, acts as a synopsis of the part of the Epic Cycle dealing with the final stages of the Trojan War and the fate of the survivors.

It comes as no surprise that, while the *Odyssey* reminiscences invoke the Fall of Troy and the Returns, those of the *Iliad* refer to the initial stages of the Trojan War. In *Iliad* 2 Odysseus reminds the Achaeans of the mustering of the troops at Aulis and the portent of the snake and the sparrows that accompanied it, whereas in *Iliad* 3 Antenor recalls the story of the embassy of Odysseus and Menelaus to Troy and the negotiations about the return of Helen and Menelaus' possessions, both having taken place at the very beginning of the war. Both accounts are closely paralleled in the *Cypria*.[10] In that they refer to events that preceded the beginning of the *Iliad*, the reminiscences of Odysseus and Antenor fulfil the same function as the reminiscences of Nestor and Menelaus in books 3 and 4 of the *Odyssey*. As a result, the reminiscences produce a comprehensive picture of the Trojan War that transcends by far the scope of events that the Homeric poems were ostensibly meant to narrate.

Re-enactments

Quite a few episodes in books 2–7 of the *Iliad*, which form a digression from the narrative sequence of the story of the Wrath of Achilles, address the beginning of the Trojan War as narrated in the Cyclic *Cypria*. The beginning of the war can be evoked in a direct reminiscence, as in Odysseus' and Antenor's reminiscences referred to above. But more frequently the *Iliad* applies a subtler strategy, in that the episodes properly belonging to the beginning of the war are incorporated into the chronological and narrative setting of its last year and become an integral part of it.[11] Thus, the seduction of Helen by Paris and Aphrodite in *Iliad* 3 provides, as was aptly put by Mark Edwards, 'a re-enactment of the original seduction', the proper context of which is again the *Cypria*: 'In the meantime Aphrodite

---

[9] Nestor: *Od.* 3.103–200; 253–312; Menelaus: 4.351–585; Agamemnon: 11.404–34; Phemius' song: 1.325–7; *Nost.* arg. lines 279–87, 291–3, 301–3 Severyns.
[10] *Il.* 2.284–332; 3.204–24; *Cypr.* arg. lines 122–4, 152–3 Severyns.
[11] Finkelberg (1998: 142–4).

brings Helen and Alexander together. And after making love they put most of [Menelaus'] possessions on board and sail away by night.'[12] In a similar way, the mustering of the troops described in *Iliad* 2 or the negotiations about Helen and the building of the Achaean Wall narrated in *Iliad* 7, both properly belonging to the beginning of the war but introduced so as to suit the context of its last year, can hardly be anything else than such re-enactments of the war's initial stages, again closely paralleled in the *Cypria* account.[13]

In fact, what we have here is a narrative strategy characteristic of the *Iliad* as a whole, for in the second half of the poem the same technique of re-enactment or, to borrow Wolfgang Kullmann's expression, 'an imitation of a narrative known to us from one of the Cyclic epics' is employed.[14] There, this strategy is used to evoke the last stages of the war which, understandably enough, could not be directly narrated in the *Iliad*. Thus, it has long been suggested that the description of the death of Patroclus and the battle over his body in books 16 and 17 of the *Iliad* evoke the circumstances of Achilles' death as narrated in the Cyclic *Aethiopis*; again, although the lamentation of Thetis and the Nereids over Achilles in *Il.* 18.22–72 is prompted by the death of Patroclus, it evokes Thetis' bewailing of Achilles, also narrated in the *Aethiopis*.[15] Likewise, although the Fall of Troy properly belongs with the events described in the Cyclic *Iliou persis*, in *Iliad* 22 Priam anticipates it in all its gruesome details, and the death of Hector is presented as if Troy were already in flames; an additional effort to evoke the outcome of the war can be discerned in the sudden emergence of Epeius, the builder of the Wooden Horse, in the Funeral Games for Patroclus in *Iliad* 23.[16]

Although the *Iliad* and the *Odyssey* relate just two single episodes from the Trojan saga, owing to their recurrent use of reminiscences and re-enactments of Cyclic subjects they act as synoptic narratives embracing the entire tradition of the Trojan War and the Returns. While the literary merits of this compositional technique were commended as early as Aristotle,[17] it has rarely been taken into account that what is being dealt with is far

---

[12] *Cypr.* arg. lines 100–2 Severyns; cf. Edwards (1987: 196); Kullmann (1991 = 1992: 110).
[13] See esp. *Cypr.* arg. lines 152–4, 169 Severyns.   [14] Kullmann (1984 = 1992: 142).
[15] *Aeth.* arg. lines 198–9 Severyns; also evoked as a reminiscence in *Od.* 24.36–97. For a recent discussion of the *Iliad* foreshadowing of the death of Achilles, see Burgess (2009: 72–92).
[16] The fall of Troy: *Il.* 22.62–71, 405–11; *Ilias parva* PEG F 16, 21 (= F 17, 20 D. = F 25, 29 W.); *Il. pers.* arg. lines 268–74 Severyns; Epeius: *Il.* 23.664–99, 838–40, *Ilias parva* arg. lines 222–3 Severyns. The Funeral Games is the only occasion on which Epeius appears in the *Iliad*; in the *Odyssey*, his name emerges twice, both times in connection with the Wooden Horse (8.492–3, 11.523).
[17] *Poet.* 1451a23–30; 1459a30–b7.

from merely a matter of composition. By isolating Cyclic episodes from their original contexts and incorporating them into the stories of Achilles' wrath and Odysseus' homecoming, Homer does not simply evoke the Cycle epics but also adapts them to his own narratives, thus appropriating their contents.[18]

HOMER'S DISACKNOWLEDGMENT OF THE CYCLE TRADITION

Reminiscences and re-enactments are far from being Homer's only means for maneuvering the Cycle tradition so as to achieve the desired effect. To see that, we have to turn to the cases where Homer applies much more aggressive intertextual strategies, in that he discredits or deliberately ignores the tradition represented by the poems of the Cycle. I mean the so-called 'lying stories' (the *Odyssey* only) and deliberate suppressions of subjects that are prominent in the Cycle tradition (both the *Iliad* and the *Odyssey*).

Lying stories

In the second half of the *Odyssey*, Odysseus is frequently found engaged in telling lying stories which place either Odysseus himself or the persona that he assumes in different locations all over the Mediterranean, especially in Crete.[19] It has been suggested more than once that Odysseus' lying stories in fact refer to alternative versions of Odysseus' wanderings, a hypothetical 'Cretan' Odyssey being the most frequently proposed candidate.[20] Yet, it is a lying story that places Odysseus in the northern parts of the Greek world that offers an identifiable parallel to one of the poems of the Trojan Cycle.

According to the story that the disguised Odysseus tells first to Eumaeus and then to Penelope, upon his arrival from Troy Odysseus left his treasure

---

[18] This is especially obvious in Homer's use of the story of Agamemnon's return, the subject of the Cyclic *Nostoi*, which acts in the *Odyssey* as a suggestive parallel running through the entire poem and thus becoming an integral part of it. Thus, Orestes' vengeance of his father's death is set as a model for young Telemachus already in book 1, whereas Clytaemnestra's perfidy is contrasted with the virtue of Penelope up to the concluding book of the poem. Telemachus and Orestes *Od.* 1.293–302, 3.301–16; Penelope and Clytaemnestra 11.405–34 and 441–53, 24.192–202.

[19] *Od.* 13.256–86, 14.192–359 and 462–506, 17.415–44, 19.165–202, 221–48 and 262–307, 24.302–14.

[20] See esp. Reece (1994); Tsagalis (2012a); cf. Marks (2003).

in Epirus with the Thesprotian king Pheidon and went to Dodona, to ask the oracle whether he should return to Ithaca openly or in secret.[21] Epirus, the Land of the Thesprotians, played a prominent part in the lost Cycle epics *Telegony* and *Thesprotis* (probably just a section of the former), both of which told a story of Odysseus' return that significantly differed from what we find in the main narrative of the Homeric *Odyssey*. According to Proclus' summary of the *Telegony*, after his return to Ithaca Odysseus migrated to Epirus where he married the Thesprotian queen Callidice; Ps.-Apollodorus adds to this that the purpose of Odysseus' journey north was to appease Poseidon's anger, thus fulfilling the prophecy given by Teiresias in the Underworld.[22] In other words, although the story is presented in the Homeric poem as a lie, it is in fact an alternative version of the story of Odysseus' return which is reasonably close to the one we find in the Cyclic *Telegony* and/or *Thesprotis* and to which Teiresias' prophecy probably also belonged.[23] In that it does not presuppose Odysseus' eventual homecoming, this version sharply disagrees with the Homeric *Odyssey*, for which the protagonist's return to Ithaca is a *sine qua non*.[24]

By the very fact of turning the Cycle version of Odysseus' wanderings into a lying story the *Odyssey* poet downgrades it and privileges the version that he offers.[25] It stands to reason that the same strategy was also at work in the case of those lying stories that cannot any longer be provided with identifiable traditional parallels.

Suppressions

On a number of occasions, the *Iliad* and the *Odyssey* can be shown to ignore themes that are prominent both in the tradition represented by the poems of the Trojan Cycle and in that associated with the name of Hesiod. This strongly speaks in favour of Homer's deliberate suppression of the subjects in question.

---

[21] *Od.* 14.316–35, 19.287–302.
[22] *Od.* 11.119–37, 23.266–84; *Tel.* arg. lines 315–323 Severyns; Ps.-Apollod. *Epit.* 7.34. According to Teiresias' prophecy, upon his return to Ithaca Odysseus should leave it again for the country of men who 'know not the sea, neither eat meat savoured with salt'.
[23] See Ballabriga (1989); Peradotto (1990: 60–76); Danek (1998: 214–20, 285–7); Malkin (1998: 120–55); Marks (2008: 100–4); Tsagalis (2011: 218, 223).
[24] Ballabriga (1989: 299): 'This Cyclic Odysseus places himself in opposition to the one of the *Odyssey*, who is fundamentally the man who returns to Ithaca' (my translation).
[25] Danek (1998: 216).

The End of the Race of Heroes. According to the Cyclic *Cypria*, Hesiod's *Works and Days* and the pseudo-Hesiodic *Catalogue of Women*, the Trojan War was devised by Zeus and other gods in order to put an end to the Race of Heroes.[26] The overall design of the Epic Cycle, which starts with the plan of Zeus to destroy the Race of Heroes and ends with the death of the last of them, conveys the same idea. Yet, although the Homeric poems formally belong to the same tradition as the poems of the Trojan Cycle, the theme of the End of the Race of Heroes is conspicuous by its absence in Homer. Among those Homeric passages for which the theme in question may be considered relevant, the following three are especially noteworthy.

(a) *Dios boulē*, the notorious 'plan of Zeus' referred to in the proem of the *Iliad* (1.3–5 'And it [the wrath of Achilles] threw down to Hades many mighty souls of heroes, and made them prey to dogs and all kinds of birds, and the plan of Zeus was being fulfilled') is strongly reminiscent of the same expression in the proem of the *Cypria* (*PEG* F 1.6–7 = D., W. 'And the heroes were being slaughtered at Troy, and the plan of Zeus was being fulfilled'). However, the theme of the destruction of the Race of Heroes is irrelevant to the rest of the poem to such a degree that many scholars, beginning with Aristarchus, have refused to take the Iliadic expression as referring to the plan of Zeus that triggered the Trojan War.[27]

(b) A passage in *Iliad* 12 referring to the future destruction of the Achaean Wall by Poseidon and Apollo contains the expression 'the race of demigods' (ἡμιθέων γένος ἀνδρῶν). This is the only case in Homer when the heroes are called 'demigods' or referred to as a special race.[28] Yet the same passage states unequivocally that after the end of the war those of the Achaeans who stayed alive simply and prosaically went home.[29] In view of this, it is difficult not to agree with Bryan Hainsworth's comment *ad locum* that 'within his narrative Homer does not recognize them [the heroes] as a separate class of being and therefore has no use for the present term, which occurs only here in the *Iliad*'.[30]

(c) Proteus' prophecy in *Odyssey* 4, according to which Menelaus will be taken after his death to the Elysian Field and the ends of the Earth where

---

[26] *Cypr. PEG* F 1 (= D., W.); Hes. *WD* 159–73; Hes. *Cat.* F 204.95–105 M.-W. = F 110.95–105 Hirsch.
[27] Discussions: Schein (1984: 59–60, with n. 34); Kirk (1985: 53); Slatkin (1991: 118–22); Edwards (2011).
[28] *Il.* 12.23. Cf. Scodel (1982: 34).
[29] *Il.* 12.15–16 and below, with n. 38. Cf. Finkelberg (2004: 14–15).
[30] Hainsworth (1993: 320).

he will enjoy a happy existence, evokes not only the Isles of the Blessed, the final abode of the heroes in Hesiod, also located at the ends of the Earth, but also the White Island where Achilles was taken after his death in the *Aethiopis* and the island of Circe where Telemachus and Penelope were led in the *Telegony*.[31] That is to say, in both Hesiod and the Cycle the heroes' immortalization seems to be the norm.[32] Yet, when taken against the rest of Homer, whose characters invariably die ordinary deaths while their souls descend to the dreary realm of Hades, the *Odyssey* version of Menelaus' afterlife appears to be exceptional.[33]

The passages adduced, as well as Homer's close acquaintance with the principal Cycle subjects as discussed above, make it highly implausible that Homer could have been unaware of such a pivotal event as the destruction of the Race of Heroes in the Trojan War. Accordingly, his failure to integrate this event into his own story of the Trojan War can only be interpreted as due to deliberate suppression.

The post-war migrations The theme of the heroes' migrations to foreign lands was prominent in the sub-genre of heroic tradition conventionally called *nostoi*.[34] Consider indeed the following. Diomedes left Argos and went to the Adriatic where he became the founder of numerous cities; Neoptolemus travelled by land to Epirus, where he became the founder of the royal dynasty of the Molossians; Philoctetes migrated to the region of Croton in Italy where he colonized Cape Crimissa; Idomeneus was expelled from Crete by his wife and her new consort and eventually went elsewhere, and so on.[35] 'The entire ethnography of the Mediterranean could be explained as originating from the Big Bang of the Trojan War and the consequent Nostos diffusion.'[36]

---

[31] *Od.* 4.561–5, Hes. *WD* 167–73, both using the expression πείρατα γαίης; cf. *Aeth.* arg. lines 198–200 Severyns, *Tel.* arg. lines 327–330 Severyns. Cf. also Hes. *Cat.* F 204.99–103 M.-W. = F 110.99–103 Hirsch.

[32] Cf. also *Aeth.* arg. lines 189–190 Severyns: 'Then Achilles kills Memnon. And Eos, after having obtained Zeus's permission, bestows immortality on him.' See further Griffin (1977: 42–3).

[33] See Griffin (1980: 167); S. West in Heubeck, S. West, Hainsworth (1988: 227); Mackie (2011). On Homer's 'grim heroic vision of the afterlife', see now Edmonds (2011).

[34] In a recent article, Anna Bonifazi (Bonifazi 2009) has drawn attention to the fact that, as Georg Curtius pointed out as early as 1874, 'returns' would be too restrictive a rendering of the Greek *nostoi*. Namely, the evidence at our disposal strongly suggests that the word's meaning implies multidirectionality, thus embracing both homecoming and migration. This of course would suit much better the actual use of the word in the *nostoi* tradition.

[35] Diomedes: Ps.-Apollod. *Epit.* 6.9, cf. Verg. *Aen.* 11.243–295; Neoptolemus: *Nost.* arg. lines 296–300 Severyns, Pind. *Nem.* 7, Eur. *Andr.* 1243–51, Ps.-Apollod. *Epit.* 6.12–13; Philoctetes: Ps.-Arist. *Mir. Ausc.* 840a15–26; Ps.-Apollod. *Epit.* 6.15b; Idomeneus: Ps.-Apollod. *Epit.* 6.9–10.

[36] Malkin (1998: 3); cf. Finkelberg (2005: 149–50).

Nothing of this will be found in Homer. Nestor's reminiscences in *Odyssey* 3, relating as they do to the same heroes whose *nostoi* were referred to above, are especially illuminating. According to Nestor's story, Diomedes' ships had safely landed in Argos, with no mention being made of Diomedes' subsequent movements; the northerners Neoptolemus and Philoctetes had also made a safe journey home; finally, Idomeneus had brought all his men back to Crete.[37] The *Iliad*, whose subject matter has ostensibly nothing to do with *nostoi*, adopts the same strategy. Thus, in the Achaean Wall passage already discussed above, the poet makes the following general statement concerning the survivors' fate after the war: 'And the city of Priam was sacked in the tenth year, and the Argives went in their ships to their dear homeland.'[38] We saw, however, that the evidence relating to the *nostoi* tradition suggests a quite different picture.

Some of the migration stories that circulated in Greek tradition might well be late, but the evidence is cumulative, the more so as we are fortunate enough to possess a piece of evidence which is supported by traditional sources and therefore can serve as an effective check.

The diviner of the Achaean fleet and personally of Agamemnon, Calchas son of Thestor is introduced in the *Iliad* as 'the best of the augurs', who knows the past, the present and the future and whose gift of prophecy, granted by Apollo, enabled him to lead the Achaean ships to Troy. Judging by Proclus' summary, Calchas was also prominent in the Cyclic *Cypria*.[39] Especially noteworthy, however, is the tradition that concerns Calchas' exploits after the Trojan War. Both the Cyclic *Nostoi* and a Hesiodic poem (probably *Melampodia*) tell us that after the war Calchas, together with other Achaeans – the Lapiths Leonteus and Polypoites in the *Nostoi* and Amphilochus son of Amphiaraus in the *Melampodia* – travelled on foot to Colophon in Asia Minor; according to the *Melampodia*, Calchas died there of a broken heart after having been defeated in a competition of divination by Mopsus, the son of Manto daughter of Teiresias.[40] Both sources are

---

[37] Diomedes: *Od.* 3.180–2, cf. *Nost.* arg. lines 283–4 Severyns; Neoptolemus: *Od.* 3.188–9, cf. 4.5–9; Philoctetes: 3.190; Idomeneus: 3.191. On the partiality of Nestor's account of the homecomings of Diomedes, Neoptolemus, and Idomeneus, see also Marks (2008: 127–9).

[38] *Il.* 12.15–16.

[39] *Il.* 1.69–72; cf. 2.299–330. According to Proclus' summary, the *Cypria* (arg. lines 122–4, 135–43 Severyns) included two episodes in which Calchas was actively involved: the portent of the snake and the sparrows that the Achaeans witnessed at Aulis (evoked also in *Iliad* 2, see above); and the sacrifice of Iphigeneia (not mentioned in Homer). I discuss the Calchas case in detail in Finkelberg (2011a).

[40] *Nost.* arg. lines 288–90 Severyns (probably also describing Calchas' death, see West (2003a: 155 n. 59)); Hes. *Melamp.* F 278 M.-W., cf. F 279. This account was also known to Callinus and

traditional, and both are sharply at variance with what we find in Homer. In the *Iliad*, Calchas is consistently presented as a humble and obedient servant of Agamemnon. This is a far cry indeed from the Cyclic and Hesiodic Calchas, who leads the survivors of the Trojan War to new places of settlement in Asia Minor. As far as I can see, the fact that here, as with the End of the Race of Heroes, the Cycle and the Hesiodic tradition coincide above the head of Homer indicates that they represent the traditional version of Calchas' story which Homer suppresses.[41]

As distinct from the explicit references to Cyclic subjects, the lying stories and suppressions are one-sided by definition and therefore heavily marked. This is especially true of suppressions. To paraphrase Ken Dowden, by the very fact of refusing reference to a given subject Homer makes the reference.[42] That is to say, when suppressing the traditional subjects of the End of the Race of Heroes and post-war migrations or marking them as false, Homer makes a statement of some kind. To inquire into the nature of this statement is our next task.

Meta-Cyclic epic[43]

Whether acknowledging the Cycle tradition and making it part of his own narrative or disacknowledging and tampering with it, Homer addresses the Cycle tradition systematically and in its entirety. This becomes especially obvious if we approach the *Iliad* and *Odyssey* not as two isolated fragments of a grand narrative of the Trojan War but, rather, as two mutually complementary parts of a single whole.

Sophocles and, in a slightly different version, to Pherecydes of Athens (Callin. *IEG* F [8]; Soph. *TrGF* F 180; Pherec. *EGM* F 142; cf. Ps.-Apollod. *Epit.* 6.2–4). An additional and probably competing version, which involved Mopsus' mother Manto but apparently did not mention Calchas, is found in a fragment from the *Epigonoi*, a traditional poem belonging to the Theban Cycle (*Epig. PEG* F 3 = D. = F 4 W.). According to yet another version, preserved by Herodotus, Calchas did not die at Colophon but travelled farther east, eventually to become, together with Amphilochus, the ancestor of the Pamphylians (Herod. 7.91; quoted in Strab. 14.4.3; also Sophocles apud Strab. 14.5.16). Calchas was also credited with founding Selge in Pisidia (Strab. 12.7.3).

[41] In view of this, the puzzling Iliadic lines 'and he led the ships of the Achaeans to Ilios in virtue of the skill of prophecy that Phoebus Apollo granted to him' (1.71–72), suggesting as they do Calchas' leading role in the Trojan expedition, may well indicate Homer's awareness of Calchas' traditional status.

[42] Dowden (1996: 53).

[43] See also Kullmann, above in this volume, p. 108.

The Trojan Cycle starts with the decision of Zeus to annihilate the Race of Heroes and ends with the death of Odysseus and transportation of Telemachus and Penelope to the island of Circe, followed by their immortalization. Thus, the very design of the Cycle, from the beginning of the *Cypria* to the end of the *Telegony*, conveys the idea of the End of the Race of Heroes. The famous passage in Hesiod's *Works and Days*, according to which those of the heroes who did not fall at Troy were transported to the Isles of the Blessed at the end of the Earth (above, with n. 31), shows clearly enough that this was also the pattern that Hesiod had in mind. It can hardly be due to mere chance that in making the *Iliad*, a poem about the Trojan War, be continued with the *Odyssey*, a poem about the Returns, the Homeric tradition follows the same pattern. That is to say, rather than introducing two separate episodes from the Trojan Cycle, Homer offers a full-scale alternative to the Cycle as a whole – an alternative which, however, suppresses the theme of the End of the Race of Heroes, the Cycle's very *raison d'être*. The question is of course what is offered instead.

In Hesiod, the myth of the End of the Race of Heroes is part of a larger teleological concept according to which the history of mankind is a process of gradual degeneration from the Race of Gold, which flourished at the dawn of humanity, to the Race of Iron, which stands for man's present condition. Needless to say, such an attitude to the past implies a distinctly negative view of the present, and Hesiod's unflattering characterisation of the Race of Iron that has replaced the Race of Heroes makes it especially manifest.[44] But the same attitude can also be discerned in the dark prophecies that conclude the description of the end of the Race of Heroes in the *Catalogue of Women*, and the poet of the *Cypria*, in that he presents Helen as the daughter of Nemesis, clearly shares the same pessimistic vision.[45] Conversely, Homer's suppression of the theme of the End of the Race of Heroes establishes a continuity between Greece of the Heroic Age and historical Greece, thus changing the pessimistic view of the present characteristic of other traditional poetry.[46]

This move is closely linked with Homer's treatment of another theme that is shared by Hesiod and the Cycle but is conspicuous by its absence in Homer, that of the heroes' posthumous immortalization. Again, nothing can be more alien to the spirit of the Homeric poems. As Jasper Griffin

---

[44] *WD* 174–8.
[45] Hes. *Cat.* F 204.102–17 M.-W. = F 110.102–17 Hirsch.; *Cypr. PEG* F 9.2 (= F 7.2 D. = F 10.2 W.), *PEG* F 10 (= F 8 D. = F 11 W.).
[46] Finkelberg (2004). Cf. Scodel (1982: 35): 'In Homer, the continuity of history from the heroes to the poet's contemporaries is complete.'

put it, 'This is what makes the *Iliad* both true and tragic, and the very different procedure of the Cycle indicates profoundly different attitudes to the fundamental nature of human life and death, and consequently to human heroism and the relation of men to the gods.'[47] At the same time, there is good reason to suppose that there is much more here than just two different attitudes. I can hardly improve on Laura Slatkin's assessment:

> Yet the Homeric poems . . . are interpreters of their mythological resources at every step; and 'destruction' as understood by the traditions represented by Hesiod, the Cycle, and Mesopotamian literature has been reinterpreted by the *Iliad* and translated into its own terms. The *Iliad* evokes these traditions, through passages that retrieve the theme of destruction, to place them ultimately in a perspective that, much as it rejects immortality, rejects utter annihilation as well. Components of the mythological complex of the end of the race survive in Iliadic allusions, and reverberate, but are transformed.[48]

As a result, the theme of immortality, ubiquitous in both the Cycle and Hesiodic tradition, is transformed in Homer into one of 'heroic experience as a metaphor for the condition of mortality, with all its contradictions'.[49] All this strongly suggests that the suppression of the traditional theme of the End of the Race of Heroes is essential to the concept of the Heroic Age that Homer develops.

The same would be true of another theme which is prominent in the Cycle but ignored by Homer, that of the heroes' post-war migrations. Note that the aftermath of the Trojan War, the Returns, is just as indispensable to the myth of the End of the Race of Heroes as the story of the war proper. The two events are inextricably linked in that, rather than returning home, most heroes who survived the war went elsewhere, eventually to disappear from the view. Yet, as we saw in the previous section, Homer either suppresses the migration theme or transforms it into that of homecoming; in a similar way, he rejects the traditions of Odysseus' settling in foreign lands, the hero's return to Ithaca being presented by him as the only option to be taken into account.

The continuity between the heroic past and the present rather than historical discontinuity; the heroes' humanization through mortality rather than their posthumous immortalization; Greece as the heroes' only destination rather than their migrations to foreign lands – these are, then, the main revisions undergone by the Cycle tradition in the hands of Homer. While

[47] Griffin (1977: 43). [48] Slatkin (1991: 121–2). [49] Slatkin (1991: 39).

it is difficult to say with certainty what concrete historical circumstances could trigger this total restructuring of the Trojan tradition,[50] we can be sure of one thing: when taken together, the revisions in question transpire as different aspects of one and the same project, a project whose objective is not so much the commemoration of the past as, rather, the establishment of usable ideological foundations for the present and the future. Judging by the evidence at our disposal, the Trojan Cycle was the only epic tradition treated by Homer in this manner. Much as Homer was aware of other epic traditions, such as the Heracles saga, the Argonauts or the Theban Cycle, all of them frequently evoked in his poems, this awareness cannot equal the total engagement that we have observed in both his accepting the Cycle tradition and rejecting it. Homer does not simply appropriate the other versions of the Trojan saga or challenge their authority: he absorbs the Cycle tradition with the purpose of superseding it. It goes without saying that a text that stands in this kind of relation to the other texts treating the same subject can no longer be regarded as just one traditional variant among many. Rather, this would be a text which deliberately positions itself beyond the tradition to which it ostensibly belongs.[51]

[50] To my mind, the Cycle emphasis on the Heroic Age, on posthumous immortalization and on migrations suggests the 'Eighth-Century Renaissance', the hero-cult and the colonization, respectively, all of the three pointing to the early archaic period; this would also agree with the evidence of vase-painting (on the latter, see esp. Burgess (2001: 53–114; 2011)). In that case, Homer's reaction to the Cycle must be late archaic. This would concur in general outline with the model, first introduced by Gregory Nagy, according to which the Cycle and Homer represent two successive stages of Panhellenism (Nagy 1990b: 70–9): this model has been effectively taken further by Christos Tsagalis in a recent publication (Tsagalis 2011: 217–18, 236–7).

[51] The implications of this conclusion from the standpoint of oral-formulaic theory are discussed in Finkelberg (2011a).

7 | Language and meter of the Epic Cycle

ALBERTO BERNABÉ

INTRODUCTION

Like the poetry attributed to Homer and Hesiod, the poems of the Cycle are written in a literary dialect which does not correspond to any real dialect of Ancient Greek. This dialect was so closely associated to the genre itself that it was used by epic poets from different periods and it remained without major changes for centuries, when dialectal variations were replaced by a common form of Greek, the *koinē*. This is, thus, a distinguishing trait of the epic genre.[1]

The dialect is basically Ionic, but with certain elements from other dialects. In general, the great majority of these features are archaisms that have been preserved in order to maintain the metrical structure.

The original date of the Cyclic poems has been much debated. Some of them have been traditionally ascribed to the early archaic period,[2] although Wilamowitz, Wackernagel, and, recently, Davies reduce this dating in a considerable way.[3] The two main linguistic arguments to support a later date (like the fifth century BC) are: the so-called Atticisms and the diction that is considered 'late'. Regarding the former, modern authors like Janko, Richardson, or Burgess[4] have revealed that many of the supposed examples are not Atticisms. With respect to diction, the label 'late' is simply based on the fact that the term is not attested in the archaic literature preserved to us. Yet, if we consider the remarkable number of Homeric or Hesiodic *hapax* that reappeared only much later, we must play down the importance of these arguments. For example, ἀλυκτοπέδαι 'bonds' is documented just once in the archaic epic (Hes. *Theog.* 521).[5] If Hesiod had decided to use another word in that verse, all the modern critics would have diagnosed the

---

[1] On the epic dialect cf. *GH*; Edwards (1971); Shipp (1972); Bernabé (1995); Horrocks (1997); Cassio (2009); Ruijgh (2011).
[2] Data provided by the Greek sources and assumed by Lesky (1971: 104). In more recent times, Parlato (2007) took them for the *Cypria*.
[3] Wilamowitz (1884); Wackernagel (1916: 178–9), whose arguments are repeated as irrefutable by Davies (1989a).
[4] Janko (1982: *passim*); Richardson (1974: 52–6); Burgess (2001: 10).
[5] Also conjectured by West in *HHom.* 1.C 5.

unequivocal Hellenistic and Imperial character of this term, since it would only appear in Apoll.Rh. 2.1249, Opp. *Hal.* 2.285, Triph. 480, and Nonn. *Dion.* 2.302. It is illusory to think that, taking into account the important number of archaic poems that are lost, we can identify a term as 'late' only because this word is not documented in Homer or Hesiod.

A good example of the risks of considering the non-attested terms as 'late' is the case of πλάτος (*Cypria* F 12), clearly regarded as 'modern' (not before the fifth century BC) by Wackernagel.[6] This is, in fact, an ancient formation of a word of Indo-European origin (*$pleth_2$-es-*, cf. Vedic *práthas*, Avestan *fraθah*), where the full-grade has been replaced by the zero-grade from the adjective in *-u-*, πλατύς < *$pl̥th_2$-ú-*, just like in τάχος or κράτος, whose antiquity is accepted by everyone because they are both documented in Homer.[7]

DIFFICULTIES

There is, as well, a series of factors that complicates the analysis of the linguistic and metrical data of the Cycle.

The first of these factors has to do with the scarcity of surviving verbatim passages, which decreases the reliability of the obtained results.

The second one derives from the Cycle's own story: the poems that make it up were composed by different authors in many places and periods; in a gradual process, whose details are not clear at all, they ended up forming a large collection to be recited in a continuous way, including the *Iliad* and the *Odyssey*[8] (in this adaptation process the texts must have been modified). So, when examining the linguistic features of every poem, we do not know which of them were ancient and which are the result of textual modifications produced in the configuration process of the whole Cycle. So, the linguistic features of a certain poem of the Cycle can have different ages, since they date back to different periods of the story of its configuration. In this way, I agree with Burgess's words:[9]

> Rather than seek a specific date, I conceive of their composition as developing in oral performance traditions over a period of time in the Archaic Age. Such a circumstance for poetic composition not only defies precise dating but also challenges the need for it.

---

[6] Wackernagel (1916: 182); Davies (1989a: 93) repeats the argument.
[7] Schmitt (1990: 17); Parlato (2007: 10–12), with more arguments.
[8] Holmberg (1998). [9] Burgess (2001: 11).

The third factor of distortion has to do with a certain lack of definition within the corpus, because none of the recent editors of the Cycle[10] have edited the same fragments, even the ones considered *dubia*. In this study I will follow my edition as a starting point, but I will accept West's verbatim fragments not included in my edition and some other contributions.[11]

THE CORPUS[12]

The number of verses that have survived as literal quotations, a small fraction of the thousands of verses making up the Cycle, can be summarized as follows:

Theban Cycle: *Titanomachy*: three literal fragments of indirect transmission (*PEG* F 4, 6, 11), five verses altogether, plus a papyrus fragment that we should probably ascribe to this work (*PEG* F 5, not in D., W.), with minimal remains of twenty-one verses, and two dubious fragments (*PEG* F °12 and °13, not in D., W.), that make four verses. *Oedipodea*: we only have a literal fragment of two verses (1). *Thebaid*: six literal fragments (*PEG* F 1–4 (4 in D. is 'Homerus' 3), 7 and 10), up to a total of twenty verses and two words from another verse (*PEG* F 11; 4* W., not in D.). West adds the end of a verse (7*), which is identical to the end of *Il.* 4.38. *Epigonoi*: two certain fragments of one verse each (*PEG* F 1 and 4, the latter was edited as Antim. 2 by D.) and two dubious fragments of two verses each (*PEG* F°6 and °7, not in D., W.), six verses altogether, one of them incomplete. *Alcmeonis*: three literal fragments (*PEG* F 1–3); seven verses altogether, one of them incomplete.

Trojan Cycle: *Cypria*: there are twelve extant literal fragments (*PEG* F 1, 4–5, 8–9, 15–18 (16 = adesp. 5 D., 7 W.), 25 (adesp. 4 D.), 32–33), plus two other dubious °38 ('Homerus' 9 D., adesp. 16 W.) and °40 (adesp. 17 W, om. D.)), in total fifty-three verses, some of them incomplete. *Aethiopis*: there are two fragments preserved, the first[13] did not originally belong to the free-standing poem, but was composed in order to be read immediately after the *Iliad*, without interruption. The first verse is made up

---

[10] *PEG*; Davies (1988). We are waiting for 'a commentary on the individual fragments which fill separately more than one volume', promised by Davies (1986: 91); on the Trojan epics, see now West (2013).

[11] Like the later edition by Bravo (2001) of *Il. parv.* °32, which substantially improves on mine.

[12] From this moment onwards I will use some conventional abbreviations: Tit(anomachy), Oed(ipodia), Theb(aïs), Epig(oni), Alcm(aeonis), Cyp(ria), Aeth(iopis), Il(ias) parv(a), Il(iou) pers(is), Nost(oi), Teleg(onia). In order to expedite my frequent lists of quotations, in the next sections I will refer only to the numbering in my edition. Like in my edition, I will distinguish the dubious fragments from those more certain by marking them with a *circellus* (°12).

[13] Transmitted by Σ *Il.* 24.804b, but considered spurious by Davies.

of *Iliad* 24.804, until the bucolic diaeresis: ὣς οἵ γ' ἀμφίεπον τάφον Ἕκτορος, and the sentence ἦλθε δ' Ἀμαζών, which introduced the episode of Penthesileia. We can confirm the secondary character of the text since we know two writings of the second verse[14] that are probably a case of the so-called 'rhapsodic variants'. There is, as well, another extant fragment of a verse (2). *Ilias parva*: we have seventeen literal fragments, with a total of sixty complete or incomplete verses: *PEG* F 1 (not in D., W.), 2, 5, 9, 21,[15] 23 (dub. 3 D.), 24, 26 (not in D.), 27 ('Hom.' 1 D.), 28–29, °32 (not in D., W.).[16] *Iliou persis*: there are three literal fragments (*PEG* F 4, 6 and 7 (Arctinus spur. D., *Aeth.* 5 W.)) with no more than twelve verses. *Nostoi*: three fragments have been preserved (*PEG* F 7, 8, 11), with a total of five verses and a half. *Telegony*: We know two literal fragments (*PEG* F 1 = 1* W., 'Hom.' 10 D. and 2 W., not in *PEG*, D.), two verses altogether.

GRAMMAR

The features that characterize the language of the Cyclic poems are, except for some cases, like those of the Homeric language.

Phonology

Vocalism

An old -ᾱ appears as η, like in Ionic, even after ε, ι, ρ (in Attic we find ᾱ in these contexts). Yet, there are also cases of ᾱ in this context, although sometimes it is improperly corrected, especially where the textual tradition is unanimous. Thus, we must read λαμπρά (nom. sg.) in *Ilias parva* 9 (rightly in 11 D., 14 W.) and not the corrected form λαμπρή.[17]

Another ᾱ that did not become η appears in λᾱῶν *Iliou persis* 6.2, °32.10. *Prima facie*, the reason would be that λᾱῶν could not be replaced by the Ionian treatment λεῶν without changing the meter, and this is why it remains

[14] 1.2a is the one transmitted by Σ *Il.* 24.804b: Ἄρηος θυγάτηρ μεγαλήτορος ἀνδροφόνοιο; 1.2b is found in PLitLond. 6, col. xxii 42: Ὀτρήρ[η]<ς> θυγάτηρ ἐυειδὴς Πενθεσί[λ<ε>ια. See Bernabé (1982: 87–9).

[15] In my edition, I consider that lines 6–11 of this fragment belong to Simias of Rhodes, just like Σ Eur. *Andr.* 14. West considers them also as a part of the *Ilias parva*. Even if this is a doubtful question, I include these verses in the grammatical commentary.

[16] Bernabé (1984) defends the position that there were two *Iliades parvae*, because two fragments seem to be the first verse of the work, but cf. Scafoglio (2006) that offers a clever solution (double invocation like in Virg. *Aen.* 1.1 and 1.8).

[17] The same prejudice led me to correct μάχας in *Ilias parva* °32.11; see Peters (1989: 229), although (Bravo 2001: 59) also prefers μάχης. About λαμπρά, see Cassio (2009: 199).

in the text. But the Ionic shows a form with η (ληός, Hippon. *IEG* F 158, Herod. 5.42), so this word is probably preserved as characteristic of the epic tradition (*GH* i.20).

With regard to the verb, in Homer, denominative verbs derived from s-stem, such as τελέ(ι)ω, νεικέ(ι)ω, πενθέ(ι)ω, present -ει- when they are placed in the princeps of the metrical foot (the long syllable) and -ε- in the biceps (the pair of short positions that may be replaced by one long). The Cycle documents ἐτελείετο *Cypria* 1.7 (cf. *GH* i.166). There is also an -ι- preserved in our texts: first, in the ancient comparative κρείων *Iliou persis* (6.1) and in the anthroponym Κρείοντος *Oedipodea* 1.2; secondly, in the derived adjective χρυσείοισι *Nostoi* 7.3.

It is characteristic of the epic dialect the alternation between the absence and (minimal) presence of vowel contraction. The examples are as follows:

Poem	No contract	Contract
Titanomachy	βαλέοντι (5.4), Τηϋγέτη (°12.1)	ὠρχεῖτο (6)
Oedipodea	–	–
Thebaid	ἄειδε (1), ἀργυρέην (2.3), χρύσεον (2.4), ἐνηέι (2.9), νόον (4.1), ἵκηαι (4.2)	ἠρᾶτο (2.8)
Epigonoi	ἐξεχέοντο (°7.2)	–
Alcmeonis	τροχοειδέι (1.1), εὐχαλκον (1.3)[18]	–
Cypria	χροΐ (4.1), ἄνθεϊ (4.4), ἡδέι (4.5), καλλιπνόου (4.6), εὐώδεας (5.2), ἄνθεα (5.2), χρυσέη (5.4), ἀείδουσαι (5.5), βασιλῆϊ (9.3), Τηϋγετον (15.2), κοίλης (15.5), ἀεθλοφόρον (15.6), ἤην (25.2), ἔπλεον (°40), Δολοπηΐδα (°40)	αἰδοῖ (9.5)[19]
Aethiopis	εὐειδής (1.2b), ἔυχ[ε]άι (2)	–
Ilias parva	ἄειρε (2.1), δηϊοτῆτος (2.1), Πηλεΐδην (2.2), χρύσεος (5.2), δίκροος (5.2), ἔην (9), κοίλας (21.2), ἐυπλοκάμοιο (21.3), πορφύρεος (21.5), ἠύζωνον (21.6), ἀριστῆες (21.7), ἀέξηται (23), Πηλεΐδην (24.1), νωλεμέως (26.4), σάωσε (26.4), ἀείδω (28.1), ἐύπωλον (28.1), Γανυμήδεος (29.4), ἐυκνήμιδες (°32.5), ἥρω]α (°32.6, Bravo 2001), νοέ]ουσι (°32.12, ibid.)	ἥρω (2.2), ἐπεφώνησω (2.3), Λαρτ]ιάδης (°32.9)
Iliou persis	ἕλκεα (4.4), ἀκριβέα (4.5), ἀναλθέα (4.6), Μενεσθῆϊ (6.2)	εὐσθενές (7.3)
Nostoi	νόον (8)	–
Telegony	–	–

[18] Although less probable, we could read τροχοειδεῖ and εὔχαλκον (West (2003a: 58) prints εὐκάλκωι).

[19] Parlato (2007: 6–7).

As in Ionic, the epic dialect presents compensatory lengthening after the simplification of clusters involving liquids/nasals before *w*. However there is no compensatory lengthening in several cases, such as Attic and Oriental or Insular Ionic. The cases of these two different treatments documented in the Cycle are:

Cluster	Long vowel	Short vowel
*-λϜ-	κᾱλάς *Tit.* 11.2, κᾱλῶι *Cypr.* 4.4, κᾱλόν *Cypr.* 5.5	–
*-ρϜ-	δουρί *Theb.* 10	Κόρον *Nost.* 7.1
*-νϜ-	–	κενώσειεν *Cypr.* 1.6

There is only one case of apocope registered: *Cypr.* ἄν(α) (5.3).

Consonants

Geminata

We observe several cases of -σσ- (coming from σ + σ or from clusters) that are not simplified to -σ-, as in Ionic (since -σ- between vowels was aspirated and finally lost). The preservation of the geminate is an archaism that bards had to maintain because the Ionic form modifies the metrical pattern. The poet, however, is free to use the simple variant for metrical reasons:

Origin	Treatment with geminate	Treatment with simple variant
-σ+σ- > -σσ-	στήθεσσιν *Il. pers.* 4.5	–
*-ds- > -σσ- (and aorists of verbs in -ίζω	πο[σσί]ν *Il. parv.* °32.16 (Bravo 2001), ῥιπίσσας *Cypr.* 1.5	ποσί(ν) *Cypr.* 15.2, *Nost.* 11.1, κουφίσαι *Cypr.* 1.4
*-ts- > -σσ-	δάσσαιντ(ο) *Theb.* 3.10	λέβησιν *Nost.* 7.3
*-dhy- > -σσ-	μέσσοισιν *Tit.* 6, [μέσσωι] *Il. parv.* °32.14 (Bravo 2001)	μεσάτη *Il. parv.* 9[20]
Etymology unknown	Ὀδυσσεύς *Il. parv.* 2.2	Ὀδυσεύς *Il. parv.* 26.3, °32.21[21]

A cluster of sibilant and resonant can become a geminate resonant, a treatment that is commonly considered an Aeolism, although it can just be an archaism:

---

[20] *Il.* 8.223, 11.6 μεσσάτω, with a suffix taken from δέκατος, *GH* i.262.
[21] In the papyrus it is mistakenly written -σσ-.

*-σμ- > -μμ-: φιλομμειδής *Cypr.* 5.1.
*-σλ- > -λλ-: ἔλλαβε *Il. parv.* 21.5.
*-νσ- > -νν-: ἔννεπε *Il. parv.* 1.1.

As we will see later on, the bards take advantage of this possibility in order to geminate or not a certain consonant (f. e. Ἀχιλλ- *Il. parv.* 21.1, but Ἀχιλ- *Il. parv.* 24.1 etc.), but also to freely lengthen an internal vowel before μ, λ, ν, or a word-final vowel before the initial μ, λ, ν of the following word. This can be the case with γέρᾱ before μέγα in *Theb.* 2.6 (cf. *infra*).

Morphology

Thematic declension

The genitive singular of the thematic inflection is frequently -οιο, a result of *-osyo*: ἀμβροσίοιο *Tit.* 4.2, Κάδμοιο *Theb.* 2.3, ἑοῖο 2.5, cf. *Epig.* °6.2, *Cypr.* 1.5, 9.8, *Il. pers.* 4.7. The epic dialect also presents the variant –ου, resulting from the contraction of *-οο: *Tit.* 11.2, *Theb.* (2.4), *Epig.* °8.1, *Alcm.* 2.1, *Cypr.* 1.2, 1.5, 4.4, 4.6, 5.5, 8.1, *Aeth.* 1.2a, *Il. pers.* 4.2, 7.2.

The dative plural in Ionic is -οισι(ν) and it is commonly documented in the poems: *Tit.* 6, *Theb.* 2.7, 2.10, 3.3, 7 W., *Epig.* 4.1, *Alcm.* 2.2, *Cypr.* 4.2, 5.1, 17.2, 9.1, 15.5, *Il. parv.* °32.11, °32.13, *Nost.* 7.3, 11.1. We have also in Homer and Hesiod the ending –οις but, even if this ending will prevail in Attic, in the fragments of the Cycle it only appears before a vowel. Actually, it could be a dative in οισι with an elided ι, for example, ἄλλοις ἀθανάτοισι (*Theb.* 3.3) or ἀμφοτέροις, ἕτερον (*Il. pers.* 4.2) can be read ἄλλοισ' ἀθανάτοισι and ἀμφοτέροισ', ἕτερον; cf. *Cypr.* 15.5, 17.2. The only exception can be found in the part that Bravo (2001) reconstructed for *Ilias parva* °32.18: ξα[νθοῖς πλοκάμοισιν.

α-Stems

A feminine θεά instead of the Ionian ἡ θεός (on this cf. *GH* i.20) is documented both in Homer (*Il.* 1.1, etc.) and in the Cycle (*Tit.* 1.1, *Cypr.* 5.3). The reason for it is that the old form could not always be replaced by the Ionian one without changing the meter.

In *Tit.* 5.2 we observe the term νεφεληγε[ρέτα, a nominative in -ᾰ of masculine α-stems, also documented in Homer (see e. g. ἱππότα *Il.* 2.236). These are normally explained as coming from vocatives.

In the case of the genitive singular of masculine α-stems, the oldest form is -ᾱο, an ending documented in Mycenaean (f. e. *su-qo-ta-o* συγʷώτᾱο 'swineherd').[22] We find it in Ἀγχίσαο *Il. parv.* 21.9. The change from ᾱ > η and the quantitative metathesis give rise to the ending -εω, realized with synizesis, as in one syllable, and also appearing in the verses of the Cycle: Τανταλίδεω *Cypr.* 15.4.

The dative plural of the -ᾱ stems presents several forms in the epic dialect: -αισιν: κεφαλαῖσιν *Cypr.* 5.3; -ῃσι: ἰδυίῃσι *Nost.* 7.2; -αις: πυκιναῖς *Cypr.* 1.3, ἀμβροσίαις *Cypr.* 4.5, ὥραις παντοίαις *Cypr.* 4.7, [ἐφ]ετ[μαῖς] *Il. parv.* °32.13, Θησείδαις *Il. pers.* 6.1. When -αῖς (which is not an Ionian ending)[23] appears before vowel, it can be an original -αισ', with an elided -ι.

The name Oedipus (Οἰδίπους) appears inflected as an α-stems masculine: Οἰδιπόδῃ *Theb.* 2.2.

Athematic declension

The Cyclic poems also present the artificial ending -εσσι, borrowed from the dative plural of the sibilant stems, but extended to other stems: πραπίδεσσι *Cypr.* 1.3, *Nost.* 7.2, καλύκεσσιν *Cypr.* 4.5, ταχέεσσι *Cypr.* 15.2. We find also the 'monster' ἐπέεσσιν *Il. parv.* 26.2 instead of ἔπεσ-σιν (*GH* i.204–207).

The σ-stems present several subtypes:

> Neuters alternating in -ος/-εσ- and adjectives in -ης/-εσ- present no other particularity than those forms without contraction, as in Ionic: ἄνθεα *Cypr.* 5.2, ἀκριβέα *Il. pers.* 4.5 which, in dative singular, can appear with no diphthong (ἄνθεϊ *Cypr.* 4.4). Also ἥρως was a form of σ-stem and not of -F-, just as the Mycenaean compound *ti-ri-se-ro-e* shows. In accusative, it appears with a contraction of -ωα in ἥρω *Cypr.* 2.2, although Bravo 2001 reconstructs [ἥρω]α in *Il. parv.* °32.6. Finally, there is a documented dative of χρώς with a maintained hiatus χροΐ *Cypr.* 4.1.

As for the neuters in -ας, we have some less clear forms, like γέρᾱ *Theb.* 2.6. In Homer, the nominative plural of γέρας is γέρᾰ, an apocopated form instead of γέραα: *Il.* 2.237, 9.334, *Od.*4.66. Thus, γέρᾱ could be the result of a contraction of γέραα[24] or, since it appears before the word μέγα, of the lengthening of a short vowel before μ- (vid. *supra*). On the other hand, the accusative κρέᾰ before a consonant (*Epig.* °6.1, *Tel.* 1) could be the remnant of an ancient formation without the word-final sigma, but also the result of an analogy with neuters of the thematic declension (cf. *GH* i.210).

Stems in -ηυ documented in the Cycle present the oldest form (resulting from the loss of F between vowels) with -η- followed by the endings, as in

---

[22] Bernabé and Luján (2006: 149–50).   [23] Wackernagel (1916: 53); cf. Parlato (2007: 27–30).
[24] As we clearly see in Eur. *Phoen.* 874 οὔτε γὰρ γέρᾱ πατρί (it is curious that this happens in the context of the same episode, which I ignore if it is fortuitous or not), or in γέρη *SIG* 1025 (Cos). There is also a rare variant γέρεα documented in Herod. 2.168, *SIG* 1037 (Miletus).

the nominative plural ἀριστῆες *Il. parv.* 21.7. In the dative, the ending does not form a diphthong with η: βασιλῆϊ *Theb.* 3.3, *Cypr.* 9.3, Ἀχιλῆϊ *Cypr.* 25.1. It is also remarkable that the name of the god Ares is declined as an -ηυ-stem: Ἄρηος *Aeth.* 1.2a, *Cypr.* 8.2 (cf. *GH* i.229).

The name of Zeus presents a double declension, (a) from the stem Δι(F)- dat. Διΐ *Theb.* 3.3, with a long vowel that probably conceals the ancient dative in *-ei* (cf. mic. *di-we*, ΔιFεί)[25], and (b) from the secondary stem resulting from re-adding the accusative ending to the ancient form Ζῆν < *dhē(u)m*: Ζῆνα *Cypr.* 18.1, from which we have the subsequent dative Ζηνί *Cypr.* 9.3.

Ἄιδος *Theb.* 3.4 is an old athematic formation, in front of the masculine of the -α stems (*GH* i.232).

The case of κᾰρη *Alcm.* 1.2 and κρᾱσίν *Alcm.* 2.3 is particularly complex.[26]

Adjectives

We find patronymic adjectives: Ἑκτορέην *Il. parv.* 21.2, Τελαμώνιον *Il. parv.* °32.9, -ε *Il. Parv.* °32.10. Also remarkable is the form Ἰλιακοῖο (*Cypr.* 1.5), not found in Homer. This is probably an adaptation of Ἰλιϊκός < Ἰλιϝικός (paralel to Ἀχαιϊκός), just as Ἀσκληπιάδης is an adaptation of Ἀσκληπιΐδης.[27]

Pronouns

We find several ancient forms, like the enclytic personal pronouns μιν *Alcm.* 1.1, reconstructed in *Il. parv.* °32.11 (Bravo 2001), and νιν *Cypr.* 9.12. We have also a genitive possesive ἑοῖο *Theb.* 2.5, dat. pl. ἑοῖσι (*Theb.* 2.7) < *sewo-*. A dative plural ᾗισιν < *sw-* is reconstructed in the formula φρεσί[ν ᾗσιν *Tit.* 5.5.

The demonstrative ὁ ἡ τό is used as a relative: *Tit.* °12.3, *Theb.* 4.2, *Cypr.* 4.1, 9.2.

Verb

The verbal augment is frequently omitted (as in Mycenaean):[28] γείνατο *Tit.* °12.3, φράσθη *Theb.* 2.5, λάνθαν' *Theb.* 2.8, δαίνυτο *Epig.* °6.1, κορέσθην *Epig.* °6.2, πλῆξε *Alcm.* 1.2, σύνθετο *Cypr.* 1.4, ποίησαν *Cypr.* 4.2, 17.1, ἀμφίεπον *Aeth.* 1.1, ἔκφερε *Il. parv.* 2.1, κάταγεν *Il. parv.* 21.2, πόρεν *Il. pers.* 4.3, μάθε *Il. pers.* 4.7, θῆκε *Nost.* 7.1, but in other cases we find forms with augment: ὠρχεῖτο *Tit.* 6, ἔτεχ' °13 (in this last case, however κήρυκ' ἔτεκε can be replaced by κήρυκα τέκε), παρέθηκε *Theb.* 2.2, ἐνόησε *Theb.* 3.1, ἔθηκεν

---

[25] Burkert (1981: 36). I do not agree with Davies' reading of Διΐ.
[26] Chantraine (2009, s.v.).
[27] Schmitt (1990: 18–19); Parlato (2007: 8–10).   [28] Bernabé-Luján (2006: 200–1).

Alcm. 2.3, ἐτελείετο *Cypr.* 1.7, ἔθεντο *Cypr.* 5.3, ἦλθε *Aeth.* 1.1, ἐγένοντο *Il. parv.* 1.1, ἐπεφωνήσω *Il. parv.* 2.3, ἔδωκε *Il. pers.* 4.1, ἔθηκε(ν) *Il. pers.* 4.2, 4.5, ἤπαφεν *Nost.* 8, ἤσθιεν *Tel.* 1.

The athematic aorists with -κ- in the three persons of the singular active forms can show the analogue extension of -κ- to plural or to middle voice: δῶκαν *Il. parv.* 21.8, ἐ[π]εθήκ[ατ'] *Il. parv.* °32.15.

As for the verbal endings, we find Aeolian infinitives in -μεν *Cypr.* 25.1, *Il. parv.* 21.11. The ending -μέναι (*Theb.* 3.4, *Cypr.* 25.1) is probably the result of adding the Ionic ending -ναι to the Aeolian -μεν.[29]

There are several remarkable verbal formations, like the full grade ἀέξηται *Il. parv.* 23, a verb in -είω with desiderative value: ὀνειδείοντες *Theb.* 3.2; a denominative in -ωω: ἰδρώοντας *Epig.* °6.2, cf. *GH* i.365; the imperfect ἤην of εἰμί *Cypr.* 25.2; the middle form ἐφάμην *Cypr.* 25.1; the optative κενώσειεν *Cypr.* 1.6; the isolated perfect, with no present τεταγών *Il. parv.* 21.4 (which corresponds to Latin *tetigi*) or the pluperfect ἔστο *Cypr.* 4.1, 4.7. And with regard to the *hapax* εὔκτο *Theb.* 3.3, it is widely discussed whether it is a pluperfect, a thematic aorist,[30] or an imperfect.[31]

In the Cycle, we also find the phenomenon of tmesis, that is, verbs modified by adverbs that work as preverbs but separated, and not combined in the same word: ἔκ... ἔλετ᾽ *Il. parv.* 21.6, ἔκ... / ... ἐλεῖν *Il. pers.* 4.3–4. The impression of the Greeks was that those words had been 'cut' and hence the name τμῆσις 'cut' with which we know this fact.

Numerals, prepositions, and particles

As for the numerals, the most relevant case is τριτάτην *Cypr.* 9.1 with superlative suffix (cf. *GH* i.261). With respect to the prepositions, we find documented the use of ἐνί, variant of ἐν: *Alcm.* 1.2, *Cypr.* 1.6, 4.4, *Il. pers.* 4.5, *Nost.* 7.3. As a modal particle they use both κεν *Theb.* 4.2, *Il. parv.* 2.4 and ἄν *Il. parv.* 2.5.

Lexicon

The number of words that are not documented in Homer or Hesiod is not very significant:[32] *Titanomachia*: χρυσώπιδες (4.1),[33] ἐλλοί (4.1),[34] δικαιοσύνη (11),[35] σχήματα (11.2). *Thebaid*: θεόφρονος (2.3),

---

[29] Horrocks (1997: 213).   [30] *GH* i.389.
[31] Narten (1968: 11–12).   [32] None in *Oed., Epig., Aeth., Tel.*
[33] Cf. Λατοῦς χρυσώπιδος Ar. *Th.* 321, χρυσῶπιν... Δίκ[ην *IEG El. adesp.* 28.4.
[34] Cf. ἔλλοπας ἰχθῦς Ps.-Hes. *Scut.* 212, ἐλλοῖς ἰχθύσιν Soph. *Aj.* 1297.   [35] Cf. Thgn. 147.

ὀνειδείοντες (3.2). *Alcmeonis*: τροχοειδέι (1.1),[36] χαμαιστρώτου (2.1), στιβάδος (2.2), ποτήρια (2.3).[37] *Cypria*: βαρυστέρνου (1.2), πλάτος (1.2), παμβώτορα (1.4), ῥιπίσσας (1.5), Ἰλιακοῖο (1.5), κενώσειεν (1.6), βάρος (1.6), αἰθέσι (4.6), καλλιπνόου (4.6), ἐξοροθύνων (9.9),[38] πολυβώλακα (9.11, *hapax*), ὄχλον (16). *Ilias parva*: ἐπεφωνήσω (2.3), δίκροος (5.2). *Iliou persis*: ἀκριβέα (4.5), ἀναλθέα (4.6), προφόρωι (7.2), εὐσθενές (7.2). *Nostoi*: κόρον (7.1), in Homer always κοῦρον, ψύας (11.2).

PROSODY AND METRICS

The Cyclic poems were written in dactylic hexameter, a quantitative verse that is based on the alternation of long (¯) syllables (those ending in a long vowel, diphthong or consonant) and short (˘) ones (ending in a short vowel), according to a basic pattern:

$$-\smile\smile \mid -\smile\smile \mid -\smile\smile \mid -\smile\smile \mid -\smile\smile \mid -\times$$

This pattern admits some flexibility, since the two short of every *metron* may be replaced by a long syllable.

We know that archaic epic poems are the result of an oral tradition dating back to the Mycenaean period and developed throughout the Dark Age. As a general rule, the bards did not turn into Ionic those archaic forms without a formal equivalent for the metrical pattern (cf. *infra*). In Ionic, for instance, the geminated sigma of a form like μέσσος is simplificated, a fact that would break the metrical structure by resolving a long syllable (μεσ-) into a short one (με-). This is why bards keep the archaism of -σσ-, as in Aeolic and other dialects. The decipherment of Mycenaean has shown that some of these Homeric archaic forms were already present in the Mycenaean dialect, like the genitives in -οιο, instead of the Ionic dialect's genitives in -ου.

On the other hand, there are some artificial forms, especially for those words that could not be fitted into the hexameter for their prosodic structure. The poets, then, must apply certain licenses, consisting in the alteration of syllables or the word structure. Here are some procedures for adapting the words to the meter:

---

[36] However, cf. Bacchyl. F 9.32 δίσκον τροχοειδέα, which can be an imitation of the passage or a sign of an epic formula.
[37] Alc. 376 Voigt, Sapph. 44.10 Voigt.   [38] But cf. Parlato (2007: 17–18).

Words that had wau

The consonantic counterpart of u, /w/ (which we are representing with the grapheme F, called digamma) was preserved in the Mycenaean dialect, but lost in Ionic in an early period. Such a loss provoked metrical alterations in the syllabic sequences that were transmitted by the oral tradition. One of these sequences consists in leaving vowels in hiatuses; so, for instance, in a sequence like *Cypr.* 4.7 τεθυωμένα εἵματα ἔστο we find two hiatuses that, originally, did not exist because, before the loss of *w*, the sequence must be pronounced τεθυωμένα Fείματα Fέστο. Another alteration produced by the loss of *w* is that a word-final closed syllable before a word beginning with F (that was originally long) becomes short. For example, in *Il. parv.* 29.1, the last syllable of ἔπορεν before Fοῦ was considered long, because -ε- stood before two consonants. However, when pronouncing ἔπορεν οὗ, it should be measured as short, something that affects the metrical structure. Subsequently, the bards were able to maintain the hiatus or the short syllable instead of the long one (a problem that they should solve by singing the verse in a particular way) but they also concealed the loss by using other strategies. In a sequence like βάλε, Fεῖπε (*Theb.* 3.1), for example, when the wau was dropped, the ε should be elided before the initial vowel of the following word βάλ', εἶπε, and this would modify the dactylic structure. Yet, the poet adds an ν ἐφελκυστικόν (the one that can appear at the end of the third person) and he restores the old pattern of long and short syllables with the new form βάλεν, εἶπε.

Sometimes, however, words that used to have a digamma do not display traces of its former presence. So, in *Il. pers.* 4.4. we read σαρκός ἑλεῖν where the final syllable of σαρκός counts as short, although ἑλεῖν comes from a word beginning with digamma. It is commonly believed that forms with no traces of digamma are indicative of a recent dating, but the fact is that we also find them in Homer and Hesiod. The distribution of facts is as follows.[39]

Work	Traces	No traces
Titanomachy	βαλέοντι (F)ἐο[ικώς (5.4)	—
Oedipodea	—	—
Thebaid	μέγα (F)οἱ (2.6), οὔ (F)οἱ (2.9)	ἔνθεν ἄνακτες (1), ἡδέος οἴνου (2.4); βάλεν εἶπε (3.1)[40]

[39] (F) indicates that the verse is measured as if F was still there and the word without (F) indicates that the verse is measured as if the word had no digamma.

[40] The -ν can be concealing βάλε (F)εῖπε.

Work	Traces	No traces
Epigonoi	–[41]	–
Alcmeonis	–	–
Cypria	δέ (F)ἰδών (1.3), χροΐ (F)ἕστο, τά (F)οἱ (4.1), τε ἵωι (4.4),-μενα (F)εἵματα (F)ἕστο (4.7), δέ (F)οἱ (8.1), ἰχθύι (F)εἰδομένην (9.9)	ἔριν Ἰλιακοῖο (1.5), ἄνθεσιν εἰαρινοῖσιν (4.2)[42], τόν τ' ἔρξαντα (18.1)[43]
Aethiopis	–	–
Ilias parva	ἔννεπε (F)ἔργα (1.1), ἔ(F)ειπες (2.3), ἀ(F)έξηται (23) τε (F)οἱ (21.7), ἀμείψασθαι (F)ἐπέεσσιν (26.2), ἀ(F)είδω (28.1) ἔπορεν (F)οὗ (29.1)	δ' ἑλών (21.3)
Iliou persis	–	σαρκὸς ἑλεῖν (4.4)
Nostoi	ἀποξύσασα (F)ἰδυίηισι (7.2)	καὶ ἔργα (8)
Telegony	μέθυ (F)ἡδύ (1)	

Epic correption

The so-called epic correption (*correptio epica*) is the shortening of a long vowel or word-final diphthong before the initial vowel of the following word:[44] καί *Tit.* °12.1, °12.2, *Cypr.* 1.3, 4.1, etc., καταβήμεναι *Theb.* 3.4, χώρωι (coni: χόρα(ι) cod. : χροιῇ West) *Theb.* 4.3, πεπαυμένοι *Epig.* °7.1 (before a lacuna), κουφίσαι *Cypr.* 1.4, κρόκωι *Cypr.* 4.3, καλλιπνόου *Cypr.* 4.6, πολυπιδάκου *Cypr.* 5.5, οἵ *Cypr.* 8.1, μιχθήμεναι *Cypr.* 9.4, τρέφει *Cypr.* 9.12, ἐπεί *Cypr.* 25.2, ἔγχ[ε]αι *Aeth.* 2, αὐτῶι *Il. parv.* 21.7, κεκορυθμένοι *Il. parv.* °32.5, [μέσσωι] *Il. parv.* °32.10 (Bravo 2001). In some cases the word-final long is not shortened: δροσερῶι ἐνί *Ilias parva* 23.

Positio debilis

Normally, to syllabify the cluster of a stop followed by a resonant (*muta cum liquida*), the stop is considered as the end of the first syllable and the resonant the beginning of the following one; therefore, the first syllable is long: Ἄτλας *Tit.* °12.3, θεόφρονος *Theb.* 2.3, πατρός *Theb.* 2.5, πατρώϊ *Theb.*

---

[41] ἱδρώοντας (°6.2), does not seem to indicate an initial F (GH 156).
[42] Although it might conceal -σι (F)εἰαρ-. [43] That could conceal τὸν Fέρξαντα.
[44] 'This conventional shortening... must have originated with the natural pronunciation of -αι and -οι as a short vowel + consonantal "y"': Horrocks (1997: 206).

2.9, λυγρά *Theb.* 7, etc. Yet, on other occasions, the poet can freely use the short scansion before the same sequences (*correptio Attica*): παρέθηκέ τράπεζαν *Theb.* 2.2, -ᾰ πλαζόμεν' *Cypr.* 1.1, Ἀφροδίτη *Cypr.* 4.6, 5.1, 5.4, πέπρωται *Cypr.* 8.1, ἐπῐ̈θρῶισκον *Tel.* 2 W.

Lengthening of short final vowel before liquid or nasal

Taking into account the cases where the initial μ- or λ- came from σμ-, σλ- and produced a geminate that lengthened the previous word-final vowel in sandhi (cf. *supra* the note on γέρᾱ *Theb.* 2.6), the bards were able to lengthen other final vowels before liquid or nasal: Μενεσθῆῐ̈ μεγαλήτορι *Il. pers.* 6.2, τεινόμενᾱ ῥώοιτο *Il. pers.* 7.3. But even without this circumstance, there can be lengthening of the final syllable: Χάριτες ἄμα *Cypr.* 5.4.

Metrical lengthening

In the case of those words with a syllabic sequence that did not fit in the hexameter pattern (for example, words consisting of three or four short syllables), the bard can lengthen one of the syllables in order to adapt the word to this structure: cf. ὕδατος *Tit.* 4.2, Κρείοντος *Oed.* 1.2, ἀθάνατος *Cypr.* 8.2, ἀθανάτοισι *Theb.* 3.3,[45] πουλύποδος *Theb.* 4.1, Ἄϊδος *Theb.* 3.4, ἐτελείετο *Cypr.* 1.7, ὕδωρ *Cypr.* 9.6, ἀείδω *Il. parv.* 28.1,[46] κατατεθν<ε>ιῶτι *Il. parv.* °32.8 (Bravo 2001). For Ἐννοσίγαιος *Il. pers.* 4.1, this lengthening of the first syllable is the result of a geminated nasal (cf. *GH* 100).

Diectasis

By using the spellings -οω- or -ωο-, the Ionian bards adapted to their verse certain forms of verbs in –αω, in which α and the rest of the vowels with o-timbre were already contracted (with the consequent loss of a syllable). These spellings indicated the timbre of the contraction, but they also were able to cover the ancient metrical pattern with ˘¯ or ¯˘, respectively. This operation is called diectasis and we find it, for example, in κομόωσαν *Il. parv.* 29.2 or in ἡβώοντα *Nost.* 7.1.

---

[45] However, an eventual link between this word and ai. *adhvanit*, could indicate traces of a wau treatment, *GH* 100.
[46] Schulze (1892: 384–5); Davies (1989a: 95).

Other syllabic adaptations

The bards were able to modify the syllabic structure by contracting two vowels of the same word (synizesis: Τανταλίδεω *Cypr.* 15.4, Πολυδεύκεα *Cypr.* 15.7) or by coalescing the final vowel of a word with the first of the following word (crasis: καὐχένας *Epig.* °6.1). Besides, they used to leave two vowels in hiatus (χαμαιστρώτου ἔπι *Alc.* 2.1,[47] ὧραι ἐν *Cypr.* 4.3, ἐνὶ ἄνθεϊ *Cypr.* 4.4,[48] νεκταρέωι ἔν *Cypr.* 4.5, χρυσέη Ἀφροδίτη *Cypr.* 5.4, Κρονίωνι ἐτείρετο *Cypr.* 9.5) or the opposite, i.e., to split a diphthong into two syllables (diaeresis: πατρώϊ' *Theb.* 2.9). There were also anomalous scansions, like the bisyllabic Τροίηι (*Cypr.* 1.6).[49]

Peculiarities of the hexameter

In general, the hexametrical behaviour of the Cyclic poems corresponds to the poetry of Homer. I merely point out a few characteristics, such as the elision in caesura κατὰ τρίτον τροχαῖον (*Theb.* 2.9), the word-end after the fourth μέτρον spondaic (*Theb.* 3.3, 4.3, 10, *Aeth.* 1.2b, *Il. parv.* 5.2, 21.1, *Tel.* 2 W.) or the word-end after the fourth trochee: *Il. parv.* °32.11.[50]

---

[47] Probably instead of χαμαιστρότοι' ἔπι.
[48] Perhaps, the text ῥόδον τ' ἐνὶ ἄνθεϊ hides a former ῥόδοιο τ' ἐν ἄνθεϊ.
[49] Schulze (1892: 406).
[50] A very important branch of metrics is the analysis of inner metric (or 'métrique verbal'), that is the study of the rules governing the distribution of word-ends in the different parts of the hexameter (two recent analyses: Fantuzzi (1995); Fantuzzi and Sens (2006)). Nevertheless, the studies of inner metric are based in statistics and statistics presuppose a more or less substantial number of lines. So, the scarce number of verses we have of the Cyclic poems prevents us from obtaining solid results from an attempt at doing some 'métrique verbal' of them.

8 | Narrative techniques in the Epic Cycle

ANTONIOS RENGAKOS

To deal with the narrative technique of works only preserved in fragments, as in the case of the poems of the Epic Cycle, is a daring task. Yet, as regards, in particular, the epics of the Trojan Cycle, i.e. the *Cypria*, the *Aethiopis*, the *Ilias parva*, the *Iliou persis*, the *Nostoi* and the *Telegony*, it is worth undertaking this task only because we are relatively well informed about the structure of these poems by Proclus' summary and their prose narration by Ps.-Apollodorus. Whereas, in the case of the epics of the Theban Cycle, i.e. the *Oedipodea*, the *Thebaid* and the *Epigonoi*, for which we totally lack such auxiliary sources and whose – strongly hypothetical – reconstruction is limited to a few essential facts about the plot of each poem, we cannot even attempt a similar undertaking.[1] Of course, even in the case of the epics of the Trojan Cycle, the nature of the sources is such that only assumptions can be made about the representation of time in these epics. For, due to the meagreness of the preserved lines from all six epics (90 genuine lines in Davies, 100 in West) one can say next to nothing about other elements of the narrative such as the narrator, the focalization or the insertion of direct speech. Still, our sources create considerable difficulties even in respect to narrative time. On the one hand, it is only natural that brief summaries such as those by Proclus or Ps.-Apollodorus tend to eliminate any deviations from the linear reproduction of the narrated story. On the other, Proclus, our main evidence, poses a very special problem to those searching for prolepses, analepses or other deviations from the linear narrative in his summary. I refer to the still unresolved question about the boundaries between the epics in the summaries of his *Chrestomathia*, and to the concomitant question of whether the fragments that seem to exceed the boundaries of each epic as set by Proclus should be seen as analeptic or proleptic passages within their respective time frame or if we are simply faced with an artificial and therefore erroneous demarcation of each epic plot on his part.[2] Within the

---

[1] See the relevant chapters by Cingano, Torres-Guerra and Debiasi, below in this volume.
[2] On the question of the limits between the poems of the Epic Cycle, see Burgess (2001: 24–5, 139); Bravo (2001: 65–6); Kullmann (2002a: 171–2).

same context, another specific problem is raised: whether Proclus tailored the events at the end of the *Cypria* to suit the plot of the *Iliad*.

Before we turn to the Cyclic epics, it is worth recalling the basic aspects of the temporal structure of the Homeric epics that will serve as a backdrop to the present discussion. The *Iliad* and the *Odyssey* begin *in medias res*: in fact, although both begin at a point towards the end of each underlying fabula (the Trojan War and the nostos of Odysseus respectively, both of which cover a 10-year time-span), they both create, each one in its own idiosyncratic way, the impression that they encompass the entire, long-standing story. To be more precise: the pre- and post-history of the 51 days covered by the plot of the *Iliad* are present in such a way in the epic that the poem on the wrath of Achilles soon becomes a full-scale portrayal of the 10-year Trojan War.[3] To achieve this effect, the poet uses first and foremost the device of the 'double temporality' (*doppelte Zeitlichkeit* in German scholarship),[4] the so-called 'reverberation' (*Einspiegelungstechnik*),[5] through which the pre-history and the beginning of the war as well as its end, the fall of Troy (in book 24), are integrated into the various segments of the plot of the *Iliad* (the ante-Homerica in books 2–7, the post-Homerica mainly in books 22–4).[6] 'Reverberation' is achieved through the incorporation of scenes which, in fact, belong to the pre- and post-history of the Iliadic plot. Some examples: the Catalogue of Ships and of the Trojan allies in book 2 points to the departure of the Greek fleet from Aulis (*Cypr.* arg. lines 122–4 Severyns) and to the scene at the beginning of the war where the Trojan allies rush to aid the besieged city (*Cypr.* arg. line 169 Severyns); the viewing from the city walls ('Teichoskopia') in book 3 points to the beginning of the siege (*Cypr.* arg. lines 153–4 Severyns), the testing of the Greek army in book 2 to the mutiny in front of the Trojan city walls (*Cypr.* arg. lines 159–60 Severyns), the so-called 'Epipolesis' in book 4 recalls the first attack against Troy (*Cypr.* arg. lines 149–51 Severyns), the death of Patroclus in book 16 points to the death of Achilles (*Aeth.* arg. lines 191–2 Severyns), the funeral games held in honour of Patroclus in book 23 to the funeral games held in honour of Achilles (*Aeth.* arg. line 201 Severyns), and so on. The degree to which this technique was used deliberately by the poet of the *Iliad* is evident from Kullmann's observation that 'the story time

---

[3] Latacz (2003: 161–6). The general characterization of the poem by Heubeck (1958) is still worth reading.
[4] Kullmann (1960: 367).   [5] For the English term 'reverberation', see Lang (1995).
[6] This technique was acknowledged and appreciated already by Aristotle (*Poet.* 1459a17–b4); later Σ ex. *Il.* 2.494–877 and Eustath. praef. to *Il.* (7.20–3, 28–37) and on *Il.* 3.230 (409.20–4): cf. Rengakos (2004: 287–292), and Fantuzzi, below in this volume, pp. 412–16.

(*erzählte Zeit*) of the Cycle seems to be crammed into the temporal frame of the *Iliad* plot... thus, the *Iliad* seems to encompass the events of the Cycle too'.[7] The presence of the ante- and post-Homerica is strongly felt also through the numerous extradiegetic analepses and prolepses, i.e. through the information given about events occurring outside the temporal span of the *Iliad* plot. A look at the catalogue of allusions of this epic to the ante- and post-Homerica shows how detailed the picture of the pre- and post-history that is reflected in the mirror of the *Iliad* is.[8]

The *Odyssey* offers a similar paradigm for the treatment of narrative time; there are however significant differences from the *Iliad*. The basic plot of the *Odyssey* covers an even shorter period of time, namely 41 days, into which an event of a slightly longer duration, namely the entire 10-year nostos of Odysseus, is incorporated. Thus, as the *Iliad* evolves into a poem about the entire Trojan War, likewise the *Odyssey* becomes an all-embracing poem recounting the nostos not only of its protagonist Odysseus but of all the significant Achaeans through the brief or more detailed nostoi narrations of the Trojan War heroes, namely Nestor, Ajax, Diomedes, Neoptolemus, Philoctetes, Agamemnon or Menelaus. Moreover, it should be noted that the *Odyssey* functions also as a continuation, at least on a temporal level, of the *Iliad* in that it includes a detailed narration of post-Iliadic events. The integration of the nostos of Odysseus and that of the Achaeans is achieved through a narrative device which is radically different from the Iliadic 'reverberation', namely the flashback technique: the pre-history of the *Odyssey* plot is offered by the narratives of Nestor and Menelaus in books 2 and 3, but first and foremost by the so-called apologoi, the narrative of Odysseus himself in books 9–12.

Another characteristic feature of both Homeric epics concerns the representation of events taking place simultaneously.[9] Simultaneity underlies the macrostructure of the poems, and specifically that of the *Odyssey*. Both storylines of the poem, the one concerning Telemachus and the other Odysseus, are suspended over and over again, and closely interlaced in several passages, as Siegmann has impressively demonstrated.[10] These storylines are interwoven so as to bring to the fore the idea of their simultaneity, i.e. to show that both threads have a common point of departure and are oriented towards the same end, namely the reunion of father and son. The

---

[7] Kullmann (1960: 366–7). See also the fine characterization in Whitman (1958: 269–71).
[8] Kullmann (1960: 6–11).   [9] Rengakos (1995); (1998).
[10] Siegmann (1987: 135–43), based on Hölscher's (1939) brilliant analysis: *passim*. On the two (or even multiple) parallel storylines upon which the Odyssey plot is structured, see de Jong (2002: 77–80).

structure of the Odyssean plot which is thus based on two storylines running parallel is modelled on the *Iliad*:[11] the two basic storylines of the Iliadic plot, namely the one concering Patroclus and the other the actual fighting, stem from the conversation between Athena and Achilles on the one hand (this corresponds to the conversation between Athena and Telemachus at the beginning of *Od.* 1), and the sending of the dream to Agamemnon on the other (which corresponds to the sending of Hermes to Calypso at the beginning of *Od.* 5). In the *Iliad* there are also two conversations between gods, namely between Hera and Athena, and Zeus and Thetis respectively (in book 1 of the *Iliad*) which correspond to the two assemblies of the gods at the beginning of *Od.* 1 and 5. From these conversations originate the two plots which until the middle of the epic take place in two different settings, but are afterwards united, first indirectly through the mediation of Patroclus (11.599), and then directly in the last third of the poem after the reconciliation of Achilles with the Greeks (from 19.57 onwards). Obviously, the simultaneity of events is not essential for the *Iliad*, because the Achilles plot-line is, strictly speaking, a 'non-plot'. It may be true that Achilles, though a 'passive' character, is always 'present' in the battle events through information given by the narrator or other characters throughout the first two thirds of the epic, and also because of his appearance in book 9; yet, it is only through the introduction of the Patroclus plot-line from 11.599 onwards that the two lines of the narrative begin gradually to converge.

In regard to the treatment of time, the Cyclic epics are not only radically different from the *Iliad* and the *Odyssey*, but in many ways simpler: due to their linear plots[12] and their plain, paratactic structure they have been traditionally described as 'chronographic epics' (in contrast to the 'dramatic epic' by which the *Iliad* and the *Odyssey* are meant).[13] As we shall see, this description is only partly correct, because these epics do not totally lack analepses and prolepses nor at times a 'dramatic' structure, i.e. a focusing on a brief time span and a core episode.[14]

Most numerous are the analepses in the *Cypria*, which swing back in the fabula and narrate the story of the Trojan War *ab ovo*, i.e. from the point in time when Zeus consults with Themis about how the Earth can be relieved from overpopulation. It appears that the anticipatory mode of narrative was

---

[11] Hölscher (1990: 76–86).
[12] Proclus ap. Photius describes this linearity with the expression διὰ τὴν ἀκολουθίαν τῶν ἐν αὐτῶι πραγμάτων (*Bibl.* 319a30); see Introduction, above in this volume, pp. 1–2, 32.
[13] Kakridis (1949: 91); Notopoulos (1964: 35, 40–1).
[14] The structure of the Cyclic epics is best described by Welcker (1865) and (1882). Kullmann (1986 = 1992: 398–9) rightly emphasizes the merits of Welcker's interpretation.

particularly characteristic of this epic. The most important (homodiegetic) prolepses are the following: the prophecies of future events made by Helenus and Cassandra when Paris departs for Sparta (*Cypr.* arg. lines 91–2 and 93–4 Severyns respectively),[15] the Delphic oracle given to Agamemnon about the sacrifice to Dionysus Sphaltes (Lyc. 206–215), the interpretation of the wonder of the sparrows in Aulis by Calchas (*Cypr.* arg. lines 122–4 Severyns), the oracle given to Telephus about his healing (*Cypr.* arg. lines 132–4 Severyns), the Delphic oracle given to Agamemnon about the quarrel between Odysseus and Achilles and the sack of Troy (*Od.* 8.79–82),[16] the prophecy of Calchas that for the Achaean fleet to depart Iphigeneia must be sacrificed first (*Cypr.* arg. lines 138–41 Severyns), the prophecy of Anius that Troy will only fall in the tenth year of war (Σ Lyc. 570, Pherec. *FgrHist* 3 F 140),[17] the prophecy of Thetis that Achilles will be killed after murdering Tenes, the son of Apollo (Ps.-Apollod. *Epit.* 3.26), and also that the first Achaean who will set foot in Troy will immediately die (Ps.-Apollod. *Epit.* 3.29).

We cannot define with any degree of certainty the narrative status of two testimonies from the *Cypria*, which seem to surpass by far the limits set by Proclus' summary.[18] I mean *PEG* F 33 (= F 25 D. = F 31 W.) about the death of Astyanax (?) and *PEG* F 34 (= F 27 D.) about the wounding of Polyxena during the sack of Troy by Odysseus and Diomedes, and her eventual death.[19] Both episodes may have been narrated in two ways. Either they were incorporated into anticipatory references or other proleptic digressions,[20] if we accept the temporal limits of the *Cypria* as set by Proclus. Or, they formed a section in this epic of which however there are no other traces and which would extend until the events that followed the sack of Troy. It seems that the linear arrangement of the narrative was also interrupted by the story of the Dioscouroi (*PEG* F 8–9 = F 6–7 D. = F 9–10 W.).[21] But, in this case too, we cannot determine any closer the exact form of the narrative – was it perhaps incorporated into a report assigned to one of the characters, e.g. in a speech addressed by Aphrodite to Paris?[22]

---

[15] For the numbering of paragraphs and the text of Proclus I have followed Kullmann (2002b).
[16] Danek (1998: 142–50) denies that this is an allusion to an event narrated in the *Cypria*.
[17] Cf. also *Od.* 6.162 and Danek (1998: 132–4).
[18] Davies (1989c: 49–50, 73); Burgess (2001: 139–40); Jouan (1966: 368–9 on *PEG* F 34, 371–2 on *PEG* F 33 = F 25 D. = F 31 W.); most recently Kullmann (2002a: 170–1).
[19] Also Wilamowitz (1884: 181 n. 27) and Bethe (1922: 213 n. 5) deny that this fragment belongs to the *Cypria*.
[20] Severyns (1928: 376).   [21] See also Currie, below in this volume, pp. 287–8.
[22] Davies (1989c: 37).

Prophecies are not at all rare in the poems treating the post-Homerica, namely the *Aethiopis*, the *Ilias parva*, the *Iliou persis* and the *Nostoi*.[23] From the *Aethiopis* we know of the prophecy of Thetis to Achilles 'about the events regarding Memnon' (*Aeth.* arg. lines 186–7 Severyns), from the *Ilias parva* the prophecy of Calchas that Helenus must be captured, because he knows the oracles that protect Troy (Ps.-Apollod. *Epit.* 5.9), the prophecy of Helenus περὶ τῆς ἁλώσεως 'about the sack' (namely that Philoctetes and Neoptolemus must be brought to Troy; *Ilias parva* arg. lines 212–13 Severyns) and of Cassandra who warns of the Wooden Horse (Ps.-Apollod. *Epit.* 5.17). In the *Iliou persis* the famous *teras* 'sign' appears to Laocoon (*Il. Pers.* arg. lines 248–9 Severyns), while in the *Nostoi* Achilles appears to Agamemnon and his people, foretells the future events and attempts to keep the Achaeans from departing (*Nost.* arg. lines 291–3 Severyns).

Another form that prolepses and analepses take in the Cyclic epics consists in the numerous correspondences of various motifs and episodes between the different epics; we may call these correspondences *Fernbeziehungen*, thus adopting the apposite term introduced by Reichel.[24] I shall only mention a few examples, since the relevant material has been exhaustively studied by Anderson.[25] The construction of the Wooden Horse may have offered a suitable opportunity to call to mind the construction of Paris' ships, 'the causes of disaster, that brought evil to all Trojans';[26] Priam's murdering by Neoptolemus may have been compared to the way in which Achilles treated the aged king of the Trojans;[27] the fathering of Neoptolemus on the island of Scyros (*Cypr.* PEG F 21 = F 16 D. = F 19 W.) had probably anticipated the episode where Odysseus fetches Achilles' son to Troy and hands the weapons of his father to him (*Ilias parva* arg. lines 217–18 Severyns);[28] the abandonment of Philoctetes in Lemnos (*Cypr.* arg. lines 144–6 Severyns) might have entailed a short mention of his return (*Ilias parva* arg. lines 212–13 Severyns);[29] the pair Neoptolemus–Eurypylus (*Ilias parva* arg. line 220 Severyns) presupposes the pair Achilles–Telephus in the *Cypria*;[30] Palamedes' murdering by Odysseus (*Cypr.* arg. line 166 Severyns) must have been linked to the celebrated story according to which Palamedes had seen

---

[23] On the oracles and prophecies in the Epic Cycle, see Stockinger (1959: 90–4); Griffin (1977); Davies (1989c: 40, 47).
[24] Reichel (1994). Bethe (1922: 287) speaks of 'merging motifs'.
[25] Anderson (1997). Anderson speaks of 'allusions' (16–17). See also Kullmann (1960: 212–14) and already Welcker (1865: 13–16, 150).
[26] Anderson (1997: 20–6) after Tryphiodorus 59–61.   [27] Anderson (1997: 28–32).
[28] Kullmann (1960: 212); Anderson (1997: 38–48) after Virg. *Aen.* 2.541–3 and *Tryph.* 636–9. See also Kelly, below in this volume, pp. 288–9
[29] Severyns (1928: 300).   [30] Kullmann (1960: 213).

through the trick that Odysseus used to evade military service against Troy (*Cypr.* arg. lines 119–21 Severyns), and so on. Of course, thematic correspondence in itself does not say much about the way these *Fernbeziehungen* were actually treated in the poems – due to the meagreness of material, we are unable to tell how intensively they were elaborated in the Cyclic epics and to what degree their connective function was made explicit.

Heterodiegetic analepses, i.e. recourse to past events that are not at all related to the main plot, are also present in the Cycle. In the *Cypria*, Nestor narrates at length (in a digression, as Proclus expressly states [*Cypr.* arg. lines 114–17 Severyns]), in his usual cosy manner the stories of Epopeus and Oedipus, the madness of Heracles and the story of Theseus and Ariadne,[31] while in the *Telegony* the story of Trophonius, Agamedes and Augeias is incorporated into an ekphrasis (*Tel.* arg. lines 311–12 Severyns).[32]

A significant simultaneous event was apparently narrated in the *Cypria*: as *Cypr.* arg. lines 106–9 Severyns informs us (see also *PEG* F 15 = F 13 D. = F 13 W.), at the time that the abduction of Helen was taking place, her two brothers, Castor and Polydeuces, were involved in a battle against Idas and Lynceus. It is not possible, of course, to determine further how these two simultaneous events were connected to each other in the poem (perhaps through the customary *men/de*?).[33]

Another narrative technique known to us from the *Iliad*, namely retardation,[34] seems to have been occasionally used in the Cycle – a fact indicating that the Cyclic epics did not lack artistic design. Thus, the beginning of the Trojan War, the principal objective of the *Cypria* plot, is repeatedly delayed: the 'wrong' landing on Teuthrania and its conquest (*Cypr.* arg. lines 125–6 Severyns, *PEG* F 20), the ensuing adventurous nostos (*Cypr.* arg. lines 129–30 Severyns), Achilles' second stay in Scyros (*PEG* F 21 = F 16 D. = F 19 W.), the second gathering in Aulis and the sacrifice of Iphigeneia, the

---

[31] Davies (1989c: 41) observes that the first and fourth story may have functioned as mythological exempla warning in the manner of the *Iliad* against 'sexual escapades', whereas we know too little about the second and the third story to decide whether these had a similar proleptic function.

[32] See Tsagalis, below in this volume, p. 380.

[33] Davies' assertion (1989c: 78) that in the *Nostoi* the travels of the Achaeans, which were conceived as happening simultaneously in reality, were narrated as if occurring one after the other according to Zielinski's law, overlooks two things. First, that Zielinski's theory does not apply to the Homeric poems either (see Rengakos (1995; 1998); and second that we cannot draw any safe conclusions about how were the various travels intertwined with each other, because Proclus' report serves the aims of his *Chrestomathy* where by necessity the different pieces of the plot were narrated in the form of a catalogue.

[34] On this point, see Reichel (1990); Davies (1989c: 42–6).

landing on Tenedos and the wounding of Philoctetes, Anius' proposal to the Achaeans to stay with him in Delos for nine years, since Troy would only fall in the tenth year of the war (*PEG* F 29 = F 19 D. = F 26 W.),[35] the quarrel between Achilles and Agamemnon – these episodes reveal a potential for a retarding narrative manner like the one used in the *Iliad*. We cannot tell any more how this retardation was actually achieved. It is worth noting, however, that the landing on Teuthrania and the subsequent difficult nostos of the Achaean army seem to imply an untimely ending of the expedition against Troy, not dissimilar from the Iliadic 'Diapeira' or the duel between Menelaus and Paris. Is perhaps here the Homeric technique of the 'misdirection' of the recipient at work?[36]

Retardation was also deployed in the *Ilias parva*. A large number of episodes was squeezed into the short period of time between the quarrel about Achilles' weapons and the trick of the Wooden Horse, the event that seals the fall of the besieged city: the plot of the poem is constantly oriented towards this aim, yet there are three conditions that must be first fulfilled (the return of Philoctetes from Lemnos and the healing of his wound, the arrival of Neoptolemus from Scyros, the construction of the Wooden Horse), before Troy can be abandoned to its eventual fate. Here too lurks the untimely end of the war through Paris' death (*Ilias parva* arg. lines 213–14 Severyns) – the poet hurries to let Deiphobus marry Helen (*Ilias parva* arg. line 216 Severyns); moreover, the deeds of Eurypylus, the last ally of the Trojans, before he gets killed by Neoptolemus (*Ilias parva* arg. lines 219–20 Severyns) represent the ultimate glimmer of hope for the Trojans and, at the same time, a brief delay of Troy's fall. Between the construction of the Wooden Horse and the use of the trick by the Greeks the *Ilias parva* allows Odysseus to penetrate twice into the city: on the first occasion, Odysseus disfigures himself and thus disguised enters Troy as a spy, but is recognized by Helen; 'he talks with her about the conquest of the city' and is able to escape, after killing some Trojans (*Ilias parva* arg. lines 224–7 Severyns) – would Odysseus have been captured, then the theme of the untimely ending of the war would again ensue. After that, the same Achaean hero returns immediately, along with Diomedes (*Ilias parva* arg. lines 228–9 Severyns), into the besieged city to abduct the Palladium.

Before closing, I would like to make some general observations about the structure and the narrative technique of the Cyclic epics. As Welcker

---

[35] It is not clear which was the exact position of the episode within the *Cypria* plot: see Severyns (1928: 309–13), Kullmann (1955b = 1992: 47); Davies (1989c: 45).
[36] Morrison (1992).

has already pointed out,[37] there is a fundamental difference between the *Cypria* and the *Ilias parva* (i.e. Stasinus and Lesches) on the one hand, and the *Aethiopis* and the *Iliou persis* (i.e. Arctinus) on the other: we may justly attribute a 'dramatic' composition technique to Arctinus, whereas the other two poems represent the 'chronographic' structure of the Cyclic epics in its purest form.[38] It is clear that both in the *Aethiopis* and in the *Iliou persis* there is a striving for unity of place and time (in both poems the plot is limited to a few days) and a focusing on an outstanding event (in the case of the *Aethiopis* on the death of Achilles, in the case of the *Iliou persis* on the conquest of the city). On the other hand, the *Cypria* extends over a long period of time, measured in years, is set against the background of the most different places (Thessaly, Ida–Troy, Sparta, Messene, the whole of Greece, Aulis, Mysia, Scyros, Argos etc.), and has a wealth of protagonists. Likewise, the torso-like *Ilias parva* with its variety of episodes following one after another does not have a unified plot – both epics were evidently designed so as to form parts of a global narration of the entire Trojan War.

The penultimate Cyclic epic, the *Nostoi*, cannot be described either as 'chronographic' or as 'dramatic'.[39] Its main features are its structuring in terms of a 'ring composition' (it begins with the quarrel between the two Atreids and closes with Agamemnon's murder, Orestes' revenge against Aegisthus and the return of Menelaus) and the 'interlacing technique' through which each nostos is interwoven and nested into the other.[40] The synchronization of the different nostoi of the Achaean heroes inevitably brings the complex arrangement of the plot in books 6 and 10 of the *Iliad* to mind.[41] We have to agree with Bethe that the *Nostoi* was 'an epic which knew how to keep together many different, divergent stories through a clever, solid disposition which consists in the protagonist roles of the two Atreids and the focusing upon their fate, and yet give the impression of artistic unity'.[42]

---

[37] Welcker (1882: 235–6).

[38] It is no coincidence that Aristotle (who does not mention the *Aethiopis*, the *Iliou persis* and the *Nostoi*) attributes to these two epics a plot that consists of 'many parts' (μίαν πρᾶξιν πολυμερῆ in *Poet.* 1459b1); it is still a mystery wherein he saw the unity of plot (*mian*). See Fantuzzi, below in this volume, pp. 413–14.

[39] I agree with Bethe (1922: 258–79) and Kullmann (1988 = 1992: 167; 1990 = 1992: 312; 2002a: 173–6) *pace* Hölscher (1990: 96–7) and Danek (1998: 79) that the 'nostoi' narratives in books 3, 4 and 11 of the *Odyssey* go back to an oral version of the Cyclic epics of the *Nostoi*, that, in other words, Proclus' summary of the *Nostoi* is not dependent on the *Odyssey*.

[40] Hölscher (1990: 98).   [41] Rengakos (1995: 17–19).   [42] Bethe (1922: 277).

The last poem of the Cycle, the *Telegony*, was clearly conceived as a continuation of the *Odyssey*, and therefore does not have a unified plot;[43] all three autonomous episodes of which the epic consists (Odysseus' trip to Elis and Thesprotia, his return and his death in Ithaca), eventually bring the life of the celebrated hero to an adventurous ending.[44]

[43] See Tsagalis, below in this volume, p. 388.
[44] Parts of this essay re-use material from my earlier article Rengakos (2004).

9 | Wit and irony in the Epic Cycle

DAVID KONSTAN

INTRODUCTION

There are two major obstacles to detecting humor in the Epic Cycle. The first is the fragmentary condition of the texts, supplemented by dry summaries that surely flatten out any flashes of wit. This we cannot remedy. The second is the abiding sense that these are inferior poems, or at best products of an oral tradition to which so individual an element as humor is foreign. The dates of various poems in the Cycle have been much discussed, and they are not uniformly regarded nowadays as necessarily post-Homeric.[1] Moreover, scholars have observed that the difference in quality that we perceive between them and the Homeric epics may well reflect a later aesthetic such as Aristotle's, who preferred the *Iliad* and the *Odyssey* because their unitary plots resembled those of tragedy, which was for him the model genre.[2] Still and all, I have not come across a discussion of the Cycle in which anyone has referred to the Monumental Poet of the *Cypria*, for example, or of the *Aethiopis*;[3] even those who are inclined to accept ancient attributions of the *Cypria* to Stasinus or Hegesias or Cyprias, or of the *Aethiopis* to Arctinus, rarely if ever put these shadowy figures in the same class as the equally shadowy Homer when it comes to subtlety and originality.[4]

In what follows, I am going to assume, for my argument's sake, that the *Cypria* and other poems in the Cycle were every bit as sophisticated as the *Odyssey*, and see whether, on such a reading, there are signs of humor in what survives – I had almost said 'deliberate humor,' but then, humor is by nature intentional; I am not referring to lapses of taste that we might find funny but are not the product of authorial wit. For humor, as we know, is entirely at home in epic, often in the form of innuendos that slyly undercut

---

[1] See Nagy (2010a) and Nagy, above in this volume, pp. 62–77; but contrast West, above in this volume, pp. 101–7.
[2] See Fantuzzi, below in this volume, pp. 411–14.
[3] For the expression 'Monumental Poet' or 'Monumental Composer' applied to Homer, see Kirk (1962: 69, 96; 1976).
[4] On the question of the authorship of the poems in the Epic Cycle, see the Introduction to this volume, pp. 21–8.

the heroic ethos – and these are perhaps the most difficult to spot. By way of preface, let me offer one such example in the *Odyssey* that I think has not been previously appreciated, and may suggest ways of interpreting some of the apparently outlandish bits in the Cyclic poems.

HUMOR IN THE *ODYSSEY*: AN UNNOTICED EXAMPLE

At the beginning of book 4 of the *Odyssey*, Telemachus, in search of news about his father's whereabouts, arrives together with Nestor's son Pisistratus at the palace of Menelaus in Sparta. While the two lads pause at the doorway to the palace, Eteoneus, a servant of Menelaus', sees them and races to report the matter to the king (4.20–5):

> ξείνω δή τινε τώδε, διοτρεφὲς ὦ Μενέλαε,
> ἄνδρε δύω, γενεῇ δὲ Διὸς μεγάλοιο ἔϊκτον.
> ἀλλ' εἴπ', ἤ σφωϊν καταλύσομεν ὠκέας ἵππους,
> ἦ ἄλλον πέμπωμεν ἱκανέμεν, ὅς κε φιλήσῃ.

> Two strangers are here, O Menelaus, nurtured by Zeus,
> two <u>men</u>, who resemble the race of great Zeus.
> Tell me, shall we unbridle their swift horses,
> or send them off to another who may receive them? (4.25–9)[5]

(I have underscored the word 'men' to reflect the position of *andres* at the beginning of the line, with enjambment). At this, Menelaus replies angrily:

> οὐ μὲν νήπιος ἦσθα, Βοηθοΐδη Ἐτεωνεῦ,
> τὸ πρίν· ἀτὰρ μὲν νῦν γε πάϊς ὣς νήπια βάζεις.
> ἦ μὲν δὴ νῶϊ ξεινήϊα πολλὰ φαγόντες
> ἄλλων ἀνθρώπων δεῦρ' ἱκόμεθ', αἴ κέ ποθι Ζεὺς
> ἐξοπίσω περ παύσῃ ὀϊζύος. ἀλλὰ λύ' ἵππους
> ξείνων, ἐς δ' αὐτοὺς προτέρω ἄγε θοινηθῆναι.

> You were not foolish, Eteoneus, son of Boethous,
> previously, but now like a child you're saying foolish things.
> We ourselves, because we ate the guest offerings
> of other men, arrived here. May Zeus
> in future put an end to our suffering. But unbridle the horses
> of the strangers, and lead the men themselves in to the feasting (4.31–6).

Menelaus and Helen are at home, reunited after Helen's elopement and the destruction of Troy, and they will receive the two young men like a good bourgeois couple, though not without a hint of malice toward one another.

---

[5] All translations are my own, and aim only at literal fidelity to the Greek.

But Eteoneus, I think, is not simply being inhospitable in proposing to dispatch the young men to someone else's house, for he has reason to be wary of visits from handsome young foreigners. In other words, I detect an allusion here to the earlier visit of Paris. Homer seems to be hinting that Helen may still be, at least in the eyes of a servant, a tad fickle. Now, a comparison between Telemachus and Paris may seem most unlikely. But young men are young men, and Telemachus is no longer a boy; he is later described as entering upon manhood, and now possessing beauty or κάλλος (18.219), a word associated with sexual attractiveness and applied in the Homeric epics particularly to Paris and Helen, as well as to Odysseus when he is rejuvenated by Athena and meant to look sexy (Nausicaa falls for him).[6] Indeed, when Helen first sees Telemachus, she wonders who he is, and says: 'Shall I lie or tell the truth? But my heart bids me: I say that no one has ever seemed more similar, neither man nor woman – awe seizes me as I gaze at him – as this man resembles... the son of great-hearted Odysseus' (4.140–3). She is right, of course: but might one not have thought for a moment that she was about to name Paris?[7]

Perhaps this is too Plautine a reading, with the significant pause, which editors tend to represent visually by a dash, before the word or phrase that constitutes the punch line. Let us turn, then, to the *Cypria*.

A WITTY PUN?

In an important article written in 1977, Jasper Griffin argued that the poems that form the Cycle had as a group a more fanciful and romantic character than the epics we ascribe to Homer.[8] Griffin did not conclude that they

---

[6] On the meaning of the noun *kallos* (more restricted than the adjective *kalos* and referring primarily to physical attractiveness), see Konstan (2014: 31–61).

[7] Alternative explanations of Eteoneus' behavior have been proposed, for example that he is reluctant to disrupt the preparations for a double wedding that are in progress inside (4.3–14). Thus S. West (1988: 195 on *Od.* 4.20ff.): 'Eteoneus' uncertainty about admitting the strangers, despite their obvious respectability, no doubt is meant to reflect the peculiar circumstance of the wedding celebrations rather than a failure to recognize the normal obligations of hospitality or a caution engendered by the disastrous results of extending a welcome to a young man of princely appearance a quarter of a century or so earlier.' Reece (1993: 78) notes that Eteoneus' cold reception 'is a very strange behavior..., the motivation for which is difficult to decipher'. Reece too suggests that the wedding celebration may be a factor (though it is entirely forgotten once the guests are inside the palace, as West remarks), as well as 'the notorious results of a previous experience with a guest in Sparta', and adds as a possible explanation that 'Eteoneus' impropriety' may act 'as a foil for Menelaus' magnanimous hospitality'. But since Homer is silent on the reasons for Eteoneus' breach of hospitality, it seems not amiss to perceive a touch of humor at the beginning of what will, after all, be rather a light-hearted episode.

[8] Griffin (1977).

were therefore funny, but a passage he notices in passing may lend itself to such a reading. According to the *Cypria*, the mother of Helen was Nemesis rather than Leda.[9] When Zeus pursued Nemesis, she transformed herself into various creatures, and finally into a goose, whom Zeus impregnated when he assumed the form of a swan (or, according to Philodemus, a goose): hence the tale that Helen was born from an egg. In seeking to avoid Zeus' attentions, Nemesis is moved, we read, αἰδοῖ καὶ νεμέσει (the formula in the dative does not seem to be Homeric, though, for the accusative, see *Il.* 13.122). Griffin sniffs at this as an incompetent pun. Might it not rather be taken as a joke, a little as though Hephaestus were to use himself to light his own cigarette (cf. Seneca, *Controversiae* 10.5.20: 'fire and mankind, Prometheus – your very own gifts – are torturing you')? The whole episode is, after all, of rather a burlesque nature (Griffin describes it as awkward), and some comic silliness is to be expected, especially when such materials are embedded in a heroic narrative.

There is something of an analogue in Menelaus' account, in the *Odyssey*, of his wrestling with the shape-changing Proteus, though the brevity of the description, in conformity with Homeric restraint in such matters, softens the absurdity of the scene (4.454–8; cf. 417–18). But the lead-up to the entrapment has a farcical tone as well, as Menelaus and three of his men lie in wait for Proteus, covering themselves with sealskins and hiding among the creatures on the beach, with Proteus' daughter protecting them against the stench by placing ambrosia under their nostrils (441–6). Menelaus' disguise as a seal is a counterpart to the transformations of Proteus, and at the same time summons up the lower bodily functions associated with smells and putrefaction, which Bakhtin argued are central to comedy. The episode is in keeping with the somewhat ambiguous representation of Menelaus in the Homeric epics, but the authors of the Cyclic poems might also have availed themselves of such parodic effects.[10] Before we leave Menelaus, we may note that Athenaeus (2.2.1–4 = 35 C) cites the following pair of verses by the 'the poet of the *Cypria*, whoever he may be':

> οἶνόν τοι, Μενέλαε, θεοὶ ποίησαν ἄριστον
> θνητοῖς ἀνθρώποισιν ἀποσκεδάσαι μελεδῶνας
>
> The gods, Menelaus, made wine as the best thing for mortal men, to scatter their cares.

---

[9] See also Currie, below in this volume, pp. 300–1.
[10] For Menelaus as a comic character, or at least a figure of mockery, see Σ Eur. *Or.* 371 ὕπουλα πάντα τὰ ῥήματα Μενελάου, ἀφ' οὗ ὁ ποιητὴς τὸ ἄστατον τῆς Λακεδαιμονίων γνώμης κωμῳδεῖ ('all the words of Menelaus are deceitful, and with this the poet ridicules the unstable character of the Lacedaemonians' judgment'); see also Σ *Or.* 643.

It is impossible, of course, to know the precise context for this observation, but it is hard not to think of the potion that Helen gives Menelaus and his visitors in *Odyssey* 4 (219–27) to make them forget their troubles. Might there not have been a similar kind of gentle irony at work in the *Cypria*?[11]

DOUBLING IN THE *CYPRIA*

I may offer one more example of ostensible humor in the *Cypria*, although I fear it will be even more dubious than the first: I am referring to the judgment of Paris. Let me begin, however, by remarking on what seems to me to be a curious feature of the *Cypria* as we know it, namely a tendency to complicate stories, presenting double or, in critical parlance, overdetermined explanations for things.[12] The birth of Helen may have been one such, whatever Leda's role in it. But it seems also to apply to the initial cause of the Trojan War, as described in the poem. The first fragment in our editions of the *Cypria*, which presumably came near the beginning of the poem, explains that Zeus felt pity for the earth, because of the heavy load of humanity that it bore; to reduce the weight of mankind, he fanned the flames of war, and so 'Zeus' plan was fulfilled' (Διὸς δ' ἐτελείετο βουλή). The echo here of the opening of the *Iliad* has aroused much discussion: are the lines in the *Cypria* somehow a take-off on the Homeric epic, or is the reverse the case, or do both go back to a common source in oral epic or folkloric tradition, deriving ultimately from a near eastern or perhaps Indo-European source? I want to set aside these speculations, stimulating as they are, and note that the Σ D to the *Iliad* that cite the lines inform us that the earth was disgusted at the impiety of humans, and requested Zeus' aid.

---

[11] If the counsel is Nestor's, the context may have been Menelaus' visit to Nestor's palace, as reported in Proclus' epitome, where Nestor related various stories, including that of Theseus and Ariadne, perhaps in an effort to console his guest; for possible reconstructions of the context, see Bernabé (1982: 6–7) and Obbink (1996: 547–48), both of whom ascribe to this passage as well (but in different locations) the verse quoted in Phil. *De pietate* (where it is put in the mouth of Socrates), οὐκ ἀπ' ἐμοῦ σκεδάσεις ὄχλον; (cf. Diogenes Laertius 2.117, where the full hexameter, ending with ταλαπείριε πρέσβυ, is attributed to Bion of Borysthenes). Nestor may even have offered Menelaus a drink from his famous wine cup, which hardly anyone else could lift when full (*Il.* 11.632–37); Marco Fantuzzi suggests to me a comparison with the inscription on the eighth-century 'Cup of Nestor,' which threatens anyone who drinks from it with passionate desire; the apparent curse in the first verse is undercut by the comic consequence in the second (cf. Fantuzzi and Hunter 2004: 286–7). Might there even be an allusion here to the *Cypria*, and Menelaus' infatuation with Helen?

[12] See Currie, below in this volume, pp. 289, 301.

Zeus first produced the Theban War, which did some of the work required. He was next prepared to use floods and thunderbolts, but Momos proposed (a) marrying Thetis to a mortal (though Philodemus in his *De pietate* gives a different account of Zeus' decision) and (b) the engendering of a beautiful daughter, and this did the trick. Was the Earth simply weighed down by the mass of humanity, or was human immorality also a factor? Well, both, perhaps: but the mechanical explanation in terms of overpopulation is odd alongside the ethical cause, and I wonder whether the author didn't perhaps mean it to be seen as somehow flippant. In passing, we may ask: why the twin allusion to Achilles and Helen here as causes of the war? Might there be an anticipation of the episode reported in Proclus' summary of the *Cypria* (arg. lines 157–8 Severyns), in which 'Achilles desires to see Helen', and Aphrodite and Thetis bring them together? The Hesiodic catalogue of women tells us that Achilles was too young to compete for Helen as his bride, else he'd surely have won out over Menelaus (F 204.89–92 M.-W. = F 110.89–92 Hirsch.). If so, it would seem to indicate a special focus on their relationship within the poem.[13] Proclus' summary adds that Achilles subsequently (εἶτα) restrained the Achaeans when they were eager to return home, a scene that recalls the flight of the Achaeans to their ships after Agamemnon tested their will to pursue the siege of Troy, when they were held back only by the quick action of Odysseus (*Il.* 2.84–210).[14] Unfortunately, we know nothing of the reason for the eagerness of the troops to leave Troy, or what motivated Achilles to check them.[15] I return below to the question of Achilles in love, and its relation to the conventions of epic narrative.

---

[13] I have not seen this connection made elsewhere. Tsagalis (2008a: 102) notes that the same verb, συνάγειν 'bring together', is used also in Proclus' summary of the *Cypria* in reference to Aphrodite leading Helen to Paris, in what is clearly an erotic context.

[14] *Cypr.* arg. lines 152–62 Severyns: 'the Greeks send negotiators to the Trojans to demand the return of Helen and the property. When the Trojans did not agree to the demands, then they began a siege. Next the Greeks go out over the country and destroy the surrounding settlements. After this Achilles has a desire to look upon Helen , and Aphrodite and Thetis bring the two of them together (Ἑλένην ἐπιθυμεῖ θεάσασθαι, καὶ συνήγαγεν αὐτοὺς εἰς τὸ αὐτὸ Ἀφροδίτη καὶ Θέτις). Then when the Achaeans are eager to return home, Achilles holds them back (εἶτα ἀπονοστεῖν ὡρμημένους τοὺς Ἀχαιοὺς Ἀχιλλεὺς κατέχει). And then he drives off Aeneas' cattle, and he sacks Lyrnessus and Pedasus and many of the surrounding settlements, and he slays Troilus.'

[15] Tsagalis (2008a: 106) argues that 'Achilles' zeal in restraining the Greeks who want to return home can be explained only in the light of a latent erotic atmosphere in the scene of his meeting with Helen' (cf. his more cautious formulation on p. 110), but what would Achilles' motive have been – to rescue Helen for Menelaus' sake? As Fantuzzi (2012: 25–6) observes, Proclus' εἶτα suggests merely a later time, not a consequence.

THE JUDGMENT OF PARIS

Proclus' epitome tells us, moreover, that Zeus took counsel with Themis concerning the Trojan War, and at the wedding of Peleus and Thetis Strife caused a clash over beauty (*kallos*) among Athena, Hera, and Aphrodite, and that Paris chose Aphrodite, aroused by marriage with Helen. I suppose that the birth of Achilles and Helen, on the advice of Momos, was not quite enough to get things going, and that Zeus needed Themis to suggest a way of triggering the conflict. But the judgment too seems to contain what looks to me like another instance of comic doubling. Despite the telegraphic nature of the text here, it would seem that the mention of Helen refers to the bribes that the three goddesses offered to Paris in order to win his vote. Martin West, in his Loeb edition, introduces at this point the account in the *Bibliotheca* of Ps.-Apollodorus of the gifts they promised, Hera offering him kingship, Athena victory in war, and Aphrodite marriage with Helen.[16] As scholars have observed, the beauty contest sits oddly with the theme of the gifts, and the two motifs may well, as Tom Stinton, for example, has argued, go back to distinct types of narrative, one based on the question of which of the goddesses, or which of their properties, is the best, the other on the more specific competition over physical beauty.[17] The elliptical allusion to this episode in the *Iliad* seems to refer to the choice of gifts, where Homer explains that Hera, Poseidon, and Athena retained their resentment against Troy from the time Paris caused strife among the goddesses and 'approved the one who afforded him grievous lust' (24.30), in contrast, presumably, to the prizes promised by the other two. Although Malcolm Davies has questioned whether the two motifs, as identified by Stinton, are strictly independent, I think the choice between rule, power, and sex is basically that of a type of life or *bios*, similar to Prodicus' version of the choice of Heracles, as reported by Xenophon, where the life of virtue and that of pleasure are represented as two women; the latter bolsters her case by her provocative attire.[18] The beauty contest is something else, and you don't have to be Euripides' Hecuba to see that it hardly befits the dignity of Hera and Athena, one a mature wife and the other a virgin, to compete with Aphrodite on this terrain. Early vase paintings of the scene show only Aphrodite naked, which can be regarded, like accompanying *erōtes*, as an identifying attribute, whereas the other two are clothed:[19] that all three were naked is apparently a later conceit even in literature (*LIMC* vii.1, p. 176; cf. e. g. Ov. *Her.* 17.118, Prop. 2.2.13–14, Luc. *Dearum iud.* 9). It

---

[16] West (2003a).   [17] Stinton (1965).   [18] Davies (2010).   [19] *LIMC* vii.1, p. 187.

is not, perhaps, surprising that visual representations of the scene should have been relatively modest, at least in respect to Hera and Athena, but they also suggest that the focus may have been on what the goddesses offered Paris rather than on their own sexual appeal – which is, as I have said, what the noun *kallos* generally implies, though of course this is Proclus' word, and may not have occurred in the *Cypria* itself. An outright rivalry over sex appeal, had it been drawn or recited, might well have been between human subjects, or at least less august deities than these.

What all this is leading up to is the suggestion that the conflation of the two motifs in the judgment of Paris – the choice among lives or values and the beauty competition – just may have been the work of the *Cypria* poet himself, that Monumental Poet whom I am hypothesizing as the author of the epic and who was, for all I know, a contemporary of Homer, whenever he lived. The image of the goddesses squabbling over which is the prettiest, rather than which can bestow the finest accomplishment, is charmingly irreverent, and might have amused audiences who expected such titillating flourishes in the otherwise sober epics. Of course, it is impossible to say whether it was really so. But taking the composer of the *Cypria* seriously may open our eyes to what may well have been funny in his poem.

ACHILLES IN LOVE

The Homeric epics are fairly chaste when it comes to representing erotic passion, and tend in particular to play down any suggestion that the principal male warriors are motivated by *erōs*. A woman such as the wife of Proetus, in the narrative concerning Bellerophon, may experience such transgressive desire (*Il.* 6.160–2), but apart from a suggestion that Paris is rather too inclined to enjoy the delights of Aphrodite (cf. *Il.* 3.58–66), heroes do not fall in love in Homer's poems. Erwin Rohde long ago observed that 'the Greeks always experienced a stormily overpowering force of love like a disabling sickness, a "pathos", to be sure, but not one that is heroic and active, but rather a purely *passive* one, which corrupts a firm will', and he added that such a passion was 'minimally suited to epic', in which the emotions of heroes tended more in the direction of rage.[20] In Apollonius' *Argonautica*, it is at least suggested that not just Medea but Jason too feels *erōs* (3.971–2), but the intense passion is clearly altogether Medea's. So too, in Virgil's *Aeneid* Dido's love for Aeneas far outweighs any sentiment that

[20] Rohde (1914: 29).

he harbors for her, which is in any case subordinate to his desire to lead the remnant of Troy into Italy. Much later, in a Latin prose narrative of the Trojan War that purports to be a translation of an eyewitness account by a certain Dictys of Crete, there is a description of Achilles' infatuation with the Trojan princess Polyxena (after the destruction of Troy, Achilles' ghost demanded that she be sacrificed at his tomb, as in Euripides' *Hecuba*). Achilles' passion is ascribed to his intemperate character (cf. 1.14, 4.13), and what is more it coincides, as Stefan Merkle has argued, with the decline of the Greeks' fortunes in the conflict, thereby confirming the negative image of love that is typical of epic.[21] Where did the author of this narrative find the inspiration for Achilles' enamorment? Apparently not in the Epic Cycle, as 'the summaries of the *Cypria* and the *Aethiopis* make no mention of Achilles' flirtation with... Polyxena', any more than they hint at a romantic attraction on his part to Troilus; so too, 'it remains rather uncertain whether already the author of the *Iliou persis* thought of an erotic relation' between Achilles and Polyxena.[22] Heroes could fall in love in lyric poetry, which stood in self-conscious contrast to the high seriousness of epic, or in tragedy, which might problematize the heroic ethos (although too little is known of Aeschylus' *Myrmidons* or of Sophocles' *Polyxena* and *Troilus* to be certain of how Achilles' love may have been represented in these plays);[23] Lycophron put in the mouth of Cassandra a vehement denunciation of the Greeks that included cryptic allusions to Achilles' passion for Troilus (309–13), Polyxena (323–9), Penthesilea (999–1001), Helen (143, 171–3), Medea (posthumously, 174–5, 798), and Iphigenia (186–96).[24] Yet we do know that Achilles was accused of being in love with the Amazon Penthesilea, who fought on the Trojan side, in the *Aethiopis*. Was this episode treated with any hint of wit or irony?

Our only evidence for this story in the *Aethiopis* comes from Proclus' *Chrestomathy*, which informs us that the *Cypria* was a prelude to Homer's *Iliad*, which in turn was followed 'by the five books of the *Aethiopis*, the work of Arctinus of Miletus'. The summary of the *Aethiopis* begins as follows:

> The Amazon Penthesilea arrives to fight alongside the Trojans – she is the daughter of Ares and Thracian in race – and Achilles kills her as she is excelling in battle (κτείνει αὐτὴν ἀριστεύουσαν), but the Trojans bury her. Achilles also slays Thersites after having been vilified by him and mocked for his alleged love for Penthesilea (λοιδορηθεὶς πρὸς αὐτοῦ καὶ ὀνειδισθεὶς τὸν ἐπὶ τῆι Πενθεσιλείαι λεγόμενον ἔρωτα). As a result strife arises (στάσις

---

[21] Merkle (1989).   [22] Fantuzzi (2012: 14, 15).
[23] Cf. also Phrynichus fragment *TrGF* F 13, on Troilus.   [24] Cf. Fantuzzi (2012: 81).

γίνεται) among the Achaeans over the murder of Thersites. After this, Achilles sails to Lesbos, and after sacrificing to Apollo, Artemis, and Leto, he is purified of the murder by Odysseus.

(*Aeth.* arg. lines 175–84 Severyns)

It is impossible to tell whether the poet himself provided any hint about Achilles' sentiments in regard to the Amazon,[25] although the term 'alleged' (*legomenon*), applied to Achilles' ἔρως, suggests that the accusation was invented by Thersites, and was designed precisely to undermine the hero's integrity or manliness by revealing him to be a slave of passion. If this is so, then the epic convention that informs Homer's *Iliad* and *Odyssey*, according to which real men don't fall in love, may have been respected as well by the author of the *Aethiopis*. And yet, there must have been some basis, however vague, for Thersites' insinuation, just as there was for his attack on Agamemnon in the *Iliad* (2.211–42), which recalled the very charges that Achilles had leveled earlier (we are also told there that Thersites was in the habit of reviling Achilles and Odysseus). Had Achilles met or conversed privately with Penthesilea, as he did with Helen, according to the *Cypria*? There was very likely some element of burlesque or low humor in the scene: Thersites will have had none of the sense of personal pain that marks Hector's censure of Paris in the *Iliad* (3.38–57). What is more, not all of the Achaeans appear to have favored Achilles' reaction, as opposed to their response when Odysseus humiliates Thersites in the *Iliad*, at which one and all take delight. I sense here a subtle undercutting of the heroic code, in which the best of the Achaeans is bested, at least rhetorically, by the worst of them.

GIRL TALK

The scholiast on Aristophanes' *Knights* 1056a explains that the expression, 'Even a woman might carry the burden, if a man were to place it on her', is adapted from the *Ilias parva*:

> 'Even a woman might carry.' The story goes this way: Ajax and Odysseus were arguing about their valorous deeds, as the poet of the *Ilias parva* says. Nestor advised the Hellenes to send some of their number beneath the walls of the Trojans and to eavesdrop about the courage of the aforementioned heroes. Those who were sent heard some girls arguing with each other,

---

[25] See Fantuzzi (2012: 274–5).

one of whom said that Ajax was much better than Odysseus, continuing as follows:

> Αἴας μὲν γὰρ ἄειρε καὶ ἔκφερε δηιοτῆτος
> ἥρω Πηλείδην, οὐδ' ἤθελε δῖος Ὀδυσσεύς

> For Ajax lifted and carried out of the combat the hero, Peleus' son, but brilliant Odysseus chose not to.

But another replied, thanks to Athena's foresight:

> πῶς ἐπεφωνήσω; πῶς οὐ κατὰ κόσμον ἔειπες;
> καί κε γυνὴ φέροι ἄχθος, ἐπεί κεν ἀνὴρ ἀναθείη,
> ἀλλ' οὐκ ἂν μαχέσαιτο

> What have you said? How shamefully you've spoken! Even a woman might carry the burden, if a man were to place it on her, but she could not fight.

I suspect that, in assigning the verse to the sausage seller, Aristophanes was not simply parodying the high style of epic but was also implicitly acknowledging the comic nature of the scene in the original. For it is rather an absurd idea to send scouts on a dangerous mission directly under the walls of Troy simply to overhear young women debate the bravery of the Greeks (were they standing on the walls?). It strikes me as the kind of deflationary treatment of epic heroism that is characteristic of the Epic Cycle – neither a lapse in taste, a kind of unintentional bathos, nor again evidence of the dominant tone of the poems, as though they were comic through and through. Rather, I take such episodes as instances of a gentle irony that depends for its effect precisely on the prevailing heroic ethos, moments in which the poet steps back briefly from the pomp and gore of war and allows a ray of humor to lighten the narrative, analogously to the way Eteoneus' momentary suspicion of Telemachus' intentions upon his arrival at the palace of Menelaus might have brought a smile to the lips of Homer's audience.

ODYSSEUS AFTER THE *ODYSSEY*[26]

Homer lets it be known that there remains one more voyage or adventure for Odysseus after he is reunited with Penelope and restores order to his household: he must carry an oar inland until he is so far from the sea that a traveler

---

[26] On the *Nostoi*, see Danek, below in this volume; on the *Telegony*, see Tsagalis, below in this volume.

mistakes it for a winnowing fan, and then he can return home, where, it is foretold, a gentle death will come upon him from the sea (11.119–37, 23.264–84). Even before he embarks on this mission, Odysseus leaves his home in order to meet his father, who has retired to a hill outside the town, where he will fend off the kinfolk of the suitors he has slain. Alexandrian critics found fault with this conclusion, perhaps because they read the epic novelistically, and expected it to end with the happy reunion of the couple. Poems in the Epic Cycle, however, in particular the *Nostoi* and the *Telegony*, carried the story still further, whether because so wily a figure as Odysseus lent himself irresistibly to exciting exploits or because tradition, or a series of local traditions, provided a variety of alternative narratives that begged to be included in his chronicle.[27] Proclus' *Chrestomathy* preserves the broad outline of the events related in the *Telegony*, a poem in two books ascribed to Eugammon of Cyrene, which is said to follow upon the *Odyssey* (itself the sequel to the *Nostoi*); the plot may be summarized as follows. After slaying the suitors, Odysseus sails to Elis to examine his cattle, and is received as a guest there by Polyxenus ('Man of Many Guests' – doubtless a *nom parlant*). He then sails back to Ithaca to perform the sacrifices stipulated by Teiresias, as recounted in the *Odyssey*, but he continues on to the land of the Thesprotians, where he marries Callidice, their queen. He leads the Thesprotians in a war with the Brygi and is routed by Ares, but Athena takes his side till Apollo separates the two deities. After Callidice's death Polypoetes, Odysseus' son, inherits the kingship, but Odysseus himself returns to Ithaca, where Telegonus, his son by Circe, comes in search of him; as Telegonus is ravaging the island, Odysseus rushes to oppose him and Telegonus, ignorant of his father's identity, slays him. When he learns of his error, Telegonus brings his father's body, and along with it both Telemachus and Penelope, to Circe; she makes them all immortal, and Telegonus marries Penelope, whereas Telemachus marries Circe.[28] Eustathius informs us that the author of the *Nostoi*, who was a Colophonian, also says that Telemachus later married Circe, and that Telegonus the son of Circe in turn married Penelope, though Eustathius adds that he regards these reports as far-fetched and the whole business as idle depravity.[29]

---

[27] Malkin (1998).
[28] *Tel.* arg. lines 306–30 Severyns. Eustath. on *Od.* 2.117.17–21 (1796.35) adds the detail that, according to the author of the *Telegony*, Odysseus had a son with Calypso named Telegonus or Teledamus and two sons with Penelope, Telemachus and Arcesilaus (ἐκ μὲν Καλυψοῦς Τηλέγονον υἱὸν Ὀδυσσεῖ ἀναγράφει ἢ Τηλέδαμον· ἐκ δὲ Πηνελόπης Τηλέμαχον καὶ Ἀρκεσίλαον).
[29] Eustath. on *Od.* 2.117.19–24 (1796.45).

The symmetrical cross-marriages of sons with their father's other wife certainly seem contrived. It is easy to imagine that the pattern reflects a folktale motif, or, if one is inclined in that direction, some prehistoric astronomical lore, such as is supposed to lie behind the story of the Dioscouri, who are said to take turns descending to Hades. But it is also perfectly reasonable to see in this arrangement the hand of the poet – or shall we say, the Monumental Poet? – of the *Telegony*. Might the finale, with its semi-incestuous couplings, have been intended as humorous, the denouement to end all denouements or, to reverse the metaphor, the tying up of loose ends to the point of absurdity? Perhaps we may see in this pat ending a deliberate contrast with the conclusion to the *Odyssey*, which leaves Odysseus suspended in mid-air, as he leaps to attack the kinsmen of the dead suitors and is stopped in mid-flight by Zeus' thunderbolt and Athena's injunction. Further speculation is unwise, but we may at least suspect that in the finale of the *Telegony* there was a shift of register from heroic narrative to a fantasy worthy of the pen of Lucian, and the juxtaposition of the two modes may well have had a comic effect.[30]

CONCLUSION

I have been suggesting that some of the more whimsical elements in the Epic Cycle may have been deliberately witty or fanciful, offsetting the heroic narratives that were part and parcel of the epic tradition. We see signs of such a complex aesthetic in the poems attributed to Homer as well, which had room for episodes such as Demodocus' song about the adultery of Aphrodite and Ares at the expense of Hephaestus, whose marriage to Aphrodite may have been an invention of the poet of the *Odyssey* with a view to just this comic effect (the anecdote as a whole was perhaps designed to echo in an openly droll vein Menelaus' recovery of Helen after her elopement with Paris, an analogy not noted by modern commentators, so far as I can tell, but appreciated by at least one ancient reader, namely Quintus of Smyrna in his *Posthomerica* 14.45–57).[31] Nor were the Cyclic poets lacking in a sense of propriety and decorum in their inventions. There is no evidence, for example, that the odd variant, according to which Penelope slept with all the suitors and gave birth to Pan (i.e., 'All'), as recorded by Douris of Samos

---

[30] See Tsagalis, below in this volume, pp. 393–5 on the conclusion to the *Telegony*.
[31] I am grateful to Calum Maciver for alerting me to this passage in Quintus.

and Servius in his commentary on the *Aeneid*, went back to the Epic Cycle, and I very much doubt that it did.[32]

I am inclined to believe that the Cyclic epics were more permissive than the Homeric poems in respect to comic dissonances within the context of heroic narrative, though always in a controlled and self-conscious way. If I may offer an analogy with another genre, we may perhaps see a roughly comparable (by no means identical) contrast between the comedies of Plautus, with their broad, occasionally slapstick humor, and the more restrained style of Terence, who was more faithful, on the whole, to the relatively demure tone of Menander. To the extent that one may judge from the meager fragments of Roman comedy, Plautus represented the dominant fashion and Terence was the exception.[33] Homer too seems to have been the exception in the genre of archaic Greek epic, and the prevailing taste might rather have approved the more extravagant compositions of his rivals.

---

[32] Douris F 42, cited by Tzetzes on Lycophr. 772, who calls the story nonsense: 'Douris the Samian, in his *On Agathocles*, says that Penelope lay with all the suitors and gave birth to the goat-footed Pan (συγγενέσθαι πᾶσι τοῖς μνηστῆρσι καὶ γεννῆσαι τραγοσκελῆ Πᾶνα). But he utters nonsense concerning Pan, for Pan was the son of Hermes and a different Penelope, and another Pan was the son of Zeus and Hybris.' Servius on Verg. *Aen.* 2.44: 'This Ulysses, of course, was the son of Laertes and husband of Penelope, who had as sons Telemachus with Penelope, but with Circe Telegonus, who, when he was seeking his father, killed him unwittingly... Another story is also told about him: for when, after his wanderings, he had returned to Ithaca, it is reported that he found Pan in his home, who is said to have been born of Penelope and all the suitors, as the name Pan itself seems to indicate (*invenisse Pana fertur in penatibus suis, qui dicitur ex Penelope et procis omnibus natus, sicut ipsum nomen Pan videtur declarare*). Others, however, say that he was born of Mercury, who, transformed into a goat, slept with Penelope (*qui in hircum mutatus cum Penelope concubuerat*). But after Ulysses saw the misshapen boy, he is said to have taken refuge in wanderings (*sed Ulixes posteaquam deformem puerum vidit, fugisse dicitur in errores*). He either died of old age, or was slain at the hand of his son Telegonus by the barb of a sea creature [sc., a sting-ray]; whereas, just as he was taking flight, he is said to have been transformed into a horse by Minerva.' It is unclear where this 'other story' might have been found, nor for that matter the version according to which Penelope slept with Hermes in the form of a goat or that Odysseus was finally metamorphosed into a horse; for a possible connection with Sanskrit mythology, see Allen (1995).

[33] See Wright (1974).

10 | The Trojan War in early Greek art

THOMAS H. CARPENTER

Images demonstrate unequivocally that by the middle of the seventh century BC the outline of the Trojan War, from the judgment of Paris to the Trojan horse and the sack of Troy, was known in many parts of the Greek world and beyond. Many episodes from that tradition appear on a variety of objects from the seventh century and early sixth century BC, mainly from the Peloponnese and the Aegean islands, while Athenian artisans seem to have had little interest in it until the 560s BC, after which Attic vases become our principal source of Trojan images.[1] Most of the early images depict episodes we know from summaries of the poems of the Epic Cycle; very few of them refer to events from our *Iliad* and *Odyssey*.[2]

To be comprehensible, most images of myth depend on prior knowledge of the event depicted, but from the images themselves it is rarely possible to determine precisely what the sources of that prior knowledge may have been. Archaic images can tell when and where a story was known but they cannot tell how it was known. Even when a text exists (e.g. *Iliad*), it is not possible to move confidently from an image to a text, much less so when all that survives are fragments of texts or summaries.

The question of whether or not an image reflects a specific text is primarily a modern one asked by students who are steeped in the textual traditions. The ancient viewers would obviously have known how they knew the stories behind the images, and on recognizing a scene, they would more likely have focused on its significance rather than on its source.

Given the small sample of archaic images that have come down to us, the fact that a story is not represented in surviving images does not necessarily tell us anything about the prevalence of that story. On the other hand, when a story is depicted, particularly when multiple examples exist, its appearance must indicate both the currency of the story in some form and the fact that it was significant for the artisans who created the images and usually for the patrons who obtained them.

In an oral culture the survival of myth depends on its cultural relevance; when it loses that relevance, it fades. As Graf has noted, 'Its capacity to adapt

---

[1] Shapiro (1990: 126–8). [2] Burgess (2001: 90); Snodgrass (1979: 120); Lowenstam (1997: 49).

to changing circumstances is a measure of its vitality.'[3] Thus, we should assume that any archaic image depicting a myth was chosen or created for a specific reason or reasons from almost unlimited possibilities and reflects and affirms a particular perspective at a particular time and place. It follows that narrative images from one area should reflect to some degree episodes that held significance for people of that area (e.g. Corinth), which could be quite different from images popular in another area (e.g. Athens).

Early images of events from the Trojan War tradition differ from surviving literary accounts of the events in two important ways. They can be assigned dates with some degree of accuracy, and they can be associated with particular locales where they were manufactured and/or where they were found. Careful attention to context (time and place) allows a differentiation in the ways myths were promoted and received.

Over the past 50 years exhaustive surveys of epic in Greek art from the Geometric to the Hellenistic periods have been published where the focus has been largely on the myths themselves and on their possible reflections of texts.[4] In what follows here the focus will be more on the contexts in which the early images appeared with an eye to the audiences for which they were produced. All of the objects discussed below were produced before the middle of the sixth century BC, and for each a place of manufacture and an intended audience can be identified. My assumption is that these images reflect aural experiences of the stories; my intent is to highlight ways that chosen myths may reflect the interests of the people who made or obtained them.

The images on a large (1.3 m) relief pithos in Mykonos from the second quarter of the seventh century BC,[5] said to be among the earliest representations of the fall of Troy, is an appropriate starting point (Fig. 10.1).[6] It was found by locals digging a well in the centre of the town of Mykonos in 1961; human bones found with it indicate that it had been used as a burial pithos, though earlier it was more likely used as a storage vessel.[7]

---

[3] Graf (1993: 3).
[4] Schefold (1964), (1978), (1993); Fittschen (1969); Schefold and Jung (1989); Ahlberg–Cornell (1992). *LIMC* includes articles on all individual figures from Greek, Roman and Etruscan myth.
[5] On the Mykonos pithos, see also Finglass, below in this volume, pp. 345–6; Noussia-Fantuzzi, below in this volume, p. 447.
[6] Mykonos, Archaeological Museum 2240. Ervin (1963: 37–77). A fragment of a relief pithos found on Tenos showing a shield between the wheeled legs of a horse, undoubtedly depicted a similar image, Fittischen (1969: 183, #100). See also London, British Museum 3205, a fragmentary Boeotian fibula circa 700 BC on which the Trojan horse probably appears, Sparkes (1971).
[7] Ebbinghaus (2005: 52–8).

Fig. 10.1 Cycladic relief pithos from Mykonos. Seventh century BC. Neck: Trojan horse. Shoulder: Massacre of women and children.

In any case it was a costly object and was the product of a Cycladic workshop most probably on the nearby island of Tenos.[8] Thus, the manufacturer and the market were both local.

The Trojan Horse depicted on the neck, with warriors peering out of windows and other warriors above and below it, has tended to determine the reading of the rest of the imagery on the shoulder and upper body of the vase where three bands of figures in relief contain a total of twenty metopes. In seventeen of those metopes a warrior attacks a woman or a woman and a child. In the initial publication of the vase, three metopes were said to contain identifiable characters from accounts of the fall of Troy: the recovery of Helen by Menelaus, death of Astyanax, and Cassandra or Polyxena.[9] Some scholars have accepted the first two identifications, while others have demurred.[10]

The principal argument for identifying specific individuals in the metopes is that in much later scenes on different fabrics similar conventions are used to depict identifiable figures. For the figure identified as Helen the argument is also supported by her clothing, which is much more elaborate than the clothing of any of the other seventeen women on the vase. These arguments obviously rely on the assumption that since the potter put the Trojan horse on the neck, he must have had in mind the specific events that followed, including the recovery of Helen, the death of Astyanax and the rape of Cassandra. In other words, he must have known what we have learned from later texts and images.

As others have noted, scenes on the body do not depict heroic subjects. One metope shows a fallen warrior; none shows males in combat. Rather, most show the massacre of women and children.[11] Particularly striking is the fact that nearly half of the metopes include scenes in which children are attacked by warriors (Fig. 10.2).[12] A similar number of metopes show a woman explicitly supplicating a warrior; in one (#4) the warrior has already mortally wounded a woman with his sword. To argue, on the basis of much later iconographic parallels, that viewers would have identified three or four out of the more than fifty figures seems like special pleading. Who might

---

[8] Caskey (1976: 21).
[9] Ervin (1963: 56–65). Metope #7 Helen and Menelaus; #17 Astyanax; #13 Cassandra or Polyxena. Caskey (1976) identifies a fallen warrior on an additional metope (#2B) recovered in 1979 as Echion; Ebbinghaus (2005) suggests that he is Hektor.
[10] E.g. Hurwitt (1985) accepts the identifications. Anderson (1997), Schefold (1964) and Morris (1995) have reservations.
[11] Schefold (1966: 46–7); Morris (1995: 226); Anderson (1997: 187).
[12] All of the children are naked and most are demonstrably male. It is unlikely that any was intended to be female: Giuliani (2003: 336 n. 20).

Fig. 10.2 Detail of Fig. 10.1. (Drawing by L. C. Lancaster.)

the other children and women be? Morris is undoubtedly right in arguing that 'specific identities would dilute the horror of universal calamity in the anonymous warriors and victims'.[13]

The probable context of the vase itself suggests that the Trojan War was used here as a vehicle to convey a broader message about war. This was a grand and costly vessel and there is nothing accidental about the imagery. In fact, each image is unique. Moulds were not used for the reliefs; rather, they were 'freely modeled' and applied to the surface of the pithos, clearly the work of a single artisan.[14] Of all the subjects that could possibly have been depicted, the potter chose repeated images of the massacre of women and children.

The restriction of the figure decorations to the neck and upper belly of one side of the pot indicates that it was intended for display, perhaps set against a wall in a prominent part of a wealthy house.[15] In other words, it was created with a Cycladic audience in mind. The unremitting brutality of the scenes makes it likely that what it conveyed to that audience had more to do with the horrors of war and its effects on civilians than it did with a particular story. The fall of Troy simply provided the frame for the discourse.

[13] Morris (1995: 226).   [14] Ervin (1963: 43–4).   [15] See Ebbinghaus (2005: 52–8).

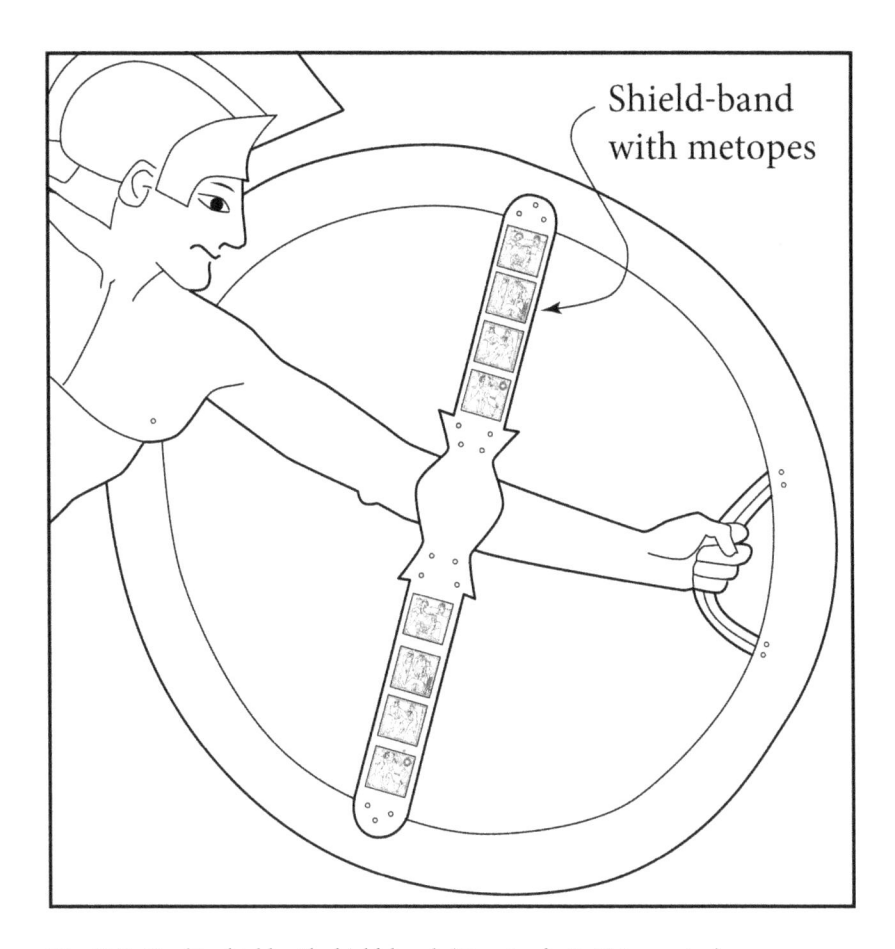

Fig. 10.3 Hoplite shield with shield-band. (Drawing by L. C. Lancaster.)

Hoplite shields dedicated at Olympia from the last quarter of the seventh century at least on through the sixth BC are an important source of archaic depictions of myth. A loop on the inside of the shield, through which the warrior thrust his left arm to 'wear' the shield, was held in place by bronze strips, usually called shield-bands, that were often decorated with small relief panels (Fig. 10.3). These shield-bands are thought to have been made primarily in Argos;[16] so, in both production and provenance, the images on them are principally a Peloponnesian phenomenon.

Though the manufacturing process allowed multiple copies of the same bands to be produced, the original choice of images must have been deliberate and carefully conceived. As Martin Robertson has written, 'these tiny

---

[16] Kunze (1950); Bol (1989); Snodgrass (1964: 63).

rectangles are austere and sparing in composition, never showing many figures and rarely any irrelevant adjuncts'.[17] The warrior who obtained the shield could see the images as he wore it and must have found them comprehensible and appropriate.

In most publications on myth in ancient art, the relief panels (metopes) are rarely shown as part of the whole shield-band but rather are used singly to illustrate a particular point; however, the warrior who obtained the shield would have seen the band as a whole and would have been aware of the juxtaposition of images. So, for example, on a well-preserved band from the first quarter of the sixth century BC (Form I) there are five metopes: on one part the murder of Troilus by Achilles adjoins the murder of Aegisthus, which adjoins Zeus attacking Typhon. On the other part of the band, Ajax dragging Cassandra from the statue of Athena adjoins a god attacking a giant.[18]

On another well preserved band (Form IV), from the second quarter of the sixth century BC there are six metopes: a more elaborate version of Ajax dragging Cassandra from the statue adjoins the suicide of Ajax, which adjoins the murder of Agamemnon, which adjoins Theseus and the Minotaur on one part, while the ransom of Hector adjoins Heracles and the Lion on the other.[19] On both bands scenes of sacrilege and murder that lead to dire consequence are juxtaposed, in one case with divine victories and in the other with deeds by the Panhellenic heroes, Heracles and Theseus. It seems not unlikely that there is an admonitory quality to these juxtapositions of scenes.

Some fourteen different episodes from the Trojan War have been identified on shield-bands,[20] and of those scenes, only one, the Ransom of Hector, depicts an event from the *Iliad*; none refers to the *Odyssey*. A naked boy attacked by a warrior, often by an altar, is one of the more numerous scenes to appear on shield-bands, starting in the first quarter of the sixth century BC.[21] (Fig. 10.4) Though he is never named, he is usually identified as Troilus, a son of Priam whose murder by Achilles was mentioned in the

---

[17] Robertson (1990: 67). [18] Kunze (1950: 7–8); Bol (1989: 138–9).
[19] Kunze (1950: 10–11); Bol (1989: 139).
[20] Kunze (1950: 139–73): Death of Troilus, Achilles and Ajax Gaming, Ransom of Hector, Achilles and Penthesilea, Ajax with the Body of Achilles or Aristodamus, Suicide of Ajax, Death of Priam, Death of Astyanax, Ajax and Cassandra, Recovery of Helen, Murder of Agamemnon, Death of Aegisthus. Bol (1989: 63–76): Peleus and Thetis, Thetis with Hephaestus with Armor.
[21] The earliest occurrence of this scene is on a late seventh-century tripod leg from Olympia B 3600. For the earliest shield-bands B 988, B 1801, B 1802, B 4962, B 1642 and Isthmia IM 3328 (*Hesperia* 28 (1959) Fig. 8). Slightly later, with a cock on the altar, B 987, B 1803, B 1912. See Bol (1989: 65).

Fig. 10.4 Panel of an Argive shield-band from Olympia. Sixth century BC. Achilles' pursuit of Troilus?

Cypria.[22] The brutality of the scene is reminiscent of the images on the Mykonos pithos, and here, when an altar is included, a sacrilegious element is added.

Achilles' murder of Troilus[23] seems to have received slight attention from archaic poets.[24] That Achilles kills Troilus is all that Proclus' summary of the *Cypria* tells. Ibycus may have told that Troilus was killed outside of the walls of Troy in the precinct of Apollo Thymbraion. Of fifth-century BC authors, Sophocles wrote a tragedy, *Troilus*, but neither Aeschylus, Pindar nor Bacchylides mentions Troilus in their preserved works, and Plautus, in

---

[22] In a few scenes where the altar is missing, the boy is sometimes identified as Astyanax e.g. B 847, B 1883. The altar is usually said to indicate the sanctuary of Apollo Thymbraion where Achilles killed Troilus.

[23] See Currie, below in this volume, p. 294; Noussia-Fantuzzi, below, pp. 445–7; Sistakou, below, p. 490; Gärtner, below, p. 553.

[24] For a review of the literary sources, see Gantz (1993: 597–603).

the second century BC, is the first surviving source to tell that Troilus' death was a necessary condition for the fall of Troy.[25]

In contrast with the meagre literary remains, depictions of the Achilles and Troilus episode are extraordinarily popular across a range of fabrics and locations from the mid seventh century on through the sixth BC and fall into three main groups – ambush, pursuit and murder. The earliest certain representation of Troilus is on a Protocorinthian aryballos from the third quarter of the seventh century BC where his name is inscribed.[26] There Achilles runs after the boy who flees on horseback. The rudimentary nature of the image with Troilus' name included implies that the story was well known in Corinth by that time.[27] The ambush of Troilus is the 'only episode from the Trojan War shown in Sparta', as well as being the most popular scene in Laconian vase painting, where all examples date from the second quarter of the sixth century BC.[28] Also from the second quarter of the sixth century is a depiction of the ambush on a Chiot Chalice, found at Pitane (modern Turkey) one of very few depictions from myth to appear on Chiot vases.[29] Recently a shield-band has been found in a tomb at Chairomonte in South Italy on which Achilles pulls Troilus from his horses.[30] The ambush is also the subject of an Etruscan tomb painting at Tarquinia from the second half of the sixth century BC and is one of the only scenes from Greek myth to appear there.

The parts of the story – ambush, pursuit and murder – are pulled together most effectively in the earliest Attic depiction of the myth, which is also the most complete version on any fabric, on the François Vase circa 570 BC found in an Etruscan tomb at Chiusi (Italy).[31] (Fig. 10.5) The degree of detail in that scene implies that the painter had a specific source in mind for the imagery. A bearded Apollo stands to the far left by a fountain house,

---

[25] Gantz (1993: 601).

[26] Athens, Canellopoulos 1319. A fragment of a relief pithos from Tenos is often cited as the earliest depiction of the subject, but the evidence for that identification is inconclusive.

[27] Depictions of the ambush and murder of Troilus also appear on other Corinthian vases from the early sixth century BC: Ambush on Athens, National Archaeological Museum 277 (NC 1072) and Tunis (NC 1404); Murder on Paris, Louvre E 638bis (NC 1196). Amyx (1988: 640–1 n. 53) rejects Zurich EHT B4 (NC 1435) as a depiction of Achilles and Troilus and questions the identity of the figures in Hephaestia (Lemnos) B-XLVI Nr. 32 often said to be Achilles pursuing Troilus.

[28] Pipili (1987: 27). Samos 1199, Stibbe #123, and Samos, Stibbe #294; London British Museum B 7.4.10–12, Stibbe #156 (from Naukratis); Rome, Villa Giulia, Stibbe #291, and Paris, Louvre E 662, Stibbe #313 (from Cerveteri).

[29] Istanbul, Archaeological Museum inv. 8904. Lemos (1991: 107–8 #800).

[30] Policoro, Museum 216208. Bottini (2008).

[31] Florence, Museo Archeologico 4209, *ABV* 76.1.

Fig. 10.5 Scene of Attic black-figure volute krater (François Vase). Sixth century BC. Achilles' pursuit of Troilus.

Fig. 10.6 Panel of an Argive shield-band from Olympia. Sixth century BC. Rape of Cassandra.

gesturing as Achilles, on foot, pursues Troilus who gallops to the right with two horses. In front of him Polyxena rushes toward the walls of Troy where Priam rises from a stool as Antenor confronts him. From a gate in the walls Hector and Polites emerge fully armed. Behind Achilles, Athena, Hermes and Thetis stand watching. The presence of Apollo and his gesture point to the ensuing sacrilege, the murder of Troilus in the sanctuary of Apollo, which ultimately contributes to the death of Achilles.

Nothing about any of these scenes carries with it heroic qualities, but it is the murder of the boy as he seeks sanctuary at an altar that is the most brutal and recalls most vividly the scenes on the Mykonos pithos.

The rape of Cassandra by the Lesser Ajax, another scene of sacrilege, is also a common subject on Argive shield-bands. On all of the examples a warrior, his sword raised, grasps the arm of a naked woman who clings to a statue of Athena (Fig. 10.6). In one type an altar is also included.[32] These scenes are in keeping with the description of the incident in Proclus' summary of the *Iliou persis*: [Ajax] 'while trying to drag Cassandra away by force, tears away with her the image of Athena' and is essentially the form used by Attic black-figure vase-painters after circa 560 BC on more than thirty vases.[33] Unlike the Troilus scene, the subject does not appear on Corinthian vases, but roughly contemporary with the shield-bands was a cedar chest from Corinth that the second-century AD traveller Pausanias saw at Olympia where it had been dedicated. He tells (5.19.5) that the scene was accompanied by the inscription 'Ajax of Locri is dragging Cassandra from Athena.'

This chest with more than thirty scenes in five bands is described in detail by Pausanias in his *Description of Greece*. He saw the chest in the temple of Hera at Olympia[34] and was told that it was the chest in which the Corinthian tyrant, Cypselus, had been hidden by his mother, a story mentioned by Herodotus (5.92), and had been dedicated at Olympia by his descendants as a thank offering. Cypselos' son, Periander, died in 587 BC, so if Pausanias is right (or if his sources were accurate), the chest would have been dedicated early in the sixth century BC. On the basis of parallels, both epigraphic and iconographic, with other late seventh- and early sixth-century BC Corinthian works, most scholars now tend to accept this date.[35] The original audience, then, would have been viewers in late seventh-century BC Corinth, and the imagery should represent, to some degree, the interests of an elite class. The apparently random ordering of the scenes in five bands would suggest that the images were chosen from a repertory already well established in Corinth by that time. Of the scenes on the chest, all based on myth, only nine are derived from the Trojan War tradition, and only two of the Trojan War scenes relate to episodes from the Homeric poems, both from the *Iliad*.[36] Achilles appears only once on the chest, in his fight with Memnon (5.19.1), an event recounted in the *Aethiopis*.[37]

---

[32] Form IV, B 1654, B 5160.
[33] Connelly (1993). For a list of Attic examples, see Oricchio (2002: 84–5 n. 10).
[34] Pausanias 5.17.5 – 5.19.10. Dio Chrysostom 11.45, who also saw the chest, says that it was in the back room (opisthodomos) of the temple.
[35] Snodgrass (2001: 128); Cossu (2005: 155).
[36] The *Iliad* scenes are: 5.19.1: Ajax's duel with Hector (*Il.* 7.225–305) 5.19.4: Agamemnon fighting Coon over the body of Iphidamas (*Il.* 11.247). Pausanias mistook two scenes as coming from the *Odyssey* and one other from the *Iliad*, but modern iconographic analyses have shown otherwise.
[37] The duel between Achilles and Memnon may be the subject of a mid-seventh-century BC Melian amphora from Melos (Athens, 3961) where the warriors are flanked by two women; Pausanias writes that on the chest, their mothers stood by them.

In three of the bands on the chest, most of the figures were identified by inscriptions, and seven scenes from those bands were accompanied by verses, most of which were written in hexameters. As Snodgrass has noted, 'the poetic quality of these verses is not high; they simply describe the content of the scenes in a banal way'.[38] Verse inscriptions accompany one of the 'Homeric' scenes (5.19.4) in which Agamemnon fights Coön over the body of Iphidamas. Above the corpse is written, 'Iphidamas, and this is Coon fighting for him', and on Agamemnon's shield, 'This is the Fear of mortals: he who holds him is Agamemnon'; however, neither verse is from the *Iliad*. The inclusion of the relatively obscure encounter between Agamemnon and Coön may point to an awareness of Homer's account, but the inclusion of non-Homeric verses would seem to distance the image from an actual text.

Three scenes on the chest depict events included in the *Cypria*.[39] Of particular note is a depiction of the Judgment of Paris (5.19.5)[40] which is accompanied by an inscription 'Here is Hermes who is showing to Alexander that he may arbitrate concerning their beauty, Hera, Athena and Aphrodite.' The earliest depiction of this subject is on a Protocorinthian oinochoe from the middle of the seventh century BC, where inscriptions guarantee the identification.[41] The same subject appears in relief on an ivory comb from Sparta from the last quarter of the seventh century BC.[42] According to Pausanias (3.18.12), the judgment also appeared on the throne by Bathycles at Amyclae near Sparta, probably dating from the mid fifth century BC. While the early depictions are all from the Peloponnesus, after circa 560 BC it becomes a common scene on Attic vases.

Two scenes are from events included in the *Iliou persis*.[43] Pausanias writes, 'Menelaus wearing a breastplate and carrying a sword is advancing to kill Helen, so it is plain that Troy has been captured' (5.18.3). Also, as noted above, Ajax dragging Cassandra from the image of Athena is shown, accompanied by the inscription.

---

[38] Snodgrass (1998: 115). See now Borg (2010).
[39] 5.19.5 Judgment of Paris; 5.18.5 Peleus subduing Thetis; 5.19.7 probably the Wedding of Peleus and Thetis rather than Odysseus and Circe as Pausanias suggests. This was a scene without an inscription.
[40] See also Currie, below in this volume, pp. 286–7.
[41] Rome, Villa Giulia 22769, 'Chigi Vase'.
[42] Athens, National Archaeological Museum 15368, Marangou (1969: 97–98 #47, figs. 78a–c).
[43] On the *Iliou persis*, see Finglass, below in this volume.

Depictions of one other Trojan subject, the suicide of Ajax,[44] demonstrates well regional preferences. The earliest certain depiction of that subject, which Proclus assigns to the *Ilias parva*, is on an early seventh century BC Protocorinthian aryballos where Ajax falls on his sword.[45] On a gem from Perachora of the second half of the seventh century BC showing Ajax's suicide, his name is inscribed as it is on several Corinthian vases from the first quarter of the sixth century BC.[46] His suicide was also the subject of a relief on an ivory comb from Sparta, dated to the first quarter of the sixth century BC,[47] as well as on shield-bands from the second quarter of the sixth century BC. (Fig. 10.7) The occurrences of the scene are predominantly from the Peloponnese while it rarely appears on Attic vases of any period.[48]

The François Vase, mentioned above, marks the beginning of an intense Attic interest in scenes from the Trojan tradition.[49] In addition to the Troilus scene, the wedding of Peleus and Thetis is the subject of the principal band that encircles the shoulder of the vase, and on each handle a named Ajax carries the body of Achilles.[50] The only scene that refers to the *Iliad* is on the neck of the vase where Achilles officiates at the funeral games of Patroclus. This scene is of particular interest both because of the inclusion of names of participants in the chariot race that do not appear in the *Iliad* and because of the absence of many names that do. In his discussion of the some 130 inscriptions on the vase, Wachter concluded that the writer was highly literate but clearly 'did not know Homer's book 23'.[51]

After the middle of the sixth century BC and for the next century and a half, images of the Trojan War are limited almost entirely to Attic vases. While made in Attica, the majority of the surviving vases have been found elsewhere and were clearly export commodities, with Etruria providing the

---

[44] On the suicide of Ajax, see Rengakos, below in this volume, pp. 307, 309; Kelly, below in this volume, p. 321.
[45] Berlin 3319. Jenkins (2002) has identified a bronze in the British Museum (1865.11–18.230) as the earliest representation of the death of Ajax, from the last quarter of the eight century BC.
[46] NY, Metropolitan Museum of Art 42.11.13 (gem); Berlin 3182, Paris, Louvre E 635, Amsterdam 1276 (vases).
[47] Athens, NM 15522, Marangou (1969: 94 #40, Fig. 69a).
[48] The Attic exception is on the famous amphora by Exekias in Boulogne (558), *ABV* 145.18. See Kannicht (1982: 81–2) for speculation on the popularity of the subject in the Peloponnese and its absence from Attica.
[49] See n. 31.
[50] A warrior carrying the enormous body of a dead warrior, usually said to be Ajax and Achilles, appears on shield-bands from the end of the seventh and beginning of the sixth centuries, see Ahlberg-Cornell (1992: 71), and it becomes a common subject on Attic black-figure vases after 560.
[51] Wachter (1991: 97 and 112).

Fig. 10.7 Panel of an Argive shield-band from Olympia. Sixth century BC. Suicide of Ajax.

major markets. As such, it is difficult to determine to what extent the choice of subjects represents Athenian interests and to what degree the markets to which the vases were regularly exported influenced the choice of subjects on them. On Attic red-figure vases from the fifth century BC the influence of the treatment of Trojan themes by tragedians can be detected, but even in the fifth century BC, as Steven Lowenstam has noted, the vases 'reveal a curious ignorance or avoidance of our *Iliad* and *Odyssey*'.[52]

Then, during the fourth century a separate iconographic tradition develops in South Italy that relies heavily on literary sources, particularly tragedies, for some images on red-figure vases, which were made there for local markets.[53] In some cases images remain incomprehensible without knowledge of specific texts, even when all of the figures are identified with

[52] Lowenstam (1997: 47). [53] See Giuliani (1996).

inscriptions.[54] The depiction of the death of Thersites on an Apulian red-figure volute krater from the second half of the fourth century BC, found in a tomb at Ceglie del Campo, an Italic (as opposed to Greek) site near Bari, is a case in point.[55] (Fig. 10.8) In the centre of side A, Achilles sits on a *kline* in a building, attended by Phoenix. The body and decapitated head of Thersites lie on the ground below the building. Agamemnon moves in from the left followed by Phorbas. Diomedes, accompanied by an Aetolian warrior, rushes in from the right, drawing his sword, but is restrained by Menelaus. At the top of the scene, to the left, Pan stands beside a seated Poina (Vengeance), and to the right Athena sits on her shield with Hermes standing by her. At the bottom of the scene, flanking the body of Thersites are Automedon and a naked youth labeled Demos. All of the figures are identified by inscriptions.

Literary sources offer some help in interpreting the episode depicted here. In his summary of the *Aethiopis*, Proclus tells that Achilles 'kills Thersites after being abused by him and insulted over his alleged love for Penthesilea. This results in a dispute among the Achaeans about the killing of Thersites. Achilles sails to Lesbos, and after sacrificing to Apollo, Artemis, and Leto, he is purified from the killing by Odysseus.' Ps.-Apollodorus adds nothing. A scholion on *Il.* 2.212 makes Thersites a kinsman of Diomedes. The fourth-century playwright, Chaeremon, wrote a play, *Achilles Thersitoktonos*, which some have suggested may have been an inspiration for this scene.[56] In short, the meaning of some of the imagery remains obscure, and there is no way to determine what the sources for the extraordinary detail of the imagery may have been, but the likelihood is that they were written texts.

Before circa 600 BC few if any depictions of scenes from the tradition of the Trojan War were produced in Athens. Rather, the majority of images come from the Peloponnese, where Corinth was the dominant producer of figure decorated pottery and Argos seems to have been the centre of production of shield-bands. Other images come from pottery workshops in the Cyclades.

---

[54] E.g. Naples, Museo Archeologico inv. 81934 (H.3255), *RVAp* 18/42 with imagery based on Euripides' *Hypsipyle*. Giuliani (2001: 33–8) attributes this change to 'the emergence of written texts in the late 5th and early 4th centuries BC'.

[55] Boston, Museum of Fine Arts 1900.03.804, *RVAp* 17/75. See Padgett (1993: #38, 99–106). Lowenstam (2008: 110–14).

[56] Padgett (1993: 105). As Lowenstam (2008: 114) notes, Aristotle's reference to Chaeremon's productions, which were written more for reading than for staging, may reinforce Giuliani's argument that vase-painters drew on texts for their images.

Fig. 10.8 Apulian red-figure volute krater from Ceglie del Campo. Fourth century BC. Murder of Thersites by Achilles.

It has long been known that non-Homeric themes were much more common than Homeric ones in archaic art. What is surprising in this review of early images depicting scenes from the Trojan War is the apparent emphasis on what might be called 'unheroic' and even sacrilegious episodes. Instead of crafting heroic duels, the potter of the Mykonos pithos chose to show repeatedly the massacre of women and children. For the artisans who produced the Argive shield-bands two scenes of sacrilege, the murder of Troilus and the rape of Cassandra, were the most common, and at least half of the fourteen Trojan scenes on them depict sacrilegious events. The popularity of scenes from the Troilus episode stretched from Asia Minor to Sparta to Corinth to Athens and even to Etruria, where it is the one subject from Greek myth that appears in Etruscan tomb paintings at Tarquinia. The suicide of Ajax, another un-Homeric subject, was long of interest to Argive artisans and Corinthian potters. We should remember that these scenes would not have maintained currency had they not spoken to the patrons who obtained them, so this emphasis on the unheroic should give us pause as we speculate on the reception of the epic cycle amongst the elite of the Peloponnese in the seventh and sixth centuries BC.

PART II

Epics

11 | *Theogony* and *Titanomachy*

GIAMBATTISTA D'ALESSIO[*]

The evidence for the presence of a *Theogony* within the Cycle rests on only two uncertain testimonies.[1] The first is a rather vague sentence of Philo of Byblos, according to whom the Greeks took over earlier traditions from other cultures, particularly that of the Phoenicians, embellished them, and eventually supplanted the originals with their own borrowings: 'hence Hesiod and the celebrated Cyclic poets fashioned Theogonies and Gigantomachies and Titanomachies of their own and castrations' (*Cyclus PEG* T 6 = *Tit.* T 1D. (= Philo, *FgrHist* 790F 2 § 40)), a sentence resonating with Xenophanes' definition of the stories of 'the wars of the Titans, the Giants and the Centaurs' as πλάσμα<τ>α προτέρων ('forgeries/fictions of previous poets') (F 1.21 G–P = *IEG*)'.[2] The second is the summary of Proclus' *Chrestomathy* in Photius (*Cyclus PEG* T 13 = T 1 D.), according to whom the Epic Cycle 'begins with the mythical story of the union of Ouranos and Ge', giving birth to the three Hundred-Handers and the three Cyclopes.

No explicit information on a free-standing theogonic narrative attached to the Cycle is preserved, but, as it has long been recognized, a summary may lurk behind the very beginning of the *Bibliotheca* falsely ascribed to Apollodorus, one of whose main sources has been identified with a prose summary of the Epic Cycle.[3] Ps.-Apollodorus' account is close to what we can reconstruct of the early stages of the Orphic *Rhapsodic Theogony*, which was in circulation from the late Hellenistic period, but which included

---

[*] I am grateful to E. Cingano, L. Battezzato and G. Ucciardello for comments on an earlier draft.
[1] On the Cyclic *Theogony*, see also Introduction, above in this volume, pp. 4, 30–1 n. 122; West, above in this volume, pp. 101–2.
[2] Cf. Philo's use of the term *plasma* further down in the same fragment, § 41. On Philo and his source, Sanchuniaton, see at least Troiani (1974); Baumgarten (1981); West (1983: 177); West (1994).
[3] Ps.-Apollodorus' passage was printed among the testimonies of the Cycle, for example, already in Kinkel's 1877 edition. Most scholars referred this to the *Titanomachy*: cf. Dietze (1914), who identified the first poem of the Cycle with the *Titanomachy*, and attributed any inconsistencies to manipulations of the mythographic sources by Ps.-Apollodorus and Proclus, Severyns (1928: 165–6) and Severyns (1938: 87–8).

elements going back to earlier versions of the poem.[4] In his seminal books on the *Orphic Poems* M. L. West argued that the two poems were closely related and accounted for a number of discrepancies between Ps.-Apollodorus and the *Rhapsodic Theogony*, explaining some of them as due to 'Apollodorus' own disposition of material', and others as 'real differences of detail between Apollodorus' immediate source and the Rhapsodies'.[5] The Cyclic *Theogony* would have gone under the name of Orpheus and was in its turn used by the compiler of the *Rhapsodic Theogony*. This identification, though highly conjectural, makes better sense of the evidence than the alternative hypothesis according to which Ps.-Apollodorus' account was based on the initial part of the *Titanomachy*.[6] That poem, as we shall see, opened not with the union of Ouranos and Ge but with Aither (*PEG* F 1/2 = F 1^A, 1^B D. = F 1 W.), and made at least one of the Hundred-Handers, Aigaion, the offspring of Ge and Pontos (*PEG* F 3 = D., W.). On both details, Ps.-Apollodorus coincides with Proclus' account, not with the *Titanomachy*.

Several details are shared by Ps.-Apollodorus' account and previous Orphic *Theogonies* now lost and only very incompletely recoverable,[7] but, given the nature of the evidence, a comparison between the two sets remains extremely uncertain. The elements attested by Proclus, i.e. the primeval union of Ouranos and Ge and the consequent birth of the Hundred-Handers and the Cyclopes, both preceding that of the Titans, are comparable with features of the so-called 'Protogonos' *Theogony*, a poem reconstructed by West and others as akin to the one used by the author of the Derveni papyrus. There Ouranos was 'the first-born king' (*PEG* ii.1 F 10.2), and was probably indicated as 'first-born' (πρωτόγονος) also in *PEG* ii.1 F 12.1, though some scholars see rather a reference to Phanes here. In that poem, however, Ouranos is generated by Night, and it is doubtful how far this would be compatible with the structure of the Cyclic *Theogony*, that, according to Proclus, 'opened' with the union of Ouranos and Ge. We have no direct evidence that in the 'Protogonos' poem the birth of the Hundred-Handers and the Cyclopes preceded that of the Titans, though this certainly was the case in the later so-called Hieronyman *Theogony* (*PEG* ii.1 F 82) where,

---

[4] See West (1983: 121–6 and West's stemma on p. 264). The relevance of the Orphic poems for the issue had already been noticed, and explained differently, by Dietze (1914). The fragments of the *Rhapsodies*, as well as those of the other Orphic *Theogonies*, are collected, with very rich bibliography, in *PEG* ii.1.

[5] West (1983: 124).

[6] Dietze (1914); Severyns (1928, 1938); above, n. 3; Brisson (1985: 405–7); F 2 D. and *PEG* F 3 (= D., W.); Carrière and Massonie (1991: 163–4). *Contra*, most recently, e.g. Debiasi (2004: 73 n. 20 and 82 n. 84).

[7] See West (1983: 126–39).

however, as in the later *Rhapsodies* (*PEG* ii.1 F 177), they were preceded by the birth of the Moirai.[8]

Other points of contact (based, in this case, on Ps.-Apollodorus' account only) concern the so-called Eudemian *Theogony*, a poem apparently known to later sources via the fourth-century Peripatetic philosopher Eudemus (*PEG* ii.1 F 19–27). In this case too, though, there are several problematic aspects. According to West, the Eudemian *Theogony*, for example, had twelve Titans generated by Ocean and Tethys (the offspring, in their turn, of Ouranos and Ge), while Ps.-Apollodorus' source would include Ocean and Tethys in a list of fourteen Titans, generated by the primeval couple.[9] In fact, however, Ps.-Apollodorus only lists thirteen Titans, his catalogue differing from that of Hesiod for the inclusion of Dione, and from that of the Eudemian *Theogony* at least for the omission of Phorcys. West's comparison is based on the assumption that the list of fourteen Titans found in the *Rhapsodies* (*PEG* ii.1 F 179) went back to the Cyclic poem, and that Ps.-Apollodorus tampered with it, by moving Phorcys to a different position. This is a plausible conjecture, but it leaves us with pretty little hard evidence regarding the actual list of Titans in the Cyclic *Theogony*. The double imprisonment of the Hundred-Handers and the Cyclopes is a remarkably artificial feature found in Ps.-Apollodorus. This may be 'an innovation of the Cyclic *Theogony* to accord with the following *Titanomachy*',[10] but it may simply be a rationalistic, if somewhat gauche way to solve a *crux* as old as Hesiod, where the condition of the fearsome Hundred-Handers brothers before and after the castration of Ouranos, and even after Zeus releases them (cf. 734–5 and 815–17) is notoriously vague.[11]

Ps.-Apollodorus' account of the birth and of the upbringing of Zeus in Crete corresponds in several details with that presupposed by Callimachus in his *Hymn to Zeus*, as well as by Aratus and Apollonius of Rhodes.[12] There is no hard evidence supporting West's suggestion that these details may constitute a further link with the Eudemian *Theogony*, though they do reappear in later Orphic tradition (for example in the *Rhapsodies*). The presence of all these details in Epimenides, the usual authority on Crete and

---

[8] See West (1983: 87, 102). West (1983: 124) attributes the omission of the Moirai to Ps.-Apollodorus' own intervention: it is remarkable that they are not mentioned in Proclus' summary of the beginning of the Cycle either. Dietze (1914: 536) had argued that Ps.-Apollodorus and Proclus represent the older version, attributing the insertion of the Moirai at this early stage to later 'Orphic' tradition.

[9] West (1983: 116–121) and *PEG* ii.1 F 21 and F 24.

[10] West (1983: 131), as an alternative to a derivation from its (entirely conjectural) presence in the 'Protogonos' *Theogony*.

[11] See Gigon (1961: xv). [12] See e.g. West (1983: 127–8).

Zeus, is uncertain, and the possibility that the Cyclic poem may have exerted its own influence, along with Epimenides, on Hellenistic poetry should not be ruled out.[13]

West's idea, therefore, that 'the author of the Cyclic version drew both [on the 'Protogonos' and the Eudemian *Theogony*] to produce a contaminated account'[14] has certainly something in its favour but, in view of the uncertainties mentioned above, should be regarded with caution. Finally, the poem must have undergone some editing when it became part of the Cycle, an event West would date to the early Hellenistic period.[15] The extent of this, again, is very uncertain. Even if obviously containing much older material, the *Theogony* in its edited form might have been one of the most recent poems in the Cycle.

TITANOMACHY[16]

Regarding the *Titanomachy* we move on slightly safer ground, inasmuch that at least its existence is certain. A handful of later sources record some details of its content, as well as quoting a very few lines.[17] Most of them refer to the *Titanomachy* as an anonymous poem, but the scholia on Apollonius of Rhodes *Arg.* 1.1165c (*PEG* F 3 = D., W.), and the source of Hyginus *fab.* 183 (*PEG* F 7 = F 4 D. = F 11 W.) attribute it to Eumelus of Corinth (thought by ancient sources to have been active in the eighth century)[18] as does Athenaeus (*PEG* F 6 = F 5 D. = F 8 W.), who once also playfully mentions its double ascription to Eumelus and Arctinus of Miletus (*PEG* T 2 = T 2 D. and *PEG* F 4 = F 8 D. = F 14 W.).[19] It was a poem in at least

---

[13] West (1983: 128) attributes the influence to the Eudemian *Theogony*. On Epimenides' influence, cf. West *loc. cit.*; Kaczyńska (1999); Mele (2001); Cozzoli (2006).

[14] West (1983: 128). Cf. 127 for possible speculative links to Orpheus' theogonic song in Ap. Rh. 1.496–511.

[15] West (1983: 129).

[16] See also Sommerstein, below in this volume, p. 463; Gärtner, below in this volume, p. 550.

[17] For recent accounts of the fragments see West (2002a: 110–18); Bremmer (2004: 35–41); Debiasi (2004: 71–108).

[18] Cf. D'Alessio (2009: 137–44).

[19] *PEG* F 6 (= F 5 D. = F 8 W.) is preserved only in the epitome of Athenaeus, and the addition in the margin of C of the alternative attribution to Arctinus may derive from a scribe familiar with the context of *PEG* F 4 (= F 8 D. = F 14 W.), rather than from independent access to a different shape of the text. On the playful introduction of the double ascription of *PEG* F 4 (= F 8 D. = F 14 W.) cf. Fraenkel on Aesch. *Ag.* 160. One of the first items in a list of epic poems possibly pertaining to the Cycle in the Borgia Table, one of the *Tabulae Iliacae*, is a -μαχία said not to have been the one composed by the otherwise unknown Telesis of Methymna (*Cyclus, PEG* T 2 = T 3 D.). The list is very fragmentary and problematic, but, given the extremely lacunose state

two books, and had a cosmogonic section where Aither was described as the origin of everything, perhaps without a consort (*PEG* F 1 = D., W.), and as father of Ouranos. This was in contradiction with the opening of the *Theogony* if we reconstruct it on the basis of Proclus and Ps.-Apollodorus. Such discrepancies between different poems are attested elsewhere within the Cycle. In this case, it is perhaps even conceivable that Book 1 of the *Titanomachy* may not have been included in the Cycle, since the matter was already covered by the *Theogony*.[20]

Ps.-Apollodorus' account of the war against the Titans may be based on this poem,[21] though it must be said that there is no certain coincidence with any of the peculiar details explicitly attributed to it by later sources. Indeed, on at least one detail Ps.-Apollodorus actually contradicts such evidence as we possess, and it is clear that he must have contaminated his account with other sources, be they the Cyclic *Theogony* or Hesiod. As we have seen, in the Cyclic *Theogony* the three Hundred-Handers were among the very first children of Ouranos and Ge, and according to Ps.-Apollodorus, and most other sources, including Hesiod, they were the most powerful allies of Zeus in his fight against the Titans. In the *Titanomachy* on the other hand, the most famous of them, Aigaion, also known as Briareus, is given a different genealogy, being a son of Ge and Pontos, and fights on the side of the Titans (*PEG* F 3 = D., W.), a version followed by Antimachus (F 14 Matthews), Virg. *Aen.* 10.565–8, and Stat. *Theb.* 2.596. Aigaion/Briareus played a prominent role also in another poem, on the history and myths of Corinth, the *Corinthiaca*, also attributed to Eumelus (*PEG* F 2 = F 12 D. = F 16* W.).[22] His allegiance to the Titans is also reflected in the link established between the cults in his honour attested at Chalcis and Carystos, in the island of Euboea, and in the appellative of Euboea as *Titanis*.[23] Differently from Ps.-Apollodorus' Cretan version, moreover, 'Eumelus' located Zeus' birthplace in Lydia (*PEG* F 18 = Eum. dub. F 4 D. = F 2 W.). This has been attributed to the *Titanomachy* by West (F 2), but the fact that Lydus

---

of the evidence, McLeod (1985) goes too far arguing that the list is certainly a fraud. Cazzaniga (1975) argues that Nic. *Ther.* 9–12 (on the birth of the snakes from the blood of the Titans: cf. possibly already Aesch. *Suppl.* 264–7; as noted by the scholiast, Acusilaus, *FgrHist* 2 F 14, linked them to the blood of Typhoeus, and Apoll.Rh. in his *Foundation of Alexandria*, *CA* F 4, to that of the Gorgon) attests an attribution of the poem to Hesiod in the early Hellenistic period.

[20] A similar possibility is envisaged regarding other Cyclic poems (after Monro) by Burgess (2001: 30–33). If this was the case, we should assume either that the book was fairly short, or that the narrative was much more detailed than in Hesiod.

[21] See Gigon (1961: xvi); West (1983: 126) and West (2002a: 114).

[22] There is no positive reason to believe that *Titanomachy PEG* F falsum 16 (on which see Debiasi 2004: 85–7) derives from our poem.

[23] Cf. the relevant sources in Bremmer (2004: 37); Debiasi (2004: 84).

(*de mensibus* 4.71) refers to this as ἐν ἱστορίαι suggests access to a prose work, such as the epitome of the *Corinthiaca* current in later ages, rather than to our poem.[24] Anyway, according to Ps.-Apollodorus, in order to release his allies from the Tartarus, Zeus has to fight the dragon Kampe (the Worm), an episode elaborated by Nonnus *Dion.* 18.235–64, that may well derive from the *Titanomachy*,[25] as might the fact that the Cyclopes gave three different weapons to Zeus, Poseidon and Pluto,[26] *and* the division of the world among the three brothers by lots at the end of the war, an Iliadic motif (15.185–93) with Near-Eastern parallels.[27] If this was the case, Callimachus' polemics against this version in his *Hymn to Zeus* 60–7 may very well be aimed in the first place at the fully fledged story of the Cyclic poem, rather than at the more casual Iliadic mention.[28]

The attribution of other details to the poem is even more conjectural and uncertain. From an ancient commentary on Virg. *Aen.* 6.580 (that does not mention either Eumelus or the *Titanomachy*) West argued that in the poem the Titan Hyperion remained neutral, and that *PEG* F 7 (= F 4 D. = F 11 W.) and *PEG* F 8 (= F 7 D. = F 10 W.) on the four-team horse-chariot of Helios and on the cauldron in which the god crosses the Ocean at night (apparently the earliest attestation for both) refer in fact to him, though in the *Corinthiaca* (*PEG* F 3.3 = F 2 D. = F 17.3 W.) Helios is the *son* of Hyperion.[29] It is not unlikely that Prometheus played an important role in the poem, and it has been conjectured that some details of the background of the *Prometheus Bound* may go back to it, though no preserved source explicitly connects him to our *Titanomachy*.[30]

Only three verbatim quotations, for a grand total of five lines, are certainly attributed to the poem. *PEG* F 11 (= F 6 D. = F 13 W.) dwells on the justice of the centaur Chiron. According to **PEG F 10 (= F 9 D. = F 12 W.)**, which has

---

[24] But cf. West (2002a: 118 n. 44), who, very tentatively, mentions the possibility that the prose paraphrase may have included the *Titanomachy* as well.
[25] Gigon (1961: xvi); Gerbeau and Vian (1992: 26–9); West (2002a: 115).
[26] Gigon (1961: xvi); West (2002a: 115).
[27] Gigon (1961: xvi); Janko on *Il.* 15.185–93 (who attributes this to the Orphic *Theogonies* too, with reference to F 56 Kern: as far as I can see, though, there seems to be no evidence for the casting of the lots in that tradition); West (2002a: 115–16).
[28] For possible echoes of the Cyclic *Theogony* in the same poem, cf. above, pp. 201–2.
[29] West (2002a: 112, 116).
[30] West (2002a: 113–14); S. West (1994: 145–9). The latter conjectures that the *Titanomachy* also featured a universal flood, another Near-Eastern motif (for which see also Bremmer 2004: 41 n. 39, with further bibliography). Entirely conjectural is also Debiasi's attribution (2004: 74–81) to the *Titanomachy* of one or both of the *aetia* about the Titans on Cercyra in Ap. Rh. 4.982–92, partly based on the circumstance that the archaic sculptures of the pediments of the local temple of Artemis may be read, in part or as a whole, as referring to the fight between Zeus and the Titans.

been attributed to a *Gigantomachy* (probably by a mere slip), he was born to the daughter of Ocean Philyra, with whom Cronus had mated in the shape of a horse. Clement of Alexandria quotes two lines which he found in the early second-century grammarian Hermippus of Berytus, who mentioned Chiron as an example of a 'wise' (σοφός) man that had instructed mankind in the understanding of the natural world. The text of the quotation has been frequently disputed:

> εἴς τε δικαιοσύνην θνητῶν γένος ἤγαγε δείξας
> ὅρκους καὶ θυσίας ἱλαρὰς καὶ σχήματ' Ὀλύμπου
>
> and he led the human race toward justice, showing oaths, and cheerful/ ingratiating (ἱλαράς) sacrifices, and the figures (σχήματα) of Olympus.

Both the adjective modifying 'sacrifices' and the final noun have been rightly suspected. The former, not attested before the late fifth century, would not be out of place in a text from the Imperial period, especially from a Christian author, but sits uneasily in an archaic text. The likeliest correction is provided by Köchly's ἱεράς, 'sacred'.[31] The 'figures of Olympus' are even more problematic. The noun is not certainly attested before the fifth century and its astronomical meaning only much later.[32] A neat and economical solution is provided by Teuffel's σήματα, which finds a good parallel already in *Il.* 13.242–4, where Zeus shakes his lightning 'from splendid Olympus, showing a sign to mortals' (ἀπ' αἰγλήεντος Ὀλύμπου δεικνὺς σῆμα βροτοῖσιν). Signs such as this one are frequently sent to mortals by Zeus in the Homeric poems, and their correct interpretation is an important prerequisite for pious behaviour (cf. e.g. *Il.* 4.381, with 405–9).

PEG F 4 (= F 8 D. = F 14 W.) is an enigmatic and graceful description of fish playing and swimming in an unspecified location (ἐν... αὐτῆι) through 'immortal water', quoted by Athenaeus from Book 2 of the poem to illustrate the sense of the adjective *elloi*, taken as a shortened form of the traditional

---

[31] See e.g. Ar. *Pax* 397. Ar. *Ran.* 455 provides a very good example for the corruption of ἱερόν (confirmed by a Hellenistic inscription) into ἱλαρόν (a correction wrongly considered 'palaeographically unconvincing and even more trivial than the MSS reading' in our passage by Lebedev (1998: 7)). Lebedev's own radical rewriting of the fragment, with ἰαχὰς κωρχήματ(α), followed by Debiasi (2004: 90 and n. 150), is entirely arbitrary, and implies that Hermippus already had a corrupt text in front of him.

[32] For this reason Gigon (1961: xix–xx) argued that the quotation was a forgery. The term *dikaiosynē* too points toward a later age (thanks to G. Ucciardello for drawing my attention to this point). The only other occurrence of the term in the 'archaic' epic *corpus* is in one of the hexameter *dicta* attributed in *Certamen* 168 (Allen), in a section sometimes attributed to Alcidamas himself; for its occurrence in Theogn. 147 (attributed also to Phocylides) cf. Kroll (1936: 213–22); Gagarin (1974: 194 n. 59).

ἔλλοπες, also used of fish at Soph. *Aj.* 1297, and as an example of Sophocles' fondness for the Epic Cycle:[33]

> ἐν δ' αὐτῆι πλωτοὶ χρυσώπιδες ἰχθύες ἐλλοί
> νήχοντες παίζουσι δι' ὕδατος ἀμβροσίοιο

> and in it there float gold-coloured fish, that swim and sport though the ambrosial water.

The present tense is used, which suggests either a direct speech, an *ekphrasis topou*, or the description of an object.[34] All other occurrences of ἀμβρόσιον ὕδωρ refer to fresh, drinking water,[35] which makes a reference to the sea or the flood unlikely.[36] A λίμνη sounds more probable,[37] but a κρήνη 'spring' or a ῥοή 'stream' would be possible too. Many scenarios are theoretically available and it may be worth pointing out that the *Titanomachy* also mentioned the golden apples of the Hesperides (*PEG* F 9 = F 10 D. = F 9 W.), whose garden famously also featured ἀμβρόσιαι κρῆναι 'immortal springs' (Eur. *Hipp.* 748).[38] Philodemus' text, to which we owe the reference, is lacunose but compatible with the possibility that in the poem the apples were guarded by a snake,[39] and, in consideration of the tragedian's alleged fondness for these lines, we may even toy with the idea that Sophocles' (*TrGF* F 226, from his *Heracles*) τρέφουσι κρήνης φύλακα, χωρίτην ὄφιν ('they nourish the spring's guardian, a rustic snake') may look back to them.

Athenaeus identifies the 'gold-coloured' fish of these lines with the well-known χρύσοφρυς (thought to correspond to our 'gilt-head bream'). This may be no more than the effect of a fanciful association between similarly sounding adjectives. It is intriguing, though, that Athenaeus himself (71b) quotes an excerpt from the second book of the *Memoirs* of Ptolemy VIII of Egypt (*FgrH* 234 F 1) on the variety of fish (including the *chrysophrys*) that abounds in the Lethon, a little river of the Cyrenaica, near Berenice: this

---

[33] In consideration of this it may be interesting to point at the possible link between πλωτοί... ἰχθύες and Soph. *TrGF* F 941.9 ἰχθύων πλωτῶι γένει, though the adjective is fairly commonly used, also in later prose, in order to indicate swimming animals in general.

[34] In this case the use of the present would imply that the object is still in existence, and therefore, most probably, the stable possession of a god: see West (2002a: 118 n. 41), with previous bibliography.

[35] See the "Homeric" hymn εἰς ξένους ap. Ps.-Herod. *Vit. Hom.* 9, Pind. F 198b; Panyass. 2.2 for ἄμβροτον ὕδωρ; cf. also Theocr. 11.48–9.

[36] Sea: Debiasi (2004: 99), and already Müller (1829: 54) and Kranz (1960: 482); flood: Bremmer (2004: 41 n. 39), with reference to Bremmer (1998: 44).

[37] West (2002a: 118).

[38] For fish (sacred and not) in sacred springs and streams, see Lightfoot on Luc. *De dea Syr.* 45 and Frazer on Paus. 7.22.4.

[39] Cf. e.g. Huxley (1969: 27).

same river is mentioned by Pliny (*Nat. hist.* 5.31) in very close proximity to the Gardens of the Hesperides: *nec procul ante oppidum (Berenicen) fluvius Lethon, lucus sacer, ubi horti memorantur* 'and not far away from the town (*sc.* of Berenice) there is the river Lethon, and a sacred grove, where there the Gardens (*sc.* of the Hesperides) are said to have been', and by Lucan, in whose text the river Lethon (said to flow from the underworld), and the by then deserted Garden of the Hesperides appear in the same sequence, in immediate proximity (9.355–8).[40]

The mention of the Golden Apples, as well as of the cauldron of the Sun, has suggested to several scholars the possibility that the poem may have included a section on Heracles, but it is not difficult to envisage different contexts (cf., for example, Hes. *Theog.* 215–16 and 334–5, where the Hesperides, the Golden Apples and the snake guarding them are mentioned within genealogical sequences).[41]

PEG F 6 (= F 5 D. = F 8 W.) is quoted, again, by Athenaeus, in a section on the importance of dance that also provides a short list of passages introducing dancing gods:

μέσσοισιν δ' ὠρχεῖτο πατὴρ ἀνδρῶν τε θεῶν τε

and among them danced the father of men and gods.

Athenaeus provides no context. Gigon's hypothesis that this might refer to the dance of Zeus among the Couretes would be attractive, if it were not for the incongruous application of the traditional formula 'father of men and gods' to the divine 'boy' (κοῦρος).[42] It is altogether more probable that it belonged to a description of the festive celebration following the victory over the Titans, as most scholars since Welcker have assumed. Later authors report that Apollo and Athena took part in these celebrations.[43] Strictly speaking, however, chronology and genealogy would not allow the presence

---

[40] On the various traditions regarding the river Lethon and the nearby Garden of the Hesperides, cf. Desanges (1980: 358–60). Tsagalis (2013: 40–4) sticks to the old interpretations of the lines of the *Titanomachy* as referring to fish in the sea, drawing on arguments I do not find convincing.

[41] Detailed discussion in D'Alessio (2014). For two divergent approaches cf. Debiasi (2004: 94–104) and West (2002a: 113, 116 n. 30). I find no compelling reason for attributing fragments PEG F °12–°14 (on the descendants of Atlas) to the *Titanomachy* rather than to any other archaic genealogical poem and/or to other Cyclic poems.

[42] Gigon (1961: xix).

[43] See Dion. Hal. *Ant. Rom.* 7.72.7 (Athena and the pyrrhic dance; for the confusion with the Gigantomachy see Ceccarelli 1998: 29–30); Tib. 2.5.9–10 and Sen. *Ag.* 332–334 (Apollo played and sang on the occasion); Diod. Sic. 6.4 ap. Tert. *de corona* 7 does not provide the name of the other gods celebrating Zeus. Cf. Kranz (1960: 482); also Lebedev (1998: 4) and West (2002a: 116 n. 28), who do not raise the chronological problem.

of the younger gods on the occasion. Other sources mention similar songs and dances following the victory over the Giants.[44] It seems that the motif of the epinician dance was applied by poets to both events, but we should hardly expect that it might have occurred twice in the same poem. The mention of Apollo and Athena in a Titanomachy context can be explained, following F. Vian, with the terminological overlap by which, already in the fifth century, the term 'Titans' was also applied to the Giants, as it emerges from the references to the iconography of the Panathenaic *peplos* in Eur. *Hec.* 472 and *I. T.* 224.[45] This, of course, would not imply that in the *Titanomachy* Athena or Apollo actually took part in the fight against Cronus and his brothers, nor that the poem featured also a Gigantomachy, a theme destined to a much greater fortune both in later literature and in the visual arts.[46]

On the other hand, a piece of evidence which has come to light only relatively recently, shows that the situation might have been more complicated and blurred already in the first half of the fifth century. A papyrus first published in 1976 preserves a fragment of an erudite mythological treatise, probably a passage of the famous work *On Gods* of Apollodorus of Athens (second century BC), discussing the origin of some epithets of Athena.[47] This includes a quotation of a few lines from a lost play of Epicharmus (PCG fr. 135), who explained the epithet Pallas with the first act she accomplished after her birth out of the head of Zeus, when the goddess killed a Pallas, flayed his corpse, and used his skin for self-protection. This story was already known thanks to other sources (*Et. Gen.* s. v. 'Παλλάς', Ps.-Apollod. *Bibl.* 1.37), who make this Pallas the son of one of the Titans, or a giant. The text of Epicharmus, however, not only shows that the episode was current already at this early date, but also locates it ἐν μάχαι τᾶι γενομέναι κατὰ Κρόνον ('in the battle that took place at the time of Cronus'), implying that, even if Pallas had been considered a Giant (according to the most common story Titans are immortals: they are punished, but not killed), the event was considered part of the same war. This cannot be explained simply as the

---

[44] See above all Eur. *Her.* 177–80; see also Pamprepius F 4.13 Livrea. Vian (1952: 210–14).
[45] See von Wilamowitz-Moellendorff (1929a: 43); Vian (1952: 173–4, who notes how the incongruence had even been flagged up in the scholia on the *Hecuba* passage), with indications of later instances of the overlap. The solution of Stamatopoulou (2012), according to whom these two passages would reveal the mythological incompetence of the characters, and who neglects some of the evidence discussed here, is, in my opinion, not convincing.
[46] Against this possibility, see Vian (1952). If the poem did include a section (be it a proper part of the sequence or a digression) on Heracles (which is far from certain: see above, p. 207), a mention of the Giants might have found place there.
[47] Koenen and Merkelbach (1976). I am grateful to L. Battezzato for discussing this with me.

consequence of a terminological overlap, and suggests that by at least this period, the two episodes were imagined as being closely and chronologically linked.[48]

This is a necessary premise to introduce a discussion of the only papyrus fragment that has been attributed to our poem. This is a strip with twenty-one fragmentary hexameters of unknown provenance (attributed to the first/second century AD), purchased by J. Rendel Harris in Egypt and transcribed with a few supplements and no commentary at all by John Enoch Powell in 1936, as *PHarr* (1.)3.[49] In his review of Powell's volume Bruno Snell pointed out that the archaic epic formula νεφεληγε[ρέτα Ζεύς 'cloud-gatherer Zeus', supplemented by Powell at line 2, was not used by poets later than Hesiod,[50] and reported Paul Maas' opinion that the verses may portray a Titanomachy, based on Snell's own supplement of the end of line 3 as Τιτῆνα μέ[γιστον ('very great Titan').[51] The attribution was subsequently dubiously accepted by A. Körte,[52] and, without any sign of doubt, by Bernabé (*Tit. PEG* F 5):[53]

---

[48] There is no evidence that the Cyclic *Titanomachy* covered also the battle against Typhoeus. Tsagalis (2013) argues that it did, mainly based on Σ Opp. *Hal.* 3.17, where the god Pan is described as 'saviour of Zeus'. There are no reliable editions of the scholia on Oppian, whose very recent origin is not a matter of dispute. As printed in current editions this garbled text reads: τῆι Τιτανομαχίαι λέγει, ὅτ' ἐκεραύνωσε τὸν Τυφῶνα ἀπατηθέντα ὑπ' αὐτοῦ τοῦ Πανός (literally: 'he says in the Titanomachy, when <Zeus> struck with his thunderbolt Typhon, who had been deceived by Pan himself'). However we restore the wording, it should be clear that the subject of 'says' must be Oppian (whose text the scholiast wants to elucidate), not another unnamed poet. According to the scholiast, Oppian calls Pan 'saviour of Zeus' because of his help in the fight against the Titans. The term 'Titanomachy' here does not refer to a poem, but to the mythical episode of the Battle against the Titans as e.g. in Ps.-Apollodorus *Bibl.* 1.2.3; note also that Typhoeus is considered as a Titan by the scholiast on the *Halieutica* passage (a very unusual definition of the monster), a fact that explains why he calls his fight with Zeus 'Titanomachy'. The scholiast provides the background details of the story (known from various sources) with the information available to him, and there is no reason to attribute any of this specifically to our poem. It goes without saying, of course, that if the *Titanomachy* dealt also with the Giants (which is uncertain) some sort of narrative about Typhoeus would be expected, but we know nothing about its possible content, and it would be incautious to attribute on the basis of the Oppian scholion the much later attested story of Pan's involvement to the Cyclic poem.

[49] Powell (1936). Cf. the interview with J.E. Powell published by *The Times Higher Educational Supplement* 1 September 1995. I have examined the fragment in the Cadbury Research Library at Birmingham in December 2011.

[50] As far as I can see this is not entirely exact, given its occurrence at Nonn. *Dion.* 8.270. Anyway, its almost exclusive confinement to archaic poetry remains noteworthy.

[51] Snell (1937: 579).

[52] A. Körte in *APF* 13 (1938): 80; cf. also Debiasi (2004: 74 n. 23).

[53] The text printed above is the one offered by Bernabé, from which I diverge in several points (see below, pp. 210–12).

```
                    ]νεκ[      ].ο.[
                    ]ς νεφεληγε[ρέτα Ζεύς
                    ].Τιτῆνα μέ[γιστον
                    ]βαλέοντι ἐο[ικώς.
              ἔχαιρ]ε μέγα φρεσί[ν ᾗσιν                    5
                    ]ντορα Φοῖβον[
                 π]ροσέφη.ευ[
                    ]φα οὔ κράτυς[
                    ]ς θ' ἵσταται.[
              δρι]μὺν χόλον[                               10
                    ]τα γε σθεν.[
                    ]ενει.απε.[
                    ]ες ἔργον δ' α[
                    ]πάντες δ[
                    ]αντη[                                 15
                    ]νωνυ[
                    ].γαπα[
                    ]σπλη[
                    ]ν ἀδικο[
                    ]σεν.[                                 20
                    ].αναֽ[
```

Regarding his supplement, Snell also mentioned the possibility of a form of τιταίνειν 'to stretch' as an alternative, to be assessed on the basis of the preceding traces in the papyrus, since only an augmented form of the verb would be compatible with Hermann's Bridge, which forbids end of word between the two short syllables of the fourth foot of the hexameter. The traces in question (end of a descending diagonal, not reaching the base of the line) do seem to rule out ἐτίτην(α-[), but the metrical issue does not clinch the question. In fact Hermann's Bridge may be infringed at least once, if not twice in the preserved lines: at line 5, if we accept, as Snell did,[54] Powell's μέγα φρεσ[ὶν ᾗσιν 'great(ly) in his mind', and at line 16, where my reading of the papyrus makes a form such as μο]νώνυχ[ες ἵπποι 'horses with uncloven hoof', however declined, all but unavoidable.[55] In

---

[54] Snell (1937: 579 n. 2). If we accept this supplement, the preceding word must end with a long α: an interesting possibility, in this case, could be θε]ὰ (see the probable mention of Hera at l. 7, with Perale's supplement discussed below).

[55] The traces of the last letter, unnoticed by Powell, show the start of two strokes at different height. The only preserved chi (line 10) is different in shape, but I cannot think of any convincing alternative. Perale suggests a form of νώνυμ[νος but this does not seem to account for the upper trace. Alternative articulations, such as]νω νυχ[, are very unlikely. This would be

consideration of βαλέοντι 'shooting' in the following line a form of the verb often used in reference to the bending of the bow would not be out of place (e.g. a form of τιτηνάμενος). Anyway Snell's articulation does retain a certain degree of plausibility, even if many other alternatives are available for the end of the line (purely *exempli gratia*: μέ[νοντ-, με[λαθρ-, μέ[δοντ-, forms of the aorist of μεθίημι, or of μεγαίρω, ἀμέ[γαρτ- or even simply μὲ[ν – x, with punctuation before Τιτῆνα). The general context is unclear: at line 4 βαλέοντι ἐο[ικώς 'like one who shoots', with its future participle suggests that somebody is described as being in the pose of threatening to throw, as is indeed the case in *Od.* 11.608 (Heracles in the Underworld, αἰεὶ β. ἐ.). The *iunctura* with a dative form of the participle followed by ἐοικώς at the end of the line is attested in *ekphraseis*[56] and short similes. At line 7 π]ροσέφη introduces a direct speech, and the best supplement for the end of the line the line seems to me Perale's λευ[κώλενος Ἥρη.[57] In the second half of the following line the words οὗ κράτος [looks like a modification of the epic

---

the only poetic occurrence of the adjective, usually substituted by the artificial μώνυχες 'with uncloven hoof'. It is, of course, also possible that in any one of these three lines (3, 5 and 16) the alignment may be misleading, and that the preserved portion of text is to be located immediately after the central caesura rather than closer to the end of the lines (for example with μέγα φρεσ[ὶ πευκαλίμῃσι 'great(ly) in his sharp mind' in line 5: note that μετὰ is not a possible reading). In this case no infringement of Hermann's Bridge would be involved.

This is a possible outline of the syllables missing at the end of the lines that lend themselves to such an analysis (based on the assumption that, unless explicitly mentioned, these lines did not have a spondaic fifth foot): 2: 3 syllables; 3: 2 syllables; 4: 1 syllable; 5: 3 (the iota is not preserved), infringing Hermann's Bridge, or 6 syllables; 6: 0 or 3 syllables; 7: 0 (?) or 5 syllables; 8: 2 or 5 syllables; 9: 2 or 5 syllables; 10: 2 (with 5 we would have a division into two equal halves); 11: 2 (with, e.g., σθένε[ϊ ᾧ or σθένο[ς ἵππων) or 5 syllables; 13: with 4 syllables missing (if –ες belongs to a separate word) we would have a bipartite hexameter, with 1 syllable missing an extremely unlikely spondaic fifth foot whose end would coincide with that of a word of two syllables (cf. West (1982: 37 n. 13): no examples): we should articulate ἐς ἔργον, following the third-foot caesura, with (regularly) postponed δ' α[, or, perhaps even articulating δα[-, and followed by 4 syllables; 16: 3, infringing Hermann's Bridge, or 6 syllables; 19: 1 or 3 syllables. All in all, both line 7 and line 13 decidedly look as if their preserved portion corresponds to the position immediately following the third-foot caesura, and this might have been the case for other lines too (in particular for lines 5 and 16).

[56] For the future participle, see also Ps.-Hes. *Scut.* 215, and also (with ἔοικε) Asclepiades or Archelaus *Anth. Plan.* 120.3 and Posidippus 63.7 A.-B.

[57] I am grateful to Marco Perale, who will include this fragment in his forthcoming edition of *adespota* hexameter fragments, for communicating this supplement to me. Snell's δ' is very unlikely: in all their formulaic occurrences the forms of προσέφη are always preceded by the direct object, and by a participle referring to the subject, making the position of the supplemented conjunction very unlikely here. On the other hand, if the uncertain letter could be reconciled with a ζ (which I very much doubt; anyway, no other zeta is preserved for comparison), Ζεὺ[ς e.g. τερπικέραυνος might provide a suitable subject, with a variation avoiding repetition of the formula used in line 2, but lambda fits the traces much better.

formulas τοῦ/οὗ/ὅ τε/γὰρ κράτος ἐστὶ (μέγιστον), and καὶ ὅου/εὖ κράτος ἐστὶ μέγιστον, often applied to Zeus in archaic poetry.[58] In this case, this line might have expanded upon the description of the Zeus, if he was indeed introduced as a speaker in the previous one, rather than being the first line of a speech.

The appearance of Phoebus at line 6[59] suggests that this might not have been actually a description of a Titanomachy *stricto sensu*, an event by whose time Apollo was not yet born. The description of the fight between Athena and Pallas in Epicharmus *PCG* 135, however, should warn against ruling out this possibility too firmly. All in all, anyway, the attribution of this fragment to the Cyclic *Titanomachy* should be considered with much caution. Possible alternative contexts would include, for example (if, indeed, a Titan was mentioned at all), an Orphic poem with Zeus entrusting to Apollo the remains of Dionysus dismembered by the Titans, or a poem featuring terminological overlap between Giants and Titans.[60] If the context was that of a battle of the gods against some supernatural or divine adversary, the use of a form of the adjective ἄδικος 'unrighteous' at line 19 would be interesting *per se*, as the word is notoriously absent in the Homeric poems, coming to the fore in Hesiod's *Works and Days*, in the *Catalogue* (mostly in contexts related to Zeus) and in the *Homeric Hymns*.[61]

---

[58] This implies that the word preceding it must have been felt as part of the second *colon*, unless we want to attribute to our poet a gauche division of the hexameter into two equal parts.

[59] If we suppose that one foot and a half are missing at the end of the line (see above, n. 55), the simple ἀμύ]ντορα 'defender' should be considered a possible alternative to Snell's ἐπαμύντορα.

[60] See above, p. 208. A reference to the Sun as 'Titan' may seem incompatible with an archaic date of the poem, but cf. possibly already Empedocles, VS 31B38.6, with Kranz (1961: 291) and Kingsley (1995: 26), and see above, p. 204, on the possibility that in this poem the Sun may be Hyperion rather than his son; but see also Kranz (1961: 291). The sequence δρι]μὺν χόλον 'bitter anger' at line 10 is noticeable, as the *iunctura* occurs elsewhere only twice: once (at the nominative) in *Il.* 18.322 (of a lion to whom Achilles is compared), and then at Call. F 380 Pf. (of a dog to whom Archilochus is compared). On the other hand the adjective δριμεῖα modifies the noun χολή 'bile' frequently enough, especially in medical texts (but cf. also Theocr. 1.18).

[61] For a list of occurrences, see Gagarin (1974: 188–9).

12 | *Oedipodea*

ETTORE CINGANO

Being placed after a *Theogony* and/or a *Titanomachy* which dealt with cosmic forces and battles between divinities, the *Oedipodea* was the first poem of the epic cycle to deal with stories of heroes. In this respect, it can safely be taken as the opening poem not just of the Theban cycle, but of the entire thematic and chronological sequel which covered four generations of heroes (five, if one includes Laius), starting with Oedipus in the Theban epics, and ending with Telemachus and Telegonus, the sons of one of the main heroes in the Trojan epics, Odysseus. Three generations of heroes out of four were covered by the Theban cycle, in spite of the smaller number of poems involved in the narrative, whereas the Trojan cycle covered only two generations: in fact, the third generation was shared by both traditions, since some of the heroes who conquered Thebes in the expedition of the Epigonoi set off to Troy a few years later. In the construction of the epic cycle the wars at Thebes and at Troy took place in the span of a few years; they were welded into one sequential string of events, according to the *akolouthia tōn pragmatōn* (Phot. *Bibl.* 319a 30);[1] the manufacture was effected probably by the Alexandrian grammarians but may have started even earlier, in pre-Hellenistic times, in the milieu of the school of Aristotle at Athens, although no piece of evidence remains to corroborate this possibility.[2]

In spite of the great popularity enjoyed from the archaic age throughout antiquity by the myths of Oedipus and of the Seven against Thebes and the Epigonoi, the precise sequence of events and the handling of characters and episodes in the Theban epics are difficult to reconstruct. The fragments of the *Oedipodea* and of the *Epigonoi* in particular are very scanty to say the least: altogether they amount to less than ten with only three verbatim fragments totalling four lines. Besides, differently from the poems of the Trojan cycle, no prose summary has survived from the second-century AD grammarian (or fifth-century AD Neoplatonist) named Proclus – who was drawing on an older source – recalling the main episodes in each poem.[3] Originally a précis

---

[1] On which see Introduction, above in this volume, pp. 1–2, 9, 32, and Fantuzzi, below, pp. 419–20.
[2] On this issue see, most recently, Burgess (2001: 12–33); West (2013: 21–5); West, above in this volume, pp. 104–5, and Introduction, above, pp. 29–30.
[3] For Proclus' summaries, see Introduction, above in this volume, p. 000.

of each poem of the Theban epics was also available, as can easily be inferred from the introductory statement by Proclus in the summary of the first poem of the Trojan cycle, the *Cypria* (arg. lines 80–1 Severyns): Ἐπιβάλλει τούτοις τὰ λεγόμενα Κύπρια ἐν βιβλίοις φερόμενα ἕνδεκα ('this is succeeded by the so-called *Cypria*, transmitted in 11 books'); τούτοις here cannot but refer to the *Epigonoi*, the last poem of the Theban cycle preceding the *Cypria* in the narrative of events.[4] But the summary of the Theban epics was dropped by Photius, who was only interested in the Trojan sequence of events.

AUTHORSHIP

The poem is variously quoted by the few extant sources as ἡ Οἰδιπόδεια, ἡ Οἰδιποδία and τὰ Οἰδιπόδια, a title indicating that it was centred on the deeds of Oedipus. Although the Theban epics were closely connected in matters of content, the *Oedipodea* seems to have been a self-contained poem, independent from the *Thebaid* and from the *Epigonoi*. It is never associated with them, and – differently from these two poems – it was ascribed by one source to another epic poet than Homer, Cinaethon of Lacedaemon; the name occurs in an inscription in the *Tabula Borgiana* (*IG* xiv.1292 = *SEG* 35.1044 = *Tab. Il.* 10K Sadurska, first century AD), whose panels are the only ones to draw mainly on Theban mythology amongst the series of pinakes of early Imperial age known as *Tabulae Iliacae*: καὶ τ]ὴν Οἰδιπόδειαν τὴν ὑπὸ Κιναίθωνος τοῦ [Λακεδαιμονίου πεποιημένην προαναγνόν]τες ἐπῶν οὖσαν ͵ϛχ´ ὑποθήσομεν Θηβαΐδα... ('reading first the *Oedipodea* [that was composed] by Cinaethon [the Lacedaemonian] in 6,600 verses we will put down the *Thebaid*').[5] Elsewhere Cinaethon is qualified as Lacedaemonian, and credited with the authorship of other poems such as the *Ilias parva*, a *Heraclea*, genealogical epics and, according to Eusebius, the *Telegony* (Cinaeth. *PEG* T 2 = T 1 D., p. 250 W.; see also *PEG* F 1–7 = F 1–5 D., W.).

Whatever one makes of the attribution to Cinaethon, the dating before the middle of the eighth century BC by Eusebius is too early: the date and

---

[4] At the beginning of the summary of the *Iliou persis* by Proclus a nearly identical expression, ἕπεται δὲ τούτοις, refers to the preceding poem, the *Ilias parva*; the same applies to συνάπτει δὲ τούτοις ('this is succeeded by...'), referring to the *Iliou persis* at the beginning of the summary of the *Nostoi*: see Welcker (1882: 499); Introduction, above in this volume, pp. 2, 32.

[5] The fillings in the lacuna are conjectured by West (2013: 3). The scepticism expressed by McLeod (1985: 157–63) on the reliability of the information conveyed by the Borgia plaque has been convincingly countered by the accurate analysis of Valenzuela Montenegro (2004: 377–80); Squire (2011: 44–7, 99, 192).

place of composition of the poem remain very uncertain, and the attempts by Bethe to posit a Boeotian origin rest on thin ground.[6] It can only be noted that the *Oedipodea* was the only poem of the Theban cycle centred mainly on Thebes and its territory, although no specific element points to a Boeotian origin. A tenuous Boeotian connection attesting the circulation of the *Oedipodea* in the first half of the fifth century BC can be posited, if one considers that at that time the final battle between Eteocles and Polynices at Thebes was represented by the painter Onasias on a wall of the temple of Athena Areia at Plataea, in Boeotia (Paus. 9.4.1–2). According to Pausanias (9.5.11), Onasias painted the queen mother bent down with grief because of the fight between her children, and named her Euryganeia, corresponding to the second wife of Oedipus in the *Oedipodea* (*PEG* F 2 = D., 1 W.).

THE STORY

The Borgia plaque states that the poem was of considerable length: 6,600 lines, more than half of the *Odyssey*. Since the *Certamen Homeri et Hesiodi* (= *Theb. PEG* T 4 = 2 D.) states that the *Thebaid* and the *Epigonoi* numbered 7,000 lines each, altogether, the Theban epics totalled more than 20,000 lines. As far as we can surmise from the titles, each poem of the Theban epics dealt with one generation of the family of Oedipus, the Labdacids.[7] In the absence of a prose summary by Proclus and given the paucity of fragments, the possibility of working out a more fully fledged account of the *Oedipodea* depends on the degree of authenticity and archaic flavour one is willing to see in the lengthy account found in the final scholium to Euripides' *Phoenissae*, whose authorship is ascribed to one Pisander at the beginning and at the end of the scholium (Σ Eur. *Phoen.* 1760 = Pisander, *FgrHist* 16 F 10). In particular, before relating diffusely the discovery of Oedipus' incest, the scholium connects the arrival of the Sphinx at Thebes with the sexual crime perpetrated by Laius, the unlawful rape of Chrysippus, which the Thebans left unpunished; it may also have motivated the fate impending over Laius, were he ever to have a child. Scholarly opinion on the reliability of the scholium as a source of the *Oedipodea* and on the identification of

---

[6] See Bethe (1891a: 142–6); the same applies to the possibility, suggested by Legras (1905: 53), that the poem had a Corinthian origin.

[7] For different attempts to reconstruct the plot of the poem see for example Welcker (1882: 313–19); Severyns (1928: 211–16); Deubner (1942: 27–38); de Kock (1961: 15–18); Davies (1989c: 19–22); for a broader and updated account of the early story of Oedipus see Gantz (1993: 488–502).

Pisander has varied considerably since the interpretation offered by Welcker and Bethe, who were willing to use it as a source for the *Oedipodea*.[8] After the criticism expressed by Robert and the reconstruction put forward by Jacoby regarding Pisander, it is now commonly believed that the scholium, albeit containing very small amounts of information which can be traced back to the *Oedipodea*, rather consists in a multilayered account compiled from several (tragic and mythographical) sources and assembled by a Hellenistic mythographer named Pisander.[9]

Leaving aside Pisander, it can safely be conjectured that the *Oedipodea* dealt with the birth of Oedipus and his exposition on Mount Cithaeron; although nothing is known regarding the role of Delphi or of the seer Teiresias in the poem, it must also have mentioned the earlier oracular response, released to his father Laius, that the birth of a son would prove fatal for him.[10] Surely the *Oedipodea* narrated at length the killing of Laius at the hands of Oedipus at a three-way crossroads in the Phocis, his arrival at Thebes and the subsequent victory over the Sphinx who had settled on a hill nearby, and was destroying the lives of many; the killing (or suicide) of the Sphinx must have been followed by the incestuous marriage of Oedipus to his unrecognized mother, named Jocaste or Epicaste (as in *Od.* 11.271; cf. Σ Eur. *Phoen.* 13; Ps.-Apollod. *Bibl.* 3.5.7), which granted him access to the throne of Thebes. When Oedipus' parricide and incest were unveiled his mother committed suicide, leaving the way open at some point for Oedipus' second marriage to a woman named Euryganeia, the daughter of Hyperphas (see *PEG* F 2 = D., 1 W.);[11] she bore four children by him, Eteocles, Polynices, Ismene and Antigone.

---

[8] This view is still shared by Bernabé, who (although cautiously) places the Pisander scholium before the fragments of the *Oedipodea* and takes it as an epitome of the poem, with the addition of later sources. It should be recalled that the account of the scholium shows inconsistencies which undermine the unity of the narrative.

[9] On the *Phoenissae* scholium and the *Oedipodea*, and on the attribution to Pisander, see especially Welcker (1865: 91–5); Bethe (1891a: 4–12); Wecklein (1901 : 667–74); Robert (1915: 149–67); Kirchhoff (1917: 128–36); Jacoby, Kommentar ad *FgrHist* F 16, 493–4; 544–7; R. Keydell, *RE* s.v. 'Peisandros', cols. 144–7; Deubner (1942: 3–27); de Kock (1962: 15–37); Valgiglio (1963: 154–66); Mastronarde (1994: 31–6); Lloyd-Jones (2002: 2–10); Sewell-Rutter (2008: 61–5); Ceccarelli (2014: 15–19).

[10] The fact that the Theban seer Teiresias is first attested in a key role in connection with Odysseus in the Trojan epics (see *Od.* 10.492, *passim*) attests to the archaicity of his status and presence in the Theban epics (see also 'Epigonoi', below in this volume, p. 251).

[11] The name of her father is Periphas in Pherec. *EGM* F 95; in Σ Eur. *Phoen.* 53 the remark that according to some she was the sister of Jocaste is clearly concocted in order to make sense of the two wives.

The *Oedipodea* may have ended with the death of Oedipus at Thebes and with the funeral games held to honour him,[12] or with his marginalization from kingdom and power, epitomized by the curses he cast upon his sons Eteocles and Polynices for neglecting his royal prerogatives, as is known from the *Thebaid* (*PEG* F 2–3 = D., W.).[13] In that poem Oedipus was still alive, and his strong reaction was triggered by what he took as an attempt by his sons to undermine his power and diminish his honour, i.e. his right to reign. Through his curses he doomed them to mutual slaughter the day they would dispute royal succession, and the expedition of the Seven against Thebes ensued.[14] In any case, the poem must have covered a considerable span of time after the suicide of Oedipus' mother, long enough for his sons from Euryganeia to grow up. The fact that in Euripides' *Phoenician Women* Oedipus is still alive and secluded behind locked doors in the royal palace at the time of the expedition of the Seven (*Phoen.* 60–8, 327–36), prevents us from drawing any conclusion as to his fate in the *Oedipodea*. In Euripides Oedipus survived both the mutual slaughter of his two sons and the suicide of Jocaste over their bodies (*Phoen.* 1454–9).

A more remote possibility must also be taken into account, that the *Oedipodea* encompassed the story of the quarrel between his two children and of the ensuing expedition of the Seven against Thebes, which ended in the mutual slaughter of the brothers. This assumption is justified if one connects the statement by Pausanias (9.5.10–11 = *Oed. PEG* F 2 = D., F 1 W.) that in the poem Euryganeia was the second wife of Oedipus, with the next sentence where he recalls as additional evidence for her name a painting by Onasias mentioned above. If Onasias was actually drawing on the *Oedipodea*, it should be assumed that the narrative of the poem incorporated the expedition of the Seven, partly overlapping in content with the narrative of the *Thebaid*.[15] Such an overlapping would not be unique or surprising, considering that the Cyclic poems were originally independent one from the other. A case in point is provided by the *Ilias*

---

[12] Cf. *Il.* 23.677–80; Hes. *Cat.* F 192 M.-W.; on the ending of the *Oedipodea* see Welcker (1882: 319).
[13] On the meaning and function of Oedipus' double curses against his sons, see Cingano (2004b).
[14] The report by Pausanias (9.5.12) on the death of Oedipus and the consequences it brought about is clearly based on an archaic source, since it closely (and uniquely) corresponds to the epic version.
[15] See Bethe (1891a: 25).

parva and the *Iliou persis*, both featuring the episodes of the Wooden Horse and of the sack of Troy.[16]

THE FRAGMENTS

In spite of their brevity, the only two extant fragments from the *Oedipodea* allow a number of remarks. The only quotation fragment of the *Oedipodea*, replete with epithets, is found at the end of the above-mentioned Σ Eur. *Phoen.* 1760, in a section preserved only by cod. Monac. 560 (***PEG* F 1 = D. = F 3 W.**):

> ἀναρπάζουσα δὲ μικροὺς καὶ μεγάλους κατήσθιεν, ἐν οἷς καὶ Αἵμονα τὸν Κρέοντος παῖδα... οἱ τὴν Οἰδιποδίαν γράφοντες †οὐδεὶς οὕτω φησί† περὶ τῆς Σφιγγός·
>> ἀλλ' ἔτι κάλλιστόν τε καὶ ἱμεροέστατον ἄλλων
>> παῖδα φίλον Κρείοντος ἀμύμονος, Αἵμονα δῖον.

[The Sphinx] seized and devoured great and small, including Haemon the son of Creon... The authors of the *Oedipodea* say of the Sphinx:
> But also the handsomest and loveliest of all, the dear son of blameless Creon, noble Haemon.

At line 1 two superlatives, *kalliston te kai himeroestaton*, stress the beauty and the youth of a prominent victim of the Sphinx, Haemon, son of Creon. The latter adjective is both the only epic occurrence of *himeroeis* in the superlative, and the only instance of attribution to a male person. The nearly erotic connotation of the line is confirmed by the occurrence of nearly the same formula in Theognis 1365 (ὦ παίδων κάλλιστε καὶ ἱμεροέστατε πάντων... 'Oh most handsome and desirable of all boys...'), whereas at Theogn. 1117 it is referred to the god Ploutos.[17]

The baneful presence of the Sphinx, the hybrid creature born from Echidna and Orthos, in a hill at the western edge of the Theban territory, was known to Hesiod, who calls her with the Boeotian form (*Th.* 326

---

[16] Davies is the only recent editor of the epic cycle to include Pausanias' mention of Onasias as part of the fragment (= F 2 D.). For a comparison of the *Oedipodea* with the *Thebaid* Legras (1905: 37–63) is still interesting, although most of his arguments are untenable. For other cases of overlapping in content in the Cyclic poems, see Burgess (2001: 21–5); West (2013: 15–16); Introduction, above in this volume, pp. 32–3.

[17] On the relation between Theogn. 1365 and the *Oedipodea* fragment, see Reitzenstein (1893: 82–3); Wilamowitz (1913: 120 n. 1).

ἡ δ' ("Εχιδνα) ἄρα Φῖκ' ὀλοὴν τέκε Καδμείοισιν ὄλεθρον 'she bore the deadly Sphinx, destruction for the Cadmeans': cf. Ps.-Hes. *Scut.* 33), and alludes to the killing of Theban citizens, as in the *Oedipodea*. Haemon was probably the last and most illustrious victim, thus preparing the way for Oedipus' arrival at Thebes and for the subsequent defeat of the Sphinx. Already in this version, Oedipus' marriage to his mother, the queen widow of Laius, and the kingdom of Thebes, were the likely reward proclaimed by Creon for pacifying the area, as can be gathered from the accounts of Ps.-Apollod. *Bibl.* 3.5.8 and of Pherec. *EGM* F 95.[18] The killing of Haemon is also recalled in the early part of the scholium to Eur. *Phoen.* 1760 quoting the *Oedipodea* fragment, with the additional information that the Sphinx devoured her victims;[19] this was the version known to Pindar, who mentions 'the riddle from the savage jaws of the maiden', αἴνιγμα παρθένοι' ἐξ ἀγρίαν γνάθων (F 117d), and to Aeschylus (*Sept.* 541: Σφίγγ' ὠμόσιτον 'Sphinx eating raw meat').

The presence of Haemon in the early stage of the myth, before the arrival of Oedipus at Thebes, shows the strong difference between the epic version and the one rearranged by Sophocles in his *Antigone*. In the *Oedipodea*, Haemon belonged to the same generation as Oedipus and died in his youth, whereas Antigone – his fiancée in the Sophoclean version – was born to Oedipus from his second marriage to Euryganeia (*PEG* F 2 = D., F 1 W.); it follows that in the archaic version of the myth Antigone was not even born at the time of Haemon's death. Besides, contrary to what happens with Ismene, who enjoyed a (tragic) life of her own in archaic Greece, no trace of Antigone is found in Greek literature before the Attic tragedians.[20] The mention of Creon, the brother of Jocaste, in *Oed. PEG* F 1.2 (= D.,

---

[18] Pherec. *EGM* F 95: Οἰδίποδι δίδωσι τὴν βασιλείαν καὶ τὴν γυναῖκα Λαΐου, μητέρα δ' αὑτοῦ Ἰοκάστην ('he gives Oedipus the kingdom and Iocasta, daughter of Laius and his mother'). According to Edmunds (1981), the Sphinx was a secondary element, introduced in the myth of Oedipus in order to motivate the hero's marriage to his mother; see also Edmunds (2007: 17–20), with bibliography.

[19] Σ Eur. *Phoen.* 1760 = Pisander, *FgrHist* 16 F 10 (2): ἡ Σφίγξ ... ἀναρπάζουσα δὲ μικροὺς καὶ μεγάλους κατήσθιεν, ἐν οἷς καὶ Αἵμονα τὸν Κρέοντος παῖδα ('the Sphinx, snatching away children and adults as well was devouring then, among whom also Haemon the son of Creon'); see also Σ Eur. *Phoen.* 45; Ps.-Apollod. *Bibl.* 3.5.8. According to this evidence, the missing verb directing the accusative Αἵμονα δῖον in *Oed. PEG* F 1 (= D., 3 W.) could refer to the Sphinx devouring her preys.

[20] Ismene appears as early as the seventh century in Mimnermus as the lover of one Pcryclimenus (or Theoclymenus), who was killed by Tydeus at the command of Athena when he caught the two lovers together (Mimn. *IEG* F 21; see also Pherec. *EGM* F 95); the scene is represented also on a Corinthian amphora (Louvre E 640; see Robert (1915: 121–6); Gantz (1993: 513–14)) and on an Attic skyphos (Acropolis 603), both from the sixth century BC.

F 3.2 W.) provides the earliest evidence of his connection to the myth of Oedipus, where probably from the very beginning he played the essential role of *Reichsverweser*, handing over the kingdom to the hero who overcame the Sphinx.[21]

Paus. 9.5.10–11 (*PEG* F 2 = D., F 1 W.)

παῖδας δὲ ἐξ αὐτῆς οὐ δοκῶ οἱ γενέσθαι, μάρτυρι Ὁμήρωι χρώμενος, ὃς ἐποίησεν ἐν Ὀδυσσείαι παῖδας (11.271–274)· 'μητέρα τ' Οἰδιπόδαο ἴδον, καλὴν Ἐπικάστην, / ἣ μέγα ἔργον ἔρεξεν ἀϊδρείηισι νόοιο / γημαμένη ὧι υἷϊ· ὁ δ' ὃν πατέρ' ἐξεναρίξας / γῆμεν· ἄφαρ δ' ἀνάπυστα θεοὶ θέσαν / ἀνθρώποισιν'. πῶς οὖν ἐποίησαν ἀνάπυστα ἄφαρ, εἰ δὴ τέσσαρες ἐκ τῆς Ἐπικάστης ἐγένοντο παῖδες τῶι Οἰδίποδι; ἐξ Εὐρυγανείας δὲ τῆς Ὑπέρφαντος ἐγεγόνεσαν· δηλοῖ δὲ καὶ ὁ τὰ ἔπη ποιήσας ἃ Οἰδιπόδια ὀνομάζουσι.

That he had children by his mother, I do not believe; witness Homer, who wrote in the *Odyssey*, 'And I saw Oedipus' mother, fair Epicaste, who unwittingly did a terrible thing in marrying her own son, who had killed his father; and the gods soon made it known among people'. How did they soon make it known, if Oedipus had four children by Epicaste? No, they had been born from Euryganeia, the daughter of Hyperphas. This is made clear also by the poet of the epic that they call *Oedipodea*.

The second fragment of the *Oedipodea*, quoted by Pausanias, stirs up multiple problems which are still debated regarding the fate of Oedipus in the epic tradition after the discovery of his parricide and incest, the possibility that he remarried, the names of his wives and the offspring issued from them. In discussing the offspring of Oedipus, Pausanias (9.5.10–11) rejects the possibility that Jocaste/Epicaste ever bore a child to her son, on the assumption that – as is stated in the Homeric Nekyia – after their incestuous wedding '... straightaway the gods made it known among men (ἄφαρ δ' ἀνάπυστα θεοὶ θέσαν ἀνθρώποισιν, *Od.* 11.273–4). The very meaning of ἄφαρ prompts Pausanias to find the proper answer to his own query: 'How could they have "made it known forthwith" if Epicaste had borne four children to Oedipus? But the mother of these children was Euryganeia, daughter of Hyperphas. Among the proofs of this are the words of the author of the poem called the *Oedipodea*; and moreover, Onasias painted a picture

---

[21] In the Homeric and Hesiodic epics Creon is connected to Heracles, not to Oedipus: cf. *Od.* 11.269–70; Ps.-Hes. *Scut.* 1–56, 83. On the role of Creon in the Theban myth as multiple *Reichsverweser* to the Labdacids see Cingano (2002–3: 81–3). An echo of the early status of Haemon can be found in *Il.* 4.391–400, if he is to be identified with the father of the only Theban survivor of an attempted ambush at Tydeus; cf. Ps.-Apollod. *Bibl.* 3.6.5.

at Plataea of Euryganeia bowed with grief because of the fight between her children.'[22]

The lines of *PEG* F 2 = D., 1 W. can be analysed in relation to a limited, and yet telling, number of epic and mythographic texts. In the extended account of the myth of Oedipus presented by Odysseus in the *Odyssey* (11.271–80) incest, parricide and the suicide of Epicaste are the only themes mentioned; there is no allusion to the children issued from the incestuous marriage, no suggestion that Oedipus blinded himself and/or went into exile; on the contrary, it is specified that he continued to rule over Thebes, albeit confronted with many pains that the Erinyes of Epicaste brought about. Regarding his death at Thebes while still a king, the epic tradition is remarkably consistent and at variance with the versions conveyed by the Attic tragedians. Apart from the *Odyssey*, a passage in the *Iliad* recalls the funeral games held at Thebes to honour him,[23] and the same version is implied in the Hesiodic *Catalogue of Women*, F 192–3 M.-W. = 90 Hirsch.[24]

The scepticism expressed by scholars in the past regarding the existence of a second marriage of Oedipus is matched by the attempts of some ancient mythographers and grammarians to account for the different wives reported for Oedipus; C. Robert called the prospect of more than one marriage 'eine Scheußlichkeit', a dreadfulness, whilst J. Bremmer is at a loss in finding a plausible explanation: 'It is hard for us to understand that a poet could let Oedipus remarry.'[25] Along the same lines, M. Davies has revived the suggestion that Euryganeia might merely be an alternative name for Jocaste.[26] It must however be pointed out that the *Oedipodea* may not have been the only epic source attesting to the second marriage of Oedipus;

---

[22] 'At once, straightaway, forthwith' is the usual meaning of *aphar* when it occurs at the beginning of a clause, followed by δέ (see *LSJ* s.v.); on the use of *aphar* in epic poetry see R. Führer, *LfgrE* s.v., 1695–8; Tsitsibakou-Vasalos (1989).

[23] *Il.* 23.679–80: (Εὐρύαλος)... ὅς ποτε Θήβας δ᾽ ἦλθε δεδουπότος Οἰδιπόδαο / ἐς τάφον· ἔνθα δὲ πάντας ἐνίκα Καδμείωνας ('(Euryalus) who on a time had come to Thebes for the burial of Oedipus, when he died, and there had worsted all the sons of Cadmus').

[24] The burial of the much-suffering Oedipus at Thebes is one of the few facts which can safely be identified in Hes. *Cat.* F 193.3–4 M.-W. = F 90 Hirsch. Interestingly, in his continuation of the story of the Labdacids (9.5.12) Pausanias is the one and only non-archaic source to relate the 'cyclic' version about Oedipus' death at Thebes as a king, probably drawing on an epic poem. The story of Oedipus was also dealt with in the *Cypria*, as can be gathered from Proclus' summary (*Cypr.* arg. lines 115–16 Severyns).

[25] See Robert (1915: 110); Rzach *RE* s.v. 'Kyklos', col. 2361; Bremmer (1987: 52).

[26] See Davies (1989c: 21–2). A trace of this conciliatory interpretation is found in the late *Etym. Magn.* s.v. Ἰοκάστη (Miller 1868: 169). Epimenides (*EGM* F 16) is the only source to call 'Eurycleia' the mother of Oedipus, while Σ Eur. *Phoen.* 13 credits Laius with two wives, Eurycleia and Epicaste: see Schneidewin (1852: 9–10).

if nothing is known about the version in the *Thebaid*, traces of a second wife of Oedipus surface in the Hesiodic *Catalogue of Women*, where the woman alluded to in F 190.13–15 M.-W. = F 89.13–15 Hirsch. is likely to be Astymedousa, daughter of Sthenelus, listed as Oedipus' third wife by Pherecydes (*EGM* F 95), and as his second wife by Σ D *Il.* 4.376 and by Eust. 484.45–8 on *Il.* 4.376–381.[27] Furthermore, apart from the *Oedipodea*, the existence of a second marriage of Oedipus to Euryganeia is well attested in a number of mythographic sources clearly drawing on an earlier tradition, and crediting Euryganeia as the mother of the four children universally known: see Pherecydes, *EGM* F 95;[28] Pisander, *FgrHist* 16 F 10 (8);[29] Σ Eur. *Phoen.* 13 and 53; Ps.-Apollod. *Bibl.* 3.5.8.[30]

It follows that the existence of a second marriage of Oedipus in the *Oedipodea* can hardly be denied: it also brings about further considerations. The marriage to Euryganeia can be accounted for in expanding on Bremmer's remark that 'The earliest stages of the Indo-European languages did not have a word for "widower"... to be a widower was not a permanent male status. So Oedipus had to remarry.'[31] This anthropological approach is all the more convincing if one considers that in the epic version (*Od.* 11.275–6) Oedipus went on reigning at Thebes after the death of Epicaste, a clear indication that – with no other successor left – the throne of the Labdacids could not be left vacant. Since, according to the *Oedipodea*, the four children of Oedipus were born to him by Euryganeia, the main purpose of introducing a second wife is that she secured legitimate children – untainted by incest – to the *genos* of the Labdacids. This version can be

---

[27] For Astymedousa as the wife of Oedipus in the *Catalogue of Women*, see Merkelbach-West, apparatus on F 190.13ff.: 'Stheneli filia Astymedusa nupsit Oedipodi'; West (1985: 110–11). Since his mother Epicaste/Jocaste is always present as Oedipus' first wife, it can be safely assumed that in this poem too Astymedousa was his second wife.

[28] ... ἐπεὶ δ' ἐνιαυτὸς παρῆλθε, γαμεῖ Οἰδίπους Εὐρυγάνειαν τὴν Περίφαντος, ἐξ ἧς γίνονται αὐτῶι... ('when the year passed, Oedipous marries Euryganeia the daughter of Periphas, from whom to him were born...'). On the archaic flavour of the detailed *EGM* F 95 by Pherecydes, who also mentions two otherwise unattested sons (Phrastor and Laonytos) borne to Oedipus by Jocaste, see Cingano (1992b: 9–10); his juxtaposition of three wives reflects the wish to record all the versions available:... ἐπεὶ δὲ Εὐρυγάνεια ἐτελεύτησε, γαμεῖ ὁ Οἰδίπους Ἀστυμέδουσαν τὴν Σθενέλου ('after Euryganeia died, Oedipous marries Asymedousa the daughter of Sthenelus').

[29] To be precise, the mention of Euryganeia as the second wife of Oedipus and mother of his four children is inserted in the final section ascribed to Pisander, but it is clearly taken from another source: φασὶ δὲ ὅτι μετὰ τὸν θάνατον τῆς Ἰοκάστης... ταῦτά φησι Πείσανδρος ('they say that after the death of Iocasta... this is what Pisander says').

[30] As was noted long ago by Müller (1844: 221), the strange silence on the children of Oedipus and Epicaste in *Od.* 11.271–80 may imply that Homer was in agreement with the version of the *Oedipodea*, that Oedipus begot them by Euryganeia.

[31] Bremmer (1987: 52).

connected to the importance of genealogies in Greece in historical times, when aristocratic families claimed descent from heroic lineage. A tradition cleared of the disturbing feature of ancestors born from incest could help in linking aristocratic families with the Labdacid dynasty, as is attested by a few cases in the fifth century. In tracing his genealogy back to Thersander the son of Polynices, Theron of Acragas apparently did not feel affected by the gloomy events of the Labdacids for many generations past (see Pind. *Ol.* 2.40–7). In Sparta, the Aegeids also claimed descent from the Labdacids (see Paus. 9.5.14), whereas at Thebes descent from Oedipus' family was boasted by the family of the Cleonymids (Pind. *Isthm.* 3.15–17).[32]

The presence in the *Oedipodea* of Euryganeia as the mother of Eteocles and Polynices shows that the shame and the burden of incest fell upon the shoulders of Oedipus' mother, Jocaste/Epicaste, whereas he went on to rule at Thebes and form a new family. Theoretically, a second marriage of Oedipus may also be assumed in the Lille papyrus of Stesichorus (*PMGF* 222b): here, the queen mother of Eteocles and Polynices, unnamed in the fragment, is alive and – before Polynices sets off in exile – she tries her best to work out a solution in order to avoid the smouldering conflict between her sons. Since no evidence is available, it remains controversial whether in the sixth century BC Stesichorus was in agreement with the version in the *Oedipodea*, and the queen mother should therefore be identified with Euryganeia, or whether he was anticipating the version found in Euripides' *Phoenissae*, where the one and only wife and mother of Oedipus, Jocaste, outlives her sons only to kill herself on the battlefield, over their bodies.[33] The image bears similarity to the scene painted by Onasias at Plataea, representing Euryganeia in grief as she watches the fight between Eteocles and Polynices.[34]

Another controversial issue in the *Oedipodea* (which also applies to the *Thebaid*) centres on the question whether Oedipus became blind after the discovery of parricide and incest; as noted above, he surely is not blind in the *Odyssey* passage, and in the fragmentary evidence from the archaic age no clear-cut evidence favours this possibility.[35] According to epic usage, the verbs φράσθη in *Theb. PEG* F 2.5 (= D., W.) and ἐνόησε in *PEG* F 3.1 (= D., W.) may refer either to seeing or to perceiving with other senses. In the (para)tragic fragment which is a clear parody of the second curse narrated in the *Thebaid*, the verb γιγνώσκειν refers to recognizing an object

[32] On this point see also Lloyd-Jones (2002: 9).
[33] See above, p. 217.   [34] See above, p. 215.
[35] Contrary to what is assumed for example by Severyns (1928: 212), who – relying on Legras (1905) – claims that in the *Oedipodea* and in the *Thebaid* Oedipus blinded himself.

by touching it (*TrGF* 458.7: ἔγνω 'παφήσας); in the following lines the blindness of Oedipus is explicitly stated (cf. *TrGF* 458.10: τυφλός· οὔ τι γνώσεται), although this detail might be a later conflation from tragedy, most of all from Sophocles' *Oedipus Tyrannus*.[36]

On the contrary, his second marriage to Euryganeia, the begetting of children and most of all the fact that he went on ruling Thebes, point to the fact that the early epic tradition did not represent Oedipus as a blind king, and it may be added that blindness does not seem to befit the status of a king in Greek archaic epic;[37] the weakening of his power at some stage may have been connected to other reasons, such as old age and the disrespectful behaviour of his two sons, with the aim of replacing their father on the throne. The only passage running against this interpretation occurs at the end of the Pisander scholium, where it is stated that 'after the death of Jocaste and his blinding he married Euryganeia' (φασὶ δὲ ὅτι μετὰ τὸν θάνατον τῆς Ἰοκάστης καὶ τὴν αὐτοῦ τύφλωσιν ἔγημεν Εὐρυγάνην παρθένον... ταῦτά φησιν Πείσανδρος, Σ Eur. *Phoen.* 1760 = Pisander, *FgrHist* 16 F 10 (8)). Yet the passage is garbled and wrongly inserted within the context referred to Pisander; it should be better considered a conflation of the epic motif of Oedipus' second marriage with the tragic motif of his blinding.[38]

The attribution to the *Oedipodea* of a third fragment which tells the riddle of the Sphinx, proposed by West (*Oed.* F 2* W. = Asclep. *FgrHist* 12 F 7a), is purely conjectural: it rests on the fact that the Sphinx's riddle in hexameters (ἔστι δίπουν ἐπὶ γῆς καὶ τετράπον, οὗ μία φωνή... 'there is a two-footed and four-footed creature with a single voice...') is quoted by Asclepiades of Tragilus (fourth century BC) who, according to West,[39] may have taken it from the *Oedipodea*. As a matter of fact the riddle may well have been earlier, as is shown by the Vatican cup (Vat 16541: first half of the fifth century BC) representing Oedipus and the Sphinx, with the beginning of an inscription which reads καὶ τρι[. It has however been noted that, although the hexameter form of the riddle could point to epic verse, in his work called *Tragoidoumena* (in eleven books) 'Asklepiades generally takes his stories from tragedy, and hexameter is the meter used for riddles on the stage.'[40] To this it may be added that evidence is also missing of the way by which Oedipus overcame the Sphinx in the *Oedipodea*: although

---

[36] On this point see also Torres-Guerra, below in this volume, p. 231 n. 16.
[37] In the Sanskrit epic *Mahabharata* controversy arises over the right of the prince Dhritarashtra to rule as a king, because of his blindness from birth (I owe this point to the courtesy of G. B. D'Alessio).
[38] See on this point Valgiglio (1963: 163–4).   [39] See West (2003c: 41 n. 1).
[40] So Gantz (1993: 496); Simon (1981: 29–30).

the riddle is implied in an earlier hydria in Stuttgart (65/15) dating from about 530 BC, the possibility remains that an earlier alternative tradition represented Oedipus fighting with the monster and finally killing her with a sword. Along with a number of vases dating from the second half of the fifth century which show the fight, an interesting piece of evidence is provided by the Boeotian poetess Corinna, who portrayed Oedipus as an 'héros civilisateur' who liberated the Theban territory from monsters: he 'killed not only the Sphinx, but also the Teumessian fox' (Corinna, *PMG* F 672).[41]

[41] See also below, pp. 258–59. See most recently Edmunds (1981: 19–21); March (1987: 124); Gantz (1993: 495–8); Lloyd-Jones (2002: 5). For the representation of Oedipus and the Sphinx on vases see most recently Simon (1981); Moret (1984); Krauskopf (1986); Krauskopf (1994).

13 | *Thebaid*

JOSÉ B. TORRES-GUERRA

In the Myth of Ages (*Works and Days* 156–73), Hesiod provides an overview of the age of heroes by making reference to two legendary tales: the Trojan War and the death at Thebes of the warlords who fought over 'the flocks of Oedipus' (163). The meaning of the expression used by Hesiod is ambiguous. Nevertheless, it is very unlikely that the Hesiodic version of the myth differs in any significant way from the established version prevalent in later times. In other words, it is likely that Hesiod's reference to the 'flocks' of Oedipus denotes the fortune – *pecunia* (μῆλα)[1] – of Oedipus, the king of Thebes, which provoked the tragic conflict between his sons, Eteocles and Polynices. Various allusions are made to this saga in both the *Iliad* and the *Odyssey*, which offer a fragmentary account of the course of events that the *Thebaid* sets out to recount in greater detail.[2]

A detailed narrative of this legend is given in Ps.-Apollodorus' *Bibliotheca* (3.5.7–3.7.1). When Oedipus relinquished the throne at Thebes (on his death or on leaving the country, as dramatized in Sophocles' *Oedipus at Colonus*),[3] his sons reached an agreement regarding their father's inheritance: either Polynices took possession of the material goods (the robe and the necklace of Harmonia) while Eteocles claimed the royal title and dignity, or the two brothers would agree to alternate the throne of Thebes.[4] Polynices arrives in Argos as an exile at the same time as Tydeus, and a fight breaks out between them. Adrastus, the king of Argos, is a witness to the scene and interprets it in terms of the prophecy that foretold he was to give his daughters' (Argia and Deipyle) hands in marriage to a lion and a wild boar, the animals depicted on the shields carried by Polynices and Tydeus, respectively. Adrastus decides to help Oedipus' son win back his

---

[1] See Cingano (1992).
[2] See *Il.* 2.572, 4.370–410, 5.115–17, 5.800–8, 6.222–3, 10.284–91, 14.113–25, 23.345–7, 23.677–80, *Od.* 11.271–80, 11.326–7, 15.243–8; and Torres-Guerra (1995a: 27–31, 65–7).
[3] The least common version of the story has Oedipus die as king of Thebes; this is the version presupposed in the *Odyssey* (11.275–6) and, perhaps, in the *Iliad* (23.677–80); see Torres (1995a: 34–7, 68).
[4] See Stesich. *PMGF* F 222 (b) 220–2; Hellanic. *FgrHist* 4 F 98; Eur. *Phoen.* 69–77; Ps.-Apollod. *Bibl.* 3.6.1.

family's throne and organizes an expedition against Thebes, a campaign which is joined by seven warlords, to whom the literary tradition attributes a variety of names.[5] A key, established member of the group is Amphiaraus, soothsayer and warrior, who takes part in the campaign against his will, pressured by his wife, Eriphyle, Adrastus' sister. On the way to Thebes, the expedition halts in Nemea, where little Opheltes, son of the local king, dies when his wet-nurse Hypsipyle[6] leaves him unprotected for a few moments to look after the outsiders. Ps.-Apollodorus (*Bibl.* 3.6.4) notes that Amphiaraus interpreted this event as a sign presaging the ignominious end of the campaign, which is why the child was renamed Archemorus, 'he who brings about disgrace'. After founding the games at Nemea in his honour, the expedition continues its march on Thebes, where the seven Argive champions join battle with seven Cadmean warlords at the city walls. Each pairing of warriors fights at one of the entryways to 'Thebes, the city of seven gates';[7] and the fratricidal brothers face one another at the final gateway. In most cases, such struggles end with the death of the Argive aggressor; but the contest between Eteocles and Polynices ends in the death of both brothers. Amphiaraus, who had an oracular shrine at Oropus, on the border between Boeotia and Attica, disappears underground. King Adrastus, who strictly speaking was not one of the Seven, escapes on his horse Arion, and later arranges to bury his dead comrades, having been granted permission to do so by the Cadmeans. The narrative of events proceeds differently in different versions of the story. The tragic version, which was to become the canonical narrative because of Sophocles' *Antigone* (442 BC), tells of the prohibition on burying Polynices, who was regarded as an enemy of his homeland, and of the conduct of his sisters, Antigone and Ismene.

DATE AND AUTHORSHIP

Although fifth-century BC tragedy reflects the typical features of Theban legend read from our contemporary perspective, its canonical status in the archaic period must have been due to the epic poems in the Theban Cycle,

---

[5] Adrastus may or may not have been regarded as one of the Seven. The established members of the group are Polynices, Tydeus, Amphiaraus, Capaneus, Hippomedon and Parthenopeus. In some instances (depending on whether or not Adrastus is included), Eteoclus and Mecisteus may be also added to the list. The full question is discussed in detail by Cingano (2002).

[6] On Hypsipyle, a character in the saga of the Argonauts, see Ps.-Apollod. *Bibl.* 1.9.17.

[7] See *Il.* 4.406, *Od.* 11.263. The set of seven gates and the company of seven leaders condition one another mutually.

one of which is the *Thebaid*, a poem comprising 7,000 verses according to the *Contest of Homer and Hesiod*,[8] and a text that encompasses the mythic account summarized in the preceding section above. The dating of this poem draws, above all, on the evidence that stems from testimonies and fragments. The first relevant testimony in this regard comes in Pausanias 9.9.5 (T 2 B = 1 D. = s. n. W.), where Callinus is said to have attributed the *Thebaid* to Homer, midway through the seventh century BC:

> ἐποιήθη δὲ ἐς τὸν πόλεμον τοῦτον καὶ ἔπη Θηβαΐς (Θηβαίοις MSS; corr. Hemsterhuys)· τὰ δὲ ἔπη ταῦτα Καλλῖνος (Καλαῖνος MSS; corr. Sylburg) ἀφικόμενος αὐτῶν ἐς μνήμην ἔφησεν Ὅμηρον τὸν ποιήσαντα εἶναι, Καλλίνωι (Καλαίνωι MSS; corr. Sylburg) δὲ πολλοί τε καὶ ἄξιοι λόγου κατὰ ταὐτὰ ἔγνωσαν.
>
> There was also an epic composed about this war, the *Thebaid*. Callinus in referring to this epic said that Homer was its author, and many worthy critics have agreed with Callinus.

However, the critical consensus nowadays is that Pausanias was articulating a personal interpretation of an elegy by Callinus, wherein the latter noted the 'Homeric' tone of some of the verses comprising the *Thebaid*; that Callinus could have explicitly cited the poem by title does not appear likely.[9] The linguistic evidence reflected in the fragments could be significant if they contained innovative features that might function as *termini post quos*. While there are no indisputable linguistic innovations in the twenty extant verses, it may be true to say that the repetition of possibly post-Homeric features suggests that the written text of the *Thebaid* postdates the *Iliad* and the *Odyssey*.[10]

Another factor that may be of interest in this regard is the consistency with which the *Thebaid* has been attributed to Homer,[11] a circumstance that might imply an acknowledgment of the poem's antiquity. The repeated attribution of the *Thebaid* to Homer certainly implies a value judgement,[12] an affirmative statement expressed in explicit terms in Pausanias 9.9.5 (T 2 B = 1 D. = s. n. W.), where the latter offers his opinion that the *Thebaid* is the third best epic poem, after the *Iliad* and the *Odyssey*.

---

[8] See *PEG* T 4 = 2 D. = F 1 W. It is also striking that an epic poem recounting the expedition of *seven* leaders should comprise *seven* thousand verses. On the *Contest of Homer and Hesiod*, see also Nagy, above in this volume, pp. 68–76.

[9] This is the explanation offered by Davison (1955 = 1968: 81–2), who concurs with e.g. West (1999: 377).

[10] See Davies (1989a).   [11] See Torres-Guerra (1998).

[12] On the use of the name 'Homer' as a 'quality seal', see Schwartz (1940).

Given the text's literary status, it is a pity our knowledge of the poem is so fragmentary. Bernabé collated eight testimonies and eleven fragments comprising twenty-one hexameters under the title *Thebaid*; Davies included four testimonies, nine fragments, sixteen verses; and West's edition comprises three testimonies and eleven fragments (twenty-two hexameters).[13] Moreover, the *Thebaid* also lacks the kind of summary transmitted by Proclus for the Trojan Cycle. Our knowledge of the poem's contents is wholly based on these fragments, although this may be complemented by careful reference to other literary texts and iconography.

FRAGMENTS

F 1: *PEG* F 1 = D., W., from the *Certamen Homeri et Hesiodi* 15 (254–7 Allen)[14]

ὁ δὲ Ὅμηρος ἀποτυχὼν τῆς νίκης περιερχόμενος ἔλεγε τὰ ποιήματα, πρῶτον μὲν τὴν Θηβαΐδα, ἔπη ,ζ, ἧς ἡ ἀρχή·

Ἄργος ἄειδε, θεά, πολυδίψιον, ἔνθεν ἄνακτες.

Homer, after his defeat in the contest, went about reciting his poems: firstly the *Thebaid* (7,000 lines), which begins:

Sing, goddess, of thirsty Argos, from where the lords.

The first fragment of the *Thebaid*, which consists of a single verse ('Sing, goddess, of thirsty Argos, from where the lords...'), frames the subject matter of the poem from the Argive perspective. This viewpoint is retained in all the extant fragments except for the two longest literal ones (2 and 3). There is a noticeable similarity between this verse and the first line in the *Iliad*: 'Sing, goddess, of the wrath of Achilles, Peleus' son'; but this does not need to imply a direct relation between the two poems as this group of words ('Sing, goddess, of...') may be a formulaic beginning.

F 2: *PEG* F 2 = D., W., from Athenaeus 11.465e

ὁ δὲ Οἰδίπους δι' ἐκπώματα τοῖς υἱοῖς κατηράσατο, ὡς ὁ τὴν κυκλικὴν Θηβαΐδα πεποιηκὼς φησιν, ὅτι αὐτῶι παρέθηκαν ἔκπωμα, ὃ ἀπηγορεύκει, λέγων οὕτως·

---

[13] *PEG*; Davies (1988); West (2003a).
[14] There is a clear consensus concerning the order of the three first fragments of the *Thebaid*. The situation is very different in relation to the rest.

αὐτὰρ ὁ διογενὴς ἥρως ξανθὸς Πολυνείκης
πρῶτα μὲν Οἰδιπόδηι καλὴν παρέθηκε τράπεζαν
ἀργυρέην Κάδμοιο θεόφρονος· αὐτὰρ ἔπειτα
χρύσεον ἔμπλησεν καλὸν δέπας ἡδέος οἴνου.
αὐτὰρ ὅ γ' ὡς φράσθη παρακείμενα πατρὸς ἑοῖο
τιμήεντα γέρα, μέγα οἱ κακὸν ἔμπεσε θυμῶι,
αἶψα δὲ παισὶν ἑοῖσι μετ' ἀμφοτέροισιν ἐπαρὰς
ἀργαλέας ἠρᾶτο, θεὰν δ' οὐ λάνθαν' Ἐρινύν,
ὡς οὔ οἱ πατρώϊ' ἐνηέι <ἐν> φιλότητι
δάσσαιντ', ἀμφοτέροισι δ' αἰεὶ πόλεμοί τε μάχαι τε ...

Oedipus cursed his sons on account of cups, as the author of the Cyclic Thebaid says, because they set before him a cup that he had forbidden. These are his words:

> But the highborn hero, flaxen-haired Polynices, firstly set beside Oedipus the fine silver table of Cadmus the godly; then he filled his fine gold cup with sweet wine. But when he became aware that his father's precious treasures had been set beside him, some great evil invaded his heart, and at once he laid dreadful curses on both his sons, which the divine Erinys did not fail to note: that they should not divide their patrimony in friendship, but the two of them ever in battle and strife ...

Fragments 2 and 3 recount the curses Oedipus issued against his sons. In fragment 2, Oedipus is angered when Polynices presents him with the table and cup of Cadmus that had belonged to Laius (an intentional evocation of the patricide he had committed). Oedipus prays to the Erinys that his two sons fail to divide his inheritance peacefully and that 'the two of them ever [be] in battle and strife' (2.10). It is clear that the first curse anticipates the ensuing quarrel between the two brothers.

It is remarkable that Oedipus has not left Thebes after the disclosure of his crime, as in the version modern readers are acquainted with (cf. n. 3). The neutral verbal expression of line 5 (*autar ho g' hōs phrasthē* ... 'But when he became aware ...') is vague with respect to whether Oedipus has blinded himself as in Sophocles' *OT* that represents the best-known version.[15] But it seems more logical that he is already blind and no longer king of Thebes,

---

[15] He is still the king in the *Odyssey* (11.275–6), so it is more probable that he was not regarded as blind in this poem; see Σ ad loc. The first explicit mention of a blind Oedipus is not to be found until Aesch. *Sept.* 783–4. On the possibility that Oedipus is blind in the *Thebaid*, see also Cingano, above in this volume, pp. 223–4.

since it would have been strange if his sons had angered an Oedipus who could still see, an Oedipus who ruled over Thebes.

F 3: *PEG* F 3 = D., W., from Σ Soph. *Oed. Col.* 1375 (54 De Marco)

οἱ περὶ Ἐτεοκλέα καὶ Πολυνείκην δι' ἔθους ἔχοντες τῶι πατρὶ Οἰδίποδι πέμπειν ἐξ ἑκάστου ἱερείου μοῖραν τὸν ὦμον, ἐκλαθόμενοί ποτε, εἴτε κατὰ ῥαιστώνην εἴτε ἐξ ὁτουοῦν, ἰσχίον αὐτῶι ἔπεμψαν· ὁ δὲ μικροψύχως καὶ τελέως ἀγεννῶς, ὅμως γοῦν ἀρὰς ἔθετο κατ' αὐτῶν, δόξας κατολιγωρεῖσθαι. ταῦτα ὁ τὴν κυκλικὴν Θηβαΐδα ποιήσας ἱστορεῖ οὕτως·

    ἰσχίον ὡς ἐνόησε χαμαὶ βάλεν, εἶπέ τε μῦθον·
    'ὤ μοι ἐγώ, παῖδες μὲν ὀνειδείοντες ἔπεμψαν...'
               *
    εὔκτο δὲ Δὶ βασιλῆι καὶ ἄλλοις ἀθανάτοισι
    χερσὶν ὑπ' ἀλλήλων καταβήμεναι Ἄιδος εἴσω.

Eteocles and Polynices, who customarily sent their father Oedipus the shoulder as his portion from every sacrificial animal, omitted to do so on one occasion, whether from simple negligence or for whatever reason, and sent him a haunch. He, in a mean and thoroughly ignoble spirit, but all the same, laid curses on them, considering he was being slighted. The author of the Cyclic *Thebaid* records this as follows:

    When he realized it was a haunch, he threw it to the
    ground and said, 'Oh, my sons have insultingly sent...'
               *
    He prayed to Zeus the king and to the other immortals that
    they should go down into Hades' house at each other's hands.

Fragment 3 intensifies the curse: on realizing[16] that Eteocles and Polynices had given him the thigh of the sacrificial animal, rather than the shoulder-blade as custom commanded, perhaps in a veiled reference to the king's incestuous relationship with his mother,[17] Oedipus calls directly for the reciprocal death of his young sons ('They should go down into Hades' house at each other's hands', F 3.4); if fragment 2 had anticipated the war

---

[16] A neutral 'realized' seems to be the best translation for *ischion hōs enoēse...* (3.2). *PEG* F 3 (= D., W.) was parodied by a paratragic text where Oedipus is decidedly blind (see *TrGFF* adesp. 458.7, 10, and Cingano, above in this volume, pp. 223–4).

[17] This interpretation was proposed by Santiago (1981: 24–5). The situation is different in the view of Cingano (2004b: 274–7), who thinks Oedipus is still the king of Thebes in the *Thebaid*; as his sons do not fulfil their ritual duties towards him, he believes they want to undermine his royal power and consequently curses them in anger.

between the two brothers, this new text and curse anticipate their mutual deaths at each other's hands.

It is noteworthy that this fragment (as was also the case with fragment 2) has the nature of a summary. Fragment 3 contains the only extant example of direct speech in the *Thebaid*, the only verse that articulates Oedipus' curse in literal terms: 'Oh, my sons have insultingly sent...' It is important to remember that the summarizing dimension of these fragments has prompted a number of scholars to conclude that the *Thebaid* was lacking in dramatic development, as would also appear to be the case with the Trojan Cycle as reflected in Proclus' summaries.[18] Nevertheless, an alternative conclusion might also be reached: in a poem that opens from an Argive perspective ('of thirsty Argos, from where the lords...', F 1), the curses may function as flashbacks in a narrative voiced by one of the characters. It could even be said, in narratological terms, that both curses were *analepses* inside a speech, including themselves as *prolepses* concerning the future development of events.[19]

F 4: *PEG* F 5 = F 8 D. = F 5 W., from Ps.-Apollod. *Bibl.* 1.8.4

Ἀλθαίας δὲ ἀποθανούσης ἔγημεν Οἰνεὺς Περίβοιαν τὴν Ἱππονόου, ταύτην δὲ ὁ μὲν γράψας τὴν Θηβαΐδα πολεμηθείσης Ὠλένου λέγει λαβεῖν Οἰνέα γέρας· Ἡσίοδος δὲ... ἐγεννήθη δὲ ἐκ ταύτης Οἰνεῖ Τυδεύς.

When Althaea died, Oeneus married Periboia the daughter of Hipponoos. The writer of the *Thebaid* says that Oeneus got her as a prize from the sack of Olenos, whereas Hesiod says... from her Tydeus was born to Oeneus.

A number of the fragments that have been handed down provide decontextualized information about different aggressors against Thebes, for example, about Tydeus, one of Adrastus' sons-in-law, who is mentioned in two of the extant fragments. The first alludes to a point of the story prior to his arrival in Argos and the war against Eteocles and Thebes, his genealogy. In the *Thebaid* (via Ps.-Apollodorus),[20] his father Oeneus received Periboea, future mother of the hero, as war booty after capturing the city of Olenos. The version attested in the *Thebaid* is only one among the four

---

[18] See Griffin (1977: 49–50); Davies (1989c: 25–6).

[19] For flashbacks included in direct speeches, see the case of the *Cypria* according to Proclus' summary, in which Nestor tells Menelaus the stories about Epopeus, the madness of Heracles, and Theseus and Ariadne (lines 114–17 Severyns).

[20] Ps.-Apollod. *Bibl.* 1.8.4: 'The writer of the *Thebaid* says...'.

possibilities Ps.-Apollodorus mentions.[21] This is also the only attested version in which Tydeus is the son of a slave woman; it is not known if this feature may have played any role in the poem.

F 5: *PEG* F 6 = F 4 D. = F 10 W., from Pausanias 9.18.6

καὶ ὁ Ἀσφόδικος οὗτος ἀπέκτεινεν ἐν τῆι μάχηι τῆι πρὸς Ἀργείους Παρθενοπαῖον τὸν Ταλαοῦ, καθὰ οἱ Θηβαῖοι λέγουσιν, ἐπεὶ τά γε ἐν Θηβαΐδι ἔπη τὰ ἐς τὴν Παρθενοπαίου τελευτὴν Περικλύμενον τὸν ἀνελόντα φησὶν εἶναι.

And this Asphodicus in the battle against the Argives killed Parthenopaeus the son of Talaos, according to what the Thebans say; the verses about Parthenopaeus' death in the *Thebaid* make Periclymenus the one who slew him.

The following fragment is also directly ascribed to the *Thebaid*[22] and refers to its decisive battle. In this fragment we are told that the hero Parthenopeus died at the hands of Periclymenus in the Cyclic poem and not at the hands of Asphodicus, as the Thebans would have it.[23]

Although there are no more fragments referring to him, Periclymenus, Parthenopeus' killer, may have played a role in the archaic versions of the legend, perhaps also in the *Thebaid*, as the lover of Ismene, the shy sister of Antigone in Sophocles. Such is the version of the story attested in Mimnermus and Pherecydes of Athens[24] and in black-figure ceramics.[25]

F 6: *PEG* F 9 = F 5 D. = F 9* W., from Σ ABDLTGen *Il.* 5.126 (ii.63 Nicole)[26]

Τυδεὺς ὁ Οἰνέως ἐν τῶι Θηβαϊκῶι πολέμωι ὑπὸ Μελανίππου τοῦ Ἀστακοῦ ἐτρώθη, Ἀμφιάρεως δὲ κτείνας τὸν Μελάνιππον τὴν κεφαλὴν ἐκόμισεν, καὶ ἀνοίξας αὐτὴν Τυδεὺς τὸν ἐγκέφαλον ἐρρόφει ἀπὸ θυμοῦ. Ἀθηνᾶ δέ, κομίζουσα Τυδεῖ ἀθανασίαν, ἰδοῦσα τὸ μίασμα ἀπεστράφη αὐτόν. Τυδεὺς δὲ γνοὺς ἐδεήθη τῆς θεοῦ ἵνα κἂν τῶι παιδὶ αὐτοῦ παράσχηι τὴν ἀθανασίαν.

---

[21] He mentions afterwards Hesiod (F 12 M.-W. = 51 Hirsch.), Peisander (*FgrHist* 16 F 1) and an anonymous version.

[22] Paus. 9.18.6: 'The verses... in the *Thebaid*...'.

[23] See Paus. 9.18.6: 'This Asphodicus in the battle against the Argives killed Parthenopaeus the son of Talaus, according to what the Thebans say.'

[24] See Mimn. *IEG* F 21; Pherec. *FgrHist* 3 F 95.

[25] Two ceramic pieces (*LIMC*, 'Ismene' 3 and 4; 575–550 BC) depict Ismene sharing a conjugal bed with Periclymenus. Tydeus discovers them together and moves to kill the young woman, while her lover escapes.

[26] See also Σ AbT *Il.* 5.126; Σ Lycophr. 1066; Tzetzes ad loc.; Ps.-Apollod. *Bibl.* 3.6.8.

Tydeus the son of Oineus in the Theban war was wounded by Melanippus the son of Astacus. Amphiaraus killed Melanippus and brought back his head, which Tydeus split open and gobbled the brain in a passion. When Athena, who was bringing Tydeus immortality, saw the horror, she turned away from him. Tydeus on realizing this begged the goddess at least to bestow the immortality on his son.

This fragment is marked by its gruesome content. According to the most common version, Tydeus was fatally wounded during his combat with his Cadmean opponent, Melanippus, who was slain in turn by Amphiaraus;[27] when Amphiaraus presented Melanippus' decapitated head to his dying comrade, Tydeus' reaction was brutal: he cut the skull in two and sucked out the brains.[28] Such an act of *hybris* did not escape the notice of Athena, protector of Tydeus according to tradition, who had just offered Tydeus the gift of immortality. The goddess withdrew the gift and Tydeus asked that the gift be granted someday to his son Diomedes.[29]

This fragment illustrates a difficulty sometimes evinced by the evidence of the *Thebaid*. Although we may assume this episode was narrated in the poem, the truth is that only one of five testimonies cited by Bernabé (*PEG*) in support of the fragment claims that 'the story is in the Cycle writers', and makes no explicit reference to the *Thebaid*. West (2003a: 50–3) regards the fragment as doubtful for this very reason.

F 7: *PEG* F 7 = F 6a D. = F 11 W., from Pausanias 8.25.7–8

τὴν δὲ Δήμητρα τεκεῖν φασιν ἐκ τοῦ Ποσειδῶνος θυγατέρα... καὶ ἵππον τὸν Ἀρίονα... ἐπάγονται δὲ ἐξ Ἰλιάδος ἔπη καὶ ἐκ Θηβαΐδος μαρτύριά σφισιν εἶναι τοῦ λόγου, ἐν μὲν Ἰλιάδι (23.346–7) ἐς αὐτὸν Ἀρίονα πεποιῆσθαι... ἐν δὲ τῆι Θηβαΐδι ὡς Ἄδραστος ἔφευγεν ἐκ Θηβῶν

εἵματα λυγρὰ φέρων σὺν Ἀρίονι κυανοχαίτηι.

αἰνίσσεσθαι οὖν ἐθέλουσι τὰ ἔπη Ποσειδῶνα Ἀρίονι εἶναι πατέρα.

They say that Demeter bore a daughter by Poseidon... and the horse Arion... And they adduce verses from the *Iliad* and from the *Thebaid* as

---

[27] According to Ps.-Apollodorus (*Bibl.* 3.6.8), Amphiaraus offered Tydeus the head of Melanippus presupposing his impious reaction. Cingano (1987: 98–9) proposed that Ps.-Apollodorus could have taken this feature from Stesichorus' *Eriphyle*.

[28] This scene is also noteworthy because stories in which men or women deliberately eat human flesh are very rare in Greek myths and legends; Tereus and Thyestes were cannibals unawares.

[29] Ibycus spoke about the divinization of Diomedes; see Ibyc. *PMGF* F 294.

evidence of their tale, saying that in the *Iliad* it is written of Arion himself... and in the *Thebaid* that Adrastus fled from Thebes,

> his clothes in sorry state, with Arion the sablehaired.

So they want the verse to hint that Poseidon was father to Arion.

The decisive battle finished with the defeat of the Argives at Thebes. Following this, Adrastus succeeded in leaving the battle-scene[30] with the help of his prodigious horse Arion.[31] Fragment 7 (numeration by Torres), consisting of a single verse ('his clothes in sorry state, with Arion the sable-haired'), refers to this flight. When Pausanias cites it, he is speaking about Arion who, according to him, was born to Poseidon and Demeter in Thelpousa (Arcadia).[32] The verse calls the horse κυανοχαίτηι ('sable-haired') and, as Pausanias indicates, this reminds us that Poseidon is his father as the epithet is used for him both in *Iliad* and in *Thebaid*.[33] The mention of the torn garments Adrastus wears puts directly before the public the disaster of the Argive warlords.[34]

F 8: *PEG* F 8 = F 6b + 6c D. = F 11 W., from Σ ABDGen *Il.* 23.346 [ii.259–60 Dindorf][35]

Ποσειδῶν ἐρασθεὶς Ἐρινύος, μεταβαλὼν τὴν αὐτοῦ φύσιν εἰς ἵππον, ἐμίγη κατὰ Βοιωτίαν παρὰ τῆι Τιλφούσηι κρήνηι. ἡ δὲ ἔγκυος γενομένη, ἵππον ἐγέννησεν, ὃς διὰ τὸ κρατιστεύειν, Ἀρείων ἐκλήθη. Κοπρεὺς δ' Ἁλιάρτου βασιλεύων πόλεως Βοιωτίας, ἔλαβε δῶρον αὐτὸν παρὰ Ποσειδῶνος, οὗτος δὲ αὐτὸν Ἡρακλεῖ ἐχαρίσατο, γενομένωι παρ' αὐτῶι. τούτωι δὲ διαγωνισάμενος Ἡρακλῆς πρὸς Κύκνον Ἄρεος υἱὸν καθ' ἱπποδρομίαν, ἐνίκησεν ἐν τῶι τοῦ Παγασαίου Ἀπόλλωνος ἱερῶι, ὅ ἐστι πρὸς Τροιζῆνι. εἶθ' ὕστερον αὖθις ὁ Ἡρακλῆς, Ἀδράστωι τὸν πῶλον παρέσχεν, ἐφ' οὗ μόνος ὁ Ἄδραστος ἐκ τοῦ Θηβαϊκοῦ πολέμου διεσώθη, τῶν ἄλλων ἀπολομένων. ἡ ἱστορία παρὰ τοῖς κυκλικοῖς.

---

[30] He must have fled and come back later to pronounce his funeral speech (see F 9 and F 12* numeration by Torres). Another interpretation is to be found in Cingano (2005b: 142–3, 150–1).

[31] Statius (*Theb.*11.442) even says that Arion could speak, which reminds us of the speech of Xanthus in the *Iliad* (19.404–17).

[32] In relation to the genealogy of Arion, see also F 8 (numeration by Torres).

[33] For this epithet in epic poetry, see Cingano (2005b: 142). For the relation of Poseidon with horses, see Burkert (2011: 215).

[34] Beck (2001) has proposed to read not εἵματα λυγρά ('clothes in sorry state') but σήματα λυγρά ('bearing the sad symbols'). This would refer to the tokens the Argive warriors should have attached to Adrastus' chariot as souvenirs for their families; see Aesch. *Sept.* 49–51, Cingano (2005b: 143–4) and, for the iconography, Krauskopf (1981a: 238).

[35] See also Σ T *Il.* 23.347, and Ps.-Apollod. *Bibl.* 3.6.8.

> Poseidon fell in love with Erinys, and changing his form into a horse he had intercourse with her by the fountain Tilphousa in Boeotia. She conceived and gave birth to a horse, which was called Arion because of its supremacy. Copreus, who was king at Haliartus, a town in Boeotia, received him from Poseidon as a gift. He gave him to Heracles when the latter stayed with him. Heracles used him to compete against Ares' son Cycnus in a horse race at the shrine of Pagasaean Apollo, which is near Troezen, and won. Then Heracles gave the foal in turn to Adrastus, and thanks to him Adrastus alone was saved from the Theban war when all the others perished. The story is in the Cyclic poets.

Fragment 8 also refers to Arion's genealogy. But it offers a different version. According to this scholium, the horse had Erinys as its mother.[36] And he was not born in Thelpousa (Arcadia) but near the Tilphousa spring, in Boeotia. We do not know with certainty which version was followed by the *Thebaid*. Actually we do not even know if the transmitted notice refers to the epic poem we are dealing with. Once again (as in F 6 numeration by Torres), the source only says that 'the story is in the Cyclic poets'.

F 9: *PEG* F 10 = F 7 D. = F 6 W., from Σ Pind. *Ol.* 6.15–17

(ἑπτὰ δ' ἔπειτα πυρᾶι νεκρῶν τελεσθέντων Ταλαϊονίδας | εἶπεν ἐν Θήβαισι τοιοῦτόν τι ἔπος· 'ποθέω στρατιᾶς ὀφθαλμὸν ἐμᾶς, | ἀμφότερον μάντίν τ' ἀγαθὸν καὶ δουρὶ μάρνασθαι' 'after the seven dead were hallowed on the pyre, the son of Talaos at Thebes said something like this: "I miss my army's seeing eye, both a good seer and good at fighting with the spear"'). Σ:

> ὁ Ἀσκληπιάδης φησὶ ταῦτα εἰληφέναι ἐκ τῆς κυκλικῆς Θηβαΐδος·
> ἀμφότερον μάντίς τ' ἀγαθὸς καὶ δουρὶ μάχεσθαι.
>
> Asclepiades (of Myrlea) says Pindar has taken this from the Cyclic *Thebaid*: (Amphiaraus), both a good seer and good at fighting with the spear.

This fragment comes from a scholium to Pindar's *Olympians*. The text of the Boeotian poet refers to the incineration in Thebes of the Argive champions after their defeat. Pindar also speaks of the speech pronounced in this occasion by Adrastus, who longed for the body of Amphiaraus,[37] 'both a good seer and good at fighting with the spear'. The scholium to this passage

---

[36] Pausanias (8.25.4) also says that Demeter was called Erinys among the Thelpousians.
[37] He had disappeared under the earth, as previously told by Pindar.

says that, according to Asclepiades (of Myrlea),[38] Pindar had taken these words 'from the Cyclic *Thebaid*'. According to tradition, Adrastus' skills in oratory (cf. F 12* numeration by Torres) were certainly best displayed in the recovery of the bodies and the funeral for the Argive warlords who were killed at Thebes. His praise of Amphiaraus contained in this fragment must have found its proper place in this context.

It is important to take into account that Amphiaraus, who had already appeared in F 6 (numeration by Torres), is the most frequently cited character in the extant fragments.[39] Although some of these fragments are dubious, a range of circumstances suggest that Amphiaraus must have played a special role in the poem. Fragment 9 (numeration by Torres), which describes him as a good fortune-teller and warrior, may be also seen as a special adaptation of the heroic ideal proclaimed in the *Iliad* by Phoenix ('speak and carry out great actions', *Il*. 9.443)[40] to the special case of a soothsayer.

F 10*: *PEG* F 4 = *Homerus* 3 D. = F 8* W., from Antigonus Carystius, *Hist. Mir.* 25 (46 Giannini) + Zenobius 1.24 (1.7 Leutsch-Schneidewinn)[41]

'πουλύποδός μοι, τέκνον, ἔχων νόον, Ἀμφίλοχ' ἥρως,
τοῖσιν ἐφαρμόζειν, τῶν κεν κατὰ δῆμον ἵκηαι,
ἄλλοτε δ' ἀλλοῖος τελέθειν καὶ χροιῆι ἕπεσθαι.'

'Pray hold to the octopus' outlook, Amphilochus my son, and adapt it to whatever people you come among; be changeable, and go along with the color.'

For line 3, Zenob. vulg. 1.24 (more or less the same in Diogenian. 1.23) explains: ἄλλοτε – ἕπεσθαι· ὅτι προσήκει ἕκαστον ἐξομοιοῦν ἑαυτὸν τούτοις ἐν οἷς ἂν καὶ γένηται τόποις· ἐκ μεταφορᾶς τοῦ πολύποδος ('Be changeable – color: meaning that one should assimilate himself to the surroundings he finds himself in. It is a metaphor from the octopus').

This fragment records some advice on travel and adaptation to other peoples apparently addressed by Amphiaraus to his son, the 'hero

---

[38] See *PEG* p. 28 and Wentzel (1896).
[39] In F 6, 9, 10*, 11*, numeration by Torres.
[40] Translation by Johnston (2007).
[41] See Athen. 7.317a; Eustath. on *Od*. 5.4321 (541.34–6), Diogenianus 1.23.

Amphilochus':[42] he should act like the octopus and adapt himself 'to whatever people you come among' (10.2).[43]

If these hexameters do indeed belong to the *Thebaid* (the testimony of Antigonus of Carystus refers to the author only as 'the poet', i.e. Homer),[44] the occasion of their declamation may have been Amphiaraus' leaving his family, an event represented in archaic art no fewer than fifteen times during the sixth century BC.[45] These scenes of Amphiaraus' departure normally depict the hero mounting his chariot and turning in a threatening way on his wife, who appears to be wearing the necklace of Harmonia. Tradition holds that Eriphyle was bribed with the necklace by Polynices,[46] who wanted to ensure Amphiaraus' participation in the expedition against Thebes. As a soothsayer, Amphiaraus refused to take part because he had already foreseen the fateful outcome of the campaign. At the same time, however, he was bound by oath to fulfil the will of his wife, who sought to settle any dispute that arose between her husband Amphiaraus and her brother Adrastus: Adrastus wanted the seven Argive warriors to march on Thebes, Amphiaraus refused to do so, and Eriphyle took Adrastus' side because she had been bribed by Polynices with the necklace of Harmonia by Polynices.

F 11*, from Σ Pind. *Nem.* 9.30b (= F 7* W.)

διαφορὰ δὲ ἐγενήθη τοῖς περὶ Ἀμφιάραον καὶ Ἄδραστον, ὥστε τὸν μὲν Ταλαὸν ὑπὸ Ἀμφιαράου ἀποθανεῖν, τὸν δὲ Ἄδραστον φυγεῖν εἰς Σικυῶνα . . . ὕστερον μέντοι συνεληλύθασι πάλιν, ἐφ' ὧι συνοικήσει τῆι Ἐριφύληι ὁ Ἀμφιάραος, ἵνα εἴ τι

μέγ' ἔρισμα μετ' ἀμφοτέροισι γένηται,

αὕτη διαιτᾶι.

A quarrel came about between Amphiaraus and Adrastus, with the consequence that Talaos was killed by Amphiaraus and Adrastus fled to

---

[42] At the time of the departure, Amphilochus is portrayed as a young boy in artistic depictions; see Krauskopf (1981c: 716–17).

[43] There is an obvious similarity with the octopus poem by Theognis (215–17). The translation here is my own.

[44] On the 'norm of the polyp', see Debiasi, below in this volume, p. 271.

[45] See Krauskopf (1981b: 706–8); Torres-Guerra (2012: 527).

[46] See e.g. D.S. 4.65.5–6; Ps.-Apollod. *Bibl.* 3.6.2.

Sicyon... But later they came to terms, it being provided that Amphiaraus should marry Eriphyle, so that if

> any great dispute should arise between the two of them,

she would arbitrate.

Fragment 11*, included as F 9 in a scholium to Pindar (*Nem.* 9.13 b (30)), alludes to the mediating role played by Eriphyle. The scholiast explains the familial origins of the rift between Adrastus and Amphiaraus. According to the tradition, Melampus and Bias had divided the power in Argos between them. As a result, their respective descendants (Amphiaraus and Adrastus) fought, and the latter was forced into exile in Sicyon. The reconciliation between the two leaders was brought about through the arranged marriage of Amphiaraus to Adrastus' sister, who was to act as the judge of any disputes between them.

The scholiast attributes this text (a part of a dactylic hexameter) neither to the *Thebaid* nor to 'the Cycle poets', nor even to 'the poet'.[47] It can only be said that a verse with this metrical structure and content must come from an epic poem. The *Thebaid* is the best candidate but not necessarily the only possibility, therefore the fragment must be regarded as dubious.

F 12*: *PEG* F 11* = F 4* W, from Plat. *Phdr.* 269a

Τί δὲ τὸν **μελίγηρυν Ἄδρηστον** οἰόμεθα ἢ τὸν Περικλέα, εἰ ἀκούσειαν ὧν νῦν δὴ ἡμεῖς διῇμεν τῶν παγκάλων τεχνημάτων, κτλ.

> How do we imagine the **honey-voiced Adrastus** or even Pericles would react, if they could hear of the wonderful rhetorical devices we were just going through, etc.,

Adrastus is also mentioned in this doubtful fragment[48] which calls him 'Adrastus the honey-voiced'. The indirect tradition for what seems to be a formulaic *iunctura* is Plato's *Phaedrus*. Plato gives the words in a different order (*meligēryn Adraston*), something that can be easily remedied through a simple change so that the expression can scan (*Adrēston meligēryn*). We cannot know for sure whether this group of words had been employed in the *Thebaid*. On the other hand, it is clear that the expression 'Adrastus the

---

[47] *Thebaid*: F 1, 2, 3, 4, 5, 7, 9 (numeration by Torres-Guerra). The Cycle: F 6, 8 (numeration by Torres-Guerra). 'The poet': F 10* (numeration by Torres-Guerra).
[48] See Merkelbach (1974: 2–3); Davies (1980).

honey-voiced' characterizes Adrastus very well, together with the role he must have played in the poem (cf. F 9 numeration by Torres).

BEYOND THE FRAGMENTS: FURTHER CONJECTURES

With regard to the significance attributed to Amphiaraus the fortune-teller in the *Thebaid*, it should also be noted that two texts included among the testimonies to the epic poem make reference to a poem by Homer entitled *Amphiaraus' departure*.[49] It is likely that this title was an alternative to the *Thebaid*; or given that the first verse of the poem tells of the leaders' departure from Argos, it may have been the title of the first canto.[50] Whatever the case may be, the existence of the title connotes Amphiaraus' significance in the poem. Indeed, if Amphiaraus was the protagonist of the *Thebaid*, a marked ambiguity about this legendary narrative might be resolved: what kind of epic tone could be struck in a poem whose characters include Polynices, who did not hesitate to bribe Eriphyle, and a monster like Tydeus?[51] West's view (2003: 5) that the sinister tenor of the Theban epics mirrors the Germanic epic tradition rather than the spirit of the *Iliad* or the *Odyssey* is meaningful in this regard. However, the sense of ambiguity that marks the subject-matter of the *Thebaid* may be resolved if Amphiaraus is read as central to the narrative and regarded as the protagonist of the poem.

An episode that is not referred to in the extant fragments, but which must be assumed to have been included in the *Thebaid*, is the foundation of the Nemean Games. The summary of the saga outlined above reported the warlords' halt in Nemea and the tragic death of Archemorus. There is a prior reason for thinking that the episode also featured in the *Thebaid*: because the event is recounted in all other versions of the legendary tale, it is more than likely that it would also be included in the Theban Cycle. A further argument in support of this hypothesis stems from iconographic

---

[49] See Ps.-Herod. *Vit. Hom.* 9, 6.22–7.10 Wilam. (*PEG* T 7 = F 9 D. = T 2 W.) and *Suda* s.v. "Ὅμηρος', ο 251 (iii. 526) Adler (*PEG* T 8 = F 9 D.). On *Amphiaraus' departure*, see also Debiasi, below in this volume, p. 279.

[50] See Torres-Guerra (1995b); West (2003a: 9). Bethe (1891a) was the most trenchant advocate of the other hypothesis (that *Amphiaraus' departure* was a separate poem); Robert (1915) critiqued his position.

[51] Given its theme, this epic poem would not appear to be an instance of the form defined by Aristotle in his *Poetics* (1452b30–1453a7), regarding the appropriate way to compose an argument.

evidence: the presence of the Seven in Nemea is attested to by at least two depictions in the sixth century BC.[52] The most plausible (albeit not wholly conclusive) explanation for the knowledge of this episode depicted in such iconographic representations is that their makers were familiar with epic sources;[53] and the *Thebaid* is the most likely provenance in this regard.

THE DATE OF THE *THEBAID* REVISITED

If the *Thebaid* tells of the mythical foundation of the Nemean Games, the poem's chronology could be explored from a new perspective. First, however, the political context of the poem must be addressed;[54] a relevant text in this regard is Herod. 5.67 (= *PEG* T 5 = D., W.), which tells of how Cleisthenes, the tyrant of Sicyon, banned the 'Homeric epics' from his city because they celebrated the Argive power he regarded as a threat to the power of Sicyon. At the same time, he also suppressed the cult of Adrastus, who had been first king of Sicyon and thereafter king of Argos. In light of the context as a whole the meaning of the reference to 'Homeric epics' in this passage becomes clearer.[55] The prohibition on the recitation of the Homeric epics and the expulsion of Adrastus are explained as being two aspects of the same anti-Argive policy. There must have been a link between Adrastus and the Homeric poems that Cleisthenes hated, and it seems quite reasonable to suppose that he was a main character in them; thus, the allusion in Herod. 5.67 must refer not to the *Iliad* or the *Odyssey* (the 'Homeric epics' par excellence) but to the *Thebaid*.[56]

On the other hand, it is important to remember that the Nemean Games may have been founded – or, rather, re-founded – in political opposition to Cleisthenes and with the assistance of Argos.[57] This is the view held by historians who interpret the scant evidence[58] as meaning that Nemea

---

[52] See *LIMC*, 'Amphiaraos' 32 and 33. See Torres-Guerra (2012).
[53] On this difficult point (where the 'sources' of archaic iconography are to be found), see Burgess (2001: 4, 61).
[54] A more detailed account of this issue is presented in Torres-Guerra (2012); see also Introduction, above in this volume, p. 11.
[55] See Cingano (1985); Burgess (2001: 129).
[56] See Cingano (1985). The same opinion had already been defended by Wilamowitz-Moellendorff (1884: 352).
[57] See e.g. Griffin (1982: 50–1); for a different point of view, see Libero (1996: 195).
[58] Plutarchus (*Moralia* 553 a–b) is the only source that speaks about the Sicyonian domination of Cleonai.

(or the city of Cleonai, which controlled Nemea) must have organized or reorganized the Nemean Games in 573 BC,[59] having escaped the control of Cleisthenes and Sicyon. In this regard, the idea that the *Thebaid* was first fixed in writing on the occasion of the reorganization of the Nemean Games is a suggestive one. The poem then acquired a layer of political meaning because it annoyed Cleisthenes for three reasons: it speaks of Adrastus and Argive power; the war is narrated from the Argive point of view; and, moreover, it recounts the mythical foundation of the Nemean Games.

This hypothesis may also find some confirmation in iconographic evidence, which discloses an increasing and striking interest in the Theban saga during the second quarter of the sixth century BC.[60] According to Cook (1983: 1–6), only a sudden rise in the number of representations of themes included in the epic poems can suggest anything about their chronology, and this is precisely the case discussed here. According to Cook's line of argument, the conclusion to be drawn is that the best explanation for renewed interest in the mythological theme of the Theban saga in the second quarter of the sixth century BC is proximity to the textual fixation or even the writing down of a major epic like the *Thebaid*, which must have happened around the time when the Nemean Games were reorganized and became a Panhellenic festival: that is, 573 BC.

This may also be an appropriate occasion on which to address a topic that has only been referred to tangentially thus far. It was asserted in the first paragraph of the article that the canonical Homeric poems presuppose an awareness of the Theban saga (cf. n. 2). Studies in the Neoanalytical school of thought have held that the author of the *Iliad* – and, less certainly, the author of the *Odyssey* – assumes that their audience's understanding of the saga is based on the version narrated in the *Thebaid*.[61] It has also been argued that linguistic analyses imply that the extant fragments of the poem date to the post-Homeric era. The resolution of this apparent *proteron hysteron* may lie in the combination of two approaches to the problem, which until recently appeared to be incompatible: oral theory and neoanalysis. Neoanalysis holds that non-traditional motifs drawn from a specific context, and thus semi-rigid in nature, have been exchanged between the poems.[62] The oral theory argument admits that the oral poems may have been sufficiently stable

---

[59] This is the date transmitted by Eusebius' *Chronicle*; see Griffin (1982: 51).
[60] See Torres-Guerra (2012).   [61] See Torres-Guerra (1995a); Kullmann (2002a: 167–9).
[62] See Kullmann (1960; 1984 = 1992; 2002a).

in form so as to enable intertextual relations between them.[63] Hence, it seems possible that an oral version of the *Thebaid* existed prior to the *Iliad*, influencing its composition, and that it was written down after the *Iliad*, possibly in the year 573 BC, in the circumstances of the political context outlined in this chapter.

[63] On the combination of orality, intertextuality and neoanalysis, the contributions of Burgess (2006) and Tsagalis (2008a, see especially 63 n. 2, and 66–8) should be noted.

14 | *Epigonoi*

ETTORE CINGANO

The *Epigonoi* is the third poem of the Theban cycle centered on the family of Oedipus: it dealt with the generation of his grandsons. The title ('Ἐπίγονοι = 'The afterborn, the younger men') and the opening line (*PEG* F 1 = D., W.: Νῦν αὖθ' ὁπλοτέρων ἀνδρῶν ἀρχώμεθα, Μοῦσαι 'and now, Muses, let us begin with the younger ones/those born after') point to a close connection with the preceding poem, the *Thebaid*, which dealt with the feud between Eteocles and Polynices and with the first war of Argos against Thebes. Consequently, the *Epigonoi* was centered on the second expedition against Thebes waged 10 years later by the sons of the Seven.[1] The continuity of the subject matter is matched by the equal length of the poems: according to the source which also quotes their beginnings, they both numbered 7,000 lines (*Certamen Homeri et Hesiodi* 15, 256–8 Allen = *Epig. PEG* T 1 = 2 D.). The poem presents a number of unsolved problems regarding its origin, dating, arrangement, and relation to other epic poems now lost (the *Thebaid*, the *Alcmeonis*, the Trojan epics).

AUTHORSHIP

The strong narrative bond with the *Thebaid* may have facilitated the attribution of the *Epigonoi* to Homer, although some doubts regarding the Homeric autorship of the poem surface as early as the fifth century BC with Herodotus: after recalling that the Hyperboreans are mentioned by 'Hesiod' (cf. Hes. F 150.21 M.-W. = F 63.21 Hirsch.), he continues '... and so does Homer in the *Epigonoi*, if Homer really composed this poem' (Herod. 4.32 = *Epig. PEG* F 2 = D., 5 W.).[2] In a later period, after quoting the opening lines of the *Thebaid* and of the *Epigonoi* (see above), the compiler of the *Certamen* casts the same doubt on Homeric paternity by adding 'some say that this

---

[1] The chronological detail is supplied by Ps.-Apollod. *Bibl.* 3.7.2. The same span of time is used to scan the course of events in the Trojan epics. On the *Thebaid*, see Torres-Guerra, above in this volume.

[2] Herod. 4.32. Cf. Wilamowitz (1884: 352): 'Bei Herodotus beginnt die Kritik...subjective Zweifel außert er.'

too is the work of Homer' (*Cert.* 15 (260 Allen) φασὶ γάρ τινες καὶ ταῦτα 'Ὁμήρου εἶναι).³

Herodotus' quotation of the poem proves that in the classical age there circulated one poem *Epigonoi* distinct from the *Thebaid*, which was believed to be Homeric. On the other hand, in the Hellenistic age the prose writer Dionysius the cyclograph still believed in the Homeric autorship of the poem(s) on the Theban wars (*FgrHist* 15 F 8); the same assumption can be drawn from the passage on the heroic past of Thebes where Pausanias, after recalling the final victory of the Epigonoi, claims that according to the poet Callinus of Ephesus (seventh century BC) and other authorities, Homer was the author of the *Thebaid* (Paus. 9.9.5 = *Theb. PEG* T 2 = 1 D.). Here Pausanias clearly considers the two Theban wars as being narrated in one single poem, which he identifies with the *Thebaid*.⁴ It follows that in antiquity this title was also used in a loose way to refer to one single poem narrating the two Theban wars; this is confirmed by a scholion to Apollonius Rhodius, where the statement 'those who wrote the *Thebaid* (οἱ δὲ τὴν Θηβαΐδα γεγραφότες) say that the daughter of Teiresias, Manto, was sent to Delphi by the Epigonoi' implies that at this time Thebes had been taken by the Argive leaders:⁵ therefore, in spite of the title mentioned by the scholiast, the episode cannot but have been narrated in the poem *Epigonoi*.

To conclude, it can be assumed from the evidence at hand that because of the strong connection between the events narrated, in antiquity the epics relating the two expeditions against Thebes could either go under the title of the more ancient and authoritative one, the *Thebaid*, or else be identified as two distinct poems (*Thebaid, Epigonoi*), each of them dealing with one war.⁶ No evidence, however, can be found in the sources to buttress the opinion expressed by Bethe, that there existed an epic poem in two parts by a single author, encompassing the *Thebaid* and the *Epigonoi*.⁷

Additional evidence suggesting doubts relating to the sources in attributing the *Epigonoi* is provided by an Aristophanic scholiast who, commenting

---

³ As was noted by Wilamowitz (1920: 399 n.1), ταῦτα here could also include the *Thebaid*; in this case it should be translated as 'these two poems', and the doubts regarding Homeric autorship should be referred to both poems.
⁴ Paus. 9.9.5; for the text and a discussion, see Torres-Guerra, above in this volume, p. 228.
⁵ Σ Apoll. Rhod. 1.308b = *Epig. PEG* F 3 = D., 4 W. On the attribution of this fragment to the *Epigonoi*, see the doubts of Welcker (1865: 194); Immisch (1889: 141 n. 1).
⁶ This point had already been made by Müller (1840: 71); Wecklein (1901: 677–8); Rzach (1922: 2374).
⁷ Bethe (1891a: 37–8) with interesting remarks, although it is nowhere attested in the ancient sources that the title *Epigonoi* could also comprehend the *Thebaid*; on this point see also Welcker (1882: 403–5); Legras (1905: 22).

on the quotation by Aristophanes of the first verse of the poem (Aristoph. *Pac.* 1270 = *Epig. PEG* F 1 = D., W., with a different ending: Νῦν αὖθ' ὁπλοτέρων ἀνδρῶν ἀρχώμεθα – Παῦσαι / ὁπλοτέρους ἄιδων, 'Stop singing of the younger men'), names one Antimachus as the author.[8] A poet bearing this name can be identified with Antimachus of Colophon, the late fifth-century poet who composed a *Thebaid* in no fewer than ten books[9]; another candidate is the shadowy Antimachus of Teos, an epic poet who allegedly lived in the eighth century BC (Plut. *Romul.* 12.2 = Antim. fr. 1 D.); elsewhere, he is credited with an epic fragment often attributed to the *Epigonoi* (Clem. Alex. *Strom.* 6.12.7 = *Epig. PEG* F 4 = 2 W. = Antim. fr. 2 D.: see below).[10] The attribution of the poem to Antimachus may result from confusion, and should be handled with care; what can be asserted, in spite of the paucity of fragments, is that the *Epigonoi* was undoubtedly circulating in fifth-century Athens as a self-standing poem, as is proved by Herodotus and Aristophanes.

THE STORY

The plot of the poem can no longer be reconstructed in detail, but its main outline can be sketched with the cautious help of Ps.-Apollodorus' *Bibliotheca* (3.7.2–5), Diodorus Siculus (4.66–67.1), and Pausanias (9.5.13, 8.6, 33.1–3). The myth of the defeat of Thebes by the Epigonoi who set from Argos was known to Homer, as is made evident most of all by Sthenelus' boast in *Il.* 4.405–6 ἡμεῖς τοι πατέρων μέγ' ἀμείνονες εὐχόμεθ' εἶναι· / ἡμεῖς καὶ Θήβης ἕδος εἵλομεν ἑπταπύλοιο ('we pride ourselves on being far braver than our fathers, since we are the ones who conquered seven-gated Thebes').[11] The *Epigonoi* can be labeled as the first instance ever of a serial in Western

---

[8] Σ Aristoph. *Pac.* 1270 ἀρχὴ τῶν Ἐπιγόνων Ἀντιμάχου ('beginning of Antimachus' *Epigonoi*').

[9] It should however be noted that, according to Matthews (1996: 20–1), we have no indication 'that Antimachus' *Thebaid* went beyond the story of the Seven against Thebes, i.e. it probably did not extend to include the campaign of the Epigonoi' (see also p. 22 on the length of Antimachus' *Thebaid*); see, however, Immisch (1889: 130–1 n. 1).

[10] On Antimachus of Teos and the *Epigonoi* see Wilamowitz (1884: 345–6 n. 26); Bethe (1891a: 36–8); Robert (1915: 182–4), who advocate the identification with this poet. See, however, Legras (1905: 67 n. 1).

[11] The myth of the Theban wars was also known to Hesiod (cf. *WD* 161–4; F 193.1–8 M.-W. + P Lit Palau Rib. 21 = F 90.1–8 Hirsch.). I am using the word 'myth' in referring to the expeditions of the Seven and of the Epigonoi, since in my opinion no decisive historical or archaeological evidence can support the idea that the two wars against seven-gated Thebes reflected a historical event in Mycenean times: see among others Dowden (1992: 68–70); Scheer (1993: 58–65); Cingano (2000: 142–3); Moggi and Osanna (2010: 263–73). For a survey of the problem see Schachter (1967), with bibliography.

literature: the story clearly presupposes to a large extent the plot of the *Thebaid*, and a number of details in its narrative point to a deliberate symmetrical arrangement in order to create doublets, parallelisms, and contrasts with the former poem. To mention one telling example, the hero and leader Adrastus was the sole survivor of the Seven in the first expedition; conversely, in the second expedition his son Aegialeus is the only leader among the Epigonoi to fall in battle, at the hands of the Theban king Laodamas, the son of Eteocles, who in turn was killed by Alcmaon, the leader of the Argives.[12] A further parallelism concerns the seminal role of Eriphyle, sister of Adrastus, in both poems: being the wife of Amphiaraus and the mother of Alcmaon and Amphilochus, Eriphyle played the pivotal role of persuading (in the *Thebaid*) her reluctant husband to go to war, having been bribed by Polynices with the necklace of Harmonia, daughter of Cadmus; years later (in the *Epigonoi*), she was bribed with the robe of Harmonia by the son of Polynices, Thersander, into convincing her sons to go to war (see Hom. *Od.* 11.326–7; 15.246–8; Σ Hom. *Od.* 11.326; Ps.-Apollod. *Bibl.* 3.6.1–2; 3.7.2, 7.5; Diod. Sic. 4.66.3).[13]

In many ways, then, the *Epigonoi* stands out as a clear (and therefore later) remake of the *Thebaid*, heavily depending on it. As recalled by Ps.-Apollodorus (*Bibl.* 3.7.2) and Diodorus Siculus (4.66.1), the aim of the Epigonoi was 'to avenge the death of their fathers'. The poem was created at some stage as a sequel to the *Thebaid*, perhaps with the intent to meet the expectations of an extended Argive audience and modify the gloomy outcome of the first expedition. In fact, albeit being centered on the traditional epic theme of the siege of a city which was bound to be captured and plundered and/or destroyed (as happens, for instance, with the *Iliupersis* and with the *Capture of Oechalia* by Creophylus of Samos), the *Thebaid* very peculiarly ended in a failure. In the sixth century BC (or even earlier) an Argive interest in the deeds of the heroes who fought against Thebes can be gathered from the famous passage in Herodotus, where the *Homēreia epea* performed at Sicyon at the time of Cleisthenes (Herod. 5.67.1) cannot but refer to the Theban epics;[14] it is confirmed in the same period by the inscription recently found in the enclosure of the heroon in the agorà of

---

[12] The correspondence between the fate of Adrastus and Aegialeus had been noted by Hellanicus, *EGM* F 100.

[13] For a survey of the relevant parallelisms and contrasts between the two poems see Welcker (1882: 399–403); Olivieri (2004: 79–91); Cingano (2011: 5–8); on Eriphyle see most recently Sineux (2007: 38–45).

[14] On the identification of the Homeric epics with the Theban epics in the Herodotus passage see Cingano (1985), with bibliography; Introduction, above in this volume, p. 11; Torres-Guerra, above, p. 241.

Argos, bearing the words ΕΡΟΟΝ ΤΟΝ ΕΝ ΘΕΒΑΙΣ, meaning 'the heroon of those in Thebes', or 'of the heroes (who fell) at Thebes' (ἡρώων τῶν ἐν Θήβαις), and referring to the Seven and the Epigonoi. The inscription, and its location in the heroon, show the intention of Argos to firmly root the Theban epics in cult.[15]

The expedition of the Seven was ill-fated from the start and ended with the death of all the Argive heroes but Adrastus;[16] on the contrary, the expedition of the Epigonoi was favored by the gods and by the oracle of Apollo at Delphi, and ended in success (cf. *Il.* 4.406–8; Ps.-Apollod. *Bibl.* 3.7.2). It is impossible to ascertain at which point of the story the poem started: perhaps with the death of the Seven and the pledge by their sons to avenge them, or else 10 years after the first expedition, when the sons had grown up and were determined to act.[17] According to the fullest accounts of the story by Ps.-Apollodorus (*Bibl.* 3.7.2–5) and Diodorus Siculus (4.66.1–67.1, with a few differences), the oracle of Apollo at Delphi predicted that the expedition against Thebes could only be successful if the leader was Alcmaon; the hero accepted reluctantly, his main urge at the time being to kill his mother Eriphyle and thus avenge the double betrayal of her husband and her sons (see above).[18]

The fact that the leadership of the expedition was not conferred upon Aegialeus, whose father Adrastus had led the first one, but upon Alcmaon, reflects both the prominence acquired by the *genos* of the seer Amphiaraus, the Melampodidai, and the growing importance of the oracle of Delphi,

---

[15] On the inscription, dating from the mid sixth century BC, see Pariente (1992); Hall (1999: 5); Boehringer (2001: 142–4). The cult of the Seven and the Epigonoi at Argos continues well into the fifth century BC: see Paus. 2.20.5; 10.10.3–4; Cingano (2002: 36–42). Pariente (1992: 218) remarks that no fewer than eight of the twenty-five heroic monuments noted by Pausanias (2.21.2; 2.23.2) at Argos are related to the Theban wars.

[16] The Seven had acted against the will of the gods: see *Il.* 4.380–1; 409; Hes. F 193.6–8 M.-W. = F 90.6–8 Hirsch.; cf. Pind. *Nem.* 9.18–20.

[17] For an attempted reconstruction of the plot of the poem see Robert (1921: 949–59); Severyns (1928: 224–8); Gantz (1993: 522–5).

[18] Conversely, Ps.-Apollodorus (*Bibl.* 3.7.5) also relates a story with a different timing of events, whereby Alcmaon found out *only after the capture of Thebes* that he (and his brother Amphilochus) had been betrayed by his mother: he killed her in accordance with the oracle of Apollo. According to another version (Asclepiades of Tragilos, *FgrHist* 12 F 29 = Σ D *Od.* 11.326–7), which is at variance with the story told by the *Epigonoi*, Alcmaon killed Eriphyle before setting off to war, and was affected by folly and persecuted by the Erinyes (cf. also Ps.-Apollod. *Bibl.* 3.7.5); on the different versions of the myth see Gantz (1993: 525); Debiasi, below in this volume, p. 264. The murder of Eriphyle is only attributed to her elder son, Alcmaon, by most sources, although Amphilochus is also occasionally involved (cf. Ps.-Apollod. quoted hereabove). The fate of Alcmaon in the Theban epics evokes a close parallelism with the story of Orestes in the aftermath of the Trojan War.

which proves central also in other episodes in the poem and in the vicissitudes of Alcmaon.[19] In keeping with the Delphic influence, the choice of Alcmaon as the leader of the expedition can be accounted for by his mantic skill, inherited from his father Amphiaraus and his ancestor Melampus; his oracular status was already well attested at the time of Pindar (see *Pyth.* 8.56–60).

Various lists with the names of the Epigonoi are preserved, including the ones from the groups of statues commissioned by Argos and described by Pausanias, one at Delphi, the other at Argos, both dating from the second quarter of the fifth century BC.[20] As happens with the lists of the Seven, the number and also some names of the heroes may differ for various reasons (local, historical, political, etc.); moreover, the inclusion of two heroes (Amphilochus and Alcmaon) replacing their father Amphiaraus cannot but prove disruptive for the traditional number of the list of the Seven.[21] The Homeric poems are the earliest source for the presence in the list of the Epigonoi of Diomedes (son of Tydeus), Sthenelus (son of Capaneus), Euryalus (son of Mecisteus), Alcmaon, and Amphilochus.[22] To these names, representing the offspring of the (presumably) original list of the *Thebaid*, Thersander, the son of Polynices, can safely be added. The other heroes fluctuate between Promachus (son of Parthenopaeus), Polydorus (son of Hippomedon), Medon (son of Eteoclus), and two more sons of Polynices, Adrastus and Timeas.[23] Two more names – unrecorded elsewhere – of heroes who 'took Thebes with the Epigonoi' (and afterwards

---

[19] Interestingly, according to Herodotus 5.61.1, the oracle of Apollo at Delphi was also connected with the Theban king Laodamas, son of Polynices, who in the final battle against the Argives dies at the hands of Alcmaon.

[20] Paus. 2.20.5; 10.10.4; the other main lists are found in Ps.-Apollod. *Bibl.* 3.7.2; Σ *Il.* 4.406a. I am not taking into account here the lists found in the Attic tragedians, since they are demonstrably influenced by other (later) circumstances. For a detailed discussion of the lists of the Epigonoi and their relation to the lists of the Seven see Cingano (2002); see also Bethe (1891a: 110–13); Robert (1921: 950–2); Kullmann (1960: 148–54); Prinz (1979: 168–74); Gantz (1993: 523–4).

[21] This explains the occasional dropping of the younger brother Amphilochus from the list of the Epigonoi, noted by Pausanias (10.10.4) in the group of statues at Delphi. Conversely, Pausanias (2.20.5) counts eleven statues of the Epigonoi at Argos, including two more sons of Polynices (see also 9.33.1); Σ *Il.* 4.406a names nine heroes, adding Medon, the son of Eteoclus, and replacing Promachus with Stratolaos as the son of Parthenopæus, whose double genealogy, debated by the ancient sources (Arcadian vs. Argive), contributes to the variations in the list.

[22] For Diomedes, Euryalus and Sthenelus as leaders of the Argive contingent at Troy see *Il.* 2.559–67, 4.365–410; 6.20–8 (Euryalus); 9.48; 23.511 (Sthenclus); only Diomedes is a steady presence in many books of the poem. *Od.* 15.244–8 implies the presence of the sons of Amphiaraus; see also Hes. F 193.1 M.-W. = F 90.1 Hirsch.; 197.6 M.-W. = 105.6 Hirsch. Alcmaon's matricide is represented on a Tyrrhenian amphora from Orvieto dating from 570/560 BC (Berlin PM VI 4841): see Gantz (1993: 526); Schefold (1993: 282–3, pl. 301).

[23] See the sources mentioned above, n. 20.

also went to Troy) are supplied by Pherecydes (*EGM* F 115): drawing on an early tradition, he names Euchenor and Cleitus, the sons of the Corinthian seer Polyidus who, like Amphiaraus, descended from Melampus.[24] The suggestion that Euchenor and Cleitus may have belonged in the epic version of the story is corroborated by the information that Alcmaon gathered allies from the neighbouring cities, including Corinth (see Paus. 9.9.4; Diod. Sic. 4.66.3–4).[25]

Laodamas too was helped by allies, but no information is left regarding the Theban side: even more drastically than with the *Thebaid*, one cannot but notice the total lack of information on the Theban defenders in the poetic, local, and antiquarian sources.[26] The only Theban opponent to stand out is the king Laodamas, who falls in battle at the hands of his peer, the commander of the Argives Alcmaon, after fighting off bravely the enemies and killing Aegialeus.[27]

The march of the Argive army towards Thebes must have been part of the poem: it was punctuated by the plunder and destruction of the surrounding villages, a theme attested also in the Trojan epics.[28] In the *Epigonoi* the private feud between the descendants of Oedipus over the throne of Thebes seems to have become a more collective issue motivated by pride and revenge (see above). Significantly (and differently from the *Thebaid*), no final clash takes place between the sons of Polynices and Eteocles, Thersander and Laodamas. Moreover, in the second expedition, no siege of the city was involved, and the seven gates play no role in the confrontation between the two armies. The Thebans advanced out of the walls and the battle with the Argives was fought at a place called Glisas, not far from Teumessos, where the graves of the Argives were still shown down to the time of Pausanias (see Hellan. *EGM* F 100; Ps.-Apollod. *Bibl.* 3.7.3; Paus. 9.5.13, 8.6, 9.4, 19.2). Although according to the mainstream tradition which can plausibly be traced back to the Theban epics, Aegialeus was the only one of

---

[24] For a tentative genealogy of Polyidus see Bernert (1952: 1647–50): he descended from Mantios, son of Melampus, whereas Amphiaraus descended from another son of Melampus, Antiphatus. It remains uncertain whether Polyidus can be identified with one Polypheides mentioned in *Od.* 15.225–55 (line 249), in a very similar genealogical context.

[25] Pherecydes adds that (like other Epigonoi) Euchenor and Cleitus also went to Troy; cf. *Il.* 13.660–5; Hes. F 136.7–14 M.-W. = F 6* Hirsch.

[26] It is noticeable that even Pindar and Pausanias are peculiarly reticent in mentioning names and stories concerning the Theban opponents in the two wars. On this matter see Cingano (2000: 145–6, 152–5).

[27] See Ps.-Apollod. *Bibl.* 3.7.5; Paus. 9.5.13. It appears from Herod. 5.61.1 that Laodamas was a fully fledged character in the archaic tradition (see above, n. 19).

[28] Cf. Ps.-Apollod. *Bibl.* 3.7.3; for the plunder of cities in the cyclic epics, see *Cypria*, arg. lines 155–6 Severyns.

the Epigonoi to fall, Pausanias (9.19.2) reports that Promachus also died in the fight along with other Argives of high rank.

Since the fate of his daughter Manto after the fall of Thebes was narrated in the *Epigonoi* (cf. *PEG* F 3 = D., 4 W.: see below), another episode very likely to have been featured in the poem after the battle is the death of the seer Teiresias at the spring Tilphussa; Teiresias seems also to have played a role in advising the Thebans to flee from their city before the arrival of the Argive army (Diod. Sic. 4.66.4–5, 67.1; Ps.-Apollod. *Bibl.* 3.7.3; Paus. 9.33.1). Finally, the death of Eriphyle must have been a major episode, rounding off the poem and contributing to the interplay between the texture of the *Thebaid* and the *Epigonoi*: by killing his mother, Alcmaon fulfilled the command imparted by his father Amphiaraus in the initial part of *Thebaid*, before reluctantly departing from Argos.

THE EPIGONOI AT THE JUNCTION BETWEEN THE THEBAN AND THE TROJAN EPICS

The ancient reports on the fate of Thebes, its inhabitants, and its conquerors after the victory of the Argives diverge to an extent that prevents any attempt at imagining how the poem ended. A scrutiny of the sources reveals ambiguities and inconsistencies: according to some, Thebes was sacked and destroyed to such an extent that – one would assume – it was abandoned by its inhabitants for a long period.[29] On the other hand, Diodorus seems to modify his earlier account by recalling (4.67.1) that some of the Thebans returned to live in the city when Creon was king (i.e. after the death of Thersander), thus implying that it had not been entirely destroyed; Ps.-Apollodorus (*Bibl.* 3.7.4) adds one more detail to the picture, by specifying that the Argives *only* 'pull down the walls' of Thebes (καθαιροῦσι τὰ τείχη), and this can only imply that the city was left more or less undamaged; Pausanias is more explicit, reporting in two passages that after capturing Thebes the Argives settled Thersander on the throne, and he welcomed back to their city the Thebans who had initially fled to Illyria (9.5.14; 9.8.7).[30]

This twofold tradition on Thebes is likely to reflect (a) the early stage of the Theban epics, and (b) the later phase when they were connected to the

---

[29] See *Il.* 4.406; Σ *Il.* 2.505 and 4.406a; Diod. Sic. 4.66.5; Strab. 9.2.32.
[30] Pausanias must be drawing on a Theban source here, since according to this version Laodamas was not killed by Alcmaon, but withdrew to Illyria with any Theban willing to follow him.

Trojan epics. When the *Epigonoi* was a self-standing poem unconnected to the Trojan cycle, the standard theme of destruction of a city by a foreign army prevailed over the original cause of the expedition – the settling of Thersander, son of Polynices, on the throne of Thebes. This version explains the absence of Thebes in the Homeric Catalogue of Ships and its replacement with the obscure and fictitious Hypothebai (*Il.* 2.505), a name unattested elsewhere: the *hapax* shows that the Homeric bard complied with the version of the destruction of the city conveyed by the Theban epics.[31] The omission of Thebes also explains the absence of Thersander from the earlier Homeric Catalogue of Ships where, given his status as the king of Thebes, one would expect to find him as the commander of the Boeotian contingent (*Il.* 2.494–510).

When at a later stage the tradition on the Theban wars and the fate of Thersander at Thebes were brought into relation with the Trojan epics, the version relating the utter destruction of the city was mitigated and reconciled with the one about his reign; somehow, 'The reign of Thersander may reflect the belief that life went on at Thebes after the war of the Epigonoi.'[32] Yet, in spite of his being a prominent character in the *Epigonoi*, his absence in the *Iliad* shows that Thersander could not be harmonized with the former established list of the five Boeotian leaders in Catalogue of Ships. Consequently, to avoid any conflict with the canonical tradition of the *Iliad*, he was inserted in the preliminaries of the Trojan expedition, in the *Cypria*, and had to undergo an early exit from the scene by dying in Mysia before he could get to Troy. The bravery in battle shown by Thersander before being killed by Telephus confirms that in the *Cypria* he had a relevant role and status (see *Cypria*, arg. lines 126–8 Severyns; Paus. 9.5.14), conforming to his kingship at Thebes and to his place among the *Epigonoi*.[33]

A similar approach can help explain the absence at Troy of two illustrious Epigonoi, the Argives Alcmaon and Amphilochus, whose popularity is well attested in early Greek poetry.[34] Although their fate after the war with Thebes

---

[31] On Hypothebai and the twofold tradition on Thebes see the discussion in Cingano (2000: 128–35). For an interpretation of the sources see, most recently, Sakellariou (1990: 210–22, to be handled with care); Vannicelli (1995: 21–4).

[32] Schachter (1967: 4).

[33] By inserting Thersander in the *Cypria*, 'The house of Cadmus... and Thebes, ill-represented by *Hypothebai* B 505, made their way into the sacred ring' of the most important event in the mythical past of the Greeks, the Trojan war (Allen (1921: 28). Still, the double status of Thersander may have contributed to hinder his entrance in the Homeric list of the Boeotian leaders at Troy: formerly living in Argos and being himself half-Argive through the marriage of the exiled Polynices with a daughter of Adrastus, after the war of the Epigonoi he was reinstalled in his Theban roots and made the king of Thebes.

[34] See *Od.* 15.248; Hes. F 193.1 M.-W. = F 90.1 Hirsch.; F 196.7 M.-W. = F 105.7 Hirsch.; F 278–9 M.-W.; Stesich. *PMGF* 193.28–31; S 148 D. (from the poem *Eriphyle*).

is differentiated in the sources, clearly the killing of their mother Eriphyle, and the ensuing madness of Alcmaon chased by the Furies, triggered a different fate of wander and adventures which took both far from the main epic track of the *Iliad*, and prevented their presence in the Catalogue of Ships. Various explanations are given to account for their absence at Troy: still, their presence amongst the suitors of Helen in the Hesiodic *Catalogue of Women* (F 197.6–9 M.-W. = F 105 Hirsch.; cf. Ps.-Apollod. *Bibl.* 3.10.8) shows that – like Thersander – at some stage they were given recognition in a significant stream of the epic tradition.[35] Interestingly, regarding Amphilochus, the importance of the *genos* of Amphiaraus, the Melampodidai, and his mantic status probably contributed to place him, at the end of the Trojan war, somehow on the route *from* Troy, in Asia Minor and farther East; this is attested by the mantic poem *Melampodia* (Hes. F 278–9 M.-W.) and by prose sources relating the returns of the Greek heroes from Troy (Herod. 3.91.1; 7.91; Thuc. 2.68.3; Ps.-Apollod. *Epit.* 6.2, 19).[36]

On the other hand, if for these reasons the above mentioned heroes were missing in the *Iliad*, when the Theban epics and the Trojan epics were brought together in a broader narrative string encompassing nearly the entire heroic age (cf. Hes. *WD* 156–65; Σ Hom. *Il.* 1.5; Σ Eur. *Or.* 1641; *Anecd. Oxon.* iv.405.27–406.1 Cramer), the Homeric Catalogue of Ships easily accommodated an adequate number of victorious Epigonoi of illustrious descent as the straightforward representatives of Argos at Troy: Diomedes, Sthenelus, and Euryalus are the natural leaders of the Argive contingent (*Il.* 2.559–68). In this way, the Epigonoi were to play a seminal role in the chronological and thematic sequel of events of the epic cycle, serving as the main junction between two traditions which were originally independent and accounted for the two major events of the mythical age.

Yet, if some heroes of the *Epigonoi* became pivotal in both traditions and shared the unique privilege of contributing to the two victorious wars, it is all the more striking to remark that they turn out undisputably unimpressive and ordinary, if contrasted not only with the traits of their fathers, the Seven (cf. Amphiaraus, Capaneus, Tydeus, Parthenopæus, Polynices, Adrastus), but also – with the exception of Diomedes in some books – with many heroes in the *Iliad*, on either side of the armies. From what we can gather, not a single Epigonos can match the prominence and fully sketched features of the Seven heroes who failed. The drabness of the plot, the lack of strength,

---

[35] On this point see Cingano (2005a: 140–3).
[36] On the wanderings of Amphilochus see Gantz (1993: 527–8); Scheer (1993: 163–71, 222–34). On the wanderings of Alcmaon see below. On Alcmaon in the *Alcmeonid* see Debiasi, below in this volume, pp. 263–6.

originality, and coherence in motivating episodes which were effectively rooted and harmonized in the *Thebaid*, did not pass unnoticed by German scholarship of the nineteenth century:[37] still, the remark by Wilamowitz (1891: 240) that 'the renown of the Epigonoi lay in the *Iliad* of Homer' can only be accepted with respect to Diomedes: it proves untenable for Sthenelus and most of all Euryalus.

It looks as if, leaving the Attic tragedians aside and with the plausible exception of the city of Argos which nurtured a primary interest in modifying the outcome of the myth, the first disastrous expedition of the Seven captured to a much greater extent the Greek archaic imagination, and left a far deeper mark than the success achieved by the Epigonoi. The same holds true with the iconography of the myth: differently from the Seven, the Epigonoi are poorly attested on vases, if at all.[38] These considerations – together with the analysis of F 1 (see below) – may help to elucidate the function performed by the *Epigonoi* and gauge the lateness and the artificiality of the poem, in spite of the familiarity of few books of the *Iliad* with its subject matter: from the evidence at hand, it seems to have been created primarily as a duplication of the *Thebaid*, with the intent to reshape the outcome of the first expedition against Thebes and to graft the tradition of the Theban wars on the Homeric tradition of the war at Troy.[39]

THE FRAGMENTS

The opening of the poem reveals that it was centered on Argos and on the deeds of the sons of the Seven: Νῦν αὖθ' ὁπλοτέρων ἀνδρῶν ἀρχώμεθα, Μοῦσαι ('And now, Muses, let us begin with those born after' (**Epig. PEG F 1 = D., W.**). Davies (1989c: 31) has plausibly suggested that the second verse may have continued with a relative and a sentence anticipating the outcome of the poem, '(the younger men) who succeeded in capturing Thebes'. The combination *nyn aute* ('and now') marks a strong transition from the time of the Seven to the time and generation of their sons, which actually proved to be 'more capable of bearing arms', as one

---

[37] See Nitzsch (1862: 449); Welcker (1882: 400–1); Wilamowitz (1891: 239–40); see also Friedländer (1914 = 1969: 42); Robert (1915: 251); Robert (1921: 949–50); Finster-Hotz (1986: 806): 'The Epigonoi stood in the shade of the generation of their fathers.'
[38] Finster-Hotz (1986: 805) lists only three vases likely to refer to the Epigonoi, against fifty-eight vases representing the Seven against Thebes. See also Cingano (2002: 32–5).
[39] On the relation between the subject matter and the written form of the cyclic poems see, most recently, West (2013: 17).

etymology of *hoploteros* would suggest.[40] The same procedure, with the adverb *nyn* at the beginning of the first verse of the poem, is attested in the Hesiodic corpus in order to effectively connect the subject matter of two poems, the *Theogony* and the *Catalogue of Women*, which originally were independent. Some manuscripts of the *Theogony* and a papyrus fragment (POxy. 2354, second century AD) present two lines with an invocation to the Muses connecting the couplet at the end of the *Theogony* (1019–20) to the very beginning of the *Catalogue* (*Theog.* [1021–2] = Hes. F 1.1–2 M.-W. = Hirsch.): αὗται μὲν θνητοῖσι παρ' ἀνδράσιν εὐνηθεῖσαι / ἀθάναται γείναντο θεοῖς ἐπιείκελα τέκνα. / νῦν δὲ γυναικῶν φῦλον ἀείσατε, ἡδυέπειαι / Μοῦσαι Ὀλυμπιάδες, κοῦραι Διὸς αἰγιόχοιο ('These are the immortal goddesses who lay with mortal men and bear them children like unto gods. But now, sweet-voiced Muses of Olympus, daughters of Zeus who holds the aegis, sing of the tribe of women').

The comparison with the Hesiodic *Catalogue of Women* also opens the possibility that the first verse of the *Epigonoi* as we have it is not the original one, but reflects a later stage in the elaboration of the epic cycle when the need was felt to present it as a natural sequel of the *Thebaid*. A similar editorial practice can be noticed in the Trojan epics: the last verse of the *Iliad* dealing with the funeral of Hector was modified in order to accomodate the mention of the Amazon Penthesileia, who was to play a key role in the following poem of the Trojan epic cycle, the *Aethiopis*.[41] The aim was probably to facilitate the insertion of the *Iliad* in the epic cycle, by creating a tighter connection with the *Aethiopis*.

F 2 *PEG* (= D. = F 5 W.), from Herodt. 4.32

Ἀλλ' Ἡσιόδωι [F 150.21 M.-W. = F 63 Hirsch.] μέν ἐστι περὶ Ὑπερβορέων εἰρημένα, ἔστι δὲ καὶ Ὁμήρωι ἐν Ἐπιγόνοισι, εἰ δὴ τῶι ἐόντι γε Ὅμηρος ταῦτα τὰ ἔπεα ἐποίησε.

But Hesiod has mention of the Hyperboreans, and so does Homer in the Epigonoi, if Homer really composed this poem.

The conciseness of the information provided by Herodotus prevents any guess as to the context where the Hyperboreans, a legendary race favourite

---

[40] On the meaning of ὁπλότερος, see S. West (1988: 189–90) and Janko (1992: 193), with bibliography; *LfgrE* s.v.; Del Freo (1994); Burkert (2002).

[41] *Aeth.* PEG 1 = W., F spur. D. (Σ *Il.* 24.804b; PLitLond 6, col. XXII 43). See Rengakos, below in this volume, pp. 312–13. In all the other manuscripts of the *Iliad* the poem ends at v. 804 with one epithet replacing the expansion, Ὣς οἵ γ', ἀμφίεπον τάφον Ἕκτορος ἱπποδάμοιο.

of Apollo and blessed with immortality, located in different places in the Far North, may have been mentioned. Their special relationship with Apollo (and in some way with Delphi) in Greek archaic poetry suggests that it may also have been mentioned in the *Epigonoi*.[42]

PEG F 3 = D. = 4 W., from Σ Ap. Rhod. 1.308b

οἱ δὲ τὴν Θηβαΐδα γεγραφότες φασίν, ὅτι ὑπὸ τῶν Ἐπιγόνων ἀκροθίνιον ἀνετέθη Μαντὼ ἡ Τειρεσίου θυγάτηρ εἰς Δελφοὺς πεμφθεῖσα, καὶ κατὰ χρησμὸν Ἀπόλλωνος ἐξερχομένη περιέπεσε Ῥακίωι τῶι Λέβητος υἱῶι Μυκηναίωι τὸ γένος. καὶ γημαμένη αὐτῶι – τοῦτο γὰρ περιεῖχε τὸ λόγιον, γαμεῖσθαι ὧι ἂν συναντήσηι – ἐλθοῦσα εἰς Κολοφῶνα καὶ ἐκεῖ δυσθυμήσασα ἐδάκρυσε διὰ τὴν τῆς πατρίδος πόρθησιν. διόπερ ὠνομάσθη Κλάρος ἀπὸ τῶν δακρύων. ἐποίησεν δὲ Ἀπόλλωνι ἱερόν.

The writers of the *Thebaid* say that Teiresias' daughter Manto was sent to Delphi by the Epigonoi and dedicated as a tithe; and she went out in obedience to an oracle of Apollo and encountered Rhacius the son of Lebes, a Mycenaean by blood. She married him – this was part of the oracle, that she should marry the first man she met – and went to Colophon, and there, overcome by sorrow, she wept for the sack of her native city. Hence the place was named Claros, from her tears. And she established a shrine for Apollo.

Of the few fragments left, this one allows an interesting insight into the subject matter of the last section of the poem. A scholion to Apollonius Rhodius (already discussed above[43]) reports that the daughter of Teiresias, Manto (a telling name for the daughter of a *mantis*), was an eminent *geras* (prize of honor) in the large booty collected by the Epigonoi at Thebes (cf. Ps.-Apollod. *Bibl.* 3.7.4); they dedicated her as a tithe to Delphi, from where she got married to one Rhacios, a Mycenean by blood; they moved out to Colophon in Ionia, and later she established a shrine of Apollo at Claros and became a priestess in the sanctuary. This picture can be integrated with other sources which differ in a few details, some adding that from their union a renowned seer, Mopsus, was born, the winner of a mantic contest with Chalcas.[44] Although the details provided seem to aim at a paretymology whereby the tears (from the verb κλαίειν, 'to weep')

---

[42] Cf. *HHom.* 7.29; Alcae. F 307c; Aristeas *PEG* F 3 = D.; Pind. *Ol.* 3.16 (Heracles); *Pyth.* 10.29–44; *Isthm.* 6.23; *Pae.* 8.63 (F 52 i); Bacchyl. 3.58–9; Herod. 4.13; 4.33–4; see Page (1955: 249–52).

[43] p. 245.

[44] Cf. Hes. *Melampod.* F 278 M.-W.; Diod. Sic. 4.66.5; Paus. 7.3.1–2; 9.33.2; Ps.-Apollod. *Bibl.* 3.7.4. Diodorus differs in giving a different name for the daughter of Teiresias (Daphne, not

of the exiled Manto account for the foundation and the name of Claros, this part of the poem shows the same antiquarian flavour found in other cyclic and minor epics and in the Hesiodic corpus: apparently the poem combined a straightforward narrative of the main event – the expedition against Thebes – with themes which are typical of mantic poetry as the Hesiodic *Melampodeia*, and with stories of traveling heroes ending in the foundation of cities and oracles, often originated from Delphi as in this fragment.[45]

Alcmaon, Amphilochus, Teiresias, Manto, Mopsus, Chalcas, all are mantic characters connected to mantic contests and/or oracles in various parts of the Greek world; they represent different areas and epic traditions and, as was the case with the *Melampodia* (F 270–79 M.-W.), their contests, marriages and journeys sketch out a broad map of the sacred places and mantic genealogies of the Greek world, connecting East and West, Acarnania and Anatolia. If one looks at the fragments and at the title, centered on the name of the protagonist, the same considerations of antiquarian and mythological lore combined with the theme of the traveling hero in a colonial world apply to the poem *Alcmeonis*, which has been identified by some with the *Epigonoi*. Notwithstanding the effort displayed mainly by Welcker and by Prinz to advocate this hypothesis, it must be stressed that not a single fragment of the poem can be brought to support the view that the *Alcmeonis* also dealt with the expedition of the Epigonoi.[46]

The subject matter of this poem can perhaps better be identified with parts of the account in Ps.-Apollod. *Bibl.* 3.7.5–7: after telling of the fall of Thebes and the killing of Eriphyle, it starts afresh with the vicissitudes and the wanderings of Alcmaon.[47] Notably, it was cited as an independent poem in relation to an episode related to the Trojan epics by a Hellenistic expert

---

Manto), and expands on her poetic skill in composing oracular responses. On this fragment see Torres-Guerra (1995a: 72–4).

[45] The account of Immisch (1889) on Claros is still unsurpassed; the mention of Claros in the *Epigonoi* also points to a later period for the poem (Robert (1921: 950). On the *Melampodia*, mantic poetry and traveling seers in general see Huxley (1969: 51–9); Schwartz (1960: 210–28); most recently, Burkert (1983b); Dillery (2005: 173–8); Lane Fox (2008: 224–3); López-Ruiz (2009).

[46] See Welcker (1865: 195–6); (1882: 380–2); Prinz (1979: 166–87; in particular 177–80), both suggesting that the *Alcmeonis* was the alternative title of the *Epigonoi*. For the opposite view see Wilamowitz (1884: 73 n. 2); Immisch (1889: 140, 154–5, 188–9); Bethe (1891a: 109–40); Friedländer (1914 = 1969: 42–8); Robert (1921: 950); Rzach (1922: 2377); Severyns (1928: 224); Sakellariou (1958: 158–9).

[47] Alcmaon in Arcadia, Psophis, Thesprotia, Aetolia, and Acarnania: Thuc. 2.102.5; Ephorus, *FgrHist* 70 F 123 a, b = Strabo, 7.7.7; 10.2.25; Ps.-Apollod. *Bibl.* 1.8.5; 3.6.2, 7.2, 7.5–7. See Robert (1921: 957–67); Gantz (1993: 525–8).

in cyclic matters, Dionysius the cyclograph (*FgrHist* 15 F 7 = Σ Eúr. *Or.* 995 = *Alcmeon. PEG* F 6 = W., 5 D.), and this may imply that Dionysius considered it a self-contained cyclic poem, although its placing in the epic cycle remains unknown. From what has been exposed here, it would appear that the best transition from the Theban to the Trojan epics could be effected by the *Epigonoi*, whose subject matter was more in tune with the theme of the war at Troy which started in the *Cypria*.[48]

The more interesting among the few fragments of the *Epigonoi* of uncertain attribution is ***PEG* F dub. °6** = F 1 inc. loci D. = F 3* W., from Phot. *Lex., Etym. gen.,* and *Suda* s. v. Τευμησία.[49] It tells the story of a ferocious Teumessian fox, located in Boeotia, which was ravaging the Theban territory and was impossible to catch:

> περὶ τῆς Τευμησίας ἀλώπεκος οἱ τὰ Θηβαϊκὰ γεγραφότες ἱκανῶς ἱστορήκασι, καθάπερ Ἀριστόδημος· ἐπιπεμφθῆναι μὲν γὰρ ὑπὸ θεῶν τὸ θηρίον τοῦτο τοῖς Καδμείοις, διότι τῆς βασιλείας ἐξέκλειον τοὺς ἀπὸ Κάδμου γεγονότας. Κέφαλον δέ φασι, τὸν Δηΐονος, Ἀθηναῖον ὄντα καὶ κύνα κεκτημένον, ὃν οὐδὲν διέφευγε τῶν θηρίων (ὃς ἀπέκτεινεν ἄκων τὴν ἑαυτοῦ γυναῖκα Πρόκριν, καθηράντων αὐτὸν τῶν Καδμείων), διώκειν τὴν ἀλώπεκα μετὰ τοῦ κυνός· καταλαμβανομένους δὲ περὶ τὸν Τευμησὸν λίθους γενέσθαι τόν τε κύνα καὶ τὴν ἀλώπεκα. εἰλήφασι δ' οὗτοι τὸν μῦθον ἐκ τοῦ ἐπικοῦ κύκλου.

> Concerning the 'Teumesian fox' the writers of Theban history have given a sufficient account, for example Aristodemus. They say that the animal was sent upon the Thebans by the gods because they were excluding the descendants of Cadmus from the kingship. They say that Cephalus the son of Deion, an Athenian who had a hunting dog that no animal could escape, after accidentally killing his wife Procris and being purified by the Cadmeans, hunted the fox with his dog; and that just as it was catching it near Teumesos, both the dog and the fox were turned to stone. These writers have taken the myth from the Epic Cycle.

The connection with Thebes and with Cadmus indicates that the story was told in one of the Theban epics, either the *Thebaid* or the *Epigonoi*. Preference is given to the latter on the ground that the exclusion from the kingship of the descendants of Cadmus is likely to have taken place after the death of Eteocles, in order to prevent further family feuds. Two motifs

---

[48] For the different opinion that the ideal link with the Trojan epics would have been better provided by the *Alcmeonis* see Debiasi, below in this volume, p. 263.

[49] Following Davies, I am not considering here *Epig. PEG* F 4 = F 2 W., attributed by Clem. Alex. (*Strom.* 6.12.7) to Antimachus of Teos (= Antim. F 2 D.).

found elsewhere in epic poetry and in folklore are originally combined here: (a) the motif of a wild beast or monster (e.g. the Calydonian boar in *Il.* 9) sent by a god/the gods against a city or region in order to ravage the land and kill the inhabitants, as a punishment for a variety of reasons (wrongful acting, lack of respect towards a god, etc.); (b) the motif of an animal endowed with the magical power of swiftness, which makes it unique and out of reach. Interestingly, apart from the story of the Teumessian fox, both motifs are found elsewhere in the Theban epics. The fox appears to duplicate the story of the Sphinx in the *Oedipodea*,[50] whereas the *Thebaid* told the story of the divine horse Arion, whose unmatched swiftness granted to his master Adrastus a safe escape from battle and made him the only survivor amongst the Seven.[51]

The gist of the story, which might have an aetiological origin connected to the Theban territory, lies in the creation – by way of standard motifs – of a puzzling dilemma, through the juxtaposition of two animals with incompatible powers: 'the fox could outrun all pursuit, the hound could overtake all fugitives'.[52] Only the intervention of Zeus could solve the logical impasse by turning both animals into stone. The myth of Cephalus and his hound was well known in Greece, as is shown by a large number of sources giving approximately the same version, with a number of variants concerning several additional events and characters, a connection with Amphitryon, the name of the angry god (Artemis, Dionysus) and of the god who put an end to the unending pursuit (Zeus).[53] It also attracted local interest: apart from the Theban writer Aristodemus (*FgrHist* 383 F 2), the story of the Teumessian fox was narrated in a most peculiar way by Corinna, *PMG* 672,[54] who credited Oedipus both with the killing of the sphinx and of the fox, apparently portraying him as a valiant fighter and monster-killer, rather than as a clever solver of riddles.

According to Welcker, the version told by Corinna was the earliest one.[55] In spite of its redundancy, since in fact Oedipus only needed to kill one monster (the sphinx) in order to be awarded the kingdom of Thebes,

---

[50] See above in this volume, pp. 215–20 *passim*.
[51] See *Il.* 23.346–7; *Theb. PEG* F 8 = F 6 b + 6 c D., F 11 W.; Torres-Guerra, above in this volume, pp. 235–6; on Arion see Cingano (2005b: 141–51). Like the sphinx, the Teumessian fox destroyed the lives of the (young) Theban citizens: cf. Ps.-Apollod. *Bibl.* 2.4.7; Anton. Lib. 41.8.
[52] Page (1953: 39).
[53] See Istr. Callim. *FgrHist* 334 F 65; Ps.-Apollod. *Bibl.* 2.4.6–7; Paus. 9.19.1; Ps.-Eratosth. *Cat.* 33; Anton. Lib. 41; Ov. *Met.* 7.672–862. On Cephalus and Procris see also Hellan. *EGM* F 169; Pherec. *EGM* F 34; Ps.-Apollod. *Bibl.* 3.15.10; Hyg. *fab.* 189.
[54] See above in this volume, pp. 224–5, 259–60.
[55] Welcker (1882: 393–6, esp. 394); on the Teumessian fox see also Schultz (1916–24); Gantz (1993: 245–7).

Corinna's version is surely more focused on the Theban myth than the cyclic version attributed to the *Epigonoi*. Here, the transfer from Oedipus to the Athenian hero Cephalus generates a different ending via his dog, and his intrusion in Theban territory is (more loosely) accounted for by his need of purification by the Cadmeans, after the accidental killing of his wife Procris.

15 | *Alcmeonis*

ANDREA DEBIASI

THE *ALCMEONIS* BETWEEN THE THEBAN AND THE TROJAN CYCLES

Seven fragments of the epic *Alcmeonis* remain that were transmitted by various sources. The work is reported anonymous, with the circumlocution 'the author of the *Alcmeonis*' (ὁ τὴν Ἀλκμαιωνίδα πεποιηκώς / ποιήσας / γράψας / γεγραφώς) being used in all the extant quotations.[1] Additional passages that have some chance belonging to the poem can be added to these relics.

The inclusion of the *Alcmeonis* to the Epic Cycle is much debated. The sources do not explicitly mention it. Yet the plot fits well in such a framework. Alcmaon, a prominent figure within the Theban saga, is the main character being the son of Amphiaraus, one of the Seven who failed the assault on Thebes (subject of the epic *Thebaid*) and himself one of the Epigonoi (the sons of the Seven) who destroyed Thebes in the subsequent campaign.[2] The thematic congruity with the epic *Epigonoi* is clear, at least in the initial part. This led some scholars to postulate an equivalence between the two epics, where the *Alcmeonis* would be an alternative title of the *Epigonoi* or a (sub)title of a specific section of it.[3] This suggestion that is consistent with a well-documented custom in the ancient epics cannot be ruled out.[4]

Nevertheless such arguments are not strong enough to dismiss the preponderant position regarding the *Epigonoi* and the *Alcmeonis* as two separate

---

[1] *PEG* F 7 (= D., W.) maintains the original form of the title (*Alkmeonis*), elsewhere changed to *Alkmaeonis*. As West (2003a: 5 n. 3) points out: 'Alcmaon is the epic form of the name, Alcmeon the Attic, Alcman the Doric; Alcmaeon is a false spelling.'

[2] For an historical and archaeological contextualization of both the expeditions, see Schachter (1967); Brillante (1980: 336).

[3] Welcker (1865: 195); more extensively Printz (1979: 166–87). See also Cingano, above in this volume, p. 257.

[4] Within the Theban Cycle, cf. the title *Amphiaraou exelasis* most likely a part of the *Thebaid*: see Davies (1989c: 29); West (2003a: 9). Discussion of similar cases, concerning epics datable to the sixth century BC, in Debiasi (2003; 2010) (poems connected to the Cypselid Corinth). The practice can be found in the corpus of Eumelus of Corinth: see Debiasi (2004: 36–7; 2013a).

poems.[5] Cases of distinct epics sharing themes and episodes are common.[6] Apart from some divergences surmised for some narrative details, the independence of the *Alcmeonis* from the *Epigonoi* is supported by its being a poem 'wide in scope and diffuse in content',[7] rich in flashbacks and digressions, to such an extent that it would be excessive as a section of a poem, the *Epigonoi*, said to have been of 7,000 lines.[8] The successful expedition against Thebes, that formed the thematic core of the *Epigonoi*, should have taken up less space in the *Alcmeonis*, being just one of several episodes of Alcmaon's heroic biography. Also, the constant and uniform quotation of the anonymous 'author of the *Alcmeonis*' appears heterogeneous with respect to the sources that allege more than one authorship (Homer, Antimachus) for the *Epigonoi*,[9] with consequent discrepancy.[10] The arrival of Teiresias' daughter Manto at Claros, in the Colophon district, as reported in *Epig*. PEG F 3 = 3 D. = 4 W., implies a background in Asia Minor compatible with the ascription of the *Epigonoi* to Antimachus of Teos,[11] whereas it hardly fits with the environment from which the *Alcmeonis* originates. This, we will see, must be placed in the Cypselid Corinth, as suggested by several data, among which the role assigned in the poem to the Delphic oracle and to Acarnania.[12]

Seen from the vantage point of an original distinction, the notion which recognizes the *Alcmeonis* as a later poem inspired by the epic *Epigonoi* is well grounded, whereas the *Epigonoi* themselves are modelled after the older *Thebaid* (a poem well-known to the author of the *Alcmeonis* as well).[13]

---

[5] See, recently, Olivieri (2010: 302–3 and n. 14); bibliographical survey in Sakellariou (1958: 159 n. 3); *PEG* p. 29.

[6] Cf. in the Theban Cycle the last section of the *Oedipodea* overlapping with the *Thebaid*: see Severyns (1928: 211–16); Cingano (2002–3: 56). For the Trojan Cycle, see Burgess (2001: 21–2).

[7] Huxley (1969: 52); cf. Gantz (1993: 527): 'The poem *Alkmaionis* covered a broad range of material.'

[8] *Epig*. PEG T 1 = W. See West (2003a: 5).

[9] *Epig*. PEG T 1–2 = F 1 D. = W. The way Herod. 4.32 (= *Epig*. PEG F 2 = D. = F 5 W.) expresses doubts about Homer's authorship of the *Epigonoi* is indicative of an opposition to a well-established belief: see Wilamowitz (1884: 352).

[10] *Epig*. PEG F 3 = D.= F 4 W.: quotation from the *Thebaid*, 'assumed to be an error for the *Epigonoi*' (West 2003c: 59 n. 14; cf. Davies 1989c: 31). Cf. *Epig*. PEG F °5 = p. 74, F 1 D. = F 3* W.

[11] West (2003a: 10). Cf. *Epig*. PEG T 3 and F 4 = Ant. F 2 D. = F 2 W.

[12] In *Epig*. PEG F 3 (= D. = F 4 W.) Manto came from Delphi to Claros, where she established a shrine for Apollo. This version seems concocted by the Clarian priesthood in opposition to the Delphic version according to which Teiresias' daughter stayed in Delphi, where she was sent from Thebes by the Epigonoi as a thanks offering: cf. Ps.-Apollod. *Bibl.* 3.7.3–4 (from the *Alcmeonis*?). See Sakellariou (1958: 152–60).

[13] Bethe (1894: 1563); Legras (1905: 91–5, 108); especially Severyns (1925: 176–81); (1928: 224–37).

Based on its fragments the *Alcmeonis* appears not only as sequel of the Theban Cycle, represented by the triad *Oedipodea – Thebaid – Epigonoi*, but also as a compelling link with the Trojan Cycle, evoked by figures such as the Epigonoi and other heroes that in the myth are connected with the siege of Troy.[14] The narrative chronology of the poem takes place between the events reported in the *Epigonoi* and those narrated in the *Cypria*. This accounts for the placing of the *Alcmeonis* between these two poems in some editions of the Greek epic fragments.[15]

Whether the inclusion of the *Alcmeonis* in the canonical Epic Cycle is admitted or not, an evaluation of the Cycle must consider such a poem, inherently placed at the crossroads between the two sagas, Theban and Trojan, which pervade the Cycle.

THE PLOT

Although not explicitly mentioning the *Alcmeonis*, some texts allow reconstructing the poem's basic plot. This must have been arranged around three main themes: the expedition against Thebes, Alcmaon's murder of his mother and the wanderings of the hero through Greece. The most comprehensive account of Alcmaon's deeds can be found in Ps.-Apollodorus (*Bibl.* 3.7.2–6), in a section which, more or less indirectly, mirrors the poem's plot, even if abridged and subjected to the intrusion of different elements (especially tragic).[16]

In *Bibl.* 3.7.2–4 Alcmaon is portrayed as the leader of the Epigonoi, a necessary condition for the victory over Thebes according to an oracle of Apollo.[17] The role of Alcmaon as the 'best of the Epigonoi' must have distinguished the *Alcmeonis* from the earlier version ascribable to the *Epigonoi*,[18] which has Aegialeus, son of Adrastus, the leader of the Seven, as

---

[14] Immisch (1889: 183–4); Severyns (1928: 224–5, 229–36); Bernabé (1979: 81). The link with the Trojan Cycle also informed the *Epigonoi*, although in a more basic way: cf. Cingano (2002–3: 58, 76; 2004a: 61).

[15] *PEG* pp. 32–6, cf. Bernabé (1979: 80–92); West (2003a: 58–63), whose text of the fragments I am using in this chapter. As Kinkel (1877: 76–7) before, the fragments of the *Alcmeonis* are separately edited by Davies (1988: 139–40), who supports a limited definition of the Epic Cycle (Davies 1986: 95–8).

[16] Sakellariou (1958: 156–7 n. 3, 159); Jouan (1990: 159). Ps.-Apollodorus quotes the *Alcmeonis* in *Bibl.* 1.8.5 (= *PEG* F 4 = D., W.).

[17] Cf. Diod. 4.66, largely drawing from the *Alcmeonis*, according to Sakellariou (1958: 156–7 n. 3, 159).

[18] For this distinction, see Bethe (1891a: esp. 136; 1894: 1563); Severyns (1928: 225); Sakellariou (1958: 159 and n. 3).

commander.[19] The list of eight Epigonoi headed by Alcmaon in *Bibl.* 3.7.2 ('Alcmaon and Amphilochus, sons of Amphiaraus; Aegialeus, son of Adrastus; Diomedes, son of Tydeus; Promachus, son of Parthenopaeus; Sthenelus, son of Capaneus; Thersander, son of Polynices; Euryalus, son of Mecisteus') is almost identical to that of the monument of the Epigonoi in Delphi commemorating the victory of the Argives over the Spartans at Oinoe,[20] and could possibly go back to the *Alcmeonis* (*PEG* F 11°).[21] Some uncertainty still remains, due to the inconsistency of the traditions concerning the names of both the Seven and the Epigonoi.[22]

Ps.-Apollodorus (*Bibl.* 3.7.5–6) further relates the madness and the vicissitudes of Alcmaon after the murder of his mother Eriphyle. Bribed by Polynices with the gift of the golden necklace of Harmonia, she forced her husband Amphiaraus to join the expedition of the Seven against his will (as a seer Amphiaraus predicted his doom).[23] It is a widespread opinion that in the *Alcmeonis* both the matricide and the related motif of the hero's being driven mad by his mother's Erinyes have occurred before the campaign against Thebes, in compliance with the injunction that Amphiaraus gave to Alcmaon, as he prepared to set out. Such an account is recorded by Asclepiades of Tragilus (*FgrHist* 12 F 29) *ap.* Σ *Od.* 11.326 (= *Alcm. PEG* F °8 [I]),[24] according to whom Amphiaraus commanded his son to avenge him before marching on Thebes.[25] If it is true that Asclepiades often summarizes the epic traditions which inspired the tragedians, in this case he rather seems to be drawing directly from a tragedy in which the sequence matricide (and subsequent madness, quickly removed by the gods 'since Alcmaon faithfully obeyed his father by slaying his mother') and expedition was not followed

---

[19] Cf. Eur. *Suppl.* 1213–26; Olivieri (2004: 82).

[20] Paus. 10.10.4. In the monument the statues of the Epigonoi are seven, Amphilochus being excluded, unless Gantz (1993: 524) is right in observing that 'Pausanias says in passing that Alkmaion was honored before Amphilochos because he was older, which may mean that the younger brother was also present.'

[21] Bethe (1894: 1563); Pomtow (1908: 321–5; 1924: 1228).

[22] Even so Cingano (2002: 39–40, 46 n. 62) seems overly sceptical. No more convincing is the hypothesis of Robert (1921: 950–1), who denies the *Alcmeonis* the expedition of the Epigonoi and regards such a list as mirroring that of the Seven in the *Thebaid*.

[23] Eriphyle's arbitration would be final, in case of disagreement between her husband Amphiaraus and her brother Adrastus, both rulers of Argos, since Adrastus was reconciled with Amphiaraus and came back from Sicyon (where he had inherited the kingdom of Polybus). Cf. Σ Pind. *Nem.* 30b, likely drawing from epics (e.g. the *Thebaid* (cf. F 7* W.), or also the *Alcmeonis*): see Hubbard (1992: 87–92, esp. 91).

[24] See Cingano, above in this volume, p. 248 n. 24; Torres-Guerra, above in this volume, pp. 237–8; Rutherford, below in this volume, p. 453.

[25] Bethe (1894: 1563); Severyns (1928: 227–8); cf. Olivieri (2013: 160).

by the hero's wanderings.[26] These wanderings represent an essential component within the epic plot and must be explained in connection with the recent bloodguilt and the subsequent need of Alcmaon to seek purification in order to free himself from madness and to settle in an uncontaminated land.[27] This is indeed what we find in Ps.-Apollodorus' account (*Bibl.* 3.7.2 and 5; cf. 3.6.2): although Alcmaon received from his father the order to avenge him, he deferred the matricide. The murder was triggered, in accordance with an oracle given by Apollo, when Alcmaon learned that Eriphyle had been bribed for a second time having persuaded him to go to the war after receiving the robe of Harmonia from Polynices' son Thersander.[28]

Once mad, Alcmaon leaves Argos, the scene of the crime, and begins his wanderings. Ps.-Apollodorus' narration from now onwards has several points of contact with Pausanias' account about Arcadia (8.24.8–10), which is both the first and the last stop of Alcmaon's travels. Alcmaon first repairs to his paternal grandfather Oicles, and thence to Phegeus at Psophis. Having been purified by Phegeus he marries his daughter Arsinoe[29] and gives her the necklace and the robe of Harmonia, which he took from his mother. Still the purification turns out to be ineffective.[30] The Pythia commands Alcmaon to seek further purification in a land not in existence at the time of his mother's murder. The quest begins and after some adventures in Aetolia and Thesprotia, Alcmaon finds the desired land in the silts recently formed at the mouth of the river Achelous, and there he founds a settlement. As Phegeus before, the river god Achelous purifies Alcmaon and gives him as wife his daughter Callirrhoe who bears him two sons, Amphoterus and Acarnan. The Delphic oracle given to Alcmaon and the figure of Acarnan, eponym of the country over which he ruled with his father, are also found

---

[26] The vicissitudes of Eriphyle and Alcmaon were popular subjects in the Attic tragedy. Sophocles, who wrote an *Alcmeon*, certainly dealt with the slaying of Eriphyle in his *Epigonoi* (also the title of a play of Aeschylus) that possibly coincides with the tragedy *Eriphyle* (*TrGF* F 187). Euripides devoted two plays to Alcmaon: *Alcmeon in Psophis* and *Alcmeon in Corinth*. See Gantz (1993: 523); Olivieri (2013); Sommerstein, below in this volume, p. 483.

[27] One might assume that the motif of the persecution by the mother's Erinyes stems from some tragedies; not so for the madness itself (a constant feature in the sources) which leads to Alcmaon's travels. See Prinz (1979: 174–6); West (2003a: 11).

[28] On the epic motif of the second bribing (most likely adopted by Stesichorus in the *Eriphyle*: cf. *PMGF* S148), see Gantz (1993: 525); Olivieri (2004: 83–5); cf. Prinz (1979: 174–6); Breglia Pulci Doria (1991–4: 129).

[29] In the tragedians and in Pausanias she is named Alphesiboea. Ps.-Apollodorus 'clearly is not always drawing from the same source as Pausanias' (Gantz 1993: 527).

[30] Because the land becomes infertile (Ps.-Apollodorus) and/or Alcmaon's disease did not grow any better (Pausanias).

in Thucydides in a section (2.102.5–6), which has been justifiably traced back to the *Alcmeonis* (*PEG* F °10).[31]

Alcmaon is finally overcome by the rivalry between his two wives. Forced to return to Psophis to get Harmonia's robe and necklace, under the pretext of dedicating them to Delphi but intending to give them to Callirrhoe, he is ambushed by the sons of Phegeus who kill him.[32] Being suddenly full-grown with Zeus' help, Amphoterus and Acarnan take vengeance on their father's slayers, by killing first the sons of Phegeus, and then both Phegeus and his wife.[33]

THE FRAGMENTS

PEG F 1 (= D., W.), from Σ Eur. *Andr.* 687

καὶ ὁ τὴν Ἀκλμαιωνίδα πεποιηκὼς φησι περὶ τοῦ Φώκου·
ἔνθά μιν ἀντίθεος Τελαμὼν τροχοειδέϊ δίσκωι
πλῆξε κάρη, Πηλεὺς δὲ θοῶς ἀνὰ χεῖρα τανύσσας
ἀξίνηι εὐχάλκωι ἐπεπλήγει μέσα νῶτα.[34]

And the author of the *Alcmeonis* says about Phocus:

There godlike Telamon hit him on the head with a
wheel-shaped discus, and Peleus quickly raised his arm
above his head and struck him in the middle of his back with
a bronze axe.

PEG F 2 (= D., W.), from Athenaeus 11.460b

καὶ ὁ τὴν Ἀλκμαιωνίδα δὲ ποιήσας φησίν·
νέκυς δὲ χαμαιστρώτου ἔπι τείνας
εὐρείης στιβάδος προέθηκ' αὐτοῖσι θάλειαν
δαῖτα ποτήριά τε, στεφάνους τ' ἐπὶ κρασὶν ἔθηκεν.

The poet who has done the *Alcmeonis* says:

And laying the bodies out on a broad pallet spread on the
ground, he set before them a rich banquet and cups, and put
garlands on their heads.

---

[31] Bethe (1891a: 136); Huxley (1969: 51). Cf. *Alcm. PEG* F 5 = F 6 D. = F 5 W.

[32] Their names diverge in the sources: Pronous and Agenor in Ps.-Apollodorus, Temenus and Axion in Pausanias, who also documents a tomb (and the related hero cult) of Alcmaon at Psophis: cf. Olivieri (2010: 307 n. 40).

[33] This section of the tale is more affected by the contributions of the tragic tradition (possibly Sophocles' *Alcmeon* and Euripides's *Alcmeon in Psophis*): see Jouan (1990: 159 nn. 21, 23); Gantz (1993: 526–7).

[34] For a different constitution of the text, see Salvador (1996), together with the translation by Burnett (2005: 24).

PEG F 3 (= D., W.), from *Etym. Gud.* s.v. 'Ζαγρεύς'

Ζαγρεύς ὁ μεγάλως ἀγρεύων, ὡς·
    πότνια Γῆ, Ζαγρεῦ τε θεῶν πανυπέρτατε πάντων,
ὁ τὴν Ἀλκμαιωνίδα γράψας ἔφη.

Zagreus: the one who greatly hunts, as the writer of the *Alcmeonis* said:
    Mistress Earth, and Zagreus highest of all the gods.

PEG F 4 (= D., W.), from Ps.-Apollod. *Bibl.* 1.8.5

Τυδεὺς δὲ ἀνὴρ γενόμενος γενναῖος ἐφυγαδεύθη κτείνας, ὡς μέν τινες λέγουσιν, ἀδελφὸν Οἰνέως Ἀλκάθοον, ὡς δὲ ὁ τὴν Ἀλκμαιωνίδα γεγραφώς, τοὺς Μέλανος παῖδας ἐπιβουλεύοντας Οἰνεῖ, Φηνέα Εὐρύαλον Ὑπέρλαον Ἀντίοχον Εὐμήδην Στέρνοπα Ξάνθιππον Σθενέλαον.

Tydeus grew into a gallant man, but was forced into exile after killing, as some say, Oineus' brother Alcathous, but as the writer of the *Alcmeonis* says, the sons of Melas, who were plotting against Oineus: Pheneus, Euryalus, Hyperlaus, Antiochus, Eumedes, Sternops, Xanthippus, and Sthenelaus.

PEG F 5 (= F 6 D. = F 5 W.), from Strab. 10.2.9

ὁ δὲ τὴν Ἀλκμεωνίδα γράψας Ἰκαρίου τοῦ Πηνελόπης πατρὸς υἱεῖς γενέσθαι δύο, Ἀλυζέα καὶ Λευκάδιον, δυναστεῦσαι δὲ ἐν τῆι Ἀκαρνανίαι τούτους μετὰ τοῦ πατρός.

But the writer of the *Alcmeonis* says that Icarius, Penelope's father, had two sons, Alyzeus and Leucadius, and that they ruled with their father in Acamania.

PEG F 6 (= 5 D. = F 6 W.), from Σ Eur. *Or.* 995

ἀκολουθεῖν ἂν δόξειεν τῶι τὴν Ἀλκμαιωνίδα πεποιηκότι εἰς τὰ περὶ τὴν ἄρνα, ὡς καὶ Διονύσιος ὁ κυκλογράφος φησί [15 F 7]. Φερεκύδης δὲ [*EGM* F 133] οὐ καθ' Ἑρμοῦ μῆνίν φησι τὴν ἄρνα ὑποβληθῆναι ἀλλὰ Ἀρτέμιδος. ὁ δὲ τὴν Ἀλκμαιωνίδα γράψας τὸν ποιμένα τὸν προσαγαγόντα τὸ ποίμνιον τῶι Ἀτρεῖ Ἀντίοχον καλεῖ.

[Euripides] would appear to be following the author of the *Alcmeonis* in regard to the story about the lamb, as Dionysius the Cyclographer also says. Pherecydes says that it was not from Hermes' wrath that the lamb was put into the flock, but from Artemis'. And the writer of the *Alcmeonis* calls the shepherd who brought the lamb to Atreus Antiochus.

PEG F 7 (= D., W.), from Philod. *De pietate* B 6798 Obbink

κα[ὶ τῆς ἐ]πὶ Κρόνου ζω[ῆς εὐ]δαιμονεστά[της οὔ]σης, ὡς ἔγραψ[αν Ἡσί]οδος καὶ ὁ τὴν [Ἀλκμ]εωνίδα ποή[σας, καὶ] Σοφοκλῆς κτλ. (*TrGF* F 278).

And the life in the time of Cronus was most happy, as [Hesi]od and the author of the [*Alcm*]*eonis* have written, and Sophocles etc.

In most cases it is difficult to determine how the surviving fragments should be placed in such a frame. We learn from Philodemus (*De piet.* B 6978 Obbink) that 'the life in the time of Cronus was most happy, as [Hesi]od and the author of [*Alcm*]*eonis* have written' (*PEG* F 7 = D., W.). The comparison with Hesiod, *Works and Days* 109–26 (golden age 'in the time of Cronus')[35] and the role of the *Alcmeonis* as a link between the Theban and the Trojan Cycle make it an attractive hypothesis that the *Alcmeonis* could hint at an epochal caesura produced by the Theban and the Trojan Wars just as the myth of the five ages does in the *Works and Days*.[36]

Athenaeus 11.460b, after claiming that Semonides of Amorgos was the first poet who spoke of 'drinking cups' (ποτήρια), quotes three lines from the *Alcmeonis* (*PEG* F 2 = D., W.).[37] The funeral banquet may have occurred in more than one context in a poem that did not lack slayings and battles, nor must we necessarily assume that Alcmaon was the subject.[38] Nonetheless the more plausible interpretation remains the one recognizing the funeral honours to be those rendered by the leader of the Epigonoi Alcmaon to the warriors fallen in the final clash at Thebes. In such case the corpses should be those of Aegialeus, the only Epigonos perished during the siege, and of his slayer Laodamas, son of Eteocles and king of Thebes, who was killed in battle by Alcmaon himself as reported by Ps.-Apollodorus (*Bibl.* 3.7.3).[39]

---

[35] See Versnel (1987: 125 ~ 1993: 96).

[36] Hes. *WD* 161–5: 'Evil war and dread battle destroyed these [*sc.* heroes (demigods)], some under seven-gated Thebes in the land of Cadmus while they fought for the sake of Oedipus' sheep, others brought in boats over the great gulf of the sea to Troy for the sake of fair-haired Helen'. See Cingano (1992: 7–9; 2002–3: 56, 68–69). Cf. Hes. *Cat.* F 204.57–65 M.-W. = F 110.57–65 Hirsch., on which see Clay (2005); Cingano (2005a: 122–4).

[37] Cf. Severyns (1928: 236–7), according to whom Aristarchus was the source of Athenaeus.

[38] Among the adventures of Alcmaon narrated by Ps.-Apollodorus the expeditions in Aetolia and Thesprotia (about which see Jouan 1990: 159–61) must have included some battle casualties; other illustrious slain were Phegeus with his family, exterminated by the sons of Alcmaon. A further group of dead in the *Alcmeonis* is represented by the sons of Melas, murdered by their cousin Tydeus (*PEG* F 4 = D., W.).

[39] Huxley (1969: 53). In another account Laodamas, having killed Aegialeus, is not slain by Alcmaon but flies to Illyria: cf. Herod. 5.61.2; Paus. 9.5.13 and 9.8.6. Olivieri (2004: 90) detects in the burial of a Theban (Laodamas) by an Argive (Alcmaon) a parallel with (and a reversal

The description of Alcmaon officiating the funeral rites at the end of the expedition of the Epigonoi would be in contrast with the motif, revisited by the tragedians but probably already present in the *Epigonoi* and/or in the *Alcmeonis* (with innovation with respect to the *Thebaid*), of the burial denied to the Seven (all perished except Adrastus).[40] The enterprise of the Seven, and especially the deeds of Alcmaon's father Amphiaraus must have been somehow mentioned in the *Alcmeonis*. In the *Thebaid* (*PEG* F 9 = F 5 D. = F 9 W.) Amphiaraus kills the Theban Melanippus, beheads him, and throws the head to Tydeus who demands it in order to take revenge of the fatal wound he received by Melanippus. Tydeus gobbles Melanippus' brain but loses the favour of Athena who turns away from him, withholding the gift of immortality. Ps.-Apollodorus (*Bibl.* 3.6.8) preserves another version: Tydeus kills Melanippus, whereas Amphiaraus, moved by hate against Tydeus who advocated the war against Thebes, on his own initiative cuts off the head of the Theban hero and gives it to Tydeus in order to provoke the condemnation of Athena. This archaic version has been plausibly traced back to Stesichorus' *Eriphyle*, 'possibly with the mediation of another source'.[41] We may conjecture such a source to be the *Epigonoi* or more likely the *Alcmeonis*.[42]

The poem gave Tydeus much room, not only in connection to the expedition of the Seven but also to its antecedents. Ps.-Apollodorus (*Bibl.* 1.8.5) records that 'Tydeus grew into a gallant man, but was forced into exile after killing, as some say, Oeneus' brother Alcathous, but as the writer of the *Alcmeonis* says, the sons of Melas, who were plotting against Oeneus: Pheneus, Euryalus, Hyperlaus, Antiochus, Eumedes, Sternops, Xanthippus, and Sthenelaus' (*PEG* F 4 = D., W.). As in the likely case of the duel between Tydeus and Melanippus, similarly here the *Alcmeonis* seems to modify the narration of the *Thebaid*, where the relatives killed by Tydeus must have been three: the uncle Melas and his sons Lycopeus and Alcathous.[43] Such

of) the Theban tradition about the Seven reported in Paus. 9.18.2, which features the burial of an Argive (Tydeus) by a Theban (Maeon).

[40] See Legras (1905: 80–3); Severyns (1928: 223–5), according to whom the *Thebaid* must have ended with the funeral of the Seven.

[41] Cingano (1987). On Stesichorus' *Eriphyle*, see Noussia-Fantuzzi, below in this volume, p. 432.

[42] 'The *Eriphyle* must have embraced pretty much the same material' of the *Alcmeonis* (Davies 1989c: 32). Steichorus' poem must as well have included a retrospection of the expedition of the Seven, as results from *PMGF* 194 (i–v), where Asclepius restores to life some of the deceased warriors. The main themes of Steichorus' poem were Eriphyle's two betrayals and the vengeance of Alcmaon, as especially *PMGF* S148 (dialogue between Adrastus and Alcmaon) leads to believe: see above, n. 28.

[43] Severyns (1928: 218, 228), based on Σ *Il.* 14.114b and Eustath. on *Il.* 14.122 (971.6–7). He regards the expansion of the components as typical of a later poem.

an episode, featuring a murder committed within the family circle in order to avenge the father, recalls that of Alcmaon and serves to explain Tydeus' move from Calydon, in Aetolia, to Argos. Like Alcmaon later, Tydeus as well went into exile and was purified in another land by a king (Adrastus) who gave him as wife his daughter (Deipyle). The importance given to the prophecy in the *Alcmeonis* leads as to believe that the poem mentioned, or at least hinted at, the encounter between Tydeus and Polynices, both having arrived to Adrastus' palace as exiles: then Adrastus recognized them as the boar and the lion who, according to an oracle by Apollo, should become his sons-in-law.[44]

A single line of the *Alcmeonis* (*PEG* F 3 = D., W.), transmitted by the *Etymologicum Gudianum* (s.v. 'Ζαγρεύς'),[45] contains the invocation 'Mistress Earth, and Zagreus highest of all the gods', which can refer to Delphi, or alternatively to the Theban background connected with the expeditions of both the Seven and the Epigonoi. A plausible explanation ascribes these words to Alcmaon, during his consultation of the Delphic oracle, as soon as his staying at Psophis proved fruitless. Among the several consultations of the Delphic oracle disseminated in the poem this one in particular, directing Alcmaon to a land that had 'not been seen by the sun at the time of his matricide',[46] is consistent with such an invocation to the Earth and to Zagreus, a god of the underworld. In a tradition, popular among the Orphics, Zagreus is Dionysus in an older guise, as son of Zeus and Persephones. He was torn to pieces by the Titans and buried by Apollo near the oracular tripod at Delphi.[47] Another possible hypothesis is that the line belongs to a prayer in which Alcmaon calls the powers of the earth to evoke the oracle of Amphiaraus.[48] During the rout of the Seven's army near Thebes, Zeus split the earth and Amphiaraus vanished with his chariot before Periclimenus could strike him in the back. He remained alive underground whence he kept on issuing prophecies.[49] In a passage of Pindar (*Pyth*. 8.39–55), most likely inspired by the *Alcmeonis*, Amphiaraus predicts to the Epigonoi the victory over

---

[44] Cf. Eur. *Suppl.* 131–6; Gantz (1993: 334, 508–9).

[45] Cf. also *Anecd. Oxon.* ii.443.8 Cramer. The etymology ζα- 'very' + ἀγρεύειν 'hunt' is doubtful: see West (1983: 153; 2003a: 61 n. 17).

[46] Cf. Thuc. 2.102.5 = *Alcm. PEG* F °10.

[47] Huxley (1969: 52). Cf. Callim. F 43b.34 Hard. and 643 Pf.; Euphor. *CA* F 13: see West (1983: 153–4); Bernabé (1998: 30 n. 5); Arrigoni (2003: 37–9 with n. 91, including previous bibliography about *Alcm. PEG* F 3 = D., W.).

[48] West (2003a: 61 n. 17), who ascribes the words to Alcmaon.

[49] Pind. *Nem*. 9.25–7, drawing from the *Thebaid* (rather than from the *Alcmeonis*, as speculated by Friedländer (1914 = 1969: 44–7); cf. Huxley (1969: 45); Davies (1989c: 29); Braswell (1998: 93, 95); West (2003a: 8).

Thebes primarily due to the bravery of the real leader of the expedition, Alcmaon.[50] The invocation addressed to both the Earth and Zagreus by Alcmaon and/or other Epigonoi may well belong to such oracular consultation.[51] Similarly some lines containing an admonishment and a precept (the so-called 'norm of the polyp') addressed by Amphiaraus to his younger son Amphilochus can possibly be traced back to this specific oracular context.[52]

The arrival to the land newly formed at the mouth of Achelous is a crucial point in the narration of the *Alcmeonis*. It is in this context that the genealogy attributed by Strabo 10.2.9 to the 'writer of the *Alcmeonis*' (*PEG* F 5 = F 6 D. = F 5 W.) must have been mentioned: for he 'says that Icarius, Penelope's father, had two sons, Alyzeus and Leucadius, and that they ruled with their father in Acarnania'. Icarius, with his sons, eponyms of the Acarnanian town Alyzea and of the nearby island of Leucas, is a sort of forerunner of Alcmaon. Like Icarius, Alcmaon rules the country with two sons: Amphoterus[53] and the eponym of the region Acarnan.[54] The reference to Odyssean characters does not surprise, since Alcmaon's biography sums up both 'Iliadic' episodes, first of all the expedition against Thebes, and 'Odyssean' episodes, characterized by the long wandering.[55] In the very same passage Strabo informs us that the mythical eponyms Alyzeus and Leucadius were also found in Ephorus (*FgrHist* 70 F 124). Soon after this Strabo provides further details concerning Icarius which, through the mediation of Ephorus, may go back to the *Alcmeonis*: Icarius and Tyndareus, after being banished by their brother Hippocoon from Lacedaemon, 'went to

---

[50] See Rutherford, below in this volume, pp. 452–3.

[51] Welcker (1882: 381–2), tracing back Pindar's passage to the *Epigonoi* (cf. Bernabé 1979: 73), in his opinion coinciding with the *Alcmeonis* (see above, n. 3.); cf. Wolff (1884–6: 300). The oracle in Pind. *Pyth.* 8.39–55 ought to be identified with the Amphiaraion mentioned by Herod. 8.134 (cf. 1.46; 49; 52; 92) rather than with the oracle in Oropos (where, according to Paus. 9.8.3, Amphiaraus issued prophecies to the Epigonoi): see Hubbard (1992: 101–7). Cf. Giannini in Gentili (2006: 573–4), who considers such consultation occurred during the siege of Thebes, when the Argives lead by Alcmaon were under the attack of the Thebans commanded by Laodamas.

[52] *Theb. PEG* F 4 = "Hom." F 3 = F 8* W. The fragment was also ascribed to the *Nostoi* (Allen 1913: 191) as well as to the *Melampodia* (Löffler 1963: 57). For a further attempt of ascription to the *Alcmeonis*, see Debiasi (2013c).

[53] 'Whose name comes from the disputed territories on either side of the wandering course of the river, at the bounds of Aitolia and Akarnania' (Huxley 1969: 51 n. 1); cf. Löffler (1963: 56).

[54] The fact that Alcmaon should have been contemporary of Alyzeus and Leucadius must have not represented a problem for the author of a poem where 'conflicting stories explaining different events may have crowded together under its aegis' (Gantz 1993: 527); cf. Jouan (1990: 162).

[55] Cf. Cingano (2002-3: 75). The only Homeric mentions of Amphiaraus and his sons Alcmaon and Amphilochus occur in the *Odyssey* (11.326–7; 15.244–248, 253).

Thestius, the ruler of the Pleuronians, and helped him to acquire possession of much of the country on the far side of the Achelous on condition that they should receive a share of it; Tyndareus however, went back home, having married Leda, the daughter of Thestius, whereas Icarius stayed on, keeping a portion of Acarnania, and by Polycaste, the daughter of Lygaeus, begot both Penelope and her brothers'.[56]

Shortly after, Strabo (10.2.25; cf. 7.7.7) recalls Ephorus (*FgrHist* 70 F 123 a–b) according to whom Alcmaon joined Diomedes, his fellow in the previous war against Thebes, in an expedition in Aetolia aiming at restoring the reign of Oeneus. Having defeated the enemies of Diomedes' grandfather, Alcmaon passed into Acarnania and subdued it. In the meantime Agamemnon attacked the Argives and prevailed over them. Later, when the expedition against Troy confronted him, Agamemnon, concerned that the heirs of Adrastus (Diomedes) and of Amphiaraus (Alcmaon) might come back and regain Argos during his absence, invited them both to resume possession of it and to take part in the war. Although Diomedes was persuaded, Alcmaon refused the invitation, and remained in Acarnania, so named after his son Acarnan. There he founded a city and named it Argos Amphilochicon after his brother Amphilochus. We are led to trace back to the poem this information as well (*PEG* F °9 [I-II]),[57] based on the parallelisms with other texts going back to the *Alcmeonis*, such as the sovereignty of Alcmaon and Acarnan over Acarnania, the foundation of a city by Alcmaon, the eponymic function exercised by Acarnan and Amphilochus,[58] and the reference to the usurpation of Oeneus' reign. This last incident was the basis for the episode, possibly mentioned in the poem in such context (*PEG* F 4 = D., W.), of the murder of his cousins by Tydeus with his subsequent exile to Argos (where Deipyles bore him Diomedes).[59] Whether the expedition in Aetolia occurred in the poem shortly before Alcmaon's arrival in Acarnania, as

---

[56] Strabo 10.2.24; cf. Ps.-Apollod. *Bibl.* 3.10.5. See Jouan (1990: 161–2). Broadbent (1968: 300–2) speculates that besides the union between Icarius and Polycaste, also the union between Telemachus and Nausicaa might have been in the *Alcmeonis* (cf. Hellan. *FgrHist* 4 F 156).

[57] Immisch (1889: 182–4); Bethe (1894: 1563); Robert (1921: 964); Kullmann (1960: 143–5); Andersen (1982: 13–6); Jouan (1990: 160–1); West (2003a: 11). Differently Breglia Pulci Doria (1991–4), who argues for an innovation by Ephorus.

[58] According to other traditions Amphilochus himself, the brother (Thuc. 2.68.3; cf. Hecat. *FgrHist* 1 F 102c) or son (Ps.-Apollod. *Bibl.* 3.7.7, drawing on Euripides' *Alcmeon in Corinth*) of Alcmaon was the founder of Argos Amphilochicon.

[59] The link between these events is confirmed by the Hellenistic *Epyllium Diomedis* (*CA* ep. adesp. 2), inspired by the *Alcmeonis*: see *CA* p. 75; Huxley (1969: 51–2 n. 2). It touched upon the slaying of the sons of Melas (line 21), the exile of Tydeus to Adrastus (cf. *Alcm. PEG* F 4 = D., W.), as well as the siege of Argos during Diomedes' absence: cf. Pellin (2007).

implied by Ephorus and as seems more straightforward from both a narrative and a geographical perspective,[60] or whether it took place in an earlier time,[61] this event served as a link between those heroes pertaining to the Theban Cycle and those pertaining to the Trojan Cycle. Agamemnon's request to join the expedition against Troy must be explained in view of the oath sworn by Helen's suitors that they would join in arms against anyone who might take her by force; this oath was imposed, following an advice of Odysseus, by Helen's father Tyndareus (the same who with his brother Icarius had been in Aetolia/Acarnania, where he married Leda, the daughter of Thestius; it is from Icarius that Tindareus obtained Penelope as wife for Odysseus).[62] Thus the *Alcmeonis* provided an explanation for Alcmaon's absence in Troy: he remained in his brand new kingdom, in the near west, whereas other Epigonoi, among whom Diomedes,[63] embarked on a further enterprise, far in the east.[64]

Likewise two fragments, transmitted by two scholia to Euripides, refer to myths and characters presenting some analogies with the story of Alcmaon, most likely being wide-ranging digressions. Σ Eur. *Andr.* 687 preserves three lines of the *Alcmeonis* (*PEG* F 1 = D., W.) describing the killing of Phocus by Telamon and Peleus. Once again we are facing a murder of kin: the tradition is that Peleus and Telamon, sons of Aeacus and Endeis, killed during an athletic contest their half-brother Phocus, born to Aeacus by Psamathe.[65] The parallelism with the tale of Alcmaon becomes even stronger in the light of the development reported by Pausanias 2.29.10: Telamon, being banished together with Peleus from Aegina, was allowed by Aeacus to plead his case provided that he did not land on the island, but remained in the ship or alternatively on a mole raised in the sea. So he sailed by night into

---

[60] Cf. Ps.-Apollod. *Bibl.* 3.17.5: Alcmaon guest of Oeneus at Calydon, presumably after the restoration of the latter's reign in Aetolia.

[61] Cf. Ps.-Apollod. *Bibl.* 1.8.6 (shortly after the quotation of *Alcm. PEG* F 4 = D., W.): Diomedes 'with another one' defeats the usurpers and later on takes part to the expeditions against Thebes and Troy. Andersen (1982: 16) maintains such a chronology for the *Alcmeonis*.

[62] Cf. Ps.-Apollod. *Bibl.* 3.10.9; Hes. *Cat.* F 197.6–8 M.-W. = 105.6–8 Hirsch. (Alcmaon and Amphilochus among the suitors of Helen), with the exegesis of Cingano (2004a: 64–5); (2005a: 140–3, esp. 141).

[63] As well as Sthenelus and Euryalus, according to *Il.* 2.559–68 (cf. 4.404–10): see Cingano (2004a: 60–4); on Thersander, see Cingano (2000: 132–41).

[64] Debiasi (2004: 111). For Acarnania and Achelous as western frontiers, see Ballabriga (1986: 35–6, 42–3).

[65] Paus. 2.29.9; cf. Pind. *Nem.* 5.6–12; Ps.-Apollod. *Bibl.* 3.12.6; Σ Eur. *Andr.* 687. See Gantz (1993: 221–3); Burnett (2005: 24–5 with n. 60: possibly the *Alcmeonis* 'showed killers who acted at their mother's instigation' (cf. Paus. 2.29.9); 69 n. 37). See also Rutherford, below in this volume, p. 452 n. 18.

the harbour called 'Hidden', and made a mole by pouring earth into the sea. The *aition* matches well the tale of the land newly formed by silting at the mouth of Achelous and may well have been in the *Alcmeonis*.[66] The poem must also have mentioned the exile of Telamon to Salamis after his plea of innocence was not accepted; Peleus fled to Thessaly instead, first at Phthia, where Eurytion purified him but later was accidentally killed by him, and then to Iolcus, where he received a further purification by Acastus:[67] this sequence of events recalls that of Alcmaon going first to Phegeus and then to Achelous. Together with the mentions of Telamon and Peleus the *Alcmeonis* could hardly lack any reference to their sons, the eminent heroes of the Trojan War Ajax and Achilles. The death of Phocus itself aims mostly to give prominence to Achilles to whom Phocus was related not only from his father's side, but also his mother's, since Psamathe was a Nereid sister of Thetis.[68] This link would become even stronger if the *Alcmeonis* provided a stemma where Chiron was the father of Endeis, i.e. the grandfather of Telamon and Peleus.[69]

Σ Eur. *Or.* 995 provides further evidence that the *Alcmeonis* (*PEG* F 6 = F 5 D. = F 6 W.) included some narrations peripheral to the main plot. We learn that 'Euripides would appear to be following the author of the *Alcmeonis*, in regard to the story about the lamb.'[70] This is the golden lamb that Hermes arranged to put into Atreus' flock in order to avenge his son Myrtilus killed by Pelops: the lamb, having become a token of the kingship at Mycenae, caused contention between the Pelopids Atreus and Thyestes.[71] The poem was generous with details, as appears from the scholium according to which 'the writer of the *Alcmeonis* calls the shepherd who brought the lamb

---

[66] Huxley (1969: 53); cf. Breglia Pulci Doria (1991–4: 131). The scepticism of Burnett (2005: 25 n. 62) is unwarranted: on the one hand the *Alcmeonis* did include extensive digressions, on the other the rationalism of the *aition* fits well a poem where some of the numerous eponyms are connected to historical settlements.

[67] Ps.-Apollod. *Bibl.* 3.12.7 (Telamon); 3.13.1–2 (Peleus). See Gantz (1993: 226–7).

[68] See Hes. *Theog.* 1003–7. See Burnett (2005: 69).

[69] Severyns (1928: 234–6), based on Philosteph. *FHG* III p. 33 F 35; Σ Pind. *Nem.* 5.12; Hyg. *fab.* 14.8. In other sources the person in question is Sciron: see Gantz (1993: 220). According to Plut. *Thes.* 10 Sciron begot Endeis by Chariclo. Yet in the myth Chariclo is Chiron's wife, whereas Chiron was born a centaur because Cronus changed into a horse in making love with the Oceanid Philyra (*Titan. PEG* F 10 = F 9 D. = F 12 W.). A metamorphosis characterizes the birth of Phocus as well, when the Nereid Psamathe tried to avoid the intercourse with Aeacus by changing into a seal (φώκη, whence the name of her son).

[70] See below, p. 278.

[71] For a link Alcmaon/Pelopids, cf. Hes. *Cat.* F 193.1 M.-W. = F 90.1 Hirsch.: Alcmaon appears in the context of the funeral of Oedipus; the latter was the husband of Astymedousa, daughter of Nicippe, a Pelopid as well as her brothers Atreus and Thyestes (*Cat.* F 190–2 M.-W. = F 89 Hirsch.).

to Atreus Antiochus'. Both the premises and the development of the myth must have been related, following a sequence of events roughly recognizable in Ps.-Apollodorus *Epit.* 2.4–14.[72] The killing of Myrtilus fits in the context of the challenge opposing Pelops to Oenomaus, king of Pisa in Elis, for the hand of the latter's daughter, Hippodamia:[73] Oenomaus would give Hippodamia as wife only to a suitor able to defeat him in a chariot race between Pisa and the Isthmus of Corinth, which already caused the death of many suitors. With the help of Oenomaus' charioteer Myrtilus, Pelops defeated the king, who, being entangled in the reins, was dragged to his death near the Isthmus. Myrtilus, having himself fallen in love with Hippodamia, was subsequently killed by Pelops, who threw him into the sea near Cape Geraestus in Euboea, called after him the Myrtoan Sea. After being cleansed by Hephaestus, Pelops succeeded Oenomaus and called the Peloponnesus after himself. The double murder, the subsequent purification and the recurrent use of the eponyms fit with the *Alcmeonis*, as well as the stage being set between Elis, Corinth (where the poem originated) and Euboea.[74] According to Pausanias, Clytius, the progenitor of a clan of renowned soothsayers operating at Olympia, was connected to the region of Elis: he was the son of Alcmaon by the daughter of Phegeus, and he migrated to Elis being afraid of his mother's brothers who killed Alcmaon.[75] The tradition preserved by Pindar according to which the founder of the Olympic Games was Pelops is also remarkable: it should not surprise us if the *Alcmeonis* mentioned it, given the tendency of early epic poetry, such as that of Eumelus of Corinth, to celebrate the heroic origins of the Panhellenic Games.[76]

With the device of the golden lamb, the vengeance of Hermes hit the progeny of Pelops. Aerope, wife of Atreus, was seduced by Thyestes and gave him the lamb. Thyestes became king of Mycenae until Atreus got this

---

[72] Severyns (1928: 229–34), based also on the Homeric scholia (cf. especially Σ *Il.* 2.104b).
[73] Ps.-Apollod. *Epit.* 2.4–9. On this episode in the sources, see Gantz (1993: 540–4).
[74] Cf. Eur. *Or.* 988–96 (Cape Geraestus). The link Euboea/Corinth goes back to the archaic age and recurs in the corpus of Eumelus: see Debiasi (2004: 19–107). According to Paus. 8.14.11 the body of Myrtilus was cast ashore by the tide near Pheneus in Arcadia, where he was buried by the locals and received a hero cult. For the tomb and the cult of Alcmaon in Arcadia, see above, n. 32.
[75] Paus. 6.17.6: cf. Löffler (1963: 55). In *Od.* 15.249 Clytius is son of Mantius having a distant relation with Alcmaon.
[76] Pind. *Ol.* 1.93–5 (immediately after the race between Oenomaus and Pelops). On the foundation of the Isthmian Games in Eumelus, see *Cor. PEG* F 8 = F 12 D. = F 22* W. For the chronological implications see, with divergent conclusions, West (2002a: 122–3; 130–1); Debiasi (2004: 33 n. 91, 35 n. 99; 2013b: 533 n. 249). West (2003a: 7) speculates that the tradition according to which the Nemean Games were instituted when the Seven paused at Nemea while approaching Thebes, may have occurred in the *Thebaid*. Assuming the year 573 as *terminus post quem*, the *Alcmeonis* cannot be entirely dismissed as alternative.

kingdom with the help of the Olympians and banished Thyestes. Afterwards, having learnt about Aerope's adultery, Atreus called Thyestes back, slaughtered his sons, and surreptitiously served them to him during a banquet. Following the advice of the oracle of Apollo, Thyestes begot by his own daughter Aegisthus who, grown to manhood, killed Atreus.[77] The contention between Atreus and Thyestes for the kingship closely recalls that between Eteocles and Polynices 'for the sake of Oedipus' sheep', i.e. for Oedipus' kingdom.[78] Aerope's betrayal of Atreus represents a striking parallel to Eriphyle's betrayal of Amphiaraus. The golden necklace given to Eriphyle by Polynices has a symbolic equivalent in the golden lamb, object of desire and source of calamities.[79] Further developments of the myth, in part already Homeric, must have been implied in the *Alcmeonis*. Aegisthus' vengeance does not spare Atreus' son Agamemnon. While Agamemnon was engaged in besieging Troy, Aegisthus seduced his wife Clytemnestra (daughter of Tyndareus and Leda), and with her help he slew Agamemnon when he came back to Mycenae. The blood chain continues with Agamemnon's son Orestes as he killed both his mother Clytemnestra and her lover Aegisthus to avenge his father; the persecution by the Erinyes, the madness, and the wanderings of the hero are consequent.[80] The analogies with the vicissitudes of Alcmaon, already noticed by the ancients, seem too strong to not assume some references or hints in the *Alcmeonis* to the story of Orestes.[81] A final hypothesis may be advanced regarding the saga of the Pelopids in the poem: the tradition records a first murder by Atreus and Thyestes, who killed their half-brother Chrysippus and hence were sent into exile. This episode represents an exact double of that involving Aeacus' sons, where Phocus is killed by Telamon and Peleus, and as such it may well go back to the *Alcmeonis*.[82]

---

[77] Ps.-Apollod. *Epit.* 2.10–4 (where the role of Hermes is played by Artemis, as in Pherec. *FgrHist* 3 F 133, who often diverges from the *Alcmeonis*: see Severyns 1928: 229, 234). On this episode in the sources, see Gantz (1993: 545–50).

[78] Hes. *WD* 163: μήλων ἕνεκ' Οἰδιπόδαο 'for the flocks of Oedipous'. See Buck (1979: 62), and above, n. 36.

[79] See Delcourt (1959: 38); West (2003a: 63 n. 19).

[80] On this myth as a whole, see Gantz (1993: 664–86).

[81] Cf. Eustath. on *Od.* 11.325 (1689.10) = *Alcm. PEG* F °8 (II). The comparative study of Delcourt (1959) remains fundamental. Based on Ps.-Apollod. *Bibl.* 3.10.6, Broadbent (1968: 302) hypothesizes a tradition built on the *Alcmeonis* where, in addition to Penelope, Leucadius and Alyzeus, Icarius would have a further son: Perileos/Perilaus, known as the prosecutor of Orestes at his trial (cf. Paus. 8.34.4).

[82] As in the murder of Phocus (see above, n. 65), the mother of the killers is involved also in that of Chrysippus, where in some sources she is depicted as the instigator. According to these sources Hippodamia either went into exile or committed suicide. On this episode (documented as early as Hellan. *FgrHist* 4 F 157; Thuc. 1.9.2), see Gantz (1993: 489–90, 544–5).

A CORINTHIAN POEM OF THE TIME OF THE CYPSELIDS

From the remaining fragments we derive a complex structure for the *Alcmeonis*, which appears abundant in myths, references, flashbacks, digressions and parallelisms.[83] The biography of the wandering hero Alcmaon entails a variety of settings through different Greek regions.[84] Numerous heroes belonging to various generations appear in the main plot or alongside it: beside the victorious warriors of the Theban and/or the Trojan War, there must have been numerous mentions of their ancestors, parents and sons. Some motifs occur very frequently: briberies, betrayals, confrontations between mother and son, murders of kin (mothers, (half-)brothers, cousins, nephews), vengeances (especially for the fate of the fathers), exiles, purifications.

The seven lines preserved by the three textual quotations (*PEG* F 1–3 = D., W.) do not allow us to date the *Alcmeonis* on the basis of linguistic and stylistic criteria. The reference to Alyzeus and Leucadius provides sound evidence of the chronology of the *Alcmeonis* (cf. *PEG* F 5 = F 6 D. = F 5 W.) in a more substantial way than the tenor of the work,[85] its possible orphic implications (cf. *PEG* F 3 = D., W.), and the lateness of the poem claimed by Athenaeus in comparison with Semonides of Amorgos (cf. *PEG* F 2 = D., W.).[86] The implied connection with Leucas, a Corinthian (or Corinthian–Corcyran) settlement established by the tyrant Cypselus and later strengthened by his son Periander,[87] points to the second half of the seventh century, if not the beginning of the sixth century, as the *terminus post quem* of the *Alcmeonis*, and locates its likely origin in the Corinthian cultural environment at the time of the Cypselids.[88] The dialectic insularity/mainland implied by the tale of the land formed by silting at the mouth of

---

[83] See Severyns (1928: 228), who regards the parallels as distinctive of the Cyclic poetry.
[84] Olivieri (2010).
[85] Which presumes the diptych *Thebaid*/*Epigonoi*, and denotes a tendency to accumulation: see above, nn. 13, 43.
[86] Wilamowitz (1884: 214 n. 13). Cf. Pellizer (1983); Pellizer and Tedeschi (1990: ix–xvii).
[87] Thus the two recorded chronologies can be made compatible: the 'earlier' after Cypselus' accession in 657, around the middle of the seventh century (Strabo 10.2.8, in the same context where he quotes *Alcm. PEG* F 5 = F 6 D. = F 5 W.; Nic. Dam. *FgrHist* 90 F 57.7); and the 'lower' during Periander's late reign, in the sixth century (Plut. *De Sera* 7 = *Mor.* 552e): see de Fidio (1997: 125–6); Piccirilli (1997: 154–5); Antonelli (2000: 87–101).
[88] This was pointed out for the first time by Wilamowitz (1884: 73 n. 2). Cf. Immisch (1889: 140, 154, 185); Bethe (1894); Legras (1905: 22–3); more recently Sakellariou (1958: 159); Jouan (1990: 163); Hilpert-Greger (1996: 66–8). Lowering the chronology by about a century suggested by West (2003a: 110, 'a sixth century or even early fifth-century date') seems

Achelous (and possibly by the tale of the artificial mole made by Telamon at Aegina) may reflect the interests of the Cypselids in digging canals through isthmi, as was planned in Corinth, and accomplished in Leucas.[89] Acarnania, with the relevant eponyms, plays a too significant role in the poem to be unrelated to the colonization conducted, with Delphic approval, by the Corinthian tyrants in Acarnania, Epirus and Illyria.[90] Likewise the prominence given to Delphi and to prophecy[91] must be connected with the period of friendly relationship between the Cypselids and Delphi documented at least until the time of the First Sacred War.[92]

A plot where the main character is played by an Argive hero, who is triumphant over Thebes[93] and then moves to Acarnania, fits with an environment in which Corinth, ruled by the Cypselids, does not hesitate to use myths and characters from the Argive legacy by ideologically connecting to the memory of Pheidon of Argos in an anti-Bacchiad perspective. In such a climate, Delphi seems to embrace a position antithetical to both Thebes and Sicyon which was then ruled by the tyrant Cleisthenes and was contending with Argos.[94] One cannot exclude the *Alcmeonis* being a reaction to the measures of Cleisthenes who banned the rhapsodic contests at Sicyon because of the epic poems, mainly the *Thebaid* and the *Epigonoi*, where the Argives and Argos were praised, and promoted instead the cult of the Theban Melanippus in opposition to the cult of the Argive Adrastus.[95]

It is also possible that the *Alcmeonis* connected specific events to Corinth. A Corinthian setting informs the *Alcmeon in Corinth* of Euripides who, in accordance with the anti-Corinth attitude of Athens at his time, must have borne in mind the *Alcmeonis* by reversing its basic perspective.[96]

---

excessive. For the chronology of the Cypselids, see Salmon (1984: 186 n. 1); de Fidio (1997: 119 n. 260); Antonelli (2000: 62 n. 10).

[89] It is significant that Strabo 10.2.8 (see above, n. 87) informs about the canal through the spit which joined Leucas to Acarnania. See Salmon (1984: 202, 210–11); Antonelli (2000: 95–9).

[90] See Braccesi (1977: 91–108); Salmon (1984: 209–17); de Fidio (1997: 125–31); on Acarnania, see Schoch (1997: 17–25).

[91] For Huxley (1969: 51, 54), who is particularly concerned with the Acarnian prophetic tradition, the *Alcmeonis* 'may well have been composed by a *mantis*'; cf. Pavese (1972: 222, 225–6).

[92] Salmon (1984: 186–7, 219–220, 227–8); Antonelli (1994); cf. Forrest (1956).

[93] Paus. 9.9.4 also counts allies from Corinth in the expedition of the Epigonoi.

[94] On such a political picture, see Braccesi (2001: 40–1, with bibliography), who traces back to it the tradition about Diomedes as the initiator of the Pythian Games for Apollo (Paus. 2.32.2). On the enmity between the Corinthian and the Sicyonian tyrants, see Nic. Dam. *FgrHist* 90 F 61.5; Salmon (1984: 227).

[95] Herod. 5.67.1–5. Cingano (1985; 2004a: 75–6) has shown that the Ὁμήρεια ἔπεα of the Herodotean account must be identified with the *Thebaid* and the *Epigonoi*; cf. Huxley (1969: 48).

[96] Eur. *TrGF* 73a–77. Cf. the plot in Ps.-Apollod. *Bibl.* 3.7.7. See Jouan (1990: 164–5); Olivieri (2013); cf. Gantz (1993: 527). An interest in Athens for the figure of Alcmaon/Alcmeon during the time of the Alcmeonids is conceivable: cf. Huxley (1969: 54 n. 1).

Ways were surely available to connect the plot and the characters to Corinth, especially considering that the author of the *Alcmeonis* is clearly in the wake of the Bacchiad poet Eumelus.[97] The corpus of Eumelus is rich in eponyms, structured (and innovative) genealogies and western backgrounds, among which stand out those centred around Corcyra and its opposite mainland, where the Achelous flows.[98] Eumelus could also have mentioned Harmonia's necklace, which became Eriphyle's, but originally belonged to Europa who gave it to Cadmus, Harmonia's husband.[99]

It is noteworthy that the 'chest of Cypselus', offered at Olympia by the house of Cypselus and described by Pausanias,[100] was decorated with scenes and hexameter inscriptions that are owed largely to the narratives of Eumelus.[101] It included also a few scenes from the Theban Cycle and we can speculate that some of them echoed themes developed in the contemporary *Alcmeonis*. In this perspective, more than the duel between Eteocles and Polynices,[102] the scene with the departure of Amphiaraus appears to be significant: Amphiaraus' sons Alcmaon and Amphilochus, and his wife Eriphyle with the necklace, stand out; Amphiaraus leaves with one foot already on the chariot and his sword drawn against Eriphyle, with an admonitory expression as claiming vengeance.[103] In the perspective of influence from the *Alcmeonis*, it is meaningful that this scene is preceded by that of the chariot race between Oenomaus and Pelops,[104] and followed by that of the funeral games of Pelias, in which Peleus also took part.[105]

Finally a probable link between the *Alcmeonis* and the epic poetry of Asius of Samos, also fragmentary, deserves some attention. Just as the author

---

[97] Jouan (1990: 165–6); Debiasi (2004: 111 n. 7).   [98] Debiasi (2004: 19–107, esp. 54–62).
[99] Cf. Pherec. *FgrHist* 3 F 89; Huxley (1969: 75); Debiasi (2013b: 529). A statuette has been found in Corinth whose gesture corresponds to that of Eriphyle 'holding up the ends of her fingers along her neck through her tunic' (Paus. 10.29.7): see Delcourt (1959: 40).
[100] Paus. 5.17.5–19.10. For a chronology during Periander's late reign, after the First Sacred War, see Salmon (1984: 227–8).
[101] Debiasi (2005).
[102] Paus. 5.19.6. The subject occurs especially in the *Oedipodea* and the *Thebaid*.
[103] Paus. 5.17.7–8. About this scene, common in the ancient iconography, see Krauskopf (1981b: 694–7); Gantz (1993: 507). The threatening gesture is lacking in Attic pottery and is to be ascribed to the Corinthian archetype from which the scene on the chest of Cypselus derives: Krauskopf (1980: 110–12). It is doubtful that the *Thebaid* described Amphiaraus commanding Alcmaon, explicitly or implicitly, to avenge him: see Legras (1905: 65–8).
[104] Paus. 5.17.7. The detail of Pelops' winged horses occurs also in Pind. *Ol.* 1.87: see above, n. 76.
[105] Paus. 5.17.9. For this episode in Eumelus, see Debiasi (2005: 51–5). According to Ps.-Apollod. *Bibl.* 3.13.3 this occurred when Peleus arrived at Iolcus, where he was purified by Pelias' son Acastus (see above, n. 67; for the mythic chronology, see Gantz 1993: 193). Ps.-Apollodorus continues by relating an episode involving Acastus, Peleus and Chiron. If we assume that Chiron and Peleus were related in the *Alcmeonis* (see above, n. 69) then the prominence that, also based on Eumelus' poetry, the chest of Cypselus gave to the Centaur appears to be meaningful (Paus. 5.19.9, on which see Debiasi 2005: 48).

of the *Alcmeonis*, Asius highlighted the eponym Phocus and mentioned his sons Panopeus and Crisus, themselves eponyms of towns in Phocis (*PEG* F 5 = D., W.); similarly he reported the offspring of Icarius, by calling Penelope's sister Meda (*PEG* F 10 = D., W.).[106] Moreover, he mentioned Icarius' brother Tyndareus whose sons were of Pleuron's stock on their mother's side, since Leda's father Thestius was the son of Agenor, himself the son of Pleuron (*PEG* F 6 = D., W.). This genealogy implies the context of the expedition of Icarius and Tyndareus in Aetolia likely narrated in the *Alcmeonis*; it also rejects Eumelus' tendentious genealogy (*Cor. PEG* F 7 = F 8 D. = F 25 W.) in which Leda was a daughter of Thestius in name only, but in fact of Glaucus. Further fragments of Asius highlight details contradicting some mythological claims formulated by Eumelus,[107] where a pro-Sicyonian and anti-Argive and anti-Corinthian attitude, consistent with the interests of the tyrant of Sicyon Cleisthenes, can be detected.[108] Accordingly one may conjecture for Asius a reaction both to some earlier narrations of Eumelus and to the contemporary ones of the *Alcmeonis*.[109] In this perspective the information that Asius also made Alcmena the daughter of Amphiaraus and Eriphyle (*PEG* F 4 = D., W.) is compelling; nor does it seem accidental that this is recorded by Pausanias in his description of the scene on the chest of Cypselus with the departure of Amphiaraus.[110]

---

[106] These two parallels are detected by Broadbent (1968: 302–3).
[107] Cf. Asius *PEG* F 1, 9, 11 = D., W.   [108] Huxley (1969: 89–98, esp. 95).
[109] This perspective is more likely than the opposite, suggested by Broadbent (1968: 302): 'the author of the *Alkmaionis* may therefore have been a younger contemporary of Asios'. Asius *PEG* F 5 (= D., W.) may imply the First Sacred War: cf. Forrest (1956: 43 n. 3); Huxley (1969: 94).
[110] Paus. 5.17.8. Alcmena, traditionally the daughter of Electryon and Lysidice (Hes. *Cat.* F 193.20 M.-W. = F 90.20 Hirsch.; Ps.-Hes. *Scut.* 3), in this way becomes Alcmaon's sister, as well as the daughter of the slayer of Melanippus, who was the hero praised by Cleisthenes. See Huxley (1969: 93, 95); see above, n. 95.

16 | *Cypria*

BRUNO CURRIE

GENERAL

The *Cypria* is first of six poems in the 'Trojan Cycle', dated sometimes to the seventh, but more usually to the late sixth century BC.[1] The later dating relies on the doubtful evidence of isolated, rarely attested forms.[2] These occur in particularly high concentration in *PEG* F1(= D., W.), but even here their implications are not clear-cut.[3] Attempts to supply a *terminus ante quem* by identifying the influence of the *Cypria* on art and poetry are also beset by methodological problems, chiefly the difficulty of identifying the source of the influence as the *Cypria* rather than another, similar, poem or the epic tradition quite generally. The Judgment of Paris is depicted on the 'Chigi Olpe' of *c.* 630 BC 'much as we see it in the *Cypria*'; but that does not make it an illustration of the *Cypria*.[4] The *Cypria* or a poem like it may have been known to the poet of the *Iliad*, Archilochus, Sappho and Alcaeus.[5] Rarely does the textual record permit one to say with any confidence that it is the *Cypria* that is known; Euripides' verbatim allusions to *Cypria PEG* F 1 (below) are exceptional.

The title *Cypria* was current in the fifth and fourth centuries BC (Herod. 2.117; Arist. *Poet.* 1459a37); an alternative *Cypriaca* is attested for a later period.[6] As with *Naupactia* alongside *Naupactica*, there was probably no difference between the two titles.[7] As those equally mean '(the epic of)

---

[1] Seventh century: Kullmann (1960: 362–3); Janko (1982: 200). Sixth century (*c.* 520 BC): Wackernagel (1916: 182–3); West (2011a: 399–400; revised in West (2013: 63–5)).

[2] Janko (2011: 24); cf. Hoekstra (1969: 11–12).

[3] Kullmann (1960: 362–3). Regarding Ἰλιακοῖο (*PEG* F 1.5 = D., W.), it should be said that the formation of adjectives in -ιακός need be no later than patronymics in -ιάδης (*GH* i.106), -ιάς (Risch 1974: 147) or verbs in -ιάζω (*Il.* 16.379 ἀνακυμβαλίαζον; cf. *HAp* 162 κρεμβαλιαστύν, presupposing κρεμβαλιάζω; (*GH* i.338); *LfrgE* v.777.48; cf. Risch 1974: 297–8). The fact that adjectives in -ιακός are next attested in Herodotus is valueless; the *Cypria* must be a hundred years earlier on its latest dating (Wackernagel's). 'Considering the paucity of our evidence for the Greek tongue until the late fifth century in Attica and even later in most regions, we should not be surprised to find a certain number of forms, usages and lexemes otherwise unattested until later' (Janko 1982: 10).

[4] Gantz (1993: 568). [5] *Iliad*: see below; West (2006: 16); West (2002b: 210–13, 232–3).

[6] Burgess (2001: 252). [7] Razch (1922: 2379.49–57).

Naupactus', so *Cypria* and *Cypriaca* (*sc. epea*) will mean '(the epic) of Cyprus'; less plausible is '(the epic of the goddess) of Cyprus', referring to the prominent role in the poem of Aphrodite.[8] The title *Cypria*, like *Naupactia*, probably indicates the region where the poem was believed to originate or to be current.[9] That does not mean that we should expect to see traces of a Cypriot vernacular in the poem.[10] The title Ἰλιακά (*The Trojan Epic*) also appears have been used, probably abbreviating Ἰλιακὰ Κύπρια (*The Cyprian Trojan Epic*), of which Naevius' *Cypria Ilias* may be a Latin rendering.[11]

Proclus reserved a separate section of his *Chrestomatheia* for a discussion of the authorship of the *Cypria*.[12] The poem was generally treated as anonymous by classical and even some much later writers.[13] The author is naturally taken to be a Cypriot.[14] The poem was attributed to Homer before Herodotus (2.117), whence the biographical tradition of a Cypriot Homer.[15] Other Cypriots, Stasinus or Hegesinus, are named in traditions discernible from the second century AD.[16] A story which may go back to Pindar has Homer on marrying his daughter to Stasinus present the *Cypria* as dowry.[17] This story attempts to reconcile the poem's purported Homeric authorship with its avowed Cyprian provenance without actually making Homer a Cypriot. We might guess that there were on Cyprus (as elsewhere) epic poets who wished to claim possession of works of 'Homer'.[18] A quite different Halicarnassan tradition, traceable to the third century BC and favoured by Proclus in the fifth (?) century AD, claimed Cyprias for the author.[19] This seems to rest solely on an interpretation of the poem's title. ΚΥΠΡΙΑ lends itself to being taken as an author's name in the genitive when accompanied by another word that could be taken for a title: ΙΛΙΑΚΑΚΥΠΡΙΑ would be interpretable either as Ἰλιακὰ Κύπρια ('*Trojan Epic of Cyprus*') or Ἰλιακὰ Κυπρία ('*Trojan Epic of Cyprias*'). The Halicarnassan epigram which speaks of 'Cyprias, author of *The Trojan Epic*' (Ἰλιακῶν Κυπρίαν ... ἀοιδοθέτην)

---

[8] Graziosi (2002: 188–9). Differently, Cassio (2012: 415 n. 10).
[9] West (1988: 172).   [10] Janko (1982: 176).   [11] Burgess (2002: 236 n. 7).
[12] Phot. *Bibl.* 239 p. 319a34–b5.   [13] Rzach (1922: 2395.9–20).
[14] *Suda* οι 135.7 Adler; cf. Athen. 8.334b = *PEG* T 9 (reading Κύπριός τις).
[15] *Homeri Vitae* Allen (1912: 244.11–12, 247.8–9, 251.17, 257.19–20).
[16] Athen. 8.334b, 15.682d; Σ D *Il.* 1.5; Σ Plat. *Euthyph.* 12b; Proclus in Phot. *Bibl.* 239 pp. 319a35–b1.
[17] Ael. *VH* 9.15; *Suda* ο 251.27–8 Adler; Proclus in Phot. *Bibl.* 239 p. 319b1–3; Tzetz. *Chil.* 13.630–5.
[18] Lloyd-Jones (1972: 116–18).
[19] Demodamas *FgrHist* 428 F1 (*On Halicarnassus*, early 3rd century BC); epigram from Halicarnassus (2nd century BC): West (2003a: 64–5). The tradition presumably postdates Herodotus (2.117). Proclus implies his acceptance of Κυπρία, paroxytone: Phot. *Bibl.* 239 p. 319b4–5.

seems to declare its own interpretation of ΙΛΙΑΚΑΚΥΠΡΙΑ: Ἰλιακά is the title, Κυπρίας the author.[20] This kind of claim implies a time when interest was shifting from title to author and when scholars were alive to the interpretative possibilities opened up by alternative accentuations.[21]

Ancient testimonia often seem to attest mutually incompatible contents for the *Cypria*. We must distinguish here between discrepant accounts specifically attributed to the *Cypria* and evidence simply of variation in mythology.[22] There are at least two cases in the former category.[23] Some have inferred from such discrepancies that the *Cypria* did not exist as a fixed text but a multiform poem.[24] Other explanations are available: it can be doubted whether one or more of the discrepant testimonia accurately reports the poem's contents; and interpolation can be suspected, especially where the testimonia attest the poem at different stages of its transmission. Some consider it likely that the *Cypria* existed as a fixed text by at least the classical period.[25] Occasional divergence between the sources on some details needs to be weighed against striking convergence on others: in particular, the convergence between Euripides and the Mythographus Homericus indicates that the text of fragment one, at least, remained fixed for half a millennium. It is thus questionable whether the discrepancies found reflect the multiformity of an oral tradition, where only a stable skeleton of narrative not the wording remains constant when a song is sung on different occasions.

Proclus knew the *Cypria* as transmitted in eleven books (*Cypr.* arg. lines 80–1 Severyns); there may originally have been more.[26] Only once is a fragment assigned to a book.[27] The scope of the narrative is contested. It is clear that it began from the very beginning of the Trojan War.[28] Its end-point, however, cannot be easily determined. The end of Proclus' summary (*Cypr.* arg. lines 167–8 Severyns) reprises themes from the beginning of the poem (*PEG* F 1 = D., W.); but that does not mean that the poem must have ended there. Some have seen the *Cypria*'s narrative as predetermined by the *Iliad*'s, with the former a prequel to the latter.[29] Others have argued that

---

[20] See also Introduction, above in this volume, p. 38.
[21] See Burkert (1972: 75); Cassio (2002: 124–6, 131–2).
[22] Burgess (2002: 238–9); Marks (2002: 4–5).
[23] See below on *Cypr.* arg. lines 84–5 and 103–4 Severyns.
[24] Finkelberg (2000); Andersen and Haug (2012b: 6); Tsagalis (2012: 26). On the question of multiformity with respect to particular Cyclic epics, see Foley and Arft, above in this volume, pp. 82–6. Gärtner, below in this volume, pp. 558–9.
[25] Burgess (2001: 20, cf. 12); Marks (2002: 5, 7); Dowden (2004: 198 n. 45).
[26] Burgess (1996: 87–90).   [27] *PEG* F 4 (= D. = F 5 W.) ap. Athen. 15.682d.
[28] Cf. POxy. 3829.ii. 8 ἐξ ἀρχῆς; Hor. *AP* 147.   [29] Bethe (1922: 282; West (2013: 57)).

the *Cypria* was independent of the *Iliad*, even that its narrative may have covered the whole Trojan War.[30]

It is barely possible to consider the *Cypria* in isolation from the *Iliad*. The *Cypria*, known through indirect transmission, is seen through a filter of scholarship that measures it explicitly or implicitly against the Homeric poem. The nature of those filters may explain why the *Cypria* seems more conformable to the *Iliad* when judged by Proclus' summary than by fragments. The summary by Proclus, included in *Iliad* manuscripts by way of a preface, was arguably primarily concerned to put at the disposal of a reader of that poem complementary (but not, on the whole, incompatible or superfluous) mythological background material,[31] while the authors who embed fragments are often explicitly interested in Homer's differences from the Cyclical poem.

There have been divergent views of the *Iliad*'s relationship with the *Cypria* from antiquity: on one view, the *Cypria* responds to the *Iliad*, is even concerned to explicate in a quasi-scholarly way 'problems' in the *Iliad*; on another, the relationship is reversed: the *Iliad* presupposes the *Cypria*, or something very like it.[32] Compromise positions are possible, such as that the *Cypria* preserves pre-Homeric mythological traditions discernible in the *Iliad*, but also responds to the *Iliad* as text. The quality and quantity of observable connections between the poems problematizes the assumption of a purely typological relationship.[33]

Appraisal of the literary qualities of the poem has suffered, since at least the time of Aristotle, from the inevitable comparison with Homer. The negative judgements of ancient and modern critics are not straightforwardly borne out by what we can see for ourselves. There is less evidence of thematic incoherence and more of direct speech than Aristotle might have led us to expect.[34] Scholars have found the fragments stylistically inferior to the Homeric epics, but judgements are often subjective and sparing in interpretive charity.[35] The *Cypria*, like other Cyclical epics, appears to

---

[30] Burgess (2001: 139–40, 143–4, 148).
[31] See Severyns (1928: 245); Kullmann (1960: 204, 209). See in general Quint. *Inst.* 1.8.18. Differently, Burgess (2001: 26–8).
[32] Burgess (2001: 149–57).
[33] Kullmann (1960: 370–3). In general on typology, Burgess (2006: 155–8).
[34] Thematic cohesion: Arist. *Poet.* 1459a29–b7; Davies (1989c: 34); differently, Marks (2010). Direct speech: Arist. *Poet.* 1460a5–11; but see *Cypria* PEG F 8? (= F 6 D. = F 9 W.), PEG F 16 (= F 5 adesp. D.), PEG F 17 (= F 15 D. = F 18 W.), PEG F 18 (= F 24 D. = F 29 W.), PEG F 25 (= F 4 adesp. D. = F 21 W.), 33; Proclus, lines 84–5, 92, 93–4, 114–17 Severyns, etc.
[35] Lloyd-Jones (1972: 121–2); Griffin (1977); Davies (1989c: 9–10). Differently, Huxley (1969: 141–2); Scaife (1995: 191); Dowden (2004: 203–4). See below on *Cypria* PEG F 4 (= D.= F 5 W.), PEG F 9 (= F 7 D.= F 10 W.), PEG F 15 (= F 13 D.= F 16 W.).

have been more receptive to folktale motifs, prophecies, romantic elements, metamorphoses, immortalizations. Such elements are, however, bound to assume greater prominence in a summary than in the poem itself, and comparative appraisals are problematic: it is easier to observe how the *Iliad* gained from its greater exclusiveness than to infer that the *Cypria* must have suffered from its greater inclusiveness.

SELECT EPISODES FROM THE SUMMARY

Zeus deliberates with Themis (MSS Thetis)[36] *concerning the Trojan War* (*Cypr.* arg. lines 84–5 Severyns). This episode is reflected in *PEG* F 1 (= D., W.). Also relevant are two testimonia which explicitly cite the *Cypria*: the 'Mythographus Homericus'[37] (in Σ D *Il.* 1.5; see *PEG* F 1 = D., W.) and Philodemus *On Piety* (*PEG* F 2 = D., W.). This complicates our understanding of the episode.

(a) In Proclus' summary, Themis is Zeus' adviser. Here and in a papyrus summary of pre-Iliadic events (POxy. 3829 ii.9–11), the deliberation of Zeus and Themis is immediately followed by the marriage of Thetis and Peleus. In various later texts Themis counsels Zeus to marry Thetis to a mortal since she is fated to have a son mightier than his father.[38] Accordingly in the *Cypria* it may have been above all Thetis' marriage to Peleus that Themis counselled.[39]

(b) According to the Mythographus Homericus, Momos ('Blame') is Zeus' adviser. He counsels the Theban and Trojan Wars as a way of lightening the burden of the overpopulated earth and punishing men's impiety. Thetis' marriage to a mortal and Zeus' begetting of a mortal daughter are proposed as the means to achieve this end (Achilles and Helen are to be catalysts of the war). Momos here may be a naturalization of Mummu in the Babylonian creation epic, who advises Apsu to eliminate a tumultous younger generation of gods who were distressing the goddess Tiamat (*Enuma elish* i.29–54).[40] Momos may be depicted at the Judgment of Paris on an Attic black-figure hydria of *c.* 510/500 BC.[41] Scholars are divided over whether the Momos-version featured in the *Cypria*.[42] On the one hand, Momos is in

---

[36] Adams (1902: 117).   [37] Montanari (1995); Van Rossum-Steenbeek (1998: 85–118).
[38] Pind. *Isth.* 8.27–46; Ps.-Apollod. *Bibl.* 3.13.5.
[39] Themis at the wedding of Peleus and Thetis on a 6th-century BC dinos: *LIMC* viii.1.1203 no. 20.
[40] Burkert (1992: 103). *Enuma elish* i.1–78 also resembles Hes. *Theog.* 116–210 (Apsu, Tiamat, Ea ~ Ouranos, Gaia, Cronus); the overcrowded Earth motif of *Cypria PEG* F 1 also resembles *Atrahasis* i.352–60.
[41] *LIMC* vi.1.649–50. Momos may have featured in a lost play of Sophocles influenced by the *Cypria*: *Momos* (*TrGF* iv pp. 351–2); cf. his *Eris* (iv p. 188).
[42] Burkert (1992: 102); West (1997: 481 n. 125). Simon (1992: 649); Scodel (2008a: 223).

place in a poem which implicated the personifications Nemesis and Eris in the outbreak of the Trojan War. Moreover, this Momos-version engages with attested themes of the *Cypria*: alleviation of the Earth's burden and a thematic linking of Achilles and Helen. On the other hand, the Mythographus Homericus links the Trojan War to the Theban to forge a 'cycle',[43] which if unobjectionable for early epic (compare Hes. *WD* 156–65) is unsupported by *Cypria PEG* F 1 (= D., W.). It is, further, hard to see why this version is absent from Proclus' summary, if it featured in the *Cypria*.[44] And Momos counselling Thetis' marriage appears incompatible with Themis doing so. Other apparent incompatibilities may be less troubling. Multiple deliberations of Zeus are not themselves problematic; Proclus' summary in any case attests two for the *Cypria* (*Cypr.* arg. 84–5, 167–8 Severyns). Even without the testimony of the Mythographus Homericus, it is clear that the *Cypria* had to accommodate distinct threats to the cosmic order: an overpopulous mankind (*PEG* F 1 = D., W.) and a prospective son of Zeus and Thetis. The solution to each is the Trojan War, but the narrative can hardly have just segued from one to the other. Did these distinct threats call for distinct deliberations, first with Momos, then with Themis?[45]

(c) According to Philodemus (*On Piety* B 7241 Obbink = *Cypria PEG* F 2 = D., W.), in the *Cypria* Zeus determined to marry Thetis to a mortal, angry that she refused him to please Hera.[46] It is hard, though not impossible, to reconcile this with the Themis-version.[47]

These are three important witnesses to the *Cypria*; their seeming incompatibility here is problematic. Possible responses are: (i) the three versions are compatible and all appeared in the *Cypria*, (ii) one or more of the testimonia misreports the *Cypria*, (iii) there were *Cypria*s with different contents, either an oral multiform or an interpolated textual tradition. Of these the easiest is probably the second (distrusting the Mythographus Homericus' attribution of the Momos-version to the *Cypria*).[48]

The goddesses repair to Paris on Mt Ida, instructed by Zeus and escorted by Hermes. Paris, induced by the prospect of marriage to Helen, judges Aphrodite most beautiful (*Cypr.* arg. lines 88–90 Severyns). The episode is covered in *PEG* F 4–5 (= D. = F 5–6 W.); compare Ps.-Apollod. *Epit.* 3.2. It is reflected in detail (with Zeus and Hermes) in vase-paintings of

---

[43] Scodel (2012: 510–11); cf. Cingano (2011).
[44] Marks (2002: 11); cf. however Simon (1992: 649).
[45] See Vos (1956: 55 and n. 2). [46] See Ps.-Apollod. *Bibl.* 3.13.5.
[47] Scodel (1982: 40 n. 15); but see Severyns (1928: 248), and Apoll. Rhod. 4.794–809.
[48] On imprecise subscriptions in the Mythographus Homericus, see Rossum-Steenbeek (1998: 112 and n. 73).

c. 630–620 BC, the chest of Cypselus (sixth century) and Attic drama.[49] The *Iliad* knows the episode, but denies it prominence (24.29–30).[50]

Ships are built under Aphrodite's supervision (*Cypr.* arg. line 91 Severyns). Phereclus may have been named in the *Cypria* as builder of Paris' ships (Σ D *Il.* 3.443 = *PEG* F dub. 37, F 8 W.; not explicitly attributed to the *Cypria*). Compare Ps.-Apollod. *Epit.* 3.2. At *Il.* 5.59–64 it is ambiguous whether Phereclus or Harmonides was the architect of the ships. If the *Cypria* can be shown here to have misread the Iliadic text and invented a mythological detail on that basis, then it can be shown to be derivative of the *Iliad*. It is, however, quite uncertain that it has done so.[51]

Hera sends a storm, Paris sacks Sidon (*Cypr.* arg. lines 103–4 Severyns). Compare Ps.-Apollod. *Epit.* 3.4; Dict. Cret. 1.5. A sojourn of Paris and Helen in Sidon is apparently alluded to at *Il.* 6.289–92. Proclus' summary here notoriously contradicts Herodotus' statement that Paris and Helen in the *Cypria* reached Troy in three days, enjoying fair weather (Herod. 2.117 = *Cypria PEG* F 14 = F 11 D. = F 14 W.). Proclus' summary may misrepresent the *Cypria*, or Herodotus may do so, or the contents of the *Cypria* may have varied, with Herodotus's and Proclus' summaries each faithfully reporting the poem they knew (we may again think either of an oral multiform or a written text subject to interpolation).[52]

In the meantime Castor and Polydeuces steal the oxen of Idas and Lynceus. Castor is killed by Idas, Lynceus and Idas are killed by Polydeuces. Zeus allots the Dioscouroi immortality on alternate days (*Cypr.* arg. lines 106–9 Severyns). The episode is covered in *PEG* F 8 (= F 6 D. = F 9 W.), F 15 (= F 13 D. = F 16 W.); compare Ps.-Apollod. *Bibl.* 3.11.2. The *Cypria*'s narrative is probably reflected in Pind. *Nem.* 10.60–90.[53] The episode is depicted on a metope of the Sicyonian treasury at Delphi (*c.* 560 BC).[54] The Dioscouroi's alternating immortality is referenced at *Od.* 11.302–4. The relevance of the story of the Dioscouroi within the Trojan War narrative is not immediately obvious. Perhaps the Dioscouroi needed to be removed from the scene so that Paris could elope with Helen. The *Cypria* may have narrated the episode, presumably in an excursus, whereby the Dioscouroi had formerly recovered

---

[49] *LIMC* vii.1.179 no. 26; cf. no. 22. Paus. 5.19.5. Cratinus *Dionysalexandros*: POxy. 663, with Bakola (2010: 332–3, 285–96); Soph. *Krisis, TGrF* F 324.
[50] Reinhardt (1997). Interpolated, according to West (2001: 12).
[51] Σ A *Il.* 5.60a (Aristarchus); Kirk (1990: 60); Kullmann (1960: 244–5 and 245 n. 1); Anderson (2004).
[52] Summary misrepresents: Kullmann (1960: 253, cf. 204); *PEG* p. 52. Herodotus misrepresents: Dowden (2004: 198 n. 45); Scafoglio (2004a: 47 and n. 26). Multiform: Finkelberg (2000: 6); Burgess (2002: 241).
[53] See Rutherford, below in this volume, pp. 458–9.   [54] *LIMC* i.1.878 no. 4.

Helen after she had been abducted by Theseus and had captured Theseus' mother Aethra and Pirithous' sister Clymene (*PEG* F 13 = F 12 D. = W.), a tradition apparently predating Homer (*Il.* 3.143–4).[55]

Menelaus goes to Nestor, who recounts four stories: how Epopeus seduced the daughter of Lycus (MSS: Lycurgus) *and was undone* (or *had his city destroyed*?), *the story of Oedipus, the madness of Heracles and the story of Theseus and Ariadne* (*Cypr.* arg. lines 114–17 Severyns). Nestor's digressions resemble those of his Iliadic namesake. This is one place where the nature of the resemblance between the *Cypria* and *Iliad* suggests a relationship between specific poems, not just traditional mythological content.[56] Of Nestor's four mythological paradeigmata, the first and last are clearly relevant to the wider narrative as stories of adulterers or abductors getting their comeuppance.

Recruitment of Odysseus, who feigned madness to avoid recruitment, but was exposed by Palamedes' pretence of violence to Telemachus (*Cypr.* arg. lines 119–21 Severyns). Compare Ps.-Apollod. *Epit.* 3.7. The recruitment of Odysseus is alluded to at *Od.* 24.115–19.[57] Palamedes was later in the *Cypria* killed by Odysseus (*Cypr.* arg. line 166 Severyns). The theme of madness, which occurs elsewhere in the Cycle (*Ilias parva* arg. line 209 Severyns), is avoided by Homer, but not by tragedy (compare below on human sacrifice).[58]

Recruitment of Achilles. Proclus' summary says nothing about the recruitment of Achilles. In the *Iliad* he is recruited from Phthia by Odysseus and Nestor (*Il.* 9.252–9, 11.765–90). But in another well-known version attributed to the Epic Cycle he is recruited from Scyros.[59] Thetis (or Peleus) had sent him there (aged nine?) disguised as a girl to avoid his being recruited to the Trojan War; while on Scyros Achilles (aged fifteen?) seduced Deidameia, daughter of King Lykomedes and future mother of Neoptolemus.[60] Achilles was recruited thence by an embassy comprising Odysseus, who exposed him through a trick. This version has been controversially assigned to the *Cypria* (*PEG* F 19 = p. 75 F 4 D. = F 19 W.).[61] The antiquity of this version is unclear; there is no decisive reason to exclude it from archaic epic.[62]

---

[55] Cingano (2007).   [56] Kullmann (1960: 257–8).   [57] Danek (1998: 477).
[58] Davies (1989c: 62–3). See Sommerstein, below in this volume, p. 476.
[59] Σ D *Il.* 19.326; Σ T *Il.* 9.668 and 19.326; Paus. 1.22.6. cf. Ps.-Apollod. *Bibl.* 3.13.8; *LIMC* i.1.55–69; Fantuzzi (2012: 21–99).
[60] For Achilles' ages, cf. Ps.-Apllod. *Bibl.* 3.13.8, *Epit.* 3.16.
[61] Differently, Davies (1988: 75); Tsagalis (2012b); cautious Fantuzzi (2012: 24–9).
[62] Stat. *Achill.* 1.1–7 does not imply that the transvestism episode has not previously been told in epic (Heslin 2005: 193), only that it has not been told by Homer. Heracles' transvestism: Gantz (1993: 439).

Disguising a boy as a girl for his preservation is a folk-tale motif.[63] Ancient ascriptions of this episode to the Cycle, coupled with fifth-century receptions of the episode by Polygnotus and Euripides (both known to exploit the Cycle) make it plausible that it featured in the *Cypria*.[64] The silence of Proclus' summary about the episode is not especially problematic.[65] More difficult is the question of its compatibility with a later episode in Proclus' summary (*Cypr.* arg. lines 130–1 Severyns, see below) in which Achilles puts in at Scyros after the Teuthranian campaign and 'marries' Deidameia: can there have been both pre-Teuthranian and post-Teuthranian Scyros episodes?[66] If *PEG* F 19 does belong in the *Cypria*, the poem and the Cycle would exhibit further doublets: both Odysseus and Achilles would be recruited reluctantly by a trick, both Achilles and Neoptolemus would be recruited as young boys from Scyros.[67] If the episode was known to Homer, he perhaps omitted it in the interests of a more heroic presentation of his hero.[68]

Muster and sacrifice at Aulis (*Cypr.* arg. lines 122 Severyns). Compare Ps.-Apollod. *Epit.* 3.11–14. Though not mentioned in Proclus' summary, the *Cypria* may have included a Catalogue of Ships here.[69] If so, it may have been omitted from Proclus' summary to avoid reduplication of Iliadic material. A similar issue arises with the Trojan Catalogue (*Cypr.* arg. line 169 Severyns), omitted from Proclus' summary in only one manuscript.[70]

Omen of snake and sparrows at Aulis and Calchas' prophecy (*Cypr.* arg. lines 122–4 Severyns). Compare Ps.-Apollod. *Epit.* 3.15; Ov. *Met.* 12.11–23. The omen and prophecy are recalled at *Il.* 2.299–330, where the *Iliad* apparently presupposes something like the context of the *Cypria*.[71]

The Greeks land at Teuthrania and lay siege to it, taking it for Troy. Telephus comes to the rescue, kills Thersander and is wounded in turn by Achilles (*Cypr.* arg. lines 125–8 Severyns). Compare Ps.-Apollod. *Epit.* 3.17–18, Σ D *Il.* 1.59; the episode was depicted on the frieze of the Pergamon altar.[72] This 'Teuthranian expedition' is arguably known to, but passed over by, the *Iliad*.[73] It is presupposed more clearly by the *Odyssey*.[74] It was mentioned

---

[63] Thompson (1955–8): K514, K1836, cf. K515.1, A511.2.3, A511.3.1.
[64] Eur. *TGrF* v.2 pp. 665–70, esp. T iia; Polygnotus ap. Paus. 1.22.6.
[65] Burgess (2001: 21); cf. Kullmann (1960: 204).
[66] Jouan (1987: 49); Burgess (2009: 15–16). Differently, Kullmann (1960: 191–2); Tsagalis (2012b); West (2013: 104).
[67] Cf. Hygin. *Fab.* 95–6. A vase of *c.* 450 BC collocates the departures from Scyros of Achilles and Neoptolemus (*LIMC* i.1.65–6 no. 176). Doublets in the *Cypria*: Cingano (2011).
[68] Σ T *Il.* 9.668; Paus. 1.22.6; Fantuzzi (2012: 3–4, 21, 23, 27–8).
[69] Burgess (2001: 241–2 n. 16).   [70] West (1966: 402).
[71] West (2011b: 32–3).   [72] *LIMC* vii.1.857–62 (ii BC).
[73] Kullmann (2012a: 213). Differently, Σ T *Il.* 1.59; Davies (1989c: 44).
[74] *Od.* 11.519–20. Cingano (2010b: 86–8).

in the *Ilias parva* and the Hesiodic *Catalogue*.[75] Its presence in epic poetry by the seventh century BC is confirmed by Archilochus' Telephus elegy, clearly influenced by epic.[76] Pindar and the tragedians probably drew on the *Cypria* for this episode. The Teuthranian campaign in the *Cypria* was modelled closely on the Trojan War: the Greeks mistook Teuthrania for Troy;[77] both campaigns started with a sacrifice on Aulis and ended with the Greeks dispersed by a storm;[78] the whole Teuthranian campaign apparently lasted ten years.[79]

Achilles puts in at Scyros and marries Deidameia (*Cypr.* arg. lines 130–1 Severyns). This post-Teuthranian Scyros episode was known also to the *Ilias parva* and possibly the *Iliad*.[80] A post-Teuthranian Scyros episode does not preclude a pre-Teuthranian one (see above). Chronological considerations suggest that a pre-Teuthranian Scyros episode was also known to pre-Homeric tradition: the *Iliad* and *Odyssey* presuppose that (a) Achilles was very young when he left for the Trojan War, (b) he fathered Neoptolemus on Scyros in the course of the expedition, (c) Achilles was killed in the ninth year of the war, (d) Neoptolemus was then fetched from Scyros and Troy was sacked within a year.[81] Without a pre-Teuthranian Scyros episode Neoptolemus is nine years old when he sacks Troy (hard to reconcile with *Od.* 11.508–37), or the mythological tradition was able to turn an entirely blind eye to its main heroes' ages (hard to reconcile with, *inter alia*, Hes. *Cat.* F 204.89 M.-W. = F 110.89 Hirsch.). If, as seems likely, pre-Homeric tradition featured the Teuthranian campaign, elongating the whole war effort by ten years, then it is hard not to think that this was coupled with a pre-Teuthranian Scyros episode, ensuring Neoptolemus was nineteen or twenty when he took to the field.[82]

If the *Cypria* featured both pre-Teuthranian and post-Teuthranian Scyros episodes, then we would get a characteristic doubling of a narrative sequence: Achilles comes to Scyros, has a liaison with Deidameia and leaves Scyros for a muster on Aulis. There is no necessary contradiction between

---

[75] Σ T and b *Il.* 19.326 = *Ilias parva PEG* F 24; Hes. *Cat.* F 165 M.-W. = F 72 Hirsch.
[76] West (2006: 16). [77] *Cypr.* arg. line 122 Severyns; cf. Σ D *Il.* 1.59; Ps.-Apollod. *Epit.* 3.17.
[78] Aulis: *Cypr.* arg. lines 122, 138–43 Severyns. Storm: *Ilias parva PEG* F 24.1 (= F 4.1 D., W.), *Od.* 3.131, *Nost.* arg. lines 294–5 Severyns.
[79] Ps.-Apollod. *Epit.* 3.18–19 (two-year muster, eight-year Teuthranian campaign). Ten years Trojan War preceded by ten years Teuthranian campaign makes a total war effort of twenty years: cf. *Il.* 24.765–6; Ps.-Apollod. *Epit.* 3.18; Σ T *Il.* 9.668; differently, Σ T *Il.* 19.326.
[80] *Ilias parva PEG* F 24 (= F 4 D. = F 4 W.); Burgess (2001: 24). *Il.* 9.668, cf. *Il.* 19.326–7, *Od.* 11.508–9; Kullmann (1960: 266). See also Kelly, below in this volume, pp. 340–3.
[81] (a) *Il.* 9.440–1. (b) *Il.* 19.326–7, cf. 24.467 (interpolated, according to West 2001: 12); *Od.* 11.508–9. (c) *Il.* 2.295, 18.96. (d) *Od.* 11.508–9, 533.
[82] The chronological problems are confronted by Σ T *Il.* 9.668, 19.326. Cf. Cingano (2010b: 79).

Achilles 'seducing' (Σ D *Il.* 19.329) then 'marrying' Deidameia (*Cypr.* arg. line 131 Severyns): we may assume the lack of opportunity for a wedding in the first Scyros episode (where Achilles' exposure was immediately followed by his departure for the war) was remedied in the second.[83]

According to Pausanias, in the *Cypria* Achilles and Deidameia's son was called Pyrrhus by Lycomedes and renamed Neoptolemus by Phoenix.[84] We can only guess when and why was he renamed (perhaps when Achilles returned to Scyros and married Deidameia, becoming *kyrios* of his son; or when Neoptolemus was himself recruited to the war). It is unclear how traditional Phoenix is: he was a member of the embassy to Achilles on Scyros, according to Σ D *Il.* 19.326; and he is buried by Neoptolemus in the *Nostoi* (*Nost.* line 299 Severyns). He may be pre-Homeric, and the *Iliad* may have novelly made him into Achilles' tutor, a role perhaps played by Cheiron in the *Cypria* (*PEG* F 35–6).[85]

The Greeks gather again at Aulis. Agamemnon kills a deer and angers Artemis. Artemis prevents them from sailing. Calchas interprets the goddess' anger and counsels the sacrifice of Iphigeneia, the Greeks send for Iphigeneia on the pretext of marriage to Achilles and try to sacrifice her. Artemis rescues her, translates her to the Taurians, makes her immortal, and substitutes a deer at the altar (*Cypr.* arg. lines 135–42 Severyns). Compare Ps.-Apollod. *Epit.* 3.21–2. The *Cypria* may be the model for Iphigeneia's sacrifice in Euripides' *Iphigeneia at Aulis* and Soph. *El.* 566–74.[86] It is attractive to see *Iliad* 1 as paralleling this episode: Agamemnon rashly angers a child of Leto, λοιμός befalls the Greeks, and a remedy proposed by Calchas compels Agamemnon to forfeit a woman he loves; the *Iliad* hints at the parallel, 1.106–9.[87] It has been questioned whether the sacrifice of Iphigeneia was known to Homer.[88] The *Iliad* ostensibly ignores Iphigeneia, mentioning a daughter of Agamemnon called 'Iphianassa' alongside Chrysothemis and Laodice (*Il.* 9.145). The *Cypria* apparently knew Iphigeneia in addition to the three daughters acknowledged by Homer (*PEG* F 24 = F 17 D. = F 20 W. *ap.* Σ Soph. *El.* 157); this has been taken as an indication of the *Cypria* responding to the *Iliad*.[89] Iphianassa and Iphigeneia may once have been alternative names for the same figure (the *Catalogue* gives 'Iphimede' as a further

---

[83] On γαμεῖ (line 131 Severyns), see Tsagalis (2012b: 7 and n. 19).
[84] *Cypria PEG* F 21 (= F 16 D. = F 19 W.) *ap.* Paus. 10.26.4. cf. Σ D *Il.* 19.326 = *PEG* F 19 (= p. 74 F 4 D. = F 19 W.).
[85] Hes. *Cat.* F 204.87–9 M.-W. = F 110.87–9 Hirsch.; Burgess (2001: 85–6 and 224 n. 145).
[86] Gantz (1993: 586–7). [87] Burgess (2001: 150 and 246 n. 63). Differently, Σ A *Il.* 1.108–9b.
[88] Σ A *Il.* 9.145; but see Dowden (1989: 11–12).
[89] Hainsworth (1993: 77). Differently, Burgess (2001: 150 and n. 62).

variant: Hes. *Cat.* F 23 a.17–26 M.-W. = F 15.17–26 Hirsch.).[90] The inclusion of Iphianassa alongside Iphigeneia looks like an attempt to synthesize variants. But that does not reveal the *Cypria*'s posteriority to the *Iliad*: the composite version is not contradicted, and could be presupposed by the *Iliad* (after the sacrifice of Iphigeneia, Agamemnon can say that he has three marriageable daughters, Chrysothemis, Laodike and Iphianassa). The theme of human sacrifice, which occurs elsewhere in the Cycle (*Il. Pers.* line 274 Severyns), is shunned by Homer, and embraced by tragedy.[91] The translation and immortalization of Iphigeneia by Artemis contrasts with the *Iliad*'s use of the motif (where it does not lead to immortalization).[92]

The Greeks disembark at Troy and Protesilaus is killed by Hector (*Cypr.* arg. lines 148–9 Severyns). Compare *PEG* F 26 (= F 18 D. = F 22 W.); Ps.-Apollod. *Epit.* 3.30. According to the *Iliad*, Protesilaus was killed by a 'Dardanian man' (*Il.* 2.698–702). The vagueness of the expression has suggested that the *Iliad* must have been ignorant of Hector as Protesilaus' killer. Accordingly this will be an instance of the *Cypria* expanding a sparse Iliadic narrative.[93] But the *Iliad* need not be ignorant of a tradition where Hector killed Protesilaus. The vagueness may be attributable to the focalization of *Il.* 2.700–2: all that matters to Protesilaus' widow left in Phylace is that 'a Dardanian man killed him'.[94] Hector is sometimes held to be an invention of the *Iliad*.[95] On the evidence of Proclus' summary, he featured in the *Cypria* as Protesilaus' killer, and it cannot be excluded that he had this role in pre-Homeric tradition. Protesilaus' wife also goes unnamed at *Il.* 2.700: presumably again Homer knew the name, but the narrator expresses sympathy by withholding it. She was apparently called Polydora in the *Cypria* (*PEG* F 26 = F 18 D. = F 22 W.), though better known as Laodameia (Ps.-Apollod. *Epit.* 3.30).[96]

Meeting between Achilles and Helen (*Cypr.* arg. lines 157–8 Severyns).[97] This meeting probably had an erotic charge. It is presumably the first time Achilles sees Helen, and compensates for Achilles' absence from the suit of Helen (cf. Hes. *Cat.* F 204.87–92 M.-W. = F 110.87–92 Hirsch.).[98] Later tradition elaborated the role of Achilles as Helen's lover and posthumous husband.[99] Achilles' son Neoptolemus later marries Helen's daughter Hermione

---

[90] Griffin (1995: 92). Differently, Burgess (2001: 150–1).   [91] Cf. Griffin (1977: 44).
[92] Kullmann (1960: 268).   [93] Huxley (1969: 137).
[94] Cf. Ov. *Her.* 13.65 *Hectora, quisquis is est*....
[95] Kullmann (1960: 182–8).   [96] Kullmann (1960: 184–5, cf. 111, 273).
[97] See Tsagalis (2008a: 93–111); West (2013: 119 n. 53–5). See also Konstan, above in this volume, p. 169.
[98] Kullmann (1960: 153).   [99] Gantz (1993: 596).

(*Od.* 4.3–9). There was a deep affinity between Achilles and Helen as joint causes of the Trojan War; there may have been more to their communion than physical attraction.

Achilles restrains the Greeks who want to return home (*Cypr.* arg. lines 159–60 Severyns). The rush for the ships is an Iliadic motif, on which the *Cypria* has been thought to depend.[100] The use of the motif in the *Iliad* is, however, not straightforward, and can be held to presuppose an earlier use – which the *Cypria* has, controversially, been argued to reflect.[101] Achilles' motivation for restraining the Greeks is not disclosed; it is often taken to be his love for Helen. Proclus' summary links Achilles' meeting with Helen and his restraining of the Greeks with a simple 'then' (*Cypr.* arg. line 159 Severyns), which is frequently used to link episodes; *post hoc* need not be *propter hoc*.[102] It cannot be excluded that Achilles had a more complex, less self-serving, motivation. Also undisclosed is the motivation for the Greeks' wanting to return home. It has been speculated that morale was low because of famine. We are told that in the *Cypria* Agamemnon sent for the daughters of Anius (Oino, Elaio, Spermo) when the Achaeans were afflicted by famine (*PEG* F 29 = F 19 D. = F 26 W.); the fetching of these 'Oinotropoi' may belong in the context of the mutiny of the troops.[103]

Achilles plunders Aeneas' cattle (*Cypr.* arg. line 160 Severyns). Compare Ps.-Apollod. *Epit.* 3.32. The episode is depicted on a Boeotian relief amphora of *c.* 625 BC, and alluded to at *Il.* 20.90–6, 188–90.[104]

Achilles sacks Lyrnessos and Pedasos and other surrounding cities (*Cypr.* arg. lines 161–2 Severyns). See *PEG* F 27–28 (= F 21–22 D. = F 23–24 W.); compare Ps.-Apollod. *Epit.* 3.33; Ov. *Met.* 13.173–6. Achilles' sacking of Lyrnessos and of Pedasos are mentioned together at *Il.* 20.92. Achilles also refers in the *Iliad* to sacking eleven cities in the Troad (9.328–9). In the *Cypria* (*PEG* F 27 = F 21 D. = F 23 W.; cf. Proclus' summary, *Cypr.* arg. lines 164–5 Severyns) Briseis was captured at Pedasos, but in the *Iliad* at Lyrnessos; arguably, the *Cypria* more faithfully transmits pre-Homeric tradition.[105] One of the other 'surrounding cities' was Thebes (*PEG* F 28 = F 22 D. = F 24 W.). The sack of Lyrnessos and Thebes are mentioned together at *Il.* 2.691. The *Cypria* furnished background details to Achilles' capture of Chryseis at Thebes: on the occasion of a sacrifice to Artemis, she had left Chryses for Thebes, where she was lodging with Iphinoe, sister of Eetion and daughter of Actor. Many scholars have seen these details in the *Cypria* as invented in

---

[100] Griffin (1977: 44). [101] Heubeck (1974: 57–8); West (2011b: 101–2).
[102] Fantuzzi (2012: 14). [103] Kullmann (1955b = 1992: 47); Gantz (1993: 596).
[104] *LIMC* i.1.95 no. 389. Moran (1975: 201–2). [105] Dué (2002: 62–3).

response to and in explanation of the sparse narrative of the *Iliad*.[106] On this view the *Cypria* aims to explicate the problem of how Chryseis was captured at Thebes, not her father's town of Chryses.[107] Conversely, the *Iliad* has been seen as presupposing the mythology of Chryseis in something like the form in which we see it in the *Cypria*.[108]

Achilles kills Troilus (*Cypr.* arg. line 162 Severyns). Compare *PEG* F dub. 41 = F 25 W. (not attributed to the *Cypria*); Ps.-Apollod. *Epit.* 3.32; Virg. *Aen.* 1.474–8.[109] The episode is frequently depicted in art.[110] The killing of Troilus (in a sanctuary of Apollo) was to have serious consequences for Achilles.[111] Aristarchus/Aristonicus assumed that the story of the pursuit by Achilles on foot of Troilus on horseback was an invention by the Cyclical poets on the basis of Troilus' Iliadic epithet ἱππιοχάρμην 'fighting from horses and chariot' (24.257).[112] It seems unlikely that this one word spawned not only an episode of the *Cypria*, but an entire mythographical tradition.[113]

Patroclus sells Lycaon on Lemnos (*Cypr.* arg. line 163 Severyns). Compare Ps.-Apollod. *Epit.* 3.32. Again, an episode in the *Cypria* resonates with one in the *Iliad*.[114] On the one hand, the *Cypria* has been taken to prepare for the *Iliad*; on the other, the details of Lycaon's history are considered more likely to be traditional than to be invented by the *Iliad*.[115] If the *Cypria* preserves pre-Homeric tradition here, then it follows that Patroclus is not a Homeric invention.[116]

Achilles receives Briseis, Agamemnon Chryseis from the spoils (*Cypr.* arg. lines 164–5 Severyns). See *PEG* F 27–28 (= F 21–22 D. = F 23–24 W.). Compare *Il.* 1.124–6, 182–5. Again, there is probably pre-Homeric tradition here.[117]

Plan of Zeus to aid the Trojans (*Cypr.* arg. lines 167–6 Severyns). Compare *PEG* F 1 (= D., W.). This 'plan of Zeus' to 'lighten' the Trojans (*Cypr.* arg. line 167 Severyns) recalls his 'plan' to 'lighten the earth' (*Cypr.* arg. line 84 Severyns, *PEG* F 1.4 (= D., W.). This second 'plan of Zeus' has been seen as designed to segue into the *Iliad*.[118] The supposed segue is problematic: the *Cypria* emphasizes a plan of Zeus to help the Trojans, not Thetis and Achilles. If either poem presupposes the context of the other, then it may be the *Iliad* just as well as the *Cypria*. Zeus in the *Iliad* states

---

[106] *Il.* 1.366–9, cf. 2.690–3, 6.414–16, 9.188, 16.153, 23.826–9.
[107] Taplin (1992: 85 and n. 4). [108] Burgess (2001: 151–2).
[109] Virgil signals his adherence to the 'Cycle' (1.457): Barchiesi (1999: 333–4).
[110] *LIMC* i.1.72–95. Gantz (1993: 597–601).
[111] Cf. the killing of Tennes: Ps.-Apollod. *Epit.* 3.26; Dowden (1989: 61–2). [112] Σ A *Il.* 24.257b.
[113] Kullmann (1960: 292–3). [114] *Il.* 21.34–138, 23.747–9, cf. 3.333, 20.81.
[115] Dowden (1996: 48); Burgess (2001: 218 n. 86, cf. 73). [116] Burgess (2001: 73–84).
[117] Dué (2002: 3–4, 12–13, 16–17, 19–20, 55–60). [118] Severyns (1928: 313).

that Hera 'always' alleges that he is aiding the Trojans (1.520); his 'always' (like Agamemnon's, 1.107) arguably references, as well as Zeus' own past experiences, a mythological 'fact' known to the audience. In that event the *Iliad* could allude to a situation like that we see in the *Cypria* (Zeus aiding the Trojans independently of Thetis'/Achilles' wishes).

Trojan catalogue (*Cypr.* arg. line 169 Severyns). Compare Ps.-Apollod. *Epit.* 3.34. It has been noted that, compared to the *Iliad* (2.816–77), the *Cypria* has the Trojan Catalogue in 'its proper place in the traditional order of events'.[119]

> *PEG* F 1 = D., W., from the so-called 'Mythographus Homericus' ap. Σ D *Il.* 1.5
>
> ἦν ὅτε μυρία φῦλα κατὰ χθόνα πλαζόμενα < ... >
> < ... ... > βαρυστέρνου πλάτος αἴης·
> Ζεὺς δὲ ἰδὼν ἐλέησε καὶ ἐν πυκιναῖς πραπίδεσσι
> <κουφίσαι ἀνθρώπων παμβώτορα σύνθετο γαῖαν,>
> ῥιπίσ<σ>ας πολέμου μεγάλην ἔριν Ἰλιακοῖο,　　(5)
> ὄφρα κενώσειεν θανάτωι βάρος· οἱ δ' ἐνὶ Τροίηι
> ἥρωες κτείνοντο, Διὸς δ' ἐτελείετο βουλή.
>
> There was a time when countless races roaming over the earth < ... > the breadth of the deep-chested land; Zeus saw it and took pity and in his shrewd mind agreed to lighten the all-nourishing earth of men, by fanning into flame the great strife of the Trojan war to deplete the burden by death; so they, the heroes, began to be slain in Troy and the plan of Zeus was being accomplished.

Euripides' close reworkings of this passage suggest that the proem was known in the fifth century BC in the same form as it was known to the Mythographus Homericus.[120] It is not clear whether the fragment was the very beginning of the poem. 'There was once a time when . . .' can function as a poetic *incipit*.[121] If it did here, there was no invocation to the muse. If, however, a muse invocation preceded, our fragment followed in asyndeton.[122] A major problem concerns the compatibility of this fragment with Proclus' summary and with the version of the Mythographus Homericus (see above).[123] While 'the plan of Zeus' (7) chimes with 'Zeus deliberates' (*Cypr.* arg. line 84 Severyns), there is no indication here of an

---

[119] Huxley (1969: 140–1).　　[120] *Hel.* 36–4, 39–40; *Or.* 1641–2; *TrGF* 1082.1–2.
[121] Theocr. 7.1; Linus *PEG* F 80.1, with D.L. 1.4; Callim. *Iambi* 2.1 Pf.
[122] For the asyndeton, cf. Hes. *Theog.* 116, *WD* 11; Kühner and Gerth (1898–1904): ii.2.346).
[123] Marks (2002: 7–8).

adviser of Zeus. The proem evidently gives only a broad-brush overview of the poem; the narrative must have back-tracked to narrate Zeus' deliberation with Momos and/or Themis.

Alongside familiar phrases ('Zeus saw it and took pity', used in the *Iliad* of Zeus pitying mortals, here of Zeus pitying Gaia and destroying mortals), we find here many lexical and prosodic features that are unparalleled in extant early Greek hexameter poetry.[124] The cumulative impression of untraditional (and advanced) diction makes this fragment stand out from the other attested fragments of the *Cypria*. The reason for this may be at least in part stylistic: the narrator's assumption here of a historical perspective may help to explain the presence of diction normally excluded from epic narrative.[125]

A key question is the relationship between the motif of the destruction of heroes by the plan of Zeus in the proems of the *Cypria* and the *Iliad*. On one view, the *Cypria* is secondary and attempts to explicate the *Iliad*'s enigmatic proem; on another, the *Cypria* exhibits the motif's primary context of use which the *Iliad* has rendered complex and allusive; both views are ancient.[126]

The destruction of heroes by the plan of Zeus is found in other early Greek hexameter poetry and is likely to be a pre-Homeric motif.[127] The 'overpopulated earth' motif, otherwise absent from extant Greek epic, is found in Mesopotamian poetry and Indic epic.[128] This makes it less likely that the *Cypria* has invented this motif simply as a rationalizing or banalizing interpretation of the proem of the *Iliad*, more likely that it reflects traditions independent of and earlier than the *Iliad*.[129]

Conversely, there is some reason to think that the *Iliad* allusively interacts with a version of the motif like that found in the *Cypria* proem. The Iliadic *mēnis*-theme evokes the whole Trojan War theme of which it is a part.[130] The anger of Achilles that leads to the destruction of many heroes evokes the Trojan War that leads to the destruction of the heroes (compare the *Cypria* proem); specifically, Briseis' abduction precipitating the *mēnis*-theme evokes Helen's abduction precipitating the Trojan War (compare the *Cypria*); attention is drawn to that parallel at *Il.* 9.339–41.

---

[124] Wackernagel (1916: 181–2). Differently, Kullmann (1960: 362–3).
[125] Cf. *Il.* 12.23 ἡμιθέων 'demi-gods'; de Jong (1987: 19, 45).
[126] Mythographus Homericus in Σ D *Il.* 1.5 (lines 4–5 van Thiel); Aristarchus in Σ A *Il.* 1.5–6, Σ D *Il.* 1.5; Montanari (1995: 162).
[127] *Il.* 12.1–34, cf. 7.442–64; Hes. *WD* 161–5; Hes. *Cat.* F 204.95–101 M.-W. = F 110.95–101 Hirsch.
[128] There is probably no 'overpopulation motif' in Hes. *Cat.* F 204.98–9 = F 110.98–9 Hirsch.; but see West (1997: 481). On *Atrahasis* i.352–6, cf. Burkert (1992: 100–4); West (1997: 481). On *Mahābhārata* 1.58, 3.142, etc., Vielle (1998).
[129] Kullmann (1955a = 1992: 28–9).   [130] Scodel (1982: 46–7).

The Iliadic 'plan of Zeus' is an ambiguous and shifting concept.[131] It is interpretable both narrowly as an intention of Zeus to inflict deaths on the Achaeans according to Thetis' and Achilles' wishes, and broadly as a desire to inflict deaths on countless heroes according to an undisclosed agenda of Zeus.[132] The *Iliad* thus seems to exploit a plan of Zeus to kill many heroes much as we see it in the *Cypria*.[133] The shared phrase 'and the plan of Zeus was being accomplished' (*Il.* 1.5, *Cypr. PEG* F 1.7 = D., W.) raises particular problems. Another phrase from the *Iliad*'s proem, 'and hurled many mighty souls of heroes to Hades' (*Il.* 1.3–4), with Achilles' wrath as subject, can plausibly be viewed as transferred from a context where the subject was Zeus purposing to destroy many heroes.[134] It is conceivable therefore that the *Cypria* reflects the more traditional context, to which the *Iliad* alludes meaningfully 'on the level of specific words'.[135] The *Cypria*'s proem, even if later than the *Iliad*, could preserve vestiges of proemial phrasing from pre-Homeric poetry.[136]

The phrase 'and the plan of Zeus was being accomplished' (and variants) is likely to be traditional; early Greek hexameter proems typically make their plots happen because of 'the plan of Zeus'. That makes it only more likely that, if there was pre-Homeric epic poetry narrating Zeus' plan to destroy the heroes, the phrase occurred there; 'the plan of Zeus' is intrinsic to the theme of his destroying the heroes or alleviating the earth's overpopulation as it is not to just any theme of early Greek epic.[137] The fact that reference was made to a 'plan of Zeus' in other poetic contexts would not preclude the phrase at *Il.* 1.5 from evoking the use of the phrase in a context like that of *Cypr. PEG* F 1 = D., W. (two very marked contexts).[138]

PEG F 4 = F 4 D. = F 5 W., from Athenaeus 15.682d

εἵματα μὲν χροῒ ἕστο, τά οἱ Χάριτές τε καὶ Ὧραι
ποίησαν καὶ ἔβαψαν ἐν ἄνθεσιν εἰαρινοῖσιν,
οἷα †φοροῦσ'† ὧραι· ἔν τε κρόκωι, ἔν θ' ὑακίνθωι,

---

[131] Allan (2008: 208).
[132] *Il.* 15.60–77, 19.270–4, cf. 3.164–5, 6.357–8, 11.79. Marks (2002: 17–18).
[133] Cf. Burgess (2001: 149–50, 246 n. 61).
[134] Cf. *Il.* 11.54–5; Hes. *Cat.* F 204.118–19 M.-W. = F 110.118–9 Hirsch.; Scodel (1982: 47); West (2011b: 82).
[135] Fowler (2004a: 229–30).
[136] Hes. *Theog.* 912–14 (*c.* 700 BC?) and *HDem.* 1–3 (*c.* 600–550 BC?) suggest the potential stability of proemial phrasing.
[137] Cf. *Od.* 8.81–2; Hes. *Cat.* F 204 M.-W. = F 110 Hirsch.; Eur. *Hel.* 36–7, *TGrF* F 1082.1–2; Enlil's plan, *Atrahasis* i.356–60, ii.3.36–9. Murnaghan (1997: 24 n. 2).
[138] Formulas as vehicles of allusion in marked contexts: Currie (2006: 5 and n. 27). Differently, Allan (2008: 211–12).

ἔν τε ἴωι θαλέθοντι ῥόδου τ' ἐνὶ ἄνθεϊ καλῶι
ἡδέι νεκταρέωι, ἔν τ' ἀμβροσίαις καλύκεσσιν (5)
†ἄνθεσι ναρκίσσου καλλιρρόου δ' οια† Ἀφροδίτη
ὥραις παντοίαις τεθυωμένα εἵματα ἔστο.

She was clothed on her body in clothes which the Charites and the Horai made for her and dipped in springtime flowers, such as the seasons bear: in crocus and in hyacinth and in blooming violet and in the beautiful flower of the rose – sweet, nectarine – and in the ambrosial buds †flowers of the beautiful-flowing narcissus; in such† clothes, scented with the various seasons, Aphrodite was clothed.

For context and interpretation, see on F5 below. The fragment's style has polarized critics.[139] We should note the ring-composition (1 *heimata ... hesto*, 7 *heimata hesto*), the 'law of increasing elements' (3–6), the different senses of *Hōrai/hōrai* 'Seasons/seasons' (1, 3, 7); the repetition of *anthos* (2, 4, ?6); the pairing (only here) of 'nectarine' with 'ambrosial' (5).

PEG F 5 = F 5 D. = F 6 W., from Athenaeus 15.682f

ἡ δὲ σὺν ἀμφιπόλοισι φιλομμειδὴς Ἀφροδίτη
πλεξάμεναι στεφάνους εὐώδεας ἄνθεα γαίης
ἂν κεφαλαῖσιν ἔθεντο θεαὶ λιπαροκρήδεμνοι,
Νύμφαι καὶ Χάριτες, ἅμα δὲ χρυσέη Ἀφροδίτη,
καλὸν ἀείδουσαι κατ' ὄρος πολυπιδάκου Ἴδης. (5)

And she, the smile-loving Aphrodite, with her attendants wove fragrant garlands, flowers of the earth, and they placed them on their heads, the goddesses of the glistening headdresses, the Nymphs and the Charites, and golden Aphrodite as well, singing beautifully over the mountain of Ida of the many springs.

Bethe, Davies and West (Loeb edn) posit a lacuna after line 1 (if so line 2 should not be taken as the beginning of a sentence, in view of the asyndeton). The combination of grammatically singular subject ('Aphrodite') with plural predicate ('they placed') is unobjectionable.[140] Line 4 seems a superfluous apposition to line 1, especially with a *further* appositional phrase intervening in line 3; but a similar, otiose-seeming repetition is found in *PEG* F 9 = F 7 D. = F 10 W. (lines 2–3 and 4–5). If the text is sound then the numerous appositional phrases should be seen as a stylistic effect: compare *PEG* F 4 (= D. = F 5 W.), where we get five appositional phrases after line 2.

---

[139] Criticized: Griffin (1977: 50–1); Davies (1989c: 36). Admired: Huxley (1969: 130, 141); Dowden (2004: 203).
[140] Braswell (1982), followed by West (2013: 77).

PEG F 4 (= D. = F 5 W.) comes 'from book 1', according to Athenaeus (emended). Evidently these are Aphrodite's preparations for the Judgement of Paris (see *Cypr.* arg. lines 88–90 Severyns). These fragments are hard to square with any view that the *Cypria* had a uniformly rapid narrative pace: we have here amplification of a theme comparable with that found in *Iliad* or *Odyssey* (a suspenseful build-up to the Judgment is intended). There are notable parallels with Aphrodite's preparations for her seduction of Anchises in *HAph* and Hera's preparations for her seduction of Zeus in the *Iliad* book 14.[141] Aphrodite prepares herself *as if* for a seduction: motifs such as the flower catalogue (*PEG* F 4 = D. = F 5 W.) and the band of female companions garlanding themselves and sporting (*PEG* F 5 = D. = F 6 W) are attached to other desirable females before a sexually charged encounter.[142] However, Paris (unlike Anchises) does not find immediate sexual gratification with Aphrodite on Ida; that gratification is deferred to another female and time and place (cf. *Cypr.* arg. line 90 Severyns).

PEG F 8 = F 6 D. = F 9 W., from Clem. Alex. *Protr.* 2.30.5

Κάστωρ μὲν θνητός, θανάτου δέ οἱ αἶσα πέπρωται,
αὐτὰρ ὅ γ' ἀθάνατος Πολυδεύκης, ὄζος Ἄρηος.

Castor is mortal and the lot of death has been allocated to him; but the other is immortal, Polydeuces, the scion of Ares.

This is generally taken to belong in the context of a narrative of the birth of the Dioscouroi (closely in conjunction with *PEG* F 9 = F 7 D. = F 10 W.).[143] The tenses make it easier to assume character-text than narrator-text. A Homeric parallel is Hera addressing Zeus at *Il.* 24.58–9: 'Hector is mortal...; but Achilles is the offspring of a goddess.' The speaker of our fragment might accordingly be Zeus addressing another god or another god addressing Zeus. We might think of a colloquy between Zeus and another deity at the encounter of the Dioscouroi and Aphraretidai (*Cypr.* arg. lines 106–9 Severyns): compare the Iliadic colloquy of Zeus and Hera at the encounter between Patroclus and Sarpedon.[144]

PEG F 9 = F 7 D. = F 10 W., from Athenaeus 8.334b

τοὺς δὲ μέτα τριτάτην Ἑλένην τέκε θαῦμα βροτοῖσι·
τήν ποτε καλλίκομος Νέμεσις φιλότητι μιγεῖσα

---

[141] Janko (1992: 185). [142] Faulkner (2008: 193).
[143] Welcker (1849: 92); West (2013: 79–80) (embedded narrative).
[144] *Il.* 16.441: πάλαι πεπρωμένον αἴσῃ ('doomed long since by fate'); *PEG* F 8.1 (F 6.1 D. = F 9.1 W.): θανάτου δέ οἱ αἶσα πέπρωται ('the destiny of death has been allotted to him').

Ζηνὶ θεῶν βασιλῆϊ τέκε κρατερῆς ὑπ' ἀνάγκης·
φεῦγε γὰρ οὐδ' ἔθελεν μιχθήμεναι ἐν φιλότητι
πατρὶ Διὶ Κρονίωνι· ἐτείρετο γὰρ φρένας αἰδοῖ (5)
καὶ νεμέσει· κατὰ γῆν δὲ καὶ ἀτρύγετον μέλαν ὕδωρ
φεῦγε, Ζεὺς δ' ἐδίωκε, λαβεῖν δ' ἐλιλαίετο θυμῶι,
ἄλλοτε μὲν κατὰ κῦμα πολυφλοίσβοιο θαλάσσης
ἰχθύι εἰδομένην πόντον πολὺν ἐξοροθύν<ω>ν,
ἄλλοτ' ἀν' Ὠκεανὸν ποταμὸν καὶ πείρατα γαίης, (10)
ἄλλοτ' ἀν' ἤπειρον πολυβώλακα· γίγνετο δ' αἰνά
θηρί, ὅσ' ἤπειρος πολλὰ τρέφει, ὄφρα φύγοι νιν.

She gave birth to Helen third after them, a wonder for men, whom Nemesis of the beautiful hair once conceived after joining in love-making with Zeus king of the gods, under strong compulsion; for she was shunning him and refusing to join in love-making with father Zeus son of Cronus, since she was afflicted in her heart with inhibition and indignation. So she was fleeing over the land and the murmuring black water, and Zeus was pursuing her and desiring in his heart to take her, now amid the surge of the resounding sea – her likening herself to a fish, he churning up a great quantity of the sea – now at the river Ocean, the ends of the earth, now on the fertile land, and she was turning into all the many dreadful beasts that the land nourishes, that she might escape him.

The fragment narrates the birth of Helen (cf. *PEG* F 10 = F 8 D. = F 11 W. ap. Philod. *Piet.* B 7369 Obbink), following on from that of the Dioscouroi (cf., perhaps, *PEG* F 8 = F 6 D. = F 9 W.). It is uncertain where in the narrative the fragment came, and whether it is narrator-text or character-text.[145]

'Them' (1) must be the Dioscouroi.[146] The subject of *teke*, 's/he bore / begot' (1) cannot be Nemesis, introduced in line 2.[147] Nor can it literally be Zeus, who did not beget both 'Dioscouroi' in the *Cypria* (*PEG* F 8 = F 6 D. = F 9 W.).[148] It is best to take Leda as subject.[149] Leda brings Helen into the world by hatching the egg (*teke*, 1) laid by Nemesis, who had conceived Helen (*teke*, 3).[150] The *Cypria* would then have given the composite version of Helen's birth recorded by Ps.-Apollodorus (*Bibl.* 3.10.7).[151]

---

[145] Welcker (1849: 93). Davies (1989c: 37).   [146] Severyns (1928: 267).

[147] *Pace* Eustath. on *Il.* 23.639 (1321.35–7), who equally relies on the indirect tradition (Herodotus, Athenaeus) for his knowledge of the *Cypria*: van der Valk (1971–1987: i p. lxxix); Scafoglio (2004a: 45).

[148] Severyns (1928: 268–9). But see *PEG* (p. 49 app.). Tyndareus as father of Castor: Pind. *Nem.* 10.80–2 with Σ 150a (where ἑτέροις τῶν ἱστορικῶν 'others of the historians' conceivably intends the author of the *Cypria*; Severyns 1928: 269–70).

[149] Huxley (1969: 133). Leda as Helen's mother is probably pre-Homeric: cf. *Il.* 3.238, *Od.* 11.298–300.

[150] Huxley (1969: 134).   [151] Kannicht (1969: ii.23).

This version was evidently well known in Attica in the fifth century.[152] A version in which Leda came upon the egg was traditional already by the time of Sappho (F 166 Voigt). Our fragment appears to suture distinct versions: one where Helen is a child of Zeus and Leda, another where Helen is daughter of Zeus and Nemesis.[153] The two narratives of Helen's birth are narratologically distinguished ('whom once' introduces a narratorial analepsis), and they were perhaps genetically distinct.[154] But it is doubtful whether we should recognize here a negotiation of Laconian (Leda) and Attic (Nemesis) traditions.[155] The *Cypria* had poetic reasons for making Nemesis co-parent of Helen, highlighting Helen's role as instrument of Zeus' plan.[156]

The figure of Nemesis (compare Themis and Eris: *Cypr.* arg. lines 84–6 Severyns) has been held to be un-Homeric and post-Homeric.[157] Several full-bodied personified abstracts occur in Hesiod, and the phenomenon is hardly a Hesiodic invention.[158] The presence of Litai (*Il.* 9.502) and Ate (9.504, 19.91) in the *Iliad* in character-text may suggest that they are rather traditional conceptions, from which the poet distances himself.[159] Eris, Demos and Phobos occur in narrator-text in the *Iliad* in a manner not unlike the personifications of the *Cypria*.[160]

Nemesis' transformations to avoid conceiving Helen by Zeus have a parallel in Thetis' transformations to avoid conceiving Achilles by Peleus, if indeed Thetis' transformations featured in the *Cypria*.[161] Like Nemesis, Thetis in the *Cypria* fled to avoid intercourse with Zeus (*PEG* F 2 = D., W.).[162] This creates further parallelism between Achilles and Helen: their mothers resisted the conception of each, and they were together destined to bring about the destruction of the heroes according to Zeus' plan (Σ D *Il.* 1.5).[163]

The fragment's style has attracted criticism. 'The total effect is incoherent', commented Griffin.[164] The perceived incoherence in line 10 disappears once καί is recognized as linking 'appositionally related ideas':[165] Oceanos is identical with 'the ends of the earth'.[166] We are left with three distinct

---

[152] Cratinus' *Nemesis*: *PCG* T ii and F 114–16 (Bakola 2010: 170–2). Pheidias' statue of Nemesis at Rhamnous ap. Paus. 1.33.7 (*LIMC* iv.1.504–5 no. 14).
[153] Kannicht (1969: ii.23).   [154] Kahil (1988: 562).   [155] Cf. Stafford (2000: 80–2).
[156] Bettini and Brillante (2002: 69).   [157] Dihle (1970: 149).
[158] Burkert (1985: 185); Burkert (2005: 17–18).
[159] See Arist. F 387 Gigon; Shapiro (1993: 19–20).   [160] Kullmann (1960: 232).
[161] Σ T *Il.* 18.434a = *Cypr.* F 3* W.; Ps.-Apollod. *Bibl.* 3.13.5. cf. Pind. *Nem.* 4.62–3; *LIMC* vii.1.251–64. Debiasi (2004: 115 n. 32).
[162] Huxley (1969: 140).   [163] Debiasi (2004: 115); Mayer (1996: 1–2, 12).
[164] Griffin (1977: 50).   [165] Denniston (1954: 291).
[166] Oceanos: *Il.* 14.200–1 ~ 301–2; cf. West on Hes. *Theog.* 133; Herod. 2.21, 4.8.2.

domains: the (salt) sea (θάλασσα/ πόντος), the (freshwater) river Ocean, and the land. Nemesis became a fish in the sea (8–9), and all the animals on the land (11–12). In lines 7–12 the organically evolving syntax, with interlaced accusative and nominative participles (line 9), mimics the sense, pursued object and pursuing subject coming in and out of view. The play on Νέμεσις/νέμεσις (enjambed for added effect, 6) resembles that on *Hōrai/hōrai* above (*PEG* F 4 = D. = F 5 W., lines 1, 3, and 7).[167] The pairing of *haidōs* and *nemesis* is traditional, and the fragment may play on a traditional use of the phrase *haidō kai nemesin* in battlefield contexts (e.g. *Il.* 13.122).[168] There is much stylistically contrived repetition throughout the passage.[169]

PEG F 15 = F 13 D. = F 16 W., from Σ Pind. *Nem.* 10.114a

... αἶψα δὲ Λυγκεύς
Τηΰγετον προσέβαινε ποσὶν ταχέεσσι πεποιθώς.
ἀκρότατον δ' ἀναβὰς διεδέρκετο νῆσον ἅπασαν
Τανταλίδ<εω> Πέλοπος, τάχα δ' εἴσιδε κύδιμος ἥρως
δεινοῖς ὀφθαλμοῖσιν ἔσω κοΐλης δρυὸς ἄμφω, (5)
Κάστορά θ' ἱππόδαμον καὶ ἀεθλοφόρον Πολυδεύκ<εα>
<... ... ...>
νύξε δ' ἄρ' ἄγχι στὰς μεγάλην δρῦν <...>

Swiftly Lynkeus started to make for Taygetos, trusting in his swift feet. He climbed up the top of it and began to survey the whole island of Pelops son of Tantalos. Soon the glorious hero glimpsed with his wondrous eyes the two of them within the hollow oak, horse-taming Castor and prize-winning Polydeuces. <...> And standing near he [*sc.* Idas] stabbed the great oak tree.

The narrative context is the battle of the Dioscouroi and Apharetidai (*Cypr. arg.* lines 106–9 Severyns). A lacuna has been posited after line 6. Without it there is a striking narrative ellipse: we must understand that Lynceus informs Idas of the Dioscouroi's whereabouts, and the two of them hasten thither (cf. Pind. *Nem.* 10.63–4). There is also a striking change of subject in line 7,

---

[167] For the play on words, cf. Γαῖα/Γαῖα (*HDem* 9, 14; cf. Hes. *Theog.* 821, 839, 841, 843); δίκη/Δίκη (Hes. *WD* 213–24). For the enjambment and sentence structure, cf. *Il.* 15.657–8.
[168] Cf. Janko (1992: 58–9); Griffin (1977: 50).
[169] *teke*: 1, 3; *pheuge*: 4, 7, cf. 12 *phygoi; allote*: 8, 10, 11; *polyphloisboio*: 8; *polyn*: 9; *polybōlaka*: 11; *polla*: 12; *philotēti migeisa / Zēni theōn basilēï* ('after joining in love-making / with Zeus king of the gods': 2–3 ~ *michthēmenai en philotēti / patri Dii Kroniōni* ('to join in love-making / with father Zeus son of Cronus'): 4–5; *allot' an' ēpeiron* ('now on the fertile land'): 11 ~ *thēri', hos' ēpeiros* ('beasts that the land ...'): 12.

for Idas, not Lynceus, was Castor's killer in the *Cypria*.[170] If the fragment is intact, Idas could only have been identified as subject late in the sentence; the narrative, if sound, is unusual and mannered (compare *PEG* F 5 (= D. = F 6 W.) for the need to recognize a lacuna or admit difficult syntax).

Lynceus' magical eyesight is a well-known instance of the fantastic elements of the Cycle eschewed by Homeric epic.[171] Stylistically, too, the passage has been unfavourably compared to Homer. Griffin called the narrative 'compressed beyond all hope of excitement'.[172] Lines 1–6 are not especially compressed; the compression results from the ellipse in lines 6–7 – *if* the text is sound. Lynceus' actions are described in numerous compound verbs not in tmesis (2–5), giving lingering emphasis to the actions described; by contrast, Idas' act of violence is described in simple verbs (7). Verbs come early in their clauses, lending a sense of urgency; proper nouns are enjambed at line-beginning (2, 4, 6). The postponement of *amphō* (5),[173] and the disposition of the names Castor and Polydeuces on the following line, again mimics the sense (the Dioscouroi tucked away from view).

PEG F 17 = F 15 D. = F 18 W., from Athenaeus 2.35c

οἶνόν τοι, Μενέλαε, θεοὶ ποίησαν ἄριστον
θνητοῖς ἀνθρώποισιν ἀποσκεδάσαι μελεδώνας.[174]

The gods made wine, Menelaus, as the best thing to disperse the cares of mortal men.

This is plainly character-text, part of an extended dialogue. Perhaps, as often assumed, these lines were spoken by Nestor to Menelaus in the former's palace at Pylos (*Cypr.* arg. lines 112–13 Severyns).[175] The fragment is sometimes associated with *PEG* 16 (not attributed to the *Cypria*).[176] That fragment may be supposed either to have preceded *PEG* F 17 (= F 15 D. = F 18 W.) as a question ('Will you not disperse the vexation from me, old man who have been through many trials?') or to have followed it as a statement ('You will not disperse etc.'). The latter is preferable.[177] The grounds for

---

[170] *Cypr.* arg. lines 106–9 Severyns; Philod. = F 14 D. / 17 W.; cf. Ps.-Apollod. *Bibl.* 3.11.2; *PEG* p. 54, note on F 15.7.
[171] Griffin (1977: 40–1).   [172] Griffin (1977: 51).
[173] See the apparatus criticus of *PEG* p. 54.
[174] On the accentuation μελεδώνας / μελεδῶνας, see *LfgrE* s.v. 'μελεδῶναι'; differently, *PEG* p. 55 in app. crit.
[175] Huxley (1969: 135); *PEG* pp. 54–5.
[176] Not assigned to the *Cypria* by Davies (1988: 160); West (2003a: 290–1).
[177] Obbink (1996: 547–8).

associating the two fragments are the correspondences and the possibility of taking 'old man' to refer to Nestor (confirming the scenario of a conversation between Nestor and Menelaus). But there are lexical peculiarities in *PEG* F 16 and there is no obligation to think that similar phrasing must point to the same narrative context.[178]

This commendation of wine has been dubbed un-Homeric.[179] The sentiment is at home in the lyric poets.[180] But the difference from Homer is exaggerated, where Hecuba can say to Hector, 'wine greatly increases a tired man's strength'.[181] Hector refused the wine; perhaps the *Cypria*'s Menelaus did likewise (he will have done, if *PEG* F 16 followed *PEG* F 17 = F 15 D. = F 18 W.). Heroes typically turn down the invitation to feast and drink when set on a serious purpose.[182] It is hard to see Menelaus here as characterized as deliberately unheroic.[183]

PEG F 18 = 24 D. = 29 W., from Plat. *Euthyphr.* 12a

Ζῆνα δὲ τόν τ' ἔρξαντα καὶ ὃς τάδε πάντ' ἐφύτευσεν
οὐκ ἐθέλει νεικεῖν· ἵνα γὰρ δέος, ἔνθα καὶ αἰδώς.

With Zeus – the perpetrator and the one who sowed the seeds of all these things – s/he has no wish to quarrel; for where there is fear, there too there is inhibition.

The passage presents textual and interpretative problems.[184] The present tense 'has no wish' and the gnomic 'where there is fear, there too there is inhibition' point to character-text. It is hard to identify the speaker; perhaps Nestor to Menelaus or a conversation between Paris and Helen.[185] As usually interpreted, *neikein* (2) is taken to mean 'criticize', and the subject of 'has no wish' taken to be a human character. However, mortals normally have no compunction about criticizing Zeus.[186] The subject of *neikein* may be a deity, with the verb meaning rather 'quarrel, pick a fight with'. Only gods are in a position to 'pick a fight with' Zeus (e.g. *Il.* 11.78); they may well, in this very immediate sense, feel 'fear' before Zeus, and they often display an 'inhibition' about opposing his will. In an extension of this, Poseidon states that Zeus 'wishes to pick a quarrel' with him (*Il.* 15.210), Athena that

---

[178] Cf. *Od.* 8.149; 'Theogn.' 883, 1323; Palladas, *AP* 11.55.   [179] Griffin (1977: 47).
[180] Cf. Archil. *IEG* F 11; Alcae. F 335, 346 Voigt.   [181] *Il.* 6.261; cf. 9.706, 19.161, 167–70.
[182] *Od.* 2.303–10; Stesich. *Eriphyle* (?) *PMGF* S148.i.1–10.   [183] Scodel (2008a: 225).
[184] The participle and relative clause are best taken as co-ordinate and both referred to Zeus. Differently, Bolling (1928: 65).
[185] Huxley (1969: 140); *PEG* p. 55 note.   [186] *Il.* 3.365, 9.18–25, 12.164–5, 13.633; *Od.* 3.161.

she 'does not wish to fight' with Poseidon (*Od.* 13.341). If a deity is the subject in line 2, then it will be one who is out of sympathy with Zeus, and feels themselves powerless to oppose his will. Who then might be speaker and addressee? The addressee should be a mortal (no deity needs to be thus enlightened): Helen speaking to Achilles (compare *Cypr.* arg. lines 157–8 Severyns) of Aphrodite, or Achilles speaking to Helen of Thetis?[187]

---

[187] West (2013: 85) suggests Helenus speaking to the Trojans of Hera.

17 | Aethiopis

ANTONIOS RENGAKOS

From the point of view of its plot, the *Aethiopis* – a Cyclic epic that must have comprised five books and that is ascribed, along with the *Iliou persis* and the *Titanomachy*, to Arctinus of Miletus – follows directly on the *Iliad* and narrates the events until the death of Achilles and the funeral games held in his honour. The structure and content of this epic can be roughly reconstructed by the plot as outlined by Proclus (*Aeth.* arg. lines 172–203 Severyns); a significant addition is offered by the only certain fragment of the epic attested in the Σ Pind. *Isth.* 4.58b, according to which the suicide of Ajax formed part of the original *Aethiopis*. This piece of information is further confirmed or supplemented by testimonies explicitly referring to this Cyclic epic, though not always certainly genuine, and assumed allusions found in the *Epitome* of Ps.-Apollodorus (5.1–6, see arg. lines 1–4 W.), the *Odyssey* (especially 24.36–92),[1] Pindar (*Pyth.* 6.28–42; *Nem.* 6.49–54), Virgil (*Aen.* 1.751; 6.57), various Homeric scholia (Σ Ariston. *Il.* 17.719 or Σ H *Od.* 11.547; Σ D *Il.* 23.660) and the *Posthomerica* of Quintus of Smyrna (third century AD), as also by the inscriptions and images of the *Tabula Iliaca Capitolina* (A), the *Tabula Veronensis* II (D) and the *Tabula Iliaca* 'Thierry' (Ti),[2] and by a number of the so-called 'Homeric Cups'.[3] Occasionally we may draw conclusions based on representations of scenes related to this Cyclic epic depicted on vases or other monuments. Not even one genuine verse from the *Aethiopis* survives (see below).

PLOT

Proclus outlines the plot of the *Aethiopis* as follows: the Amazon Penthesilea, a daughter of Ares of Thracian provenance, comes to assist the Trojans as their ally. After having excelled in battle, she is killed by Achilles and eventually buried by the Trojans. Thersites scoffs at Achilles for his supposed love for Penthesilea; Achilles kills him and as a result a quarrel arises among

---

[1] Detailed analysis in Danek (1998: 466–70).
[2] Sadurska (1964); Valenzuela Montenegro (2004: 26–149, 192–8, also 199–203).
[3] From the third or second century BC; cf. Sinn (1979: 92–3 = MB 23–6).

the Achaeans. Thereupon, Achilles must sail to Lesbos, sacrifice to Apollo, Artemis and Leto and be purified of the murder by Odysseus. Memnon, the son of Eos (= the goddess of Dawn), who possesses an armour made by Hephaestus, comes also to assist the Trojans as their ally. Thetis prophesies to Achilles the events related to Memnon. During a battle Memnon kills Antilochus, the companion of Achilles and son of Nestor, and is thereupon killed by Achilles. His mother, Eos, makes a plea to Zeus to give her son immortality, and it is granted. Achilles puts the Trojans to flight and enters the city, but is killed by Paris and Apollo. A fierce battle erupts over his dead body; Ajax carries it off to the ships, while Odysseus fights back the Trojans. Then Antilochus is buried and Achilles' body lies in state. Achilles' mother, Thetis, accompanied by the Muses and her sisters, the Nereids, comes and laments her son; she then snatches the body from the pyre and carries it off to the island of Leuce. The Achaeans build for him a grave mound and hold funeral games in his honour. A quarrel breaks out between Odysseus and Ajax over the armour of Achilles. From *Aeth. PEG* F 5 (= F 1 D. = F 6 W.), as also from the *Tabula Capitolina* (*PEG* T 8 II = T 3 (i) D.), it can be inferred that the suicide of Ajax, an event taking place after he was defeated in the quarrel by Odysseus, was also narrated in the *Aethiopis*.

The plot of the *Aethiopis*, as outlined above, can be supplemented by various other sources; I shall only quote the most important and the most certain ones.[4]

1. The details concerning the killing of Antilochus by Memnon are provided by Pindar. In *Pyth*. 6.28–39 it is said that Paris injures one of the horses of Nestor's carriage with an arrow and, while the old king struggles to release the dead horse from its harness, Memnon draws near threateningly. In imminent danger of being killed, Nestor summons his son Antilochus to help him, who, after enabling his father to flee, is himself killed by Memnon. (For a similar scene in *Il*. 8.80–91, see below.[5])
2. It seems that in Aeschylus' lost tragedy *Psychostasia* (*TrGF* F 279–80), the weighing of the fates of Achilles and Memnon by Zeus, the so-called *kērostasia*, preceded the decision about the outcome of the combat

---

[4] All eight basic motifs of the Achilles-fabula (this is what Burgess calls the plot of the *Aethiopis*) are assembled in Burgess (2009: 30–42).
[5] Pindar does not draw on the *Ilias parva*, as has been suggested by certain scholars in the past (see Wilamowitz (1884: 154; 1920: 45)), but on the *Aethiopis*; cf. already Welcker (1882: 174); Fraenkel (1932: 244–8); Kullmann (1960: 314–16, 335 n. 2); Erbse (1993: 394); Heitsch (2008: 2–3 n. 9) against Kelly (2006: 13–24), who claims that Pindar's source was the *Iliad* and not the *Aethiopis*; see also West (2003c: 1–2) and Cook (2009: 133–61).

between them.[6] This evidence is confirmed by several representations of the *psychostasia* on vases dating from the last third of the sixth century BC (i.e. already before Aeschylus' time: *LIMC* s.v. 'Memnon', no. 16–25; s.v. 'Achilleus', 172).[7] Similar scenes are also found in the *Iliad* (22.209–13; 8.69–74), on which see below.

3. According to Ps.-Apollodorus' *Epitome* (5.3), the death of Achilles occurs 'at the Scaean Gates'; the Greek hero receives the fatal wound in his ankle. The exact place of this event is also testified by the so-called *Tabula Veronensis* (T 3 (ii) D.). In the *Iliad*, the dying Hector prophesies to Achilles that 'Paris and Phoebus Apollo, valiant though you be, shall slay you at the Scaean Gates' (*Il.* 22.359–60).

4. According to Ps.-Apollodorus' *Epitome* (5.4), Ajax kills Glaucus during the battle over Achilles' body. The scene was represented on a now lost amphora from Chalcis (dating from the middle sixth century BC; with indication of the figures' names) as follows: on the ground lies the still armed dead body of Achilles; arrows are still stuck in his flank and left ankle; Glaucus attempts to drag the body away using a loop of rope, which is fixed around Achilles' heel; Ajax defends the body and gives Glaucus a fatal blow with his spear; Paris attempts to rescue Glaucus, yet his arrows rebound off Ajax's shield. Apart from these, Athena (protecting Ajax) and the Trojans Aeneas and Laodocus participate in the scene (*LIMC* s.v. 'Achilleus', no. 850, pp. 182–3).[8] During the fighting over Patroclus' body in book 17 of the *Iliad* Ajax is covering the retreat of his comrades, killing the Trojan Hippothoos, while the latter tries to drag off the dead body of Patroclus by the foot (17.288–300).

THE FRAGMENTS

Genuine

PEG F 5 = F 1 D. = F 6 W., from Σ Pind. *Isth.* 4.35/36b (ἴστε μὰν Αἴαντος ἀλκὰν φοίνιον τὰν ὀψίαι ἐν νυκτὶ ταμὼν περὶ ὧι φασγάνωι μομφὰν ἔχει παίδεσσιν Ἑλλάνων ὅσοι Τροίανδ' ἔβαν, 'You surely know of the bloodstained strength of Ajax which he cut late in the night with his sword

---

[6] See West (2000: 343–7); cf. Kullmann (1960: 32–47, 316–35).
[7] See Heitsch (2001: 241–2; 2005: 434–5).
[8] Quintus of Smyrna, who narrates in detail the fighting over Achilles' body in the third book of his *Posthomerica* and who is partially indebted to the divergent version of *Od.* 24.37–42, seems also to take into account Arctinus in that he mentions the three most important Trojans (Glaucus, Paris, Aeneas). Not entirely right is Vian (1959: 33).

and made the target of reproach the children of the Greeks, those who went to Troy'):

> τὸ δὲ ὀψίαι ἐν νυκτὶ τριχῶς νοεῖται· ἢ γὰρ τὴν ὀψίαν τῆς ἡμέρας· ὅτε γὰρ ὀψὲ τῆς ἡμέρας ἐστί, τότε ἀρχὴ τῆς νυκτός· οἷον ἀφ' ἑσπέρας· ἢ κατὰ τὸ ὀψὲ τῆς νυκτός, οἷον τὸ μεσονύκτιον, μετὰ τὴν ὀψίαν ὥραν τῆς νυκτός, ὥστε ὅλον ὅμοιον εἶναι τῶι ἐν νυκτὸς ἀμολγῶι, ὅτε ἀμέλγουσι πρὸς ἑσπέρας· ἢ πρὸς ἕω, ὅτε ἐστὶ τῆς νυκτὸς ὀψὲ πρὸ τοῦ ὄρθρου. τοῖς δὲ τὸν ὄρθρον ἀκούουσι καὶ τὰ ἀπὸ τῆς ἱστορίας συνᾴδει· ὁ γὰρ τὴν Αἰθιοπίδα γράφων περὶ τὸν ὄρθρον φησὶ τὸν Αἴαντα ἑαυτὸν ἀνελεῖν.

> the phrase 'late in the night' has a triple meaning; (it denotes) either late in the day; for when it is late in the day, it is then the beginning of the night; i.e. after evening; or during late in the night, i.e. at midnight, after the late hours of the night, with the result that it is completely similar to 'at the dead of night', when they milk towards evening; or at the coming of dawn, when it is late in the night before early morning. The details of the story agree with those who take the expression as denoting the morning; for the author of the *Aethiopis* says that Ajax killed himself around the time of early morning.

This is the only fragment that can be attributed to the *Aethiopis* with certainty. Moreover, it contains the additional important information to Proclus' summary that in this epic Ajax's suicide occurred in the morning of the day following the quarrel over the armour of Achilles. As noted above, the information given by the Pindar scholion is confirmed by the inscription of the *Tabula Capitolina*: Αἴας [μανι]ώδης (the *Tabula* names explicitly its source: Αἰ[θ]ιοπὶς κατὰ Ἀρκτῖνον τὸν Μιλήσιον).

Dubious

Several other fragments which may be attributed to the *Aethiopis* are dubious for different reasons.

PEG F 2 = F dub. D. = F 2 W., from POxy. 1611 F 4 col. II 145–148, third century AD; 13.135 Grenfell-Hunt

>] 'σύ, γύναι, τίνος ἔκγον[ος] εὔχ[ε]αι εἶναι;'
> καὶ τ[ὰ ἑ]ξῆς καὶ ὡς ἐκτίθετ[αι Ἀρκτῖ]νος ὅλον αὐτῆ[ς τὸν] θάνατον.

>] 'you, woman, whose offspring do you boast to be?'
> And the following and how Arctinus presents her entire death.

The fragment originates from a school commentary (?): Allen has ascribed it to the *Aethiopis*, yet not only is the supplementation Ἀρκτῖ]νος dubious

(Grenfell and Hunt have also suggested e.g. the reading [Ἀχ ?]αιος) but also the attempt of Allen to read, in the previous severely mutilated verses of the text (F 3, 135–41), twice (139, 141) the name Πενθεσίλεια; on the other hand, the first editors of the text have pointed out that, due to the different colour of the papyrus, the joining of fragments 3 and 4 is 'improbable'. According to West, Penthesilea is addressed here either by Priam (upon her arrival in Troy) or Achilles (during their first encounter on the battlefield?).[9]

PEG F 4 = Fragm. inc. loci intra cyclum epicum 3 D.
(p. 74) = F 4 W. ('uncertain attribution'), from Σ D *Il.* 23.660

Φόρβας ἀνδρειότατος τῶν καθ' αὑτὸν γενόμενος, ὑπερήφανος δέ, πυγμὴν ἤσκησεν, καὶ τοὺς παριόντας ἀναγκάζων ἀγωνίζεσθαι ἀνῄρει, ὑπὸ δὲ τῆς πολλῆς ὑπερηφανίας ἠβούλετο καὶ πρὸς τοὺς θεοὺς τὸ ἴσον φρόνημα ἔχειν. διὸ Ἀπόλλων παραγενόμενος καὶ συστὰς αὐτῶι ἀπέκτεινεν αὐτόν. ὅθεν ἐξ ἐκείνου καὶ τῆς πυκτικῆς ἔφορος ἐνομίσθη ὁ θεός· ἡ ἱστορία παρὰ τοῖς κυκλικοῖς.

After he became the bravest of those of his time, and arrogant, he practiced boxing, and by forcing those who came to him to compete he destroyed them, and then because of his great arrogance he wished to have the same spirit towards the gods. For this reason Apollo, after coming and standing next to him, killed him. Whence because of him the god was considered to be an overseer of boxing; the story is attested in the Cyclic poets.

According to Allen,[10] this Phorbas, the son of Panopeus of Phocis, is the same man as Panopeus, the father of Epeius. It seems that his genealogy was recounted in detail in the *Aethiopis* on the occasion of the funeral games held in honour of Achilles, in which Epeius participated in the boxing match according to Q. S. 4.323–74 (Epeius takes part in a similar contest during the funeral games in honour of Patroclus in *Il.* 23.664–99). However, the connection between Phorbas and Epeius' father is purely hypothetical; a weak indication that this fragment actually belonged to the *Aethiopis* is only the motif of the boxing match.

F 5 W. = Arctinus 1 D. ('dubia et spuria') = *Ilii excidium PEG*
F 7 = *Iliou persis* F 16 Bethe ('dubious' p. 181), from Diomedes, *Gramm. Lat.* 1.477.9 Keil

Alii a Marte ortum Iambum strenuum ducem tradunt, qui cum crebriter pugnas iniret et telum cum clamore torqueret, ἀπὸ τοῦ ἱεῖν καὶ βοᾶν [West: *apo tu eim και ban* codd.] Iambus appellatur. Idcirco ex brevi et longa

---

[9] West (2013: 139); see also Vian (1959: 22).
[10] Allen (1913: 190); see also Welcker (1865: 61).

pedem hunc esse compositum, quod hi qui iaculentur ex brevi accessu in extensum passum proferuntur, ut promptiore nisu telis ictum confirment. Auctor huius vibrationis [Schneidewin: *librationis* codd.] Arctinus [Scaliger: *Arctinius, Artinius, Agretinus* codd.] Graecus his versibus perhibetur {ὁ Ἴαμβος} [del. Welcker]:

ἐξ ὀλίγου διαβὰς προφόρωι ποδί, γυῖά οἱ ὄφρα
τεινόμενα ῥώοιτο καὶ εὐσθενὲς εἶδος ἔχησιν.

Others report that Iambus as a vigorous leader was the son of Mars, who is called Iambus from ἱεῖν and βοᾶν (West: *apo tu eim και ban* codd.), because he repeatedly entered battle and hurled his spear with a shout. On that account, the iambic foot is made up of a short and a long, since those who hurl a javelin take a short step forward followed by a long stride, in order to strengthen the blow of the spear by a more resolute effort. The author of this method of brandishing is said to be the Greek Arctinus [Scaliger: *Arctinius, Artinius, Agretinus* codd.] in the following verses [{ὁ Ἴαμβος} del. Welcker]:

With legs slightly apart and one foot forward, so that his limbs should move vigorously at full stretch and have a good appearance of strength.

Welcker ascribed both verses to the *Iliou persis*;[11] West, on the contrary, notes (2013: 158): 'the fragment suggests an athlete rather than a warrior, though it is not clear what he is preparing to do. He might be getting set for a foot race... The emphasis on strength would better suit boxing, wrestling, or hurling a discus or a javelin... An athletic setting looks more likely... the games for Achilles make the obvious one.' The epithet *euthenes* is not attested elsewhere in archaic epic and the expression *ex oligou* is likewise unepic in diction (it is first found in Thucydides).

PEG F 3 = F 3 W. = *Ilias parva* F 3.7 Bethe (p. 171), from Σ Ariston. *Il.* 17.719

ὅτι ἐντεῦθεν τοῖς νεωτέροις ὁ βασταζόμενος Ἀχιλλεὺς ὑπ' Αἴαντος, ὑπερασπίζων δὲ Ὀδυσσεὺς παρῆκται. εἰ δὲ Ὅμηρος ἔγραφε τὸν Ἀχιλλέως θάνατον, οὐκ ἂν ἐποίησε τὸν νεκρὸν ὑπ' Αἴαντος βασταζόμενον, ὡς οἱ νεώτεροι.

[The critical sign is] because from this passage [*Il.* 17.719] more recent writers have derived Achilles being carried by Ajax with Odysseus defending him. But if Homer had been describing the death of Achilles, he would not have the body carried by Ajax, as the later writers do.

---

[11] See Welcker (1882: 529–30). Likewise *PEG*; Bethe (1922: 181) also thinks of the *Titanomachy*.

Cf. also Σ *Od*. 11.547

> οἱ φονευθέντες ὑπὸ Ὀδυσσέως ὅτε Αἴας τὸ πτῶμα Ἀχιλλέως ἐβάσταζεν. ἀθετεῖ Ἀρίσταρχος. ἡ δὲ ἱστορία ἐκ τῶν κυκλικῶν.
>
> The people killed by Odysseus when Ajax carried the body of Achilles. Aristarchus athetizes. The story comes from the Cyclic authors.

Proclus ('a fierce battle develops over his body, in which Ajax takes up the body and carries it towards the ships, with Odysseus fighting the Trojans off') and the information provided by the *Epitome* ('a fight taking place for the corpse, Ajax... carried the body, though shot by darts, through the midst of the enemies, while Odysseus fought his assailants') suggest the possibility that the criticism exercised by Aristarchus on the representation of Ajax as the bearer of the corpse and not as a fighter (as he is represented in the fighting over Patroclus' body in *Il*. 17.717–21) was aimed at the *Aethiopis*. The rescuing of Achilles' body by the same characters was also represented in the *Ilias parva* (see *PEG* F 2 = D., W.); moreover, in this version of the event the fact that Ajax functioned only as the bearer of a heavy weight was crucial for the awarding of Achilles' armour to Odysseus. Therefore, the hypothesis that by *neōteroi* or *kyklikoi* not only Arctinus but also Lesches is meant is a possibility that cannot be excluded. The *Odyssey* (5.309–12 and 24.37–9, 41–3) cannot enlighten us further as to who played which role in this episode; yet, the representation of Ajax with the body of Achilles belongs to the earliest and most popular reconstructions of the myth (see *LIMC* s.v. 'Achilleus', 185–193).[12]

Spurious

1. Σ ex. (Did. ?) *Il*. 24.804a

> 'ὣς οἵ γ' ἀμφίεπον τάφον Ἕκτορος ἱπποδάμοιο'· τινὲς γράφουσιν·
>
> ὣς οἵ γ' ἀμφίεπον τάφον Ἕκτορος· ἦλθε δ' Ἀμαζών
> Ἄρηος θυγάτηρ μεγαλήτορος ἀνδροφόνοιο.
>
> 'So they busied themselves with Hector's, the tamer of horses, funeral'. Some write:
>
> So they busied themselves with Hector's funeral. And an Amazon came, a daughter of Ares the great hearted, the slayer of men.

---

[12] Severyns (1928: 320–2) and Vian (1959: 32) think wrongly that Aristarchus' criticism is directed only against Arctinus.

Cf. PLitLond. 6 (inv. 1873; first century AD)

ὣς οἵ γ' ἀμφίεπον τάφον Ἕκτορος· ἦλθε δ' Ἀμαζών
Ὀτρήρ[η] <ς> θυγάτηρ ἐϋειδὴς Πενθεσίλ<ε>ια.[13]

So they busied themselves with Hector's funeral. And an Amazon came, a daughter of Otrere, the beautiful Penthesilea.[14]

Welcker's assumption that both these distichs which have come down to us by the *Iliad* scholia belong to the opening of the *Aethiopis*[15] has been rejected by the majority of scholars, and rightly so,[16] because it is highly improbable that Arctinus had introduced his epic not by the typical proem but by a slight variation of the closing verse of the *Iliad*. It is beyond doubt that these verses originated from the tendency to connect the *Iliad* and the *Aethiopis* within the tradition of the Epic Cycle.[17]

DATE AND AUTHORSHIP

The testimonies concerning the date and authorship of the *Aethiopis* are far from illuminating. The epic has been ascribed to Arctinus quite late: the earliest testimony is the Tabula Capitolina (early imperial period; *PEG* T 8 II = T 1 D.), followed by Eusebius (fourth century AD; *PEG* T 4) and Proclus. Arctinus is characterized as a poet first by the Peripatetics Pha(i)nias of Eresos (fourth century BC) and Artemon of Klazomenai (also fourth century BC) in *PEG* T 5 and *PEG* T 1 respectively, and then by Dionysius of Halicarnassos (*PEG* T 7). Date is also doubtful: Artemon and Eusebius date the *Aethiopis* back to the middle of the eighth century (*PEG* T 1, 2, 4),

---

[13] See West (2001: 283–5; 2013: 137).   [14] See West (2001: 283–5; 2013: 137).
[15] Welcker (1865: 199). West (2011b: 428–30) agrees on the point.
[16] Cf. Burgess (2001: 140–3 with further bibliography in 242 n. 23).
[17] Von der Mühll (1952: 390) speaks of 'the Cyclic connection to the *Aethiopis*'. It is difficult to say how old this connection is; see Burgess (2001: 141): 'the two lines may be created by rhapsodes in performance of parts of the *Iliad* and the *Aethiopis*... the join would not testify to the beginning of the *Aethiopis* in its earlier fixed manifestation, but rather would have resulted from rhapsodic presentation of a part of the Cyclic poem in conjunction with the end of the *Iliad*'. Kopff (1983) assumes, on the basis of the Homeric cups (see Squire, below in this volume, pp. 497–500) no. 23–6 Sinn, on which three scenes from the *Iliad* and the *Aethiopis* are depicted (Priam begs Achilles to give him the body of Hector – Priam receives Penthesilea at the tomb of Hector – the duel between Achilles and Penthesilea), that initially the *Aethiopis* represented the release and burial of Hector's body before the arrival of Penthesilea and that both verses bring the connection between the Iliadic and the Penthesilea section of the *Aethiopis* to the fore. However, it is more likely that the representations on the vases derive from two different epics, namely the *Iliad* and the *Aethiopis*. Cf. Fantuzzi (2012: 268).

whereas Pha(i)nias places it after Archilochus (*PEG* T 5). Modern scholarship considers both the ascription to Arctinus (or the historicity of this poet in general) and the early dating of the epic to be unreliable.[18] Obviously, the problem of the date depends on the broader question about the relationship between the *Iliad* and the *Aethiopis* (see below). It is the *communis opinio* today that the material of the *Aethiopis* is pre-Iliadic, however, the concrete form which this material took in the Cyclic epic known to us is post-Iliadic.[19] Thus, if the *Iliad* is dated back to the first third of the seventh century and the *Odyssey* (which already knows Memnon: 4.188; 11.522) slightly later, then the *Aethiopis* as we know it must belong to the last third of the seventh century.[20]

THE CHARACTER OF THE POEM

'On the whole, it seems that the work of Arctinus was, after the *Iliad* and the *Odyssey*, the most significant among the epics of the Trojan Cycle and also that its unity was greater and more solid than in the other epics of the Cycle thanks to its leading character.'[21] In effect, the *Aethiopis* is characterized by a solid structure and a linearly developing plot, which, after the narration of the two preparatory episodes about Achilles' victory over Penthesilea and Memnon, reaches its climax with the death of the Achaean hero by Paris and Apollo.[22] We cannot say how the plot was divided into each of its five books;[23] however, it is unlikely that Quintus of Smyrna who divides the same material into the first five books of his *Posthomerica* (B. I: Penthesilea, B. II: the episode of Memnon, B. III: the death and burial of Achilles, B. IV: the funeral games in honour of Achilles, B. V: the quarrel over the armour of Achilles, the insanity, suicide and burial of Ajax) had direct access to the *Aethiopis*.[24] In general, we can follow Schadewaldt's judgement: 'The

---

[18] On the question of authorship, see Wilamowitz (1884: 344–50, differently in 1920: 405 n. 1); Burgess (2001: 142); Davies (1989c: 5); Kullmann (1960: 215–16) considers Arctinus to be a genuine name.

[19] See for instance West, above in this volume, pp. 97–9.

[20] West (2003c: 12); he now (2013: 136) dates the *Amazonis* more precisely to 640–630 and the *Memnonis* to 630–610. This dating is consistent with the fact that Achilles' transfer to the island of Leuce generally thought to be related to the colonization by Miletus (and with Arctinus' descent from this particular city of Asia Minor) of the northern coast of the Black Sea; Burgess (2001: 160–71, with further bibliography) and (2004a: 33 n. 2) remains sceptical.

[21] Welcker (1882: 235). [22] A fair judgement of the poem in Monro (1884: 14).

[23] Schadewaldt (1952 = 1965: 159–63) offers a hypothetical scenario for the four books of the so-called 'Memnonis' in twenty scenes.

[24] Vian (1959: 90).

Aethiopis, with its strongly accentuated structure, its drama and pathos, the plasticity of its imagery, the element of surprise and its taste for the marvellous, the rhythmic climax towards its closing, in which death and life, downfall and exaltation unite, proves the saying: more with less. Thus, the *Aethiopis*, functioning as a solid block, diverges significantly from the other epics of the Cycle, in which each scene is linearly arranged next to the other.'[25]

THE *ILIAD* AND THE *AETHIOPIS*

Even a fleeting glance at the plot of the *Aethiopis* reveals its striking similarity to the plot of the *Iliad*.[26] This fundamental similarity underlies the plot of the so-called *Memnonis* or *Aethiopis*, which forms the core of the neoanalytical or *motivgeschichtlich* approach to the Homeric question. In Wolfgang Kullmann's words 'the depiction of Patroclus' sacrifice and Achilles taking revenge on Hector which foreshadows the death of Achilles is modelled upon the depiction of Antilochus' sacrifice and Achilles taking revenge on Memnon which is followed by Achilles' murdering by Paris, as these events had been represented in the *Aethiopis*'.[27] This fundamental similarity is further supported by a series of parallel motifs that are listed below in the same order in which they appear in the *Aethiopis*: the making of Memnon's armour by Hephaestus and the Iliadic *hoplopoiia*; the death warning addressed by Thetis (in the *Aethiopis* within the context of the Memnon episode and in *Iliad* 18.96 when she warns Achilles that he is going to die 'shortly' after Hector's death); Nestor's rescuing by Diomedes in *Il.* 8.80–171 and Antilochus' sacrifice in the Cyclic epic; the *kērostasia* that decides on the battle between Achilles and Memnon and was narrated in detail in the *Aethiopis*, and the *kērostasia* in *Il.* 22.209–13, where the same motif has no dramatic function, because the fate of Hector has been decided upon long before; the carrying off of Memnon and that of Sarpedon by Sleep and Death (*Il.* 16.666–75); Achilles' attack on Troy in the *Aethiopis* and his interrupted attack against the same city in *Il.* 22.378–94; the formulaic phrase αὐτὸς δ'ἐν κονίῃσι μέγας μεγαλωστὶ τανυσθεὶς / κεῖτο ('and he himself, mighty in might, in the dust lay at length'), which is used in *Il.* 18.26–7 in reference to Achilles as he lies prostrate due to his pain for Patroclus' death and which, to judge from *Od.* 24.39–40, was probably used in the *Aethiopis* in regard to the dead Achilles

---

[25] Schadewaldt (1952 = 1965: 175–6).
[26] See already West, above in this volume, p. 98.   [27] Kullmann (1991 = 1992: 104).

(cf. also *Il.* 16.775 where the same phrase occurs in relation to Cebriones, Hector's charioteer); the fighting over Achilles' body in the *Aethiopis* and that over Patroclus' body in book 17 of the *Iliad*; the lament of Thetis and the Nereids for Achilles while he, still alive, mourns for his friend Patroclus in *Il.* 18.35–64, and the lament of Thetis, the Nereids and the Muses for the dead Achilles in the *Aethiopis*;[28] the funeral games in honour of Patroclus in book 23 of the *Iliad* and those in honour of Achilles in the *Aethiopis*. Classic neoanalysis has decided that (an oral pre-stage) of the *Aethiopis* predated the *Iliad* and served as its source.[29] This view, which was strongly opposed at the beginning by D. Page, U. Hölscher, A. Dihle and K. Reinhardt, is now widely accepted by scholars, at least with regard to Nestor's rescuing, Patroclus' death, the lament of Thetis and the funeral games in honour of Patroclus.[30] More recently J. Burgess has attempted to shift from 'classic neoanalysis' to an orally reshaped 'post-neoanalysis'.[31] The main differences between these methods have been sketched out as follows: first in regard to the type of the 'sources', 'whereas neoanalysis has looked for specific Cyclic epics, whether oral or textual, as the source for motifs transferred into a Homeric context, it is more credible to view oral mythological traditions as the primary or source material. The Homeric poems would have also been aware of Cyclic epic that exemplifies such myth, but allusion to specific poems should not be expected'; due to post-neoanalytical readings the role of the audience in the transference of motifs comes into play: 'whereas classic neoanalysis has reserved discernment of motif transference to the scholar, it is more probable that the reflection would be recognized by a mythologically informed audience. In this case, motif transference is more than coincidental, casual or merely vestigial. It is significant allusion, at least in the manner that oral intertextuality can be understood in the archaic Age.'[32] Burgess also views the *Aethiopis* as the primary model for the

---

[28] See the classic interpretation of this scene by Kakridis (1949: 65–75).

[29] Kullmann (1960; 1981; 1991); the matter is summarized with the basic bibliography in Willcock (1997) as also in Currie (2006: 23–41).

[30] Neoanalysis has definitely become a mainstream theory after its positive reception in the Cambridge *Iliad* commentary: cf. e.g. Edwards (1991: 16–19, 140); Janko (1992: 312–14, 372 etc.). The neoanalytical *Memnonis* theory has been recently criticized by West (2003c; 2011b: 202, 322, 369, 398), according to whom Memnon and the *Memnonis* (*Aethiopis*) are post-Iliadic; partly in agreement with West is Heitsch (2005); this view is rejected by Kullmann (2005); Currie (2006: 27–8); Burgess (2009: 28 with n. 6).

[31] See Burgess, above in this volume, with bibliography.

[32] Both quotations from Burgess (2009: 60 and 71) respectively. On reception, see also Currie (2006: 4) and Danek (1998: *passim*).

Iliad. However, he rejects the so-called 'vengeance theory', i.e. he does not believe that Achilles' murdering of Memnon was represented as an action of vengeance for the murder of Antilochus in the *Aethiopis*; therefore, it cannot have served as a model for Achilles' vengeance on Hector for the murder of Patroclus.

18 | *Ilias parva*

ADRIAN KELLY*

Though it is the one of the best attested members of the 'Epic Cycle', and the only poem of that group to have taken its title from one of the Homeric epics, the *Ilias parva* illustrates how difficult it is to reconstruct, let alone understand, the history of Greek epic poetry after Homer.

AUTHOR – TITLE – DATE

The author most widely named in modern literature, Lesches from the city of Pyrrha[1] on Lesbos, is also the most cited figure in ancient discussions, but only from the middle of the fourth century BC; as with other 'Cyclic' poems, the earliest attestations take the form of 'the one who made the *Ilias parva*', while the inevitable Homeric attributions are few and late.[2] The poem's epithet is therefore doubly surprising, for such differentiations usually qualify works by the same author,[3] and yet the title was settled as early as Aristotle.[4] A range of similarities with the *Iliad* (and *Odyssey*) can reasonably be invoked as the cause, as perhaps can the first word of

---

* I would like to thank the editors of this volume, and Bill Allan, Bob Corthals, Patrick J. Finglass, Nick Sekunda and Bert Smith for their help with this article and its contents.
[1] Mytilene, according to Proclus.
[2] The making formula is used 15x (*PEG* T 7 = T 5 D. = p. 118 W.; *PEG* T 10 = T 2 / F 6 D. = F 6 W.; *PEG* F 2 = D., W.; *PEG* F 3 = D., W.; *PEG* F 5[I] = D., W.; *PEG* F 7–9 = F 8, 10 and 11 D. = F 8, 12 and 14 W.; *PEG* F 21 = F 20 D. = F 29–30 W.; *PEG* F 24 = F 4 D. = F 4 W.; *PEG* F 25 = F 9 D. = F 11 W.; *PEG* F 28–31 = F 1, 6, 7, and 22 D. = F 1, 6, 7 and 20 W.), Lesches 23x (*PEG* T 1–6 = T 3, 4^B 6, and 7 D. = pp. 118 and 120 W.; *PEG* T 10–11 = T 2 / F 6 D. = F 6 W.; *PEG* F 5[II], 9–23 = D., W.) and Homer only 2x (*PEG* T 8–9 (= T 1 D. = p. 120 W.) = *Suda* and Ps.-Herodotean *Life of Homer*; cf. also *PEG* F 27 (= "Hom." F 1 D. = F 32 W.). The crucial figure in advancing Lesches' claims seems to have been his fellow Lesbian, the fourth-century Phaenias of Eresos; cf. Mosshammer (1979: 229–33); Davies (1989c: 5–6); West (2013: 35–7) opts for an earlier Lesbian, Hellanicus (*EGM* F (dub) 202c), but relies on both emendation and addition to the fragment to do so.
[3] Cf. West (1978: 22 n. 4); also Hirschberger (2004: 26–30).
[4] The epithet is twice qualified (*PEG* T 3 = T 3 and 6 D. = p. 118 W.; *PEG* F 31 = F 22 D. = F 20 W.), and the poem is once the '*Lesser Iliad*' (*PEG* T 8 = T 1 D.), but there is no indication that it was generally understood as a qualitative rather than quantitative description.

PEG F 28 (= F 1 D. = F 1 W.), though it may not have been the poet's own choice.[5]

The meagre linguistic evidence of the fragments does not help to determine the date of the *Ilias parva*, for none of those features usually judged to be 'late' lack some genuinely Archaic epic parallel or explanation.[6] A post-Homeric genesis is overwhelmingly likely, tallying with the ancient chronographers[7] and the poem's title, and modern scholars' datings therefore range rather freely between the seventh and sixth centuries BC.[8] The earliest reliable *terminus ante quem* comes with its first, roughly contemporaneous quotations, (i) in Aristophanes' *Knights* (1056–7) of 424 BC (*PEG* F 2 = D. = F 2 W.) and (ii) on two potsherds (*PEG* F 28 = F 1 D. = F 1 W.) from the Black Sea region, one (420–410 BC) from Chersonesos and another (less precisely datable) from Olbia.[9] Getting back beyond this point, as we shall see, is fraught with difficulty.

PREDECESSORS AND COMPETITORS

The material covered in the *Ilias parva*, from the quarrel between Ajax and Odysseus over Achilles' arms to the sack of the city, was popular from the very beginning of the visible record. In terms of other epic representations, the poem was competing with at least the *Iliou persis* in covering the city's destruction, and also with the *Aethiopis* in treating the fate of Ajax. These narratives are undated and undatable, and so their precise relationship with our poem will remain unknown,[10] but Homer was already familiar with most of the episodes later attested for the *Ilias parva*: Ajax's disgrace

---

[5] Cf. Nachmanson (1941); also below, pp. 326–7, esp. n. 57 for the Homeric intertexts. West (2013: 163) ascribes the title to a 'currency in the region of Ilion' shared with the *Iliad*, and thinks the epithet a secondary development. For *PEG* F 28 (= F 1 D. = F 1 W.) as the opening line, cf. below, pp. 329–31.

[6] *Contra* Wackernagel (1916: 181–2), Davies (1989a: 95–8); and cf. below, pp. 329–43 for examples.

[7] According to whom Lesches is to be placed in either the eighth (Phaenias: F 33 Wehrli) or seventh century (Eusebius: *PEG* T 5 = T 4[B] D.) BC, but these dates are unreliable; cf. Mosshammer (1979), Davies (1989c: 5–6); also Most (2006: 186) and Kivilo (2010: 23–4) for Plutarch's report of Lesches' connection with the *Contest of Homer and Hesiod*.

[8] For example, Griffin (1977), *PEG* and West (2003a) opt for different parts of the seventh century; Wackernagel (1916), Davies (1989a) and West (2013: 171–2) for the sixth; cf. Burgess (2001: 8–12).

[9] See Vinogradov (1969=1997: 385; 1990=1997: 408 n. 59, 419), who cites Milesian involvement in the area to explain the poem's popularity there; see also Burgess (2001: 165–6).

[10] Bethe (1929: 211–16) argued that the *Ilias parva* originally included the *Aethiopis* and *Iliou persis*, but the more likely conception (e.g. Davies 1989c: 60–1) is that the *Ilias parva* overlapped with both of these originally independent poems, before the creation of the Cycle; see Burgess, above in this volume; also Severyns (1928: 357–9).

and suicide (*Od.* 11.543–65), the retrieval of Philoctetes (*Il.* 2.716–25, *Od.* 8.219–20), Deiphobus' marriage to Helen (*Od.* 4.276, 8.517), Neoptolemus' arrival and defeat of Eurypylus (*Od.* 11.519–22), Epeius' construction of the wooden horse and its deployment (*Od.* 8.492–8, 11.523–32), Odysseus' spying mission into Troy (*Od.* 4.242–59), the death of Astyanax (*Il.* 24.735)[11] and, more generally, the city's sack (*Od.* 1.2 etc.). None of this proves that Homer knew these tales from a fixed text or even a single orally circulating poem,[12] but it does show a well-known epic background within which the poet of the *Ilias parva* was able to work.

The early melic poets similarly reflect a continuing taste for this material:[13] in the seventh to sixth centuries BC, both Sappho (F 16, 44 Voigt) and Alcaeus (F 42, 44 Voigt) detail several episodes from the broader Trojan War, the latter including a narrative of Cassandra's rape (306 A(h) V), a story also treated by Ibycus in the mid sixth century (*PMGF* 303(a)), along with the meeting of Menelaus and Helen (*PMGF* 296). His elder contemporary Stesichorus wrote an *Iliou persis* (*PMGF* 196–205), but the state of this text makes it impossible to detect any influence.[14]

The fifth-century Athenian tragedians generally avoided retelling stories from the two Homeric epics,[15] but many plays covered material also known in the *Ilias parva*, and yet the same problems recur. Consider, for instance, Odysseus' frequently negative reception in tragedy:[16] in Euripides he is the instigator or perpetrator of the murder of Astyanax (*Trojan Women*), Polyxena (*Hecuba*) and Iphigeneia (*IA* and *IT*), and the 'corruptor' of Neoptolemus in Sophocles' *Philoctetes*.[17] This might represent a reaction against the *Ilias parva*'s depiction of Odysseus (see below), but equally it could reflect the negative character known from Pindar (*Nem.* 7.21–7, 8.26–34; cf. also F 260, esp. 1–7),[18] with the same mixture of qualities for which

---

[11] *Contra* Kullmann (1960: 186–7); cf. Burgess (2012) and below in this volume, p. 338.

[12] *Contra* West (2012: esp. 230), but his chronology of early Greek epic is unconvincing.

[13] Cf. Pallantza (2005: 17–89); Bowie (2010b).

[14] See Pallantza (2005: 94–7); Finglass and Noussia-Fantuzzi, below in this volume, pp. 344–54 and pp. 430–9; Finglass and Davies (forthcoming). Tantalizingly, the little-known *Iliou persis* of the sixth century Argive elegiac poet Sacadas may have taken an anti-Odysseus line, and thus could be linked with the *Ilias parva*'s pro-Odysseus position (see below); cf. Bowie (2010b: 81–2; 2014).

[15] For tragedy and the Trojan War, cf. Anderson (1997: 105–76); Fantuzzi (2006: 140–8); Pallantza (2005: 201–310); Zeitlin (2009); Sommerstein, below in this volume.

[16] See Stanford (1968: 102–17); Montiglio (2011: 1–19). Equally, his depiction in the *Ajax* points to a more favourable reception; see Blundell (1989: 95–105); also Garassino (1930) for the many lost plays.

[17] See, e.g., Blundell (1989: 184–93, 205–14); *contra* Heath (1999: 145–7).

[18] See also *Isth.* 4.49–60, and Kirschkowski (2009). For Pindar's relationship with Homer, see Mann (1994), Kelly (2006: 13–24).

he was later excoriated in Gorgias' *Palamedes* (*VS* 82B 11a).[19] The specific influence(s) of, or on, the *Ilias parva* in this period cannot be traced with any confidence, for Odysseus' currency is too widespread.

Early pictorial art also reflects the popularity of the poem's material, within the general preponderance of non-Homeric Trojan War themes in the Archaic period,[20] but it is again very difficult to see the *Ilias parva*'s precise influence. For example, the suicide of Ajax finds no fewer than six separate representations before the end of the seventh century,[21] but the popularity of the theme has no necessary link with the *Ilias parva* (even if more than Proclus' rather terse summary had survived), because the episode was also treated in the *Aethiopis* (*PEG* F 5 = F 1 D. = F 6 W.) and known already to Homer (see above).[22] So too with the widespread images of Astyanax's death, most notably the seventeenth metope of the 'Mykonos pithos' (second quarter of the seventh century BC),[23] for the adult figure – if it is not a generic illustration – could be Neoptolemus (*PEG* F 21 = F 20 D. = F 29–30 W.) or Odysseus (*Il. Pers.* arg. line 268 Severyns), or it could represent a widespread story rather than a specific version.[24]

In sum, many of the stories found in the *Ilias parva* were prominent from the beginning of Greek myth's visible history, and attest to a rich culture of storytelling, in several media, from which the poem emerged at some point before, or during, the fifth century BC.

---

[19] See Stanford (1968: 96); Montiglio (2011: 8–9, 30). This negativity does not (*contra* Stanford) begin with Pindar, even laying aside the epic *Iliou persis* (see above, n. 14), nor probably with Epicharmus (*contra* Mahaffy (1873–4); cf. Phillips (1959: esp. 58–9) and now Kerkhof (2001: 123–9), but must have been possible, for such a complex character, from the earliest period. For defences of Odysseus' character in fifth- and fourth-century literature, see Stanford (1968: 96–9, Alcidamas and Antisthenes); Montiglio (2011: 20–37, Antisthenes, 38–65 Plato). For a recent discussion of Odysseus in Archaic and Classical art, see von den Hoff (2009).

[20] See, e.g., Cook (1983), Snodgrass (1998); *contra* Friis Johansen (1967), Ahlberg-Cornell (1992).

[21] *LIMC* 'Aias' I 110, 118, 120–1, 125–6; cf. Friis Johansen (1967: 30–1); Ahlberg-Cornell (1992: nos. 52–6, 74–5); Gantz (1993: 633–4); Finglass (2011: 28–9).

[22] The same qualifications apply to the emergence of the contest over Achilles' arms as a popular artistic theme around the first quarter of the fifth century BC; cf. von den Hoff (2009: 58–9).

[23] *LIMC* 'Astyanax' 27; cf. Anderson (1997: 188–9, and 182–91 more generally).

[24] Similarly, in Menelaus' encounter with Helen (*PEG* F 19 = D. = F 28 W.), found first on the same pithos (met. 7: *LIMC* 'Helene' 225; Ahlberg-Cornell (1992: no. 62, 78–80, fig. 120, 327); Anderson (1997: 187)), his sword is drawn threateningly as she uncovers herself, but supplication in this form is so well and early evidenced that the artist need not have relied on our, or indeed any single, poem; see Ahlberg-Cornell (1992: 79, 186); *contra* Kahil (1988: 499–500, 537–48). On more general reasons to treat the evidence of art with extreme caution when reconstructing the history of early Greek epic, see Lowenstam (1997), Hedreen (2001: 3–10).

CONTENTS OF THE POEM

The usual method for reconstructing any Cyclic poem is to match its fragments with Proclus' summary (supplemented by Ps.-Apollodorus or not), and in our record of Proclus the *Ilias parva* extended only from the quarrel between Odysseus and Ajax over Achilles' arms to the moment when the Trojans take the horse into Troy. However, our poem certainly went further, since an impressive range of ancient sources (*PEG* T 2 = T 7 D. = p. 118 W.; *PEG* T 7 = T 5 D. = p. 118 W.; *PEG* F 10–18 = F 12–18 D. = 15, 16, 21–7 W.; *PEG* F 20–22 = F 20, 22–3 = F 17, 19, 29–30 W.; *PEG* F 31 = F 22 D. = F 20 W.) indicate that it included the sack. Truncation occurs between the time of Pausanias and Proclus, or in the process of the latter's work being excerpted, and so we may doubt his assertion that the *Ilias parva* contained four books.[25] Proclus' report of the poem's beginning is more secure; quarrels are a standard epic introduction, and no ancient source clearly attributes any earlier episode to the *Ilias parva*.[26]

The plot of the poem moved in regular stages of increasing Trojan defeat, with the opening quarrel, killing of the Greeks' flocks, and Ajax's subsequent suicide (*Ilias parva* arg. lines 208–10 Severyns, *PEG* F 2–3 = D., W.) followed by the capture of Helenus and his revelation of the importance of Philoctetes, who is fetched from Lemnos and kills Paris in a duel; his body being despoiled, the Trojans bury him (arg. lines 211–15 Severyns). After Deiphobus marries Helen (arg. line 216 Severyns, *PEG* F 4), the second stage seems to have been the arrival of Neoptolemus (arg. lines 217–18 Severyns, *PEG* F 5 = D., W.), the 'appearance' of Achilles to him and his combat with, and killing of, the most recent Trojan allied arrival, Eurypylus (arg. lines 218–20 Severyns). The Trojans are besieged, the wooden horse is planned and constructed (arg. lines 221–3 Severyns, *PEG* F 8 = F 10 D. = F 12 W.), and there are two missions into Troy, one where Odysseus scouts alone after disguising himself as a beggar (*PEG* F 6–7 = F 8 D. = F 8–9 W.), the second in which he, together with Diomedes, removes the Palladium from the city

---

[25] *Contra* West (2013: 168–9). This might also explain Sinon's absence from Proclus' summary, despite the fact that he did appear in the poem; cf. *PEG* T 3 = T 3 and 6 D. = p. 118 W. (an illustration on the *Tabulae Iliacae* (tablet 1A): Squire (2011: 36–7, fig. 5)) and *PEG* F 9[III] (= F 11[C] D. = F 14 W.); West (2013: 204–5). On the process by which Proclus' work has survived, see Davies (1986); West (2013: 1–51).

[26] Cf., however, Burgess (2001: 24–5), also on *PEG* F 24 = F 4 D. = F 4 W. (concerning Achilles being blown off course to Scyros after the encounter with Telephus), though this probably fell in a flashback: see below, pp. 340–2. For introductory quarrels, see *Il.* 1.6–7, *WD* 27–41, *Od.* 8.75–82 etc. West (2013: 167) thinks the quarrel was chosen 'to establish a mood of despair among the Achaeans as a starting-point'.

(arg. lines 224–9 Severyns), though this seems also to have occasioned a quarrel between the Iliadic companions (*PEG* F 25 = F 9 D. = F 11 W.). The final stage is the actual loading of the horse (*PEG* F 8 = F 10 D. = F 12 W.) and the Greek removal to Tenedos, while the Trojans take the horse into the city and celebrate their apparent victory (arg. lines 230–6 Severyns). Here Proclus stops, but other sources continue – it was the middle of the night (*PEG* F 9 = F 11 D. = F 14 W.), a series of people killed (or saved) during the course of the fighting (*PEG* F 10–15 = F 12–16 D. = F 15–16 and 21–4 W.; *PEG* F 17–18 = F 18 D. = F 26–7 W.), Priam slain at the doors of his own house (*PEG* F 16 = F 17 D. = F 25 W.), Helen reclaimed by Menelaus (*PEG* F 19 = D. = F 28 W.), Aethra rescued (*PEG* F 20 = F 23 D. = F 17 W.), Astyanax murdered (*PEG* F 21 = F 20 D. = F 29–30 W.), Aeneas and Andromache taken as booty by Neoptolemus (*PEG* F 21 = F 20 D. = F 29–30 W.; cf. *PEG* F 22 = F 22 D. = F 19 W.).

This breathless outline immediately reveals three connected features.[27] The first is a focus on night-time and ambush:[28] Ajax's destruction of the flocks, Helenus' capture, the making, filling and deployment of the horse, Odysseus' spying mission into Troy, the theft of the Palladium, the destruction of the city after the retreat to Tenedos. These episodes anticipate Troy's last night in a series of preliminary Greek successes, using equally underhanded and indirect means. The second feature is the horse's function as a narrative frame for the two missions into Troy, linked with the Palladium as a votive for Athene that is vital for the destruction of the city through theft and deception.[29] Similarly important is the third feature, the quasi-magical token required for Troy's overthrow:[30] the summonings of Neoptolemus (and the restoration of his father's divinely made arms) and Philoctetes (with Heracles' bow),[31] and the theft of the Palladium.[32] The possession of each token is followed by Trojan death of numerically increasing importance (Paris in a duel, Eurypylus and a number of his men, the

---

[27] West (2013: 167–9) ventures a somewhat speculative reconstruction into twelve days of action, does not see any structural connection between episodes, and faults the poem for its lack of organic unity.

[28] See Dué and Ebbott (2010: 82).

[29] Anderson (1997: 18–20, esp. 190). On the Palladium, see Severyns (1928: 349–52); Bethe (1929: 254–6); Smith (1981: 26–7); Gantz (1993: 641–6). Its thematic significance is also noted in the motif's repetition on tablet 1A of the *Tabulae Iliacae*; see Squire (2011: 172–4).

[30] See Hedreen (2001: 154–5) for others.

[31] See Anderson (1997: 96–7) on its thematic significance.

[32] See Davies (1989c: 63). Helenus' capture is only explicitly linked with the first event (arg. lines 211–13 Severyns), but the structural parallels suggest a strong correlation, and Philoctetes' importance was already known to Homer (*Il.* 2.724–5, *Od.* 8.219–20); see also West (2013: 181–4).

citizenry), and the equivalence between the horse and the Palladium thus combines the token-sequence with an ambush-sequence at Troy's final moment.[33]

But perhaps the narrative's most important characteristic is that Odysseus comes out of the *Ilias parva* very well:[34] he captures Helenus and the secret(s) to taking Troy, brings Neoptolemus to the army and restores his father's arms to him, sneaks into Troy (twice) at night, bringing back information and the Palladium as preparation for the sack, persuades the leading Greeks to get into the horse (*PEG* F 8 = F 10 D. = F 12 W.) and then commands them (*PEG* F 26 = F13 W.), saves the wounded Trojan Helicaon during the sack (*PEG* F 12 = F 13 D. = F 22 W.), thus repaying the hospitality of the aged Agenor (*Il.* 3.123–4, 205–8), and he does *not* kill Astyanax (*PEG* F 21 = F 20 D. = F 29–30 W.). Even the story that Odysseus tried to murder Diomedes during their mission to steal the Palladium (*PEG* F 25 = F 9 D. = F 11 W.), upon which the latter forced him back to the camp (the proverbial 'compulsion of Diomedes'), may have been told so as to flatter Odysseus.[35] Unsurprisingly for a poem so concerned with ambush and trickery, the *Ilias parva* celebrates Odysseus' military effectiveness and heroic stature, from his victory over Ajax in the opening contest to his stratagem's triumph in the city's destruction, and it does so in such a sustained manner as to suggest that its author may have been responding to a specific, negative treatment of this slippery character.[36]

This may be related to the poem's engagement with its tradition in more general ways. For instance, the *Ilias parva* places Priam's death (*PEG* F 16 = F 17 D. = F 25 W.) at the door of his house, after being dragged from the altar of Zeus Herkeios, where he is usually killed.[37] This seems to be a combination of Priam's vision of his own death in Homer (*Il.* 22.59–71,

---

[33] *Contra* West (2013: 200): '. . . it lacks all connection with the surrounding episodes'.

[34] See, e.g., Welcker (1849: 269–76); Monro (1884: 23–4); Holt (1992: 327–8).

[35] *PEG* F 25[III] (= F 9 D. = F 11 W.) has Diomedes as the driver, but F 25[II] = F 9 D. = F 11 W. (from the Augustan mythographer Conon) has Odysseus in that role, which would fit better with the *Ilias parva*'s general programme; cf. West (2013: 202–3).

[36] Cf. above, pp. 319–21, but which treatment? The *Ilias parva*'s depiction of Odysseus might suggest a generally positive view of the entire sack (see Castriota (1992: esp. 117–18) for a similar purpose to Polygnotus' depiction of these events in Delphi), since *PEG* F 21[II] (= D. = F 18 W.) has Neoptolemus kill Astyanax ἰδίαι, while arg. lines 217–18 Severyns makes no mention (*pace* Anderson (1997: 60 n. 21)) of Achilles' shade demanding Polyxena's sacrifce. The epic *Iliou persis* could, then, have been the *Ilias parva*'s target, as it focused on Greek sacrilege (see Finglass, below in this volume, pp. 344–54), but Neoptolemus' role as Astyanax' killer was central to artistic representations (cf. Castriota (1992: 97–9); Anderson (1997: 53–9, 192–3)), and the sacrilegious element is already known to Homer; see Clay (1983).

[37] *Il. pers.* arg. lines 257–8 Severyns; cf. Kullmann (1960: 217 n. 1); also *LIMC* s.v. 'Priamos', 85–114.

esp. 66, 71) with the rest of the poetic and artistic tradition,[38] though the *Ilias parva* is also capable of open disagreement with its Homeric predecessor, e.g. substituting the immortal horses given by Zeus as compensation for Ganymedes' rape (*Il.* 5.265–7) with a golden vine made by Hephaestus (*PEG* F 29 = F 6 D. = F 6 W.), in that fragment also making Ganymede the son of Laomedon, not Tros (*Il.* 5.266, 20.252).[39]

Competitiveness of this sort is in fact typical of the poem: Odysseus fights while Ajax lifts Achilles' corpse (*PEG* F 2 = D., W.), whereas in some sources the roles shift;[40] Odysseus was not self-wounded before his mission, but by Thoas (*PEG* F 7 = F 8 D. = W.);[41] there were thirteen[42] men in the horse, not fifty *vel sim.* (*PEG* F 8 = F 10 D. = F 12 W.); the Trojan ally Coroebus is killed by Diomedes, not Neoptolemus (*PEG* F 15 = F 16 D. = F 24 W.), the Greek healer Machaon by Eurypylus, not Penthesileia (*PEG* F 30 = F 7 D. = F 7 W.), and Astyanax by Neoptolemus, not Odysseus (*PEG* F 21.3–5 = F 20.3–5 D. = F 29.3–5 W.); Aeneas was taken as a prisoner by Neoptolemus and so did not escape before or during the sack of the city (*PEG* F 21.9–11 = F 20.9–11 D. = F 30.4–6 W.);[43] Aeneas' wife was called Eurydice, not Creousa (*PEG* F 22 = D. = F 19 W.); and Achilles was not hidden on Scyros by Thetis, but came there after the failed attack on Mysia (*PEG* F 24 = F 4 D. = F 4 W.). These are all precise points of difference, suggesting an engagement with relatively fixed traditions or versions of these tales, and several (*PEG* F 2 = D., W.; *PEG* F 8 = F 10 D. = F 12 W.; *PEG* F 21.3–5 = F 20.3–5 D. = F 29.3–5 W.) seem to be weighted in Odysseus' favour.[44] In short, the poet of *Ilias parva* worked hard to create his own, distinctive version of this popular material.

Finally, the *Ilias parva* also contained a great deal of combat narrative, to judge from the list of killed and wounded given by Pausanias: Meges was wounded in the arm (*PEG* F 10 = F 12 D. = F 15 W.), Lycomedes on the

---

[38] Kullmann (1960: 216–17); Anderson (1997: 28–38). [39] See below, pp. 342–3.
[40] See, e.g. *PEG* F 32 dub. (POxy. 2510) which has Odysseus lift the body; also Edwards (1991: 131–2); West (2013: 175–6); see also below, p. 332.
[41] Cf., however, arg. lines 224–5 Severyns (Ὀδυσσεύς τε αἰκισάμενος ἑαυτὸν κατάσκοπος εἰς Ἴλιον παραγίνεται 'Odysseus disfigures himself and enters Ilion to reconnoitre'); Proclus' extant summary shows the influence of the Odyssean version (4.244–6), though West (2013: 196) feels no contradiction. This is not unknown elsewhere in the *Ilias parva*, for the first solo mission into Troy (arg. lines 24–6 Severyns) looks like it was modelled on Helen's story (*Od.* 4.242–64) rather than drawing upon an independent tradition; cf. Severyns (1928: 347–9).
[42] Severyns' emendation for the 3000 cited in Ps.-Apollod. *Epit.* 5.14; see Severyns (1928: 355–6), West (2013: 203–4).
[43] See below, p. 336.
[44] Perhaps also Thoas' wounding of Odysseus (*PEG* F 7 = F 8 D. = W.), since self-harm may have been less admirable, as Herod. 3.154.2–160.2 (a servile act); see Liapis (2011: 206).

wrist (*PEG* F 11 = F 12 D. = F 16 W.), a supplicating Astynous was killed by Neoptolemus (*PEG* F 13 = F 14 D. = F 21 W.), Eioneus[45] by Neoptolemus, Admetus by Philoctetes (*PEG* F 14 = F 15 D. = F 23 W.), Coroebus by Diomedes (*PEG* F 15 = F 16 D. = F 24 W.), Axion by Eurypylus (*PEG* F 17 = F 18 D. = F 26 W.) etc. Though any poem dealing with events before and during the sack would have this kind of narrative, its extent and detail may have been one reason for the poem's titular comparison with the *Iliad*.[46]

HOMERIC AND UN-HOMERIC

Modern scholars have deemed much of the *Ilias parva* 'un-Homeric', e.g. in its use of quasi-magical tokens like the Palladium or Heracles' bow, the prominence of oracles (though cf. *Od.* 8.79–82) or the stress on ambush and deception (though cf. *Od.* 14.258–70).[47] Aristotle famously compared Homer's structural unity ('one part with many episodes') to the narratives of the *Cypria* and *Ilias parva*, since their poets 'composed about one hero, or one time or one action, with many parts' (*Poetics* 1459a30–b7 = *PEG* T 7 = T 5 D. = p. 118 W.) and, however meaningful we find it, this must reflect real differences in the authors and in their audiences' tastes. Yet, as with the linguistic features mentioned earlier and discussed in the commentary, a separative comparison can be overdone: for example, the *Ilias parva*'s 'frank avowal of Zeus' homosexual abduction of Ganymedes'[48] (*PEG* F 29 = F 6 D. = F 6 W.) is neither so frank nor removed from Homer's mention of both the rape and its purpose (*Il.* 20.232–5), and produces its own gift (a golden vine) to parallel or replace the compensation of divine horses (*Il.* 5.265–7).[49] Here 'unHomeric' means little more than 'not by Homer', despite its usual negative connotation.

The more disparaging critical tendency becomes clear in discussions of the *Ilias parva*'s most substantial fragment (*PEG* F 21 = F 20 D. = F 29–30 W.),[50] in which Astyanax's death is briefly summarised (*PEG* F 21.3–5 = F 20.3–5 D. = F 29.3–5 W.). Little should be extrapolated about

---

[45] For the suggestion that this figure (Rhesus' father at *Il.* 10.435) may be linked with Cimonian military activity in Thrace in the 470s–460s BC, see Castriota (1992: 90–1).

[46] See Graziosi (2002: 175–80).

[47] See, e.g., Severyns (1928) *passim* but esp. 333–4, Griffin (1977) (though the requisite portion is not reproduced) and Davies (1989c: 60–70, esp. 66–7) on ambush; *contra* Dué and Ebbott (2010), who suggest that Homer used (and not only in the suspect *Doloneia*) a tradition of ambush poetry.

[48] Davies (1989c: 65), where he also claims that Homer knew nothing of the cupbearer story, though cf. *Il.* 20.234 (οἰνοχοεύειν).

[49] See below, pp. 342–3.   [50] See below, pp. 335–40.

the poem as a whole,[51] firstly because the two sources which quote the lines (Σ Lycophr. 1268, Σ Eur. *Andr.* 14) only do so to illustrate the fact that Neoptolemus took Andromache and Aeneas as his prisoners. We have no way of knowing, therefore, whether the quoted passage was the actual narration of the event in the *Ilias parva* rather than a summary contained in a speech or flashback.[52] On the other hand, if this was the entirety of the child's demise in the poem, its author may have aimed deliberately to compress and thus sideline the whole story, and its usual association with Odysseus, in keeping with his pro-Odysseus programme.[53] Whatever the original context, *PEG* F 21 (= F 20 D. = F 29–30 W.) should not lead us to 'suspect that a poem which handled such a scene in such a style as this contained, in Iliadic terms, no high points at all'.[54]

Indeed, the summary above suggests that the *Ilias parva* had an exciting narrative, sprinkled with quarrels, ambushes, oracles and lots of fighting, but it could interpose quieter events as well. The fall of Ajax, the rescue of Aethra by Theseus' sons (*PEG* F 20 = F 23 D. = F 17 W.), the reclaiming of Helen (*PEG* F 19 = D. = F 28 W.) – a highlight in itself[55] – and Helicaon's sparing (*PEG* F 12 = F 13 D. = F 22 W.) all suggest considerable variety amidst the fighting, while the overheard (and then quoted?) conversation between two Trojan women about the relative merits of Odysseus and Ajax displayed in the battle over Achilles' corpse (cf. *Od.* 11.547) sounds fascinating. Their opposition – the first speaker spins Odysseus' action as cowardice (*PEG* F 2.2 = D., W.), the second as a typically brave and manly endeavour (*PEG* F 2.3–5 = D., W.) – is not only Homeric in its dynamic (if not its speakers; cf. *Il.* 7.345–64) but shows, as Homer does, considerable sophistication in its awareness of the ways in which the same narrative event may be turned to different rhetorical ends.[56]

However the relationship is to be understood in other cases, Homer was already a giant to the poet of the *Ilias parva*: he incorporates specific scenes from both the *Iliad* (Priam's fear of death) and the *Odyssey* (the spying mission), revels in combat narrative, and generally approves of Odysseus.[57]

---

[51] *Contra* Davies (1989c: 69–70), Griffin (1977: 51–2), West (2013: 219–22).
[52] See Bravo (2001).   [53] See above, p. 324, for other such indications.
[54] Griffin (1977: 51). West (2013: 169–71) is similarly dismissive of the poem's 'more comical and romantic elements' (170). For indication that the poet was, nonetheless, both aware of the emotional potential in this event, see below, p. 339 n. 108.
[55] See above, n. 24.
[56] Compare the hostile spin put on Odysseus' actions by Eupeithes (*Od.* 24.425–37) and the differences between Odysseus' various accounts of his adventures; cf. Kelly (2008); also below, pp. 331–2.
[57] Further points of similarity with the *Iliad* include the opening quarrel over τιμή, Paris' unsuccessful involvement in a duel (arg. lines 213–15 Severyns), the chief Trojan/ally killed by

But this should not count against the later poem – even the title suggests an ancient opinion about its qualities and affiliations for which modern critics should have more regard.

ONE POEM OR MANY?

The existence of more than one *Ilias parva* may be suggested by a second opening Muse invocation (*PEG* F 1), Tzetzes' claim that many people wrote '*Iliads*' (*PEG* T 11 = T 2 D.), and several small factual differences within the record.[58] Most interesting is the evidence of a first-century AD papyrus which contains a fragmentary summary of a Trojan War narrative.[59] The extant portion of this papyrus is reminiscent of Proclus' précis of the *Ilias parva* in both style and content, but (i) places the theft of the Palladium before the summoning of Neoptolemus and right after the capture of Helenus, and (ii) has Coroebus killed by Diomedes and Odysseus well before the city's destruction, much like Rhesus in *Iliad* book 10. The similarities suggest a connection with a poetic text covering the same events, in much the same way, as our poem.[60]

Much of this evidence could be reconciled with a single tradition,[61] but the *Ilias parva*'s transmission was so tenuous that we cannot preclude the concurrence of different versions. Though not great, these differences are telling, and show the influence of the Homeric poems,[62] e.g. in using the story of Odysseus' self-wounding (*Od.* 4.244–6, *Ilias parva* arg. lines 224 Severyns) rather than the original wounding by Thoas (*PEG* F 7 = F 8 D. = F 8 W.), or making Coroebus into a late-arriving ally killed, like Rhesus, by Odysseus and Diomedes on a mission (*PEG* arg. 2.3–4 (PRylands 22.3–4)) rather than a victim of the final night's fighting (*PEG* F 15 =

---

a Peleid (arg. lines 219–20 Severyns), and a closing focus on Trojan mourning and suffering; cf. also Anderson (1997: 39–40, 53–4). Given the perennial scholarly fascination with the Homeric simile, we note here the *Ilias parva*'s cucumber simile (*PEG* F 23 = F. dub. 3 D. = F 31 W.), though it is an image not found in Homer; cf. below, p. 340.

[58] Cf. esp. Bernabé (1984); the relevant section of his *PEG* edition is entitled '*Iliades Parvae*'.
[59] PRylands 22; cf. Hunt (1911). Neither Davies nor West include this summary in their editions, but *PEG* prints it as the *Ilias parva*'s second argument.
[60] Bernabé (1984: 148); cf. also West (2013: 166–7).
[61] For multiple (re-)invocations (*PEG* F 1; *PEG* F 28 = F 1 D. = F 1 W.) in the same poem, see below, pp. 329–31.
[62] See Finkelberg (2000: esp. 6–11); Burgess (2001: 19–21, 201–2 nn. 64–8) on the analogous and notorious case of the agreement between the *Cypria* (according to Proclus) and Homer on Paris' voyage to Troy from Sparta, *against* Herodotus' report (2.117); see above, p. 325 and n. 41.

F 16 D. = F 24 W.).[63] In effect, the papyrus' source treats the *Ilias parva* much as that poem treated its forebears, recomposing through recombination. Whether it proves the existence of another *Ilias parva* or not, this evidence is at least a salutary reminder of how much of this kind of poetry has been lost.

COMMENTARY ON SELECTED FRAGMENTS

PEG F 1, from Plut. *Sept. sap. conv.* 154a

Μοῦσά μοι ἔννεπε ἔργα, τὰ μήτ' ἐγένοντο πάροιθε
μήτ' ἔσται μετόπισθεν.

Muse, sing to me the deeds [West; 'those things' MSS], which never occurred before and will not be hereafter . . .

PEG F 28 = F 1 D. = W., from Ps.-Herod. *Vita Homeri* 9.31 Wilamowitz

Ἴλιον ἀείδω καὶ Δαρδανίην εὔπωλον,
ἧς πέρι πολλὰ πάθον Δαναοὶ θεράποντες Ἄρηος.

Ilion do I sing and Dardania well-foaled, for which the Danaans suffered much, servants of Ares.

The existence of two *incipits* has suggested to some scholars multiple poems,[64] but the latter is more likely to be the opening of the *Ilias parva*: while *PEG* F 1 is only linked in a general – and disputed – manner with Lesches, *PEG* F 28 is identified explicitly as the start of the *Ilias parva* itself, and is also inscribed on two fifth-century Black Sea

---

[63] Cf. Verg. *Aen.* 2.341–6, 407–8, 424–6. Coroebus has also been plausibly identified on the early fifth-century BC 'Vivenzio hydra' (*LIMC* 'Koroibos' I 2), lying at the feet of Oilean Ajax as the latter pursues Cassandra (see Serbeti (1992: 103)), but he later becomes a byword for foolishness; see Langerbeck (1958: 45–7); Ambühl (1992 s.v. (2)). An Iliadic role in this recomposition is suggested by his similarity to Rhesus in being killed by Odysseus and Diomedes, and to Othryoneus in coming to Troy to marry Cassandra (see Janko (1992: 93 on *Il.* 13.361–82)), a motive which may have been shared with Eurypylus in the *Ilias parva* (cf. *PEG* F 29 F 6 D. = F 6 W., and *Od.* 11.519–21 with Σ *Od.* 11.521, which explicitly links him with Othryoneus). The papyrus' Coroebus is thus a recreation of both the *Ilias parva's* Eurypylus and the *Iliad's* Othryoneus and Rhesus, rather than an independent 'late-arriving ally' (as Memnon, Penthesileia, Eurypylus etc.).

[64] Bernabé (1984); see also above for PRylands 22. Of modern editors, only Bernabé takes *PEG* F 1 as the incipit, and only West fails to include it.

ostraca.[65] Yet the poem may have found room for *PEG* F 1 as well: the *Iliad* had an alternative beginning[66] and on several occasions addresses or reinvokes the Muse (*Il.* 11.218, 14.508, 16.112), while the rhetorical positioning of both fragments is well paralleled in Archaic epic (Muse invocation (*PEG* F 1): cf. *Il.* 1.1–2, *Od.* 1.1, *WD* 1–2, *Thebais PEG* F 1 (= D., W.), *HHomHerm* 1, *HHom* 9.1, 14.1–2, etc.; first person statement (*PEG* F 28): cf. *Th.* 1, *HHomDem.* 1, *HHomAp.* 1, *HHomAphr.* 1–2, etc.), and can easily be combined within the same text, even the same passage (cf. *Il.* 2.484–9 (Muses 484 > first person 493), *Theog.* 1–110 (first person 1 > Muses 104–15), *WD* 1–10 (Muses 1–2 > first person 10), and sometimes the same line (*Epigonoi PEG* F 1 = D., W.).[67]

There is nothing in the language of either fragment to indicate lateness or an untraditional quality: the heavy first syllable in *aeidō* (*PEG* F 28.1) is paralleled at *Od.* 17.519 (with light first syllable at 520), while the fact that *PEG* F 1.1a = *HHomAphr.* 1a may suggest direct influence, but it may of course be merely an underrepresented formula.[68] In *PEG* F 28 (= F 1 D. = W.), the expressions *Danaoi, therapontes Arēos* (4x Hom.) and *poll' epathon* (21x, 4x* Hom.) are formulaic, while the epithet *eupōlon* is confined in Homer (5x) to a formula for Troy. Given the consistent rivalry between the two lines of the royal family (and the priority of Dardania's foundation: *Il.* 20.216–18), the transfer of *eupōlon* may be intended to contrast the survival of Dardanian Aeneas[69] and the success of his descendants next to the demise of Priam's line.[70] The epithet would have additional point in this context, since Anchises secretly sired Aeneas' team from Laomedon's divinely given horses (*Il.* 5.265–72; cf. also 23.291–2, 348). *PEG* F 29 = F 6 D. = F 6 W. (see below) replaces these horses with another gift, and we do not know whether the *Ilias parva* retained this or a similar story in some other form; if not, then *eupōlon* would effectively allude to the Homeric story whilst opposing

---

[65] As Lowenstam (1997: 47 with n. 83) notes, poetic inscriptions almost always come from the beginnings of texts.

[66] For the text see Introduction, above in this volume, n. 6.

[67] On the Douris cup (Μοῖσα μοι ἀ⟨μ⟩φὶ Σκάμανδρον ἐύρ⟨ρ⟩οον ἄρχομ' ἀεί[ν]δε⟨ι⟩ν), see most recently Lowenstam (1997: 46–7) and Sider (2010). Scafoglio (2006) also argues that both *PEG* F 1 & 28 are authentic, but implausibly relates them (à la Snell) to different stages in Greek thought, and so treats them as evidence for an evolving text.

[68] For imperative verb + *erga ta*, cf. Hes. *WD* 398.

[69] Cf. below, p. 336 and n. 90 on *PEG* F 21 (= F 20 D. = F 29–30 W).

[70] For significant epithet alteration of this sort, cf. *WD* 653 (Ἑλλάδος ἐξ ἱερῆς Τροίην ἐς καλλιγύναικα 'from sacred Greece to Troy of the beautiful women') with Edwards (1971: 80–1). For West (2013: 173), the generality of *PEG* F 28 is a function of the 'diffuse' nature of the poem's contents.

it, figuring Dardania as 'well-foaled' for other reasons. Though the relative expression in line 2 (*hēs peri*) could apply simply to both cities in line 1, its attraction into the singular lends an emphasis to Dardania which may also be suggestive in this context.[71]

PEG F 2 = D., W., from Σ Aristoph. *Eq.* 1056 a

Αἴας μὲν γὰρ ἄειρε καὶ ἔκφερε δηϊοτῆτος
ἥρω Πηλείδην, οὐδ' ἤθελε δῖος Ὀδυσσεύς.

*

πῶς ἐπιφωνήσω; πῶς οὐ κατὰ κόσμον ἔειπες;
<καί κεν γυνὴ φέροι ἄχθος, ἐπεί κε ἀνὴρ ἀναθείη,
ἀλλ' οὐκ ἂν μαχέσαιτο.>

For Ajax raised and bore out of the fighting the hero Peleus' son, nor was godlike Odysseus willing...

*

How have you spoken? How have you not spoken in accordance with order? '<Even a woman could carry the burden, when a man should put it upon her, but she would not fight.>'[72]

Comprising a quotation from Aristoph. *Knights* 1056–7 (lines 3–4) and the back-story in the scholia ad loc. (lines 1–2), this fragment comes from the discussion between two Trojan women about the relative virtues of Ajax and Odysseus. The scholia provide the context: once Ajax and Odysseus quarrelled over the arms of Achilles, Nestor proposed to solve the dispute by sending a spy to eavesdrop on the Trojans and see which of the two they valued more. The *Odyssey* knows a similar story: Thetis sets out the arms and 'the children of the Trojans made the decision (viz, in Odysseus' favour) and Pallas Athene' (*Od.* 11.546–7). Scholars generally separate the two, on the grounds (i) that Homer's expression 'made the decision' (*dikasan*) requires a more formal setting; and (ii) 'children of the Trojans' (*paides Trōōn*) is an unusual way of referring to two (or more) Trojan women. The second objection is certainly stronger than the first: the H scholiast on *Od.* 11.547 suggests an analogy with *huies Achaiōn*, before relating it to the Trojans

---

[71] Cf. *Il.* 14.66–7 (τεῖχος δ' οὐκ ἔχραισμε τετυγμένον, οὐδέ τι τάφρος, / ἧ ἔπι πολλὰ πάθον Δαναοί 'and the wall we built has done us no good, nor the ditch either / where the Danaans endured so much', transl. by Lattimore), where the relative refers to both antecedents (Janko (1992: 158)), but in our fragment both antecedents are of the same gender; the examples collected by GH 21 are not comparable.

[72] The Aristophanic quotation of lines 4–5 continues 'for she would shit (χέσαιτο), if she fought', which may conceal an original 'she would withdraw' (χάσαιτο); cf. *PEG* p. 76.

slain by Odysseus during the battle, whilst the HVQ scholia add the detail that Agamemnon questioned Trojan prisoners, who judged Odysseus to the best 'because he grieved his enemies the most'. At any rate, it is not the same version as told in the *Ilias parva*, the propensity of which to differ from established tradition was noted earlier. It would be particularly apt for this poem to use yet another, secretive night mission towards Troy, especially in so doing to grant the prize to Odysseus, the master of such activity.

The roles played by each figure in the rescue of Achilles' corpse are also interesting.[73] All iconographic and most literary sources (starting with *Aeth.* arg. lines 193–5 Severyns) agree with this fragment in having Odysseus fight whilst Ajax carries the body, though the battle over Patroclus' corpse – which is often held to be an allusion to the struggle over Achilles – sees the Aiantes fight whilst Menelaus and Meriones lift the body (*Il.* 17.715–21). Probably not uninfluenced by this Iliadic scene, the BPQ scholia to *Od.* 5.310 assign Odysseus the carrying role, as does a fourth-century papyrus (*PEG* F (dub.) 32). Since all surviving versions give Odysseus the greater glory and success because he 'harmed' his enemies the most (either in general or because he killed many Trojans during the fight), the reversal of roles in these latter sources may have been purposed to lessen his credit.[74]

PEG F 5 = D., W., from Σ Hom. *Il.* 16.142b

ἀμφὶ δὲ πόρκης
χρύσεος ἀστράπτει, καὶ ἐπ' αὐτῶι δίκροος αἰχμή.

and about it a collar of gold flashes as lightning, and on it a two-fold spear-head

Invoked (by an Homeric scholion) to explain the fact that only Achilles could wield the famous ash spear of Peleus (*Il.* 16.142–3), and (by a Pindaric scholion) to justify its description as 'very angry' (*Nem.* 6.53) on the grounds that it could inflict two wounds at once, *PEG* F 5 is probably reacting directly to Homer's choice of verb (ἐπίστατο: not 'knew' but 'was able') to refer to Achilles' privileged ability; both scholia cite the *Ilias parva* as authority for the notion that the spear required special knowledge or skill, and instruction thereto may have been part of the purpose behind the appearance of Achilles' shade to his son (*Ilias parva* arg. line 218 Severyns).[75] The weapon itself had

---

[73] See Edwards (1991: 132); West (2013: 175–6).
[74] See above, pp. 324–5, for the reputation of Odysseus.
[75] See Severyns (1928: 338–42); also West (2013: 189).

a long prehistory, probably imagined as early as the *Iliad* as Cheiron's gift to Peleus on the occasion of his marriage to Thetis,[76] but Homer describes neither this nor any other spear as having a double-headed point.[77] Though there are some limited literary reflexes of this feature (Aesch. *TrGF* F 152, Soph. *TrGF* F 152), it has left no discernible iconographic footprint.[78]

The fragment's phrasing most closely matches the description of Hector's spear (*Il.* 6.319–20 = 8.494–5), and it could have occurred in a number of contexts: a depiction of Achilles' panoply in the *Hoplôn krisis* (arg. lines 208–10 Severyns), Odysseus giving his father's arms to Neoptolemus (arg. lines 217–18 Severyns), the appearance of Achilles to his son (see above), an arming scene in preparation for Neoptolemus' combat with Eurypylus (arg. lines 219–20 Severyns), or perhaps the extensive combat scenes during Troy's final night (cf. *PEG* F 10–17 = F 12, 13–18 D. = F 15–16, 21–6 W.). The verb 'flashes as lightning' (*astraptei*) is usually confined to Zeus in early Greek epic, whether his direct actions (*Il.* 2.353, 9.237, 8.75, 10.5, 17.595) or his weaponry (Hes. *Theog.* 689), but the *Ilias parva*'s striking metaphor is merely a development of a common Homeric combination;[79] the present tense (*astraptei*), though easily emended to a past, would indicate that the description was found in a speech, which would fit very well in the first or third situations above.[80]

---

[76] Whilst Homer explicitly describes Peleus' horses and armour as wedding gifts on several occasions (*Il.* 16.381–2, 17.194–7, 17.443–4, 18.84–5, 23.276–8), the spear is not so sourced (cf. *Il.* 16.140–4, 19.387–91); cf. Kullmann (1960: 234–5, 232–6 more generally), with *Cypr. PEG* F 3 = D. = F 4 W. (= Σ *Il.* 16.140).

[77] The formula ἔγχεσιν ἀμφιγύοισιν (9x Hom.) is generally held to refer instead to the shape of a single spear-point; cf. *LfgrE* s.v. ἀμφίγυος; Janko (1992: 64 on *Il.* 13.147). Double spear-points are not unknown in the material record of the Mycenaean and later periods (see Cook (1925: 798–806); also Sekunda (1992: 24) for a (now lost) fifth-century Lycian relief of a 'sickle-soldier' so armed) but they receive no mention in Trümpy (1950), Snodgrass (1964) or Höckmann (1980). Bert Smith suggests to me a misinterpretation of the common two-spear motif from Mycenaean art onwards; some role may also have been played by 'spear-pairs' in Homeric poetry (*Il.* 3.18 etc.) and funerary deposits from the Geometric period onwards; cf. Höckmann (1980: 301–2, 308, 311–12).

[78] Pausanias 3.3.8 locates a bronze spear of Achilles in the temple of Athene at Phaselis, though he speaks only of 'its spear head and butt-spike'.

[79] Cf. the formula χαλκοῦ... στεροπήν 'the shining... of bronze' (*Il.* 11.83, 19.363 ~ *Od.* 4.72, 14.268, 17.437); also τῆλε δὲ χαλκὸς | λάμφ' ὥς τε στεροπὴ πατρὸς Διός 'and the bronze afar off / glared, like the lightning of Zeus father' (*Il.* 10.153–4 ~ 11.65–6, transl. by Lattimore). Davies (1989a: 95–6) calls it a 'post-Homeric... extension', but the poet did not have to stretch the language very far.

[80] Homer usually describes the prizes in the funeral games in his own voice (and in the past tense), but cf. e.g. *Il.* 23.560–2, 832–5, and more generally 9.121–57, *Od.* 4.613–9, 8.403–5 (a sword!), 430–2 for such descriptions of objects, with present and future orientation, in character speech; see also Grethlein (2008). West (2013: 188–9) notes that Odysseus does

PEG F 9 = F 11 D. = F 14 W., from Clement of Alex. *Strom.* 1.21.104

νὺξ μὲν ἔην μέσση, λαμπρὰ δ' ἐπέτελλε σελήνη.

Night was in its middle, and a bright moon was rising.

This fragment accompanied the description of Troy's sack, and apparently marked the hour when Sinon raised the torch to the Greeks on Tenedos (Σ Lycophr. 344). In early epic, the moon's appearance facilitates vision (*Il.* 8.555–6) and is linked with the sun (*Od.* 4.45 = 7.84, 24.148; also *HHomAphr.* 89), whilst its absence indicates the opposite (*Il.* 17.367, *Od.* 9.144–5), so presumably the poet was here underlining the nocturnal visibility required for the work at hand.[81]

As the fall of Troy was an obvious target for early chronological speculation, there was much discussion about precisely which date is revealed here: probably because of its epithet, some argued for a full moon in the middle of the month (12th day: Hellanicus *EGM* F 152), others that a moon rising at or around midnight falls in the last part of the month (24th: Damastes *EGM* F 7).

The latter view seems now to hold the field, but the imperfect *epetelle* need not mean that the rising began at midnight (Hes. *WD* 567, 597–8 uses a form of *prōtos* to mark the start of astronomical phenomena), merely that it was in process and had not yet been completed, which could indicate the period closer to the full moon (as Hellanicus thought). In either case, the poet was unconcerned with this kind of calculation.[82]

The dialect of the second hemistich (*lamprē d' epetelle selēnē*) is interesting, since most sources read *lamprā* for *lamprē*, with final alpha usually interpreted as an Atticism and therefore another sign of the 'lateness' of this poem.[83] However, the early archaic formula *lamprān te Selēnēn* (Hes. *Theog.* 19, 371)[84] shows that *lamprā* in *PEG* F 9 cannot support such a conclusion. Other (very late) sources (Clement, Eusebius) extend the alpha

---

describe the armour in Quintus of Smyrna (7.194–204), though he is inclined towards emendation.

[81] For the narrative associations of night, see above, p. 323.

[82] As Grafton and Swerdlow (1986: 217–18) term it, 'the application of a marvellously precocious | scientific method to entirely fantastic data'. On the entire issue, cf. West (2013: 208–12), though he daringly combines *Titanomachia PEG* F 14 with this fragment, and endorses the very tentative speculation of Grafton and Swerdlow (1986: 216–8) that the *Ilias parva* specified that the Greeks sacked Troy for seventeen days before sailing home.

[83] See Wackernagel (1916: 181–2), Davies (1989a: 95–8, esp. 96–7).

[84] See West (1966: 81), Edwards (1971: 102–3), both of whom also judge it a sign of Attic influence on Hesiod's dialect, but not a corruption in the transmission.

throughout the verse (*selana* for *sēlēnē*; *mesata* for *mesatē*), perhaps as a result of hypercorrection.⁸⁵

PEG F 21 = F 20 D. = F 29–30 W., from Σ Lycophr. 1268

αὐτὰρ Ἀχιλλῆος μεγαθύμου φαίδιμος υἱός
Ἑκτορέην ἄλοχον κάταγεν κοίλας ἐπὶ νῆας
παῖδα δ' ἑλὼν ἐκ κόλπου ἐϋπλοκάμου τιθήνης
ῥῖψε ποδὸς τεταγὼν ἀπὸ πύργου, τὸν δὲ πεσόντα
ἔλλαβε πορφύρεος θάνατος καὶ μοῖρα κραταιή (5)
{ἐκ δ' ἕλετ' Ἀνδρομάχην, ἠΰζωνον παράκοιτιν
Ἕκτορος, ἥν τε οἱ αὐτῶι ἀριστῆες Παναχαιῶν
δῶκαν ἔχειν ἐπίηρον ἀμειβόμενοι γέρας ἀνδρί·
αὐτόν τ' Ἀγχίσαο κλυτὸν γόνον ἱπποδάμοιο
Αἰνείαν ἐν νηυσὶν ἐβήσατο ποντοπόροισιν (10)
ἐκ πάντων Δαναῶν ἀγέμεν γέρας ἔξοχον ἄλλων}.

But great-hearted Achilles' glorious son led away Hector's wife to the hollow ships. And seizing his son from the fold of the well-tressed nurse he hurled him, grabbing by the foot, from the tower, and when he fell dark death and powerful fate took him. {And he took out Andromache, the well-belted wife of Hector, whom the best of the all-Greeks gave to him, granting a pleasing prize to the man, and him, the glorious son of Anchises the horse-tamer Aeneas, he embarked on [MSS; 'planned' Schwartz] his sea-faring ships of all the Danaans to take as a prize outstanding beyond others.}

Homer knew that Neoptolemus left Troy with his 'noble prize' (*Od.* 11.533–5), the nature of which is subject of this fragment, though its extent, authenticity and placement have been questioned: Σ Eur. *Andr.* 14 attributes lines 6–11 to the Hellenistic poet Simias of Rhodes (F 6 Powell), and the return to Andromache in line 6 seems rather strange after lines 1–2. Some, therefore, follow the scholion⁸⁶ or rearrange the lines to avoid the problem,⁸⁷ but an economical hypothesis is that two passages from different parts of the poem have been run together, the first (lines 1–5) from the destruction of the city (e.g.), and the second (lines 6–11) from the later division of spoils.⁸⁸

---

⁸⁵ i.e., 'restoring' all the alphas for the normal epic eta. Otherwise still unexplained, the alphatized verse has been considered the result of Doric or Aeolic influence (West 1966: 80 n. 2; *contra* West 2013: 209), and Bowie (2014) argues that the citations in Clement are to be ascribed to the *Iliou persis* of the sixth-century Argive elegist Sakadas.
⁸⁶ Debiasi (2005: 180–1).
⁸⁷ Huxley (1969: 199) reorders the lines 6, 7, 8, 3, 4, 5, 1, 2, 9, 10, 11.
⁸⁸ West (2003a: 139–40; 2013: 219–20).

Aeneas' captivity is told only here, but it is later reflected in Hellanicus' story (*EGM* F 84) that he founded Rome after travelling with Odysseus to Italy from the Molossians,[89] who presumably comprised or were within Neoptolemus' realm (cf. *Nost.* arg. lines 299–300 Severyns). Within the poem, the event parallels the earlier capture of Helenus (*Ilias parva* arg. lines 211–12 Severyns), who also survives the sack and leaves the Troad, but it does not contradict the widespread story that Aeneas' dynasty would continue in sovereignty (*Il.* 20.307–8, *HHomAphr.* 196–7),[90] since neither passage specifies the location for that future rule.[91] The bondage must therefore have been temporary in the *Ilias parva*, as in the case of Helenus and in the later tale that Neoptolemus released Hector's descendants to return to the Troad so as to rejoin Aeneas' son Ascanius and resettle Troy (Hellanicus *EGM* F 31.24–7). That Neoptolemus is associated with all of these stories may suggest a common epic source. One may further speculate that the *Ilias parva* was deliberately figuring Aeneas in the role of Helenus as Neoptolemus' primary male captive, since this would concord with the poem's characteristic continuity factor, i.e. in having the man unwillingly spared by the father in the *Iliad* now spared, captured and then apparently freed by the son.[92]

As the poem's most substantial fragment(s), *PEG* F 21 allows some cautious appreciation of its style and merits.[93] Firstly, there is a heavy preponderance of formular units:

1 Ἀχιλλῆος μεγαθύμου φαίδιμος υἱός: = *Od.* 3.189; Ἀχιλλῆος μεγαθύμου: 2x* Hom. φαίδιμος υἱός: 10x* Hom., (acc.) 5x* Hom., 2x Hes.; 2 κοίλας ἐπὶ νῆας: 14x (11x*) Hom. (esp. *Il.* 5.26, 21.32 κατάγειν); 4 τὸν δὲ πεσόντα: 3x Hom.; πεσόντα: 9x* Hom.; 5 ἔλλαβε πορφύρεος θάνατος καὶ μοῖρα κραταιή: 3x* Hom. (always prec. by τὸν δὲ κατ' ὄσσε in prev. line); θάνατος καὶ μοῖρα κραταιή: 6x* Hom; μοῖρα κραταιή: 9x* Hom.; 7 Ἕκτορος: 20x* Hom.; ἀριστῆες Παναχαιῶν: 6x* Hom., (acc.) 2x* Hom.; 9 ἱπποδάμοιο: 22x* Hom., 2x* Hes. (F); 10 νηυσίν ... ποντοπόροισιν: 6x (4x*) Hom.; 11

---

[89] Though cf. *EGM* F 31.19–33, where Aeneas leaves the area under treaty and sails to Pallene.
[90] *Contra* West (2013: 220–1), who thinks it 'very un-epic' as well. For the pro-Dardanian leanings of *PEG* F 28 (= F 1 D. = F 1 W.) and *PEG* F 29 (= F 6 D. = F 6 W.), see my comments ad loc.
[91] Homer says only that Aeneas and his children 'will rule over the Trojans' (Τρώεσσι ἀνάξει *Il.* 20.307), the *Hymn* that his son 'will rule among the Trojans' (ἐν Τρώεσσι ἀνάξει 196) and will have lots of descendants; see Olson (2012: 1–9, esp. 4 and 9); also Edwards (1991: 298–301) more generally.
[92] See below, p. 339 on *PEG* F 21.1–2 (= F 20.1–2 D. = F 29.1–2 W.), p. 341 on *PEG* F 24 (= F 4 D. = F 4 W.) and p. 343 on *PEG* F 29 (= F 6 D. = F 6 W.) for other examples of this tendency.
[93] See also above, pp. 326–7 for the usual negative judgements, esp. with regard to Astyanax's death, and reasons not to follow them.

πάντων Δαναῶν: 1x* Hom., also *Il.* 1.90 (συμπάντων Δαναῶν); ἀγέμεν: 7x (3x*) Hom.; ἔξοχον ἄλλων: 9x* Hom., 1x* *HHom.*, 2x Hes. (F).

There are also several other, less definitely formulaic, parallels with Archaic epic:

1 Ἀχιλλῆος μεγαθύμου: cf., e. g., Ἰφίτου μεγαθύμου (2.518) etc., 32x* Hom.; 2 Ἑκτορέην: cf. *Il.* 2.416, 10.46; Ἑκτορέην ἄλοχον: cf. *Od.* 3.264 (Ἀγαμεμνονέην ἄλοχον); 3 κόλπου ἐυπλοκάμοιο τιθήνης: cf. *Il.* 6.466 (πάϊς πρὸς κόλπον ἐυζώνοιο τιθήνης), also 6.400, 483, *HHomDem.* 187; 4 ῥῖψε ποδὸς τεταγὼν ἀπὸ πύργου: ~ *Il.* 1.591* (ἀπὸ βηλοῦ), 24.735* (ῥίψε χειρὸς ἑλὼν ἀπὸ πύργου; cf. *HHomAp.* 318 ῥίψ' ἀνὰ χερσὶν ἑλοῦσα), also *Il.* 8.13, Hes. *Theog.* 868, *HHomHerm.* 256; 6 ἐκ δ' ἕλετ': ~ *Il.* 1.369* (ἐκ δ' ἕλον), 9.130* (ἐξελόμην), 9.272* (ἐξέλεθ'), also *HHomAp.* 489 (ἐκ δὲ κτήμαθ' ἕλεσθε), *Il.* 11.696–7; ἠΰζωνον παράκοιτιν: cf. *Il.* 9.590 (ἐΰζωνος παράκοιτις), also *HHomDem.* 212, 234, 243, 255; 8 δῶκαν ἔχειν: cf. Theogn. 1.1057 (ἔδωκαν ἔχειν), also *HHomAphr.* 212, Mimn. *IEG* 4.1, Theogn. 2.1387 (ἔδωκεν ἔχειν), also Hes. *Theog.* 219, 905–6.

This is the language of a poet fluent in the oral-traditional style of composition, with one telling sign of the strains imposed thereby: the form *ēüzōnon* (line 6) (for Homeric *eü–*) seems to violate 'the traditional formulaic system' (i.e. for καλλίζωνος),[94] yet such violations are well known in Homer[95] and necessitated here by unique location of *eüzōnos* at the strong caesura, the placement and spelling *ēü–* being paralleled by Homer's alternation in the adjective *ēüs*/*eüs*, the former at strong medial caesura (6x, (acc.) 3x), the latter weak (3x, (acc.) 2x).[96] Given Andromache's story and associations, one also suspects the specific influence of *eüzōnoio tithēnēs* (*Il.* 6.467) and

---

[94] West (2013: 171).
[95] Cf. Friedrich (2007). This alternation is probably not a formula system anyway, for it is only found once (Hes. *Cat.* F 26 M.-W. = F 17 Hirsch.) and the words are otherwise used in different conditions: *kallizōnos* qualifies unnamed groups to the verse-end (*gynaikes Il.* 7.139; *gynaikas HHomAp.* 154 (acc); *gynaikōn Il.* 24.298, *Od.* 23.147; *thygatres HHomAp.* 446), while *eüzōnos* qualifies only one of these words (*gynaikas*) from the start of the verse (*Il.* 9.366, 23.261), being otherwise deployed to the verse-end with singular nouns (*gynaikos Il.* 1.429, 23.760; Hes. *Cat.* F 195.31 M.-W. = 91 Hirsch.; Ps.-Hes. *Scut.* 31; *tithēnēs Il.* 6.467; *parakoitis Il.* 9.590) and names (*Il.* 9.667 (verse-initial), *HHomDem.* 212, 234, 243, 255, Hes. *Cat.* F 26.23, 33a.7, 221.1 M.-W. = F 17.23, 25.7, *10.1 Hirsch.). This distribution reflects individual prosody and word-placement. Of course, a formula system is a reified combination of these factors, but it can violate them if required, as e.g. in declining *meropōn anthrōpōn* (9x Hom.) into unmetrical *meropes anthrōpoi* (*Il.* 18.288); cf. Parry (1928 = 1972: 191–239).
[96] ἐΰς is also used after the strong caesura before a vowel to close the foot (5x Hom., scanned ⏑ ⏑ |), and so enabling different following conditions from those of ἐΰς (scanned – | –). West (2013: 171) thinks it significant that the alternation *ēü–*/*eü–* occurs 'only where the second syllable is short, as in ἠΰκομος, ἠϋγένειος, and the like'.

eüzōnos parakoitis (9.590),[97] indicating that specific reminiscences helped to shape the way in which formular units (viz, *eüzōnos* + sing. noun to verse-end from medial caesura: 4x Hom., 4x *HHom.* etc.) were manipulated and regenerated.

This may also be supposed in the similarities between *PEG* F 21.3–4 and two particular Iliadic passages foreshadowing the death of Astyanax (6.467–70 and 24.736–9). Some scholars have concluded that there was a tradition surrounding the death of Hector's son[98] – a popular theme in early Greek art[99] – but two Homeric examples of the verse-initial expression *rhipse(i) podos/cheiros* (1.591, 24.735; cf. *PEG* F 21.4), especially when one of them refers to Hephaestus, do not prove the existence of formulae explicitly associated with Astyanax. The poet instead seems to be consciously reworking the language of the *Iliad* in order to renovate his own traditional dialect.

This suggests that the oral epic tradition evolves with the appearance of fixed texts, assimilating them into its compositional processes. Such a continuity may also be observed in several features in the language of *PEG* F 21, sometimes judged as straightforwardly 'late' or 'untraditional'.[100] The use of *nu* mobile to 'make position' (*katagen koilas* line 2) is a frequent occurrence in Homer.[101] For *te* in a relative clause denoting non-habitual action (*hēn te* line 7), cf. *Il.* 5.467–8, 7.452, 12.236, 17.174, 19.88, 22.116, *Od.* 4.136.[102] The epithet *epiēron* (line 8) is not found elsewhere before the fifth century (cf. *epiēranos Od.* 19.343),[103] but adjectival compounds of adverbial and prepositional expressions are extremely common in Homer.[104] For noun–epithet separation in *auton t' Agkhisao klyton gonon hippodamoio* (line 9), cf. *Il.* 2.23 = 60, 4.370, 7.38, 11.450);[105] *hippodamoio* is not elsewhere applied to Anchises, but it is very frequently applied to the Trojans (*Il.* 2.230 etc.) and to several other characters of his generation (e.g. Antenor

---

[97] For other signs of direct interaction with the *Iliad*, see above, p. 327 n. 57.
[98] Burgess (2012: 176–82); cf. Anderson (1997: 54–6). [99] See above, p. 321.
[100] See Wackernagel (1916: 181–2), Davies (1989a: 95–8), West (2013: 171–2, 221–2).
[101] See also *PEG* F 29.1 and 4 (= F 6.1 and 4 D. = F 6.1 and 4 W.). Janko (1982: 66) notes that the *Ilias parva* concords with Homeric statistics, though the sample is too small for any firm conclusion about the poem as a whole (1982: 189 and 273–4).
[102] 'An oddity': Davies (1989a: 96), citing Ruijgh (1971: 916) (as West 2013: 221); cf. also Ruijgh (1971: 421–3): 'plus irrégulier', though he concludes (918) that 'l'emploi de τε épique dans les fragments épiques entre Homère et l'épopée hellénistique semble s'accorder avec l'emploi homérique'.
[103] See West (2013: 171), with some diffidence: 'no logical reason... why ἐπίηρος should not already have been coined by a sixth-century poet'. Homer's compound *epiēra* (2x) is a 'fossilised' result of the more common expression *epi* (dat.) *ēra* + *pherein* (4x).
[104] Risch (1974: 187–9 (§ 69a), 112–15 (§ 40)).
[105] *Contra* Dihle (1970: 148). West (2013: 221) surprisingly thinks the whole verse typically Cyclic in its 'prolixity'.

Il. 6.299, 14.473), as well as being used as a name in itself (*Il.* 11.335); *kl-* (in *klyton* line 9) fails to 'make position' as it sometimes does in Homer (cf. *Od.* 1.366 = 18.213, 12.215, 12.421, 20.92).[106] Some of these are minority phenomena in Homer, but the indirect parallels are easy extensions of traditional resources, and the size of the sample is too small to be sure that the snapshot is representative of the poem as a whole. That the language of this fragment reflects a post-Homeric stage of development is in any case probable, given the evidence for direct interaction with the *Iliad*, but these cases do not indicate an especially late date for the poem, nor that its poet was untraditional.

In the relationship between sentence and verse structure, *PEG* F 21 (= F 20 D. = F 29–30 W.) shows a relatively high proportion of lines with necessary enjambment (lines 1–2, 3–4, 4–5, 7–8, 9–10), which may (once more, if representative) be a function of a post-Homeric date.[107] More likely, enjambment expresses the poet/speaker's awareness of the emotional potential of the subject matter, notwithstanding the brevity of its description (note especially the cluster in lines 3–5).[108]

Artistry of other sorts is evident: the pointed reminders of Achilles (*Achilleos*) and Hector (*Hektoreēn*) in lines 1–2 highlight the continuity of their antipathy in the *Ilias parva*, as the former's son now claims the latter's wife before killing his son;[109] that none of these figures is given their own name (if not a misleading impression of the wider passage) highlights the relational aspect of their identities.[110] Furthermore, note the structural sophistication of lines 6–11, where three verses are allotted to each prize, with considerable syntactical and phraseological variation balancing out the patterned similarities: the last verse in each case describes the gift in general terms and uses an infinitive to denote possession (*echein* 8 / *agemen* 11), whilst the first two verses naming the gifts are also linked chiastically, with Andromache's name (line 6) followed by her husband's (line 7) finding its response in Anchises' name (line 9) appearing before Aeneas' (line 10). Finally, the status of that second prize is reinforced (line 11) by sonant

---

[106] *Contra* West (2013: 221).
[107] For a comparison between archaic and later epic in these terms, cf. Barnes (1979: esp. 7–8). Notopoulos (1964: 30–1) hastily takes this as evidence of the poem's orality.
[108] For necessary enjambment expressing 'urgency and animation' in Homer, see Graziosi and Haubold (2010: 13), drawing on the work of Bakker (2005). This effect is particularly noticeable in speeches, which might lead one to speculate that lines 1–5 were contained in a speech; cf. above, p. 327. On the criticism that the death of Astyanax did not receive a proper treatment here, see above, pp. 326–7.
[109] See above, p. 336 on *PEG* F 21.9–11, and below, p. 341 on *PEG* F 24 and p. 343 on *PEG* F 29 for other examples.
[110] See Anderson (1997: 54).

repetitions, with central *agemen geras* enclosed by *ek pantōn Danaōn... exochon allōn*. However successful or appealing one judges these features to be, their presence suggests that the poet was not unaware of verbal art.

PEG F 23 = F dub. 3 D. = F 31 W., from Athenaeus 3.73a

ὡς δ' ὅτ' ἀέξηται σικυὸς δροσερῶι ἐνὶ χώρωι

and as when a cucumber grows in a watery place...

The ascription of this fragment to Lesches depends on a relatively certain emendation in Athenaeus (3.73e Olson),[111] but there is no indication of context. While the syntax is too common to need exemplification, the image is certainly unique in early Greek epic,[112] as are many images of peaceful human collaboration with nature in the Homeric poems.[113] The development of the young is often compared there to saplings (*Il*. 18.56–7 = 437–8, *Od*. 6.162–8, 14.175), and frequently with location specified (cf. also *Il*. 17.54), so it is not impossible that West is right to link this rather unusual image to Neoptolemus' growth (in conjunction perhaps with *PEG* F 24 = F 4 D. = F 4 W.: see below).[114]

PEG F 24 = F 4 D. = F 4 W., from Σ Hom. *Il*. 19.326

Πηλεΐδην δ' Ἀχιλῆα φέρε Σκῦρόνδε θύελλα,
ἔνθ' ὅ γ' ἐς ἀργαλέον λιμέν' ἵκετο νυκτὸς ἐκείνης.

and a storm bore Peleus' son Achilles to Scyros, where he came into the difficult harbour during that night.

This fragment is invoked by an Homeric scholiast to explain Achilles' reference to his son's presence on Scyros (*Il*. 19.326), and explicitly set against the version of 'some' who relate the story that Achilles was hidden there by his mother before the Trojan War. The *Cypria* (arg. lines 125–31 Severyns

---

[111] Olson (2006: 45) cautiously restores the author's name as 'Dieuches' (*SH* 379).

[112] It is first found elsewhere in dactylic hexameter poetry in Praxilla *PMG* F 1.3, where the dead Adonis enumerates things he misses most and includes the 'seasonal cucumbers' after the sun, stars and moon (lines 1–2 ∼ *Il*. 18.484–5). Zenobius, who quotes the fragment to illustrate the proverb 'foolish as the Adonis of Praxilla', suggests that the effect of the third verse is bathetic, but it may rather have played on the similarity between 'cucumbers' (σικύους) and Praxilla's home city of Sicyon, thus alluding – perhaps in an erotic way (*hōraious*) – to the local participants of the festival at which this poem may have been performed; see Snyder (1989: 57–8) and (more speculatively) Sumler (2010: 468–9).

[113] Edwards (1991: 35); see also Scott (2009: 205).

[114] West (2013: 185); see also above, p. 328 n. 57.

and F 20) tells us that Achilles married (*gamei*) Deidameia, daughter of king Lycomedes, in the aftermath of the Teuthranian setback, arriving in the *Ilias parva* apparently on the day (*nyktos ekeinēs* line 2) they set out from Mysia.[115] Though this would make Neoptolemus barely old enough to hold a weapon, early epic can treat long periods of time in a very imprecise manner (Odysseus' ten years' wandering leaves a considerable gap after seven years with Calypso (*Od.* 7.259–60) and one with Circe (10.469), as does Helen's reference (*Il.* 24.765–6) to her twenty years since leaving Menelaus, while the story of Iphitus and his bow (*Od.* 21.11–41) seems to synchronize Heracles and Odysseus),[116] and the story adds greatly to the poem's 'continuity' factor, since Neoptolemus is now begotten directly after his father's encounter with Telephus.[117] Storms were a constant threat for the journeying hero, and frequently linked with erotic encounters: aside from the overtures made to Odysseus by Nausicaa and Alcinous, and his extended sojourn with Calypso, cf. e.g. *Il.* 14.249–56, 15.26–8 (Heracles), *Cypria PEG* arg. lines 98–100 Severyns (Paris and Helen).

PEG F 24 (= F 4 D. = F 4 W.) must be a flashback set in the context of Neoptolemus' arrival or summoning (arg. lines 216–18 Severyns), but it is unclear whether it was contained in character- or narrator-text: the latter might be indicated by *PEG* F 23 (= F dub. 3 D. = F 31 W.) as similarly concerned with Neoptolemus' backstory,[118] were it not for (i) the uncertainty of the simile's reference, and (ii) the use of similes in Homeric character-speech, especially in youthful comparisons (see above). If in character speech, then possible candidates could include Helenus' revelations (arg. lines 211–12 Severyns), a subsequent council scene in the Greek camp, or self-identification on Scyros.

The language is once again traditional: verse-initial *Pēleïdēn Achilēa* only occurs 1x Hom. (*Il.* 23.542), but in other cases is formulaic (9x*); *thyella* is frequently linked with forms of *pherō* (9x Hom., 1x Hes.); though *ekeinēs* (line 2) may be a 'very recent arrival'[119] in Homer (i.e. with *e–*), it is there (18x), and therefore only a much larger sample of verses from the *Ilias parva* than we currently have could make any point about proportions. Strikingly,

---

[115] Severyns (1928: 288–91) separates the *Cypria* and the *Ilias parva*, the former containing the story of youthful confinement as well as the formal marriage (under the influence of the latter), thus creating a more coherent story; differently West (2013: 104, 184).

[116] See Severyns (1928: 288–91); Brügger (2009: 259–60); Crissy (1997).

[117] See Anderson (1997: 38–48) for the poet's construction of the Achilles – Neoptolemus/Telephus – Eurypylus nexus. For other examples of this feature, see above, pp. 336 and 339 on *PEG* F 21.9–11 and *PEG* F 21.1–2, and below, p. 343 on *PEG* F 29.

[118] West (2013: 184–5).   [119] Davies (1989a: 95–6), citing Janko (1982: 237).

the harbour at Scyros is 'difficult' (*argaleon*) in that it was hard to attain; cf. the common 'difficult' road/seas/winds etc.[120]

PEG F 29 = F 6 D. = F 6 W., from Σ Eur. *Tr.* 822

ἄμπελον ἣν Κρονίδης ἔπορεν οὗ παιδὸς ἄποινα
χρυσείην, φύλλοισιν ἀγαυοῖσιν κομόωσαν
βότρυσί θ' οὓς Ἥφαιστος ἐπασκήσας Διὶ πατρὶ
δῶχ', ὃ δὲ Λαομέδοντι πόρεν Γανυμήδεος ἀντί.

the vine which the son of Cronus provided as recompense for his son, golden, plumed with leaves brilliant [Jortin; 'gentle' MSS] and grape clusters, which Hephaestus adorned and gave to father Zeus, and he provided it to Laomedon for Ganymedes.

This description must have been associated with the arrival of the Trojan ally Eurypylus (son of Telephus), since Σ *Od.* 11.520 relates that this vine was given by Priam to Eurypylus' mother, Astyoche, so that she would send her son to Troy. The *Ilias parva* makes him a prominent figure,[121] with his victims including Machaon (*PEG* F 30 = F 7 D. = F 7 W.) and Axion (*PEG* F 17 = F 18 D. = F 26 W.), whilst his death at the hands of Neoptolemus begins the final stage of the Trojan siege (arg. lines 219–21 Severyns). Divinely made heirlooms or gifts are well known in early Greek epic (cf., e.g., *Il.* 2.100–8; *Od.* 4.613–19 etc.),[122] and the ring-composition between *eporen hou paidos apoina* (line 1) and *poren Ganymēdeos anti*[123] (line 4) neatly surrounds the physical description and Hephaistian origin (lines 2–3), emphasising the purpose for which it was given.

PEG F 29 diverges from the *Iliad* on two points: the first in making Ganymedes the son of Laomedon and not Tros (*Il.* 5.265–6, 20.231–5), and the second in making the 'recompense' for this rape (*hou paidos apoina PEG* F 29.1. ~ *huios poinēn Il.* 5.266) an Hephaistian vine instead of divine horses (*Il.* 5.265–7).[124] The mistaken notion that the *Ilias parva*'s depiction of Ganymedes' rape is unhomeric in its 'frank avowal of homosexual desire' has been already discussed above,[125] but of more interest is the poet's decision to make Ganymedes Priam's brother: while the story casts Eurypylus as a

---

[120] See *LFGE* s.v., B1c; also *Od.* 11.101, 22.137. West (2003a: 127) translates 'with difficulty'.
[121] See West (2013: 190–1).   [122] See further Latacz *et al.* (2003: 37–8).
[123] For anastrophe of *anti* (another 'late' feature acc. to Wackernagel (1916: 181–2), cf. *Il.* 13.447, 14.471, 23.650; also 8.163, 24.254, Hes. *Theog.* 893.
[124] *HHomAphr.* 202–4, 210–17 agrees with the *Iliad* on both points; cf. also Severyns (1928: 342–7).
[125] See above, p. 326.

tragically noble figure (already at *Od.* 11.519–22), duped by a greedy mother into going to war (as Amphiaraus by Eriphyle; cf. 15.246–7, 11.326–7),[126] the new genealogy isolates the infection, as it were, within the line of Laomedon and Priam as the prime arena for the events which eventually doom the city (cf. *Il.* 20.301–8). Certainly, the ring-compositional emphasis on the gift's purpose ironically underscores Priam's responsibility and limited vision: an item given to compensate a parent for a child's loss is now used, by that child's brother, to bribe another parent into losing her child.[127] Moreover, in a poem which opens with the topic *Dardaniēn eupōlon* (*PEG* F 28 = F 1 D. = F 1 W.), this new gift may also have cancelled the Homeric slur that Aeneas' father had surreptitiously bred from Laomedon's horses (*Il.* 5.265–72), though it is possible that the story was retained elsewhere in the poem, or that Aeneas had an immortal team sourced in some other way. On the other hand, it would be entirely characteristic of the *Ilias parva* to downplay the divine origin of Aeneas' team so as to undermine the significance of their capture by Diomedes.[128]

CONCLUSION

At some point after the creation of the Homeric poems in the eighth or seventh centuries BC, and (at least) before the last quarter of the fifth century, the *Ilias parva* was composed by someone whom later antiquity knew as Lesches of Lesbos. Its narrative was so engaged with the *Iliad* and *Odyssey* as perhaps to have earned – or justified – the title which prioritized that relationship. Its central figure was Odysseus, whose triumphs characterize and determine the poem's focus on ambush and deception. Its poet was inventive and skilled: he had a noticeable talent for striking metaphor and expressive syntax, he was traditionally trained and fluent, whilst at the same time interacting directly with the Homeric poems. Though the smaller and lesser of the *Iliads* famous in antiquity, its meagre remains give us reason enough to regret its loss.

---

[126] See West (2013: 191) for further parallels, esp. the expression *gynaiōn heineka dōrōn* (*Od.* 11.521 of Astyoche, *Od.* 15.247 of Eriphyle).

[127] See above, pp. 336 and 339 on *PEG* F 21.9–11 (= F 20.9–11 D. = F 30.4–6 W.) and *PEG* F 21.1–2 (= F 20.1–2 D. = F 30.1–2 W.), and p. 341 on *PEG* F 24 (= F 4 D. = F 4 W.) for this type of generational continuity.

[128] See above, pp. 330–1 and n. 69 on *PEG* F 28.1 (= F 1.1 D. = F 1.1 W.).

19 | *Iliou persis*

PATRICK J. FINGLASS

THE MYTH IN POETRY AND ART

For as long as the Trojan War was the subject of Greek song, the sack of that city must have provided bards with some of their most memorable poetry. The recovery of Helen required the destruction of an ancient and mighty city, with dramatic consequences for victors and vanquished. The Greeks won great glory,[1] but their impiety during the sack tainted that achievement, and led to many warriors experiencing a perilous or even fatal return. The Trojans suffered annihilation: their men killed, their women enslaved. Yet a group led by Aeneas escaped destruction and propagated the Trojan race. The events of such a momentous night cry out for poetic treatment. Yet in what survives of classical literature, the earliest extended narrative of the sack is owed to . . . Publius Vergilius Maro, in the second book of the *Aeneid*. For earlier periods, mere fragments remain.

The first extant poems which deal with the Trojan saga are set respectively before and after the fall of Troy. The *Iliad*, which describes events in the tenth and final year of the siege, conspicuously fails to pursue its narrative as far as the destruction of the city. Hector is sure that the sack will take place; indeed, his death will be its proximate cause.[2] But the epic ends not with the sack, but with his funeral. The poet's decision to stop short of what seems a more obvious terminus springs from his concentration on a single theme: the anger of Achilles, its consequences and resolution. Adding a narrative of the sack of Troy would have seriously unbalanced the work, preventing the poet from giving prominence to the profound meeting between Achilles and Priam. More generally, accounts of the sack were no doubt already familiar when the *Iliad* was being composed; Homer decides to fashion his poem from less obvious material.[3] In his hands, the low-key encounter between two enemies forms a more moving ending than the sack could ever have been.

---

[1] Cf. *Od.* 9.263–6.
[2] *Il.* 6.447–9; cf. Zeus' prophecy at 15.68–71 and the pregnant simile at 22.410–11.
[3] The poem also knows of the earlier sack of the city, by Heracles, which receives some coverage in archaic literature and art; see *Il.* 5.638–42, 648–51, etc., and Finglass (2011) on Soph. *Aj.* 434–6.

The *Odyssey* is the first extant poem to narrate the destruction of Troy. The gods brought about the sack of the city, Alcinous tells Odysseus, so that it would be a subject of song among men.[4] As he speaks those words, the epic poet has just demonstrated the impact of that song. Odysseus asks Demodocus to tell of the Wooden Horse (made by Epeius with the help of Athena, and brought by Odysseus to the Trojan acropolis), but is reduced to tears by the story.[5] The bard describes how the Greeks set fire to their huts and sail off, leaving Odysseus and other warriors inside the horse. The Trojans drag it to their acropolis and set it in the agora. They then debate what to do with it – whether to pierce it with their weapons, to cast it off a cliff, or to let it be, to secure the goodwill of the gods. Fate had determined that the city was doomed, and so the third course prevails. Later the Greeks leave the horse and sack the city, with Athena's support. Demodocus specifies only one of the many dire events of that night known from later accounts: the visit by Odysseus and Menelaus to Deiphobus, presumably to kill him and recover Helen.[6]

This is not the only reference to the sack in the poem – or, at least, to the events leading up to it. The horse also features during Telemachus' visit to Sparta. Menelaus describes how Helen called out to the beast in the voices of the Greek warriors' wives. Only the intervention of Odysseus prevented the other Greeks inside the horse (three of whom are named: Menelaus, Diomedes, and Anticlus) from responding and thus revealing the stratagem.[7] A third reference to the horse occurs in Odysseus' speech to Agamemnon in the underworld. Odysseus remarks on how Neoptolemus, unlike the other Greek leaders, kept hold of his emotions as they waited to launch their ambush.[8] All these narratives shed light on wider themes within the poem.[9]

The decision of both these poets to avoid a full-scale account of the sack is all the more remarkable when we consider how popular the topic was in archaic art.[10] The horse is attested as early as the late eighth century, on a fragmentary bronze Boeotian fibula. A relief pithos from Mykonos, dating to the second quarter of the seventh century, shows a particularly impressive specimen.[11] The horse is on the neck of the vessel, with several warriors

---

[4] *Od.* 8.579–80.   [5] *Od.* 8.482–531.

[6] The poem nevertheless avoids explicitly mentioning Deiphobus' marriage to Helen; see Schischwani (1994: 111).

[7] *Od.* 4.266–89.   [8] *Od.* 11.523–37.   [9] See Davies (2000).

[10] See further Sadurska (1986); Anderson (1997: 179–265); Hedreen (2001); Giuliani (2003: 77–95); Davies and Finglass (2014: 395–6).

[11] See Carpenter, above in this volume, pp. 179–82.

visible through windows, and men fighting outside; the rest of the pithos displays the violent scenes of that bloody night, including two panels which might represent Menelaus confronting Helen and the death of Astyanax, although neither identification is certain. Such images are testimony to the popularity of the myth in the archaic period. Hence the absence of a major written poetic treatment presented others with an opportunity. An enterprising bard now had the chance to immortalise in writing this central event of one of the great Greek sagas.[12] One such poet was the author of what we know as the epic *Iliou persis*. But he was not alone. The same title was used for lyric poems by Stesichorus and Sacadas of Argos;[13] and the sack was also prominent in the epic *Ilias parva*. Stesichorus and Sacadas were both active probably in the first half of the sixth century. The dating of the Cyclic works depends among other things on when the Homeric poems were composed, a subject beyond the scope of this chapter. Their composition may well have lasted some time; their essentially episodic nature might well have invited frequent interpolation, and so it may be a mistake to posit a specific date of composition. Nor can we assume that the *Iliou persis* and *Ilias parva* preceded Stesichorus and Sacadas on the ground that epic treatments of the myth ought to come before lyric ones. As Bethe remarks, 'one speaks of the replacement of epic by the lyric poets, but I would prefer to speak of their concurrence with epic poets in the contemporary treatment of the same material'.[14] Even if we do prefer to think that epic had more impact on lyric than the reverse, lyric poets may have been influenced by various epic treatments of the story, not necessarily by the work that we know as the *Iliou persis*.[15]

The subject retained its popularity in art from the mid sixth century until the mid fifth century, with three scenes from the sack particularly prominent on Attic pottery: the recovery of Helen, the death of Priam (usually accompanied by the killing of Astyanax), and Ajax's rape of Cassandra.[16] Eventually it found its way into tragedy: Sophocles' son Iophon wrote an

---

[12] Note however West (2012: 230–1), who argues that 'the *Odyssey* poet must have known a poem similar to the *Iliou persis* in scope and content. It is hardly going too far to say that he represents Demodocus as singing the *Iliou persis*'; cf. *ibid.* 233–4 'the fact that the *Odyssey* poet knew poems closely related to the canonical *Aethiopis*, *Ilias parva*, *Iliou persis*, and *Nostoi* makes it all the more likely that these poems enjoyed some general currency by the end of the seventh century'. That would place our poem before the *Odyssey* as dated by West.

[13] See Stesich. F 98–164 Finglass (previous edition of the fragments then known: *PMGF* pp. 183–205); Sacadas ap. Athen. 13.610c as emended by Casaubon (1600: 559.10–14), on which see Bowie (2010a: 152–3); (2014).

[14] Bethe (1929: ii.382): 'Man redet von Umsetzung des Epos durch die Lyriker, ich möchte lieber von ihrer Concurrenz mit den Epikern in gleichzeitiger Behandlung derselben Stoffe sprechen.'

[15] See West (2002b: 212–13 = 2011a: 398–400), on Alcaeus.

[16] See the works cited in n. 10 above.

Iliou persis, and a *Persis* is credited to Cleophon and Nicomachus.[17] But overall, tragedy is more interested in the terrible consequences of the sack, whether for the conquerors (Aeschylus' *Agamemnon*) or the conquered (Euripides' *Andromache*, *Hecuba*, *Trojan Women*).

SOURCES AND PLOT

Sources for the epic *Iliou persis* are few, even in comparison to other poems of the Cycle. At the start of his plot summary Proclus calls the work the Ἰλίου πέρσις, attributes it to Arctinus of Miletus,[18] and states that it was two books long.[19] Five further fragments are preserved, as well as one fragment of uncertain attribution. Three are attributed to Arctinus (*PEG* F 2 = D. = F 1 W., *PEG* F 4 = F 1 D. = F 2 W., *PEG* F 1 = F dub. D. = F 4 W.), of which one (*PEG* F 4 = F 1 D. = F 2 W.) also names the poem, calling it the Ἰλίου πόρθησις. Two other fragments refer to the author anonymously as ὁ τὴν Πέρσιδα συντεταχὼς κυκλικὸς ποιητής ('the Cyclic poet who composed the *Sack*') (*PEG* F 5 = F 3 D. = W.) and ὁ τὴν Πέρσιδα πεποιηκώς ('the author of the *Sack*') (*PEG* F 6 = F 4 D. = F 6 W.). A further fragment (*PEG Tit*. F 14 = p. 74 D. = F 5 W.) comes from a source that simply states ἡ ἱστορία παρὰ τοῖς κυκλικοῖς. Its content (a reference to how Electra, mother of Zeus' son Dardanus, left the place in heaven where she had been a star because she did not want to watch the destruction of Troy) comes from an account of the sack, but that account might have been that of the *Ilias parva* rather than our poem.

These fragments come chiefly from scholia: on the *Iliad* (*PEG* F 4 = F 1 D. = F 2 W., *Tit. PEG* F 14 = p. 74 D. = F 5 W.), on Euripides' *Andromache* (*PEG* F 5 = F 3 D. = W.) and *Troades* (*PEG* F 6 = F 4 D. = F 6 W.), cited by the scholiast on the authority of Lysimachus), and on Virgil's *Aeneid* (*PEG* F 2 = D. = F 1 W.). The one remaining fragment is owed to Dionysius of Halicarnassus (*PEG* F 1 = F dub. D. = F 4 W.). The same author provides one of two testimonia for the poem.[20] In the course of a discussion of the Trojan penates, he refers to Arctinus (and by implication our poem) as the

---

[17] Iophon 22 F 2b, Cleophon 77 F 10, Nicomachus 127 F 8 in *TrGF* i. See further Anderson (1997: 105–76).

[18] Arctinus is also credited with the *Aethiopis* and (by one source) the *Titanomachy*, though nothing else is known of him. No early source refers to him by name, so we cannot place much faith in the attribution. See further Burgess (2001: 9–10).

[19] Perhaps the Alexandrian editor placed the book division so that the first book contained the preliminaries to the sack, the second the sack itself.

[20] See West (2003a: 143).

oldest of the sources known to him. The other testimonium, an inscription on a relief plaque dating to the reign of Augustus or Tiberius, refers to the poem as the Ἰλίου πέρσις.[21] A final likely source is the epitome of the *Bibliotheca* ascribed to Apollodorus.[22] Although the author does not refer explicitly to the *Iliou persis*, or indeed to any earlier account of the story, some of his summary is probably taken from that poem.

Proclus begins his account of the plot with the Trojans standing round the horse and wondering what to do with it. This is most unlikely to have been the opening of the work. The Neoplatonist has probably omitted the construction of the horse to avoid overlap with the end of his account of the *Ilias parva*.[23] Three views are expressed: that it should be cast over a cliff, set on fire, or dedicated to Athena as a sacred object. The third view prevails, as in the *Odyssey*, and the Trojans celebrate their freedom. As they do so, two serpents appear, killing Laocoon and one of his sons.[24] This disconcerting event leads Aeneas and his companions to leave Troy for Ida.

Prompted by firebrands held by Sinon, who had entered the city under a false pretext, the Greeks sail back from Tenedos, and together with the men in the horse they launch their assault. In the course of the sack Neoptolemus kills Priam, who had fled to the altar of Zeus Herceios for refuge; Menelaus kills Deiphobus, finds Helen, and takes her to the ships; and the lesser Ajax drags off Cassandra, dislodging the status of Athena. The Greeks consider stoning him, but he saves himself by taking refuge at Athena's altar; she herself takes vengeance on him during his voyage home.[25] Odysseus kills Astyanax;[26] Neoptolemus receives Andromache as his prize, and the rest of

---

[21] The plaque is one of the *Tabulae Iliacae*, for which see Squire, below in this volume, p. 504. A further possible testimonium, another relief plaque (recorded by Davies (1988: 61)), refers to various warriors at the Sack, but it is not certain that the item is meant to illustrate our poem.

[22] Ps.-Apollod. *Epit.* 5.14–23.

[23] Admittedly, Proclus does allow some overlap between the two poems. By the end of his account of the *Ilias parva*, the Trojans have brought the horse into the city and are celebrating their deliverance, whereas in his summary of the *Iliou persis*, they have not made up their minds what to do with the beast. Still, even here we can see how he avoids repetition: only in his summary of the latter does he mention the various options discussed by the Trojans, when we may presume that they debated their course of action in the *Ilias parva* too. (The *Tabula Iliaca*, on which see n. 21 above, in its illustration of the *Ilias parva* shows Sinon accompanying the horse into Troy, hands bound behind his back; this suggests the story familiar from Virgil, in which he is left behind by the Greeks to persuade the Trojans to accept the horse, and so implies a discussion or debate.) Stesichorus' poem almost certainly began with Epeius and the construction of the horse (see Finglass (2013b)).

[24] For the different accounts of Laocoon's death see Coo (2011: 49–52).

[25] It is not clear whether the poem contained a (brief) account of the Greeks' return home, or whether the poet referred proleptically to Ajax's future trauma.

[26] For Astyanax in epic, tragedy, and art see further Kern (1918).

the spoil is divided up. Theseus' sons Demophon and Acamas find their grandmother Aethra and take her back with them.[27] The Greeks then set fire to Troy and sacrifice Polyxena at Achilles' tomb.[28]

Ps.-Apollodorus goes into more detail in several places. Some of these may be taken from our poem, such as the three possible fates for the horse, which differ slightly from those found in Homer. But other passages had an alternative origin: for example, in Ps.-Apollodorus, Aeneas flees during the sack, whereas in the *Iliou persis* he departs after seeing the portent of the serpents. Hence we must be cautious in supplementing Proclus' narrative with material taken from Ps.-Apollodorus. For example, he tells us that Cassandra, supported by Laocoon, wanted to destroy the horse. The intervention of the serpents in the *Iliou persis* makes it certain that Laocoon was involved at that early stage, but it does not follow that Cassandra was too. She may have featured at the end of the poem, too, since Ps.-Apollodorus mentions that she was assigned to Agamemnon. Equally, the poet may have omitted her entirely; Ps.-Apollodorus could have taken the references to her from other accounts of the fall of Troy.

The fragments add little flesh to the bare bones offered by Proclus:

The horse was a hundred feet long and fifty feet wide, and its tail and knees could move (*PEG* F 2 = D. = F 1 W.).[29]

The brothers Machaon and Podalirius featured in the poem as sons of Poseidon,[30] the one an expert surgeon, the other skilled in making diagnoses. See ***PEG* F 4 = F 1 D. = F 2 W.**, from Σ T Hom. *Il.* 11.515 ἰούς τ' ἐκτάμνειν ἐπί τ' ἤπια φάρμακα πάσσειν ('the cutting out of arrows and the spreading of soothing medicines'):

ἔνιοι δέ φασιν ὡς οὐδὲ ἐπὶ πάντας τοὺς ἰατροὺς ὁ ἔπαινος οὗτός ἐστι κοινός, ἀλλ' ἐπὶ τὸν Μαχάονα, ὃν μόνον χειρουργεῖν τινες λέγουσι· τὸν γὰρ Ποδαλείριον διαιτᾶσθαι νόσους... τοῦτο ἔοικε καὶ Ἀρκτῖνος ἐν Ἰλίου πορθήσει νομίζειν, ἐν οἷς φησι·

αὐτὸς γάρ σφιν ἔδωκε πατὴρ <γέρας> Ἐννοσίγαιος
ἀμφοτέροις, ἕτερον δ' ἑτέρου κυδίον' ἔθηκεν
τῶι μὲν κουφοτέρας χεῖρας πόρεν ἔκ τε βέλεμνα

---

[27] For this episode in early literature see Finglass (2013a).
[28] Archaic and classical traditions concerning Polyxena and her sacrifice are discussed by Coo (2011: 160–8).
[29] Σ Monac. on Verg. *Aen.* 2.15 'Arctinus says that it was 100 feet long and 50 feet wide, and that its tail and knees could move.' Servius auctus on Verg. *Aen.* 2.150 '"the huge horse": some record that this horse was 120 feet long and 30 wide, and that its tail, knees, and eyes could move'.
[30] Elsewhere their father is Asclepius.

σαρκός ἑλεῖν τμῆξαί τε καὶ ἕλκεα πάντ' ἀκέσασθαι,
τῶι δ' ἄρ' ἀκριβέα πάντα ἐνὶ στήθεσσιν ἔθηκεν
ἄσκοπά τε γνῶναι καὶ ἀναλθέα ἰήσασθαι·
ὅς ῥα καὶ Αἴαντος πρῶτος μάθε χωομένοιο
ὄμματά τ' ἀστράπτοντα βαρυνόμενόν τε νόημα.

But some say that this commendation does not apply generally to all doctors, but specially to Machaon, who certain people say was the only one to do surgery, as Podalirius tended illnesses... This seems to be the view also of Arctinus in the *Sack of Ilion*, where he says:

> For their father the Earth-shaker himself gave them both the healing gift; but he made one higher in prestige than the other. To the one he gave defter hands, to remove missiles from flesh and cut and heal all wounds, but in the other's heart he placed exact knowledge, to diagnose what is hidden and to cure what does not get better. He it was who first recognized the raging Ajax's flashing eyes and burdened spirit.

This refers to the greater Ajax, who killed himself before the beginning of the poem.

Astyanax was killed by being hurled from the walls of Troy (***PEG* F 5 = F 3 D. = W.**, from Σ Eur. *Andr.* 10):

<οἳ δέ> φασιν ὅτι <οὐκ ἔμελλεν> ὁ Εὐριπίδης Ξάνθωι προσέχειν περὶ τῶν Τρωϊκῶν μύθων, [*FgrHist* 765 F 21], τοῖς δὲ χρησιμοτέροις καὶ ἀξιοπιστοτέροις· Στησίχορον μὲν γὰρ [F 107 Finglass = *PMGF* F 202] ἱστορεῖν ὅτι τεθνήκοι, καὶ τὸν τὴν Πέρσιδα συντεταχότα κυκλικὸν ποιητὴν ὅτι καὶ ἀπὸ τοῦ τείχους ῥιφθείη, ὧι ἠκολουθηκέναι Εὐριπίδην.

But others say that Euripides was not likely to pay attention to Xanthus on the myths about Troy, but only to the more serviceable and trustworthy sources: Stesichorus records that Astyanax was dead, and the Cyclic poet who composed the *Sack* that he was in fact hurled from the wall, and Euripides has followed him.

Agamemnon includes the sons of Theseus (i.e. Demophon and Acamas) and Menestheus among the recipients of spoil after the sack (***PEG* F 6 = F 4 D. = F 6 W.**), from Σ Eur. *Tr.* 30–1 τὰς δὲ Θεσσαλὸς λεώς / εἴληχ' Ἀθηναίων τε Θησεῖδαι πρόμοι ('... and some the Thessalian army has received, and the sons of Theseus, lords of the Athenians'). The scholiast comments:

ἔνιοι ταῦτά φασι πρὸς χάριν εἰρῆσθαι, μηδὲν γὰρ εἰληφέναι τοὺς περὶ Ἀκάμαντα καὶ Δημοφῶντα ἐκ τῶν λαφύρων ἀλλὰ μόνην τὴν Αἴθραν, δι' ἣν καὶ

> ἀφίκοντο εἰς Ἴλιον Μενεσθέως ἡγουμένου. Λυσίμαχος δὲ [*FgrHist* 382 F 14]
> τὸν τὴν Πέρσιδα πεποιηκότα φησὶ γράφειν οὕτως·
>
>> Θησείδαις δ' ἔπορεν δῶρα κρείων Ἀγαμέμνων
>> ἠδὲ Μενεσθῆϊ μεγαλήτορι ποιμένι λαῶν.
>
> Some say that this is said to please the audience, as Acamas and Demophon took nothing from the booty but only Aethra, on whose account they went to Ilion in the first place under Menestheus' leadership. But Lysimachus says that the author of the *Sack* writes as follows:
>
>> To the sons of Theseus the lord Agamemnon gave gifts, and to great-hearted Menestheus, shepherd of peoples.[31]

A further fragment describes how the Palladium, given by Zeus to Dardanus, remained hidden in Troy; the Greeks stole a replica that had been placed in public as a decoy (***PEG* F 1 = F dub. D. = F 4 W.**), from Dion. Hal. *Ant. Rom.* 1.69.3:

> Ἀρκτῖνος δέ φησιν ὅτι ὑπὸ Διὸς δοθῆναι Δαρδάνωι Παλλάδιον ἓν καὶ εἶναι τοῦτο ἐν Ἰλίωι τέως ἡ πόλις ἡλίσκετο, κεκρυμμένον ἐν ἀβάτωι· εἰκόνα δ' ἐκείνου κατεσκευασμένην ὡς μηδὲν τῆς ἀρχετύπου διαφέρειν ἀπάτης τῶν ἐπιβουλευόντων ἕνεκεν ἐν φανερῶι τεθῆναι, καὶ αὐτὴν Ἀχαιοὺς ἐπιβουλεύσαντας λαβεῖν.
>
> Arctinus says that a single Palladium was given by Zeus to Dardanus, and that this remained in Ilion while the city was being taken, concealed in an inner sanctum; an exact replica had been made of it and placed in the public area to deceive any who had designs on it, and it was this that the Achaeans schemed against and took.

The authenticity of the fragment has been doubted,[32] with Horsfall suggesting that the extra Palladium was invented by the Romans to bolster their claim that they possessed this venerable statue; Aeneas took it with him on his voyage to found Rome.[33] But as West counters, 'the same claim may have been made in Arctinus' time by the Aineiadai in the Troad';[34] Aeneas' escape was recounted in the *Iliou persis*, and so perhaps was his foundation of a local

---

[31] See also Ps.-Demosth. 60.29: 'The Acamantids recalled the verses in which Homer says that Acamas went to Troy on account of his mother Aethra. He, then, experienced every danger for the sake of rescuing his own mother.'

[32] First by Bethe (1929: ii.254–5, pp. 250–1 in the first edition); cf. Horsfall (1979a: 374–5; 2008) on Verg. *Aen.* 2.165–6, and Davies (1988: 65–6), who includes this fragment as a *fragmentum dubium*.

[33] Horsfall compares Dion. Hal. *Ant. Rom.* 2.66.5, where Aeneas is said to have taken the real Palladium with him, the Greeks stealing a mere copy.

[34] West (2003a: 151 n. 53).

dynasty. The idea of a false Palladium is also associated with Demophon, son of Theseus, in a myth which is unlikely to have a Roman origin.[35] The format of the story also recalls another work, Stesichorus' *Palinodes*, in which the real Helen remains in Egypt while the Greeks recover a mere εἴδωλον from Troy.[36] Those poems provide an unquestionably archaic parallel for an account of two Palladia, one genuine, one false.

THE CHARACTER OF THE POEM

Extant early accounts of the sack are so brief that there is little room for significant comparison. Nevertheless, we can follow up a few details. For example, in the *Odyssey* the debate over what to do with the horse takes place after the Trojans have dragged the Greeks' gift inside the city; Stesichorus, by contrast, sets their discussion outside, an altogether more logical course.[37] Proclus does not reveal where the debate takes place in the *Iliou persis*. A location inside the city is more likely, for the following reasons.[38] First, Proclus' κατακρημνίσαι makes better sense if the horse is inside; there are no cliffs in the vicinity of the seashore, whereas it would be possible to cast the device off the walls of the city.[39] Second, Proclus states that the Trojans began to feast after taking their decision. A decision taken inside the walls is naturally followed by feasting throughout the city. If the Trojans were outside the walls, they would have to feast on the beach (an improbable location), or first return to the city (yet Proclus makes no reference to such a return). Third, Ps.-Apollodorus (*Epit.* 5.16) locates the debate inside the city, and we may imagine that this is an episode where he has been influenced by our poem.

In the *Odyssey* Deiphobus is killed by Odysseus and Menelaus, whereas in Proclus' summary, only Menelaus is named. Perhaps the *Odyssey* includes Odysseus as one of the killers to glorify the protagonist of that epic;[40] perhaps the *Iliou persis* features only Menelaus to emphasize the particular antagonism between the wronged husband and his wife's lover. (This could

---

[35] Polyaen. *Strat.* 1.5; Sourvinou-Inwood (2011: 225–62).
[36] For this connexion see Zeitlin (2010: 277–8), who cites earlier literature.
[37] See F 103.33 Finglass = *PMGF* S88 F 1 col. ii.6: 'hurrying to a temple onto the acropolis...', a line which comes from the debate on what to do with the horse. These words imply that the Trojans are not already in either of these locations, and so are most likely outside the city; see Noussia-Fantuzzi, below in this volume, p. 437.
[38] I owe these observations to Professor Tsagalis.
[39] Cf. *Od.* 8.508 κατὰ πετράων βαλέειν ἐρύσαντες ἐπ' ἄκρης ('to drag it to the height and cast it down the rocks'); Proclus' word seems to evoke the same picture.
[40] Thus West (2012: 230).

be the poet's innovation, or he might be returning to an already-existing version of the myth that Homer changed for his own purposes.) It is possible but unlikely that Proclus has abbreviated the perpetrators, and that Odysseus takes part in the killing in the *Iliou persis* too.[41] The poem tends to attribute one wrongdoing to each hero: Menelaus kills Deiphobus, Odysseus kills Astyanax, Neoptolemus kills Priam, Ajax rapes Cassandra. And when two men are involved (Demophon and Acamas), Proclus mentions both of them.

In the *Odyssey*, the three courses of action discussed by the crowd are to pierce the horse, to cast it from a cliff, or to let it be. Proclus' account shows a slight variation: the first option is the same as the second in the *Odyssey*, and the second to set it on fire. The difference is unlikely to be significant. In the *Iliou persis* Astyanax is thrown from the walls of Troy by Odysseus, but by Neoptolemus in the *Ilias parva*. Each poet may have had a reason for assigning this grim task to a particular warrior, but without the complete text, which would enable us to examine questions of motive and characterization, we cannot tell. The *Ilias parva* also includes the theft of the Palladium, by Odysseus and Diomedes, but there is no indication that the statue is a mere copy, as in the *Iliou persis*.

Amid all this uncertainty, I venture three tentative points about the overall presentation of the sack in the epic.

(i) The sheer number of events that have to be fitted into two books means that the narrative was probably somewhat breathless. As a consequence, the emotional impact of any one scene is likely to have been muted. Contrast Virgil's account in the *Aeneid*, where (for example) the death of Priam is described at length with such pathos. The one surviving extended quotation from the *Iliou persis* spends a surprisingly long time delimiting the respective expertise of a pair of medics. One has to wonder whether the poet was wise to use eight lines in this way, given his decision to recount such a detailed narrative within so brief a poem.

(ii) In Homer Demodocus omits the grim deeds of the sack. The only specific event that he mentions is the visit of Odysseus and Menelaus to Deiphobus, a reasonable enough mission given that Helen fell to him after Paris' death; his mutilation and killing, prominent in later accounts, is not mentioned.[42] By contrast, the *Iliou persis* goes out of its way to to depict the Greek assault in an unflattering light. Neoptolemus

---

[41] The argument that follows is owed to Professor Tsagalis.　[42] Cf. e.g. Verg. *Aen.* 6.494–7.

kills Priam at Zeus' altar; Ajax rapes Cassandra despite her clinging to Athena's statue; death is meted out to infants (Astyanax) and women (Polyxena).[43] Little here glorifies the Greek conquerors.[44]

(iii) The poem seems especially interested in the house of Aeneas. He slips away before the sack; the two Palladia may be connected with him, as discussed above; and the survival of one of Laocoon's children may symbolize the preservation of one line of the Trojan royal house (that of Anchises), while the other is destroyed (Priam's).[45] The survival of Aeneas' family is briefly noted elsewhere in early epic, and seems to have been prominent in Stesichorus.[46] Our poet may have given particular emphasis to this motif because of a connexion with a dynasty claiming descent from Aeneas, or (for purely literary reasons) to emphasize the survival of the Trojans despite the violence and cruelty of the Greeks. The potential for such a sophisticated contrast between slaughter and salvation was certainly there. But without the original text, we cannot tell whether the poet took advantage of it. The same difficulty frustrates any attempt to assess the character of this enigmatic poem.

---

[43] The *Odyssey* knows of Ajax's death at the hands of the gods, but 'is reticent as to the reason for Athena's wrath' (S. West (1988: on 1.325–7, with discussion).

[44] All these events took place in Stesichorus, and several in the *Ilias parva*.

[45] Thus Robert (1881: 192–3).

[46] Cf. *Il.* 20.300–8 and *HHomAphr.* 196–7, with Faulkner (2008: 3–18), and the discussion of the *Tabula Iliaca* in Davies and Finglass (2014: 428–36); Finglass (2014).

20 | *Nostoi*

GEORG DANEK

If we can trust the plot structure given by Proclus, the *Nostoi* closely corresponded to the scattered return accounts of Nestor, Menelaus, Odysseus and Agamemnon (and Proteus) in the *Odyssey*:[1] following a quarrel caused by Athena, the Achaeans split up right at their departure from Troy and sailed off at different times and on different routes. Nestor and Diomedes who were first reached their homes safely. Menelaus who was second lost most of his ships and was driven to Egypt. Agamemnon and the Locrian Ajax sailed off last and met a storm that caused Ajax's death, while Agamemnon reached his home only to find his death by Aegisthus and Clytaemnestra. Later on Orestes took revenge, and Menelaus arrived at home.

Proclus includes two more storylines, untold in the *Odyssey*: Calchas and other heroes walked along the coastline of Asia Minor up to Colophon, where Calchas died; and Neoptolemus walked along the coastline of Thrace, joined the Molossians in Epirus and finally met his grandfather Peleus. But Proclus leaves no doubt that the *Return of the Atreidai*[2] constituted the main storyline of this epic, occupying the beginning, the dramatic centre, and the end of the narrative.[3]

Ps.-Apollodorus (*Epit.* 6.1–30) follows the same sequence of events as Proclus, with fuller wording and more details. He leaves out a few details told by Proclus, gives a sense of the full stories of Calchas and Neoptolemus which are just adumbrated in Proclus, and adds (parts of) storylines which clearly interrupt the stream of narrative. Apart from these additions, and with necessary caution, we may take his account as a fuller version of the same source used by Proclus: the text of the *Nostoi*, or rather a handbook prose version of it. As there are no other sources for the plot of the *Nostoi*,[4]

---

[1] The main reports are: *Od.* 3.130–98 and 3.254–312 (Nestor); 4.351–586 (Menelaus, including Proteus' reports, 492–537 and 555–60); 9.39–81 (Odysseus); 11.409–34 (Agamemnon); for important minor remarks see 4.81–94, 4.120–36, 4.219–32, 9.39–81, 11.533–7.

[2] Athenaeus twice attests an epic titled Ἀτρειδῶν κάθοδος ('Return of the Atreidai'). West (2003a: 17) sums up a long discussion (see Bethe 1929: 270–5) stating that this was an alternative title for the *Nostoi*.

[3] This was first shown by Bethe (1929: 262–83).

[4] The few fragments (for which see below) give no hint at the plot structure.

we should trust Proclus when he calls the epic he summarizes 'The Returns, by Agias of Troizen, in five books'.

Different explanations have been proposed for the striking similarities between the *Nostoi* and the *Odyssey*. Scholars in antiquity, following Aristarchus, posited that the *Epic Cycle* was written after the Homeric epics and the *Nostoi* simply followed the lead of the *Odyssey*.[5] Opinions changed with Analysts who held that the *Telemachy*, which contains the return accounts, belongs to the last layers of the *Odyssey* and thus follows the text of the *Nostoi*.[6] Neoanalysts modified this thesis assuming that both the *Odyssey* and the *Nostoi* were modelled on an oral Nostos epic that had already found a stable shape of content and plot (Kullmann's 'Faktenkanon').[7] This view matches recent currents of oral theory claiming that traditional epic singers never aim at challenging or changing stories sanctioned by tradition.[8] Thus, for many scholars nowadays the congruence of the *Odyssey* and the *Nostoi* proves that in oral tradition the story of the Achaeans' Return had been told long before the *Odyssey* precisely in this way.[9]

Now the *Odyssey* unmistakably presupposes the knowledge of the story of the Achaeans' Return: the highly allusive and elliptical style of Nestor's and Proteus' accounts is directed at primary narratees who are able to put together and complement the piecemeal distributed information units. After all, the λυγρὸς νόστος Ἀχαιῶν ('sad return of the Achaeans') (*Od.* 1.326–7, cf. 3.312–3) is presented as being familiar to the persons of the story. This enables us to reconstruct a catalogue of story elements sanctioned by the pre-Homeric tradition: Ajax's rape of Cassandra; Athena's wrath as cause for the Achaeans' failed return; Ajax's death in the storm; Agamemnon's murder by Aegisthus, and Orestes' revenge; Menelaus' stay in Egypt (possibly), and Odysseus' wanderings (certainly).

But this *Faktenkanon* was not automatically bound to the plot structure that we find in the *Odyssey*. That the Achaeans split up right at Troy belongs to the *Odyssey*'s narrative strategy of relegating the return stories to the prehistory of the plot and distributing them among several eyewitness narrators.[10] Unlike omniscient narrators, Nestor and Menelaus only

---

[5] Cf. *Suda* v 500 Adler, s.v. 'νόστος': 'The poets of the *Returns* follow Homer as far as possible, too.' For a full discussion of Aristarchus and the *Epic Cycle*, see Severyns (1928).

[6] Bethe (1929: 262–83).

[7] Kullmann (2002a: 173–4) refers to the PhD thesis of Schischwani (1994).

[8] This postulate of Lord (1960) and Nagy (1990b, and later) is not confirmed by the South Slavic tradition, see Danek (2012).

[9] See generally Burgess (2001), without specific arguments for the *Nostoi* (for a detail, see 154–5); most recently Anderson (2011); Petropoulos (2012); West (2012: 231).

[10] See de Jong (2001: 76–7).

tell what they experienced or what they heard by hearsay;[11] thus the homecomings of most heroes are not touched at all. Still we are left with the impression of 'getting the whole story', thanks to Proteus who, as a god, is able to add details about the deaths of Ajax and Agamemnon, who have left no surviving eyewitnesses.

Those heroes who are treated in full offer a variety of comments on, and comparison with, the fate of Odysseus:[12] Ajax insults Poseidon and is killed by him, as opposed to Odysseus who also offended this god but can rely on Athena's help;[13] Agamemnon is slain by a rival who managed to seduce his wife, while Penelope still resists her suitors; Orestes kills his father's slayer, which prompts Telemachus to oppose, and finally kill, the suitors; Menelaus must overcome a final divine obstacle to find his way home, while Odysseus still has to escape from Poseidon's wrath.

The return of the Achaeans is split up both in space and time: Nestor and Diomedes sail across the open sea; Agamemnon and Ajax take their way through the Cyclades; Odysseus sails along the coastline. Concerning time, the single narrative units seemingly follow the time order of the single returns:[14] Nestor first recounts his own group's homecoming, which took place first; in a second narrative unit he reports how Menelaus' journey was delayed; then he mentions Agamemnon's homecoming and death, the full record of which is only given when Menelaus reports Proteus' account. Finally, we must wait until *Odyssey* 9 for learning how Odysseus set off from Troy, which suggests that he departed last.

But the impression that the Achaeans met their respective fates one after the other is delusive.[15] By calculating how many days it takes each hero to reach his home or to be thrown off course, we learn that Menelaus, Ajax, Agamemnon and Odysseus are affected by a storm at different places within the Aegean, but at the same day. Thus there was only one storm, i.e. the storm that caused the death of Ajax.[16]

The split-up of the Achaeans' returns was thus conceptualized precisely to meet the requirements of the *Odyssey*'s narrative strategy, i.e. to present the

---

[11] For hearsay accounts, see *Odyssey* 3.186–92, where Nestor mentions the successful homecomings of Neoptolemus, Philoctetes and Idomeneus.
[12] See Hölscher (1990: 300–5); Olson (1995: 24–42).
[13] Athena as protector of Odysseus at Troy: 3.219 (see Hölscher (1990: 98)); as initiator of his return: 1.48–95, and *passim*. Clay (1983) has argued that Athena's anger was directed against Odysseus, too. But see Danek (1998) s.v. 'Athena, Zorn der' in the index.
[14] Hölscher (1990: 98–9).
[15] I discussed what follows at length in Danek (1998: 165–71; 2005: 48–50).
[16] Athena as the author of the storm is only alluded to with καὶ ἐχθόμενός περ Ἀθήνηι ('though he was hated by Athena') (4.502).

return tales as flashbacks and eyewitness accounts, and to disguise Athena as the cause of the Achaeans' failed return. Above all, an omniscient narrator who was not bound to such requirements could follow a much easier path to tell the tale of the Achaeans' Return. If we try, as a *Gedankenexperiment*, to condense this tale to the outline of a 'Simple Story',[17] we get this hypothetical script:

> *The Achaeans start together from Troy. Athena sends a storm which affects them all, with varying results: some of them die, some lose most of their ships, and most of them are thrown off course and 'lose their return'.*

This plot structure is condensed in a quasi-formulaic expression of the *Odyssey* (3.130–1 = 13.316–17; cf. 14.241–2):

> αὐτὰρ ἐπεὶ Πριάμοιο πόλιν διεπέρσαμεν αἰπήν,
> βῆμεν δ᾽ ἐν νήεσσι, θεὸς δ᾽ ἐκέδασσεν Ἀχαιούς...
>
> but when we destroyed Priam's high city
> and stepped in the ships and a god dispersed the Achaeans...

The underlying plot structure is even better expressed when Hermes gives to Calypso a condensed summary of Odysseus' failed return (*Od.* 5.105–11):

> φησί τοι ἄνδρα παρεῖναι ὀιζυρώτατον ἄλλων,
> τῶν ἀνδρῶν, οἳ ἄστυ πέρι Πριάμοιο μάχοντο
> εἰνάετες, δεκάτωι δὲ πόλιν πέρσαντες ἔβησαν
> οἴκαδ᾽· ἀτὰρ ἐν νόστωι Ἀθηναίην ἀλίτοντο,
> ἥ σφιν ἐπῶρσ᾽ ἄνεμόν τε κακὸν καὶ κύματα μακρά.
> ἔνθ᾽ ἄλλοι μὲν πάντες ἀπέφθιθεν ἐσθλοὶ ἑταῖροι,
> τὸν δ᾽ ἄρα δεῦρ᾽ ἄνεμός τε φέρων καὶ κῦμα πέλασσεν.
>
> ...[Zeus] says, there is a man here, more miserable than all others, one of those men who fought over the city of Priam for nine years, and sacked it in the tenth and went home, but offended on their return (ἐν νόστωι) Athena, who excited against them an evil wind and high waves. Then all others perished, his excellent comrades, but as for him, the wind and waves brought him near here...

Hermes suppresses Odysseus' wanderings by connecting the beginning and the end of his travels, and Calypso immediately corrects him (Zeus, and not Athena, caused Odysseus' final shipwreck). Still we sense that the highly allusive character of Hermes' summary is meant to remind us of the

---

[17] For the narratological concept of the 'einfache Geschichte' see Hölscher (1990: 25–34).

well-known story of how Athena's storm damaged *all* the Achaeans and caused the beginning of Odysseus' wanderings.[18]

That this was the quasi-canonical version of the traditional Return Tale is confirmed by the observation that this version prevailed from the archaic period through late antiquity, in spite of the authority of the *Odyssey*: the storm in the Aegean is given as explanation why the Achaeans were dispersed in texts like Alcaeus F 298 Voigt; Sappho F 17 Voigt; Aesch. *Ag.* 650–80 and 841–4; Eur. *Tro.* 77–94; *Hel.* 123–32, 766–7 and 1126–31; Virg. *Aen.* 11.255–65; Ov. *Met.* 14.466–82; Hyg. *Fab.* 116; Ps.-Apollod. *Epit.* 6.15–22; Dictys 6.1–2. There can thus be no doubt that this version of the Achaeans' Return prevailed already in the pre-Homeric oral tradition. The poet who composed our *Odyssey* used this traditional version as an intertextual foil for his novel version, urged by his specific narrative requirements (flashbacks, eyewitness accounts) and interpretive aims (downplaying of Athena's role).[19]

Consequently, the pre-Homeric Nostos epic of the oral tradition was not the only source of inspiration of the *Nostoi*, as its plot construction followed exactly the lead of the *Odyssey*. The close correspondence between the *Nostoi* and the *Odyssey* is thus best explained by assuming that the poet of the *Nostoi* aimed at sticking closely to the main data of the *Odyssey*, and transforming the piecemeal elliptical flashback accounts into a continuous full account by an omniscient narrator.

But what about those storylines of the *Nostoi* which do not stem from the *Odyssey*? Here we may ask once again how the *Odyssey* represents the Return of the Achaeans. When Phemius sings of 'the dreadful return of the Achaeans from Troy which Pallas Athena had imposed' (*Od.* 1.326–7), the phrasing evokes the traditional plot as sketched above: the Achaean return ended in a collective disaster, caused by Athena, the most prominent result of which was the death of Agamemnon[20] and the disappearance of many heroes, including Odysseus. This explains why Penelope reacts with despair to Phemius' song, and it opens the way for the eyewitness accounts of Nestor, Menelaus and Odysseus, who know how things really happened, and thus correct Phemius, the *aoidos autodidaktos* ('selftaught') (*Od.* 22.347) who relies on *kleos*, i.e. hearsay, which is identical with the narrative tradition.

But neither Phemius nor Nestor knows about the fates of those heroes who did not arrive home but ended up somewhere else. Here we might hope to learn more from Proteus, who announces to tell how 'many of them died,

---

[18] See Danek (1998: 126–7).

[19] It may have become clear by now that I firmly believe in a single poet who was responsible of the precise plot composition and phrasing of the *Odyssey* as we have it. See Danek (1998; 2012).

[20] Agamemnon's death and Orestes' revenge are already known in Ithaca (*Od.* 1.298–300).

and many were left behind' (*Od.* 4.495);[21] but he, too, restricts his account of those 'left behind' to Odysseus alone (4.498). The *Odyssey* thus omits a whole category of heroes, those who never returned home but settled somewhere else. But this does not mean that those heroes did not exist, i.e. that there were no such stories stored in tradition, even before Homer.

Post-Homeric tradition abounded in such stories. Most of them look like local legends, invented by *poleis* that wanted to trace back their origins to prominent founding heroes, and have thus been dated to the time after the Greek colonization. But, as Malkin has shown, many of them may well have existed earlier.[22] This can best be seen in those cases where Greek *poleis* claimed a kind of double *ktisis*, one by the 'historical' *oikistēs* who performed the ritual act of *apoikia* in the name of his mother city, and the other one by a 'mythical' *oikistēs*, preferably a Trojan War hero. In this perspective, the end of the Age of Heroes became the beginning of the historical age leading to Greek settlements all over the Mediterranean.[23]

The most prominent wandering hero was Odysseus, whose presence is attested all over northwestern Greece and southern Italy. The *Odyssey* betrays a profound knowledge of his traditional centrifugal bias. But as it runs counter to Homer's presentation of him as a centripetal hero par excellence, it is concealed in his lying tales and in Teiresias' prophecy of his inland journey after his arrival at Ithaca.[24] In the *Odyssey*, the wandering Odysseus is relegated to the world of counterfactual alternative versions – while all the other heroes who had similar fates are simply excluded from the narrative (e.g. Teucer and Calchas) or treated in such a truncated way that their wanderings, or post-return fates, are left out (as we will see for Diomedes and Neoptolemus).

We are now in the position to understand how Agias situated the *Nostoi* between the broad stream of floating, ever-changing traditional Return Tales, on the one hand, and the *Odyssey* as an authoritative attempt at monopolizing this tradition, on the other hand. I will now go on to discuss some aspects of this intertextual process, first by elucidating the main

---

[21] 'They were left' (ἐλίποντο) does not mean 'they survived', as translators and commentators understand it, but 'they were left away from home'.

[22] Malkin (1998).

[23] This perspective is epitomized in Ps.-Apollodorus (*Epit.* 6.15): 'The Greeks, driven apart, landed and settled here and there, some in Libya, some in Italy, others in Sicily, some on the close-by Iberian Islands, others at the river Sangarios. Some of them even colonized Cyprus.'

[24] See Danek (1998: 224–5).

characters of the plot, and then by focussing on aspects of narrative technique: time, space, key motifs, style, and plot construction.

But first I will examine the contribution of the fragments to our understanding of the narrative strategy of the *Nostoi*, following the sequence of events given in Proclus.

THE FRAGMENTS

PEG F 1 (= D. = F 11 W.), from Ps.-Apollodorus *Bibl.* 2.1.5

ἔγημεν [Ναύπλιος], ὡς μὲν οἱ τραγικοὶ λέγουσι, Κλυμένην τὴν Κατρέως, ὡς δὲ ὁ τοὺς Νόστους γράψας, Φιλύραν... καὶ ἐγέννησε Παλαμήδην Οἴακα Ναυσιμέδοντα.

Nauplius married Clymene the daughter of Catreus, according to the tragedians, but according to the author of the *Returns* he married Philyra... and he fathered Palamedes, Oeax, and Nausimedon.

Ps.-Apollodorus tells us that in the *Nostoi* Philyra, the wife of Nauplius, was mentioned, which means that Nauplius himself played a role in the *Nostoi*.

PEG F 2 (= D. = F 13 W.), from Σ Hom. *Od.* 4.12

αὕτη, ὡς μὲν Ἀλεξίων... ὡς δὲ ὁ τῶν Νόστων ποιητής, Γέτις.

She was, as Alexion says, ... but as the poet of the *Returns* says, a Getic.

I prefer to think that the poet of the *Nostoi* christened the mother of Megapenthes (who is nameless in the *Odyssey*) Getis.

PEG F 3 (= D. = F 1 W.), from Pausanias 10.28.7

ἡ δὲ Ὁμήρου ποίησις ἐς Ὀδυσσέα καὶ ἡ Μινυάς τε καλουμένη καὶ οἱ Νόστοι (μνήμη γὰρ δὴ καὶ ἐν ταύταις Ἅιδου καὶ τῶν ἐκεῖ δειμάτων ἐστίν) ἴσασιν οὐδένα Εὐρύνομον δαίμονα.

But Homer's poem about Odysseus and the so-called *Minyas* and the *Returns* (for in these too there is mention of Hades and the terrors in it) know of no demon Eurynomus.

Starting from this note by Pausanias, the following fragments can be best allocated to the plot of the *Nostoi* if we assume that the named persons figured in catalogical entries of a Nekyia comparable to that of the *Odyssey*.

PEG F 4 (= F 9 D. = F 3 W.), from Athenaeus 7.281b

φιλήδονον δὲ οἱ ποιηταὶ καὶ τὸν ἀρχαῖον φασι γενέσθαι Τάνταλον. ὁ γοῦν τὴν τῶν Ἀτρειδῶν ποιήσας κάθοδον ἀφικόμενον αὐτὸν λέγει πρὸς τοὺς θεοὺς καὶ συνδιατρίβοντα ἐξουσίας τυχεῖν παρὰ τοῦ Διὸς αἰτήσασθαι ὅτου ἐπιθυμεῖ· τὸν δέ, πρὸς τὰς ἀπολαύσεις ἀπλήστως διακείμενον, ὑπὲρ αὐτῶν τε τούτων μνείαν ποιήσασθαι καὶ τοῦ ζῆν τὸν αὐτὸν τρόπον τοῖς θεοῖς. ἐφ᾽ οἷς ἀγανακτήσαντα τὸν Δία τὴν μὲν εὐχὴν ἀποτελέσαι διὰ τὴν ὑπόσχεσιν, ὅπως δὲ μηδὲν ἀπολαύῃ τῶν παρακειμένων ἀλλὰ διατελῇ ταραττόμενος, ὑπὲρ τῆς κεφαλῆς ἐξήρτησεν αὐτῶι πέτρον, δι᾽ ὃν οὐ δύναται τῶν παρακειμένων <ἡδονῆς> τυχεῖν οὐδενός.

The poets say that old Tantalus too was a voluptuary. At any rate the author of the 'Return of the Atreidai' tells that when he came to the gods and spent some time with them, and was granted the liberty by Zeus to ask for whatever he wanted, he, being insatiably devoted to sensual pleasures, spoke of these, and of living in the same style as the gods. Zeus was angry at this, and fulfilled his wish, because of his promise, but so that he should get no enjoyment from what was set before him but suffer perpetual anxiety: he suspended a boulder over his head. Because of this he is unable to get <pleasure from> anything set before him.

The detailed version of the story of Tantalus which Athenaeus reports from the *Atreidōn kathodos,* may be read as the prehistory of what we read about Tantalus in the *Odyssey*.

PEG F 5 (= F 4 D. = F 4 W.), from Pausanias 10.29.6

ἔστι δὲ πεποιημένα ἐν Νόστοις Μινύου μὲν τὴν Κλυμένην θυγατέρα εἶναι, γήμασθαι δὲ αὐτὴν Κεφάλῳ τῷ Δηίονος, καὶ γενέσθαι σφίσιν Ἴφικλον παῖδα.

It is written in the poem *Returns* that Clymene was the daughter of Minyas, that she married Cephalus the son of Deion, and that their child was Iphiclus.

Pausanias refers to a picture of Clymene in Hades, with more details than in the *Odyssey*.

PEG F 6 (= F 5 D. = F 5 W.), from Pausanias 10.30.5

ὑπὲρ τούτους Μαῖρά ἐστιν ἐπὶ πέτραι καθεζομένη. περὶ δὲ αὐτῆς πεποιημένα ἐστὶν ἐν Νόστοις ἀπελθεῖν μὲν παρθένον ἔτι ἐξ ἀνθρώπων, θυγατέρα δὲ αὐτὴν εἶναι Προίτου τοῦ Θερσάνδρου, τὸν δὲ εἶναι Σισύφου.

Above these is Maira, sitting on a rock. Concerning her it is written in the poem *Returns* that she departed from mankind still a virgin, and that she was the daughter of Proitos son of Thersander, and that he was a son of Sisyphus.

Here too, Pausanias refers to a picture of Maera in Hades, with genealogical details.

PEG F 7 (= F 6 D. = F 6 W.), from the hypothesis (a) to Euripides *Medea*, p. 88 Diggle

περὶ δὲ τοῦ πατρὸς αὐτοῦ (Ἰάσονος) Αἴσονος ὁ τοὺς Νόστους ποιήσας φησὶν οὕτως·

αὐτίκα δ' Αἴσονα θῆκε φίλον κόρον ἡβώοντα,
γῆρας ἀποξύσασα ἰδυίῃσι πραπίδεσσιν,
φάρμακα πόλλ' ἕψουσα ἐνὶ χρυσέοισι λέβησιν.

About Jason's father Aison the poet of the *Returns* says:

And straightway she [Medea] made Aeson a nice young lad, stripping away his old skin by her expertise, boiling various drugs in her golden cauldrons.

In the *Nostoi*, Medea rejuvenated her father-in-law Aeson (quotation of three verses). She may have been found in Hades.

PEG F 8 (= F 7 D. = F 7 W.), from Clement of Alex. *Strom.* 6.2.12

Ἀντιμάχου τε τοῦ Τηίου εἰπόντος·

ἐκ γὰρ δώρων πολλὰ κάκ' ἀνθρώποισι πέλονται (*Epig.* PEG F 4 = Antim. 2 D. = F 2 W.),

Ἀγίας ἐποίησεν·

δῶρα γὰρ ἀνθρώπων νόον ἤπαφεν ἠδὲ καὶ ἔργα

And where Antimachus of Teos had said:

For from gifts much ill comes to mankind,

Agias wrote:

For gifts delude people's minds and (corrupt) their actions.

Clement quotes a verse of Agias (the manuscripts have Aug[[e]]ias), which possibly may have been said of Eriphyle staying already in Hades.

PEG F 9 (= p. 75 D. = F 8 W.), from Σ Hom. *Od.* 2.120

Μυκήνη Ἰνάχου θυγάτηρ καὶ Μελίας τῆς Ὠκεανοῦ, ἧς καὶ Ἀρέστορος Ἄργος, ὡς ἐν τῶι κύκλωι φέρεται.

Mycene was the daughter of Inachus and the Oceanid Melia. She and Arestor were the parents of Argos, as it is related in the Cycle.

Mycene, too (with more details than in *Od.* 2.120) in the *Nostoi* may have stayed in Hades.

PEG F 10 (= T 2 D. = F 10 W.), from a second-century beaker (MB36: Sinn (1979: 101))

(a) [Ἀ]γαμέμνων
(b) [κατὰ τὸν ποιητὴν] Ἀ[γίαν] ἐκ τῶν [Ν]όστων Ἀχα[ι]ῶν. θάνατος Ἀγαμέμ[νο]νος.
(c) Κλυταιμήστρα / Κασσάν[δρα] / Ἀγαμέμνων
(d) ΝỊỊỊΑΣ (?)/ Ἀλκμέων / Μήστωρ / Αἴαντος / Ἀντ[ί]οχος / Ἀργεῖος.

(a) Agamemnon.
(b) [After the poet] A[gias], from the [*Re*]*turns of the Achaeans*: the death of Agamemnon.
(c) Clytaemestra, Cassandra, Agamemnon.
(d) ?, Alcmaon, Mestor son of Ajax, Antiochos, Argeios.

One of the Macedonian 'Homeric Cups'[25] shows the death of Agamemnon, naming as its source the *Nostoi* and, possibly, the first letter of its poet, 'A'. One scene has Clytaemnestra killing Cassandra over the body of Agamemnon; on the other one Agamemnon, lying on a sofa, is attacked by (supposedly) Aegisthus, while three of his companions (Alcmaon, Mestor, son of Ajax, and an illegible EIIICHS or NIIIAS (?)), are attacked by two aggressors named Antiochus and Argeius. So we have the same scene as described in the Odyssey, but enriched with specified names of fighters on both sides.

PEG F 11 (= F 8 D. = 12 W.), from Athenaeus 9.399a

Ἶσον δ' Ἑρμιονεὺς ποσὶ καρπαλίμοισι μετασπών
ψύας ἔγχεϊ νύξε

Hermioneus reached Isos with his swift feet and stabbed him in the groin with his spear.

Athenaeus cites from the *Atreidōn kathodos*. The battle scene may have belonged to the killing of Agamemnon.

PEG F 12 (= p. 75 D. = F 2 W.), from *Etymologicum Gudianum* 405.1 Sturz s.v. 'νεκάδες'

παρὰ μὲν τοῖς κυκλικοῖς αἱ ψυχαὶ νεκάδες λέγονται

In the Cyclic poets the souls of the dead are called *nekades*.

---

[25] See Squire, below in this volume, pp. 497–500.

F 9 W., from Philodemus, *De pietate* B 4901 Obbink

τὸν Ἀσκλ[ηπιὸν δ' ὑ]πὸ Διὸς κα[τακταν]θῆναι γεγρ[άφασιν
Ἡ]σίοδος... λ[έγεται] δὲ καὶ ἐν το[ῖς Νόσ]τοις.

He]siod has written that Ascl[epius] was killed by Zeus... [It is sai]d also in t[he *Ret*]*urns*.

As far as the reconstruction of the text can go, Philodemus would have reported that in the *Nostoi* Asclepius was killed by Zeus. Possibly he stayed in Hades, too.

Most of these fragments contain additional information about persons who are mentioned in the *Odyssey* just by name (11.326: Maera, Clymene; 2.120: Mycene; 11.259: Aeson, 4.12: Megapenthes' mother) or in an allusive way (the killing of Agamemnon and Aegisthus; 11.326–7: Eriphyle; 11.582–92: Tantalos). So we may ponder whether some other mythological details can be allocated to the *Nostoi*, too.

Pausanias (1.22.6) describes a painting on the Acropolis in which Orestes killed Aegisthus, and Pylades killed 'the sons of Nauplius who came to assist Aegisthus'. The names of Nauplius' sons on the painting (which Pausanias does not cite, but must have read) may have stemmed from a detailed battle description in the *Nostoi* (see West 2003a: 163 n. 65).

Ps.-Apollodorus (*Epit.* 6.30) tells us that Menelaus was deified by Hera. As this detail is not contained in the *Odyssey* (see 4.563–4), it may stem from the *Nostoi*.

Σ *Od.* 3.188 tells how Neoptolemus was directed by Helenus away from Phthia towards Epirus. Although we are told that the story was related by Eratosthenes, this may be limited to the last sentence of the story, which says that the kings of Molossia went back to Molossus, son of Neoptolemus and Andromache. The story as a whole may well go back to the *Nostoi*.

Taken as a whole, the fragments support the assumption that the poet of the *Nostoi* worked in the footsteps of the *Odyssey* and tried to fill in the gaps left open in the earlier epic. This impression will be confirmed in our discussion of the characters.

CHARACTERS

I will discuss all characters who appear in Proclus' summary, adding Nauplius, and closing with Hades who does not appear in Proclus and is, strictly speaking, not a character at all, but deserves discussion anyhow.

Menelaus: Proclus and Ps.-Apollodorus show no significant difference from the scattered accounts of the *Odyssey*. Ps.-Apollodorus makes us guess that here, too, Menelaus was delayed due to the death of Phrontis at Sounion, as in the *Odyssey* (3.276–85), and sailed off only after Nestor and Diomedes reached their homes, as Proclus seems to imply. One fragment shows that his son Megapenthes was mentioned, probably at the occasion of his marriage (*Od.* 4.5–9), which may imply that Hermione was wedded to Neoptolemus, too. We may ask if the *Nostoi* gave a full record of Menelaus' travels or just a summary account, as in the *Odyssey*.[26] It can be ruled out that Agias used the motif of Helen's stay in Egypt during the Trojan War, even if we assume that it was not 'invented' by Stesichorus but already stored in tradition and alluded to in the *Odyssey*.[27] Otherwise, it would have been inevitable that Proclus and Ps.-Apollodorus remark on that motif. The *Nostoi* thus stuck closely to the time frame and the plot version defined in the *Odyssey* and excluded competing versions.

Agamemnon: Here, too, we get full accordance with the *Odyssey*, but no details. Nothing can be said about the circumstances of Agamemnon's arrival at home, nor about Clytaemnestra's role in the ambush. Proclus and Ps.-Apollodorus suggest that his assassination was told only after the report of Neoptolemus' journey, just before the account of Orestes' revenge. This implies that Agias left Agamemnon's fate open after the storm in the Aegean, inserted the Neoptolemus story, and only then harked back in time to resume Agamemnon's story. Athenaeus, however, mentions a brief passage on Hermioneus and Isos from book 3 of the *Return of the Atreidai*, *PEG* F 11 = F 8 D. = 12 W. quoted above. Neither name points at any known myth. West suggests Hermioneus was 'a son of Menelaus who assisted Orestes in the battle against Aigisthos' men'.[28] But if Orestes' revenge was told already in book 3, what content was left for books 4 and 5? It seems more plausible to assign the fragment to the battle between Agamemnon and Aegisthus, which implies that Agamemnon's homecoming was told right after Athena's storm, and that Agias strove for epic colouring in a fully described battle scene.

Nestor: He was destined to return home, because tradition had it that some generations later the Neleids, his descendants were driven out of Pylos by the returning Heracleidai, came to Athens and participated in the

---

[26] See below, p. 375.
[27] For allusions to 'Helen in Egypt' in the *Odyssey* see Danek (1998: 101–6).
[28] West (2003a: 163 n. 66).

'Ionian Migration'. Our earliest witness of this narrative tradition is Mimnermus,[29] which means that it was well established in the seventh-century and known to the authors of the *Odyssey* and the *Nostoi*. We have no means for judging how, if at all, Nestor's arrival at Pylos and the fate of his descendants were related in the *Nostoi*. Most probably the *Nostoi* did not add to what we read in the *Odyssey*.

Diomedes: He returns to Argos safely both in the *Odyssey* and in the *Nostoi* (Proclus, confirmed by Ps.-Apollodorus). Later sources, however, had him leave again and settle in the Adriatic or in Italy where he enjoyed hero cult at several places.[30] He left Argos when he learnt that Aphrodite, avenging his wounding her on the battlefield (*Il*. 5.330–430), had instigated his wife Aegialeia to commit adultery during his absence.[31] Some sources combine his departure from Argos with his intervention in Calydon to help his grandfather Oeneus. Parts of the story are attested for Mimnermus, which has been doubted on good grounds.[32] But scholars have seen a pointed allusion to this tale already in *Il*. 5.406–15, where Dione talks about Aegialeia's presumed grief over her husband in case he should die at Troy ('things will come out the other way round...'), and the re-elimination of the Aetolian intruder Diomedes from the Argive royal house may have been prescribed by pre-Homeric tradition, anyhow. If Aegialeia's adultery, caused by Aphrodite, and Diomedes' flight from Argos were treated in the *Nostoi*,[33] this episode interrupted the succession of narrative time. Now it cannot be ruled out that his future fate was mentioned in passing, perhaps in a narratorial prolepsis like this: 'he arrived happily at home, fool that he was, who did not know what awaited him at home...'. But it seems more probable that the poet of the *Nostoi* followed the lead of the *Odyssey* in suppressing the traditional tales about Diomedes' post war career.[34]

Calchas: The text of Proclus makes little sense: Calchas, Leonteus and Polypoites walked on foot to Colophon and buried Teiresias who died

---

[29] Mimn. *IEG* F 10 has Andraemon of Pylos as the founder of Colophon. Mimn. *IEG* F 9 has new settlers coming from the 'Neleid Pylos' replace former inhabitants of Colophon. Pherecydes (Strab. 14.1.3) called them Carians; mythological thinking may have identified them as the Achaeans who arrived with Calchas.

[30] For Diomedes in the West, see Malkin (1998: 234–57).

[31] Alternative versions had Aigialeia instigated by Nauplius (see below, p. 369).

[32] Mimn. *IEG* F 22. West corrects the authority cited by Σ Lycophr. 610 from Μίμνερμος to καὶ Ὅμηρος (as in Eustathius who reports the same tale), and refers it only to the wounding of Aphrodite.

[33] Thus Severyns (1928: 371–6).

[34] Paranoid readers of the *Odyssey* might point out that Nestor does not say that Diomedes himself arrived at Argos, but only his comrades (*Od*. 3.180–1).

there. The full story is told in Ps.-Apollodorus: Amphilochus, Calchas, Leonteus, Podaleirius and Polypoites left their ships in Troy, walked on foot to Colophon and buried Calchas, not Teiresias. Why Calchas died is told at some length: Mopsus, grandson of Teiresias, challenged Calchas to a mantic contest which lasted for several rounds each of which was won by Mopsus. In the end Calchas died from distress. The story was told in the Hesiodic *Melampodia* (F 278–9; Strabon cites six verses). In other sources (as early as Herod. 7.91), the remaining Achaeans continued their journey together with Mopsus and settled in Caria (Podaleirius), Pamphylia (Polypoites and Leonteus) and Cilicia (Amphilochus). As Proclus and Ps.-Apollodorus do not mention this continuation of the tale, the most remarkable feat about the presentation of the story in the *Nostoi* may have been that it stopped right after the burial of Calchas, thus limiting the geographical horizon to Aeolia and Ionia.

Ajax: Proclus does not mention Ajax's crime at the beginning of the *Nostoi*, apparently because he has just told the episode in his summary of the *Iliou persis*.[35] Perhaps the *Nostoi* started with an assembly scene, in typical epic manner,[36] which gave room for presenting the prehistory of the plot and resulted in Calchas' decision to evade the goddess' anger on foot.[37] The *Odyssey* offers some details on Ajax's death: shipwrecked, and hated by Athena, he saved himself on a rock with the help of Poseidon. Only when he insulted all the gods, Poseidon shattered the rock and brought him to death. This strange combination conforms to the theology of the *Odyssey*, where Athena's wrath does not cause any hero's death. In Ps.-Apollodorus' account, to the contrary, Athena herself crashes Ajax's ship with a thunderbolt. When he boasts to have saved himself in spite of Athena's wrath, Poseidon shatters the rock and drowns him. Thetis buries his corpse on Mykonos. This version shows a simpler theology than the *Odyssey*, as Athena tries everything to cause Ajax's death and gets additional help from Poseidon. The motif of divine burial, however, suggests ritual afterlife, which runs counter to the theology of the *Odyssey* and may stem from local (Locrian) tradition.

Nauplius: He does not figure in the *Odyssey*.[38] Proclus sums up the events in the Aegean in a single sentence: 'Then the storm at the Capherean Rocks

---

[35] Ps.-Apollodorus presents the events in due order (*Epit.* 5.25–6.1): 'When they wanted to sail off having destroyed Troy, Calchas stopped them saying that Athena was angry with them due to Ajax's crime. And they wanted to kill Ajax, but he took refuge to an altar and they let him go. Subsequently they joined an assembly, and Agamemnon and Menelaus started a quarrel...'

[36] See Petropoulos (2012).   [37] Davies (1989c: 78).

[38] Odysseus' heinous murder of Palamedes and its consequences are deliberately omitted in the *Odyssey*, see Danek (1998 s.v. 'Palamedes' in the index), and Maronitis (1973: 160–77).

is narrated, and the death of the Locrian Ajax.' Elsewhere the storm which caused Ajax's death is located at Tenos, Mykonos or Andros,[39] while the Capherean Rocks (Euboea) are the place where Nauplius, in revenge of his son Palamedes' murder, ambushed the returning Achaeans by making their ships crash on the rocks. Nauplius' revenge functions as a double of the divine wrath of Athena: one could tell the Trojan War either as a story of conflict between Odysseus and Palamedes, with Nauplius' vengeance as the cause for Odysseus' wanderings, or as a prolonged series of divine wrath and punishment which extinguished first the Trojan and then the Achaean party. Later authors, including Ps.-Apollodorus, combine both motifs: the Achaeans were struck by Athena's storm and consequently driven to the Capherean Rocks where, due to Nauplius' beacons, their ships were clashed or dispersed in all directions. Nauplius was mentioned in the *Nostoi*.[40] Maybe the *Nostoi* poet was first in linking the version followed in the *Odyssey* with the Nauplius tradition. Ps.-Apollodorus (*Epit.* 6.8–11) adds in a digression another part of Nauplius' vengeance: he convinced the wives of several heroes, among them Clytaemnestra and Aegialeia, to commit adultery. But it is improbable that it was contained in the *Nostoi* where it could figure only as an external analepsis.[41]

Neoptolemus: In the *Odyssey* he sails off from Troy with his share of booty (11.533–7), leads the Myrmidons home safely (3.188–9), and is ruling 'in the city of the Myrmidons' ten years later (4.5–9). How he managed to get there is left open, as Nestor does not specify whether Neoptolemus crossed the Aegean by himself or in a different way. Things sound different in the *Nostoi* (Proclus and Ps.-Apollodorus here complement each other): Neoptolemus and Agamemnon first stay in Troy, detained by the ghost of Achilles. Then they sail to Tenedos where Thetis advises Neoptolemus to wait two more days and then make his way on foot, accompanied by the Priamid Helenus.[42] He meets Odysseus at Maroneia in Thrace, on his way buries Phoenix, joins the Molossians, defeats them and becomes their king. He has a son with Andromache, Molossus. When Peleus is expelled from Phthia by the sons of Acastus he leaves Helenus in Molossia and weds him to Deidameia, 'is recognized by Peleus' and 'takes over his father's kingdom',

---

[39] The location of the *Gyrai petrai* (*Od.* 4.500) was disputed in antiquity.
[40] Fragment 11 (West) only says that in the *Nostoi* Nauplius' wife was named Philyra. West links this with a painting on the Acropolis described by Pausanias (1.22.6) where Nauplius' sons, fighting on the side of Aegisthus, were killed by Pylades.
[41] Severyns (1928: 371–6) argues that the tale was included in the *Cypria*.
[42] Neoptolemus thus parts company with Agamemnon only at Tenedos, in imitation of (or allusion to) the *Odyssey* where Odysseus parts company with Nestor at Tenedos and sails back to Agamemnon at Troy (*Od.* 3.159–64).

which implies that he overcomes the sons of Acastus and leaves Molossia for Phthia.[43] The presence of Neoptolemus in Molossia, close to the Ionian Sea, far from his father's kingdom in Phthia, was sometimes explained by ambitions of the Molossian ruling dynasty to trace back their origins to a prominent Trojan War hero. But politically motivated appropriation of the mythical ancestor Molossus may well go back to the seventh century,[44] and there are traces of a close connection between Achilles and Dodona (*Il.* 16.233–5), as well as connections between Epirus (Dodona) and Thessaly, apparently rooted in population movement in (pre-)archaic times.[45] Stories about the presence of Neoptolemus in Epirus may thus have circled in epic tradition long before Homer. In other versions Neoptolemus' ship was carried off by the Big Storm as far as Epirus, where he became king of the Molossians (Pind. *Nem.* 7.36–40). Neoptolemus' wandering on foot is paralleled in a story told by Herodotus (7.20): before the Trojan War, wandering forces of the Teucrians and Mysians conquered the whole of Thrace and Northern Greece as far as the Ionian Sea. But the *Nostoi* may rather have been inspired by the *Odyssey*, where Odysseus sails along the coast of Thrace, evidently in order to evade the open sea.[46] Neoptolemus, then, becomes in the *Nostoi* a kind of heir to Odysseus whom he meets right at the beginning of his march through Thrace. The dynastic conflict between Peleus and (the sons of) Acastus is alluded to already in the *Iliad* (24.488–52) and the *Odyssey* (11.494–503).[47] Agias has thus not 'invented' the motif but taken it over from the pre-Homeric tradition. Perhaps the poet of the *Odyssey* knew most of these traditional tales of Neoptolemus but suppressed them on purpose, at the same time trying not to contradict them: Odysseus just knows that Neoptolemus sailed off from Troy, and Nestor just knows that he arrived at home, sometime later. What came in between is kept in silence. The poet of the *Nostoi*, in contrast, filled in the gaps left in the *Odyssey* but took pains not to contradict his model text.

Odysseus: Proclus says that Neoptolemus 'when he reached Thrace came across Odysseus at Maroneia'. Burgess ventures the idea 'that the *Nosti* once also narrated the return of Odysseus', presumably in a flashback by Odysseus in Hades at the end of the plot.[48] This idea can be ruled out as soon as we

---

[43] We cannot tell how much of this was told in the *Nostoi*. Ps.-Apollodorus goes on to recount Neoptolemus' conflict with Orestes about Hermione, and his death at Delphi, both of which do not fit in the time-frame of the *Nostoi*.
[44] See Malkin (1998: 136–8); Funke (2000).
[45] See the evidence discussed in Janko (1992: 348–9), and Malkin (1998: 147–50).
[46] See Danek (1998: 165–71).   [47] See Danek (1998: 240–1).   [48] Burgess (2001: 142–3).

accept that the *Nostoi* tried not to contradict the *Odyssey*. The meeting of Neoptolemus and Odysseus alludes to the episode of the Cicones in *Odyssey* 9 that has been shown to be no part of the pre-Homeric tradition but a free adaptation of an expedition of Odysseus to Thrace during the Trojan War.[49] The poet of the *Nostoi* thus signalled that he was well aware of the authority of the *Odyssey* and did not want to compete with it, but to supplement it.

Orestes: In the *Odyssey*, Orestes 'came back from Athens, killed his father's murderer ... and gave a funeral feast for the Argives on behalf of his hateful mother and the coward Aegisthus' (3.306–10). No more details. Proclus has just 'Then follow Orestes' and Pylades' avenging of Agamemnon's murder by Aegisthus and Clytaemestra' (West). Ps.-Apollodorus recounts the full biography of Orestes, well known from tragedy, starting from the point when Electra handed him over to the Phocian Strophius, and ending only with his death. How much of this was contained in the *Nostoi* must remain guesswork. I doubt, at least, that in the *Nostoi* Orestes married Hermione, as this contradicts the *Odyssey* where Hermione is wedded to Neoptolemus. I prefer to think that the *Nostoi* ended shortly after the homecoming of Menelaus, and therefore had no place for the further biography of Orestes. There remains one divergence from the *Odyssey*.[50] In the *Nostoi*, Orestes comes from Delphi together with Pylades; in the *Odyssey* Orestes comes from Athens, and no companion is mentioned. The difference is best explained if we assume that Homer knew Pylades but left him out on purpose in the *Odyssey*, where his mention would imply that Telemachus, too, should return to Ithaca with a companion. On the other hand, the role of Peisistratus in the *Telemachy* may have been modelled on Pylades. The poet of the *Nostoi* has then added a traditional detail, which in the *Odyssey* was left out on purpose.

Missing characters: Several heroes who are reported to 'have lost their returns' are not mentioned in the *Odyssey* and did not figure in the *Nostoi*. Teucer was expelled from Salamis by his father Telamon and settled on Cyprus (Pind. *Nem.* 4.46). Philoctetes arrived home according to Nestor (*Od.* 3.190), but most sources had him settled in Italy.[51] Idomeneus arrived home according to Nestor (*Od.* 3.191–2) but ended up in Italy, too, in later sources. Eurypylus was driven to Lydia (Lyc. 901–2). Ps.-Apollodorus

---

[49] Kakridis (2001).

[50] The *Odyssey* avoids specifying that Orestes killed his mother because Telemachus must not be encouraged to kill Penelope. But in the *Odyssey*, too, Clytaemnestra died together with Aegisthus (3.309–10).

[51] Malkin (1998: 214–26).

(*Epit.* 6.15 a) lists several heroes who settled elsewhere, including Antiphus, Pheidippus, Agapenor, Menestheus, Acamas and Demophon, while Prothous was drowned at the Capherean Rocks.

Hades: Pausanias (10.28.7 = *PEG* F 3 = F 3 D. = F 1 W.) reports that in the *Nostoi* there was 'mention of Hades and the monsters in it'. Several persons are attested to have figured in the *Nostoi* who find no place in the main plot.[52] Their presence is best explained if they were mentioned on the occasion of a Katabasis, or at the arrival in Hades of a hero who had just died.[53] Scholars have speculated at which point of the plot, and connected with whose entrance in Hades, and with what, if any, function for the plot, the 'monsters in Hades' were inserted. Several prominent heroes 'go to Hades' in the *Nostoi*, even in Proclus' summary,[54] and we may add, as a guess, that Neoptolemus consulted the Thesprotian νεκυομαντεῖον.[55] But we may content ourselves with stating that the Nekyia obviously did not influence the overall plot structure of the *Nostoi*.

TIME

The biggest challenge for epic singers who wanted to tell the traditional story of the Return of the Achaeans as a narrative unity consisted in how to manage narrative time. As all the heroes were sent on their respective journeys through the storm in the Aegean, they experienced their fates at different places, but at the same time. This ruled out the possibility of following the events in chronological order. Singers who wanted to comprise the fates of all the return heroes had to rely on the form of a catalogue, and were thus limited to comprehensive remarks on each hero. But they could not present the single return stories as an extended all comprising epic tale

---

[52] Tantalus (possibly offering the background of *Od*. 11.582–92); Maera, Clymene and possibly Eriphyle (expanding on their mention in a single verse of the *Odyssey*'s Nekyia, 11.326), Medea and Aeson (Aeson: *Od*. 11.259), Mycenae (possibly expanding on her mention in *Od*. 2.120), and Asclepius. See Severyns (1928: 387–99).

[53] Severyns (1928: 385–6) argues that the *Nekyia* of the *Nostoi* was a first-person account of Odysseus during his meeting with Neoptolemus at Maroneia. This runs counter to the time scheme of the plot.

[54] Calchas, Ajax, Agamemnon, Phoenix, Aegisthus, Clytaemnestra.

[55] See West (2003a: 18): 'The least unlikely suggestion is perhaps that the souls of Agamemnon and those killed with him were described arriving in the underworld, like the souls of the Suitors in *Odyssey* 24.1–204.' More sceptical Bethe (1929: 281): 'Es ist zwecklos, zu raten.'

claiming internal coherence.[56] It seems plausible, therefore, that oral singers rarely tried to present the returns of all the Achaeans in a single epic story.

The poet of the *Odyssey* solved this problem, as we have seen, by shifting the split up of the Achaeans from the middle of the Aegean to their departure from Troy, by treating only a limited choice of heroes, and by making them have their return travels one after another – actually the apparent sequence of events in chronological order conceals the fact that some of the return travels overlap in time and thus veil a disguised simultaneity.

Agias adopted the time-frame of the *Odyssey* for the plot of the *Nostoi*. But minor differences to the *Odyssey* reveal that he aimed at transforming the pretended continuity of time into a real one, and that he avoided to include simultaneous events. We can thus reconstruct the time schedule of the *Nostoi* as a continuous sequence of events following one after another:

- *In medias res*: Assembly, quarrel of Agamemnon and Menelaus (Day 0)
- [Calchas foresees the forthcoming catastrophe and sets off on foot]
- Nestor and Diomedes sail as far as Tenedos (Day 1), then Lesbos (Day 2) and Euboea (Day 3). They leave Menelaus at Sounion, while Diomedes reaches Argos 'on Day 4' (*Od.* 3.180). Nestor [rounds Malea and] arrives safely at Pylos (Day 5)
- Menelaus starts from Sounion and is driven off course at Malea (Day 6), and once again when he passes Crete (Day 7) on his way to Egypt[57]
- Calchas arrives at Colophon (Day 7)[58] and meets his destiny
- Agamemnon and the rest of the army, having been detained by the phantom of Achilles,[59] set off for Tenedos (Day 8)
- Thetis instructs Neoptolemus to stay there for two more days
- In the meantime, Agamemnon's party sets off and meets the storm at the *Gyrai petrai*. Ajax dies. They are driven to the Capherean Rocks (Day 9)
- Agamemnon continues his journey and is slain by Aegisthus (Day 10)

---

[56] Lesky (1966: 81) extends this verdict to the *Nostoi*, too: 'The element of catalogue must have been very prominent in the construction of such a poem.'

[57] Either the narrator left Menelaus after passing Crete (Day 7), or he accompanied him as far as Egypt, which takes five more days (see *Od.* 14.257) (Day 12). On this assumption, we must add five days to the rest of our time schedule.

[58] Or (Day 12) which seems more plausible: on modern roads, the distance between Troy and Colophon amounts to 340 km (Google Maps).

[59] The appearance of Achilles has found no comment so far. Has the poet of the *Nostoi* moved back the sacrifice of Polyxena, which was initiated by the phantom of Achilles, from its traditional position to the time after the departure of Nestor, Diomedes and Menelaus, in order to explain the delay of Agamemnon's departure?

- Now Neoptolemus starts from Tenedos (Day 11), sails to the Thracian coast, and at Maroneia meets Odysseus, who has started directly from Troy, has already fought the Cicones, and is just being entertained by the priest Maron
- Neoptolemus leaves his ships and walks on foot (Day 12). His march takes several weeks,[60] and his ensuing adventures may span several years (fighting and kingship in Molossia; fighting and regaining of the kingdom in Phthia)
- Eight years after Agamemnon's death (*Od.* 3.306), Orestes and Pylades kill Aegisthus and Clytaemnestra
- On the day of Aegisthus' funeral, Menelaus arrives at Mycenae, wins back his kingdom in Sparta and weds his daughter Hermione to Neoptolemus

This time schedule offers a clear-cut criterion for deciding which parts of Ps.-Apollodorus can be labelled additional insertions: Nauplius' fraud on the heroes' wives (§ 8–11, external analepsis), the final part of Neoptolemus' life (§ 14, external prolepsis), the fates of those heroes who were carried off by the big storm (§ 15–22, internal analepsis, combined with internal and external prolepses), and the fate of Orestes after his matricide (§ 25–8, external prolepsis).

The time schedule can be refined if we assume that the poet of the *Nostoi* imitated Homer in presenting simultaneous lines of action by hopping to and fro between different scenes.[61] On this assumption we may compose this script:

> *Agamemnon sails off, leaving Neoptolemus on Tenedos, and passes by Tenos and Caphereus. While he is sailing on towards Mycenae, the narrator switches to Neoptolemus who is just starting from Tenedos. While he is on his way to the Thracian coast (which takes him a whole day) Agamemnon reaches Mycenae, and we get a full account of his murder by Aegisthus. After all the blood has been spilt the narrator switches back to Neoptolemus who is just landing at Maroneia and facing another enemy, the Cicones whose city has just been plundered by Odysseus...*

Similar solutions may be suggested for other transitions. This would bring about even closer connections between the narrative strands, and a high thematic coherence between the single return stories.

---

[60] The distance from Maroneia to Dodona amounts to 550 km (Google Maps).
[61] On this narrative technique, first described by Zielinski (1899–1901), see Rengakos (1995). On 'Zielinski's Law', see now Scodel (2008b).

Our synchronization model helps us decide if Menelaus' adventures, which covered eight years, were told in full or not: if the narrator continued his report on Menelaus after bringing him to Egypt, he had to hark back in time for resuming the storyline of Calchas; if he told it at the end of the plot, he had to cover the time between the very beginning and the end of the plot through an internal completing narratorial analepsis, both narrative techniques unheard of in the *Iliad* and the *Odyssey*. Even an internal completing personal analepsis would run counter to Zielinski's rule. So, Menelaus' travels may have been subsumed in the *Nostoi* in a short cut similar to the *Odyssey* (3.300–2; 4.81–9).

SPACE

In the (pre-)Homeric narrative tradition, the return of the Achaeans caused an expansion of the geographical space from mainland Greece to large areas of the Mediterranean. The final generation of heroes conquered the geographical space that was still occupied by Greeks in historical times.

In the *Odyssey*, the returning heroes re-established their former reigns in mainland Greece and Crete. Geographical space outside of this zone offered no room for new settlements, but remained reserved for wandering, merchandising and raiding activities – apart from the fantasy world of Odysseus' wanderings.

In the *Nostoi*, the boundaries of the settlement area of Greek heroes got slightly expanded in two directions, to the northwest of mainland Greece, and to Ionia in the east. But this expansion did not persist, as Calchas died at Colophon, and Neoptolemus returned back home after ruling in Molossia for a short time. The world of heroes remained bound to its tight geographical limits.

PROPHECIES, BURIALS AND HERO CULTS

In contrast to the *Iliad* and the *Odyssey*, the *Nostoi* abounded both in prophecies and hero cults. Plot relevant prophecies included Calchas who foretold the fatal consequences of Ajax's crime;[62] Calchas and Mopsus during their mantic contest; Achilles who foretold the forthcoming disaster; Thetis who

---

[62] Calchas' prophecy which was part of the *Iliou persis* according to Proclus and Ps.-Apollodorus must have played a deciding role in the quarrel between Agamemnon and Menelaus.

warned Neoptolemus against crossing the Aegean; Helenus who advised Neoptolemus where to settle;[63] and Proteus who foretold an afterlife in Elysium to Menelaus and Helen.[64]

Proclus and Ps.-Apollodorus mention burials of several heroes, none of which furthers the plot progress. Thus we may look for some other function they had in the poem. The instalment of hero cult may be the answer. Phrontis was buried at Sounion (*Od.* 3.278–85 and Ps.-Apollodorus *Epit.* 6.29),[65] perhaps an echo of his ritual worship there.[66] Calchas was buried at Colophon, which points at the foundation of the oracle at Claros. Podaleirius who followed Calchas ended up in the Carian Chersonesos, certainly an *aition* for the cult of Asclepius at Cnidos and Cos.[67] Thetis buried Ajax on Mykonos, which may point to an established hero cult of Ajax. Neoptolemus buried Phoenix on his way, which may point to a hero cult of Phoenix in Thrace.[68] Neoptolemus may have buried Peleus, too. Orestes buried Aegisthus (*Od.* 3.309–10), which may reflect a hero cult of Aegisthus at Mycenae.

This all attests to a manifest interest by the poet of the *Nostoi* in supernatural motivation, contrary to the rationalistic spirit which dominates in the *Iliad* and the *Odyssey*, and characteristic of the *Epic Cycle*.[69]

STYLE

About the style of the *Nostoi* we can say next to nothing. The five and a half verses which survive in citations show the usual epic diction, interspersed with 'Homeric' phrases. The longest fragment (*PEG* F 7 = F 6 D. = W.) has been criticized as containing 'a number of infelicities of expression'.[70]

---

[63] According to the Σ *Od.* 3.18, Helenus interpreted a portent according to which Neoptolemus should settle at a place where he sees a house with iron fundaments, wooden walls and a woollen roof. In Epirus he met people living in tents made of their own spears and garments, and conquered them. We cannot tell if the story was contained in the *Nostoi*.

[64] *Od.* 4.561–9 (Proteus' prophecy). In Ps.-Apollod. *Epit.* 6.30, the text runs: 'after being immortalized by Hera, he goes to Elysium with Helen'. As Hera is not mentioned in the *Odyssey*, Ps.-Apollodorus follows here the *Nostoi*.

[65] In the *Odyssey*, the sudden death of Menelaus' helmsman explains why Menelaus is caught up in the storm, although he crosses the Aegean as fast as possible. See Danek (1998: 93).

[66] See Currie (2006: 53–4): 'The archaeological findings may suggest a hero cult of Phrontis at Sounion going back to about 700 BC.'

[67] See Bethe (1929: 278). See, however, above, p. 368, where I suggest that this storyline stopped short before Podaleirius set off for Caria.

[68] Bethe (1929: 277) suggests 'thrakische Siedlungssagen'.

[69] Griffin (1977).   [70] See also Davies (1989c: 81).

This reminds us of the fact that the excellence of phrasing which we find in the *Iliad* and the *Odyssey* is not nearly matched by the poets of the Hesiodic corpus, the Hymns, or the *Epic Cycle*. This does not come as a surprise to anyone familiar with a living oral epic tradition, where you find few, if any, brilliant poets, in contrast to a broad mass of average singers who stick closely to prefabricated formulas, contents and plots, coined and transmitted by the anonymous tradition.

PLOT

We can now read the plot of the *Nostoi* as a symmetrical structure in five parts, like five acts of a tragedy.[71] Parts one, three, and five contain the main storyline, concerned with the fates of the Atreidai: part 1 is framed by the quarrel between the two brothers and the failed return of Menelaus;[72] part 3 contains Agamemnon's fatal return; part 5 includes Orestes' revenge and Menelaus' final return. Parts 2 and 4 offer interludes, each of them occupied by heroes who travel on foot, not by ship, and occupy regions on the fringes of the heroic world. The interludes are interlaced with the main storyline so as to avoid the impression of a catalogical enumeration of unconnected travels: the Calchas story of part 2 points back to Calchas' interpretation of Athena's wrath which led to the Atreidai's quarrel at the beginning of part 1; the Neoptolemus story of part 4 is prepared for at the beginning of part 3, when his father's ghost warns Agamemnon against crossing the Aegean, and when Thetis advises Neoptolemus to delay his departure until Agamemnon has met his fate. Neoptolemus may have turned up again at the end of part 5 when, after Menelaus' successful homecoming, his marriage with Hermione was narrated or, at least, announced.

The *Nostoi* thus exemplified a variety of (almost) all possible outcomes of returns: some heroes returned safely (Nestor, Diomedes), some returned after a long delay (Menelaus), some died on their way home (Ajax), some on their return (Agamemnon), some died although they tried to evade their fates (Calchas), and some found a new home, but then regained their inherited kingdom (Neoptolemus). Thus the *Nostoi* broadened the spectrum of the *Odyssey* but, like the *Odyssey*, avoided treating those heroes who permanently settled somewhere else.

---

[71] West (2003a) aptly arranges Proclus' summary in five paragraphs. The five parts need not have been identical with the five books.

[72] In the *Odyssey* (3.247–312) the delay of Menelaus' return explains why he could not prevent his brother's death.

The poet of the *Nostoi* offered an extensive narrative of those return heroes who figured in the *Odyssey*. Thus he presented a kind of prequel to the *Odyssey*: people who heard or read the *Nostoi*, gathered all the needed information to understand the allusive and elliptical return accounts of the *Odyssey*. To this fuller version of the Odyssean return accounts he added a limited choice from a broad mass of return stories stored in tradition. The poet of the *Nostoi* refrained from including even a representative part of those stories – which forced Ps.-Apollodorus to insert a whole series of them in catalogue form. This may partly explain why the *Nostoi* obviously had no success in antiquity, which is evidenced by the fact that they are even less cited or referred to in ancient literature than most other epics of the *Trojan Cycle*: the *Nostoi* were not representative enough of the tradition of Return Stories as a whole to be read on their own merits.

IDEOLOGY

Different attempts at representing the traditional tales of the Achaean Return resulted in different visions on continuity and identity, centred on the question how the gap between the age of heroes and the historical period was bridged.

In the pre-Homeric as well as post-Homeric tradition the failed return of the Achaeans led to internal strife, displacement, expulsion, exile, and in the end (via the Return of the Heracleidai and the Ionian migration) to a total reorganization of the Greek mainland and the distribution of new settlements all over the Mediterranean, as a prelude to the historical process later called colonization. The end of the Heroic Age brought about the beginning of the historical period.

The *Odyssey* strongly opposed this perspective. Here there is no end of the Heroic Age, but a reinstatement of that political order which was valid before the War. Stability is reached by a utopian freezing of the Heroic Age.[73] The gaze of Odysseus is not that of a colonial settler, but of a pre-colonial wanderer, raider and merchant, who strives to bring his booty back to his own kingdom. The *Odyssey* leaves no room for the beginning of the historical period. The gap between the race of mythical heroes and the race of historical mankind, 'such as human beings are now', is not bridged.

---

[73] Danek (1998: 504–5).

In the *Nostoi* the consequences of the Trojan War appear as the controlled reorganization of political order, which is used to expand the geographical and political horizon within well-defined limits. Compared with the *Odyssey*, the geographical view is broadened only to a limited degree. No bridge is spanned between the age of heroes and the contemporary world of the poet and his audience. Ideologically seen, thus, the *Nostoi* pursued a compromise between the 'progressive' return tales of the oral tradition and the 'conservative' *Odyssey*, but added nothing to the vision of the *Odyssey*.

21 | *Telegony*

CHRISTOS TSAGALIS

The *Telegony* (Τηλεγονία or Τηλεγόνεια)[1] by Eugammon of Cyrene in two books brings the Epic Cycle to an end. Our knowledge of its content is largely, but not solely, based on the summary of Proclus,[2] with Ps.-Apollodorus[3] offering some supplementary information that should be treated with caution.[4] The *Telegony* poses various problems for anyone wishing to reconstruct its plot, the more so since the three principal critical editions available significantly differ with respect to the number of fragments they ascribe to the actual poem.[5] Having said this, I will offer my own classification of the relevant fragments and discuss them in due course.

Plot[6]

After the burial of the suitors by their relatives, Odysseus sacrifices to the Nymphs and sails off to Elis in order to inspect his oxen-stables there. Polyxenus, who supervises his stables, offers him hospitality and gives him a bowl as a gift. The epic must have departed on a digression at this point, featuring an extended *ekphrasis* with respect to the story of Trophonius, Agamedes, and Augeas. After the completion of his inspection, Odysseus sails back to Ithaca and carries out the sacrifices Teiresias had told him to

---

[1] The former spelling (Τηλεγονία) is given by Proclus, while the latter (Τηλεγόνεια) by Herodianus (from Choeroboscus), *Gramm. Gr.* iii.1.249.9, iii.2.451.20 Lentz and Eustath. on *Od.* 16.118 (1796.48), who explains (on *Il.* 10 praef. (785.21)) this divergence in the following manner: προπαροξύνονται δὲ καὶ ἄμφω αἱ τοιαῦται λέξεις [scil. Δολώνεια, Πατρόκλεια] ὥσπερ καὶ Τηλεγόνεια κατὰ τὴν παλαιὰν ὀρθογραφίαν ἡ κατὰ Τηλέγονον πραγματεία, καὶ Ἡράκλεια ἡ κατὰ Ἡρακλέα ('both such words are accented on the antepenultimate syllable [scil. Doloneia, Patrocleia], as it is the case with *Telegoneia*, the treatment of the myth of Telegonus, according to the old spelling, and *Heracleia*, the treatment of the story of Heracles'). The spelling in –ια seems to be the correct one, despite a considerable number of variants in -εια; see West (2013: 288).

[2] *Chrest.* lines 306–30 Severyns.   [3] *Epit.* 7.34–8.

[4] On the reservations and limitations concerning the use of Ps.-Apollodorus' mythographical collection, see the pertinent remarks by Davies (1989c: 7).

[5] *PEG*, Davies (1988), and West (2003a).

[6] The reconstruction of the plot follows closely (with some additions, mainly but not solely from Ps-Apollodorus' *Epitome*) Proclus' summary.

perform. He then travels to the land of the Thesprotians. After marrying Callidice, queen of the Thesprotians, Odysseus becomes king and decides to stay there. He has a son with her, whose name is Polypoites. When a war breaks out between the Thesprotians and the Brygians he leads the Thesprotian army but fails to defeat the enemy. Ares and Athena support the Brygians and the Thesprotians respectively, but it is Apollo who brings the war to an end by calling for a truce. After Callidice's death, Odysseus gives the throne to Polypoites and returns to Ithaca. It is at this point that Telegonus, who has been told by his mother Circe that he is the son of Odysseus, arrives at Ithaca in search of his father and ravages the island. Odysseus tries to avert the danger but is killed by the ignorant Telegonus, who uses as a weapon a spear barbed with the spine of a sting-ray. When he realizes that he has killed his own father,[7] Telegonus laments and brings the body of Odysseus together with Telemachus and Penelope to Aeaea, Circe's island. Then, Telegonus is married to Penelope and Telemachus to Circe, who makes them all immortal.

THE QUESTION OF AUTHORSHIP

The attribution of the *Telegony* to Eugammon of Cyrene is based on Proclus,[8] Eusebius,[9] Syncellus,[10] and Clement.[11] Eustathius[12] refers to an anonymous poet from Cyrene, while Cinaethon's authorship is supported by a single reference of Eusebius.

---

[7] For the motif 'son kills his father without knowing his identity', see Potter (1902).
[8] Procl. *Chrestom.*: μετὰ ταῦτά ἐστι Ὁμήρου Ὀδύσσεια· ἔπειτα Τηλεγονίας βιβλία δύο Εὐγάμμωνος Κυρηναίου περιέχοντα τάδε ('after this [scil. *Nostoi*] comes Homer's *Odyssey*, and then the two books of the *Telegony* by Eugammon of Cyrene, with the following content, etc.').
[9] Euseb. (Hieron.) *Chron. Ol.* 56.2 year 555 BC p. 102^B 1 Helm (cf. eundem (Armen.) *Chron. Ol.* 53.2 year 567 BC p. 188 Karst: *Eugamon Cyrenaeus, qui Telegoniam fecit, agnoscitur* ('Eugamon the Cyrenean, who composed the *Telegony*, is recognized').
[10] Syncelli *Eclog. Chronogr.* 454 sine anno (p. 286 Mosshammer): Εὐγάμων Κυρηναῖος ὁ τὴν Τηλεγονίαν ποιήσας ἐγνωρίζετο ('Eugamon the Cyrenean, who composed the *Telegony*, is recognized').
[11] Clem. Alexandr. *Stromat.* 6.25.1 (2.442 Stählin) = Euseb. *Praep. Evang.* 10.2.7 (1.559 Mras): αὐτοτελῶς γὰρ τὰ ἑτέρων ὑφελόμενοι ὡς ἴδια ἐξήνεγκαν, καθάπερ Εὐγάμμων [Dindorf: Εὐγάμων Clem., Εὐγράμμων Euseb.] ὁ Κυρηναῖος ἐκ Μουσαίου [VS 2 B6] τὸ περὶ Θεσπρωτῶν βιβλίον ὁλόκληρον ('by their own initiative [the Greeks] have stolen other people's works and brought them out as their own; as Eugammon [Dindorf: Εὐγάμων Clem., Εὐγράμμων Euseb.] of Cyrene stole from Musaeus his entire book about the Thesprotians').
[12] Eust. on *Od.* 16.118, p. 1796.48: ὁ τὴν Τηλεγόνειαν γράψας Κυρηναῖος ('the Cyrenean who wrote the *Telegony*').

With the notable exception of Wilamowitz, most modern editors consider Eugammon to be the author of the *Telegony*. The almost unanimous agreement of ancient testimonia on his authorship seems to turn the scales against Cinaethon from Lacedaemon, whose false authorship has been explained through an elaborate argument by Hartmann (see below).[13] Although Eusebius (via Hieronymus) is notorious for confusing authors of the Cyclic epics (Arctinus and Eumelus being the best-known example), misattribution may in this case be very instructive with respect to the shaping of the *Telegony*. Today it is generally agreed that we are not dealing with a change of *Genealogias* into *Telegoniam* in Eusebius' (via Hieronymus) text,[14] but with a reflex of the complex process through which the *Telegony* of Eugammon came into being.

The attribution of the *Telegony* to Eugammon of Cyrene or a Cyrenean poet or redactor is based on the following argument and reflects the effort to associate one of the ancestors of the Cyrenaean dynasty with Odysseus.[15] The first wave of immigrants from Greece must have arrived in Libya at some point in the late second millennium BC. These settlers, who came from the Peloponnese and must have departed from Cape Taenarum, had already been mingled with other Thessalian immigrants in the Peloponnese and brought with them traditions about Euphemus, their mythical leader.[16] When, after 631 BC, a new wave of Dorian settlers from Thera came to Libya, their leader Aristoteles who founded Cyrene decided to be named after the Libyan title Βάττος. It is at this point that the new dynasty in its search for links with the past tried to associate itself not only with Odysseus, the paragonal traveler who in the *Odyssey* refers to a journey to Libya,[17] but also with Euphemus, the mythical leader of the first colonization.[18] The introduction of Arcesilaus as Odysseus' son from Penelope (next to Telemachus) in the *Telegony* indicates both a Cyrenaean interest and a Spartan element: the arrival of new settlers after 570 BC coincides with the reign of Battus II whose real name was Arcesilas and Odysseus' son Arcesilaus was linked though his mother's side to Sparta, since her father Icarius was

---

[13] Hartmann (1917: 78–86).

[14] See Rzach *RE* s.v. 'Kinaithon', cols. 462–3. Differently, West (2013: 32, 38).

[15] See Rzach *RE* s.v. 'Kyklos', 2431; (2013: 38–9).

[16] On the relations between Thessaly, pre-Doric Peloponnese, Crete, and Libya, see Malten (1911: 126–42).

[17] On the association between the *Odyssey* and Libya, see Debiasi (2004: 260), who draws attention to certain place names with clear Odyssean coloring (see *Etym. magn.* s.v. 'Κύκλωπες'; Herod. 4.177 (Lotus-Eaters); Ps.-Scyl. 110 (Lotus-Eaters)). He also argues, on the basis of the Hyrieus version of the Trophonius and Agamedes tale (Paus. 9.35.5–7) and Hyrieus being 'un eponimo di un centro collegato all'Eubea', that Euboea was the 'bridge' through which Odyssean features were brought to Cyrene. See also Vürtheim (1901: 22–41).

[18] In Herod. 4.150 Aristoteles-Battus is called Εὐφημίδης τὸ γένος. See Malten (1911: 151).

settled there. Another link to Sparta may be seen in the tradition presenting Euphemus as son of Poseidon and Mecionice, daughter of Eurotas[19] as well as the association of Telemachus with Thera[20] and of a certain Tainarus as son of Icarius.[21] In fact, there is also information concerning a Spartan instead of a Theran colonization of Cyrene[22] and – along the same lines – specific references to Battus as a Spartan.[23] We can see here that the Peloponnesian settlers the Therans found in Cyrene upon their arrival in 631 BC considered Euphemus their mythical leader and had no place in their myths for Icarius and Penelope. So it is not unthinkable that, when genealogical material strengthening or suggesting a Spartan connection was brought into the picture, Cinaethon, who was famous for composing genealogies, started becoming associated with a developing tradition aiming at a fusion of Spartan, Cyrenean, and local elements (see below). In tandem with this, it is possible that the misattribution of the *Telegony* to the Lacedaemonian Cinaethon is a distant echo of the complex situation described above. In other words, it is the Spartan influence that we should trace behind Cinaethon instead of looking for a real poet. Although the same may be the case with Eugammon, i.e. Cyrenean elements may explain the attribution to a Cyrenaean poet, the fact that we do not know him independently from the *Telegony* is an argument *ex silentio* against the falsification of the attribution. Other features have played their role too: the *Schauplatz* tale of Trophonius, Agamedes, and Augeas with its Egyptian coloring and Peloponnesian background,[24] as well as the insertion of Telegonus, half-brother of Arcesilaus, into the Inachid genealogy (as a king of Egypt who married Io[25] or as a son of Epaphus and brother of Libye)[26] strongly indicate that the author of the *Telegony* must be

---

[19] See Hes. *Meg. Ehoiai* F 53 M.-W. = F 14 Hirsch.

[20] In Σ Pind. *Ol.* 2.82 Telemachus is called Thera's uncle.

[21] Steph. Byz. *Ethn.* 598.6–11 Mein.: '<Taenarum> [is a] city, [named] after Taenarus, brother of Geraestus, son of Zeus. After sailing together with his brother Calabrus and taking possession of some area in the Peloponnese, he founded a sanctuary of Poseidon, which is called <Taenarum>. Taenarus is also the name of Icarius' son "after whom the city is named and the citadel and the port".'

[22] Isocr. *Phil.* 5: 'such as the place the Lacedaemonians have settled the Cyrenaeans'; Josephus, *bellum Judaicum* 2.16.4: 'neither the Cyreneans, the Laconian race'.

[23] Amm. Marc. 22.16.4: 'Cyrene is situated at the Libyan Pentapolis. It is an ancient but deserted city, which the Spartan Battus has founded'; Solin. 27, 125.10 Mommsen (2nd edn): 'greater Syrtis exhibits a city they call Cyrene, which Battius [sic] the Lacedaemonian founded in the fourty-fifth Olympiad'.

[24] See Huxley (1969: 171), who reminds us of the ample importation of laconic pottery to Cyrene during the lifetime of Eugammon and in particular of a shard on which Trophonius has been identified.

[25] Ps.-Apollod. *Bibl.* 2.9.   [26] Σ Eur. *Or.* 932.

Eugammon or an unknown Cyrenaean poet or redactor.[27] This line of argument is much more convincing than the aetiological explanation of the name Euga[m]mon through the *Doppelheirat* at the epic's end, since it explains sufficiently how the confusion between Euga(m)mon and Cinaethon may have originated.

DATE OF COMPOSITION

The *Telegony* was probably composed in the sixth century, with 570 BC operating as a *terminus ante quem*. This chronology rests on the following grounds:

(a) A Cyrenaean poet records that one of Odysseus' sons was Arcesilaus. This name is irrelevant to the poetic tradition of the *Telegony*, unless it is associated with the Cyrenaean kings Arcesilaus I and II who ruled in the sixth century.[28]
(b) Eusebius dates Eugammon in the fifty-third Olympiad (568–564 BC).
(c) In 570 BC King Arcesilaus II enlisted new settlers from various Greek cities, brought them to Cyrene, and was then able to defeat Pharaoh Apries in the battle of Irasa.[29] Given (a) and (b), it is not unthinkable that the arrival of new, Peloponnesian colonists may have functioned as a catalyst for the creation of an epic poem aiming at associating the Cyrenaean Arcesilaus with Odysseus' family through Sparta, where Penelope's father came from (see above).[30]

COMMENTARY ON SELECTED FRAGMENTS

F 1* (a) = *PEG* F 2, from Σ Aristoph. *Nu.* 508a = Charax *FgrHist* 103F 5; (b) from Paus. 9.37.5–7[31]

(a) Οὕτως ὁ Χάραξ ἐν τῷ δ´· Ἀγαμήδης ἄρχων Στυμφήλου τῆς Ἀρκαδίας ἐγάμει Ἐπικάστην, ἧς παῖς ἦν Τροφώνιος σκότιος. Οὗτοι τοὺς τότε πάντας ὑπερέβαλλοντο εὐτεχνίαι, τόν τε ἐν Δελφοῖς ναὸν ἠργολάβησαν, ἐν Ἤλιδι <δὲ> ταμιεῖον χρυσοῦν κατεσκεύασαν Αὐγείαι· ὧι καταλείψαντες ἁρμὸν λίθινον, νυκτὸς εἰσιόντες ἔκλεπτον τῶν χρημάτων <ἅμα Κερκυόνι,

---

[27] See West (1985: 88–9). In his recent commentary on the Trojan epics of the Cycle, West (2013: 289) has suggested that the name Εὐγάμμων may be 'the Hellenized form of a non-Greek name containing Ammon, who as Zeus Ammon was a principal god of Cyrene'.
[28] Herod. 4.159–60. [29] On Cyrene and Egypt during this period, see Malten (1911: 270).
[30] See Hartmann (1917: 83–4); Rzach *RE* s.v. 'Kyklos', 2431.
[31] An asterisk is attached to a fragment number of uncertain attribution.

ὃς γνήσιος Ἀγαμήδους καὶ Ἐπικάστης υἱός. Ὡς δὲ ἠπόρει λίαν Αὐγείας, ἐπιδημήσαντα Δαίδαλον διὰ <φυγῆς> Μίνωος ἐλιτάνευσεν ἐξιχνεῦσαι τὸν φῶρα. Ὁ δὲ> παγίδας ἔστησεν, αἷς περιπεσὼν Ἀγαμήδης ἀναιρεῖται. Τροφώνιος δὲ τὴν κεφαλὴν αὐτοῦ τεμὼν πρὸς τὸ μὴ γνωρισθῆναι, <ἅμα Κερκυόνι φεύγει εἰς Ὀρχομενόν. Αὐγείου δὲ κατὰ κέλευσιν Δαιδάλου πρὸς τὴν τῶν αἱμάτων ἔκχυσιν (πρὸς τὴν τῶν χρημάτων ἔκδοσιν [Vürtheim]) ἐπιδιώκοντος, καταφεύγουσιν ὁ μὲν Κερκυὼν εἰς Ἀθήνας – Καλλίμαχος -, ὁ δὲ Τροφώνιος Ἐργίνου> εἰς Λεβάδειαν τῆς Βοιωτίας φεύγει· οὗ κατωρυχὴν ποιησάμενος οἰκήσας διετέλει. Τελευτήσαντος δὲ αὐτοῦ μαντεῖον ἀτρεκὲς ἐφάνη αὐτοῖς καὶ θύουσιν αὐτῶι ὡς θεῶι. περιέλιπε δὲ υἱὸν Ἄλκανδρον.

(a) Thus Harax in book 4. Agamedes, lord of Stymphalus in Arcadia, married Epicaste, whose bastard son was Trophonius. These men surpassed all others of their time in craftsmanship. They undertook by contract the construction of the temple at Delphi and built the golden treasury for Augeas in Elis. After leaving open a made-of-stone joint, they entered at night and started stealing the treasures <together with Cercyon, who was the legitimate son of Agamedes and Epicaste. Since Augeas was at a great loss, he begged Daedalus who had come to him after fleeing from Minos to trace the thief. He then> set traps, in which Agamedes fell and died. Trophonius cut his head so that he is not recognized and <together with Cercyon fled to Orchomenus. While Augeas started chasing them, in accordance with Daedalus' advice with respect to the shedding of blood (with respect to returning the treasures [Vürtheim]), Cercyon found refuge in Athens – Calimachus –, and Trophonius son of Erginus> in Lebadea in Boeotia. At this place he dug a cavern and made it his home. After his death, an oracle that speaks the truth appeared to them and they offer sacrifices to him (Trophonius) as to a god. He left a son, Alcandros.[32]

(b) λαβόντι δὲ γυναῖκα αὐτῶι νέαν κατὰ τὸ μάντευμα Τροφώνιος γίνεται καὶ Ἀγαμήδης. Λέγεται δὲ ὁ Τροφώνιος Ἀπόλλωνος εἶναι καὶ οὐκ Ἐργίνου· καὶ ἐγώ τε πείθομαι καὶ ὅστις παρὰ Τροφώνιον ἦλθε ἤδη μαντευσόμενος. τούτους φασίν, ὡς ηὐξήθησαν, γενέσθαι δεινοὺς θεοῖς τε ἱερὰ κατασκευάσασθαι καὶ βασίλεια ἀνθρώποις· καὶ γὰρ τῶι Ἀπόλλωνι τὸν ναὸν ὠικοδόμησαν τὸν ἐν Δελφοῖς καὶ Ὑριεῖ τὸν θησαυρόν. ἐποίησαν δὲ ἐνταῦθα τῶν λίθων ἕνα εἶναι σφίσιν ἀφαιρεῖν κατὰ τὸ ἐκτός· καὶ οἱ μὲν ἀεί τι ἀπὸ τῶν τιθεμένων ἐλάμβανον· Ὑριεὺς δὲ εἴχετο ἀφασίαι, κλεῖς μὲν καὶ σημεῖα τὰ ἄλλα ὁρῶν ἀκίνητα, τὸν δὲ ἀριθμὸν ἀεὶ τῶν χρημάτων ἐλάττονα. ἵστησιν οὖν ὑπὲρ τῶν ἀγγείων, ἐν οἷς ὅ τε ἄργυρος καὶ ὁ χρυσός οἱ, πάγας ἤ τι καὶ ἄλλο ὃ τὸν ἐσελθόντα καὶ ἁπτόμενον τῶν χρημάτων καθέξειν ἔμελλεν. ἐσελθόντος τοῦ Ἀγαμήδους τὸν μὲν ὁ δεσμὸς κατεῖχε, Τροφώνιος δὲ ἀπέτεμεν αὐτοῦ τὴν κεφαλήν, ὅπως μὴ ἡμέρας ἐπισχούσης ἐκεῖνος γένοιτο ἐν αἰκίαις καὶ αὐτὸς

---

[32] All translations are my own, unless otherwise stated.

μηνυθείη μετέχων τοῦ τολμήματος. καὶ Τροφώνιον μὲν ἐνταῦθα ἐδέξατο ἡ γῆ διαστᾶσα, ἔνθα ἐστὶν <ἐν> τῶι ἄλσει τῶι ἐν Λεβαδείαι βόθρος τε Ἀγαμήδους καλούμενος καὶ πρὸς αὐτῶι στήλη.

(b) Obeying the oracle he took to himself a young wife, and had children, Trophonius and Agamedes. Trophonius is said to have been a son of Apollo, not of Erginus. This I am inclined to believe, as does everyone who has gone to Trophonius to inquire of his oracle. They say that these, when they grew up, proved clever at building sanctuaries for the gods and palaces of men. For they built the temple for Apollo at Delphi and the sanctuary of Hyrieus. One of the stones in it they made so that they could take it away from the outside. So they kept on removing something from the store. Hyrieus was dumbfounded when he saw keys and seals untampered with, while the treasure kept on getting less. So he set over the vessels, in which were his silver and gold, snares or other contrivance, to arrest any who should enter and lay hands on the treasure. Agamedes entered and was kept fast to the trap, but Trophonius cut off his head, lest when day came his brother should be tortured, and he himself be informed of as being concerned in the crime. The earth opened and swallowed up Trophonius at the point in the grove at Lebadea where is what is called the pit of Agamedes, with a slab beside it.[33]

Only through a combination of the two versions of the story of Trophonius and Agamedes can we reasonably guess about the content of the *ekphrasis* on the bowl offered by Polyxenus to Odysseus,[34] for the former story contains some 'late and rationalizing elements'[35] that can be easily omitted without damaging the tale's kernel,[36] while the latter does not include Augeas (who clearly belongs to the version offered by the *Telegony*). If we omit Cercyon and Daedalus on the one hand, and Hyrieus on the other, then we can safely reconstruct the content of the *ekphrasis* narrated in Odysseus' Elis journey in the *Telegony*. Comparison with the Rhampsinitus story in Herod. 2.121 shows that only the first part of the Greek version, that is the deceit–theft–punishment triad, bears striking similarities to its Egyptian counterpart. Since the story of Trophonius, Agamedes, and Augeas that featured in the *Telegony* ends with the foundation of Trophonius' oracle in Lebadea, it must have been shaped only after the rise of the hero cult under the influence of epic poetry.[37] Its marked difference from another version

---

[33] Translation by W. H. S. Jones (Loeb Classical Library).
[34] *Tel.* arg. lines 310–12 Severyns: 'and is entertained as a guest by Polyxenus and receives a bowl, and on it [is depicted] the story concerning Trophonius and Agamedes and Augeas'.
[35] Davies (1989c: 86). [36] Hartmann (1917: 66). [37] See Burkert (1985: 205).

of the Trophonius and Agamedes tale related by Pindar is very instructive.[38] Agamedes and Trophonius after completing the construction of Apollo's temple at Delphi asked for their wages from the god, who replied that they would receive their payment on the seventh day until which they could enjoy themselves in feasting. The two skilled architects followed the god's advice, but on the seventh night and after going to sleep they died peacefully. The former version that functions as an aetiology for the foundation of the oracle of Trophonius in Boeotia is slightly later than the one ending with the death of Trophonius and Agamedes in Delphi and reflects two rival traditions between these major cult sites. In tandem with the Peloponnesian and Cyrenaean backgrounds of the *Telegony*, it is not unthinkable that the deceit–theft–punishment version of the Trophonius and Agamedes myth was transferred by Peloponnesian colonists from Greece to Cyrene; it was later transferred to Egypt, where it was enriched and expanded with certain Egyptian features, like the sealing of the doors[39] and the prostitution of the king's daughter (that Herodotus tellingly refuses to accept).[40] Augeas may have been introduced in the story by Eugammon himself, since his wealth was both enormous and well known and, most evocatively, he could function as a bridge to the episode of Polyxenus, who was his grandson.[41] Charax had taken the story from Eugammon or a plot summary and had added some further elements, like Cercyon and Daedalus. Pausanias' version with its clear Boeotian coloring had no place for Augeas, since it had been shaped by the influence of the foundation of Trophonius' oracle in Lebadea in Boeotia and did not aim at creating a link with Odysseus.

What was the point of this long *ekphrasis*? Given that (a) like Augeas, Odysseus punished the suitors who were destroying his household, and (b) Augeas lived a long happy life honored by his people, Polyxenus' offering of the mixing-bowl to Odysseus would have functioned as a gesture expressing his wish that his guest will also, in the manner of Augeas, live in happiness.[42] Since the punishment of the suitors had already taken place, the story of Trophonius and Agamedes would have functioned as an

---

[38] See Pind. *Paean* 8 = 52i (100–111) and Plut. *consol. Apoll.* 109a; also Luc. *Dial. mort.* 10.
[39] See Asheri, Lloyd, and Corcella (2007: 327) on Herod. 2.121. Hartmann thinks that the shaving of the guards' beards is an Egyptian feature but he is likely to be mistaken. In fact, this detail is an argument *ex silentio* that the guards may have been foreign mercenaries in Egypt, for growing a beard was a very rare phenomenon in Egypt after the New Kingdom; see Kees (1933: 90 n. 8); Asheri, Lloyd, and Corcella (2007: 263) on Herod. 2.36. On the Rhampsinitus story in Herodotus, see S. West (2007: 322–7).
[40] See Hartmann (1917: 69).   [41] *Il.* 2.623–4.
[42] Differently West (2013: 294), who thinks that this story 'has no perceptible relevance to Odysseus'.

introduction to the basic theme of the entire *Telegony*, the post-Odyssean future of Odysseus.[43]

F 2 = F 1 D. = F 3 W., from Pausanias 8.12.5

> ... καὶ ἐν δεξιᾶι τῆς ὁδοῦ γῆς χῶμα ὑψηλόν· Πηνελόπης δὲ εἶναι τάφον φασίν, οὐχ ὁμολογοῦντες τὰ ἐς αὐτὴν ποιήσει <τῆι> Θεσπρωτίδι ὀνομαζομένηι. ἐν ταύτηι μέν γέ ἐστι τῆι ποιήσει ἐπανήκοντι ἐκ Τροίας Ὀδυσσεῖ τεκεῖν τὴν Πηνελόπην Πτολιπόρθην παῖδα.

> ...and on the right of the road is a high mound of earth. It is said to be the grave of Penelope, but the account of her in the poem called *Thesprotis* is not in agreement with this saying. For in it the poet says that when Odysseus returned from Troy he had a son Ptoliporthes from Penelope.

Pausanias goes on by saying that the Mantinean story, according to which Odysseus upon his return from Troy found Penelope responsible for bringing the suitors into the palace and exiled her, stands in contrast to a lost *Thesprotis*, in which Penelope bore to Odysseus upon his return from Troy a son, whose name was Ptoliporthes. This *Thesprotis* should not be taken as identical with an archaic epichoric tradition about Odysseus' adventures in Thesprotia.[44] It was, in all probability, a name for the first book of the *Telegony*.[45] Given that Ptoliporthes features as Odysseus' son in Ps.-Apollodorus (*Epit.* 7.35–6: καὶ εὑρίσκει ἐκ Πηνελόπης Π<τ>ολιπόρθην αὐτῶι γεγεννημένον 'and there he found Ptoliporthes, whom Penelope had borne to him'), without any specification of the source he is using, and that naming a son after a quality of his father[46] was common epic practice,[47] we can safely conclude that, despite Proclus' silence on this issue, Odysseus had a second son from Penelope after his return to Ithaca, who was named Ptoliporthes.

F 3 = *PEG* F 3 = F 2 D. = F 4 W., from Eustath. on *Od.* 16.118 (1796.48–9)

> Ὁ δὲ τὴν Τηλεγονίαν γράψας Κυρηναῖος ἐκ μὲν Κίρκης [Muetzell: codd. Καλυψοῦς] Τηλέγονον υἱὸν Ὀδυσσεῖ ἀναγράφει ἢ Τηλέδαμον, ἐκ δὲ Πηνελόπης Τηλέμαχον καὶ Ἀρκεσίλαον.

---

[43] See Tsagalis (2008a: 80).   [44] I am designating this tradition as **Thesprotis*.
[45] See Hartmann (1917: 59), who argued that the title *Thesprotis* may have been used for the entire poem in the manner of the *Aethiopis*, which designates a whole epic poem although it refers only to a part of it. See also West (2013: 288).
[46] Πτολιπόρθης ('Sacker of cities') recalls Odysseus' designation as πτολίπορθος.
[47] See Davies (1989c: 89), who observes that Telemachus was named after his father's fighting in a distant land and Neoptolemus after his father's participation in the Trojan War.

> The Cyrenean author of the *Telegony* reports that Telegonus or Teledamus was the son of Odysseus from Circe, and Telemachus and Arcesilaus his sons from Penelope.

Since the Cyrenaean association of Arcesilaus,[48] who must have been another name for Ptoliporthes,[49] points to an innovation by Eugammon, it should be explained why the name Ptoliporthes had been created.[50] It may be the case that when an older *Thesprotis*, in which Odysseus died peacefully in Thesprotia, started to be linked to the Telegonus myth that necessitated Odysseus' return to Ithaca, certain changes had to be made with respect to Odysseus' offspring. The introduction of a son from Circe into the tale of Odysseus' last days may, therefore, have resulted in the proliferation of Odysseus' sons.[51] When the older story of the 'Sailor and the Oar' was replaced by Odysseus' marriage with Callidice, a new son named Polypoites was invented, who would become king of the Thesprotians, when Odysseus would return to Ithaca after Callidice's death.[52] In like manner, the prospect of the double marriages at the end of the play[53] and the transfer of Telemachus, Telegonus, and Penelope to Aeaea necessitated that a second son to Penelope be left in Ithaca as the sole heir to Odysseus' throne.[54] This son was Ptoliporthes-Arcesilaus. In this way, after Odysseus' death two of the sons born to him by different wives (Callidice and Penelope) were left to rule *alone* in Thesprotia and Ithaca respectively, while two other sons born to him by Penelope and Circe (Telemachus and Telegonus) were immortalized. It is obvious that the aural similarity in the first part of the two pairs of names (Πολυποίτης–Π[τ]ολιπόρθης/Τηλέμαχος–Τηλέγονος) given

---

[48] Vürtheim (1901: 49 n. 3); Phillips (1953: 55); Huxley (1960: 24; 1969: 172).

[49] First suggested by Schmidt (1885: 430); see also West (2003a: 171 n. 72).

[50] Hartmann's suggestion (1917: 86) that the Cyrenaean genealogy of Arcesilaus is an external accessory to the epic's subject matter fails to explain why the name Ptoliporthes was invented in the first place, since he seems to play no role in the epic's plot.

[51] Eugammon was no doubt aware of various traditions concerning the non-Homeric proliferation of Odysseus' sons: according to Hesiod, 1011–18, Odysseus had two sons from Circe (Agrius and Latinus) and two more from Calypso (Nausithoos and Nausinoos); on the interpolated verse 1014 introducing Telegonus as Odysseus' son from Aphrodite (!), see West (1966: 434–5).

[52] I am extremely skeptical about any latent associations of Callidice and Polypoites with the Underworld; see Vürtheim (1901: 49–51).

[53] Differently Hartmann (1917: 86), who states that the double marriages at the end of the *Telegony* leave no room for a second son of Odysseus from Penelope.

[54] It should be noted that Ps.-Apollodorus' formulation (*Epit.* 7.35–6: καὶ εὑρίσκει ἐκ Πηνελόπης Π<τ>ολιπόρθην αὐτῷ γεγεννημένον 'and he finds Ptoliporthes born to him from Penelope') indicates that Penelope had given birth to Ptoliporthes before the long absence of Odysseus in Thesprotia. Since he stayed there for many years (when he left Thesprotia, Polypoites, his son from Callidice, was old enough to take the throne), it is clear that Ptoliporthes was at least of an age that allowed him to take the throne in Ithaca after his father's death and the subsequent departure of Telemachus for Aeaea.

to Odysseus' sons reflects Eugammon's plan to couple their fate after the death of Odysseus. In this light, it is not unthinkable that while the name Arcesilaus reflects Cyrenaean political concerns of the Battiad dynasty, the name Ptoliporthes may have been invented in order to create an analogy with Polypoites, in the manner Eugammon had shaped Telegonus' name after that of Telemachus. Moreover, all these *nomina loquentia* are associated with features pertaining either to Odysseus (Πολυποίτης < πολυποινίτης < πολύ + ποινή 'much-punished',[55] Πτολιπόρθης < πτολίπορθος < πτόλις + πέρθω 'sacker of cities') or to Ptoliporthes'/Arcesilaus' future role (Ἀρκεσίλαος < ἀρκεῖν + λαοῖς 'protector of the people').[56]

F 4(a), from Σ *Od.* 11.134; F 4(b), from Σ *Od.* 11.134; (c) = *PEG* F 4 = F 5 W., from Ps.-Apollod. *Epit.* 7.36[57]

(a) Ἔνιοι δέ... φασιν ὡς ἐντεύξει τῆς Κίρκης Ἥφαιστος κατεσκεύασε Τηλεγόνωι δόρυ ἐκ τρυγόνος θαλασσίας, ἣν Φόρκυς ἀνεῖλεν ἐσθίουσαν τοὺς ἐν τῇ Φορκίδι λίμνηι ἰχθῦς· οὗ τὴν μὲν ἐπιδορατίδα ἀδαμαντίνην, τὸν δὲ στύρακα χρυσοῦν εἶναι, τὸν Ὀδυσσέα ἀνεῖλεν.[58]

(a) Some... say that on a visit to Circe Hephaestus made Telegonus a spear from a sting-ray that Phorcys had killed when it was eating the fish in Phorcys' lake. Its head was of adamant, and its shaft of gold. With it he killed Odysseus.[59]

(b) οἱ νεώτεροι τὰ περὶ Τηλέγονον ἀνέπλασαν τὸν Κίρκης καὶ Ὀδυσσέως, ὃς δοκεῖ κατὰ ζήτησιν τοῦ πατρὸς εἰς Ἰθάκην ἐλθὼν ὑπ' ἀγνοίας τὸν πατέρα διαχρήσασθαι τρυγόνος κέντρωι.

(b) Post-Homeric writers invented the story of Telegonus the son of Circe and Odysseus, who is supposed to have gone to Ithaca in search of his father and killed him in ignorance with the barb of a sting-ray.[60]

---

[55] It has been argued that Odysseus' Thesprotian journey was a rationalistic reinterpretation of his journey to Hades and that it was from this association that Eugammon used the name Πολυποίτης (also employed for Peirithoos' son) for his son with Callidice, whose name also has been regarded as a euphemism for Persephone (*quae bene ius dicit* 'who sets forth justice'); see Höfer (1897–1909: 2717).

[56] See West (2013: 305).

[57] On the *Nachleben* of Odysseus' death by Telegonus in ancient Greek and Roman literature, see *PEG*, p. 105; for analysis of this episode, see Wilamowitz-Moellendorff (1884: 194–8); Vürtheim (1901: 55–8); Hartmann (1917: 106–35).

[58] I do not quote Eustath. on *Od.* 11.134 (1676.43), since his version is clearly based on Σ *Od.* 11.134 (see above F 4 a+b).

[59] Translation by M. L. West (Loeb Classical Library).

[60] Translation by M. L. West (Loeb Classical Library).

(c) καὶ Ὀδυσσέα βοηθοῦντα τῷ μετὰ χεῖρας δόρατι Τηλεγόνος <τρυγόνος> κέντρον τὴν αἰχμὴν ἔχοντι τιτρώσκει, καὶ Ὀδυσσεὺς θνήισκει.

(c) and Telegonus with the spear in his hands, which was tipped with a sting-ray spine, wounded Odysseus when he tried to stop him. Odysseus died.[61]

Fragment 4 points to the third and last part of the *Telegony* that includes the story of Telegonus. Not much later than Odysseus' return to Ithaca, Telegonus, his son from Circe, sails from Aeaea in search of his father,[62] whom he has never met. After landing at Ithaca, probably following the advice of his mother on how to find this island, he ravages the land (Proclus)[63] and raids the cattle (Ps.-Apollodorus).[64] Though Proclus' expression does not explicitly refer to a cattle-raid, which was after all a traditional epic theme, Ps.-Apollodorus' information on this particular point may well be right, since it creates a symmetrical effect, almost as a thematic ring, to Odysseus' visit to his oxen-stables in Elis in the beginning of the epic, which he had entrusted to Polyxenus. Since the latter represents a conflation of the Iliadic Polyxenus with a Polyxenus from Heracles' mythical saga (to whom the Taphians/Teleboans entrusted the stolen cows of Electryon),[65] it is not unthinkable that the cattle-raid by Telegonus may have been shaped under the influence of an analogous reference in the episode of Polyxenus during Odysseus' journey to Elis. In this way, Odysseus was presented trying to look after his cattle in both beginning and end of the *Telegony*. According to Oppian,[66] when Telegonus set out in search of his father he carried with him the very weapon he was going to use to kill Odysseus, that is a spear barbed with the spine of a sting-ray, which he had received from his mother Circe. The scholia to the *Odyssey*[67] and Eustathius[68] add the significant detail that this was a Hephaestus-made weapon that Circe had asked the smith–god to manufacture. Although it is difficult to contemplate about this gift from

---

[61] Translation by Scott Smith and Trzaskoma (2007: 93).
[62] Hyginus' version (*fab.* 127.1–2) that Telegonus was driven to Ithaca by a storm (*tempestate in Ithacam est delatus* 'he was brought off to Ithaca because of a storm') is not incompatible with Circe's advice. See Davies (1989c: 89). On the dependence of Hyginus' version on Sophocles' Ὀδυσσεὺς ἀκανθοπλήξ 'Odysseus wounded by the prickle', see Hartmann (1917: 115–22) and West (2013: 303).
[63] *Tel.* arg. line 325 Severyns: τέμνει τὴν νῆσον ('he lays waste the island').
[64] Ps.-Apollod. *Epit.* 7.36: ἀπευλάνει τινὰ τῶν βοσκημάτων ('he drives away some of the cattle').
[65] See Ps.-Apollod. *Bibl.* 2.54–5. Polyxenus' name as well as the fact that he was not killed in the *Iliad* made him ideal for his new role. See Severyns (1962: 18–19); Davies (1989c: 86) rightly observes that 'the expansion of a secondary figure from Homer is thoroughly typical of the Epic Cycle'.
[66] *Hal.* 2.497.   [67] Σ *Od.* 11.134.   [68] Eustath. on *Od.* 11.134 (1676.43).

mother to son, it is plausible to detect a general cyclic influence duplicating the motif of the divine weapons given to Achilles by his father Peleus before his departure to Troy (*Cypria*),[69] as well as the Hephaestus-made weapons of Achilles and Memnon delivered by their mothers Thetis and Eos in the *Iliad* and the *Aethiopis* respectively.[70] Eugammon had exploited this particular kind of weapon,[71] so as to fit his reinterpretation of the Homeric expression ἐξ ἁλός,[72] which he read as 'from the sea' and not in its Odyssean meaning 'away from the sea' (*Od.* 11.134 = 23.281). Circe, who could not have possibly known that Telegonus would kill his own father, may have given her son this precious weapon[73] to protect himself on his journey. The *Telegony* may have thus employed a traditional motif or riddle,[74] according to which a set of conditions that seem impossible to meet have to be fulfilled, so that a certain result may be achieved. In our case, Odysseus as the typical hero 'of the sea' will die by something coming 'from the sea' but 'outside of the sea'. The combination of these two conditions seems impossible, but for a sea-weapon used on land. In this light, Telegonus was equipped upon his departure with a weapon that made one recall his father's sea adventures, but which, ironically, would cause Odysseus' death. Long have scholars pondered on the cryptic words of Teiresias in *Od.* 11.134–7 (= 23.281–4), mainly because they thought it was necessary to explain how a death inflicted by a spear barbed with the spine of a *trygōn* ('sting-ray')[75]

---

[69] *Cypr. PEG* F 3 = D. = F 4 W.; see also Ps.-Apollod. *Bibl.* 3.13.5. The same topic is reflected a number of times in the *Iliad* (16.140–4; 17.194–7; 18.84–5; 19.277; 19.388–91; 21.162; 22.133; 23.276–8).

[70] See *Il.* 18; *Aeth.* arg. lines 185–6 Severyns: Μέμνων δὲ ὁ Ἠοῦς υἱὸς ἔχων ἡφαιστότευκτον πανοπλίαν παραγίνεται τοῖς Τρωσὶ βοηθήσων ('Memnon comes, the son of Eos having an armor made by Hephaestus, in order to assist the Trojans').

[71] Σ *Od.* 11.134 = F 4 a+b (this chapter). On the use of this motif in classical, Hellenistic, and Roman poetry, especially tragedy, see Hartmann (1917: 106–35).

[72] This is the standard view that has been adopted by most scholars: see Scheliha (1943: 415–16); Burkert (1983a: 157–9); Edwards (1985: 227 n. 28); Ballabriga (1990: 26); Nagy (1990a: 214); Peradotto (1990: 63–74); Edmunds (1997: 423–4). Differently Burgess (2001: 153): 'the prediction of the death of Odysseus seems to employ the motif of the misunderstood oracle. The Cyclic poem has not misused a Homeric passage; the Homeric poem is alluding to a traditional story of misinterpreted oracle that the *Telegony* happened to narrate'.

[73] Its spear-head (*epidoratis*) was made of adamant, while its spike (*styrax*) was golden. These details point to the divine craftsman who made it. West (2013: 303 and n. 18) thinks that this may derive from an epic source.

[74] See West (2004: 1–9; 2013: 307–14).

[75] On *trygōn* (*trygon pastinaca*), see Thompson (1947: 270–1). Differently Hadjicosti (2005: 79), who argues that the use of the modifier *thalassia* ('of the sea') for *trygōn* in Σ *Od.* 11.134 and by Eustath. on *Od.* 11.134 (1676.43) indicates that 'the species that he referred to also had varieties that lived on land' (79) and, therefore, it could be a turtle. This is not unthinkable but not on the grounds Hadjicosti argues, for: (a) another scholium (Σ *Od.* 11.134), Ps.-Apollodorus (*Epit.* 7.36), and Oppian (*Hal.* 2.505) do not employ *thalassia*; (b) the use of the backbone of a turtle as a hard sharp point is incompatible with the 'gentle death' of

could be called *ablēchros* ('gentle').[76] Both problems though are based on the assumption that Eugammon did not only alter the meaning of *ex halos*,[77] but changed the entire prophecy of Teiresias as expressed in *Od.* 11.134–7 (= 23.281–4). Three solutions are possible with respect to *ablēchros*: it either refers to the soft flesh of the sting-ray[78] or we should understand the sting-ray to be poisonous[79] or it does not mean 'gentle' but 'feeble', 'easily penetrable', 'mild' and points to Odysseus in his old age dying at Telegonus' hands.[80]

F 5 (a), from Eustath. on *Od.* 16.118 (1796.52); (b), from Ps.-Apollod. *Epit.* 7.37; (c) = *PEG* F 5 = F 2 D. = F 6 W., from Hygin. *fab.* 127

(a) ὁ δὲ τοὺς Νόστους ποιήσας Κολοφώνιος Τηλέμαχον μέν φησι τὴν Κίρκην ὕστερον γῆμαι, Τηλέγονον δὲ τὸν ἐκ Κίρκης ἀντιγῆμαι Πηνελόπην.

Odysseus; (c) in Oppian's *Halieutica* (2.497–505), *trygōn*, which is designated as ἀλγινόεσσα (505: 'painful') and μιῇ κατενήρατο ῥιπῇ (505: 'brought death [to Odysseus], with one blow'), causes ἅλιον μόρον (499: 'death from the sea') but is not modified by the epithet *thalassia*.

[76] *pephnēi* ('shall kill') has also caused some trouble, because it seems awkward to have 'death' as its subject, instead of a human or divine agent. According to Ballabriga (1989: 294–5), this is sufficient indication that there is a play on the obscurity of Teiresias' oracle and an allusion to a tradition relating a violent death of Odysseus by Telegonus. In my view (Tsagalis 2008a: 69–75), there is even an irony in Penelope's reply (*Od.* 23.286–7) to Odysseus when he repeats Teiresias' oracle to her (*Od.* 23.264–84). See also Vürtheim (1901: 51–2).

[77] See Welcker (1865: 307–8).   [78] Davies (1989c: 90).

[79] See Burgess (2001: 153), who argues that 'the stingray has a venomous tail that at least one ancient source (Ael. *NA* 1.56) thought inflicted incurable wounds'.

[80] See Marks (2008: 95 and n. 15), giving various examples (*Il.* 5.337; 8.178) where *ablechros* means 'feeble' or 'easily penetrated'. See also Peradotto (1990: 66 and 74); West (2013: 307–14) claims that *ex halos* can *only* mean 'from the sea' (307) and argues extensively (by drawing attention, among other passages, to Aesch. *Psychagogoi*, *TrGF* F 275) that Odysseus' death was 'gentle' because 'Odysseus is not subjected to the agonies of being stung by the fish; the residual toxicity of its digested remains seeps into his balding scalp and he succumbs to it without pain. He has grown vulnerable because of his sleek (λιπαρόν) old age' (314). I am skeptical about this interpretation; for one thing, the Odyssean passage explicitly refers to a 'gentle death' for Odysseus 'surrounded by his prosperous people' (11.136–7 = 23.283–4). How can his people surround him *in happiness* when Odysseus dies? See Tsagalis (2008a: 63–90) and Tsagalis (2014: 460): 'In an older Thesprotian tradition, Odysseus may have died peacefully in Thesprotia *ex halos* ("away from the sea"), as Teiresias had prophesied in *Od.* 11.134. When the myth of Telegonus, which belonged to the typical story-pattern "son kills his father by accident", was added to the older Thesprotian lay and the expression *ex halos* was reinterpreted so as to mean "from the sea", Eugammon had to invent a reason for Odysseus' departure from Thesprotia and return to Ithaca. This reason was Callidice's death, which allowed Odysseus to leave the throne to Polypoites, the son he had by her.' Moreover, *ek/ex* can regularly denote position (as well as place) in Homer; *Od.* 15.272 is very instructive on this, since Theoclymenus uses the phrase ἐκ πατρίδος 'away from my country' to answer Telemachus' ἐξ Ἰθάκης γένος εἰμί ('my family comes from Ithaca', 15.267). In this case, we have ample evidence for the two meanings of *ek/ex* used in the same context.

(a) The Colophonian poet of the *Returns* says that Telemachus afterwards married Circe, while Telegonus, the son from Circe, married Penelope.[81]

(b) κἀκεῖ τὴν Πηνελόπην γαμεῖ [Τηλέγονος]. Κίρκη δὲ ἑκατέρους αὐτοὺς εἰς μακάρων νήσους ἀποστέλλει.

(b) There he married Penelope. Circe sent them both off to the Isles of the Blessed.[82]

(c) Quem postquam cognovit qui esset, iussu Minervae cum Telemacho et Penelope in patriam reduxerunt, in insulam Aeaeam; ad Circen Ulixem mortuum deportaverunt. Ibique sepulturae tradiderunt. Eiusdem Minervae monitu Telegonus Penelopen, Telemachus Circen duxerunt uxores.

(c) When he learned whom he had killed, Telegonus on Minerva's orders returned to his home on the island of Aeaea along with Telemachus and Penelope. They returned Ulysses' dead body to Circe and there laid him to rest. Again on Minerva's orders, Telegonus took Penelope and Telemachus took Circe in marriage.[83]

Comparison of Eustathius (on *Od.* 16.118 (1796.52)) with Ps.-Apollodorus (*Epit.* 7.37) and Hyginus (*fab.* 127), as well as with F 3[84] (Eustath. on *Od.* 16.118 (1796.48–9)), shows the kind of mistakes Eustathius has made: whereas in F 3[85] he had confused Κίρκη with Καλυψώ, this time he is right about the mother of Telegonus, with whom Telemachus is married, but wrong about the poem.[86] The double marriages have been often treated with contempt but this may well be an impression created by the fact that we basically possess a plot summary of the *Telegony*,[87] which deprives each episode from its context and offers only the 'bare bones' of its content. In this respect, a possible reconstruction may be telling: when Telegonus realized that he had killed his own father,[88] he began to lament.[89] After this rather moving scene, which may have been filled with compassion for the unwilling patricide, Athena appeared and advised[90] Telegonus, Telemachus,

---

[81] Translation by M. L. West (Loeb Classical Library).
[82] Translation by Scott Smith and Trzaskoma (2007: 93).
[83] Translation by Scott Smith and Trzaskoma (2007: 142).   [84] Numeration by Tsagalis.
[85] Numeration by Tsagalis.   [86] Severyns (1928: 416); West (2003: 171 nn. 2–3).
[87] Malkin (1998: 126); Burgess (2001: 170). See also Kullmann (1960: 46), who emphasizes that we should not treat erotic features as proof or even indications of late composition. Love stories stand at the very center of early Greek myth and of even earlier non-Greek literature.
[88] *Tel. arg.* line 327 Severyns Τηλέγονος δ' ἐπιγνοὺς τὴν ἁμαρτίαν ('Telegonus realizing his mistake'); Ps.-Apollod. *Epit.* 7.37 ἀναγνωρισάμενος δὲ αὐτὸν ('after recognizing him'); Hyg. *fab.* 127 *quem postquam cognovit qui esset* ('when he realized who he was').
[89] Ps.-Apollod. *Epit.* 7.37 (καὶ πολλὰ κατοδυράμενος 'and after excessive lamentation').
[90] Hygin. *fab.* 127.

and Penelope about what they should do: they all had to leave Ithaca, whose throne would be left to Ptoliporthes–Arcesilaus, and travel to Aeaea, Circe's island. Odysseus' two sons would marry Odysseus' two wives/concubines (Circe and Penelope) and be subsequently all immortalized in Aeaea.[91] In this way, Odysseus' Odyssean world would be emblematically immortalized, while the hero's new offspring would be left to rule the places their father had also ruled in the past, Polypoites in Thesprotia and Ptoliporthes–Arcesilaus in Ithaca. Under this perspective, the double marriages acquire a very different, and not at all contemptuous and disrespectful function. In tandem with this line of thought, the stress on mortality in the Homeric epics that stands in marked contrast to the recurrent immortalization of heroes in the Cyclic epics should not be interpreted in chronological terms, for it is a matter pertaining to dramatic impact and not to the literary taste of a later age.[92] In this light, we need not regard the immortalization of the two couples at the end of the *Telegony* simply as a post-Homeric concept.

DUBIOUS

There is no verse fragment that can be safely attributed to the *Telegony*. I hereby explain why the two anonymous verse fragments conjecturally assigned to the poem can hardly come from it.[93]

> **1. *PEG* F 1 = "Hom." 10 D. = F 1* W., from Athenaeus 10.412b26-d16**
>
> γέρων τε ὢν [Ὀδυσσεύς]
> ἤσθιεν ἁρπαλέως κρέα τ' ἄσπετα καὶ μέθυ ἡδύ.
>
> And even as an old man [sc. 'disguised as a beggar'] Odysseus
> was eating avidly abundant meat and sweet wine.

1. Since Athenaeus quotes his Cyclic or archaic epic source more than thirty times, it seems unlikely that he would not have done the same thing for Eugammon and the *Telegony*.

---

[91] *Tel.* arg. lines 327–30 Severyns. The information (Ps.-Apollod. *Epit.* 7.37) about immortalized Odysseus who was transferred to the Isles of the Blessed as well as the placement of Penelope and Telegonus there probably reflects a tendency to locate in the Μακάρων νῆσοι all immortalized heroes. It is unlikely that this is what happened at the end of the *Telegony*; see West (2013: 306).
[92] See Burgess (2001: 167 and 255–6 nn. 148–51).
[93] For a detailed analysis, see Tsagalis (2014), where I argue extensively that neither of these two fragments belongs to the *Telegony*. West (2013: 297–8, 300) remains skeptical.

2. Having explicitly indicated to his readers that his quotations in 10.412b26–d16 are from Homer at the very beginning of this section (καὶ τὸν Ὀδυσσέα δὲ Ὅμηρος πολυφάγον καὶ λαίμαργον παραδίδωσιν ὅταν λέγηι 'Homer presents Odysseus too as eating a lot and greedy, when he says'), Athenaeus includes the verse under discussion within an Odyssean context.[94] Since he indicates change of context and author by giving the author's name (10.412d17: Θεαγένης δ' ὁ Θάσιος... 'Theagenes of Thasos...'), it becomes clear that he regards the line ἤσθιεν ἁρπαλέως κρέα τ' ἄσπετα καὶ μέθυ ἡδύ ('he was eating avidly abundant meat and sweet wine') as Homeric, and in particular as Odyssean.

3. The 'problem' has originated from the fact that γέρων does not designate Odysseus' old age but the disguised Odysseus, who quite often is called a γέρων ('old fellow') in the second half of the *Odyssey* (for example in 14.37, 14.122, 14.166, 14.386, 14.508; 18.21, 18.74). Some of these uses of γέρων are attested within a context pertaining to excessive eating and drinking (in the hut of Eumaeus and in the episode with the glutton Irus).

4. What has probably happened is that influenced by the formulaic line ἤμεθα δαινύμενοι κρέα τ' ἄσπετα καὶ μέθυ ἡδύ ('we lingered eating avidly abundant meat and sweet wine') employed for Odysseus and the comrades five times in the *Odyssey* (9.162 = 9.557 = 10.184 = 10.477 = 12.30), Athenaeus made one of his banqueters create a line reading ἤσθιεν ἁρπαλέως κρέα τ' ἄσπετα καὶ μέθυ ἡδύ ('he was eating avidly abundant meat and sweet wine') that sounds perfectly Odyssean. This line of thought becomes further strengthened, if one takes into account that it emphasized the theme of gluttony that was the topic of discussion in this particular part of the *Deipnosophistae*. A crucial point is that Odysseus had been presented as a glutton in the very same Odyssean context that he was called a γέρων, namely in Eumaeus' hut. In fact, if Athenaeus had made one of the banqueters use the expression ἤσθιεν ἁρπαλέως ('he was eating ravenously')[95] that is employed in alternate lines in *Od.* 14.109–10 for *Odysseus alone*,[96] then the phrasing γέρων τε ὤν ('and even as an old man') for Odysseus would become evident: for

---

[94] He also gives two other citations from book 7 of the *Odyssey* (215–18 and 219–21).
[95] Interestingly enough, κρέα also features in the same Odyssean context.
[96] ὣς φάθ', ὁ δ' ἐνδυκέως κρέα τ' ἤσθιε πῖνέ τε οἶνον / ἁρπαλέως ἀκέων, κακὰ δὲ μνηστῆρσι φύτευεν ('so he spoke, and Odysseus kept eating and drinking wine ravenously in silence, brooding his revenge against the suitors'); see also *Od.* 6.249–50 ἦ τοι ὁ πῖνε καὶ ἦσθε πολύτλας δῖος Ὀδυσσεύς / ἁρπαλέως· δηρὸν γὰρ ἐδητύος ἦεν ἄπαστος ('and indeed much-enduring Odysseus drank and ate ravenously; for he had not tasted food for a long time').

in *Od.* 18.21–2 (immediately before facing the glutton Irus), almost the same expression had been used by Odysseus with respect to his own self (μή σε γέρων περ ἐών στῆθος καὶ χείλεα φύρσω / αἵματος 'lest, though an old man, I stain your breast and lips with blood').

2. F 2* W., from Synesius, *Epist.* 148

οὐ γὰρ σφᾶς ἐκ νυκτὸς ἐγείρει κῦμ' ἐπιθρῶισκον

for the rising wave does not awaken them at night

It is unlikely that the dactylic hexameter οὐ γὰρ σφᾶς ἐκ νυκτὸς ἐγείρει κῦμ' ἐπιθρῶισκον comes from Eugammon's *Telegony*.[97] I hereby present the basic arguments against such an attribution.

1. Synesius could hardly have access to a genuine verse from the *Telegony*. In the very same letter he refers to a post-Odyssean adventure of Odysseus (the wandering with the oar episode in his attempt to appease Poseidon's anger) by using a one-and-a-half lines from *Od.* 11.122–3 (= 23.269–70): οἳ οὐκ ἴσασι θάλασσαν / ἀνέρες, οὐδέ θ' ἅλεσσι μεμιγμένον εἶδαρ ἔδουσιν ('men who do not know of the sea nor do they eat food mixed with salt'). This piece of evidence shows that, if Synesius knew the actual text of the *Telegony*, he would have referred to a post-Odyssean adventure of Odysseus with a verse of the *Telegony*, and not by an Odyssean verse.
2. Synesius' diction shows that with respect to the wandering with the oar episode he is employing his general knowledge of the Homeric text: he uses the word πηδάλιον[98] ('steering paddle', 'rudder') instead of ἐρετμόν ('oar') (εὖῆρες ἐρετμόν 'well-fitted oar', *Od.* 11.121 = 23.268). In fact, he may be mixing expressions like πηδάλιον μετὰ χερσὶ θεούσης νηὸς ἔχοντα ('having the steering paddle of a running ship in his hands', *Od.* 3.281) with ἐν χείρεσσιν ἔχοντ' εὖῆρες ἐρετμόν ('having in his hands a well-fitted oar', *Od.* 23.268).[99] It is noteworthy that Synesius does not substitute the Homeric word ἐρετμόν ('oar') with κώπη ('oar'), which is synonymous, widely employed in later Greek, and also regularly employed by Synesius himself in his *Epistles*.[100]

---

[97] Livrea (1998: 2).
[98] The word πηδάλιον ('steering paddle', 'rudder') is also regularly used by Synesius in the *Epistles*; see e.g. *Ep.* 5.15, p. 15; 5.11, p. 16, 5.15, p. 21 (Garzya).
[99] See *Od.* 11.121: λαβὼν εὖῆρες ἐρετμόν ('after taking a well-fitted oar').
[100] See *Ep.* 4.26, *Ep.* 148.38 in Hercher (1873).

3. Livrea draws attention to the violation of Naeke's rule,[101] in order to argue that the verse is pre-Hellenistic. The diction of this line suggests otherwise: σφᾶς with a long α is attested *once* in the extant corpus of archaic Greek poetry (Hes. *Theog.* 34: σφᾶς δ' αὐτάς 'themselves'), and even there it is placed in proclitic position,[102] whereas in Synesius it is not. If the verse is archaic, we have to consider the possibility that Synesius has substituted an original σφέας with synizesis by σφᾶς, but then how are we to explain the fact that ἐγείρω ('rouse', 'stir up') and ἐπιθρώσκω ('spring', 'leap upon') never occur with κῦμα ('wave') as subject in the extant corpus of archaic Greek epic?

4. The expression ἐκ νυκτός ('after night-fall') is puzzling; it seems to recall ἐκ νυκτῶν ('after night-fall') in *Od.* 12.286, where it is employed in the context of the Thrinacia episode. When Odysseus suggests to his comrades that they should depart immediately telling them of Teiresias' advice not to eat the cattle of the Sun (*Od.* 11.107–15), Eurylochus disagrees and stresses how dangerous it is *to sail away at night*. Being trapped in Thrinacia because the winds sent by Zeus do not allow them to sail away, they run out of food. When Odysseus falls asleep, his comrades slaughter and eat the cattle of the Sun (*Od.* 12.279–396). This whole passage is marked by the emphasis given to the sound made by the sheep and cattle on the Sun's island, both when Odysseus and his men first arrive (*Od.* 12.265–6 μυκηθμοῦ τ' ἤκουσα βοῶν αὐλιζομενάων / οἰῶν τε βληχήν 'I heard both the bellowing of the cattle lying in the court-yard and the bleating of sheep') and most tellingly when the comrades roast and eat them (*Od.* 12.395–6 κρέα δ' ἀμφ' ὀβελοῖσι μεμύκει, / ὀπταλέα τε καὶ ὠμά, βοῶν δ' ὡς γίγνετο φωνή 'the flesh, both roasted and raw, bellowed on the spits, and the sound was as of cattle'). The same is the case, mutatis mutandis, with Synesius' context: the dactylic hexameter under discussion is immediately followed by a statement that the people who are ignorant of the sea are only awakened at night by 'the neighing of horses, and the bleating of goats and sheep and the bellowing of bulls' (ἀλλ' ἵππων χρεμετισμοὶ καὶ μηκάζον αἰπόλιον, καὶ προβατίων βληχὴ καὶ ταύρου μύκημα 'only the neighings of horses, the bleating of a herd of goats, the cry of sheep, or the bellowing of a bull').[103] In this light, it becomes all the more likely that Synesius is exploiting his general knowledge of the Homeric text,[104] where equivalent themes were used.

---

[101] According to this rule, diaeresis after a spondaic fourth foot is generally avoided.
[102] See Wackernagel (1916: 4–6); West (1966: 166 on line 34).
[103] Translated by Fitzgerald (1926).
[104] See also the story of the Cyclops, in which some of these features appear: (a) the 'they do not know of the sea' motif (9.125–7); (b) the noise made by various animals (9.166–7; see in

5. There is not a single example of Synesius mentioning a Cyclic poet by name or quoting a single verse from the Cyclic epics. This observation should not be confused with his knowledge of episodes featuring in the Cyclic epics, as *Ep.* 123.9–10 (cf. *Nost.* PEG F 7 = F 6 D. = W.) shows.
6. Scholars who are sympathetic to Livrea's suggestion believe that the episode of Odysseus wandering with an oar on his shoulder and his appeasement of Poseidon by means of sacrifices after arriving at a land where people are ignorant of the sea would have been included in Eugammon's *Telegony*. For the refutation of this argument, see Tsagalis (2008a: 75–90; 2014); and above.

In my view, it is possible that Synesius had made up this verse. There are other cases where an author has created a metrical sequence or even an entire hexameter.[105] West argues that it is not clear why Synesius may have composed this line.[106] Perhaps the answer is that it was unintentional (a reflex of his mind operating within an Odyssean context), as the syntax of the entire quotation suggests: καὶ εἰκότα γε ἀγνοοῦσιν. οὐ γὰρ σφᾶς ἐκ νυκτὸς ἐγείρει κῦμ' ἐπιθρῶισκον πελάγους, ἀλλ' ἵππων χρεμετισμοὶ καὶ μηκάζον αἰπόλιον, καὶ προβατίων βληχὴ καὶ ταύρου μύκημα, πρώτης δὲ ἀκτῖνος ἐπιβαλλούσης τῶν μελιττῶν ὁ βόμβος, εἰς ἡδονῆς λόγον οὐδεμιᾶι παραχωρῶν μουσικῆι ('And yet their ignorance is natural. "For the onrushing wave" of the sea "awakens them not in the night" – only the neighings of horses, the bleating of a herd of goats, the cry of sheep, or the bellowing of a bull; then at the first ray of sunshine the humming of bees, yielding the palm to no other music in the pleasure it gives').[107]

THE MAKING OF THE *TELEGONY*

The epic is divided into three parts that are narrated in two books: a journey to Elis and the adventure in Thesprotia were presented in the first book, while Odysseus' return and subsequent death in Ithaca occupy the second.[108] Eugammon has used material from various sources, which he has

---

particular 9.439: θήλειαι δὲ μέμηκον ἀνήμελκτοι περὶ σηκούς 'but the unmilked females bleated around their pens'); (c) (uninterrupted) sleep (9.150–1); and (d) movement of a wave (9.147–8). The very end of his letter, in which the Cyclops' episode is explicitly mentioned, makes it clear that Synesius has also the episode of the Cyclops in his mind (p. 267, 1–6 [Garzya]).

[105] See Davies (1980: 129–32; 1982: 267–9).
[106] West (2013: 296), *contra* D. Russell (oral communication), who draws attention to a fragment of Aristeas' *Arimaspeia* (Ps.-Long. *subl.* 10.4).
[107] Translated by Fitzgerald (1926).
[108] See Wilamowitz (1884: 187); Hartmann (1917: 73) has argued that at the end of book 1, the poet's attention may have turned to Circe's island and the beginning of Telegonus' search for

molded into a new synthesis bearing the marks of some personal contributions. In particular, we can detect the following sources: (a) western-Greek local traditions about Odysseus; (b) a lost *Thesprotis narrating Odysseus' journey to Thesprotia in order to appease the anger of Poseidon; (c) the story of Telegonus pertaining to the death of Odysseus; (d) Cyrenaean and Egyptian elements, which the poet wanted to insert into Odysseus' post-*Odyssey* afterlife so as to validate historical claims of the Battiad dynasty that aimed at tracing its past to Odysseus.[109]

Western epichoric traditions about Odysseus are reflected in the Elis episode, which may have echoed in a *proto-Odyssey and has left some vague traces in our *Odyssey*. It is possible that Eugammon had employed some of these features that may have been brought to Cyrene by Peloponnesian settlers and combined them with Egyptian elements, as in the tale of Agamedes and Augeas. The bridge for this fusion may have been the figure of Polyxenus, who was known from both the *Iliad* and from Heracles' mythical saga. With respect to an older, oral *Thesprotis, Eugammon decided to use its subject matter but made profound changes as far as the reason for Odysseus' journey and subsequent long stay in Thesprotia is concerned. Having aimed at presenting an Odysseus who travels willingly,[110] he decided to separate the journey to Thesprotia from Odysseus' appeasement of and reconciliation with Poseidon.[111] He, therefore, got rid of the

---

his father. See also Vürtheim (1901: 43); Malkin (1998: 127); Debiasi (2004: 252). West (2013: 290–1) draws attention to Clement's assertion (*Strom.* 6.25.1) that Eugammon took wholesale from Musaeus the entire book on the Thesprotians. See West (1983: 43–4). Differently, Bethe (1929: 135). On balance, it should be noted that Ps.-Apollodorus' narrative (*Epit.* 7.34–8), omitting the Elis journey, is given in such a way as to suggest that he is excerpting his material from a single book of the *Telegony*.

[109] On the shaping of the *Telegony*, see Hartmann (1917: 218–21).

[110] See Ballabriga (1989: 299–300), who claims that Odysseus' errance is a voluntary one and suggests that it stems from a cyclic tendency that is reflected even in the hero's false tales in the *Odyssey* (e.g. 14.244–6).

[111] Merkelbach's suggestion (1969: 145–6) that Odysseus went to Elis and then to Thesprotia, because he was exiled after the killing of the suitors (as covertly indicated by the initial phrase of Proclus' summary) is based on his reading Proclus' εἰς Ἰθάκην ('to Ithaca') as εἰς τὴν Ἤπειρον ('to Epirus'). For a refutation of this thesis, see Tsagalis (2008a: 87–8) and (2014.) It is important that Ps.-Apollod. *Epit.* 7.40 refers to Odysseus' exile *only* in a version (7.40: εἰσὶ δὲ οἱ λέγοντες 'some say') that is clearly distinct from the one pertaining to the *Telegony* (7.34–37); see also Plut. *Aetia Rom. et Graeca* 14, 294cd = Arist. F 51.1 Gigon. One should not fail to draw the line between the *motivation* and the *function* of Odysseus' long absence from Ithaca. Its motivation may be an almost cyclic impulse for more adventures and traveling, but its function is linked to Eugammon's aim to introduce a story of Cyrenaean associations with respect to his visit to Elis on the one hand, and prolong Odysseus' stay in Thesprotia so that his son Ptoliporthes–Arcesilaus comes of age when he returns to Ithaca on the other. On the difference between *motivation* and *function*, see Peradotto (1985: 434–5).

story of the 'Sailor and the Oar' and replaced it with a troubling stay of Odysseus among the Thesprotians, since he wanted his hero to return to Ithaca for the continuation of the saga. The old theme of the 'Sailor and the Oar' and a peaceful death among the Thesprotians that featured in the *Thesprotis* were, therefore, eliminated, only to be substituted by a new marriage and especially a new son, Polypoites, who was to become the heir to the Thesprotian throne after Callidice's death and Odysseus' return to Ithaca. By changing the reason for Odysseus' long stay among the Thesprotians, Eugammon was able to exploit it in order to introduce a second son from Penelope, Ptoliporthes–Arcesilaus, as a tribute to the Battiad dynasty of Cyrene. In this way, this new son would be of age upon Odysseus' return to Ithaca from Thesprotia, and subsequently could receive the throne, after Odysseus' death and the transfer of Telemachus, Telegonus, and Penelope to Aeaea. Last, the Cyrenaean poet invented the myth of Telegonus by means of the combination of two folk-tale motifs, i.e. that of 'the son who kills his father through ignorance' and that of 'death away from the sea'.[112] In order to put together these two motifs, Eugammon had to reinterpret the 'death away from the sea' motif that now acquired the meaning 'from the sea'. This change was made possible by the borrowing of a third motif, that of 'the poisonous barbed spine of the sting-ray' weapon that would cause Odysseus' death.[113]

---

[112] Teiresias' prophecy in *Od.* 11 represents a reflection of the 'Sailor and the Oar' story from the *Thesprotis* with an Odyssean ending. Instead of dying peacefully among the Thesprotians, as it may well have been the case in the *Thesprotis* with its marked local viewpoint, in the version given in the *Odyssey* the hero returns to Ithaca and dies there peacefully. Needless to say, the *Odyssey* has no room for the story of Telegonus, which may have been Eugammon's own invention.

[113] See West (2013: 290, 307–15).

PART III

The Fortune of the Epic Cycle in the Ancient World

22 | The aesthetics of sequentiality and its discontents

MARCO FANTUZZI

The aesthetics of the *Iliad* and *Odyssey* represented something most probably unusual in the archaic age, with their detailed narrative pace, their selection of chronologically limited and unified time-spans, and their frequent deviations from the chronological order of events. In contrast to (what we now label) the 'Homeric' poems, the narrative strategies of the other poems in the Epic Cycle may have been the norm – strategies well suited to an audience's horizon of expectations at the time when the poems were first performed. In the pages that follow, I will try to investigate when and why the Epic Cycle could no longer satisfy the aesthetic expectations of both later readers and post-archaic literary critics. As we shall see, the Epic Cyclic poems turned into a practical (and indispensable) reference for Theban and Trojan mythology, and yet they seem to have been less and less read; above all, they came to function as a poetic foil against which the different mechanics of Homeric narrative were defined. Of course, the fact that the poems were condensed into epitomizing summaries – transformed into easy-to-swallow pills that were widely consulted from the Hellenistic age onwards – does not by itself prove that the 'originals' were no longer read. But the phenomenon does demonstrate that – differently from the summaries – the original poetic form of the Cyclic poems ended up being seen as dispensable, at least for many post-classical readers.

BEFORE ARISTOTLE

If we are ready to believe that vase-painters drew their inspiration not only from oral and more or less non-canonical versions of the Trojan-War myths, but also from canonical poems such as the *Iliad*, the *Odyssey*, and the Cycle they heard performed in public,[1] then 'we should have to assume that Arctinus of Miletus, who wrote the *Aethiopis*, and Stasinus, author

---

[1] The great freedom of sixth- and fifth-century iconography from specific textual models – in terms of both contamination and variation of the motifs we know from Homer or the Cycle – has recently been reconsidered by Giuliani (2003: 158–280) and Squire (2009: 122–39).

of the *Cypria*, were far more beloved than Homer'.[2] The impression that the Homeric poems did not receive any privileged attention in the archaic age as models for the iconographical imagination, and that the Cyclic texts were at least as dominant as Homer, has been amply confirmed in the last decades. At least down to the late sixth century, pictures more or less certainly inspired by the Homeric poems comprised less than one-third of all visual depictions focusing on myths of the Trojan Cycle.[3] By contrast, Macedonian beakers of the second century BC decorated with Trojan-War scenes (and relevant captions) display a marked inbalance *in favor* of Homer over the Cyclic authors: twenty-two of the vessels depict scenes from the *Iliad* and the *Odyssey*, whereas only four deal with the *Aethiopis*, seven with the *Ilias parva*, two with the *Iliou persis*, and one with the *Nostoi*.[4] This is usually assumed to parallel the editorial activity of third-century scholars, and their concentration on the Homeric poems.

The observation that there may have been a preference for 'Cyclic' over 'Homeric' material during the archaic age is seconded by Greek drama as well. By the peak of the classical era, an age in which it is usually assumed that the 'superiority' of Homer was firmly established, the Epic Cycle still exerted a greater influence on Attic tragedy than the *Iliad* or *Odyssey*. Among those tragedies by the three major tragedians that dealt with the events of the Trojan War, the majority derived their plots from poems of the Epic Cycle. There are in fact only two cases in which enough of a tragic text reworking the Homeric *Iliad* survives for us to figure out substantive features of its content. First, there are the fragments of an Aeschylean trilogy on the death of Patroclus and the death of Hector (or, alternatively, the deaths of Patroclus and Hector, plus the death of Achilles[5]); second, the *Rhesus* tragedy ascribed to Euripides survives whole. To consider briefly those tragedies of which only fragments or the name survives: forty-three of Sophocles' titles (more than one-fourth of the Sophoclean titles that we know) deal with myths of the Trojan War, and, of this number, thirty-six or thirty-eight plays are derived from the Epic Cycle, while only five or seven take up Homeric subjects. Euripides shows a similar bias in favor of Cyclic stories, and of his plays dealing with Trojan myths only three draw on Homeric myths (one is the

---

[2] Shapiro (1989: 46).

[3] See now Carpenter, above in this volume; Fittschen (1969); Kannicht (1982); Cook (1983); Ahlberg-Cornell (1992); Scaife (1995); Snodgrass (1998: 127–50).

[4] According to the catalogue provided by Sinn (1979). On the Macedonian Homeric beakers and a review of the substantial presence of the Epic Cycle in Pompeii paintings and the *Tabulae Iliacae*, see Squire, below in this volume.

[5] For bibliography, Fantuzzi (2012: 215 n. 63) and Sommerstein below in this volume, p. 461 n.5.

satyr play *Cyclops*), while fourteen focus on Cyclic events. Aeschylus' plays are more evenly distributed between the Epic Cycle and Homer: of his Trojan plays, ten develop Homeric myths, and fourteen develop myths of the Epic Cycle.[6]

An Aristotelian answer to this disproportion of attention among the tragedians might be a quantitative one: the *Iliad* narrated one single event concerning one main character (Achilles and his wrath), and thus from the *Iliad* as a whole only 'one or two' tragedies could be derived. By comparison, the poems of the Epic Cycle would have lacked unity, so several tragedies could be drawn from each. This answer is of course very idiosyncratically Aristotelian: the claim that one can make 'only one or two tragedies' out of the *Iliad* or *Odyssey*, is an oddity in contrast with at least the trilogy of Aeschylus on Achilles and Patroclus.[7] Besides, Aristotle himself admitted that the single event described in the *Iliad* is *polymythos* 'with a multiple plot' (1456a12–3; see below); it incorporates a multiplicity of scenes that are memorable and can potentially inspire iconographic or literary reworking.[8] Perhaps the relatively small number of tragic enactments of the *Iliad* instead reflects the fact that varying the model of the *Iliad* seemed a more daunting task, considering the absolute centrality of Homer to fifth-century culture. The remolding of events narrated in the Cyclic poems might also have been easier because of their narrative pace, which is usually assumed to have been faster than that of the Homeric poems.[9] In other words, by focusing on the poems of the Epic Cycle, the tragedians perhaps thought to construct a tragedy simply by choosing from among the relatively numerous narrative opportunities left unexploited by the Cyclic poems. They 'just' had to fill in details that these poems had not provided. Conversely, dealing with the *Iliad* would have required the more demanding task of finding out the relatively few details of the characters' actions or characterization that had been left untold, or were but briefly expressed, in the *Iliad*. It would also have been very challenging to reuse the structure the *Iliad* imposes on the events, which at least some Hellenistic readers perceived as extremely non-linear in comparison to Cyclic sequentiality. At least in the cases of the *Rhesus* and the *Myrmidons*, to reuse an Iliadic tale meant also to significantly reshape the narrative prototype. The *Rhesus*, as a consequence, represents the night of *Iliad* 10 from the perspective not of the Greeks but of the Trojans and their

---

[6] According to the data produced by Radt (1983: 197–8), Kannicht (2004b: 189–96), and now Tsagalis (2008c: 112–15). See also Sommerstein, below in this volume, pp. 461–5.
[7] See Sommerstein, below in this volume, p. 461.
[8] Twenty-two of these scenes/stories are listed by Snodgrass (1998: 69–72).
[9] See Griffin (1977).

Thracian ally Rhesus. This contrasts strongly with the 'philhellenic' agenda that Homer seems to have pursued in the *Iliad*, as the ancient scholiasts already remarked (see for instance Σ T 10.13, bt 10.14–16). Similarly, the *Myrmidons*, the first play of Aeschylus' Iliadic trilogy, rewrote the events leading up to the death of Patroclus, and Achilles' reactions to it to match an erotic interpretation of the bond between the two heroes – an explicit interpretation which contrasts with the *Iliad*'s total silence on this subject.

Hints that the tragedians may have preferred the Epic Cycle over Homer can also be found in the writings of ancient critics. According to Athenaeus, Zoilus the Ὁμηρομάστιξ ('Homer-whipper') commented that (*TrGF* T 136) 'Sophocles was pleased (ἔχαιρε) with the Epic Cycle, to the extent that he composed entire plays closely following the construction of the myth told in it (κατακολουθῶν τῆι ἐν τούτωι μυθοποιίαι).'[10] Sophocles could thus give the impression, at least to one ancient critic, that the plot of some of his tragedies had 'closely followed' the model of the 'construction of the myth' already adopted in the Epic Cycle. Of course, we do not know whether Sophocles followed the Epic Cycle closely because he actually loved it, as Zoilus says, or simply because it was easy to follow and easier to remold than other sources – certainly, attributing Sophocles' choice to his *love* for the Cyclic authors would have been a logical strategy for the biased 'Homer-whipper', which we do not have to share.

A different ancient critic confirms our suspicion why the Epic Cycle may have been more easy to follow than the Homeric poem. There is a telling silence on the subject of aesthetic value in the evaluation of the merits of these poems as consisting mainly of their ordered *akolouthia tōn . . . pragmatōn*, which was expressed by Proclus (the author of the summaries) according to Photius' *Bibliotheca* (319a30) – for the text, see Introduction above.

It is probable that Proclus' analysis – which seems mainly synchronic (= focused on his own age)[11] but hints also at the historical aspect of transmission in *diasōizetai* – emphasized the format of the Cyclic summaries

---

[10] Zoilus' consideration may seem to be contradicting the statement in the *Vita* of Sophocles (*TrGF* T A1.20) that this playwright τούς τε γὰρ μύθους φέρει κατ' ἴχνος τοῦ ποιητοῦ· καὶ τὴν Ὀδύσσειαν δὲ ἐν πολλοῖς δράμασιν ἀπογράφεται ('in fact he presents the myths following in the footsteps of the poet; and in many of his plays he also produces a copy of the *Odyssey*'). But only three of Sophocles' plays draw on the *Odyssey*. The *Vita* instead may thus point to allusions to single motifs, scenes, stylistic features, or linguistic usages of the *Odyssey* and Homer that Sophocles adopted in non-Homeric plots; the fact that the *Vita* continues by appreciating in Soph. *TrGF* F 965 the paretymology of the name Odysseus familiar from *Od*. 19.406–9 clearly supports this reading. See Radt (1983: 199–202).

[11] Severyns (1928: 76).

Proclus himself produced in pursuit of a complete/continuous outline of the wars of the gods and the heroes. This idea of an orderly sequence of events will however reflect a feature already present in the original poems, though at a lower level of consistency. Despite the presence in the original Cyclic poems of occasional incongruities, contradictions, and overlappings, that Proclus and/or pre-Proclian summaries may have smoothed out, the *akolouthia tōn pragmatōn* must already have informed the 'Cyclic impulse'[12] to fix late-archaic epic in writing – though it may have been less likely that the idea of *akolouthia* was already consistent in the epic tales when they circulated orally.[13]

A poet who wanted to become part of this gradually forming encyclopedic narrative of the Trojan War (and so to win attention by association) had necessarily to look for mythological narratives that could fit in with those that had already been established;[14] to fill the gaps between these gradually fixed texts, and thus to become a segment of a more and more systematic continuum, must have been a main motivation for any author acting on the post-'Homeric' cyclic impulse. Of course, acknowledging the existence of the available texts also involved competing with them, exploiting them, and claiming their territory; but this was just another way of accepting the idea of coming after or together with a series of other texts. In other words, when the texts of the *Iliad* and the *Odyssey* were progressively fixed in a more or less standardized form, it may not have been difficult to select a specific plot and allude to other episodes of the Trojan myth that still circulated as oral tales. Of course the poets of the Epic Cycle had to cope with the need to tailor their work more or less precisely to the remaining slots that were not yet formalized in the form of fixed texts. The results of this synchronization may not have always been perfect, and there were probably versions of the Cyclic poems with overlaps between the boundaries of the various poems, and also with contradictions. These would have been pruned in later – more cyclically self-conscious – versions or in the summaries. In fact, we do not have to assume that the poems were all heavily episodic in structure and lacking in organic unity, and some may have adopted the task of 'filling a slot' in the sequence of events in a more elastic way than others.[15]

---

[12] The concept, and much of its definition in the terms I provide in this paragraph, derive from Scodel (2012).
[13] See Introduction, above in this volume, pp. 1–2, 9–12, 20–1, and 32–3, and West, above, pp. 97–101.
[14] The fight about narrative territories between the *Ilias parva* and the *Iliou persis* is an especially telling case: see Introduction, above, pp. 28–9.
[15] See West, above, pp. 97–101.

The mapping of these narrative slots in the frame of the whole myth of the war at Troy, and the resultant task of pursuing the events in each slot sequentially (the only form of plot 'unity' noticeable in most of the Cyclic plots), may have 'taught' the poets of the Epic Cycle to produce versions of their stories which, despite possible overlaps and contradictions, were generically destined to be parts of a whole; they were meant to belong to a collective unity (the Cycle), rather than to constitute a series of discrete, individual units.[16]

ARISTOTLE

Herodotus (2.117) observes a discrepancy between the *Cypria* and the *Iliad* concerning the route Paris' ship took from Sparta to Troy, and he maintains that this shows 'most clearly' (οὐκ ἥκιστα ἀλλὰ μάλιστα) that the *Cypria* are by the hand not of Homer but of another.[17] The adverbs may mean, in principle, that there were other reasons to doubt the common authorship, but nothing in Herodotus' words leads us to suppose that among these he included a difference in aesthetic quality between the *Cypria* and the *Iliad*. There is, in fact, not a single disparaging statement about the aesthetic value of the Epic Cycle attested before the fourth century BC. Rather, as we have seen above, there is plenty of evidence about their very large diffusion.[18]

However, both Plato's and Aristotle's foundational contributions to the birth of a technical literary criticism established criteria of evaluation that were potentially in conflict with the goal of strict narrative sequentiality, and thus with the poetics of the Cyclic authors. The most 'dangerous' criterion for the Cyclic poetics, in particular, was the idea of unity as a technical requisite for (good) literary texts, that is paramount in the aesthetics hinted at in Plato's *Phaedrus* and, above all, in the systematic treatment of the poetics of tragedy (and epic) offered by Aristotle in the *Poetics* (*Phaedr.* 264; *Poet.* chap. 7–8 and in particular 23). As it has been correctly observed, even Aristotle's requirements for unity are much more flexible than the modern prominence of this idea leads us to suppose, and give room to centrifugal trends.[19] Besides, many other literary critics of the ancient world

---

[16] See Burgess (2004b: 3): 'before the textualization of the Epic Cycle, then, oral performance of epic could on any given occasion be organized according to a notional "cycle" of myth. When the mythological cycle was actualized by epic performance, oral prototypes of the Epic Cycle would have resulted.'

[17] See above in this volume, pp. 33–4, 52–3, 61–2, 287.

[18] As Burgess (2004b: 3) correctly remarks, 'Cyclic poetry can be seen as representing a type of epic that functioned successfully in its own temporal-local parameters.'

[19] See above all Heath (1987: 98–111; 1989: 38–55).

appear to pay little (if any) attention to the idea of unity. But this idea, in its basic requirements of continuity and completeness, seems structural in Aristotle's system of aesthetical thought, and may even be the reflection of the need for necessary or probable clarity in the logic of the dramatic action.[20] And the aesthetical parameters of Aristotle or the Peripatos appear to have been extremely influential on the Homeric scholarship of the Hellenistic age and in general the literary criticism of epic and drama.[21]

Quite tellingly, just as the visual dimension of an object makes more conspicuous and unappealing any lack of unity and wholeness, both *Phaedrus* and *Poetics* transform the unity and order of a successful plot from its natural dimension of duration and successive vision of chronologically successive events into a spatial scheme.[22] They compare the whole and unified work to an animal that is well developed, with all its parts in the right places, and is complete in itself.[23] Aristotle in particular considers the 'structure of the events' (*systasis tōn pragmatōn*) as 'the first and greatest thing in tragedy' (1450b22–3) and elaborates on this biological teleology in detail, reaching the conclusion that wholeness presupposes 'a beginning, a middle, and an end' (1450b24–5).[24] By 'beginning' (*archē*) he meant 'that which does not itself follow necessarily from something else'; by 'end', 'that which itself naturally occurs, whether necessarily or usually, after a preceding event, but which need not be followed by anything else' (1450b28–30). Wholeness and unity are thus very strongly connected in his thought, as the 'whole' *praxis* that both tragedy and epic should pursue turns out to be a self-contained series of interdependent events[25] – 'it makes a great difference whether things happen because of, or only after, their antecedents', as Aristotle states in 1452a21–2, expressing at the same time an obvious preference for the causal kind of interdependence over chronology. From this viewpoint the selective narrative technique practiced by Homer, centered around a single centripetal motif, was predictably to be viewed as a great achievement,

---

[20] If we agree with Halliwell (1998: 98–108 and 210) that unity is helpful to the understanding of human action and thus has a cognitive relevance in the *Poetics*.
[21] See Meijering (1987); Grisolia (2001); Fantuzzi (forthcoming).   [22] Klimis (1997: 57–8).
[23] Heath (1989: 18–21, 38–55); Ford (2002: 241–3); Purves (2010: 24–32).
[24] As Ford (2002: 265) correctly comments, 'Aristotle's conception of organic composition had a payoff for critical practice as well: if we place the arts within a teleological nature that "does nothing in vain", good poets might be held to similar standards; critics are then justified in examining each perceived detail of a literary text and asking what role it plays in the overall design.'
[25] See Heath (1989: 41).

whereas the poetics of the Cyclic poems (or of other poems of archaic epic) were doomed to seem quite problematic.

It is telling that in both passages in which the unity of the plot is discussed (chaps. 7–8 and 23), Aristotle adduces archaic epic (excluding Homer) as a negative paradigm to have it contrast with the positive paradigm of Homer. Chapter 8 deals with 'biographic' epic. The authors of *Heracleids* and *Theseids* are berated for their misguided belief that focusing on a single character could provide their works with sufficient unity (1451a16–25):

> μῦθος δ' ἐστὶν εἷς οὐχ ὥσπερ τινές οἴονται ἐὰν περὶ ἕνα ἦι· πολλὰ γὰρ καὶ ἄπειρα τῶι ἑνὶ συμβαίνει, ἐξ ὧν ἐνίων οὐδέν ἐστιν ἕν· οὕτως δὲ καὶ πράξεις ἑνὸς πολλαί εἰσιν, ἐξ ὧν μία οὐδεμία γίνεται πρᾶξις. διὸ πάντες ἐοίκασιν ἁμαρτάνειν ὅσοι τῶν ποιητῶν Ἡρακληΐδα Θησηΐδα καὶ τὰ τοιαῦτα ποιήματα πεποιήκασιν· οἴονται γάρ, ἐπεὶ εἷς ἦν ὁ Ἡρακλῆς, ἕνα καὶ τὸν μῦθον εἶναι προσήκειν. ὁ δ' Ὅμηρος ὥσπερ καὶ τὰ ἄλλα διαφέρει καὶ τοῦτ' ἔοικεν καλῶς ἰδεῖν, ἤτοι διὰ τέχνην ἢ διὰ φύσιν· Ὀδύσσειαν γὰρ ποιῶν οὐκ ἐποίησεν ἅπαντα ὅσα αὐτῶι συνέβη, κτλ.

> a plot is not unified, as some think, if built round an individual. Any entity has innumerable features, not all of which cohere into a unity; likewise, an individual performs many actions which yield no unitary action. So all those poets are clearly at fault who have composed a *Heracleid*, a *Theseid*, and similar poems: they think that since Heracles was an individual, the plot too must be unitary. But Homer, in keeping with his general superiority, evidently grasped well, whether by art or nature, this point too: though composing an *Odyssey*, he did not include every feature of the hero's life, etc.

Similarly, and not without a precise cross reference to chap. 8 in 1459a30, chap. 23 highlights the difference between real unity of action and the false impression of unity which can derive from the linear treatment of a particular span of time. The examples of this chronological pseudo-unity that Aristotle provides are from historiography, the *Cypria* and the *Ilias parva*, and both of these negative Cyclic paradigms are opposed to Homer's successful preference for selectivity in delimiting the extension of the plot (1459a17–b4):

> περὶ δὲ τῆς διηγηματικῆς καὶ ἐν μέτρωι μιμητικῆς, ὅτι δεῖ τοὺς μύθους καθάπερ ἐν ταῖς τραγωιδίαις συνιστάναι δραματικοὺς καὶ περὶ μίαν πρᾶξιν ὅλην καὶ τελείαν ἔχουσαν ἀρχὴν καὶ μέσα καὶ τέλος, ἵν' ὥσπερ ζῶιον ἓν ὅλον ποιῆι τὴν οἰκείαν ἡδονήν, δῆλον, καὶ μὴ ὁμοίας ἱστορίαις τὰς συνθέσεις εἶναι, ἐν αἷς ἀνάγκη οὐχὶ μιᾶς πράξεως ποιεῖσθαι δήλωσιν ἀλλ' ἑνὸς χρόνου, ὅσα ἐν τούτωι συνέβη περὶ ἕνα ἢ πλείους, ὧν ἕκαστον ὡς ἔτυχεν ἔχει πρὸς

ἄλληλα... διὸ ὥσπερ εἴπομεν ἤδη καὶ ταύτηι θεσπέσιος ἂν φανείη Ὅμηρος παρὰ τοὺς ἄλλους, τῶι μηδὲ τὸν πόλεμον καίπερ ἔχοντα ἀρχὴν καὶ τέλος ἐπιχειρῆσαι ποιεῖν ὅλον· λίαν γὰρ ἂν μέγας καὶ οὐκ εὐσύνοπτος ἔμελλεν ἔσεσθαι ὁ μῦθος... νῦν δ' ἓν μέρος ἀπολαβὼν ἐπεισοδίοις κέχρηται αὐτῶν πολλοῖς, οἷον νεῶν καταλόγωι καὶ ἄλλοις ἐπεισοδίοις οἷς διαλαμβάνει τὴν ποίησιν. οἱ δ' ἄλλοι περὶ ἕνα ποιοῦσι καὶ περὶ ἕνα χρόνον καὶ μίαν πρᾶξιν πολυμερῆ, οἷον ὁ τὰ Κύπρια ποιήσας καὶ τὴν μικρὰν Ἰλιάδα. τοιγαροῦν ἐκ μὲν Ἰλιάδος καὶ Ὀδυσσείας μία τραγωιδία ποιεῖται ἑκατέρας ἢ δύο μόναι, ἐκ δὲ Κυπρίων πολλαὶ καὶ τῆς μικρᾶς Ἰλιάδος πλέον[26] ἢ ὀκτώ, οἷον ὅπλων κρίσις, Φιλοκτήτης, Νεοπτόλεμος, Εὐρύπυλος, πτωχεία, Λάκαιναι, Ἰλίου πέρσις καὶ Ἀπόπλους.

As regards narrative mimesis in verse, it is clear that plots, as in tragedy, should be constructed dramatically, that is, around a single, whole, and complete action, with beginning, middle, and end, so that epic, like a single and whole animal, may produce the pleasure proper to it. Its structures should not be like histories, which require an exposition not of a single action but of a single period of time, with all the events (in their contingent relationships) that happened to one person or more during it... Homer's inspired superiority over the rest can be seen here too: though the war had a beginning and an end, he did not try to treat its entirety, for the plot was bound to be too large and not easily taken by the eye in one view... instead he has selected one section, but has used many others as episodes, such as the Catalogue of the Ships[27] and other episodes, by which he diversifies the composition. But the others compose poems around a single figure or single period, hence an action of many parts, like the author of the *Cypria* and of the *Ilias parva*. Therefore out of the *Iliad* and *Odyssey* respectively only one or two tragedies are made, while from the *Cypria* there can be many and from the *Ilias parva* eight – say, the *Award of the Arms, Philoctetes, Neoptolemus, Eurypylus, Beggar Mission, The Laconian Women, Iliou persis* and *Departure.*

The last statement of Aristotle is concentrated on the task of drawing a contrastive distinction between Homeric epic, Epic Cycle, and tragedy and is obviously aprioristic, as it is in contrast with the fact that Aeschylus wrote a trilogy on Achilles and Patroclus, and Sophocles derived three tragedies from the *Odyssey*.[28] It is true that in other passages of the *Poetics* the *Iliad* is also said to be πολύμυθος, in the sense that it has the 'multiple plot' structure that is typical of epic (1456a12–3; but see more below), and Aristotle notes of both Homeric poems that they display 'a structure of multiple

---

[26] πλέον may be interpolated: see Sommerstein, below in this volume, p. 461 n. 1.
[27] See below, pp. 414–15.   [28] See Sommerstein, below in this volume, pp. 461–2.

actions... and have many parts of individual magnitude' (1462b7–10). But in these passages Aristotle must be referring to the digressive expansions, the ἐπεισόδια, whose presence he also appreciates in 1459a36;[29] differently, the *Cypria* and *Ilias parva* are described as simply and irrecoverably *polymerē* 'formed of many parts' – nor are their 'parts' subordinated in some way to a prevailing action, like the *epeisodia*. In any case, Aristotle specifies (1462b10–11) that, despite the presence of these parts of individual magnitude, the poems of Homer 'are structured as well as could be, and are as close as possible to mimesis of a unitarian action'. By contrast, in 1456a10–18, just after stressing the fact that the Iliadic plot is *polymythos*, Aristotle highlights the difference between tragedy and epic *tout-court* – the latter being structurally less μία 'unified' than the former. He justifies epic *polymythia* as follows: 'the poet must remember to avoid turning a tragedy into an epic structure (by "epic" I mean a structure with a multiple plot), say by dramatizing the entire plot of the *Iliad*. In epic, because of its length, the sections take on an apt magnitude, but in plays [the plot of epic scope] goes quite against expectation. An indication of this is that those who have treated the entire fall of Troy, rather than part of it (like Euripides)... either founder or do badly in competition.' This last passage seems to confirm Aristotle's statement at 1459a17–b4 (quoted above), though nuancing it by considering not only good but also bad real or potential tragedies. The resulting picture is that only bad tragedies can be derived from single parts of the *Iliad* (= only one good tragedy can come from the *Iliad*, and/but it should not be a systematic dramatization of the whole), whereas more than one good Euripidean tragedy can be derived from the *Iliou persis*. However the tragedy whose plot tries to coincide with the whole of the plot of the *Iliou persis* is doomed to failure. Epic can reach only seldom the delicate balance that Aristotle pursues between its inherent *polymythia* and the unity of the best tragedies, and finds it with Homer, whereas in particular the poems of the Epic Cycle present an obvious counterweight to this balance.

Σ b *Il.* 2.494–877, which seems a later development along the Aristotelian line of thought, also proves that the *Poetics*' emphasis on 'unity' of the plot can be read as including a dialectical dynamic between the events of the main action and worthwhile digressions that are capable of providing amusing variations:

> θαυμάσιος ὁ ποιητὴς μηδ' ὁτιοῦν παραλιμπάνων τῆς ὑποθέσεως, πάντα δ' ἐξ ἀναστροφῆς κατὰ τὸν ἐπιβάλλοντα καιρὸν διηγούμενος, τὴν τῶν θεῶν ἔριν, τὴν τῆς Ἑλένης ἁρπαγήν, τὸν Ἀχιλλέως θάνατον· ἡ γὰρ κατὰ τάξιν διήγησις νεωτερικὸν καὶ συγγραφικὸν καὶ τῆς ποιητικῆς ἄπο σεμνότητος.

---

[29] I agree with Heath (1989: 50–4, 114–18), to whom this paragraph and the next owe a lot.

εὔκαιρον τοίνυν ἐπιθεὶς Νέστορι ῥητορείαν τὸν Κατάλογον ἐμνηστεύσατο, ὅπως μὴ ἐν τῶι αὐτῶι λόγωι λέγων τὰ πρακτικὰ καὶ γενεαλογικὰ τὴν ἀκοὴν ἐπιταράσσοι.

> Homer is admirable in his not leaving out anything of the subject matter, and narrating everything in inverse order at the right moment: the contention of the goddesses, the abduction of Helen, the death of Achilles. In fact the narration in a straightforward order is modern and historiographical, and removed from the sublimity of poetry. Therefore opportunely, after introducing the speech of Nestor [namely the speech of 2.362–8, where Nestor had advised Agamemnon to 'separate men by tribes and by clans, so that clan may bear aid to clan and tribe to tribe,' thereby creating the incentive to each man to do his best in defense of his clan/tribe], he joined to it the 'Catalogue', in order not to confuse the audience by expressing in the same speech the practical plans and the genealogical details.

The 'Catalogue of the Ships' is thus seen as an informative digression about the forces on the field. It may mainly concern the narrative of the whole war (*hypothesis*) rather than the *Iliad* proper, but Homer helpfully produces it at a point where it seems 'motivated' by Nestor's hint at the various ethnic subdivisions of the Greek army and does not undermine the epic's overall unity. The scholiast's appreciation for this digression's unitarian quality does not surprise: it is a digression from the main narrative action, but a digression that points centripetally to the superstructure of the war of Troy, to which the *Iliad* belongs.[30] Compare the digression by, again, Nestor, that from the length of Proclus' summary appears to have been one of the longest to be found in a Cyclic poem. According to Proclus

---

[30] Most similar to the aesthetics of Σ 2.494–877 is the viewpoint expressed many centuries later by Eustathius in his introductory essay to the *Iliad* (7.14–42). Homer is lauded because, of the ten years of the war for Troy, he 'made the *Iliad* from the last events, namely the tenth year, and not from the whole of it, but from a part of it...' He adopted this principle both for the novelty and the surprise deriving from the unexpected – in fact beginning from the first events is not new, as the listener expects this approach as the most common, (ἅμα μὲν διὰ τὸ καινοπρεπὲς καὶ τῶι ἀνελπίστωι ξενίζον, τὸ γὰρ κατὰ φύσιν ἀπὸ τῶν πρώτων ἄρξασθαι οὔτε καινόν τι ἔχει καὶ ὁ ἀκροατὴς δὲ ὡς ἐπὶ πολὺ οὕτως ἐλπίζει γενέσθαι). But Homer is also appreciated because he takes into consideration a possible 'gluttonous listener' (τις λίχνος τὴν ἀκοήν), who may be upset about the poet's selective approach and eager to learn only about the end, not about what happens before the end (ὅτι τὸ τέλος μαθὼν ἀνήκουστος ἔσται τῶν πρὸ τοῦ τέλους), and therefore disseminates in his narrative events that precede the action of the *Iliad*, or follow it. According to Eusthatius (7.37–9), who seems to develop Peripatetic material (cf. *Poet.* 1456a10–8 quoted above), Homer was imitated by later authors, in particular by Euripides, who ἐκ τοῦ μέσου τῶν δραματικῶν ἀρχόμενος ὑποθέσεων, εἶτα καὶ τὰ φθάσαντα παρεισάγει καὶ τὰ μέλλοντα δὲ ὕστερον εὐφυέστατα παρενείρει τῶι λόγωι ('beginning from the middle of the dramatic stories, introduces preceding events and intrudes on the side future events, in the most suitable way for the narrative').

(§ 4), 'Nestor in a digression (ἐν παρεκβάσει) relates to him (scil. Menelaus) how Epopeus seduced the daughter of Lycurgus [or Lycus: emend. Heyne] and had his city sacked, and the story of Oedipus, and the madness of Heracles, and the story of Theseus and Ariadne.' The first and the last narratives are stories of erotic abduction (~ Paris), while the two central myths seem connected to the main narrative action only as paradigms for the madness induced by eros.[31] Though Nestor's paradigms are not incompatible with the style of his tales in the *Iliad* and the *Odyssey*, which often 'situate the Homeric epics with respect to other epic traditions',[32] ancient interpreters might well have questioned their relevance to the narrative, just as some modern readers do.[33] Certainly there are as many as four stories in a row, and none of them belongs to the superstructure of the war of Troy, but to the broader network of pre-Trojan myths. Ancient scholars like the one(s) behind Σ *Il.* 2.494–877, who appreciated the selective unity of the Iliadic plot (first level: internal unity), and also its capacity to hint, through the digression of the Catalogue, at the larger unity of the superstructure of the war of Troy (second level: external unity[34]), may have dismissed Nestor's digression in the *Cypria* as an irrelevant tangent leading beyond even the second level of unity into extra-Cyclic myths. It could thus have served as a hair-raising example of an utterly non-unitarian narrative style.

CALLIMACHUS

The Cyclic poems must have seemed, in poetological terms, radically incompatible with the aesthetics of unity and/but selectivity that were widely enforced by some poets and critics after Aristotle. Accordingly, the Cyclic poems became a staple target of readers who were (more or less by Aristotelian predilection) fond of these ideals. And the *cahiers de doléances* on their alleged aesthetical faults also came to include new developments.

---

[31] See Scaife (1995: 167).   [32] Marks (2010).
[33] Their relevance has been argued spiritedly by Marks (2010). I rather sympathize with Rengakos (2004: 285), who considers Nestor's digression in the *Cypria* one of the 'heterodiegetische Analepses, Rückgriffe also auf Vergangenes, das mit der Haupthandlung in keiner Beziehung steht', and Scodel (2008a: 225), who infers from their irrelevance: 'we have to consider the possibility that our poet lacks respect for Nestor. While I would argue that all Nestor's speeches in the *Iliad* are significant, when Telemachus at *Od.* 15.194–201 seeks to avoid having to stay with him, the poet seems to hint that Nestor likes the sound of his own voice too much. The *Cypria* seems to have developed this possibility by having him tell irrelevant stories.'
[34] Kullmann (1960: 257–8) and above in this volume, p. 123; correctly observes the Cyclic concern of the Catalogue within the *Iliad*.

The Cycle's obvious popularity as a source or model in iconography, tragedy, and epic of the late archaic and classical age made it acquire a taste of 'commonality'. From at least the early Hellenistic age this commonality of reuses, joined to the consequent accusation of fastidious repetitiveness resulting in a sense of déjà vu, appears often to have been blamed on the Cyclic inability to select a single sequence of events within a myth; and so, somewhat ironically, the Cycle's very popularity became another mark of its supposedly poor quality and lack of distinction.

Callimachus is the first author known to depict the archaic Epic Cycle, or later poetry written in imitation of the Epic Cycle,[35] as something too conventional and/or something that was *too* easy to imitate for everyone. *AP* 12.43 = *ep.* 28 Pf. = *HE* 1041ff. is one Callimachean passage where poetological statements are justified through widely agreed-upon ethical standards:

> Ἐχθαίρω τὸ ποίημα τὸ κυκλικὸν οὐδὲ κελεύθωι
>   χαίρω, τίς πολλοὺς ὧδε καὶ ὧδε φέρει·
> μισέω καὶ περίφοιτον ἐρώμενον οὐδ' ἀπὸ κρήνης
>   πίνω· σικχαίνω πάντα τὰ δημόσια.
> Λυσανίη, σὺ δὲ ναίχι καλὸς καλός· ἀλλὰ πρὶν εἰπεῖν
>   τοῦτο σαφῶς, ἠχώ φησί τις· 'ἄλλος ἔχει'.

> I hate Cyclic poetry, and get no pleasure from a road that drives many travelers here and there. I cannot stand a gadabout lover, do not drink at public fountains, and loathe everything vulgar. Now you, Lysanies, surely are handsome. But before I have repeated 'handsome', Echo's 'and someone else's' cuts me off.

Conventional experience of eros leads most people not to prefer promiscuous lovers but to opt for a beloved who is loyal and monogamous. In turn, hygiene leads one to want to drink from springs of the purest water. Sadly, fountains or lovers of this sort are much harder to find than public wells or gadabout boys. Many of Callimachus' readers would have remembered that this negative priamel was reminiscent of two quite similar statements in Theognis' elegies: 579–82: 'I hate a scoundrel (ἐχθαίρω κακὸν ἄνδρα), and I veil myself as I pass by, with as little thought for him as a small bird would have. And I hate (again *echthairō*) a woman who runs around... As long as I was drinking myself from the spring's dark water, it seemed sweet

---

[35] Despite Ps.-Acro's and Porphyrio's commentaries to Horace's *Ars poet.* 136–7 (where the *scriptor cyclicus* mentioned by Horace is identified as Antimachus), Cameron (1995: 393–9) spiritedly argues against the idea that Callimachus hints here at imitators of the Epic Cycle – especially recent or contemporary imitators such as Antimachus or Apollonius of Rhodes.

and good to me. But now it has become dirty, and water is mixed with earth. I will drink from another spring rather than a river.' Callimachus' epigram seems to present itself as a new piece of archaic elegy: in this genre, the practice of sympotic performance customarily consisted of the recitation and recreation/updating of previous poetic material. Our Ps.-Theognidean Callimachus expresses a new metaliterary voice, which raises the ethical/erotic priamel of Theognis to the intellectual level of poetics. Callimachus illustrates the desirability of his poetics through widely shared feelings in erotic life that had already found poetic validation in Theognis; his new poetological creed thus takes on the obvious agreeability of traditional ethical behaviors, which had also been sanctioned by the most famous archaic gnomic poet. To return to our specific interests, being acquainted with promiscuous lovers is compared to the practice of traditional Cyclic poetry – all under the sign of excessive easiness – while the taking of uncommon paths is associated with non-banal (= not too well known and not too frequently imitated) sources of inspiration: 'lack of exclusiveness' is therefore the main fault for which Callimachus blames the Epic Cycle, 'as it touches on too many subjects, just as a busy road, a promiscuous lover, and the parish pump serve too many needs'.[36] 'Easy to find/follow' and 'publicity' are thus the negative values that most openly liken the 'Cyclic poem' to the promiscuous lover, the common path, and the public fountain. But 'commonality' is not the only issue at stake in this epigram. Both the common path and the promiscuous lover also hint at another dimension of the 'Cyclic poem', one which has perhaps not attracted enough attention. Callimachus defines the promiscuous lover as *periphoitos*, an epithet whose prefix points to a circular movement. The possible influence of Theognis' *peridromos* or the parallel of the hetaera *periphoitos* of Callim. *AP* 13.24.2 = *ep.* 38.2 Pf. = *HE* 1144 are not to be ignored, of course, but it may be telling that Callimachus chooses to confirm Theognis' definition of the promiscuous lover as someone who 'roams in a circle' or 'around' in order to attract the attention of old and new lovers.[37]

The motion of the unbridled lover who roams 'around' again and again in the public space and woos and tries to conquer one lover after another (with the same techniques and the same roaming), without selecting enough and instead of dwelling in the more private spaces typical of decent reserve,

---

[36] Quotations from Henrichs (1979: 211).
[37] Thomas (1979: 182–4) connects this wandering lover of Callimachus to the frustrated lovers of New Comedy.

comes to be assimilated with the 'circular' motion from the beginning to the end of the Trojan-War myths and its precedents, which is the etymological quintessence of the poems of the Epic Cycle. Going in circles, both as a social/erotic behavior and as the narrative drift of the Cyclic variety of epic, turns out to be a very disreputable choice, as it becomes the geometrical dimension – the dishonorable badge – typical of the 'too common' both at a sexual and aesthetical level.

A similar, equally malicious hint at the 'faults' of the Cyclic poems may underlie, I suggest, Callimachus' definition of the detestable common path: this path is detestable because too many people take it, as modern interpreters have usually observed; but it is also telling that it is said to lead this mob *hōde kai hōde*. This phrase was perhaps idiomatic in the age of Callimachus (it became common in the imperial age), but the fact that it amounts to the repetition of the same adverb goes to show how repetitive these paths' fixed starting and end points are perceived to be: only a single route is marked on these paths, as well as in the narratives of the 'Cyclic' *akolouthia*, and this route may have felt even more monotonous, if Callimachus also perceived the language of the cyclic poems to be heavily repetitive – an accusation that is not expressed nor perhaps involved in Callimachus but is fully voiced by Pollianus, to whom we will come back soon.

In any case, if *AP* 12.43 is the manifesto of Callimachus' rejection of, specifically, the commonality of 'cyclic poetry', his prologue to the *Aetia* most explicitly rejects the typical narrative principles of linearity/completeness that had already been in the sights of the criticism of Aristotle: Callimachus explains in fact that his adversaries, the Telchines, have often accused him (1.3–5 Harder)

> εἵνεκε]ν οὐχ ἓν ἄεισμα διηνεκὲς ἢ βασιλ[ήων
>   ...]ας ἐν πολλαῖς ἤνυσα χιλιάσιν
> ἢ.....].ους ἥρωας ἔπος δ' ἐπὶ τυτθὸν ἑλ[ίσσω
>   [πα]ῖς ἅτ]ε, τῶν δ' ἐτέων ἡ δεκὰ[ς] οὐκ ὀλίγη

> because I did not complete one single continuous song [on the glory of?] kings... in many thousands of lines or on... heroes, but turn around words a little in my mind like a child, although the decades of my years are not few.

The phrase *en pollais chiliasin* ('in many thousands of lines') points to the opposition between big quantity (preferred by Telchines) and small quantity (preferred by Callimachus), and probably also *ouch hen*, if it means 'not even one single' in opposition to 'many'.[38] But certainly *diēnekes* refers to features of the narrative. It is a Homeric word which in Homer and the critics of Callimachus had a positive sense and designated an object, operation, or narration (especially in direct speeches) characterized by continuity, completeness, uninterruptedness, and chronological order of its phases.[39] These features, that Callimachus rejects, and already Aristotle had connected to the Cyclic narrative style and rejected as proper to history more than poetry (*Poet.* 1459a20–b7), practically coincide with the *akolouthia tōn . . . pragmatōn*, that Proclus was going to mention as the most widely acknowledged positive merit of the Cyclic poems.

AFTER ARISTOTLE AND CALLIMACHUS

In *Ars poet.* 128–52, while discussing whether it is better to deal with established plots, or to invent new ones, Horace goes for the former option, but specifies in detail how an author can and should be original in this reapplication (128–49):

> . . . tuque
> rectius Iliacum carmen deducis in actus
> quam si proferres ignota indictaque primus.   130
> publica materies privati iuris erit, si
> non circa vilem patulumque moraberis orbem,
> nec verbo verbum curabis reddere fidus
> interpres nec desilies imitator in artum,
> unde pedem proferre pudor vetet aut operis lex.   135
> nec sic incipies, ut scriptor cyclicus olim:
> 'Fortunam Priami cantabo et nobile bellum'.
> quid dignum tanto feret hic promissor hiatu?
> parturient montes, nascetur ridiculus mus.
> quanto rectius hic, qui nil molitur inepte: 140
> 'Dic mihi, Musa, virum, captae post tempora Troiae

---

[38] I find very appealing the suggestion by Heath (1989: 56) and Asper (1997: 217) that *ouch hen* simply means 'not even one' (almost as if it were the answer to the critics' question 'how many poems *diēnekea* did you compose?'); likewise Harder (2012: 18), to be seen also for a discussion of the bibliography. But *hen* may also perhaps point to the convenience of unity presupposed elsewhere by Aristotle's or Plato's esthetical discussions (see above, pp. 410–11) – as it is more commonly assumed. In this case, since *hen* = 'endowed with unity' is a value for Aristotle, and *diēnekes* is a disvalue, Callimachus may insidiously point that the ignorant Telchines do not understand that both qualities cannot coexist in the same poem (Hunter (1993: 192–3)).

[39] See, e.g., van Tress (2004: 31–8).

qui mores hominum multorum vidit et urbes'.
non fumum ex fulgore, sed ex fumo dare lucem
cogitat, ut speciosa dehinc miracula promat,
Antiphaten Scyllamque et cum Cyclope Charybdim.   145
nec reditum Diomedis ab interitu Meleagri,
nec gemino bellum Troianum orditur ab ovo;
semper ad eventum festinat et in medias res
non secus ac notas auditorem rapit.

It's better to weave a play from the poem of Troy, than be first to offer something unknown, unsung. You'll win private rights to public themes, if you don't keep slowly circling the broad beaten track, or, pedantic translator, render them word for word, or, following an idea, leap like the goat into the well from which shame, or the work's logic, denies escape. And don't start like the old writer of epic cycles: 'Of Priam's fate I'll sing, and the greatest of Wars.' What will he produce to match his opening promise? Mountains will labor: What's born? A ridiculous mouse! How much better the man who doesn't struggle, ineptly: 'Tell me, Muse, of that man, who after the fall of Troy, had sight of the manners and cities of many peoples.' He intends not smoke from flame, but light from smoke, so as then to reveal striking and marvelous things: Antiphates, Charybdis and Scylla, the Cyclops. He doesn't start Diomede's return from Troy with Meleager's death, or the Trojan War with two eggs. He always hastens the outcome, and snatches the reader into the midst of the action, as if all were known.[40]

The first suggestion is that one should not linger on the 'easy and large pathway', a fault that Horace sets in parallel to the obvious and negative un-originality of the author who clings too slavishly to his model. The epithet *vilem*, qualifying *orbem*, here has an obviously derogatory relevance. As for *orbem*, this noun hints at the notion of a circular piece of ground, thus evoking sameness and completeness of movement, but also possibly the 'unremitting and tediously complete narrative' of the Epic Cycle.[41] Most explicitly, Horace's author has to avoid being the *scriptor cyclicus* who had once begun his poem with the line: *Fortunam Priami cantabo et nobile bellum*. It has been widely debated whether this line is Horace's invention or translates a Greek Cyclic incipit (by Antimachus, according to

---

[40] Translation by A. S. Kline.
[41] See Brink (1971: 210). Porphyrio commented on Horace's lines 131–2: *in eos dixit, qui a fine Iliados Homeri scripserunt <et κυκλικοί> appellantur. Ideo et patulum orbem dixit* ('He said that against those who wrote from the end of Homer's *Iliad* onwards <and are called Cyclic>. That is why he also speaks of the wide circuit').

Ps.-Acro and Porphyrio); whatever the case, its out-of-focus quality resembles the surviving incipit of the *Ilias parva*, which goes: 'Of Ilios I sing, and the Dardanian land of fine colts, over which the Danaans suffered much, servants of Ares' (*PEG* F 28 = F 1 D. = F 1 W).[42] What Horace appears to dislike in this kind of incipit is that it refers to the whole myth to which the given poem belongs as a mere part: it fails to admit the fact that it narrates only a portion of the war. Thus, in contrast to the incipit of the *Odyssey*, which points precisely to Odysseus and his return after the war (and specifies the chronology and protagonist of the poem), proems like *Fortunam Priami cantabo* are the total negation of intriguing selective choices and throw around megalomaniac promises that are destined not to be fulfilled. Hence Horace's depiction of the readers' disappointed reaction to the discovery of the limited chronological span of the poem: *mons parturit murem*, etc. Likewise, Horace adds, proems that introduce the war of Troy by mentioning the 'twin eggs' and the birth of Helen would be ill-adapted to the *mediae res* of the action, into which, instead, a good author should immediately lead the reader. The specific unity inherent in a poem, which Horace exhorts us to pursue, is thus set in contrast to the 'Cyclic impulse', to the pride of belonging as a segment to the whole myth of the war of Troy – a pride that Horace does not appreciate as a form of homage to the overarching 'Cyclic' unity of the war story, but presents as a lack of compatibility with the core action of the specific poem, and thus a crime of lèse-majesté against its internal unity.

The same acknowledgement of the diffusion of the Epic Cycle as a 'reference work', but also the same elitist disdain for its supposed 'vulgarity' and inability to properly arrange the plot, can be found in Virgil's descriptions of the pictures that Aeneas sees in the temple of Juno at Carthage.[43] At the beginning of his *Aeneid*, Virgil is ready to construct a new poem that celebrates the fame of Aeneas in his post-Trojan existence, but he presents the Trojan past of Aeneas as connected to the events of the war that the Trojan Cycle (inclusive of the *Iliad*) had narrated (*Aen.* 1.456–7):

> ... videt Iliacas ex ordine pugnas,
> bellaque iam fama totum vulgata per orbem
>
> he sees in due order the battles of Ilion, the warfare now known by fame throughout the world.[44]

---

[42] For Greek text and a discussion of the fragment, see Kelly, above in this volume, pp. 329–31.

[43] Other discussions of these pictures in Squire and Gärtner, below in this volume, pp. 520 and 552–4.

[44] The epithet *Iliacus* also hints at the *Iliad*, and the references among the pictures at Carthage to Memnon (*Aen.* 1.489) and Penthesileia (1.490–3), from the *Aethiopis*, and to Troilus (1.474–8),

In terms similar to Horace's, Virgil's *orbem*, ambiguously suspended between 'world' and 'circle', highlights first of all that this Trojan story of Aeneas is now known everywhere in the 'world' (Aeneas acknowledges this fact in front of the pictures he has found in non-Greek and non-Trojan Carthage). But *orbem* also allusively reminds us that the literary medium through which it had become known was the Epic Cycle. And if the wide distribution of the Cycle could, at least after Callimachus' epigram on the 'Cyclic poem', be deemed to have made it *too* common, and thus 'vulgar', then the participle *vulgata* of Virgil (as well as the epithet *vilem* of Horace) suggestively connotes this negative programmatic value. Besides, the sequential, memorialistic 'order' that Aeneas seems to appreciate in the record of the events leading to the fall of Troy depicted on the walls of the temple, and later the chronological order of the events of the battles represented on the shield of Aeneas (*Aen.* 8.629: *pugnataque in ordine bella*[45]), belong to an annalistic narrative that has nothing to do with the elaborately thoughtful disposition of the events in the plot of the *Aeneid*.[46] At any rate, the order of the events in the pictures of the temple is tellingly reversed in Virgil's report: the killing of Rhesus in *Iliad* 10 precedes the death of Troilus that had taken place in the *Cypria*, and is followed by the procession of the Trojan women with Athena's *peplos* in *Iliad* 6; Memnon is mentioned before Penthesileia, whereas the Amazon appears to have made her appearance before him in the *Aethiopis*.[47] Furthermore, Virgil's reading turns out to be a radical subjectivization of the Cyclic *ordo* of the pictures, as it dwells on scenes which are more or less closely paralleled in the

---

from the *Cypria*, leave no doubt that the literary texts underlying the majority of these pictures include the non-Iliadic poems on the Trojan War.

[45] As Hardie (1986: 347) correctly remarks, history is usually presented according to the temporal order of its events, whereas *ekphrasis* does not necessarily need to follow a chronological order – 'but chronological order *is* essential to create an impression of growth and expansion on both the historical and the cosmic levels'.

[46] See first of all Barchiesi (1999; but the original Italian version dates from 1994). Also Boyd (1995: 77), who in particular observes that thanks to the focalization according to which Aeneas' eyes select and describe the scenes of the past Trojan (= Cyclic) history, which is most complex and non-linear, Aeneas 'becomes participant in and observer of his own history simultaneously, both the same as the Trojan Aeneas and different from him'. With his emphasis on Penthesileia, which closes the *ekphrasis* of the pictures, Aeneas' focalization also makes room for the tragic role of Dido and, through her, for her people, the future defeated enemies of Aeneas' descendants; see Putnam (1998a: 34–45); La Penna (2000: 7–8).

[47] Squire correctly observes (below in this volume, p. 520) that within an *ekphrasis* sketching the *Aeneid*'s own relation to the literary lineage of Homer and the Homeric Cycle, Virgil's descriptive order departs from both Homer and the Epic Cycle, as it does not adopt the 'natural'–chronological order of the Cycle but is also different from the 'artificial' order that had been appreciated in Homer.

Aeneid,[48] and which reflect the viewpoint of Aeneas, not that of the Carthaginians. On their temple, the events would likely have been depicted from the viewpoint of the Greek winners (and we of course remember that the temple was a temple of Juno, the enemy of Aeneas).[49]

Virgil's opposition between the Cyclic *ordo* and the *Aeneid*'s non-Cyclic and non-chronological *ordo* remains implicit in the *ekphrasis* of the pictures of the temple, but it seems to belong to a widely shared lexicon of literary criticism that must have been easily understood by every reader of Virgil – and not only by the well-read ones who will have known Callimachus by heart. A few decades after Virgil, one of the *Tabulae Iliacae* (*IG* xiv.1284 = 1A Sadurska) displays the caption-epigram:

[τέχνην τὴν Θεοδ]ώρηον μάθε τάξιν Ὁμήρου
ὄφρα δαεὶς πάσης μέτρον ἔχηις σοφίας.[50]

Understand [the *techne* of Theod]orus so that, knowing the order of Homer, you may have the measure of all wisdom.

As has been recently observed, the *Tabula Iliaca Capitolina* trains its viewer to appreciate the infinite variety of viewing strategies and sequences they *and* their sources pursue (often with different narrative results). The phrase *taxis Homērou* encapsulates in its ambiguity two polar aspects of its relation to the Homeric poems, as it may refer to the original 'order' of the *Iliad* and to the artistic rearrangement that Theodorus has imposed on Homer. The phrase may also ask its readers to undergo a sort of exercise in comparative judgment, and to appreciate the difference between the arrangement of the events in Homer on the one hand, and on the other his successors in the Epic Cycle and Stesichorus, authors whose names are explicitly mentioned as sources for the pictures in the *Tabula Capitolina* together with the *Iliad*.[51] It seems, then, that Virgil's readers were well trained for the kind of comparative exercise that Aeneas' description of the Carthaginian temple asks of them.

This interpretation is compatible with the observation that the Homeric interpreters of the Hellenistic age also appear to have used the Epic Cycle mainly as a foil to acknowledge (and to educate the readers on) the comparatively greater significance of Homer or his occasional defaillances, and

---

[48] Penthesileia anticipates Dido and Camilla, Pallas is a second Troilus, and the raid of Odysseus and Diomedes reminds of Nisus and Euryalus. See Clay (1988: 200–5); Bartsch (1998: 337–8).
[49] Elsner (2007: 81).   [50] See Squire, below in this volume, pp. 516–28.
[51] See Squire (2011: 87–126, 195–6, 248–59). Squire here below, p. 538 and (2014) also interprets, most interestingly, the rearrangement of Iliadic scenes in the Pompeii oecus of Octavius Quartio as another exercise in *taxis*.

to remember what a good author to their mind should not do. It is telling that individual poems of the Epic Cycle are sometimes quoted in the Homeric scholia, but only to introduce quotations of fragments or the occasional summary of mythical tales, and thus to point to specific portions of text.[52] More frequently, the scholia use general terms like *kyklikoi* or *kyklikōs* (adverb). These terms define first of all the subcategory of archaic epic to which they belong – a convenient 'other pole' of archaic epic that has to be kept distinguished and quarantined from Homer, not only in order to better highlight the uncontaminated uniqueness of Homer's aesthetical greatness, but also – if the frequent use of *kyklikōs/-oi* in the scholia derives from Aristarchus, as well as the large use of the broader category of the *neōteroi*[53] – in order to keep the text of the 'real' Homer as pure as possible from later cyclic interpolations[54] and thus enable Aristarchus and his pupils to 'interpret Homer from Homer'. But on other occasions these terms may also involve a negative connotation which is not part and parcel of their etymology, and which finds an obvious parallel in Callimachus' *poiēma kyklikon* or Horace's *scriptor cyclicus*. This is especially evident in some scholia where the adverb *kyklikōs* is found, mentioning the Cycle in their discussion of Homer either to show why the Homeric alternative is better than Cyclic practice or – on some occasions – to show how Homer erred on the side of less acceptable, Cyclic modes of composition. Σ BEPT *Od*. 7.115, commenting on the epithets that qualify the trees in the gardens of Alcinoos' palace, observes: 'the epithets are not thrown down in the manner of the Cyclics (οὐ κυκλικῶς τὰ ἐπίθετα προσέρριπται), but the peculiarity (τὸ ἰδίωμα) of each plant is carefully respected through the epithet'. We might compare with this the consideration of an ancient commentator of *Il*. 11.805 '(Patroclus) set out to run along the line of the ships to Achilles, son of Aeacus' (παρὰ νῆας ἐπ' Αἰακίδην Ἀχιλῆα). Σ T ad loc. observes that Homer 'showed the

---

[52] *Tit. PEG* F 7 (= F 4 D. = F 11 W.); *Cypr. PEG* F 1 (= D., W.), *PEG* F 3 (= F 3 D. = F 4 W.), *PEG* F 27 (= F 21 D. = F 23 W.); *Il. parva PEG* F 3 (= D., W.), *PEG* F 5 (= D., W.), *PEG* F 24 (= F 4 D. = W.); *Il. pers. PEG* F 4 (= F 1 D. = F 2 W.); *Nost. PEG* F 2 (= D. = F 13 W.).

[53] Aristarchus was perhaps not the first to use the term *neōteroi* for the post-Homeric authors, but appears to have been the first to systematize its use; in fact, as was pointed out by Severyns (1928: 42–7), in our Homeric scholia the term includes all sorts of authors from Hesiod to Euphorion = the age of Aristarchus. It is appealing to suppose that in parallel to *neōteroi* he may have also used the general term *kyklikoi* for the archaic non-Homeric epos that he strove to keep well distinguished from Homer (see below). Of course references to the *neōteroi* tend to include the *kyklikoi*; a few times however the *kyklikoi* are opposed to the *neōteroi*. See Severyns (1928: 66–70).

[54] We know that in some cases Aristarchus athetized lines of Homer simply for the reason that they reflected lexicon (Σ *Od*. 4.248) or versions of myths attested in the Cycle (Σ *Od*. 11.547; 4.285).

rush of the run... good is also that he did not say "[ships] of the Achaeans"'. This phrase would have been typical of the Cycle, while the other text has emphasized the rush of Patroclus towards Achilles (εὖ δὲ καὶ τὸ μὴ 'Ἀχαιῶν χαλκοχιτώνων' φάναι· τὸ μὲν γὰρ τοῦ Κύκλου, τὸ δὲ τὴν ὁρμὴν ἐνέφηνε τὴν ἐπὶ τὸν Ἀχιλλέα).' Homer is thus appreciated for *not* using for the last part of the line the formulaic phrase *nēas Achaiōn chalkochitōnōn* (*Il.* 1.371, etc.), as the avoidance of this predictable formula and the prompt mention of Achilles emphasize the swiftness of Patroclus' rush towards his companion. This remark attests to a taste for expressive variation in and contextual motivation for lexical choices – a taste which Cratinus must have presupposed as more or less widespread among his audience when he mocked Homer for using the formula τὸν δ' ἀπαμειβόμενος προσέφη ('to him answering he said') too frequently (*PCG* 355).

The scholia to *Od* 7.115 appreciate Homer precisely for *not* sticking to the 'aesthetics of regularity' that in fact underlay both the Homeric and the Cyclic use of formulaic language.[55] In this instance, the scholia are – expectably – ready to criticize the stylistic standard of the Cycle for dully avoiding any variation and adjustment to the context in its use of epic's stereotypical phrases. Conversely, Homer is at times criticized for his 'Cyclic' sloppiness when he is supposed to be misusing a word. In *Il.* 6.325 a speech of Hector is introduced with the words νείκεσσεν ἰδὼν αἰσχροῖς ἐπέεσσιν ('rebuked him with words of shame') and Σ A ad loc. comments: 'it is a misuse in the manner of the Cyclics (ὅτι κυκλικῶς κατακέχρηται); in fact nothing offensive is said'. Again, at 9.222 'when they (the ambassadors) had put from them the desire for food and drink', Σ A ad loc. comments: 'the line is misused in too cyclic a way (κυκλικώτερον κατακέχρηται τῶι στίχωι), as they had been eating a short time before' (namely in Agamemnon's hut at 9.177–8). Finally, Σ A *Il.* 15.610–14 observes that 'these five lines are athetized' (by Aristarchus, as often in the scholia A, when the author of the intervention is not named[56]), and lists some reasons, among them the fact that 'there is a tautology in the manner of the Cyclics (κυκλικῶς ταυτολογεῖται)', because the intervention of Zeus to urge Hector to the battle (the main topic of these lines) had already been mentioned at 15.603–4.

In these passages the adverb *kyklikōs* appears to denote simply or primarily a connection to the Epic Cycle, or a similarity with its stylistic practice. The

---

[55] On the aesthetics of 'regularity', see Russo (1978) and Fantuzzi (1988: 7–27).

[56] It may not be a sheer coincidence that all of the three passages in the Iliadic scholia where *kyklikōs* or the excess-comparative *kyklikōteron* appear to criticize Homer come from A, the manuscript Ven. Graec. 822 that most directly reflects the 'commentary of the four' (Didymus, Aristonicus, Nicanor, and Herodian), who were close pupils of Aristarchus. See above, n. 53.

epithet *kyklikos* is attested with some certainty in the sense of 'standard', 'commonly used' in Numenius fr. 20 Des Places, but the attempt to suggest that the same sense was operative in Callimachus' *poiēma kyklikon* does not seem to have met with much favor.[57] Instead, the fact that the adverb 'in the Cyclic way' is always used in the context of derogatory remarks exemplifying the stylistic sloppiness of the Cycle gives the impression that at a connotative level being sloppy and/or repetitive and/or insufficiently thoughtful/selective was a feature matter-of-factly ascribed to the Epic Cycle.[58]

An epigram by Pollianus (*AP* 11.130; first/second century AD) confirms in a brilliant synthesis that the Hellenistic scholiasts' charge of stylistic sloppiness/un-originality stuck to the Epic Cycle no less than Aristotle's original charge of narrative inferiority:

> Τοὺς κυκλίους τούτους τοὺς 'αὐτὰρ ἔπειτα' λέγοντας
>   μισῶ, λωποδύτας ἀλλοτρίων ἐπέων.
> καὶ διὰ τοῦτ' ἐλέγοις προσέχω πλέον· οὐδὲν ἔχω γὰρ
>   Παρθενίου κλέπτειν ἢ πάλι Καλλιμάχου.
> 'θηρὶ μὲν οὐατόεντι' γενοίμην, εἴ ποτε γράψω,
>   εἴκελος, 'ἐκ ποταμῶν χλωρὰ χελιδόνια.'
> οἱ δ' οὕτως τὸν Ὅμηρον ἀναιδῶς λωποδυτοῦσιν,
>   ὥστε γράφειν ἤδη 'μῆνιν ἄειδε, θεά'.

> I hate these Cyclic poems who say 'then afterwards', filchers of the verses of others, and so I pay more attention to elegies, for there is nothing I can steal from Callimachus or Parthenius. May I become like an 'eared beast' [Callim. F 1.31 Hard.] if I should ever write 'from the rivers yellow celandine' [Parthen. F 32 Lightfoot]. But these epic poets strip Homer so shamelessly that they already write 'Sing, goddess, the wrath.'

The epigram is, in my opinion, just another of the post-Hellenistic encomia of elegiac poetics.[59] Here, elegy is appreciated as a tradition in which the aesthetics of variation or originality leave no room for what is seen as lazy indulgence in formulaic repetition. It is clear from the whole epigram that

---

[57] Blumenthal (1978). [58] See e.g. Pfeiffer (1968: 230); Cameron (1995: 396).
[59] Mersinias (1993: 19–20) expresses a radically different view, and considers the epigram 'an attack on Callimachean theories besides an attack on cyclic poets', isolated in its age in combining 'adversely criticism against epic poetry and elegy simultaneously'. But the opposition between the practice of authors who 'steal' stereotypical phrases in the manner of the cyclic poets, and the impossibility of stealing from Callimachean poets such as Parthenius seems however to be sure, and favor the poetics of elegy with its inimitable language.

the main accusation that Pollianus levels against the 'Cyclic' poets[60] is that they are 'thieves' of phrases belonging to their models, i.e. they are unable to rid themselves of epic's formulaic style, which – after the end of the genre's oral stage – felt no longer justifiable. This same accusation lurks behind the observation of Σ *Il.* 11.805 (quoted above), which appreciates the Homeric passage's relative freedom from the constraints of formulaic composition. Significantly, the formulaic phrase that Pollianus chooses as his example is *autar epeita* 'then afterwards', and this choice points to the old charge of narrative inadequacy. The phrase was commonly used to introduce an action or scene successive to a previous one, not just in Cyclic poetry, but also in Homer. But it may feel like an effective swipe at the sequential *taxis* that structured the narratives of the Epic Cycle – thus marring their pursuit of internal unity, at least from an Aristotelian viewpoint.

In conclusion, independently from other possible stylistic flaws of some (or all) individual Cyclic poems, some poetological features shared by all of them qua unitarian 'cycle' were doomed to receive a more or less bad press from critics who, at least from Aristotle onwards, widely endorsed the ideas of internal narrative unity and selectivity of subject matter. At least from the third century onwards, critics cherished the pursuit of stylistic originality, or at least of originality in one's imitation of the models of the past. Centuries after the poems' composition, the variance between the narrative target of overarching external unity involved in the very idea of the Epic Cycle and the Aristotelian target of selective and self-contained unity led Aristotle and Horace to see the Cyclic poets as incapable of creating this desired internal unity (a perhaps unavoidable lack of understanding for the inherently Cyclic pride of coming after or before, or after and before, another poem). Furthermore, the Hellenistic interpreters, with their microstylistic analyses, emphasized the Cyclic language's mindless attachment to the thesaurus of the epic formulae. Hellenistic sensibilities labeled the meager attention that the Cyclic poets seemed to pay to the contextual motivation of their linguistic choices as thoughtlessly inappropriate, or as lazily indulgent in the inherited tradition.

---

[60] The extension of the term is difficult to ascertain, in this case as well as for Callimachus' *poiēma kyklikon* (see above). I agree with Cameron (1995: 399) that for him 'Cyclic poetry meant Cyclic poetry, not epic poetry in general.' But at least in the third century Pisander of Laranda did write an epic poem overarching Greek mythology (*Herōikai theogoniai* 'Heroic marriages of the gods') that according to Philoponus (see Introduction, above in this volume, p. 34 n. 137; and pp. 549 and 604–5 below) met with so much favor that 'the writing of the poets before his time fell out of favour, and this is why the poems listed in the Cycles are not even found'. We cannot rule out that a kind of poetry existed in the age of Pollianus, that could have been written in the tradition of the archaic Cycle and thus attracted Pollianus' darts no less than the archaic Cycle.

It is no surprise, then, that perhaps already long before Pollianus (Proclus may have drawn on pre-existing summaries) or at the very least soon after him (if the initiative of the summaries belongs to Proclus, and he dates from the second century), the conjunction of post-Aristotelian and post-Callimachean criticism made the poetics of the Cyclic poems seem so mediocre or awkward that even amateurs of mythology or aspiring poets preferred to access the Cyclic plots stripped of their original poetical form.

23 | The Epic Cycle, Stesichorus, and Ibycus

MARIA NOUSSIA-FANTUZZI

We do not know whether the seventh-/sixth-century poets of the Epic Cycle really saw it as their role to simply fill in the gaps left by the magisterial Homer. Indeed, our impression of their structural reliance on the *Iliad* and *Odyssey* may be due simply to the bad press they enjoyed with some critics after Aristotle, or the compact form their narratives took in the summaries that we know them from. But there is sufficient evidence to surmise that at least the sixth-century retellings of the Epic Cycle by the poets Stesichorus and Ibycus approach these tales in a manner that was innovative and cannot be reduced simply to a complementary relationship. Although Stesichorus and Ibycus were often confused with each other in antiquity and ancient commentators disagreed regarding the authorship of many of their works,[1] as far as their approaches to the *Iliad*, the *Odyssey* and the broader epic tradition is concerned their differences are rather clear. In this chapter, I will examine both of them – first Stesichorus, then Ibycus – against the backdrop of their literary forerunners.

For pseudo-Longinus (*Subl.* 13.3) Stesichorus is 'most Homeric', and for Dio Chrysostom he was 'an imitator of Homer' (*Or.* 2.33), while Quintilian 10.1.62 speaks of Stesichorus as *epici carminis onera lyra sustinentem*. Simonides *PMG* F 564.4 also comments on the thematic similarity between the poems of Homer and Stesichorus and Antipater hails Stesichorus as the reincarnation of Homer (*A.P.* 7.75). Such references by the ancient critics highlight the typically epic nature of Stesichorus' diction, the relevance of the dactylic foot to his versification, the frequent occurrence of epic myths and characters in his works, as well as the expansive dimension of his narrative style, all of which can be labelled 'Homeric' features.[2] Of course, for Stesichorus, as for probably everyone down to the fifth century, 'Homeric'

---

[1] E.g. a title Ἆθλα 'Contests' was attributed to both: Athen. 4.172d (= *PMGF* F 179(i)); see Cingano (1992: 191–4). POxy. 2735 (= Ibycus *PMGF* S166–219) is ascribed by some scholars to the *Helen* of Stesichorus. For the attribution of glosses to both poets, see Sisti (1967: 61 n. 20).

[2] The bibliography on these aspects of Stesichorus' style is vast. On diction, see e.g. Schade (2003) for the Homeric and epic parallels in POxy. 2619; Haslam (1978) for the Lille papyrus (PLille 76 abc). The *Oresteia* and the *Geryoneis* are examples of extensive length. Other works of Stesichorus have been suspected to have been similarly voluminous: see e.g. Stoneman (1981) for the *Eriphyle* as covering *all* the events of the expedition against Thebes.

meant 'referring to the *Iliad*, the *Odyssey and* the Cyclic poems'.[3] Accordingly, what little remains from the poems shows that it would be mistaken to view them as derived solely from Homeric poetry and offers sufficient clues to suggest that Stesichorus was 'Cyclic' almost as much as 'Homeric' (in our sense). As has recently been observed,[4] Stesichorus' version of the Trojan War seems to have resembled the Cycle in that it was 'less complex, less synthetic, than the version of Homer'. In fact, Stesichorus seems to show a great interest in the Cyclic way of telling a story.[5] His is a capacious type of composition that develops through various poems a sort of narration in installments of a series of events connected according to principles of cause and effect.[6] This produces a predominantly linear narrative[7] that is largely uninterested in multiple layers and the usual paraphernalia of foreshadowing, flashbacks and similar departures from the principle of linearity that characterize the *Iliad* and the *Odyssey*. Unlike Stesichorus' comprehensive – and therefore 'Cyclic' – poems, the introductions of the *Iliad* and the *Odyssey* contextualize their narratives within the frame of the Trojan War rather eclectically. Although both poems allude to numerous events that could have been the subject of their narratives (*Il*. 1.2, 3, *Od*. 1, 3, 4),[8] they were composed with a view to telling a single story (this is especially true of the *Iliad*), and therefore they contain little that is extraneous to the main action.

Unlike the *Iliad* or *Odyssey*, Stesichorus' poetics thus often follow the artistic aim of presenting a series of poems that belong to mythic wholes (e.g. the heroes who perished at Troy and Thebes).[9] From the fragments we can grasp that the events were linked together by clear connections from their beginning to their end,[10] whereas both the *Iliad* and the *Odyssey* begin *in medias res*. Furthermore, while the unity of the *Iliad* is that of a single poem,

---

[3] See Schwartz (1940) and Introduction, above in this volume, pp. 21–8.

[4] Nagy (1990b: 421–2).

[5] According to Photius' (319a30) Proclus in the Χρηστομαθία γραμματική says that the poems of the Epic Cycle are preserved and studied not because of their quality (ἀρετή) but because of the ἀκολουθία τῶν ἐν αὐτῶι πραγμάτων; see Introduction and Fantuzzi, above in this volume, pp. 1–3, 8–9, 32, 408–9, 419–20.

[6] There are insightful remarks in Arrighetti (1996: esp. 25–6).

[7] For exceptions to the narrative technique of the Cyclic epics, see Rengakos, above in this volume, pp. 157–8; Carey (2015).

[8] See Rengakos, above in this volume, pp. 155–6 besides, for the *Iliad*, Heiden (1996) and, for the *Odyssey*, Camerotto (2003: esp. 24).

[9] Stesichorus is also interested in several other, extra-Cyclic myths, including Heracles and the Argonautic legend, which are very much present in his poetry. On Stesichorus' panhellenic poetic agenda, i.e. his attempt to generate a narrative corpus that at least touches on all the major cycles of Greece, see Carey (2015).

[10] Arrighetti (1996: 29).

the unity that Stesichorus pursues seems to be 'cyclic' in its nature: namely, it is realized through serialized compositions that – while they can stand on their own – still jointly develop a larger mythological theme. For instance, the Lille poem of unknown title (*PMGF* 222(b)) narrates Polynices' exile from Thebes; the *Eriphyle*, *PMGF* 194, includes the reference to Stesichorus' mention of Asclepius as raising from the dead some of those who fell at Thebes; in *PMGF* S 148 the figures of Adrastus and Alcmaon seem to point to the *Epigonoi. Europeia* (*PMGF* 195), which covers the Theban foundation myths, may have belonged to this group too. This proves that the poet dealt with distinct chapters of the Theban saga in separate poems.[11] Similarly there is a group of his poems that cover Trojan themes from the origins to the consequences of the war: a *Helen* (*PMGF* 187–91), the *Palinode(s)* (*PMGF* 192–3), a *Sack of Troy* and/or a *Wooden Horse* (perhaps a section of the *Sack of Troy*?: *PMGF* S 88–147, 196–205), and the *Returns* (*PMGF* 208 and ?209). It is thus worth noting that in retelling Trojan tales Stesichorus does not rework the *Iliad* or the *Odyssey* but focuses (as far as we can tell) on Cyclic content.[12] Furthermore, his tendency to structure his poems in a Cyclic manner can also be observed at a micro level. Here, the poet's fondness for catalogues is a telling example: see *PMGF* S 105.10–12 with its miniature catalogue of the gods friendly to Troy,[13] or *PMGF* 179(i) with the list of cakes, or *PMGF* 222 with the lists of the various participants in the Calydonian boar hunt in the first column of the papyrus and the list of different Greek peoples who joined the expedition in the second.

Yet in spite of his relative closeness to the Cycle, Stesichorus' innovations in the treatment of Cyclic themes – such as his inclusion of one Clymene among the captive women at Troy[14] (*PMGF* 197) and his having Hecuba carried off by Apollo to Lycia (*PMGF* 198) in his *Sack of Troy* or his making Hector a son of Apollo[15] (and thus a semi-divine hero like the Iliadic Achilles) (*PMGF* 224)[16] – reveal his creative departure from relatively

---

[11] Burnett (1998: 112); Haslam (1978: 37 n. 15).

[12] As also observed by Carey (2015), who comments that the *Iliad* and *Odyssey* had to have established themselves already, in some form, at the time of Stesichorus.

[13] By cataloguing the gods who leave Troy, Stesichorus would exasperate the drama of the imminent destruction of the city according to Pallantza (2005: 96).

[14] Bowie (2010b: 80) calls attention to Stesichorus' eye for detail in recalling that Clymene was a named chaperone of Helen at *Il.* 3.144. On Demophon's visit to Egypt as an innovation that reflects Athenian political interests see Finglass (2013a).

[15] A point of confusion with Ibycus in some sources: see Σ D *Il.* 3.314 that ascribed this version to Ibycus, Alexander Aetolus, Euphorion and Lycophron.

[16] According to the reconstruction of Garner (1993), POxy. 3876 F 37–77 seems to come from Stesichorus' treatment of the death and burial of Achilles, but the state of the text makes it impossible to detect any influence from the *Aethiopis*, although Haslam reads the name Μέμνων in *PMGF* Appendix F 56.5; for this Μέμνων as a reflex of the *Aethiopis*, see West (2013: 41–2).

The Epic Cycle, Stesichorus, and Ibycus

well-established 'standard' versions of the myth. Most famously, Stesichorus did not take up the Homeric and Cyclic tradition of Helen's flight with Paris (*PMGF* 193; POxy. 2506 F 26), but had her stay behind in Egypt while a mere 'phantom' fled to Troy. This 'discourse of denial'[17] seems to emphasize Stesichorus' disagreement with the *Iliad* and *Cypria*:[18] the Iliadic Helen did make it to Troy and participated in the famous *teichoscopia*, whereas Stesichorus' Helen never reached the citadel (*PMGF* 192.3), nor did she go on the well-benched ships, i.e. Paris' ships whose building was supervised by Aphrodite in the *Cypria* (arg. line 91 Severyns). Through the story of the 'image' (εἴδωλον) Stesichorus exonerates his Helen from having gone to Troy but she still retains some portion of the stain of adultery since she travelled up to Egypt with Paris before Proteus robbed her from him (*PMGF* 193). Plato's remark (*Rep.* 9.586c) that Helen's phantom was fought over by the warriors at Troy 'in ignorance of the truth' (ἀγνοίαι τοῦ ἀληθοῦς) hints at the fact that Stesichorus' treatment of the myth took root and introduced a radical change into the Trojan War myth, and it foregrounds the overtone of tragic ἁμαρτία that the phantom introduced into the story of the war.

It seems safe to conclude that Stesichorus described the early part of the traditional Helen story – her courting, the oath her father exacted from the suitors and her marriage with Menelaus: see *PMGF* 187 – most probably on a magnificent scale, and also that in the *Helen* or in the *Oresteia* or *Sack of Troy* or in all of these poems (*PMGF* 191 and 223) he may have made the most of Helen's matrimonial misadventures. See in particular *PMGF* 223:

> οὕνεκα Τυνδάρεος
> ῥέζων ποκὰ πᾶσι θεοῖς μόνας λάθετ' ἠπιοδώρου
> Κύπριδος· κείνα δὲ Τυνδαρέου κόρας
> χολωσαμένα διγάμους τε καὶ τριγάμους ἐτίθει
> καὶ λιπεσάνορας

> Because Tyndareus when sacrificing one day to all the gods forgot the Cyprian only, kindly in her giving; and she in anger made the daughters of Tyndareus twice-wed and thrice-wed and husband-deserters.[19]

---

[17] Bassi (1993: 51) introduces the term 'discourse of denial' and defines it as 'a mode of self-conscious textual antagonism in which one text affirms its own authority or validity by contrastively representing the inadequacy, untruthfulness or insufficiency of another'.

[18] POxy. 2506 F 26 = *PMGF* 193 informs us that Stesichorus also opposed Hesiod's account of Helen, without providing further details.

[19] This fragment is quoted by its source, Σ Eur. *Or.* 249, together with a passage from the Hesiodic *Catalogue* (F 176 M.-W. = F 8 * Hirsch.) that reflects the same tradition and gives the detail of the 'curse' affecting the daughters of Tyndareus: 'Smile loving Aphrodite was angry with them when she saw them, and she cast bad repute upon them. Then Timandra left behind

Helen is most probably the τρίγαμος wife among Tyndareus' daughters. Prior to Menelaus and Paris, she married Theseus, who had abducted her, and she gave birth to his child, Iphigeneia; alternative versions of the myth have her marry Paris' brother Deiphobus when Paris died before the fall of Troy.[20] If Stesichorus included Deiphobus (rather than Theseus) in the count, then he agreed with the standard version of Helen's biography, which was also recounted in the *Ilias parva* according to Proclus' summaries. Be that as it may, it is certain that Stesichorus did discuss Helen's rape by Theseus. Pausanias (2.22.6 = *PMGF* 191) specifically names Stesichorus, Alexander Aetolus and Euphorion as the authors who 'agree with the Argives that Iphigeneia was Theseus' daughter'. Stesichorus thus probably established a parental connection between two heroines, Helen and Iphigeneia, who already had such a specific *trait d'union* as an *eidolon* in common (that Artemis replaced Iphimede = Iphigeneia with an *eidolon* when she rescued her from the sacrifice is already in Hes. F 23a.17–24 M.-W. = F 15.17–24 Hirsch.;[21] for Helen, Hes. F dub. 358 M.-W.). Differently, the *Cypria* did not handle the myth of Iphigeneia's birth from Helen (*PEG* F 24 = F 17 D. = F 20 W.), even though it hinted at the rape of Helen by Theseus (*PEG* F 13 = F 12 D. = W.; cf. *Il.* 3.144).[22] Besides, in the *Cypria* Helen is the daughter of Zeus and Nemesis (see Athen. 334b, Philodemus, *De piet.* B 7369 Obbink, Ps.-Apollod. *Bibl.* 3.10.7) and not, as in Stesichorus, the daughter of Tyndareus.

However, in the *Oresteia* Stesichorus seems (according to Philodemus) to have followed the standard (and Hesiodic) version according to which Iphigeneia was the daughter of Menelaus: *PMGF* 215. This discrepancy is not unlikely, and we do not have to surmise that one of our two reports on Stesichorus' treatment of Iphigeneia's paternity is incorrect. After all, if *PMGF* 191 comes from the Helen poem, and Iphigeneia's sacrifice also featured there, then the idea that Helen's adultery also led to the killing of her own child may have surfaced: this compromising picture of Helen

---

Echemus and ran away, and came to Phyleus, who was dear to the blessed gods; so too Clytaemnestra, leaving behind godly Agamemnon, lay beside Aegisthus and preferred a worse husband; so too Helen shames the marriage-bed of blond Menelaus.'

[20] It is difficult to say whether Stesichorus' τρίγαμος 'thrice married' alludes to Deiphobus or Theseus. Grossardt (2012: 16–18) suggests that Deiphobus is a more probable candidate, since in the case of Theseus it was never a regular marriage, but rather a rape. However in light of the uncertain distinction between formal marriage and sexual intercourse (γαμεῖν means both in ancient Greek) it is difficult to confidently agree with him.

[21] On which see Solmsen (1981).

[22] On the reception of this Stesichorean innovation in the Hellenistic age, see Massimilla (1990: 380–1).

would have created a sharp contrast with Helen as protagonist of the 'Palinode'.[23]

By focusing on Helen's matrimonial misadventures, Stesichorus represents the Trojan War as caused by sexual passion; instead of Eris who arrives at the wedding feast of Peleus and instigates a beauty contest between Athena, Hera and Aphrodite, as in the *Cypria* (arg. lines 86–8 Severyns), it is now Aphrodite who is implicated in the outbreak of the war. The Trojan War may be the outcome of both narratives, but Stesichorus' choice of Aphrodite as its instigator reflects his tendency to accentuate the erotic elements in the tales he narrates. It has been suggested[24] that Stesichorus' innovations introduce clearer connections between the narrated facts and their motivations. No doubt, Stesichorus' particular emphasis on Aphrodite and her ambiguous gifts creates more obvious and suitable associations in a Helen poem than the rather abstract personification of Nemesis.

The relatively broad and linear sweep of Stesichorus' narratives – which of course can only be fully appreciated in cases where his models have survived and make a comparison possible – seems to have been a recognizable and deliberate characteristic of his style. For example, *PMGF* 209, his song about Telemachus at Sparta, proves 'that he knew parts, at least, of the *Odyssey* by heart'.[25] The possibility that the fragment does not belong to a general *Nostoi* poem as has been assumed and that it instead belongs to a separate *Odyssey* or a *Telemachy* has to remain open. Stesichorus may have shown interest in this part of the Homeric epic because it involved an erotic potential: cf. *Od.* 15.4–5 where Telemachus and the son of Nestor are described as lying in the fore-hall of the palace of Menelaus, a scene which has often been used by modern scholars as proof of Homer's acknowledgement of homosexual love.[26] In any case, Stesichorus does not seem to have followed the complex narrative structure of the *Odyssey*, where Telemachus' departure from Sparta in book 4 is interrupted by ten books of narration of Odysseus' adventures. Instead he appears to have narrated Telemachus' visit to Sparta and his departure therefrom (cf. the description of Menelaus' guest-gift to Telemachus in the second column of the papyrus) without interruption,[27] thus reconstituting the linear sequence of a narrative that Homer had disrupted.

---

[23] As Grossardt (2012: 10) has observed.
[24] Arrighetti (1996: 27).   [25] Burnett (1998: 138).
[26] See Fantuzzi (2012: 190 n. 8). Athen. 13.601a credits Stesichorus with the composition of 'boy-songs' (παίδεια καὶ παιδικὰ ἄισματα).
[27] Reece (1988: 8).

What else is clear from the scanty remains is the way Stesichorus moves beyond Homer's presentation of Helen and expands her role into a sympathetic and motherly figure concerned about Penelope's feelings for her son Telemachus. She urges him home for reasons that are more appropriate for a mother (and a mother who understands another mother's anxiety over her departed son) than the *Odyssey*'s account, where Helen sends Telemachus home with fears that his mother might be about to remarry. In Stesichorus' poem, she gets introduced as νύμφα ('bride'), a word that immediately evokes the idea of marriage and focuses on Helen's present status and relationships[28] by neutralizing her past transgressions. Certainly, Stesichorus knows his *Iliad* too: his presentation of Helen as reproaching herself as a λακέρυζα κορώνα ('a chattering crow': an un-Homeric expression) is consistent with her characterization in the *Iliad*.[29] There she castigates herself most memorably as a 'chilling, evil-devising (κακομήχανος) bitch' (cf. *Il.* 6.344, 3.180 (to Priam); 6.356 (to Hector); *Od.* 4.145 (to the assembled company).[30] In these Iliadic passages her words cast her as a menacing, destructive figure, magnifying her lethal qualities by associating her with strife, fear, war and death.[31] Helen's self-abasement in Stesichorus is less heavy than in the *Iliad*, and it refers to her talkativeness rather than her destructive potential.

Another specifically Stesichorean feature is the poet's effort to flesh out characters that the epos of Homer had largely ignored. Epeius from Stesichorus' *Iliou persis* can serve as an example.[32] Homer dealt with the depiction of characters who are σπουδαῖοι ('noble'),[33] as Arist. *Poet.* 1448a27 had already observed. Epeius does not fit this description, and even the Cycle, possibly lacking interest in character development, may have merely named him. Thus, in contrast with the rather flat mention of his exploits in the *Ilias parva* (arg. lines 222–3 Severyns), καὶ Ἐπειὸς κατ' Ἀθηνᾶς προαίρεσιν τὸν δούρειον ἵππον κατασκευάζει ('and Epeius, following an initiative of Athena, constructs the wooden horse'), and also in contrast with the *Odyssey*'s all-too-brief summary ἵππου κόσμον ἄεισον / δουρατέου, τὸν Ἐπειὸς ἐποίησεν σὺν Ἀθήνηι, / ὅν ποτ' ἐς ἀκρόπολιν δόλον ἤγαγε δῖος Ὀδυσσεύς ('sing of the building of the wooden horse, which Epeius made with Athena's help,

---

[28] She is referred as such only once in the *Iliad*. In the *Odyssey* this is a characterization for Penelope.

[29] Cf. δυσώνυμος 'bearing an evil name' in S 107, if this is part of a scene in which Helen is speaking to Menelaus, as West suggests.

[30] On which see Blondell (2010).   [31] Clader (1976: 17–23).

[32] On Epeius in the *Iliad*, see Howland (1954).

[33] On Stesichorus' ability to give nobility to his characters, see the example of the monster Geryon in the *Geryoneis*, with Noussia-Fantuzzi (2013).

the horse which once Odysseus led up into the citadel as a thing of guile',
8.492–94), Stesichorus 'sets a dramatized motivation of Epeius' demiurgic
capacity, tracing it back to Athena's pity and intervention',[34] and explicitly
depicts for this 'new' hero a talent which is opposed to the usual martial
excellence of epos:

> νῦν δ' ἄ[σ]εν [χα]λεπῶς πα[ρὰ καλλιρόου
> δίνα[ς] Σιμόεντος ἀνὴρ [
> θ]εᾶς ἰ[ό]τατι δαεὶς σεμν[ᾶς Ἀθάνας
> μέτ[ρα] τε καὶ σοφίαν του[
> [ ]ος ἀντὶ μάχα[ς   (5)
> καὶ] φυ[λόπ]ιδος κλέο[ς].[
> εὐρυ]χόρ[ο]υ Τρο<ί>ας ἁλώσι[μον ἆμαρ
> [ ]ν ἔθηκεν   [
> [ ]. εσσι πόνοι[

> But now by the (fair-flowing) eddies of the Simois a man has grievously
> misled us, taught his measurements and skill by the will of the august
> goddess Athena, a man by whose (devices trickery?) instead of fighting
> and the battle-cry (will have) fame (that it) brought the capture of spacious
> Troy... hardships.

However, he may not necessarily have been the first to adopt this mode of
presentation, as the detail that Epeius was the water-carrier for the Atreids
suggests that Stesichorus may not necessarily have been the first or the only
one to adopt this presentation.[35]

In short, the poet worked consciously to create his own distinctive version
out of the popular legendary tales he had at his disposition. *PMGF* S89
simultaneously introduces and conceals its protagonist Epeius; by calling
him just ἀνήρ as it mentions Athena's will that the destruction of Troy be
achieved through trickery and not force, it clearly sets Epeius as a lesser
parallel to Odysseus, who was also described in this way in the proem of
the *Odyssey*.[36] Stesichorus, however, departs from the Odyssean version
at 8.505–10 and also differs from the Cycle in more plausibly locating
the debate of the Trojans on the plain and not on the acropolis (cf. the
opposing definitions of locality in *PMGF* S89 ii.6 and ii.11). Even more

---

[34] Tsitsibakou-Vasalos (2010: 8). See also Pallantza (2005: 97) who explains the characterization of Epeius in Stesichorus as a result of his role as a cultural hero and founder of Metapontum.

[35] This is more likely to have been in the Epic Cycle as well. Cf. Athenaeus (10.456 F 457 A), who, quoting from Stesichorus, says that an image of Epeius as water-carrier was in the temple of Apollo in Carphaia, on Ceos.

[36] There is another implicit similarity between the two men: Odysseus is a kind of carpenter, too, as he has fashioned his own bed in the *Odyssey*.

significantly, in Stesichorus Astyanax has already died when the city is taken (*PMGF* 202 = Σ Eur. *Andr.* 10). This detail may reveal Stesichorus' sensitive and humane touch: 'he suppresses this moment of intolerable cruelty, and subtly mitigates the atrocities of the Achaeans',[37] unlike both the *Ilias parva* (which had Neoptolemus kill Astyanax) and the *Iliou persis* (which focused on Greek sacrilege and had Odysseus kill the child). There is a tendency in Stesichorus to ignore the nastier side of the Achaeans as it appears in the Cyclic epics, which is also complemented by greater attention to the Trojan side: e.g. Stesich. *PMGF* 199 does not offer any name for the one hundred warriors inside the Wooden Horse – the *Ilias parva* had three thousand (thirteen? West (2003: 133)) warriors within the Horse (*PEG* F 8 = F 10 D. = F 12 W.); the *Odyssey* mentions only fifty out of the πάντες ἄριστοι Ἀργείων (4.271–273; 8.512–513; 11.523) – but he seems to have named the daughters of Priam (*PMGF* 204). It is reasonable to believe that he also dealt with the flight of Aeneas,[38] given his interest in the Western Mediterranean and what we know from the first-century-AD tablet *Tabula Iliaca Capitolina* (1 A Sadurska) which claims to portray the sack of Troy 'according to Stesichorus' and has Aeneas fleeing, together with other scenes that we know to have been included in his poem. By contrast, Aeneas is captured and given to Achilles' son Neoptolemus in the *Ilias parva* (*PEG* F 21 = F 20 D. = F 29–30 W.), while the *Iliou persis* mentions that he and his party slipped away to Ida.[39]

More innovations can be claimed for the Lille poem. In it, Stesichorus has set up a typical ruler–prophet conflict, familiar from the Homeric epics.[40] But instead of the Iliadic Agamemnon or Hector or the *Odyssey*'s suitors and their corresponding seers, we find a female figure in Iocasta,[41] a queen mother whom Stesichorus economically establishes 'as head of her house and also as a fighter of heroic quality'[42] by making her take on language appropriate to male warriors in her epic wish to die before witnessing the fall of her city or her *genos*. In making the queen survive the discovery of the incest and continue the reign at Thebes, Stesichorus is likely to have followed the tradition of the *Thebaid* (in contrast with *Od.* 11.271–80,

---

[37] Tsitsibakou-Vasalos (2010: 43).
[38] Our earliest literary reference to Aeneas' voyage westwards comes from the *Trōika* of Hellanicus, the fifth-century logographer.
[39] Cf. Lehnus (1972: 53), who identifies Stesichorus' propensity for colonial myths; Noussia-Fantuzzi (2013) on Stesichorus and Iberia.
[40] Macinnes (2007: 99).
[41] This has some similarity with Stesichorus' treatment of Hecuba's death in the *Iliou persis*, where he reworks a scene that Homer had reserved for a male character, i.e. the dead Sarpedon who is transported to Lycia by Apollo.
[42] Burnett (1998: 115).

which mentions her hanging, or *Il.* 23.679–80 and Hesiodic F 192–193 M.-W. (cf. F 90 Hirsch.), which affirm that Oedipus remained at Thebes as king after the incest was discovered). Stesichorus has not however simply reproduced the *Thebaid*. For instance, he makes no use of Oedipus' curses upon his sons Eteocles and Polynices (*PEG* F 2–3 = D., W.), which were so important in that epic in that they triggered their quarrel. Instead, he frames the plot around the prophecy of Teiresias. As has been correctly remarked, the queen's response to Teiresias' predictions 'makes it plain that the only supernatural factors to be dealt with are Apollo's responsibility to his prophet's words and Zeus' power over the time-scheme of destiny. In the second place, it is clear that Stesichorus' song did not reflect the pro-Argive stance of the *Thebaid*, since his lot-chosen Polynices can have no future claim on the Theban throne.'[43] Note 'according to the Moirae' of line 273 or 'under the escort of the gods' of line 299, where the narrator emphasizes the legitimacy of Eteocles' position; this is a feature which separates Stesichorus as a narrator from the Homeric narrator's remote and dispassionate style.[44]

The surviving fragments of Stesichorus contain direct speech,[45] and this may reveal some predilection for it within the narrative, a feature that suggests his poems were stylistically quite similar to the Homeric epics.[46] Such a similarity was already noticed by the scholiast on *Il.* 21.65–6, at least according to Wilamowitz's extensive emendations: 'those who are on the point of dying all talk at great length, in order to gain so much time at least; for example, in Stesichorus ...' There are, however, also differences from the speeches in the *Iliad*. While the Iliadic speakers most frequently use paradigmatic stories as a form of argument, Stesichorean speakers often use speeches that are rather based on the logic of everyday-life experience rather – for example, in the Lille poem the queen argues that, in principle, strife does not have to last a lifetime (PLille 76 A ii + 73 i, lines 204–6):

> οὔτε γὰρ αἰὲν ὁμῶς
> θεοὶ θέσαν ἀθάνατοι κατ' αἶαν ἱράν
> νεῖκος ἔμπεδον βροτοῖσιν

for the immortal gods did not for all time alike establish over the holy earth strife unending for mortals.

---

[43] Burnett (1998: 125).
[44] For other Stesichorean authorial intrusions, see Garner (1994: 28–9).
[45] See Auger (1976).
[46] Page (1973: 49); Maingon (1989: 45–6). Cf. Griffin (2004: 156): *Iliad* 15,690 lines, speeches 7,018. *Odyssey* 12,103 lines, direct speech: 8,225. Direct speech thus amounts to some 55 per cent of the total of the two epics.

Her words are in tune with the recommendation of Phoenix to Achilles in *Il.* 9.527–605, who however differently had relied on the paradigm of Meleager and his wife, whereas the Queen's speech seems to lack paradigmatic stories or digressions altogether.[47] Indeed, Stesichorus seems to favour speeches in which a speaker in the grip of an emotion must make either an argument or a decision. These speeches do more than 'just' permit the expression of the characters' individual thoughts or statements. Rather, they become the vehicle of dramatic irony and create proto-tragical passages of a sort.[48] For instance, it has been pointed out that the Lille poem contains strong situational irony in its 'moment of false *peripeteia*, for Jocasta sets herself against fate and schemes with apparent success to keep the destined future at bay'.[49] Similarly a strong situational irony is created by the Trojans' debate about the Wooden Horse in the *Iliou persis* (POxy. 2619 F 1 = *PMGF* S 88), where they decide whether or not to take it into the city – according to Proclus this scene was the end of the Cyclic *Ilias parva* and the beginning of the *Iliou persis*. In the *Iliou persis* the courses of action are three: some Trojans want to push the Trojan Horse over a cliff, and some to set fire to it, while others want it to be dedicated to Athena. Differently Stesichorus appears to focus on the frequent tragic motif of the undue split between successful and righteous, as his speaker who strongly advocates acting out of respect for the gods (*PMGF* S88 col. ii) is the one who gives the wrong advice, and it is this opinion that prevails in the end. Last but not least, in a particularly strong instance of tragic irony that highlights the embarrassing 'wrongness' of even the most pious religiosity, the Wooden Horse is considered an ἁγνὸν ἄγαλμα by the Trojans, namely a sacred gift for Athena (col. ii, line 10). Let us now move on to Ibycus. Evidence for his Trojan tales is much scantier, but we can easily suppose that he shared with Stesichorus a similar emphasis on the erotic/sentimental dimension. It is telling, for instance, that both authors (Stes. in the *Iliou persis*, POxy. 2619 F 14 = *PMGF* S 103.5 Ib. *PMGF* S 151.5) apply an epithet to Helen, ξανθά ('blonde'), that is attested nowhere in the texts of archaic epos, but had appeared in Sapph. F 23.5 Voigt.[50] Both Stesichorus and Ibycus also dealt with the encounter of Helen and Menelaus and its great erotic potential, as already the *Ilias parva* had done. Accordingly, Ibycus shows a quite different metapoetic self-awareness from Homer, especially from what we can infer from his least fragmentary poem, *PMGF* S151 in praise of Polycrates:

---

[47] Burnett (1998: 113); for the logic of the queen's argument see Macinnes (2007: 99).
[48] On the less explicit and straightforward ways the tragedians exploited motifs of Stesichorus, see e.g. Thalmann (1982).
[49] Burnett (1998: 113).   [50] See Grossardt (2012: 36–9).

...]ου Δαρδανίδα Πριάμοιο μέ-
γ' ἄσ]τυ περικλεὲς ὄλβιον ἠνάρον
Ἄργ]οθεν ὀρνυμένοι
Ζη]νὸς μεγάλοιο βουλαῖς
ξα]νθᾶς Ἑλένας περὶ εἴδει (5)
δῆ]ριν πολύυμνον ἔχ[ο]ντες
πό]λεμον κατὰ δακρ[υό]εντα,
Πέρ]γαμον δ' ἀνέ[β]α ταλαπείριο[ν ἄ]τα
χρυ]σοέθειραν δ[ι]ὰ Κύπριδα.
νῦ]ν δέ μοι οὔτε ξειναπάταν Π[άρι]ν (10)
..] ἐπιθύμιον οὔτε τανί[σφ]υρ[ον
ὑμ]νῆν Κασσάνδραν
Πρι]άμοιό τε παῖδας ἄλλου[ς
Τρο]ίας θ' ὑψιπύλοιο ἁλώσι[μο]ν
ἆμ]αρ ἀνώνυμον· οὐδεπ[(15)
ἡρ]ώων ἀρετὰν
ὑπ]εράφανον οὕς τε κοῖλα[ι
νᾶες] πολυγόμφοι ἐλεύσα[ν
Τροί]αι κακόν, ἥρωας ἐσθ[λούς·
τῶν] μὲν κρείων Ἀγαμέ[μνων (20)
ἄ]ρχε Πλεισθ[ενί]δας βασιλ[εὺ]ς ἀγὸς ἀνδρῶν
Ἀτρέος ἐσ[θλοῦ] πάις ἔκγ[ο]νος.
καὶ τὰ μὲ[ν ἂν] Μοίσαι σεσοφ[ισμ]έναι
εὖ Ἑλικωνίδ[ες] ἐμβαίεν †λόγω[ι,
θνατὸς †δ' οὔ κ[ε]ν ἀνὴρ (25)
διερὸ[ς] τὰ ἕκαστα εἴποι
ναῶν ὅ[σσος ἀρι]θμὸς ἀπ' Αὐλίδος
Αἰγαῖον δ[ιὰ πό]ντον ἀπ' Ἄργεος
ἠλύθο[ν ἐς Τροία]ν
ἱπποτρόφο[ν, ἐν δ]ὲ φῶτες (30)
χ]αλκάσπ[ιδες υἷ]ες Ἀχα[ι]ῶν
τ]ῶν μὲν πρ[οφ]ερέστατος α[ἰ]χμᾶι
...]. πόδ[ας ὠ]κὺς Ἀχιλλεύς
καὶ μέ]γας Τ[ελαμ]ώνιος ἄλκι[μος Αἴας
. . . . . .]. ατ[. . . . . . .]γυρος. (35)
. . . . κάλλι]στος ἀπ' Ἄργεος
. . . . .Κυάνι]ππ[ο]ς ἐς Ἴλιον
. . . .]
. . . .].[.].
. . . .]α χρυσόστροφ[ος (40)
Ὕλλις ἐγήνατο, τῶι δ' [ἄ]ρα Τρωίλον
ὡσεὶ χρυσὸν ὀρει-
χάλκωι τρὶς ἄπεφθο[ν] ἤδη

Τρῶες Δ[α]ναοί τ' ἐρό[ε]σσαν
μορφὰν μάλ' ἐίσκον ὅμοιον.   (45)
τοῖς μὲν πέδα κάλλεος αἰὲν
καὶ σύ, Πολύκρατες, κλέος ἄφθιτον ἑξεῖς
ὡς κατ' ἀοιδὰν καὶ ἐμὸν κλέος.

. . . . destroyed the great, glorious, blessed city of Priam, son of Dardanus, setting off from Argos by the plans of great Zeus, enduring much-sung strife over the beauty of auburn Helen in tearful war; and ruin mounted long-suffering Pergamum thanks to the golden-haired Cyprian; but now it was not my heart's wish to sing of Paris, deceiver of his host, or of slim-ankled Cassandra and Priam's other children and the unmentionable day of the capture of high-gated Troy, nor shall I recount the proud valour of the heroes whom hollow, many-bolted ships brought to be an evil to Troy, fine heroes: they were commanded by lord Agamemnon, Pleisthenid king, leader of men, fine son born to Atreus. On these themes the skilled Muses of Helicon might embark in story, but no mortal man [untaught?] could tell each detail, the great number of ships that came from Aulis across the Aegean sea from Argos to horse-rearing Troy, with bronze-shielded warriors on board, sons of the Achaeans; among them foremost with the spear went swift-footed Achilles and great valiant Telamonian Ajax [who threw strong fire on Troy?]; [with them also went] from Argos to Ilion Cyanippus, the most handsome man, [descendant of Adrastus], [and Zeuxippus, whom the Naiad,] golden-girdled Hyllis, [conceived and] bore [to Phoebus]; and to him Trojans and Greeks likened Troilus as gold already thrice-refined to orichalc, judging him very similar in loveliness of form. These have a share in beauty always: you too, Polycrates, will have undying fame as song and my fame can give it.

Ibycus' declaration of not being able to narrate ἕκαστα in lines 25–6 reflects a strong contrast between his and Homer's narrative styles. Far from the Homeric *kata kosmon* manner of narration[51] or the Stesichorean tendency for historical (mythic) narrative, Ibycus chooses a manner of composition that 'involves a strict and consistent selection of contents in relation to the occasion of the song'.[52] This completely de-emphasizes the narrative of traditional epic tales, by suppressing whatever is not in line with his poetic strategies and occasions for song. In this poem Homeric and Cyclic material 'has become a catalogue enumerated and passed over, a *praeteritio* with the purpose of moving beyond an epic litany to some new focus'.[53] As has been

---

[51] On which see most recently Finkelberg (1998: 124–6); Worman (2002: 21–9).
[52] Gentili (1978: 397).   [53] MacLachlan (1997: 192).

well pointed out[54] 'after some remarkable beating about the bush he makes his poem end in a eulogy of the beauty of a boy called Polycrates'.

The poem as we have it starts with a *hysteron proteron* that hints immediately at the final event of the Trojan War, the 'unmentionable day of the capture of high-gated Troy', lines 14–15. The Trojan perspective is dealt with in a compassionate and abundant way, after a rather stark initial reference to the Greek forces. Despite the absence of any substantial narrative of the Greek deeds that brought about the capture of Troy, Paris, 'the deceiver of his host', 'slim-ankled' Cassandra and, more generally, the other children of Priam (lines 10–14) hold the field. They are the first subjects of the war of Troy to attract the poet's attention, and are in fact the first that he recuses himself from singing about (*nyn de moi oute* ... *ēn epithymion*, lines 10–11). In turn, the martial story of the victory of the Greek army led by Agamemnon (the only Greek hero to be described with a sequence of seven nouns and adjectives in three verses in the epode) surfaces only later in the poet's words, only to be rejected as a theme of song (lines 15–24). Ibycus will not sing about the entire number of the Greeks who came to Troy, but leaves this to the Iliadic Catalogue of Ships or Hesiod's Muses. This *recusatio* of epic models separates Ibycus as an (epic) poet both from Homer and Hesiod and puts emphasis on his own divergences from the epic tradition. At the same time it serves to highlight the distinctiveness of his ode.

The matchless beauty of a woman (Helen) as well as the nature, power and role of the goddess Aphrodite *are* worthy of Ibycus' mention (lines 5–9) even before and more emphatically than the fall of Troy or the victorious Greek heroes. Furthermore, the poem's general vocabulary is not conventionally and specifically Homeric. For instance, although the phrase *Zēnos megaloio boulais*[55] (line 4) 'belongs to a larger continuum of heroic songs'[56] and is often found in Homer,[57] it is the proem of the *Cypria* (*PEG* F 1.7 = D., W.) that Ibycus most probably wants to evoke. And indeed, the epode's references to Helen's appearance and to Aphrodite[58] also point in this allusive direction. Ibycus may not explicitly allude to specific contents of the *Cypria*,[59] but he certainly starts from the earliest causes of the war, just as the *Cypria* did. Besides, he chooses to focus on the less Iliadic, more erotic aspects of the Trojan myth. Among these choices is Ibycus' probable adoption of the motif of Zeus' *boulai*, as mentioned above from the *Cypria*. In fact this

---

[54] Fränkel (1975: 288).   [55] On which see Marks (2002).   [56] Allan (2008: 204).
[57] *Il.* 1.5, 12. 241 (with μεγάλοιο), *Od.* 8.82 (with μεγάλου), 11.297.
[58] On Aphrodite's role in the *Cypria*, see Scaife (1995: 173).
[59] As suggested by Barron (1969: 133 and n. 62).

poem, decidedly non-Iliadic and often erotic in many of its themes, ties nicely with the occasion and the purpose of the ode.[60]

It is in keeping with these observations that the outward beauty (*eidos*) of Helen hints at the beauty contest that involved the judgment of Paris and Aphrodite, a theme which figures again at line 36 and is the real leitmotif of the ode. The amorous 'crime' of Paris, strongly emphasized in *xeinapatas*, line 10 (see *Cypria* arg. lines 96–8 Severyns, and Hom. *Il.* 3.354, 13.624–5, on Menelaus' hospitality to Paris) is then juxtaposed with the loveliness of his τανίσφυρος 'slim-ankled' sister Cassandra. A contrast is thereby created between the innocent beauty that her epithet highlights[61] and the fact that (as we know from Proclus' summary of the *Cypria*) Paris' departure from home occurred at the bidding of Aphrodite and that it was accompanied by predictions from Helenus and Cassandra, who surely foretold the dire consequences of bringing Helen to Troy (*Cypr.* arg. lines 91–4 Severyns).

Ibycus thus develops the theme of the Trojan War by emphasizing the centrality of love to it[62] and declaring his relative lack of interest in the prominent themes of the epic tradition on the war of Troy. In creating this distance from Homer, the personal pronoun that reinforces the role of the speaker and the adverb that highlights the newness of the poem (*nyn de moi*, 10) further separate the ode from the narrative modes of the Homeric epics.

As has been mentioned before[63] the poet may have had in mind particularly the second book of the *Iliad* with the catalogue of the Greeks at Troy. The two bravest Achaeans are mentioned in 2.768–9 (Ajax and Achilles) and the two most handsome in 2.671–74 (Achilles with Nireus of Syme). The thought of Ibycus' lines 23–7 ('on these themes the skilled Muses of Helicon might embark in story, but no mortal (untaught?) could tell each detail') is parallel to *Il.* 2.484–6 ('tell me now, you Muses that have dwellings on Olympus – for you are goddesses and are at hand and know all things, whereas we hear but a rumor and know not anything …'). But Ibycus borrows from Homer the rhetorical motif of the homage to the Muses only in order to do something different from the larger Homeric catalogue, albeit

---

[60] As Graziosi (2002: 187) notes, the subject of the poem can explain why a certain distance was often postulated between Homer and the *Cypria* regarding the authorship. See also Scaife (1995).

[61] Cf. Hutchinson (2001: 241): 'set against Paris's epithet, and in this context, the adjective displays a beauty which was separate from the amorous crime, and was destroyed by it'. See also the praise of Cassandra already in *Il.* 13.365 and again in Ibyc. *PMGF* 303(a).

[62] Hutchinson (2001: 249).

[63] Fränkel (1975: 290 n. 27), among other scholars, noted the allusion.

something similar to the brief comparison between Achilles and Nireus at 2.671–74. With the Muses' help Homer had sung the long catalogue of the warriors, while Ibycus appears to limit himself to a very selective catalogue of few names with a very specific orientation. For example, after listing only Achilles and Ajax, the two most valiant Greek warriors already mentioned by Hom. *Il.* 2.768–9, he is mainly concerned with the question of the most handsome among Greeks and Trojans in a putative beauty contest that leads up to a playfully un-Homeric list of the most beautiful warriors of the Trojan War, Cyanippus from Argos and Zeuxippus from Sicyon (lines 36–46). On Zeuxippus Ibycus comments that 'to him Trojans and Greeks likened Troilus as gold thrice-refined to orichalc, judging him very similar in loveliness of form' (lines 39–43) – we do not know whether the *Cypria* had already told of Achilles' love for Troilus, but it may at least have featured Troilus as a beautiful boy (see below).

After the poet's shift from the martial (for which he has no inclination) to the erotic, the poem moves to an explicit statement on appearance (and fame). As has been very nicely observed,[64] the first of the three sections on myth in the ode includes the epic traditional 'beauties' (Helen, Paris, Cassandra); then there is a sort of parenthesis between the kind of beauty most praised in Homer and the ephebic one, followed by the forceful address to Polycrates, which brings the narrative to the present moment of performance. A visual link is created between the goddess with the golden mane (Aphrodite), the fair-haired Helen and the gold to which the Trojan Troilus and the Greek Zeuxippus are likened, and it is an imposing link because of its circularity. As has been noted,[65] the phrase *Trōes Danaoi te* (line 44) is an association that, if it does not have a totalizing function (that is, it means: 'everybody'), is not easily understood. The phrase is used here of judging beauty (and not of fighting as in Hom. *Il.* 16.764) and shows the equal appreciation of both the Greeks and the Trojans for the heroes' physical beauty. Beauty bridges divisions and creates a single aesthetic community in which the Iliadic warriors are transformed into spectators of physical beauty. In fact, the ecumenical significance of eros[66] and Ibycus' certainty that his heroes '*always* (αἰέν) have a share in beauty' (line 46) contrast with the austere atmosphere of blood and death of the Homeric *Iliad*, via the

---

[64] Bonanno (2004: 91).   [65] Giannini (2004: 57).
[66] This emphasis on the power of love certainly contributes to establishing Ibycus' poetics as those of an erotic author. It may also take on added significance if it suggests that 'the presence of the beautiful Polycrates has too powerful a claim on the poet's heart and senses' (Fränkel (1975: 289)).

less austere pre-Iliadic or extra-Iliadic characters and atmospheres of the *Cypria*, and provide the poem and its addressee Polycrates with their own *kleos*, which is *aphthiton* like the Iliadic one,[67] but different in substance (lines 47–8).

A few other surviving fragments and testimonies that mainly involve minor mythological figures merit brief mention, although not much can be gathered. *PMGF* S 224 (POxy. 2637 F 12) includes a quotation stating that Achilles kills Troilus in the sanctuary of Apollo Thymbraeus outside the walls of Ilion 'after waiting for him/ambushing him' (ἐπιτηρήσας).[68] Apart from defining the action as an ambush, Ibycus seems to have also referred to a 'sister' of Troilus (line 13). If this sister was Polyxena (absent from Homer), it would mean that Ibycus inserted her, side by side with her brother Hector (line 15), into the story of the death of Troilus. Achilles' ambush (an un-Homeric way of fighting) certainly degrades the hero's *kleos*[69] (even more so if an erotic, and thus un-Homeric, tone was involved or added). It also prefigures the inappropriate end of Troilus' slayer, Achilles, at the hand of the god Apollo as a punishment for the sacrilege. Troilus' youthful beauty and desirability is highlighted in the phrase θεοῖς ἴκελον (line 8),[70] which suggests that he was Achilles' *eromenos*,[71] in tune with Ibycus' tendency to give myths an erotic/homoerotic slant.[72] Troilus' death may, however, have been discussed by Ibycus merely as paradigmatic of the dangers inherent in godlike beauty (cf. the fate of Cassandra).[73] In any case, this representation of Troilus clashes with the *Iliad*, where he is a mature warrior (cf. Σ *Il*. 24.257). The *Cypria*, on the other hand, may have been one of Ibycus' inspirations. It is true that according to Proclus (arg. line 162 Severyns), the *Cypria* merely said that Achilles killed Troilus, but this Cyclic poem is the main text that we can surmise either to have triggered the well-established sixth-century iconography of Achilles in love for Troilus,

---

[67] Cf. *Il*. 9.413. For the combination see Nagy (1999: 175–89).

[68] On the iconography of Troilus' death, see Gantz (1993: 598–600); Scaife (1995: 189–91). On Troilus and Polyxena, see Robertson (1990).

[69] See further Boitani (1989: 10).

[70] Cf. *PMGF* S 151.41–6 again on Troilus' beauty. Another example of extraordinary male beauty in Ibycus is Ganymedes: see *PMGF* 289(a), where Ibycus writes that Ganymedes was carried off by Zeus who was in love with the youth; the homosexual abduction of Ganymedes was first introduced in the *Ilias parva*. Homer (*Il*. 20.234) emphasizes the position of Ganymedes in Olympus as the gods' cup-bearer, an element that does not seem to have appeared in Ibycus.

[71] Cavallini (1994). One cannot exclude, however, that the erotic motif was present also in Stesichorus' *Iliou persis*.

[72] The homoeroticism in Ibycus' myths is noted by Dover (1989: 197 and 199). See also Jenner (1998: 9); Cavallini (1994: 42).

[73] Robertson (1990: 12). Jenner (1998: 12).

or to have paralleled it (as we do not have to presuppose a poetic origin for every iconographic motif).[74]

Then, there is *PMGF* 291, which speaks of the death of Achilles, his arrival in the Elysian Fields and his subsequent marriage to Medea, whom various sources ascribed to Achilles as a wife after his death. The *Iliad* includes no hint at a life for Achilles after his death, nor does the *Aethiopis*, which described the hero's actual demise. It is telling of Ibycus' amorous poetics that he decided to adopt the post-Iliadic and post-Cyclic attention to the erotic life of Achilles in the afterworld, which parallels fifth-century and later attention to Achilles' erotic life before his death.[75]

Next, the encounter between Menelaus and Helen was described in the *Little Iliad* (*PEG* F 19 = D. = F 28 W.). According to Σ Aristoph. *Lys.* 155, the relevant Aristophanic lines 155–6 – 'Ὁ γῶν Μενέλαος τᾶς Ἑλένας τὰ μᾶλα πᾳ / γυμνᾶς παραϊδὼν ἐξέβαλ', οἰῶ, τὸ ξίφος ('Like Menelaus! As soon as he peeked at bare Helen's melons, he threw his sword away, I reckon') – are a parody of this scene, and 'the same story' was also found in Ibycus, *PMGF* 296. From another source (Σ Eur. *Or.* 1287) we know that this scenario also appeared in Stesichorus (*PMGF* 201: 'Stesichorus indicates something similar in connection with the men who are on the point of stoning her [Helen]: he says that the moment they saw her face, they dropped their stones on the ground'). The scene of Menelaus dropping his sword for love was later alluded to in Eur. *Andr.* 629–30, and *Or.* 1287. Σ Eur. *Andr.* 630, without specifying the author, also adds a narrative detail that may derive from either the *Little Iliad* or Ibycus or Stesichorus or all of the above: 'Helen takes refuge in the temple of Aphrodite and there she speaks to Menelaus, and he drops the sword for love' (διαλέγεται τῶι Μενελάωι, ὁ δ' ὑπ' ἔρωτος ἀφίησι τὸ ξίφος). Ibycus will have turned to the *Little Iliad* as he revisited this scene (it seems to have been well known; see a possible iconographical parallel in a pithos from Myconos of the end of the seventh century BC[76]). He would likely have emphasized the idea that the power of love (cf. *hyp' erōtos*) can *stop* war – a theme symmetrical to the Polycrates poem's idea that the power of seduction can *provoke* it. Aristophanes' parody envisions a rather explicitly sexual form of seduction, but this may just be the usual vantage point of comedy.[77] If Ibycus' *PMGF* 316, which focuses on the colourful nature of dyed garments, and conveys an intensity that suits an erotic context, is to be ascribed to the encounter between Helen

---

[74] See e.g. Carpenter, above in this volume, p. 178.   [75] On this, see Fantuzzi (2012: 1–20).
[76] *LIMC* 'Helene' 225; Ahlberg-Cornell (1992: 78–80); West (2013: 219).
[77] As West (2013: 219) correctly observes, 'if Helen uncovered her breast on purpose, the motif recalls Hekabe's exposure of hers for a different purpose in *Il.* 22.80'.

and Menelaus,[78] then we can surmise that the atmosphere of the scene in Ibycus will have been characterized by a much more refined eroticism than the one in Aristophanes. In this context, if the detail narrated by the Σ Eur. *Andr.* 629–30 belongs to Ibycus, or to both Ibycus and the *Little Iliad*, we can surmise that Aphrodite may also have played some role in granting Helen shelter in her temple and by supporting her successful seductive operation.

Another fragment supporting our study of Ibycus' poetics is *PMGF* 297, which proves that Ibycus further investigated Helen's erotic life. The source of the fragment, Σ *Il.* 13.516, notes that Ibycus made Deiphobus and Idomeneus rivals for the hand of Helen, and it emphatically denies the truth of Ibycus' story noting that Idomeneus was advanced in his years. It may be the result of the scholiast's confusion from a reference to the suitors of a young Helen (a topic that the *Cypria* certainly dealt with) rather than to the events regarding her life in Troy after Paris' death.

Finally, we can note that Ibycus' interest in events and characters that were in the Cyclic *Iliou persis* – like Cassandra and Polyxena – makes it likely that he composed his own '*Iliou persis*'[79] and shows, in any case, his emphasis on retelling the War of Troy from the Trojans' viewpoint. As in the Polycrates poem, this is a strategy Ibycus chose in order to 'complement' Homer. *PMGF* 303(a) describes Cassandra. Her name is placed between two epithets, γλαυκῶπις ('bright-eyed') and ἐρασιπλόκαμος ('with lovely locks'), each in the emphatic initial position in its respective line (lines 1 and 2), and each stressing aspects of Cassandra's beauty such as her eyes and hair; actually, they transform what might have been just a conventional patronymic (see 'daughter of Priam' at the end of line 2) into a full physical description of Cassandra's face. The phrase 'daughter of Priam' also links Cassandra's fate to the demise of Troy, a connection usually made in the poetic tradition to stress the sadness of her life, which is also found again in *PMGF* S151.12–15. Ibycus' Polyxena, on the other hand, is sacrificed to Achilles, as *PMGF* 307, from Σ Eur. *Hec.* 41, suggests by stating that Euripides was following Ibycus' version in his play.[80] The *Iliou persis* (arg. line 274 Severyns) also stated that Polyxena was slain on Achilles' tomb. It is not possible to ascertain whether or not an erotic interpretation (which for instance would depict Polyxena as a posthumous victim of Achilles' love) is

---

[78] Cingano (1992: 217 n. 92).   [79] See Sisti (1967: 60–1).

[80] By contrast, the *Cypria* would have said that Polyxena died of her wounds at the hands of Odysseus and Diomedes during the sack of the city and was buried by Neoptolemus (*PEG* F 34 = F 27 D.). See above, pp. 446, 448–9 for the difference of Polyxena's fate in Ibycus and *Cypr. PEG* F34 = F 27 D. Polyxena's name also may be reconstructed in Stesich. *PMGF* S 135, but we do not know in which context.

involved here.[81] This is certainly the case with Achilles' erotic desires in the tragedians of the fifth century, interested as they were in exploring human passions and, more specifically, the passion of love,[82] and may have already been the case of Ibycus.[83]

[81] On the story of Achilles' love for Polyxena, see Jenner (1998: 12–15).
[82] Fantuzzi (2012: esp. 16–18).
[83] I would like to thank David Sider for his suggestions, Chris Carey for allowing me to see an unpublished paper of his on Stesichorus, and the editors for comments on an earlier draft.

24 | Pindar's Cycle

IAN RUTHERFORD

OVERLAPS BETWEEN PINDAR AND CYCLIC EPIC

Most choral songs of the sort composed by Pindar included a narrative based on the established themes of Greek mythology (usually a unique one for each song), or at least brief mythological references. The subjects were most often ones belonging to Panhellenic or common-Greek traditions; ones of purely local interest and disconnected from Panhellenic tradition are rarer. Since the Trojan and Theban Cycle are primary repositories of such myths, it is no surprise to find that there are many overlaps between choral narratives and the Epic Cycle, as indeed there are with the Hesiodic *Catalogue of Women*.[1] Obviously, an overlap does not in itself prove borrowing, or that Pindar knew the Cycle.[2]

The Trojan Cycle is well represented in Pindar, particularly when he is composing for victors from Aegina, in whose mythology the Aeacidae play a major role. Overlaps with the *Cypria* include: the wedding of Thetis and Peleus;[3] perhaps the infancy of Achilles, and his being raised by Cheiron;[4] the conflict between the Dioscuri and the Apharetidae (see below); the battle with Telephus in Teuthrania during the first and abortive expedition,[5] where the military cooperation between Achilles and Patroclus was first displayed;[6]

---

[1] D'Alessio (2005).
[2] Burgess (2001: 45, with n. 133): 'Pindar was very much interested in "Cycle" material and perhaps depended on the poems we know in the Epic Cycle as a source.'
[3] *Cypr. PEG* F 2–3 (= D. = F 2 and 4 W.); Pind. *Pyth.* 3.91, *Nem.* 3.35–6, *Nem.* 4.62–5 etc.; Burnett (2005: 131 n. 25) thinks the metamorphotic wrestling match was in the *Cypria*, ascribed to the *neōteroi* in F 3*W. = Σ *Il.* 18.434a.
[4] The *Cypria* may have had Thetis abandon Achilles at the age of 12 (Σ Hom. *Il.* 16.574b = *PEG* F dub. 35; assigned to *neōteroi*) and Pindar would follow the latter (*Pyth.* 6.21–7; *Nem.* 3.43–58). The *Iliad* is sometimes said to have an alternate version that Thetis and Peleus were waiting for Achilles at home together (Stoneman (1981: 62); Mann (1994: 316)), but all these come down to the statement that Thetis helped in preparations for war (*Il.* 16.222–4), and will not welcome Achilles home from Troy (*Il.* 18.330–32). For the gasping bodies of animals, see below p. 459.
[5] *Ol.* 9.73; *Isth.* 5.41; *Isth.* 8.50. The third of these passages refers to the episode of Dionysus tripping up Telephus with the vine, which could perhaps have come from the *Cypria*: see Burnett (2005: 97 n. 14).
[6] *Ol.* 9.70–5.

and Achilles' slaying Cycnus the son of Poseidon early on in the war.[7] Another striking overlap with the *Cypria* can also be found in the Odes of Bacchylides, whose short Ode 15 has as its subject the 'Demand for Helen' made by Menelaus and Odysseus, when they were protected by Antenor and Theaino.[8] Overlaps between the *Aethiopis* and Pindar include the killing of Memnon,[9] the mourning for Achilles,[10] and his immortalization on the White Island.[11] Here too belongs the suicide of Ajax, apparently dealt with in both *Aethiopis* and *Ilias parva*; a scholiast discussing Pindar's account of it at *Isth*. 4.35–9, and his specification that it happened ὀψίᾳ ἐν νυκτὶ, says that if this phrase means 'in the last part of the night', i.e. just before dawn, this is parallel to the account in the *Aethiopis* (*PEG* F 5 = F 1 D. = F 6 W.).[12]

Overlaps with the rest of the Trojan Cycle are less striking, but it is worth paying attention to Achilles' son Neoptolemus: Pindar follows the *Ilias parva* in having him brought from Scyros (though Pindar differs in having multiple messengers);[13] he follows the Milesian *Iliou persis* (but disagrees with the Mytilenean *Ilias parva*) in situating Neoptolemus' killing of Priam at the altar of Zeus Herceios (by contrast, the *Ilias parva* had it occur at the palace gates);[14] and, like the *Nostoi*, he narrates Neoptolemus' return from Troy, though the itinerary is completely different (see below). Σ *Nem.* 6 finds a parallel for Pindar's description of Achilles spear as 'angry' in the 'double-tipped' spear of the *Ilias parva*, but the idea must have been common.[15]

No extant Pindaric Ode uses as its primary narrative the story of the *Iliad* (although the death of Hector is mentioned alongside Achilles' other

---

[7] *Ol.* 2.82; *Isth.* 5.39.

[8] Angeli Bernardini (2005: 21–2); Fearn (2007: 269–87) thinks rather of the *Iliad*.

[9] *Ol.* 2.83, *Pyth.* 6.32, *Nem.* 3.63, *Nem.* 6.52–5, *Isth.* 5.40–1, *Isth.* 8.54–5.

[10] *Pyth.* 3.101–2; *Isth.* 8.56–9. Another intertext is clearly Hom. *Od.* 24.56–8; Sotiriou (1997: 242–4) explores the latter model, but ignores the *Aethiopis* (I thank B. Currie for pointing this out).

[11] *Nem.* 4.4.   [12] 3.231.7–8 (Drachmann).

[13] In *Paean* 6.102, ἄγγελοι 'messengers' bring Neoptolemus. In Proclus' summary of the *Ilias parva* and also the *Odyssey* (11.508–9) Odysseus fetched Neoptolemus, though in PRylands 22, which *PEG* assigns to the *Ilias parva* (p. 75), it seems to be [Odysseu]s and Phoenix; in Sophocles' *Scyrians*, it was Odysseus and Phoenix (*TrGF* F 154 n. 1).

[14] Anderson (1997: 28–9); Hedreen (2001: 66). Neoptolemus and Zeus Herceios: *Ilias parva PEG* F 16 (I) = F 17 D. = F 25 W., but *PEG* F 16 (II) = F 17 D. = F 25 W. (Paus. 10.27.2) says it was not in Lesches. See also *Iliou persis* (arg. lines 257–8 Severyns); cf. Davies (1989c: 71). For conflict between *Ilias parva* and *Iliou persis*, see Nagy (1990b: 76).

[15] Achilles' ζάκοτος ('exceeding wroth') spear at *Nem.* 6.85: Σ b ad loc. connects with *Ilias parva PEG* F 5 (= D., W.). For possible parallels in Stesichorus POxy. 3876, F 64a2 and 67a5, see Schade (2003: 42).

conquests)[16] or that of the *Odyssey*. Here we may contrast Bacchylides, whose Ode 13 contains a sort of mini-*Iliad*. If Pindar avoided the *Iliad* and *Odyssey*, it may have been because his aim in the epinicia was to create for each patron a unique memorial, and that could only be done with a myth that had not achieved such a fixed form in the Panhellenic tradition.[17]

Precise overlaps with the Theban Cycle are harder to find, not only because we know the *Thebaid*, *Epigonoi* and *Alcmeonis* less well but also because Pindar, despite his Theban origins, devotes less space to these myths in the extant poems. The summary of the myth of the campaign of the Seven in *Nem.* 9 (lines 13–27) no doubt draws in part on the Cyclic *Thebaid* and perhaps also the *Alcmeonis* (see below),[18] just as Amphiaraus' prophecy in the context of the second expedition narrated in *Pyth.* 8.39–56 may well sample the *Epigonoi*. One of the best specific parallels is the detail in the catalogue of the glories of Argos in the proem of *Nem.* 10 (line 7) that Athena made Diomedes immortal; this can be connected with a story ascribed in Σ *Il.* 5.126 to the *kyklikoi* that Tydeus lost his promised immortality when Athena saw him eating the brains of Melanippus (*PEG* F 9 = F 5 D. = F 9* W.), and that he asked Athena to give it instead to Diomedes.[19]

In addition, two reworkings of the language of the Theban Cycle have been alleged. According to an ancient scholar called Asclepiades (cited by the scholiast), Adrastus' description of the late Amphiaraus as: ἀμφότερον μάντιν τ' ἀγαθὸν καὶ δουρὶ μάρνασθαι ('both a good seer and good at fighting

---

[16] At *Ol.* 2.81 alongside Cycnus and Memnon, at *Isth.* 5.39–41 alongside Cycnus, Memnon and Telephos, and at *Isth.* 8.55 alongside Memnon. Notice also that the funeral of Achilles, described in *Isth.* 8.56–8, was in the *Odyssey* (24.60) as well as the *Aethiopis*.

[17] Mann (1994: 325, 334–5). By contrast Nagy (1990b) argued that there is no qualitative difference between the way Pindar uses 'Homeric' and 'Cyclical' material, on the grounds that the lyric tradition, represented by Pindar, had from earliest times contained within itself prototypes of all the mythical narratives of the Trojan Cycle; the epic realizations of these myths would on this model be later, as would be the process whereby some versions achieve Panhellenic status (i.e. Homeric ones), and others remain local (i.e. Cyclical ones). The improbable implication of Nagy's somewhat mystical approach is that the lyric versions are always primary and epic ones secondary, perhaps even that epic ones adapt/allude to lyric ones.

[18] The *Alcmeonis* (*PEG* F 1 = D., W.) also contained the earliest attestation of a detail from Aeginetan mythology, namely the killing of Phocus by his half-brothers Telamon and Peleus (*Nem.* 5.12).

[19] Cf. Braswell (1998: 33, n. 28). Diomedes: Davies (1989c: 28), *Thebaid PEG* F 9 (= F 5 D. = F 9 W.), followed by Pindar and Ibycus, *PMG* F 294 (= Σ *Nem.* 10.12). Bacchylides F 41; also Nagy (1999: 163–4); worshipped as a god in Italy, Bethe in *RE* 9: 822–3, Malkin (1998: 252–4). Braswell (1982: 81) suggests that the lack of omens at *Nem.* 9.18–19 may come from the *Thebaid*.

with the spear', *Ol.* 6.17)[20] was taken from the *Thebaid*, and scholars have produced a good hexameter by a minor change in the last word (*PEG* F 10 = F 7 D. = F 6 W.: ἀμφότερον μάντιν τ' ἀγαθὸν καὶ δουρὶ μάχεσθαι).[21] However, this could be a more general formula, since something similar is said of Amphiaraus in the Hesiodic *Catalogue of Women*: F 25.37 M.-W. ὅς ῥ' ἀγαθὸς μὲν ἔην ἀγορῆι, ἀγαθὸς δὲ μάχεσθαι ('he was good in assembly, and good at warfare').[22] Another possible resonance of *Thebaid* may be found in a dactylo-epitrite Pindaric fragment (F 43) in which Amphiaraus advises his son Amphilochus:

> ὦ τέκνον, ποντίου θηρὸς πετραίου
> χρωτὶ μάλιστα νόον
> προσφέρων πάσαις πολίεσσιν ὁμίλει·
> τῶι παρεόντι δ' ἐπαινήσαις ἑκών
> ἄλλοτ' ἀλλοῖα φρόνει.

> Child, consort with all cities by adapting your mind as closely as possibly to the skin of the rocky sea creature. And willingly praising the one who is present, think different things on different occasions.[23]

The fragment has a general resemblance to some lines of Theognis (215–19), and the same comparison is made in several dramatic sources (see *PEG* apparatus), but it is also found also in a three-line hexameter fragment, in which Amphiaraus addresses his son:

> Πουλύποδός μοι, τέκνον, ἔχον νόον, Ἀμφίλοχ' ἥρως,
> τοῖσιν ἐφαρμόζειν, τῶν κεν κατὰ δῆμον ἵκηαι,
> ἄλλοτε δ' ἀλλοῖος τελέθειν καὶ χροίηι (West; χώρηι MS) ἕπεσθαι.

> Pray, hold to the octopus' outlook, Amphilochus my son, and adapt it to whatever people you come among; be changeable, and go along with the colour.

This fragment has been confidently ascribed to the *Thebaid* by Bernabé (*PEG* F 4), hesitatingly by West (2003a: F 8*); to the *Alcmeonis* by Debiasi.[24]

---

[20] For Pindar and the *Thebaid* see Stoneman (1981: 49–50); for this passage see Tsagalis (2008b: 262–3).

[21] Leutsch; on the whole passage, Stoneman (1981: 50–1).

[22] Braswell (1998: 28–9). For the relation between the *CAT.* and the *Thebaid*, see Rutherford (2012: 156).

[23] Amphilochus mentioned in Athenaeus 12.513c, Amphiaraus in Philodemus, *Rhet.* 2, F12 (2.74.1 [Sudh]); see also Stoneman (1981: 48–9).

[24] Above, in this volume, pp. 237–8, 270–1 with n. 52. It had been attributed to the *Nostoi* by Allen (1913: 191); to an '*Amphiarai Exilium*' by Powell in *CA*: 246 Stoneman (1981: 49); Braswell (1998: 36 n. 35). For the 'norm of the polyp', see Gentili (1990: 132–3). See also Davies ("Hom." 3).

In both the hexameter fragment and the Pindar fragment, the occasion for the advice could have been the departure of Amphiaraus for Thebes (though Amphilochus was a baby then), or it could have been later, in the context of an oracular consultation. In the latter case, there would be a parallel with Amphiaraus' words on the occasion of the second expedition by the *Epigonoi* as reported in *Pyth*. 8.44–55 and these may have had a similar source.

One general feature where Pindar is in agreement with the Cyclic poems and in disagreement with the *Iliad* and *Odyssey* is that he allows that heroes may in exceptional cases become immortal: so Achilles in the *Aethiopis* and Diomedes in the *Thebaid*. Castor in the *Cypria* is a more difficult case, because even in the *Odyssey* he enjoys some sort of enhanced afterlife.[25]

DIFFERENCES

In a few cases, Pindar's version of a myth is manifestly different from that of the Cycle. A good case is the *nostos* of Neoptolemus, who in *Nemean* 7 (lines 36–7) and *Paean* 6 (lines 109–17) returned from Troy by sea and was driven off course, ending up in Molossia. This contrasts with the Cyclic *Nostoi*, where he was explicitly told by Thetis to avoid the sea-route, and so went by land across Thrace, where he encountered Odysseus at Maroneia. The *Odyssey* too (3.188–90) implies that he got back to the Myrmidons in safety. The sea-voyage in Pindar does not have to be later – it may even be that the *Nostoi* is innovating here – but the idea that the final destination was Molossia may well be an innovation, reflecting a new association between Neoptolemus and that region.[26] The full account in the *Paean* where he 'does not escape the winds or Apollo' seems to imply that being driven off course was part of Neoptolemus' punishment for killing Priam at the altar of Zeus Herceios – a sequence perhaps modelled on the story of Locrian Ajax's punishment for raping Cassandra.[27] Neoptolemus' later death at Delphi, which Pindar puts so much emphasis on, along with the tragedians, was not in the Epic Cycle either, and may well reflect a subsequent development of Delphic cult.

More complex is the case of the conflict between Ajax and Odysseus for the arms of Achilles. According to a scholium on Aristophanes' *Knights* 1056 (*PEG* F 2 = D., W.), the *Ilias parva* said that the issue was decided at Nestor's

---

[25] Currie (2006: 44): deaths of Achilles, Diomedes, Amphiaraus; see Davies (1989c: 28). For Castor, see below pp. 457–9.
[26] For the Molossi, see Strauch in *DNP* 9.131–2, s.v.
[27] Radt (1958: 158); Rutherford (2001: 313 n. 31).

suggestion by sending messengers to eavesdrop on some Trojan girls, one of whom favoured Ajax for carrying the body of Achilles off the field while Odysseus guarded the retreat, while another, influenced by Athena, objected that carrying a body was not man's work. There is no clear evidence that the version of the *Aethiopis* survives. Homer's Odysseus (*Od.* 11.547) reports the judges were 'the children of the Trojans and Pallas Athena', which would be just about compatible with the *Ilias parva*, though the Homeric scholia here say that it refers to Trojan captives whom Agamemnon asked which of the heroes had hurt them more.[28] In Pindar we find the completely different story of a secret ballot by the Greeks, rigged in some way by Odysseus (*Nem.* 7.22–7; *Nem.* 8.26). Sophocles' *Ajax* (1135–7) has something similar except that the ballot-rigger was Menelaus. The introduction of the ballot implies a completely different explanation for the injustice against Ajax: it was not that divine forces were manipulating the minds of the Trojan girls or men; rather, the decisive factor was human psychology and those who manipulated it: as Pindar puts it, 'envy and hateful deception, the companion of flattering tales, guileful contriver, evil-working disgrace, which represses what is illustrious, but holds up for obscure men a glory that is rotten' (lines 32–4).[29] This idea fits perfectly into Pindar's epinician text-world, since the reputation of the athletes who were his patrons was subject to similar human distortion. For that reason, it is tempting to draw the conclusion that Pindar came up with the mytheme of the secret ballot himself. However, a ballot, if not a secret one, is already illustrated on vases from around 500 BC, and in fact we cannot be certain that this was not already mentioned in the *Aethiopis*.[30]

Some myths connected to the Trojan Cycle that Pindar narrates were not, as far as we know, included in the canonical Cycle, and we do not know what the source was, if any. One example is Aeacus' assisting Poseidon and Apollo in building the walls of Troy in *Ol. 8*, with the prophecy about the two sacks of the city,[31] another is the expedition of Heracles and Telamon against Laomedon of Troy narrated in *Isth.* 6. Similar is Pindar's explanation in *Isth.* 8 (478 BC) for why Thetis married the mortal Peleus and not Zeus.

---

[28] Severyns (1928: 331) thinks the *Odyssey*'s version was the same as the *Aethiopis*. See Holmberg (1998: 467 n. 41); Nisetich (1989: 18); Davies (1989c: 60) thinks that Pindar's version could be that of the *Aethiopis*. See further Burnett (2005: 173 n. 29).

[29] See Nisetich (1989: 18); Scodel (2001: 130–1), from whom I draw the translation; Miller (1982).

[30] See Henry (2005: 80–1); Hedreen (2001: 106). The voting is illustrated on vases from about 500 BC; see Williams (1980). In Aeschylus' *Hoplon Krisis* (*TrGF* F 174) the judges may have been Nereids. See Touchefeu (1981: 326–7).

[31] For speculation of what the source may have been, if there was one, see Burnett (2005: 213 n. 15).

Whereas the *Cypria* seems to have represented her as rejecting Zeus out of respect for Hera, in response to which Zeus was enraged and married her to a mortal (*PEG* F 2 = D., W.), in Pindar's version the marriage to a mortal comes about after Themis warns Zeus and Poseidon of the consequences if one of them were to father a son by her. Closely related is the version of the Ps.-Aeschylean *Prometheus Bound*, where knowledge of this prophecy is attributed to Prometheus (768, 924–5). There is no sign of 'Themis' Advice' in the *Cypria*,[32] although Themis (restored by Heyne) is probably involved with Zeus at the beginning in deliberations about the Trojan War. Albin Lesky traced the motif back to a hypothetical epic poem, which he called the 'Themis-Gedicht'.[33] Another possibility is that Pindar invented Themis' Advice, perhaps using as his model Hesiod's account of the advice of Ge and Ouranos to Zeus not to allow Metis to bear a son (*Theog.* 886–900).[34]

DID PINDAR KNOW THE CYCLE?

These overlaps do not prove that Pindar knew the Cyclic epics as a whole or individually, merely that he was familiar with similar mythology. The clearest evidence for knowledge of them on his part comes from the imperial author Aelian (*VH* 9.15) who attributes to him (F 265) the tradition that an impoverished Homer gave his daughter the *Cypria* as a dowry. The husband must have been Stasinus of Cyprus, as we see from the Hesychian Life (c. 5) that identifies their sons as Eriphon and Theolaus. Pindar was interested in earlier poets, and there is no reason to think he would have shared Herodotus' scepticism about the authorship of the *Cypria*.[35] This story is obviously meant to reconcile two rival claims.[36]

The only passage in the extant poems where there may be a reference to the Cycle is *Nem.* 6.55, where the expression 'those of old' (παλαιότεροι), used of those who have told the story of Achilles and Memnon, has been thought to refer to the *Aethiopis*.[37] It has sometimes been thought that on two occasions where Pindar refers to Homer in the context of the suicide

---

[32] Contrast the view of Stoneman (1981: 61) that Themis' prophecy was in the *Cypria*; at Apoll. Rh. 4.790–809 the 'refusal of Thetis' and the 'prophecy of Themis' are combined.
[33] Kossatz-Deissmann (1981: 41); Lesky (1937: 297); cf. Latte (1934: 1627). See also Slatkin (1991: 74–5).
[34] For theories, see Burnett (2005: 115 n. 30).
[35] Herod. 2.53, 117; 4.32; Lloyd-Jones (1972) defends its attribution to Pindar.
[36] So West (1982: 1438), cited by Graziosi (2002: 187). [37] Nisetich (1989: 22).

of Ajax, he meant Homer as poet of the *Aethiopis*. These are *Isth.* 4.35–9, where the statement that Ajax's suicide shames all the Greeks at Troy, but his virtue was glorified by Homer comes immediately after the detail that Ajax died late at night, which, as we saw, the scholiast links to the *Aethiopis*; similarly at *Nem.* 7.22–30 Pindar says that Homer has given Odysseus too much fame, and that men are blind, which also explains why Ajax was not awarded the arms of Achilles. If Pindar regarded the *Cypria* as Homeric, it is not impossible that he believed the same of the *Aethiopis*. But in fact, both passages make adequate sense if we understand 'Homer' as the author of the *Iliad* (*Isth.* 4) and the *Odyssey* (*Nem.* 7); there is no need to infer reference to the Cycle here.[38]

THE EPIC CYCLE AS A PRIMARY SOURCE FOR PINDAR: THE CASE OF *NEMEAN* 10?

In one case an argument can be made for a systematic adaption by Pindar of a specific narrative in the Cycle. The *Cypria* included the story of how Castor and Pollux attempted to steal the cattle of the Aphareditae Idas and Lynceus.[39] Proclus represents this as happening in the period when Paris seduces Helen and elopes with her. Immediately before, Paris had been entertained first in Lacedaemon by the Dioscouroi themselves and then in Sparta by Menelaus, who afterwards went off to Crete. The episode of the Aphareteдae thus serves the narratological function of getting the Dioscouroi off the scene, so that they cannot pursue Helen, as they had on the earlier occasion when she had been abducted by Theseus (*Cypr. PEG* F 13 = F 12 D. = W.).[40] In one of the longest extant fragments of the *Cypria* (*PEG* F 15 cited by the Pindar scholia) the sharp-eyed Lynceus goes up Mt Taugetos and sees Castor and Pollux in the hollow of an oak tree. In the subsequent battle the mortal[41] Castor is speared by Idas (*Cypr. PEG* F 15 = F 14 D. = F 17 W.; *EGM* F 127 A), and the Aphareditae are killed by the immortal Pollux. After this Zeus grants the Tyndaridae the gift of 'immortality every other day' (ἑτερήμερος... ἀθανασία). Other early sources give a slightly different outcome: the *Odyssey* (11.301–4) says that though held by the

---

[38] For the older view that Pindar saw the Cycle as Homeric, see Fitch (1924); *contra* Mann (1994); Kelly (2006: 14 n. 60).
[39] *Cypr.* arg. lines 106–9 Severyns.   [40] Cf. Lyc. 512–43; cf. Gantz (1993: 325).
[41] Castor is mortal, Pollux immortal in the *Cypria* (*PEG* F 8 = F 6 D. = F 9 W.). Contrast the *Odyssey* which says that they are both children of the mortal Tyndareus (11.299), while Hesiod said that they are both sons of Zeus (F 24 M.-W.).

ground 'alive', they are in the Underworld sometimes alive and sometimes dead, holding honour equal to the gods (so Alcman, *PMG* F 7), whereas in *Iliad* 3.236–44, when Helen notices that the Dioscouroi are not among the Greek army, the poet comments that they were both already dead in Lacedaemon.

Pindar makes this episode the subject of the narrative-section of his victory ode for Theaeus of Argos (*Nem*.10), the link to Theaeus being that Pamphaes, one of his ancestors, had performed a *theoxenia*-ritual for them in the past (lines 49–50).[42] This section is introduced with an anticipation of the result, which seems to come right from the *Cypria*: they are on Olympus one day and at Therapnai the next, enjoying the same fate (lines 5–6).[43] The first half of the narrative, occupying the fourth triad of the poem, deals with the combat between the two sides: Idas stabbed Castor; Lynceus and Idas tried to kill Pollux with a slab from the tomb of their father Aphareus, but it bounced off without injuring him;[44] then Lynceus was killed by Pollux's javelin, and Idas by Zeus' thunderbolt. After the stabbing of Castor, Pindar inserts the background detail that (before the combat) Lynceus, gazing from Taygetos, had seen the Tyndaridae sitting on an oak stump.[45] Most of this is clearly parallel to the *Cypria*; the only demonstrable differences are that in Pindar the Tyndaridae are not sitting inside a tree trunk but on a stump (so that Lynceus' eyesight does not have to be quite so superhuman) and that in the *Cypria*, Pollux killed both the brothers himself.[46]

The second half of the narrative, in the fifth and final triad, begins with Pollux's return to find his brother dying, and his appeal to Zeus to let him die as well. There follows an extraordinary confrontation with Zeus, who 'came to meet him' (ἀντίος ἤλυθέ οἱ), observed that Pollux, unlike his brother, was immortal, and offered him the choice of life on Olympus, free of death and old age, or a mixed existence half below the earth and half above with Castor (lines 80–8). Pollux makes his decision, and the effect is to 'free the eye and the voice' of Castor, which provides an unusually abrupt end to the

---

[42] See Flückiger-Guggenheim (1984: 65–6). Notice that *Paean* 18, a prosodion for the Argives, (Rutherford 2001: S5), begins with a reference to the local sanctuary of the Tyndaridae, on which see D'Alessio (2004: 111–13).

[43] Henry (2005: 110).

[44] Ps.-Apollodorus (3.11.2.5–6) has Idas throw a stone at Pollux's head, rendering him unconscious (σκότωσε); in Pindar, the stone bounces off; see Henry (2005: 113). Wilamowitz (1922: 429) thought that this was a Pindaric innovation, to make clear that Pollux was divine, and Idas a sinner.

[45] *Nem*. 10.61–2; see Henry (2005: 112–13) for the text here. Whether we read ἡμένους (Boeckh) or ἡμένος (Didymus), both brothers are in the tree; for discussion, see Henry (2005: 112–13).

[46] See Huxley (1975: 20–1), who perhaps overstates the differences.

ode.[47] Neither Pollux's choice nor the meeting with Zeus appears in Proclus' brief summary; however, in Ps.-Apollodorus' version, which is sometimes thought to follow the *Cypria*, the meeting takes place on Olympus, where Pollux was taken and where he refuses to accept immortality as long as Castor is dead. If that is indeed the *Cypria*'s version (and not a garbled adaptation of Pindar), then Pindar innovated by having the dialogue with Zeus take place on earth, and in proximity to Castor's body. This could be seen as an example of a common Pindaric technique of focusing on episodes of direct contact between god and man, such as Pelops' appeal to Zeus in *Ol.* 1, Poseidon's gift to Iamus in *Ol.* 6 or Athena's to Bellerophon in *Ol.* 13.

To sum up, Pindar's version of the myth of the Tyndaridae and Apharetidae in *Nem.* 10 may well draw on, elaborate and adapt the version in the *Cypria*. Even here, however, it is impossible to be certain, and it cannot be ruled out that his primary source was something different, such as the narrative of an otherwise unknown traditional cult hymn to the Tyndaridae.

USING PINDAR TO RECONSTRUCT THE CYCLE

Despite the evidence that Pindar did not follow the Cyclic poems in every respect,[48] the assumption is widely made that his use of them is so consistent that his narratives can be used as evidence for them. For example, since it is known that the wedding of Peleus and Thetis was in the *Cypria*, it has been suggested that related mythemes mentioned by Pindar were as well, such as Achilles being educated by Cheiron, and in particular the detail of his bringing back to his teacher the bodies of recently killed animals still gasping (with the implication that he ate them raw).[49]

More complex issues are generated by the episode of how Antilochus was killed by Memnon while he was trying to defend his father Nestor's chariot, which is narrated in *Pyth.* 6 (lines 28–39; the so-called 'Nestorbedrängnis'). Proclus' summary of the *Aethiopis* mentions Antilochus' death by Memnon, followed by Achilles' killing of Memnon, but not the defence of Nestor's chariot. While it would be possible to argue that Pindar has invented Antilochus' action to illustrate the theme of the service of sons to their fathers which runs through this ode, its attribution to the *Aethiopis* is not

---

[47] See Young (1993: 129 n. 23).   [48] See above pp. 454–6.
[49] Gasping bodies at *Nem.* 3.48: Robinson (1940); Beazley (1986: 9–10) suggested that the motif is from the *Cypria*; Bowra (1964: 283–4, 287 n. 1); Kossatz-Deissmann (1981: 45 n. 21); in general Robbins (1993); Huxley (1975: 19); Scaife (1995: 181–3).

implausible. In fact this has become a point of great importance to neoanalysts who see it as pivotal step in the argument that the plotline of the *Iliad* imitates the *Aethiopis*: just as the overall sequence 'Hector kills Patroclus, Patroclus kills Hector' would be modeled on the Memnon story, so the episode where Antilochus defends the chariot is supposed to be the model for the episode of the *Iliad* where Nestor's horse has been shot by Paris, and Diomedes rescues him (8.78–99).[50] This reconstruction has, however, recently been challenged, first by Martin West, for whom the *Aethiopis* postdates the *Iliad*, and secondly by Adrian Kelly who argues incidentally that *Pyth.* 6.28–39 in fact shows the direct influence not of the *Aethiopis* but of the scene in the *Iliad* where Diomedes rescues Nestor.[51]

Pindar has also been mined for evidence for the Theban Cycle. The narrative of the Seven Against Thebes in *Nem.* 9 overlapped with the *Thebaid* and may well be influenced by it, but it has been suggested that one detail in it goes back to the *Alcmeonis*, which is assumed to be later. This is the story that Adrastus came to Sicyon at a point before the expedition of the Seven, when he was exiled from Argos, which is referred to briefly at the start of the narrative (*Nem.* 9.13–15). Paul Friedländer argued that Cleisthenes of Sicyon (early sixth century BC), who according to Herodotus (5.67) wanted to expel the cult of Adrastus from his city, promulgated this story as a way of reducing the status of Adrastus in Sicyonian history. If the *Thebaid* itself predates Cleisthenes, the story of the exile could be attributed to the *Alcmeonis*.[52] There are many uncertainties in this reconstruction, however, and in particular it is doubtful whether it is a safe assumption that every detail of Pindaric myth can be traced to an earlier source, let alone to the Cycle.

---

[50] Willcock (1997: 179–80).   [51] West (2003c); Kelly (2006).

[52] Friedländer (1914 = 1969: 44–7); Stoneman (1981: 44–6); *contra* Hubbard (1992: 91). For possible echoes of the *Epigonoi*, see Stoneman (1981: 54–5).

25 | Tragedy and the Epic Cycle

ALAN H. SOMMERSTEIN

INTRODUCTION

In the twenty-third chapter of his *Poetics*, Aristotle is arguing that an epic, as much as a tragedy (if not quite in the same way), ought to be composed around 'a single, whole, complete action, having a beginning, a middle and an end' (1459a20–1), and he praises Homer (i.e. the poet of the *Iliad* and *Odyssey*) for perceiving this and choosing for his subject, not even the whole of the Trojan War, but just one cohesive part of it (the events arising from the quarrel between Achilles and Agamemnon).

> The others compose poems of many parts about one person, one period, or one action, like the author of the *Cypria* and of the *Ilias parva*. Therefore out of the *Iliad* and *Odyssey* respectively only one or two tragedies are made, while from the *Cypria* there can be many and from the *Ilias parva* eight[1] – say, the *Award of the Arms*, *Philoctetes*, *Neoptolemus*, *Eurypylus*, the *Beggar Mission*,[2] *The Laconian Women*,[3] the *Iliou persis* and the *Departure*.[4]

The claim that one can make 'only one or two tragedies' out of the *Iliad* or *Odyssey* does not quite stand up. Aeschylus, after all, created a complete trilogy out of each of the two epics.[5] Sophocles may have written three plays based on episodes from the *Odyssey* – *Nausicaa or The Washerwomen*

---

[1] The manuscripts say 'more than eight' and add to the list 'and *Sinon* and *The Trojan Women*'; but these are generally regarded as later additions to Aristotle's text – the last two plays are out of order, and if Aristotle had had ten plays in his list he would have written 'ten', not 'more than eight'.

[2] Literally 'Beggary', referring to the occasion when Odysseus entered Troy disguised as a beggar and made contact with Helen (*Ilias parva* arg. lines 224–7 Severyns and *PEG* F 6 = F 9 W., with Ps.-Apollod. *Epit*. 3.13).

[3] Sophocles' play of this name seems to have combined this clandestine infiltration of Troy with the subsequent one in which Odysseus and Diomedes together stole the Palladium (*Ilias parva* arg. lines 224–9 Severyns and *PEG* F 25 = F 9 D. = F 11 W.); Ps.-Apollod. *Epit*. 3.13 likewise combines the two missions. See above in this volume, p. 322, and below, p. 468.

[4] See above, p. 1 for the Greek text.

[5] The trilogy based on the *Iliad* comprised *The Myrmidons*, *The Nereids* (see Michelakis (2002: 31 n. 21, 53 n. 71), Sommerstein (2010: 253 n. 4); *contra* West (2000: 341–3)) and *The Phrygians*; that based on the *Odyssey* comprised *The Ghost-Raisers*, *Penelope* and *The Bone-Gatherers*, and was followed by a satyr-play, *Circe*, whose story was also taken from the *Odyssey*.

(from book 6), *The Phaeacians* (presumably from books 7–12 or some part thereof), and *The Foot-Washing* (from book 19, unless – as has also been suggested[6] – it was actually about events leading to Odysseus' death and identical with Sophocles' *Odysseus and the Fatal Spine*). But the *Odyssey* does, much more than the *Iliad*, contain within its overall unity many episodes that can if desired be treated as self-contained stories. The relevant thing about the Cyclic epics, and especially the two that Aristotle singles out, was that they consisted almost entirely of such episodes, with little if any overall unity. And they were indeed, as Aristotle implies, massively exploited by the great tragedians,[7] to the extent of about twenty-two plays in the corpus of Aeschylus, twenty-three in that of Euripides, and no less than forty-seven (about two-fifths of his total output) in that of Sophocles. As we shall see, however, it was the *Cypria* rather than the *Ilias parva* that was the most popular source.

It is noteworthy that the tragedies based on stories told in the Cyclic epics include six of the seven surviving plays of Sophocles, and four of the six genuine surviving plays of Aeschylus. In the case of Euripides, the ten 'select' plays – those which owe their survival to the late antique and Byzantine school curriculum rather than to the good fortune of their position in the alphabet – include five based on Cyclic stories, still a much higher proportion than would have resulted from a random selection. However, this apparent bias may well be due to a focus, on the part of those responsible for making the selections, not so much on the Cycle as such, as on particular characters and stories. Of the fifteen plays concerned, five are centred on Oedipus, the conflict between his sons, and its immediate consequences, and six more on the murder of Agamemnon, Orestes' revenge, and its immediate consequences.[8] The other four – Sophocles' *Ajax* and *Philoctetes*, Euripides' *Hecuba* and *Trojan Women* – are all based on the *Ilias parva* or the *Iliou persis* (whose content overlapped), and all of them, remarkably, are centred

---

[6] By Brunck and many others, including Pearson (1917: ii.105–10), on the ground that the *Niptra* of Pacuvius (F 199–200 Schierl, cited by Cic. *TD* 2.48–50) did include Odysseus' death; but see Lucas de Dios (1983: 229–31); Radt, *TrGF* p. 373); Schierl (2006: 392–4); Jouanna (2007: 650).

[7] Such evidence as we have suggests that it was Aeschylus who first exploited the Cycle on a large scale as a source of tragic plots. Of some twenty-five surviving titles of plays by his predecessors and contemporaries (Thespis, Choerilus, Phrynichus and his son Polyphrasmon, Pratinas and his son Aristias) none indicates a Cyclic source, though one fragment of Phrynichus (*TrGF* F 13) does show that he wrote a play based on an episode (that of Troilus) from the *Cypria*. By contrast, with one exception (Dionysius I of Syracuse), every tragic dramatist contemporary with or later than Sophocles, down to 300 BC, for whom at least three play-titles survive, is known to have written at least one play derived directly or indirectly from the Cycle.

[8] Including Euripides' *Andromache*, in which Orestes takes revenge on Neoptolemus for robbing him of his fiancée Hermione.

on persons who are, or see themselves as, victims of Agamemnon, Menelaus and Odysseus.

No tragedy of Aeschylus, Sophocles or Euripides was based on the *Titanomachy*, so far as we can tell. This is hardly surprising: the stuff of tragedy is the tribulations of *human* life. The contribution of the other Cyclic epics to the works of these dramatists is summed up in the following table.[9]

Epic	Aeschylus	Sophocles	Euripides	Total
Oedipodea	2.5[10]	1	2	5.5
Thebaid	4.5	3	4	11.5
Epigonoi	1	1	0	2
Alcmeonis	0	1	2	3
Cypria	4	16	6	26
Aethiopis	2	1	0	3
Ilias parva and *Iliou persis*	3	10.5[11]	3	16.5
Nostoi	5	6.5	5	16.5
Telegony	0	2	0	2
Uncertain	0	5	0	5
Total	22	47	23	92

In all three dramatists the Trojan saga figures more strongly than the Theban, but – contrary to what might be expected by one who knew the tragedians only from their extant plays – this predominance is much stronger in Sophocles (41: 6) than in Aeschylus (14: 8) or Euripides (15: 8). In Sophocles and Euripides, though not in Aeschylus, the *Cypria* contributes more than any other single epic; in the three corpora together it provides 29 per cent of all the Cyclic material. The *Aethiopis* is poorly represented, probably because it is among the most tightly structured of the Cyclic poems – apart from its initial Penthesileia episode, it narrated a continuous, causally connected series of events leading to the death and funeral of Achilles. Poorly represented also are the 'sequel' poems – the *Epigonoi*, the *Alcmeonis* (which was,

---

[9] A detailed list of these plays, and of the known Cycle-based plays of other fifth- and fourth-century tragedians, is given in the Appendix.

[10] Aeschylus' *Oedipus* appears to have included some events (Oedipus' discovery of the truth about himself) which one would have expected to be part of the *Oedipodea*, and at least one (his curse on his sons) which was described in detail in the *Thebaid*.

[11] Sophocles' *Polyxene* included both the sacrifice of Polyxene (which formed part of the *Iliou persis*) and the quarrel between Agamemnon and Menelaus over whether to sail immediately for home (which was an early incident in the *Nostoi*).

however, very popular with other contemporary and later dramatists)[12] and the *Telegony*. Only Sophocles dramatized at least one story from every one of the epics.

Within each of the saga-cycles, certain stories were particularly favoured, and seven of them were used by all three of the great tragedians:

> *The discovery of Oedipus' parricide and incest* (from the *Oedipodea*).
>
> *The mutual fratricide of Eteocles and Polynices* (from the *Thebaid*) – though, whereas Aeschylus and Euripides made this the climax of a play, Sophocles began his *Antigone* with the brothers already dead.
>
> *The healing of Telephus* (from the *Cypria*).
> *The sacrifice of Iphigeneia* (also from the *Cypria*).
> *The murder of Palamedes* (again from the *Cypria*).
> *The bringing of Philoctetes from Lemnos to Troy* (from the *Ilias parva*).
> *The revenge of Orestes and its consequences* (from the *Nostoi*).

By no means all of these are obvious tragic material. Four of them involve that quintessentially tragic event, the killing of a close relative (cf. Arist. *Poet.* 1453b19–4a9), but in the other three (Telephus, Palamedes, Philoctetes) no such horror is perpetrated or even, as happens in many tragedies, narrowly averted. Probably it was simply found by experience that these stories made good theatre; as we shall see, at least one of them (that of Palamedes) had to be completely transformed for this purpose, and its new pattern, once established by Aeschylus, was followed fairly closely by both his successors.

In all cases it will have been necessary to reshape the epic story considerably to make it suitable for theatrical presentation. The change from narrative to mimetic mode would require more words to be put into the characters' mouths than even the poet of the *Iliad* had done, let alone the Cyclic poets.[13] The dramatist would have to select for direct representation only those parts of the episode which an audience could reasonably be expected to accept as a continuous action, normally in a single location, bringing in earlier events by way of retrospective narrative and events taking place away from the dramatic scene through messenger-speeches and

---

[12] Aristotle (*Poet.* 1453a20) names Alcmaon first among the favourite subjects of the tragedians of his time. In addition to the Alcmaon plays of Sophocles and Euripides, we know of others by six fifth- and fourth-century tragedians – Achaeus, Agathon, Timotheus, Astydamas II, Theodectas and Euaretus – and there were almost certainly more which have disappeared without trace; Agathon, Timotheus and Chaeremon also wrote plays named after Alcmaon's Psophidian wife, Alphesiboea.

[13] Who were much more reluctant to give their characters speeches in *oratio recta*; see Arist. *Poet.* 1460a5–11; Griffin (1977: 49–50).

similar devices. And the story itself may need to be altered to provide the tension and excitement, or the 'pity and fear', necessary to a successful tragedy – or simply to devise a coherent sequence of events of sufficient length and complexity to make a drama.

Often we cannot clearly see the traces of this process, because of the scantiness of our information about one or more of the relevant tragedies, or about its Cyclic model, or about both. Sometimes, however, we are more fortunate.

THREE EPISODES FROM THE *CYPRIA*

Of the healing of Telephus, in Proclus' summary of the *Cypria* (arg. lines 132–4 Severyns), we hear only that Telephus, instructed by an oracle, came to Argos, and Achilles healed him in return for a promise that he would guide the fleet on its voyage to Troy (a very important function, considering the disastrous error they had made on their first attempt to sail there). Here the outcome seems like a straightforward bargain offering advantages to both sides. Yet we know that in Euripides' play, Telephus at one stage seized the infant Orestes as a hostage and threatened to kill him if the Greeks refused to heal his wound; and there is both textual and artistic evidence[14] that there was already a scene of the same kind in Aeschylus' play at least twenty years earlier. If so, it would appear that Aeschylus' invention, being successful, came to be regarded (at least at Athens) as part of the canonical form of the myth, and Euripides, when he came to create *his* play, thought of it no longer as modified *Cypria* but as modified Aeschylus. We shall see later that this is often the position Euripides occupies in relation to his predecessors.

In the *Iphigeneia* and *Palamedes* plays, too, Aeschylus seems to have set the tragic pattern. In the *Cypria* there is no reason whatever to believe that Iphigeneia's mother, Clytaemnestra, came with her to Aulis. But Aeschylus, Sophocles and Euripides all seem to have felt that one of the best ways of making tragic capital out of the story was to present it partly through the eyes of the woman who, as their audience knew, would one day take revenge for what her husband was now doing. Euripides' treatment in *Iphigeneia at Aulis* is well known (and for this purpose it does not matter how much of the play is actually Euripides' work). In Aeschylus' play (*TrGF* 94) someone said 'It is not right to revile women' – which sounds as if it ought to be

---

[14] Textual evidence: Σ Aristoph. *Ach*. 332. Artistic evidence: see Csapo (1990); Preiser (2000: 51–9).

the utterance of a woman sure of herself and refusing to be subservient to men, not unlike the Clytaemnestra of *Agamemnon*. In Sophocles' play it appears that Clytaemnestra was brought into the action in a different way, in a way, indeed, that might be considered to be implicit (and may even have been explicit) in the epic account. Two mythographic accounts (Hyg. *fab.* 98 and Ps.-Apollod. *Epit.* 3.22) speak of Odysseus being sent to Clytaemnestra (accompanied either by Diomedes or by the herald Talthybius) to fetch Iphigeneia on the pretence that she was to be married to Achilles; and in a line quoted from Sophocles' play (*TrGF* F 305) it is, we are informed, Odysseus who congratulates Clytaemnestra on having 'gained the greatest of in-laws'. It seems, therefore, that Sophocles' play was set at Argos/Mycenae and centred on the persuasion of Clytaemnestra; Iphigeneia herself must also have played a significant role (she was, after all, the title character) – but in contrast with the Iphigeneia of Euripides (and presumably of Aeschylus) she will probably have done so not knowing what fate awaited her, unless one of Odysseus' companions revealed the truth to her.

We do know how the *Cypria* treated the murder of Palamedes: he was drowned by Diomedes and Odysseus when out on a fishing expedition (*PEG* F 30 = F 20 D. = F 27 W.). One might reasonably ask why so clever a hero took the risk of going out in a boat with two men one of whom, at least, was an old enemy of his; but the Cyclic poet may well have provided an explanation (e.g. that Odysseus had pretended to be reconciled to him, or that Palamedes had gone out alone and his murderers took another boat and intercepted him). At any rate, this was not a suitable scenario for a drama. We possess four versions of the story – two from mythographers, two from ancient commentators on Euripides and Virgil[15] – which *do* seem well adapted for dramatic presentation, and it is widely, and probably rightly, believed that all of them go back to the three fifth-century tragedies.[16] If so, Aeschylus created a new form of the story which proved so effective that both Sophocles and Euripides were content to play variations on it and increase its sophistication. In all three tragedies, Odysseus, alone or with confederates, engineered the death of Palamedes by getting him condemned on a false charge of treason, with the aid of fabricated evidence (a letter alleged to have been sent to, or by, the Trojan king; a quantity of gold planted in Palamedes' tent or hut). This gave scope for a trial that pitted against each other in forensic battle the two subtlest intellects in the Greek army – though in

---

[15] Hygin. *Fab.* 105; Ps.-Apollod. *Epit.* 3.7–8; Σ Eur. *Or.* 432; Servius on Virg. *Aen.* 2.81.
[16] See my discussion in Sommerstein and Talboy (2012: 114–24), which gives references to earlier work.

Sophocles it appears that Odysseus neutralized his enemy's eloquence by himself speaking in Palamedes' defence, ending with an offer (such as an innocent man would naturally make) to have his tent searched! At the end of Aeschylus' play, and of Euripides' also, Palamedes' father Nauplius came to Troy, demanding (in vain) justice for his son's death (Sophocles made a separate play, *The Arrival of Nauplius*, out of this episode);[17] we do not know whether this incident was narrated in the *Cypria*.

PHILOCTETES

The fetching of Philoctetes from Lemnos was a long-established part of the Trojan War saga, and is duly mentioned in Proclus' summary of the *Ilias parva* (arg. lines 211–14 Severyns), in which we are told that the mission was carried out by Diomedes and that it resulted from a prophecy 'about the taking of the city' by the captured Trojan seer Helenus. In all three of the tragic versions, we know, Odysseus was the leader of the mission; in Aeschylus he was alone, and only in Euripides did Diomedes accompany him. Ps.-Apollodorus (*Epit.* 5.8) says that Philoctetes was brought to Troy by 'Odysseus with Diomedes'. Is he contaminating the epic account with that of Euripides, or has Odysseus' name been omitted from Proclus' text? Otherwise put, did Aeschylus *omit* Diomedes from what in the epic had been a two-man mission, or did he *replace* him by Odysseus? If the former, he may simply have been effecting a simplification necessary at a time when tragedies were performed by only two actors. If the latter, he will have judged Odysseus a more suitable character than Diomedes for a tragic presentation of the story, in which so much must depend on the spoken word, Odysseus being famously eloquent and crafty: he made Odysseus concoct an elaborate false tale of disasters that had befallen the army, including the death, as criminals, of Agamemnon and of Odysseus himself.[18] There is, in fact, evidence that a version of the story with a two-man mission existed in Aeschylus' time: Pindar in the *First Pythian* (performed in 470) says (52–3) that Philoctetes was brought from Lemnos by 'godlike *heroes*', so it is perhaps most likely that already in the *Ilias parva* Odysseus had a hand in this episode as he did in almost every other action (off the battlefield itself) between the death of Ajax and the taking of the city (the capture of Helenus, the mission

---

[17] Aesch. *TrGF* F 181; Nauplius' appearance in Euripides' play is now known from PMich. inv. 3020 (A); see Luppe (2011).
[18] Dio Chrys. 52.10.

to Scyros to fetch Neoptolemus, the two secret missions into Troy, and the manning – though not the making – of the Wooden Horse).[19] If so, Aeschylus by removing Diomedes has removed the possibility of using force to take Philoctetes and left Odysseus, on his own, entirely dependent on persuasion, deception and theft. Euripides and Sophocles (in that order)[20] both made major innovations. Euripides had the Trojans send a delegation to Lemnos to persuade Philoctetes to aid *their* side. He also brought Diomedes back into the story[21] – not merely, we may be sure, because he had three actors available, but because his design called for Diomedes to play a crucial role in the plot. Unfortunately we do not know for certain what this role was, since our considerable evidence for Euripides' play tells us nothing about Diomedes except that he was present; it is even compatible with our evidence that Euripides kept him silent, like Pylades in the Orestes revenge plays, and used him only to supply a convenient pair of hands (e.g. to steal Philoctetes' bow, or to apply physical force to Philoctetes himself). Sophocles makes an equally drastic change by introducing Neoptolemus, who according to the *Ilias parva* (arg. lines 217–21 Severyns) was still, at the relevant time, on Scyros with his mother and her parents, and making much of the action take place, as it were, in his mind.

ORESTES

We know a good deal about the treatment of Orestes' revenge, both in poetry and in art, before Aeschylus' *Oresteia*.[22] Of its presentation in the *Nostoi* we know only that Pylades took part in it (*Nost.* arg. lines 301–3 Severyns), and in this all three tragic poets follow suit – but except for one famous moment in Aeschylus (*Choeph.* 900–2), they all keep Pylades silent throughout (whereas in *Iphigeneia in Tauris* and *Orestes* Euripides is happy to let him speak). Aeschylus' motive for doing this is clear enough: he wanted to maximize the effect of the one utterance that Pylades does make, when Orestes is temporarily unable to steel himself to kill his mother and Pylades reminds him that if he does not, he will make an enemy of Apollo. It

---

[19] *Ilias parva* arg. lines 211–29 Severyns and *PEG* F 7 (= F 8 D., W.), *PEG* F 6 (= F 9 W.), *PEG* F 25 (= F 9 D. = F 11 W.), *PEG* F 8 (= F 10 D. = F 12 W.).
[20] Euripides' play was produced in 431 BC (Hypothesis of 'Aristophanes of Byzantium' to *Medea*), Sophocles' in 409 BC.
[21] Dio Chrys. 52.14.
[22] See especially Prag (1985); also March (1987: 79–98); Gantz (1993: 664–86); Shapiro (1994: 125–48); Sommerstein (2010: 136–45).

is less obvious why Euripides and Sophocles[23] do the same. It is true that a speaking Pylades, on stage with Orestes in almost every scene, would tie up one of the three actors more or less permanently; but in that case, why bother to have Pylades as a character at all? He gives Orestes a crucial two-to-one advantage in his two confrontations, but a young and vigorous slave (rather than Sophocles' elderly *paidagōgos*) would have done that equally well. In Aeschylus, it seems likely that Pylades does not even appear in the final scene, when all attention must be concentrated on Orestes – the avenger of his father, the killer of his mother, the quarry of the pursuing Erinyes, the suppliant of Apollo. In Euripides and Sophocles he is on stage till the end, or almost the end. In Sophocles he is needed to help force Aegisthus indoors to his death, in what is the last action of the play;[24] in Euripides he leaves with Electra, Orestes having been instructed by the *dei ex machina* to give him his sister in marriage (this marriage is mentioned no less than four times in the final scene,[25] presumably to contrast it with the inappropriate and unconsummated 'marriage' in which Electra was trapped at the beginning of the play). Probably this marriage is the real clue to Pylades' importance. Although it is never spoken of in Aeschylus' or Sophocles' play, it was probably traditional – Hellanicus (*EGM* F 155) can give the names of two sons born to the couple – and may well have been mentioned in the *Nostoi*: in all the tragedians Electra's improperly prolonged virginity is prominent among the wrongs inflicted on the house of Agamemnon, and the presence of Pylades may be a reminder that this wrong too will be put right, along with the unavenged murder, the disinheritance of Orestes, and the tyrannical rule of Aegisthus and Clytaemnestra over the Argives/Mycenaeans.

NEW MYTH IN THE CYCLIC FRAMEWORK

The dramatists may not only modify, sometimes drastically, the stories they find in the Cycle; they may introduce, within its framework, stories entirely unknown to the Cycle. Aeschylus seems to do this only in order to accommodate specifically Athenian versions of myths properly belonging to other cities – Theseus' intervention to secure the burial of the Seven against Thebes (*The Eleusinians*), Orestes' trial on the Areopagus (*The Eumenides*). Sophocles can do this too, as in *Oedipus at Colonus*, but he

---

[23] Euripides' *Electra* is likely to be the earlier of the two; see March (2001: 20–2).
[24] Pylades' presence in this final scene is attested by the plural imperative χαλᾶτε ('take away') in 1468.
[25] Eur. *El.* 1249, 1284–5, 1311, 1340–2.

is also ready to create new myth without such excuse. The most striking example is *Antigone*. There is no evidence that the story of Antigone's defiance of an edict denying burial to Polynices existed before Sophocles (for the last scene of Aeschylus' *Seven against Thebes* is spurious). Sophocles has interpolated it into the story between the battle in which Eteocles and Polynices kill each other (which must have been the climax of the *Thebaid*) and the burial of the Seven through the intervention of Theseus (not in the *Thebaid* but well known to all Athenians and a great source of Athenian pride).[26] It fits into that position without difficulty; for though it contains many terrible events, none of them affects the subsequent course of the saga. Antigone, it seems, has to die, and has to die childless (at least until Euripides gives her a son);[27] but about the nature and even the time of her death there seems to have been no fixed tradition, and at least one early poet seems to have placed it *before* the death of her brothers, the elegist Mimnermus; for we read in one of the Hypotheses to Sophocles' play:[28]

> The tales told about the heroine, and about her sister Ismene, are in conflict with each other. Ion in his *Dithyrambs* [*PMG* F 740] says they were both burned to death in the temple of Hera by Leodamas, son of Eteocles [one of the Epigonoi]; but Mimnermus [*IEG* F 21] says that Ismene, on the one hand, perished at the hands of Tydeus, at the urging of Athena, when she was having sexual relations with Theoclymenus...

At which point there must be a lacuna in which is lost Mimnermus' account of how Antigone (on the other hand) died, for the next sentence begins 'Such are the outlandish tales told about *the heroines.*'

The story of Tydeus, Ismene and Theoclymenus (or Periclymenus) is also known, in somewhat varying forms, from archaic art[29] and from the fifth-century mythographer Pherecydes,[30] and it may well be derived from the *Thebaid*, since Periclymenus was a character in that poem, one of the seven Theban champions, who killed Parthenopaeus (*Th. PEG* F 6 = F 4 D. = F 10 W.). If so, Sophocles has kept Ismene alive to play a new role, and has very likely done the same for Antigone. He has certainly done so for Haemon, who in the epic account (*Oed. PEG* F 1 = D. = F 3 W.) was slain

---

[26] Lys. 2.7–10; Plat. *Menex.* 239b; Isocr. 4.55, 10.31; Dem. 60.8.
[27] Hypothesis of 'Aristophanes of Byzantium' to Soph. *Ant.*
[28] Hypothesis of 'Salustius' to Soph. *Ant.*
[29] Paris, Louvre E640 = *LIMC* 'Ismene' i.3 (Corinthian amphora, c. 560 BC), where the fleeing man is named as Periclymenus; Athens, Nat. Mus. Acr. 603 = *LIMC* 'Ismene' i.4 (Attic black-figure skyphos, 575–550 BC).
[30] Pherec. *EGM* F 95 (Ismene killed by Tydeus at a spring, thenceforth named after her; no further details given).

by the Sphinx, before Oedipus had come to Thebes and therefore before Antigone was even born. The only other irrevocable event that occurs in *Antigone* is the death of Creon's wife, Eurydice; but she, like many another female in mythical genealogies, has nothing essential to do after bearing her children and can die whenever it suits a particular storyteller's convenience. As to Creon himself, he is spiritually crushed, but he lives on (having narrowly escaped death at the hands of his maddened son), and there is not even any sign that he ceases to be the ruler of Thebes (where, according to a well-established story, he will later become the first father-in-law of Heracles).[31] Thus at the end of *Antigone* everything is ready for the events that traditionally followed, including the expedition of Theseus and, later, the war of the Epigonoi (either or both of which may be foreshadowed in *Antigone* 1080–3).

Sophocles' lost play *Euryalus* is probably another such interpolation in the story of a Cyclic poem, in this case the *Telegony*. Proclus gives quite a detailed summary of this poem (particularly considering that it only consisted of two books), and it seems to keep Odysseus pretty busy, with an absence in Thesprotia lasting long enough for a son born to him there to grow up and become king, and hardly to offer any opportunity for the occurrence of the events narrated by Parthenius (*Erot. path.* 3) in the story he ascribes to Sophocles' *Euryalus*:

> Odysseus... when he had killed the suitors went to Epirus because of certain oracles, and violated Euippe, the daughter of Tyrimmas, after Tyrimmas had welcomed him like a friend and entertained him with great enthusiasm; she bore him a son named Euryalus. When he came to manhood, his mother sent him to Ithaca, giving him certain tokens sealed in a folded tablet. Odysseus happened to be absent at the time, and Penelope, learning of this [Euryalus' arrival] and having already by other means come to know of Odysseus' relationship with Euippe, persuaded Odysseus, as soon as he returned and before he knew anything of what had happened, to kill Euryalus, saying he was plotting against him. And Odysseus, because he was not by nature in control of himself and not in general of sound moral character, became the murderer of his son.[32] Not long after he had done this, he was wounded by his own offspring with the spine of a sting-ray and died.

---

[31] His daughter was Megara, whom, and whose children, Heracles killed in a fit of madness; early references include *Od.* 11.269–70, Stesich. *PMGF* F 230, Panyass. F 1 Matthews, Pherec. *EGM* F 14 and Pind. *Isthm.* 4.62–6.

[32] Eustath. ad *Od.* 16.118 (1796.52) says that in Sophocles' play Euryalus was killed by Telemachus; this is quite consistent with Parthenius' narrative, if Odysseus (who must by now have been an old man) ordered Telemachus to kill the stranger.

Thus the Euryalus story may well be Sophocles' invention. Once again, the interpolation leaves the structure of the saga – and, here, of the *Telegony* – unaltered. The only change on the mythological chessboard has been the death of Euryalus, who had never existed in the *Telegony* in the first place. But the innovation has fundamentally changed our view of other events that did exist in the earlier poem. Parthenius' last sentence seems to indicate that the impending death of Odysseus at the hand of Telegonus was prophesied at the end of *Euryalus*, doubtless by a *deus ex machina* or equivalent. In the *Telegony* itself, so far as we can tell, no attempt was made to 'make sense' of Odysseus' death, to show it either as being the 'inevitable or probable' consequence of previous human actions or as resulting from intelligible divine action. Telegonus was searching for his father, landed on Ithaca, began ravaging the country (presumably not knowing it was his father's homeland), was confronted by an Ithacan army led by Odysseus, and killed him not knowing who he was. What has Odysseus done, that we could be enabled to accept this as anything other than a monstrosity? Sophocles' play provided the answer, maybe quite explicitly: he had himself, not very long ago, killed an innocent man who was also in fact his son, and Parthenius' remarks about his character suggest that he should have known he was doing so on inadequate evidence (and probably that he did not give Euryalus the chance to contest the allegations against him). Penelope is also represented as blameworthy (in the traditional style of the stepmother or equivalent), but she had the excuse that Odysseus had concealed his infidelities from her (just as he does in the *Odyssey* when, in bed on the night of their reunion, he tells her 'everything' about his wanderings – but mentions Circe only as one who craftily plotted against him, and gives the strong impression that he had never become Calypso's lover).[33] A perceived inadequacy in the Cyclic story is thus put right.

Euripides takes this tendency much further. Of twenty-three plays of his whose setting involves characters from a Cyclic epic within the period of mythical time covered by that epic, something like nine present stories which, as far as we can tell, were entirely, or almost entirely, absent from the Cycle. The plot of his *Hypsipyle* is tied to a story about the expedition of the Seven against Thebes, the death of the child Archemorus (or Opheltes), and the founding of the Nemean Games, which had already been used by Aeschylus in his *Nemea* (probably a satyr-drama) and which surfaces twice in sixth- and fifth-century lyric poetry;[34] it is reasonable to suppose that

---

[33] *Od.* 23.306–43 ('everything', 306–9 ὅσα ... ὅσα ... πάντ' ... ἅπαντα; Circe, 321; Calypso, 333–7). See de Jong (2001: 563).
[34] Simon. *PMG* F 553; Bacchyl. 9.10–20.

this story figured already in the *Thebaid* as an incident on the expedition's march from Argos to Thebes. But Euripides' play is dominated by the figure of Hypsipyle and her reunion with her sons, and Hypsipyle of Lemnos has nothing to do with the Seven against Thebes – she belongs to a completely different saga-cycle, that of the Argonauts, and the father of her long-lost sons was Jason – and there is no sign that she had any role in the Nemea story before Euripides.

Euripides' *Chrysippus* presented the tale of the abduction and rape by Laius[35] of Chrysippus, son of Pelops, ending probably with the suicide of Chrysippus and a curse by Pelops on Laius which was made the cause of the subsequent disasters in Laius' family.[36] Earlier accounts either give no clear causal explanation of these disasters or (like Aeschylus' *Seven against Thebes*) trace them to Laius' defiance of an oracle from Apollo which, in varying terms, warned him against begetting a son, without offering any explanation of the oracle itself, and it has often been found tempting to use this story about Chrysippus to fill the gap.[37] Certainly we would expect that some 'first cause' or 'beginning of evils' would have been placed at the beginning of the *Oedipodea*, as the desire of Zeus to cull the earth's human population was placed at the beginning of the *Cypria*. But it is unlikely to have been this one. There is no trace of the Laius–Chrysippus story before Euripides, and the best-known story about Chrysippus' death in his time seems to have been an entirely different one. Hellanicus (*EGM* F 157) presented a version which did not involve Laius at all:

In Hellanicus' version Pelops, having a son Chrysippus by his first wife,[38] married Hippodameia, daughter of Oenomaus, by whom he had several children. But he made Chrysippus his particular favourite, and the lad's stepmother and her children grew jealous, fearing he might leave him his royal power, and plotted his death, giving the eldest of Hippodameia's children, Atreus and Thyestes, the leading role. After they had killed Chrysippus, Pelops came to know of it and banished those of his sons who had

---

[35] This story made Laius the prototype, and the mythical paradigm, of pederasty. He was also the earliest known example of the randy driving instructor (Ps.-Apollod. 3.5.5; Strattis F 55).

[36] Ael. *NA* 6.15 shows that Euripides' play included the death of Chrysippus; there is no explicit evidence that it also included Laius' curse, but some recent discussions have cautiously favoured the view that it did (Jouan and van Looy (2002: 373–82); Collard and Cropp (2008: ii. 459–63)).

[37] The first to be tempted appears to have been a certain Peisander, whose account is preserved in Σ Eur. *Phoen.* 1760; but this account, which has Hera send the Sphinx to Thebes and presupposes that homosexual passion is an offence against her, is likely to be of later origin.

[38] Or perhaps 'by an earlier woman', since some sources speak of Chrysippus as a bastard (Σ Eur. *Or.* 4, cf. Σ Pind. *Olymp.* 1.144d; Hyginus *fab.* 85).

committed the murder with their own hands, cursing them with the prayer that they and their offspring might be murdered.

And Thucydides (1.9.2), who had no great fondness for Hellanicus,[39] treated this as the standard account, almost as if he had never heard of the Laius story. There was an early version of Chrysippus' story in which he was the victim of a homosexual abduction, but the abductor was Zeus (Praxilla *PMG* 751). It looks as though Euripides in *Chrysippus*, as in *Hypsipyle*, took a character from one saga-cycle and foisted him into another – conveniently, a character who died young without offspring – to create what was effectively a new myth (and in this case a very influential one).

THREATENING TO RUIN THE SAGA

One of the basic constraints on mythical innovation by tragic (and other) poets was that they could not create new stories that undermined the integrity of *other* parts of the existing mythical corpus; they could not, for example, allow Thebes to be captured and destroyed by the Seven, or Agamemnon's expedition to sail home without having captured Troy. But the invention of the *deus ex machina* made it possible for them, in this respect, to have their cake and eat it, to alter established myth in fundamental ways and yet leave it unaltered. In Sophocles' *Philoctetes*, when Neoptolemus' final attempt to persuade Philoctetes to come to Troy has failed, Philoctetes claims the fulfilment of Neoptolemus' earlier promise to take him home to Greece (1367–72, 1398–1401), and they are about to set out on this voyage (which will make the capture of Troy impossible) when Heracles appears and orders his old friend Philoctetes to go to Troy where both he and Neoptolemus will win glory. A year later, in *Orestes*, Euripides does the same thing in a far more spectacular way. We do not know what was said in the *Nostoi* about the aftermath of Orestes' revenge, but it certainly was not this! Orestes, in this play, after killing Aegisthus and Clytaemnestra, has not left Argos for Delphi or elsewhere; an immediate attack of both mental and physical sickness has confined him to his bed, and meanwhile he and Electra are to be judged by the Argive people for the murder of his mother. They get no effective help from the recently arrived Menelaus, and after an assembly debate (not a trial) they are condemned to death, but the sentence is commuted from stoning to compulsory suicide. Together with Pylades (who has been disowned and expelled by his

[39] See Thuc. 1.97.2.

father, and has returned to help his friend Orestes) they plot to secure their safety by killing Helen (who is almost as unpopular in Argos as they themselves are), taking Hermione hostage, and threatening to burn down the palace with her and themselves in it if they are not given a free pardon. Just as they are about to carry out their threat, Apollo appears as *deus ex machina* and, as it were, presses the reset button, giving a series of instructions that have the effect of cancelling the entire action of the play. He has Helen with him; she was saved from Orestes' sword and has been made immortal. Orestes is to go into temporary exile, be tried and acquitted on the Areopagus, and then become king of Argos and marry Hermione (at whose neck his sword has been poised for the last quarter of an hour); Electra will marry Pylades, and everyone will live happily ever after (except Neoptolemus, previously betrothed to Hermione, who has had no role in the play, and who will be killed at Delphi).

AESCHYLUS AND SOPHOCLES: CONTRASTING APPROACHES

While Euripides was certainly often ready to make radical innovations in myth and plot, it was not necessarily – perhaps not even normally – the Epic Cycle's version of a story that he took as his point of departure. *Orestes* is the heir to a long tragic tradition (itself heavily indebted to earlier poetry, notably Stesichorus' *Oresteia*) which includes not only plays of Aeschylus and Sophocles but Euripides' own *Electra*; *Hypsipyle* is based partly on a story which, as we have seen, had previously been treated by Aeschylus, and partly on a pattern of mother–child reunion which had already become hackneyed in late fifth-century tragedy;[40] Euripides' *Antigone* builds directly on that of Sophocles... and so on. Aeschylus and Sophocles, on the other hand, both do often seem to place themselves in direct relation to the Cycle, and they have different characteristic responses to it.

Aeschylus is the great practitioner of the connected trilogy, whereby a single myth, or a sequence of myths causally connected, is presented through a series of plays forming together a single production (together with a satyr-drama usually presenting a different portion of the same mythical complex). Aeschylus treated both the *Iliad* and the *Odyssey* in this way, and he did likewise with many parts of the Cycle. The greater part of the Theban saga, down to the expedition of the Epigonoi and the

---

[40] Particularly in Euripides (*Ion, Antiope, Cresphontes, Melanippe the Captive*).

matricide of Alcmaon, was covered in two productions, one extending as far as the mutual killing of Eteocles and Polynices (*Laius, Oedipus, Seven against Thebes*, plus *The Sphinx*) and one picking up the story immediately thereafter (*The Eleusinians, The Women of Argos, The Epigonoi*). The central story of the *Aethiopis* was dramatized in *Memnon* and *The Weighing of Souls*, which may either have been preceded by *The Carians* (in which the mother of another half-divine hero, Sarpedon, learned of his death at Troy) or followed by a play about the death of Achilles.[41] The first major episode of the *Ilias parva* was the subject of a trilogy about the death of Ajax and its consequences (*The Award of the Arms, The Thracian Women, The Women of Salamis*). And the *Oresteia* is based on two sections of the *Nostoi* which so dominated ancient perceptions of the poem that it was sometimes actually referred to as *The Return of the Atreidae* (the second Atreid, Menelaus, is frequently mentioned in *Agamemnon* and was a major character in the satyr-drama *Proteus*). The *Cypria* was not treated in this way, perhaps because it was exceptionally episodic even by Cyclic standards; we can identify a sequence containing *The Mysians* and *Telephus*, but it is not clear whether there was a third play (*Iphigeneia* has been suggested,[42] but there would then be little connection between the third play and the first).

Sophocles' favourite practice seems to be to take two episodes from a Cyclic epic, which did not necessarily have any organic relation to each other, and combine them into one play. *The Laconian Women* is a good example. Some of our evidence about it[43] suggests that its subject was the theft of the Palladium (*Ilias parva* arg. lines 228–9 Severyns and *PEG* F 25 = F 9 D. = F 11 W.), while other features (such as the evident involvement of Helen – the 'Laconian women' must have been her servants) point rather to Odysseus' earlier mission into Troy when he established contact with her and 'made an agreement … about the taking of the city' (*Ilias parva* arg. lines 224–7 Severyns and *PEG* F 7, 6 = F 8 D. = F 8–10 W.). Other plays in which Sophocles has done something like the same thing include:

- *The Diners* (a quarrel between Agamemnon and Achilles at Tenedos, from the *Cypria* (arg. lines 146–7 Severyns),[44] and a quarrel between Achilles

---

[41] For the former view, see West (2000: 347–50); for the latter, Gantz (1980: 220–1), Sommerstein (1996: 56–7) and Lucas de Dios (2008: 664–5).

[42] Mette (1959: 259; 1963: 77–8).

[43] Notably *TrGF* F 367 (where someone says 'we entered a narrow, slimy drain') taken together with Servius on Virg. *Aen.* 2.166 who speaks of Diomedes and Ulysses entering Troy by a tunnel or sewer to steal the Palladium.

[44] See my discussion in Sommerstein *et al.* (2006: 84–100).

and Odysseus at an unspecified location, mentioned in the *Odyssey* (8.75–8); Sophocles seems to have made Odysseus intervene in the Agamemnon-Achilles confrontation and divert the anger of Achilles on to himself)
- *The Shepherds* (the first two battles of the Trojan War, involving first the death of Protesilaus and then that of Cycnus (*Cypr.* arg. lines 148–51 Severyns)[45]
- *Philoctetes* (the bringing to Troy of Philoctetes and of Neoptolemus (*Ilias parva* arg. lines 211–21 Severyns) – Sophocles reverses the order of these events, in order to bring Neoptolemus into the Philoctetes story)
- *Polyxene* (the sacrifice of Polyxene from the *Iliou persis* (arg. line 274 Severyns),[46] and the quarrel between Agamemnon and Menelaus over when to set sail, from the *Nostoi* (arg. lines 279–80 Severyns, also *Odyssey* 3.130–64); Sophocles places the latter before the former, and unifies his drama by having Achilles prevent the fleet from sailing until the sacrifice has been performed)
- *Teucer* (the return of Teucer,[47] the arrival of news of the death of the lesser Ajax,[48] and an apparently invented visit of Odysseus to Salamis[49])

OEDIPUS AND HIS CHILDREN

We may end by briefly reflecting on what the three tragedians have made of the story of Oedipus and his sons, narrated in the *Oedipodea* and the *Thebaid*. In typical fashion, Aeschylus presented the story in a trilogy, Sophocles and Euripides each in three separate plays.

Aeschylus certainly made at least some changes to the story as it had been told in the epics – for example, he replaces Periclymenus[50] by Actor as the opponent of Parthenopaeus; but we cannot identify any *major* changes,

---

[45] See my discussion in Sommerstein and Talboy (2012: 174–83).
[46] See my discussion in Sommerstein *et al.* (2006: 41–65).
[47] This is not mentioned either in Proclus' summary of the *Nostoi* or in the other surviving quotations from and references to the poem; but neither are the returns home of some other major figures such as Philoctetes and Idomeneus, whom the *Nostoi* can hardly have ignored since their safe return is noted in the *Odyssey* (3.190–2).
[48] Soph. *TrGF* F 576 with Cic. *Tusc.* 3.71.   [49] Soph. *TrGF* F 579a.
[50] Perhaps because Periclymenus was too closely identified with the story of the seduction of Ismene, which Aeschylus did not want to use? Actor ('leader') is a common name for minor figures in various myths, some of them (like the kindly Lemnian in Euripides' *Philoctetes*, see Dio Chrys. 52.8) certainly or probably *ad hoc* creations.

except that Aeschylus did not follow the *Oedipodea* in providing Oedipus with a second wife so that his children were not the fruit of incest.[51] We can, however, identify at least one place where he appears to have followed the epic closely: Oedipus' curse against his sons is said to have been uttered because he was 'angry about his wretched maintenance' (*Seven against Thebes* 785–6),[52] which corresponds to one of the two motives cited from the *Thebaid* (that he thought they had insulted him by sending him an inferior cut of meat from a sacrifice: *PEG* F 3 = D., W.). In the play that survives, *Seven against Thebes*, he has shaped the story to emphasize particular features, and above all to make the conflict develop from an attack on a city by a hostile army, through a series of individual duels at the seven gates, to focus finally and completely on the two brothers who kill each other. Much of the background, which there would have been no scope to explain in the previous plays, is taken for granted, the audience being presumed to know it – that Tydeus and Polynices were sons-in-law of Adrastus, why Amphiaraus was a member of an expedition which he believed (*Seven* 570–89, 609–12) to be immoral, who was the mother of Parthenopaeus; the *Thebaid* will have been the only poem that contained *all* this information, and Aeschylus may well have followed it fairly closely for the 'facts' of the story except where he had specific reason to diverge.

That Oedipus discovered his own guilt by his own efforts is assumed to be known in Sophocles' *Antigone* (which was produced earlier than *Oedipus the King*);[53] that he put out his own eyes is stated in Aeschylus' *Seven against Thebes* (784); evidently then in Aeschylus' *Oedipus* he did both those things, and the self-blinding, at least, may reasonably be ascribed to the epic *Oedipodea*. In *Oedipus the King* Sophocles doubtless created a new mechanism for the discovery, and he almost certainly also invented an incident that makes an enormous difference to our understanding of the story, the oracle given to Oedipus (*OT* 788–93) that he would kill his father and marry his mother. (The earlier oracle to Laius,[54] that any son he had would kill him, was certainly part of the story from the first, since it is needed to motivate the exposure of his son and the pinning or

---

[51] For it is said that the mother of Eteocles and Polynices 'made her own son her husband' (*Seven* 929–30).

[52] For a defence of this interpretation of †ἀραιᾶς† ἐπίκοτος τροφᾶς see Sommerstein (1989: 440–5).

[53] Soph. *Ant.* 51 αὐτοφώρων ἀμπλακημάτων 'self-detected crimes'.

[54] *OT* 711–14, cf. Eur. *Phoen.* 17–20; in Aeschylus (*Seven* 743–9) the oracle tells him that in order to keep his city safe he must die without issue. That in Sophocles, as in Aeschylus and Euripides, the oracle predicts disaster only conditionally, 'leav[ing] Laius the option of having no child', is demonstrated by Kovacs (2009: 366).

binding of his feet.) He also left it uncertain at the end whether Oedipus would remain in Thebes (as he certainly did in Aeschylus, where he is assumed to be buried there,[55] and probably in the epic) or would go into exile.

In *Antigone*, as we have seen, Sophocles created a completely new story within the *Thebaid* framework, keeping at least one and probably several characters alive longer than was traditional in order to do so. He still, however, assumes a quite detailed knowledge of the inherited story. Today we have no idea precisely what is referred to when Eurydice is reported (*Ant.* 1302–5, cf. 1312–13) as having lamented 'the bed of Megareus, who died before' and cursed Creon as 'the killer of his son(s)': we gather that Megareus is dead, and that Creon was somehow responsible for this, but we do not know the nature of his responsibility. Sophocles' audience will have known this, and they did not know it from Aeschylus – though in *Seven against Thebes* (473–9) Megareus is the only one of those defending the gates, except Eteocles himself, whose death is envisaged in advance as a possibility. Presumably then they knew it from the epic, which once again is presupposed as background when not clearly being departed from. Earlier hints in Sophocles' play (but they are only hints)[56] indicate, when taken together with the later passages, that Teiresias had at some time (perhaps even the previous day) declared that Thebes could be saved only if a son of Creon perished, and Creon had obeyed him – the son being Megareus. In the epic this would be a terrible moment, for Haemon, as we have seen, had already been slain by the Sphinx. Sophocles has reversed the effect: Megareus dies first, and Haemon is now Creon's only son[57] – something that Creon quickly forgets when Haemon gently criticizes him.

Oedipus at Colonus, on the other hand, bears little direct relation to the Cycle: its main intertexts are rather Sophocles' own two earlier plays, to one of which it is a sequel and to the other a prequel. We are assumed to know the detailed facts (given by Oedipus in *Oedipus the King*)[58] that make it legitimate for him to claim that in killing Laius he was acting in self-defence; we are assumed to know that Antigone's determination to return

---

[55] Aesch. *Seven* 1004. Cf. *Iliad* 23.679–80, Hes. *Cat.* F 192 M.-W. (cf. F 90.1–4 Hirsch.).
[56] Soph. *Ant.* 993–5, 1058; see Griffith (1999: 350–1). Perhaps we should add 182–3: Creon's condemnation of anyone who 'reckons a loved one as of more account than his fatherland' would be all the more powerful if not long ago he had deliberately sent a son to death in order to save his city.
[57] Cf. *Ant.* 626–7 with Griffith (1999: 232).
[58] The claim by Harris (2010) that these facts would not, in Athenian law, exonerate Oedipus from a charge of wilful homicide is refuted by Sommerstein (2011).

to Thebes, and her promise to bury Polynices should he die in the war,[59] will be the cause of her own death; we are not assumed to know anything of significance that was not contained in the two earlier plays, except indeed the topography of the suburban village of Colonus.

Euripides dramatized parts of the story in four plays – in the sequence of the legend, *Oedipus, Hypsipyle* (on which see above), *The Phoenician Maidens* and *Antigone*. There is much uncertainty about the plot of *Oedipus*, but nothing suggests that at any point Euripides was harking back to the *Oedipodea*, unless perhaps it was in the detailed narrative which Oedipus or another gave of his confrontation with the Sphinx (Eur. *TrGF* F 540, 540 a). Rather, he was constantly concerned to vary from Sophocles, as he does in the two other features of the play of which we can be most certain – that Oedipus did not blind himself but was forcibly blinded by the servants of Laius (*TrGF* F 541), and that Iocasta chose to live on and share her son/husband's tribulations.[60]

In *Antigone*, too, Euripides' point of departure was Sophocles – in this case, both the attempt to bury Polynices and the intended marriage of Antigone and Haemon. In Sophocles, Haemon was not even mentioned until Antigone had already been condemned to death; in Euripides he took part in the burial of Polynices, and in the end, contrary to all precedent, the marriage took place and they had a son, Maeon.[61] A Maeon, son of Haemon, is mentioned in the *Iliad* (4.391–8) as having been one of the leaders of an ambush set for Tydeus on his way back from Thebes to his army, spared when his forty-nine comrades were killed, and sent home with the news of the slaughter; it is certainly possible that he was a grandson of Creon (if the story presupposed included the slaying of Haemon by the Sphinx) and that the episode was included in the *Thebaid*, but if so, Euripides owed nothing here to the epic except a name.

In *The Phoenician Maidens* the background text is Aeschylus' *Seven against Thebes*, which at some points is explicitly recalled. However, Teiresias' demand for the death of a son of Creon, not mentioned by Aeschylus and only obscurely alluded to by Sophocles, now reappears as a major, if rather isolated, episode. Shortly after Polynices has asked Creon to make sure that Antigone's marriage to Haemon is carried through, Teiresias,

---

[59] In *OC* 1405–13 (cf. 1435–6) Polynices begs her and her sister to do this. Antigone never explicitly accedes to his request by word, and we cannot tell whether she did so by gesture (e.g. clasping his hand); but we know that she is in fact going to carry it out.

[60] Eur. *TrGF* F 545, 545a; see Jouan and van Looy (2000: 443); Collard (2004: 107, 109, 128–9); Kannicht, *TrGF* pp. 577–8).

[61] Hypothesis of 'Aristophanes of Byzantium' to Soph. *Ant*.

summoned to give advice about the war, says that to save Thebes, Creon must sacrifice his other son. This is not an elder son like the warrior Megareus but a younger one, little more than a boy, given the obviously invented name of Menoeceus (that of his paternal grandfather): if lines 944–6 are genuine,[62] Haemon is spared because he has a (betrothed) wife. Creon refuses, and tells Menoeceus to flee to Dodona; Menoeceus pretends to agree, but then sacrifices himself. Menoeceus' death is mentioned several times in the next few scenes (1080–2, 1204–7, 1310–21, 1327); but once news arrives of the mutual slaying of Eteocles and Polynices, and the suicide of Iocasta, Menoeceus is forgotten, and the arrangements for his burial, which Creon was about to initiate (1317–21), are never carried any further within the play.[63]

Later tragic dramatists[64] continued to rework Cyclic episodes already exploited by their predecessors, and occasionally to add new ones to the repertoire – new, at least, so far as our information goes – such as Achilles' killing of Thersites (from the *Aethiopis*), dramatized by the fourth-century poet Chaeremon. But these were mere gleanings after a harvest which, as we have seen, had largely been gathered in, in their different ways, in the course of the fifth century, by Aeschylus and Sophocles.

APPENDIX: TRAGEDIES BASED ON THE CYCLIC EPICS[65]

Aeschylus

Oedipodea: Laius, *The Sphinx*[s], Oedipus (in part)
Thebaid: Oedipus (in part), *Nemea*[s?], The Seven against Thebes, The Eleusinians, The Women of Argos (*Argeiai*)

---

[62] The lines were deleted by Willink (1990: 192–3); but see Mastronarde (1994: 418 n.1).
[63] Mastronarde (1994: 512–15) shows that, contrary to what has often been supposed, Creon when he comes on stage at 1308 does not bring Menoeceus' body with him.
[64] The most striking case, before the Hellenistic period, is that of the fourth-century dramatist Theodectas, six of whose nine known titles indicate a plot derived ultimately from the Cycle.
[65] This listing covers all tragic dramatists assigned by Snell in *TrGF* to the sixth, fifth or fourth century BC; the minor tragedians are listed in the sequence in which they appear in Snell's volume. The plays of each author are listed, as far as possible, in the order in which the episodes dramatized in them appeared in the epics. The superscripts [s] or [s?] indicate respectively that the play so designated was certainly or probably satyric. Where the identification of the mythical episode on which a play was based is in doubt, I follow Sommerstein (2008) for Aeschylus, Jouanna (2007) for Sophocles, and Collard and Cropp (2008) for Euripides, unless otherwise stated. In the case of the minor tragedians, I have also included references to fragments which provide evidence of Cycle-based plays of theirs whose titles have not survived.

Epigonoi: *The Epigonoi*
Alcmeonis: none
Cypria: *The Chamber-Makers (Thalamopoioi), Telephus, Iphigeneia, Palamedes*
Aethiopis: *Memnon, The Weighing of Souls (Psychostasia)*
Ilias parva/Iliou persis: *The Award of the Arms (Hoplōn Krisis), The Thracian Women (Thrēissai), Philoctetes*
Nostoi: *Proteus??, The Women of Salamis (Salaminiai), Agamemnon, The Libation Bearers (Choephoroi), The Eumenides*
Telegony: none

Sophocles

Oedipodea: *Oedipus the King*
Thebaid: *Amphiaraus??, Oedipus at Colonus, Antigone*
Epigonoi: *The Epigonoi*[66]
Alcmeonis: *Alcmaon*
Cypria: *Alexandros, Momus??, Eris??, The Lovers of Achilles?? (Achilleōs Erastai), The Judgement?? (Krisis), The Abduction of Helen (Helenēs Harpagē), The Madness of Odysseus (Odysseus Mainomenos), Telephus, Iphigeneia, The Diners (Syndeipnoi),*[67] *The Demand for Helen (Helenēs Apaitēsis), The Shepherds (Poimenes), Troilus, The Captive Women (Aichmalōtides),*[68] *Palamedes, The Arrival of Nauplius (Nauplios Katapleōn)*[69]
Aethiopis: *The Ethiopians (Aithiopes)*[70]
Ilias parva/Iliou persis: *Ajax, The Scyrians (Skyrioi),*[71] *Eurypylus, Philoctetes, Philoctetes at Troy, The Laconian Women (Lakainai), Sinon, Laocoon, Ajax the Locrian (Ajax Locros), The Sons of Antenor (Antēnoridai), Polyxene* (in part)

---

[66] Probably identical with *Eriphyle*: see my discussion in Sommerstein and Talboy (2012: 34–8).

[67] Probably identical with *The Assembly of the Achaeans (Achaiōn Syllogos)*; see my discussion in Sommerstein *et al.* (2006: 84–90).

[68] I take these to be the women whose distribution as prizes to the Greek leaders caused the crisis with which the *Iliad* begins; see Lloyd-Jones (1996: 24–5); *contra*, Jouanna (2007: 614).

[69] I place *The Arrival of Nauplius* here on the provisional assumption that, as in Aeschylus and Euripides (both of whom brought Nauplius to Troy at the end of their *Palamedes* plays), its action was set soon after the death of Palamedes; but it is quite possible that Sophocles made Nauplius' arrival coincide with some later crisis in the war, specifically the coming of a new ally for the Trojans (note Soph. *TrGF* 426, 427); see my discussions in Sommerstein and Talboy (2012: 129–30, 162–3).

[70] Probably identical with *Memnon*; see Pearson (1917: i.22–3); Lloyd-Jones (1996: 22–3).

[71] Or *The Women of Scyros (Skyriai)*; the authors who quote our fragments give the title now in one gender, now in the other.

Nostoi: *Polyxene* (in part), *Nauplius and the Beacon (Nauplios Pyrkaeus), Teucer, Peleus, Hermione,*[72] *Electra, Erigone*[73]
Telegony: *Euryalus, Odysseus and the Fatal Spine (Odysseus Akanthoplēx)*
Uncertain: *Andromache, Helen's Wedding*[s?] *(Helenēs Gamos), Clytaemnestra, Priam, Tyndareos*

Euripides

Oedipodea: *Chrysippus, Oedipus*
Thebaid: *Hypsipyle, The Phoenician Maidens, The Suppliants, Antigone*
Epigonoi: none
Alcmeonis: *Alcmaon in Corinth, Alcmaon at Psophis*
Cypria: *Alexandros, The Scyrians (Skyrioi), Telephus, Iphigeneia at Aulis, Tennes,*[74] *Protesilaus, Palamedes*
Aethiopis: none
Ilias parva/Iliou persis: *Philoctetes, Epeius*[s]*, Hecuba*
Nostoi: *The Trojan Women, Helen, Electra, Orestes, Andromache*
Telegony: none

Minor Tragedians[75]

Phrynichus
    Troy: cf. *TrGF* F 13 (Troilus)
Aristarchus of Tegea
    Thebes: cf. *TrGF* F 5 (Parthenopaeus)
Euripides the Younger
    Troy: *Polyxene, Orestes*

---

[72] Probably identical with *The Women of Phthia (Phthiotides)*; see my discussion in Sommerstein et al. (2006: 14–17).

[73] I omit the *Aletes* ascribed to Sophocles, which likewise dealt with a conflict between Orestes and a child of Aegisthus and Clytaemestra, since its authenticity is in doubt (Wilamowitz 1929b: 465–6); it is mentioned at the end of this Appendix as a play of unknown authorship.

[74] This play was alternatively ascribed to Critias.

[75] In listing plays of the minor tragedians I have not attempted to distinguish among the various epics composing the Theban and Trojan cycles, since we often do not have sufficient information to be able to associate a play with a particular epic. Plays named simply *Achilles* or *Odysseus* have been assumed, unless there is evidence to the contrary, to have been based on the *Iliad* and *Odyssey* respectively. The listing beautifully illustrates Aristotle's statement (*Poet.* 1453a18–22) that in his time tragedy had come to concentrate heavily on a few families; of the first three individuals he names in that passage, Oedipus gives his name to nine known plays by these dramatists, Alcmaon to six (and his wife Alphesiboea to three more), Orestes to four, and no other figure from the Theban or Trojan cycles to more than three.

Ion of Chios
    Troy: *The Watchmen (Phrouroi)*,[76] *Teucer, Agamemnon*
    Uncertain: *The Argives*
Achaeus I
    Thebes: *Oedipus, Adrastus, Alcmaon^s, Alphesiboea*[77]
    Troy: *Momus (?), Cycnus (?), Philoctetes*
Iophon
    Troy: *Telephus*, the *Iliou persis (Iliou persis)*[78]
Philocles
    Thebes: *Oedipus*; cf. also *TrGF* F 3 (Parthenopaeus)
    Troy: *Priam, Nauplius, Philoctetes, Erigone*; cf. also *TrGF* F 2 (Hermione)
Theognis
    Troy: cf. *TrGF* F 2 (Hermione)
Xenocles I
    Thebes: *Oedipus*
Nicomachus I
    Thebes: *Oedipus*
Callistratus
    Thebes: *Amphilochus*[79]
Agathon
    Thebes: *Alcmaon*
    Troy: *Telephus*; cf. also *TrGF* F 17 (Pylades)

[76] This play, like Sophocles' *Laconian Women*, dealt with Odysseus' entry into Troy in disguise and his meeting there with Helen (cf. Σ Aristoph. *Frogs* 1425).

[77] Alphesiboea is the name usually given (e.g. Paus. 8.24.8; title of Latin play by Accius; Propertius 1.15.5) to the daughter of Phegeus, king of Psophis (also sometimes called Arsinoe, e.g. Ps.-Apollod. *Bibl.* 3.7.5), who became the wife of Alcmaon and was probably a character in Euripides' *Alcmeon at Psophis*.

[78] Two further plays, one from the Theban cycle (*Amphiaraus*) and one from the Trojan (*Erigone*), are ascribed by *Suda* (κ 1730 Adler) to one Cleophon. However, the overlap between Cleophon's play-titles and Iophon's, also listed by *Suda* (ι 451), is so extensive (six of the seven listed Iophon titles also appear in the Cleophon list) that Snell (*TrGF*: 132, 246) is likely to be right in his suspicion that these two poets are actually one. If so, the ghost of the pair is certainly Cleophon, since Iophon is very well attested as a son of Sophocles and a dramatist himself.

[79] Amphilochus was Alcmeon's brother, the younger son of Amphiaraus; he was a character in the *Thebaid* (*PEG* F 4 = "Hom." F 3 D. = F 8 W.) and doubtless also in the *Epigonoi*. Euripides gave the same name to a son of Alcmeon who was a character in his *Alcmeon in Corinth* (Ps.-Apollod. *Bibl.* 3.7.7; cf. Eur. *TrGF* F 73a, 75). It is just conceivable that Alcmeon might have been the central figure in a play based on the Trojan rather than the Theban cycle: we find his name on a Tyrrhenian black-figure vase (London BM 1897.7–27.2 = *LIMC* 'Polyxene' 26) among those taking an active part in the sacrifice of Polyxene, and in the Hesiodic *Catalogue of Women* (F 197.6–8 M.-W. = F 105.6–8 Hirsch.) both he and, more surprisingly, his brother Alcmeon are listed among the suitors of Helen.

Meletus II
    Thebes: *Oedipodea* (tetralogy)
Antiphon
    Troy: *Andromache*
Timotheus
    Thebes: *Alcmaon, Alphesiboea*
Astydamas II
    Thebes: *Parthenopaeus, Antigone, The Epigonoi, Alcmeon*
    Troy: *Palamedes, Nauplius, The Madness of Ajax (Aiax Mainomenos)*
Ps.-Apollodorus
    Troy: *The Greeks (Hellenes) (?), The Fatal Spine (Akanthoplēx)*
Carcinus II
    Thebes: *Oedipus, Amphiaraus*
    Troy: *Ajax, Orestes*
Chaeremon
    Thebes: *Alphesiboea*
    Troy: *The Slaying of Thersites (Achilleus Thersitoktonos)*
Theodectas
    Thebes: *Oedipus, Alcmeon*
    Troy: *Helen, Ajax, Philoctetes, Orestes*
Aphareus
    Troy: *Orestes*
Euaretus
    Thebes: *[Alc]me[o]n.* (?)
    Troy: *Teucer*
Timocles
    Thebes: *Oedipus*
Diogenes of Sinope
    Thebes: *Chrysippus, Oedipus*
    Troy: *Helen*
Sosiphanes
    Thebes: cf. *TrGF* F 4 (Laius)
Troy: cf. *TrGF* F 5 (children of Menelaus and Helen), *TrGF* F 7 (son of Neoptolemus and Hermione)

A few titles not otherwise known are attested in our sources without any dramatist's name being attached to them; these are *The Beggar Mission, The Departure, Neoptolemus* and *Aegisthus*, to which may be added the *Aletes* sometimes ascribed to Sophocles (see above, p. 483 n. 73). The first three are mentioned by Aristotle (see above, pp. 461–2); the *Aegisthus* referred to by Philodemus[80] was probably also of classical date, and so doubtless was *Aletes*, since it is unlikely that a drama composed in Hellenistic times would have gained even limited acceptance as a work of Sophocles.

[80] *On Piety* i p. 22 Gomperz (*TrGF* F 327c).

26 | The Hellenistic reception of the Epic Cycle

EVINA SISTAKOU

Contrary to the ringing declaration of Callimachus ἐχθαίρω τὸ ποίημα τὸ κυκλικόν, the Epic Cycle seems to hold a strong attraction for Hellenistic poets.[1] As expected, the Homeric myth with its Panhellenic flair is bypassed by those who follow the untrodden paths of arcane mythology and its tellings; in this respect, the 'invention' of mythography may be seen as a by-product of the Hellenistic penchant for obscure and original versions of the Greek myths.[2] So, apart from the *Theseids* and the *Heracleids*, the Pre-Hellenic mythological traditions, the stories of gods and heroes or the local traditions of Attica and Argos, of Greece and the Mediterranean, the narrations deriving from the Epic Cycle – which, according to Proclus (*Chrest.* apud Phot. *Bibl.* 319a21 = *Cycli epitoma Procli PEG* T 13 = T 1 D.), begins with the union of Ouranos and Gaia, and ends with the unwanted killing of Odysseus by his son Telegonus – are of utmost importance for the making of Hellenistic poetry. To support this argument, I shall first give an outline of the reception of the Epic Cycle by mostly referring to Hellenistic poets and poems; in the second part of this study, I shall focus on the devices by which the Hellenistic poets have transformed the Cyclic myths into neoteric material.

THE EPIC CYCLE IN HELLENISTIC POETRY: A ROUGH OUTLINE

To give an overview of the Hellenistic reception of the Epic Cycle is a daunting task, and not primarily due to the philological problems associated with the textual tradition and the exact plots of these, lost long ago, epics. The temporal and geographical distance separating the various poets, the

---

[1] The complex relation of Hellenistic poetry and scholarship to the notion of *kyklikos* is discussed by Cameron (1995: 394–402); see Fantuzzi, above in this volume, pp. 405–29, and Squire, below in this volume, pp. 512–16. That Apollonius seems to have written a 'Cyclic' epic, at least from a narratological viewpoint, is convincingly argued by Rengakos (2004).

[2] To avoid retelling the Homeric myths and, conversely, to explore unknown myths from the entire Epic Cycle is a fundamental tenet of Hellenistic poetics, on which see Sistakou (2008). On the main features of Hellenistic mythography, see Higbie (2007).

differences in their aesthetics and style, and the fragmentary preservation of a good part of Hellenistic poetry place many obstacles in the way of scholars trying to address complex questions, such as: which myths and which poems of the Epic Cycle attracted the attention of Hellenistic poets? Did they show a preference for Trojan myth as opposed to other mythic cycles and/or the Homeric myth? How are the Cyclic episodes, motifs or characters reworked under the influence of new genres and narrative forms developed during Hellenistic times?

Some preliminary remarks may serve as an introduction, albeit not as an answer, to the above-mentioned questions.[3] Callimachus may loathe the continuous epicizing narrative, but he makes sure that a big part of 'Cyclic' mythology is integrated either into episodes explaining an *aition* or into compact phrases in his poems. An example for the former is why the statue of Athena has a bandage on its thigh: the *aition* is dated back to the time when the Greeks had gathered at Aulis, when a quarrel broke out between Agamemnon and Teuthis (*SH* 276 = F 190a–b Hard.). The latter is exemplified by numerous allusions to well-known incidents from the entire Cycle, such as the judgment of Paris (*HLav. Pall.* 18 οὐδ' ὅκα τὰν Ἴδαι Φρὺξ ἐδίκαζεν ἔριν 'not even when the Phrygian was judging the contest on Mount Ida', cf. *Cypr.* arg. lines 88–90 Severyns), the hybristic behaviour of Agamemnon against Artemis over deer-hunting (*HArt.* 262–3 μηδ' ἐλαφηβολίην μηδ' εὐστοχίην ἐριδαίνειν – οὐδὲ γὰρ Ἀτρεΐδης ὀλίγωι ἐπὶ κόμπασε μισθῶι 'nor dispute her skill in shooting of deers nor in archery – since not even the son of Atreus could boast without paying a high price', cf. *Cypr.* arg. lines 135–8 Severyns) or the mourning of Thetis for the dead Achilles (*HAp.* 20 οὐδὲ Θέτις Ἀχιλῆα κινύρεται αἴλινα μήτηρ 'nor does Thetis sing a dirge for Achilles', cf. *Aeth.* arg. lines 198–9 Severyns). In Callimachus the 'Cyclic' allusions are scattered and only scarcely do they form coherent narratives.

However, Callimachus is the exception rather than the rule among his contemporaries. Lycophron of Chalcis, if he should be credited with the writing of the bizarre *Alexandra*, offers a linear, albeit enigmatic to the highest degree, narration of the Trojan myth starting from the early history of Troy and stretching over the war and well beyond, into the wanderings of the homecoming heroes. In attempting to include all the Trojan War events into a single narrative (and the entire range of Greek literature from Homer to the poets of the Cycle, and from archaic lyric to tragedy), Lycophron is, in effect, dramatizing the idea of the Cycle *per se*.[4] Apollonius, on the other

---

[3] For a thorough account of the Hellenistic reception of the Epic Cycle, see Sistakou (2008).

[4] Lycophron's experiment with the Cycle in the *Alexandra* (on which see Sistakou (2008: 100–20)) should be seen in the light of another philological hypothesis: that the Epic Cycle was

hand, proposes something quite different with the *Argonautica*. Though narrating a myth that officially does not belong to the Cycle, Apollonius crosses the Argonautic with the Trojan myth (both in its Cyclic and in its Homeric version) by using three devices: the Argonautic expedition is rendered as a pre-phase to the Trojan War myth; scenes and motifs in the *Argonautica* are modelled on celebrated episodes from the Trojan myth; three characters, Peleus, Thetis and Achilles, common in both cycles, closely link the plot of the *Argonautica* with that of the *Cypria*.[5]

Hellenistic genres, such as the epyllia and the idylls, consisting of small-scale narrations of single episodes, are ideal for the treatment of marginal stories from the Epic Cycle and Homer. Philitas wrote his own version of Odysseus' adventure on the island of Aeolus in one of the first poems of the kind, the epyllion *Hermes*.[6] Yet although the 'romantic' potential of the *Odyssey* inspired various adaptations during the Hellenistic era,[7] it was a Cyclic epic, the *Cypria*, that primarily attracted the poets for its novelistic qualities and aetiological focus.[8] The following list supports the assumption: Euphorion's two lost epyllia *Philoctetes* (*CA* 44, cf. *Cypr.* arg. lines 144–6 Severyns) and *Anius* (*CA* 2, not mentioned by Proclus but only by the Σ Lycophr. 570 = *PEG* F 29 = F 19 D. = F 26 W.); the hexametric poem of Apollonius *Lesbou ktisis* narrating the love affair between Achilles and Peisidice during the siege of Methymna (F 12 CA; the general context is given by Proclus in *Cypr.* arg. lines 160–2 Severyns); the *Telephi Epyllion* attributed to an unknown author (*CA Epica Adesp.* 3, cf. *Cypr.* arg. lines 126–8 Severyns); and several love stories (in prose summaries) set against the background of the Trojan War from Parthenius' *Erotica pathēmata* (4 *On Oenone*, 16 *On Laodice*, 21 *On Peisidice*, 26 *On Apriate*, 34 *On Corythus* and 36 *On Arganthone*). The picture cannot be complete without reference to Theocritus and the poets of the bucolic corpus. Theocritus wrote two idylls referring to pre-Iliadic events, the *Epithalamion for Helen* (*Id.* 18) and the *Dioscuri* (*Id.* 22, directly referring to *Cypr.* arg. lines 106–9 Severyns). Also an idyll with bucolic frame entitled *Epithalamion for Achilles*

'manufactured' (i.e. edited, abridged and arranged into one collection) by the scholars of the Hellenistic era, as plausibly argued by Burgess (2001: 12–33).

[5] Sistakou (2008: 88–100).
[6] On Philitas' *Hermes*, see especially Sbardella (2000: 16–28 and 105–12), and Spanoudakis (2002: 95–141).
[7] In his prose summaries of the *Eroti pathēmata*, Parthenius foregrounds the erotic element in three of his 'Odyssean' stories (2 *On Polymela*, 3 *On Euippe* and 12 *On Calchus*).
[8] On this facet of the *Cypria*, see Scaife (1995); cf. Griffin (1977: 40) who speaks of 'the fantastic, the miraculous and the romantic' as the features that distinguish the Homeric epics from the Epic Cycle. Or perhaps because the *Cypria* were embodying local traditions of the Trojan War, as Burgess (1996) believes, a tendency which equals the Hellenistic taste for local mythology. A general overview of the Hellenistic reception of the *Cypria* in Sistakou (2007).

and Deideia has come down to us in fragments, sometimes attributed to Bion of Smyrna, where Achilles' Σκύριος ἔρως is dramatized (*Cypr.* arg. lines 130–1 Severyns). Last but not least, Simias' technopaegnion *Axe* represents the famous axe by which Epeius once constructed the Wooden Horse (a story also treated by Callimachus in his seventh *Iamb*).[9]

THE NEOTERIC TRANSFORMATIONS OF THE 'CYCLIC' MYTH

In what follows I attempt to categorize the mechanisms by which the Hellenistic poets have transformed the archaic myths of the Cycle to suit their own aesthetic ends. After a brief description, I shall provide a characteristic example for each one of them.

Compression

To provide a summary or an elliptical narration instead of the full-scale narrative of an episode is what I have termed *compression*. Mythological examples, such as the ones quoted above from the *Hymns* of Callimachus, are typical cases of compression.[10] In a different manner, Lycophron has compressed all the Cyclic stories of the *Alexandra* into micro-narratives. Verses 307–64 of the *Alexandra* are dedicated to the events which, according to Proclus' summary, were included in the *Iliou persis*.[11] Though Lycophron seems to have composed a great part of the *Alexandra* under the influence of the Epic Cycle, it is notable that the chronological sequence of the Cyclic episodes is distorted in this Hellenistic poem. Thus, within the context of Alexandra's tragic lament, the following episodes are referred to: the deaths of Troilus (307–13), Laodice (316–22), Polyxena (323–9), Hecuba (330–4)

---

[9] Although the references to the Trojan War myth are numerous, the contrary holds true for the Theban part of the Cycle, very rarely treated by the Hellenistic poets. Two notable exceptions: (1) the Theban *aition* about 'Antigone's Dragging' of Polynices' body to the pyre of Eteocles from Callimachus' *Aetia* 4 (F 105–105b Hard.); and (2) the *Diomedis Epyllion* by an unknown author (*CA Ep. adesp.* 2).

[10] Other versions of compression are the epic catalogues (like those found in Theocr. *Id.* 15–17, 22) and the proverbial expressions, especially in low poetic genres and the epigrams: on both, see Sistakou (2008: 37–61).

[11] With two exceptions: (1) the section begins with the death of Troilus (307–13) which was originally part of the *Cypria* (*Cypr.* arg. line 162 Severyns), and (2) the drowning of Ajax the Locrian (*Nost.* arg. lines 294–5 Severyns; see also *Il. pers.* arg. lines 266–7 Severyns) is postponed for verses 387–407.

and Priam (335–6), then the betrayal of Antenor and Sinon, the Greeks coming out from the Wooden Horse and the attack of the serpents against Laocoon (340–7)[12] and finally the rape of Cassandra by Ajax on the altar of Athena (348–64). The order in the summary of Proclus is Laocoon (*Il. pers.* arg. lines 248–9 Severyns), Sinon *Il. pers.* arg. lines 252–3 Severyns), the Wooden Horse (*Il. pers.* arg. lines 254–6 Severyns), Priam (*Il. pers.* arg. lines 257–8 Severyns), Cassandra (*Il. pers.* arg. lines 261–2 Severyns) and Polyxena (*Il. pers.* arg. lines 273–4 Severyns), whereas the fates of Laodice and Hecuba are not mentioned at all. More importantly the episodes in Lycophron are reworked into key images, focusing on the most critical or graphic detail of each one of them. Thus, for example, Priam is depicted lying slain on the altar of Zeus (335–6 ὁ δ' ἀμφὶ τύμβωι τἀγαμέμνονος δαμεὶς / κρηπῖδα πηγῶι νέρθε καλλυνεῖ πλόκωι 'and he killed at Zeus' altar shall beautify the pedestal with his silver locks') and Sinon at the critical moment when he gives a fire signal to the Greek fleet (344–5 τῆς Σισυφείας δ' ἀγκύλης λαμπούριδος / λάμψηι κακὸν φρύκτωρον αὐτανέψιος 'and he, the cousin of that crooked Sisyphean fox, shall light his baneful beacon').[13]

Expansion

To turn a Cyclic episode into a self-contained plot and to rework it into an epyllion or idyll is one of the greatest challenges of Hellenistic aesthetics: this is what I have termed *expansion*. The abandonment of Philoctetes by the Achaeans on the island of Lemnos was part of the *Cypria*, but, if Proclus' summary is accurate, it may have been narrated *en passant* in this Cyclic epic (arg. lines 144–6 Severyns: καὶ εὐωχουμένων αὐτῶν Φιλοκτήτης ὑφ' ὕδρου πληγεὶς διὰ τὴν δυσοσμίαν ἐν Λήμνωι κατελείφθη 'and while they were feasting, Philoctetes was bitten by a snake and left behind on the island of Lemnos because of the stench of his wound'). We know, moreover, that all three tragedians expanded on the initial episode yet with one critical difference: whereas Aeschylus and Sophocles stressed the desolation of the wounded hero, Euripides introduced a new character into the story, the Lemnian Actor, as an acquaintance of Philoctetes (Dio Chrys. 52.8). Euphorion took a step further in his epyllion *Philoctetes*, by adding

---

[12] The latter only indirectly through the phrase παιδοβρῶτος Πορκέως ('of Porceus the eater of children'), which alludes to the one of the two dragons that devoured Laocoon and his sons (see *Il. pers. PEG* F 3 Πόρκις καὶ Χαρίβοια).

[13] For the formation of these micro-narratives under the influence of the Epic Cycle, see Hurst and Kolde (2008: 144–54).

a marginal figure (inspired, as so many other Hellenistic figures, by the sphere of low, everyday life), the shepherd Iphimachus as a comrade and helper of Philoctetes (*CA* 44–45, cf. *SH* 428 and 440). It was with him that Philoctetes returned to Troy; and it was Iphimachus who, during Philoctetes' homecoming, had drowned by the Capherean Rocks. The expansion of the Cyclic episode had also a distinctly Alexandrian feature. As the surviving fragment *CA* 44 reveals, Euphorion recorded in detail the actual moment of Iphimachus' drowning which he had rendered with an undertone of tender sentimentality.[14]

Inversion

By *inversion* I mean any kind of antithesis in plot or characterization, any dramatic difference in the ending of a story. A nice example for the latter is the Hellenistic version of Diomedes' homecoming. Whereas in the Cyclic *Nostoi* it is expressly stated that Diomedes and Nestor return safely at home and are saved at the end (*Nost.* arg. lines 283–4 Severyns), Lycophron adopts a rare local tradition according to which the hero, upon arriving at Argos, is nearly murdered by his wife, the adulteress Aegialeia, and is hence doomed to leave Greece and wander in Daunia of Italy (*Alex.* 592–632).[15] Numerous similar examples where a common 'Cyclic' version is replaced by an obscure variation from Hellenistic mythography may be listed here. Yet I wish to point out a striking case of inversion in characterization, concerning the hero *par excellence* of the Trojan War myth, namely Achilles. According to the *Cypria* (arg. lines 130–1 Severyns) Achilles has a relation with Deidameia on the island of Scyrus, although the exact details of this episode are not given by Proclus. The depiction of Achilles not as a fierce warrior but as a passionate lover is featured by many non-Homeric poems.[16] What differentiates the lover Achilles in the *Epithalamion for Achilles and Deidameia* is that he is almost caricatured. He is the protagonist of an erotic bucolic song (an equal to Paris the shepherd and the Sicilian Cyclops), and an effeminate lover to the highest degree (in effect he has lost his status as a warrior and he takes on feminine habits and activity), while his sole 'masculinity' is oriented towards sex and not war.[17]

---

[14] Essential for the reading of the epyllion is Livrea (2002).
[15] On Diomedes in Daunia, see Hurst and Kolde (2008: 183–8).
[16] E.g. by Euripides' *Scyrians*, on which see Jouan (1966: 204–22). Hellenistic versions include the story of Achilles and Peisidice in the *Lesbou ktisis* and Achilles' depiction as a melancholic lover by Lyc. 171–201.
[17] For a thorough discussion of the episode, see Sistakou (2008: 171–6); Fantuzzi (2012: 39–58).

Conversion

To transfer a recognizable story-pattern into a new mythological context is what I have termed *conversion*. An outstanding example is the core pattern of the *Iliad*, i.e. the *eris* between Agamemnon and Achilles, the anger of the latter and his withdrawal from the Trojan War, as exploited by Callimachus in the *Aetia*. Upon explaining the 'bandaged' statue of Athena in Arcadia, Callimachus narrates a rare local tradition involving Agamemnon and an unknown hero, Teuthis, the leader of the Arcadians (*SH* 276, F 190a–b Hard.).[18] The setting is Cyclic, as the story is set against the background of the gathering of the Greek forces at Aulis.[19] Here the Iliadic scenario, adapted to the plot of the *Cypria*, repeats itself in *variatio*. The analogy between the Iliadic and Callimachean plot must have been extraordinary – if Pausanias' testimony is accurate as regards Callimachus' account (8.28.4–6): Teuthis quarrels with Agamemnon and, as a consequence, leads his men back to Arcadia; Athena in disguise tries to prevent Teuthis from withdrawing, whereupon the latter strikes the thigh of the goddess with his spear; after this incident disease and famine fall on Arcadia and its people, until Athena is eventually appeased.[20] Even a superficial reading of the Callimachean episode reveals its common motifs especially with *Iliad* 1. And the most striking variation of Callimachus pertains to the intervention of Athena in the quarrel, who not only fails to restrain the angered Teuthis from drawing his weapon (unlike what happens with Achilles in *Il.* 1.188–222) but is herself wounded by it.

Supplementation

Supplementation is a mechanism by which either the past of a character whose future is well known is explored – a device termed by Barchiesi 'future reflexive'[21] – or new characters and episodes are seen as add-ons to

---

[18] The tradition is known to Pausanias but perhaps dates back to the third/second century BC *periegetes* Polemo of Ilion (who however calls the Arcadian leader Ornytus not Teuthis; Polemo *Fr.hist.Gr.* F 24 Müller): for the testimonies see Pfeiffer (1949: on F 667) and Lloyd-Jones and Parsons on *SH* 276.

[19] At least in the account given by Pausanias 8.28.4; slightly different is the scholion found on PMich. inv. 6235 F 1.11–12, according to which the incident occurred 'when the Greeks were on their way to Troy' (Koenen, Luppe and Pagán 1991: 160).

[20] For a discussion of the story of Teuthis in the *Aetia*, see Koenen, Luppe and Pagán (1991: 160–4) and Hollis (1992).

[21] Barchiesi (2001: 105–6). For this popular device of intertextuality as exploited by the Hellenistic poets, and especially Callimachus, see Ambühl (2005: 23–30).

an old scenario. The Hellenistic taste for innovation underlies the depiction of 'old' epic heroes as children and youths (just like baby Achilles in Apoll. Rh. 1.557–8), the introduction of heroes 'on the margins' (like Menelaus' captain in Apollonius' lost poem *Canobus CA* 1–3) and the writing of prequels to famous episodes. The wedding song for Helen and Menelaus in Theocritus' *Id.* 18 is a case in point for the last category. According to Proclus, in the first part of the *Cypria* two weddings were narrated, namely that of Peleus and Thetis (*Cypr.* arg. lines 86–8 Severyns) and that of Paris and Helen (*Cypr.* arg. lines 104–5 Severyns). Perhaps inspired by these Cyclic episodes – and modelled on the lyric tradition of the *epithalamion*[22] – Idyll 18 not only brings the portrayal of the domestic Helen to the fore;[23] it moreover mirrors the kind of celebration that took place during that event in Sparta (by analogy to the feast given in honour of Paris in Sparta in the *Cypria* (arg. lines 96–8 Severyns) and of course it functions as an ironic alternative to the future of the fatal heroine that motivated the Trojan War.

Redirection

By *redirection* I mean a shift in emphasis or 'aim' of the narrative: the Cyclic episode is thus not narrated for its own sake, but functions as a digression, explanation or flashback within another context, mainly aetiological. It is a neoteric feature that the *nostoi* of the Greeks in Lycophron's *Alexandra* are contextualized as *ktisis*-stories, thus serving as a bridge between the mythical and the historical/political section of the poem (365–1089). The Cyclic episode, filtered through aetiology, thus becomes a fragment, a relic from the (epic) past.[24] It is a plausible hypothesis that the hybris of Ajax the Locrian against Athena which ended with the drowning of the hero by Poseidon was a favourite Cyclic story among the Hellenistic poets – yet not *per se* but as a background against which the custom of the sacrifice of the Locrian maidens at Troy was set. Callimachus, who is said to have included the story in *Aetia* F 35 Hard., probably drew on the Cyclic *Nostoi* (arg. lines 294–5 Severyns, cf. *Od.* 4.499–511) and on the Sicilian historiographer Timaeus.

---

[22] Including among others Sappho's wedding song for Hector and Andromache (F 44 Voigt) and of course Stesichorus' *Helen* (*PMGF* F 187–191; cf. Σ Theocr. 18 Arg. 'this idyll has the title *Epithalamion for Helen* and some elements in it are taken (εἴληπται) from Stesichorus' first poem on Helen'): on both see Contiades-Tsitsoni (1990: 64–109); on the latter Noussia-Fantuzzi, above in this volume, pp. 430–4.

[23] As known from *Odyssey* 4: see Pantelia (1995).

[24] On the concept of the *aition* as a fragment from the past, see Sistakou (2009).

The reworking of the *aition* by Lycophron (*Alex.* 1141–73), rendered in dark, dramatic tones,[25] is a valuable clue as to the emphasis and atmosphere of the Callimachean narrative too:[26] though it cannot be proved, Callimachus must have paid less attention to the death of Ajax and much more to the description of the Locrian custom itself.[27]

[25] The ritual and cultural context of the *aition* of the Locrian maidens, as also of other 'Trojan' *Aetia* in Lycophron is explored by Mari (2009).
[26] The same dark tonality is featured in a fragment by Euphorion on the same topic (*CA* 53).
[27] As Pfeiffer (1949: on F 35 = Hard. notes: 'Quid in Callimaco fuerit non constat (caveas ne universas scholiastarum 'historias' ei tribuas) . . . fortasse de Locrensium tributo . . . de virginum fato . . . narravit Callimachus.'

27 | Running rings round Troy: Recycling the 'Epic Circle' in Hellenistic and Roman art

MICHAEL SQUIRE

Literary responses to (what we call) the 'Epic Cycle' are not always literally 'literary'. In addition to the numerous Greek and Roman poets who engaged with the poems and their stories, artists offered distinctive visual interpretations of their own. Right from the beginnings of Late Geometric Greek figurative art, we find sculptors and painters responding to the tales of Troy, actively adding new twists and variations – necessarily changing the stories as much as passively 'following' them.[1]

This visual interest in Epic Cyclic stories intensified in the Hellenistic world. Although – as with the Epic Cycle poems themselves – we have only a tiny fraction of the original paintings, mosaics and sculptures produced, we know that the Epic Cycle played a major role. Textual sources confirm that such subjects appealed right to the top of the political and social orders: when decorating his famous ship in the third century BC, for example, Hieron II is said to have commissioned a series of mosaics 'on which the entire story of the *Iliad* was wonderfully wrought' (ἐν οἷς κατεσκευασμένος πᾶς ὁ περὶ τὴν Ἰλιάδα μῦθος θαυμασίως: Athen. 5.207 c).[2] Related cycles of paintings were also collected in Rome: Pliny the Elder records how a series on 'the Trojan War in many panels' (*bellumque Iliacum pluribus tabulis*, HN 35.144) came to be displayed in the Portico of Philip, attributed to a certain Theorus.[3]

Works like these might be lost. But extant Hellenistic and Roman visual materials nonetheless testify to the popularity of Epic Cycle themes, and across a broad range of different media. My aim in this chapter is to offer

---

[1] For a review of bibliography, see Burgess (2001: 35–44); Carpenter, above in this volume, pp. 178–95. The most important discussion remains Schefold (1975: 27–42), dividing the 'Ikonographie der Trojasaga' into 11 chronological 'Tendenzen' (p. 42).

[2] On Athenaeus' discussion of the ship (itself derived from an earlier account by Moschion: Athen. 5.206d), see Pollitt (1986: 281). The precise phrasing – *pas ho peri tēn Iliada mythos* – appears somewhat ambiguous: does it refer solely to episodes drawn from the *Iliad*, or might it also possibly nod to the story 'surrounding' it?

[3] For Hieron II's mosaics, see e.g. Webster (1964: 257–8); Pollitt (1986: 281); Kazansky (1994: 74–9, arguing, unpersuasively, for a close connection with the *Tabulae Iliacae*). Although Theorus' painted panels are lost, the theme was certainly famous enough to be lampooned – as, for example, at Petr. *Sat.* 89 (on which see Rimell (2002: 60–81) and Elsner (2007: 194–6)).

a brief preliminary survey of those surviving objects and paintings. At the same time, I also want to rethink exactly what these 'testimonia' attest. Rather than use the material record to reconstruct the content or narrative mode of the poems, the chapter aims at something both less and more ambitious: to show how pictorial engagements with the Epic Cycle could parallel and develop the literary concerns of contemporary poetic texts.

CIRCUMSCRIBING THE EVIDENCE

Let me begin by saying something about the sorts of Hellenistic and Roman materials that survive.[4] All manner of objects and installations could be cited here: stories relating to the Epic Cycle are a recurrent theme on Roman sarcophagi reliefs, for example;[5] they also crop up in larger-scale sculptural settings – as in the Imperial grotto at Sperlonga, where a variety of epic themes (and indeed different epics) were brought together on a single pseudo-theatrical stage.[6] Given the limitations of space, this chapter instead focuses on just three classes of Hellenistic and Roman materials: first, the so-called 'Megarian' or 'Homeric' relief bowls (most datable to the second century BC); second, Pompeian cycles of wall painting (from the late first century BC and first century AD); and third, the *Tabulae Iliacae*, or 'Iliac tablets' (the earliest of which likewise seem to date to around the late first century BC).

Homeric bowls

My first set of objects is a group of second-century, moulded terracotta relief bowls.[7] Although most often referred to in English as 'Homeric bowls' or

---

[4] The best single-volume introduction to the Epic Cycle in Classical and Hellenistic art remains Schefold and Jung (1989), with their inventory of Epic Cyclic episodes on pp. 426–7.

[5] For a short guide (focusing on the question of iconographic derivation), see Schefold (1976).

[6] For a review of bibliography, see e.g. Squire (2009: 209–15). The Skylla and Polyphemus groups from Sperlonga are the most famous, but other sculptures took events beyond Homer (e.g. the Theft of the Palladium – an episode dealt with in the *Ilias parva*); still other installations looked beyond Troy altogether – as, for example, with the ship carved out of the rock to the north of the triclinium, labelled (in mosaic) as the *navis Argo*. Private displays like these served as prompts for not only recalling but also retelling epic; as such, they find parallels in the still grander commissions of Hellenistic public sculpture (cf. e.g. Simon (1975) on the supposed 'Hesiodic' inscriptions on the external frieze of the Pergamon Altar of Zeus, with further comments in Ridgway (2000: 34–9)).

[7] For an overview of these objects and their origins, see Rotroff (1982: 6–13). The best discussion of their visual–verbal relations is Giuliani (2003: 263–280, arguing for a second-century BC date), but there are well-referenced English discussions in e.g. Webster (1964: 147–153);

'Homeric cups' (after the German *homerische Becher* – 'Homeric beakers' might be a more appropriate translation), these vessels engaged with a variety of epic and non-epic subjects. In his important study of 1979, Ulrich Sinn surveyed 137 cups in total, of which fourteen are deemed to engage with the *Iliad*, eight with the *Odyssey* and fourteen with the *Aethiopis*, *Ilias parva*, *Iliou persis* and *Nostoi*.[8] Sometimes these cups paraded their individual Epic Cyclic subjects explicitly. Three bear inscriptions relating them to Lesches' *Ilias parva* (κατὰ ποιητὴν Λέσχην ἐκ τῆς Μικρᾶς Ἰλιάδος), for instance, of which Fig. 27.1 is just one example (in this case, a description of the action is sandwiched between two scenes of Priam – we first see Priam kneeling before Neoptolemus, and second his murder, as witnessed by Hecuba);[9] a further cup bears a fragmentary inscription apparently relating it to an anonymous *Nostoi* (ἐκ τῶν [Νό]στων).[10] Other examples claim no such textual derivation. But by looking closely at the iconography, scholars have been confident about various Epic Cyclic connections.[11]

Vessels like these are best understood as opportunities to showcase literary erudition, above all in sympotic contexts.[12] As we shall see, the very selection of scenes invited drinkers to ponder the cups' mode of episodic excerption, which transformed the weighty poems of a larger epic set into miniature, self-contained 'extracts', designed for individual consumption: epic texts are converted into lightweight, almost epigrammatic objects (albeit often requiring considerable philological *gravitas* to be understood). As such,

---

Brilliant (1984: 41–3); Small (2003: 80–90). In what follows, I refer to the edition of Sinn (1979), which incorporates earlier references to Hausmann (1959).

[8] Many more comparanda have been found since Sinn's catalogue, and many of them on related Epic Cyclic themes: e.g. *SEG* 45.785 (sixteen moulded second-century clay vessels from Pella, including five of the *Iliou persis*); *SEG* 48.805 (two relief cups with Homeric scenes from Kelle); *SEG* 50.533 (seven additional Hellenistic relief cups from Pherai). Compare also Schmid (2006: 53–69) on seventeen cups from the Eretrian Sanctuary of Apollo Daphnephoros, of which some clearly relate to Epic Cyclic themes (e.g. p. 27, no. B7).

[9] See Sinn (1979: 94–7, nos. MB 27, MB 31 and MB 32). The inscriptions are discussed by West (2013: 14, 165), who compares the formulations of the epitomizing summaries with those of Paus. 10.27.2, and infers 'a compendium of digests of the Cyclic poems current no later than the Hellenistic period' (14).

[10] See Sinn (1979: 101, no. MB 36), with West (2013: 268–9).

[11] For one example, see e.g. Weitzmann (1959: 43), on a cup depicting the rape of Helen (Sinn 1979: 101–2, no. MB 37), supposing a link with the *Cypria*.

[12] See Burn (2004: 133), on how the cups cater to a 'scholarly clientele who may, perhaps, have enjoyed the cups at literary symposia, turning them in their hands and taking it in turns to recite the stories shown'. In the interests of space, I pass over debates about the original repertoire produced – above all, Weitzmann's argument, derived from the ratio of image to text on the surviving Odyssean cups, that 'all twenty-four books together would require about 168 cups in order to illustrate the *Odyssey* by roughly five hundred scenes': Weitzmann (1947: 38); cf. Giuliani (2003: 271–2).

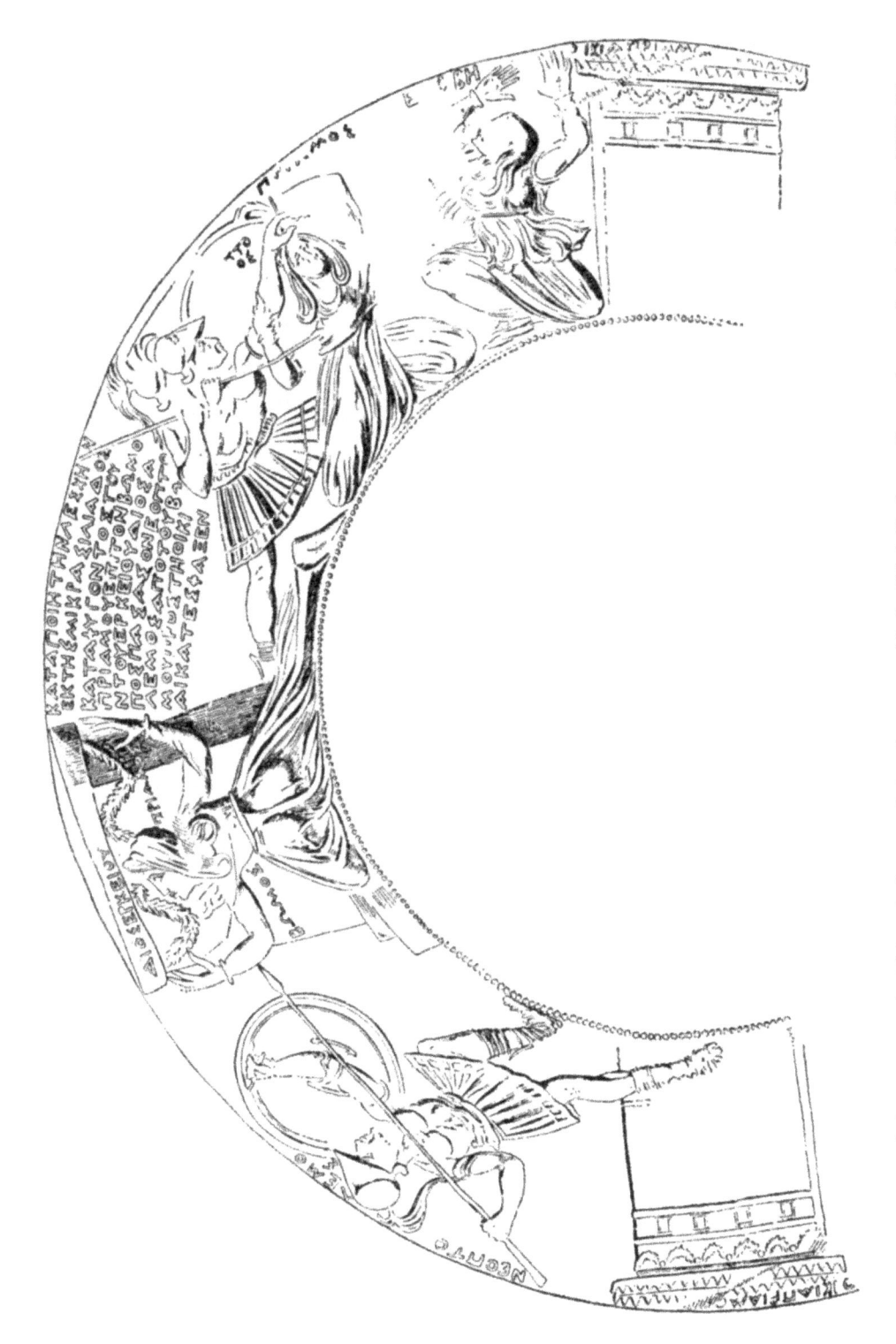

Fig. 27.1 Drawing of a 'Homeric cup', with inscription associating the scenes with the *'Little Iliad'* according to the poet Lesches (= Sinn (1979: 94, no MB 27)).

the terracotta 'beakers' bear comparison with the sorts of cup evoked in Theocritus' first *Idyll* (at once replicating epic and departing from it), or indeed later imitations of that passage (most famously in Virgil's third *Eclogue*).[13]

In practical terms, the Homeric cups seem to have been relatively inexpensive to produce. Because they were cast in moulds, the objects could be manufactured in bulk, and they were certainly exported all over the Mediterranean. Despite their number, we should be wary of judging the cups wholly lowbrow objects. We know of related vessels in other materials, and it is at least possible that the surviving terracotta cups reflect more costly metal prototypes.[14] Our terracotta cups might look like humble objects, in other words. But they tap into a culture of philological exhibitionism. Indeed, some examples went beyond their epic prototypes in labelling the various figures depicted: one cup from Volos in Thessaly, for instance, names each of the various companions of Odysseus whom Circe turned into swine, even though those characters go unspecified in the Homeric 'original'.[15]

Pompeian wall painting

Where my first group of objects were mobile miniatures, my second amounts to a series of domestic installations from Pompeii. Scholars had long known from Vitruvius that, at least by around the end of the first century BC, 'the battles of Troy or the wanderings of Odysseus through landscapes' were popular themes for contemporary Roman mural decoration (*Troianas pugnas seu Ulixis errationes per topia*, Vitr. 7.5.2). But Pompeian finds confirm the general picture: Campanian wall painting engaged not only with the *Iliad* and *Odyssey*, but also with narrative cycles drawn from other epics too.

Three major Trojan cycles from Pompeii were published in 1953. Two were displayed in separate rooms within what was once the same house: the first was installed around 30 BC, complete with Greek labels, in the large

---

[13] On Theocr. 1.26–60 and its reception, see e.g. Halperin (1983: 176–83); Goldhill (1991: 240–6); Männlein-Robert (2007b: 303–7).

[14] For different versions of the argument, see e.g. Hausmann (1959: 40–5); Sinn (1979: 46–51); Rotroff (1982: 6–13). Suetonius records how Nero owned two 'favourite drinking-cups' made out of glass, 'which he called "Homeric" because they were carved with scenes from Homer's poems' (*quos Homericos a caelatura carminum Homeri uocabat*, Suet. *Ner.* 47; cf. Plin. *HN* 37.29); compare also Athen. 11.782b.

[15] See Webster (1964: 153), on Hausmann (1959: 55, no. 27 = Sinn 1979: 126, no. MB 73). Name inscriptions like these are paralleled by those inscribed on the Esquiline 'Odyssey frieze', many of which go unattested in the *Odyssey*: introducing such names evidently provided a way of getting one's philological own back on the epic, not least its cataloguing mode; for a review of bibliography, see O'Sullivan (2007: 500–4), and compare Coarelli (1998, especially p. 25 for the relation to the 'erudite elaborations of Hellenistic philology').

U-shaped cryptoporticus of the eponymous Casa del Criptoportico (Pompeii I.6.2) (see Figs. 27.17 and 27.18, below); the second was installed almost a century later, this time rendered in painted stucco and left uninscribed (the space is now usually referred to as the Sacellum or Sacrarium, at the south-west end of the atrium in the Casa di Sacello Iliaco, Pompeii I.6.4). A third series of 'Fourth Style' paintings was found in the Casa di Octavius Quartio (also known as the Casa di Loreius Tiburtinus), Pompeii II.2.2: these paintings adorn an oecus overlooking an elaborate pergola complex and landscaped gardens to the south, and were probably installed c. AD 70; in contrast to the eponymous room in the Casa del Criptoportico, the labels were here inscribed in Latin.[16]

Like the Homeric bowls, some of these wall paintings dealt with events beyond the narrative frame of the *Iliad*. The paintings from the Casa del Criptoportico are the most interesting example. Although the surviving panels are highly fragmentary (just over a quarter of the estimated eighty-six panels survive),[17] the frieze evidently combined scenes from the *Iliad* with others drawn from the *Aethiopis*: in the west wing of the cryptoporticus, on the east and south walls, viewers were faced first with Penthesilea's arrival at Troy (Fig. 27.2),[18] then a fragmentary scene that has been interpreted as either Thetis sitting at Achilles' tomb or Helen sitting at the walls of Troy, and finally (adjacent to the house's rear entrance and exit, on the southern wall of the western wing) a single scene of Aeneas' departure from Troy (see Figs. 27.17–19, below).[19] Something similar happens in the eponymous

---

[16] The three Pompeian cycles are published by Aurigemma (1953), and further discussed by e.g. Schefold (1975: 129–34); Brilliant (1984: 60–5); Croisille (2005: 154–65); Santoro (2005). For other, single tableaux of Trojan Epic Cyclic themes from Pompeii, see Hodske (2007: 33–5): Hodske counts 106 examples in all (14 per cent of his total calculated Pompeian 'mythological' themes), and notes the occasional significance of arrangement and juxtaposition (pp. 111–12). One particularly enlightening case study is the series of Fourth Style paintings from the portico of the Temple of Apollo at Pompeii, now lost, but documented by Morelli in the nineteenth century (Schefold 1957: 192–3; cf. *PPM* 7: 295–6, nos. 15. along with *PPM Disegnatori* 112–13).

[17] See Aurigemma (1953: 968–70).

[18] Despite the fragmentary nature of the evidence, epigraphic testimonia confirm that this east wall of the west wing was adorned with other scenes relating to the *Aethiopis*: see Aurigemma (1953: 965–8) on fragments inscribed with the names of, *inter alios*, Penthesilea and Achilles (the scenes go without reference in West (2013: 129–62)). The surviving panel of Penthesilea's arrival at Troy is the first or second to feature on this eastern wall of the western wing (cf. Spinazzola (1953: Tav. LXXXVII)). Aurigemma (1953: 970) supposes eight panels in total. On the difficult archaeology of the house, see below, n. 80.

[19] The scenes were set into a high-level frieze which comprised panels of varying lengths, but which measure a consistent 34 cm in height. Following Aurigemma (1953: 970), Schefold (1975: 129) estimates that there were originally as many as eight *Aethiopis* scenes on this eastern wall of the west wing, perhaps combined with other scenes from the *Ilias parva* and *Iliou persis*; supposing up to seventy-five Trojan scenes in total, he adds that the first three or so scenes on the west wall of the west wing might have been drawn from the *Iliad*'s 'unmittelbarer

Fig. 27.2 Reconstruction of the painting of Penthesilea arriving at Troy, from the east wall of the west wing of the eponymous room of the Casa del Criptoportico (Pompeii II.2.2). See Fig. 27.17, below.

Sacellum of the Casa di Sacello Iliaco (see Fig. 27.20, below). Although the stucco friezes deal with *Iliad* 22–24 alone, other scenes relate the moulded imagery to a broader cycle of stories: the Iliadic frieze is situated beneath a lunette of Endymion and Selene on the back wall, and a vaulted ceiling emblazons a central medallion of Ganymede seized by an eagle. No less interesting are the 'Fourth Style' scenes from oecus h of the Casa di Octavius Quartio. This room in fact juxtaposes two narrative subjects in its single space – a small 30-cm frieze dealing with events told in *Iliad* 1–24 below, and a larger 80-cm frieze with narrative scenes from the life of Heracles above (Figs. 27.3 and 27.21, below).[20] I return to all three cycles at the end of the chapter.

Tabulae Iliacae

My third group of Hellenistic–Roman objects is arguably the most explicit in bringing together different Epic Cyclic stories: the so-called *Tabulae Iliacae*,

Vorgeschichte' in the *Cypria* ('denn links von der erhaltenen Pestszene ist noch Raum für drei bis fünf Bilder'); for the precise location of the extant scenes, see Spinazzola (1953: Tav. LXXXVII). For parallel combinations of Cyprian and Iliadic scenes, see below, n. 84.

[20] For the Heraclean scenes, see Coralini (2001: 78–81; 2002), with further bibliography.

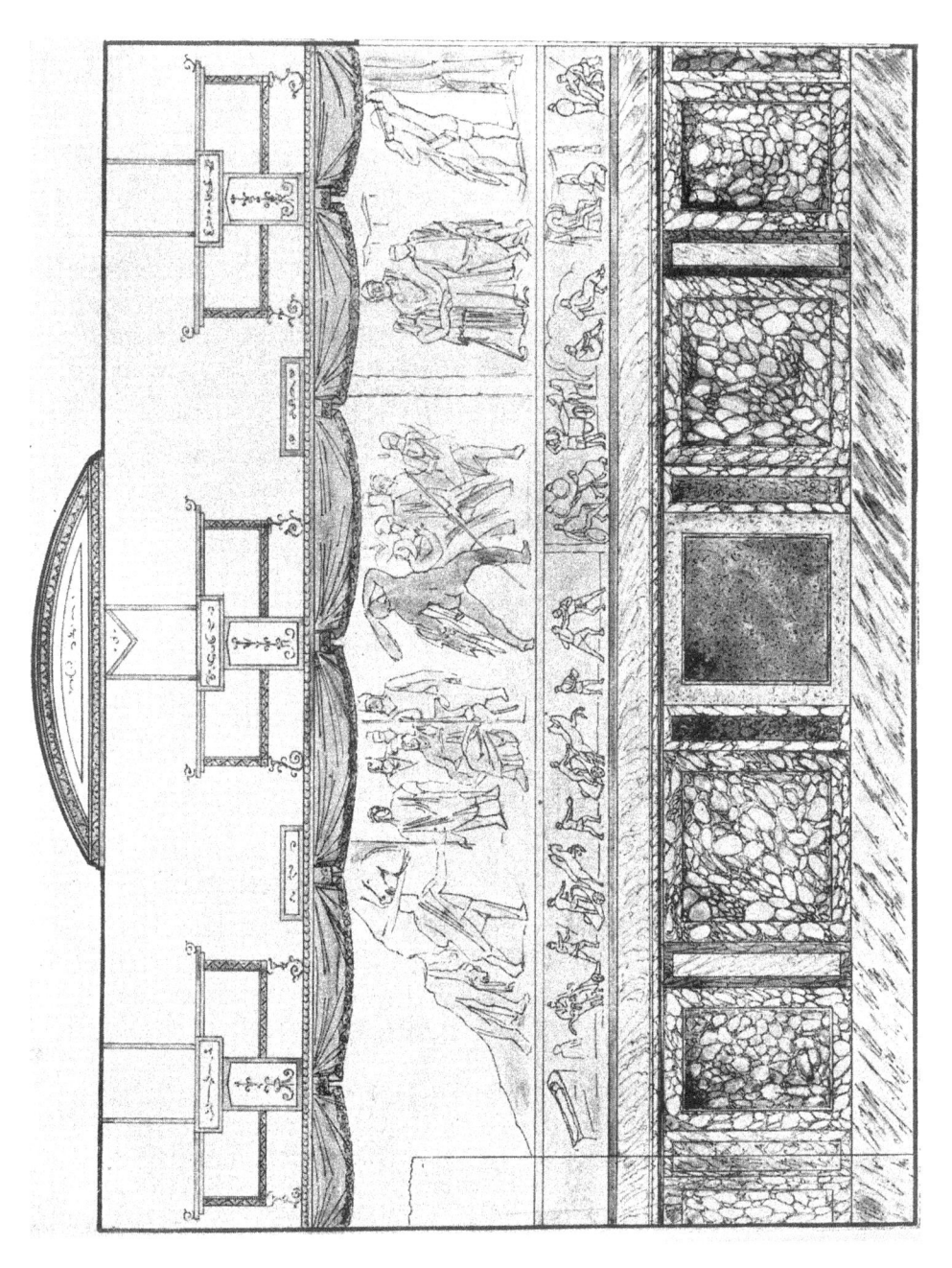

Fig. 27.3 Drawing of the east wall of oecus h in the Casa di Octavius Quartio (Pompeii II.2.2), with the Heracles frieze above, and the smaller Iliadic frieze below. (For the order of scenes, see Fig. 27.21: the lower, Iliadic frieze shows first scenes from the end of the poem – the funerary games of Patroclus at the left, and the embassy to Achilles to the central right; it then switches to earlier episodes – Phoenix beseeching Achilles, and Achilles sulking alone in his tent.)

or 'Iliac tablets'. This collection of twenty-two miniature marble reliefs date (for the most part) from the late first century BC or early first century AD. Because most of the tablets survive as piecemeal fragments, the precise subjects are often difficult to reconstruct; Table 27.1 nonetheless provides a simplified chart on the basis of surviving reliefs and inscriptions.[21]

Of the twenty-two extant reliefs, some fifteen or so clearly engaged with Iliadic and Trojan themes, most of them combining the *Iliad* with other Epic Cyclic subjects. At least one small fragment (10K) deals with a Theban Cycle, and it is just possible that two further puzzling fragments (9D, 10K) originally combined Theban and Trojan subjects.[22] Sometimes the tablets openly declare their purported textual sources. The most famous example comes on the *Tabula Capitolina*, or 'Capitoline tablet' (1A), in Rome (Fig. 27.4). Underneath a central scene of the sack of Troy is a Greek inscription which names its various epic subjects:

> Ἰλίου πέρσις
> κατὰ Στησίχορον.
> Τρωϊκός.
> Ἰλιὰς
> κατὰ Ὅμηρον,
> Αἰθιοπὶς κατὰ Ἀρκτῖ-
> νον τὸν Μιλήσιον,
> Ἰλιὰς ἡ μικρὰ λε-
> γομένη κατὰ
> Λέσχην Πυρραῖον

Iliou persis according to Stesichorus. Trojan. Iliad, according to Homer. Aethiopis, according to Arctinus from Miletus. Ilias parva, according to Lesches from Pyrrha.[23]

The surrounding scenes of the tablet – reproduced here both as a line drawing of the extant fragment (Fig. 27.5), and as a reconstruction of the original whole (Fig. 27.6) – bear out the inscription's promise. At the original centre we see the sack of Troy, explicitly related to the lyric *Iliou persis* of

---

[21] My combined numerical and alphabetical system for referring to the tablets follows those of *IGUR* 4: 93–8, nos. 1612–33. There are three major catalogues: Jahn (1873), Sadurska (1964) and Valenzuela Montenegro (2004); I offer a more detailed analysis of these objects in Squire 2011 (with appendix catalogue on pp. 387–412), and Petrain (2014), which appeared while this book was in progress. For a supposed tablet 23Ky, discovered in Cumae in 2006, see Gasparri (2009) with Squire (2011: 413–16).

[22] For these two tablets, see Valenzuela Montenegro (2004: 192–8, 264–7), along with Squire (2011: 399–400) for cross-references.

[23] For the inscription (*IG* 14.1284), see Mancuso (1909: 670–1); for a more detailed analysis of the tablet and its inscriptions, see Maras (ed.) (1999: 17–67) and Valenzuela Montenegro (2004: 22–149).

Table 27.1 Table detailing the various subjects of the Tabulae Iliacae, based on the identification of their surviving sections; (ins.) refers to extant inscriptions that pertain to non-extant parts of the fragments

	1 A	2 NY	3 C	4 N	5 O	6 B	7 Ti	8 E	9 D	10 K	11 H	12 F	13 Ta	14 G	15 Ber	16 Sa	17 M	18 L	19 J	20 Par	21 Fro	22 Get
Iliad (Books)	• 1, 13–24	• 19–24	• 1–5	• 18	• 18	• 1–9			• 22–24			24	• 22 (+?)	• 14–18	• ?3					• 17–20	• 22–24	
Iliou persis	•	•				•	•	•	•													
Aethiopis	•						•	•	•											•		
Little Iliad	•						• (ins.)															
Odyssey (Books)						• (ins.)					• 10					• ?3–16						
Theban cycle									? (ins.)	•												
Heraclean cycle																			•			
Historical subjects																	•	•				•

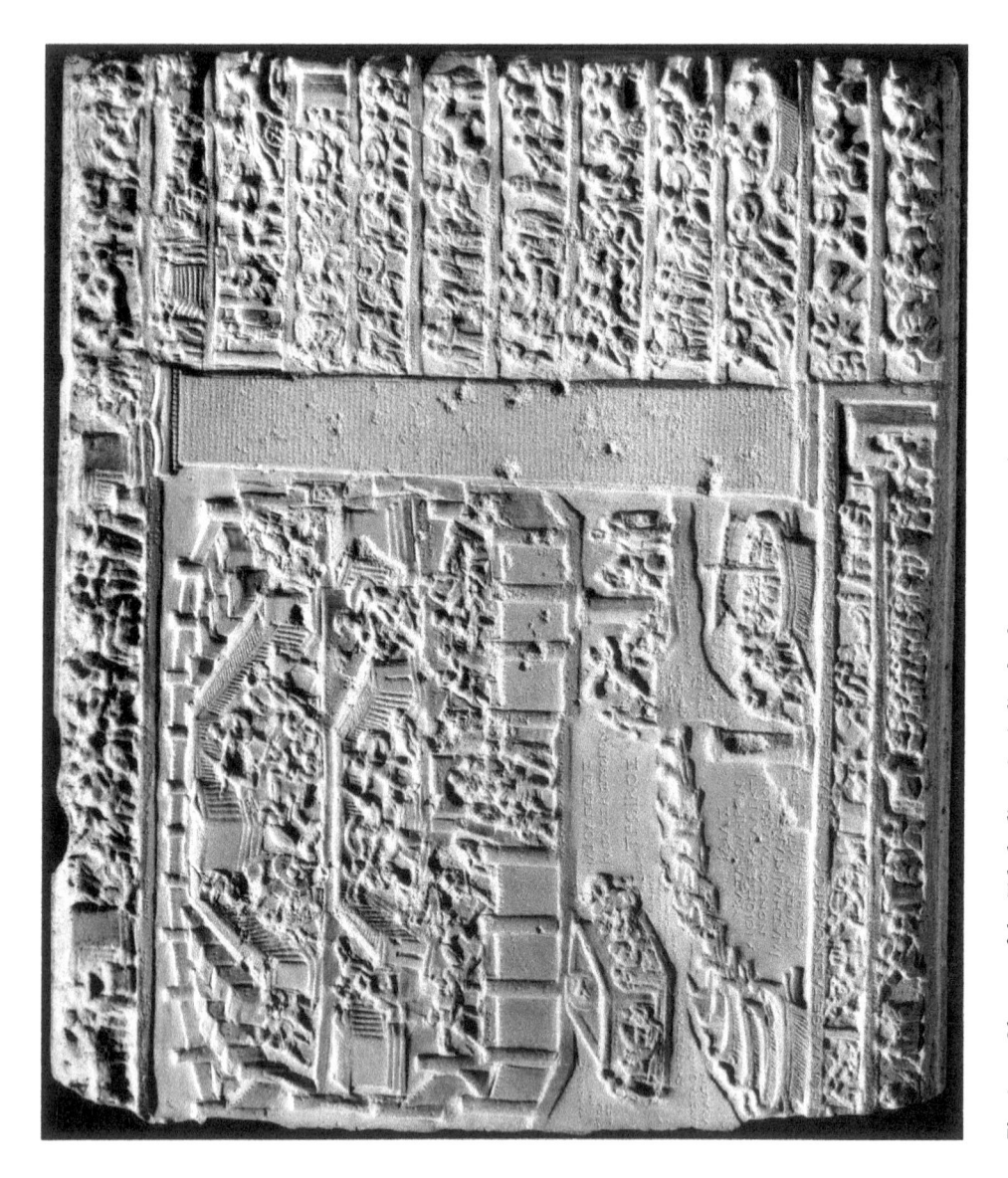

Fig. 27.4 Obverse of the *Tabula Iliaca Capitolina* [1A], as it survives today.

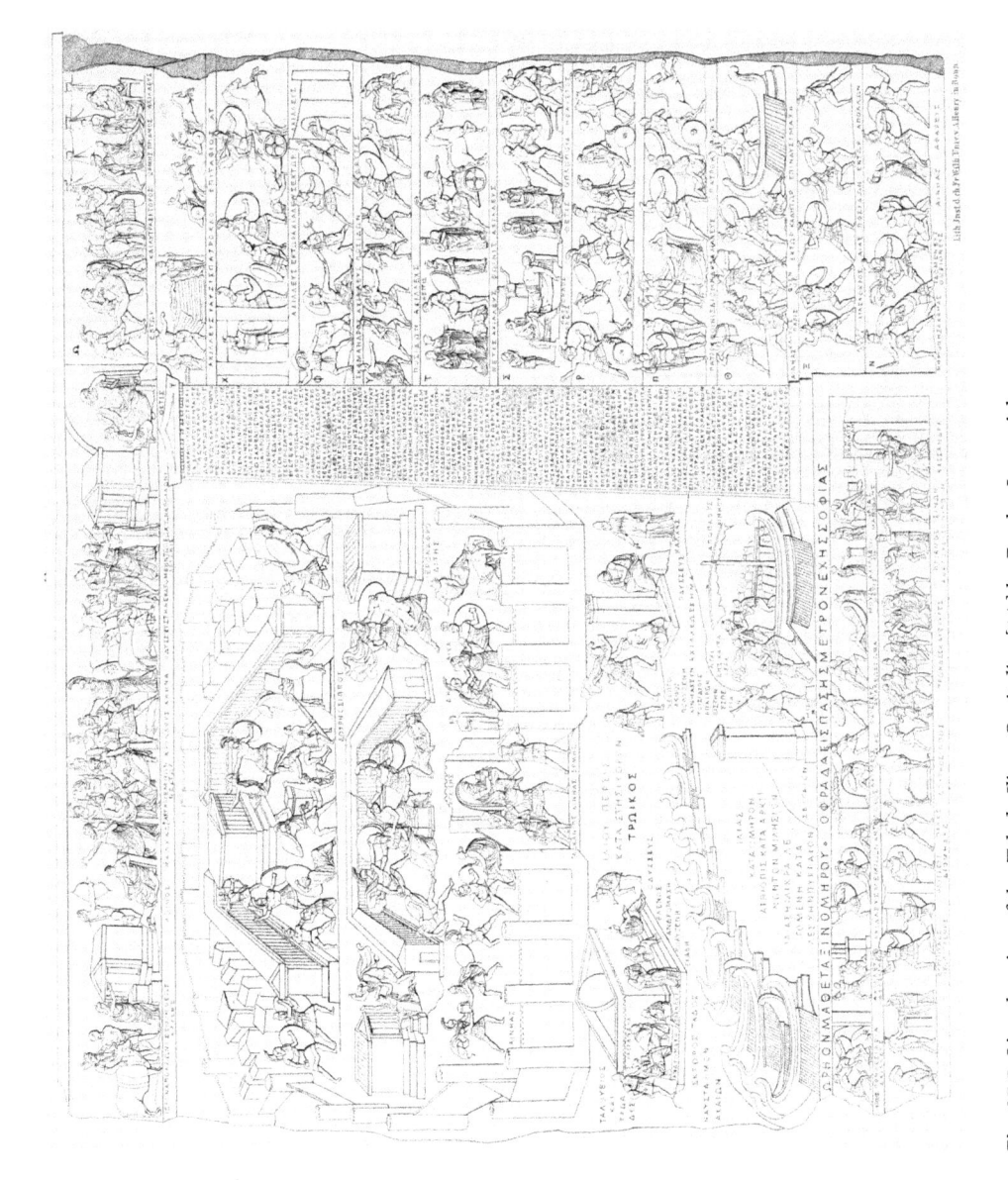

Fig. 27.5 Line drawing of the *Tabula Iliaca Capitolina* [1A] by Feodor Ivanovich.

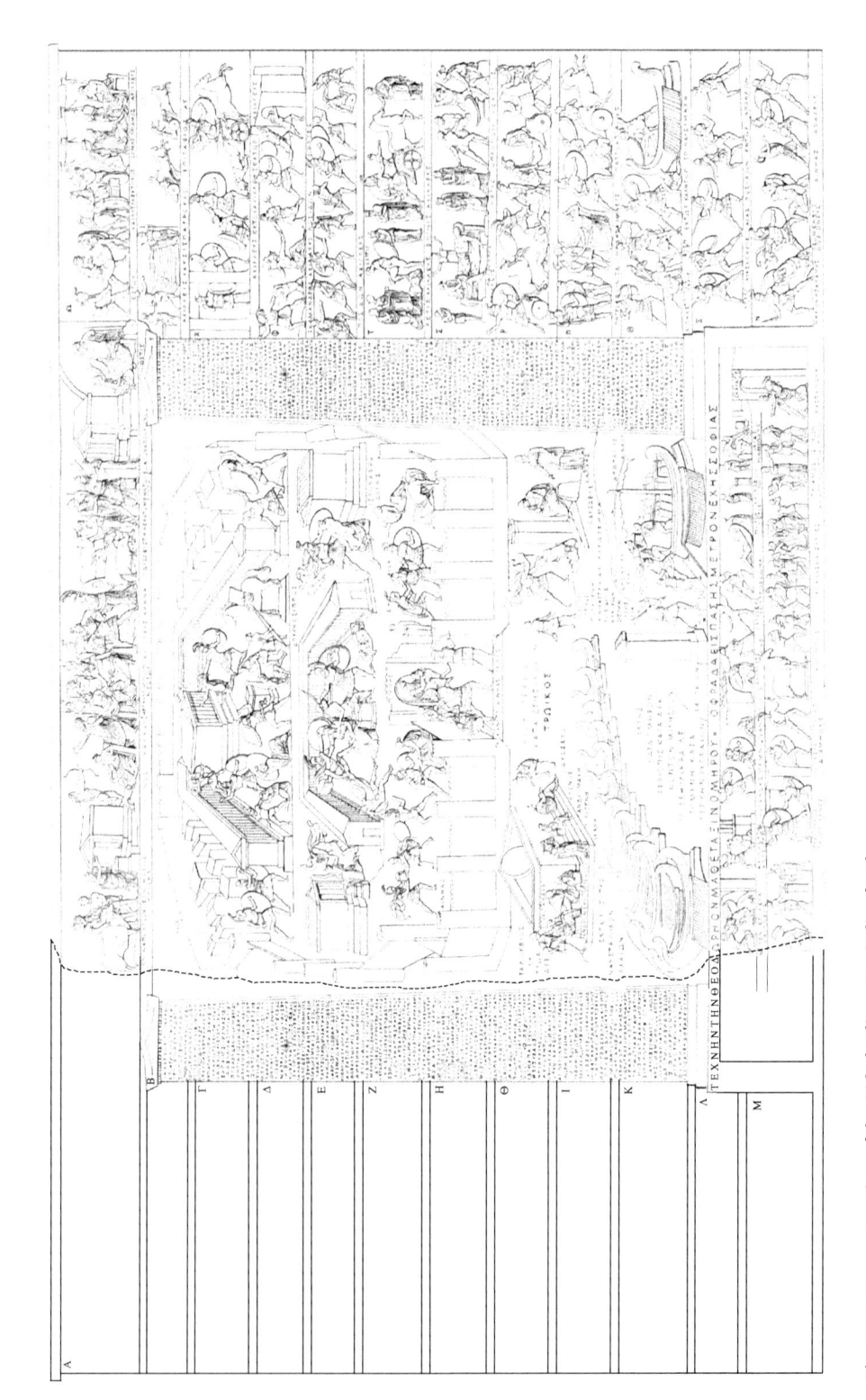

Fig. 27.6 Reconstruction of the *Tabula Iliaca Capitolina* [1A].

Stesichorus;[24] beneath the city itself we find the ships in which the Greeks will return home (the ship to the right is marked out as that of Aeneas, shown departing πρὸς τὴν Ἑσπερίαν, 'to the Western land').[25] These are events to which the *Iliad* of course refers only obliquely, as in Hector's famous speech to Hecuba (*Il.* 6.447–9); here, though, that endpoint is visualized for us all to see, and at the very centre of the composition. As for the individual books of the *Iliad*, these are laid out in lateral friezes on either side of the central scene, with book 1 stretched over the tablet's top (leading directly to the final book at the upper right); each of the twenty-four friezes is labelled with the corresponding letter of the alphabet, from alpha to omega. The two pilasters flanking the centre provide an additional verbal synopsis: while the words proceed from left to right, they are often split across individual lines (only the right-hand pilaster survives, inscribed with 108 lines of text pertaining to books 7 to 24 of the *Iliad*, of which some sixty-nine have words divided between lines). At the bottom of the tablet are two additional friezes, this time relating to events known from the *Aethiopis* and *Ilias parva* (as again declared in the central inscription). With the exception of the band relating to *Iliad* 17, all of the scenes are accompanied by Greek inscriptions which name the characters and sometimes label the action.

Although more fragmentary, other *Tabulae* evidently paraded their Epic Cyclic subjects in related fashion. A tablet in New York (2NY) labels its central scene as an *Iliou persis*, for example, despite leaving the authorship unspecified; similarly, the lost *Tabula Thierry* (7Ti) referred to the *Ilias parva* on its recto and mentioned the *Iliou persis* on a verso inscription. Additional fragments clearly once juxtaposed Iliadic scenes with episodes from other epic poems, even though those poems went unnamed: in total, at least seven tablets presented a central depiction of Troy's sack (1A, 2NY, 3C, 6B, 7Ti, 8E, 9D), the majority framing it with Iliadic scenes; of the twenty-two fragments, moreover, at least three or possibly four seem to have engaged with stories from the *Aethiopis* (1A, 7Ti, 9 D and probably 20Par).[26]

---

[24] The little 'Stesichorean' claim has attracted a large bibliography (see Squire 2011: 18–19, n. 54): the best guide is Scafoglio (2005). Whatever else we make of the reference, we should note the express interest in Stesichorus specifically, and in his *Iliou persis* in particular (see Arrighetti (1996); Finglass (2013a: esp. 6)): while heralded as 'most Homeric' in style ('Longin.' 13.3; see Quint. *Inst.* 10.1.62), Stesichorus was also famous for reconciling epic models with poetic innovation – not least via his genre-crossing lyric metre.

[25] For discussion, see Valenzuela Montenegro (2004: 143–5, 387–91).

[26] For tablet 20Par, see Squire (2011: 187–91). Valenzuela Montenegro (2004: 358–81) offers a much more detailed analysis of these Epic Cyclic engagements.

Vicious circles

Most scholarly responses to our three sets of materials have followed a standard academic pattern: the tendency has been to put together this trio of 'evidence', and then to compare the overarching assemblage with extent textual testimonia. In doing so, the straightforward aim has been to reconstruct the content, structure and themes of lost Epic Cyclic poems. Proclus' summaries of the Cycle have been particularly important here, enabling scholars to chart both correspondences and discrepancies between image and text. Where the two media match, the picture is heralded as an illustration of the poem; when there are differences between image and text, scholars have concocted elaborate explanations to account for the 'corruption' – in terms of textual transmission, for example, or else with reference to artistic 'ignorance' and 'incompetence'.[27]

One example can suffice to demonstrate the methodology: Kopff's analysis of extant sources for the *Aethiopis*. Examining four Homeric bowls, and comparing these with related imagery from the Casa del Criptoportico and the Capitoline *Tabula Iliaca*, Kopff (1983: 57–8) constructs a wholly philological argument to explain divergences: 'our knowledge of the poems of the so-called "epic cycle" is split into two quite distinct and separate, but related traditions', Kopff explains. According to this 'stemmatic' mode of analytical reconstruction, branch 'H' is represented by the Homeric bowls, whereas branch 'C' is reflected first in the *Tabulae* and wall paintings, and then in later mythographic summaries – 'it is derived from an attempt to show the events of the Trojan War as a continuous narrative from its origins to the *Sack of Troy* and the *Returns* of the Greek Heroes'. 'We need both traditions, H and C, to reconstruct the poems of the epic cycle,' Kopff concludes, 'but we must be aware of the different traditions' strengths and weaknesses.'

Many Classicists will no doubt approve of this method and its underlying philological logic. But to my mind there are at least two general problems with such an approach. The first lies in our sheer lack of knowledge about the poems and their literary forms: of the twelve ancient testimonia to the *Aethiopis* cited in Bernabé's *PEG*, for example, no fewer than three are taken from the *Tabulae Iliacae* themselves.[28] Even with Proclus' description of the poem's content, there is a clear danger of

---

[27] For Proclus' text, see Burgess (2001: 177–80), Davies (1989c: 6–8) and West (2013: esp. 1–16).
[28] *PEG* p. 66, nos. 8–10, referring to tablets 1A, 7Ti, and 9D.

circular argumentation.[29] A second problem exacerbates the first: namely, the assumption that images must – or indeed can – faithfully follow the details of the text in the first place. Where we are able to compare Homeric cups, Pompeian wall painting and the *Tabulae Iliacae* with surviving texts – as, for example, with the *Iliad* and the *Odyssey* – it is clear that these objects knowingly disrupt narrative order for their own visual effect: Hellenistic and Roman visual materials change and adapt the stories with which they actively engage.[30]

Where classical scholars have usually looked to visual materials to reconstruct lost Epic Cyclic poems, classical archaeologists have tended to take a different but related tack: they have used these objects to reconstruct a supposed tradition of Alexandrian book illustration. Although there were numerous nineteenth-century philological precursors (foremost among them, perhaps, Wilamowitz-Moellendorff), Weitzmann proved the most influential exponent of this theory, concluding in 1959 that 'the κύκλος ἐπικός was prolifically illustrated in its entirety and that it took a pre-eminent position among the illustrated epic poems'.[31] Analysing the Homeric bowls, Pompeian paintings and *Tabulae Iliacae*, Weitzmann argued that each medium reflected the iconographic models of Hellenistic illustrated papyri. Once again, Weitzmann adopted a wholly philological interpretive mode: when faced with a discrepancy between the images of the *Ilias parva* on the Homeric bowls and Capitoline Iliac tablet, for example, Weitzmann concluded in favour of different archetypal 'recensions', each giving rise to its own iconographic derivatives.[32]

---

[29] As Sistakou (2008: 19) writes, 'it should always be borne in mind that the picture we have of the Epic Cycle is very much the result of multiple intermediaries'; I would add that this holds especially true when it comes to pictures themselves. Foley (1999b: 105) is also right to criticize related assumptions about these poems as 'texts', even after the poems were written down: 'Based on models developed in the nineteenth century, this Epic Cycle reconstructs the past anachronistically by appeal to unexamined – and distinctively post-Gutenberg – assumptions about texts, transmission, influence, and reception.' More sanguine about the problems of reconstruction is West (2013: esp. 51–54), examining literary testimonia alongside the archaeological evidence, albeit focusing more on the tablets' epigraphy than on their iconography, and relying in part on Feodor Ivanovich's nineteenth-century drawing of the *Tabula Capitolina* (130–2, 165–6).

[30] For two examples from among the *Tabulae Iliacae*, see e.g. Squire (2011: 143–5) on the depiction of *Il*. 24.448–71 and ibid. 165–6 (on scenes from *Il*. 15).

[31] Weitzmann (1959: 31–62, quotation from p. 62); cf. idem (1947: 37–46, esp. p. 44).

[32] Compare e.g. Weitzmann (1959: 46–8). Although four Homeric bowls depict the death of Priam (Sinn 1979: 94–6, nos. MB 27–30), this scene is not found in the corresponding *Ilias parva* frieze of the *Tabula Capitolina*: in Weitzmann's view, 'one can only surmise that, in analogy to what has been said about the illustrations of Homer's *Iliad* and the *Aethiopis*,

This is not the place to revisit Weitzmann's 'illustration' hypothesis.[33] Suffice it to say, perhaps, that his is an argument from silence: there is no evidence for Hellenistic papyri juxtaposing the Homeric poems with cycles of imagery, and no extant papyrus fragment can securely be associated with the *Aethiopis*, *Ilias parva* and *Iliou persis* (never mind any 'illustrated' example).[34] The earliest examples of literary texts complete with painted miniatures are all much later in date, and they appear to respond to a specific cultural and intellectual development within later antiquity. To talk of ancient 'illustrations' is therefore – in my view – to talk in anachronistically modern terms.

Rather than match up our Hellenistic and Roman material case studies with posthumous descriptions of the lost Epic Cyclic poems, or indeed use them to reconstruct a hypothetical tradition of book illustration, the remainder of this chapter attempts something different. Comparing Hellenistic and Roman images with the sorts of literary critical responses found in contemporary texts, my aim is to show how artists, like poets, could turn to Epic Cyclic stories to reflect upon the narrative unity of the 'Epic Cycle' itself. As we shall see, the very notion that these poems amount to a *kyklos* ('circle') is important here. Hellenistic artists, like their poetic counterparts, seem to have been interested in the figure of the circle as a means not only of uniting different subjects, but also of raising questions about their structural and narratological organization: by engaging with the Epic Cycle, and differently figuring that 'circle' in their figurative compositions, these material objects and paintings invited viewers to think critically about the underlying trope, and in all sorts of provocative and creative ways.

EPIC AS CYCLE

Before proceeding, we should perhaps say something more about this term 'Epic Cycle' (*kyklos epikos*) and its derivation. As others in this volume have explored, Aristotle provides the earliest testimony to the metaphor. Aristotle uses the term in a figurative manner within a discussion about

---

the bowls represent also in this case a recension different from that of the Iliac tablets' (Weitzmann 1959: 47).

[33] For some preliminary comments, see Squire (2009: 122–39 and 2011: 127–96, esp. 129–48). Weitzmann's thesis still has its loyal supporters, especially with reference to the materials examined in this chapter (e.g. Reinhardt 2008).

[34] As West (2013: 47) rightly reminds us, 'it is striking that not a single papyrus fragment of any of the Cyclic poems has yet been identified'.

whether or not ἡ Ὁμήρου ποίησις σχῆμα διὰ τοῦ κύκλου ('Homeric poetry is a figure because it forms a circle', *Soph. Elench.* 171a = *Cyclus epicus PEG* 8).[35] What makes the passage especially puzzling is the fact that *kyklos* is used not in association with a larger collection of epic poems, but rather to describe the poems of Homer specifically. Of course, Aristotle knew the poems that subsequent ancient and modern scholars group together under the 'Cyclic' banner; indeed, his *Poetics* discusses the superiority of Homeric epic outright – comparing the *Iliad* and *Odyssey* with self-confessed non-Homeric poems like the *Cypria* and *Ilias parva*. But while Aristotle was evidently familiar with these poems individually, he does not mention any sort of conjoined collective. The 'cyclic' figure is reserved for Homer alone.[36]

Within two centuries of Aristotle's writing something appears to have changed. By around the third century BC or so, it seems to have become standard to refer to a self-contained band or 'ring' of epic poems. Whatever the earlier archaic/classical oral-cum-textual tradition, this particular development surely reflects a Hellenistic editorial intervention, whereby a series of individual poems were brought together and compared as part of a larger collective.[37] Among second-century scholars and critics, the noun *kyklos* and the adverb *kyklikōs* seem to have become the *lingua franca* for referring to these texts: we find them among the likes of Aristarchus and the scholiasts,[38] for example, as well as in Callimachus' programmatic dismissal of 'the Cyclic' *tout court* (*AP* 12.43 = *ep.* 28.1 Pf. = *HE* 2).[39] When

---

[35] See Pfeiffer (1968: 73) and Davies (1986: 94–5). Nagy (1996b: 38, 89–91) considers the metaphor to be much older, stemming from 'the ancient pre-Aristotelian tradition of applying the metaphor of cycle to the sum total of epic poetry, as if all of it were composed by Homer' (p. 38).

[36] For discussion and further references, see Sistakou (2008: 11–13) and Introduction, above in this volume, pp. 1–7, also for Aristotle's image of epic as 'circle' in *Anal. Post.* 77b34 = *Cyclus epicus PEG* T 1.

[37] See Sistakou (2008: 25: 'both the compilation of the Epic Cycle and its systematic comparison with the Homeric epics was the work of Hellenistic philology'); compare also West (1983: 129; 2012: 21–6, associating the development with an epitome by Phyallos, c. 350–320 BC); Burgess (1996; 2001: 12–33, esp. 15–16); Davies (1989c: 1–2). For a masterful review of scholarly attempts to date the poems and trace their textual traditions, see Davies (1989a; 1989c: 2–5). Davies is surely right to conclude that 'the *Iliad* and the *Odyssey* would appear to have been preserved in written texts earlier than the other poems of the Epic Cycle' so that 'by the time they took on the stable and permanent form of which we possess fragmentary knowledge, they would have been accurately termed post-Homeric' (1989c: 5).

[38] See *PEG* pp. 7–8, 30–5, with discussion in Severyns (1928: 155–9); Pfeiffer (1968: 227–31); Davies (1986: 95); and Cameron (1995: 396). For the connotations of the scholastic 'Cyclic' label, serving as a convenient 'other pole of archaic epic' among Hellenistic critics, see Fantuzzi, above in this volume, p. 425.

[39] On Callimachus' epigram, and the precise meaning of τὸ ποίημα τὸ κυκλικὸν, see especially Blumenthal (1978) and Cameron (1995: 387–402). As Fantuzzi reminds us (above, in this

Athenaeus talks of the 'Epic Cycle' specifically, he is certainly drawing upon that scholastic literary critical tradition (*Deipn.* 7.5). According to one suggested reading (albeit, it has to be said, an optimistic one at best), we even find the term paraded on the verso of one of the *Tabulae Iliacae* themselves.[40]

Much later, when John Philoponus wrote his sixth-century commentary on Aristotle's *Posterior Analytics*, the idea of epic as 'circle' seems to have been so widespread as to elicit express discussion as to why 'both epic and a geometrical figure are called 'circle'' (λέγοιτο κύκλος καὶ τὰ ἔπη καὶ τὸ σχῆμα).[41] Many things (and not just figurative shapes) are labelled 'circles', as the commentary later puts it – hence the idea of a 'so-called "rounded" education' (τὰ ἐγκύκλια λεγόμενα μαθήματα), one which includes everything within its circumscribing embrace. Responding to Aristotle's question as to whether 'epics are circles' in the first book's twelfth chapter (*Post. Anal.* 77b34), Philoponus notes that the same word has been used to delineate both epic and geometric figure: 'concerning the epic circle', Philoponus continues, 'some have written about how many poets there were, what each of them wrote, how many verses were contained in each poem and their order, as well as about which one a person needs to learn first, which second, and so on'.[42]

In their introduction to this book, the editors have related this new critical vocabulary to a multi-stage development in the Epic Cycle's ancient evolution. They have also offered some important comments about the various associations at stake – relating this *kyklos* to a perceived unity of compositional form, for example, a supposed ring formation, as well as to the tropes of cyclic completion, the Homeric pivot, and the hypothetical perfection of the circle as geometrical unit. As a 'ring' or 'circle', the term

---

volume, p. 418), the epigram's resounding allusions to Theognis establish it as 'a new piece of archaic elegy'. At the same time, the third verse's ensuing reference to the promiscuous lover as περίφοιτος – 'roaming around in a circle' (developing the Theognian περίδρομος) – appears to develop the specifically anti-cyclical imagery of Callimachus' opening invective (*pace* Cameron 1995: 393–9).

[40] For the supposed inscription on the reverse of tablet 10K (τὸν κύκλ[ον), see *IG* 14.1292; Sadurska (1964: 60); *Cyclus epicus PEG* T 2; Valenzuela Montenegro 2004: 265). Petrain (2010: 52) is probably right to challenge the reading. For references to other Hellenistic 'cyclic' projects, see West (2013: 1) on a citharode named Menekles, credited with performing a Cretan narrative 'cycle' (*Inscr. Cret.* 1.280), and Dionysius of Samos' Κύκλος ἱστορικός (*FgrHist* 15), 'presumably modelled on Κύκλος ἐπικός'.

[41] See Wallies (ed.) (1909: 155.5–6), with McKirahan (2012: 55). I am grateful to Marco Fantuzzi for alerting me to this fascinating reference.

[42] Wallies (ed.) (1909: 157.11–14): γεγράφασι γοῦν τινες περὶ τοῦ κύκλου ἀναγράφοντες πόσοι τε ποιηταὶ γεγόνασι καὶ τί ἕκαστος ἔγραψε καὶ πόσοι στίχοι ἑκάστου ποιήματος καὶ τὴν τούτων τάξιν, τίνα τε πρῶτα δεῖ μανθάνειν καὶ δεύτερα καὶ ἐφεξῆς. My translation adapts that of McKirahan (2012: 57).

kyklos is as old as Homeric poetry itself (referring, for instance, to the concentric rings of brass around Agamemnon's shield at *Il.* 11.33). But by at least the classical period, the term had taken on a broader cosmological sense, describing 'any natural movement that recurs periodically: time, the motion of the planets, the change of seasons of the succession of birth and death'.[43] Through a similar process of semantic extension, the word came to encompass a range of additional rhetorical nuances, both positive and negative alike. For Hermogenes (admittedly writing much later), *kyklos* came closest to what we today label 'ring-composition', describing the use of repeated words, rhythms or concepts that bound together the beginning and end of a verbal unit.[44] As an emblem of geometrical perfection, the circle served to define the 'well-rounded' spoken or written form.[45] And yet not everything 'circular' was worthy of praise: the same figure could also be used to refer to writers who 'go round in circles', running around a theme rather than sticking to a linear progression or argument.[46]

We shall perhaps never know where, when or why this descriptive 'cyclic' label was chosen to describe a 'set' of epic poems. But it is at least plausible that the delineation *kyklos epikos* came to reflect (and indeed helped construct) some of the various positive and negative ideas about non-Homeric epic poetry already mentioned. As self-confessed 'circle', the *kyklos epikos* was both all-encompassing and marginal at the same time. On the one hand, it could imply a sort of holistic, integrated, systematic completeness (in line with Ovid's idea of the *carmen perpetuum*).[47] On the other, it could imply a kind of peripheral fringe – a series of lesser poems orbiting around

---

[43] Quotation from Sistakou (2008: 4).

[44] See Hermogenes, *De inventione* 4.8 (=Rabe 1913 = 196), where the analysis of ring-composition (which opens and closes with the word *kyklos*) itself practises what it preaches: κύκλος ἐστὶ τὸ ἀφ' ὧν ἂν ἄρξηταί τις ὀνομάτων ἢ ῥημάτων εἰς τὰ αὐτὰ καταλήγειν δύνασθαι πάλιν· τοῦτο γάρ ἐστιν ὁ κύκλος ('the *kyklos* occurs whenever one can conclude with the same noun or verb with which he begins'). For further discussion, see Nünlist (2009b: 319–20).

[45] On the virtues of 'rounded' (στρογγύλος/ *rotundus*) expression, see Brink (1963) ad Hor. *Ars poet.* 323 (*ingenium... ore rotundo*), with further references.

[46] Sistakou (2008: 4 n. 14) cites Arist. *Rh.* 1415b (slaves 'never answer questions directly but go all round them' (οὐ τὰ ἐρωτώμενα λέγουσιν ἀλλὰ τὰ κύκλωι), and indulge in preambles'), and compares e.g. Dion. Hal. *Dem.* 19.6. The underlying rhetoric of circularity seems to have persisted well into Roman times. Glossing Horace's mention of 'a cyclic poet' (*scriptor cyclicus*) at *Ars poet.* 136, one scholiast commented upon the metaphor explicitly, likening him to 'one who passes around his poems like one circling round the forum' or to 'those who move from one city to the other performing': *Cyclicus poeta est... uel qui carmina sua circumfert quasi circumforaneus... Aliter: cyclici dicuntur poetae, qui ciuitates circummeant recitantes* (*Cyclus epicus PEG* T 25; no. 25).

[47] For Ovid's phrase, see especially Herter (1948: 141–8); Otis (1970: 45–90); Cameron (1995: 359–61); and van Tress (2004: 24–71).

a central core (which was in turn associated with Homer). When Photius sums up Proclus' evaluation of the self-confessed 'Epic Cycle', the image arguably implies the positive and the negative connotations alike. If it suggested a sense of completeness (a linear sort of progression – from the union of Uranus and Gaea all the way through to the wanderings of Odysseus), it also implied a sort of peripheral circumlocution, encompassing poems 'of interest to most not for their worth but for the sequentiality of events (*akolouthia tōn pragmatōn*)', 319a30.[48]

That there was a literary critical dimension to this delineation of the 'Epic Circle' is clear from the programmatic responses of Hellenistic poets. Whether responding to it positively or negatively, Hellenistic authors evidently found the figure of the Cycle useful for negotiating their own poetic agendas. Callimachus provides the most famous example. While, as we have said, one of Callimachus' epigrams rallied against *to poiēma to kyklikon*,[49] the poet's reply to the Telchines returns to the same essential dismissal of narrative linearity and thematic unity when he responds to those criticising him for 'not [accomplishing] one single continuous poem on kings or heroes in many thousands of verses' (1.3–4 Pf.).[50] Already by the third century, the critical language for theorizing epic poetry appears bound up with the figurative metaphor of circle.

THE *TAXIS* OF THE *TABULAE ILIACAE*

This poetological backdrop seems important for making sense of Hellenistic and Roman visual engagements with epic. To demonstrate the point, let me return first to the *Tabulae Iliacae*, and to the *Tabula Capitolina* in particular (Figs. 27.4–6). As we have said, the tablet brings together a series of different Greek epic poems, offering an 'all-in-one' panoramic guide to their themes and subjects.[51] A programmatic elegiac couplet, inscribed underneath the

---

[48] See Introduction, above in this volume, pp. 9, 19, 32.
[49] Callim. *Ep.* 28.1 Pf. (see above, n. 39).
[50] The *Aetia* prologue has attracted a very substantial bibliography, but there are two excellent guides in Acosta-Hughes and Stephens (2002) and Fantuzzi and Hunter (2004: 66–76). On the phrase ἓν ἄεισμα διηνεκές ('one single continuous poem') specifically, see Hunter (1993: 190–5: 'With tongue firmly in cheek, Callimachus suggests that his poem is both and neither', p. 193), along with Asper (1997: 217–24) and Harder (2012: ii.25–6, ad loc.); for the view that Callimachus' polemic pertains to elegy rather than epic, see Cameron 1995: 339–61. For other Hellenistic responses, see especially Rengakos (2004), discussing the Aristotelian backdrop on pp. 287–90, and relating this to Apollonius' *Argonautica* ('Apollonios hat also eine auch äußerlich abgerundete Form, die als "kyklisch" bezeichnet werden konnte, geflissentlich gesucht', p. 301).
[51] As such, the tablet might be compared with a project like Ps.-Apollodorus' *Bibliotheca*. As an epigram attributed to Apollodorus (and preserved by Photius) puts it, the *Bibliotheca* brought

two pilasters in the lower frame, draws out that agenda explicitly. Although it makes no reference to a 'cycle', the epigram does flag an associated idea of arrangement:

[τέχνην τὴν Θεοδ]ώρηον μάθε τάξιν Ὁμήρου
ὄφρα δαεὶς πάσης μέτρον ἔχηις σοφίας.

Understand the Theodorean *technē* so that, knowing the order of Homer, you may have the measure of all wisdom.

Nineteenth-century scholars took the tablet's inscription at its word: they supposed that the object functioned as a sort of 'schoolboy crib' – an elaborate learning aid for teaching the mythology of the Trojan War.[52] This seems most unlikely. The various literary allusions, not to mention the knowing plays on the combined language of artistic and literary criticism (*technē, metron, sophia*), leave little doubt about the programmatic sophistication of both the inscribed epigram and epigraphic object.[53]

There is much to say about this epigram and its relationship with another fragmentary couplet inscribed on a tablet in New York (tablet 2NY). For our purposes, though, I limit discussion to the inscription's delineation of the *taxis Homērou* ('order of Homer').[54] As we have said, the other inscriptions on the Capitoline tablet make explicit reference not only to the Homeric *Iliad*, but also to the *Iliou persis*, *Aethiopis* and *Ilias parva* (each named along with its respective author). In this programmatic elegiac distich, however, all other poetic sources have been eclipsed by the Homeric: Homer is made to exert the greatest gravitational pull.

No less intriguing is the talk of *taxis* in the first place.[55] This is hardly a neutral delineation. Rather, the epigram's very language of linear 'order'

---

together all manner of genres (Homer, elegy, tragedy, lyric, even the κυκλικῶν... πολύθρουν στίχον, 'clamorous verse of the Cyclic poets') so that the reader now required only one volume (εἰς ἐμὲ δ' ἀθρῶν / εὑρήσεις ἐν ἐμοὶ πάνθ' ὅσα κόσμος ἔχει, 'look at me: in me you will find every story in the world'); for discussion, see Cameron (1995: 397–8).

[52] See Squire (2011: 70–1). The interpretation was premised on a spurious reconstruction of the hexameter, corrected by Mancuso (1909: 729–30 [ὦ φίλε παῖ, Θεοδ]ώρηον μάθε τάξιν Ὁμήρου...).

[53] For my own views, see Squire (2010: 72–7; 2011: 102–21, and compare ibid. 283–302 on the significance of the 'Theodorean' name); cf. also Petrain (2012: 615–19; 2014: 49–68). One might contrast the still prevalent view that the tablets delight in 'the obvious, the trivial and the false' (Horsfall 1979b: 46), serving as 'tawdry gewgaws intended to provide the illusion of sophistication for those who had none' (McLeod 1985: 164–5).

[54] The formulation is deeply ambiguous, all the more so given the lack of definite article: the genitive could be read in both 'subjective' and 'objective' senses, referring at once to Homer's original 'order', as well as to an order imposed on Homeric poetry (not least by the object in hand).

[55] I offer a more detailed discussion of the rhetorical significance of the term *taxis* (Latin *ordo*) in Squire (2014).

or 'arrangement' frames responses to the tablet in terms of rhetorical-cum-poetological debates about the most effective modes of narrative (*diēgēsis*).[56] Literary critical concerns with *taxis* hark back at least to Aristotle, who famously compared the *taxis* of a poem to that of a living creature in the seventh chapter of his *Poetics* (1450b34–1451a6).[57] But the concept remained an important one among subsequent rhetoricians and scholiasts, used above all for reflecting upon the unity of a text or speech: *taxis* provided a means of theorizing the relationship between the order of events and the order in which events were narrated.[58]

Questions of *taxis* were also critical to the project of poetic criticism, and a habitual concern among commentators upon Homer. Again and again, we find Homer being praised for having inverted the 'natural order' of the events he describes. Instead of narrating events in real time, according to their chronological sequence (*kata taxin*), Homer was celebrated for pioneering a system of *analepses* and *prolepses* that defied 'real' time, according to a so-called 'anastrophic' narrative mode (*ex anastrophēs*).[59] Roman critics were no less interested in this aspect of Homeric narrative, translating Greek concepts of *taxis* into the Roman language of *ordo*.[60] When Horace came to comment on the arrangement of the *Iliad* in his *Ars Poetica*, it seems to have been almost cliché to comment on the *Iliad*'s opening *in medias res*; similarly, Greek and Roman rhetoricians likewise had recourse to Homeric paradigms in order to explain the different narratological options open to an orator.[61]

Even more significantly, I think, the language of *taxis* provided a way of pitching Homeric poetry against that of the Epic Cycle at large. Where

---

[56] My own views have learned especially from Meijering (1987: 138–48); Hunter (2008: 127–40); Nünlist (2009a: 65–9; 2009b: 69–93, esp. 87–92); compare also Hunter (2009: esp. 52–5), nicely demonstrating how Dio's eleventh ('Trojan') *Oration* has recourse to the critical language of Homeric *taxis* only to turn it on its head...

[57] For discussion (and further bibliography), see Meijering (1987: 138–9), who notes that 'even before Aristotle's days, rhetoricians had been dealing with the parts of a speech, τὰ μέρη τοῦ λόγου, under the heading of τάξις' (138); cf. Purves (2010: 24–32); Squire (2011: 250–3).

[58] See Meijering (1987: 138–42): 'τάξις should arrange the constituents of a text to a harmonious whole suited to its purpose' (142); later rhetoricians would sometimes label this order οἰκονομία, crafted to suit the rhetorical purpose of persuasion (see Nünlist 2009b: 24–5).

[59] See especially Meijering (1987: 146–8), citing *inter alia* Ps.-Plut. *Vit. Hom.* 162. For ancient discussions of Homer's 'anastrophic' narratological mode, see the numerous passages cited by Nünlist (2009b: 89 n. 52).

[60] For rhetorical discussions of *ordo*, see Meijering (1987: 140–1, citing e.g. *Ad Herenn.* 3.16; Cic. *de orat.* 2.307; Sulp. Vict. 14), and above all Lausberg (1998: 209–214 nos. 443–452).

[61] On Hor. *Ars poet.* 146–50, see e.g. Meijering (1987: 146); on the *ordo* of the *Iliad* specifically, cf. Quint. 7.10.11, and compare Theon's use of the *Odyssey* in outlining the various narratological strategies open to an orator (Patillon and Bolognesi (eds.) (1997: 48–9)).

Homer succeeded in developing the most effective means of ordering events – or so the common critical trope ran – other epic poets were deemed much more pedestrian in their modes of narrative organisation. Once again, Aristotle provides the earliest critical reflection on the trope. According to the *Poetics*, Homer's inspired superiority in relation to other poets (θεσπέσιος... παρὰ τοὺς ἄλλους) can be seen in the selectiveness of his plots, which nonetheless incorporate other stories into their overarching structure. This is a feature of the *Iliad* and *Odyssey* which Aristotle explicitly contrasts with the *Cypria* and *Ilias parva*. Unlike the poems of Homer, these lesser epics were said to centre around a 'single figure and single period and hence a single action of many parts' (περὶ ἕνα χρόνον καὶ μίαν πρᾶξιν πολυμερῆ): the result, Aristotle continues, is that a single tragedy, 'or at most two', can be made from the poems of Homer, whereas 'many can be made from the *Cypria*, and more than eight from the *Ilias parva*' (1459a30–7).[62]

A much-cited scholiast takes up the same essential trope, developing it in light of the Homeric 'Catalogue of Ships':[63]

> The poet is admirable: he omits no part of the story, but narrates all events at the appropriate moment in inverse order – the strife of the goddesses, the seizure of Helen, the death of Achilles. For chronological narrative (κατὰ τάξιν) is typical of later epic poets and of historians and lacks grandeur.[64]

Although this particular scholiast compares Homer with 'more recent' poets rather than with 'Cyclic' poets specifically, other contemporary commentators framed their tirades in expressly 'cyclic' terms. Take a famous epigram by Pollianus (penned in the first or second century AD), responding to Callimachus' own dismissal of the 'Cycle' *tout court*:[65] 'I hate these cyclic poets with their declarations of "and then... and then" (αὐτὰρ ἔπειτα), stealing the epic verses of others.'[66] For Pollianus, writing in the first or second century AD, the Cyclic poems are once again defined by their narrative mode, whereby individual episodes are strung together in an endless succession (hence their use of the phrase *autar epeita*). Where Homer was celebrated for his anachronic plots – breaking the natural sequence of events – Cyclic poets are understood to have proceeded from one episode to the next

---

[62] For Aristotle's critique of Homer and other epic poets, see Heath (1989: 38–55), along with Fantuzzi, above in this volume, pp. 412–14.

[63] See Erbse (ed.) (1969–88:1: 288 (=Σ b *Il.* 2.494–877)). For discussion and further parallels, see e.g. Sistakou (2008: 20); Nünlist (2009a: 67–8; 2009b: 88–9).

[64] For discussion and the Greek text, see Fantuzzi, above in this volume, pp. 414–16.

[65] *AP* 11.130.1–2, helpfully discussed by Cameron (1995: 396–9, commenting on the textual problems of the first line).

[66] For discussion and the Greek text, see Fantuzzi, above in this volume, pp. 427–8.

in simple linear progression. By the time Virgil was writing his *Aeneid*, this critical language of *taxis* could itself be appropriated within epic's own self-conscious retelling of epic events. Virgil famously tells how Aeneas surveyed a variety of battle scenes amid the decoration of the Carthaginian Temple of Juno at *Aen.* 1.441–93, even recognizing himself among the 'Trojan battles laid out in order' (*Iliacas ex ordine pugnas, Aen.* 1.456). In putting the scenes together, as part of a set-piece *ekphrasis* which moves self-consciously from epic text to image and back again, Aeneas is made to reconstruct an 'order' that is both like and unlike that of the larger inherited cycle.[67]

This critical idea of epic *taxis* was no less important to the *Tabulae Iliacae*. Explicitly heralded in the *Tabula Capitolina*'s programmatic inscription, *taxis* proves fundamental to the object's pictorial–poetic games. Like other *Tabulae*, the Captitoline tablet might be said to comprise a material counterpart to the 'Trojan battles laid out in order' in Virgil's Carthaginian ecphrastic description. Of course, *taxis* and *ordo* denote a linear sort of seriality quite distinct from the circular arrangement implied in the figure of *kyklos*. While juxtaposing the events of Homeric epic alongside those drawn from a larger cycle of epic stories, however, the tablet raises similar questions about its own linear-cum-circular rationale: although the individual books of the *Iliad* are laid out in individual 'rank and file' rows (just as the *Aethiopis* and *Ilias parva* occupy their own independent friezes in the lower centre), the tablet monumentalizes a programme of linear progression only to raise questions about underlying cyclical connections.

Despite its rectilinear shape, the *Tabula Capitolina* can be interpreted in a series of circular ways. For one thing, we might observe how the figure of the circle is emblazoned in the mural *kyklos* surrounding the city of Troy at the heart of the tablet. Still more revealingly, perhaps, we find – just below that ring-fenced Trojan citadel, after the inscribed reference to Stesichorus (but before the list of other poetic sources) – the single word ΤΡΩΙΚΟΣ ('Trojan'): the adjective is inscribed in large letters, leaving its precise referent unspecified.[68] Floating in the lower centre of the original tablet, the word acts as a sort of pivot for the scenes inscribed around it: the subjects of this tablet are said to be not just Iliadic, but 'Trojan' in the

---

[67] The bibliography on the Virgilian passage is extensive, but see in particular Johnson (1976: 99–105); Laird (1996: 87–94); Putnam (1998a: 23–54). I return to it in Squire (2014: 387–95). For the parallels with the talk of *taxis* on the *Tabulae Iliacae*, see Leach (1988: 321); Barchiesi (1994: 275); La Penna (2000: 3–4).

[68] For the various scholarly attempts to explain the adjective, see Petrain (2010: 51–3), concluding that 'the artisan of the *Capitolina* may purposefully have left the adjective's referent undetermined' (Petrain 2010: 53; cf. Squire 2011: 253).

broadest sense. Most significant of all, I think, is the decision to arrange the Iliadic scenes so as to form a 'ring' of their own. Figuratively speaking, it is the *Iliad* that is here moved to the sidelines, while the sack of Troy takes centre stage: the Epic Cycle does not orbit around the *Iliad*, but rather the individual Iliadic friezes run rings around an all-encompassing 'Trojan' subject. And yet, for all the linear sequentiality of each individual frieze, running from left to right, the bands are nonetheless crafted to form a circular unit.

When perceived from this angle, the tablet's *taxis* appears wholly ambiguous. The arrangement may at first appear straightforward, running in numbered sequence from alpha to omega:[69] according to this view, the friezes proceed in anticlockwise order from the upper top-left corner, moving first down, and then up, ending at the top right-hand side (with the *Aethiopis* and *Ilias parva* stretched in between) (Fig. 27.7). But the fact that the first book of the *Iliad* extends over the top of the composition rather complicates matters, enabling viewers – as the twenty-fourth chapter of Aristotle's *Poetics* prescribes – quite literally 'to see together (συνορᾶσθαι) the beginning and the end together'.[70] The organization has the effect of turning the first and last Iliadic books into a single frieze (structured around a series of cyclical iconographic and compositional repeats), which in turn raises questions about the arrangement of this single line, and its relationship to the object at large. Is there not an alternative 'cycle' to be had, one which moves *directly* from alpha to omega, proceeding to revisit in reverse cyclical order the various books bypassed in between (including the *Aethiopis* and *Ilias parva*, which at once completes and breaks the circle) (Fig. 27.8)?

However viewers proceed, the inscription's promise of linear *taxis* proves at odds with the visual suggestion of a more complex narrative mode. While seeming to delineate a series of poetic and sub-poetic units, the tablet exploits its visual arrangement to undermine that notion, crafting something that is at once curtailed *and* continuous: we are prompted to think about the cyclical narrative integrity – or indeed incongruity – of the whole. Rather than illustrate a 'cycle' of epic in any straightforward sense,

---

[69] One might note in passing here that the partitioned layout literalizes Aristotelian prescriptions about epic's 'multiple plot' (τὸ πολύμυθον, *Poet.* 1456a). Epic's extended length makes for less unified plots than those of tragedy (see Fantuzzi, above in this volume, pp. 407, 412–14): 'in epic, the narrative mode enables the poem to include many simultaneous parts' (διὰ τὸ διήγησιν εἶναι ἔστι πολλὰ μέρη ἅμα ποιεῖν περαινόμενα, 1459b). On the *Tabula Capitolina*, the *Iliad*'s 'many parts', rendered as twenty-four partitioned friezes, can be seen both collectively and in isolation; whatever else we make of it, though, the Iliadic whole is shown to amount to something 'greater' (in every sense) than the *Aethiopis* and *Ilias parva*.

[70] Cf. Squire (2011: 165–76).

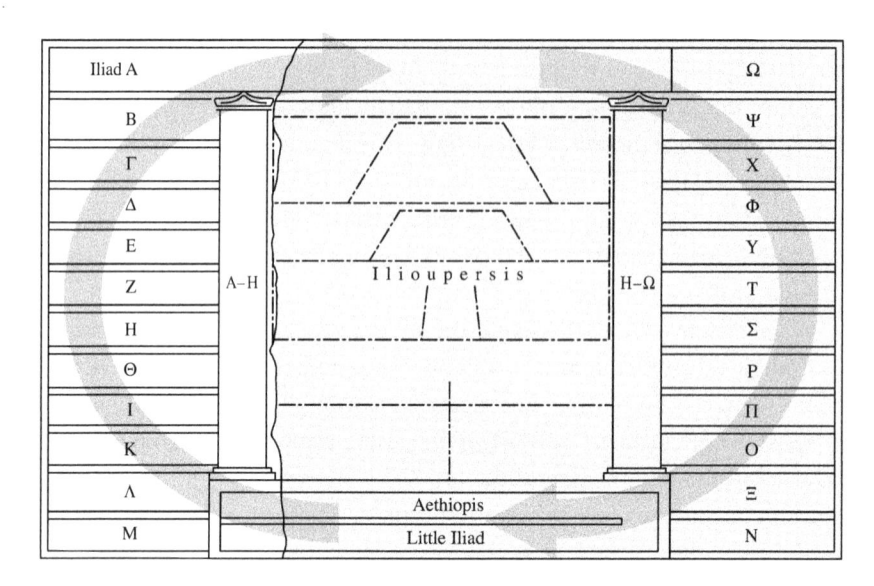

Fig. 27.7 Cyclical arrangement of scenes on the *Tabula Iliaca Capitolina* [1A], with suggested clockwise viewing of the Iliadic scenes.

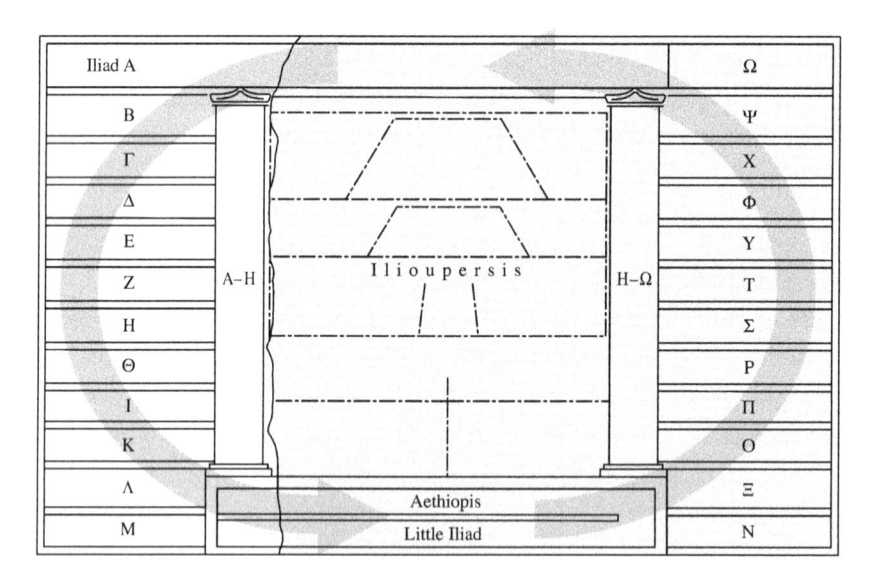

Fig. 27.8 Cyclical arrangement of scenes on the *Tabula Iliaca Capitolina* [1A], with suggested anticlockwise viewing of the Iliadic scenes.

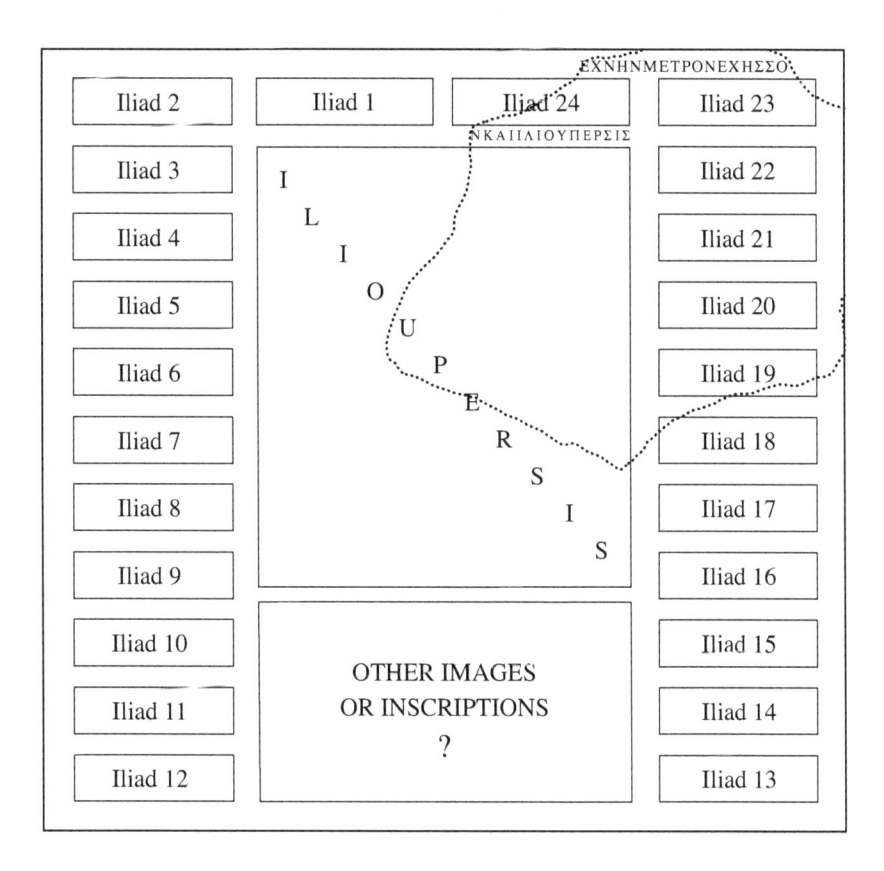

```
┌─────────────────────────────────────────────────────────────┐
│                              ΕΧΝΗΝΜΕΤΡΟΝΕΧΗΣΣΟ               │
│  ┌────────┐  ┌────────┐  ┌────────┐  ┌────────┐             │
│  │ Iliad 2│  │ Iliad 1│  │Iliad 24│  │Iliad 23│             │
│  └────────┘  └────────┘  └────────┘  └────────┘             │
│                         ΝΚΑΙΙΛΙΟΥΠΕΡΣΙΣ                      │
│  ┌────────┐       I                  ┌────────┐             │
│  │ Iliad 3│                          │Iliad 22│             │
│  └────────┘      L                   └────────┘             │
│  ┌────────┐    I                     ┌────────┐             │
│  │ Iliad 4│                          │Iliad 21│             │
│  └────────┘       O                  └────────┘             │
│  ┌────────┐       ⋰                  ┌────────┐             │
│  │ Iliad 5│      U                   │Iliad 20│             │
│  └────────┘                          └────────┘             │
│  ┌────────┐       P                  ┌────────┐             │
│  │ Iliad 6│                          │Iliad 19│             │
│  └────────┘      E                   └────────┘             │
│  ┌────────┐         R                ┌────────┐             │
│  │ Iliad 7│                          │Iliad 18│             │
│  └────────┘          S               └────────┘             │
│  ┌────────┐              I           ┌────────┐             │
│  │ Iliad 8│                          │Iliad 17│             │
│  └────────┘             S            └────────┘             │
│  ┌────────┐                          ┌────────┐             │
│  │ Iliad 9│                          │Iliad 16│             │
│  └────────┘                          └────────┘             │
│  ┌────────┐  ┌────────────────────┐  ┌────────┐             │
│  │Iliad 10│  │                    │  │Iliad 15│             │
│  └────────┘  │   OTHER IMAGES     │  └────────┘             │
│  ┌────────┐  │   OR INSCRIPTIONS  │  ┌────────┐             │
│  │Iliad 11│  │         ?          │  │Iliad 14│             │
│  └────────┘  │                    │  └────────┘             │
│  ┌────────┐  └────────────────────┘  ┌────────┐             │
│  │Iliad 12│                          │Iliad 13│             │
│  └────────┘                          └────────┘             │
└─────────────────────────────────────────────────────────────┘
```

Fig. 27.9 Reconstruction of the obverse of the *Tabula New York* [2NY] (cf. Fig. 27.15).

the Capitoline tablet spurs viewers into thinking about both the linearity and circularity of its juxtaposed epic poetic subjects. Like Aeneas before the imaginary Carthaginian temple, viewers consequently find themselves acting as dynamic players in the stories that they spin, reflecting upon their own mode of narrative *taxis* in the process.

Although the *Tabula Capitolina* offers the best-preserved example of such poetic–pictorial games, other reliefs develop its circular conceits in no less complex ways. On tablet 2NY, for example, the first Iliadic metope begins in the relief's upper centre rather than at its upper left-hand edge, underscoring the cyclical arrangement (Fig. 27.9, and cf. Fig. 27.15); tablet 6B, by contrast, juxtaposed the central ringed city of Troy with a cyclical image of Achilles' shield, while also apparently originally interrupting the Iliadic friezes with a cycle drawn from the *Odyssey* below (Fig. 27.10). Still more interesting are two tablets (9D, 20Par) which evidently reversed the cyclical order of the *Tabula Capitolina*'s Iliadic scenes, with *Iliad* 24 now occupying the top-left

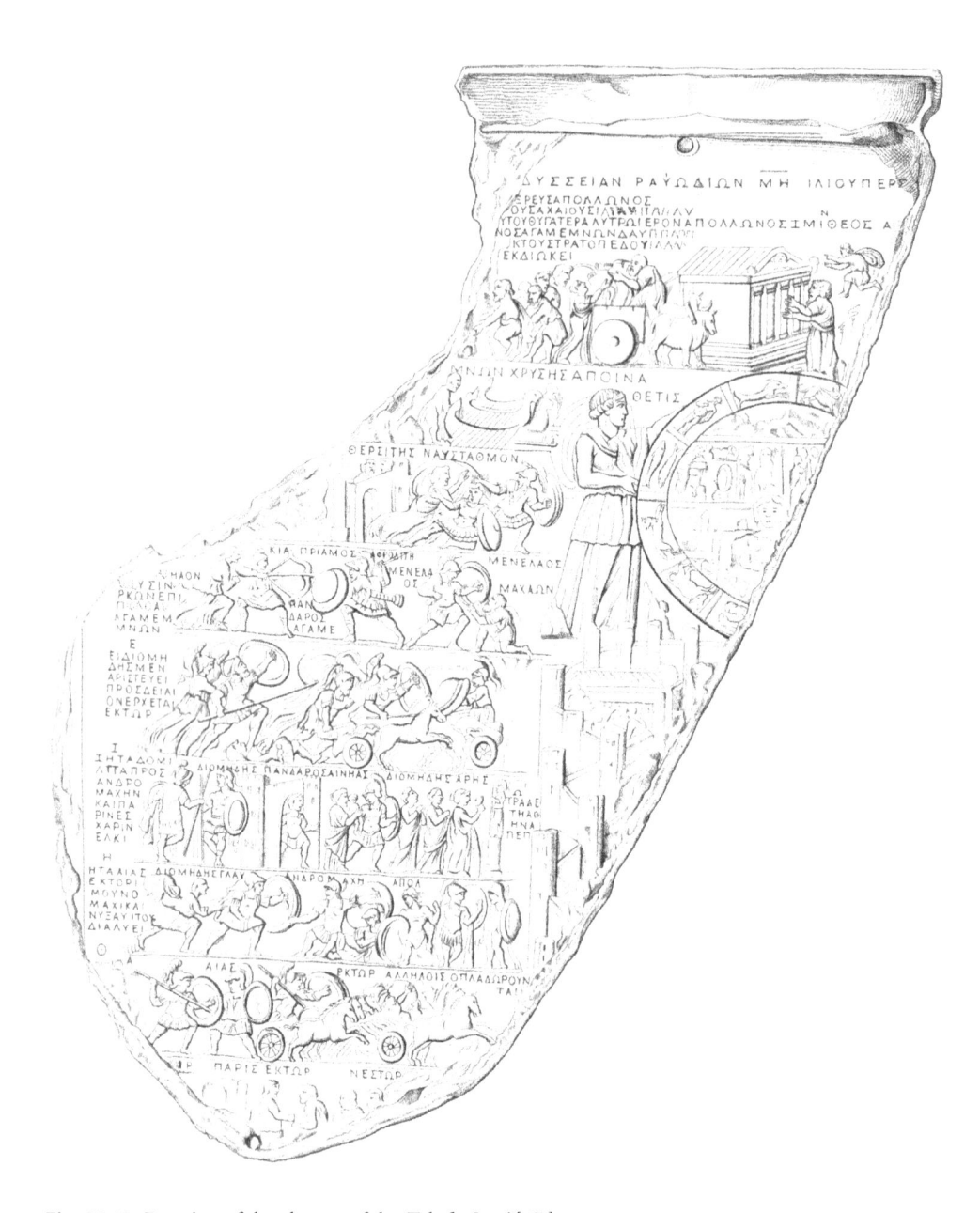

Fig. 27.10 Drawing of the obverse of the *Tabula Sarti* [6B].

rather than top-right space.[71] The surviving fragment 9D, for instance, set scenes from the *Iliad* and *Aethiopis* in two vertical columns to the left of the central *Iliou persis* (Fig. 27.11): viewers had to read one miniature cycle

[71] For more detailed discussions of these and other tablets, see Squire (2011: 176–94).

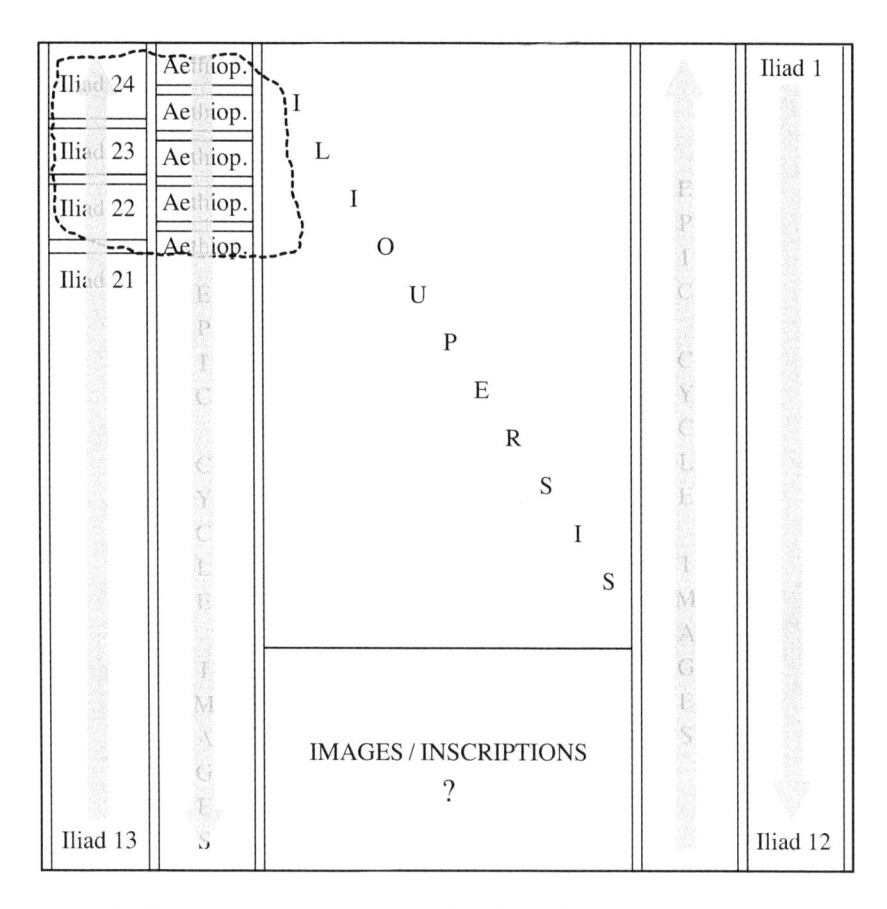

Fig. 27.11 Reconstruction of the obverse of the *Tabula Veronensis II* [9D].

against the other, with the two circles in fact revolving in opposite directions (the left-hand Iliadic scenes progress from bottom to top, while the *Aethiopis* scenes proceed from top to bottom).[72] Rather than place the *Aethiopis* scenes *between* the *Iliad* and *Iliou persis*, tablet 20Par goes still further in breaking the chronological and narrative sequence (Fig. 27.12). First, in the left-hand column, it is the chronologically later events of the *Aethiopis* which seem to have been displayed; then, to the right of these vertical scenes, we find their antecedents in the *Iliad*. Only in the centre of tablet 20Par do we see the culmination of events in the *Iliou persis*, a tableau framed on either side by the narratives that foreshadow it. With each unique tablet, the game seems to lie in putting the individual cycles together: to construct, in

---

[72] For the *Aethiopis* inscriptions (*IG* 14.336, no.1285), see *PEG Aeth*. T 9 and Valenzuela Montenegro (2004: 196–8).

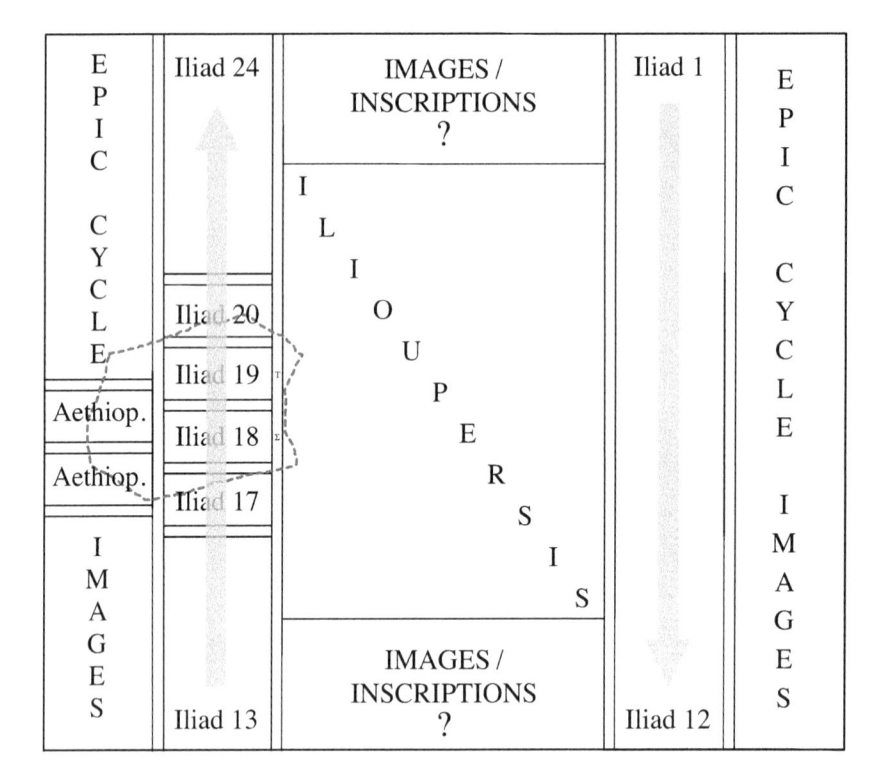

Fig. 27.12 Reconstruction of the obverse of the *Tabula Froehner* [20Par].

the mind's eye, a narrative that circumscribes all the smaller circular units within.[73]

The inscribed reverse sides of seven different tablets developed such poetic–pictorial games still further. Of the twenty-two tablets, eleven are inscribed on both recto and verso alike, and seven of these are inscribed with a so-called 'magic square' diagram.[74] In each case, the verso provides a titular text for the recto scenes depicted, and four refer to Homer specifically. But what is especially interesting about these verbal inscriptions is their visual mode of presentation [e.g. Fig. 27.13]. As a hexameter epigram on two tablets explicitly instructs, the objective was: γράμμα μέσον καθ[ελὼν παρολίσθα]νε οὗ ποτε βούλει ('seize the middle letter, and turn whichever

---

[73] Such taxing games might remind one of John Philoponus' express discussion of the figure of epic as 'circle', in his commentary on the twelfth chapter of Aristotle's first book of *Posterior Analytics* (see above, p. 514): as Philoponus puts it, much had been written on the *taxis* of the poems, 'as well as about which one a person needs to learn first, which second, and so on'.

[74] For the texts and their significance, see Bua (1971), along with Squire (2010: 77–84; 2011: 197–246, with further bibliography).

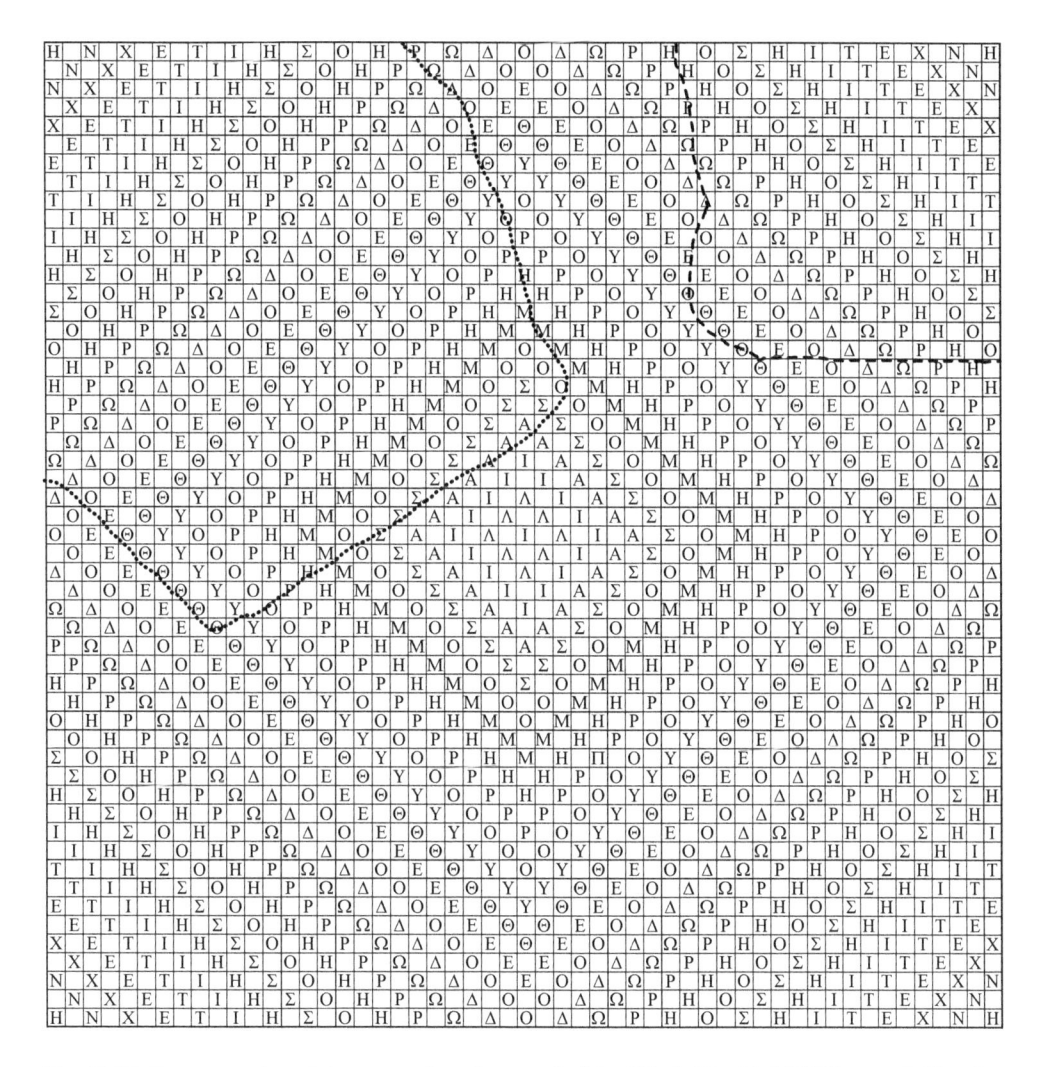

Fig. 27.13 Reconstruction of the reverse 'magic square' of the *Tabula New York* [2NY, upper left] and *Tabula Veronensis I* [3C, upper right].

way you like').[75] Starting from the *iota* at the centre of Fig. 27.13, one could proceed to any of the four outer edges, varying one's horizontal, vertical and diagonal *taxis* along the way. Regardless of the specific path chosen, the literal text from centre to outer corners remains the same: Ἰλιὰς Ὁμήρου Θεοδώρηος ἡ{ι} τέχνη ('The *Iliad* is Homer's, but the *technē* is Theodorean'). The interpretative freedom of each readerly view extends and legitimates

---

[75] For the reconstruction of the text (and other suggestions regarding the central *lacuna*), see Squire (2011: 202–5).

528   MICHAEL SQUIRE

Fig. 27.14 Reverse of the *Tabula New York* [2NY].

that of approaching the *grammata* on the recto (Figs. 27.14 and 27.15). In each case, though, the arrangement of letters also figures a related theme of circularity: whatever else we make of them, these bands of letters run literal and metaphorical rings around the proclaimed '*gramma* in the middle'.

THE SEMANTICS OF CIRCULARITY

Whether we look to the obverse or reverse sides of the *Tabulae Iliacae*, my suggestion is that their provocative games with epic resonate against contemporary critical ideas about narrative mode. The figure of the circle plays an important underlying role here. In one sense, the tablets might be said to visualize precisely the sort of 'single unending poem' against which Callimachus took so programmatic a poetic stand. At the same time

Fig. 27.15 Obverse of the *Tabula New York* [2NY].

that they arrange their images and texts in linear sequence, however, the tablets also exploit compositional layout to undermine any sense of single narrative end. In this sense, the riddlesomely small details of the tablets measure up to other Hellenistic retellings of the Epic Cycle. Like Lycophron's *Alexandra* (1–2 λέξω τὰ πάντα νητρεκῶς ἅ μ' ἱστορεῖς, / ἀρχῆς ἀπ' ἄκρας, 'I will tell everything you ask directly from the beginning'), the *Tabulae* might promise to relay the stories of the Cycle 'straight'; as with Lycophron, though, the miniature conundrums encountered along the way encourage readers to forge new narrative connections, championing innovative sorts of association between the stories evoked and displayed.[76]

[76] Cf. Sistakou (2008: 100–20), concluding of Lycophron's poem (p. 118) that 'the narrative is not actually a straight line, it is not merely interrupted by embedded *analepses* and *prolepses* as is

As the epigram on the *Tabula Capitolina* reminds us, coming to visual terms with these visual epic cycles also involves pitching the '*taxis* of Homer' against that of other epic poets. If the tablet prompted audiences to evaluate how Homer 'orders' events like and unlike other epic poets, its talk of the 'order of Homer' invites viewers in turn to 'rank' Homer (and the anastrophic texture of his narrative arrangements) in relation to Lesches, Arctinus and Stesichorus. Such is the 'Theodorean *technē*' of the tablet that it visualizes Homer's orderings of events on the one hand, and allows us to see how his poetry fits within a hierarchical *taxis* or *ordo* of poets on the other: in its implicit calls to comparative judgement, the talk of the '*taxis* of Homer' consequently serves, in every sense, as a 'measure of all wisdom'.

The narratological complexity with which the *Tabulae* treat the poems of the Epic Cycle finds parallels among the other Hellenistic and Roman objects surveyed at the beginning of this chapter. Whatever else we make of Hellenistic 'Homeric cups' and Pompeian wall paintings, they offer no straightforward evidence for the content of lost Epic Cyclic poems. Like the tablets, they also play with related ideas of narrative structure, and in particular with the figure of circularity.

As self-consciously circular entities, the Homeric cups are an excellent case in point. Of course, the circular compositions of the cups in one sense monumentalise the idea of a 'single, unending song'. Here, though, the very selection of Epic Cyclic episodes undermines that suggestion, dismantling the poems into a series of bite-size (which is to say *drink*-size) units. These were entities to be turned in one's hands as one quaffed the wine contained within: 'the more diverse the images and the more riddlesome the citations', as Giuliani puts it, 'the more appealing the game'.[77] In this connection, it is worth observing how certain cups exploit their compositional arrangement for innovative narrative effect. A cup in Berlin (now lost, but known from drawings) provides just one example, whereby the end of the *Iliad* is set alongside events from the *Aethiopis* [Fig. 27.16]: as we revolve between the three scenes, we move from Priam kneeling before Achilles in the final book of the *Iliad*, through a scene of Penthesilea and Priam at the grave of Hector, to the ensuing battle between Achilles and Penthesilea.[78] But

---

the case with the Homeric text, but it is presented rather as moving freely between past and present by means of digressions and codified allusions'.

[77] Giuliani (2003: 277: 'Je vielfaltiger die Bilder und je ratselhafter die Zitate, desto reizvoller das Spiel').

[78] For the cup (=Sinn 1979: 92, no. MB 23), see Robert (1890: 25–9: 'Für diese enge bildliche Verknüpfung des Anfangs der Aithiopis mit dem Schluss der Ilias ist der Becher das älteste Beispiel', p. 29); Weitzmann (1959: 43–4); Webster (1964: 152: 'a possible explanation of the

Fig. 27.16 Drawing of a 'Homeric cup' juxtaposing scenes from the *Iliad* and *Aethiopis*. (= Sinn (1979: 92, no. MB 23)).

'fold-out' images of the sort reproduced in Fig. 27.16 are somewhat misleading. Because the cup is in fact circular, each 'scene' moves seamlessly from one episode to the next. Just as we move from the story at the end of the *Iliad* to that opening the *Aethiopis*, in other words, so too does the Aethiopic scene of Achilles fighting Penthesilea move full circle back to the *Iliad*. Faced with the cup, viewers are free to rotate the object in *either* direction, whether in turn reconsidering the *Iliad* in light of the *Aethiopis*, or indeed contemplating the *Aethiopis* in light of the *Iliad*. The circle of hermeneutic possibilities is never-ending: as with the *Tabulae Iliacae*, viewers are faced with a range of cyclical opportunities – and thereby with a series of questions about *taxis*.[79]

Similar interests can be detected in the three extant Pompeian Trojan cycles. In the earliest ('Second Style') example, from the Casa del Criptoportico,[80] the inscribed panels served to guide the viewer around the space of the U-shaped, covered portico; audiences had to navigate en route not only the windows (which illuminate the space from above), but also various doorways in the east wing, a stairway and niche in the north wing,

---

dislocations is that the cups were ordered at short notice... If the bowls were to be used at a single great party it was not very serious if a scene at the end of the *Iliad* overlapped on to the *Aithiopis* cup').

[79] For related order games on Homeric cups, see e.g. Giuliani (2003: 264–9) on Sinn (1979: 89–90 no. MB 21). In contrast to e.g. Small (2003: 80–2, concluding simply that the scenes are 'out of narrative order'), Giuliani draws out the evident sophistication with which text and inscriptions could be laid out and combined.

[80] I am indebted to Anna Anguissola here for her help with the house's problematic archaeology, which still awaits full discussion (see Spinazzola 1953: 435–593; Aurigemma 1953: 905–8; Schefold 1957: esp. 17–18; *PPM* 1: 193–277). Because of current restoration works, I have been unable to visit the house in person, and remain somewhat puzzled about numerous aspects of both chronology and layout (especially the south wall of the cryptoporticus' west wing and the walls of the adjoining room, which are omitted from Spinazzola (1953: Tav. LXXXVII). The cryptoporticus was evidently adapted in the first century AD, with two fragmentary 'grandi muri grezzi' (Aurigemma 1953: 906) constructed in the east and west wings (as seen in Fig. 27.17). Already by this time, many of the Epic Cyclic panels had been severely damaged, and the cryptoporticus seems to have been converted into a makeshift wine-cellar (hence the numerous extant amphorae found *in situ*); other panels, although photographed, were destroyed during the allied bombings of the Second World War (Aurigemma 1953: 906). While some of the rooms off the cryptoporticus remain enigmatic (not least the set of so-called 'rustic' rooms squaring the south end of the cryptoporticus), it seems that those to the east of the cryptoporticus functioned as a private bathing suite, with an additional corridor at the eastern extremity of the house (cf. Coarelli (ed.) 2002: 257–8, *pace* e.g. Richardson 1988: 167–8); the elaborately decorated oecus, accessed from the south of the cryptoporticus' east wing, functioned as a grand triclinium (*PPM* 1: 250–73 nos. 99–143). The house could once be entered and exited via the south-west corner of the cryptoporticus, via a small 'vestibule guided by a porter's lodge' (Coarelli (ed.) 2002: 257): this gave access to the Vicolo del Menandro, running parallel to the Via dell'Abbondanza.

and other painted distractions [Fig. 27.17].[81] Considered as a collective, this cycle of images both is and is not circular, at once spinning and springing its cyclical course along segregated panels that twist and turn around a series of connected walls (Fig. 27.18): from the room's southern entrance, we proceed first clockwise (the west wall of the west wing preserves an image of Apollo's plague),[82] through Hector's challenging of the Achaeans in *Iliad* 7 (on the north wall of the north wing), and on to the removal of Patroclus' body in *Iliad* 17 (on the east and south walls of the east wing);[83] at this stage, though, the scenes turn cyclically back in on themselves on the adjacent wall, proceeding in what might be called an anticlockwise motion through Achilles' return to battle (*Iliad* 20 and 21: west wall of the east wing), Patroclus' funerary games (*Iliad* 23: south wall of the north wing), and finally scenes drawn from the *Aethiopis* (including Penthesilea's arrival at Troy and a possible scene of Thetis at Achilles' tomb, on the east wall of the west wing). As on the Iliadic–Aethiopic drinking cup (Fig. 27.16), the pictorial cycle brings together episodes which poets had dispatched to different poetic units.[84] While monumentalizing a single storyline, moreover, the visual medium allows the viewer to operate in a spatial way that works quite differently from the linearity of texts: he can walk backwards as well as forwards, or else stop and compare the scenes all around him at any given moment; from any single viewpoint, there were a multiplicity of pictures to be seen, stretching across different Iliadic books, and even across different Cyclic poems.

---

[81] Among those distractions are a series of herms and masked pilasters, themselves interrupting the panels and influencing (through the direction of the masked figures' gazes) how viewers put the Trojan panels together. Among the most thought-provoking analysis of the scenes and their arrangement is Corlàita Scagliarini (1974–6: 20–1): 'Il percorso suggerito dai *pinakes* iliaci si distribuisce lungo tutti i lati del criptoportico, iniziandosi e concludendosi presso la porta sud-occidentale . . . : si tratta perciò di un percorso in sé stesso, non finalizzato a una meta, ma solo alla contemplazione del lungo e avvincente ciclo narrativo'; cf. Brilliant (1984: 62–3).

[82] For the suggestion of additional scenes on this western wall of the western wing, drawn from the *Iliad*'s prehistory in the *Cypria*, see above, n. 19: although only one recognizable scene survives here, relating to the opening events of the *Iliad*, there seems to have been space to the south for several earlier scenes which are now lost (cf. Spinazzola 1953: Tav. LXXXVII).

[83] It is worth noting that the order of painted scenes is sometimes out of sync with the Homeric account (cf. Aurigemma 1953: 907–8): the scenes labelled 2 and 3 in Fig. 27.17 have been reversed (so that events relating to the sixth book of the *Iliad* now precede those from the fifth); likewise, the scenes labelled 13 and 14 are in inverse narrative order.

[84] Something similar can be said of at least some of the *Tabulae Iliacae*: although the Capitoline tablet (Figs. 27.3–27.6) makes a series of formal spatial distinctions between the *Iliad*, *Iliou persis*, *Aethiopis* and *Ilias parva*, the frieze of the first book of the *Iliad* seems originally to have opened with scenes drawn from the *Cypria* (a composition mirrored on the surviving scenes of tablet 3C); see Squire (2011: 170–1).

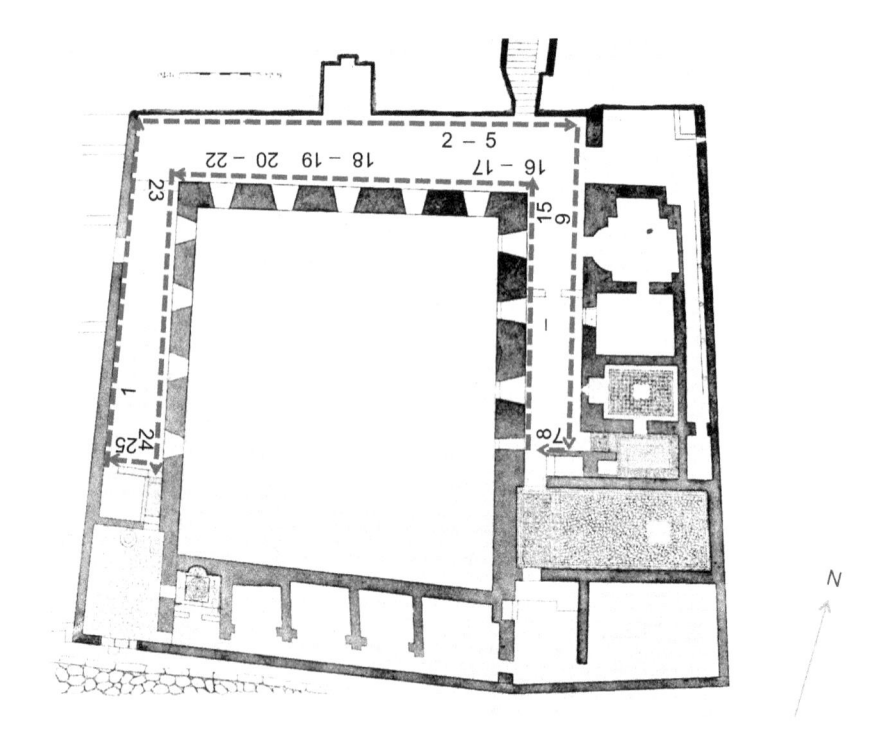

Fig. 27.17 Ground plan of the Casa del Criptoportico (Pompeii I.6.2), after Corlàita Scagliarini (1974–6: 34, Fig. 30), following Spinazzola (1953: 455, Fig. 517). Identification and order of extant scenes mostly follow those of Aurigemma (1953: 903–70); for the precise location of scenes, see Spinazzola (1953: Tav. LXXXVII–LXXXIX).

West wing, west wall

1. Apollo and the plague in the Greek camp, relating to *Iliad* 1. [The layout suggests several earlier scenes, probably drawn from events narrated in the *Cypria*, arranged to the left of this one.]

North wing, north wall

2. Exchange of armour between Diomedes and Glaucus, relating to *Iliad* 6.
3. Diomedes with Athena, and Diomedes' combat with (?) Mars or Aeneas, relating to *Iliad* 5.
4. Departure of Hector from Andromache and Astyanax, relating to *Iliad* 6.
5. Counsel of Greek leaders after the challenge of Hector, relating to *Iliad* 7.

East wing, east wall

6. Combat of Hector and the Greeks over the body of Patroclus, relating to *Iliad* 17.

East wing, south wall

7. Removal of the body of Patroclus, relating to *Iliad* 17.

Fig. 27.17 (*cont.*)
East wing, west wall

8. Thetis seated in the workshop of Hephaestus, relating to *Iliad* 18 (with female figure holding the shield of Achilles, labelled as Euanthe).
9. (?) Achilles beside the body of Patroclus.
10. Three unlabelled and unidentified standing male heroic figures.
11. Return of Briseis to Achilles and a group of seated Greeks, relating to *Iliad* 19.
12. (?) Athena and other gods intervening in the battle between Trojans and Greeks/council of the gods, relating to *Iliad* 20.
13. Achilles' return to battle and combat between Achilles and Hector (alongside other scenes), relating to *Iliad* 20.
14. Combat between Achilles and Aeneas (who is saved by Poseidon), relating to *Iliad* 20.
15. Achilles raging against the Trojans and the capture of Trojan prisoners, relating to *Iliad* 21.

East wing, south wall

16. Death of Lycaon next to the Scamander river, relating to *Iliad* 21.
17. (?) Pursuit of the Trojans.
18. Lost panel (but inscriptions naming Achilles and Xanthos).
19. Mourning of Andromache, relating to *Iliad* 22.
20. Women mourning Hector's death, possibly relating to *Iliad* 24.
21. Achilles offering a libation before Patroclus' pyre, relating to *Iliad* 23.
22. Funerary games of Patroclus, relating to *Iliad* 23.

West wing, east wall

23. Penthesilea's arrival at Troy (received by Priam), drawn from the *Aethiopis*.
24. (?) Thetis at the tomb of Achilles or Helen on the walls of Troy.

West wing, south wall

25. Aeneas, Anchises and Ascanius fleeing Troy, guided by Hermes.

Most interesting of all is what happens on the south wall of the cryptoporticus' west wing. Here – at what was once the house's entrance and exit (also encasing a 'janitor's' vestibule behind)[85] – we find a single surviving panel that tied together the clockwise and anticlockwise orders around the room. Just as at the centre of numerous *Tabulae Iliacae* (e.g. Figs. 27.4 and 27.15), visitors were confronted with a scene of Aeneas, Anchises and

---

[85] Cf. Aurigemma 1953: 970: 'La larghezza dell'ala in questo punto è di m. 2,84; va peraltro tenuto presente che nella parete, a questa estremità dell'ala, si aprivano tanto la porticina che dava accesso alla stanzetta dello *ianitor*, come la porta da cui si giungeva all'uscita verso la via parallela e a sud di Via dell'Abbondanza.'

Fig. 27.18 Reconstruction of the north wing of the eponymous cryptoporticus in the Casa del Criptoportico (Pompeii I.6.2); the drawing shows the view across to the western wing of the room (with the Trojan cycle occupying the upper grey frieze).

Ascanius leaving Troy, guided by Hermes (Fig. 27.19).[86] While Aeneas' exit from Troy could signpost the viewer's own exit from the house, the subject

---

[86] On the centrality of Aeneas on the obverse of *Tabulae Iliacae* 1A and 2NY (and most likely also on 3C, 6B, 7Ti, 8E, 9D and 20Par), see Squire (2011: esp. 148–58, 240–3).

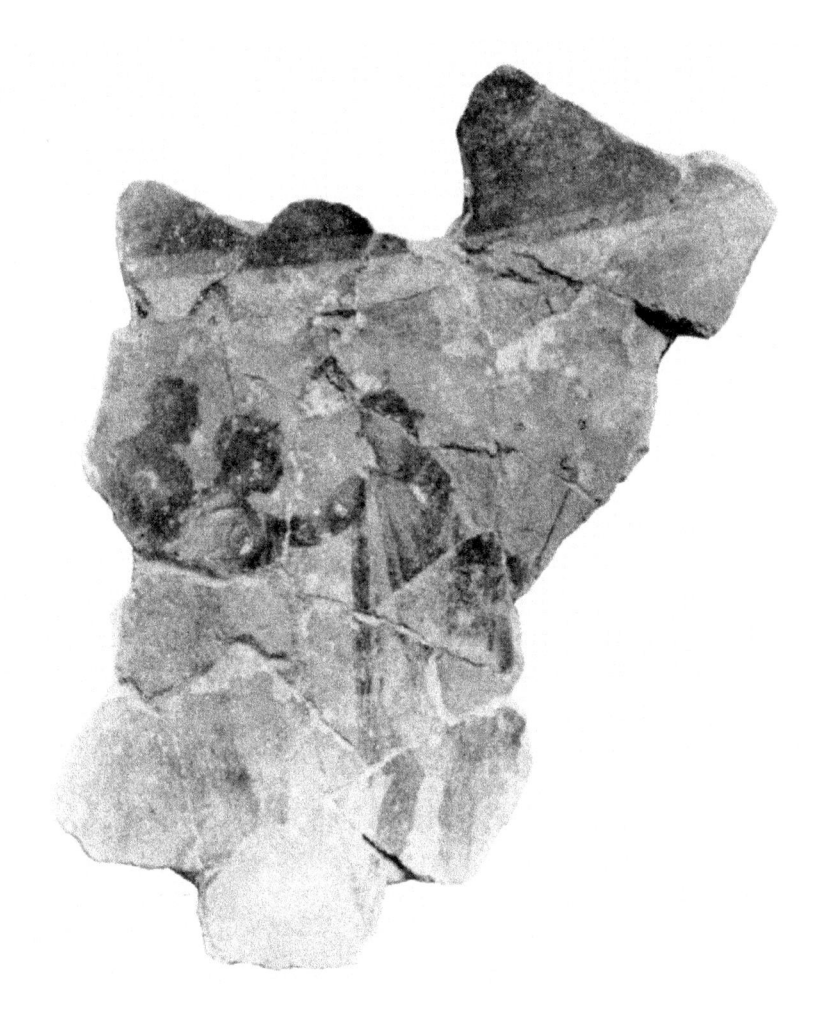

Fig. 27.19 Image of Hermes with Aeneas and Anchises, from the south wall of the west wing of the Casa del Criptoportico (Pompeii I.6.2).

also provides a new focalizing perspective for making sense of the room's various scenes. If the frieze monumentalizes a single unending circle of events, the privileged location of this particular scene provides a literal and metaphorical way out, as well as a poignant way in.[87]

---

[87] See Galinsky (1969: 31–2), on how this scene 'provides an ennobling mythological parallel to the ordinary, everyday act of leaving the house'. Compare also Schefold (1975: 129): 'Der Eintretende sah zu seiner Linken die ersten Szenen aus der Ilias und konnte ihrer Fortseztung, immer zu seiner Linken, durch den ganzen Gang folgen, bis er wieder zur Tür zurückkam, und neben dieser, als einziges Bild allein auf einer Wand, das Bild mit Aeneas' Flucht fand.' The

Although the scenes from the Casa di Sacello Iliaco and Casa di Octavius Quartio in Pompeii do not contain the same breadth of epic scenes, they arguably play with cyclical arrangement in equally nuanced ways. The stucco scenes from the Sacrarium of the Casa di Sacello Iliaco constitute a more concentrated circle, this time focusing on events at the end of the *Iliad* (and without the epigraphic aid of labelling inscriptions). As in the Casa del Criptoportico, though, the designer or patron has evidently thought carefully about the circular order, so that opening and closing events are here made to occupy the single wall to the east – ending the Homeric story, as it were, before it has even begun (Fig. 27.20).[88] Something related can be found in the oecus of the Casa di Octavius Quartio.[89] As we have said, the room's lower Trojan frieze restricts itself to events from the *Iliad*, whereas the bigger frieze above pertains to a different narrative cycle (or perhaps several), concerning the deeds of the larger-than-life Heracles (Fig. 27.3). In physical terms, the two friezes make up two segregated cycles, extending over all four sides of the room. But the arrangement goes out of its way to *break* the impression of any 'single unending song' (ἓν ἄεισμα διηνεκές), not only by the dual format of one frieze on top of the other, but also via their ordered arrangement. A reconstruction of the scenes (Fig. 27.21) shows how the two cycles seem to have begun at opposite corners of the room, the one snaking anticlockwise and then clockwise, the other by contrast proceeding first in clockwise direction and then in an anticlockwise order. As the off-kilter entrance of the east wall testifies, this room was laid out to accommodate three couches, and viewers sat amid the scenes looking out to the landscaped gardens visible through the south door: the spatial riddles were clearly intended as a stimulus for erudite dinner conversation.

What might all this mean within a companion to the Epic Cycle at large? Above all, the sorts of visual–verbal games traced here demonstrate some of the close-knit connections between art and poetry in the Hellenistic and Roman worlds. Rather than use extant visual culture to try and reconstruct the forms of lost Epic Cycle poems, or indeed to evaluate how well they were known at any given place or moment, my objective has been to showcase the interplay between literary, critical and artistic responses. Whether we turn to humble terracotta objects like the Homeric cups, or to costly

---

panel seems to have been the only one on this south wall of the west wing (cf. Aurigemma 1953: 970; the wall goes unillustrated in Spinazzola (1953: Tav. LXXXVII)).

[88] See Aurigemma (1953: 869–901, esp. 873, Fig. 870 (= Tav. LXXXVI)).

[89] For further discussions, see Squire (2011: 145–7), developed in idem (2014: 374–86); compare also Lorenz (2008: 539; 2013).

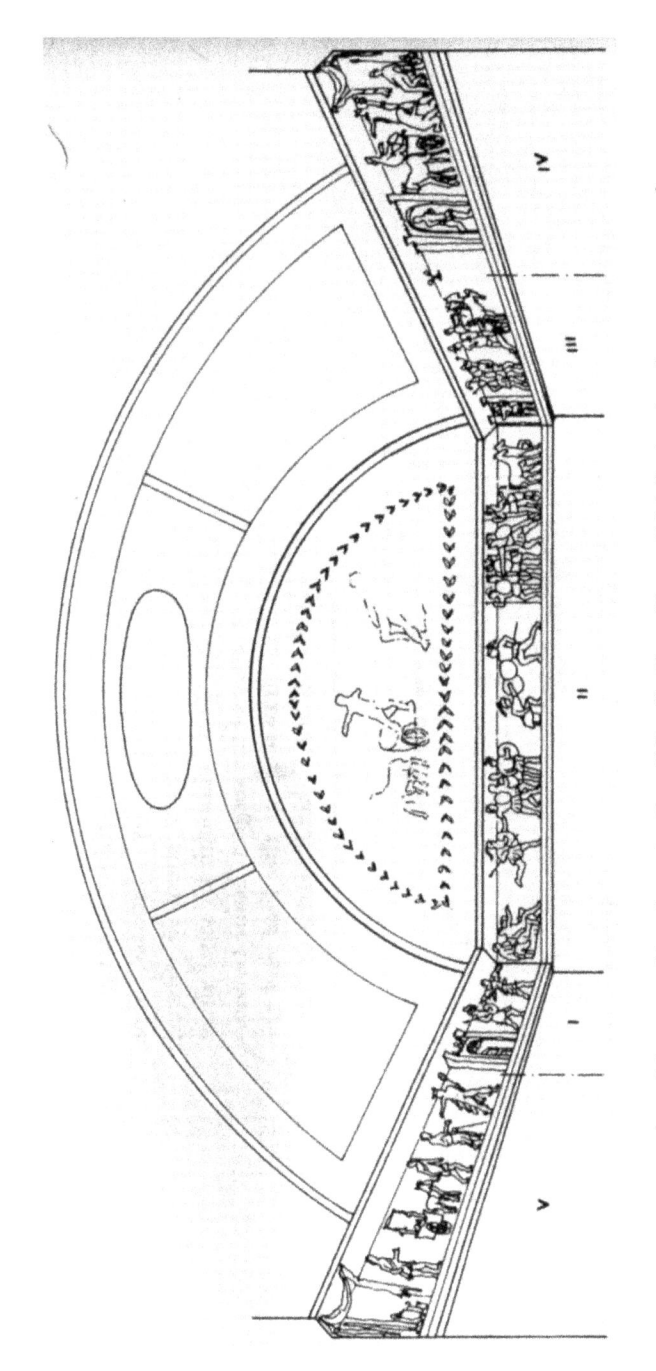

Fig. 27.20 Reconstruction of the stucco frieze from the Casa di Sacello Iliaco (Pompeii I.6.4), showing the arrangement of scenes.

Large frieze (scenes from the life of Heracles)

I Heracles kills the monster and rescues Hesione (?)
II Heracles and Telamon at the court of Laomedon (Heracles asks for the horses promised for freeing Hesione)
III Heracles kills Laomedon (who is defended in vain by Hesione)
IV Wedding of Telamon and Hesione (witnessed by Heracles)
V Heracles crowns the child Priam as prince of Troy
VI Heracles and Nessus (?)
VII Deianeira and Nessus
VIII Heracles on the pyre
IX Apotheosis of Heracles (?)

Small frieze (scenes from the *Iliad*)

1 Apollo shoots arrow into the Greek camp, beginning the plague
2 Horses are led to water
3 Odysseus, Ajax and Phoenix go to negotiate with Achilles
4 Achilles seated in front of his tent
5 Phoenix depicted on his knees, beseeching the seated Achilles
6 Combat below the walls of the Greek camp
7 Combat near the ships
8 Trojans try to recover the body of a fallen warrior (?)
9 Patroclus dresses in the armour of Achilles and fights the Trojans
10 Achilles arms himself in the presence of Thetis
11 Achilles drags Hector's body around the walls of Troy
12 Patroclus' funerary games
13 Priam depicted on his knees, beseeching the seated Achilles
14 Priam and Idaeus guard the body of Hector

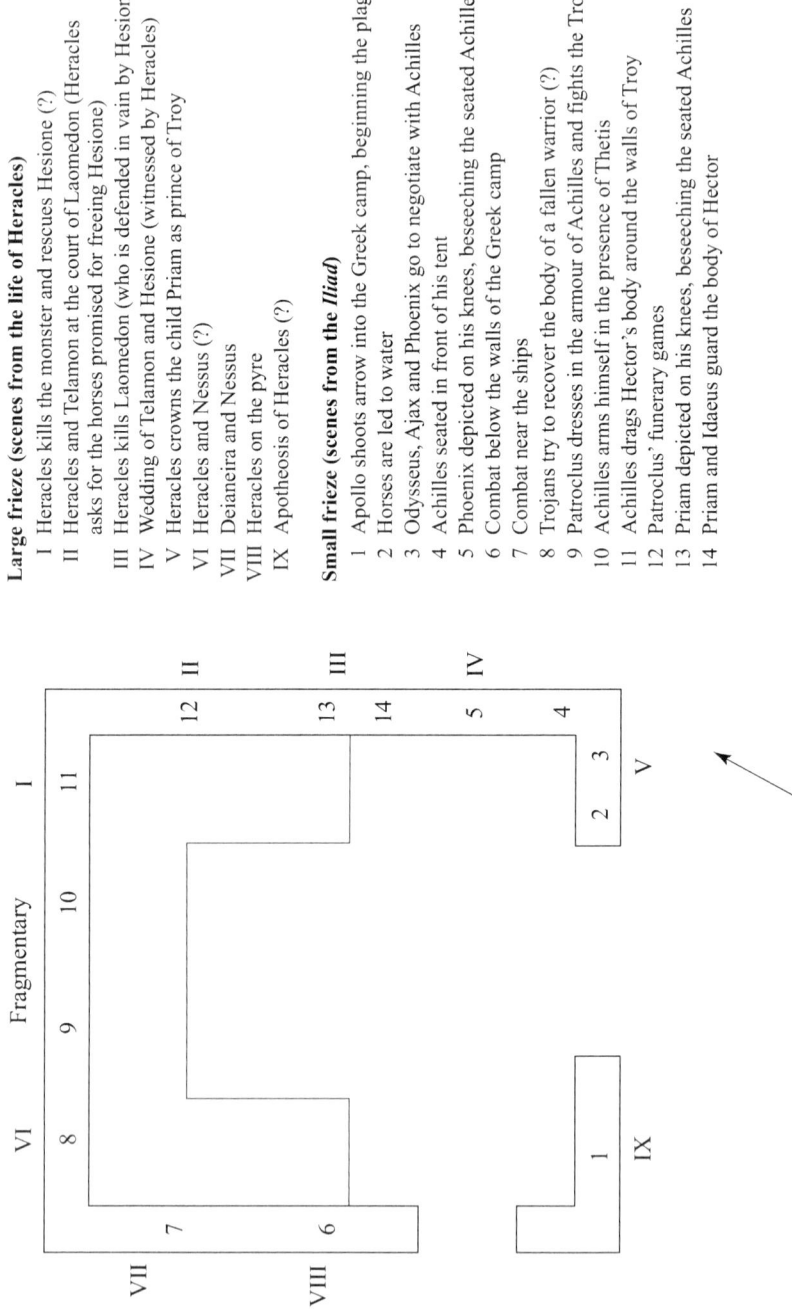

Fig. 27.21 Plan of the Iliadic and Heracles scenes in the Casa di Octavius Quartio (Pompeii II.2.2); see Fig. 27.3.

marble reliefs like the *Tabulae Iliacae*, we find artists not simply 'illustrating' the Epic Cycle, but instead probing the narrative connections, playing upon the 'circular' semantics of their overall arrangement.

This is something equally pertinent to the production of (what we label) 'Roman' visual culture as to the art of the earlier Hellenistic world. With that in mind, it seems appropriate to end with the opening of Statius' *Achilleis*, a poem that comments on the critical stakes with particular sophistication (1.3–10):

> ... *quamquam acta uiri multum inclita cantu*
> *Maeonio, sed plura uacant nos ire per omnem*
> *(sic amor est) heroa uelis Scyroque latentem*
> *Dulichia proferre tuba nec in Hectore tracto*
> *sistere, sed tota iuuenem deducere Troia.*
> *Tu modo, si ueterem digno depleuimus haustu,*
> *da fontes mihi, Phoebe, nouos ac fronde secunda*
> *necte comas.*

> Although the man's deeds are much famed in Maeonian song, still more is missing: suffer me (for such is my desire) to traverse the whole hero, bringing him forth with Dulichian trump from his hiding-place in Scyros and – not stopping with the dragging of Hector's body – to spin out the youth instead through the *complete* tale of Troy. If, Apollo, I have worthily drained the old source with my draught, grant me springs that are new, binding my hair with a second garland.

My interpretation of Hellenistic and Roman visual culture is very much in tune with Statius' cyclical take on the Epic Cycle – his self-confessed avowal to 'traverse the whole hero' (*ire per omnem... heroa*), carrying the story of Achilles through the entire history of Troy (*sed tota iuuenem deducere Troia*), and offering thereby a new sort of 'director's cut'.[90] Of course, the visual medium of our Homeric bowls, Pompeian paintings and Iliac tablets operates differently from Statius' verbal poem (and each class of object works differently from every other). At the same time, though, all these materials reflect a closely related interest: literary and visual cultures both exhibit a similar concern with re-cycling the Epic Cycle, challenging established stops and starts, re-spinning old stories in new and distinctive ways. For Hellenistic and Roman readers and viewers alike, the old stories of the Epic

---

[90] On the significance of Statius' programmatic (and highly allusive) opening, see Barchiesi (1996), together with Heslin (2005: 71–86). One might note in particular the significance of the verb *deducere*, implying at once 'drawing out' in linear sequence, and figuratively 'spinning' a yarn...

Cycle could serve to spin out something new and experimental, and in all manner of self-referential ways.[91]

[91] I am grateful to Richard Hunter and John Henderson for their feedback on an earlier version of this chapter, and above all to the editors for their help, patience and encouragement.

28 | Virgil and the Epic Cycle

URSULA GÄRTNER

Anyone addressing Virgil's relation to the Epic Cycle is faced above all with questions: did Virgil and his public read the epics in the original and, if so, did they read them all or only some of them, and in what version? Or was the material known only through later texts and primarily from handbooks? Or did the poet know the epics, but paid them no attention? Virgil is renowned for his allusive technique, but is his engagement with Homer or Apollonius Rhodius enough to prove that he used the Cyclic epics in the same way? And if he did, in whatever way, refer to them, which readers or listeners were able and expected to respond, and how were the relevant passages marked out for them?[1]

One can begin from different angles: if the focus is placed on the *Aeneid*, we can evaluate the Cyclic epics as sources (of both motifs and structure) and as subtexts; if the main interest is the epics themselves, we can ask if the *Aeneid* permits inferences about these lost texts. Both approaches will be pursued here, but the latter much more briefly because its validity depends on the results of the first approach. Given the lost and fragmentary character of the epics, it is clear that we should not expect definitive answers to our questions.

THE BACKGROUND: THE EPIC CYCLE AMONG VIRGIL'S CONTEMPORARIES

It is generally assumed that Proclus did not know the epics at first hand, but views differ about testimonia in early imperial authors. It is argued that when Pausanias and Athenaeus claim that they 'read' something in a particular author, they should not be taken literally.[2] However, there are no real grounds to challenge the statements of such well-read authors.[3] The

---

[1] Similar general questions were raised about Virgil in antiquitiy, see e.g. Macrob. 5.18.1; 6.1.7; Sen. *Suas.* 3.7. On Virgil's intertextuality, see Farrell (1997).
[2] E.g. Wilamowitz (1884: 338–49); Rzach (1922: 2349).
[3] On these statements, see Allen (1908a; 1908b); cf. Kopff (1981: 921); West (2003a: 4; 2013: 47–51); critical Horsfall (2003: 469–70).

same holds for the – rare – remarks in scholia and commentaries on other authors.[4] Admittedly this general conclusion sidesteps the question of the form the Epic Cycle took at this time and where it was available.[5]

Can anything be deduced from Augustan art? The *Tabulae Iliacae* should be mentioned, panels found in and around Rome dating in part from the late first century BC or the early first century AD.[6] Panel IA shows scenes from the conquest of Troy accompanied by 'source citations', which mention not only Homer, but also Lesches, Arctinus and even Stesichorus. Unfortunately the panel may not have been modelled directly on the poems named but on handbooks of stock images, in combination with summaries of the literary works. The artistic freedom used to transpose successive events in a story into a single, simultaneous image should also be remembered. Finally, it cannot be ruled out that other common motifs have contributed elements to the images, or that there is contemporary influence at work, perhaps even from Virgil himself. The *Tabula* should therefore not be overestimated as a testimony to lost literary works.[7] The arrangement of the scenes and texts is nonetheless remarkable, because the label Τρωικός (sc. κύκλος?) is placed in the middle, beneath the central scene in which Aeneas leaves Troy: the episode that was central for the Augustan period is thus 'encircled' by the preceding events of the Epic Cycle.[8]

Ovid's relation to the Epic Cycle is addressed in a separate chapter and so will not be discussed here.[9] Horace, however, needs to be examined more closely, especially the statement in the *Ars poetica* that refers both explicitly and implicitly to the Epic Cycle.[10] In these verses (136–7), he appears to be citing the first line of an epic poem:

---

[4] Servius refers to parallels to Virgil in 'Homer' that are not present in the *Iliad* and *Odyssey*, which may therefore refer to the Cyclic epics, some of which circulated under Homer's name; cf. Knight (1932a: 181 n. 7; 1932b: 77). Given the large quantity of lost epic, it is hardly possible to assign these verses; further, they may derive from later indirect tradition, especially if the Homeric epics themselves long continued to exist in different forms; cf. Nagy (2001).

[5] On the variety of versions, see Bernabé (1984); Finkelberg (2000); Nagy (2001).

[6] The basic treatment is Sadurska (1964); Horsfall (1979b; 2008: 587–91); Valenzuela-Montenegro (2004a; 2004b); Squire (2011); cf. Debiasi (2004: 161–77). The *Tabulae Iliacae* are discussed by Squire, above in this volume, pp. 502–28. Concerning our question they are often referred to as testimonia; therefore it seemed useful to outline just some of the difficulties.

[7] Cf. Horsfall (1979b: 43 and 47–8); see Squire, above in this volume on 'Vicious circles', pp. 510–16.

[8] Horsfall (1979b: 37): 'here Theodorus *may* be perpetrating a minor verbal/visual pun'. On the noun to be supplied, see West and Squire, above in this volume, respectively pp. 101 n. 8 and 520–1. On the significance of *taxis/ordo* and in particular the figure of circularity, see Squire, above, pp. 516–28.

[9] See Rosati, below in this volume.

[10] Horace's *Ars* is also discussed by Fantuzzi, above in this volume, pp. 420–5; it is touched here because one needs to have the contemporary statement in mind considering the question of the Epic Cycle as a reference work for the *Aeneid*.

> nec sic incipies, ut scriptor Cyclicus olim:
> 'fortunam Priami cantabo et nobile bellum.'
>
> And you are not to begin as the Cyclic poet of old: 'Of Priam's fate and famous war I'll sing.'

This may be a Latin version of a genuine opening line or an invented – and perhaps exaggerated – example.[11] The criticism is clearly directed at a proem where sweeping claims are made but not fulfilled in the actual content, whereas the first two lines of the *Odyssey* are cited in contrast as ideal. The criticism is raised again in lines 146–7, which refer to the subject matter of the Epic Cycle and cite long pre-histories that Homer omits:

> nec reditum Diomedis ab interitu Meleagri,
> nec gemino bellum Troianum orditur ab ovo;
>
> Nor does he begin Diomede's return from the death of Meleager, or the war of Troy from the twin eggs.

Here too it is unclear if the lines refer to a particular epic and, if so, to which one,[12] but the criticism of the expansive approach of the Cyclic epics seems the most important aspect. Contemporaries must have associated the term *scriptor Cyclicus* (line 136) with something – generally something negative.[13] Some earlier lines (131–2) gain a quite specific meaning in retrospect:

> publica materies privati iuris erit, si
> non circa vilem patulumque moraberis orbem, etc.
>
> In ground open to all you will win private rights, if you do not linger along the easy and open pathway, etc.

That is, it is acceptable to treat known material, but not if one dawdles on the cheap and frequently travelled *orbis*. *orbis* could mean 'closed, unchanging

---

[11] See e.g. Kopff (1981: 927–8), who, like most commentators, suggested the *Cypria*; contra Brink (1971: 214): 'one specific proem of a Cyclic epic'. Horace's *cantabo*, unlikely to come from a Greek future, might also render the line-one ending of some Homeric Hymns, ἄρχομ' ἀείδειν ('I begin to sing').

[12] Porphyrio commenting on line 146 cited the Cyclic *Thebaid* of Antimachus: *Antimachus fuit Cyclicus poeta. Hic adgressus est materiam, quam sic extendit, ut viginti quattuor volumina imple<r>it, antequam septem duces usque ad Thebas perduceret* ('Antimachus was a Cyclic poet. He took up a theme that he stretched out so far that he filled twenty-four books before he had the seven leaders arrive at Thebes'). Although most commentaries accept this, it seems more apt for the argumentation to consider instead the Cyclic *Nostoi*, cf. Brink (1971: 442). Line 147 may refer to *Cypria PEG* F 10 (= F 8 D. = F 11 W.), but it is unclear whether there the twins were born from an egg (*PEG* F 8 = F 6 D. = F 9 W.), because in the *Cypria* Nemesis and Zeus unite in the form of geese, and it is Helen who is born from the egg. In both cases Horace may be exaggerating to illustrate a point.

[13] See Fantuzzi, above in this volume, pp. 417 n. 35, 420–2, 425.

circuit of themes', but Horace is at the same time referring to the Epic Cycle, and putting it down.[14] He implicitly cites Callimachus' poetic criticism of 'I hate the Cyclic poem, etc.' (*Epigr.* 28.1–2 Pf. = *HE* 1041f.).[15] Even if nobody read the epics any more, people with literary interests must have known the ideas and content, and apparently also the usual criticisms made, of these epics.

Whether wider educated circles also knew the Cyclic epics seems doubtful. They have no role in education, and Quintilian, who can cite poets like Nicander or Euphorion in his survey of literature (10.1.45–72), does not list them.

QUESTIONS OF METHOD: VIRGIL'S 'USE' OF THE EPIC CYCLE

The signs that one text is being 'used' in another are generally taken to be verbal similarities, parallels in motifs, structural analogies and intertextual references. Verbal parallels are the most obvious form of link, but none can be demonstrated between Virgil and the Cyclic epics.

To enquire whether the Cyclic epics had a role as source, model or subtext, we must therefore rely on their subject matter and structure. Research remains divided on this issue, but it is often based on unsound methods.[16] It is sometimes founded simply on reflections, such as those sketched out above, about the likelihood that the Epic Cycle circulated in Virgil's time. Depending on how one treats that issue, it is concluded either that Virgil only knew the subject matter of the epics through a handbook,[17] or else that he was indeed able to track down a copy of them, as befits his thorough craftsmanship.[18] Kopff even asserted that the burden of proof rests with

---

[14] The connection of *orbis* and Cyclic epic is made explicit by Porphyrio, see Fantuzzi, above in this volume, p. 421 n. 41.

[15] Cf. *Aet.* 1.1.27–8; and, further, Arist. *Poet.* 8 and 23; Phot. *Bibl.* 319a30–3; *A.P.* 11.130 (Pollianus). On Callimachus and Pollianus, see Fantuzzi, above in this volume, pp. 427–9.

[16] For an overview, see Gärtner (2005: 27–9); Bär (2009: 78–84).

[17] E.g. Bethe (1891b: 607 n. 1; 1891c: 516); Kroll (1902: 161–9); Heinze (1915: 198–9); Norden (1957: 261); Horsfall (1979b: 46–7; 1995: 184); Gransden (1991: 22); von Albrecht (2007: 142).

[18] Ehwald (1894: 732–3); Knight (1932a: 181–2 n. 7; 1932b: 77); Fraenkel (1932) is cautious, but has been exceptionally influential; Assereto (1970); Kopff (1981); La Penna (1988: 222); Burgess (2001: 44–5); West (2013: 48). Philodemus seems to be familiar with the Epic Cycle (e.g. in *De pietate*); considering the personal link between him and Virgil one might come to the conclusion that Virgil could have known the Cycle first hand, but it is still no proof, as Philodemus himself might have taken over the citations from earlier writers; cf. West (2013: 48).

those who deny that Virgil read the original.[19] Much work on the subject is remarkably unclear about whether direct or indirect knowledge is assumed, or else the arguments for direct knowledge would be just as valid in support of an indirect one.[20] The assertion that Virgil will have used the Cyclic epics in the same way as we know he used the *Iliad*, *Odyssey* and *Argonautica* of Apollonius[21] cannot be demonstrated and ignores the issue of the reception of any such references.

Reliable indications of whether Virgil used the Cyclic epics can only be found by analysing all accessible testimonia for affinities in motifs, but this kind of source analysis is soon revealed as a thankless task. With such poor transmission of the epics and the unquantifiable number of lost works, it seems an essentially dubious proposition to trace a motif in Virgil directly to the Epic Cycle. Detailed comparison with the fragments and the summaries in Proclus reveals that many small details are treated differently in Virgil, and that there are many major differences and many motifs that can also be found in other traditions as well as in the Epic Cycle, above all in Greek tragic and lyric poetry and early Latin literature. *Imitatio/aemulatio* has built up a web of references that we can only decipher here and there. Motifs in the *Aeneid* that differ or are absent in Homer or subsequent literature have been too easily assigned to the Cyclic epics. Coincidence in a motif is not evidence that Virgil read the Epic Cycle. Nor is variation in a given motif evidence that he did *not* know the epics, as he may have preferred to present a rival version. And until it has been demonstrated that Virgil certainly knew the Epic Cycle, it cannot be said in such a case that he is intentionally rejecting these works either.

Two other aspects are relevant. Firstly, Homer himself may have drawn on older material for his subject matter and may have taken it as his model in other respects.[22] So if, as Knauer suggests, Virgil took his subject matter from the Epic Cycle but his structure from the *Iliad* or *Odyssey*, it must be remembered that this structure may be older than Homer. The difficulty of tracing the source of motifs thus doubles. Secondly, literature *after* Virgil needs to be considered more fully.[23] The key question here is whether and, if so, how the Greek epic poets Quintus Smyrnaeus and Triphiodorus, whose

---

[19] Kopff (1981: 921).
[20] E.g. Knauer (1979); Manton (1962: 13); Debiasi (2004: 125); this is true also of the 'methods' listed by Kopff (1981: 932).
[21] Kopff (1981: 921).
[22] On the results of neoanalytic approaches, see Kullmann, above in this volume; on newer approaches, see Burgess, Foley and Arft, and Finkelberg, above in this volume.
[23] The problem is dismissed too lightly by Kopff (1981: 922). On imperial Greek epic, see Bär and Baumbach, below in this volume.

work overlaps with the *Aeneid* in its subject matter, used the *Aeneid* itself.[24] There are such close parallels right down to the level of formulas that, if one chooses to exclude the possibility that a Greek poet drew on Latin literature, it must be accepted that all three poets have one or more shared sources.[25] The idea that each scene has a single source shared e.g. by Quintus Smyrnaeus and Virgil quickly leads *ad absurdum* when all the comparable episodes are examined in detail. Viewing one scene at a time, it may be convincing to posit dependence on a lost epic, but the number of parallel passages in these works makes this implausible: one would need to maintain that both poets drew on all the different epics at exactly the same points. If it is argued instead that the poets drew on a single prior model for the whole material, it must have matched the *Posthomerica* in subject matter and must already have included all the motifs and new combinations that appear in both Virgil and Quintus Smyrnaeus. One is then forced to ask what exactly Virgil's innovations were – not to mention how we should judge his relation to Homer and Apollonius Rhodius. All these problems are insufficiently recognized in investigations of shared motifs. However, given that Virgil and Quintus Smyrnaeus share variants and differences even from Proclus, it can at least be concluded securely that the Cyclic epics are not *the* shared source. They are at most one among many subtexts.

Great confusion has been caused by the puzzling statement by Macrobius (*Sat.* 5.2.4) that Virgil in the second book of the *Aeneid* followed *paene ad verbum* ('almost word for word') a version by Pisander. This is complicated further by a statement of John Philoponus in the sixth century AD, who claims that Pisander drove the Cyclic epics out of popularity.[26] Pisander of Camirus, of the sixth century BC, is said to have written a *Heraclea* in two books; Pisander of Laranda, whose sixty books of ἡρωικαὶ θεογαμίαι are not extant, reportedly lived in the third century AD.[27] Keydell's theory, that Macrobius was mistaken and it was not Virgil who followed Pisander but

---

[24] On methodological difficulties concerning Latin literature as possible subtexts for these Greek texts, see Gärtner (2005); for a different approach see e.g. Bär and Baumbach, below in this volume, p. 605 with n. 4.

[25] 'Common sources' proposed included extant works such as Homer, Sophocles, Euripides, Apollonius Rhodius and Theocritus, lost or fragmentary works such as Cyclic epics, Stesichorus, Euphorion and the mysterious Pisander, and also, from the Hellenistic period, works whose existence was only assumed: a Penthesileia epic, an *Amazonomachy*, *Aethiopis*, *Iliou persis*, *Heracleis*, *Thebaid*, *Nostoi* and *Gigantomachy* as well as more general depictions of the sacking of cities.

[26] Cf. Kopff (1981: 921), who accepts the report too easily; Horsfall (2003: 470–1) is rightly critical.

[27] Cf. *Suda* π 1466 Adler; *A.P.* 9.598; Athen. 11.38p.469d; Zos. *Hist.* 5.29.3.

vice versa, may indeed be a 'simplification illusoire', but Vian's proposed solution is no less of a simplification: he proposes that this Pisander is one – or even the – lost Hellenistic common source of Quintus and Virgil.[28] The expression *paene ad verbum* should not be given too much weight, however: in the same context Macrobius cites Theocritus as the model of the *Bucolics* and Hesiod and Aratus as models for the *Georgics*, and elsewhere (5.17.4) he asserts that in the fourth book of the *Aeneid* Virgil has followed the third book of the *Argonautica* of Apollonius Rhodius *totum paene*.

The result is soberingly limited: to date, it has not been possible to demonstrate that Virgil or his audience knew the Epic Cycle in the original; they did know its subject matter and they knew it *as* the subject matter of the Epic Cycle, which is to say that they knew the Epic Cycle *in its tradition in literature and art*, as it had been transmitted to them.

THEMATIC LIMITATION: VIRGIL AND NON-TROJAN CYCLIC MOTIFS

The discussion presented here will refer almost exclusively to the Trojan cycle of myths, as is natural when investigating the thematic links with the *Aeneid*, but the broader Cycle certainly cannot be ignored. Consider the following simile, in which Aeneas in his *aristeia* in book 10 is compared to Aegaeon (10.565–70):

> Aegaeon qualis, centum cui bracchia dicunt
> centenasque manus, quinquaginta oribus ignem
> pectoribusque arsisse, Iouis cum fulmina contra
> tot paribus streperet clipeis, tot stringeret ensis:
> sic toto Aeneas desaevit in aequore victor
> ut semel intepuit mucro.

> Like Aegaeon, who, men say, had a hundred arms and a hundred hands, and flashed fire from fifty mouths and breasts, when against Jove's thunders he clanged with as many like shields, and bared as many swords; so Aeneas over the whole plain gluts his victorious rage, when once his sword grew warm.

---

[28] Keydell (1935); Vian (1959: 99–100, 107). Reference to the Hellenistic mythographer of the same name (*FgrHist* i.16) does not help because an epic remains the most likely model, especially if one chooses not to explain the verbal parallels between Quintus and Virgil as the result of direct knowledge.

The motif of the hundred-armed giant is found in a wide range of variants. In the *Iliad* (1.401–6) the hundred-armed giant 'whom the Gods call Briareos, but all mortals call Aegaeon' (403)[29] is brought by Thetis to support the Father of the Gods against the other Olympians; in Hesiod's *Theogony* (713–25) he is Zeus' ally in the battle against the Titans. Here, however, he is fighting against Iuppiter, a version of the story that probably derives from an old *Titanomachy*.[30] It is no longer possible to reconstruct whether Virgil is referring to a particular text and, if so, which one.[31] What can be established is that, through the simile, he inscribes the *Titanomachy* like a miniature into his text, and thus into the Trojan material. The striking decision to use the non-Homeric variant catches the attention of the reader who is, at the least, provoked to reflect on how Aeneas' *aristeia* is being judged.[32] This inclusion of the subject matter of the *Titanomachy* is also worth remarking in light of the significance – including political significance – of the matter of the Titans (and Giants) in Augustan art and literature, e.g. as a typical element of a *recusatio*.[33]

The epics that treated themes other than the Trojan cycle may have provided structural models too. In the siege scenes in the *Aeneid* there are parallels to the attack of the Seven against Thebes, for instance in repelling the *testudo* attack on Troy (2.440–52) and later on the Trojan camp (9.505–24). If the parallels in Quintus Smyrnaeus (11.358–439) are not accepted as a direct borrowing from the *Aeneid*, they could go back to a shared source in the Theban cycle, especially considering the treatment in Euripides (*Phoen.* 1104–86).[34] These epic treatments of the Theban material and the period in which they originated remain entirely unknown.[35]

---

[29] In the description of the underworld, Virgil calls the hundred-armed giant Briareos (6.287).

[30] *PEG* F 3 = D., W. (Σ Apoll. Rh. 1.1165c; Serv. auct. *Aen.* 6.287; 10.565; cf. Antim. F 14 Matthews); see D'Alessio, above in this volume, pp. 202–4. On the question of whether and when this *Titanomachy* came to be counted part of the Epic Cycle, or if it belongs in the Corinthian cycle of myths, see West (2002a: esp. 111–12).

[31] Cf. Horsfall (1995: 114 and 184): 'Not that Virgil read that text'.

[32] On the ambiguity of the image, see e.g. Hardie (1986: 154–6).

[33] See Hardie (1986: 87–90); Hor. *Carm.* 2.12.5–12; 3.4.42–80; Prop. 2.1.19–20, 39–40; 3.9.47–8; Ov. *Am.* 2.1.11–16; *Trist.* 2.69–72, 331–4; Tib. 2.5.9–10; and further Hardie *passim* on the theme of Gigantomachy as a key characteristic of the *Aeneid*.

[34] See also Apoll. Rh. 2.1047–89; see Gärtner (2005: 114–32).

[35] Did Quintus Smyrnaeus follow the basic structure in Euripides? Or did Euripides follow the Cyclic *Thebaid* or even the *Iliou persis*? Vian (1959: 52–5) considered as examples a Hellenistic *Thebaid* or a Hellenistic *Iliou persis* influenced by the Cyclic *Thebaid*. This is pushing the limits of useful speculation. On the Cyclic *Thebaid*, see Torres-Guerra, above in this volume.

SEARCHING FOR CLUES: THE EPIC CYCLE BEHIND THE *AENEID*

After what has been said so far, it will not be a surprise that no analysis will be made here of passages in the *Aeneid* where there is obvious thematic overlap with the Epic Cycle but no indications about sources.[36] One thinks especially of the *Iliou persis* in the second book of the *Aeneid* with the following shared motifs: design and construction of the Wooden Horse; departure of the Greeks; council of the Trojans in/below the city; the role of Sinon (he secretly slips towards Troy, is captured, and tortured, advises that the Horse be brought into the city, and that the walls be torn down, gives only a fire signal); the role of Cassandra (gives warning in/below the city); the role of Laocoon (gives warning in/below the city, is priest of Apollo or Poseidon); snake prodigy; death of Laocoon and/or his sons; death of Priam; death of Coroebus; escape of Aeneas, among much else.

If we compare only those accounts of the fall of Troy that are still in some way accessible (e.g. in the *Odyssey*, the *Iliou persis*, the *Ilias parva*, in Stesichorus, Bacchylides, Sophocles, Lysimachus, Euripides, Hellanicus, Euphorion, Lycophron, Livius Andronicus, Naevius, Ennius, Accius, Plautus, Ps.-Apollodorus, Petronius, Dictys Cretensis, Hyginus, Dares Phrygius, Palaephatus, Dio Chrysostomus, Quintus Smyrnaeus, Triphiodorus, Cedrenus, Tzetzes),[37] we will admire the *Aeneid*'s artful design,[38] but for the history of the motifs, as far as the Cyclic epics are concerned, we are confronted with a near-insoluble tangle of sources. All that can be established securely is that Virgil in his *Iliou persis* aims to rival the entire tradition of the Epic Cycle and that, drawing especially on the tragedians, he creates something entirely new by having Aeneas present the story from the Trojan point of view, as a victim of the events described.[39]

It would serve no purpose to discuss all the passages in the *Aeneid* that merely mention figures or content attested in the Epic Cycle (or that may have appeared there but also elsewhere), in which the context in Virgil creates no reference to the old epics or where a knowledge of them does not seem necessary. This is even less convincing when the version given of the mythical theme departs entirely from the Cyclic epics. A brief mention of Venus and Anchises (1.617–18) or Astyanax (3.489–91) need not refer to the

---

[36] *Contra* Kopff (1981: 928): 'The only clear place where the Cyclic epics provided a partial source for Virgil's narrative is A. 2.' Cf. Horsfall (2008: xix–xx).
[37] See Gärtner (2005: 134–60).
[38] See e.g. Heinze (1915: 3–81); Zintzen (1979); for an overview, Horsfall (2008: xiii–xxvii).
[39] See below.

epics; the same holds for the fate of Antenor (1.242–9), of whom we know nothing in the *Nostoi* while Virgil's version is derived via Accius probably from Sophocles, or the mention of Palamedes (2.81–5), whose betrayal by Odysseus was recounted in the *Cypria* (*PEG* F 30 = F 20 D. = F 27 W.) differently from Virgil and most of the later tradition.

MARKED REFERENCES: THE EPIC CYCLE IN THE *AENEID*

It is more interesting to look for passages that feature a type of intertextual reference that demands that the reader bring the Cyclic epics to mind. Let us first consider the one marked most strongly, which also seems to be significant in terms of poetics: the images on the temple at Carthage.

After Aeneas lands in Libya, before meeting Dido herself, he sees the new city of Carthage under construction and sees images on its temple of Iuno presenting scenes from the Trojan War in sequence (*ex ordine*, 1.453–93, 466). He is astonished and moved, and concludes that in this place there must be pity (*sunt lacrimae rerum et mentem mortalia tangunt*, 'Here there are tears for misfortune, and human suffering touches the senses', 462) and salvation (*feret haec aliquam tibi fama salutem*, 'This fame will bring you some kind of salvation', 463). In what follows, the reader sees through the eyes of the viewer Aeneas individual scenes that form part of the subject matter of the *Iliad*, but also of the Epic Cycle.[40] Like every *ekphrasis*, this initially produces a pause in the narrative, but it is above all a point that prompts the reader to reflect upon the medium itself, i.e. not only on the relation between image and text, but also on the manner of presentation or narrative, on perception, emotional effect and interpretation.[41] Virgil has also used the passage to present to the reader alternative narrative strategies. When later, in the description of the shield, he presents the future history of Rome in sequence (*in ordine*, 8.629), he will provide a miniature version of annalistic historical epic in the manner of an Ennius, leading to Augustus, who may have wanted a work of that kind though Virgil did not provide it. The temple images engage with the entire material of the Trojan cycle, which can be seen as a reference to the Epic Cycle, given the sequential

---

[40] Barchiesi (1997; 1999) are essential discussions; see also Clay (1988); Putnam (1998b) among many other discussions. The passage is also discussed by Fantuzzi and Squire, above in this volume, respectively pp. 422–4 and 520.

[41] For reflection upon the artist's capabilities, cf. the *ekphrasis* of the doors to the temple of Apollo made by Daedalus (6.18–33).

narrative style for which it was criticized in antiquity. The scenes described are admittedly viewed through the eyes of Aeneas and we follow where his gaze falls in a very realistic way; Virgil specifically presents them out of temporal sequence. This new sequence proleptically sets out the narrative structure of the later books of the *Aeneid*, as the scenes foreshadow what is to come, especially Aeneas' experiences in Latium.[42] The initial scenes are connected in general to the Trojan War (466–8). The Rhesus episode (469–73) draws on *Iliad* 10 and prepares the way for the nocturnal fight for Troy in book 2 (especially as his death is a necessary step for the fall of Troy), but above all for the night sortie of Nisus and Euryalus in book 9. The killing of Troilus by Achilles (474–8) must have been treated in the *Cypria*. In Proclus (arg. line 162 Severyns) we read only that Achilles killed him; one of the key features of later accounts was that he was young and unarmed when he was ambushed and killed by Achilles beside or in the temple of Apollo. As his early death was also a condition for the fall of Troy (Plaut. *Bacch.* 953–6), this too announces book 2. Further, the unequal fight (*impar* 475) prefigures the defeat of Pallas and Lausus in book 10 and of Turnus himself (cf. 12.216), and the death scene itself is perhaps a model for the death of Camilla in book 11. It should also be noted that it is not only Turnus who becomes a second Achilles (cf. 6.89–90) and, like the Greek hero, must surrender his life for his guilt in the death of a young warrior, but also Aeneas himself at the end of the *Aeneid*.[43] The vain sacrifice of the Trojan women (479–82) can be read in *Iliad* 6. It foreshadows the sacrifice of Amata in book 11 and that of Turnus in book 12. In the representation of Achilles dragging Hector round the walls of Troy[44] and trading the body for money (483–7), Virgil does not follow the *Iliad*; the scene itself suggests the end of the *Aeneid*. Aeneas' sight of himself in battle (488) stands for his role in the whole struggle for Troy and announces book 2, but also the approaching battles in Latium. The two figures in the last images were the protagonists of the *Aethiopis*: the representation of Memnon (489) is picked up again in the forging of the weapons in book 8; Penthesileia (490–3) foreshadows Dido, but above all Camilla in books 7 and 11. It is striking that Achilles is implicitly present in almost all images and is a foil for Turnus, as he will later be also for Aeneas.

The temple images as a whole create a link to the songs of Demodocus – and the emotional reaction of Odysseus to them – in book 8 of the

---

[42] See e.g. Knauer (1979: 349–50); Putnam (1998b: 265–7).   [43] See e.g. Clay (1988: 204).
[44] This version is already found in Euripides (*Andr.* 107–8); whether it derives from the *Aethiopis* cannot be determined. From this starting point, Kopff (1981: 930–1; 1983) goes quite far in speculating about the *Aethiopis*.

Odyssey.⁴⁵ There too themes from the Epic Cycle are presented, with the contest for the weapons of Achilles (72–82) and the capture of Troy with the Wooden Horse (499–520). However, while in the *Odyssey* the epic is in a certain sense mirrored by Demodocus' oral presentation, the reflection on the medium prompted by the temple images draws attention to the *Aeneid*'s new conception of the entire Epic Cycle.

It has often been remarked that Aeneas misreads the scenes or interprets them in a way that is consoling to himself (*animum pictura pascit inani*, 'he feeds his soul on the vain picture', 464), because this temple of a goddess hostile to the Trojans displays not their suffering but the Greeks' victory, and in especially savage and treacherous scenes. This creates a reference not only to the issue of how art is interpreted, but also to the character of the *Aeneid* itself, which presents the familiar material from a new perspective, that of the Trojans or Romans; this is cast into sharp focus when in book 2 Aeneas himself becomes the involved narrator of the *Iliou persis*.

Against this background it is, while not demonstrable, at least very tempting to read lines 456–7 *videt Iliacas ex ordine pugnas / bellaque iam fama totum vulgata per orbem* ('he sees in sequence the Iliadic battles and wars, that have already been spread by report through the whole world/Cycle') with Barchiesi as a metapoetic reference to the Epic Cycle (*orbem*) with its account that is not only known but even hackneyed (*vulgata*), especially in light of the passage of Horace discussed above.⁴⁶ This interpretation does not require that the old epics themselves were in wide circulation. A bigger influence for the formation of the Troilus story may have been Sophocles' tragedy, and the motifs are realized in ways that reveal later characteristics; however, the subjects of the temple images were known as a whole as elements of the Epic Cycle.

Other passages, too, clearly signal to the reader that material is from the Epic Cycle. The comparison of Penthesileia and Camilla in the temple image mentioned above is picked up again in a simile in book 11 (659–63).

> quales Threiciae cum flumina Thermodontis
> pulsant et pictis bellantur Amazones armis,
> seu circum Hippolyten seu cum se Martia curru
> Penthesileia refert, magnoque ululante tumultu
> feminea exsultant lunatis agmina peltis.

---

[45] Putnam (1998b: 268–75); Barchiesi (1999: 332–3).
[46] Cf. *Georg.* 3.4 *omnia iam vulgata*; cf. Barchiesi (1999: 334). Admittedly, the spreading of glory is a topos; cf. already *Od.* 8.73–4; 9.263–4. On *orbis* as a common term for the world in the Augustan period, see Christ (1938: 4–18).

> Such are the Amazons of Thrace, when they tramp over Thermodon's streams and war in blazoned armour, whether round Hippolyte, or when Penthesileia, child of Mars, returns in her chariot, and, amid loud tumultuous cries, the army of women exult with crescent shields.

Mention of Hippolyte will have called to mind her defeat by Hercules or Theseus and will therefore have suggested Camilla's death. That the figure of Camilla exhibits characteristics of Penthesileia needs no discussion, but it is not clear whether and to what extent the depiction of Penthesileia in the *Aethiopis* should be seen as a background to this.[47] In Proclus (arg. lines 175–7 Severyns) we read that she was a daughter of Ares, came from Thrace to help the Trojans, was killed by Achilles and buried by the Trojans. Her origin has been debated, as has the female warriors' battle-mode (chariots, horseback or on foot). As this ultimately yields little, we should accept simply that Virgil in his battle-scenes draws on different variants and so creates a new, striking mixture in his depiction. The figure of Camilla includes Italic elements; much of the story reveals structures from the *Iliad*, such as the final combats of Patroclus or Sarpedon; the death in an ambush is reminiscent of the death of Troilus (see above) or of Achilles himself. Influence from tragedy should also be noted. Given the state of the transmission, we cannot say what, if anything, derives from the *Aethiopis* or the *Cypria*.[48] The Penthesileia simile is a prompt to the reader to call to mind the subject matter as a whole (the female warrior, her wildness, bravery and overconfidence) and to recognize against this foil the new creation of an Italic female warrior.

The second main figure of the *Aethiopis*, Memnon, has a similar role. When Venus asks Vulcanus for weapons for her son Aeneas, she reminds him that both Thetis and Aurora persuaded him to forge arms for their sons (8.383–4); the theme of weapons was already emphasised in the temple images (*Memnonis arma* 1.489). Proclus (arg. lines 185–6 Severyns) cites the arms made for Memnon by Hephaestus, so it is plausible that these and a comparable request scene may have featured in the *Aethiopis*.[49] On the other hand, arms and armour were a popular characteristic of Memnon at an early stage (cf. Hes. *Theog.* 984 χαλκοκορυστής 'bronze-armed'; Aristoph. *Ran.* 963 Μέμνονας κωδωνοφαλαροπώλους 'people like the bells-and-bridle-mounted Memnon'), so that this is in itself already a literary allusion. In

---

[47] Cf. e.g. Arrigoni (1982); La Penna (1988); Horsfall (1988: esp. 46–7 ; 2003: 465–72 ; 2004); Fantuzzi (2012).
[48] For a detailed study of Penthesileia in Quintus Smyrnaeus, see Bär (2009); on the relation between Camilla and Penthesileia in Quintus, see Gärtner (2005: 43–66).
[49] See Welcker (1882: 173); Kopff (1981: 935); Davies (1989c: 53); West (2013: 144).

the present passage, it is enough that the naming of the two goddesses recalls for the reader the typically epic element of a description of a shield, a literary challenge taken up by the *ekphrasis* that follows. The metapoetic engagement with the narrative technique of epic itself, as discussed above, gives special weight to the reference to the older epics.

A similar technique of signalling a reference is found at the start of the *Aeneid*, where again a goddess compares her situation to that of a goddess from the subject matter of the Epic Cycle. Iuno refers angrily to Athena (1.39–45), who was able to destroy the fleet of the Greeks on account of the transgression of Ajax Oileus. Ajax's assault on Cassandra at the cult-statue of Athena was recounted in the *Iliou persis* (arg. lines 261–5 Severyns), his downfall in the *Nostoi* (arg. lines 294–5 Severyns). Did these epics serve as sources, or as model or subtext? The storm at sea is in itself a very common motif, and the great storm in *Odyssey* book 5 is central for the understanding of book 1 of the *Aeneid*; the reader recognized that Odysseus had just escaped from the woman trying to prevent his return home, while Aeneas' encounter with Dido is yet to happen. The storm on the Greeks' return journey is presented differently in the *Odyssey* (4.499–511), as Ajax's guilt is not mentioned explicitly there; the tragic tradition presumably had a strong influence on Virgil.[50] Here again, the parallel draws attention to the innovative design of the *Aeneid*, with the distinctive *nostos* of Aeneas, and quite directly of course to the approaching storm. The reader must have at least been sufficiently familiar with the material of the *Nostoi* to recognize that there Athena destroys the ships with Zeus' permission, whereas here Iuno knowingly acts against Iuppiter and Fate; that Ajax was punished for sacrilege, whereas Aeneas has shown himself to be *pius*; that Ajax at first boasts of his escape to safety, whereas Aeneas, despite his worries, tries to console his companions by referring to fate; and finally that Poseidon helps to kill Ajax, whereas he saves Aeneas.[51] But did the reader need to know the Cyclic *Nostoi* for this, or Hellenistic *Nostoi* together with a *Gigantomachy*?[52]

Just before this (1.23–32), the poet gives us an insight into Iuno's intentions: she recalls not only the war that she fought for her Greeks, which is the subject matter of the Cycle from *Cypria* to the *Iliou persis* (23–4), but also the insult done to her by the judgment of Paris and the rape of Ganymede, subjects from the *Cypria* (25–8), and the victory of the Greeks (30), a subject from the *Ilias parva* or *Iliou persis*. Thus at the start of the

---

[50] Cf. Aesch. *Ag.* 648–60; Eur. *Tro.* 77–97; Sen. *Ag.* 421–578; Q.S. 14.370–658.
[51] See Kopff (1981: 933).   [52] Thus Vian (1959: 84–5).

Aeneid the reader is given a sketch of the entire Cycle – once again *ex ordine* – and is led to expect a novel version. *reliquias Danaum* (30) could then be understood metapoetically.

Things come full circle when Dido at the end of book 1 (750–6) asks about Priam and Hector, about which weapons the son of Aurora brought (again here the theme of weapons is emphasized with Memnon: *quibus Aurorae venisset filius armis* 751; cf. 489), what the horses of Diomedes were like, and how tall Achilles was, and finally asks the guest to tell of the Greeks' ruse and his own wanderings. The material is already known in Carthage, but Dido wants to hear Aeneas' own version. In this way, the first book encompasses the entire material of the Epic Cycle and at the same time announces a new *nostos*, and a new design of the entire cycle.[53]

Similar points could be demonstrated in many other passages where the material of the Epic Cycle is used as a comparison or is directly mentioned. However, these references are for the most part so general that they do not suggest that the Epic Cycle was a source or that a particular epic is being signalled to the reader. Thus in book 7 Amata voices her fear that Aeneas will take Lavinia away overseas, and compares Paris and Helen (7.359–64), but here again only the subject matter need be known, and it must in fact be (too) well-known (cf. 10.92–3) if even Amata can use it as an argument.

Other passages are less strongly marked. It has been claimed that Euander and Pallas, or Mezentius and Lausus, create a reference to Nestor and Antilochus in the *Aethiopis*.[54] In Proclus (arg. lines 188–9 Severyns) we read only that in the *Aethiopis* Antilochus was buried after Achilles' death. Pindar recounts (*Pyth.* 6.28–43) that Antilochus fell trying to defend his elderly father Nestor from Memnon's attack.[55] The motif of Nestor bewailing his fate on the death of his son is widespread in Latin literature.[56] The laments of Euander for Pallas in books 8 (508–19; 579–83) and 11 (160–1) could thus hint at Nestor, and the self-sacrifice of Lausus at that of Antilochus. This is picked up again in Turnus' boasting that he will cause Euander pain (10.441–3; 491–5). It can be demonstrated that Virgil is here drawing on

---

[53] See also Fantuzzi, above in this volume, pp. 422–3.
[54] See Fränkel (1932); Manton (1962); Assereto (1970: 55–6); Kopff (1981: 936).
[55] The question of the priority of Nestor's distress in *Iliad* 8 or of the scene sketched here can only be mentioned in passing. Here too the solution offered by neoanalytic approaches seems the most convincing, namely that the motif itself is older, and that it was picked up both in the *Iliad* and, later, in the *Aethiopis*. The version presented by Quintus Smyrnaeus includes fewer parallels to Pindar than are present in Virgil; see Gärtner (2005: 67–8); to *Iliad* and *Aethiopis*, see West (2003c) and Kullmann (2005); to Pindar and *Aethiopis*, see Kullmann and Rutherford, above in this volume, respectively pp. 114 and 451–7 *passim*.
[56] Prop. 2.13.46–50; Hor. *Carm.* 2.9.13–15; Juv. 10.246–55; Auson. *Epitaph.* 7, 8.

Pindar, but whether he used the *Aethiopis* in this passage is an open question. However, in this passage too a familiarity with the subject matter is all the reader needs to admire the new form of presentation and to guess the death of Pallas already in book 8. Admittedly this is marked via the *Iliad*, because Euander's lament *o mihi praeteritos referat si Iuppiter annos, / qualis eram cum, etc.* ('O if Iuppiter would return to me the years gone by, as I was when, etc.') (8.560–1) will at once remind the reader of the opening lines of the garrulous Nestor's frequent speeches in the *Iliad*, who bewails his current weakness in comparison to the strength he once had: εἴθ' ὣς ἡβώοιμι βίη δέ μοι ἔμπεδος εἴη, | ὡς ὁπότ'… ('if I were only as young and my strength so firm as when…') (11.670–1 = 23.629–30; cf. 7.132–3, 157). Once the association with Nestor had been called to mind, however, the well-known non-Iliadic material of the Cycle could be recalled via the old man.

There is a strikingly large number of deaths of young warriors in the *Aeneid*, in particular Pallas, Lausus and Camilla. After what has been said above, this may seem to recall Troilus in the *Cypria*[57] and Antilochus in the *Aethiopis*, though the manner of presenting the scenes has been taken from the *Iliad*, especially from Sarpedon and Patroclus. Despite strong arguments in favour,[58] one should still be cautious as long as the relation between the *Iliad* and the Epic Cycle remains unclear. Perhaps these combinations of supposedly 'Homeric' styles of presentation with 'Cyclic' content appeared already in the Cycle or in later lost epics.

It would go too far to address passages that neither name material from the Epic Cycle nor suggest it by a comparison, but that merely lead one to suspect a parallel. For example there is a potential parallel in the single combat between Memnon and Achilles in the *Aethiopis* and between Turnus and Aeneas at the end of the *Aeneid*, especially if the version in Quintus book 2 is borne in mind.[59] However, this moves us into the realm of speculation.

THROUGH THE *AENEID* TO THE EPIC CYCLE

Can we infer anything from the *Aeneid* about the Epic Cycle? After the discussion above, this will seem somewhat unlikely. However, one hypothesis may be mentioned.

---

[57] See Currie, above in this volume, p. 294.
[58] See e.g. Knauer (1979: 298–315); Kopff (1981: 938–44).
[59] The single combat between Achilles and Hector in *Il.* 22.131–366 must of course be kept in mind. See Gärtner (2005: 68–76).

The beginning of the *Ilias parva* is generally believed to be the 'beginning' cited in the *Life of Homer* (*Ilias parva PEG* F 28 = F 1 D. = F 1 W.): Ἴλιον ἀείδω καὶ Δαρδανίην εὔπωλον / ἧς πέρι πολλὰ πάθον Δαναοὶ θεράποντες Ἄρηος ('Of Ilium I sing, and Dardania land of fine colts, over which the Danaans suffered much, servants of the War god'). The matter is complicated by the following verses, transmitted in Plutarch as – probably – by Lesches, referring to a proem (*Ilias parva PEG* F 1 = dub. 2 D.): Μοῦσά μοι ἔννεπε κεῖνα, τὰ μήτ' ἐγένοντο πάροιθε / μήτ' ἔσται μετόπισθεν ('Muse, tell me of those things that never occurred before nor will do again'). Explanations have included that there were two or more *Iliades parvae* or that the poem was multiform, or else one of the two fragments has been suspected, usually the second as it is judged to lack the self-confidence of the first fragment and also to be simplistic, banal and hackneyed.[60] Attempts have also been made to harmonize the two fragments by reference to the proem of the *Aeneid*.[61] After the author's prominence at the start (*arma virumque cano*, 'arms I sing and the man'), there is a second beginning, with a clear reference to the *Iliad* and *Odyssey* in that the Muse is invoked as the source of knowledge (*Musa, mihi causas memora*, 'Muse, tell me the causes', 1.8), and the causes named (1.12–49) encompass the entire Epic Cycle, as described above. Perhaps therefore there was a similar structure in the proem of the *Ilias parva*, in which the poet first steps forward confidently as an individual,[62] and then in a second move the poem inscribes itself in the Homeric tradition.[63] Virgil would thus have combined this pattern with the content of the *Iliad*, *Odyssey* and Cycle.

CONCLUSION

The result may seem disappointing: verbal parallels between the works of Virgil and the Epic Cycle cannot be identified. Evidence that Virgil read the epics in the original cannot be found either. It must be accepted that all further hypotheses about the epics as sources, models or subtexts are speculative, and are made even more so by the uncertain relation of these epics to Homer, by the unknown number of lost works and by the popularity of mythographical summaries.

---

[60] On the two incipits see Kelly, above in this volume, pp. 328–31. [61] See Scafoglio (2006).
[62] Cf. Hor. *Ars poet.* 137, on which see above, pp. 544–6.
[63] We find this in Apollonius Rhodius (1.1–2) in similar form: ἀρχόμενος ... | μνήσομαι ('Beginning with ... I will tell'); 22: Μοῦσαι δ' ὑποφήτορες εἶεν ἀοιδῆς ('The Muses shall be the helpers with the song').

It can probably be accepted that, even if Virgil had access to the text of these works, he could not assume that they would be present to his public as a verbally recognisable subtext. Nonetheless, the material of the epics was present in people's minds, and probably also in a narrower sense as the material of the Cyclic epics. Further, as we can tell from Horace, people knew the criticisms levelled at this type of poetry. Traces of this at least, it seems, can be identified in the *Aeneid*: Virgil draws on the material in his epics, surpasses it and at the same time creates a new – Roman – view of the cycle, or indeed a new cycle.

LIST OF MOTIFS[64]

The following list gives a survey of places which have been thought of as references to the Cyclic epics as sources or models. It is of course no proof in any way. To keep it manageable, passages concerning the *Iliou persis* in *Aeneid* 2 were left out almost completely.[65]

↔ different
~ similar
? uncertain

Virgil	Motifs	Source/Model
1.1–11	two-part proem: *cano – Musa*	*Ilias parva* F 28; F 1; cf. Apoll. Rh. 1.1–22
	cano	cf. Hor. *Ars P.* 137: *cantabo*
1.27	judgment of Paris	*Cypr.*
1.28	Ganymede	*Ilias parva* F 29.
	both as reasons for Juno's hatred	*Cypr.*
1.39–45	Juno: storm, death of Ajax Oileus	*Nostoi*
1.223–96	Jupiter / Venus ~ Zeus / Thetis	*Cypr.*
1.242–9	Antenor in Italy	? *Nostoi*
1.450–93	pictures on Juno's temple (gen.): *Iliacas in ordine pugnas*	epic Cycle; *Il.*; *Od.* gen.
1.474–8	death of Troilus	*Cypr.*
1.479–82	women of Troy sacrifice peplos to Pallas (see below 1.648–52)	*Il.* 6.288–312
1.483–4	mutilation of Hector (three times dragged around the city – alive?) (see below 2.272–3; 285–6)	? *Aeth.* (cf. Soph. *Aj.* 1029–31; Eur. *Andr.* 107–8. 399; *A.P.* 7.151, 152; Curt. 4.28) ↔ *Il.* 22.395–404

---

[64] Because of lack of space in the following table only the numbering used in Bernabé's edition of the epic fragments (*PEG*) is provided.

[65] Cf. the tabular summary in Gärtner (2005: 159–60).

Virgil	Motifs	Source/Model
1.489	Memnon	*Aeth.*
1.490–3	Penthesileia	*Aeth.*
1.617–8	Venus / Anchises	? *Cypr.*
1.619–20	Teucer being exile in Sidon and Cyprus	? *Nostoi*
1.648–52	Helen's mantle and veil (brought from Mycenae to Troy) (see above 1.479–82)	? *Cypr.*
1.657–722	Dido / Cupido ~ Helen / Eros (cf. 10.92–3)	? *Cypr.*
1.750–6	Dido asks about Priam, Hector, Memnon (cf. *Aen.* 8), Diomedes' horses, Achilles' tallness, treachery of the Greeks, Aeneas' own wandering and fate	*Il.*; *Aeth.*; *Il. pers.*; *Ilias parva*
2	gen.	*Il. pers.*; *Ilias parva*
2 gen.	Aeneas' exodus to Mt. Ida	*Il. pers.*
	Creusa	↔ *Ilias parva*: Neoptolemus takes Aeneas as a special prize
		↔ Eurydice: *Cypr.* F 31; *Ilias parva* F 22
2.15	size of the wooden horse	*Il. pers.* F 2
2.81–93	death of Palamedes because of the false accusations of Odysseus	↔ *Cypr.* F 30: drowned by Odysseus and Diomedes on a fishing expedition; in tragic tradition he is the victim of a mistrial
2.116	Iphigenia	*Cypr.* arg. lines 135–43 Severyns; F 24.
2.162–75	Odysseus and Diomedes steal the Palladium	*Ilias parva* arg. ll. 228–9 Severyns; F 25; *Il. pers.* F 1
2.198	1000 ships	?
		Aesch. *Ag.* 45
2.246–7		? *Ilias parva* (Ps.-Apollod.; Hyg. *fab.*)
	Cassandra unbelieved (gen.)	?
2.268–97	Hector's demand to leave ~ Achilles' warning not to leave	*Nostoi*
2.272–3 285–6	mutilation of Hector (see above 1.483–4)	*Aeth.* ↔ *Il.*
3.19–68	Polydorus	?
		Eur.
3.80	Anius (king of Delos, priest of Apollo)	?
		cf. Σ Lycophr. 578
3.121–3	Idomeneus being exile from Crete	? *Nostoi*

(*cont.*)

(*Cont.*)

Virgil	Motifs	Source/Model
3.294–351	Helenus / Andromache	? *Nostoi*
3.321–4	Polyxena	*Il. pers.* arg. line 274 Severyns ? *Nostoi*
3.398–402	Greeks in Italy	? *Nostoi*
3.489–91	Andromache compares Iulus to Astyanax	? *Nostoi*
3.708–11	death of Anchises ~ death of Calchas / Phoenix	*Nostoi*
5	funeral games for Anchises ~ funeral games for Achilles	*Aeth.* (cf. *Il.* 23: for Patroclus) *Nostoi*: for Calchas / Phoenix
5.370	Paris as boxer	? (cf. Hyg. *fab.* 91; 273)
5.535–8	Hecuba's father: Cisseus (see below 7.319–20; 10.702–5)	cf. Eur. *Hec.* 3; Serv. *Aen.* 7.320: Ennius/Pacuvius follow Euripides ↔ *Il.* 16.718: Dymas; 11.223–4: Cisses: father of Theano
6	Catabasis gen. ~ Catabasis of Hercules	? *Heracleis*
6.57–8	Achilles killed by Paris and Apollo	*Aeth.* arg. lines 191–2 Severyns
6.121–2	Castor and Pollux: immortality on alternate days	*Cypr.* arg. lines 106–9 Severyns
6.494–547	Deiphobus	*Ilias parva* arg. line 216 Severyns (Deiphobus marries Helen); *Il. pers.* arg. lines 259–60 Severyns (Menelaus kills Deiphobus)
6.518–9	Helen's fire-signal	↔ *Il. pers.* arg. lines 252–3 Severyns: Sinon
7.293–7	Juno's hatred: –Trojans survive Sigeum –Trojans survive the sack of Troy –Trojans find their way	? *Il. pers.*; *Ilias parva*
7.319–20	Hecuba: daughter of Cisseus (see above 5.535–8) –conceives a firebrand, gives birth to nuptial flames	see above ? (cf. Eur. *Tro.* 921–2; Cic. *Div.* 1.42; Ps.-Apollod. *Bibl.* 3.12.5)
7.321–2	Juno: second Paris (= Aeneas) will destroy new Troy	gen.
7.363–4	Amata: Paris abducts Helen ~ Aeneas will abduct Lavinia	*Cypr.*

Virgil	Motifs	Source/Model
7.723–32	Halaesus: companion of Agamemnon, in Turnus' army, leader of the Falerii	? *Nostoi* cf. Verg. *Aen.* 10.411–25; Serv. *Aen.* 7. 695. 723; Ov. *Am.* 3.13.31–2; *Fast.* 4.73–4; *Met.* 12.462
7.808–9	Camilla could fly over unmown corn without bruising it ~ Penthesileia	? *Aeth.*
8.9–17	Diomedes in Italy (see below 11.225–95)	? *Nostoi*
8.383–4	Venus at Vulcanus; ~ Thetis and Aurora at Hephaestus	*Il.*; *Aeth.*
8.560–84	Euander's lament because of Pallas ~ Nestor / Antilochus (see below 11.152–81)	*Aeth.* (cf. *Il.* 7.132–3; 11.670–1; 23.629–30)
9	*aristeia* of Turnus ~ *aristeia* of Achilles before his death	*Aeth.*
9.151	Palladium = 2.166 (see above)	
9.152	Turnus: he will not lurk in a wooden horse	gen.
9.176–458	Nisus / Euryalus ~ theft of the Palladium	*Ilias parva*; cf. *Il.* 10: *Rhesus*
10/11	death of Pallas, Lausus, Camilla ~ death of Sarpedon, Patroclus, Troilus	*Il.*; *Cypr.*
10	landing of Aeneas – death of Pallas ~ landing of the Greeks – death of Protesilaus	*Cypr.*
10.28–9	Venus: Diomedes rises against the Trojans	gen.
10.68	Juno: Aeneas came *fatis auctoribus... Cassandrae impulsus furiis*	gen.
10.92–3	Juno: Helen's abduction	*Cypr.*
10.565–70	simile: Titanomachy: Aegaeon against Jupiter / Aeneas' aristia	*Tit.* F 3 ↔ Hes. *Theog.* 713–25; *Il.* 1.401–6
10.702–5	Mimas born by Theano to Amycus the same day as Paris by Cisseis (= Hecuba) (see above 5.535–8)	
10.769–832	death of Lausus / Mezentius ~ Antilochus / Nestor	*Aeth.* cf. Pind. *Pyth.* 6.27–8
10.831–2	Aen. holds dead Lausus in his arms ~ Achilles / Penthesileia	? *Aeth.*

(*cont.*)

(*Cont.*)

Virgil	Motifs	Source/Model
11.152–81	Euander's lament because of Pallas ~ Nestor / Antilochus (see above 8.560–84)	*Aeth.*
11.175–81	Euander demands revenge from Aeneas ~ Nestor / Achilles	*Aeth.*
11.225–95	Diomedes	?
11.252–74	Diomedes tells his nostos ~ Nostoi ? new: penalties for guilt	? ↔ *Od.* 3.130–83; *Nost.* arg. lines 283–4 Severyns: Diomedes and Nestor διασῴζονται
11.259–60	Minerva, Caphereus (= Ajax Oileus)	*Nostoi*
11.261–3	Menelaus in Egypt	*Nost.* arg. lines 285–7 Severyns
11.264–5	fates of Neoptolemus, Idomeneus and the Locri	? post-'*Nostoi*'
11.266–8	death of Agamemnon	*Nost.* arg. lines 301–2 Severyns
11.269–74	Diomedes being exile; metamorphosis of his companions into birds	? *Nost.*; *Theb.*
11.498–835	Camilla ~ Penthesileia	*Aeth.*
	death of Camilla ~ death of Patroclus, Sarpedon, Troilus	*Il.*; *Cypr.*
11.581–2	Etruscan women wish Camilla as daughter-in-law ~ Greeks wish Penthesileia as wife	? *Aeth.* ? (cf. Q.S. 1.669–70)
11.648–9	end of line: *Amazon*	*Aeth.* F 1: end of line 1: Ἀμαζών
11.659–63	simile: Penthesileia / Camilla	*Aeth.*
	'Thracian' amazons ~ genealogy from *Aeth.*	*Aeth.*
11.836–67	–Opis / Diana taking revenge for Camilla ~ Penthesileia receives honourable funeral, acknowledged by Achilles	*Aeth.*
	~ Oupis: epithet of Artemis	Callim. *Hymn.* 3.237–58
12	single combat of Aeneas / Turnus ~ Achilles / Memnon ?	*Aeth.* Q. S. 2

29 | Ovid and the Epic Cycle

GIANPIERO ROSATI

AN EPIC WITHOUT BOUNDARIES

If the adjective 'Cyclic' describes a kind of epic that aspires to be universal, all-inclusive, that is to say, based on an essentially anti-Homeric aesthetic, then it is difficult to imagine a more Cyclic oeuvre than Ovid's. Throughout his whole career, Ovid remained an ecumenical and inclusive writer. He is the only elegiac poet who refused to restrict himself to this single literary genre. Instead, he experimented with many others, even those that seem incompatible with elegiac sensibility, such as tragedy and epic, and he is nowhere more inclusive than in his major poem. The *Metamorphoses* is a decidedly comprehensive, omnivorous, non-selective, all-encompassing epic that accumulates, and does not exclude, anything that is *narrabile*.[1] As the proem states, the narrative style of the poem is continuous (*perpetuum*, 1.4), that is to say: not Homeric, but Hesiodic, or, rather, Cyclic. After all, the notion of 'continuity' had long since been linked to the name of Hesiod, both because the genealogical *Theogony* was structured in this manner and because it was perceived as part of a Hesiodic *Theogony–Catalogue–Erga* sequence. In turn, scholars have often pointed out the evident influence of the Epic Cycle on the structural organization of the Trojan section of the *Metamorphoses*.[2] More generally speaking, the idea of cyclicity is a necessary presupposition for the kind of 'universal history' that Ovid's poem presents. Its structure openly contradicts Aristotle's norm (*Poet.* chap. 23) that epic needs to be selective – like the Homeric and unlike the Cyclic model – and needs to make some *a priori* exclusions.[3] Ovid in fact goes well beyond the *scriptor Cyclicus* who, as Horace deplores, *gemino bellum Troianum orditur ab ovo* (*Ars* 147: 'begin[s]...the war of Troy from

---

[1] On 'narrability' as the inspiring criterion of the poem, see Barchiesi (2002: 180–2 and *passim*); valuable observations on this aspect can also be found in Calvino (1995).

[2] See e.g. Ludwig (1965: 60–5); Ellsworth (1980); Croisille (1985: 61–8); Dippel (1990: 19–21); Papaioannou (2007: 3). However, despite the excellent contribution of Papaioannou (2007), the topic still lacks an adequate, exhaustive discussion; as Ziogas (2008) observes, 'the Cyclic nature of Ovid's *Metamorphoses* in general and his Trojan War in particular calls for an extensive analysis of the poetics of the Epic Cycle vis-à-vis Homeric epic'.

[3] See Fantuzzi, above in this volume, pp. 412–14.

the twin eggs'): he begins much earlier, and ends much later, delineating the broadest narrative arc imaginable (*prima... ab origine mundi ad mea... tempora* 'from nature's first remote beginning to our modern times',[4] *Met.* 1.3–4). In Ovidian as in Cyclic epic, there is no well-defined, circumscribed, 'Homeric' narrative arc, or any functional organization that assigns to the single narrative unit a role subordinate to the hierarchic structure that governs the larger story. Rather, the structural principle that seems to have inspired the Cyclic poems, that is, to provide a chronological sequence of single episodes that are autonomous in themselves,[5] finds a correspondence in the predominantly chronological frame that contains the narrative of Ovid's poem. The *Metamorphoses* lacks a teleological organization that has single episodes serve a function in the poem's overall organization. If there is any difference, it lies in the care Ovid takes to create, on every occasion, some link between the episodes, with that virtuosity typical of an illusionist that aroused Quintilian's admiration (4.1.77).[6] Yet the exhibited artificial nature of that 'fil rouge' is a clear indication of how hard the author had to work to create the causal connections that make the *Metamorphoses* a consistent, coherent plot.

If organic unity was essential to Aristotle's definition of Homeric epic as a normative model, if he praises Homer precisely because he avoids narrating the whole of the Trojan War, seeing that 'it would have been too vast a theme, and not easily embraced in a single view' (*Poet.* chap. 23), then it is not difficult to imagine how Aristotle would have judged the *Metamorphoses*, a poem that makes the continual proliferation of narrative topics and the multiplication of points of view its main driving force, a poem that does not have any centre, or any unifying hero, and that does not exclude anything, either early or late, 'high' or 'low', rational or irrational–fantastic–marvellous.

Among the various definitions which scholars, from Aristotle on, have applied to distinguish Homer's epic from the Cycle, there is also the one according to which Homeric epic excludes aspects of reality that are 'common' and everyday, foreign to the heroic dimension, while Cyclic epic makes room for characters who refuse heroism, as well as for 'humble' aspects or activities.[7] It is from this point of view, too, that Ovid is decidedly closer to this second kind of epic: while martial heroism, and war in general,

---

[4] Translations from the *Metamorphoses* are by A. D. Melville.   [5] Finkelberg (1998: 137).

[6] However, also from this point of view, Ovid could have found a precedent in the way in which the various Cyclic poems were linked on the occasion of their performance: as regards this procedure, see Burgess (2002).

[7] Griffin (1977: 45–6).

are noticeably absent from this 'epic of peace', the *Metamorphoses* presents, on various occasions, modest characters and humble workers, like seamen, farmers, shepherds, artisans: e.g., there is Idmon, the artisan dyer and father of the 'little' Arachne (6.8–13), who herself lacks any resources other than her *ars*; or the father of Acoetes (3.582–96), a fisherman who has no wealth but his *ars* (*ars illi sua census erat,* 3.580) and whose 'crude vision of the life of workers on the sea'[8] even led scholars to speak of 'a truly disconcerting realism and an unexpected social truth';[9] last, not least, we have to remember Philemon and Baucis (see esp. 8.624–702), memorable characters who illustrate that this dimension is far from irrelevant to Ovid's poem.

A modest, non-heroic reality thus finds ample space in the poem, as does the monstrous or fantastic.[10] This latter presence, Ovid's rational reader does not find disturbing, mediated as it is, somewhat, by expressions like *si credere dignum est*; *vix ausim credere*; *res . . . fide maior*; *quis hoc credat, nisi sit pro teste vetustas?*, etc. Examples include monsters like Argus (1.624–9), the Chimaera (9.648–9), and the two Graiae, the horrifying sisters who stand guard at the house of the Gorgons, passing back and forth their single eye (4.774–7); or the narration of miraculous events like the rejuvenation of Aeson by Medea (7.159–296), or the prodigious speed of the fox on Mount Teumessus (7.763–93), two stories that, not by chance, are also documented in Cyclic epic (in *PEG* F 7 (= F 6 D. = W.) of the *Nostoi* and in *PEG* F 5 (= F inc. 1 D. = F 3* W.) of the *Epigonoi*, respectively).[11] No less significant is the way in which the 'Centaurs in love', Cyllarus and Hylonome, are presented: their description is, in fact, designed to straightforwardly refute Lucretius' 'scientific' demonstration of the impossibility of such absurd *portenta* as the hybrid men–horses of myth.[12] Also, the theme of divinities disguised in some animal form, especially for the purpose of erotic seduction, which is so common in the *Metamorphoses* (and central in the tapestry of Arachne), maintained a presence in the Cycle, whereas it is significantly absent from Homer.[13]

---

[8] Thus Barchiesi (2005: 225), who speaks of 'a sort of low realism' (227) as a characteristic feature of this episode.
[9] Bilinski (1959: 110–11). On fishing as an 'uncharacteristic activity for epic', but attested in the *Cypria*, see West (2013: 123).
[10] On the importance of this aspect in Cyclic epic, see Griffin (1977: 40–2).
[11] See Bömer (1980: 241 and 385).   [12] See Debrohun (2004: esp. 422–7).
[13] See Davies (1989c: 17): 'Homer characteristically has no time for shape-changing deities and it is no coincidence that when Zeus lists his various mortal amours at *Il.* 14.315–28, though Europe and Danae are among them, nothing is said of his metamorphosis into bull or golden shower.'

Together with the fantastic or monstrous, there is also no lack of the grotesque in Ovid, as e.g. in the horrendous autophagy of Erysichthon (8.875–8), or in the minute, macabre description of mutilated, dismembered or skinned bodies, like that of Marsyas (5.104–6; 6.255–60, 387–91, 556–60; 12.268–70, 390–2; 15.524–9),[14] or in the disturbing personifications/allegories of abstract concepts like Hunger (8.799–808) or Envy (2.768–82).

But in the field of the fantastic, one particularly elaborate case is that of Cycnus, a warrior at Troy, whose story is among the antecedents leading up to the Great War. And it is in this Cyc-lic environment that Ovid sets the story of Cyc-nus (who seems almost a symbol of it).

OVID'S *ILIAS PARVA*

If by 'Cyclic Epic' we mean that series of traditions relating to the Trojan War of which the Homeric poems only constitute a limited selection, then Ovid's relationship with that narrative patrimony is to be investigated above all in the *Metamorphoses*' own '*Ilias parva*', that is to say, the section of the poem that covers the Trojan War and the characters, Homeric or non-Homeric ones, that are associated with it (12.1–13.622).[15] Among these, Cycnus, the hero with the invulnerable body, receives special attention and a 'programmatic' place at the beginning of the *Metamorphoses'* Iliadic section. His duel with Achilles (the first in the Iliadic portion: 12.72–145) gives rise to the latter's frustration in seeing his own valour as a warrior lessened by the miraculous property that protects the body of his enemy (who only wears armour for aesthetic reasons: 12.90). Cycnus' invulnerability in fact undermines the whole of the heroic code that governs the Iliadic world. The clash between Achilles, the central hero of Homeric epic, and a hero with fantastic characteristics like Cycnus actually typifies the difference between the two worlds: the Iliadic one and that of more remote, magical or fabulous heroes and scenarios contained in a more archaic kind of epic that easily passes into the supernatural (that different world, peopled by monsters and extraordinary figures, at which Homeric epic had taken various glances

---

[14] On this satisfied attention to the physical violence inflicted on the human body, which recalls the 'over-heated taste for sadistically coloured scenes' of the Cyclic poems (Griffin (1977: 45)), see Segal (2005: esp. LIV–LXII).

[15] The most wide-ranging, detailed study of the subject, after Ellsworth (1980) and Dippel (1990), is that of Papaioannou (2007); much that is useful can be found in Hopkinson (2000).

during the adventurous *nostos* of Odysseus).[16] The uselessness of traditional arms, and the necessity for Achilles to resort to an 'irregular', primitive, savage combat to defeat Cycnus (in order to kill him, he has to suffocate him), marks the retrogression into a more marginal, non-Homeric region of ancient epic (the story of Cycnus was narrated in the *Cypria*).[17]

The fact that we are taking a look back at pre-Homeric epic, even at the very beginning of Ovid's '*Ilias parva*,' is metapoetically marked by the presence of Nestor, the long-lived hero *par excellence* whose life has lasted three generations. This enables him to remember the most remote past (*quamvis obstet mihi tarda vetustas / multaque me fugiant primis spectata sub annis*, 'despite the impediments of my slow years, and although much seen in my youth escapes me now', 12.182–3). Before an audience of Homeric heroes, including Achilles himself, and in the context of a banquet that alludes not only to precise epic models (*Odyssey* 8 and *Aeneid* 2) but even to the very origins of the genre,[18] Nestor takes the floor.[19] He proceeds to narrate a more archaic epic, the Centauromachy, a savage, brutal clash between men–beasts like the Centaurs on the one hand, and the fierce Lapiths on the other (169–535). The world of the *Iliad* is thus the diegetic background from which the memory of Nestor's *spatiosa senectus* ('great length of years', 186)

---

[16] Excellent observations now on this aspect in Labate (2010: esp. 21–7, with preceding bibliography), who emphasizes the influence of Apollonian and Virgilian epic (as well as the Theocritean epyllion), highlighting Ovid's difference from the purely epic, Iliadic code and his preference for the grotesque, the eccentric and the fantastic; see also Keith (1999: 231–3) and Papaioannou (2007: 50–86).

[17] Möller (2003) gives a reading of the episode in a poetological key, focusing on Ovid's reflexion on his own epic poetry in relation to the genre's tradition. As Mathias Hanses suggests *per litteras*, 'that Achilles suffocates Cycnus could be a statement about literary history: by Ovid's day, Homeric epic had suffocated Cyclic epic'.

[18] According to a theory of which conspicuous traces remain in Roman antiquarianism: cf. Varro F 394 Salv. (= Non. 77.4–5 M.) *carmina antiqua, in quibus laudes erant maiorum et assa voce et cum tibicine* ('ancient songs in praise of their ancestors, both for solo voice and with the flute'); Cato, *Orig.* 1.4 Cugusi in Cic. *Tusc.* 4.3 *gravissimus auctor in Originibus dixit Cato morem apud maiores hunc epularum fuisse, ut deinceps qui accubarent canerent ad tibiam clarorum virorum laudes atque virtutes* ('Cato, a writer of great authority, in his *Origines* said that our ancestors used at banquets to sing in turn with flute accompaniment in praise of the merits and virtues of illustrious men'); 1.3 *quamquam est in Originibus solitos esse in epulis canere convivas ad tibicinem de clarorum hominum virtutibus* ('though it is stated in the *Origines* that guests at banquets used to sing with flute accompaniment about the virtues of famous men'); *Brutus* 19.75 *illa carmina, quae multis saeclis ante suam aetatem in epulis esse cantitata a singulis convivis de clarorum virorum laudibus in Originibus scriptum reliquit Cato* ('those songs of which Cato in his *Origines* recorded that many centuries before his time guests at banquets used to sing in turn the praises of illustrious men').

[19] A pause in the fighting after the death of Cycnus was also present in the *Cypria*; on the striking analogy in the narrative structure between the passage in Ovid and the *Cypria*, see Bömer (1982: 31–2).

opens up a window to a more ancient world, towards another epic, quite different in its essence from that of Homer. Ovid's poem, in whose narrative economy the *Centauromachia* (concluding in the death of Caeneus, just as Homer's poem concludes in that of Hector) actually substitutes the *Iliad*,[20] thus offers his reader the story of a decidedly anomalous battle, conducted by means of improper arms, without any formalization of the fighting as we know it from Homer's epic: a primitive, indeed, primordial epic, which focuses on the battle's ferocious characteristics and leaves ample space for the grotesque and the macabre (e.g. 238–40, 248–57, 268–89, 320–49, etc.).[21] The conclusion of the bloody battle, which features the death of another invulnerable fighter, the Lapith Caeneus (12.459–531), confirms that Ovid invites us to compare and contrast the *Iliad*.[22] Even the ambiguity of gender that characterizes this latter, transsexual hero highlights the *Metamorphoses*' indifference to the machismo, and the ideology of masculinity, that was notoriously dominant in traditional epic[23] and in the entire system of values associated with it.[24]

The description of the house of Fame (12.39–63) right at the beginning of the Iliadic section, and the effect of distortion that it produces (53–5), already seems to address the multiplicity of the epic tradition, in which history and legend overlap (57), and the importance of a different literary region, alternative to the voice of Homer, like that of the Cyclic epic.[25]

After the *Centauromachia* (12.169–535), and arranged symmetrically to it within the Iliadic section of the poem, we find another markedly Cyclic episode in the *Armorum iudicium* (13.1–398), i.e. the narration of the dispute between Ajax and Ulysses over the arms of Achilles, a story only outlined in the *Odyssey* (11.543–62),[26] but narrated in detail in the *Aethiopis* and in the *Ilias parva*.[27] This long, non-Homeric episode is told through the voices of the two rivals and thus provides an illuminating view on minor and often much less heroic characters and events of the Trojan War. Such narratives

---

[20] See Due (1974: 150); Hopkinson (2000: 10); Keith (1999: 232).

[21] See Newlands (2005: 482).

[22] The analogies between Cycnus and Caeneus are marked (see e.g. 12.82–131 and 479–89), and this is precisely why (cf. 169–75) Nestor tells the latter's story; see also Keith (1999: 237).

[23] It is clear e.g. that the scorn for the sexual identity of Caeneus (470–6) alludes to the words with which Numanus Remulus mocks the Trojans in *Aen.* 9.598–620; on the male-chauvinistic ideology intrinsic in Roman epic, cf. e.g. Keith (2000: esp. chap. 2).

[24] It is precisely this dissociation that seems to motivate the particular interest in listening to the story of Caeneus shown by Achilles (12.177–82), the Homeric hero who – outside Homeric epic, of course – had experienced transvestism at Scyros: see Rosati (2002: 288–9).

[25] See especially Zumwalt (1977), also Rosati (2002: 297–9).

[26] See however Hopkinson (2000: 13 n. 40), on the possible derivation from the Cycle.

[27] For a detailed analysis see Papaioannou (2007: 153–206).

were typical of the poems of the Cycle and would later prove immensely popular with the tragedians. They include, e.g., the folly of Ulysses, simulated in order to avoid leaving for Troy, but unmasked by Palamedes, who for this reason suffered Ulysses' fatal retaliation (13.34–9). This story was narrated in the *Cypria*, as was the stranding of Philoctetes at Lemnos (45–54),[28] or the wounding of Telephus (171–2).[29]

Besides making room for a kind of epic different from that of Homer,[30] Ovid's 'Little Iliad' also sees the Homeric world in a different light: Ajax's perspective restores to us an image of Ulysses that is far darker than the Homeric one (as in the episode of the theft of the Palladium, maliciously alluded to by Ajax at 99–100, and retold from a completely different angle by Ulysses at 335–49; this was narrated in the *Ilias parva*, *PEG* F 25 = F 9 D. = F 11 W.). Similarly, the portrait that Ulysses himself gives us of Achilles is far more complex and controversial than the one offered by the *Iliad*.[31] For example, the far from heroic story of his stay at Scyros (13.162–80) and his transvestism (*virgineos habitus*, 167) are completely foreign to Homer, but may have been handed down by the *Cypria* or other Cyclic poems (*Ilias parva*).[32]

In Ovid's representation of Nestor, the admittedly partial and tendentious narrator (cf. 12.542–8), there is an implicit criticism of the claim of truth that Homeric epic assigns to itself.[33] This thesis finds confirmation in the allegory of Fame as the agent of 'confusion', and the manipulation of the messages that it transmits. This Ovidian criticism acquires a far more complex meaning if we remember that an alternative epic voice already existed, a voice that has nothing of the official character of Homer's voice. Ovid's polyphonic poem takes it upon itself to help this other narrative voice re-emerge. It may thus be said that Ovid's '*Ilias parva*' is to be measured not only against Homer, but also against the Epic Cycle:[34] in the

---

[28] See Hopkinson (2000: 86 and 89).
[29] See Davies (1989c: 44); Papaioannou (2007: 77–8 and n. 166); Preiser (2000: 41–8).
[30] Different, but not necessarily more recent: against the presupposition that the poems of the Epic Cycle are less ancient than those of Homer, cf. Burgess (2001: 158, 169–71, and *passim*); Burgess (2005: 347–8).
[31] Important observations on this aspect in Papaioannou (2007: chap. 5, esp. 171–87).
[32] Davies (1989c: 43–4) and Heslin (2005: 202–5). For sceptical views, see Fantuzzi (2012: 23–7); Tsagalis (2012b).
[33] See Rosati (2001: 56–9).
[34] Statements like that of Ellsworth (1980) seem to beg the question: 'I contend that this neglect of the *Iliad* is only a pretence, and that it, not the Epic Cycle, is the actual organizing principle for Ovid's presentation of the Trojan war' (25); 'it is Homer's *Iliad* which is the integrating principle in the organization of his [scil. Ovid's] Trojan story, whereas the Epic Cycle merely provides the chronological framework' (28). It is, on the contrary, undoubtedly true that Ovid wants to *differentiate* his work from Homer's. There is no reason to assume that while he

absence of sufficient documentation referring to the poems of the Cycle, it is difficult for us to evaluate their impact on Ovid's text, and yet there is reason to believe Ovid drew from the Cycle not only particularly attractive thematic material to include in his non-warlike epos, but also tones and moods much closer to those of the *Metamorphoses* than to those of Homer.[35]

For Ovid, in short, 'Troy' is not a world that is automatically identified as 'Homeric', but a pole around which events and characters are set into motion that are, it is true, associated with the Great War, but that are far removed from the Homeric warrior ethos. We have already seen several instances of Ovid highlighting this approach as his narrative leads up to Troy and his own '*Ilias parva*'. For another example, we can turn to the story that brings on to the scene the first Trojan of the *Metamorphoses*, Aesacus (11.749–52), who is one of Hector's brothers. Aesacus is a character who is foreign to the world of Troy, and to power (764–6); a character who dedicates himself to a sequestered, 'elegiac' life devoted to love, and whose destiny is determined by his passion for the nymph Hesperie. In this episode, the contrast between warlike and erotic language is stark. Examples include the metaphor *nec inexpugnabile amori / pectus* ('he was not a boor at heart nor unassailable by love', 767–8) or the description of a *Troius heros* who *insequitur celeremque metu celer urget amore* ('followed in pursuit, she swift in fear, he swift in love', 773–4). Significantly, martial language is here employed to describe Aesacus chasing after his beloved, instead of the enemy on the battlefield (he is a sort of Hector-turned-Paris). Aesacus is a man who acts in the name of love (*indignatur amans*, 787), who out of love vows to commit suicide, but fails in the attempt (783–6), and whose condition as an unhappy lover even determines his metamorphosis into a cormorant (*fecit amor maciem* 'love made him lean', 793).

Thus it is a moving love story, and not the blaring of war trumpets, that introduces Ovid's readers into the Trojan world. Their entrance, furthermore, has been delayed (this is metaphorically represented by the absence of navigable winds that postpones the Greek expedition: 12.8–10), which leaves room to describe the prodigy of the sparrows devoured by the snake (11–34) and the sacrifice of Iphigenia (both present in the *Cypria*).[36] It is

sought an antagonistic comparison with the great epic model, Ovid could not *also* be engaging with the poems of the Cycle, be it directly or through the intermediator of tragedy and the visual arts.

[35] Papaioannou (2007: 3): 'as a matter of fact, the narrative strategy adopted in the composition of the "Ilias parva" points to the Cyclic rather than the Homeric poems'.

[36] See Bömer (1982: 14).

only after this that Fame (39–63) makes her appearance in the poem and spreads the news of the arrival of the enemy fleet on Trojan soil (64–6). After the paradoxical initial duel between Achilles and Cycnus (71–145), the narration of the Homeric section of the *Iliad* is omitted (that is to say, substituted with the '*Centauromachia*', 169–535). With the death of Achilles (580–619) we are already beyond Homer, in Cyclic territory (it was narrated in the *Aethiopis* and in other poems of the Cycle), where other *Posthomerica* follow, such as the '*Armorum iudicium*' (12.620–13.398) and the '*Iliou persis*' (399–428), leading up to the tragic destinies of Polydorus, Polyxena and Hecuba (429–575) and the metamorphosis of the sisters of Memnon (576–622), whose death was narrated in the *Aethiopis*. Ovid's '*Ilias parva*' is thus actually a sequence of *Antehomerica* and *Posthomerica*, whereas the Homeric section is outstanding for its absence: there is no room for the Great War in the pacifist epic of the *Metamorphoses*.

A WORLD WITHOUT DEATH

Beyond certain marked thematic affinities that connect the *Metamorphoses* to the Cycle, there is another aspect that is characteristic of Cyclic epic and similarly crucial for the planning and organization of Ovid's poem: as Griffin observes (1977, 42), 'in the accommodating world of the Cycle death itself can be evaded'. The same is not true for the world of Homeric epic, where – on the contrary – death plays a decisive role not only in the development of events, but also in the very conception of the human condition. Yet the absence of death *is* an essential characteristic of the *Metamorphoses*. The peculiarity of Ovid's poem is continuity: in the world where *omnia mutantur, nil interit* ('everything changes, nothing dies', 15.165), the break that death necessarily introduces into the flow of events is assigned such a secondary position that it actually disappears from the individual and collective horizon. This kind of continuity is an 'inclusive' feature because, in reality, no character ever disappears definitively, but continues to live in a new form, perpetuating aspects of the previous life that have determined the metamorphosis, and thus enriching the fabric of Ovid's world. Thus Lycaon maintains his ferocity in the form of a wolf, or Arachne continues to weave her web as a spider, Niobe lives in perennial mourning as a weeping rock, and so on.

Losing their original form in this 'partial death' that is metamorphosis, the characters end up in a kind of intermediary space: this is that neutral condition, which is no longer life (that is to say, the first form of life), but it is not death, either, as Myrrha puts it in her appeal to the gods (10.484–7):

> ... merui nec triste recuso
> supplicium, sed ne violem vivosque superstes
> mortuaque exstinctos, ambobus pellite regnis
> mutataeque mihi vitamque necemque negate!
>
> ... I've well deserved – I'll not refuse – the pain of punishment, but lest I outrage, if I'm left alive, the living, or, if I shall die, the dead, expel me from both realms; some nature give that's different; let me neither die nor live!

The epic inevitability of death, which hangs threateningly over the destiny of all mortals, even the greatest heroes, is substituted by metamorphosis, which very often acts as a sort of 'compensation' for, or attenuation of death. The adverb *tamen* constitutes a frequent linguistic marker of this fact, highlighting as it does what remains of the original nature, or what alleviates the pain suffered: e.g. 2.485 *mens antiqua tamen facta quoque mansit in ursa* 'she was a bear, but kept her woman's heart'; 4.164 *vota tamen tetigere deos* 'but the gods received her prayer'; 4.251 *tanges tamen aethera* 'yet you shall touch the sky'; 5.561–3 etc. This typical formulation is reversed in the words of Minerva to Arachne: *vive quidem, pende tamen* ('Live', she said, 'yes, live but hang', 6.136). As Griffin observes,[37] it is our destiny of old age and death, compared with the eternal youth of the gods, that makes the human condition a tragedy in Homeric epic, whereas the metamorphosis that 'concludes' life (or life in its original form) in Ovid's poem undoubtedly attenuates the drama of an ending that is not absolute, but partial. This rather relative, and far from definitive sense of death means that e.g. even Hercules, who confirmed the Homeric inevitability of death dying at *Iliad* 18.117, may die in the ninth book of the *Metamorphoses* (272), but subsequently reappears, a couple of books later, on the scene at Troy (11.212–15): an anomaly[38] that might be perceived as intolerable in a Homeric–Virgilian kind of epic, but proves to be substantially innocuous in a universe with a fluctuating chronology like that of Ovid's poem.

Another contribution to this fluid dimension, which causes the chronological structure of the *Metamorphoses* to be more indistinct, is its highly 'mimetic' character: the continuous, giddy network of changing narrative voices (more than one third of the poem is told, not by the voice of the external narrator, but by that of the many characters who take over his role)[39]

---

[37] (1977: 42–3).   [38] See Wheeler (1999: 135–9); Cole (2008: 26–8).
[39] On this subject see especially Wheeler (1999).

reveals a poetic strategy that may have been influenced by the probably oral origin of the Cycle.[40] The extreme variety of Ovid's narrators might also reflect in some ways the diversity and local character of the traditions present in the Cycle.[41] Indeed, the voice of Nestor, which selects the material for its stories with declared tendentiousness (achieving a *damnatio memoriae* of his enemies)[42] seems to reflect a polycentric epic like that of the Cycle, whose main thematic nuclei are indeed present in Ovid (wars with giants, Theban cycle, Theseid, Trojan War with all its complex antecedents and consequences).[43]

But one additional aspect that will undoubtedly have exerted a strong attraction on the 'elegiac' epic of the *Metamorphoses* is the 'proliferation of intrigues and episodes of romance'[44] that is characteristic of the Epic Cycle. Even if we limit ourselves to Achilles, it is well known that most of the romantic novels of his private life were born inside the Epic Cycle: his love at first sight for Penthesilea was narrated in the *Aethiopis*, his stay at Scyros and the connected liaison with Deidameia may have been included in the *Cypria*, and to a Cyclic tradition must date back his falling in love with Polyxena; Helen too, according to Proclus' summary of the *Cypria*, could have been an object of desire for Achilles. So, the overall eroticization of Achilles' life (and afterlife), familiar to Ovid and Roman readers even before Statius' *Achilleid*, must have been a typical feature of the Cyclic poems.[45] By contrast, the severe restraint of eros and sex is a well-known feature of Homeric epic (examples are the elusive figure of Nausicaa, or the evanescent relationships of Odysseus with Calypso and Circe), which insists on the exemplary nature of the matrimonial relationship between Hector and Andromache (seen in contrast to the guilty relationship between Paris and Helen). This near-exclusion is indirectly confirmed by the provocatively erotic reading of Homeric epic that Ovid composed in exile (*Trist.* 2.371–80):

> Ilias ipsa quid est aliud nisi adultera, de qua
>   inter amatorem pugna virumque fuit?
> quid prius est illi flamma Briseidos, utque
>   fecerit iratos rapta puella duces?
> aut quid Odyssea est nisi femina propter amorem,
>   dum vir abest, multis una petita viris?

---

[40] The thesis of a rhapsodic performance as the original form of circulation of the Cycle, before its textualisation in the Hellenistic age, is well argued by Burgess (2004b).
[41] On this aspect see Burgess (2001: 162–6).   [42] See Rosati (2002: 301–3).
[43] Burgess (2004b: 6) notes as an oddity the absence, among the poems of the Cycle, of a sub-cycle on the 'labours of Hercules'; it is remarkable, then, that Ovid's poem also lacks a Herculean sage (this is attributed to the censure of a tendentious narrator like Nestor: 12.542–8).
[44] Griffin (1977: 43).   [45] For the details see Fantuzzi (2012).

> quis nisi Maeonides Venerem Martemque ligatos
>   narrat, in obsceno corpora prensa toro?
> unde nisi indicio magni sciremus Homeri
>   hospitis igne duas incaluisse deas?

> The *Iliad*, what's that but an adulteress, husband and lover and the war they wage? What comes before the passion for Briseis, the rape that caused commanders so much rage? Or what's the *Odyssey* except a woman wooed by the suitors while her man's away? And who but Homer tells of Mars and Venus ensnared as in the bed of shame they lay? Without his evidence who'd know the love of two goddesses who wished their guest to stay?

Ovid's tendency to read even Homeric epic in an erotic key must have made the poems of the Cycle extremely attractive for him. The story of Achilles appears to be exemplary in this connection: his 'romantic intrigue' with Deidameia at Scyros, which is totally absent from Homer (and possible hints at it were 'removed' by the scholiasts who insisted on his exclusively heroic dimension),[46] probably goes back to the *Cypria*[47] and is decisive in the development of this Homeric hero's heterodox afterlife (starting from Statius' *Achilleid*).[48] This story, removed from or censured in Homer's texts, proves to be a *fabula nota* for the Ovid of the *Ars* (1.681–706), and is expressly recalled in the *Metamorphoses* (13.162–9).

The background against which the events of Ovid's poem take place is crowded with erotic plots and adventures, a complex web in which desire – that is to say, a kind of eros not at all conjugal, ubiquitously pervasive – represents the dominant energy. The emblem of this central theme is the recurring image of a god pursuing a woman (goddess, nymph or mortal) who is the object of his erotic intentions: this image, wholly foreign to Homer, is found to be well attested in a fragment of the *Cypria* (*PEG* F 9 = F 7 D. = F 10 W.) that relates Nemesis' flight from Zeus. In order to escape from god's erotic assault the goddess assumes various animal forms:

> ... whom lovely-haired Nemesis once bore, united in love to Zeus the king of the gods, under harsh compulsion. For she ran away, not wanting to unite in love with father Zeus the son of Kronos tormented by inhibition and misgiving: across land and the dark, barren water she ran, and Zeus

---

[46] See Griffin (1977: 44).

[47] Fantuzzi (2012: 13 and 21–9) is sceptical on this point. The presence of narrative material of a more or less directly erotic nature is no surprise in a poem that, already in its name, recalled the power of Aphrodite. Cf. Scaife 1995: 173.

[48] Fantuzzi (2012) is now the key work on this subject.

> pursued, eager to catch her; sometimes in the noisy sea's wave, where she had the form of a fish, as he stirred up the mighty deep; sometimes along Ocean's stream and the ends of the earth; sometimes on the loam-rich land; and she kept changing into all the fearsome creatures that the land nurtures, so as to escape him

For every reader of Ovid, this fragment[49] evokes the recurrent animal metamorphoses that Jupiter assumes in his adventures as a serial rapist (some of which are portrayed by Arachne in *Met.* 6.103–14), as well as the countless transformation by means of which the victims try to escape divine predators (cf. e.g. 1.547–52, 704; 2.578–88; 5.632–6, etc.).[50]

Once again, we have confirmation of the profound affinity linking Ovid's poem to an epic that not only offered an extremely rich mythical reservoir of Trojan stories, but whose world-view was also open, digressive and polyphonic like the *Metamorphoses*. To sum up, if we agree that the typical characteristics of the Cyclic epic included 'monsters, miracles, metamorphoses, and an un-tragic attitude towards mortality, all seasoned with exoticism and romance, and composed in a flatter, looser, less dramatic style',[51] then we can say that here Ovid's *Metamorphoses* could find a model no less important, and perhaps more productive, than the great Homeric poems.

It is obviously impossible for us to know whether, and to what extent, Ovid knew the poems of the Cycle, but if a knowledge of them has been convincingly hypothesized for Virgil,[52] then there is undoubtedly no reason to exclude it for Ovid. Conversely, it is thanks to him, and to his different kind of epic, that we can perhaps open up a window into the fascinating world of the Cycle that has otherwise largely disappeared.

---

[49] On which see also West (2013: 80–3).
[50] Also the insistence on the 'geography of the flight' recalls e.g. the way in which Ovid describes in detail the long flight of Arethusa pursued by Alpheus (5.604–13).
[51] Griffin (1977: 53).
[52] See Kopff (1981) and Gärtner, above in this volume, pp. 559–60 (who is more sceptical). Barchiesi (1999) reads, in the *ekphrasis* of the temple of Carthage, Virgil's desire to underline the distance from the tradition of the Cycle epic, and the originality of his poetic project (see also Barchiesi 1997: 273–4).

30 | Statius' *Achilleid* and the *Cypria*

CHARLES MCNELIS

The proem of the *Achilleid* explicitly mentions Homeric poetry as a precursor in treating the deeds of Achilles:

> Magnanimum Aeaciden formidatamque Tonanti
> progeniem et patrio vetitam succedere caelo,
> diva, refer. Quamquam acta viri multum inclita cantu
> Maeonio (sed plura vacant), nos ire per omnem
> – sic amor est – heroa velis Scyroque latentem
> Dulichia proferre tuba nec in Hectore tracto
> sistere, sed tota iuvenem deducere Troia.

> Goddess, tell of the great-hearted Aeacides and the offspring that caused fear for the Thunderer and was forbidden to be the successor to his father's heaven. Although the man's acts have been much celebrated in Homeric poetry, there are more, and may you wish for me to go through the entirety of the hero (that is my desire), to bring him out by Odysseus' trumpet as he hides on Scyros, nor to stop with the dragging of Hector, but to describe the youth in the entire Trojan saga.

Maeonio is a periphrastic but unambiguous reference to Homer (e.g. Hor. *C.* 1.6.2), and the Homeric frame is reinforced by the invocation that dubs the Muse a *diva*, a Latin translation for the goddess who appears at the start of the *Iliad*.[1] Statius also claims that he wants to tell Achilles' story without stopping at the dragging of Hector's body in the dust, one of the most prominent events in the *Iliad*. That the poet articulates his aims in seven verses and then turns to the divine source of his inspiration in the eighth verse (1.8. *tu modo... Phoebe*) mimics the structure of the proem of the *Aeneid*, but Virgil's preface reworks the proem of the *Iliad* and its own seven-verse opening sentence.[2] In this regard, Statius operates within the tradition of the Homeric proem. The heroic context is also reinforced by words such as *inclita*, which is etymologically connected to the Greek

---

[1] Cf. the translation of the opening line of *Il.* 1.1 by the poet of the *Ilias Latina*: *iram pande mihi Pelidae, diva, superbi*. Livius Andronicus (*FPL* F 21) uses *diva* for the Homeric muse in his translation of the *Odyssey*.

[2] See Austin on *Aen.* 1.1; Weber (1987).

kleos and cognate Homeric epithets,[3] and *acta*, which recalls the exploits of famous Greeks such as the Argonauts (Val. Flac. 1.40) and Hercules (Ov. *Met.* 9.134, 247; Stat. *Theb.* 4.826). Yet Statius is clear that this Homeric and heroic backdrop is only part of Achilles' story (*sed plura vacant*), and his goal is to treat the hero's entire life, particularly his time hiding in Scyros. Homeric poetry is in fact silent about Achilles' time on Scyros save for glancing references to the fact that Achilles sacked the island (*Il.* 9.666–8) and that his son Neoptolemus lives there (*Il.* 19.326). By Statius' day, however, a number of poets had briefly alluded to or even elaborated upon the myth.[4] Without seeking to diminish the importance of any predecessors for Statius' treatment of Achilles on Scyros, this paper argues that the epic Cycle and particularly the *Cypria* significantly contribute to the *Achilleid*'s strategies.

The case for the importance of the Cycle for the *Achilleid* may initially seem to be manifest in light of the D-scholia on *Iliad* 19.326 (the verse in which Achilles mentions that he has a son on the island of Scyros), which records what is essentially an outline of the myth that is found in Statius' *Achilleid* and then attributes this version to the Cycle. To be sure, Statius' account deviates in some respects from that recorded in the scholion: he has Thetis, not Peleus, hide Achilles on Scyros, and instead of Phoenix and Nestor joining Odysseus on the mission to fetch Achilles, Statius pairs Odysseus with his traditional comrade Diomedes. But the many similarities between Statius and the account contained in the scholia may seem more trenchant than their differences: a parent hides the youthful hero on Scyros in order to prevent his death at Troy; the cross-dressing; the oracle that declared that Achilles must be present in order for the Greek army to succeed at Troy; the seduction of Deidameia; the birth of a child from that union; Odysseus' plan to lure the youthful soldier out of hiding; and, finally, Achilles' departure from Scyros with Odysseus and Diomedes. Nonetheless, the D-scholia as a whole are often suspect,[5] and in this case, the version reported therein is at odds with the other archaic evidence that refers to the Scyrian episode without mentioning Achilles' cross-dressing or any attempt

---

[3] Serv. on *Aen.* 6.781 connects *inclutus* with the Greek κλυτόν, which is cognate to κλέος.
[4] Our earliest extant treatment of the cross-dressing story comes from Euripides' *Scyrioi* (*TrGF* ii pp. 665–666); according to Pausanias (1.22.6), Polygnotos (fifth century BCE) painted in Athens a scene in which Achilles lives with girls. Outside of these attestations from classical Athens, there are references to or even sustained treatments of the myth in Lycophron (276–7), Ps.-Bion, *Epithalamium*, Horace (*C.* 1.8) and Ovid (*Ars.* 1.681–704; *Met.* 13.162–9). See now Fantuzzi (2012: 21–71).
[5] Erbse (1969–88: i.11).

to hide from war.[6] Since the summary found in the D-scholia thus seems worrisomely isolated, a treatment of the *Achilleid* and its relation to the Epic Cycle that relies heavily upon this scholium and focuses on the motif of cross-dressing seems doomed.

It is best, then, to move beyond this scholion in order to assess the relation of the Cycle for Statius' poem. The fragmentary nature of the poems that made up the Cycle as well as their controversial origins and survival make it difficult (and perhaps pointless) to identify them as a 'direct source' for Statius. A more productive route is to trace the Cyclic tradition as reflected in myth. While indirect sources such as Greek drama or vase-painting provide useful insights about what was (potentially) Cyclic, information about the Cycle also comes from ancient critics who sought to dissociate aspects of mythology from Homeric poetry. For example, the myth of Achilles' lengthy stay as a child with Chiron is, according to the Pindaric scholia (on *Nem.* 3.76), a version found in the 'more recent' poets (a designation that often refers to the Cyclic poets) and distinct from the brief mention in the *Iliad* that Chiron taught Achilles medicine (*Il.* 4.219). In the case of the *Achilleid*, the poem not only narrates Achilles' stay with the Centaur (1.147–97), it even has Diomedes ask Achilles to elaborate upon his life with Chiron (2.89–91). Diomedes' curiosity reflects his ignorance, and it is tempting to view his lack of knowledge in a meta-textual manner: the character who wants to know more about Achilles' life calls attention to the Homeric silence about his instruction by Chiron. Achilles complies and brings up points of detail that themselves may come from the Cycle (2.96–167).[7] Whether or not Achilles' own narrative includes Cyclic elements, the myth that he was educated in Chiron's cave follows what some ancients thought was a Cyclic tradition. This handling of 'Cyclic' mythological material is one example of Statius' strategy, openly declared in the proem, of augmenting Homeric poetry.[8]

It may seem natural or even coincidental that Statius' mythic content would overlap with the Cycle in as much as both relate events that occurred before the temporal moment of the *Iliad*. But Statius' deployment of Cyclic myth does not result in a linear movement through the

---

[6] Heslin (2005: 204–5) argues that it is a serious mistake to use the scholion as evidence for the existence of the story of cross-dressing in the archaic period. See most recently the discussions of the problem in Fantuzzi (2012: 23–6) and Tsagalis (2012b).

[7] Beazley (1986: 10) connects Achilles' eating of animal marrow with the Cycle.

[8] Ancient sources suggest that the Cycle provided accounts of what happened before and after the Homeric poems (*Cyclus ep. PEG* TT 11, 12 = T 6, 10 D.). It is not clear how widely accepted such a view would have been, but the proem of the *Achilleid* seems consonant with it.

pre-Homeric mythology of the Trojan War. Rather, his use of the Cycle contributes to his poetic agenda. For instance, at the start of the poem, Statius draws upon the *Cypria* in a way that casts Thetis as a new Hera in that she seeks to raise a storm against a fleet. In addition, Thetis acts with a keen awareness of her son's future, and her knowledge operates within the prophetic tradition as represented in the *Cypria*. The Cyclic content, then, enhances an understanding of Thetis' situation at the outset of the poem, and, consequently, the plot of the poem. As for Achilles himself, he starts the poem in Chiron's cave, but is then pointedly transferred to Scyros. Both locales feature in the Cycle, but Statius constructs the two sites in such a way that they symbolize Achilles' childhood development under the guidance of Thetis and Chiron. Each instructs the young Achilles and exerts a strong influence upon him, yet since each has distinct aims (one prepares Achilles for masculine endeavors, the other for feminine), the two compete in their methods of rearing the child. In the end, against the wishes of his mother, Achilles puts aside his feminine garb, leaves Scyros, and pursues his heroic mission. Thus it seems that Chiron's instruction has prevailed. But ancients such as Plato pointed out that some of Achilles' behavior that is depicted in the *Iliad* is problematic and even womanish. Certainly Achilles does not put on women's clothes once he leaves Scyros, but if, as Plato and others argued, he exhibited feminine behavior even after ten years at Troy, it seems that his initial experience with the opposite sex must have been influential. Barchiesi has argued that tales of childhood allow poets, particularly those that come in late in the tradition, to construct narratives that depict heroes in the process of becoming their canonical selves.[9] That dynamic is played out in Statius' reworking of the Cyclic material. The *Achilleid* supplements Homeric material by rewriting the Cyclic account of the Trojan war, but it also reworks the *Cypria* in ways that present an aetiology of the Homeric hero and that show a full range of Achilles' nascent values.

THETIS AND SEA STORMS

Statius' narrative proper begins with Paris' return to Troy after his seizure of Helen (1.20–5):

> Solverat Oebalio classem de litore pastor
> Dardanus incautas blande populatus Amyclas

[9] Barchiesi (1993: 335).

> plenaque materni referens praesagia somni
> culpatum relegebat iter, qua condita ponto
> fluctibus invisis iam Nereis imperat Helle
> cum Thetis...

> The Trojan shepherd had launched a fleet from the shores of Sparta after he seductively laid waste to unsuspecting Amyclae. Bringing to fruition the premonitions his mother had in her sleep, he was retracing the guilty path where Helle, now a Nereid hidden in the sea, commands the hateful waves when Thetis...

Statius does not, as Horace imagines a Cyclic poet would do (*Ars poet.* 147), begin his narrative with the wedding of Thetis and Peleus, nor with any of the events that were the fallout of that wedding (e.g. the Judgment, etc.). By opening in the middle of things, Statius replicates the start of the *Aeneid*, where the narrative proper also starts with an account of a Trojan fleet sailing (*Aen.* 1.34–5). Both poems then turn, via a *cum* clause, to a goddess's emotional response to the progress of the ships. While this opening is manifestly Virgilian, Statius' revisiting of Paris' journey simultaneously engages with a moment of deep literary history. With little elaboration or development, the *Iliad* states that Paris sailed back to Troy by way of Phoenicia (*Il.* 6.290–2). The Homeric text offers no explanation as to why Paris stopped in Phoenicia, but ancient commentators tried to explain that Paris and Helen had tried to confuse the Greeks who might have been following them, or even that a storm had blown them off course (Σ AbT *Il.* 6.291). Nor was it simply the logistics of the Homeric narrative that attracted ancient attention. Herodotus, for example, lumped this Iliadic passage together with accounts from the *Odyssey* in which Helen sails to Egypt in order to suggest that Homer knew that Paris stopped in Egypt and among the neighboring Phoenicians (2.117). Herodotus then adds that, according to the *Cypria*, Paris' trip did not entail any diversions and that it took only a rather astonishing three days because of a favorable wind and calm sea (2.116–17).

Herodotus' account, which seeks to dissociate the author of the *Cypria* from Homer, raises several problems.[10] For my purposes, the larger point is that interest in the circumstances under which Paris sailed back finds a number of parallels in ancient literature. The Ovidian Paris claims that Venus, in as much as she has jurisdiction over the seas, gave him calm

---

[10] Herodotus' version of the story conflicts with Proclus' summary of the *Cypria;* for the matter, see Burgess (2001: 19–21) and above in this volume, pp. 52–3. Herodotus also seems to miss the point that the passages from the *Odyssey* do not concern Helen and Paris.

breezes and favorable winds (*Her.* 16.23). Admittedly, Paris here speaks about his trip to (not from) Sparta, but the inversion responds to the larger tradition surrounding the journey.[11] The favorable winds that blew during Paris' second leg of the trip also appear in Horace *C.* 1.15, where Paris had been enjoying helpful winds when Nereus stopped the swift breezes (1.15.3–4 *celeris... ventos*). The winds, in turn, find their imposed rest to be irksome (1.15.3 *ingrato... otio* 'unwelcome calm').[12] In sum, despite (or perhaps because of) the fact that the *Iliad* does not elaborate upon Paris' return trip, ancients were intrigued by the conditions under which Paris sailed back to Troy, and Herodotus' testimony reveals that this interest appeared as early as the *Cypria*.[13]

Against this rich literary historical backdrop, the opening of the *Achilleid* takes on special point. Since Paris has already approached the Hellespont, it seems that there will be no detour to Sidon. Moreover, he has made the trip from Sparta to the eastern Aegean in just five verses. Implicitly, then, he has enjoyed favorable conditions on his second leg of the trip, as he did in Herodotus' version of the *Cypria* and in the subsequent accounts. The importance of the Cyclic tradition of the journey in the face of the Homeric version is thus marked at the very start of the poem.

But the narrative turns to Thetis' reaction and soliloquy before it reaches the completion of Paris' travels. The position of this speech at the start of the epic corresponds to the location of Juno's speech in *Aeneid* 1, and the diction and themes of this speech repeatedly draw upon Virgil's depiction of Juno. One of Thetis' initial phrases, for instance, mentions that Bellona brings a new daughter-in-law to Priam (1.33–4 *ecce novam Priamo facibus de puppe levatis / fert Bellona nurum* 'raising her torch from the stern, behold, Bellona brings Priam a new daughter-in-law'). Pointedly, Thetis' juxtaposition of the war-goddess Bellona with *nurum* conflates marriage and warfare in terms similar to those that Juno had used when comparing Aeneas and Lavinia to

---

[11] Cf. Kenney on *Her.* 16.126–7.

[12] Interestingly, the ancient commentator Porphyry notes that Hor. *C.* 1.15 is an imitation of Bacchylides except for the fact that the Greek poet had Cassandra recount the events of the Trojan War. If Porphyry is right, then Paris' journey served as a key moment for Bacchylides as well. One suspects, however, that Bacchylides' poem likely plays with mythological chronology. For if Cassandra delivered the prophecy, presumably she did so upon Paris' departure, as she did in the *Cypria* (arg. lines 93–4 Severyns).

[13] All sorts of details about the return trip attracted attention. Thus in the *Iliad*, Helen herself indicates that she and Paris consummated their union on the island of Kranae (3.445), a location just off the Spartan shore. Ancients debated that point and offered alternative locations for the union; others argued that the word κρανέη was not a location but an epithet. The Σ Lycophr. 101 note that there were nine ships, a detail that surely points to some sort of debate about Paris' fleet.

Paris and Helen (*Aen.* 7.319–22 *at Bellona manet te pronuba. nec face tantum / Cisseis praegnas ignis enixa iugalis / quin idem Veneri partus suus et Paris alter / funestaeque iterum recidiua in Pergama taedae* 'but Bellona awaits you as your bridal matron. Nor was it only Cisseus' daughter who conceived a firebrand and gave birth to nuptial flames. No, Venus has the like in her own child, a second Paris, another funeral torch for reborn Troy'). Further, Thetis' lament that she did not overwhelm Paris' fleet (1.43 *non potui infelix* 'Unhappy that I am, I could not...') replicates Juno's frustration with her inability to overwhelm Aeneas' fleet (*Aen.* 7.309 *quae potui infelix* 'unhappy that I am, I could...').[14] Thetis' designation of Paris as an *incesti praedonis* 'foul pirate' is not strictly Virgilian, but *incestus* does recall Hor. *C.* 3.3.19, where Juno calls Paris *incestus*. Moreover, *praedo* is a highly charged word for Paris: Amata uses it of Aeneas (*Aen.* 7.362), then immediately compares him to Paris (7.363).[15] Finally, Thetis' use of *furto* echoes Juno's derisive description of the abduction of Helen as the cause of the Trojan war (*Aen.* 10.90–1 *... quae causa fuit, consurgere in arma / Europamque Asiamque et foedera soluere furto* 'what cause was there that Europe and Asia should rise up in arms and break the bonds of peace by treachery?').

Thetis' language also specifically picks up upon diction from the storm scene in *Aeneid* 1. The phrase *fas sit / ... mihi* ('let it be lawful for me', 1.73–4) mimics Aeolus' words to Juno after she beseeches him to create a storm (*Aen.* 1.76–77 *tuus, o regina, quid optes, / explorare labor; mihi iussa capessere fas est* 'your task, O queen, is to search out your desire; my duty is to do your bidding'). Further, *obrue puppes* ('drown the sterns', 1.72) echoes Juno's order that Aeolus destroy Aeneas' fleet (*Aen.* 1.69). Thetis' request for one storm (1.51 *unam hiemem* 'one storm') brings to mind the description of the storm at the start of the *Aeneid* (1.125). Similarly the use of *iniuria* to describe an action that has offended the goddess and motivates her desire for a storm evokes the explanation for Juno's desire to raise a storm (*Aen.* 1.26–7 *manet alta mente repostum / iudicium Paridis spretaeque iniuria formae* 'deep in her heart remain the judgment of Paris and the outrage to her slighted beauty').

Statius' construction of Thetis as a second Juno underscores the basic point that both goddesses want to engender a storm in order to destroy a Trojan fleet. But Statius grafts a Cyclic dimension onto this Virgilian superstructure. According to Proclus' summary of the *Cypria*, it is Hera who introduces the storm that drives Paris to Sidon during his journey home.

---

[14] Mulder (1955: 124); Aricò (1986: 2933 n. 45).
[15] For Aeneas as a second Paris, cf. also *Aen.* 4.215; 7.321; Donatus on *Aen.* 11.485 *ex facto Paridis omnis Troianos esse raptores* 'As a result of what Paris did, all the Trojans are abductors.'

Statius' temporal layout (i.e. the possible creation of a storm to thwart Paris' return to Troy as opposed to stopping the Virgilian exodus of Trojans from it) thus mirrors that of (Proclus' version of) the *Cypria*. Two distinct strands of the literary tradition (the Virgilian Juno; the Cyclic Hera) are brought together in a single character, and their co-presence puts the models in a truly intertextual and dialogic relationship. From this perspective, Statius' Thetis is modeled upon Virgil's Juno, but his intense reworking of that goddess at the moment of Paris' journey aligns her with the Cyclic Hera as well.

Another allusive parallel reinforces Thetis' composite nature. When Thetis expresses her frustration about the state of events, she claims that she could have killed Paris while he cut down the trees that became his ships (1.43–4). The felling of these trees stems from the *Cypria*, which mentions that Aphrodite drove Paris to make these ships and that Aeneas should sail with Paris (*Cypr.* arg. lines 92–3 Severyns). It was also well recognized that Paris has Aphrodite as a special advocate during all phases of his expedition (e.g. Hor. *C.* 1.15.13 *Veneris praesidio* 'under Venus' protection'; Ov. *Her.* 16.23). In the *Achilleid*, then, Thetis' reference to the felling of the trees recalls the patronage of Venus from the start of the story, and in this sense, Thetis' anger against the sea-faring favorite of Aphrodite is parallel to the hatred Juno feels towards another moment when Aeneas' sailing is of special interest to Venus.

So while it had seemed that Paris would arrive home safely (as in Herodotus' account of the *Cypria*), Thetis' sudden intrusion into the narrative and her desire to sink the fleet opens up the possibility of a storm (as in Proclus' version of the *Cypria*). The opening verses of the *Achilleid* thus gesture towards the alternative outcomes that were contained in the *Cypria*. Admittedly, it is not clear when these variant versions concerning Paris' trip in the *Cypria* took root; there may have been multiple versions of the *Cypria* available for the ancients,[16] or ancients may have attempted to square mythological details that led to these alternative versions.[17] However that may be, Ps.-Apollodorus, who is usually assumed to follow the Cycle for much of his mythological account of the Trojan War,[18] does mention the storm (*Epit.* 3.4), so perhaps the storm was associated with the Cycle earlier than Proclus. At the least, the testimony from Ps.-Apollodorus and the Homeric scholia on 6.291 reveal that the storm version was available during Statius' day. In this light, Thetis' deliberations have special point: will she, à la Hera/Juno, be able to stop the journey, or will Paris continue on his

---

[16] Both the scholia to Lycophron and to the *Iliad* use the plural when discussing the authors of the *Cypria*; see also Huxley (1967: 25–7).
[17] Burgess (2001: 19–21).   [18] West (1983: 124–6).

way? Statius' narrative turns upon this dramatization of which version of the mythological tradition will be enacted, and, at the minimum, a central part of that tradition comes from the Cycle.

Thetis and Hera conventionally have a close relationship in myth (e.g. *Il.* 24.59–60), but here Statius' mapping of Thetis onto the Hera/Juno character imputes the goddess' tempestuous personality to Thetis. Pointedly, the *Iliad*, which allows for Paris' diversion to Sidon but not the tumult associated with a storm incited by Hera, does not inform the behavior of Statius' Thetis at the start of the poem. Indeed, Thetis in the *Achilleid* is hardly the resigned (*Il.* 18.62) and obedient goddess that appears in the *Iliad* (e. g. 18.433: ἔτλην... οὐκ ἐθέλουσα, 'I endured...though very much against my will'). At this early moment in the Trojan saga, she still endeavors to change fate, and the Cyclic backdrop of her more aggressive behavior now merits attention.

PROPHECY

The prophetic nature of the entire *Achilleid* is established in the opening verses, where Achilles is labeled an offspring who was 'forbidden to succeed his father's sky' (1.2). The phrase refers to a myth in which, though details diverge in various accounts, Jupiter is warned by Themis (or Proteus, according to Ov. *Met.* 11.221) not to pursue a sexual encounter with Thetis since the child that will be born to the goddess is destined to be greater than his father. In the *Prometheus Bound* (907–12), Prometheus specifically informs Jupiter that if Thetis bore a son to Jupiter, the child would supplant him as ruler of the heavens. As a result of this potential threat to his rule (and, in addition, because he was angry that Thetis had continually rejected his advances; cf. Apoll. Rh. 4.797), Jupiter insists she be married to a mortal (e.g. Apoll. Rh. 4.802–4) and that her child thus die (Pind. *Isth.* 8.35–6). This explanation for Thetis' marriage to a mortal differs from that attested for the *Cypria*, where, according to Philodemus (*de piet.* 1678–81 Obbink), Thetis' marriage to Peleus is a reward from Hera because Thetis spurned Zeus' advance. In this sense, the *Achilleid* creates an overall context for Thetis' marriage that is distinct from the Cycle.

But the opening scene with Thetis establishes that other prophecies are part of the fabric of the poem, and the Cycle provides a model for these forecasts. The Cycle is full of prophecies,[19] but Paris' journey, whether it

---

[19] Kullmann (1960: 221). Predictions specifically about the life of Achilles and the Trojan war are pervasive in the Cycle as well as in Hellenistic and Roman poetry (e.g. Lycophron; Catullus 64;

be to or from Sparta, is a moment that is surrounded by a rich prophetic tradition. Two predictions in the *Cypria* – one by Helenus and another by Cassandra – accompany Paris' departure (arg. lines 92–4 Severyns). Later literature also connects Paris' journey with prophecies about the fate of Troy (Lyc. 20–30; Hor. *C.* 1.15.1–5). In the *Achilleid*, however, as is fitting for a character at the end of such a tradition, Thetis is represented at the moment of Paris' sailing as having received insights about the future. Thus immediately before her soliloquy in which she articulates her desire for a storm, the narrative indicates that her sense of the future (1.26 *auguria*) is not wrong, and the second verse that she speaks mentions Proteus' prophecy (1.32). Moreover, she begins her soliloquy by saying that the fleet threatens her (1.31 '*me petit haec, mihi classis*' ait '*funesta minatur*' '"This fleet" she says "is after me, to me a deadly menace"'). This idea of a fleet attacking Thetis is familiar from Virgil, who, in the prophetic *Eclogue* 4, describes ships assaulting Thetis, a metonym for the sea (*E.* 4.32 *temptare Thetin ratibus* 'to attack the sea in ships'). Virgil himself, as Clausen notes, takes over this metonymy from Lycophron (22), who also employs it within a prophecy. But whereas Thetis is a metonym for the sea in Virgil and Lycophron, in Statius' account, Thetis speaks for herself, and the repetition of the personal pronouns (*me, mihi*) personalizes the image that his predecessors had used. That is, in the *Achilleid*, sailing is not just an unnatural act that symbolizes human transgression, but it also challenges Thetis in a real and personal way. Coming after the mention of her fears (1.26 *auguria*) and right before the mention of Proteus' prophecy (1.32), Statius' rewriting of his models repositions them in a new prophetic context that emphasizes Thetis' personal stake. The goddess' awareness of the prophetic tradition surrounding Paris' journey and its consequences is thus established, and provides an explanation for her desire to raise a storm.

In the Cycle, the only time Thetis informs Achilles of future events concerns Memnon (*Aeth.* arg. lines 186–7 Severyns), but from other sources it is clear that before Achilles goes to Troy, his mother informs him of a number of fated events: she tells him not to be the first to leap from the boats onto the Trojan soil lest he perish (Ps.-Apollod. *Epit.* 3.29); she sends (to no end) Mnemon to tell Achilles not to kill Tennes (e.g. Lyc. 240–1); and she tells him that he will not take Troy (*Il.* 17.401–9).[20] Traditionally, then, Thetis is aware of the fate of her child and of events that will happen at Troy, and

---

Virg. *Ecl.* 4; Hor *C.* 1.15; cf. Virg. *Aen.* 6.90–1), so Statius's scene also fits with this familiar kind of discourse.

[20] Burgess (2009: 43–4) discusses Achilles' knowledge of the future from his mother.

her warnings to him indicate that she tries to keep him alive. In the opening scene of his poem, Statius takes over this model of the protective mother.[21] By contrast, in the *Iliad*, Thetis is aware of Achilles' impending doom, but she does not aggressively seek to preserve her son until he loses his armor, and until after he makes the choice to fight Hector and face his death.[22] In fact, even when Thetis turns to Hephaestus to make new weapons for Achilles, it is clear that his doom is sealed (*Il.* 18.464–7). Moreover, whereas archaic Greek art suggests that Thetis presented Achilles with divine armor before the war, the *Iliad* explicitly states that Achilles received his initial set of armor from Peleus (*Il.* 17.194–7).[23] Homeric poetry thus downplays Thetis' protection of her child. By contrast, the *Achilleid* emphasizes the importance of prophecies for motivating Thetis' attempts to circumvent fate. In broad terms, these two aspects of the opening scene operate within the tradition of the cycle.

CHIRON'S CAVE

For all of Thetis' efforts, she fails to convince Neptune to create a storm. Pointedly, he argues that he cannot subvert fate, which is exactly what Thetis had been trying to circumvent. Though frustrated, she immediately turns to fetch her son from Chiron, and it quickly emerges that he is a foil to the overprotective Thetis. She herself had expressed regret that she (and Peleus; cf. 1.39 *commisimus*) entrusted her son to the Centaur (1.38–9), and when she arrives at his cave, she upbraids Chiron about the fact that he is not with Achilles (1.127–9). Not only does she have doubts about Chiron's supervision of Achilles, she also recognizes that he would never allow her to pursue her plan to disguise Achilles (1.141–3). Two distinct modes of raising a child are in play, and the cave, situated away from humanity in the woods of Thessaly, symbolizes one of those methods.

Statius' use of the literary past enhances this dynamic of competing parental influences. The relationship between the Centaur and Achilles is treated only cursorily and with no special emphasis in the *Iliad* (4.219). Yet the earliest Greek art regularly depicts Achilles' stay with Chiron,[24] so the story was certainly known and available. To judge from the previously

---

[21] It is useful to remember here that Statius' version is not the sole account of how Achilles ends up on Scyros: Σ D *Il.* 19.326 record that Peleus, kowing what would happen at Troy, was responsible for hiding Achilles, whereas Lycophron suggests that Achilles, fearing his fate, hit upon the plan.

[22] Slatkin (1991: 44).   [23] Friis Johansen (1967: 92–127).   [24] Robbins (1993: 7–20).

discussed Pindaric scholia ad *Nem.* 3.76, the episode probably came from the Cycle (cf. *PEG* F 36). From this perspective, Achilles' tutelage under Chiron exemplifies Statius' strategy of supplementing Homeric poetry, but this augmentation serves a greater purpose. After all, the Homeric suppression of the story of Chiron's role in raising Achilles highlights Peleus and thus the motif of the aged father.[25] By contrast, Peleus is essentially absent from the *Achilleid*,[26] and Chiron plays the part of the father figure.

Chiron's role as Achilles' tutor has great symbolic value. The Centaur is not just a superhuman tutor, but he is also Achilles' great-grandfather. Moreover, he saved his grandson Peleus from death (Ps.-Apollod. *Bibl.* 3.13.3) and taught him how to capture Thetis. He has thus watched over multiple generations of the Aeacids, though his relationship with Thetis would not seem to be particularly amicable. Hence Achilles' education is, for his family, a traditional one, and a host of literary sources reveal that Chiron indeed taught Achilles traditional values: he should display reverence to the gods and parents (Pin. *Pyth.* 6.23–6); he will kill many Trojans and die in Troy (Bacch. F 27; cf. Phil. *Imag.* 2.2); he should not make hasty decisions (Plut. *Mor.* 1034e); and the Centaur also sings war-songs that fired the imagination of Achilles' famous anger (Sen. *Tro.* 832–5). Achilles' instruction in the *Achilleid* is of a similarly hyper-masculine, martial type in that he plays war, and in roaming far and wide he comes close to provoking a fight with the Centaurs (1.151–5).[27] In sum, Pelion is where Achilles learns epic values without the interference of any women.

Within the structure of the *Achilleid*, then, the scene with Chiron establishes what Thetis must offset. She does so by taking her son to Scyros and then instructing him about feminine behavior and comportment. Pelion and Scyros thus represents gendered polarities. Like Achilles' stay with Chiron, Scyros also has a Cyclic heritage, and his encounter there with love counters Achilles' early training with Chiron. As such, it invites further examination.

FALLING IN LOVE

The poems of the Cycle recount more romantic episodes for Achilles than do the Homeric poems.[28] In the Cycle, Achilles is connected with Helen

---

[25] Cf. Janko (1992) on *Il.* 16.141–4.
[26] Statius' strategy is in sharp contrast with the Σ D *Il.* 19.326 which has Peleus hide Achilles.
[27] Advice of a somewhat different sort is mentioned in Horace's *Epode* 13.
[28] Griffin (1977: 44–5); Burgess (2001: 169–70) qualifies this view.

and Penthesileia, and if his encounter with Troilus in the *Cypria* included the erotic subtext that appears in later authors, then Achilles' sexuality was greatly amplified in the cycle. For certain, the sexual encounter between Achilles and Deidameia fits in with and is attested in the *Cypria* (arg. lines 129–31 Severyns). Though the cross-dressing is not for certain a Cyclic detail, it certainly strengthens the contrast between his masculine education and his feminine experience in Scyros. And just as he used *Aeneid* 1 as a backdrop to reinforce the Cyclic dimensions of Thetis, so too here Statius heavily reworks another part of *Aeneid* 1 in ways that mark the importance of the Cycle.

When Thetis and Achilles arrive at Scyros, Achilles initially rejects Thetis' plan to dress him as a girl, but he changes his mind when he sees the beautiful Deidameia amidst her sisters. It is important, then, that Achilles himself submits to the plan in order to pursue Deidameia. For him, the cross-dressing is a means to an end, and he subordinates the pursuit of warfare to that end.[29] Deidameia is compared to Diana among the Naiads or Venus among the sea-nymphs (1.293–6), and she is finally compared to Minerva (1.299–300). As the goddess of love and sexual desire, Venus provides an apt point of comparison. Minerva, however, is a less obvious goddess to invoke, and her role here seems ironic given that Deidameia is worshipping a virgin goddess. But Minerva was part of the beauty contest that Paris adjudicated, so she is hardly a homely goddess. Moreover, a passage from Callimachus' *Bath of Pallas* discusses Athena's preparation of her hair for the Judgment (31–2 with Bulloch) in sensual terms that rework the Homeric passage in which Hera prepares to seduce Zeus.[30] Statius also concentrates upon Minerva's hair. When he describes the cult statue of Minerva that the girls decorate, Statius refers to the goddess' virginal hair (1.288–9 *severas...comas*). As the narrative proceeds, however, and the intensity of Achilles' erotic feelings increases, Statius likens Deidameia to Minerva when she has taken off her helmet in addition to putting aside her shield (1.299–300). Most naturally, the phrase refers to Minerva putting aside her martial visage, but the removal of the helmet also exposes her hair. Statius refers to Minerva's hair twice within close compass, the first of which marks Minerva's chastity, the second her beauty. Minerva's hair is thus linked to her sexuality, and in this sense may build upon the Callimachean passage in which Athena's hair is a central feature of her sexuality. If so, then it is intriguing that, in addition

---

[29] In this sense, Statius seems to build upon the treatment of the cross-dressing Achilles as it relates to the enamored Sybaris in Horace, *C.* 1.8.

[30] For fuller treatment of Callimachus' Athena, see Hadjittofi (2008: 9–37).

to the model of the Homeric Hera, Callimachus's depiction of Athena likely draws upon the representation of Aphrodite preparing for the Judgment, a common enough scene but one that was also depicted in the *Cypria* (*PEG* F 4 = D. = F 5 W.). If Statius does follow Callimachus, then, his inclusion of Minerva also implicates the Cyclic tradition.

Statius' comparison of Deidameia to Diana engages with the Cycle in more direct fashion as well. Comparisons of a nubile girl to Artemis/Diana are ubiquitous in epic (e.g. Nausicaa (*Od.* 6.102–8); Medea (Apoll. Rh. 3.875–84; Val. Flac. 5.343–7)), but Virgil's comparison of Dido to this goddess (*Aen.* 1.498–502) is particularly important for the *Achilleid*. For instance, the word *regina* may describe any woman of a royal household, but in this context of a simile comparing Deidameia to Diana, it recalls the Virgilian designation of Dido as such right before the simile that compares her to Diana (*Aen.* 1.496). Moreover, the one time that Vergil treats the quantity of the –*i* in Diana's name as long occurs in the Dido simile (*Aen.* 1.499), and it is long in Statius' simile as well (1.294). The initial meeting between Dido and Aeneas thus forms the backdrop for the encounter between Achilles and Deidameia.

As Achilles gazes at Deidameia, he falls deeply in love, and to describe this reaction, Statius employs diction that stems from the various moments in the relationship between Aeneas and Dido. Thus Statius' phrase *totisque novum bibit ossibus ignem* 'he drank novel flame in all his bones' (1.303) describes the symptoms of love in Virgilian terms. The metaphorical sense of *ignis* for erotic feeling is common (*OLD* s.v. 9) but *ossibus ignem* at verse-end appears in both an account of the destructive power of love on a youth (*Georg.* 3.258–9 *quid iuuenis, magnum cui uersat in ossibus ignem / durus amor ?* 'what of the youth, in whose marrow fierce love fans the mighty flame?') and in Venus' plan for Dido (*Aen.* 1.659–61 *donisque furentem / incendat reginam atque ossibus implicet ignem* '(how Cupid may) by his gifts kindle the queen to madness and send the flame into the very marrow'); cf. *Aen.* 4.66). The idea of Achilles drinking in the flame of love (1.303 *bibit*) also echoes the description of the love-struck Dido (*Aen.* 1.749 *infelix Dido longumque bibebat amorem* '… unhappy Dido, and drank deep draughts of love') though Statius' present tense points to Achilles' instantaneous love. *nouum*, however, emphasizes Achilles' virginity and sexual inexperience, whereas Dido's passion is old (*Aen.* 4.23 *ueteris uestigia flammae* 'I feel again a spark of that former flame'). Moreover, at 1.306, Statius' use of *impulsam* in an erotic sense comes from Virgil (*Aen.* 4.22–3 *solus hic inflexit sensus animumque labantem / impulit* 'he alone has swayed my will and overthrown my tottering soul'). Finally, *primusque … amor* (1.316–17) echoes a description of the enamored Dido (*Aen.* 4.17 *postquam primus amor deceptam morte fefellit* 'since my first love, turning traitor, cheated me to death').[31] In fundamental ways, then, the entire Virgilian erotic episode concerning the two leaders is a model for the encounter between Achilles and Deidameia.

In this scene that depicts the initial encounter between the lovers, Statius also draws upon the verses that set up the first meeting of Dido and Aeneas. When Achilles sees Deidameia, she is described as leading her cohort (1.301 *ducentem . . . socia agmina* '(when the boy saw) her leading her attendant column'). In a context that is predicated upon the relationship between Dido and Aeneas and particularly their introduction in *Aeneid* 1, Statius' diction recalls the depiction of Penthesileia on the walls of Juno's temple in Carthage (*Aen.* 1.490 *ducit Amazonidum lunatis agmina peltis* '(Penthesileia) in fury leads the crescent-shielded ranks of the Amazons'). The entire Virgilian tableau contains a number of events that stem in part from the Epic Cycle,[32] and the position of Penthesileia, who features in the *Aethiopis*, at the end of the sequence prepares for the immediate arrival of Dido, another strong woman who leads her people.[33] There is an implicit comparison, then, between the social status of Dido and of the Amazon queen, but the larger point is that, just as an erotic relationship – and indeed Cupid himself – is about to be introduced to the epic, Vergil treats Penthesileia in decidedly non-erotic terms that correlate to Dido's attempts to live and rule without a husband.

In the *Achilleid*, however, Statius adapts this Vergilian treatment of the Amazon to an erotic context. Deidameia is like Penthesileia in that she leads a female troupe, but here the leader's beauty causes Achilles to fall in love with her. The allusive comparison of the attractive Deidameia to the Amazon queen evokes the story in the *Aethiopis*, in which Achilles was said to have fallen in love with Penthesileia (arg. lines 175–7 Severyns). Intriguingly, Achilles fell in love with her after he removed her helmet (e. g. Prop. 3.11.15–6), a detail that recalls the comparison in Statius' preceding verse of Deidameia to the helmet-less Minerva. Though the mention of Minerva removing her helmet does not refer to Penthesileia, the likening of Deidameia to both figures in such close proximity creates a triangular relationship that blurs attributes of each. Deidameia is like Minerva and Penthesileia. Before he reaches Troy, then, Statius' Achilles is attracted to a character comparable to the one that he is attracted to on the Trojan battlefield.

---

[31] Lyne (1989: 31–2).
[32] For the Cyclic background to the scene, see Barchiesi (1997: 273–7).
[33] Pöschl (1962: 147).

In the Cycle, Thersites mocked Achilles for his feelings towards Penthesileia (*Aeth.* arg. lines 178–81 Severyns). The ugliest man to come to Troy is hardly a reliable guide for appropriate and inappropriate behavior, but his mockery implies that Achilles' erotic feelings were improper. Indeed, Propertius plays upon the myth in such a way that the Amazon's erotic conquest of Achilles disrupts the masculine paradigm that conflates martial and sexual prowess in that Achilles the martial victor becomes the erotically vanquished (Prop. 3.11.16). In the *Achilleid*, Achilles' erotic feelings similarly prevail in that they keep him from going to war. Achilles' passion puts him at odds with Chiron's training, and the female clothing amplifies the problematic nature of his feelings. The poem consistently balances these polarities, but the end of Achilles' time on Scyros poignantly represents the conflicting feelings. For instance, when it seems that Achilles is headed to Troy after Odysseus exposes Achilles' identity, Deidameia cries out (1.885–6). Achilles immediately (1.886 *cum . . . primum*) alters his intentions. Her huge laments (1.886–7 *grandia . . . lamenta*) both counteract the martial blare of Odysseus' tuba (1.875 *grande*) and cause Achilles to stand still (1.888 *haesit*; cf. 1.867 *haeres*). What is more, Achilles' *virtus* – the masculine, martial virtue par excellence – is broken (1.888 *infracta*). Similar language appears in a passage from Virgil in which female lamentation confounds martial desire (*Aen.* 9.499 *torpent infractae ad proelia vires* 'their strength for battle is numbed and crushed'), but at this moment in Roman literary history, the language also recalls Ovid's reference to a dramatic portrayal of the erotic (and sexually passive) Achilles at the expense of his heroic deeds (*Tr.* 2.411–12 *nec nocet auctori, mollem qui fecit Achillem, / infregisse suis fortia facta modis* 'and the author who depicted Achilles tender with love does not suffer for having weakened by his verses deeds of valour'). Statius' moment has a heterosexual focus, but he uses the diction of his predecessors in a way that reinforces the tension between love and the pursuit of martial accomplishment. Indeed, Achilles' *occultus amor*, a synecdochic reference to his time on Scyros, had vanished (1.857), but after he hears Deidameia, another hidden heat returns and counters the martial spirit that Achilles had displayed (1.881–2). In fact, Achilles lowers his shield (1.889), an act that undoes his taking up of the shield (1.879) and symbolizes a waning interest in warfare. Indeed, *demittit* is the verb used of someone who has abandoned a fight (*Theb.* 5.739; 9.237; 10.423). Love for Deidameia has softened Achilles' martial drive and caused him to hesitate in joining the expedition to Troy – even after he has cast off his feminine disguise.

As he sails away from Scyros, Achilles thinks about Deidameia's laments and loses his spirit to fight (2.27–9). Twice, then, female lamentation undermines Achilles' heroism, and it is worth recalling that the Platonic Socrates condemns the Homeric passage in which Achilles weeps over Patroclus because the hero acts like a woman (*Rep.* 387e–388e; cf. *Rep.* 605d9–e1). Mourning compromises Achilles' heroism, though in the *Achilleid*, Achilles is the audience rather than the performer. In other respects as well, Achilles' departure from Scyros hardly marks an end to the influence of feminine activity. To be sure, he does not don female garb at any other point, but the Platonic Socrates argues that fouling the body of an enemy by dragging it in the dust reflects a womanish mind (*Rep.* 469d6–e2).[34] Though Achilles is not explicitly mentioned in the latter passage, there is no doubt that he is the subject. The feminized Achilles is thus not defined simply by his cross-dressing. At the broadest level, however, Scyros provides a powerful analogy for Achilles' behavior at Troy in that his feelings for a woman will lead to his segregation from the rest of the Greek army and from fighting. In fact, his divided sense of purpose presages that his Homeric incarnation will never lose his passion and interest in his beloved women. As Richard Martin has argued, the Homeric Achilles is unique among Greek heroes in that he speaks of tenderness and compatability between lovers.[35] Indeed, Achilles claims that it is not the sons of Atreus alone who love their women (*Il.* 9.337–9), and thus he questions the very reason for fighting with the Trojans (*Il.* 9.337–8). In the *Achilleid*, Odysseus is able to redirect Achilles' melancholy about leaving Deidameia when he asks what he would do if someone had stolen away Deidameia the way Paris has Helen (2.81–2). Odysseus' astute rhetoric uses Achilles' amorous devotion to drive him to war, but the irony is that it is precisely that sort of affection for Briseis that will keep Achilles out of the war in the *Iliad*.

Odysseus' speech also self-referentially marks that the broader narrative, while operating within the tradition of Cyclic poetry, approaches it circuitously. The Cycle was notoriously famous for proceeding in linear fashion. Statius' focus on Achilles, however, has meant that the pre-Trojan war saga has been filtered through the hero. Indeed, Achilles' segregation means that he has no real sense of what has been happening in the larger Greek world, and thus his desire to know how the war started (2.46–8) prompts Odysseus to fill him in on the events through a flashback (2.50–83). Intriguingly, Odysseus relates (in nearly linear fashion) events from the *Cypria* that were omitted or mentioned only allusively in the earlier part of the *Achilleid*. So when Odysseus informs Achilles about the Judgment

---

[34] Zoilus of Amphipolis (*FgrHist* 71 F 11) also attacks Achilles' effeminate weeping.
[35] Martin (1989: 184).

(2.50–4), the wedding of Peleus and Thetis (2.56–7), Paris' preparations for his journey to Sparta (2.59–63), the seizure of Helen (2.63–4), and the marshaling of the Greeks (2.64–71), he virtually narrates to Achilles a *Cypria*. Achilles' childhood and the birth of his son, two aspects of the *Cypria*, had been addressed in the main narrative, and Odysseus' account fills in other aspects of the *Cypria* that concern the Greeks as whole. From a meta-textual perspective, then, by having Odysseus recount the activities that took place while Achilles was apart from the Greeks, Statius achieves a temporal coincidence that frames his subject matter within the Cycle.

31 | The Epic Cycle and the ancient novel

DAVID F. ELMER

The 'ancient novel' is a diffuse phenomenon, comprising a core of clearly fictional texts generally acknowledged (by classicists, at least) as meeting the criteria for designation as 'novels', and a 'fringe' of prose texts that flirt with fictionality to varying degrees.[1] If, for the purposes of this brief discussion, we restrict our gaze to the seven extant texts typically assigned to the core – the five Greek romances (Chariton's *Chaereas and Callirhoe*, Xenophon's *Ephesiaca*, Achilles Tatius' *Leucippe and Cleitophon*, Longus' *Daphnis and Chloe*, Heliodorus' *Aethiopica*) and the two 'comic' novels in Latin (Petronius' *Satyrica*, Apuleius' *Metamorphoses*) – we will find that, in spite of certain promising convergences, it is not easy to identify direct connections between the Epic Cycle and this corpus.[2] Obvious references to the content of the Cycle are relatively infrequent,[3] while arguably the most prominent display of Cyclic themes in the novels, the 'Iliou persis' recited by Petronius' Eumolpus, is, first and foremost, a parodic reworking of Roman texts (Virgil and Seneca), and only residually (if at all) an evocation of Greek models.[4] The difficulty, to be sure, is compounded by the very fragmentary state of our evidence for the Cycle itself, which makes it virtually impossible to say whether any given reference to the stories reported in the Cycle is

---

[1] See Holzberg (1996). Philostratus' *Life of Apollonius of Tyana*, which fictionalizes the career of a historical individual, is a good example of a 'fringe' text. The modern study of the novel begins with Rohde's *Der griechische Roman und seine Vorläufer* (1876; 3rd edn 1914). The literature has grown exponentially in the last decades; I can do no more here than direct the reader to a few works providing useful overviews: Hägg (1983); Tatum (1994); Swain (1999); Harrison (1999); Whitmarsh (2008).

[2] I refer to the novels by the titles in most common use in contemporary scholarship. For titling conventions in antiquity, see Whitmarsh (2005). By distinguishing the Greek 'romances' from the Latin 'novels', I follow the usage of Whitmarsh (2011: 1 n. 1); elsewhere in this essay I apply the term 'novel' to the Greek romances as well.

[3] In addition to the passages discussed below, examples include: Chariton's use of the story of Ariadne and Dionysus, which may echo the lost *Thebaid*(s) (which I include in the Epic Cycle broadly defined); the duel between the brothers Thyamis and Petosiris in book 7 of Heliodorus' *Aethiopica*, which evokes Theban legend, and possibly the *Thebaid*; Apuleius' treatment of the 'Judgment of Paris' pantomime in *Metamorphoses* 10.

[4] See Sullivan (1968: 186–9). The Virgilian orientation of Eumolpus' poem, which is essentially a rewriting of parts of *Aeneid* 2 in Senecan iambic trimeters, can be seen particularly clearly in the speaker's markedly Trojan perspective.

intended as an allusion to a specific Cyclic text, or instead draws merely on general knowledge of heroic legend. All the same, the Cycle makes a disappointing showing in the extant novels – especially considering the many good reasons for supposing that traces of its influence might be there to be found.

There is, first of all, the suggestive chronological proximity of literary trends. The mid to late first century AD is a period that sees not only the birth of the Greek romance (so far as we can tell), but also a renewed interest in the penumbra of Trojan legends surrounding the Homeric poems. Much uncertainty surrounds the dating of the novels, but there is now broad consensus that *Chaereas and Callirhoe*, the earliest of the extant Greek texts, should be placed roughly around AD 50, and there is a strong likelihood that the earliest fragmentary romances (the so-called *Ninus* and *Metiochus and Parthenope*) were composed in the decades immediately thereafter.[5] Meanwhile, Petronius' poem on the sack of Troy is only one indicator of a noticeably more intense engagement in the same period with the more obscure details of Trojan legend.[6] Others include the *Trojan Oration* of Dio of Prusa, the Trojan War trivia collected in Ptolemaeus Chennos' *New* (or *Novel*) *History*, Statius' *Achilleid*, and possibly Lucan's *Iliaca* (of which only two certain fragments remain). This interest is sustained into the second and third centuries, when it develops a distinctly novelistic cast: witness the Greek texts translated into Latin as the *Diary of the Trojan War*, pseudepigraphically attributed to a certain Dictys of Crete, and the *History of the Fall of Troy* supposedly by the Trojan priest Dares, as well as Philostratus' *On Heroes*.[7] Works such as these speak to the fundamental

---

[5] Detailed discussion of the dating of Chariton's *Chaereas and Callirhoe* at Tilg (2010: 36–79), who also believes that Chariton was the 'inventor' of the Greek romance, and the author of *Metiochus and Parthenope* as well; his arguments on both points are not, in my view, conclusive. Bowie (2002) makes a well-founded, though sometimes speculative, case for the mid-first-century dating of *Ninus* and *Metiochus and Parthenope*, arguing also that the next earliest novels might be dated somewhat earlier than has generally been accepted (Xenophon after 65; Antonius Diogenes in the years 98–130; Achilles Tatius before 164). For an overview of the 'current orthodoxy' on the dating of the Greek novels, see Whitmarsh (2011: 261–4).

[6] See Milazzo (1984: 16); Pavano (1998: 211–12).

[7] The Greek original for 'Dictys' has long been known in papyrus fragments; Merkle (1994: 192) fixes the date of composition between AD 66 and 200. The existence of a Greek original for 'Dares' has been a matter of some dispute, but has now been confirmed by the discovery of an ostracon bearing text that corresponds to part of the extant Latin version: see Pavano (1998) and Mheallaigh (2008: 412), who asserts that the Greek version must have been in circulation in the second century AD. The novelistic qualities of these texts are frequently stressed. Mheallaigh, for instance, relates their pseudo-documentary strategies to the *Beglaubigungsapparat* of Antonius Diogenes; see also Haight (1947); Milazzo (1984). On Philostratus' connection to this tradition, see Merkle (1989: 254–9; 1994: 193–4).

amenability of Trojan (and thus Cyclic) themes to treatment according to the narrative predilections of imperial prose fiction. There is no obvious reason to discount the possibility that first-century experimenters with the form would not likewise have perceived the potential inherent in the Cycle.

Indeed, the extant novels – especially the five Greek romances – are far from reluctant to exploit epic models. All of them engage, sometimes directly, sometimes indirectly, with the Greek epic tradition. Chariton's *Chaereas and Callirhoe* illustrates the range of possibilities in this regard. After the marriage of the protagonists, the story's complicating action is set in motion by the plotting of Callirhoe's frustrated suitors, who are angered by the fact that Chaereas has succeeded where they have failed. The malicious suitors, their conspiratorial meeting to hatch a fatal scheme (1.2), even the contemptuous terms in which they characterize their rival, whom they describe as a πένης ('beggar', 1.2.3), all plainly evoke the *Odyssey*. At the same time, the destabilizing force they represent, the force that sets the plot in motion, is equated by explicit allusion with the event that sets in motion the entire Trojan saga: 'Such was the wedding of Thetis on Pelion, according to the poets' hymns; but on this occasion, too, a certain envious power was present, as they say Strife was then' (1.1.16). This might be counted as a rare example of allusion to one of the poems of the Cycle (the *Cypria*); more likely it is simply a reference to the more amorphous body of Trojan legend. There can be no doubt, however, about Chariton's many quotations from the Homeric poems, taken in roughly equal measure from the *Iliad* and the *Odyssey*.[8]

The whole of the epic tradition thus lies within the novel's reach. Without a doubt, Chariton is especially eager to situate his text in relation to epic models: the range and frequency of his epic references are exceptional. Nevertheless, all of the extant Greek erotic novels can be seen to engage more or less substantially with the master text for the romance of return, the *Odyssey*: 'To greater or lesser degree, and with varying degrees of specificity, all the novels are descants on the second Homeric epic.'[9] The *Odyssey* is a principal intertext for the novels of Petronius and Apuleius as well. Encolpius' wanderings and apparent persecution by Priapus, for instance, are commonly understood as comic transformations of the suffering imposed on Odysseus by a wrathful Poseidon, while the central scene of the *Metamorphoses* – the

---

[8] E.g. 1.1.14 (= *Il.* 21.425, *Od.* 4.703, etc.), 1.4.6 (= *Il.* 18.22–24), 2.3.7 (~ *Od.* 17.485, 487), 2.9.6 (= *Il.* 23.66–67), etc. On Chariton's Homeric quotations, see Müller (1976); Biraud (1985); Létoublon (2008); Morgan (2008: 219 n. 2); on poetic citations in the novels more generally, Fusillo (1990) and Robiano (2000).

[9] Morgan (2008: 220).

episode in the robbers' cave, which frames the Cupid and Psyche novella – simultaneously evokes both Odysseus' encounter with the Cyclops and his vanquishing of the suitors on Ithaca.[10] The prominence of the *Odyssey* as a point of reference can be explained by the fact that it provides such a rich matrix of novelistic preoccupations and techniques. The narrative of return outlines a basic trajectory and a closural paradigm that are as relevant to Lucius' struggle to recover his human form as they are to the more literal homecomings of the Greek romances; Odysseus' dalliances and his longing for Penelope establish the utility of eros as a motive force for both 'centripetal' and 'centrifugal' modes of narrativity;[11] the episodic structure, particularly of Odysseus' '*Apologoi*', offers a model for the composition of an extended, self-renewing plot; the insertion of Odysseus' first-person perspective in a third-person frame exposes the contrasting possibilities represented by homodiegetic, heterodiegetic, and embedded narrators; and, finally, the contrast between the plausibility of Odysseus' 'Cretan lies' and the fantastic quality of his apparently truthful tales in Alcinous' palace signals an interest in exploring the very nature of fictionality.[12]

The *Odyssey*'s pre-eminent position as a point of reference for the novelists is, therefore, guaranteed by its particular combination of formal and thematic properties. But many of the poems of the Cycle would appear to have equal claims in these regards. Aristotle famously contrasts the *Cypria* and the *Ilias parva* with the *Iliad* and *Odyssey* precisely on the basis of the episodic character of the former (*Poet*. 1459a30–b7).[13] So, for instance, the compositional structure of Xenophon's *Ephesiaca*, with its lengthy concatenation of discrete episodes exhibiting minimal causal links, bears a stronger resemblance to the *Cypria*, so far as we can tell, than to the *Odyssey* – although the *Odyssey* itself is more 'Cyclic' in this regard than the *Iliad*.[14] With respect to themes, Rohde already identified the Cycle as a potential

---

[10] Petronius: Klebs (1889), who first proposed the analogy between Priapus and Poseidon, Sullivan (1968: 92–8); Harrison (2008: 229); Morgan (2009: 32–8). Apuleius: Frangoulidis (1992); Harrison (1990: 198–200; 2008: 231).

[11] On the tension between 'centrifugal' and 'centripetal' elements in the Greek romances, see Whitmarsh (2011: esp. Ch. 5).

[12] For the importance of plausibility to the concept of fictionality, see Gallagher (2006: esp. p. 339): 'Plausible stories are thus the real test for the progress of fictional sophistication in a culture.'

[13] 'Episodic' in our sense of the word: Aristotle actually speaks of the *praxis polumerēs* of these Cyclic poems, while expressing admiration for Homer's incorporation of *epeisodia* in his more unified epic. On the meaning of *epeisodion* in this passage, see Friedrich (1983) and Heath (1989: 51–2); on the 'essentially episodic' character of the Cycle, Richardson (1992: 37), as well as Scaife (1995: 170 on the *Cypria*) and Holmberg (1998: 459).

[14] See Scaife (1995: 173).

source for the kinds of erotic narratives that would later exert an influence on the novel (in his view, through the intermediary of Hellenistic poetry).[15] These seem to have been especially prominent in the *Cypria*, a poem that may have derived its name from the prominent role played by Aphrodite in the direction of the action:[16] in addition to the love affair of Helen and Paris – a story that may lie somewhere in the background of Xenophon's tale of Aegialeus, whose love affair with Thelxinoe resulted in their precipitous flight from Sparta (*Eph.* 5.1.4–11) – that poem also included a series of inset erotic tales narrated by Nestor (*Cypr.* arg. lines 114–17 Severyns) and several romantic episodes featuring Achilles (the affair with Deidameia, the ruse of marriage with Iphigenia, and the encounter with Helen, engineered in part by Aphrodite). Erotic motifs can also be traced in the *Aethiopis*,[17] possibly in the *Iliou persis*,[18] and in the *Telegony*, which recounted Odysseus' marriage with the Thesprotian princess Callidice and brought the Trojan cycle as a whole to a conclusion with a convenient set of marriages. This happy ending through marriage even prompted Severyns to declare that the *Telegony* 'marks the end of the epic genre, and announces a new genre, that of the prose romance'.[19] Another staple of the novel, travel in foreign lands, was presumably much in evidence in the *Nostoi*, which featured, in the course of recounting the journeys of numerous heroes, an account of the time spent in Egypt by the reunited lovers Helen and Menelaus.[20] Egypt, of course, is the novelistic setting par excellence.[21]

This rich store of material, as noted above, has left few verifiable traces in the novelistic corpus. But the *Nostoi* and especially the *Telegony*, by virtue

---

[15] Rohde (1914: 110–11 (102–4 in the 1st edn); cf. Welcker (1849: 227).
[16] Huxley (1969: 126); Davies (1989c: 33).
[17] In Thersites' claim that Achilles harbored a romantic passion for Penthesileia (*Aeth.* arg. lines 178–81 Severyns). It is possible that this episode, or some later elaboration on it, also lies in the background of Xenophon's Aigialeus, who has the rather remarkable habit of enjoying an erotic relationship with his wife's embalmed corpse (*Eph.* 5.1.9). According to the scholia to Sophocles and Lycophron, Thersites claimed that Achilles sought erotic contact with Penthesileia's corpse (Σ Soph. *Phil.* 445; Σ Lycophr. 999).
[18] Later writers make the sacrifice of Polyxena a consequence of Achilles' desire for her, but it is unclear what, if anything, this story owes to the Cycle. Förster (1883: 447) argued that the Cycle knew of Achilles' passion for Polyxena, but later scholarship has tended to see this story as a Hellenistic or later invention (cf. Rohde 1914: 111 n. 3; Merkle 1989: 207).
[19] Severyns (1928: 409); cf. Davies (1989a: 94).
[20] The Egyptian Menelaus who appears in Achilles Tatius' novel is a playful recasting of this epic prototype. Achilles' Menelaus is a lover just like his epic counterpart, but one with decidedly different tastes: his wanderings away from his Egyptian homeland are the result of an unhappy love affair with a young man (2.34.1–6).
[21] On Egypt as a virtually obligatory *topos* within the novels, and as a metonym for novelistic discourse, see Brioso Sánchez (1992: esp. p. 204), Plazenet (1995), and Elmer (2008: 429).

of their position as collateral narratives that circulated beside and contextualized the master-romance of the *Odyssey*, point to a form of indirect influence that the Cycle may have exerted on at least some novels.

One of the most distinctive features of the core group of ancient novels, which differentiates them from the bulk of ancient literature, is their avoidance of any direct reliance on external frames of reference – historical facts or literary traditions – to provide contextual support for their narratives. (Chariton – exceptionally, but perhaps not insignificantly, as we shall see – does construct certain links between his narrative and the history of Syracuse.) This autonomy vis-à-vis other narratives is in fact constitutive of fiction (and ancient fiction) as such.[22] The difference from the *Odyssey* could not be more extreme: that text binds itself particularly closely to the contextualizing narrative represented by the Cycle.[23] The tales of Nestor and Menelaus in books 3 and 4 introduce embedded versions of the *Nostoi*, implying that the story of Odysseus' return is only the latest episode in a sequential narrative that begins well outside the limits of the poem. And Teiresias' prophecy, recapitulated by Odysseus in book 23 (248–84), emphasizes that Odysseus' story will not conclude with the end of the poem, but will extend beyond – into the events narrated in the *Telegony*. The *Odyssey*, then – perhaps even more than the *Iliad*, which has its own set of internal connections to the surrounding Cyclic narratives – draws attention to its position within a larger narrative continuum, in a way that would seem precluded by the fundamental autonomy of the novels.

Two of the Greek romancers, however, strive deliberately to create the impression that the stories of their fictional protagonists escape the limits of their texts. It is tempting to think that they do so in part because their archetype, the *Odyssey*, suggested to them the desirability of introducing a 'centrifugal' counterpoint to their 'centripetal' acts of closure, and that they look to the *Telegony*, Severyns' 'romance' in verse, as a means of conjuring an extension of a story world that is, by its nature, strictly bounded by a single narrative.

---

[22] See Konstan (1998) on the relationship between referentiality and fictionality: the novels pursue a strategy of auto-referentiality that suspends reference to any external body of facts or knowledge.

[23] From the point of view of the novelists in the first century and later, it is immaterial whether or not the poems of the Cycle were fixed in writing after the *Odyssey*: the close connection between them is evident in any case. I assume, following Nagy (1990b: 72–3), that the Cycle, though textualized at a later date than the Homeric poems, nevertheless represents traditions that evolved alongside those of the *Iliad* and *Odyssey*. This assumption, however, has no bearing on my arguments here.

The problems presented by the conclusion of Achilles Tatius' novel are well known.[24] At the beginning of the text, the anonymous narrator encounters in Sidon a solitary Cleitophon, whose narrative of his adventures constitutes the rest of the novel; but Cleitophon concludes his story by telling only of his return with Leucippe to Tyre, and their intention to travel to Byzantium in the spring. The unclosed frame leaves open the question of what Cleitophon is doing (by himself!) in Sidon. Is it too much to see in this man who has 'suffered so much on account of love' (τοσαύτας ὕβρεις ἐξ ἔρωτος παθών, 1.2.1) and is now wandering apart from his beloved – a man, moreover, who will soon distinguish himself as an artful (and unreliable) narrator of his sufferings – an image of the Odysseus of the *Telegony*?

More suggestive still is the sequel predicted in Chariton's romance. At the novel's end, Callirhoe has returned to Syracuse with her first husband Chaereas, but she has left their son (whom Chaereas has never seen) in Miletus, in the care of her second husband Dionysius, who believes the child to be his own. Callirhoe, who compares herself to Odysseus early on (2.5.11), shares with her predecessor a multiplicity of conjugal ties, and she scripts for her unconventional family an eventual reunion that recalls the one that brings together Odysseus' nearest and dearest in the last poem of the Cycle. Callirhoe directs Dionysius to send her son to Syracuse after marrying him to his own daughter, so that he may be reunited with his maternal grandfather – and of course with his father, although she cannot mention this to Dionysius (8.4.6). This reunion is presumably to be happier than the one reported in the *Telegony*, in which Telegonus mistakenly killed his father, but it is similarly accompanied by the fusion, through marriage, of the distinct branches of the family.

Perhaps, however, the darker undertones of this Cyclic intertext ought not to be so quickly discounted in the complex interplay Chariton sets up between his fiction, its literary models, and history. Several scholars have suggested that Callirhoe's child, left in the care of Dionysius (whose name he might reasonably inherit) – a strange and apparently unnecessary anti-closural detail – is meant to be the tyrant Dionysius I, who succeeded Hermocrates (Callirhoe's father in Chariton's fictional world) as ruler of Syracuse.[25] This historical Dionysius in fact married a daughter of Hermocrates, who suffered greatly as a result of the union – according to Plutarch, eventually taking her own life (*Dio* Chrys. 3). Chariton has clearly

---

[24] For a survey of these problems and proposed solutions, see Repath (2005).
[25] First suggested by Naber (1901: 98–9); cf. Perry (1967: 137–9); Connors (2002: 14, 16–17); Tilg (2010: 46).

tried to connect his tale with Syracusan history, but here a seemingly irremediable discrepancy arises – is Callirhoe to be understood as the mother or as the wife of Dionysius I? Or somehow as both? The discrepancy is, if not resolved, at least reduced on a 'Telegonic' reading of Chariton's blend of fiction and history, for the *Telegony* authorizes both roles: in a composite view that blends all the literary and historical sources, Callirhoe may be understood as a Penelope figure (the woman who marries the returning child) or/and as an Odysseus figure (the parent who suffers on account of the child). The last of the Trojan epics charts a possible interchange between the worlds of fiction and history; and the Epic Cycle, as a narrative that both inhabits and escapes the Homeric master-text, provides a vehicle by which the novel may transcend the limits of its own fiction.

32 | The Epic Cycle and imperial Greek epic

SILVIO BÄR AND MANUEL BAUMBACH

The Greek world from the third to the sixth century AD enjoyed a rich and continuous production of hexameter poetry, ranging from the didactic poems *Halieutica* and *Cynegetica* (second century AD) by the two Oppians, Quintus of Smyrna's large-scale *Posthomerica* and Triphiodorus' small-scale *Capture of Troy* (third century AD), to Nonnus of Panopolis' gargantuan *Dionysiaca* (fifth century AD), as well as those poets who are indebted to Nonnus and are therefore often (however inappropriately) called his 'disciples' (e.g. Musaeus, Colluthus, or Christodorus of Coptos; fifth/sixth century AD). In addition to this, mention has also to be made of the multitudinous (longer and shorter) fragments of hexameter poems of various lengths and sorts which were not transmitted through our mediaeval manuscript tradition, but are known to us only via papyri and parchment, most of them preserved in the deserts of Egypt. Finally, we also have to think of those epics which are entirely lost to us now, such as Nestor of Laranda's *Metamorphoses*, his son's Pisander of Laranda's Ἡρωϊκαὶ θεογαμίαι 'Heroic Marriages of the Gods', or Scopelianus' *Gigantia*.[1]

When considering the possible influences of the poems of the Epic Cycle upon the hexameter poetry of the imperial period, we must therefore, first and foremost, bear in mind that the poems with which we will be dealing represent only a small section of an extremely diversified and rich poetic production, within which the Trojan saga played a doubtlessly important, but by no means singular, role. At the same time, however, even those texts which re-enact the Trojan saga were numerous, and only a small fraction of them has survived, whereas much textual material is lost or available to us only in fragments. Further, essentially three caveats have to be expressed with regard to the potential engagement of later epic with the Cyclic poems. First, the date of the Cycle's loss is still a moot point, depending, inter alia, on the dating and/or identification of Proclus (the author of the Cycle's prose summaries), and the assessment of Ioannes Philoponus' notice that the Cycle was no longer available at the time of Pisander of Laranda (viz. the

---

[1] For a general survey of Greek imperial epic, see e.g. Vian (1986); Brioso Sánchez (1999); Carvounis and Hunter (2008); Miguélez Cavero (2008: 3–105).

third century AD; cf. *Epicus Cyclus* T 2 D.). Hence, the 'loss question' poses a challenge to everyone who wishes to consider the intertextual engagement of an imperial text with the Cycle – and it is important for the dating of poems which might have been written in order to replace lost parts of the Cycle.[2] On the whole, it is generally assumed that the Cycle (or at least larger parts of it) may still have been available to Quintus and Triphiodorus, but is more likely to have been entirely lost at the times of Nonnus and Colluthus (but still formed part of their epic memory). Second, we must not forget that 'the Epic Cycle' was not one coherent piece of literature, but, rather, a conglomeration of different (and differing) hexameter texts that were thematically arranged 'around' the Homeric epics. Therefore, it is possible that parts of the Cycle were already lost in certain places of the then known world, whereas other parts were still available.[3] Third, we have to be aware of the fact that the aims and methods of traditional source criticism are limited and partially inappropriate with regard to questions relating to the intertextual engagement of a later text with an earlier one. In short, we must not restrict our analysis to the mere goal of noting similarities and differences and hence draw conclusions as to whether or not a later author made use of a specific earlier 'source'. Rather, we always have to take into account the fact that intertextuality is a much more complex matter. For one thing, when considering the composition of a scene, a motif, etc., any similarity between two texts can as much be coincidental (rather than a piece of evidence for the author's knowledge of a particular hypotext), as a specific dissimilarity can be read as a purposeful intertextual reference *ex negativo* (rather than as a token of the author's ignorance of the supposed source). For another, the possible net of intertextual points of reference is probably hardly ever as linear as to reach from a 'late' (viz. imperial) hexameter text back to the Epic Cycle in a direct way. We may only think of the classical tragedians, the Hellenistic poets, or canonical Latin texts such as Virgil's *Aeneid* or Ovid's *Metamorphoses*,[4] which are all, in one way or another, important hypotexts to imperial epics and thus are likely to act

---

[2] For the date of the possible loss of the Cycle, see above in this volume, pp. 34–6, 107; for the identification of Proclus, p. 35; for Pisander of Laranda and Ioannes Philoponus, pp. 34 n. 137, 428 n. 60, 548–9.

[3] On the relative (non-)coherence of the Epic Cycle, see Introduction, above in this volume, pp. 32–4, 98–100. Latacz (1997: 1155) rightly points to the fact that there is not even a consensus (ancient or modern) as to the scope of the Cycle, which is sometimes thought to have included theo-/cosmogonic epics and/or the Theban saga, sometimes not.

[4] The question as to whether or not imperial epic poetry intertextually engages with earlier Latin poetry is a controversial topic. There is no room to enter into this debate here; however, as a rule, we are of the opinion that a Latin text can be regarded as an intertext of a Greek text as much as any Greek text can.

as intermediaries between them and the Cyclic poems. Therefore, it seems virtually impossible to decide whether any potential intertextual relation between these texts and the Epic Cycle is a concrete intertextual allusion, or, rather, broadly participates in a theoretically endless reference system of texts and hypotexts.[5]

QUINTUS OF SMYRNA, *POSTHOMERICA*

Quintus of Smyrna's *Posthomerica* (Τὰ μεθ' Ὅμηρον / Τὰ μετὰ τὸν Ὅμηρον 'The [events] after Homer') is an epic poem in fourteen books of a total of c. 8,700 lines, to be dated to approximately the third century AD and thus most probably pre-dating Triphiodorus' short-scale epic *Capture of Troy*.[6] It fills the narrative gap between the two Homeric epics, setting off as a sequel to the *Iliad* after Hector's death and retelling the post-Iliadic events in episodic succession; hence it largely covers those parts of the Trojan saga which in the Epic Cycle were contained in the *Aethiopis*, the *Ilias parva* and the *Iliou persis*, while the beginning of the *Nostoi* is touched upon too.[7] A quasi-Homeric authorship is implemented by the lack of a proem at the beginning of Book 1 in favour of a direct narrative continuation, as well as an intertextual outlook towards the proem of the *Odyssey* at the end of Book 14.[8] Thus, the narrator of the *Posthomerica* indirectly, but clearly, stages himself as a second Homer – so much so that we can actually perceive Homer as the work's implied author.[9] Consequently, the question

---

[5] In what follows, translations from Homer and the Cyclic poems are our own; from Quintus by James (2004); for Triphiodorus/Colluthus and Nonnus respectively by A. W. Mair and W. H. D. Rouse (Loeb Classical Library).

[6] On Quintus' dating, see James and Lee (2000: 4–9); James (2004: xvii–xxi); Gärtner (2005: 23–6); Bär and Baumbach (2007b: 1–8); Bär (2009: 14–23). That Quintus pre-dates Triphiodorus is broadly, but not universally, accepted in scholarship; for an overview, see Dubielzig (1996: 11); Gärtner (2005: 25 n. 16); Tomasso (2012: 372–3). On the dating of Triphiodorus see also the according paragraph below.

[7] Penthesileia (Book 1), Memnon (Book 2), Achilles' death (Book 3), the funeral games for Achilles (Book 4), the contest over Achilles' armour (Book 5), Eurypylus (Book 6), Neoptolemus (Book 7), Eurypylus' death (Book 8), Philoctetes (Book 9), Paris' death (Book 10), last unsuccessful assault on the Trojan walls (Book 11), the Wooden Horse (Book 12), the sack of Troy (Book 13), the *nostos* of the Greek warriors (Book 14).

[8] Cf. Q. S. 1.1–2: Εὖθ' ὑπὸ Πηλείωνι δάμη θεοείκελος Ἕκτωρ / καί ἑ πυρῇ κατέδαψε καὶ ὀστέα γαῖα κεκεύθει ('Hector the equal of gods had been killed by the son of Peleus. Consumed by the funeral pyre, his bones were under the ground') – Q. S. 14.630–31: ἄχνυτ' Ὀδυσσῆος πινυτόφρονος, οὕνεκ' ἔμελλε / πάσχειν ἄλγεα πολλὰ Ποσειδάωνος ὁμοκλῇ ('[Athena] was torn on account of prudent Odysseus, because he was destined to suffer many woes through Poseidon's hostility').

[9] See Bär (2007) on the lack of the initial proem and the metapoetic consequences arising from this fact.

as to whether or not Quintus may have had access to the poems of the Epic Cycle, and, if so, to what extent he may have used (and followed) them, is important not only in view of the fact that the topics of the *Posthomerica* are so ostentatiously 'Cyclic', but also because of the narrator's programmatic staging as a second Homer – which may be seen as a reference not only to the author of the *Iliad* and the *Odyssey*, but also to the widespread notion of Homer as the author of some of the Cyclic poems.[10] Up to 1850, it was indeed *communis opinio* that Quintus must have known and made use of the Cycle; however, this stance was heavily opposed by Hermann Köchly, the most eminent Quintus expert of the nineteenth century; ever since, the question has been subject to hot debate.[11] First, it was linked to the *Posthomerica*'s supposed *Werkmotivation*. Noack claimed that 'the mere existence of such a late epic poem' was evidence enough for the non-existence of the Epic Cycle at that time, since 'the *Iliad* and the *Odyssey* were there; [Quintus] adds his *Posthomerica*, as there was no longer another epic about these episodes'.[12] The very same argument, however, was also used in the opposite direction by others who argued that Quintus must have known the various and disparate poems of the Cycle and deliberately have composed his *Posthomerica* as a coherent, large-scale counter draft.[13] Second, the comparison of similarities and differences was used to argue for Quintus' acquaintance with, or ignorance of, the Cycle. In most cases, ignorance was assumed, since Quintus' account does not agree with that of the Cycle in a number of instances. For example, Vian concluded that 'Quintus did not borrow the frame of his plot from the Cyclic Epics directly; he does not even seem to have known them'.[14] Others, however, have been more positive; for example, Burgess (2001: 45) firmly states that 'the Cycle also seems to be an important source for the narration of post-Iliadic events in the Trojan War by Quintus of Smyrna'.

[10] On the ancient notion of Homer as the author of some poems of the Epic Cycle, see Introduction, above in this volume, pp. 21–8.

[11] See Köchly (1850: viii–xxxii). For an overview of the pro's and contra's in scholarship, see Vian (1959: 87–9); Gärtner (2005: 28–9, with n. 10); Bär (2009: 78–9).

[12] Noack (1892a: 770): 'Dafür [viz. that Quintus no longer knew the Epic Cycle] spricht vor allem schon die bloße Existenz einer solchen späten Dichtung. Ilias und Odyssee waren da; er dichtet seine Posthomerika dazu... weil es kein andres Epos über dieses Sagen mehr gab'. The last to reiterate this hypothesis was James (2004: xix): 'the main motive and justification of Quintus' work is likely to have been replacement of the recently lost Trojan constituents of the Epic Cycle'.

[13] Cf. e.g. Wolf (1831: 181–2). Further, cf. Paley (1879) who 'developed the unequivocally wrong, yet stimulating theory that Quintus' *Posthomerica* "represented" the texts of the Epic Cycle and were therefore to be considered the sources of Virgil and other later poets' (Baumbach and Bär 2007b: 20).

[14] 'Ce n'est pas... aux Cycliques que Quintus a emprunté directement la trame de son récit; il ne semble même pas les avoir connus...': Vian (1963: i.xxviii).

In what follows, some of the most eminent differences between the *Posthomerica* and the Epic Cycle as suggested by scholars and commentators are discussed.[15]

Book 1 The killing of Thersites by Achilles is attested in both Arctinus' *Aethiopis* (arg. lines 178–81 Severyns) and Quintus' *Posthomerica* (Q. S. 1.741–6); however, Achilles' ritual cleansing on Lesbos which is mentioned in the *Aethiopis* (arg. lines 182–4 Severyns) is not contained in Quintus' version. Hence, James (2004: 268) argues that the expiation of Penthesileia, who, according to Q. S. 1.21–5, had come to Troy after involuntarily killing her sister, may also have been part of the *Aethiopis* (although not mentioned in Proclus' summary).

Book 2 According to the *Aethiopis* (arg. lines 186–7 Severyns), Thetis foretells Achilles' destiny, that is, that he is to die after Memnon's death; this prediction is not contained in the *Posthomerica*. In addition to this, Vian (1966: ii.50) and James (2004: 275, 281) argue that a further difference could be seen in the fact that in the *Aethiopis*, Achilles' death allegedly followed that of Memnon immediately, whereas in the *Posthomerica*, one or two days are in between.[16] However, this is not conclusive: for one thing, Proclus' summary does not explicitly state that one death followed the other at once; for another, 'immediacy' is a relative term.

Book 3 In the *Posthomerica*, the burial of Antilochus' corpse (Q. S. 3.1–5) precedes Achilles' death and the fierce battle over his dead body, whereas in the *Aethiopis*, Antilochus is buried after these events (arg. lines 190–7 Severyns). Thus, according to James, in the *Posthomerica* 'Achilles' death [is given] a separate and central position in the first major part of the epic', which he assumes to be 'an innovation made by Quintus himself'.[17] Further, whereas Proclus' summary (ibid.) insinuates that in the *Aethiopis*, Ajax and Odysseus were on an equal footing when fighting over Achilles' dead body – the former dragging the corpse to the ships, the latter repelling the Trojans – in Quintus' account it is clearly Ajax who plays the major part in the defence (Q. S. 3.217–95; 3.321–81), whereas Odysseus is wounded at an early stage and has to retreat from the battlefield (Q. S. 3.296–321). Thus, the Posthomeric account characterizes Odysseus as a lesser warrior

---

[15] Cf. Vian (1959: 87–94), who mainly discusses linguistic issues and attempts to find traces of Cyclic vocabulary in Quintus of Smyrna; he also provides an overview of previous scholarship; Vian (1963: i.xxviii–xxix); Vian (1963; 1966; 1969: *passim*); James (2004: 268–347, *passim*). Our list is not meant to be comprehensive.

[16] See further Kakridis (1949: 81–2) for some more speculation on the *Aethiopis* as a potential source of *Posthomerica* 2.

[17] James (2004: 281).

in comparison to Ajax and in so doing prepares the depiction of the contest over Achilles' armour (Book 5) as an unfair enterprise in which Odysseus is unjustifiably privileged.[18] Moreover, the killing of Achilles was a joint enterprise between Paris and Apollo in the *Aethiopis* (arg. line 192 Severyns), but is left to Apollo alone in the *Posthomerica* (Q. S. 3.60–6).[19] Last, a small difference can be seen in the fact that the Cyclic account has Thetis take her son's corpse off the funeral pyre and carry it to the island of Leuke by herself, while in the Posthomeric narrative it is Poseidon who promises to Thetis that he 'will present him [sc. Achilles] with an island fit for a god' (Q. S. 3.775: καί οἱ δῶρον ἔγωγε θεουδέα νῆσον ὀπάσσω), without explicitly naming the island.

Book 4 No details on the funeral games for Achilles are given in Proclus' account except for the mere mention that they take place (*Aeth.* arg. line 201 Severyns), whereas a whole book of the *Posthomerica* is devoted to them. Vian, based on a comparison of the Posthomeric account with Ps.-Apollodorus' renarration (*Epit.* 5.6–7), which he assumes to be an excerpt of the Cyclic versions, argues that 'Quintus is independent from this Cyclic tradition',[20] while Fantuzzi tentatively suggests that 'Quintus may... have relied on the *Aethiopis* for the description of the funeral of Achilles... and included precise allusions to this Cyclic poem which we cannot now detect because we do not have its text.'[21]

Book 5 Proclus only gives a brief reference to the quarrel of Ajax and Odysseus over Achilles' armour in his summary of the *Aethiopis* (arg. lines 202–3 Severyns), but does not mention Ajax's madness and suicide, which seems to have formed the opening scene of Lesches' *Ilias parva* (arg. lines 208–10 Severyns).[22] Proclus mentions the detail that in the *Ilias*

---

[18] See Bär (2010: 296–308). The imbalance between Ajax and Odysseus in the rescue of Achilles' armour seems to have featured already in the *Ilias parva*; cf. *PEG* F 2 (= D., W.): Αἴας μὲν γὰρ ἄειρε καὶ ἔκφερε δηϊοτῆτος / ἥρω Πηλεΐδην, οὐδ' ἤθελε δῖος Ὀδυσσεύς, 'For Ajax lifted the [corpse of] the hero Achilles and carried it off the battlefield, whereas the divine Odysseus did not want [to help?].'

[19] See Vian (1963: i.91 n. 3) for an overview of the two traditions. The version which features Apollo as the sole killer was the more widespread. Notably, the *Iliad* mentions both traditions: in 21.277–8, Achilles in a prolepsis speaks of Apollo as his sole murderer, whereas in 23.358–60, Hector reminds his fatal enemy of his destiny to die by the hands of both Apollo and Paris.

[20] Vian (1963: i.134): 'Quintus est indépendant de cette tradition cyclique.'

[21] Fantuzzi (2012: 155). It has to be noted that it has not remained unchallenged as to whether or not Ps.-Apollodorus' *Bibliotheca* is, in fact, indebted to the poems of the Epic Cycle (cf. Dräger 2005: 872–5); but cf. Burgess (2001: 16): 'The description of the Trojan War in Apollodorus' *Epitome* is essentially a summary of the Epic Cycle'. See also Burgess, above in this volume, p. 48.

[22] On the possible narrative overlap between *Aethiopis* and *Ilias parva*, see Davies (1989c: 60–5). Cf. also *Ilias parva*, *PEG* F 2 (= D., W.), with Davies' (1989c: 64–5) brief commentary.

parva, Odysseus is awarded the armour 'at the behest of Athena' (κατὰ βούλησιν Ἀθηνᾶς), while the Posthomeric account has Trojan prisoners make the allotment (Q. S. 5.318–20). However, according to an analepsis in *Odyssey* 11.547, the contest was decided by both 'children of the Trojans and Pallas Athena' (παῖδες δὲ Τρώων δίκασαν καὶ Παλλὰς Ἀθήνη); therefore we cannot necessarily conclude that the *Ilias parva* did not contain a reference to the Trojan judges, too.[23]

Books 6–10 The succession of events in the second third of the *Posthomerica* most conspicuously differs from that of the *Ilias parva*.[24] According to Proclus, Lesches put the fetching of Philoctetes from the isle of Lemnos, as well as the death of Paris, before the arrival of Neoptolemus and his rival Eurypylus, whom Neoptolemus subsequently kills (arg. lines 219–20 Severyns). In the *Posthomerica*, however, the arrival of Neoptolemus (Q. S. 6.57–115; 7.169–252), into which Eurypylus' arrival is embedded (Q. S. 6.116–90), comes first, and it is only after Eurypylus' death (Book 9) that Philoctetes is brought to Troy (Book 10) and Paris dies (Book 11). Hence, James (2004: 301) convincingly argues that 'Quintus' version, with the decision to send for Neoptolemus followed by Eurypylus' arrival and initial success, from which the Greeks are saved by Neoptolemus in the nick of time, is dramatically far superior and may well be original'. Further, the death of Paris is depicted differently: while Lesches has him killed by Philoctetes and recovered by the Trojans after being abused by Menelaus (arg. lines 213–15 Severyns), Quintus follows a different tradition, according to which Paris is not shot to death, but only mortally wounded so as to be able to seek help from his first wife Oenone (and die since she refuses to help, Q. S. 10.223–331).[25] Finally, three minor incidents which are part of the Cyclic main narrative are postponed and removed to a prolepsis in *Posthomerica* 10, namely, the capture of the Trojan seer Helenus by Odysseus (Q. S. 10.346–9; in the *Ilias parva* directly following Ajax's suicide and preceding the fetching of Philoctetes etc., cf. arg. line 211 Severyns), the marriage of Deiphobus and Helen (Q. S. 10.345–6; in the *Ilias parva* immediately preceding Neoptolemus' arrival at Troy, cf. arg. line 216 Severyns), and the

---

[23] On the different versions and narrative traditions to do with the allotment of the arms, cf. Vian (1966: ii.7–10), and Kelly and Rutherford, above in this volume, pp. 331–2, 454–5. Also Kullmann (1960: 217–18) on *Odyssey* 11.547.

[24] Cf. Vian (1963: i.xxviii–xxix); Vian (1966: ii.49); James (2004: 301–2).

[25] Oenone does not feature in what remains of, and is known to us about, the Epic Cycle. Quintus' account of Paris' death is conspicuously similar to that offered by Dictys Cretensis (4.19–20); cf. Vian (1969: iii.6–12); James (2004: 319).

theft of the Palladion (Q. S. 10.353–60; in the *Ilias parva*, a joint enterprise between Odysseus and Diomedes after Odysseus has managed to invade Troy as a spy, cf. arg. lines 224–9 Severyns).[26]

Book 11 The content of *Posthomerica* 11 (the Greeks' last unsuccessful assault on the Trojan walls) is reflected in Proclus' summary by only one short sentence: καὶ οἱ Τρῶες πολιορκοῦνται ('and the Trojans are besieged'). The *aristeia* of Aeneas, which occupies a major part of *Posthomerica* 11 (Q. S. 11.129–501), is not mentioned in Proclus' summary of the *Ilias parva*.[27]

Books 12–13 The story with the Wooden Horse and the subsequent capture of Troy is at the overlap between Lesches' *Ilias parva* (arg. lines 222–36 Severyns) and Arctinus' *Iliou persis* (arg. lines 241–7 Severyns). According to Proclus, the *Ilias parva* ended with the Greeks feasting and celebrating their victory over the Trojans (arg. lines 235–6 Severyns). However, one of the extant fragments of the *Ilias parva* contains the narration of Astyanax' killing by Neoptolemus, which takes place when Andromache is brought as a slave to Neoptolemus' ship (*PEG* F 21 = F 20 D. = F 29–30 W.).[28] Hence, the *Ilias parva* must have been renarrating at least the day after the sack of, and massacre in, the city of Troy, too, and Proclus' summary is clearly not comprehensive at that point.[29] In contrast, the *Iliou persis* according to Proclus attributes Astyanax's murder not to Neoptolemus, but to Odysseus (arg. line 268 Severyns).[30] In the *Posthomerica*, Astyanax's murder is placed after Neoptolemus has killed Priam and three of his sons (Q. S. 13.251–7).

---

[26] James (2004: 319) argues that 'the curious interlude at lines 334–62 ... amounts to acknowledgment that Quintus chose to omit this part of the canonical story, most probably because he saw it as problematic in terms of the morally edifying picture of the heroic world that he tried to present'.

[27] However, Aeneas was part of the Cyclic narrative; cf. e.g. *Ilias parva PEG* F 21.10 (= F 20.10 D. = F 30.5 W.); *Il. persis* arg. lines 250–1 Severyns.

[28] On this fragment cf. Davies (1989c: 69–70, 74) and above, in this volume, pp. 33, 326–7, 335–40.

[29] One of the several inconsistencies between Proclus' summary and the existing fragments and testimonia; cf. pp. 9, 20–21, 32–4 in this volume.

[30] Proclus' summary does not make it clear when exactly in the course of the narrative Astyanax' killing by Odysseus was placed. The genitive absolute καὶ Ὀδυσσέως Ἀστυάνακτα ἀνελόντος ('and after Odysseus had killed Astyanax') follows a sentence which points to the *nostos* of the Greek heroes – which would be illogical in terms of the narrative development. Therefore, we have to assume that at this point, Proclus no longer summarizes the events in their chronological order as originally presented in Arctinus' *Iliou persis*. – Odysseus as Astyanax' murderer is the version followed by Triphiodorus in the *Capture of Troy* (645–6; cf. discussion below). *Il.* 24.734–5 (ἤ τις Ἀχαιῶν / ῥίψει χειρὸς ἑλὼν ἀπὸ πύργου ('or one of the Achaeans will fetch [you] by the arm and throw [you] from the tower': Andromache addressing her little son) seems to imply that differing versions as to who kills Astyanax may have existed early. See Kullmann (1960: 186–7).

Two non-trivial Posthomeric differences to the Cyclic account are to be remarked: for one thing, Quintus does not place Astyanax' death in the context of the allotment of the enslaved women to the Greek leaders; for another, he has some anonymous Greek soldiers, and not Neoptolemus, commit the gruesome murder of the baby. With regard to the latter, Boyten has argued that Quintus' deviation from this traditional motif be regarded in the context of his general tendency to portray Neoptolemus in a more positive light and thus to stage him as a morally 'improved' version of his father Achilles.[31]

Another issue in the context of the Wooden Horse story is the Sinon and Laocoon scene, which displays significant differences between its depiction in the *Posthomerica* and in the *Iliou persis* (following Proclus): in the Cyclic version, it is insinuated (yet not entirely clear) that the assault of the two snakes on Laocoon happens *after* the Trojans' council about whether or not to take in the Wooden Horse has already been held and decided; and the snakes kill Laocoon and one of his two sons. In contrast, in the Posthomeric account, Laocoon is first blinded by Athena (Q. S. 12.395–415); only afterwards, does she send the two snakes, who do not kill Laocoon himself, but both of his sons (Q. S. 12.447–77). As far as Sinon is concerned, the *Iliou persis* mentions him only briefly as the one who gives the fire signal to the Greeks to come back from Tenedos (arg. lines 252–3 Severyns; cf. also *PEG Ilias parva* F 9 (III) = F 11^C D. = F 14 W.), but it does not give an account of his torture, which is recounted at great length in the *Posthomerica* (12.353–94). A comprehensive evaluation of the differences between the Cyclic and the Posthomeric account is particularly problematic in the case of this scene since, for one thing, Proclus' summary of the *Iliou persis* seems partly unreliable with regard to the chronology of the events which he gives.[32] For another, the whole matter is further complicated by the highly complex, and hotly disputed, intertextual relation between *Posthomerica* 12 and *Aeneid* 2: simply put, the dissimilarities in the Sinon and Laocoon scene between these two epics are so blatant and systematic that they do not seem to prove Quintus' ignorance or non-observance of the *Aeneid* as his 'source', but, rather, that the *Posthomerica* seems to be a *deliberate* rewriting and 'de-Romanization' of the *Aeneid*. Consequently, any attempt at evaluating the relationship between the Cyclic and the Posthomeric versions must necessarily fail, as Quintus' primary point of

---

[31] Boyten (2007: 326). On the different literary traditions of this motif, see Vian (1969: iii.125–6); James (2004: 333–6); Gärtner (2005: 241–3).

[32] See Finglass, above in this volume, pp. 348–9; also our n. 30 above.

intertextual relation is, most probably, not Arctinus' *Aethiopis*, but Virgil's *Aeneid*.[33]

Book 14 James (2004: 340) notes that Quintus 'follows a simplified version favored by the tragedians – departure as a single fleet, which is then separated and partly destroyed by Athena's storm'. In particular, Proclus mentions an argument between Agamemnon and Menelaus about the departure, caused by Athena, which the *Nostoi* contained (arg. lines 279–80 Severyns), but which does not feature in the *Posthomerica*. James (ibid.) consequently argues that 'Quintus' version has the advantage of a simple, dramatic denouement, but it is marred by lack of an adequate link between Ajax's offense and the punishment of the whole army.'

As this overview shows, there are numerous, and in parts considerable, dissimilarities between what we know of the Epic Cycle and Quintus' *Posthomerica*. The question therefore arises as to how we should evaluate these differences. In this context, we have to bear in mind the appraisal of the quality of the *Posthomerica* as a literary work. Until recently, Quintus was regarded as a notoriously unoriginal imitator of a (pseudo-)Homeric narrative style, who supposedly followed his models slavishly.[34] Consequently, any deviation from what was considered to be one of Quintus' potential sources was regarded as a piece of evidence that Quintus did in fact not have access to a certain source. It is only most recently that the specific poetic qualities of the *Posthomerica* as a 'belated' epic poem have been radically re-evaluated. When seen from this angle, it seems tempting to assume that the many cases in which Quintus 'deviates' from the Cyclic version are deliberate choices made for reasons pertaining to narrative and plot. Along those lines, Tomasso goes so far as to suggest that the dissimilarities between the *Posthomerica* and the corresponding Cyclic poems be read as a metapoetic statement, in the sense that the Cyclic poets are rejected and Homer re-emerges as Quintus' sole and principal authority and a locus for Greek identity.[35] However, this hypothesis seems problematic not only because of the scarcity of our knowledge about the Epic Cycle, but also in view of

---

[33] A meticulous comparison of the Sinon and Laocoon scene in *Posthomerica* 12 and *Aeneid* 2 is offered by Gärtner (2005: 161–226). However, her tentative conclusion that 'one can recognise [Quintus'] independent dealings with his sources, amongst which the *Aeneid* cannot be excluded' ('kann man ein eigenständiges Umgehen mit den Vorlagen erkennen, aus denen die Aeneis nicht auszuschließen ist', 226) seems feeble and unsatisfactory. On the idea of the *Posthomerica* as a 'de-Romanization' of the *Aeneid*, cf. Cuypers (2005: 607); Bär (forthcoming). On the relation between the *Aeneid* and the Epic Cycle, cf. Kopff (1981) and Gärtner, above in this volume. On the great impact of Virgil's Laocoon on later reception see Most (2010).

[34] See Schmidt (1999); Baumbach and Bär (2007b: 23–5); Bär (2009: 33–6).

[35] Tomasso (2010: 15). See also Paschal (1904: 73).

the fact that in antiquity, some of the Cyclic poems were in fact attributed to Homer, too. Moreover, Quintus at times 'deviates' from his Homeric 'source' as much as he does from any other 'source'. Thus, he demonstrates his poetic abilities as a *Homerus novus* who does not slavishly adhere to *any* model, and metapoetically states that he is able – and prepared – not even to follow his Homeric predecessor in certain instances.[36] All in all, therefore Quintus 'provides no safe and easy route for the reconstruction of the Cyclic epic', as Kopff (1981: 922) puts it, since we are unable finally to decide upon the role which an almost entirely lost corpus of texts may have played in the virtually infinite net of possible hypotexts within which Quintus navigates in a creative manner.

TRIPHIODORUS, *CAPTURE OF TROY*

Triphiodorus' *Capture of Troy* (Ἰλίου ἅλωσις) is a short-scale epic poem of c. 691 lines that portrays the conquest of Troy, from Epeius' construction of the Wooden Horse to the Greeks massacring the Trojans in their own city. Hence, the poem is to be compared with the parts of the Trojan saga covered by the final part of the *Ilias parva*, and the whole of the *Iliou persis*. Triphiodorus used to be regarded as a follower in the so-called 'school of Nonnus'; however, on the basis of a papyrus fragment published in 1972 (POxy. 2946), he is now to be antedated some hundred years, that is, to the very early fourth century at the latest. Nevertheless, his poem is still commonly (yet not universally) regarded as intertextually indebted to Quintus of Smyrna's *Posthomerica*.[37] In contrast (and perhaps open opposition) to Quintus, the narrator of the *Capture of Troy* does not dispense with the epic tradition of an initial proem, but, in an invocation of the Muse Calliopeia, asks for a 'swift song' (5), beginning with the Wooden Horse and leaving aside the whole prehistory. In so doing, he programmatically

---

[36] This is programmatically demonstrated at the very beginning of the *Posthomerica* (Q. S. 1.12), where the narrator states that Achilles 'dragged [Hector's body] *round* the city' (ἀμφείρυσσε πόληι). This is a clear deviation from the Homeric notion that Hector was dragged *in front of* the city walls and *to* the ships (cf. *Il.* 22.395–404, 463–5; 24.14–18), attested in other, non-Homeric sources (Eur. *Andr.* 107–8; Virg. *Aen.* 1.483–4); cf. Bär (2009: 158–9). It was argued that this version might stem from the Cycle (see Vian (1963: i.12 n. 1); Kopff (1981: 930–1)), but this is pure speculation.

[37] On Triphiodorus' dating, see Gerlaud (1982: 6–9); Dubielzig (1996: 7–11); Miguélez Cavero (2008: 14–15). POxy. 2946 was edited by Rea (1972). On the chronology of Quintus and Triphiodorus, cf. our n. 6 above; on the intertextual engagement between the two authors, see most recently Ypsilanti (2007); Tomasso (2012). On the problematic term 'school of Nonnus', see below our n. 47.

inscribes his poem into a tradition of small-scale epic poetry, opposing himself to the tradition of large-scale epic that covers the whole Trojan saga at great length (Triph. 1–5):[38]

> Τέρμα πολυκμήτοιο μεταχρόνιον πολέμοιο
> καὶ λόχον, Ἀργείης ἱππήλατον ἔργον Ἀθήνης,
> αὐτίκα μοι σπεύδοντι πολὺν διὰ μῦθον ἀνεῖσα
> ἔννεπε, Καλλιόπεια, καὶ ἀρχαίην ἔριν ἀνδρῶν
> κεκριμένου πολέμοιο ταχείηι λῦσον ἀοιδῆι.

> Of the long delayed end of the laborious war and of the ambush, even the horse fashioned of Argive Athena, straightway to me in my haste do thou tell, O Calliopeia, remitting copious speech; and the ancient strife of men, in that war now decided, do thou resolve with speedy song.

Tomasso (2012) convincingly argues that Triphiodorus thus challenges the great Homeric epics, but also the competitive product of his quasi-Homeric contemporary Quintus, by 'produc[ing] a text that is both ultra-Homeric and at the same time para-Homeric' (p. 408). Also, Tomasso is certainly right in stating that 'the known fragments [of the Epic Cycle], which amount to less than two hundred lines', are 'hardly enough for us to comprehend the relationship they have with later receptions' (p. 373). Nonetheless, it might be argued that Triphiodorus' call for a 'swift song' that concentrates on the narrative peak in the final days of the long war could in fact also point to the poems of the Epic Cycle, which included the whole of the Trojan saga and were at times criticized in antiquity for their merely episodic, unvaried pace of narration.[39]

However, as much as in the case of Quintus, the question as to whether or not Triphiodorus knew, and made concrete use of, the poems of the Epic Cycle is a matter of unsolvable dispute. Whereas some scholars regard Homer as his principal (or sole) intertextual model,[40] others claim that Triphiodorus did use Cyclic material. Gerlaud makes such an assumption on the basis of similarities between the *Capture of Troy* and Ps.-Apollodorus' Trojan account in the *Epitome*, which he takes to be an excerpt of the Cycle.[41]

---

[38] On Triphiodorus' programmatic brevity, see Leone (1968: 64); Gerlaud (1982: 103); Tomasso (2012: 385–90).

[39] Cf. e.g. Pollianus' famous epigram (*A.P.* 11.130 = *Cyclus epicus PEG* T 21 = T 8 D.), on which see Fantuzzi and Squire, above in this volume, respectively pp. 427–9 and 519–20. On the estimated lengths of the Cyclic poems, see e.g. Burgess (2005: 345); on their narrative pace and style, Burgess (2005: 350–1).

[40] For example, Noack (1892b); Orsini (1974).

[41] Gerlaud (1982: 37–9; see in particular 37–8: 'Que Triphiodore se soit servi du Cycle est suggéré par les nombreux points communs qui existent entre son poème et l'*Épitomé* d'Apollodore: la

Further, he argues that the central part of the poem (57–546) is 'borrowed' from Lesches' *Ilias parva*, whereas the actual description of the sack of Troy (547–691) is not. Concludingly, he states that Triphiodorus' 'knowledge of [Lesches'] work must have been fragmentary or indirect' (viz. acquired via a prose summary like that of Proclus),[42] whilst the possibility that Triphiodorus, for whatever reason, may have deliberately chosen *not* to follow a specific model at some point in his narrative is not considered.

In what follows, we discuss a few passages where Cyclic influence on the *Capture of Troy* has been claimed by scholars and commentators:[43]

198–9 ὡς οἵ γε γλαφυροῖο διὰ ξυλόχοιο θορόντες / ἀτλήτους ἀνέχοντο πόνους ἀκμῆτες Ἀχαιοί, 'Even so the unwearied Achaeans leapt through the carven wood and supported travail beyond enduring.' These verses are compared by Gerlaud (1982: 125) to the beginning of the *Ilias parva* (*PEG* F 28 = F 1 D., W.): Ἴλιον ἀείδω καὶ Δαρδανίην εὔπωλον / ἧς πέρι πολλὰ πάθον Δαναοὶ θεράποντες Ἄρηος ('Of Ilion I sing, and of Dardania, well equipped with horses, for which the Danaans, the servants of Ares, suffered [so] much'). However, neither the wording nor the context (getting into the Wooden Horse under great distress versus general remark on the afflictions caused by the war) are comparable so as to suggest an intertextual relation.

219, 228–9, 259–61 The motif of Sinon's *self*-mutilation is not found either in the *Posthomerica* or in the *Aeneid*, but is emphasized in the *Capture of Troy*. Hence, Gerlaud (1982: 22) argues that the motif may be traced back to Lesches' *Ilias parva*. However, this is purely speculative, and the motif may as well be Triphiodorus' innovation, or perhaps even a response to Quintus' depiction of Sinon who heroically withstands the tortures inflicted on him by the Trojans (Q. S. 12.363–90, 418–20).

318–22 The Wooden Horse's groaning when being pulled into Troy is argued to be 'the imitation of a famous comparison which appeared in Lesches' poem'.[44] However, this is mere speculation, as the extant Cyclic sources do not testify to this.

498–505 The motif of the peaceful silence of the night, in the midst of which the Greeks unexpectedly intrude to start their massacre, is compared

---

chronologie des événements est identique; beaucoup d'épisodes sont semblables chez les deux auteurs.' On the relation between the Cycle and Ps.-Apollodorus, see our n. 21 above.

[42] Gerlaud (1982: 39): '[S]a connaissance de l'œuvre devait être fragmentaire ou indirecte.'

[43] See Leone (1968: 103–4); Cuartero (1973); Gerlaud (1982: 16–41); Dubielzig (1996: 19–20). Again, what follows is not meant to be comprehensive. A brief overview on earlier scholarship is provided by Dubielzig (1996: 20).

[44] Gerlaud (1982: 27): '[I]l s'agit de l'imitation d'une comparaison célèbre qui figurait dans le poème de Leschès.'

to a fragment of the *Ilias parva* (*PEG* F 9 = F 11ᴬ D. = F 14 W.): νὺξ μὲν ἔην μεσάτη, λαμπρὴ δ' ἐπέτελλε σελήνη 'It was the middle of the night, and the moon was shining bright.' However, the fact that the elaboration of the 'silent night motif' is unique to Lesches, Ps.-Apollodorus and Triphiodorus, as Gerlaud (1982: 148–9) notes, does not allow the conclusion that the *Ilias parva* must have been Triphiodorus' direct source, since the motif is too unspecific and too universal.

645–6 This is an example of a (seeming) deviation from Lesches' model, as stated by Gerlaud (1982: 39): the killing of Astyanax, whose murderer is Odysseus in accordance with the *Iliou persis* (arg. line 268 Severyns), not Neoptolemus as in the *Ilias parva* (*PEG* F 21.1–4 = F 20.1–4 D. = F 29.1–4 W.). While the passage can be seen as a trace of a (direct or indirect) reception of the *Iliou persis* indeed, it may as well be read as Triphiodorus' comment on Quintus' unorthodox version (where Astyanax is precipitated into the abyss by some anonymous Greek soldiers, Q. S. 13.251–7), and/or on Quintus' generally negative depiction of Odysseus (cf. above).

667 Dubielzig (1996: 20) tentatively suggests an allusion to the Epic Cycle in the adjective ἀμφιέλισσαν ('wheeling about') with the connotation of *kyklikon* ('Cyclic') towards the end of the poem (Triph. 664–7):

> πᾶσαν δ' οὐκ ἂν ἔγωγε μόθου χύσιν ἀείσαιμι
> κρινάμενος καθ' ἕκαστα καὶ ἄλγεα νυκτὸς ἐκείνης·
> Μουσάων ὅδε μόχθος, ἐγὼ δ' ἅπερ ἵππον ἐλάσσω
> τέρματος ἀμφιέλισσαν ἐπιψαύουσαν ἀοιδήν

> All the multitude of strife and the sorrows of that night I could not sing, distinguishing each event. This is the Muses' task; and I shall drive, as it were a horse, a song which, wheeling about, grazes the turning-post.

However, Dubielzig does not specify the kind of metapoetic implication this allusion entails. Apart from that, even if we wish to accept his assumption, it does not allow us to jump to the conclusion that Triphiodorus must necessarily have known, and made use of, the Epic Cycle; the supposed allusion could, at best, be indicative of the fact that the Epic Cycle was part of Triphiodorus' epic memory.

As this brief discussion shows, there may be traces of a reception of the Epic Cycle in the *Capture of Troy* in a few instances; however, none of them is compelling. Moreover, the intertextual engagement does not only work with the most obvious point of reference, the Homeric *Iliad*, but Triphiodorus' epic arguably also responds to Quintus' *Posthomerica*. Thus, it is virtually impossible to decide upon the role a potential Cyclic hypotext might play. Rather, it seems fruitful to pursue further the intertextual relation between Quintus and Triphiodorus – be it in a way that looks at how Triphiodorus concretely 'responds' to Quintus, or be it in a more general manner that investigates the position of the two epics in their specific imperial context, and with one another, without paying too much attention to the strict chronological relation between the two.[45]

NONNUS OF PANOPOLIS, *DIONYSIACA*

Nonnus of Panopolis is the author of the longest coherent hexameter poem in antiquity, the *Dionysiaca* (48 books, c. 21,000 lines), a gargantuan epic on the birth, life, adventures and apotheosis of the wine-god Dionysus.[46] He is generally dated to the fifth century AD; however, his precise dating is subject to controversy.[47] While Quintus of Smyrna and Triphiodorus may still have had (partial) access to the original poems of the Epic Cycle, it is very unlikely that Nonnus had more than second-hand knowledge of it (viz. via prose summaries such as that by Proclus).[48] Content-wise, the *Dionysiaca* differs significantly from Quintus' *Posthomerica* and Triphiodorus' *Capture of Troy* inasmuch as it does not renarrate the stories of the Trojan saga. However, the narrator of the *Dionysiaca* ostentatiously inscribes himself into the Trojan tradition, nonetheless: on the one hand, he programmatically refers

---

[45] See Tomasso (2012: 373): 'Ultimately, it does not matter whether Triphiodorus was responding specifically to the *Posthomerica* (or any other imperial Greek text, for that matter) or the other way around; both poets wrote their compositions to position themselves within or against the continuum of epic tradition that surrounded them.'

[46] For a plot summary, see Vian (1976: i.xxii–xxix); Shorrock (2001: 7–11; 2005: 375–6); Miguélez Cavero (2008: 19–21). Nonnus is also the author of the lesser-known hexameter *Paraphrase of St. John's Gospel* (22 books, c. 3,600 lines).

[47] On Nonnus' dating, cf. Vian (1976: i.xvii); Miguélez Cavero (2008: 16–18). The fact that Nonnus wrote poems both on a pagan and a Christian topic has long been seen as irreconcilable; hence it was assumed that he must have converted to Christianity at some point in his life, having written the *Dionysiaca* before, the *Paraphrase* afterwards. However, this ambiguity is not contradictory, but typical of the late antique amalgamation of paganism and Christianity; see Shorrock (2011). Further, Nonnus has often been thought to have been the 'head' of a 'school' of epic poets and poetasters (some of his disciples for example having been Musaeus, Colluthus, or Christodorus of Coptos). However, Miguélez Cavero (2008) was able to show that the idea of a 'school of Nonnus' is a modern construct that does not do justice to the geographical and temporal diversity and richness of Greek hexameter production in the imperial period.

[48] See Shorrock (2001: 28–31), who suggests that Pisander of Laranda's lost Ἡρωϊκαὶ θεογαμίαι must have been an important hypotext to the *Dionysiaca*. On Nonnus' sources, see in more detail Vian (1976: i.xli–l).

to Homer as his father in his second call to the Muse, at the beginning of the second part of his epic (*Dion*. 25.264–5):

ἀλλά, θεά, με κόμιζε τὸ δεύτερον εἰς μέσον Ἰνδῶν,
ἔμπνοον ἔγχος ἔχοντα καὶ ἀσπίδα πατρὸς Ὁμήρου.

Then bring me, O goddess, into the midst of the Indians again, holding the inspired spear and shield of Father Homer.

On the other hand, the central narrative of the entire *Dionysiaca*, that is, the march to India and the war against the Indians (Books 13–40), is clearly modelled on the genre of the archaic war epic, featuring typical scenes such as, for example, catalogues of troops (*Dion*. 13.35–568; 14.1–227), a deceptive dream sent to the leader (Book 26), or funerary games (Book 37).[49] However, Nonnus does not follow the subtle, non-linear mode of narration which is so artfully employed in the *Iliad*. Rather, as Shorrock (2007: 380) puts it, he 'recasts material that Homer had artfully compressed into the narrative of the final year of the war... and fashions a linear narrative by restoring Homeric analepses and prolepses to their "true" chronological sequence', so much so that 'the traditional cycle of Greek mythology... is adapted... to form a broad and overarching framework to support the specific narrative of the hero Dionysus'.[50] Therefore, it could be argued that Nonnus enters into an intertextual dialogue with the tradition of the Epic Cycle from a structural/generic point of view, since although the Cyclic poems were probably no longer known to him, they still belonged to his cultural heritage and therefore formed part of his epic memory. Nonnus fashions an epic narrative which not only combines large-scale and short-scale epic, but also reconciles the seemingly irreconcilable, that is, a Homeric and a Cyclic mode of narration.[51] In so doing, he not only enhances his own poetic achievement, but equally manages to surpass the greatness and importance of the Trojan War, which falls short of the Indian War according to *Dion*. 25.25–6: οὐδὲ τόσος στρατὸς ἦλθεν ἐς Ἴλιον, οὐ στόλος ἀνδρῶν / τηλίκος ('No such army came to Ilion, no such host of men.') Further, Shorrock considers the possibility of an allusion to the Cyclic poet Arctinus in *Dion*. 40.284–6, that is, after the Indian War, in the context of the *nostos* of the Dionysiac heroes: ἀντὶ δὲ πάτρης / Ἀστέριος τότε

---

[49] On Nonnus' in-text proem, see Hopkinson (1994a: 12–13); Shorrock (2001: 170–4). On Nonnus as a 'Homeric' poet in general, see Hopkinson (1994a) at length; brief summary in Hopkinson (1994b: 122–3).
[50] See in depth Shorrock (2001: 25–111).
[51] See our n. 39 above on the ancient *topos* of the Cycle as a solely episodic, unvaried, 'boring' type of narrative.

μοῦνος ἀνιπτοπόδων σχεδὸν Ἄρκτων / Φάσιδος ἀμφὶ ῥέεθρον ('Asterios alone did not now return to his own country; instead, he settled near the foot-unwashed Bears, about the river Phasis.')[52] As Phasis was a Milesian colony, and Arctinus a native of Miletus, Shorrock (ibid.) claims that 'Nonnus has included a reference to one of the most famous sources for the story of the fall of Troy at the end of his own version', punning on the name of Arctinus and the constellation of the Great Bear, Ἄρκτος. If we wish to follow this line of thought, we can read Nonnus' allusion as an Alexandrian footnote with which the poet points out that he not only equals (or even surpasses) his 'father Homer', but at the same time has also accomplished his own, new version of the Epic Cycle, with regard to both content and style, as the poetological reflections in the proem to Book 1 indicate (*Dion.* 1.10–15):

> ἄξατέ μοι νάρθηκα, τινάξατε κύμβαλα, Μοῦσαι,
> καὶ παλάμηι δότε θύρσον ἀειδομένου Διονύσου.
> ἀλλὰ χοροῦ ψαύοντι Φάρωι παρὰ γείτονι νήσωι
> στήσατέ μοι Πρωτῆα πολύτροπον, ὄφρα φανείη
> ποικίλον εἶδος ἔχων, ὅτι ποικίλον ὕμνον ἀράσσω.

> Bring me the fennel, rattle the cymbals, ye Muses! put in my hand the wand of Dionysus whom I sing: but bring me a partner for your dance in the neighbouring island of Pharos, Proteus of many turns, that he may appear in all his diversity of shapes, since I twang my harp to a diversity of songs.

On the one hand, Nonnus' *Dionysiaca* inscribes itself into the Homeric tradition by referring to the Homeric figure of Proteus (*Odyssey* 4) and intertextually alluding to the proem of the *Odyssey* (1.1) in taking up πολύτροπον in line 14. On the other hand, Proteus is elevated by Nonnus to the role of a muse for new poetry who no longer proclaims Homeric narration and wisdom but is the source of the Dionysiac transformations in the *Dionysiaca*.[53] Thus, Proteus can be read as the symbolic embodiment of the creative potential of epic poetry, which is in principle infinite and may assume, in terms of both content and form, many shapes, that is, many variations of the Epic Cycle.

---

[52] Shorrock (2007: 389 n. 24).

[53] On the poetological dimension of the proem see Schmitz (2005: 202–8); Baumbach (2013). The fact that Homer is mentioned at the end of the proem (*Dion.* 1.37–8) in connection with the 'rank skin of the seals' (βυθίηι δὲ παρ' Εἰδοθέηι καὶ Ὁμήρωι / φωκάων βαρὺ δέρμα φυλασσέσθω Μενελάωι) underlines the poetic distance between the *Dionysiaca* and Homer's epic.

CONCLUSION

Long epic poems were popular in the third century AD, as not only Quintus of Smyrna's *Posthomerica*, but also the now lost *Metamorphoses* by Nestor of Laranda, the Ἡρωϊκαὶ θεογαμίαι by Pisander of Laranda or the *Gigantia* by Scopelianus demonstrate. Triphiodorus may have written his 'swift song' as a response to this trend, confining his *Capture of Troy* to the climax of the Trojan War and, in doing so, reiterating the opposition between long-scale and short-scale epic.[54] Instead of speculating about whether or not any of these authors may – or may not – have used the poems of the Epic Cycle as their 'sources', it seems more fruitful to ask how the Cycle fits into this overall picture. In other words, we ought to consider the Cycle's structural intertextuality with imperial epic, instead of merely looking for material intertextuality by making problematic attempts at retracing sources which are, for the most part, lost. As we have seen, both Quintus' and Triphiodorus' epics can be looked upon as re-enactments of the Epic Cycle. Quintus achieves this end by assuming a quasi-Homeric identity and composing a full-scale epic poem as a counter draft to the various and disparate poems of the Cycle, while Triphiodorus chooses the opposite path by focusing on the climax of the Cyclic stories and thus reduces their multitude and heterogeneity to a small, one-episode poem. Some time later, Nonnus of Panopolis reopens this intertextual dialogue in his own way, by abandoning the Trojan saga and restricting his dialogue with the Epic Cycle to structural intertextuality. Like his protagonist Dionysus, who is the son of Zeus, the father of the gods, he stages himself as the son of the godlike Homer,[55] and thus accomplishes his own version of the Cycle by combining Homeric and Cyclic modes of narration. To this, we might want to add one other poet, namely, the post-Nonnian Colluthus, author of an epyllion on the *Kidnapping of Helen* (Ἑλένης ἁρπαγή; c. 392 lines). Writing under the reign of Anastasius I (AD 491–518), he restages the *pre*-Iliadic events that led to the Trojan War, beginning with the wedding of Thetis and Peleus, and ending with the arrival of Paris and Helen in Troy. With near certainty, Colluthus had no more direct knowledge of Stasinus' *Cypria*, the relevant poem of the Epic Cycle.[56] However, he complements yet another blank in

---

[54] On the generic tradition and self-reflections of short-scale epic see Baumbach and Bär (2012b).
[55] The divinity of Homer is a widespread late antique *topos*; cf. e.g. *A.P.* 2.321 (Christodorus).
[56] On Colluthus' dating, see Orsini (1972: v–vi). On his sources, Livrea (1968: xiv–xxiii); Orsini (1972: viii–xxvii); Schönberger (1993: 9–11); Miguélez Cavero (2008: 28–9). Magnelli (2008) emphasizes Colluthus' Homeric heritage, whereas Prauscello (2008) puts his focus on the pastoral tradition that shapes the *Kidnapping of Helen*.

his predecessors' structural response to the Cycle by structurally resorting to that part of the Cycle which dealt with the events *before* the *Iliad*. Thus, the *Kidnapping of Helen* can be seen as the last in a row of 'belated' texts that re-enact and reshape the Cyclic tradition – a tradition which was most probably lost at that time in a material sense, but nevertheless continued to form part of epic memory.

Works cited

Acosta-Hughes, B., and S. A. Stephens. 2002. 'Rereading Callimachus' *Aetia* Fragment 1', *CPh* 97: 238–55.
  2012. *Callimachus in Context: From Plato to the Augustan Poets*, Cambridge.
Adam, L. 1889. *Die Aristotelische Theorie vom Epos nach ihrer Entwicklung bei Griechen und Römern*, Wiesbaden.
Adams, J. 1902. *The* Republic *of Plato*. i, Cambridge.
Ahlberg-Cornell, G. 1992. *Myth and Epos in Early Greek Art. Representation and Interpretation*, Jonsered.
Albis, R. 1996. *Poet and Audience in the* Argonautica *of Apollonius*, Lanham, MA.
von Albrecht, M. 2007. *Vergil. Bucolica, Georgica, Aeneis: Eine Einführung*. 2nd edn, Heidelberg.
Alden, M. J. 2000. *Homer Beside Himself. Para-Narratives in the Iliad*, Oxford.
ALGRM = Roscher, W. H. (ed.) 1884–1937. *Ausführliches Lexikon der griechischen und römischen Mythologie*, 6 vols., Leipzig.
Allan, W. 2008. 'Performing the Will of Zeus. The Διὸς βουλή and the Scope of Early Greek Epic', in Revermann and Wilson 2008: 204–16.
Allen, N. J. 1995. 'Why Did Odysseus Become a Horse?', *JASO* 26: 143–54.
Allen, T. W. 1908a. 'The Epic Cycle', *CQ* 2.1: 64–74.
  1908b. 'The Epic Cycle (Continued from p. 74)', *CQ* 2.2: 81–8.
  1912. *Homeri opera*. v. *Hymni, Cyclus, fragmenta, Margites, Batrachomyomachia*, Oxford.
  1913. 'Homerica. ii. Additions to the Epic Cycle', *CR* 27: 189–91.
  1921. *The Homeric Catalogue of Ships*. Oxford.
Ambühl, A. 1992. 'Koroibos', in *Der Neue Pauly*. vi, Stuttgart: 755.
  2005. *Kinder und junge Helden. Innovative Aspekte des Umgangs mit der literarischen Tradition bei Kallimachos*, Leuven.
Amyx, D. 1988. *Corinthian Vase-painting of the Archaic Period*, Berkeley, CA.
Andersen, Ø. 1982. 'Thersites und Thoas vor Troia', *SO* 57: 7–34.
Andersen, Ø. and D. T. T. Haug (eds.) 2012a. *Relative Chronology in Early Greek Epic Poetry*, Cambridge.
  2012b. 'Introduction', in Andersen and Haug 2012: 1–19.
Anderson, M. J. 1997. *The Fall of Troy in Early Greek Poetry and Art*, Oxford.
  2004. Review of West 2003a, *BMCR* 2004.04:35.
  2011. 'Returns', in Finkelberg 2011b: 743–5.

Angeli Bernardini, P. (ed.) 2004. *La città di Argo. Mito, storia, tradizioni poetiche* (Atti del Convegno Internazionale, Urbino, 13–15 giugno 2002), Rome.
  2005. 'Trittico bacchilideo. *Epinicio* 3; *Ditirambo* 1 (15); *Ditirambo* 3', *QUCC* 79: 11–28.
  (ed.) 2013. *Corinto, luogo di azione e luogo di racconto* (Atti del convegno internazionale, Urbino, 23–25 settembre 2009), Pisa.
Antonelli, L. 1994. 'Cadmo ed Eracle al cospetto di Apollo. Echi di propaganda intorno a Delfi arcaica', in L. Braccesi (ed.), *Hespería. Studi sulla grecità di occidente.* iv, Rome: 13–48.
  2000, *Kerkyraiká. Ricerche su Corcira alto-arcaica tra Ionio e Adriatico*, Rome.
Aricò, G. 1986. 'L' *Achilleide* di Stazio. Tradizione letteraria e invenzione narrativa', *ANRW* ii.32.5: 2925–64.
Arrighetti, G. 1996. 'L'arte di Stesicoro nel giudizio degli antichi', in L. Dubois (ed.), *Poésie et lyrique antiques*, Lille: 55–72.
Arrigoni, G. 1982. *Camilla. Amazzone e sacerdotessa di Diana*, Milan.
  2003. 'La maschera e lo specchio. Il caso di Perseo e Dioniso a Delfi e l'enigma dei Satiri', *QUCC* 73: 9–53.
Asheri, D., A. Lloyd, and A. Corcella. 2007. *A Commentary on Herodotus, Books i–iv*, Oxford.
Asper, M. 1997. *Onomata allotria. Zur Genese, Struktur und Funktion poetologischer Metaphern bei Kallimachos*, Stuttgart.
Assereto, A. M. 1970. 'Dall'Etiopide all'Eneide', in *Mythos. Scripta in honorem M. Untersteiner*, Genoa: 51–8.
Auger, D. 1976. 'Discours et récit chez Stésichore', in *Cahiers de recherch. de l'Inst. de papyrol. et d' égyptol. de Lille* 4: 335–7.
Aurigemma, F. 1953. 'Appendice: tre nuovi cicli di figurazioni ispirate all'*Iliade* in case della Via dell'Abbondanza in Pompei', in Spinazzola 1953: ii.867–1008.
Bär, S. 2007. 'Quintus Smyrnaeus und die Tradition des epischen Musenanrufs', in Baumbach and Bär 2007a: 29–64.
  2009. *Quintus Smyrnaeus: Posthomerica. 1: Die Wiedergeburt des Epos aus dem Geiste der Amazonomachie. Mit einem Kommentar zu den Versen 1–219*, Göttingen.
  2010. 'Quintus of Smyrna and the Second Sophistic', *HSCPh* 105: 287–316.
  forthcoming. 'Sinon and Laocoon in Quintus of Smyrna's *Posthomerica*. A Rewriting and De-Romanization of Virgil's *Aeneid*'.
Bakker, E. J. 2005. *Pointing at the Past. From Formula to Performance in Homeric Poetics*, Washington DC.
Bakola, E. 2010. *Cratinus and the Art of Comedy*, Oxford.
Ballabriga, A. 1986. *Le Soleil et le Tartare. L'image mythique du monde en Grèce archaïque*, Paris.
  1989. 'La prophétie de Tirésias', *Métis* 4: 291–304.
  1990. 'La question homérique. Pour une réouverture du débat', *REG* 103: 16–29.

1998. *Les fictions d'Homère. L'invention mythologique et cosmographique dans l'*Odyssée, Paris.

Barchiesi, A. 1993. 'Future Reflexive. Two Modes of Allusion in Ovid's *Heroides*', *HSCPh* 95: 333–65.

1994. 'Rappresentazioni del dolore e interpretazione nell'*Eneide*', *A&A* 40: 109–24.

1996. 'La guerra di Troia non avrà luogo. Il proemio dell'*Achilleide* di Stazio', *Annali dell'Istit. Univ. Orient. Napoli* 18: 45–62.

1997. 'Vergilian Narrative – Ecphrasis', in C. Martindale (ed.), *The Cambridge Companion to Virgil*, Cambridge: 271–81.

1999. 'Representations of Suffering and Interpretation in the *Aeneid*' (trans. of Barchiesi 1994), in P. Hardie (ed.), *Virgil. Critical Assessments of Classical Authors.* iii, London 1999: 324–44.

2001. *Speaking Volumes. Narrative and Intertext in Ovid and Other Latin Poets*, London.

2002. 'Narrative Technique and Narratology in the *Metamorphoses*', in P. Hardie (ed.), *The Cambridge Companion to Ovid*, Cambridge: 180–99.

2005. *Ovidio,* Metamorfosi. i. *Libri I–II*, Milan.

Barnes, H. R. 1979. 'Enjambement and Oral Composition', *TAPhA* 109: 1–10.

Barron, J. P. 1969. 'Ibycus. To Polycrates', *BICS* 16: 119–49.

Bartsch, S. 1998. 'Ars and the Man. The Politics of Art in Virgil's *Aeneid*', *CPh* 93: 322–42.

Bassi, K. 1993. 'Helen and the Discourse of Denial in Stesichorus' Palinode', *Arethusa* 26: 51–75.

Baumbach, M. 2013. 'Proteus and Protean Epic: From Homer to Nonnus', in I. Gildenhard and A. Zissos (eds.), *Transformative Change in Western Thought. A History of Metamorphosis from Homer to Hollywood*, s.l. (but London): 153–62.

Baumbach, M. and S. Bär (eds.) 2007a. *Quintus Smyrnaeus. Transforming Homer in Second Sophistic Epic*, Berlin and New York.

2007b. 'An Introduction to Quintus Smyrnaeus' *Posthomerica*', in Baumbach and Bär 2007a: 1–26.

(eds.) 2012a. *Brill's Companion to Greek and Latin Epyllion and Its Reception*, Leiden and Boston.

2012b. 'A Short Introduction to the Ancient Epyllion', in Baumbach and Bär 2012a: ix–xvi.

Baumgarten, A. I. 1981. *The Phoenician History of Philo of Byblos. A Commentary*, Leiden.

Beazley, J. D. 1986. *The Development of Attic Black Figure.* 2nd edn, Berkeley, CA.

Beck, W. 2001. '*Thebais* Fr. 6A Davies (Pausanias 8.25.8)', *MusHelv* 58: 137–9.

Beekes. R. 2010. *Etymological Dictionary of Greek*, Leiden.

Belcher, S. 1999. *Epic Traditions of Africa*, Bloomington, IN.

Bergk, T. 1883. *Griechische Literaturgeschichte.* ii, Berlin.

Bernabé, A. 1979. *Fragmentos de épica griega arcaica. Introducción, traducción y notas*, Madrid.
　1982. 'Cyclica I', *Emerita* 50: 81–92.
　1984. '¿Más de una Ilias parva?', in L. Gil and R. M. Aguilar (eds.), *Apophoreta philologica E. Fernández-Galiano a sodalibus oblata* i (= *Estudios Clásicos* 87), Madrid: 141–50.
　1995. 'La lengua de Homero en los últimos años: problemas, soluciones, perspectivas', *Tempus* 11: 5–38.
　1998. 'Nacimientos y muertes de Dioniso en los mitos órficos', in C. Sánchez Fernández and P. Cabrera Bonet (eds.), *En los límites de Dioniso*, Murcia: 29–39.
Bernabé, A. and E. R. Luján. 2006. *Introducción al griego micénico*, Zaragoza.
Bernert, E. 1952. 'Polyidos 1', in *RE* xlii: 1646–57.
Bethe, E. 1891a. *Thebanische Heldenlieder. Untersuchungen über die Epen des thebanisch–argivischen Sagenkreises*, Leipzig.
　1891b. 'Proklos und der epische Cyclus', *Hermes* 26: 593–633.
　1891c. 'Vergilstudien', *RhM* 46: 511–27.
　1894. 'Alkmaionis', *RE* i.2: 1562–4.
　1922. *Homer. Dichtung und Sage*. ii. *Odyssee-Kyklos-Zeitbestimmung, nebst den Resten des troischen Kyklos*, Leipzig and Berlin.
　1929. *Homer. Dichtung und Sage*. ii.2. *Kyklos-Zeitbestimmung, nebst den Resten des troischen Kyklos*. 2nd edn, Leipzig and Berlin (repr. Darmstadt 1966 with the title: *Der troische Epenkreis, nebst den Resten des troischen Kyklos*).
Bettini, M. and C. Brillante. 2002. *Il mito di Elena*, Turin.
Beye, C. R. 1993. *Ancient Epic Poetry. Homer, Apollonius, Virgil*, Ithaca, NY.
Biebuyck, D. and K. C. Mateene. 1969. *The Mwindo Epic from the Banyanga*, Berkeley, CA.
Bilinski, B. 1959. 'Elementi esiodei nelle Metamorfosi di Ovidio', in Atti del convegno internazionale ovidiano (Sulmona, Maggio 1958), Rome: ii.101–23.
Biraud, M. 1985. 'L'hypotexte homérique et les rôles amoureux de Callirhoé dans le roman de Chariton', in A. Goursonnet (ed.), *Sémiologie de l'amour dans les civilisations méditerranéennes*, Paris: 21–7.
Blondell, R. 2010. '"Bitch that I Am": Self-Blame and Self-Assertion in the *Iliad*', *TAPhA* 140: 1–32.
Blumenthal, H. J. 1978. 'Callimachus, Epigram 28, Numenius fr. 20, and the Meaning of κυκλικός', *CQ* 28: 125–7.
Blundell, M. W. 1989. *Helping Friends and Harming Enemies. A Study in Sophocles and Greek Ethics*, Cambridge.
Boehringer, D. 2001. *Heroenkulte in Griechenland von der geometrischen bis zur klassischen Zeit. Attika, Argolis, Messenien*, Berlin.
Boitani, P. (ed.) 1989. *The European Tragedy of Troilus*, Oxford.
Bol, P. 1989. *Argivische Schilde*, Berlin.
Bolling, G. M. 1928. 'Homeric Notes', *CPh* 23: 63–5.

Bömer, F. 1976. *P. Ovidius Naso*. Metamorphosen *VI–VII*, Heidelberg.
　1980. *P. Ovidius Naso*. Metamorphosen *X–XI*, Heidelberg.
　1982. *P. Ovidius Naso*. Metamorphosen *XII–XIII*, Heidelberg.
Bonanno, M. G. 2004. 'Come guarire dal complesso epico. L'Ode a Policrate di Ibico', in E. Cavallini (ed.), *Samo. Storia, letteratura, scienza = AION* (filol.) 8: 67–96.
Bonifazi, A. 2009. 'Inquiring into Nostos and Its Cognates', *AJPh* 130: 481–510.
Bonnechere, P. 2003. *Trophonios de Lébadée. Cultes et mythes d'une cité béotienne au miroir de la mentalité antique*, Leiden.
Borg, B. 2010. 'Epigrams, Art, and Epic. The "Chest of Kypselos"', in I. and A. Petrovich and M. Baumbach (eds.), *Archaic and Classical Greek Epigram*, Cambridge: 81–99.
Bottini, A. 2008. 'Nuovi schildbänder in contesti Italici della Basilicata', *Ostraka* 17: 11–24.
Bowie, E. L. 2002. 'The Chronology of the Earlier Greek Novels since B. E. Perry. Revisions and Precisions', *Ancient Narrative* 2: 47–63.
　2010a. 'Historical Narrative in Archaic and Early Classical Greek Elegy', in D. Konstan and K. A. Raaflaub (eds.), *Epic and History*, Malden, MA: 145–66.
　2010b. 'The Trojan War's Reception in Early Greek Lyric, Iambic and Elegiac Poetry', in L. Foxhall, H.-J. Gehrke, and N. Luraghi (eds.), *Intentional History. Spinning Time in Ancient Greece*, Stuttgart: 57–88.
　2014. 'Rediscovering Sacadas', in A. Moreno and R. Thomas (eds.), *Patterns of the Past. Epitēdeumata in the Greek Tradition*, Oxford: 39–55.
Bowra, C. M. 1964. *Pindar*, Oxford.
Boyd, B. W. 1995. '*Non enarrabile Textum*. Ecphrastic Trespass and Narrative Ambiguity in the *Aeneid*', *Vergilius* 41: 71–92.
Boyten, B. 2007. 'More "Parfit Gentil Knyght" than "Hyrcanian Beast". The Reception of Neoptolemos in Quintus Smyrnaeus' *Posthomerica*', in Baumbach and Bär 2007a: 307–36.
Braccesi, L. 1977. *Grecità adriatica. Un capitolo della colonizzazione greca in occidente*. 2nd edn, Bologna.
　2001. *Hellenikòs kólpos. Supplemento a 'Grecità adriatica'*, Rome.
Brann, E. 1962. *Late Geometric and Protoattic Pottery* (*Agora* 8), Princeton, NJ.
　1959. 'A Figured Geometric Fragment from the Athenian Agora', *Antike Kunst* 2: 35–7.
Braswell, B. K. 1982. 'A Grammatical Note on *Cypria*, Fr. 4 K', *Glotta* 60: 221–5.
　1998. *A Commentary on Pindar*, Nemean *Nine*, Berlin and New York.
Bravo, B. 2001. 'Un frammento della *Piccola Iliade* (P. Oxy. 2510), lo stile narrativo tardo-arcaico, i racconti su Achille immortale', *QUCC* 67: 49–114.
Breglia, L. and A. Moleti (eds.) 2014. *Hesperia. Tradizione, rotte, paesaggi*, Paestum.
Breglia Pulci Doria, L. 1991–4. 'Argo Amfilochia, l'*Alkmaionis* e la tradizione di Eforo', *Ann. Ist. ital. studi stor*. 12: 123–40.

Bremmer, J. N. 1987. 'Oedipus and the Greek Oedipus Complex', in J. Bremmer (ed.), *Interpretations of Greek Mythology*, London: 41–59.
  1998. 'Near Eastern and Native Traditions in Apollodorus' Account of the Flood', in F. G. Martínez and G. P. Luttikhuizen (eds.), *Interpretations of the Flood*, Leiden: 39–55.
  2004. 'Remember the Titans', in Ch. Auffarth and L. Stuckenbruck (eds.), *The Fall of the Angels*, Leiden: 35–61.
Brillante, C. 1980. 'Le leggende tebane e l'archeologia', *Stud. Micen. Eg. Anat.* 21: 309–40.
Brilliant, R. 1984. *Visual Narratives. Story-telling in Etruscan and Roman Art*, Ithaca, NY.
Brink, C. O. 1963. *Horace on Poetry*. i. *Prolegomena to the Literary Epistles*, Cambridge.
  1971. *Horace on Poetry*. ii. *The* Ars poetica, Cambridge.
Brioso Sánchez, M. 1992. 'Egipto en la novela griega antigua', *Habis* 23: 197–215.
  1999. 'La épica griega en la Antigüedad Tardía (siglos III–VII d.C.)', in J. González (ed.), *El Mundo Mediterráneo (Siglos III–VII)*, Madrid: 11–46.
Brisson, L. 1985. 'Les Théogonies orphiques et le papyrus de Derveni. Notes critiques', *Rev. hist. relig.* 202: 389–420.
Broadbent, M. 1968. *Studies in Greek Genealogy*, Leiden.
Brügger, C. 2009. *Homers* Ilias. *Gesamtkommentar*. VIII: *24. Gesang*; Fasz. 2: *Kommentar*, Berlin.
Bua, M. T. 1971. 'I giuochi alfabetici delle *tavole iliache*', *MemLinc* 16: 1–35.
Buck, R. J. 1979. *A History of Boeotia*, Edmonton.
Burgess, J. S. 1996. 'The Non-Homeric *Cypria*', *TAPhA* 126: 77–99.
  1997. 'Beyond Neo-Analysis. Problems with the Vengeance Theory', *AJPh* 118: 1–19.
  2001. *The Tradition of the Trojan War in Homer and the Epic Cycle*, Baltimore, MD.
  2002. 'Kyprias, the *Kypria*, and Multiformity', *Phoenix* 56: 234–45.
  2004a. 'Early Images of Achilles and Memnon', *QUCC* 76: 33–51.
  2004b. 'Performance and the Epic Cycle', *CJ* 100.1: 1–23.
  2005. 'The Epic Cycle and Fragments', in Foley 2005a: 344–52.
  2006. 'Neoanalysis, Orality, and Intertextuality. An Examination of Homeric Motif Transference', *Oral Tradition* 21: 148–89.
  2009. *The Death and Afterlife of Achilles*, Baltimore, MD.
  2010. 'The Hypertext of Astyanax', *Trends in Classics* 2: 211–24.
  2011. 'Iconography, Early', in Finkelberg 2011b: 391–4.
  2012. 'Intertextuality without Text in Early Greek Epic', in Andersen and Haug 2012: 168–83.
Burkert, W. 1972. 'Die Leistung eines Kreophylos. Kreophyleer, Homeriden und die archaische Heraklesepik', *MusHelv* 29: 74–85.

1981. 'Seven against Thebes. An Oral Tradition between Babylonian Magic and Greek Literature', in C. Brillante, M. Cantilena and C. O. Pavese (eds.), *I poemi epici rapsodici non omerici e la tradizione orale*, Padua: 29–46.

1983a. *Homo necans* (trans.: Berlin 1972), Berkeley, CA.

1983b. 'Itinerant Diviners and Magicians. A Neglected Element in Cultural Contacts', in Hägg 1983: 115–19.

1985. *Greek Religion* (trans.: Stuttgart and Berlin 1977), Cambridge, MA.

1987. 'The Making of Homer in the Sixth Century B.C. Rhapsodes versus Stesichorus', in *Papers on the Amasis Painter and his World* (Colloquium Sponsored by the Getty Center for the History of Art and the Humanities and Symposium sponsored by the J. Paul Getty Museum), Malibu, CA: 43–62.

1992. *The Orientalizing Revolution. Near Eastern Influence on Greek Culture in the Early Archaic Age*, Cambridge, MA.

2002. 'Die Waffen und die Jungen. Homerisch ὁπλότεροι', in M. Reichel and A. Rengakos (eds.), *EPEA PTEROENTA. Beiträge zur Homerforschung: Festschrift für W. Kullmann*, Stuttgart: 31–4.

2005. 'Hesiod in Context. Abstractions and Divinities in an Aegean-Eastern Koiné', in E. Stafford and J. Herrin (eds.), *Personification in the Greek World from Antiquity to Byzantium*, London: 3–20.

2011. *Griechische Religion der archaischen und klassischen Epoche*. 2nd edn, Stuttgart.

Burn, L. 2004. *Hellenistic Art from Alexander the Great to Augustus*, London.

Burnett, A. P. 1998. 'Jocasta in the West. The Lille Stesichorus', *CA* 7: 107–54.

2005. *Pindar's Songs for Young Athletes of Aigina*, Oxford.

CA = Powell, J. U. 1925. *Collectanea Alexandrina*, Oxford.

Calvino, I. 1995. 'Ovidio e la contiguità universale', in M. Barenghi (ed.), *Saggi 1945–1985*, Milan: 904–16.

Cameron, A. 1995. *Callimachus and his Critics*, Princeton, NJ.

Cameron, A. and A. Cameron. 1966. 'The Cycle of Agathias', *JHS* 86: 6–25.

Camerotto, A. 2003. 'Le storie e i canti degli eroi', *QUCC* 74: 9–31.

Campanile, E. 1977. *Ricerche di cultura poetica indoeuropea*, Pisa.

Canfora, L. 1971 = 1999. 'Il ciclo storico', *Belfagor* 26: 653–670 (= Id., *La storiografia greca*, Milan 1999: 61–91).

Carey, C. 2015. 'Stesichoros and the Epic Cycle', in P. J. Finglass and A. Kelly (eds.), *Stesichorus in Context*, Oxford (forthcoming).

Carrière, J. C. and B. Massonie. 1991. *La Bibliothèque d'Apollodore*, Besançon.

Carter, J. B. and S. P. Morris (eds.) 1995. *The Ages of Homer. A Tribute to E.T. Vermeule*, Austin, TX.

Carvounis, K. and R. Hunter (eds.) 2008. *Signs of Life? Studies in Later Greek Poetry* = *Ramus* 37.

Casaubon, I. 1600. *Animadversionum in Athenaei Dipnosophistas libri XV*, Lyon.

Caskey, M. E. 1976. 'Notes on Relief Pithoi of the Tenian–Boiotian Group', *AJA* 80: 19–41.
Cassio, A. C. 2002. 'Early Editions of the Greek Epics and Homeric Textual Criticism in the Sixth and Fifth Centuries BC', in Montanari and Ascheri 2002: 105–36.
  2003. 'Ospitare in casa poeti orali: Omero, Testoride, Creofilo e Staroselac', in R. Nicolai (ed.), *Rysmos. Studi di poesia, metrica e musica greca offerti dagli allievi a L. E. Rossi*, Rome: 35–46.
  2009. 'The Language of Hesiod and the Corpus Hesiodeum', in F. Montanari, A. Rengakos, and C. Tsagalis (eds.), *Brill's Companion to Hesiod*, Leiden: 179–202.
  2012. 'Kypris, Kythereia and the Fifth Book of the *Iliad*', in Montanari, Rengakos, and Tsagalis 2012: 413–26.
Castriota, D. 1992. *Myth, Ethos and Actuality. Official Art in 5th-century BC Athens*, Madison, WI.
Cavallini, E. 1994. 'Il παῖς Troilo (fr. S224 Dav.)', *Eikasmos* 5: 39–42.
Cazzaniga, I. 1975. 'Per Nicandro Colofonio la Titanomachia fu opera autentica di Esiodo', *Rend. Ist. Lomb.* 109: 173–80.
Ceccarelli, P. 1998. *La pirrica nell'antichità greco-romana. Studi sulla danza armata*, Pisa and Rome.
  2014. 'Peisandros', in *Brill's New Jacoby* (BrillOnline.com).
CEG = Hansen, P. A. 1983–9. *Carmina epigraphica Graeca*. 2 vols., Berlin and New York.
Chaniotis, A. 1988a. *Historie und Historiker in den griechischen Inschriften*, Stuttgart.
  1988b. 'Als die Diplomaten noch tanzen und sangen. Zu zwei Dekreten kretischer Städte in Mylasa', *ZPE* 71: 154–6.
  2010. 'The Best of Homer: The Homeric Texts, Performances and Images in the Hellenistic World and Beyond. The Contribution of Inscriptions', in H. Walter-Karydi (ed.), Μύθοι, κείμενα, εικόνες. ομηρικά έπη και αρχαία ελληνική τέχνη. *Proceedings of the 11th International Symposium on the Odyssey (Ithaki, September 15–19, 2009)*, Ithaki 2010: 257–78.
Chantraine, P. 2009. *Dictionnaire étymologique de la langue grecque*. New edn. by J. Taillardat, O. Masson, and J.-L. Perpillou, Paris.
Choitz, T. and J. Latacz 1981. 'Zum gegenwärtigen Stand der "Thalysien"-Deutung (Theokrit Id. 7)', *WJA* 7: 85–95.
Christ, F. 1938. *Die römische Weltherrschaft in der antiken Dichtung*, Stuttgart.
Cingano, E. 1985. 'Clistene di Sicione, Erodoto e i poemi del Ciclo Tebano', *QUCC* 20: 31–40.
  1987. 'Il duello tra Tideo e Melanippo nella *Biblioteca* dello Ps.-Apollodoro e nell'altorilievo etrusco di Pyrgi. Un'ipotesi stesicorea', *QUCC* 54: 93–102.
  1990. 'L'opera di Ibico e Stesicoro nella classificazione degli antichi e dei moderni', in *Lirica greca e latina. Atti del convegno di studio polacco-italiano (Poznań 2–5 maggio 1990) = AION* (filol.) 12: 189–224.

1992. 'The Death of Oedipus in the Epic Tradition', *Phoenix* 46: 1–11.
2000. 'Tradizioni su Tebe nell'epica e nella lirica greca arcaica', in P. Angeli Bernardini (ed.), *Presenza e funzione della città di Tebe nella cultura greca* (Atti del Convegno Internazionale, Urbino, 7–9 luglio 1997), Pisa: 127–161.
2002. 'I nomi dei Sette a Tebe e degli Epigoni nella tradizione epica, tragica e iconografica', in A. Aloni, E. Berardi, G. Besso, and S. Cecchin (eds.), *I Sette a Tebe. Dal mito alla letteratura* (Atti del Seminario Internazionale, Torino, 21–22 febbraio 2001), Bologna: 27–62.
2002–3. 'Riflessi dell'epos tebano in Omero e in Esiodo', in L. Cristante and A. Tessier (eds.), *Incontri triestini di filologia classica*. ii, Trieste: 55–76.
2004a. 'Tradizioni epiche intorno ad Argo da Omero al VI sec. a.C.', in Angeli Bernardini 2004: 59–78.
2004b. 'The Sacrificial Cut and the Sense of Honour Wronged in Greek Epic Poetry: Thebais, frgs. 2–3 D.', in C. Grottanelli and L. Milano (eds.), *Food and Identity in the Ancient World*, Padua: 57–67.
2005a. 'A Catalogue within a Catalogue. Helen's Suitors in the Hesiodic *Catalogue of Women* (frr. 196–204)', in Hunter 2005: 118–52.
2005b. 'Il cavallo "aiutante magico" nella Grecia eroica', in E. Cingano, A. Ghersetti, and L. Milano (eds.), *Animali tra zoologia, mito e letteratura nella cultura classica e orientale*, Padua: 139–54.
2007. 'Teseo e i Teseidi tra Troia e Atene', in P. Angeli Bernardini (ed.), *L'epos minore, le tradizioni locali e la poesia arcaica*, Pisa: 91–102.
(ed.) 2010a. *Tra panellenismo e tradizioni locali Generi poetici e storiografia*, Alessandria.
2010b. 'Differenze di età e altre peculiarità narrative in Omero e nel ciclo epico', in Cingano 2010a: 77–90.
2011. 'Aporie, parallelismi, riprese e convergenze. La costruzione del ciclo epico', in A. Aloni and M. Ornaghi (eds.), *Tra panellenismo e tradizioni locali. Nuovi contributi*, Messina: 3–26.
Clader, L. L. 1976. *Helen. The Evolution from Divine to Heroic in Greek Epic Tradition*, Leiden.
Clark, M. E. 1986. 'Neoanalysis. A Bibliographical Review', *CW* 79: 379–94.
Clay, D. 1988. 'The Archaeology of the Temple to Juno in Carthage (*Aen.* 1.445–493)', *CPh* 83: 195–205.
Clay, J. S. 1983. *The Wrath of Athena. Gods and Men in the Odyssey*, Princeton, NJ.
2005. 'The Beginning and the End of the *Catalogue of Women* and its Relation to Hesiod', in Hunter 2005: 25–34.
Coarelli, F. 1998. 'The Odyssey Frescoes of the Via Graziosa. A Proposed Context', *PBSR* 66: 21–37.
(ed.) 2002. *Pompeii*, New York.
Colbeaux, M.-A. 2005. *Raconter la vie d'Homère dans l'antiquité*, Diss., Lille.
Cole, T. 2008. *Ovidius Mythistoricus. Legendary Time in the* Metamorphoses, Frankfurt/Main.

Collard, C. 2004. '*Oedipus*', in C. Collard, M. J. Cropp, and J. Gibert (eds.), *Euripides. Selected Fragmentary Plays*, Oxford: ii.105–32.

Collard, C. and M. J. Cropp. 2008. *Euripides. Fragments.* 2 vols., Cambridge, MA.

Connelly, J. 1993. 'Narrative and Image in Attic Vase Painting. Ajax and Kassandra at the Trojan Palladion', in P. Holliday (ed.), *Narrative and Event in Ancient Art*, Cambridge: 80–129.

Connors, C. 2002. 'Chariton's Syracuse and Its Histories of Empire', in M. Paschalis and S. Frangoulidis (eds.), *Space in the Ancient Novel*, Groningen: 12–26.

Contiades-Tsitsoni, E. 1990. *Hymenaios und Epithalamion. Das Hochzeitslied in der frühgriechischen Lyrik*, Stuttgart.

Coo, L. M.-L. 2011. *Sophocles' Trojan Fragments. A Commentary on Selected Plays*, Diss. Cambridge.

Cook, A. B. 1925. *Zeus: A Study in Ancient Religion II: Zeus God of the Dark Sky (Thunder and Lightning)*. i: *Text and Notes*, Cambridge.

Cook, E. 2009. 'On the "Importance" of *Iliad* Book 8', *CPh* 104: 133–61.

Cook, R. M. 1983. 'Art and Epic in Archaic Greece', *Bull. Vereen. Bevord. Kennis Ant. Beschaving* 58: 1–10.

Coralini, A. 2001. *Hercules Domesticus. Immagini di Ercole nelle case della regione vesuviana (I sec. a.C. –79 d.C.)*, Naples.

   2002. 'Una stanza di Ercole a Pompei. La sala del doppio fregio nella Casa di D. Octavius Quartio (II 2,2)', in I. Colpo, I. Favaretto, and F. Ghedini (eds.), *Iconografia. Studi sull' Immagine (Atti del convegno, Padova, 30 maggio–1 giugno 2001)*, Rome: 331–43.

Corlàita Scagliarini, D. 1974–6. 'Spazio e decorazione nella pittura pompeiana', *Palladio (Rivista di storia dell'architettura)* 23–5: 3–44.

Cossu, T. 2005. 'Il programma figurativo dell'arca di Cipselo e la propaganda politica di Periandro', in M. Giuman (ed.), *L'arca invisibile. Studi sull'arca di Cipselo*, Cagliari: 81–164.

Cozzoli, A.-T. 2006. 'L'Inno a Zeus. Fonti e modelli', in A. Martina and A.-T. Cozzoli (eds.), *Callimachea*. i, Rome: 115–36.

Crissy, K. 1997. 'Herakles, Odysseus, and the Bow: *Odyssey* 21.11–41', *CJ* 93: 41–53.

Croisille, J.-M. 1985. 'Remarques sur l'épisode troyen dans les *Métamorphoses* d'Ovide (*Met.*, XII–XIII, 1–622)', in J.M. Frécaut and D. Porte (eds.), *Journées Ovidiennes de Parménie* (Actes du colloque sur Ovide, 24–26 juin 1983), Bruxelles: 57–81.

   2005. *La peinture romaine*, Paris.

Csapo, E. G. 1990. 'Hikesia in the *Telephus* of Aeschylus', *QUCC* 63: 41–52.

Cuartero, F. J. 1973. 'Las fuentes de Trifiodoro', *Boletín Inst. Estud. Helénicos* 7: 39–43.

Currie, B. 2006. 'Homer and the Early Epic Tradition', in M. J. Clarke, B. G. F. Currie, and R. O. A. M. Lyne (eds.), *Epic Interactions. Perspectives on Homer, Virgil, and the Epic Tradition Presented to J. Griffin by Former Pupils*, Oxford: 1–46.

Cuypers, M. P. 2005. 'Review of James and Lee (2000)', *Mnemosyne* 58: 605–13.

D'Alessio, G. B. 2004. 'Argo e l'Argolide nei canti cultuali di Pindaro', in Angeli Bernardini 2004: 107–25.
　2005. 'Ordering from the Catalogue. Pindar, Bacchylides, and Hesiodic Genealogical Poetry', in Hunter 2005: 217–38.
　2009. 'Defining Local Identities in Greek Lyric Poetry', in R. Hunter and I. Rutherford (eds.), *Wandering Poets in Ancient Greek Culture*, Cambridge: 137–67.
　2014. 'L'estremo Occidente nella *Titanomachia* ciclica', in Breglia and Moleti 2014: 87–97.
Danek, G. 1998. *Epos und Zitat. Studien zu den Quellen der* Odyssee, Vienna.
　2002. 'Traditional Referentiality and Homeric Intertextuality', in Montanari and Ascheri 2002: 3–19.
　2005. 'Nostos und Nostoi', *Aevum Antiquum* 5: 45–54.
　2012a. 'The Doloneia Revisited', in Andersen and Haug 2012: 106–21.
　2012b. 'Homer und Avdo Mededuvić als "post-traditional" singers', in M. Meier-Brügger (ed). *Homer, gedenet durch eine grosses Lexikon*, Berlin: 27–44.
Darmesteter, J. 1878. 'Une métaphore grammaticale de la langue indo-européenne', *MSLP* 3: 319–21.
Davies, M. 1980. 'Poetry in Plato. A New Epic Fragment?', *MusHelv* 37: 129–32.
　1982. 'Tzetzes and Stesichorus', *ZPE* 45: 267–9.
　1986. 'Prolegomena and Paralegomena to a New Edition (with Commentary) of the Fragments of Early Greek Epic', *Nachr. Akad. Wissensch. Göttingen (Phil.-hist. Kl.)* 2: 91–111.
　1988. *Epicorum Graecorum fragmenta*, Göttingen.
　1989a. 'The Date of the Epic Cycle', *Glotta* 67: 89–100.
　1989b. 'Kinkel redivivus', *CR* 39: 4–9.
　1989c. *The Epic Cycle*, Bristol.
　2000. 'Climax and Structure in *Odyssey* 8.492–520. Further Reflections on Odysseus and the Wooden Horse', *SO* 75: 56–61.
　2002. 'The Folk-Tale Origins of the *Iliad* and *Odyssey*', *WS* 115: 5–43.
　2010. 'Folk-tale Elements in the Cypria', *Classics@* 6 (ed. E. Karakantza, The Center for Hellenic Studies of Harvard University; online edn. of December 21, 2010).
Davies, M. and P. J. Finglass. 2014. *Stesichorus. The Poems*, Cambridge.
Davison, J. A. 1955=1968. 'Quotations and Allusions in Early Greek Literature', *Eranos* 53: 125–40 (= Id., *From Archilochus to Pindar*, New York: 70–85).
Debiasi, A. 2003. 'Ναυπάκτια ~ Ἀργοῦς ναυτιηγία', *Eikasmos* 14: 91–101.
　2004. *L'epica perduta. Eumelo, il ciclo, l'occidente*, Rome.
　2005. 'Eumeli Corinthii fragmenta neglecta?', *ZPE* 153: 43–58.
　2010. 'Orcomeno, Ascra e l'epopea regionale "minore"', in Cingano 2010a: 255–98.
　2012. 'Homer ἀγωνιστής in Chalcis', in Montanari, Rengakos, and Tsagalis 2012: 471–500.

2013a. 'Riflessi di epos corinzio (Eumelo) nelle *Dionisiache* di Nonno di Panopoli', in Angeli Bernardini 2013: 107–37.

2013b. 'Trame euboiche (arcaiche ed ellenistiche) nelle *Dionisiache* di Nonno di Panopoli. Eumelo ed Euforione', in F. Raviola, M. Bassani, A. Debiasi and E. Pastorio (eds.), *L'indagine e la rima. Scritti per L. Braccesi*, Rome: 503–45.

2013c. 'The "Norm of the Polyp", the *Alcmeonis* and the oracle of Amphiaraus', *Trends in Classics* 5: 195–207.

Debrohun, J. B. 2004. 'Centaurs in Love and War. Cyllarus and Hylonome in Ovid *Metamorphoses* 12.393–428', *AJPh* 125: 417–52.

De Fidio, P. 1997. 'Corinto e l'occidente tra VIII e VI secolo a.C.', in *Corinto e l'occidente* (Atti del trentaquattresimo Convegno di studi sulla Magna Grecia, Taranto, 7–11 ottobre 1994), Naples: 47–141.

de Kock, E. L. 1961. 'The Sophoklean Oidipus and its Antecedents', *AClass* 4: 7–28.

1962. 'The Peisandros Scholium. Its Sources, Unity and Relationship to Euripides' *Chrysippos*', *ActaClass* 5: 15–37.

Delarue, F. 2000. *Stace, poète épique*, Paris.

Delcourt, M. 1959. *Oreste et Alcméon. Étude sur la projection du matricide en Grèce*, Paris.

Del Freo, M. 1994. 'Osservazioni su gr. ὁπλότερος', *RCCM* 36: 104–111.

De Libero, L. 1996. *Die archaische Tyrannis*, Stuttgart.

Denniston, J.D. 1954. *The Greek Particles*. 2nd edn by K. J. Dover, Oxford.

De Rijk, L. M. 1965. 'ἐγκύκλιος παιδεία. A Study of its Original Meaning', *Vivarium* 3: 24–94.

Desanges, J. 1980. *Pline l'Ancien, Histoire naturelle. Livre V, 146, 1ère partie*, Paris.

Deubner, L. 1942. 'Oedipusprobleme', *Abhandl. Preuß. Akad. Wiss. (Philol-hist. Kl.)*, Berlin.

Diels, H. 1888. 'Atacta II', *Hermes* 23: 279–88.

Dietze, J. 1914. 'Zur kyklischen Theogonie', *RhM* 69: 522–37.

Dihle, A. 1970. *Homer-Probleme*, Opladen.

Dillery, J. 2005. 'Chresmologues and Manteis: Independent Diviners and the Problem of Authority', in S. I. Johnston and P. T. Struck (eds.), *Mantike. Studies in Ancient Divination*, Leiden: 167–231.

Dippel, M. 1990. *Die Darstellung des trojanischen Krieges in Ovids* Metamorphosen *(12,1–13,622)*, Frankfurt/Main.

Dover, K. J. 1989. *Greek Homosexuality*. 2nd edn, London.

Dowden, K. 1989. *Death and the Maiden. Girls' Initiation Rites in Greek Mythology*, London.

1992. *The Uses of Greek Mythology*, London.

1996. 'Homer's Sense of Text', *JHS* 116: 47–61.

2004. 'The Epic Tradition in Greece', in Fowler 2004b: 188–205.

Dräger, P. 2005. *Apollodor. Bibliotheke: Götter- und Heldensagen*, Düsseldorf and Zurich.

Dubielzig, U. 1996. Τριφιοδώρου Ἰλίου ἅλωσις. *Triphiodor. Die Einnahme Ilions*, Tübingen.

Due, O. S. 1974. *Changing Forms. Studies in the* Metamorphoses *of Ovid*, Copenhagen.

Dué, C. 2002. *Homeric Variations on a Lament by Briseis*, Lanham, MD.

Dué, C. and M. Ebbott. 2010. Iliad *10 and the Poetics of Ambush. A Multitext Edition with Essays and Commentary*, Washington DC.

Düntzer, H. 1840. *Die Fragmente der epischen Poesie der Griechen bis zur Zeit Alexander's des Großen*, Cologne.

Ebbinghaus, S. 2005. 'Protector of the City, or the Art of Storage in Early Greece', *JHS* 125: 51–72.

Edmonds, R.G. III. 2011. 'Afterlife', in Finkelberg 2011b: 11–14.

Edmunds, L. 1981. *The Sphinx in the Oedipus Legend*, Königstein im Taunus.

(ed.) 1990. *Approaches to Greek Myth*, Baltimore, MD.

1997. 'Myth in Homer', in I. Morris and B. Powell (eds.), *A New Companion to Homer*, Leiden: 415–441.

2007. *Oedipus*, New York.

Edwards, A. 1985. 'Achilles in the Underworld. *Iliad*, *Odyssey*, and *Aethiopis*', *GRBS* 26: 215–28.

Edwards, G. P. 1971. *The Language of Hesiod in its Traditional Context*, Oxford.

Edwards, M. W. 1987. *Homer, Poet of the* Iliad, Baltimore, MD.

1990. 'Neoanalysis and Beyond', *ClAnt* 9: 311–25.

1991. *The* Iliad. *A Commentary.* v. *Books 17–20*, Cambridge.

2011. 'Dios Boulê', in Finkelberg 2011b: 212.

EGM = Fowler, R. 2000. *Early Greek Mythography*, Oxford.

Ehwald, R. 1894. 'Vergilische Vergleiche', *Philologus* 53: 729–44.

Eichgrün, E. 1961. *Kallimachos und Apollonios Rhodios*. Diss., Berlin.

Ellsworth, J. D. 1980. 'Ovid's *Iliad* (*Metamorphoses* 12.1–13.622)', *Prudentia* 12: 23–9.

Elmer, D. F. 2008. 'Heliodoros's "Sources". Intertextuality, Paternity, and the Nile River in the *Aithiopika*', *TAPhA* 138: 411–50.

Elsner, J. 2007. *Roman Eyes. Visuality and Subjectivity in Art and Text*, Princeton, NJ.

Erbse, H. (ed.) 1969–88. *Scholia Graeca in Homeri* Iliadem *(scholia vetera)*. 6 vols., Berlin and New York.

1992. *Studien zum Verständnis Herodots*, Berlin.

1993. 'Nestor und Antilochos bei Homer und Arktinos', *Hermes* 121: 385–403.

Ervin, M. 1963. 'A Relief Pithos from Mykonos', *Archaiologikon Deltion* 18: 37–77.

Fantuzzi, M. 1988. *Ricerche su Apollonio Rodio. Diacronie della dizione epica*, Rome.

1995. 'Variazioni sull'esametro in Teocrito', in M. Fantuzzi and R. Pretagostini (eds.), *Struttura e storia dell'esametro greco*, Rome: i.221–64.

2006. 'The Myths of Dolon and Rhesus from Homer to the 'Homeric/Cyclic' Tragedy *Rhesus*', in Montanari and Rengakos 2006: 135–76.

2012. *Achilles in Love. Intertextual Studies*, Oxford.

2014. 'Tragic Smiles: When Tragedy Gets Too Comic for Aristotle and Later Hellenistic Readers', in R. Hunter, A. Rengakos, and E. Sistakou (eds.), *Hellenistic Studies at a Crossroads. Exploring Texts, Contexts and Metatexts*, Berlin and New York: 215–33.

forthcoming. 'Dionysius (*Comp. verb.* 19) and Graeco-Roman Critics on Variety and Unity', in C. C. Casper de Jonge (ed.), *Dionysius of Halicarnassus and Augustan Rome*, Leiden.

Fantuzzi, M. and R. Hunter. 2004. *Tradition and Innovation in Hellenistic Poetry*, Cambridge.

Fantuzzi, M. and A. Sens. 2006. 'The Hexameter of Inscribed Hellenistic Epigram', in M. A. Harder, R. F. Regtuit, and G. C. Wakker (eds.), *Beyond the Canon*, Leuven: 105–22.

Farrell, J. 1997. 'The Virgilian Intertext', in C. Martindale (ed.), *The Cambridge Companion to Virgil*, Cambridge: 222–38.

Faulkner, A. 2008. *The Homeric Hymn to Aphrodite*, Oxford.

Fearn, D. 2007. *Bacchylides. Politics, Performance, Poetic Tradition*, Oxford.

Fenik, B. 1964. *Iliad X and the Rhesus. The Myth*, Brussels.

1968. *Typical Battle Scenes in the Iliad*, Wiesbaden.

FgrHist = Jacoby, F. *et al.* 1923–. *Fragmente der griechischen Historiker*, Berlin.

Fick, A. 1886. *Die homerische Ilias nach ihrer Entstehung betrachtet und in der ursprünglichen Sprachform wiederhergestellt*, Göttingen.

Finglass, P. J. 2011. *Sophocles. Ajax*, Cambridge.

2013a. 'Demophon in Egypt', *ZPE* 184: 37–50.

2013b. 'How Stesichorus began his *Sack of Troy*', *ZPE* 185: 1–17.

2014. 'Stesichorus and the West', in Breglia and Moleti 2014: 29–34.

Finkelberg, M. 1998. *The Birth of Literary Fiction in Ancient Greece*, Oxford.

2000. 'The *Cypria*, the *Iliad*, and the Problem of Multiformity in Oral and Written Tradition', *CPh* 95: 1–11.

2002. 'The Sources of *Iliad* 7', in H. M. Roisman and J. Roisman (eds.), *Essays on Homeric Epic* (= *Colby Quarterly* 38): 151–61.

2003a. 'Neoanalysis and Oral Tradition in Homeric Studies', *Oral Tradition* 18.1: 68–9.

2003b. 'Homer as a Foundation Text', in Ead. and G. G. Stroumsa (eds.), *Homer, the Bible and Beyond. Literary and Religious Canons in the Ancient World*, Leiden: 75–96.

2004. 'The End of the Heroic Age in Homer, Hesiod and the Cycle', *Ordia Prima* 3: 1–24.

2005. *Greeks and Pre-Greeks. Aegean Prehistory and Greek Heroic Tradition*, Cambridge.

2011a. 'Homer and His Peers. Neoanalysis, Oral Theory, and the Status of Homer', *Trends in Classics* 3: 197–208.

(ed.) 2011b. *The Homer Encyclopedia*, Malden, MA. and Oxford.

Finsler, G. 1924. *Homer.* i. *Der Dichter und seine Welt.* 3rd edn, Leipzig and Berlin.
Finster-Hotz, U. 1986. 'Epigonoi', in *LIMC* iii.1, 803–6.
Fitch, E. 1924. 'Pindar and Homer', *CPh* 19: 57–65.
Fittschen, K. 1969. *Untersuchungen zum Beginn der Sagendarstellungen bei den Griechen,* Berlin.
Fitzgerald, A. 1926. *Letters of Synesius of Cyrene,* London.
Flückinger-Guggenheim, D. 1984. *Göttliche Gäste. Die Einkehr von Göttern und Heroen in der griechischen Mythologie,* Bern.
Förster, R. 1883. 'Zu Achilleus und Polyxena', *Hermes* 18: 475–8.
Foley, J. M. 1988. *The Theory of Oral Composition. History and Methodology,* Bloomington, IN.
  1990. *Traditional Oral Epic. The Odyssey, Beowulf, and the Serbo-Croatian Return Song,* Berkeley, CA.
  1991. *Immanent Art. From Structure to Meaning in Traditional Oral Epic,* Bloomington, IN.
  1995. *The Singer of Tales in Performance,* Bloomington, IN.
  1999a. *Homer's Traditional Art,* University Park, PA.
  1999b. 'Epic Cycles and Epic Traditions', in J. N. Kazazis and A. Rengakos (eds.), *Euphrosyne. Studies in Ancient Epic and its Legacy in Honor of D. N. Maronitis,* Stuttgart: 99–108.
  2002. *How to Read an Oral Poem,* Urbana, IL.
  2004a. 'Epic as Genre', in R. Fowler (ed.), *The Cambridge Companion to Homer,* Cambridge: 171–87.
  2004b. *The Wedding of Mustajbey's Son Bećirbey as Performed by Halil Bajgorić,* Helsinki.
  (ed.) 2005a. *A Companion to Ancient Epic,* Malden, MA.
  2005b. 'Analogues. Modern Oral Epics', in Foley 2005a: 196–212.
  2012. *Oral Tradition and the Internet. Pathways of the Mind,* Urbana, IL.
Forbes Irving, P. M. C. 1990. *Metamorphosis in Greek Myths,* Oxford.
Ford, A. 2002. *The Origins of Criticism. Literary Culture and Poetic Theory in Classical Greece,* Princeton, NJ.
Fornara, C. W. 1983. *The Nature of History in Ancient Greece and Rome,* Berkeley, CA.
Forrest, G. 1956. 'The First Sacred War', *BCH* 80: 33–52.
Fowler, R. L. 2004a. 'The Homeric Question', in Fowler 2004b: 220–32.
  (ed.) 2004b. *The Cambridge Companion to Homer,* Cambridge.
Fraenkel, E. 1932. 'Vergil und die *Aithiopis*', *Philologus* 87: 242–8.
Fränkel, H. 1975. *Early Greek Poetry and Philosophy* (trans.: Munich 1962, 2nd edn.), New York and London.
Frangoulidis, S. A. 1992. 'Homeric Allusions to the Cyclopeia in Apuleius' Description of the Robbers' Cave', *PP* 47: 50–8.
Friedländer, P. 1905. *Argolica. Quaestiones ad Graecorum historiam fabularem pertinentes.* Diss., Berlin.

1914 = 1969. 'Kritische Untersuchungen zur Geschichte der Heldensage,' *RhM* 69: 299–341 (= Id., *Studien zur antiken Literatur und Kunst*, Berlin 1969: 19–53).

Friedrich, R. 1983. 'ΕΠΕΙΣΟΔΙΟΝ in Drama and Epic. A Neglected and Misunderstood Term of Aristotle's Poetics', *Hermes* 111: 34–52.

2007. *Formular Economy in Homer. The Poetics of the Breaches*, Stuttgart.

Friis Johansen, K. 1967. *The Iliad in Early Greek Art*, Copenhagen.

Funke, S. 2000. *Aiakidenmythos und epeirotisches Königtum. Der Weg einer hellenistischen Monarchie*, Stuttgart.

Fusillo, M. 1985. *Il tempo delle Argonautiche. Un'analisi del racconto in Apollonio Rodio*, Rome.

1990. 'Il testo nel testo. La citazione nel romanzo greco', *MD* 25: 27–48.

Gärtner, U. 2005. *Quintus Smyrnaeus und die Aeneis. Zur Nachwirkung Vergils in der griechischen Literatur der Kaiserzeit*, Munich.

Gagarin, M. 1974. 'Dikē in Archaic Greek Thought', *CPh* 69: 186–97.

Galinsky, K. 1969. *Aeneas, Sicily, and Rome*, Princeton, NJ.

Gallagher, C. 2006. 'The Rise of Fictionality', in F. Moretti (ed.), *The Novel*, Princeton, NJ: ii.336–53.

Gantz, T. N. 1980. 'Aischylos' Lost Plays. The Fifth Column', *RhM* 123: 210–22.

1993. *Early Greek Myth. A Guide to Literary and Artistic Sources*, Baltimore, MD.

Garassino, A. 1930. 'Ulisse nel teatro Greco', *Atene & Roma* 11: 219–51.

Garner, R. 1993. 'Achilles in Locri? P.Oxy. LVII.3876. frr. 37–77', *ZPE* 96: 153–65.

1994. 'Stesichorus' Althaia: P.Oxy. LVII.3876. frr. 1–36', *ZPE* 100: 26–38.

Gasparri, C. 2009. '23 Ky. Un nuovo rilievo della serie delle tabulae iliacae dal Foro di Cuma', in C. Gasparri and G. Greco (eds.), *Cuma. Indagini archeologiche e nuove scoperte*, Pozzuoli: 251–7.

Gehrke, H.-J. and M. Kirschkowski (eds.) 2009. *Odysseus. Irrfahrten durch die Jahrhunderte*, Freiburg/Bresgau.

Gentili, B. 1978. 'Poeta-committente-pubblico. Stesicoro e Ibico', in E. Livrea and G.A. Privitera (eds.), *Studi in onore di A. Ardizzoni*, Rome: 393–401.

1990. *Poetry and its Public in Ancient Greece from Homer to the Fifth Century* (trans.: Rome and Bari 1988), Baltimore, MD.

Gentili B., P. Angeli Bernardini, E. Cingano, and P. Giannini 2006. *Pindaro. Le Pitiche*. 4th edn, Milan.

Gerbeau, J. and F. Vian. 1992. *Nonnos de Panopolis. Les Dionysiaques. vii. Chants 18–19*, Paris.

Gerlaud, B. 1982. *Triphiodore. La prise d'Ilion*, Paris.

GH = Chantraine, P. *Grammaire homerique*. 5th edn, 2 vols., Paris 1973–86.

Giannini, P. 2004. 'Ibico a Samo', in E. Cavallini (ed.), *Samo. Storia, letteratura, scienza* (Atti delle giornate di studio, Ravenna, 14–16 novembre 2002), Pisa: 51–64.

Gigon, O. 1961. 'Die epische Titanomachie', in O. Gigon and J. Dörig, *Der Kampf der Götter und Titanen*, Olten-Lausanne: iv–xxiv.

Giuliani, L. 1996. 'Rhesus between Dream and Death. On the Relation of Image to Literature in Apulian Vase-Painting', *BICS* 41: 71–86.
  2001. 'Sleeping Furies. Allegory, Narration and the Impact of Texts in Apulian Vase-Painting', *Scripta class. Israel.* 20: 17–38.
  2003. *Bild und Mythos. Geschichte der Bilderzählung in der griechischen Kunst*, Munich.
Goldhill, S. D. 1991. *The Poet's Voice. Essays on Poetics and Greek Literature*, Cambridge.
Graf, F. 1993. *Greek Mythology*, Baltimore, MD.
Grafton, A. T. and N. M. Swerdlow. 1986. 'Greek Chronography in Roman Epic: The Calendrical Date of the Fall of Troy in the *Aeneid*', *CQ* 36: 212–18.
Gransden, K. W. 1991. *Virgil. Aeneid. Book XI*, Cambridge.
Graziosi, B. 2002. *Inventing Homer. The Early Reception of Epic*, Cambridge.
Graziosi, B. and J. Haubold. 2010. *Homer. Iliad. Book VI*, Cambridge.
Grethlein, J. 2006. 'How Old is Nestor?', *Eikasmos* 17: 11–16.
  2008. 'Memory and Material Objects in the Iliad and the Odyssey', *JHS* 128: 27–51.
Grethlein, J. and A. Rengakos (eds.) 2009. *Narratology and Interpretation. The Content of Narrative Form in Ancient Literature*, Berlin and New York.
Griffin, A. 1982. *Sikyon*, Oxford.
Griffin, J. 1977. 'The Epic Cycle and the Uniqueness of Homer', *JHS* 97: 39–53.
  1980. *Homer on Life and Death*, Oxford.
  1995. *Homer. Iliad IX*, Oxford.
  2004. 'The Speeches', in R. Fowler (ed.), *The Cambridge Companion to Homer*, Cambridge: 156–67.
Griffith, M. 1999. *Sophocles. Antigone*, Cambridge.
Grisolia, R. 2001. *Oikonomia. Struttura e tecnica drammatica negli scoli antichi ai testi drammatici*, Naples.
Grossardt, P. 2012. *Stesichoros zwischen kultischer Praxis, mythischer Tradition und eigenem Kunstanspruch. Zur Behandlung des Helenamythos im Werk des Dichters aus Himera*, Tübingen.
Gruppe, O. 1906. *Griechische Mythologie und Religionsgeschichte*, Munich.
Guarducci, M. 1935–50. *Inscriptiones Creticae*. 4 vols., Rome.
Habicht, C. 1985. 'An Ancient Baedeker and His Critics. Pausanias' *Guide to Greece*', *PAPS* 129: 220–4.
Hadjicosti, I. L. 2005. 'Death by a Turtle. The Route of a Motif from *Telegonia* to the *Vita* of Aeschylus', *Eranos* 103: 78–82.
Hadjittofi, F. 2008. 'Callimachus' Sexy Athena. The *Hymn to Athena* and the *Hymn to Aphrodite*', *MD* 60: 9–37.
Hägg, R. (ed.) 1983. *The Greek Renaissance of the 8th Century B.C.*, Stockholm.
Hägg, T. 1975. *Photius als Vermittler antiker Literatur. Untersuchungen zur Technik des Referierens und Exzerpierens in der Bibliotheke*, Uppsala.
  1983. *The Novel in Antiquity*, Berkeley, CA.

Haight, E. H. 1947. 'The Tale of Troy. An Early Romantic Approach', *CJ* 42: 261–9.
Hainsworth, J. B. 1993. *The* Iliad. *A Commentary.* iii. *Books 9–12*, Cambridge.
Hall, J. M. 1999. 'Beyond the Polis: the Multilocality of Heroes', in R. Hägg (ed.), *Ancient Greek Hero Cult*, Stockholm: 49–59.
Halliwell, S. 1998. *Aristotle's* Poetics. 2nd edn, Chicago, IL.
Halperin, D. M. 1983. *Before Pastoral. Theocritus and the Ancient Tradition of Bucolic Poetry*, New Haven, CT.
Harder, A. 2012. *Callimachus.* Aetia. 2 vols., Oxford.
Hardie, P. R. 1986. *Virgil's* Aeneid. *Cosmos and Imperium*, Oxford.
Harris, E. M. 2010. 'Is Oedipus Guilty? Sophocles and Athenian Homicide Law', in E. M. Harris, D. F. Leão, and P. J. Rhodes (eds.), *Law and Drama in Ancient Greeece*, London: 122–46.
Harrison, S. 1990. 'Some Odyssean Scenes in Apuleius' *Metamorphoses*', *MD* 25: 193–201.
  (ed.) 1999. *Oxford Readings in the Roman Novel*, Oxford.
  2008. 'Intertextuality. The Roman Novel', in Whitmarsh 2008: 227–36.
Hartmann, A. 1917. *Untersuchungen über die Sagen vom Tod des Odysseus*, Munich.
Haslam, M. 1978. 'The Versification of the New Stesichorus (P. Lille 76 abc)', *GRBS* 19: 29–57.
Hausmann, U. 1959. *Hellenistische Reliefbecher aus attischen und boötischen Werkstätten*, Stuttgart.
Heath, M. 1987. *The Poetics of Greek Tragedy*, London.
  1989. *Unity in Greek Poetics*, Oxford.
  1999. '"Sophocles" *Philoctetes*, a Problem Play?', in J. Griffin (ed.), *Sophocles Revisited. Essays Presented to Sir H. Lloyd-Jones*, Oxford: 137–60.
Hedreen, G. M. 2001. *Capturing Troy. The Narrative Functions of Landscape in Archaic and Early Classical Greek Art*, Ann Arbor, MI.
Heiden, B. 1996. 'The Three Movements of the *Iliad*', *GRBS* 37: 5–22.
Heinze, R. 1915. *Virgils epische Technik.* 3rd edn, Leipzig.
Heitsch, E. 1990 = 2001. 'Homerische Dreigespanne', in W. Kullmann and M. Reichel (eds.), *Der Übergang von der Mündlickeit zur Literatur der Griechen*, Tübingen 1990: 153–74 = Heitsch 2001: 210–31.
  1991 = 2001. 'Die epische Schicksalswaage', *Philologus* 136: 143–57 (= Heitsch 2001: 232–46).
  2001. *Gesammelte Schriften.* i. *Zum frühgriechischen Epos*, Munich and Leipzig.
  2005. '*Ilias* und *Aithiopis*', *Gymnasium* 112: 431–41.
  2008. 'Neoanalytische Antikritik', *RhM* 151: 1–12.
Henrichs, A. 1979. 'Callimachus Epigram 28, a Fastidious Priamel', *HSCPh* 83: 207–21.
Henry, W. B. 2005. *Pindar's* Nemeans. *A Selection*, Munich.
Hercher, R. 1873. *Epistolographi Graeci*, Paris.
Hermann, G. 1827–77. *Opuscula.* 8 vols., Leipzig.

Herter, H. 1948. 'Ovids Kunstprinzip in den *Metamorphosen*', *AJPh* 69: 129–48.

Heslin, P. J. 2005. *The Transvestite Achilles. Gender and Genre in Statius' Achilleid*, Cambridge.

Heubeck, A. 1958. 'Zur inneren Form der Ilias', *Gymnasium* 65: 37–47.

  1974. *Die homerische Frage. Ein Bericht über die Forschung der letzten Jahrzehnte*, Darmstadt.

Heyne, C. G. 1797. *P. Virgilius Maro varietate lectionis et perpetua adnotatione illustratus*. ii. Aeneidis *libri i–iv*. 3rd edn, Leipzig.

Higbie, C. 2007. 'Hellenistic Mythographers', in R.G. Woodard (ed.), *The Cambridge Companion to Greek Mythology*, Cambridge: 237–54.

Hillgruber, M. 1990. 'Zur Zeitbestimmung der Chrestomathie des Proclos', *RhM* 133: 397–404.

Hilpert-Greger, R. 1996. 'Die Gründungsmythen des Akarnanischen Ethnos', in P. Berktold, J. Schmid, and C. Wacker (eds.), *Akarnanien. Eine Landschaft im antiken Griecheland*, Würzburg 1997: 61–8.

Hirschberger, M. 2004. *Gynaikon Katalogos und Megalai Ehoiai. Ein Kommentar zu den Fragmenten zweier hesiodischen Epen*, Munich.

  2008. 'Die Parteiungen der Götter in der Ilias. Antike Auslegung und Hintergründe in Kult und epischer Tradition', *WS* 121: 5–28.

Hodske, J. 2007. *Mythologische Bildthemen in den Häusern Pompejis. Die Bedeutung der zentralen Mythenbilder für die Bewohner Pompejis*, Stendal.

Höckmann, O. 1980. 'Lanze und Speer', in H.-G. Buchholz (ed.), *Kriegswesen*. ii. *Angriffswaffen* (*Archaeologia Homerica* I E 2), Göttingen: 275–319.

Höfer, O. 1897–1909. 'Polypoites', in *ALGRM*: iii.2715–17.

Hoekstra, A. 1969. *The Sub-Epic Stage of the Formulaic Tradition. Studies in the Homeric Hymns to Apollo, to Aphrodite and to Demeter*, Amsterdam.

Hölscher, U. 1939. *Untersuchungen zur Form der* Odyssee. *Szenenwechsel und gleichzeitige Handlungen*, Berlin.

  1990. *Die* Odyssee. *Epos zwischen Märchen und Roman*. 3rd edn, Munich.

von den Hoff, R. 2009. 'Odysseus in der antiken Bildkunst', in Gehrke and Kirschkowski 2009: 39–64.

Hollis, A. S. 1992. 'Teuthis in Callimachus' *Aetia* (P.Mich.Inv. 6235)', *ZPE* 92: 115–17.

Holmberg, I. 1998. 'The Creation of the Ancient Greek Epic Cycle', *Oral Tradition* 13.2: 456–78.

Holt, P. 1992. 'Ajax's Burial in Early Greek Epic', *AJPh* 113: 319–31.

Holzberg, N. 1996. 'The Genre. Novels Proper and the Fringe', in G. Schmeling (ed.), *The Novel in the Ancient World*, Leiden: 11–28.

Hommel, H. 1980. *Der Gott Achilleus*, Heidelberg.

Honko, L. 1998. *Textualising the Siri Epic*, Helsinki.

Hopkinson, N. 1994a. 'Nonnus and Homer', in Id. (ed.), *Studies in the* Dionysiaca *of Nonnus*, Cambridge: 9–42.

  1994b. *Greek Poetry of the Imperial Period. An Anthology*, Cambridge.

  2000. *Ovid.* Metamorphoses *Book XIII*, Cambridge.

Horrocks, G. 1997. 'Homer's Dialect', in Morris and Powell 1997: 193–217.
Horsfall, N. 1979a. 'Some problems in the Aeneas legend', *CQ* 29: 372–90.
   1979b. 'Stesichorus at Bovillae?', *JHS* 99: 26–48.
   1988. 'Camilla, o i limiti dell'invenzione', *Athenaeum* 66: 31–51.
   1995. 'Aeneid', in Id. (ed.), *A Companion to the Study of Virgil*, Leiden: 101–216.
   2003. *Virgil, Aeneid 11. A Commentary*, Leiden.
   2004. 'Arctinus, Virgil and Quintus Smyrnaeus', in P.-A. Deproost and A. Meurant (eds.), *Images d'origines, origines d'une image*, Paris: 73–80.
   2008. *Virgil, Aeneid 2. A Commentary*, Leiden.
Howland, R. L. 1954. 'Epeius, Carpenter and Athlete', *PCPhS* 183: 15–16.
Hubbard, T. K. 1992. 'Remaking Myth and Rewriting History. Cult Tradition in Pindar's Ninth *Nemean*', *HSCPh* 94: 77–111.
Huber, L. 1965. 'Herodots Homerverständnis', in H. Flashar and K. Gaiser (eds.), *Synusia. Festgabe für W. Schadewaldt*, Pfullingen: 29–52.
Hunt, A. S. 1911. *Catalogue of the Greek Papyri in the John Rylands Library, Manchester*. i. *Literary Texts (Nos. 1–61)*, Manchester.
Hunter, R. 1993. *The* Argonautica *of Apollonius. Literary Studies*, Cambridge.
   (ed.) 2005. *The Hesiodic* Catalogue of Women. *Constructions and Reconstructions*, Cambridge.
   2008. 'The Poetics of Narrative in the *Argonautica*', in T. D. Papanghelis and A. Rengakos (eds.), *A Companion to Apollonius Rhodius*. 2nd edn, Leiden: 115–46.
   2009. 'The *Trojan Oration* of Dio Chrysostom and Ancient Homeric Criticism', in Grethlein and Rengakos 2009: 43–61.
Hurst, A. and A. Kolde. 2008. *Lycophron. Alexandra*, Paris.
Hurwitt, J. 1985. *The Art and Culture of Early Greece*, Ithaca, NY.
Hutchinson, G. O. 2001. *Greek Lyric Poetry. A Commentary on Selected Larger Pieces*, Oxford.
Huxley, G. L. 1960. 'Homerica II. *Eugamon*', *GRBS* 3: 23–8.
   1967. 'A Problem in the *Cypria*', *GRBS* 8: 25–7.
   1969. *Greek Epic Poetry from Eumelos to Panyassis*, London.
   1975. *Pindar's Vision of the Past*, Belfast.
IEG = West, M. L. 1989–92. *Iambi et elegi Graeci ante Alexandrum cantati*. 2nd edn, 2 vols., Oxford.
IG = 1873–. *Inscriptiones Graecae*, Berlin.
IGUR = Moretti, L. 1968–1990. *Inscriptiones Graecae urbis Romae*, Rome.
Immisch, O. 1889. *Klaros. Forschungen über griechische Stiftungssagen*, Leipzig.
   1894. 'Kyklos bei Aristoteles', in *Griechische Studien H. Lipsius zum sechzigsten Geburtstag dargebracht*, Leipzig: 108–19.
Irigoin, J. 1962. 'Les manuscript grecs 1931–1960', *Lustrum* 7: 5–93.
Jacoby, F. 1909. 'Über die Entwicklung der griechischen Historiographie und den Plan einer neuen Sammlung der griechischen Historikerfragmente', *Klio* 9: 80–123.
Jahn, O. 1873. *Griechische Bilderchroniken* (ed. A. Michaelis), Bonn.

James, A. W. 2004. *Quintus of Smyrna. The Trojan Epic*, Posthomerica, Baltimore, MD.
James, A. W. and K. Lee. 2000. *A Commentary on Quintus of Smyrna*, Posthomerica V, Leiden.
Janko, R. 1982. *Homer, Hesiod, and the Hymns*, Cambridge.
  1992. *The* Iliad. *A Commentary*. iv. *Books 13–16*, Cambridge.
  1998. 'The Homeric Poems as Oral Dictated Texts', *CQ* 48: 1–13.
  2011. 'πρῶτόν τε καὶ ὕστατον αἰὲν ἀείδειν. Relative Chronology and the Literary History of the Early Greek epos', in Andersen and Haug 2012a: 20–43.
Jenkins, I. 2002. 'The Earliest Representation in Greek Art of the Death of Ajax', in A. Clark and J. Gaunt (eds.), *Essays in Honor of D. von Bothmer*, Amsterdam: 153–6.
Jenner, E. A. B. 1998. 'Troilus and Polyxena in Archaic Greek Lyric: Ibycus fr. S 224 Dav.', *Prudentia* 30: 1–15.
Jensen, M. S. 1980. *The Homeric Question and the Oral–Formulaic Theory*, Copenhagen.
  2011. *Writing Homer. A Study Based on Results from Modern Fieldwork*, Copenhagen.
Johnson, J. W. 1980. 'Yes, Virginia, There is an Epic in Africa', *Review of African Literatures* 11: 308–26.
Johnson, J. W., T. A. Hale, and S. Belcher (eds.) 1997. *Oral Epics from Africa. Vibrant Voices from a Vast Continent*, Bloomington, IN.
  2003. *Son-Jara, the Mande Epic*. 3rd edn, Bloomington, IN.
Johnson, W. R. 1976. *Darkness Visible. A Study of Vergil's* Aeneid, Berkeley, CA.
Johnston, I. 2007. *Homer. The* Iliad, Arlington, VA.
Jones, B. 2010. 'Relative Chronology within (an) Oral Tradition', *CJ* 105: 289–318.
  2011. 'Relative Chronology and an "Aeolic Phase"', in Andersen and Haug 2011a: 44–64.
Jong, I. J. F. de. 1987. *Narrators and Focalizers. The Presentation of the Story in the* Iliad, Amsterdam.
  1999. 'Aspects narratologiques des *Histoires* d'Hérodote', *Lalies* 19: 217–75.
  2001. *A Narratological Commentary on the* Odyssey, Cambridge.
  2002. 'Developments in Narrative Technique in the *Odyssey*', in Reichel and Rengakos 2002: 77–91.
Jouan, F. 1966. *Euripide et les légendes des Chants Cypriens*, Paris.
  1987. 'Les reprises d'épisodes dans le cycle épique', in J. Servais, T. Hackens, and B. Servais-Soyez (eds.), *Stemmata. Mélanges de philologie, d'histoire et d'archéologie grecques offerts à J. Labarbe*, Liège: 39–54.
  1990. 'Les Corinthiens en Acarnanie et leurs prédécesseurs mythiques', in F. Jouan and A. Motte (eds.), *Mythe et politique* (Actes du Colloque, Liège, 14–16 septembre 1989), Paris: 155–66.
Jouan, F. and H. van Looy. 2000. *Euripide. Tragédies*. viii.2. *Fragments*. Bellérophon-Protésilas, Paris.

    2002. *Euripide. Tragédies.* viii.3. *Fragments.* Sthénébée-Chrysippos, Paris.
Jouanna, J. 2007. *Sophocle*, Paris.
Kaczyńska, E. 1999. 'The Panacra Mountains in Callimachus and Epimenides', *Eos* 86: 33–7.
Kahil, G. 1988. 'Helene', in *LIMC* iv.1: 498–572.
Kakridis, J. T. 1944. Ομηρικές έρευνες, Athens.
    1949. *Homeric Researches*, Lund.
Kakridis, Ph. J. 1961. 'Achilleus' Rüstung', *Hermes* 89: 288–97.
    1995. 'Odysseus und Palamedes', in Ø. Andersen and M. Dickie (eds.), *Homer's World: Fiction, Tradition, Reality*, Bergen: 91–100.
    2001. 'Κίκονες', in M. Païsi-Apostolopoulou (ed.), *Eranos.* (Proceedings of the 9th International Symposium on the *Odyssey*, 2–7 September 2000), Ithaca: 481–7.
Kannicht, R. 1969. *Euripides Helena.* 2 vols., Heidelberg.
    1982. 'Poetry and Art. Homer and the Monuments', *ClAnt* 1: 70–86.
    2004a. *Tragicorum Graecorum Fragmenta.* v. *Euripides.* 2 vols., Göttingen.
    2004b. 'Scheiben von den grossen Mahlzeiten Homers: Euripides und der Troische Epenkreis', in A. Bierl, A. Schmitt, and A. Willi (eds.), *Antike Literatur in neuer Deutung. Festschrift für J. Latacz anlässlich seines 70. Geburtstages*, Munich: 185–202.
Karakantza, E. 2010. 'Eating from the Tables of Others. Sophocles' *Ajax* and the Greek Epic Cycle', *Classics@* 6 (ed. E. Karakantza, The Center for Hellenic Studies of Harvard University; online edn of December 21, 2010).
Kay, M. W. 1995. *The Index of the Milman Parry Collection 1933–1935. Heroic Songs, Conversations and Stories*, New York.
Kazansky, N. N. 1997. *Principles of the Reconstruction of a Fragmentary Text*, St Petersburg.
Kees, H. 1933. *Kulturgeschichte des alten Orients.* iii.1. *Ägypten*, Munich.
Keith, A. M. 1999. 'Versions of Epic Masculinity in Ovid's *Metamorphoses*', in P. Hardie, A. Barchiesi, and S. Hinds (eds.), *Ovidian Transformations. Essays on Ovid's* Metamorphoses *and its Reception*, Cambridge: 214–39.
    2000. *Engendering Rome. Women in Latin Epic*, Cambridge.
Kelly, A. 2006. 'Neoanalysis and the *Nestorbedrängnis.* A Test Case', *Hermes* 134: 1–25.
    2008. 'Performance and Rivalry. Homer, Odysseus and Hesiod', in Revermann and Wilson 2008: 177–203.
Kerkhof, R. 2001. *Dorische Posse, Epicharm und Attische Komödie*, Munich.
Kern, H. 1918. 'Der antike Astyanax-Mythus und seine späteren Auswüchse', *Philologus* 75: 183–201.
Keydell, R. 1935. 'Die Dichter mit Namen Peisandros', *Hermes* 70: 301–11.
Kim, L. 2011. *Homer between History and Fiction in Imperial Greek Literature*, Cambridge.
Kingsley, P. 1995. 'Notes on Air. Four Questions of Meaning in Empedocles and Anaxagoras', *CQ* 45: 26–9.

Kinkel, G. 1877. *Epicorum Graecorum fragmenta*. i, Leipzig.
Kirchhoff, A. 1879. *Die homerische* Odyssee, 2nd edn, Berlin.
Kirchhoff, C. 1917. *Der Kampf der Sieben vor Theben und König Oedipus*. Diss., Münster.
Kirk, G. S. 1962. *The Songs of Homer*, Cambridge.
  1965. *Homer and the Epic (A Shortened Version of* The Songs of Homer*)*, Cambridge.
  1976. *Homer and the Oral Tradition*, Cambridge.
  1985. *The* Iliad. *A Commentary*. i. *Books 1–4*, Cambridge.
  1990. *The* Iliad. *A Commentary*. ii. *Books 5–8*, Cambridge.
Kirschkowski, M. 2009. 'Die Gestalt des Odysseus bei Pindar', in Gehrke and Kirschkowski 2009: 65–78.
Kivilo, M. 2010. *Early Greek Poets' Lives. The Shaping of the Tradition*, Leiden.
Klebs, E. 1889. 'Zur Composition von Petronius *Satirae*', *Philologus* 47: 623–35.
Klimis, S. 1997. *Le statut du mythe dans la* Poétique *d'Aristote. Les fondements philosophiques de la tragédie*, Brussels.
Knauer, G. N. 1979. *Die Aeneis und Homer. Studien zur poetischen Technik Vergils mit Listen der Homerzitate in der* Aeneis. 2nd edn, Göttingen.
Knight, W. F. J. 1932a. 'Iliupersides', *CQ* 26: 178–89.
  1932b. *Vergil's Troy: Essays on the Second Book of the* Aeneid, Oxford.
Köchly, H. 1850. Κοΐντου τὰ μεθ' Ὅμηρον. *Quinti Smyrnaei Posthomericorum libri XIV*, Leipzig.
Koenen, L., W. Luppe, and V. Pagán. 1991. 'Explanations of Callimachean αἴτια', *ZPE* 88: 157–64.
Koenen, L. and R. Merkelbach. 1976. 'Apollodoros (ΠΕΡΙ ΘΕΩΝ), Epicharm und die Meropis', in A. E. Hanson (ed.), *Collectanea Papyrologica. Texts Published in Honor of H.C. Youtie*, Bonn: i.3–26.
Konstan, D. 1998. 'The Invention of Fiction', in R. F. Hock, J. B. Chance, and J. Perkins (eds.), *Ancient Fiction and Early Christian Narrative*, Atlanta, GA: 3–17.
  2014. *Beauty. The Fortunes of an Ancient Greek Idea*, Oxford.
Kopff, E. C. 1981. 'Virgil and the Cyclic Epics', *ANRW* ii.31.2: 919–47.
  1983. 'The Structure of the Amazonia (*Aethiopis*)', in Hägg 1983: 57–62.
Kossatz-Deissmann, A. 1981. 'Achilleus', in *LIMC* i.1: 37–200.
Kovacs, P. D. 2009. 'The Role of Apollo in *Oedipus Tyrannus*', in J. R. C. Cousland and J. R. Hume (eds.), *The Play of Texts and Fragments. Essays in Honour of M. Cropp*, Leiden: 357–68.
Kranz, W. 1960. 'Titanomachia', in *Studi in onore di L. Castiglioni*, Florence: 475–86.
  1961. 'Die Sonne als Titan', *Philologus* 105: 290–5.
Krauskopf, I. 1980. 'Die Ausfahrt des Amphiaraos auf Amphoren der tyrrhenischen Gruppe', in H. A. Cahn and E. Simon (eds.), *Tainia. Festschrift für R. Hampe*, Mainz: 105–16.
  1981a. 'Adrastos', *LIMC* i.1: 231–40.

1981b. 'Amphiaraos', in *LIMC* i.1: 691–713.

1981c. 'Amphilochos', in *LIMC* i.1: 713–17.

1986. 'Edipo nell'arte antica', in B. Gentili and R. Pretagostini (eds.), *Edipo. Il teatro greco e la cultura europea*, Rome: 327–41.

1994. 'Oidipous', in *LIMC* vii.1: 2–9.

Kroll, J. 1936. *Theognis-Interpretationen*, Leipzig.

Kroll, W. 1902. 'Studien über die Komposition der *Aeneis*', *Jahrbücher für das classische Altertum* Suppl. 27: 135-69.

Kühner, R. and B. Gerth. 1898–1904. *Ausführliche Grammatik der griechischen Sprache*. 2 vols., Hanover.

Kullmann, W. 1955a = 1992. 'Ein vorhomerisches Motiv im Iliasproömium', *Philologus* 99: 167–92. (= Kullmann 1992: 11–35).

1955b = 1992. 'Die Probe des Achaierheeres in der *Ilias*', *MusHelv* 12: 253–73 (= Kullmann 1992: 38–63).

1956 = 1992. *Das Wirken der Götter in der* Ilias, Berlin.

1958 = 1992. Review of M. Treu, *Von Homer zur Lyrik*, *Gymnasium* 65: 545–8.

1960 = 1992. *Die Quellen der* Ilias *(Troischer Sagenkreis)*, Wiesbaden.

1981 = 1992. 'Zur Methode der Neoanalyse in der Homerforschung', *WS* 15: 5–42 (= Kullmann 1992: 67–99).

1984 = 1992. 'Oral Poetry Theory and Neoanalysis in Homeric Research', *GRBS* 25: 307–24 (= Kullmann 1992: 140–155).

1986 = 1992. 'F. G. Welcker über Homer und den epischen Kyklos', in W. M. Calder III, A. Köhnken, W. Kullmann, and G. Pflug (eds.), *Friedrich Gottlob Welcker. Werk und Wirkung*, Stuttgart: 105–30 (= Kullmann 1992, 373–99).

1988 = 1992. '"Oral Tradition/Oral History" und die frühgriechische Epik', in J. von Ungern-Sternberg and H. Reinau (eds.), *Vergangenheit in mündlicher Überlieferung*, Stuttgart: 184–96 (= Kullmann 1992: 156–69).

1990 = 1992. 'Die poetische Funktion des Palastes des Odysseus in der *Odyssee*', in Πρακτικά του Ε' Συνεδρίου για την Οδύσσεια (11–14 Σεπτεμβρίου 1987), Κέντρο Οδυσσειακών Σπουδών, Ithaki: 41–55 (= Kullmann 1992: 305–16).

1991 = 1992. 'Ergebnisse der motivgeschichtlichen Forschung zu Homer (Neoanalyse)', in J. Latacz (ed.), *200 Jahre Homerforschung. Rückblick und Ausblick*, Stuttgart: 425–55 (= Kullmann 1992: 100–34).

1992. *Homerische Motive* (ed. R. J. Müller), Stuttgart.

2002a. 'Nachlese zur Neoanalyse', in A. Rengakos (ed.), *Realität, Imagination und Theorie. Kleine Schriften zu Epos und Tragödie in der Antike*, Stuttgart: 162–76.

2002b. 'Procli Cyclicorum enarrationes paragraphis divisae', in A. Rengakos (ed.), *Realität, Imagination und Theorie. Kleine Schriften zu Epos und Tragödie in der Antike*, Stuttgart: 156–61.

2005. '*Ilias* und *Aithiopis*', *Hermes* 133: 9–28.

2009. 'Poesie, Mythos und Realität im Schiffskatalog der *Ilias*', *Hermes* 137: 1–20.

2011a. 'The Relative Chronology of the Homeric Catalogue of Ships and of the Lists of Heroes and Cities within the Catalogue', in Andersen and Haug 2011a: 210–23.

2011b. '*Ilias*' in A. Rengakos and B. Zimmermann (eds.), *Homer-Handbuch*, Stuttgart: 78–120.

2012. 'Neoanalysis between Orality and Literacy. Some Remarks Concerning the Development of Greek Myths Including the Legend of the Capture of Troy', in Montanari, Rengakos, and Tsagalis 2012: 13–25.

Kunze, E. 1950. *Archaische Schildbänder*, Berlin.

Labate, M. 2010. *Passato remoto. Età mitiche e identità augustea in Ovidio*, Pisa and Rome.

Laird, A. 1996. '*Ut figura poesis*. Writing Art and the Art of Writing in Augustan Poetry', in J. Elsner (ed.), *Art and Text in Roman Culture*, Cambridge: 75–102.

Lane Fox, R. 2008. *Travelling Heroes: Greeks and their Myths in the Epic Age of Homer*, London.

Lang, A. 1893. *Homer and the Epic*, London.

Lang, M. L. 1995. 'War Story into Wrath Story', in Carter and Morris 1995: 149–62.

Langerbeck, H. 1958. 'Margites. Versuch einer Beschreibung und Rekonstruktion', *HSCPh* 63: 33–63.

La Penna, A. 1988. 'Gli archetipi epici di Camilla', *Maia* 40: 221–50.

2000. 'L'ordine delle raffigurazioni della guerra Troiana nel tempio di Cartagine (*Aeneid* I.469–493)', *Maia* 52: 1–8.

Latacz, J. 1996. *Homer, His Art and His World* (trans.: Düsseldorf. 1989, 2nd edn), Ann Arbor, MI.

1997. 'Epischer Zyklus', in *Der Neue Pauly*. vi, Stuttgart: 1154–6.

2003. *Homer. Der erste Dichter des Abendlands*. 3rd edn, Düsseldorf.

Latacz, J. et al. 2003. *Homers Ilias. Gesamtkommentar*. Band II: *2. Gesang*, Fasz. 2: *Kommentar*, Munich.

Latte, K. 1934. 'Themis', *RE* A 5: 1626–30.

Lausberg, H. 1998. *Handbook of Literary Rhetoric. A Foundation for Literary Study* (trans.: Munich 1973, 2nd edn), Leiden.

Leach, E.W. 1988. *The Rhetoric of Space. Literary and Artistic Representations of Landscape in Republican and Augustan Rome*, Princeton, NJ.

Lebedev, A. 1998. 'The Justice of Chiron (Titanomachia, fr. 6 and 11 B.)', *Philologus* 142: 3–10.

Legras, L. 1905. *Les légendes thébaines dans l'épopée et la tragédie grecques*, Paris.

Lehnus, L. 1972. 'Note stesicoree (Pap.Oxy. 2506 e 2619)', *SCO* 21: 52–5.

Lemerle, P. 1986. *Byzantine Humanism. The First Phase. Notes and Remarks on Education and Culture from First Origins to the 10th century* (trans.: Paris 1971), Canberra.

Lemos, A. 1991. *Archaic Pottery of Chios*, Oxford.

Lendle, O. 1992. *Einführung in die griechische Geschichtsschreibung*, Darmstadt.

Leone, P.L. 1968. 'La *Presa di Troia* di Trifiodoro', *Vichiana* 5: 59–108.

Lesky, A. 1937. 'Peleus', *RE* xix.1: 271–308.
  1966. *A History of Greek Literature* (trans.: Bern 1963 2nd edn), London.
  1971. *Geschichte der griechischen Literatur*. 3rd edn, Bern.
Létoublon, F. 2008. 'Λύτο γούνατα. D'Homère aux romans grecs', in D. Auger and J. Peigney (eds.), *Phileuripidès. Mélanges offerts à F. Jouan*, Nanterre: 711–23.
LfgrE = *Lexikon des frühgriechischen epos*, Göttingen 1955–2010.
Liapis, V. 2011. *A Commentary on the* Rhesus *Attributed to Euripides*, Oxford.
LIMC = *Lexicon iconographicum mythologiae classicae*, Zurich and Munich 1981–97.
Livrea, E. 1968. *Colluto. Il Ratto di Elena*, Bologna.
  1998. 'Nuovi frammenti della *Telegonia*', *ZPE* 122: 1–5.
  2002. 'Il *Philoctetes* di Euforione', *ZPE* 139: 35–9.
Lloyd-Jones, H. 1972. 'Stasinos and the *Cypria*', *Stasinos* 4: 115–22.
  1996. *Sophocles. Fragments*, Cambridge, MA.
  2002. 'Curses and Divine Anger in Early Greek Epic. The Pisander Scholion', *CQ* 52: 1–14.
Löffler, I. 1963. *Die Melampodie. Versuch einer Rekonstruktion des Inhalts*, Meisenheim am Glan.
López-Ruiz, C. 2009. 'Mopsos and Cultural Exchange between Greeks and Locals in Cilicia', in U. Dill and Chr. Walde (eds.), *Ancient Myth. Media, Transformations and Sense-Constructions / Antike Mythen. Medien, Transformationen und Konstruktionen*, Berlin: 487–501.
Lord, A. B. 1954. 'General Introduction', in Parry, Lord, and Bynum 1954: i.3–20.
  1960. *The Singer of Tales*, Cambridge, MA (2nd edn 2000 by S. Mitchell and G. Nagy).
  1986. 'The Merging of Two Worlds. Oral and Written Poetry as Carriers of Ancient Values', in J. M. Foley (ed.), *Oral Tradition in Literature*, Columbia, MO: 19–64.
Lorenz, K. 2008. *Bilder machen Räume. Mythenbilder in der pompeianischen Häusern*, Berlin.
  2013. 'Split-screen Aficionados. Heracles on Top of Troy in the Casa di Octavius Quartio', in H. Lovatt and C. Vout (eds.), *Epic Visions. Visuality in Greek and Latin Epic and its Reception*, Cambridge: 218–47.
Lowenstam, S. 1997. 'Talking Vases. The Relationship between the Homeric Poems and Archaic Representations of Epic Myth', *TAPhA* 127: 21–76.
  2008. *As Witnessed by Images. The Trojan War Tradition in Greek and Etruscan Art*, Baltimore, MD.
Lucas de Dios, J. M. 1983. *Sófocles. Fragmentos*, Madrid.
  2008. *Esquilo. Fragmentos, Testimonio*, Madrid.
Ludwig, W. 1965. *Struktur und Einheit der* Metamorphosen *Ovids*, Berlin.
Luppe, W. 2011. 'Die *Palamedes* und die *Polyidos*-Hypothesis P. Mich. inv. 3020 (A)', *ZPE* 176: 52–5.
Lyne, R. O. A. M. 1989. *Words and the Poet*, Oxford.

Macinnes, D. 2007. 'Gainsaying the Prophet. Jocasta, Tiresias, and the Lille Stesichorus', *QUCC* 86: 95–108.
Mackie, C. J. 2011. 'Elysium', in Finkelberg 2011b: 246–7.
McKirahan, R. 2012. *On Aristotle* Posterior Analytics 1.9–18, Bristol.
MacLachlan, B. C. 1997. 'Personal Poetry', in D. E. Gerber (ed.), *A Companion to the Greek Lyric Poets*, Leiden: 135–213.
McLeod, W. 1985. 'The "Epic Canon" of the Borgia Table. Hellenistic Lore or Roman Fraud?', *TAPhA* 115: 153–65.
Magnelli, E. 2008. 'Colluthus' "Homeric" Epyllion', *Ramus* 37: 151–72.
Mahaffy, J. P. 1873–4. 'The Degradation of Odysseus in Greek Literature', *Hermathena* 1: 265–75.
Maingon, A. D. 1989. 'Form and Content in the Lille Stesichorus', *QUCC* 31: 31–56.
Malkin, I. 1998. *The Returns of Odysseus. Colonization and Ethnicity*, Berkeley, CA.
Malten, L. 1911. *Kyrene. Sagengeschichtliche und historische Untersuchungen*, Berlin.
Mancuso, U. 1909. 'La "*Tabula Iliaca*" del Museo Capitolino', *Mem. Accad. Lincei* 5.14: 661–731.
Mann, R. 1994. 'Pindar's Homer and Pindar's Myths', *GRBS* 35: 313–37.
Männlein-Robert, I. 2007. *Stimme, Schrift und Bild. Zum Verhältnis der Künste in der hellenistischen Dichtung*, Heidelberg.
Manton, G. R. 1962. 'Virgil and the Greek Epic. The Tragedy of Euander', *AUMLA* 17: 5–17.
Marangou, L. 1969. *Lakonische Elfenbein- und Beinschnitzereien*, Tübingen.
Maras, D. F. (ed.) 1999. *La Tabula Iliaca di Bovillae*, Boville.
March, J. R. 1987. *The Creative Poet. Studies on the Treatment of Myths in Greek Poetry*, London.
  2001. *Sophocles*. Electra, Warminster.
Mari, M. 2009. 'Cassandra e le altre. Riti di donne nell'*Alessandra* di Licofrone', in C. Cusset and É. Prioux (eds.), *Lycophron, éclats d'obscurité*, Saint-Étienne: 405–40.
Marincola, J. 2001. *Greek Historians*, Oxford.
  (ed.) 2007. *A Companion to Greek and Roman Historiography*, Oxford.
Marks, J. 2002. 'The Junction between the *Kypria* and the *Iliad*', *Phoenix* 56: 1–24.
  2003. 'Alternative Odysseys. The Case of Thoas and Odysseus', *TAPhA* 133: 209–26.
  2008. *Zeus in the Odyssey*, Washington, DC.
  2010. 'Inset Narratives in the Epic Cycle'. *Classics@* 6 (ed. E. Karakantza, The Center for Hellenic Studies of Harvard University; online edn. of December 20, 2010).
Maronitis, D. N. 1973. Ἀναζήτηση καὶ Νόστος τοῦ Ὀδυσσέα. Ἡ Διαλεκτικὴ τῆς Ὀδύσσειας, Athens.
Martin, R. P. 1989. *The Language of Heroes. Speech and Performance in the* Iliad, Ithaca, NY.

Massimilla, G. 1990. 'L' *Elena* di Stesicoro quale premessa ad una ritrattazione', *PP* 45: 370–81.
Mastronarde, D. J. 1994. *Euripides*. Phoenissae, Cambridge.
Matthews, V. J. 1996. *Antimachus of Colophon. Text and Commentary*, Leiden.
Mayer, K. 1996. 'Helen and the ΔΙΟΣ ΒΟΥΛΗ', *AJPh* 117: 1–15.
Meijering, R. 1987. *Literary and Rhetorical Theories in Greek Scholia*, Groningen.
Mele, A. 2001. 'Il corpus epimenideo', in E. Federico and A. Visconti (eds.), *Epimenide cretese*, Naples: 227–76.
Merkelbach, R. 1969. *Untersuchungen zur Odyssee*. 2nd edn, Munich.
  1974. *Kritische Beiträge zu antiken Autoren*, Meisenheim/Glan.
Merkle, S. 1989. *Die Ephemeris belli Troiani des Diktys von Kreta*, Frankfurt/Main.
  1994. 'Telling the True Story of the Trojan War. The Eyewitness Account of Dictys of Crete', in J. Tatum (ed.), *The Search for the Ancient Novel*, Baltimore, MD: 183–96.
Mersinias, S. 1993. 'The Epigrams of Pollianus', *Dodone (Philologia)* 22: 9–30.
Mette, H. J. 1959. *Die Fragmente der Tragödien des Aischylos*, Berlin.
  1963. *Der verlorene Aischylos*, Berlin.
Mheallaigh, K. N. 2008. 'Pseudo-Documentarism and the Limits of Ancient Fiction', *AJPh* 129: 403–31.
Michelakis, P. 2002. *Achilles in Greek Tragedy*, Cambridge.
Miguélez Cavero, L. 2008. *Poems in Context. Greek Poetry in the Egyptian Thebaid 200–600 AD*, Berlin and New York.
Milazzo, A. M. 1984. 'Achille e Polissena in Ditti Cretese. Un romanzo nel romanzo', *Le forme e la storia (Riv. quadrimestr. di studi stor. e lett., Catania. CUECM)* 5: 3–24.
Miller, A. 1982. 'Phthonos and Parphasis. *Nemean* 8.190–4', *GRBS* 23: 111–20.
Miller, M. 1868. *Mélanges de littérature grecque*, Paris.
Mitchell, S. and G. Nagy. 2000. 'Introduction to the Second Edition', in A. B. Lord, *The Singer of Tales*. 2nd edn, Cambridge, MA: vii–xxix.
Möller, M. 2003. 'Der staunende Achill. Eine poetologische Lektüre der *Cygnus*-Episode (Ov. met. 12, 64–176)', *Göttinger Forum Altertumswiss.* 6: 51–66.
Moggi, M. and M. Osanna. 2010. *Pausania. Guida della Grecia. Libro IX. La Beozia.* Milan.
Monro, D. B. 1883. 'On the Fragment of Proclus' Abstract of the Epic Cycle Contained in the Codex Venetus of the *Iliad*', *JHS* 4: 305–34.
  1884. 'The Poems of the Epic Cycle', *JHS* 5: 1–41.
  1901. 'Homer and the Cyclic Poets', in Id., *Homer's Odyssey. Books XIII–XXIV*, Oxford: 340–84.
Montanari, F. 1995. 'The Mythographus Homericus', in J. G. Abbenes, S. R. Slings, and I. Sluiter (eds.), *Greek Literary Theory after Aristotle. A Collection of Papers in Honour of D. M. Schenkeveld*, Amsterdam: 135–72.
Montanari, F. and P. Ascheri (eds.) 2002. *Omero tremila anni dopo*, Rome.

Montanari, F. and A. Rengakos (eds.) 2006. *La poésie épique grecque*, Vandoeuvre–Geneva.
Montanari, F., A. Rengakos, and C. Tsagalis (eds.) 2012. *Homeric Contexts. Neonalysis and the Interpretation of Oral Poetry*, Berlin.
Montiglio, S. 2011. *From Villain to Hero. Odysseus in Ancient Thought*, Ann Arbor, MI.
Moran, W. S. 1975. 'Μιμνήσκομαι and "Remembering" Epic Stories in Homer and the Hymns', *QUCC* 20: 195–211.
Moret, J.-M. 1984. *Œdipe, la Sphinx et les Thébains. Essai de mythologie iconographique*, Geneva.
Morgan, J. 2008. 'Intertextuality. The Greek Novel', in Whitmarsh 2008: 218–27.
  2009. 'Petronius and Greek Literature', in J. Prag and I. Repath (eds.), *Petronius. A Handbook*, Malden, MA: 32–47.
Morris, I. and B. Powell (eds.) 1997. *A New Companion to Homer*, Leiden.
Morris, S. 1995. 'The Sacrifice of Astyanax. Near Eastern Contributions to the Siege of Troy', in Carter and Morris 1995: 221–45.
Morrison, J. 1992. *Homeric Misdirection. False Predictions in the* Iliad, Ann Arbor, MI.
Mosshammer, A. 1979. *The Chronicle of Eusebius and Greek Chronographic Tradition*, Lewisburg, PA.
Most, G. W. 2006. *Hesiod*. Theogony, Works and Days, Testimonia, Cambridge, MA.
  2010. 'Laocoons', in J. Farrell and M. C. Putnam (eds.), *A Companion to Vergil's* Aeneid *and Its Tradition*, Chicester: 325–40.
Mülder, D. 1910. *Die* Ilias *und ihre Quellen*, Berlin.
Mulder, H. 1955. 'Fata vetant. De imitandi componendique in Achilleide ratione Statiana', in P. de Jonge *et al.* (eds.), *Ut pictura poesis. Studio latino P. J. Enk septuagenario oblata*, Leiden: 119–28.
Müller, K. W. 1829. *De Cyclo Graecorum epico et poetis cyclicis*, Leipzig.
Müller, C. W. 1976. 'Chariton von Aphrodisias und die Theorie des Romans in der Antike', *A&A* 22: 115–36.
Müller, K. O. 1840. *History of the Literature of Ancient Greece*. i, London.
  1844. *Orchomenos und die Minyer*. 2nd edn, Breslau.
Murnaghan, S. 1997. 'Equal Honor and Future Glory. The Plan of Zeus in the *Iliad*', in D. H. Roberts, F. M. Dunn, and D. Fowler (eds.), *Classical Closure. Reading the End in Greek and Latin Literature*, Princeton, NJ: 23–42.
Murray, G. 1934. *The Rise of the Greek Epic*. 4th edn, Oxford.
Naber, S. A. 1901. 'Ad Charitonem', *Mnemosyne* 29: 92–9.
Nachmanson, E. 1941. *Der griechische Buchtitel. Einige Beobachtungen*, Göteborg.
Nagy, G. 1990a. *Greek Mythology and Poetics*, Ithaca, NY.
  1990b. *Pindar's Homer. The Lyric Possession of an Epic Past*. Baltimore, MD.
  1996a. *Homeric Questions*, Austin, TX.
  1996b. *Poetry as Performance*, Cambridge.
  1999. *The Best of the Achaeans*. 2nd edn; 1st edn 1979, Baltimore, MD.

2001. 'Homeric Poetry and Problems of Multiformity. The "Panathenaic Bottleneck"', *CPh* 96: 109–19.

2003. *Homeric Responses*, Austin, TX.

2009a. *Homer the Classic*, Washington, DC.

2009b. 'Hesiod and the ancient biographical tradition', in F. Montanari, A. Rengakos, C. Tsagalis (eds.), *The Brill Companion to Hesiod*, Leiden: 271–311.

2010a. *Homer the Preclassic*, Berkeley, CA.

2010b. 'Aristarchus and the Epic Cycle', *Classics@* 6 (ed. E. Karakantza, The Center for Hellenic Studies of Harvard University; online edition of December 20, 2010).

Narten, J. 1968. 'Zum "proterodynamischen" Wurzelpräsens', in *Pratidānam. Indian, Iranian and Indo-European Studies presented to F. B. J. Kuyper*, Leiden: 9–19.

Neils, J. 1987. *The Youthful Deeds of Theseus*, Rome.

1992. 'The Panathenaia. An Introduction', in Ead. (ed.), *Goddess and Polis. The Panathenaic Festival in Ancient Athens*, Princeton, NJ: 13–27.

Neils, J. and S. Woodford. 1994. 'Theseus', in *LIMC* vii.1: 922–51.

Nelson, S. 2005. 'Hesiod', in Foley 2005a: 330–43.

Newlands, C. E. 2005. 'Ovid', in Foley 2005a: 476–91.

Nisetich, F. J. 1989. *Pindar and Homer*, Baltimore, MD.

Nitzsch, G. W. 1830–7. *De Historia Homeri maximeque de scriptorum carminum aetate meletemata*. i–ii, Hanover.

1852. *Die Sagenpoesie der Griechen*, Braunschweig.

1862. *Beiträge zur Geschichte der epischen Poesie der Griechen*, Leipzig.

Noack, F. 1892a. 'Review of F. Kehmptzow, *De Quinti Smyrnaei fontibus et mythopoeia*, Kiel 1891', in *Götting. gel. Anz.* 1.20: 769–812.

1892b. 'Die Quellen des Tryphiodoros', *Hermes* 27: 452–63.

Norden, E. 1957. *P. Vergilius Maro: Aeneis Buch VI*. 4th edn, Darmstadt.

Notopoulos, J. A. 1964. 'Studies in Early Greek Oral Poetry', *HSCPh* 68: 1–77.

Noussia-Fantuzzi, M. 2013. 'A Scenario for Stesichorus' Portrayal of the Monster Geryon in the *Geryoneis*', *Trends in Classics* 5: 234–59.

Nünlist, R. 1998. *Poetologische Bildersprache in der frühgriechischen Dichtung*, Stuttgart and Leipzig.

2009a. 'Narratological Concepts in Greek Scholia', in Grethlein and Rengakos 2009: 63–83.

2009b. *The Ancient Critic at Work. Terms and Concepts of Literary Criticism in Greek Scholia*, Cambridge.

Obbink, D. 1996. *Philodemus On Piety. Part 1*, Oxford.

2005. '4708. Archilochus. Elegies (More of VI 854 and XXX 2507)', in *The Oxyrhynchus Papyri*. lxix, London: 18–42.

Oinas, F. J. 1978. 'Russian byliny', in F. J. Oinas (ed.), *Heroic Epic and Saga*, Bloomington, IN: 236–56.

O'Keeffe, K. O'B. 1990. *Visible Song. Transitional Literacy in Old English Verse*, Cambridge.

Olivieri, O. 2004. 'Analogie e rovesciamenti tra i Sette e gli Epigoni', in Angeli Bernardini 2004: 79–91.
  2010. 'La geografia mitica delle imprese di Alcmeone dall'epica minore alla lirica corale', in Cingano 2010a: 299–314.
  2013. 'Alcmeone, un eroe itinerante a Corinto. I frammenti dell'omonima tragedia di Euripide', in Angeli Bernardini 2013: 157–68.
Olson, S. D. 1995. *Blood and Iron. Stories and Storytelling in Homer's* Odyssey, Leiden.
  2006. *Athenaeus: The Learned Banqueteers*. i. *Books 1–3.106e*, Cambridge, MA.
  2012. *The Homeric Hymn to Aphrodite and Related Texts*, Berlin.
Olson, S. D. and A. Sens. 1999. *Matro of Pitane and the Tradition of Epic Parody in the Fourth Century BCE*, Atlanta, GA.
  2000. *Archestratus of Gela. Greek Culture and Cuisine in the Fourth Century BCE*, Oxford.
Oricchio, A. 2002. 'Il mito di Aiace e Cassandra attraverso le immagini', in L. Cerchiai (ed.), *L'iconografia di Atena con elmo frigio in Italia meridionale (Atti della giornata di studi, Fisciano, 12 giugno 1998)*, Naples: 81–99.
Orsini, P. 1972. *Collouthos. L'enlèvement d'Hélène*, Paris.
  1974. 'Tryphiodore et la μίμησις', *Pallas* 21: 3–12.
O'Sullivan, T. 2007. 'Walking with Odysseus. The Portico Frame of the *Odyssey* Landscapes', *AJPh* 128: 497–532.
Otis, B. 1970. *Ovid as an Epic Poet*. 2nd edn, Cambridge.
Padgett, J. (ed.) 1993. *Vase Painting in Italy. Red-Figure and Related Works in the Museum of Fine Arts, Boston*, Boston, MA.
Page, D. L. 1953. *Corinna*, London.
  1955. *Sappho and Alcaeus. An Introduction to the Study of Ancient Lesbian Poetry*, Oxford.
  1973. 'Stesichorus. The Sack of Troy and the Wooden Horse (P.Oxy. 2619 and 2803)', *PCPhS* 19: 47–65.
Paley, F. A. 1879. *Quintus Smyrnaeus and the "Homer" of the Tragic Poets*. 2nd edn, London.
Pallantza, E. 2005. *Der troische Krieg in der nachhomerischen Literatur bis zum 5. Jahrhundert v. Chr.*, Stuttgart.
Pantelia, M. C. 1995. 'Theocritus at Sparta. Homeric Allusions in Theocritus' *Idyll* 18', *Hermes* 123: 76–81.
Papaioannou, S. 2007. *Redesigning Achilles. 'Recycling' the Epic Cycle in the 'Little Iliad' (Ovid*, Metamorphoses *12.1–13.622)*, Berlin.
Pariente, A. 1992. 'Le monument argien des *Sept contre Thèbes*', in M. Piérart (ed.), *Polydipsion Argos*, Athens and Paris: 195–229.
Parlato, G. 2007. 'I "modernismi" linguistici dei *Cypria*. Una diversa valutazione', *RFIC* 135: 5–36.
Parmentier, L. 1914. 'L'Épigramme du tombeau de Midas et la question du cycle épique', *Bull. Acad. royale de Belgique (Classe des Lettres)*: 341–94.

Parry, A. (ed.) 1972. *The Making of Homeric Verse: The Collected Papers of M. Parry*, Oxford.
Parry, M. 1928. *Les formules et la métrique d'Homère*, Paris (trans. in Parry 1972: 191–239).
  1930. 'Studies in the Epic Technique of Oral Verse-Making. i. Homer and Homeric Style', *HSCPh* 41: 73–147 (= Parry 1972: 266–324).
Parry, M., A. B. Lord and D. Bynum (eds.) 1954. *Serbocroatian Heroic Songs*, Cambridge, MA.
Paschal, G. W. 1904. *A Study of Quintus of Smyrna*, Diss., Chicago.
Patillon, M. and G. Bolognesi (eds.) 1997. *Aelius Théon*. Progymnasmata, Paris.
Pavano, A. 1998. 'Le redazioni latine e il presunto originale greco dell'opera di Darete Frigio', *Sileno* 24: 207–18.
Pavese, C. O. 1972. *Tradizioni e generi poetici della Grecia arcaica*, Rome.
Payne, H. 1931. *Necrocorinthia*, Oxford.
PCG = Kassel, R. and C. Austin. 1983–. *Poetae comici Graeci*, Berlin.
Pearson, A. C. 1917. *The Fragments of Sophocles, Edited with Additional Notes from the Papers of Sir R. C. Jebb and Dr W. G. Headlam*, Cambridge.
PEG = Bernabé, A. 1996. *Poetae epici Graeci. Testimonia et fragmenta*. i, 2nd edn (1st edn 1987), Stuttgart and Leipzig.
PEG ii.1 = Bernabé, A. 2004. *Poetae epici Graeci*. Pars II. Fasc. 1. *Orphicorum et Orphicis similium testimonia et fragmenta*, Munich and Leipzig.
Pellin, A. 2007. 'Un epos ellenistico su papiro, l'*Epyllium Diomedis* (fr. ep. adesp. 2 Powell = *P. Berol.* 10566)', in G. Cresci Marrone and A. Pistellato (eds.), *Studi in ricordo di F. Broilo* (Atti del Convegno, Venezia, 14–15 ottobre 2005), Padua: 471–85.
Pellizer, E. 1983. 'Sulla cronologia, la vita e le opere di Semonide Amorgino', *QUCC* 14: 17–28.
Pellizer, E. and G. Tedeschi (eds.) 1990. *Semonides. Testimonia et fragmenta*, Rome.
Peradotto, J. 1985. 'Prophecy Degree Zero', in B. Gentili and G. Paioni (eds.), *Oralità. Cultura, letteratura, discorso*, Rome: 429–59.
  1990. *Man in the Middle Voice. Name and Narration in the* Odyssey, Princeton, NJ.
Perale, M. 2010. '*Il. Parv.* Fr. 21 Bernabé e la *Gorgo* di Simia di Rodi', in Cingano 2010: 497–518.
Perry, B. E. 1967. *The Ancient Romances. A Literary–Historical Account of Their Origins*, Berkeley, CA.
Pestalozzi, H. 1945. *Die Achilleis als Quelle der* Ilias, Erlenbach and Zurich.
Peters, M. 1989. 'Indogermanische Chronik 33', *Die Sprache* 33: 228–30.
Petrain, D. 2010. 'More Inscriptions from the *Tabulae Iliacae*', *ZPE* 174: 51–6.
  2012. 'The Archaeology of the Epigrams from the *Tabulae Iliacae*. Adaptation, Allusion, Alteration', *Mnemosyne* 65: 597–635.
  2014. *Homer in Stone: The Tabulae Iliacae in their Roman Context*, Cambridge.

Petropoulos, I. 2012. 'The Telemachy and the Cyclic Nostoi', in Montanari, Rengakos, and Tsagalis 2012: 291–308.
Pfeiffer, R. 1949. *Callimachus*. i. *Fragmenta*, Oxford.
　1968. *History of Classical Scholarship*. i. *From the Beginnings to the End of the Hellenistic Age*, Oxford.
Phillips, E. D. 1953. 'Odysseus in Italy', *JHS* 73: 53–67.
　1959. 'The Comic Odysseus', *G&R* 6: 58–67.
Piccirilli, L. 1997. 'Corinto e l'occidente. Aspetti di politica internazionale fino al V secolo a.C.', in *Corinto e l'occidente* (Atti del trentaquattresimo Convegno di studi sulla Magna Grecia, Taranto, 7–11 ottobre 1994), Naples: 143–76.
Pipili, M. 1987. *Laconian Iconography of the Sixth Century B.C.*, Oxford.
　2006. 'Laconian Pottery' in N. Kaltsas (ed.), *Athens–Sparta*, New York: 123–7.
Plazenet, L. 1995. 'Le Nil et son delta dans les romans grecs', *Phoenix* 49: 5–22.
PMG = Page, D. L. 1962. *Poetae melici Graeci*, Oxford.
PMGF = Davies, M. 1991. *Poetarum melicorum Graecorum fragmenta*, Oxford.
Pollitt, J. J. 1986. *Art in the Hellenistic Age*, Cambridge.
Pomtow, H. von 1908. 'Studien zu den Weihgeschenken und der Topographie von Delphi III–IV', *Klio* 8: 186–205 and 302–25.
　1924. 'Delphoi', *RE* Suppl. iv: 1189–432.
Pöschl, V. 1962. *The Art of Vergil* (trans.: Wiesbaden 1950), Ann Arbor, MI.
Potter, M. A. 1902. *Sohrab and Rustem. The Epic Theme of a Combat between Father and Son*, London.
Powell, B. 1991. *Homer and the Origin of the Greek Alphabet*, Cambridge.
Powell, J. E. 1936. *The Rendel Harris Papyri of Woodbrooke College, Birmingham*, Cambridge.
PPM = Pugliese Carratelli, G. (ed.) 1990–2003. *Pompei. Pitture e mosaici*. 10 vols., Rome.
Prag, A. J. N. W. 1985. *The Oresteia. Iconographic and Narrative Traditions*, Warminster.
Prauscello, L. 2008. 'Colluthus' Pastoral Traditions. Narrative Strategies and Bucolic Criticism in the Abduction of Helen', *Ramus* 37: 173–90.
Preiser, C. 2000. *Euripides. Telephos*, Hildesheim.
Prinz, F. 1979. *Gründungsmythen und Sagenchronologie*, Munich.
Purves, A. C. 2010. *Space and Time in Ancient Greek Narrative*, Cambridge.
Putnam, M. C. J. 1998a. *Virgil's Epic Designs. Ekphrasis in the* Aeneid, New Haven, CT.
　1998b. 'Dido's murals and Virgilian ekphrasis', *HSCPh* 98: 243–75.
Rabe, H. 1913. *Hermogenis opera*, Leipzig.
Radloff, W. 1885 = 1990. *Samples of Folk Literature from the North Turkic Tribes*. 'Preface' to Volume v: *The Dialect of the Kara-Kirgiz* (trans. by G. Böttcher Sherman and A. B. Davis), *Oral Tradition* 5: 73–90.
Radt, S. L. 1958. *Pindars zweiter und sechster Paian*, Amsterdam.

1983. 'Sophokles in seinen Fragmenten', in J. de Romilly (ed.), *Sophocle (Entret. Ant. class.* 29), Vandoeuvres–Geneva: 185–222.

1999. *Tragicorum Graecorum fragmenta*. iv. *Sophocles*. 2nd edn, Göttingen.

RE = *Real-Encyclopädie der classischen Altertumswissenschaft*, Stuttgart–Munich 1893–1980.

Rea, J. R. 1972. 'Triphiodorus, Fall of Troy, 391–402', in Id., *The Oxyrhynchus Papyri vol. XLI*, London: 9–10.

Ready, J. 2005. '*Iliad* 22.123–128 and the Erotics of Supplication', *CB* 81: 145–64.

2007. 'Toil and Trouble. The Acquisition of Spoils in the *Iliad*', *TAPhA* 137: 3–43.

Reckford, K. J. 1964. 'Helen in the *Iliad*', *GRBS* 5: 5–20.

Reece, S. 1988. 'Homeric Influence in Stesichorus' *Nostoi*', *Bull. Amer. Soc. Papyrologists* 15: 1–8.

1993. *The Stranger's Welcome. Oral Theory and the Aesthetics of the Homeric Hospitality Scene*, Ann Arbor, MI.

1994. 'The Cretan Odyssey. A Lie Truer than Truth', *AJPh* 115: 157–73.

2011. 'Penelope's "Early Recognition" of Odysseus from a Neoanalytic and Oral Perspective', *College Literature* 38: 101–17.

Reichel, M. 1990. 'Retardationstechniken in der Ilias', in W. Kullmann and M. Reichel (eds.), *Der Übergang von der Mündlichkeit zur Literatur bei den Griechen*, Tübingen: 125–51.

1994. *Fernbeziehungen in der Ilias*, Tübingen.

2011. 'Epische Dichtung', in B. Zimmermann (ed.), *Handbuch der griechischen Literatur der Antike*, Munich: 7–77.

Reichel, M. and A. Rengakos (eds.) 2002. *Epea pteroenta. Beiträge zur Homerforschung. Festschrift für W. Kullmann zum 75. Geburtstag*, Stuttgart.

Reichl, K. 1992. *Turkic Oral Epic Poetry. Traditions, Forms, Poetic Structure*, New York.

2000. *Singing the Past. Turkic and Medieval Heroic Poetry*, Ithaca, NY.

Reinhardt, K. 1961. *Die* Ilias *und ihr Dichter*, Göttingen.

1997. 'The Judgement of Paris', in G. M. Wright and P. V. Jones (eds.), *Homer. German Scholarship in Translation* (trans.: Frankfurt 1938), Oxford: 170–91.

Reinhardt, U. 2008. 'Hellenistische Reliefbecher mit Szenen aus Dramen des Euripides und die antiken Anfänge textbegleitender Illustrierung', *WS* 121: 85–102.

Reitzenstein, R. 1893. *Epigramm und Skolion. Ein Beitrag zur geschichte der Alexandrinischen Dichtung*, Giessen.

Rengakos, A. 1995. 'Zeit und Gleichzeitigkeit in den homerischen Epen', *A&A* 41: 1–32.

1998. 'Zur Zeitstruktur der *Odyssee*', *WS* 111: 45–66.

2004. 'Die Argonautika und das "kyklische Gedicht". Bemerkungen zur Erzähltechnik des griechischen Epos', in A. Bierl, A. Schmitt, and A. Willi (eds.), *Antike Literatur in neuer Deutung*, Munich and Leipzig: 277–304.

2006. 'Homer and the Historians. The Influence of Epic Narrative Technique on Herodotus and Thucydides', in Montanari and Rengakos 2006: 183–209.

- 2007. 'The Smile of Achilles, or the *Iliad* and its Mirror-Image', in M. Païzi-Apostolopoulou, A. Rengakos and C. Tsagalis (eds.), *Contests and Rewards in the Homeric Epics (Proceedings of the 10th International Symposium on the Odyssey, 15–19 September 2004)*, Ithaki: 101–10.
- Repath, I. D. 2005. 'Achilles Tatius' *Leucippe and Cleitophon*. What Happened Next?', *CQ* 55: 250–65.
- Revermann, M. and P. Wilson (eds.) 2008. *Performance, Reception, Iconography. Studies in Honour of O. Taplin*, Oxford.
- Reynolds, D. F. 1995. *Heroic Poets, Poetic Heroes. The Ethnography of Performance in an Arabic Oral Epic Tradition*, Ithaca, NY.
- Richardson, L. Jr. 1988. *Pompeii. An Architectural History*. Baltimore, MD.
- Richardson, N. J. 1974. *The Homeric Hymn to Demeter*, Oxford.
  - 1992. 'Aristotle's Reading of Homer and Its Background', in R. Lamberton and J. J. Keaney (eds.), *Homer's Ancient Readers. The Hermeneutics of Greek Epic's Earliest Exegetes*, Princeton, NJ: 30–40.
  - 1993. *The* Iliad. *A Commentary*. vi. *Books 21–24*, Cambridge.
  - 2010. *Three Homeric Hymns: to Apollo, Hermes, and Aphrodite (Hymns 3, 4, and 5)*, Cambridge.
- Ridgway, B. S. 2000. *Hellenistic Sculpture*. ii. *The Styles of* ca. *200–100 BC.*, Madison, WI.
- Rimell, V. 2002. *Petronius and the Anatomy of Fiction*, Cambridge.
- Risch, E. 1974. *Wortbildung der homerischen Sprache*. 2nd edn, Berlin.
- Robbins, E. 1993. 'The Education of Achilles', *QUCC* 45: 7–20.
- Robert, C. 1881. *Bild und Lied*, Berlin.
  - 1890. *Homerische Becher*, Berlin.
  - 1915. *Oidipus. Geschichte eines poetischen Stoffs im griechischen Altertum*, Berlin.
  - 1921. *Die griechische Heldensage*. iii. *Die grossen Heldenepen*. i: *Die Argonauten. Der Thebanische Kreis*. 4th edn, Berlin.
- Robertson, M. 1970. 'Ibycus: Polycrates, Troilus, Polyxena', *BICS* 17: 11–15.
  - 1990. 'Troilos and Polyxene. Notes on a Changing Legend', in J.-P. Descoeudres (ed.), *Eumousia. Ceramic and Iconographic Studies in Honour of A. Cambitoglou*, Sydney: 63–70.
- Robiano, P. 2000. 'La citation poétique dans le roman érotique grec', *REA* 102: 509–29.
- Robinson, D. S. 1940. 'The Food of Achilles', *CR* 54: 177–82.
- Rohde, E. 1914. *Der griechische Roman und seiner Vorläufer*. 3rd edn, Leipzig.
- Rosati, G. 2001. 'Mito e potere nell'epica di Ovidio', *MD* 46: 39–61.
  - 2002. 'Narrative Techniques and Narrative Structures in the *Metamorphoses*', in B. W. Boyd (ed.), *Brill's Companion to Ovid*, Leiden: 271–304.
- Rotroff, S. I. 1982. *Hellenistic Pottery. Athenian and Imported Moldmade Bowls*, Princeton, NJ.
- Ruijgh, C. J. 1971. *Autour de 'τε épique'. Études sur la syntaxe grecque*, Amsterdam.

2011. 'Mycenaean and Homeric Language', in Y. Duhoux and A. Morpurgo Davies (eds.), *A Companion to Linear B. Mycenaean Greek Texts and their World*, Leuven: ii. 253–98.

Russo, J. A. 1978. 'How, and What, Does Homer Communicate? The Medium and Message of Homeric Verse', in E. A. Havelock and J. P. Hershbell (eds.), *Communication Arts in the Ancient World*, New York: 37–52.

Rutherford, I. 2001. *Pindar's Paeans. A Reading of the Fragments with Survey of the Genre*, Oxford.

2012. 'The Catalogue of Women within the Greek Epic Tradition. Allusion, Intertextuality and Traditional Referentiality', in Andersen and Haug 2012a: 152–67.

Rzach, A. 1921. 'Kinaithon', *RE* xi: 462–3.

1922. 'Kyklos', *RE* xi: 2347–435.

Sachs, J. 2010. 'On the Road. Travel, Antiquarianism, Philology', in S. Gurd (ed.), *Philology and Its Histories*, Columbus, OH: 127–47.

Sadurska, A. 1964. *Les Tables Iliaques*, Warsaw.

1986. 'Equus Troianus', in *LIMC* iii. 1: 813–17.

Sakellariou, M. B. 1958. *La Migration grecque en Ionie*, Athens.

1990. *Between Memory and Oblivion. The Transmission of Early Greek Historical Traditions*, Athens.

Salmon, J. B. 1984. *Wealthy Corinth. A History of the City to 338 BC*, Oxford.

Salvador, J. A. 1996. 'Nota crítica a *Alcmaeonis*, fr. 1 Bern. = 1 Dav.', *Eikasmos* 7: 21–4.

Santiago, R. A. 1981. 'La fusión de dos mitos tebanos', *Faventia* 3: 19–30.

Santoro, S. 2005. 'I temi iliaci nella pittura pompeiana', in G. Burzacchini (ed.), *Troia tra realtà e leggenda*, Parma: 97–123.

Saussure, F. de 1916 = 1972, *Cours de linguistique générale* (ed. T. De Mauro; 1st edn 1916), Paris.

Sbardella, L. 2000. *Filita. Testimonianze e frammenti poetici*, Rome.

Scafoglio, G. 2004a. 'Proclo e il ciclo epico', *Göttinger Forum Altertumswiss.* 7: 39–57.

2004b. 'La questione ciclica', *RPh* 78: 289–301.

2005. 'Virgilio e Stesicoro. Una ricerca sulla *Tabula Iliaca Capitolina*', *RhM* 148: 113–25.

2006. 'Two Fragments of the Epic Cycle', *GRBS* 46: 5–11.

Scaife, R. 1995. 'The *Kypria* and its Early Reception', *ClAnt* 14: 164–91.

Schachter, A. 1967. 'The Theban Wars', *Phoenix* 21: 1–10.

Schade, G. 2003. *Stesichoros. Papyrus Oxyrhynchus 2359, 3876, 2619, 2803*, Leiden.

Schadewaldt, W. 1952 = 1965. 'Einblick in die Erfindung der *Ilias*. *Ilias* und *Memnonis*', in *Varia variorum. Festgabe für K. Reinhardt*, Münster and Cologne: 13–48 (= Id., *Von Homers Welt und Werk*. 4th edn, Stuttgart 1965: 155–202).

1966. *Iliasstudien*. 3rd edn, Darmstadt.

Scheer, T. S. 1993. *Mythische Vorväter: zur Bedeutung griechischer Heroenmythen im Selbstverständnis kleinasiatischer Städte*, Munich.

Schefold, K. 1957. *Die Wände Pompejis. Topographisches Verzeichnis der Bildmotive*, Berlin.
  1964. *Frühgriechische Sagenbilder*, Munich.
  1975. *Wort und Bild. Studien zur Gegenwart der Antike*, Mainz.
  1976. 'Bilderbücher als Vorlagen römischer Sarkophage', *MÉFRA* 88: 759–814.
  1978. *Götter- und Heldensagen der Griechen in der spätarchaischen Kunst*, Munich (trans. Cambridge 1992).
  1993. *Götter- und Heldensagen der Griechen in der früh- und hocharchaischen Kunst*, Munich.
Schefold, K. and F. Jung. 1989. *Die Sagen von den Argonauten, von Theben und Troia in der klassischen und hellenistischen Kunst*, Munich.
Schein, S. L. 1984. *The Mortal Hero. An Introduction to Homer's Iliad*, Berkeley, CA.
Scheliha, R. von. 1943. *Patroklos*, Basel.
Schierl, P. 2006. *Die Tragödien des Pacuvius*, Berlin.
Schischwani, S. 1994. *Mündliche Quellen der Odyssee*. Diss., Freiburg.
Schmid, S. G. 2006. *Boire pour Apollon. Céramique hellénistique et banquets dans le Sanctuaire d'Apollon Daphnéphoros*, Gollion.
Schmidt, E. G. 1999. 'Quintus von Smyrna – der schlechteste Dichter des Altertums?', *Phasis* 1: 139–50.
Schmidt, J. L. 1885. 'Ulixes posthomericus', *Berliner Studien für classische Philologie und Archäologie* 2: 399–497.
Schmitt, R. 1967. *Dichtung und Dichtersprache in Indogermanischer Zeit*, Wiesbaden.
  1990. 'Zur Sprache der Kyklischen Kypria', in W. Görler and S. Koster (eds.), *Pratum Saraviense. Festgabe für P. Steinmetz*, Stuttgart: 11–24.
Schmitz, T.A. 2005. 'Nonnos und seine Tradition', in S. Alkier and R. B. Hays (eds.), *Die Bibel im Dialog der Schriften. Konzepte intertextueller Bibellektüre*, Tübingen: 195–216.
Schneidewin, F. W. 1852. 'Die Sage vom Ödipus', *Abhandl. König. Gesellsch. Wiss. Göttingen*: 1–50.
Schoch, M. 1997. *Beiträge zur Topographie Akarnaniens in klassischer und hellenistischer Zeit*, Würzburg.
Schoeck, G. 1961. Ilias *und* Aithiopis, Diss., Zurich.
Schönberger, O. 1993. *Kolluthos. Raub der Helena*, Würzburg.
Schultz, W. 1916–24. 'Teumessischer Fuchs', in *ALGRM*: v. 429–35.
Schulze, W. 1892. *Quaestiones epicae*, Gütersloh.
Schwartz, E. 1924. *Die* Odyssee, Munich.
  1940. 'Der Name Homeros', *Hermes* 75: 1–9.
Schwartz, J. 1960. *Pseudo-Hesiodeia. Recherches sur la composition, la diffusion et la disparition ancienne d'œuvres attribuées à Hésiode*, Leiden.
Scodel, R. 1982. 'The Achaean Wall and the Myth of Destruction', *HSCPh* 86: 33–50.
  2001. 'Poetic Authority and Oral Tradition on Hesiod and Pindar', in J. Watson (ed.), *Speaking Volumes. Orality and Literacy in the Greek and Roman World*, Leiden: 109–38.

2008a. 'Stupid, Pointless Wars', *TAPhA* 138: 219–35.
2008b. 'Zielinkski's Law Reconsidered', *TAPhA* 138: 107–25.
2012. 'Hesiod and the Epic Cycle', in Montanari, Rengakos and Tsagalis 2012: 501–16.
Scott Smith, R. and S. Trzaskoma. 2007. *Apollodorus' Library and Hyginus' Fabulae. Two Handbooks of Greek Mythology*, Indianapolis, IN.
Scott, W. C. 2009. *The Artistry of the Homeric Simile*, Hanover, NH.
SEG = 1923–. *Supplementum epigraphicum Graecum*, Amsterdam.
Segal, C. 2005. 'Il corpo e l'io nelle *Metamorfosi* di Ovidio', in Barchiesi 2005: xv–ci.
Sekunda, N. 1992. *The Persian Army 560–330 BC*, London.
Sens, A. 2006. 'Τίπτε γένος τοὐμὸν ζητεῖς; The *Batrachomyomachia*, Hellenistic Epic Parody, and Early Epic', in Montanari and Rengakos 2006: 215–44.
Serbeti, E. 1992. 'Koroibos I', in *LIMC* vi.1: 103.
Severyns, A. 'Review of Bethe 1922'. *Revue Belge philol. hist.* 5: 132–40.
  1925. 'L'*Éthiopide* d'Arctinos et la question du Cycle épique', *RPh* 49: 153–83.
  1928. *Le Cycle épique dans l'école d'Aristarque*, Paris.
  1932. 'Pindare et les *Chants Cypriens*', *AC* 1: 261–71.
  1938. *Recherches sur la* Chrestomathie *de Proclos. Le Codex 239 de Photius.* ii. *Texte, Traduction, Commentaire*, Paris.
  1953. *Recherches sur la* Chrestomathie *de Proclos.* iii. *La* Vita Homeri *et les sommaires du Cycle*, Paris.
  1962. 'Ulysse en Élide', *AC* 31: 15–24.
Sewell-Rutter, N. J. 2008. *Guilt by Descent. Moral Inheritance and Decision Making in Greek Tragedy*, New York.
SH = Lloyd-Jones, H. and P. J. Parsons. 1983. *Supplementum Hellenisticum*, Berlin.
Shapiro, H. A. 1989. *Art and Cult under the Tyrants in Athens*, Mainz.
  1990. 'Old and New Heroes. Narrative, Composition, and Subject in Attic Black-Figure', *ClAnt* 9: 114–48.
  1993. *Personifications in Greek Art. The Representation of Abstract Concepts 600–400 BC*, Zurich.
  1994. *Myth into Art. Poet and Painter in Classical Greece*, London.
Shipp, G. P. 1972. *Studies in the Language of Homer.* 2nd edn, Cambridge.
Shorrock, R. 2001. *The Challenge of epic. Allusive engagement in the* Dionysiaca *of Nonnus*, Leiden.
  2005. 'Nonnus', in Foley 2005a: 374–85.
  2007. 'Nonnus, Quintus and the Sack of Troy', in Baumbach and Bär 2007a: 379–91.
  2011. *The Myth of Paganism. Nonnus, Dionysus and the World of Late Antiquity*, London.
Sider, D. 2010. 'Greek Verse on a Vase by Douris', *Hesperia* 79: 541–54.
Siegmann, E. 1987. *Homer. Vorlesungen über die* Odyssee, Würzburg.
Simon, E. 1975. *Pergamon und Hesiod*, Mainz.
  1981. *Das Satyrspiel* Sphinx *des Aischylos*, Heidelberg.

 1992. 'Momos', in *LIMC* vi.1: 649–50.

Sineux, P. 2007. *Amphiaraos. Guerrier, devin et guérisseur*, Paris.

Sinn, E. 1979. *Die Homerischen Becher. Hellenistische Reliefkeramik aus Makedonien*, Berlin.

Sistakou, E. 2007. 'Cyclic Stories? The Reception of the *Cypria* in Hellenistic Poetry', *Philologus* 151: 78–94.

 2008. *Reconstructing the Epic. Cross-Readings of the Trojan Myth in Hellenistic Poetry*, Leuven.

 2009. 'Fragments of an Imaginary Past. Strategies of Mythical Narration in Apollonius' *Argonautica* and Callimachus' *Aitia*', *RFIC* 137: 380–401.

Sisti, F. 1967. 'L'ode a Policrate. Un caso di *recusatio* in Ibico', *QUCC* 4: 59–79.

Slatkin, L. 1991. *The Power of Thetis. Allusion and Interpretation in the* Iliad, Berkeley, CA.

Small, J. P. 2003. *The Parallel Worlds of Classical Art and Text*, Cambridge.

Smith, J. D. 1991. *The Epic of Pābūjī. A Study, Transcription, and Translation*, Cambridge.

Smith, P. 1981. 'Aineiadai as Patrons of *Iliad* XX and the Homeric Hymn to Aphrodite', *HSCPh* 85: 17–58.

Snell, B. 1937. Review of Powell 1936, *Gnomon* 13: 577–86.

Snodgrass, A. M. 1964. *Early Greek Armour and Weapons*, Edinburgh.

 1979. 'Poet and Painter in Eighth-Century Greece', *PCPhS* 205: 118–30.

 1998. *Homer and the Artists*, Cambridge.

 2001. 'Pausanias and the Chest of Kypselos', in S. Alcock, J. Cherry, and J. Elsner (eds.), *Pausanias. Travel and Memory in Roman Greece*, Oxford: 127–41.

Snyder, J. M. 1989. *The Woman and the Lyre. Women Writers in Classical Greece and Rome*, Carbondale, IL.

Solmsen, F. 1981. '*The Sacrifice of Agamemnon's Daughter in Hesiod's' Ehoeae*', *AJPh* 102: 353–8.

Sommerstein, A. H. 1989. 'Notes on Aeschylus' *Seven against Thebes*', *Hermes* 117: 432–45.

 1996. *Aeschylean Tragedy*, Bari.

 2008. *Aeschylus. Fragments*, Cambridge, MA.

 2010. *Aeschylean Tragedy*. 2nd edn, London.

 2011. 'Sophocles and the guilt of Oedipus', *CFC(G)* 21: 93–107.

Sommerstein, A. H. and T. H. Talboy. 2012. *Sophocles. Selected Fragmentary Plays*. ii, Oxford.

Sommerstein, A. H., D. G. Fitzpatrick, and T. H. Talboy. 2006. *Sophocles. Selected Fragmentary Plays*. i, Oxford.

Sotiriou, M. 1997. *Pindarus Homericus. Homer-Rezeption in Pindars Epinikien*, Berlin.

Sourvinou-Inwood, C. 2011. *Athenian Myths and Festivals. Aglauros, Erechtheus, Plynteria, Panathenaia, Dionysia*, Oxford.

Spanoudakis, K. 2002. *Philitas of Cos*, Leiden.
Sparkes, B. 1971. 'The Trojan Horse in Classical Art', *G&R* 18: 54–70.
Spinazzola, V. 1953. *Pompei alla luce degli scavi nuovi di Via dell'Abbondanza (anni 1920–23)*, 2 vols., Rome.
Squire, M. 2009. *Image and Text in Graeco-Roman Antiquity*, Cambridge.
  2010. 'Texts on the Tables. The *Tabulae Iliacae* in Their Hellenistic Literary Context', *JHS* 130: 67–96.
  2011. *The* Iliad *in a Nutshell. Visualizing Epic on the Tabulae Iliacae*, Oxford.
  2014. 'The *ordo* of Rhetoric and the Rhetoric of *ordo*', in M. Meyer and J. Elsner (eds.), *Art and Rhetoric in Roman Culture*, Cambridge: 353–417.
Stafford, E. 2000. *Worshipping Virtues. Personification and the Divine in Ancient Greece*, London.
Stamatopoulou, Z. 2012. 'Weaving Titans for Athena: Euripides and the Panathenaic Peplos (*Hec.* 466–74 and *IT* 218–24)', *CQ* 62: 72–80.
Stanford, W. B. 1968. *The Ulysses Theme. A Study in the Adaptability of a Traditional Hero*, Oxford.
Stansbury-O'Donnell, M. D. 1989. 'Polygnotus' *Iliupersis*. A New Reconstruction', *AJA* 93: 203–15.
  1999. *Pictorial Narrative in Ancient Greek Art*, Cambridge.
Stewart, A. 1983. 'Stesichoros and the François Vase', in W. Moon (ed.), *Early Greek Art and Iconography*, Madison, WI: 53–74.
Stinton, T. C. W. 1965. *Euripides and the Judgement of Paris*, London.
Stockinger, H. 1959. *Die Vorzeichen im homerischen Epos. Ihre Typik und ihre Bedeutung*, St Ottilien.
Stoneman, R. 1976. 'Mythology and Interpretation. Two Notes on Pindar's *Nemeans*', *Maia* 28: 227–32.
  1981. 'Pindar and the Mythological Tradition', *Philologus* 125: 44–63.
Strasburger, G. 1954. *Die kleinen Kämpfer der* Ilias. Diss., Frankfurt.
Sullivan, J. P. 1968. *The* Satyricon *of Petronius. A Literary Study*, Bloomington, IN.
Sumler, A. 2010. 'A Catalogue of Shoes: Puns in Herodas Mime 7', *CW* 103: 465–75.
Swain, S. (ed.) 1999. *Oxford Readings in the Greek Novel*, Oxford.
Taplin, O. 1992. *Homeric Soundings. The Shaping of the* Iliad, Oxford.
Thalmann, W. G. 1982. 'The Lille Stesichorus and the "Seven against Thebes"', *Hermes* 110: 385–91.
Thomas, R. 1979. 'New Comedy, Callimachus, and Roman Poetry', *HSCPh* 83: 179–206.
Thompson, D'A. W. 1947. *A Glossary of Greek Fishes*, London.
Thompson, S. 1955–8. *Motif Index of Folk Literature*. 2nd edn, Copenhagen.
Tilg, S. 2010. *Chariton of Aphrodisias and the Invention of the Greek Love Novel*, New York.
Tomasso, V. 2010. *'Cast in Later Grecian Mould': Quintus of Smyrna's Reception of Homer in the Posthomerica*, Diss. Stanford, CA.

2012. 'The Fast and the Furious. Triphiodorus' Reception of Homer in the *Capture of Troy*', in Baumbach and Bär 2012a: 371–409.

Torres-Guerra, J. B. 1995a. *La* Tebaida *homérica como fuente de* Ilíada *y* Odisea, Madrid.

1995b. 'Die homerische *Thebais* und die *Amphiaraos-Ausfahrt*', *Eranos* 93: 39–48.

1998. 'Homero, compositor de la *Tebaida*', *CFC* 8: 133–45.

2012. 'The Writing Down of the Oral Thebaid that Homer Knew. In the Footsteps of Wolfgang Kullmann', in A. Rengakos and C. Tsagalis (eds.), *Homer in the 21st Century. Orality, Neoanalysis, Interpretation*, Berlin: 517–30.

Touchefeu, O. 1981. 'Aias I', in *LIMC* i.1: 312–36.

Treadgold, W. T. 1980. *The Nature of the* Bibliotheca *of Photius*. Washington DC.

TrGF = Kannicht, R., Radt, S. and Snell, B. 1981–2004. *Tragicorum Graecorum fragmenta*. 5 vols. (vols. 1 and 3 in 2nd edn), Göttingen.

van Tress, H. 2004. *Poetic Memory. Allusion in the Poetry of Callimachus and the* Metamorphoses *of Ovid*, Leiden.

Troiani, L. 1974. *L'opera storiografica di Filone da Byblos*, Pisa.

Trümpy, H. 1950. *Kriegerische Fachausdrücke im griechischen Epos. Untersuchungen zum Wortschatze Homers*, Basel.

Tsagalis, C. 2005. 'Detextualizing Homer. Intonation Units, Background Knowledge, and the Proems of the *Iliad* and the *Odyssey*', *Eranos* 103: 55–62.

2008a. *The Oral Palimpsest. Exploring Intertextuality in the Homeric Epics*, Cambridge, MA.

2008b. *Inscribing Sorrow. Fourth-Century Attic Funerary Epitaphs*, Berlin.

2008c. 'Μεταμορφώσεις του μύθου. Ο Τρωικός Κύκλος στους τρεις μεγάλους τραγικούς', in A. Markantonatos and C. Tsagalis (eds.), Αρχαία Ελληνική τραγωδία. Θεωρία και πράξη, Athens: 33–115.

2011. 'Towards an Oral, Intertextual Neoanalysis', *Trends in Classics* 3: 209–44.

2012a. 'De-Authorizing the Epic Cycle. Odysseus' False Tale to Eumaeus (*Od.* 14.199–359)', in Montanari, Rengakos and Tsagalis 2012: 299–336.

2012b. 'Cypria fr. 19 (Bernabé, West). Further considerations', *RFIC* 140: 257–89.

2013. 'Typhon and Eumelus' *Titanomachy*', *Trends in Classics* 5: 19–48.

2014. 'Verses Attributed to the *Telegony*,' *CQ* 64: 448–61.

Tsitsibakou-Vasalos, E. 1989. 'The Homeric ἄφαρ in the Oedipus Myth and the Identity of the Lille Mother', *Glotta* 67: 60–88.

2010. 'Stesichorus' Ἰλίου Πέρσις and the Epic Tradition', in *Classics@* 6 (ed. E. D. Karakantza, The Center for Hellenic Studies of Harvard University, edition of December 21, 2010).

Usener, K. 1990. *Beobachtungen zum Verhältnis der* Odyssee *zur* Ilias, Tübingen.

Valenzuela Montenegro, N. 2004. *Die Tabulae Iliacae. Mythos und Geschichte im Spiegel einer Gruppe frühkaiserzeitlicher Miniaturreliefs*, Berlin.

Valgiglio, E. 1963. 'Edipo nella tradizione pre-attica', *Riv. Studi Class.* 11: 18–43 and 153–71.

van der Valk, M. 1949. *Textual Criticism of the* Odyssey, Leiden.
  1971–1987. *Eustathii Archiepiscopi Thessalonicensis commentarii ad Homeri Iliadem pertinentes.* 5 vols., Leiden.
Vannicelli, P. 1995. 'La fuga da Tebe dei Cadmei dopo la spedizione degli Epigonoi', in M. Sordi (ed.), *Coercizione e mobilità nel mondo antico*, Milan: 17–26.
van Rossum-Steenbeek, M. 1998. *Greek Readers' Digests? Studies on a Selection of Subliterary Papyri*, Leiden.
van Tress, H. 2004. *Poetic Memory. Allusion in the Poetry of Callimachus and the* Metamorphoses *of Ovid*, Leiden.
Versnel, H. S. 1987. 'Greek Myth and Ritual. The Case of Kronos', in J. Bremmer (ed.), *Interpretations of Greek Mythology*, London: 121–152.
  1993. *Inconsistencies in Greek and Roman Religion.* ii. *Transition and Reversal in Myth and Ritual*, Leiden.
Vian, F. 1952. *La guerre des Géants. Le mythe avant l'époque hellénistique*, Paris.
  1959. *Recherches sur les* Posthomerica *de Quintus de Smyrne*, Paris.
  1963, 1966, 1969. *Quintus de Smyrne: La suite d'Homère.* 3 vols., Paris.
Vian, F. et al. 1976–2006. *Nonnos de Panopolis: Les Dionysiaques.* 19 vols., Paris.
  1986. 'La Poésie antique tardive (IVe–VIe siècles). i. L'Épopée grecque de Quintus de Smyrne à Nonnos de Panopolis', *Bullet. Assoc. G. Budé*: 333–43.
Vielle, C. 1998. 'Les correspondences des prologues divins de la guerre de Troie et du Mahābhārata', in L. Isebaert and R. Lebrun (eds.), *Quaestiones Homericae (Acta Colloquii Namurcensis habiti diebus 7–9 mensis Septembris anni 1995)*, Louvain: 275–90.
Vinogradov, J. 1969 = 1997. 'Kyklische Dichtung in Olbia', in Id., *Pontische Studien* (see above): 385–96 (original Russian text in *Vestnik drevnej istorii* 1969: 142–50).
  1990 =1997. 'La Chersonèse de la fin de l'archaisme', in O. Lordkipanidze and P. Lévêque (eds.), *Le Pont-Euxin vu par les Grecs. Sources écrites et archéologie (Symposium de Vani (Colchide), Sept. –Oct. 1987)*, Paris: 85–119 = Id., *Pontische Studien* (see above): 397–419.
Von der Mühll, P. 1940. 'Odyssee', *RE* Supp. vii: 696–768.
  1952. *Kritisches Hypomnema zur Ilias*, Basel.
Vos, H. 1956. *Themis*, Assen.
VS = H. Diels and W. Kranz, *Die Fragmente der Vorsokratiker.* 6th edn, Berlin, 1951–2.
Vürtheim, J. 1901. 'De Eugammonis Cyrenaei *Telegonia*', *Mnemosyne* 29: 23–58.
Wachter, R. 1991. 'The Inscriptions on the François Vase', *MusHelv* 48: 86–113.
Wackernagel, J. 1916. *Sprachliche Untersuchungen zu Homer*, Göttingen.
  1953–79. *Kleine Schriften.* 3 vols., Göttingen.
Wade-Gery, H. T. 1952. *The Poet of the* Iliad, Cambridge.
Wagner, R. 1886. 'Ein Excerpt aus Apollodors *Bibliothek*', *RhM* 41: 134–50.
  1891. *Epitoma Vaticana ex Apollodori* Bibliotheca. *Accedunt Curae Mythographae de Apollodori fontibus*, Leipzig.

Wallies, M. (ed.) 1909. *Joannis Philoponi in Aristotelis Analytica posteriora commentaria cum anonymo in librum II*, Berlin.
Weber, C. 1987. 'Metrical Imitatio in the Proem to the *Aeneid*', *HSCPh* 91: 261–71.
Webster, T. B. L. 1964. *Hellenistic Poetry and Art*, London.
Wecklein, N. 1901. 'Die Kyklische Thebaid, die *Oedipodee*, die *Oedipussage* und der *Oedipus* des Euripides', *Sitzungsber. königl. bayerischen Akad. Wiss.*: 661–92.
Weitzmann, K, 1947. *Illustrations in Roll and Codex*, Princeton, NJ.
   1959. *Ancient Book Illumination*, Cambridge, MA.
   1970. *Illustrations in Roll and Codex*. 2nd edn, Princeton, NJ.
Welcker, F.G. 1849. *Der epische Cyclus, oder die homerischen Dichter*. ii. 1st edn, Bonn.
   1865. *Der epische Cyclus, oder die homerischen Dichter*. i. 2nd edn, Bonn.
   1882. *Der epische Cyclus, oder die homerischen Dichter*. ii. 2nd edn, Bonn.
Wentzel, G. 1896. 'Asklepiades. 28', *RE* ii.2: 1628–31.
West, M. L. 1966, *Hesiod*. Theogony, Oxford.
   1971. 'Greek Epic Poetry', *CR* 85: 67–9.
   1978. *Hesiod*. Works and Days, Oxford.
   1982. *Greek Metre*, Oxford.
   1983. *The Orphic Poems*, Oxford.
   1985. *The Hesiodic Catalogue of Women. Its Nature, Structure, and Origins*, Oxford.
   1988. 'The Rise of the Greek Epic', *JHS* 108: 151–72.
   1994. 'Ab ovo. Orpheus, Sanchuniaton, and the Origins of the Ionian World Model', *CQ* 44: 289–307.
   1996. 'Stasinos', in *Oxford Class. Dict.* 3rd edn: 1438.
   1997. *The East Face of Helicon. West Asiatic Elements in Greek Poetry and Myth*, Oxford.
   1999. 'The Invention of Homer', *CQ* 49: 364–82.
   2000. '*Iliad* and *Aethiopis* on the Stage. Aeschylus and Son', *CQ* 50: 338–52.
   2001. *Studies in the Text and Transmission of the* Iliad, Munich.
   2002a. '"Eumelus", a Corinthian Epic Cycle?', *JHS* 122: 109–33.
   2002b. 'The View from Lesbos', in Reichel and Rengakos 2002: 207–19.
   2003a. *Greek Epic Fragments From the Seventh to the Fifth Centuries BC*, Cambridge, MA.
   2003b. *Homeric Hymns. Homeric Apocrypha. Lives of Homer*, Cambridge MA.
   2003c. '*Iliad* and *Aethiopis*', *CQ* 53: 1–14.
   2004. 'The Death of Baldr', *J. Indo-Europ. Stud.* 32: 1–9.
   2005. '*Odyssey* and *Argonautica*', *CQ* 55: 39–64.
   2006. 'Archilochus and Telephus', *ZPE* 156: 11–17.
   2011a. *Hellenica. Selected Papers on Greek Literature and Thought*. i. *Epic*, Oxford.
   2011b. *The Making of the* Iliad. *Disquisition and Analytical Commentary*, Oxford.
   2012. 'Towards a Chronology of Early Greek Epic', in Andersen and Haug 2012: 224–41.

2013. *The Greek Epic Cycle. A Commentary on the Lost Troy Epics*, Oxford.
West, S. 1988. *A Commentary on Homer's* Odyssey. i. *Introduction and Books I–VIII*, Oxford.
  1994, 'Prometheus Orientalized', *MusHelv* 51: 129–49.
  2007. 'Rhampsinitos and the Clever Thief (Herodotus 2.121)', in Marincola 2007: 322–7.
Wheeler, S. M. 1999. *A Discourse of Wonders. Audience and Performance in Ovid's* Metamorphoses, Philadelphia, PA.
Whitman, C. H. 1958. *Homer and the Heroic Tradition*, Cambridge, MA.
Whitmarsh, T. 2005. 'The Greek Novel. Titles and Genre', *AJPh* 126: 587–611.
  (ed.) 2008. *The Cambridge Companion to the Greek and Roman Novel*, Cambridge.
  2011. *Narrative and Identity in the Ancient Greek Novel. Returning Romance*, Cambridge.
Wilamowitz-Moellendorff, U. von 1884. *Homerische Untersuchungen*, Berlin.
  1891. 'Die sieben Thore Thebens', *Hermes* 26: 191–242.
  1893. *Aristoteles und Athen*, Berlin.
  1913. *Sappho und Simonides. Untersuchungen über griechische Lyriker*, Berlin.
  1920. *Die Ilias und Homer*. 2nd edn, Berlin.
  1922. *Pindaros*, Berlin.
  1925. 'Lesefrüchte', *Hermes* 60: 280–316.
  1929a. 'Kronos und die Titanen', *Sitz. Preuss. Akad. Wiss.* 1929: 35–53.
  1929b. 'Lesefrüchte', *Hermes* 64: 458–90.
Willcock, M. 1987. 'The Final Scenes of *Iliad* XVII,' in J. M. Bremer, I. F. de Jong, and S. Kalf (eds.), *Homer beyond Oral Poetry. Recent Trends in Homeric Interpretation*, Amsterdam: 185–94.
  1997. 'Neoanalysis', in Morris and Powell 1997: 174–89.
Williams, D. 1980. 'Ajax, Odysseus and the Arms of Odysseus', *Antike Kunst* 23: 137–45.
Willink, C. W. 1990. 'The Goddess Εὐλάβεια and Pseudo-Euripides in Euripides' *Phoenissae*', *PCPhS* 36: 182–201.
Wolf, F. A. 1831. *Vorlesungen über die Alterthumswissenschaft*. ii. *Vorlesung über die Geschichte der griechischen Literatur* (ed. J. D. Gürtler), Leipzig.
Wolff, O. 1884–6. 'Amphiaraos', in *ALGRM*: i.293–303.
Woodford, S. 1993. *The Trojan War in Ancient Art*, London.
  2003. *Images of Myths in Classical Antiquity*, Cambridge.
Worman, N. 2002. *The Cast of Character. Style in Greek Literature.* Austin, TX.
Wright, J. 1974. *Dancing in Chains. The Stylistic Unity of the Comoedia Palliata*, Rome.
Wüllner, F. 1825. *De cyclo epico poetisque cyclicis commentatio philologica*, Diss., Münster.
Young, D. C. 1993. '"Something Like the Gods". A Pindaric Theme and the Myth of *Nemean* 10', *GRBS* 34: 123–32.

Ypsilanti, M. 2007. 'Triphiodorus Homericus. People in the Ἰλίου Ἅλωσις and their forebears in the Iliad and Odyssey', *WS* 120: 93–114.

Zeitlin, F.I. 2009. 'Troy and Tragedy. The Conscience of Hellas', in F. Graf, U. Dill, and C. Walde (eds.), *Antike Mythen. Medien, Transformationen und Konstruktionen*, Berlin: 678–95.

2010. 'The Lady Vanishes. Helen and Her Phantom in Euripidean Drama', in P. Mitsis and C. Tsagalis (eds.), *Allusion, Authority, and Truth. Critical Perspectives on Greek Poetic and Rhetorical Praxis*, Berlin: 263–82.

Zielinski, T. 1899–1901. 'Die Behandlung gleichzeitiger Ereignisse im antiken Epos', *Philologus* Suppl. 8: 404–49.

Zintzen, C. 1979. *Die Laokoonepisode bei Vergil*, Wiesbaden.

Ziogas, I. 2008. 'Review of Papaioannou 2007', *BMCR* 2008.10.33.

Zumwalt, N. 1977. '*Fama Subversa*. Theme and Structure in Ovid *Metamorphoses* 12', *CSCA* 10: 209–22.

Index of principal passages

Aethiopis
    F 5 W. (= Arctinus 1 D. ['dubia et spuria'] = *Ilii excidium* PEG F 7) 310–11
    PEG F 1 141–2
    PEG F 2 (= F dub. D., F 2 W.) 309–10
    PEG F 3 (= F 3 W.) 311–12
    PEG F 4 (= Fragm. inc. loci intra cyclum epicum 3 D. [p. 74] = F 4 W. ['uncertain attribution']) 310
    PEG F 5 (= F 1 D., F 6 W.) 33, 308–9

Alcmeonis
    PEG F 1 (= D., W.) 266, 273–4, 277
    PEG F 2 (= D., W.) 266, 268–9, 277
    PEG F 3 (= D., W.) 267, 270–1, 277
    PEG F 4 (= D., W.) 267, 269–70, 272
    PEG F 5 (= F 6 D. = F 5 W.) 267, 271, 277
    PEG F 6 G (= F 5 D. = F 6 W.) 267, 275
    PEG F 7 (= D., W.) 268
    PEG F °8 [I] 264
    PEG F °8 [II] 276n81
    PEG F °9 [I–II] 272–3
    PEG F °10 266
    PEG F °11 264

Antimachus
    F 14 (Matthews) 203

Aristotle
    Analytica posteriora
        77b32 30, 34n137, 103n37, 104n20
    De sophisticis elenchis
        171a7 30
        171a10 104n20
    Poetica
        1451a16–25 412
        1459a17–b4 412–14
    Rhetorica
        1417a12 104

Asclepiades of Tragilus
    FgrHist 12 F 29 264

Asius
    PEG F 4 (= D., W.) 280
    PEG F 5 (= D., W.) 280
    PEG F 6 (= D., W.) 280
    PEG F 10 (= D., W.) 280

Callimachus
    Aetia
        F 1.3–5 Hard. 419–20
        F 35 Hard. 494
    Anthologia Palatina
        12.43 417–19
    Hymn to Zeus
        60–7 204
    SH 276 = F 190a–b Hard. 488

Corinna
    PMG 672 225, 259, 260

Cypria
    PEG F 1 (= D., W.) 281, 283, 285–6, 294, 295–7
    PEG F 1.2 (= D., W.) 140
    PEG F 1.6–7 (= D., W.) 132
    PEG F 2 (= D., W.) 285–6, 301
    PEG F 4 (= F 4 D. = F 5 W.) 283n27, 286–7, 297–8
    PEG F 4.7 (= D. = F 5 W.) 150
    PEG F 5 (= F 5 D. = F 6 W.) 286–7, 298–9, 303
    PEG F 8 (= F 6 D. = F 9 W.) 287, 299, 300
    PEG F 9 (= F 7 D. = F 10 W.) 298, 299–302
    PEG F 10 (= F 8 D. = F 11 W.) 300
    PEG F 13 (= F 12 D. = F 12 W.) 288
    PEG F 14 (= F 11 D. = F 14 W.) 287
    PEG F 15 (= F 13 D. = F 16 W.) 287, 302
    PEG F 16 (= F 5 D. = F 7 W.) 303
    PEG F 17 (= F 15 D. = F 18 W.) 303–4
    PEG F 18 (= F 24 D. = F 29 W.) 304–5
    PEG F 19 (= F 4 D. = F 19 W.) 288
    PEG F 24 (= F 17 D. = F 20 W.) 291
    PEG F 26 (= F 18 D. = F 22 W.) 292
    PEG F 27 (= F 21 D. = F 23 W.) 293, 294
    PEG F 28 (= F 22 D. = F 24 W.) 293, 294
    PEG F 29 (= F 19 D. = F 26 W.) 293
    PEG F 35–6 291
    PEG F dub. 37 (= F 8 W.) 287
    PEG F dub. 41 (= F 25 W.) 294

Index of principal passages

Ephorus
   FgrHist 70 F 123a–b 272, 273
   FgrHist 70 F 124 271
Epicharmus
   F 135 K.-A. 208
Epigonoi
   PEG F 1 (= D., W.) 244, 246, 254
   PEG F 2 (= D., W.) 244, 255–6
   PEG F 3 (= F 3 D. = F 4 W.) 251, 256–8, 262
   PEG F 4 (= F 2 W. = Antim. F 2 D.) 246
   PEG F dub. °6 (= F 1 inc. loci D. = F 3* W.) 258–9
Epithalamion for Achilles and Deidameia 489, 492
Epithalamion for Helen 489, 494
Eumelus
   Corinthiaca
      PEG F 7 (= F. 8 D. = F 25 W.) 280
      PEG F 8 (= F. 12 D. = F 22* W.) 275n76
Euphorion
   Philoctetes CA 44–45 489
Euripides
   Hippolytus 748 206
Eustathius
   Praefatio to the *Iliad* 415n30

Hellanicus
   EGM F 202c 106n5
Herodotus
   2.117 52, 281, 282, 410
   7.20 370
   7.91 368
Hesiod
   Catalogue of Women
      F 1.1–2 M.-W. 3, 255
      F 23a.17–24 M.-W. 434
      F 190.13–15 M.-W. 222
      F 192–3 M.-W. 221
      F dub. 358 M.-W. 434
   Theogony
      1–110 330
      19 334
      215–16 207
      334–5 207
      371 334
      521 139
      567 334
      597–8 334
      689 333
      713–25 550
      886–900 456

      984 555
      1019–20 3, 255
   Works and Days
      1–10 330
      156–73 12–14, 226
      167–73 133n31
Homer
   Iliad
      1.3–5 132
      5.406–15 367
      6.289–92 52
      12.15–16 132n29, 134n38
      12.23 132n28
   Odyssey
      1.326–6 356
      3.130–1 358
      3.180–2 134n37
      3.188–9 134n37
      3.312–3 356
      4.20–5 165
      4.495 360
      4.561–5 133n31
      5.105–11 358
      11.71–80 221
      11.119–37 131n22
      11.271–4 220
      14.316–35 131n21
      19.287–302 131n21
      23.266–84 131n22
Horace
   Ars poetica
      128–49 420–2
      136–7 544–6

Ibycus
   PMGF 291 447
   PMGF 296 447
   PMGF 297 448
   PMGF 303a 448
   PMGF 316 447
   PMGF S 151 440–5
   PMGF S 224 446–7
Ilias Parva
   PEG F 1 328, 329–31
   PEG F 2 (= D., W.) 319, 327, 331–2
   PEG F 5 (= D., W.) 333
   PEG F 8 (= F 10 D. = F 12 W.) 323
   PEG F 9 (= F 11 D. = F 14 W.) 323, 334–5, 612
   PEG F 10 (= F 12 D. = F 15 W.) 325
   PEG F 11 (= F 12 D. = F 16 W.) 326
   PEG F 13 (= F 14 D. = F 21 W.) 326
   PEG F 15 (= F 16 D. = F 24 W.) 326

Ilias Parva (*cont.*)
  PEG F 19 (= F 19 D. = F 28 W.) 323
  PEG F 21 (= F 20 D. = FF 29–30 W.) 53–5, 321, 335–40
  PEG F 23 (= F dub. 3 D. = F 31 W.) 340
  PEG F 24 (= F 4 D. = F 4 W.) 340–2
  PEG F 25 (= F 9 D. = F 11 W.) 323
  PEG F 28 (= F 1 D. = F 1 W.) 319, 329–31, 559
  PEG F 29 (= F 6 D. = F 6 W.) 326, 342–3

Iliou Persis
  PEG F 1 (= F dub. D. = F 4 W.) 351–2
  PEG F 4 (= F 1 D. = F 2 W.) 349–50
  PEG F 5 (= F 3 D. = F 3W.) 350–1

Lucan
  Bellum civile
    9.355–8 207

Lycophron
  Alexandra
    307–364 490
    592–632 492

Mimnermus
  F 9 367n29
  F 10 367n29

Nicander
  Theriaca
    9–12 203n19

Nonnus
  Dionysiaca 18.235–64 204

Nostoi
  F 9 W. 365
  PEG F 1 (= F 1 D. = F 11 W.) 361
  PEG F 2 (= F 2 D. = F 13 W.) 361
  PEG F 3 (= F 3 D. = F 1 W.) 361, 372
  PEG F 4 (= F 9 D. = F 3 W.) 362
  PEG F 5 (= F 9 D. = F 3 W.) 362
  PEG F 6 (= F 5 D. = F 5 W.) 362–3
  PEG F 7 (= F 5 D. = F 5 W.) 363, 376
  PEG F 8 (= F 5 D. = F 5 W.) 363
  PEG F 9 (= p. 75 D. = F 8 W.) 363–4
  PEG F 10 (= T 2 D. = F 10 W.) 364
  PEG F 11 (= F 8 D. = 12 W.) 364, 366
  PEG F 12 (= p. 75 D. = F 2 W.) 364

Oedipodea
  F *2 W. 224
  PEG F 1 (= F 1 D. = F 3 W.) 218–20
  PEG F 2 (= F 2 D. = F 1 W.) 220–4

Papyrus Harris: see Titanomachy PEG F 5
Papyrus Lille 76A ii + 73 i, ll. 204–6 439–40
Pausanias
  1.22.6 365
  2.22.6 434
  2.29.10 273
  5.17.5–19.10 279
  5.19.5 189
  6.17.6 275
  8.24.8–10 265
  8.25.7–8 234–5
  8.28.4–6 493
  9.5.10–11 217, 220–5
  9.5.11 215
  9.5.13 246, 250
  9.9.5 228, 245
  9.19.2 251
  10.28.7 372

Philodemus
  On Piety: see Cypria PEG F 2 (= D., W.)

Philoponus
  On Arist. *Analytica posteriora* p. 157.11 Wallies: see Aristotle (*Analytica posteriora* 77b32)

Pindar
  Olympian
    1.93–5 275n76
  Pythian
    8.39–55 270
  Nemean
    7.36–40 370

Pisander
  FGrHist 16 F 10 215, 216, 222, 224

Plato
  Phaedrus 264 410–11

Pollianus
  Anthologia Palatina
    11.130 427–9, 519, 546n15, 615n38

Pseudo-Apollodorus
  Bibliotheca
    1.8.4 232–3
    3.5.7–3.7.1 216, 226
    3.6.8 269
    3.7.2–6 263, 264, 265
  Epitome
    2.4–14 275

Ptolemy VIII of Egypt
  Memoirs (*FgrH* 234 F 1) 206

Quintus Smyrnaeus
  Posthomerica
    1.21–5 608
    1.741–6 608

Index of principal passages

3.1–5 608
3.60–6 609
3.217–95 608
3.296–321 608
3.321–81 608
3.775 609
4.323–74 310
6.57–115 610
6.116–90 610
7.169–252 610
10.223–331 610
10.345–6 610
10.346–9 610
10.353–60 611
11.29–501 611
12.353–94 612
12.395–415 612
13.251–7 611

Scholia Homerica
  Iliad
    2.494–877 414–16
    6.325 426
    11.805 425–6
    15.610–14 426
  Odyssey
    7.115 425
Sophocles
  Ajax 1297 206
  TrGF F 226 206
Statius
  Achilleid
    1.1–8 578
    1.20–5 581–2
    1.299–300 590
  Thebaid
    2.596 203
Stesichorus
  PMGF 209 435–6
  PMGF 223 433–4
  PMGF S 89 437

Thebaid (Cyclic)
  F 1 Torres (= *PEG*, D., W.) 229, 232
  F 2 Torres (= *PEG* F 1, D., W.) 229–31
  F 3 Torres (= *PEG*, D., W.) 230–2
  F 4 Torres (*PEG* F 5 = F 8 D. = F 5 W.) 232–3
  F 5 Torres (*PEG* F 6 = F 4 D. = F 10 W.) 233
  F 6 Torres (*PEG* F 9 = F 5 D. = F 9* W.) 233–4, 236, 237
  F 7 Torres (*PEG* F 7 = F 6 a D. = 11 W.) 234–5
  F 8 Torres (*PEG* F 8 = F 6 b + c D. = 11 W.) 235–6
  F 9 Torres (*PEG* F 10 = F 6 D. = 6 W.) 236–7
  F 10* Torres (= *PEG* F 4 = Homerus 3 D. = F 8* W.) 237–8
  F 11* Torres (= F 7* W.) 238–9
  F 12* Torres (= *PEG* F 11 = F 4* W.) 237, 239–40
  PEG F 4 (= F. "Hom." 3 D. = F 8* W) 271n52
  PEG F 9 (= F. 5 D. = F 9 W.) 269
  PEG FF 2–3 (= D., W.) 217, 223
  PEG T 2 (T 1 D. = s. n. W.) 228
  PEG T 4 (T 2 D. = 1 W.) 228n8
  PEG T 5 (= D., W.) 241
  PEG T 7 (F 9 D. = T 2 W.) 240n50
  PEG T 8 (F 9 D.) 240n50
Telegony
  arg. lines 315–323 Severyns 131–5
  F 1* a Tsagalis (= *PEG* F 2) 384–8
  F 2 Tsagalis (= F 1 D. = F 3 W.) 388
  F 2* W. 397–9
  F 3 Tsagalis (= *PEG* F 3 = F 2 D. = F 4 W.) 388–90
  F 4 a + b + c Tsagalis (= *PEG* F 4 = F 5W) 390–3
  F 5 a + b + c Tsagalis (= *PEG* F 5 = F 2 D. = F 6 W.) 393–5
  PEG F 1 (= "Hom." 10 D. = F 1* W.) 395–7
Theocritus
  Idyll 18: see *Epithalamion for Helen*
Theogony (Cyclic)
  Cyclus ep. PEG T 6 (= *Tit.* T 1 D.) 199
  Cyclus ep. PEG T 13 (= *de epico cyclo* T1 D.) 199
Titanomachy
  F 2 W. 203
  PEG F 1/2 (= F 1A, 1B D. = F 1W.) 200, 203
  PEG F 3 (= D., W.) 202, 203
  PEG F 4 (= F 8 D. = F 14 W.) 202, 205–7
  PEG F 5 209–12
  PEG F 6 (= F 5 D. = F 8 W.) 202, 207–9
  PEG F 7 (= F 4 D. = F 11 W.) 204
  PEG F 8 (= F 7 D. = F 10 W.) 204
  PEG F 10 (= F 9 D. = F 12W.) 204
  PEG F11 (= F 6 D. = F 13 W.) 204
  PEG T 2 (= T 2 D.) 202

Virgil
  Aeneid
    1.12–49 559
    1.23–32 556–7
    1.39–45 556

Virgil (*cont.*)
   1.453–93 552–4
   1.456–7 422–4
   6.580 204
   8.383–4 113, 555
   8.629 423, 552
   10.565–8 203
   10.565–70 549–50
   11.659–63 554–5

Xenophanes
   F 1.21 G–P (= *IEG*^{2}) 199

Index nominum et rerum

absence of death 573
Aesacus 572
Achilles
  afterlife of 51, 575, 576
  and Helen 22, 110, 169, 172, 173, 285, 286, 292–3, 301, 305, 589
  and Memnon: *see* Memnon
  and Penthesileia: *see* Penthesileia (and Achilles)
  and Phoenix: *see* Phoenix
  and Scyros: *see* Scyros
  and Troilus: *see* Troilus
  arms/armor of 11, 33, 99, 111, 113, 116, 120, 307, 309, 312, 314, 319, 322, 331, 454, 457, 554, 570, 588, 609
  cult worship of 51
  death of 98, 99, 111, 114, 115, 118, 129, 155, 162, 308, 314, 315, 406, 415, 447, 463, 476, 519, 557, 608
  funeral of 127, 314
  recruitment of 288–9
  story of 98, 117, 118, 576
  wrath of 49, 128, 130, 132, 155, 229, 296, 297, 407, 477
Adrastus 12, 226, 232, 235, 236, 237, 238, 239, 240, 241, 242, 247, 248, 249, 253, 259, 263, 264, 270, 272, 278, 432, 452, 460, 478
Aegaeon 200, 203, 549, 550
Aeneas 53, 54, 110, 122, 171, 308, 323, 325, 327, 330, 336, 339, 343, 344, 348, 349, 351, 354, 422, 423, 424, 438, 501, 509, 520, 523, 535, 544, 549, 550, 551, 552, 553, 554, 555, 556, 557, 558, 583, 584, 585, 591, 592, 611
Aethiopis
  and the *Iliad* 315–17
  character of 314–15
  date and authorship of 313–14
  plot 306–8
aetiology 75, 387, 494, 581
African oral epic 88–9

Ajax Locrian/Oileus 100, 119, 120, 124, 355, 369, 454, 494, 556
Ajax Telamonian
  and arms of Achilles: *see* arms/armor of Achilles
  madness of: *see* madness (of Ajax)
  quarrels with Odysseus: *see* arms/armor of Achilles
  rescues Achilles' body 116, 307, 311, 312, 325, 332, 455, 608
  suicide of 33, 98, 99, 184, 191, 195, 306, 309, 314, 321, 322, 451, 457, 476, 610
  wrestles with Odysseus 120
akolouthia tōn… pragmatōn 1, 9, 19, 32, 34, 104, 213, 408–9, 414, 420, 431, 516
Alcmaon 247, 248, 249, 250, 251, 252, 257, 261, 262, 263, 264, 265, 266, 268, 269, 270, 271, 272, 273, 274, 275, 276, 277, 279, 364, 432, 476
allusion 10, 35, 53, 93, 94, 96, 97, 101, 104, 108, 112, 118, 120, 121, 124, 137, 156, 166, 169, 170, 172, 221, 226, 241, 281, 306, 316, 332, 367, 488, 517, 555, 597, 598, 606, 617, 619, 620
alternative versions 10, 130, 131, 360, 434, 585
ambush 186, 266, 323, 324, 326, 327, 343, 345, 366, 369, 446, 480, 553, 555, 615
Amphiaraus 134, 227, 234, 236, 237, 238, 239, 240, 247, 248, 249, 250, 251, 253, 261, 264, 269, 270, 272, 276, 279, 280, 343, 452, 453, 454, 478
Amphilochus 134, 237, 238, 247, 249, 252, 253, 257, 264, 271, 272, 279, 368, 453, 454
Anius 158, 161, 293
Apharetidae: *see* Idas; Lynceus
Aphrodite 22, 49, 109–10, 128, 158, 169, 170–1, 176, 282, 286, 287, 298, 299, 305, 367, 433, 435, 443–8, 585, 591, 600
Arabic oral epic (or, Sirat Bani Hilal epics) 88
Arcesilas 384
Arcesilaus 51, 382–4, 389, 390, 395, 401

674 *Index nominum et rerum*

Archemorus 227, 240, 472
Arctinus 21, 23, 24, 28, 29, 39, 51, 59, 61, 63,
    65, 67, 74, 75, 76, 77, 98, 102, 105, 106,
    116, 162, 164, 172, 202, 306, 309, 311,
    312, 313, 314, 347, 350, 351, 382, 405,
    504, 530, 544, 608, 611, 613, 619, 620
Argive shield-bands 183–5, 188–9, 191, 193,
    195
Arion 227, 236, 259
Aristarchus 425–6
Aristotle 5–6, 7, 18, 27, 29, 30, 32, 44, 61, 73,
    80, 97, 99, 104, 105, 129, 164, 213, 284,
    318, 326, 410–16, 428, 461–5, 512–13,
    514, 518, 519, 521, 565, 566, 599
Astyanax 33, 54, 55, 56, 65, 158, 181, 320, 321,
    323, 324, 325, 326, 338, 346, 348, 350,
    353, 354, 438, 551, 611, 612, 617
Aulis 97, 99, 121, 128, 155, 158, 160, 162, 289,
    290, 291–2, 465, 488, 493
autar epeita 428

blindness 221, 223–4
book divisions in Cycle 29n113, 35, 105n23,
    347n19
Briareus: *see* Aegaeon
Briseis 122, 123, 293, 294, 296, 576, 594

Calchas 121, 134, 135, 158, 159, 257, 289, 291,
    355, 360, 367–8, 373, 376, 377
Callidice 131, 175, 381, 389, 401, 600
Callimachus 416–20
Catalogue of Ships 97, 121, 155, 252, 253, 289,
    415, 416, 443, 444, 519
Catalogue of Trojans 33, 123, 155, 295
Cebriones: 116, 316
Central Asian oral epic (or Kirghiz oral epic)
    89–90
Chest of Cypselus 279, 280, 287
Chiron 204, 205, 274, 291, 332, 450, 459, 580,
    581, 588–9, 593
Chryseis 122, 124, 293, 294
Cleisthenes of Sicyon 11, 241, 242, 247, 278,
    280, 460
colonization 116, 122, 278, 314n20, 360, 378,
    382, 383
compensatory lengthening 144
contemporary oral cycles (or, living cycles)
    85–91
Cretan lies: *see* lying tales
curse 217n13, 223
Cycle
    Hellenistic reception of 487–90
    prosody and metrics 149–53

'Cyclic'
    defined 1–7, 17, 30, 32, 34–6, 43, 60, 61,
    97–101, 104, 406, 419, 422, 425, 426,
    431, 432, 488, 512–16, 519, 558, 565,
    580, 599, 607
Cycnus
    son of Ares 236
    son of Poseidon 110, 451, 477, 568, 569, 573
Cypria 99–100, 101, 281–305
    abstractions, personified (in *Cypria*) 286,
        301
    authorship of 282–3
    date of 281
    doublets and parallels in 289, 291, 296, 299,
        301
    relationship with *Iliad* 284 and Chapter
        16 *passim*
    style of 284–5, 295–6, 298–9, 301–2, 303
    title of 281
Cyprias 38, 50, 164, 282, 286

date of the Cyclic poems 51–2, 57, 139–40
Deidameia 288, 289, 290–1, 341, 369, 492, 579,
    590–4, 600
Demeter 235–6
dikaiosynē 205n32
Diomedes 14, 33, 86, 114, 115, 117, 118, 133,
    134, 156, 158, 161, 193, 234, 249, 253,
    254, 264, 272, 273, 315, 322, 324, 325,
    326, 328, 343, 345, 353, 355, 357, 360,
    366, 367, 373, 377, 452, 454, 460, 466,
    467–8, 492, 557, 579, 580, 611
Dionysus 158, 212, 259, 270, 618, 619, 621
Dios boulē 132, 443
Dioscouroi 121, 158, 176, 287–8, 299, 300,
    302–3, 450, 457, 458

Egypt 352, 356, 366
Epigonoi 244–60
epinician dance 207–8
Erinys 230, 236
Eriphyle 227, 238–40, 247, 248, 251, 253, 257,
    264, 265, 276, 279, 280, 343, 365
eris 493
erotic dimension (in Ibycus) 440–4, 445, 446,
    447, 448
Eteocles 215, 216, 217, 223, 226, 227, 231, 244,
    247, 250, 258, 268, 276, 279, 439, 464,
    470, 476, 479, 481
Eugammon 24, 39, 101, 105, 175, 381–4, 389,
    390, 392, 393, 397, 399–401
Eumelus 24, 28, 102, 202, 203, 204, 275, 279,
    280, 382

fixity of text 8, 11, 16, 29, 31, 32, 78, 79, 81, 82, 83, 85, 94, 242, 283, 320, 338, 409, 601n2
folktale 101, 176, 285

Gigantomachy: confusion with *Titanomachy* 208–9, 212

Hector
   and Polites 188
   and Protesilaus 292
   censuring Paris 173
   death/fate of 114, 115, 129, 308, 315, 344, 406, 451, 553, 570, 578, 606
   funeral of 255, 312, 530
   invention of the poet of the *Iliad* 119
   ransom of 184
   refusing to drink wine 304
Hegesias 23, 50, 164
Hegesinus 282
Helen
   and Achilles: *see* Achilles
   in Egypt: *see* Egypt
   and Menelaus 33, 128, 165, 168, 176, 181, 190, 320, 323, 341, 345, 346, 376, 433, 440, 447, 448, 451, 494, 600
   and Odysseus 99, 127, 128, 451
   and Paris 22, 52, 97, 121, 128, 129, 160, 166, 170, 286, 287, 288, 296, 304, 432, 445, 457, 557, 575, 582, 584, 594, 600, 621
   daughter of Nemesis 136, 167, 298–9
   in Ibycus: *see* Ibycus (inspiration from the *Cypria* in)
   in Stesichorus 433–6
   phantom 433
   suitors of 253, 273
Hera 115, 120, 157, 170, 190, 286, 287, 295, 365, 456, 581, 584, 585, 586, 590
Heracles
   and Odysseus 341
   and Philoctetes: *see* Philoctetes
   cycle of 9, 10, 96
   deeds/saga 24, 96, 138, 211, 391, 400, 455, 502, 538
   madness of 160, 232, 288, 416
Hermione 292, 366, 371, 374, 377, 475
hero cult 12, 367, 375–6, 386
Heroic Age
   end of 102, 378
Hesperides 206, 207
"Homeric cups" 26, 106, 306, 364, 497–500, 511, 530, 538

Horace 420–2
House of Fame 570
human sacrifice 80n11, 292
humor 164–77
Hundred-Handers 199, 200, 201, 203

Ibycus
   inspiration from the *Cypria* in 443, 446
   metapoetic self-awareness in 440, 554, 556, 557, 569, 613, 614, 617
   narrative style of 442–3
iconography 52, 208, 229, 254, 405–6, 417, 446, 498
Idas 160, 287, 302–3, 457, 458
Iliad, alternative incipit and ending 103
Ilias parva
   and *Iliades parvae* (?) 328–9
   author, title, and date 318–19
   contents of 322–6
   Homeric and un-Homeric 326–8
   influence of *Iliad* and *Odyssey* (upon) 328, 330
   predecessors and competitors 319–21
Iliou persis
   character of the poem 352–4
   the myth in poetry and art 344–7
immortality/immortalization 4, 115, 116, 117, 133, 136, 137, 234, 256, 269, 285, 287, 292, 307, 395, 451, 452, 457, 459
incest 220
Indian oral epic (or Pābūjī epic) 90–1
intertextuality 83, 93, 94, 95, 243, 316, 355–61, 365, 605, 621
Iphianassa 291, 292
Iphigeneia 121, 158, 160, 172, 291, 292, 320, 434, 464, 465, 466, 572, 600
Iphinoe 293

Judgment of Paris 97, 98, 99, 121, 168, 170, 178, 190, 281, 285, 299, 444, 488, 556, 582, 584, 590, 591, 594
Juno 422, 424, 520, 583, 584, 585, 586, 592

kyklikoi/kyklikōs 424–9
kyklos: *see* 'Cyclic'

language, of the Epic Cycle
   α-Stems 145–6
   athematic declension 146–7
   diectasis 152
   epic correption 151
   geminata 144–5
   pronouns 147

language, of the Epic Cycle (*cont.*)
    syllabic adaptations 153
    verb 147–8
    wau 150–1
Laodameia 292
Leda 167, 168, 272, 273, 276, 280, 300, 301
Lesches 24, 26, 28, 29, 33, 39, 51, 54, 55, 59, 61, 65, 67, 74, 75, 76, 77, 99, 105, 106, 162, 312, 318, 329, 340, 343, 498, 504, 530, 544, 559, 609, 610, 611, 616, 617
Lycaon 122, 294, 573
Lycomedes 291, 325, 341
lying tales 130–1, 135, 599
Lynceus: *see* Idas

Macedonian cups/bowls: *see* "Homeric cups"
madness
    of Ajax 350, 609
    of Alcmaon 253, 264, 265
    of Dido 591
    of Heracles: *see* Heracles (madness of)
    of Odysseus: 288
    of Orestes: 276
magical elements/motif/token
    in *Cypria* 303
    in *Epigonoi* 295
    in *Ilias parva* 323, 326
Manto 134, 245, 251, 256, 257, 262
marginal characters 492, 494
Melanippus 12, 234, 269, 278, 452
Memnon 111, 113–19, 120, 159, 189, 307, 314, 315, 317, 392, 423, 451, 456, 459, 460, 553, 555, 557, 558, 587, 608
Menelaus
    afterlife 133
    and Agamemnon 49, 156, 477, 613
    and Deiphobus 345, 348, 352, 353
    and Diomedes 193
    and Helen: *see* Helen (in Egypt: and Menelaus)
    and Nestor 121, 288, 303, 304, 357, 601
    combat with Paris 122, 161
    deification of 365
    in *Odyssey* 127–8, 132, 165, 167, 174, 359
    offers hospitality to Paris 444, 457
    return of 100, 162, 355, 366, 371, 373, 374, 377
Mesopotamian poetry (*Atrahasis, Enuma elish*) 137, 285, 296
metamorphosis 167, 177, 274n69, 285, 572, 573, 574, 577
migrations 133–5, 137, 367, 378
Momos 169, 170, 285, 286, 296

Mopsus 134, 256, 257, 368, 375
multiformity 78, 79, 84, 90, 92, 93, 94, 95, 283, 286, 287, 559
Mykonos pithos 179–82, 188, 195, 321, 345, 346, 447
Mythographus Homericus 283, 285, 286, 295

Nauplius 124, 361, 365, 368–9, 374, 467
necklace of Harmonia 226, 238, 247, 264, 265, 266, 276, 279
Nemean Games 227, 240–2, 472
Nemesis 300–1
    mother of Helen: *see* Helen (in Egypt: daughter of Nemesis)
Neoanalysis 46, 47, 56, 79, 108, 111, 112, 126, 316
    and oral poetics: 91–5, 242–3
Neoptolemus
    and Epirus 133, 336, 355, 365, 369–70, 375, 454
    and Peleus 100
    and Scyros 99, 121, 124, 159, 161, 288, 289, 290, 291, 322, 323, 328, 341–2, 468
    kills Eurypylus 320
    kills Priam 348, 353, 451, 498, 610
    takes Andromache as prisoner (and kills Astyanax) 33, 56, 327, 348, 376, 438, 611, 612
    takes his father's arms 333
neōteroi 425
Nestor 10, 100, 114, 115, 121, 156, 160, 288, 303, 304, 307, 316, 355, 356, 357, 359, 366–7, 369, 370, 371, 373, 415, 416, 454, 459, 460, 492, 557, 558, 569, 571, 575, 579, 600
Nostoi
    characters 365–72
    ideology 378–9
    plot of 377–8
    relation to *Odyssey*: *see Odyssey* (relation to *Nostoi*)
    style of 376–7

Ocean 13, 201, 204, 205, 300, 301, 577
Odysseus
    after the *Odyssey* 174–6, 355–79, 471–2
    and Achilles' armor: *see* Achilles (arms/armor of)
    and Antenor 128
    and Neoptolemus: *see* Neoptolemus (and Scyros)
    and Thersites 124, 173
    and the Wooden Horse 345

death of 2, 10, 48, 101, 462, 487
enters into Troy in secret 99, 161, 320, 322, 323, 476, 611
immortalization 4
in the Underworld 127
kills Astyanax 56, 348, 438, 451, 611, 617
murders Palamedes 159, 466–7
narrates lying tales: *see* lying tales
purifies Achilles 193, 307
quarrels with Achilles 121, 158, 312
quarrels with Ajax: *see* Achilles (arms/armor of)
recruitment of 288
saves the body of Achilles 116, 325, 332, 455
Odyssey
and Theban saga 226, 228, 235, 240–3
'Cyclic' edition of 103
relation to *Nostoi* 100
Oedipus 146, 160, 213–25, 226, 230, 231, 232, 244, 250, 259, 260, 276, 416, 439, 462, 471, 477–81
Oinotropoi 293
Opheltes: *see* Archemorus
oral theory 82–5, 91–5, 138n51, 242–3
Orestes 100, 162, 276, 355, 356, 357, 365, 366, 371, 374, 376, 377, 462, 464, 465, 468–9, 474, 475
Oropos 227
Orphic *Theogonies* 199–202
Ovid
and eroticization of Achilles' life 575
and his '*Ilias parva*' 568–73
and the *Metamorphoses* as a non-Homeric epic 565, 566, 567, 573, 575, 577
and Nestor as symbol of a pre-Homeric epic 569, 575

Palamedes 49, 288, 464, 552, 571 *see* Odysseus (murders Palamedes)
Paris: *see* Hector (censuring Paris); Helen (in Egypt: and Paris); Judgment of Paris; Menelaus (combat with Paris), (offers hospitality to Paris)
Parry (and Lord) 44, 80, 84, 85, 86, 89
pars pro toto 15, 84–5, 90
Parthenopaeus 233, 249, 253, 470, 477, 478
patronymic adjectives 147, 448
Penthesileia
and Achilles 49, 52, 98, 123, 124, 142, 172, 173, 193, 255, 306, 310, 314, 325, 423, 463, 501, 530, 532, 533, 553, 555, 575, 590, 592, 593, 608
and Camilla 114, 554

Periclymenus 233, 470, 477
Phayllus 104–6
Phereclus 287
Philoctetes 97, 121, 124, 133, 134, 159, 161, 320, 322, 323, 326, 464, 467–8, 474, 477, 491, 492, 571, 610
Phoenix 193, 237, 291, 369, 376, 440, 579
Photius 1, 22, 23, 35, 38, 48, 101, 102, 103, 199, 214, 408
Polites: *see* Hector
Polydora 292
polymythos 407, 414
Polynices: *see* Eteocles; necklace of Harmonia
Poseidon 131, 132, 170, 204, 234, 235, 304, 305, 349, 357, 368, 383, 397, 399, 400, 451, 455, 456, 459, 494, 551, 556, 598, 609
positio debilis 151
Proclus 1, 2, 3, 9, 21, 29, 32, 33, 34, 35, 36, 37, 38, 39, 40, 47–8, 50, 52, 53, 55, 56, 57, 98, 100, 101–6, 108, 119, 123, 126, 131, 134, 154, 155, 158, 160, 169, 170–1, 172, 175, 185, 189, 191, 193, 199, 200, 203, 213, 214, 215, 229, 232, 282, 283, 284, 286, 287, 289, 293, 295, 306, 309, 313, 322, 348, 349, 352, 353, 355, 356, 361, 366, 367, 368, 369, 370, 371, 372, 376, 380, 388, 391, 408, 409, 415, 420, 429, 434, 440, 457, 459, 465, 467, 471, 487, 489, 490, 491, 492, 494, 510, 516, 543, 547, 548, 553, 555, 557, 585, 604, 609, 612, 613, 616, 618
Prometheus Bound and the *Titanomachy* 204
prophecy: *see* Calchas; Manto; Mopsus; Tiresias
Protesilaus: *see* Hector

Race of Heroes
the end of 132–3, 135, 136–7
re-enactments, of epic / Cyclic poems 127, 128–30, 621
reminiscences 127–8, 129, 130, 134, 338
Russian oral epic (or, *byliny*) 87–8

scriptor cyclicus 420–2, 425, 515, 545–6, 565
Scyros
and Achilles 159, 160, 288, 289, 290, 291, 325, 541, 571, 575, 576, 578, 579, 581, 589, 590, 593, 594
and Neoptolemus: *see* Neoptolemus
selectivity, narrative: *see* unity
Seven champions 213–23, 452, 460, 469, 470, 472, 473, 474, 550

Sicyon: *see* Cleisthenes
and *Thebaid* 239
in Ibycus 445
South Slavic oral epic 86–7
space (narrative space) 19, 262, 357, 361, 375, 452
Sphinx 215, 216, 218–20, 224–5, 259–60
Stasinus 22, 23, 50, 99, 101, 105, 162, 164, 282, 405, 456, 621
Stesichorus
   character development 436
   direct speech 439
   erotic dimension 435, 440, 443
   'Homeric' 430–1
   image (εἴδωλον) 433, 434
   innovations in myth 432, 435, 438–9
   irony 440
   linear narrative 431, 435
sting-ray 381, 390, 391, 392, 393, 401, 471
suppression 40, 130, 131–5, 136, 137, 589

Tabula Borgiana 5, 102, 214
Tabula Capitolina 5, 306, 307, 309, 313, 424, 438, 504, 516, 520, 523, 530
Tabulae Iliacae 105, 106, 214, 424, 497, 502–9, 510, 511, 514, 516–28, 532, 535, 541, 544
taxis/ordo, narrative 424
Telegonus 4, 101, 175, 213, 380–401, 472, 487, 602
Tennes 294n111, 587
Teumessian fox 225, 258–9
Teuthranian expedition 121, 123, 289, 290, 341
textualization 45, 66–7, 80, 82, 83, 84, 92
Thebaid
   chronology 227, 241–3
   direct speech 232, 236
   flashback 232n19
Thebes 11, 14, 43, 96, 213, 293, 294, 431, 432, 438, 439, 469, 471, 473, 474, 479, 480, 481, 550

Themis 157, 170, 285, 286, 296, 301, 456, 586
Thesprotia 131, 163, 175, 265, 372, 381, 388, 389, 393, 395, 399, 400, 401, 471, 600
Thetis 22, 99, 114, 115, 117, 120, 123, 129, 158, 169, 188, 191, 274, 285, 286, 288, 294, 295, 297, 301, 307, 315, 316, 325, 331, 368, 369, 373, 375, 376, 377, 392, 450, 454, 455, 459, 488, 489, 494, 501, 533, 555, 579, 581–6, 587, 588, 589, 590, 595, 598, 608, 609, 621
Tilphousa 236, 251
time (narrative time) 154, 156, 367, 372–5
Tiresias 101, 131, 175, 216, 251, 257, 360, 367, 368, 380, 392, 393, 398, 439, 479, 480, 601
tragedy
   and the Epic Cycle 406–9, 410, 411, 414, 461–2
Triphiodorus 547, 551, 604, 605, 606, 614–18, 621
Troilus 122, 172, 184, 185, 186, 188, 189, 191, 195, 294, 423, 445, 446, 490, 553, 554, 555, 558, 590
Trojan War myth 405, 419, 489
Tydeus 12, 226, 232, 233, 234, 240, 253, 267, 269, 270, 272, 452, 470, 478, 480
Typhoeus/Typhon 184, 209n48

unity, poetic 408–9, 414, 422
Universal Flood 204n30, 206

wine 167, 303–4, 395, 530, 618

Zeus 13, 25, 99, 100, 115, 116, 117, 123, 132, 157, 165, 167, 168, 176, 201, 202, 203, 204, 205, 207, 209, 212, 259, 266, 270, 285, 286, 287, 294, 295, 296, 297, 299, 300, 301, 304, 305, 307, 324, 325, 326, 333, 348, 351, 354, 365, 398, 426, 439, 451, 454, 456, 457, 458, 459, 473, 474, 491, 550, 556, 576, 586
Zoilus the Homer-Whipper 408

Lightning Source UK Ltd.
Milton Keynes UK
UKHW051154240722
406270UK00015B/443